Civil Rights since 1787

Civil Rights since 1787

A Reader on the Black Struggle

EDITED BY

Jonathan Birnbaum and
Clarence Taylor

New York University Press

NEW YORK AND LONDON

NEW YORK UNIVERSITY PRESS
New York and London

© 2000 by New York University

Library of Congress Cataloging-in-Publication Data
Civil rights since 1787 : a reader on the Black struggle / edited by
Jonathan Birnbaum and Clarence Taylor.
p.   cm.
Includes bibliographical references and index.
ISBN 0-8147-8215-9 (alk. paper) —
ISBN 0-8147-8249-3 (pbk. : alk. paper)
1. Afro-Americans—Civil rights—History—Sources. 2. Civil rights
movements—United States—History—Sources. 3. United States—Race
relations—Sources.   I. Birnbaum, Jonathan, 1956– II. Taylor, Clarence.
E184.6 .C595 1999
323.1'196073'009—dc21   00-008112

New York University Press books are printed on acid-free paper,
and their binding materials are chosen for strength and durability.

Manufactured in the United States of America

10 9 8 7 6 5 4 3 2 1

For Jason and Amanda
— C. T.

and Michael, Jaime, Shana, Danny, Stephanie, and Liza
— J. B.

We hold these truths to be self-evident, that all men are created equal, that they are endowed by their Creator with certain unalienable Rights, that among these are Life, Liberty and the pursuit of Happiness.

—Declaration of Independence

"We the People." It is a very eloquent beginning. But when that document [the Constitution] was completed on the 17th of September in 1787 I was not included in that "We the People."

—Representative Barbara Jordan

Let me give you a word of the philosophy of reforms. The whole history of the progress of human liberty shows that all concessions yet made to her august claims have been born of struggle. . . . If there is no struggle there is no progress. Those who profess to favor freedom and yet deprecate agitation, are men who want crops without plowing up the ground. They want rain without thunder and lightning. They want the ocean without the awful roar of its many waters. The struggle may be a moral one; or it may be a physical one; or it may be both moral and physical, but it must be a struggle. Power concedes nothing without a demand. It never did and it never will.

—Frederick Douglass

In 1919 "FBI agents visited [W. E. B.] Du Bois' office, asking him, 'what he was up to?' Du Bois replied that he was trying to get the Constitution enforced; he added to the men from the Justice Department: 'What are you up to?'"

—Herbert Aptheker

Contents

PART III: **Segregation**

The Repression of Free Blacks

Acknowledgments

No book is ever really the result of only one person or even—as in this case—two. Along with thanking, most obviously, our contributors and the overworked and underpaid permissions editors at the many presses who have assisted us, we'd also like to mention some of the many other folks who have offered us help at various points with this project.

Those who assisted us in our efforts include Eric Foner, Carol Berkin, Manning Marable, Clay Carson, Dan T. Carter, Gerald Horne, Nell Gutman, Jesse Lemisch, Aldon Morris, Judy Stein, Judy Pasternak, Carleton Mabee, Vicky Wells, Kimberlé Crenshaw, Mert Chernoff, Rose Boghasen, and Mickey Beslow.

Thanks for funding assistance from William Walker, chair of the Department of History at Florida International University (FIU); Ivelaw Griffith, associate dean of Arts and Sciences at FIU, and Carol Boyce-Davies, director of African/New World Studies at FIU.

Thanks to Cathe Barnabee, Samantha Lawrence, Toshiko Hiramatsu, and Mary Mullins for meticulously word-processing an ocean of essays.

Particular thanks to Cindy Kurman for p.r. advice.

Special thanks to Marsha Taylor, Asher Birnbaum, and Irene Birnbaum for their loving support for this and other projects.

Credit to our late professor, Herb Gutman, whose work and friendship continues to inspire us.

And finally, thanks to the boundless enthusiasm and support of our editor, Niko Pfund.

Introduction: It Didn't Start in 1954

Jonathan Birnbaum and Clarence Taylor

The struggle for civil rights has a long history in the United States—much longer than we are usually taught, or than we pause to consider. Textbooks traditionally designate the landmark 1954 Supreme Court case *Brown v. Board of Education* as the beginning of the civil rights movement. But even if we accept *Brown* as a starting point, we must ask, Why 1954? Couldn't the Supreme Court just as easily have come to the same conclusion in 1944, 1934, or 1904? To understand how and why it happened in 1954 requires a longer historical time frame. After all, why was there even a question that the Supreme Court had to decide?

The more complete story of civil rights, as virtually every historian acknowledges, must start at least as far back as the arrival of the first African slaves to the land Europeans called the New World. After all, what greater denial of civil rights—or human rights—exists than slavery?

This book begins—after a brief discussion of the international slave trade—in 1787, with the writing and ratification of the Constitution. In a sense, this book represents a history of the United States from the vantage point of the black struggle for civil rights.

So much for beginnings, what about the conclusion of the story? Some journalists and historians point to the passage of the 1965 Voting Rights Act or the assassination of Martin Luther King, Jr., in 1968. Others argue that the movement ended when the objectives of some of its participants changed from integration and interracial coalition protest to black power politics. Still others say the end came with the backlash of the 1970s or 1980s.

The primary documents and secondary assessments contained in this volume effectively demonstrate that civil rights is an ongoing story in which such rights may continue to advance—or retreat. For this reason, our book concludes with a set of current discussions on the possible future trajectory of the civil rights movement.

Answering the question of the time frame of the civil rights movement leads us to another question: Who were its primary actors? Historians often present history as the story of a handful of great (usually white) men. These men, we're told, made (and make) great decisions and discoveries, leading forward, while the rest of us ordinary folks quietly follow in their giant footsteps. In this version of history, most people are just background characters, the wallpaper of history. With only slight revision, the story of civil rights is sometimes written as the story of a handful of great white *and* black men—Abraham Lincoln, Frederick Douglass, Martin Luther King, Jr., Lyndon Johnson, and a few others. The rest of the men and generally all of the women and children are again left with the minor, essentially irrelevant, roles.

But where would our history be without the young students who risked their lives on Freedom Rides and sitting in at lunch counters? Where would we be without the Rosa Parkses, Ella Bakers, and Septima Clarks? Such people, and many more lesser known folks in every city and town, have played—and continue to play—primary, not secondary parts. Civil rights, as more than one author has noted, had to be fought for in every city and town. Martin Luther King, Jr., *was* a great man, but many other people whose tales usually go unsung also have played pivotal roles. Restricting our vision to a handful of great men narrows our understanding of the real dynamics of history.

Textbooks also tend to present civil rights as a blandly middle-of-the-road project. The politics of the participants—especially left-wing and progressive blacks and whites—are often sanitized almost out of existence. Even more ignored is the long history of Red Scares and other anti-left hysterias that have undermined, delayed, and derailed the civil rights project. A more complete version of the story must include not only more of the participants but also a fuller discussion of their politics—and the politics of their opponents.

And what about the objective of this struggle? The "prize" that the movement has sought has often been reduced to a quest for the vote in the South. But everyone involved in the struggle has always known that it is about much more than the vote. The prize has been economic as well as political, which explains the significant role of labor and the left, as well as much of the repression the movement has experienced. This also helps explain why the struggle has been fought in both the North and the South.

This anthology incorporates other running themes. For example, in the usual textbook tale, the issue of education arises from nowhere with *Brown v. Board of Education.* But education did not suddenly become a burning issue for the black community in 1954—or even in 1896 with *Plessy v. Ferguson,* the decision that *Brown* overturned. As selections in this anthology demonstrate, education has been a central concern of the black community throughout this country's history.

The long involvement of religion in the civil rights struggle has also been underemphasized. Every year, on January 20, we celebrate the birthday of a great religious and political leader, the Rev. Dr. Martin Luther King, Jr., who helped lead the struggle for civil rights. We're told that civil rights made a great leap forward once the churches and their leaders finally became involved in the 1950s. There is truth to that claim, but the more complete story, as with education, is that, whether positively or negatively, religion has always played a pivotal part.

History is not a straight line. Sadly, it is not simply the story of the inevitable unfolding of progress. The cause of civil rights has not simply moved forward; it has gone through periods of progress and periods of regress. The fight for civil rights, as Roger Baldwin said about civil liberties, never stays won. In fact, even during the most progressive periods, it never has been fully won.

So, the story of the civil rights movement is not over. And it is not just a story about high-profile advocates and politicians and their historians. It is a story that all of us continue to write and participate in every day. We hope that this book contributes to a better understanding of that project.

EDITORIAL NOTE ON LANGUAGE: The authors brought together in this volume have employed a wide variety of spelling, punctuation, and capitalization over the past two hundred years. This is especially evident in each author's decision about whether to refer to "African Americans," "Afro-Americans," "Blacks," "Negroes," "Coloreds," or variations thereof, including whether or not to adopt capitalized or hyphenated forms. For the sake of historical accuracy, we have chosen not to impose changes on the original texts except in occasional instances, which are clearly indicated.

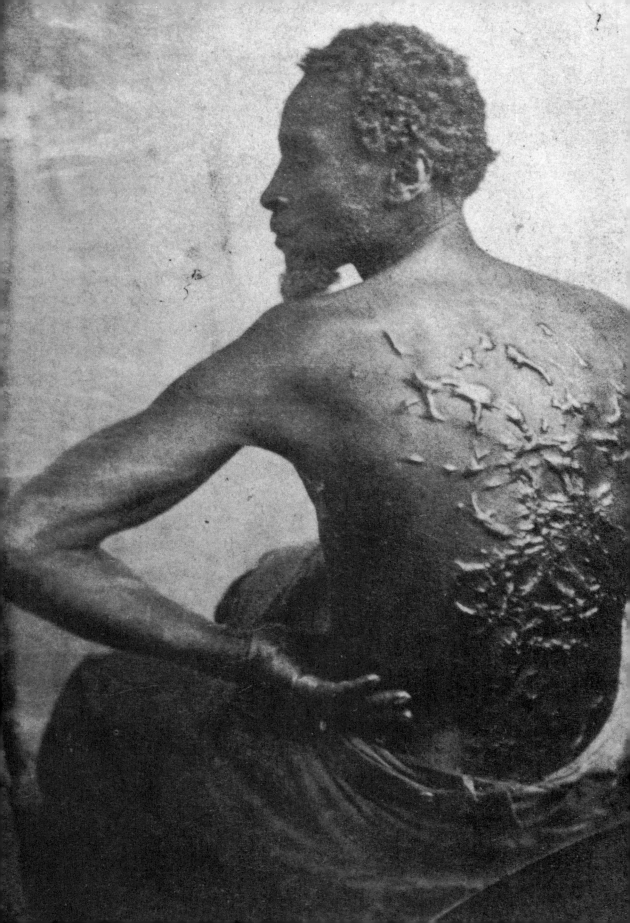

1

Slavery
America's First Compromise

Gordon, an escaped slave from Mississippi. Southern law allowed slave owners to punish their slaves physically. "Slave men and women were whipped frequently enough," according to the historian Herbert Gutman, "to reveal to them (and to us) that whipping regularly served as a negative instrument of labor discipline." This photograph was the basis for an engraving and a brief story that appeared in *Harper's Weekly,* 4 July 1863. After his escape, Gordon joined the Union army and served as a guide in Louisiana. (Photo courtesy of Culver Pictures.)

Chapter 1

Introduction: Original Sin

Jonathan Birnbaum and Clarence Taylor

"Globalization" has become a popular buzzword. Practically every day some U.S. workers lose their jobs or are forced to accept lower wages because of competition, we're told, from low-wage workers in less-developed countries in Latin America, Asia, and Eastern Europe. The pundits promise that consumers will reap the benefit with lower prices at their local Wal-Mart. (Few of these writers mention that workers and consumers are usually the same people.) And why is all this happening? The explanation, we're told, is a new phenomenon—globalization.

But globalization isn't new; it's a slowly unfolding process that simply has taken a longer time to reach some parts of the world than others—more than five hundred years, in fact. Globalization—the integration of the far corners of the world into a single, expanding global capitalist system—began at least as far back as the fifteenth-century European voyages of discovery.

Perhaps the best example of this process in its earlier years was the transatlantic slave trade, in which Europeans purchased (kidnapped) 10 million or more Africans for slave labor in North and South America. It was the expansion of the capitalist system—under which everything has a price, even people—across the globe that brought Africans to the Americas. Africans were forcibly transported across enormous distances to labor in the fields, manufactures, and homes of the New World. The profits from their labor enriched Western Europe and its colonies. And those profits helped finance the Industrial Revolution that catapulted the countries of Western Europe ahead of other countries financially, technologically, and militarily.

Black history in the Americas began as labor history. And for the same reason, the history of the black struggle for civil rights, originating as a struggle against slave labor, began as labor history. This explains, among many other things, Herbert Aptheker's argument (see chapter 7) that "the Emancipation Proclamation and the [13th] Amendment abolishing slavery are great documents in the history of the labor movement."

The Declaration of Independence proudly declared, in 1776, that "All men are created equal," despite the fact that its principal author, Thomas Jefferson, like many other signers, owned slaves. Slavery was the country's founding contradiction. Jefferson did suggest a paragraph—ultimately rejected—that would have condemned King George for his role in the slave trade. But, in another lapse, Jefferson failed to criticize or even mention the colonists' contribution to that infamous business.

After the American Revolution, some states incorporated the Declaration's proud proclamation about equality into their own constitutions, but only Massachusetts, when challenged in court, considered the phrase's claim serious enough to require the end of slavery within its jurisdiction.[1] Other northern states phased out slavery gradually, while the South maintained and expanded the system.

The Constitution framed in Philadelphia in 1787 continued the Declaration's compromises over slavery. It is generally forgotten that the country's first constitution, the Articles of Confederation,[2] included no mention of slavery. Nothing in the Articles endorsed slavery. Of course, nothing condemned it either, and slavery continued. But while slavery could be justified during this early period on the basis of custom, practice, and state laws, its proponents could not rely on national constitutional support and endorsement. This changed in the aftermath of Shays's Rebellion, an armed revolt against taxation that terrified the propertied classes and helped inspire the writing of our current Constitution.[3]

The 1787 Constitution included three clauses that directly discussed slavery,[4] although the actual words "slave" and "slavery" did not appear in the document. Through subsequent periods of amendment, upheaval, enforcement, and neglect, the Constitution has been the law of the land. So, it is with 1787, and the contradictions and challenges that our central legal document has inspired, that this book begins.

Of course, modern ears are not the only ones to hear the contradiction echoing between the high promise of freedom and the low practice of slavery. People at the time recognized the contradiction—most especially blacks themselves. So it should not be surprising, as the following texts demonstrate, that blacks would take the lead in changing their condition.

NOTES

1. See Arthur Zilversmit, *The First Emancipation: The Abolition of Slavery in the North* (Chicago: University of Chicago Press, 1967).

2. For a general discussion of the Articles of Confederation period, see Merrill Jensen's classic history, *The New Nation* (Madison: University of Wisconsin Press, 1950).

3. See David P. Szatmary, *Shays' Rebellion: The Making of an Agrarian Insurrection* (Amherst: University of Massachusetts Press, 1980). For other discussions of the Articles of Confederation and Shays's Rebellion, see *The United States Constitution: Two Hundred Years of Criticism*, ed. Bertell Ollman and Jonathan Birnbaum (New York: New York University Press, 1991).

4. Abolitionist Wendell Phillips argued that other clauses also indirectly supported slavery. For a discussion of this position, see chapter 3 below.

Chapter 2

The International Slave Trade

Philip Foner

Philip Foner (1910–1994) was a prolific Marxist labor historian. In 1941, during New York's Rapp-Coudert hearings, he was accused of membership in the Communist party and of not cooperating by informing on other members. Foner and his three brothers were among fifty academics fired by the City College of New York. Blacklisted, he was unable to find another academic position until 1967. The Board of Trustees of the City University of New York formally apologized in 1981. In 1994, he received a Special Education Award for Lifetime Achievement in the field of labor history from the New York State Labor History Association.

Foner's works on black history include Business and Slavery *(1941),* Frederick Douglass: A Biography *(1964),* Organized Labor and the Black Worker *(2d ed., 1982),* History of Black Americans *(3 vols., 1975–1983), and* Essays in Afro-American History *(1978). He also edited* The Life and Writings of Frederick Douglass *(5 vols., 1950–1975),* The Black Panthers Speak *(1970),* The Voice of Black America *(1972),* The Black Worker: A Documentary History *(8 vols., 1978–1984),* Paul Robeson Speaks *(1978), and* Proceedings of the Black State Conventions, 1840–1865 *(2 vols., 1978–1979).*

The following selection is excerpted from History of Black Americans, *vol. 1,* From Africa to the Emergence of the Cotton Kingdom *(Westport, Conn.: Greenwood Press, 1975), 100, 106–8, 108–12, 112–13. Copyright © 1975 by Philip Foner. All rights reserved. Reprinted with permission.*

The discovery of America added an entirely new dimension to the demand for slaves. By the sixteenth century the demand for cheap labor to exploit the new continent's resources had created an enormous market for slaves, and the slave traffic in Africa changed from an accessory to the older trades into a major economic enterprise, providing enormous profits for the rising European capitalist class. Africa would continue to supply gold dust, ivory, dye, woods, animal skins, tortoise shells, beeswax, and bamboo canes, but so lucrative was the slave trade that no other form of commerce could compete with it. Henceforth what money-thirsty European merchants demanded from Africa was human beings for slaves, and the demand did not slacken for two hundred years. . . .

In a number of European possessions in the New World, especially in the English

West Indian and North American colonies, the immediate successor of the Indian slave was not the Negro but the landless poor white of Europe. Promoters of colonization appealed to hard-pressed tenants, craftsmen, farm hands, unemployed artisans, and agricultural laborers to start a new life in the New World. Many responded eagerly and came over under the terms of a labor contract or indenture that bound them to service for a specified term, usually from five to seven years, in return for their passage. But there were others who came, not of their own volition, but as victims of a highly organized, thriving kidnapping business, which dragged them off the streets of large cities—grown men and women and young boys and girls—and brought them in chains aboard a ship. Many more, victims of the heavy sentences of that day for petty misdemeanors or destitution, were sold out of the crowded prisons by a government eager to rid itself of costly public charges. Still others received court sentences for deportation or, given their choice, preferred indenture to long prison terms or the gallows.

A constant stream of poor whites from Spain, Portugal, France, and especially England moved to the colonies of the New World. But they failed to satisfy the tobacco and sugar plantations' voracious appetite for labor. Many ran away into the wilderness or countryside and were lost to their masters. Most had come over hoping to become landowners; at the end of seven years, when they became free, many acquired land. Others, leaving before their contracts had expired, had little difficulty disappearing into the mass of free citizens.

What the plantations needed was a cheap and stable labor supply, and slavery met this need. Slavery was a lifetime status; moreover, it was passed on to the slaves' children. The owner was not limited by the expiration of the indenture or by the inconvenience of hiring a new worker. Men and women with black skins could be held for a lifetime of service. An indentured white worker, after eluding his master, might be assimilated in the mass of free workers. Because of their color, runaway Negro slaves could more easily be recognized and captured. Even when they had attained freedom, they were viewed with suspicion when seeking work, and sometimes were thrown back into slavery. As blacks they were held to be descended from Ham, the accursed son of Noah; as pagans, their "savagery" and "barbarism" placed them beyond the pale of civilization, and the usual rites of Christian conduct did not apply to them. As Eric Williams points out, the owners of plantations "would have gone to the moon, if necessary, for labor." But they had Africa, with its seemingly unlimited cheap labor supply. In an essay entitled "On the Populousness of Africa," a British official on the Gold Coast wrote in 1764: "Africa not only can continue supplying the West Indies in the quantities she has hitherto, but, if necessity required it, could spare thousands, nay, millions more, and go on doing the same to the end of time." It was to Africa that the European colonists turned.

The Atlantic Slave Trade

For a short time the Portuguese were preeminent in deriving profits from the transportation of slaves to the New World. In 1493 the Pope had issued a series of papal bulls that established a line of demarcation between the colonial possessions of Spain and Portugal. The West, including the New World, went to Spain, and the East, including Africa and most of the lands in Asia, to Portugal. (A year later, in the Treaty of Tordesillas, Portugal was permitted ownership of Brazil, her sole possession in the New World.) Since the papal judgment excluded Spain from Africa, she was never able to supply her own colonies with slaves. Even if she had been inclined to ignore the papal division, Spain would have found it difficult to engage in the slave trade. [Although] her gold and silver helped to finance the European economic revolution then in progress, Spain's own social system remained basically feudal, and she lacked the capital and industry to make her independent. She had to rely on foreigners to populate her colonies with slaves. . . .

After 1640 the official Spanish contract to supply slaves to her colonies, the *Asiento do Negros,* was awarded to various contractors in turn, and although Portuguese merchants were often able to purchase the exclusive privilege, their monopoly over the trade with the Spanish possessions was broken. While an illegal trade in slaves flourished, and the official policy of exclusiveness was difficult to enforce, the *Asiento* became a highly coveted and bitterly contested prize among nearly all the European powers. There is some question as to whether the *Asiento* was prized for the profits to be made on the slave trade or for the opportunity it provided for illicit sale of other goods in Spanish America in return for silver. Probably both were factors.

England and Holland emerged earliest as capitalist countries; during the sixteenth century the merchant capitalists in both countries achieved preeminence over the landed aristocracy, and during the revolutions of the seventeenth century, they became the dominant force in the state and assumed direction of its policies. For this rising class, the slave trade and the slave plantations in the New World provided an important source of wealth in the crucial period of primitive (or original) accumulation of capital. Nevertheless, in the early years of the slave trade, none of the maritime countries of northern Europe showed much interest in becoming directly involved. Not that they had any scruples. But the high cost of the African slave trade made it unattractive until the end of the sixteenth century. Between 1620 and 1650 the English, Dutch, and French all established colonies in the Caribbean. Sugar cultivation was introduced into these colonies during the 1640s, and the Caribbean islands rapidly developed into large-scale sugar producers. As sugar consumption soared, the vast profits from sugar production quickly justified the high cost of slave importation from Africa. The demand for slaves increased at a phenomenal rate. Having now become a highly profitable business, the slave trade inevitably attracted all maritime Europe. "Strange," writes Eric Williams, "that an article like sugar, so sweet and necessary to human existence, should have occasioned such crimes and bloodshed!"

As early as the sixteenth century, the British and French were already staging occasional raids on Portuguese slavers, but they posed no real threat to Portuguese dominance of the slave coast. The arrival of the Dutch in the seventeenth century, with a formidable navy and the capital and shipping resources of the Dutch West Indian Company, was another matter. The Dutch seized Portuguese vessels on the high seas, established contacts with Africans who opposed the Portuguese, and set up permanent settlements of their own on the Guinea Coast. By the middle of the seventeenth century, the Dutch navy had seized all of the Portuguese forts on the Gold Coast and had even added Luanda and northeastern Brazil to their overseas dominions. Although Portugal lost her preeminent commercial position in West Africa, she soon regained control of Angola and Brazil. The Congo and Angola remained in the hands of the Portuguese and continued to supply Brazil until the end of the slave trade.

In the course of the seventeenth century, other European nations competed for African slaves and built posts along the West African coast: Sweden, Denmark, France, England, even Brandenburg, a province of present-day Germany. Jean Baptiste Colbert's West Indian Company, representing the France of Louis XIV, occupied the mouth of the Senegal River and established an important center there. Although the company failed, a successor was formed that in 1677 captured the important island base of Gorée (near Cape Verde) from the Dutch. By the last quarter of the seventeenth century, the Dutch position on the slave coasts, so strong in midcentury, was being challenged by both England and France.

The English were the chief competitors of the Dutch, and they soon replaced them as the dominant power in the slave trade. English merchants were slow to enter the traffic, for they enjoyed a lucrative trade in gold and ivory with the African tribes and feared that the slave trade might cause a disruption in this commerce. When in the mid-sixteenth century an Englishman, John Lok, carried off five Negroes from the Guinea Coast under the justification that they "were a people of beastly living, without God, law, religion or commonwealth," the trade in gold and ivory was halted, and the London merchants forced Lok to return his booty in order to help them reestablish their trade. No such difficulty, however, confronted Sir John Hawkins in 1562, when he encroached on the Portuguese monopoly of Africa, acquired three hundred Negroes on the Guinea Coast and carried his "good merchandise," as it was described, across the Atlantic on a ship called the Jesus. Aboard this vessel, the psalms of David, the Lord's prayer, and the Creed were recited every evening in the English tongue. Amid these religious surroundings, the Negroes were herded together in pest-ridden holes. Those who survived were sold to the Spaniards in Hispaniola.

Queen Elizabeth, when she first heard of Hawkins' venture, commented that it "was detestable and would call down vengeance from the heavens upon the undertakers. . . ." But when Hawkins came to see her and informed her of his "prosperous success . . . and much gaine to himselfe," she not only forgave him but became a shareholder in his second slaving voyage. After his first venture, Hawkins formed an African company with the leading citizens of London. According to Philip II's Spanish envoy to London, Hawkins' second voyage "brought him 60 per cent profit." As a result, his chronicler happily wrote, "His name therefore be praised, for evermore! Amen."

On three separate occasions Hawkins sailed with his human cargo to the New World—in 1562, 1564, and 1568—and while he attracted increasingly wealthy and powerful backers, he did not inspire many Englishmen to emulate him. As yet

England had no colonies, and when, in the early seventeenth century, she did acquire such colonies in the West Indies and in North America, the colonists obtained their small numbers of Africans from the slave traders of other European nations. But with the introduction of sugarcane in the Barbados in 1641, and the occupation of Jamaica by the British in 1655, the demand for Negroes grew to the point where the English themselves began to transport large numbers of slaves from Africa. The lucrative business was handled by chartered companies. The Royal African Company, chartered in 1672 with the backing of the Duke of York (later King James II), was given a monopoly of the English trade between Cape Blanco on the north and the Cape of Good Hope on the south for one thousand years. No subject of the crown, other than the company, was to visit West Africa except with the company's permission, and the company was authorized to seize ships and cargo infringing on its monopoly. In return, the company promised each year to supply England's American colonial possessions with three thousand slaves.

The Royal African Company established forts along the African coast, but the Dutch opposed the English intrusion, and the two European nations fought an undeclared war over the African trade, with the British emerging victorious. Between 1673 and 1711 the Royal African Company delivered about ninety thousand slaves to England's West Indian and North American colonies. But the company was powerless against the competition of freebooters. The coast was too long and the number of forts too few to prevent interlopers from operating. Some traders bought licenses from the company, but many successfully evaded the attempts to enforce the monopoly privilege and profitably carried slaves to the West Indies. After a long and bitter controversy waged between the Royal African Company and the separate traders, Parliament, in 1712, refused to confirm the company's monopoly. In 1731 the Royal African Company abandoned the slave trade and specialized only in trade in ivory and gold dust. After 1712 any Englishman, including those in the colonies, was free to engage in the African trade.

In the first edition of the *Encyclopaedia Britannica,* published in London in 1771, there is the following entry under *African company*: "A society of merchants, established by King Charles II for trading to Africa; which trade is now laid open to all his majesty's subjects, paying 10 *per cent,* for maintaining the forts." The fact that this trade was in human merchandise was thus concealed.

With the ever-increasing demands of the sugar plantations, the volume of the British slave trade skyrocketed. The British colonies imported 2,130,000 Africans from 1680 to 1786, and the island of Jamaica absorbed as many as 610,000 slaves from 1700 to 1786. Between 1712 and 1721, Bristol ships alone carried 160,950 slaves to the sugar plantations.

But British slave traders did not stop at providing laborers for England's colonial possessions. In 1713, as a result of her victory in the War of Spanish Succession, England was conceded the *Asiento,* the exclusive right to carry slaves to the Spanish colonies for thirty years. British traders were quick to take advantage of the privilege. At the same time, they were furnishing slaves to the French West Indian colonies. It was estimated in 1788 that of the annual British export of slaves from Africa, two-thirds were sold to foreigners, and according to one authority, during the whole of the eighteenth century British slave traders furnished the sugar planters of France and Spain with half a million Africans.

With her powerful navy, her industries capable of supplying the necessary goods, and her unlimited resources in capital for investments, England emerged as the most powerful nation in the slave trade. For most of three centuries, from early in the sixteenth until the middle of the nineteenth, the English dominated the trade, although at various times the French, Dutch, Portuguese, and Americans were active competitors. . . .

If Liverpool was practically built on traffic in slavery, so too was the African trade a key factor in the rise of British industry. The triangular trade, of which the slave trade was the cornerstone, involved the barter of manufactured goods for African slaves; these in turn were sold in the West Indies in exchange either for sugar or for bills of exchange payable in England. The New England slave trade in the mid-eighteenth century was three-cornered, like the British trade. But only three commodities were usually involved: rum, slaves, and molasses. Rum was shipped from Newport, Salem, Boston, and New York to the west coast of Africa. Here it was exchanged for Negroes, who were shipped across the Atlantic to the West Indies and sold mainly for molasses, which would be carried back to New England to be distilled into more rum, to buy more slaves, and so on and on.

The triangular trade stimulated the growth of the shipping, iron, woolen, linen, and cotton goods industries; and the manufacture of cotton goods for the purchase of slaves provided the initial stimulus for the emergence of Manchester as the great cotton-manufacturing center of the world. The trade in slaves provided employment for thousands of British seamen, ship carpenters, riggers, sail makers, ironmongers, rope makers, and makers of cotton, linen, and woolen goods, silk handkerchiefs, guns and ammunition, hardware and household utensils of all kinds. Even though there were some Europeans who saw that the huge sale of firearms to Africans in exchange for slaves might boomerang by enabling Africans to resist, the inexorable requirements of the slave trade overcame such concerns. As Basil Davidson notes, "huge quantities of firearms were poured into West Africa during the major period of the slave trade. . . . At the height of the eighteenth century commerce, gunsmiths in Birmingham (England) alone were exporting muskets to Africa at the rate of between 100,000 and 150,000 a year."

The profits from the triangular trade provided one of the major sources for the accumulation of capital that financed the Industrial Revolution in England. Merchants who made money in the African trade invested their profits in a variety of other industries and in banking, and provided the capital necessary for the "take-off" of England's great industrial development. In the first volume of his classic work, *Capital,* Karl Marx pointed out that, together with the discovery of gold and silver in America, the enslavement of the Indian population, the beginning of "the conquest and lotting" of the East Indies, "the turning of Africa into a warren for the commercial hunting of black skins, signalized the rosy dawn of the era of capitalistic production. These idyllic proceedings are the chief moments of primitive accumulation." As Marx pointed out, all capitalist societies have needed as a condition for their early development what he called "the primitive accumulation of capital." This was a relatively swift, open plundering of wealth to prime the pump, to launch the building of the factory system. In the European countries the slave trade was a primary source of the primitive accumulation of capital, and upon this to no small extent the British, French, and Dutch capitalist systems were built. Thus Marx speaks in *Capital* of European capitalism emerging out of the "bloody womb" of African slavery.

Chapter 3

Slavery, the Constitution, and the Founding Fathers

Mary Frances Berry

Mary Frances Berry, professor of history and law at the University of Pennsylvania and past president of the Organization of American Historians (1990–1991), has been a member of the U.S. Commission on Civil Rights since 1980 (despite President Ronald Reagan's efforts to dismiss her). She currently chairs the commission. Berry previously served as assistant secretary for education in the Department of Health, Education, and Welfare during the Carter Administration. Among her many works, Berry is the author of Black Resistance/White Law: A History of Constitutional Racism in America *(rev. ed., 1994),* Why ERA Failed *(1986),* Military Necessity and Civil Rights Policy *(1977), and* The Politics of Parenthood: Child Care, Women's Rights, and the Myth of the Good Mother *(1993), and co-author of* Long Memory: The Black Experience in America *(1982).*

The following selection is from African Americans and the Living Constitution, *edited by John Hope Franklin and Genna Rae McNeil; "Slavery, the Constitution and the Founding Fathers" by Mary Frances Berry; copyright © 1995 by the Smithsonian Institution. Used by permission of the publisher.*

Neither the U.S. Constitution nor American slavery can be fully understood without examining the proslavery compromises worked out at the Constitutional Convention in 1787. Slavery was expressly sanctioned in three places. [First,] in Article I, Section 2, under the three-fifths clause, three-fifths of a state's slaves—euphemistically referred to as "other persons"—were to be counted for purposes of representation in Congress. Another provision required that any direct tax levied in the states be imposed according to population, but only three-fifths of the slaves were to be counted in determining each state's tax levy. Counting slaves helped the South, but taxing slaves partly nullified this benefit. In Article I, Section 9, Paragraph 4, any capitation (head tax) or other direct tax had to be consistent with the provision of the three-fifths clause. This meant that slaveholders could pay less. [Second,] Article I, Section 9, Paragraph 1 stipulated that the slave trade was not to end before 1808. States that needed more slaves wanted to continue importing them, whereas the older slave states would have preferred terminating importation immediately. [Third], the Constitution sanctioned slavery through the fugitive slave clause in Article IV, Section 2, and the Article V provision prohibiting any amendment of the paragraph on slave importation before 1808. The cumulative effect of these provisions was the direct ratification of slavery.

Other parts of the original Constitution were also helpful to the institution of slavery. Particularly important were the provisions in Article I that prohibited taxes on exports, because slaveholders depended on the agricultural exports produced by slaves. Furthermore, the electoral college provision on its face gave whites in slave states a disproportionate influence in the election of the president. The three-fifths ratio, which enabled slave states to count nonvoting slaves, increased a slave state's representation and thereby its influence in the electoral college, since the electors were chosen on the basis of congressional representation. The significant point to recognize in this discussion is its impact on the power of slaveholders.

Another constitutional provision useful to the slave states was that requiring agreement of three-quarters of the states to ratify a constitutional amendment. Slave states could refuse to ratify any constitutional amendment that curtailed or adversely affected the institution of slavery. The U.S. Supreme Court interpreted Article III's accord of diversity jurisdiction to "citizens" of different states as a prohibition on a slave's right to sue in federal court. If the language had said "inhabitants" of different states—assuming that slaves would be inhabitants and not property—there might have been a stronger basis for jurisdiction. But this assumption may be inappropriate on the basis of the evidence.

After [James] Madison's notes became available in 1836, some abolitionists, led by Wendell Phillips, argued that the Constitution was essentially a proslavery document and pointed out still other proslavery provisions.[1] The military clauses in Article IV, Section 4, Phillips said, called on the federal government to protect the states from domestic violence, including slave rebellions; and Article I, Section 8, required the Congress to call forth the militia to suppress insurrections, including slave rebellions.

When I first read Phillips in law school, I was persuaded by his arguments that we had missed a most important proslavery compromise. I researched the debates in the 1787 convention and ratifying conventions and in 1971 published the results in a book focusing on the federal government's role in suppressing black rebellions, *Black Resistance/White Law: A History of Constitutional Racism in America*.[2] (Perhaps the title of the book was too harsh. A senior scholar in the field of constitutional history insisted I had erred, and that everyone already knew there were only three proslavery compromises.)[3] I am still persuaded that Phillips and the other abolitionists who shared these more expansive views were correct. Beyond the three traditionally cited compromises, these other features are correctly considered the framers' handiwork on the subject of slavery.

These slavery provisions have profoundly affected the predominant African American vision of the Constitution over the past two hundred years, African Americans' status, and aspirations. We know a great deal about the thoughts of free Negroes in the period before the Civil War from newspapers, letters, pamphlets, lectures, and speeches. In the first federal census of 1790, taken three years after the Constitution was approved in Philadelphia, most blacks were slaves, but about 59,000 free Negroes were counted, 27,000 in the North and 32,000 in the South. Their numbers grew rapidly between 1790 and 1810, but subsequently the rate of increase dropped sharply because of restraints on manumission and other hardships. By the time the Constitution was written, blacks in the United States were aware that the unequal political, social, and economic opportunities of their group were a consequence of whites' identification of African ancestry with inferiority and subordination. Arguing for greater opportunities for persons of African descent and for the abolition of slavery, numbers of blacks noted that in ratifying slavery the Constitution had betrayed the promises of the Declaration of Independence, which had stated that everyone had a right to life, liberty, and the pursuit of happiness. At the same time, many denounced the hypocrisy of the Declaration for not including blacks as beneficiaries of its promises.

In the years immediately after the Convention, African Americans did not have access to Madison's notes and other materials that have come to light since then, but they were contemporaries of the Constitution makers. In the absence of records of the debates at the Convention, they could, when it suited their purposes, use the very vagueness of some of the Constitution's wording to support arguments that the Constitution stood for freedom and rights. As petitioners, they noted the potential for antislavery action in the Fifth Amendment of the Bill of Rights and the clauses in the original document pertaining to interstate commerce, general welfare, and the guarantee of a republican form of government. They could—and did—assert that Congress could, therefore, manumit contraband slaves, prohibit the coastal and interstate slave trade, ban slavery from the territories and other property of the United States, enlist slaves in the armed forces, and even take private property for public use by purchasing and emancipating slaves. Although there was not doubt that the Constitution had ratified slavery in the states, it was certainly still open to debate whether some antislavery objectives could be achieved under its provisions.

Most African Americans avoided choosing emigration or attacking the Constitution, preferring instead to advance the antislavery cause by swaddling themselves in arguments emphasizing the Constitution's potential.[4] In short, these African Americans, like some literalists and original-intent adherents today, chose to base their arguments only on the words in the document, insisting that their interpretation of original intent was the only one possible. They asserted that the Constitution could be interpreted in such a way as to support abolition, or at least the containment of slavery.

In those early years of the nation, there was an overriding impression of consensus among African Americans: no matter how one interpreted the language of the Constitution, the slaveholders held the reins of power. To unseat this class would require political action and moral suasion, or, as many others eventually came to agree, it could only be accomplished through the violence of a civil war.[5] African Americans looked to other provisions of the Constitution as they considered their predicament and the means for improvement. They and their white allies were very fond of the First Amendment because it led them to hope that their right to petition the Congress and to assemble in protest would be protected. They were decidedly unimpressed with the Tenth Amendment and the federalism it promoted because states' rights then, as today, permitted discrimination and subordination in the states without interference by the national government. They found, unfortunately, that their protests were not protected automatically from state suppression because in those days the First Amendment applied to federal and not to state action.

Frederick Douglass, a former slave and ardent abolitionist, perhaps best summed up the antebellum view of the Constitution. In 1849 he pointed out that the Constitution's words could be taken to express antislavery sentiment, but that the meaning of the Constitution given to it by the framers and those with the power to interpret it made it a proslavery document. He explained:

> Had the Constitution dropped down from the blue overhanging sky, upon a land uncursed by slavery, and without an interpreter, although some difficulty might have occurred in applying its manifold provisions, yet so cunningly is it framed, that no one would have imagined that it recognized or sanctioned slavery. But having a terrestrial, and not a celestial origin, we find no difficulty in ascertaining its meaning in all the parts which we allege to relate to slavery. . . . [The Constitution] was made in view of the existence of slavery, and in a manner well calculated to aid and strengthen that heaven-daring crime.[6]

When as a result of the bloodshed and violence of the Civil War and Reconstruction, the Constitution was amended to include the Thirteenth, Fourteenth, and Fifteenth Amendments, the legacy of slavery remained prominent in the African American vision of the new reality. This vision was apparent at the centennial of the Constitution's writing, observed in 1887. Among the approximately seven million African Americans in the country at that time, most of whom lived in the South, the badges of slavery persisted. Frederick Douglass pointed out how much they relied on the Constitution when the promise of freedom seemed abandoned forever:

> I now undertake to say that neither the original Constitution nor the Constitution as amended since the War is the law of the land. That Constitution has been slain in the house of its friends. So far as the colored people of the country are concerned, the Constitution is but a stupendous sham . . . keeping the promise to the eye and breaking it to the heart. . . . They have promised us law and abandoned us to anarchy.[7]

Yet there was more to celebrate in 1887 than there had been in 1787. Slavery was depicted in the centennial exposition floats in Philadelphia, and despite offers of payment, organizers could not find blacks to play the role of plantation slaves. Incongruously, some of the banners in the African American part of the exposition proclaimed enfranchisement and full political rights.[8] Even so, the trend in the South, where most blacks lived, was already well on the way toward almost total disfranchisement.

Slavery was also visible in the African American vision of the Constitution as interpreted by the Supreme Court of the United States. The Court's influence permeated the *Slaughterhouse Cases* that acknowledged the one pervading purpose of the Fourteenth Amendment.[9] The *Civil Rights Cases* further weakened the ability of the Fourteenth Amendment to remove badges and incidents of slavery.[10] Tragically, *Plessy v. Ferguson* reduced the badges of slavery to a figment of the black imagination.[11]

Slavery was fundamental in the rationale of white Southerners for the political disfranchisement, economic oppression, and punishment of African Americans. White Southerners argued that African Americans were still not far enough removed from the slave condition to be positive participants in the political process. In the Southern states, where the majority of the black population lived, the recent history of slavery loomed large in the decisions handed down during military reconstruction. Some, for example, prohibited whites from reenslaving black children as "apprentices," and others protected blacks from disproportionately harsh punishment in the criminal justice system. Slavery as context, as definition for all that occurred to African Americans, was prevalent even in the highest state courts.

Throughout the late nineteenth century, when racial fairness appeared impossible, slavery remained an ever-present force both in legal and social affairs. The North Carolina Court, just in time to set the right tone for the centennial celebrations, struck down the statute earmarking taxes paid by Negroes only for the Negro schools and by whites only for the white schools, explaining that because of slavery, "the vast bulk of property yielding the fruits of taxation belongs to the white people of the state and very little is held by the emancipated race." The court hastened to say, however, that it was not questioning the constitutionality of separate schools, or laws forbidding the intermarriage of the races; these were made more necessary by the abolition of slavery.[12]

The centennial period notwithstanding, state courts at the highest levels, the most visible representatives of a justice system in the South, continued to hand down decisions acknowledging the ideals of slavery. The Alabama high court, in refusing to convict, as demanded by "her mistress, a colored girl, 17 or 18 years of age," for burning down the house in which she lived and worked, noted that her confession could be attributed to the fact that "her mistress" routinely disciplined her by whipping. The court did not find whipping, which was a routine punishment administered to slaves, unusual in 1887 but thought since there was no other evidence that the girl set the fire at the house, being locked up and whipped might have meant the confession was false.[13]

Cases declaring the illegitimacy of intimate relations between whites and blacks were common, indicating there were many such relationships and an eagerness to end them. White men were often involved. A case in Yazoo County, Mississippi, decided in the centennial year, involved a white man and "a colored woman" who had been jointly convicted. They had been seen together in bed; he was frequently at her house. She had two mulatto children and he "had been heard to call them his children." The court upheld the conviction. Before slavery became illegal, she could have been his concubine, as was not unusual. After the Thirteenth Amendment was passed, it became important, as the prosecutor told the jury, to maintain appropriate social relations by punishing miscegenation "as a stigma on both races."[14] As in so many things, the North had already shown the importance of strictures concerning interracial sex in a state of so-called freedom, by its law and policies concerning relationships between blacks and whites.

The courts spoke most directly about slavery in the numerous cases from 1870 to 1900 involving legacies and bequests to freedmen. In a case decided by the Virginia high court in 1887, the descendants of slaves filed a lawsuit after failing repeatedly in their attempts to collect a promised legacy. A plantation owner in Danville had left his fifteen slaves to his heirs in an 1862 will with the understanding that they would be set free seven years after his death and taken to a free state. They were also to be given one half of what they would be worth to his estate and $3,000. He instructed his heirs to pay the money out of a surplus he had in his estate in 1865. He added this provision to this will, and shortly thereafter he died. A few months later, the slaves were freed by the war's results, and they asked for their legacy. The high court decided that the end of the war did not automatically invalidate the former slaves' right to the legacy. As it turned out, however, the heirs did not have to pay them because the legacy, unlike the rest of the estate that the heirs could keep, was to be taken out of the surplus, which was in worthless Confederate money.[15]

Race and the badges of slavery entered into every type of legal matter during the centennial era and thereafter. A court describing the routine issuance of a summons emphasized that it was given to "a white person over the age of sixteen years."[16] All during the proceedings of a tort case in which the value of the life of a black man who was killed accidentally as a result of turning on the light switches for the company where he worked, the court described everyone in racial terms, as did the lawyers and the witnesses: X "a white man" was a witness for the "colored widow," X "(white)" testified that the deceased whose wife was his house servant "was . . . of average intelligence for a colored man."[17] But at least blacks could bring lawsuits and appear as parties—and could sometimes win—which would have been impossible under pre–Civil War restrictions.[18]

The African American vision of the Founding Fathers, of the meaning of slavery, and of the Constitution in 1787 and 1887 was shaped by political, economic, and legal conditions. That vision was consistently suffused with both hope and suspicion of a kind that persists to this day. The Founding Fathers created a framework of government that has served many purposes. In protecting slavery and assuming racial inequality, they made African Americans outsiders from the beginning. They also provided a rationale that could be used by non-African Americans to assume the basic worthlessness, powerlessness, and inhumanity of African Americans as a part of the nation's legacy. Even though by the time of the centennial there had been a great deal of violence and their work had been modified and improved upon, the pall of slavery's influence remained. The pall was still present at the Constitution's bicentennial, although it had diminished somewhat.

An unstated premise of many discussions about intelligence and qualifications is that blackness is associated with inferiority and subordination. In recent years, discussions about African Americans and legal rights under the Constitution have often turned on how far away blacks are from slavery. Many a conversation with a white American has begun, "My grand-daddy did not have any slaves, and anyway slavery was a long time ago and why do we still need to remedy vestiges and discuss redress." But many have also revolved around the economic disparities that continue to plague black communities. In some of these conversations, speakers emphasize the reality of legally enforced slavery, which means blacks should not expect to close the gap and become equal, except for a few extraordinary individuals who ought to be thankful instead of complaining.

The African American vision of the Constitution as it was written in 1787 can be characterized as an affirmation of exploitation and exclusion. By 1887 the Constitution had come to represent inclusion in language but exclusion in reality. Today African Americans see in it a continuing struggle for inclusion. Our lives begin and end taking into account that vision of us crafted by the Founding Fathers in the Constitution. The role we have today they might not have envisioned, but certainly our African American ancestors did.

Because there was slavery, the free Negroes bore the burden of having blackness identified with subordination. Because there was slavery, the Thirteenth, Fourteenth, and Fifteenth Amendments came into being, and because some of the slaves were women, the Nineteenth Amendment was not made fully effective for women of minority groups until the Voting Rights Act of 1965. Because there was slavery, there was Jim Crow and segregation and a race-imbued justice system. Because there was slavery, there were civil rights movements; there was litigation for rights and jail for those who fought for those rights. There were lost jobs and death in the name of improving our lives and the constitutional imperatives under which we live. Because there was slavery, there is debate over remedies and correctives such as affirmative action, school busing, self-help, and black community organization designed to overcome the lingering effects of slavery. Because there was slavery, the most important features of the Constitution are the amending clause in Article V and the power of interpretation by the Supreme Court under Article III. Because there was slavery, the appointment power for Supreme Court justices under Article II, providing for a sharing of power between the president and the Senate, has to be kept constantly on our minds.

We need to remember that, interpreting the same Constitution, one group of judges said forced segregation was wrong in 1954 but another said it was perfectly legal in 1896. We must worry about who is appointed to the courts and what they will say in the future. Because there was slavery, we read and hear every day that the United States is not ready for a black man to become president, not just Jesse Jackson. Because there was slavery, we have race and slavery on our minds, and we are likely to keep it on our minds until it is obviously on no one's minds in ways that constrict the freedom and opportunities of African Americans. Therefore, when we think about everything important to our well-being, including the Constitution and the Founding Fathers, our vision, our African American vision, remains preoccupied and on guard. But perhaps it is not simply because there was slavery, but because the vision of others was shaped by slavery, and because most African Americans still experience unpleasant reminders that we are the descendants of those who were enslaved.

NOTES

1. "The Constitution—a Pro-slavery Compact," in *Selections from the Madison Papers,* ed. Wendell Phillips, 2d ed. rev. (New York: Anti-slavery Society, 1845), 5–9.

2. Mary Frances Berry, *Black Resistance/White Law: A History of Constitutional Racism in America* (Englewood Cliffs, N.J.: Prentice Hall, 1971).

3. Staughton Lynd advances a similar interpretation in *Slavery, Class Conflict, and the Constitution* (Indianapolis: Bobbs-Merrill, 1967). Lynd also suggests that the Northwest Ordinance, outlawing slavery in the Northwest territory, passed while the convention was in session, was part of the pattern of compromises concerning slavery. See also Staughton Lynd, "The Compromise of 1787," *Political Science Quarterly* 81 (1966): 225–50.

4. David Brion Davis, *The Problem of Slavery in the Age of Revolution* (Ithaca: Cornell University Press, 1975), 130. See also John Hope Franklin and Alfred A. Moss Jr., *From Slavery to Freedom: A History of Negro Americans,* 6th ed. rev. (New York: Alfred Knopf, 1987), 76–77.

5. Mary Frances Berry and John W. Blassingame, *Long Memory: The Black Experience in America* (New York: Oxford University Press, 1982), 60–66.

6. Frederick Douglass, "The Constitution and Slavery" (*North Star,* March 16, 1849), in *The Life and Writings of Frederick Douglass,* ed. Philip S. Foner, 4 vols. (New York: International Publishers, 1950–), I, 363.

7. Frederick Douglass, "Speech on the Occasion of the Twenty-Fourth Anniversary of Emancipation in the District of Columbia, Washington D.C., 1886," in *The Life and Writings of Frederick Douglass,* ed. Philip S. Foner, IV, 431.

8. Leon Litwack, "Trouble in Mind: The Bicentennial and the Afro-American Experience," *Journal of American History* 74 (September 1987): 315–37, and notes cited on p. 315. See also Leon Litwack, *Been in the Storm So Long: The Aftermath of Slavery* (New York: Alfred Knopf, 1979), chap. 5.

9. 16 Wallace 36 (1873).

10. 109 U.S. 3 (1883).

11. 163 U.S. 437 (1896).

12. *Puitt v. Gaston County,* 94 North Carolina 709 (1886).

13. *Hoober v. State,* 81 Ala. 51 (1887).

14. *Steward v. State,* 64 Miss. 626 (1887).

15. *Allen et al. v. Patton Als.,* 83 Va. 255 (1887).

16. *Stolz v. Collins,* 83 Va. 824 (1887).

17. *Piedmont Electric Illinois Co. v. Patteson's Adm.,* 84 Va. 18 (1887).

18. This material on state courts is drawn from my ongoing research on how white women and black males as well as females fared in cases in the state courts in the South from Reconstruction to 1900.

Chapter 4

Our Pro-Slavery Constitution

William Lloyd Garrison

William Lloyd Garrison (1805–1879) founded and edited the Liberator *(1831–1865), an abolitionist weekly, and was a founder of the American Anti-Slavery Society. At an 1854 Independence Day gathering in Framingham, Massachusetts, he burned a copy of the Constitution, saying: "So perish all compromises with tyranny!" The masthead for his newspaper restated his point: "[T]he compact which exists between the North and the South is a 'covenant with death, and an agreement with hell,'—involving both parties in atrocious criminality,—and should be immediately annulled." For biographies, see Henry Mayer,* All on Fire: William Lloyd Garrison and the Abolition of Slavery *(1998) and James Brewer Stewart,* William Lloyd Garrison and the Challenge of Emancipation *(1991).*

The following selection is excerpted from "The United States Constitution," Selections from the Writings and Speeches of William Lloyd Garrison *(1852).*

For another selection by Garrison, see chapter 12.

There are some very worthy men, who are gravely trying to convince this slave-holding and slave-trading nation, that it has an Anti-Slavery Constitution, if it did but know it—always has had it since it was a nation—and so designed it to be from the beginning! Hence, all slaveholding under it is illegal, and ought in virtue of it to be forthwith-abolished by act of Congress. . . .

'To ascertain the meaning of the Constitution,' we are told, 'we are to subject it, as we do any other law, to the strict rules of legal interpretation.' It seems to us that this statement is extremely fallacious. The Constitution is not a statute, but a UNION, a COMPACT formed between separate and independent colonies, with conflicting interests and diverse sentiments, to be reconciled in the best manner possible, by concession and compromise, for the attainment of a common object—their own safety and welfare against a common enemy. What those concessions and compromises were, all knew when the compact was framed and adopted: they related to the prosecution of the foreign slave trade for twenty years, to the allowance of a slave representation in Congress, to the hunting of fugitive slaves, and to the suppression of domestic insurrections, for the special benefit of the slave States; and to direct taxation and the navigation laws, in behalf of the free States. . . . The people of this country have bound themselves by an oath to have no other God before them than the CONSTITUTIONAL GOD, which their own hands have made, and to which they demand homage of every one born or resident on the American soil, on peril of imprisonment or death! His fiat is 'the supreme law of the land.'

It is said, that with the intention of the framers of the Constitution, we do not need to concern ourselves, 'any more than with the intention of the scrivener whom we employ to write the deed of a parcel of land.' We see no pertinency in the illustration: the analogy is defective. A scrivener employed to write a deed—to write as ordered by us—to write according to an approved and established form; in the name of common sense, is he, or his avocation, or his deed, or all together, to be compared with a deliberative assembly, chosen by popular suffrage, and invested with powers to frame a new government, in some shape or other endurable, if not every thing desirable! . . .

Again it is said, we are to look after the intention of the adopters, not that of the framers of the Constitution. We do not see that any thing is gained by this distinction. That the adopters and framers of that instrument understood its conditions and requirements in precisely the same manner is historically certain; and especially as to whatever is in it relating to slavery and the slave trade. The law of Congress, providing for the recapture of fugitive slaves, was passed almost immediately after the adoption of the Constitution: who cried out against it as unconstitutional? When Southern representatives of the slave population (on the three-fifths basis) first made their appearance in Congress, who raised his voice against them in the name of the Constitution? The foreign slave traffic was prosecuted under our star-spangled banner more vigorously after than before the adoption of that instrument: who dreamed of its being an illegal trade? There were at least six hundred thousand slaves in the country, at the adoption of the Constitution: who thought, believed, or proclaimed, that they were made free by it? If, then, they who adopted it so understood and so designed it, how came the slaveholding South to vote for it? and how came it to pass, that, under the 'supreme law of the land,' not a single slave thereby became free? When was the will, yes, the very purpose of a people, so instantly nullified before? 'The slave system, it was supposed, (!) could not extend beyond that generation'; but though the Constitution demanded its abolition, neither during that generation was it applied, nor has it been at any subsequent period, in any other manner than to extend and perpetuate what it was framed to suppress! All logical gravity terminates here in loud and long-protracted laughter.

But this is not the height of this folly. We are told, that it was thought better to let slavery live on in sufferance through that generation, at least, than to disturb the infant and unconsolidated nation by putting an immediate stop to it! So, then, even at that period, an attempt to give the slaves the benefit of the Anti-Slavery Constitution aforesaid would have convulsed the land, and blown the Union sky high! Undoubtedly; because no such Constitution was ever adopted, and for no other reason! And is any one so infatuated as to believe, that what could not be done sixty years ago, with only six hundred thousand slaves to be liberated, without convulsing the country, can now be done 'by the strict rules of legal interpretation,' in utter disregard of all the facts and all the precedents in our national history, with fifteen instead of six slave States, and three millions of slaves, without filling the land with a deluge of blood? Supposing—what is not within the scope of probabilities—that we could win over to their view of the Constitution a majority, ay, the entire body of the people of the North, so that they could control the action of Congress through their representatives, and in this manner decree the abolition of slavery throughout the South— could we hope to witness even the enactment of such a decree, (to say nothing of its enforcement,) without its being accompanied by the most fearful consequences? Does any reply, that a fear of consequences should not deter us from doing right? This is cheerfully granted: but are these Anti-Slavery interpreters ready for a civil war, as the inevitable result of their construction of the Constitution? What reason have they to believe, from the past, that a civil war would not immediately follow, in the case supposed? . . .

Away with all verbal casuistry, all legal quibbling . . . to prove that the United States Constitution is an Anti-Slavery instrument! It is worse than labor lost, and, as a false issue, cannot advance, but must rather retard, the Anti-Slavery movement. Let there be no dodging; no shuffling, no evasion. Let us confess the sin of our fathers, and our own sin as a people, in conspiring for the degradation and enslavement of the colored race among us. Let us be honest with the facts of history, and acknowledge the compromises that were made to secure the adoption of the Constitution, and the consequent establishment of the Union. Let us, who profess to abhor slavery, and who claim to be freemen indeed, dissolve the bands that connect us with the Slave Power, religiously and politically; not doubting that a faithful adherence to principle will be the wisest policy, the highest expediency, for ourselves and our posterity, for the miserable victims of Southern oppression, and for the cause of liberty throughout the world. . . .

We charge upon the present national compact, that it was formed at the expense of human liberty, by a profligate surrender of principle, and to this hour is cemented with human blood.

We charge upon the American Constitution, that it contains provisions, and enjoins duties, which make it unlawful for freemen to take the oath of allegiance to it, because they are expressly designed to favor a slaveholding oligarchy, and, consequently, to make one portion of the people a prey to another.

It was pleaded at the time of its adoption, it is pleaded now, that, without such a compromise, there could have been no union; that, without union, the colonies would have become an easy prey to the mother country [Great Britain]; and, hence, that it was an act of necessity, deplorable indeed when viewed alone, but absolutely indispensable to the safety of the republic.

To this we reply: The plea is as profligate as the act was tyrannical. It is the . . . doctrine, that the end sanctifies the means. It is a confession of sin, but the denial of any guilt in its perpetration. This plea is sufficiently broad to cover all the oppression and villainy that the sun has witnessed in his circuit, since God said, 'Let there be light.' It assumes that to be practicable which is impossible, namely, that there can be freedom with slavery, union with injustice, and safety with blood-guiltiness. A union of virtue with pollution is the triumph of licentiousness. A partnership between right and wrong is wholly wrong. A compromise of the principles of justice is the deification of crime.

Better that the American Union had never been formed, than that it should have been obtained at such a frightful cost! If they were guilty who fashioned it, but who could not foresee all its frightful consequences, how much more guilty are they, who, in full view of all that has resulted from it, clamor for its perpetuity! . . .

The fact is, the compromise alluded to, instead of effecting a union, rendered it impracticable; unless by the term union we are to understand the absolute reign of the slave-holding power over the whole country, to the prostration of Northern rights. It is not certain, it is not even probable, that if the present Constitution had not been adopted, the mother country would have reconquered the colonies. The spirit that would have chosen danger in preference to crime, to perish with justice rather than live with dishonor, to dare and suffer whatever might betide [happen] rather than sacrifice the rights of one human being, could never have been subjugated by any mortal power. Surely, it is paying a poor tribute to the valor and devotion of our revolutionary fathers in the cause of liberty, to say that, if they had sternly refused to sacrifice their principles, they would have fallen an easy prey to the despotic power of England. . . .

It is absurd, it is false, it is an insult to the common sense of mankind, to pretend that the Constitution was intended to embrace the entire population of the country under its sheltering wings; or that the parties to it were actuated by a sense of justice and the spirit of impartial liberty; or that it needs no alteration, but only a new interpretation, to make it harmonize with the object aimed at by its adoption. As truly might it be argued, that because it is asserted in the Declaration of Independence, that all men are created equal, and endowed with an inalienable right to liberty, therefore none of its signers were slaveholders, and since its adoption slavery has been banished from the American soil! The truth is, our fathers were intent on securing liberty to themselves without being very scrupulous as to the means they used to accomplish their purpose. They were not actuated by the spirit of universal philanthropy; and though in words they recognised occasionally the brotherhood of the human race, in practice they continually denied it. They did not blush to enslave a portion of their fellow-men, and to buy and sell them as cattle in the market, while they were fighting against the oppression of the mother country, and boasting of their regard for the rights of man. Why, then, concede to them virtues which they did not possess? . . .

Three millions of the American people are crushed under the American Union! They are held as slaves, trafficked as merchandise, registered as goods and chattels! The government gives them no protection—the government is their enemy, the government keeps them in chains! Where they lie bleeding, we are prostrate by their side—in their sorrows and sufferings we participate—their stripes are inflicted on our bodies, their shackles are fastened on our limbs, their cause is ours! The Union which grinds them to the dust rests upon us, and with them we will struggle to overthrow it! The Constitution which subjects them to hopeless bondage is one that we cannot swear to support. Our motto is, 'NO UNION WITH SLAVEHOLDERS,' either religious or political. They are the fiercest enemies of mankind, and the bitterest foes of God! We separate from them, not in anger, not in malice, not for a selfish purpose, not to do them an injury, not to cease warning, exhorting, reproving them for their crimes, not to leave the perishing bondman to his fate—O no! But to clear our skirts of innocent blood—to give the oppressor no countenance—and to hasten the downfall of slavery in America, and throughout the world! . . .

The form of government that shall succeed the present government of the United States, let time determine. It would be a waste of time to argue that question, until the people are regenerated and turned from their iniquity. Ours is no anarchical movement, but one of order and obedience. In ceasing from oppression, we establish liberty. What is now fragmentary shall in due time be crystalized, and shine like a gem set in the heavens, for a light to all coming ages.

Chapter 5

Slave Religion, Rebellion, and Docility

Albert J. Raboteau

Albert J. Raboteau, professor of religion at Princeton University, is the author of
A Fire in the Bones: Reflections on African American Religious History *(1995)*
and co-editor of African American Religion: Interpretive Essays in History and
Culture *(1997).*

The following selection is reprinted with permission from Slave Religion: The
"Invisible Institution" in the Antebellum South *(New York: Oxford University*
Press, 1978), footnotes deleted.

The tendency of Christianity to support the established order has long been noted
and criticized by some. It has been alleged that Christianity, and its otherworldly,
compensatory emphasis, is a religion particularly fitted for slaves. . . . [M]issionar-
ies from the colonial S[ociety for the] P[ropagation of the] G[ospel] to the antebellum advocates of plantation missions labored long and hard to convince masters
that this was so. Yet temporal rulers—from provincial governors in the late
Roman empire, to medieval kings and emperors, down to presidents of modern
states—have had abundant opportunity to ponder the disruptive implications of a
religious conscience owing ultimate allegiance to a "higher authority" than their
own. Clerical and civil leaders have appealed for centuries to the sayings of
Jesus—"My kingdom is not of this world," "Blessed are the meek," "Render to
Caesar the things that are Caesar's, to God the things that are God's"—to validate
obedience to authority. Yet Christians individually and in groups have disagreed,
sometimes violently, with their rulers, ecclesiastical and political, about what was
legitimately Caesar's and what God's. Revolutionary interpretations of the Bible
by such slaves as [Denmark] Vesey and [Nat] Turner were proof to American
slaveholders that slave Christianity could become a double-edged sword.

As early as 1774 American slaves were declaring publicly and politically that
they thought Christianity and slavery were incompatible. In that year the governor
of Massachusetts received "The Petition of a Grate Number of Blacks of this
Province who by divine permission are held in a state of slavery within the bowels
of a free and Christian Country." The petitioners protested that "we have in common with other men a natural right to our freedoms without being deprived of
them by our fellowman. . . . There is a great number of us sencear . . . members of

the Church of Christ. . . . Bear ye onenothers Bordens How can the master be said to Beare my Borden when he Beares me down with the Have [heavy] chanes of slavery and operson [oppression] against my will . . . how can the slave perform the duties of a husband to a wife or parent to his child . . . [?]" In arguing for their freedom, these New England slaves combined the political rhetoric of the [American] Revolution with appeals to the claims of Christian fellowship. Most slaves had to keep publicly silent about their attitudes, but in private they condemned the hypocrisy of Christian slaveowners. Frederick Douglass, who himself composed a bitterly ironic attack on slaveholding Christianity as an appendix to his *Narrative,* claimed that "Slaves knew enough of the orthodox theology of the time to consign all bad slaveholders to hell." And Charles Ball recorded that in his experience, slaves thought that heaven would not be heaven unless slaves would be avenged on their enemies. "A fortunate and kind master or mistress, may now and then be admitted into heaven, but this rather as a matter of favour, to the intercession of some slave, then as a matter of strict justice to the whites, who will, by no means, be of an equal rank with those who shall be raised from the depths of misery in this world." Ball concluded that "The idea of a revolution in the conditions of the whites and blacks, is the cornerstone of the religion of the latter . . ."

. . . . [T]he slaves' confidence in the ultimate condemnation of slaveholders was supported by manifestations of their masters' guilt. John Brown recalled his master's deathbed attempt to save his soul:

> There was my old master Thomas Stevens. Ever so many times before his time was come. But though he . . . recovered from his illnesses, in his frights he sent for us all and asked us to forgive him. Many a time he would exclaim, that he wished 'he'd never seen a nigger.' I remember his calling old Aunt Sally to him and begging and praying of her to get the devil away from behind the door, and such like.

Brown goes on to generalize: "It is a common belief amongst us that all the masters die in an awful fright, for it is usual for the slaves to be called up on such occasions to say they forgive them for what they have done. So we come to think their minds must be dreadfully uneasy about holding slaves . . . All this may seem to be trifling, but it is the truth . . . and I only give what I have myself experienced." Brown's observation is certainly not "trifling." For slaves to perceive their master's guilt-filled dread and to see him begging for their prayers and forgiveness vindicated their belief in final retribution and demonstrated not only their moral superiority to whites but also a serious measure of psychological and emotional control over them.

In the slaves' moral judgement, ministers in particular were deserving of condemnation. "The ministers used to tell us not to be disorderly on taking the sacrament," observed James Sumler. "I thought he was disorderly himself, for he kept slaves." . . .

Slaves distinguished the hypocritical religion of their masters from true Christianity and rejected the slaveholder's gospel of obedience to master and mistress. Ex-slave Douglas Dorsey reported that after the minister on his plantation admonished the slaves to honor their masters, whom they could see, as they would God, whom they could not see, "the driver's wife who could read and write a little" would say that the minister's sermon "was all lies." Lunsford Lane recounted an incident when a "kind-hearted clergyman . . . who was very popular with the colored people" made the mistake of preaching "a sermon to us in which he argued from the Bible that it was the will of Heaven from all eternity that we should be slaves, and our masters be our owners, [and] many of us left him . . ." From the other side of the pulpit, Charles Colcock Jones recalled a similar reaction to a sermon he gave before a slave congregation in 1833:

> I was preaching to a large congregation on the *Epistle of Philemon*: and when I insisted upon fidelity and obedience as Christian virtues in servants and upon the authority of Paul, condemned the practice of *running away*, one half of my audience deliberately rose up and walked off with themselves, and those that remained looked any thing but satisfied, either with the preacher or his doctrine. After dismission, there was no small stir among them; some solemnly declared 'that there was no such an Epistle in the Bible'; others, 'that they did not care if they ever heard me preach again!' . . . There were some too, who had strong objections against me as a Preacher because I was a *master,* and said, 'his people have to work as well as we.'

According to Lewis and Milton Clarke, slaves believed that there existed somewhere a real Bible from God, "but they frequently say the Bible now used is master's Bible," since all that they heard from it was "Servants, obey your masters."

Some slaves' inner rejection of "white folks religion" was expressed outwardly by their rejection of their masters' denomination. The slaves of a mean master named Gooch, according to Moses Roper, figured that their master was such "a bad sample of what a professing Christian ought to be" that they refused to "join the connexion [Baptist] he belonged to thinking they must be a very bad set of people" and joined instead the Methodist Church.

Nowhere is the slaves' rejection of the master's religion clearer than in their refusal to obey moral precepts held up to them by whites, especially commands against stealing. While white preachers repeatedly urged "Don't steal," slaves just as persistently denied that this commandment applied to them, since they themselves were stolen property. Josephine Howard demonstrated how the structure of white morality could collapse when examined from the slaves' point of view: "Dey allus done tell us it am wrong to lie and steal, but why did de white foks steal my mammy and her mammy? Dey lives clost to some water, somewheres over in Africy, and de man come in a little boat to de sho' and tell dem he got presents on de big boat . . . and my mammy and her mammy gits took out to dat big boat and dey locks dem in a black hole what mammy say so black you can't see nothin'. Dat de sinfulles' stealin' dey is." Charles Brown, a fugitive slave from Virginia, claimed that he had expressed the same argument to his master's face: "I told my master one day—said I, 'You white folks set the bad example of stealing—you stole us from Africa, and not content with that, if any got free here, you stole them afterward, and so we are made slaves.'" According to George Womble, who had been a slave in Georgia, "slaves were taught to steal by their masters. Sometimes they were sent to the nearby plantations to steal chickens, pigs and other things that could be carried away easily. At such times the master would tell them that he was not going to mistreat them and that he was not going to allow anyone else to mistreat them and that by taking the above mentioned things they were helping him to be more able to take care of them." . . .

Religious faith sometimes sustained the decision of slaves to flee or to revolt. Slave rebelliousness should not be thought of exclusively in terms of acts such as arson, sabotage, flight or revolt, for religion itself, in a very real sense, could be an act of rebelliousness—an assertion of slave independence, which sometimes required outright defiance of the master's command. . . .

When the master's will conflicted with God's, slaves faced a choice which was simultaneously an opportunity to assert their own free will and to act virtuously, even heroically, in the context of Christianity, in which disobedience to white authority, no matter the consequence, could seem morally imperative. When Thomas Jones, for example, grew concerned about the state of his soul, his master told him to stop moping about, forbade him to attend prayer meetings, and ordered him to stop praying. In spite of repeated and severe whippings, Jones persisted in attending Methodist class meetings and refused to promise that he would abandon prayer. Eli Johnson claimed that when he was threatened with five hundred lashes for holding prayer meetings, he stood up to his master and declared, "In the name of God why is it, that I can't after working hard all the week, have a meeting on Saturday evening? I'll suffer the flesh to be dragged off my bones . . . for the sake of my blessed Redeemer." . . .

Prayer was such an effective symbol of resistance because both masters and slaves believed in the power of prayer. Hence the desperate need of some masters and mistresses for slaves to pray for the success of the Confederacy, and hence their anger when slaves dissembled or refused outright to do so. . . .

Slaves prayed for the future day of deliverance to come, and they kept hope alive by incorporating as part of *their* mythic past the Old Testament exodus of Israel out of slavery. The appropriation of the Exodus story was for the slaves a way of articulating their sense of historical identity as a people. That identity was also based, of course, upon their common heritage of enslavement. The Christian slaves applied the Exodus story, whose end they knew, to their own experience of slavery, which had not ended. In identifying with the Exodus story, they created meaning and purpose out of the chaotic and senseless experience of slavery. Exodus functioned as an archetypal event for the slaves. . . .

The story of Israel's exodus from Egypt helped make it possible for the slaves to project a future radically different from their present. From other parts of the Bible, especially the prophetic and apocalyptic books, the slaves drew descriptions which gave form and, thus, assurance to their anticipation of deliverance. The troublesome question, according to Aunt Ellen, a freed woman in North Carolina, had not been *if* the slaves would be free, but *when*: "When we used to think about it, it 'peared like de Judgement, sure to come, but a powerful step off." As that "powerful step" loomed closer with the beginning and progress of the war, slaves turned, as had generations of Christians before them in time of crisis, to the biblical promises of God for reassurance. . . .

Not all slaves took solace in religion. Some slaves would not accept belief in a supposedly just God who could will or permit slavery. If God was all-just and all-powerful, why did the innocent suffer and injustice reign? was a question which devastated faith in the minds of some slaves. "I pretended to profess religion one time," recalled one. "I don't hardly know what to think about religion. They say God killed the just and unjust; I don't understand that part of it. It looks hard to think that if you ain't done nothing in the world you be punished just like the wicked. Plenty folks went crazy trying to get that straightened out." Nor did all slaves distinguish true Christianity from that practiced by their masters: for them it remained a white man's religion. . . .

Two poles of behavior, accommodation and rebelliousness, have been the foci for discussion about slave personality and slave-master relationship. Slave testimony indicates that Christianity supported both, influencing some slaves to accept and others to rebel against their enslavement. But these were not the only alternatives. Religion, especially the revivalistic, inward, experientially oriented religion to which many slaves and masters adhered, had an egalitarian tendency which occasionally led to moments of genuine religious mutuality, whereby blacks and whites preached to, prayed for, and converted each other in situations where the status of master and slave was, at least for the moment, suspended. In the fervor of religious worship, master and slave, white and black, could be found sharing a common event, professing a common faith and experiencing a common ecstasy. "I have witnessed . . . many a season of refreshing in which master, mistress, and slave alike participated, and seen them all rejoice together," remarked H. J. Harris, a Methodist missionary to Mississippi plantations after 1839. On the Frierson plantation, in Sumter County, South Carolina, the front yard of the big house was set aside for the slaves' Sunday worship. Black preachers were always invited to conduct these services, according to former slave Irving Lowery. A table covered with a white cloth on which lay a Bible was set up to serve as a pulpit, and chairs were arranged for the slave congregation. Overlooking the yard was the piazza, or gallery, of the big house where white families sat and watched the services. . . .

Occasionally religious mutuality between white and black Christians included personal recognition and respect. Reverend C. C. Jones, for example, felt that he was put to shame by the sincerity and eloquence of the prayers said by Dembo, a native African and a member of Jones' Midway Church: "I can never forget the prayers of *Dembo*. . . . There was a depth of humility, a conviction of sinfulness . . . an assurance of faith . . . a flowing out of love, a being swallowed up in God, which I never heard before nor since; and often when he closed his prayers, I felt as weak as water, and that I ought not to open my mouth in public, and indeed knew not what it was to pray." On the other side of the racial line, William Wells Brown acknowledged that he had "the greatest respect" for "the Christian zeal" of one planter in his area, Dr. John Gaines, "a truly pious and conscientious man, willing at all times to give of his means . . . in spreading the Gospel." . . .

Slave religion has been stereotyped as otherworldly and compensatory. It was otherworldly in the sense that it held that this world and this life were not the end, nor the final measure of existence. It was compensatory to the extent that it consoled and supported slaves worn out by the unremitting toil and capricious cruelty of the "peculiar institution." To conclude, however, that religion distracted slaves from concern with this life and dissuaded them from action in the present is to distort the full story and to simplify the complex role of religious motivation in human behavior. It does not always follow that belief in a future state of happiness leads to acceptance of suffering in this world. It does not follow necessarily that a hope in a future when all wrongs will be righted leads to acquiescence to injustice in the present. Religion had different effects on the motivation and identity of different slaves and even dissimilar effects on the same slave at different times and in different circumstances.

To describe slave religion as merely otherworldly is inaccurate, for the slaves believed that God had acted, was acting, and would continue to act within human history and within their own particular history as a peculiar people just as long ago he had acted on behalf of another chosen people, biblical Israel. Moreover, slave religion had a this-worldly impact, not only in leading some slaves to acts of external rebellion, but also in helping slaves to assert and maintain a sense of personal value—even of ultimate worth. The religious meetings in the quarters, groves, and "hush harbors" were themselves frequently acts of rebellion against the proscriptions of the master. In the context of divine authority, the limited authority of any human was placed in perspective. By obeying the commands of God, even when they contradicted the commands of men, slaves developed and treasured a sense of moral superiority and actual moral authority over their masters.

Chapter 6

1787 Petition for Equal Educational Facilities

Rev. Prince Hall et al.

Rev. Prince Hall (1748–1807), born in Barbados, was a Revolutionary War veteran and early abolitionist. He was an advocate of black education and a founder of the first black Masonic lodge, an institution which eventually became involved in a wide array of black social and political activity.

Petition from black citizens to the Massachusetts State Legislature, 17 October 1787. The petition was not granted. This version is excerpted from Herbert Aptheker, A Documentary History of the Negro People in the United States, *vol. I (1951), 19–20.*

To the Honorable [members of] the Senate and House of Representatives of the Commonwealth of Massachusetts Bay, in General Court assembled.

The petition of a great number of blacks, freemen of this Commonwealth, humbly sheweth, that your petitioners are held in common with other freemen of this town and Commonwealth and have never been backward in paying our proportionate part of the burdens under which they have, or may labor under; and as we are willing to pay our equal part of these burdens, we are of the humble opinion that we have the right to enjoy the privileges of free men. But that we do not will appear in many instances, and we beg leave to mention one out of many, and that is of the education of our children which now receive no benefit from the free schools in the town of Boston, which we think is a great grievance, as by woful experience we now feel the want of a common education. . . .

We therefore pray your Honors that you would in your wisdom [find] some provision may be made for the education of our dear children. And in duty bound shall ever pray.

Chapter 7

The Abolitionist Movement

Herbert Aptheker

Herbert Aptheker, a Marxist historian and the literary executor for W. E. B. Du Bois, has been a prolific American historian. A past member of the Central Committee of the Communist Party, he is currently active with the Committees of Correspondence.

Aptheker's works on black history include The Negro in the Civil War *(1938),* Negro Slave Revolts in the United States, 1526–1860 *(1939), "Maroons within the Present Limits of the United States,"* Journal of Negro History *(April 1939),* American Negro Slave Revolts *(1943),* Nat Turner's Revolt *(1968),* Annotated Bibliography of the Writings of W. E. B. Du Bois *(1973),* Abolitionism: A Revolutionary Movement *(1989), and* Anti-Racism in U.S. History: The First Two Hundred Years *(1992). His edited works include* A Documentary History of the Negro People in the United States *(7 vols., 1951–1994),* The Selected Correspondence of W. E. B. Du Bois *(3 vols., 1973–1978), and* Selections from "Phylon" *(1980). For a collection of essays on Aptheker's work, see* Nature, Society, and Thought *(January/April 1997).*

The following selection is reprinted from "The Abolitionist Movement," Political Affairs, *February 1976. Reprinted with permission of* Political Affairs.

The abolitionist movement in the United States was the second great revolutionary effort to succeed in our history—the first, of course, being that movement which resulted in the establishment of the nation. The abolitionist movement had three interrelated purposes: 1) to abolish slavery immediately and without compensation to the owners; 2) to combat racism and racist practices in the North; 3) to assist the free Black population. Certainly the first goal was the basic one in the nineteenth century, but the other two were consciously part of the Movement and their historical treatment has been very meager.

Generally in the literature, the Abolitionist has been presented as a reform effort, with white people as inspirers, strategists and leaders. This is erroneous. The Abolitionist effort was a revolutionary one and therefore necessarily was a Black-white movement, for in the United States no democratic effort—let alone a revolutionary one—can be anything but a united struggle of people of all colors and ethnic origins. Furthermore, since the movement was especially concerned with the position of Black people, it naturally was those people who were its grand strategists, most effective tacticians, most persevering adherents and especially its pioneers.

The movement was a revolutionary one because it sought the overthrow of the ruling class—the ruling class not only in the South but also in the nation as a whole. Of course, the slaveowners utterly dominated the economics, ideology and politics of the South—though not without significant challenge from the slaves and, increasingly as the years rolled on, from the nonslaveholding whites. But that class, which numbered not more than about 175,000 at its high point in 1860, also constituted the greatest single economic interest in the nation as a whole prior to the Civil War. Their ownership of some 3,500,000 slaves worth perhaps three and a half billion dollars, plus their ownership of the cotton, tobacco, rice, sugar, hemp, [and] lumber-products that they produced, and of the land which that labor made fruitful, plus the buildings and tools and animals, made of that interrelated, highly class-conscious oligarchy by far the greatest single vested interest in the nation as a whole. Based upon that foundation, that class dominated both political parties—Democratic and Whig (while tending to favor the former)—and therefore dominated the Congress and the Presidency. It dominated the judiciary and its ideology was the ruling one not only in Mississippi but in the nation as a whole. That is, the major publishing houses would print nothing offensive to the slaveholding class, the major universities would not hire professors who condemned slavery and the leading newspapers of the nation—with extremely rare and partial exceptions—at least acquiesced in slavery's existence and excoriated the "fanatical" Abolitionists.

The Abolitionist movement, then, stood opposed to all of that; it was in principled opposition to the ruling class and the state and all its apparatus of persuasion, domination and coercion. That movement was revolutionary exactly in the sense that it sought the overthrow of the ruling class in the only way in which a ruling class can be overthrown; i.e., it sought the elimination of that form of private property the ownership of which defined that ruling class and gave it its power. The slaveowners were the ruling class and the Abolitionists sought the immediate, uncompensated abolition of slave property; nothing else could *end* slavery and nothing else could *terminate* the power of the slaveowners. That is not a reform movement; it is a revolutionary one.

The available literature is meager, too, on the *movement* feature of the Abolitionist struggle. Most of the available works—and especially the textbooks—give readers an impression of a rather formless, nebulous conglomeration of (generally white) people of benevolent feelings (or malevolent, if the author opposes Abolitionism, as many books still do) who somehow were able to stir up considerable commotion and influence significant political developments. The reality is otherwise. The Abolitionist movement was a *movement*; that is, it was highly organized on national, regional, state-wide, and local levels. In addition, it contained organizations of particular components of the population, as of women and of youth. It was served by a professional revolutionary cadre—men and women who devoted their lives to the movement; it held regular meetings and conventions, had formal constitutions and organs of agitation and propaganda. Its points of concentration and its campaigns did not simply "happen"; on the contrary, they were the results of collective and prolonged discussions and debates and on the basis of such efforts would be determined a policy of concentrating upon ending the domestic slave-trade, for example, or petitioning Congress to abolish slavery in the District of Columbia, or in the federal territories, or fighting in Massachusetts, for instance, to abolish [J]im-[C]row schools, or [J]im-[C]row transportation. In this way, there came into being—especially among the Afro-American people, but always with white allies—vigilance committees and the underground railroad and major rescue attempts, which helped capture the attention of the nation and, indeed, of the world.

The abolitionist movement, like all revolutionary efforts, had its inner struggles against opportunism, sectarianism and racial and sexual chauvinism. This movement, too, like all revolutionary movements, not only was Black-white but also reflected male and female joint struggle. Indeed it is reflective of the deeply revolutionary nature of the struggle to abolish slavery that it was exactly that movement which witnessed the first appearance of significant public participation by women and which in turn helped inspired the organized movement in the United States for the liberation of women.

The abolitionist movement also was a basic component of the overall democratic struggle of humanity. That is, its effort to abolish slavery, its commitment to oppose racism, its male-female reality, all reflected a new definition of "people." When the Fathers of this Republic wrote "people" they had in mind what propertied white males of the eighteenth century had in mind by that word—i.e., people like themselves, and not people of other colors, and not women and not the propertyless. But the Abolitionist movement of the nineteenth century broadens the meaning of people; its usage is anti-elitist and anti-racist and anti-male-chauvinist. When the Abolitionist movement sought freedom it sought freedom for the least among the people and therefore its blows were directed toward human emancipation.

Hence, too, one sees in the struggle against slavery a significant effort to preserve and extend freedom of press and speech and assembly and to oppose aggressive, expansionistic foreign policies emanating from Washington—as that which made war upon Mexico and threatened war upon Spain in order to annex Cuba.

Furthermore, this battle to abolish slavery is part of the whole history of the labor movement in this country and in the world. Most of the Black people labored as slaves—skilled and unskilled and not only in the field but also in the city and not only raising cotton but also digging coal and not only producing hemp but also making iron. In this very real sense, the Emancipation Proclamation and the [13th] Amendment abolishing slavery are great documents in the history of the labor movement. This is at the heart of Marx's insistence that labor in a white skin cannot be free while labor in a black skin is branded. This is the point, negatively, in the insistence by the leading ideologists of the slaveholders—as George Fitzhugh, for example—that only slavery "solves" the class struggle for it makes of the worker so much "capital" in the pockets of the owners.

Abolitionism struck at the heart of so-called "civilization" as envisaged from John Locke to John C. Calhoun; that is, government exists to secure private property and the security of the private ownership of the means of production is the fundamental function of the state. Our slaves, insisted their owners, belong to us by the same right and the same law and with the same justification that the land and the factories belong to you in the North. If on Monday, they warned, the flames of Abolition should light up our plantations and consume our property in slaves, then on Tuesday you had better watch out that the tenants on your lands do not treat you similarly and that on Wednesday the workers in your factories do not feel it is their turn to emulate the slaves and the landless farmers. Once yield the precedent in any form of property rights, and then the ownership of all private property is in jeopardy and its sanctity is vitiated. When that goes, there goes also the sacredness of contract and if that goes then what has become of "civilization"? This is why the proslavery propagandists insisted that the Abolitionists were communists and socialists as well as atheists and barbarians.

One of the essential purposes of the racism which bulwarked slavery was to hide this anti-elitist, basically revolutionary quality of Abolitionism.

Abolitionism, then, was part of the democratic, egalitarian, anti-elitist quality of the entire fabric of human history. Further, it was fundamental to the liberation of the Afro-American people and while that liberation is a basic part of the history of the United States and of the world, it also is a history in and of itself. In this sense, then, Abolitionism is part of the liberation struggles of the especially oppressed peoples and nationalities of the earth. In our country, because of the organic character of Black-white unity, one sees the merging of all these struggles; this is dramatized in the Civil War where the original avowed purpose of the salvation of the Union was only possible if there occurred the emancipation of the Black people—and the emancipation of the Black people in turn was only possible if one saved the Union. To save the Union it was necessary to end slavery; to end slavery it was necessary to save the Union.

Another feature of the revolutionary quality of the Abolitionist movement was its internationalism. The effort to end slavery in the United States was part of the effort to end slavery in Mexico and all Latin-America and the West Indies.

The struggles of the slaves in Virginia and the slaves of Jamaica, of the slaves of Mississippi and of Haiti, of South Carolina and Cuba—these are all one mighty component of the inspiring human resistance to insult and enslavement. The antislavery men and women in the United States had comrades in the same struggles in Mexico and Brazil, in France and England, in Ireland and Cuba. These revolutionaries knew each other, visited each other and helped each other.

And, of course, the humanistic essence of antislavery and its anti-elitist and basically labor component made all Marxists friends of the struggle to abolish slavery, with the leadership of that undertaking falling upon Marx himself. This brought decisive results during the Civil War with the key role played in the diplomacy of that War by the working classes of Europe.

In this great crusade within the United States there appeared some of the noblest figures not only in the history of our nation but in that of the world. From the best among the Black and white people who preceded us in this country came such colossal figures as the indomitable Harriet Tubman, the clear-visioned Wendell Phillips, the stalwart Sojourner Truth, the brilliant Frederick Douglass, the magnificent John Brown.

Someday a dramatist will appear among us and he or she will be able to do full justice to that moment when the jailed and chained Nat Turner faces the court-appointed questioner who comes seeking an admission from the 30 year old slave-rebel that what he had attempted was foolish and wrong. It was important to the slave-holders that this rebel, whose uprising had rocked their society to its heels, be made to confess failure and fault. This slaveowners' representative came to Nat Turner the day before he was to be hanged. He told Turner that all was lost, that his comrades had been hanged and that he himself would be executed the next day. Tell us, he demanded and implored, that you know that your act was stupid and wrong.

That lackey of the masters reports, himself, what the rebel did and said. He [Turner] raised himself from his cot, there in the county jail in Virginia back in 1831, stood up, and with one hand shackled to the cement wall he spread his other arm wide and, looking at the inquisitor, said to him: "Was not Christ crucified?"

I believe that in all the record of the history of the United States—with its many moments of high drama, from Bunker Hill to Harper's Ferry, from the Boston Massacre to the Haymarket martyrdom, there is no single moment so filled with drama and with meaning as that one instant of immortal defiance and challenge.

Such were the struggles of our Abolitionist comrades; such is the heritage of valor and of effectiveness that they have bequeathed to us.

Chapter 8

Too Long Have Others Spoken for Us

Freedom's Journal

Freedom's Journal (1827–1829) was the first black newspaper in the United States. The editors, John Rosswurm and the Rev. Samuel Cornish, began publishing four years before William Lloyd Garrison launched his abolitionist weekly, the Liberator.

The following selection is reprinted from the newspaper's opening editorial, 16 March 1827, 1.

To Our Patrons

In presenting our first number to our Patrons, we feel all the diffidence of persons entering upon a new and untried line of business. But a moment's reflection upon the noble objects, which we have in view by the publication of this Journal; the expediency of its appearance at this time, when so many schemes are in action concerning our people—encourage us to come boldly before an enlightened publick. For we believe, that a paper devoted to the dissemination of useful knowledge among our brethren, and to their moral and religious improvement, must meet with the cordial approbation of every friend to humanity.

The peculiarities of this Journal, renders it important that we should advertise to the world our motives by whic[h] we are actuated, and the objects which we contemplate.

We wish to plead our own cause. Too long have others spoken for us. Too long has the publick been deceived by misrepresentations, in things which concern us dearly, though in the estimation of some mere trifles; for though there are many in society who exercise towards us benevolent feelings; still (with sorrow we confess it) there are others who make it their business to enlarge upon the least trifle, which tends to the discredit of any person of colour; and pronounce anathemas and denounce our whole body for the misconduct of this guilty one. We are aware that there [are] many instances of vice among us, but we avow that it is because no one has taught its subjects to be virtuous: many instances of poverty, because no sufficient efforts accommodated to minds contracted by slavery, and deprived of early education have been made, to teach them how to husband their hard earnings, and to secure to themselves comforts.

Education being an object of the highest importance to the welfare of society, we shall endeavour to present just and adequate views of it, and to urge upon our brethren the necessity and expediency of training their children, while young, to habits of industry, and thus forming them for becoming useful members of society. It is surely time that we should awake from this lethargy of years, and make a concentrated effort for the education of our youth. We form a spoke in the human wheel, and it is necessary that we should understand our pendence on the different parts, and theirs on us, in order to perform our part with propriety.

Though not desirous of dictating, we shall feel it our incumbent duty to dwell occasionally upon the general principles and rules of economy. The world has grown too enlightened, to estimate any man's character by his personal appearance. Though all men acknowledge the excellency of [Benjamin] Franklin's maxims, yet comparatively few practise upon them. We may deplore when it is too late, the neglect of these self-evident truths, but it avails little to mourn. Ours will be the task of admonishing our brethren on these points.

The civil rights of a people being of the greatest value, it shall ever be our duty to vindicate our brethren, when oppressed, and to lay the case before the publick. We shall also urge upon our brethren, (who are qualified by the laws of the different states) the expediency of using their elective franchise; and of making an independent use of the same. We wish them not to become the tools of party.

And as much time is frequently lost, and wrong principles instilled, by the perusal of works of trivial importance, we shall consider it a part of our duty to recommend to our young readers, such authors as will not only enlarge their stock of useful knowledge, but such as will also serve to stimulate them to higher attainments in science.

We trust also, that through the columns of the FREEDOM'S JOURNAL, many practical pieces, having for their bases, the improvement of our brethren, will be presented to them, from the pens of many of our respected friends, who have kindly promised their assistance.

It is our earnest wish to make our Journal a medium of intercourse between our brethren in the different states of this great confederacy: that through its columns an expression of our sentiments, on many interesting subjects which concern us, may be offered to the publick: that plans which apparently are beneficial may be candidly discussed and properly weighed; if worthy, receive our cordial approbation; if not, our marked disapprobation.

Useful knowledge of every kind, and every thing that relates to Africa, shall find a ready admission into our columns; and as that vast continent becomes daily more known, we trust that many things will come to light, proving that the natives of it are neither so ignorant nor stupid as they have generally been supposed to be.

And while these important subjects shall occupy the columns of the FREEDOM'S JOURNAL, we would not be unmindful of our brethren who are still in the iron fetters of bondage. They are our kindred by all the ties of nature; and though but little can be effected by us, still let our sympathies be poured forth and our prayers in their behalf, ascend to Him who is able to succour them.

From the press and the pulpit we have suffered much by being incorrectly represented. Men whom we equally love and admire have not hesitated to represent us disadvantageously, without becoming personally acquainted with the true state of things, nor discerning between virtue and vice among us. The virtuous part of our people feel themselves sorely aggrieved under the existing state of things— they are not appreciated.

Our vices and our degradation are ever arrayed against us, but our virtues are passed by unnoticed. And what is still more lamentable, our friends, to whom we concede all the principles of humanity and religion, from these very causes seem to have fallen into the current of popular feeling and are imperceptibly floating on the stream—actually living in the practice of prejudice, while they abjure it in theory, and feel it not in their hearts. Is it not very desirable that such should know more of our actual condition, and of our efforts and feelings, that in forming or advocating plans for our amelioration, they may do it more understandingly? In the spirit of candor and humility we intend by a simple representation of facts to lay our case before the publick, with a view to arrest the progress of prejudice, and to shield ourselves against the consequent evils. We wish to conciliate all and to irritate none, yet we must be firm and unwavering in our principles, and persevering in our efforts.

If ignorance, poverty and degradation have hitherto been our unhappy lot; has the Eternal decree gone forth, that our race alone, are to remain in this state, while knowledge and civilization are shedding their enlivening rays over the rest of the human family? The recent travels of [explorers Dixon] Denham and [Hugh] Clapperton in the interior of Africa, and the interesting narrative which they have published; the establishment of the republic of [Haiti] after years of sanguinary warfare; its subsequent progress in all the arts of civilization; and the advancement of liberal ideas in South America, where despotism has given place to free governments, and where many of our brethren now fill important civil and military stations, prove the contrary.

The interesting fact that there are FIVE HUNDRED THOUSAND free persons of colour, one half of whom might peruse, and the whole be benefitted by the publication of the Journal; that no publication, as yet, has been devoted exclusively to their improvement—that many selections from approved standard authors, which are within the reach of few, may occasionally be made—and more important still, that this large body of our citizens have no public channel—all serve to prove the real necessity, at present, for the appearance of the FREEDOM'S JOURNAL.

It shall ever be our desire so to conduct the editorial department of our paper as to give offence to none of our patrons; as nothing is farther from us than to make it the advocate of any partial views, either in politics or religion. What few days we can number, have been devoted to the improvement of our brethren; and it is our earnest wish that the remainder may be spent in the same delightful service.

In conclusion, whatever concerns us as a people, will ever find a ready admission into the FREEDOM'S JOURNAL, interwoven with all the principal news of the day.

And while every thing in our power shall be performed to support the character of our Journal, we would respectfully invite our numerous friends to assist by their communications, and our coloured brethren to strengthen our hands by their subscriptions, as our labour is one of common cause, and worthy of their consideration and support. And we most earnestly solicit the latter, that if at any time we should seem to be zealous, or too pointed in the inculcation of any important lesson, they will remember, that they are equally interested in the cause in which we are engaged, and attribute our zeal to the peculiarities of our situation; and our earnest engagedness in their well-being.

Chapter 9

Education for Black Women

Matilda

The following selection is one of the first published articles by a black woman discussing education for black women. Reprinted from Freedom's Journal, *10 August 1827, 2. Herbert Aptheker, in his* Documentary History of the Negro People, *speculates that "Matilda" was a pseudonym.*

Messrs. Editors,

Will you allow a female to offer a few remarks upon a subject that you must allow to be all-important? I don't know that in any of your papers, you have said sufficient upon the education of females. I hope you are not to be classed with those, who think that our mathematical knowledge should be limited to "fathoming the dish-kettle," and that we have acquired enough of history, if we know that our grandfather's father lived and died. 'Tis true the time has been, when to darn a stocking, and cook a pudding well, was considered the end and aim of a woman's being. But those were days when ignorance blinded men's eyes. The diffusion of knowledge has destroyed those degrading opinions, and men of the present age, allow, that we have minds that are capable and deserving of culture. There are difficulties, and great difficulties in the way of our advancement; but that should only stir us to greater efforts. We possess not the advantages with those of our sex, whose skins are not colored like our own, but we can improve what little we have, and make our one talent produce two-fold. The influence that we have over the male sex demands, that our minds should be instructed and improved with the principles of education and religion, in order that this influence should be properly directed. Ignorant ourselves, how can we be expected to form the minds of our youth, and conduct them in the paths of knowledge? [H]ow can we "teach the young idea how to shoot," if we have none ourselves? There is a great responsibility resting somewhere, and it is time for us to be up and doing. I would address myself to all mothers, and say to them, that while it is necessary to possess a knowledge of cookery, and the various mysteries of pudding-making, something more is requisite. It is their bounden duty to store their daughters' minds with useful learning. They should be made to devote their leisure time to reading books, whence they would derive valuable information, which could never be taken from them. I will not longer trespass on your time and patience. I merely throw out these hints, in order that some more able pen will take up the subject.

Chapter 10

Walker's Appeal

David Walker

David Walker (1785–1830), the son of a free black woman and a slave father, was born in North Carolina. He moved to Massachusetts in the 1820s, where he joined the Boston Colored Association and became involved with Freedom's Journal.

After the publication of Walker's Appeal to the Coloured Citizens of the World *(1829), the governor of Georgia wrote to Boston mayor Harrison Otis requesting the suppression of further editions. The mayor declined. In Georgia, a reward was offered for his murder. The cause of Walker's death, at age thirty-four, is unknown. For a biography, see Peter Hinks,* To Awaken My Affiliated Brethren *(1997).*

The following selection is excerpted from Walker's Appeal.

My dearly beloved Brethren and Fellow Citizens:

Having travelled over a considerable portion of these United States, and having, in the course of my travels taken the most accurate observations of things as they exist—the result of my observations has warranted the full and unshakened conviction, that we, (colored people of these United States) are the most degraded, wretched, and abject set of beings that ever lived since the world began, and I pray God, that none like us ever may live again until time shall be no more. . . .

I am fully aware, in making this appeal to my much afflicted and suffering brethren, that I shall not only be assailed by those whose greatest earthly desires are, to keep us in abject ignorance and wretchedness, and who are of the firm conviction that heaven has designed us and our children to be slaves and *beasts of burden* to them and their children.—I say, I do not only expect to be held up to the public as an ignorant, impudent and restless disturber of the public peace, by such avaricious creatures, as well as a mover of insubordination—and perhaps put in prison or to death, for giving a superficial exposition of our miseries, and exposing tyrants. But I am persuaded, that in any of my brethren, particularly those who are ignorantly in league with slave-holders or tyrants, who acquire their daily bread by the blood and sweat of their more ignorant brethren—and not a few of those too, who are too ignorant to see an inch beyond their noses, will rise up and call me cursed—Yea, the jealous ones among us will perhaps use more abject subtlety by affirming that this work is not worth perusing; that we are well situated and there is no use in trying to better our condition, for we cannot. I will ask one question here.—Can our condition be any worse?—Can it be more mean and abject? If there are any changes, will they not be for the better, though they may appear for the worse at first? Can they get us any lower? Where can they get us? They are afraid to treat us worse, for they know well, the day they do it they are gone. But against all accusations which may or can be preferred against me, I appeal to heaven for my motive in writing—who knows that my object is, if possible, to awaken in the breasts of my afflicted, degraded and slumbering brethren, a spirit of enquiry and investigation respecting our miseries and wretchedness in this *Republican Land of Liberty*!!!!! . . .

Men of colour, who are also of sense, for you particularly is my appeal designed. Our more ignorant brethren are not able to penetrate its value. I call upon you therefore to cast your eyes upon the wretchedness of your brethren and to do your utmost to enlighten them—*go to work and enlighten your brethren!*—let the Lord see you doing what you can to rescue them and yourselves from degradation. . . .

There is a great work for you to do, as trifling as some of you may think of it. You have to prove to the Americans and the world, that we are MEN, and not *brutes* as we have been represented, and by millions treated. Remember, to let the aim of your labours among your brethren, and particularly the youths, be the dissemination of education and religion.

. . . I pray that the Lord may undeceive my ignorant brethren, and permit them to throw away pretensions, and seek after the substance of learning. I would crawl on my hands and knees through mud and mire, to the feet of a learned man, where I would sit and humbly supplicate him to instill into me, that which neither devils nor tyrants could remove, only with my life—for the Africans to acquire learning in this country, makes tyrants quake and tremble on their sandy foundation. Why what is the matter? Why, they know that their infernal deeds of cruelty will be made known to the world. Do you suppose one man of good sense and learning would submit himself, his father, mother, wife and children, to be slaves to a wretched man like himself, who, instead of compensating him for his labours, chains, handcuffs and beats him and family almost to death, leaving life enough in them, however, to work for, and call him master? No ! no! he would cut his devilish throat from ear to ear, and well do slaveholders know it. The bare name of educating the coloured people, scares our cruel oppressors almost to death.

. . . What the American preachers can think of us, I aver this day before my God, I have never been able to define. They have newspapers and monthly periodicals, which they receive in continual succession, but on the pages of which, you will scarcely ever find a paragraph respecting slavery, which is ten thousand times more injurious to this country than all the other evils put together; and which will be the final overthrow of its government, unless something is very speedily done; for their cup is nearly full.—Perhaps they will laugh at, or make light of this; but I tell you Americans! that unless you speedily alter your course, *you* and your *Country are gone*!!!!!! For God Almighty will tear up the very face of the earth!!!! . . .

See your declaration, Americans!! Do you understand your own language? Hear your language, proclaimed to the world, July 4, 1776—"We hold these truths to be self evident—that ALL MEN ARE CREATED EQUAL! *that they are endowed by their Creator with certain unalienable rights; that among these are life, liberty, and the pursuit of happiness!!"* Compare your own language above, extracted from your Declaration of Independence, with your cruelties and murders inflicted by your cruel and unmerciful fathers on ourselves on our fathers and on us, men who have never given your fathers or you the least provocation!!!

Hear your language further! [The Declaration says] "But when a long train of abuses and usurpations, pursuing invariably the same object, evinces a design to reduce them under absolute despotism, it is their *right,* it is their *duty,* to throw off such government, and to provide new guards for their future security."

Now, Americans! I ask you candidly, was your sufferings under Great Britain one hundredth part as cruel and tyrannical as you have rendered ours under you? Some of you, no doubt, believe that we will never throw off your murderous government, and "provide new guards["] for our future "security." If Satan has made you believe it, will he not deceive you? Do the whites say, I being a black man, ought to be humble, which I readily admit? I ask them, ought they not to be as humble as I? or do they think they can measure arms with Jehovah? Will not the Lord yet humble them? or will not these very coloured people, whom they now treat worse than brutes, yet under God, humble them low down enough? Some of the whites are ignorant enough to tell us, that we ought to be submissive to them, that they may keep their feet on our throats. And if we do not submit to be beaten to death by them, we are bad creatures and of course must be damned, &c. If any man wishes to hear this doctrine openly preached to us by the American preachers, let him go into the Southern and Western sections of this country—I do not speak from hearsay—what I have written, is what I have seen and heard myself. No man may think that my book is made up of conjecture—I have travelled and observed nearly the whole of those things myself, and what little I did not get by my own observation, I received from those among the whites and blacks, in whom the greatest confidence may be placed.

The Americans may be as vigilant as they please, but they cannot be vigilant enough for the Lord, neither can they hide themselves, where he will not find and bring them out.

Chapter 11

On African Rights and Liberty

Maria W. Stewart

In the eighteenth and nineteenth centuries, the public sphere—the realm of politics—was overwhelmingly male. Politicians, speakers, and audiences were almost exclusively male. Maria W. Stewart (1803–1879), a middle-class black woman who took up public speaking after the death of her husband in 1829, was the first native-born woman to deliver a public address in U.S. history (only a non-native, Frances Wright from Scotland, is known to have spoken earlier). From 1832 to 1833, Stewart delivered a series of four harsh, strongly religious speeches that were so poorly received that she was driven from public life. "I find it is no use for me, as an individual, to try to make myself useful among my color in this city. . . . I have made myself contemptible in the eyes of many," Stewart said in her "Farewell Address." Although Stewart left the public realm, a small group of women inspired by the abolitionist cause, including Mary Ann Shadd Cary and Sojourner Truth, soon followed.

Stewart's four speeches were published in the Liberator *and later compiled in book form, together with earlier writings, as* Meditations of Mrs. Maria W. Stewart *(1879).*

The following selection is excerpted from her address at the African Masonic Hall in Boston on 27 February 1833.

African rights and liberty is a subject that ought to fire the breast of every free man of color in these United States, and excite in his bosom a lively, deep, decided and heart-felt interest. When I cast my eyes on the long list of illustrious names that are enrolled on the bright annals of fame among the whites, I turn my eyes within, and ask my thoughts, "Where are the names of our illustrious ones?" It must certainly have been for the want of energy on the part of the free people of color, that they have been long willing to bear the yoke of oppression. It must have been the want of ambition and force that has given the whites occasion to say that our natural abilities are not as good, and our capacities by nature inferior to theirs. They boldly assert that did we possess a natural independence of soul, and feel a love for liberty within our breasts, some one of our sable race, long before this, would have testified it, notwithstanding the disadvantages under which we labor. We have made ourselves appear altogether unqualified to speak in our own defence, and are therefore looked upon as objects of pity and commiseration. We have been imposed upon, insulted and derided on every side; and now, if we complain, it is considered as the height of impertinence. We have suffered ourselves to be considered as dastards, cowards, mean, faint-hearted wretches; and on this account (not because of our complexion) many despise us, and would gladly spurn us from their presence.

These things have fired my soul with a holy indignation, and compelled me thus to come forward, and endeavor to turn their attention to knowledge and improvement; for knowledge is power. . . .

I am sensible that there are many highly intelligent men of color in these United States, in the force of whose arguments, doubtless, I should discover my inferiority; but if they are blessed with wit and talent, friends and fortune, why have they not made themselves men of eminence, by striving to take all the reproach that is cast upon the people of color, and in endeavoring to alleviate the woes of their brethren in bondage? Talk, without effort, is nothing; you are abundantly capable, gentlemen, of making yourselves men of distinction; and this gross neglect, on your part, causes my blood to boil within me. Here is the grand cause which hinders the rise and progress of people of color. It is their want of laudable ambition and requisite courage. . . .

History informs us that we sprung from one of the most learned nations of the whole earth; from the seat, if not the parent, of science. Yes, poor despised Africa was once the resort of sages and legislators of other nations, was esteemed the school for learning, and the most illustrious men in Greece flocked thither for instruction. But it was our gross sins and abominations that provoked the Almighty to frown thus heavily upon us, and give our glory unto others. Sin and prodigality have caused the downfall of nations, kings and emperors; and were it not that God in wrath remembers mercy, we might indeed despair. . . .

Let our money, instead of being thrown away as heretofore, be appropriated for schools and seminaries of learning for our children and youth. We ought to follow the example of the whites in this respect. Nothing would raise our respectability, add to our peace and happiness, and reflect so much honor upon us, as to be ourselves the promoters of temperance, and the supporters, as far as we are able, of useful and scientific knowledge. The rays of light and knowledge have been hid from our view; we have been taught to consider ourselves as scarce superior to the brute creation; and have performed the most laborious part of American drudgery. Had we as a people received one-half the early advantages the whites have received, I would defy the government of these United States to deprive us any longer of our rights.

I am informed that the agent of the Colonization Society has recently formed an association of young men for the purpose of influencing those of us to go to Liberia who may feel disposed. The colonizationists are blind to their own interest, for should the nations of the earth make war with America, they would find their forces much weakened by our absence; or should we remain here, can our "brave soldiers" and "fellow citizens," as they were termed in time of calamity, condescend to defend the rights of whites and be again deprived of their own, or sent to Liberia in return? Or, if the colonizationists are the real friends to Africa, let them expend the money which they collect in erecting a college to educate her injured sons in this land of gospel, light, and liberty. . . .

It is of no use for us to wait any longer for a generation of well educated men to arise. We have slumbered and slept too long already; the day is far spent; the night of death approaches; and you have sound sense and good judgment sufficient to begin with, if you feel disposed to make a right use of it. Let every man of color throughout the United States, who possesses the spirit and principles of a man, sign a petition to Congress to abolish slavery in the District of Columbia, and grant you the rights and privileges of common free citizens; for if you had had faith as a grain of mustard seed [Matthew 13:31], long before this the mountain of prejudice might have been removed. We are all sensible that the Anti-Slavery Society has taken hold of the arm of our whole population, in order to raise them out of the mire. Now all we have to do is, by a spirit of virtuous ambition, to strive to raise ourselves. . . .

It appears to me that America has become like the great city of Babylon, for she has boasted in her heart: "I sit a queen and am no widow, and shall see no sorrow!" [Revelation 18:7]. She is, indeed, a seller of slaves and the souls of men; she has-made the Africans drunk with the wine of her fornication; she has put them completely beneath her feet, and she means to keep them there; her right hand supports the reins of government and her left hand the wheel of power, and she is determined not to let go her grasp. But many powerful sons and daughters of Africa will shortly arise, who will put down vice and immorality among us, and declare by Him that sitteth upon the throne that they will have their rights; and if refused, I am afraid they will spread horror and devastation around. I believe that the oppression of injured Africa has come up before the majesty of Heaven; and when our cries shall have reached the ears of the Most High, it will be a tremendous day for the people of this land; for strong is the hand of the Lord God Almighty. . . .

The unfriendly whites first drove the native American from his much loved home. Then they stole our fathers from their peaceful and quiet dwellings, and brought them hither, and made bond-men and bond-women of them and their little ones. They have obliged our brethren to labor; kept them in utter ignorance, nourished them in vice, and raised them in degradation; and now that we have enriched their soil, and filled their coffers, they say that we are not capable of becoming like white men, and that we can never rise to respectability in this country. They would drive us to a strange land [Liberia]. But before I go, the bayonet shall pierce me through. African rights and liberty is a subject that ought to fire the breast of every free man of color in these United States, and excite in his bosom a lively, deep, decided, and heartfelt interest.

Chapter 12

The *Liberator:* Opening Editorial

William Lloyd Garrison

William Lloyd Garrison (1805–1879) was the founder and editor of the Liberator *(1831–1865), an abolitionist weekly.*

The following selection is excerpted from the first editorial of the Liberator, *1 January 1831, 1.*

For another selection by Garrison, see chapter 4.

During my recent tour for the purpose of exciting the minds of the people by a series of discourses on the subject of slavery, every place that I visited gave fresh evidence of the fact, that a greater revolution in public sentiment was to be effected in the free states—*and particularly in New England*—than at the south. I found contempt more bitter, opposition more active, detraction more relentless, prejudice more stubborn, and apathy more frozen, than among the slave owners themselves. Of course, there were individual exceptions to the contrary. This state of things afflicted, but did not dishearten me. I determined, at every hazard to lift up the standard of emancipation in the eyes of the nation, *within sight of Bunker Hill and in the birth place of liberty.* That standard is now unfurled; and long may it float, unhurt by the spoliations of time or the missiles of a desperate foe—yea, till every chain be broken, and every bondman set free! Let southern oppressors tremble—let their secret abettors tremble—let their northern apologists tremble—let all the enemies of the persecuted blacks tremble.

I deem the publication of my original Prospectus unnecessary, as it has obtained a wide circulation. The principles therein inculcated will be steadily pursued in this paper, excepting that I shall not array myself as the political partisan of any man. In defending the great cause of human rights, I wish to derive the assistance of all religions and of all parties.

Assenting to the 'self-evident truth' maintained in the American Declaration of Independence, 'that all men are created equal and endowed by their Creator with certain inalienable rights—among which are life, liberty and pursuit of happiness,' I shall strenuously contend for the immediate enfranchisement of our slave population. In Park-street Church, on the Fourth of July, 1829, in an address on slavery, I unreflectingly assented to the popular but pernicious doctrine of *gradual* abolition. I seize this opportunity to make a full and unequivocal recantation, and thus publicly to ask pardon of my God, of my country, and of my brethren the poor slaves, for having uttered a sentiment so full of timidity, injustice and absurdity. A similar recantation, from my pen, was published in the *Genius of Universal Emancipation* at Baltimore, in September, 1829. My conscience is now satisfied.

I am aware, that many object to the severity of my language; but is there not cause for severity? I *will be* as harsh as truth, and as uncompromising as justice. On this subject, I do not wish to think, or speak, or write, with moderation. No! no! Tell a man whose house is on fire, to give a moderate alarm; tell him to moderately rescue his wife from the hands of the ravisher; tell the mother to gradually extricate her babe from the fire into which it has fallen;—but urge me not to use moderation in a cause like the present. I am in earnest—I will not equivocate—I will not excuse—I will not retreat a single inch—AND I WILL BE HEARD. The apathy of the people is enough to make every statue leap from its pedestal, and to hasten the resurrection of the dead.

It is pretended, that I am retarding the cause of emancipation, by the coarseness of my invective, and the precipitancy of my measures. *The charge is not true.* On this question my influence,—humble as it is,—is felt at this moment to a considerable extent, and shall be felt in coming years—not as a curse, but as blessing; and posterity will bear testimony that I was right. I desire to thank God, that he enables me to disregard 'the fear of man which bringeth a snare,' and to speak his truth in its simplicity and power.

Chapter 13

An Address to the Slaves of the United States

Rev. Henry Highland Garnet

Rev. Henry Highland Garnet (1815–1881) was born into slavery in Maryland. After escaping in 1824, he and his parents moved to New York City. Garnet began preaching in 1842.

Independent northern black churches—first formed in the 1790s in response to the segregation of blacks in separate pews—were regular meeting places for abolitionists and other reformers. Church-affiliated African Americans were central in launching the colored convention movement, "to ameliorate the condition of the colored people." The movement had its first national meeting in 1830 at Bethel Church in Philadelphia.

In August 1843, speaking before the National Convention of Negro Citizens in Buffalo, New York, Garnet called for slave rebellions as the best way to end slavery. The delegates turned down his proposal by a margin of one vote. The abolitionist John Brown later had the speech reprinted.

The following selection is an excerpt from Garnet's "Address to the Slaves of the United States of America" (1843).

Nearly three millions of your fellow citizens are prohibited by law and public opinion (which in this country is stronger than law) from reading the Book of Life [the Bible]. Your intellect has been destroyed as much as possible, and every ray of light they have attempted to shut out from your minds. The oppressors themselves have become involved in the ruin. They have become weak, sensual and rapacious; they have cursed you; they have cursed themselves; they have cursed the earth which they have trod.

The colonies threw the blame upon England. They said that the mother country entailed the evil [of slavery] upon them, and they would rid themselves of it if they could. The world thought they were sincere, and the philanthropic pitied them. But time soon tested their sincerity. In a few years the colonists grew strong and severed themselves from the British government. Their independence was declared, and they took their station among the sovereign powers of the earth. The [D]eclaration [of Independence] was a glorious document. Sages admired it, and the patriotic of every nation reverenced the Godlike sentiments which it contained. When the power of government returned to their hands, did they emancipate the slaves? No; they rather added new links to our chains. Were they ignorant of the principles of Liberty? Certainly they were not. The sentiments of their revolutionary orators fell in burning eloquence upon their hearts, and with one voice they cried, "Liberty or death." Oh, what a sentence was that! It ran from soul to soul like electric fire and nerved the arms of thousands to fight in the holy cause of Freedom. Among the diversity of opinions that are entertained in regard to physical resistance, there are but a few found to gainsay the stern declaration. We are among those who do not. . . .

Brethren, it is as wrong for your lordly oppressors to keep you in slavery as it was for the man thief [slave traders] to steal our ancestors from the coast of Africa. You should therefore now use the same manner of resistance as would have been just in our ancestors when the bloody footprints of the first remorseless soul thief was placed upon the shores of our fatherland. The humblest peasant is as free in the sight of God as the proudest monarch that ever swayed a scepter. Liberty is a spirit sent out from God and, like its great Author, is no respecter of persons.

Brethren, the time has come when you must act for yourselves. It is an old and true saying that, "if hereditary bondmen would be free, they must themselves strike the blow." You can plead your own cause and do the work of emancipation better than any others. The nations of the Old World are moving in the great cause of universal freedom, and some of them at least will, ere long, do you justice. The combined powers of Europe have placed their broad seal of disapprobation upon the African slave trade. But in the slaveholding parts of the United States the trade is as brisk as ever. They buy and sell you as though you were brute beasts. . . . You had far better all die—*die immediately*—than live slaves and entail your wretchedness upon your posterity. If you would be free in this generation, here is your only hope. However much you and all of us may desire it, there is not much hope of redemption without the shedding of blood. If you must bleed, let it all come at once—rather *die freemen than live to be the slaves. . . .*

Fellow men, patient sufferers, behold your dearest rights crushed to the earth! See your sons murdered, and your wives, mothers and sisters doomed to prostitution. In the name of the merciful God, and by all that life is worth, let it no longer be a debatable question, whether it is better to choose liberty or death.

In 1822, Denmark [Vesey], of South Carolina, formed a plan for the liberation of his fellow men. In the whole history of human efforts to overthrow slavery, a more complicated and tremendous plan was never formed. He was betrayed by the treachery of his own people, and died a martyr to freedom. Many a brave hero fell, but history, faithful to her high trust, will transcribe his name on the same monument with Moses, [John] Hampden, [William] Tell, [Robert the] Bruce and [William] Wallace, Toussaint L'Ouverture, [Marquis de] Lafayette and [George] Washington. That tremendous movement shook the whole empire of slavery. The guilty soul thieves were overwhelmed with fear. It is a matter of fact that at this time, and in consequence of the threatened revolution, the slave states talked strongly of emancipation. But they blew but one blast of the trumpet of freedom, and then laid it aside. As these men became quiet, the slaveholders ceased to talk about emancipation; and now behold your condition today! Angels sigh over it, and humanity has long since exhausted her tears in weeping on your account!

The patriotic Nathaniel Turner followed Denmark [Vesey]. He was goaded to desperation by wrong and injustice. By despotism, his name has been recorded on the list of infamy, [but] future generations will remember him among the noble and brave.

Next arose the immortal Joseph Cinque, the hero of the *Amistad*. He was a native African, and by the help of God he emancipated a whole shipload of his fellow men on the high seas. And he now sings of liberty on the sunny hills of Africa and beneath his native palm trees, where he hears the lion roar and feels himself as free as the king of the forest.

Next arose Madison Washington, that bright star of freedom, and took his station in the constellation of true heroism. He was a slave on board the brig *Creole,* of Richmond, bound to New Orleans, that great slave mart, with a hundred and four others. Nineteen struck for liberty or death. But one life was taken, and the whole were emancipated, and the vessel was carried into Nassau, New Providence.

Noble men! Those who have fallen in freedom's conflict, their memories will be cherished by the true-hearted and the God-fearing in all future generations; those who are living, their names are surrounded by a halo of glory.

Brethren, arise, arise! Strike for your lives and liberties. Now is the day and the hour. Let every slave throughout the land do this, and the days of slavery are numbered. You cannot be more oppressed than you have been; you cannot suffer greater cruelties than you have already. *Rather die freemen than live to be slaves.* Remember that you are *four millions!* . . .

Let your motto be Resistance! *Resistance!* RESISTANCE! No oppressed people have ever secured their liberty without resistance. What kind of resistance you had better make you must decide by the circumstances that surround you, and according to the suggestion of expediency. Brethren, adieu! Trust in the living God. Labor for the peace of the human race, and remember that you are *four millions!*

Chapter 14

Free Blacks and Suffrage

Alexis de Tocqueville

In the nineteenth century, European travelers often visited the United States to study what was then referred to as the country's "experiment with democracy." The number of books they published constitute an entire genre. The most famous and most frequently reprinted of these studies is Alexis de Tocqueville's Democracy in America *(1839).*

For more on the denial of political and civil rights in the North, see Leon Litwack, North of Slavery: The Negro in the Free States, 1790–1860 *(1961).*

I said one day to an inhabitant of Pennsylvania, "Be so good as to explain to me how it happens, that in a State founded by Quakers, and celebrated for its toleration, freed Blacks are not allowed to exercise civil rights. They pay the taxes; is it not fair that they should have a vote?"

"You insult us," replied my informant, "if you imagine that our legislators could have committed so gross an act of injustice and intolerance."

"What, then, the Blacks possess the right of voting in this country?"

"Without the smallest doubt."

"How comes it, then, that at the polling-booth this morning I did not perceive a single Negro in the whole meeting?"

"This is not the fault of the law: the Negroes have an undisputed right of voting; but they voluntarily abstain from making their appearance."

"A very pretty piece of modesty on their parts!" rejoined I.

"Why, the truth is that they are not disinclined to vote, but they are afraid of being maltreated; in this country the law is sometimes unable to maintain its authority, without the support of the majority. But in this case the majority entertains very strong prejudices against the Blacks, and the magistrates are unable to protect them in the exercise of their legal privileges."

"What, then, the majority claims the right not only of making the laws, but of breaking the laws it has made?"

Chapter 15

Silencing Debate:
The Congressional Gag Rule

In the early nineteenth century, as a further defense of the institution of slavery, southern congressmen—together with their northern allies—passed a rule banning any discussion in Congress of the abolition of slavery or the slave trade, effectively silencing debate on the most critical problems facing the Union. Former president John Quincy Adams (the only president to serve in Congress after his tenure) played a major role in the eventual overturning of the rule.

The following selection is reprinted from "Standing Rules and Orders for Conducting Business in the House of Representatives of the United States," A Manual of Parliamentary Practice Composed Originally for the Use of the Senate of the United States by Thomas Jefferson (Philadelphia: Hogan and Thompson, 1843).

For a history of the gag rule, see William Lee Miller, Arguing about Slavery: John Quincy Adams and the Great Battle in the United States Congress *(1995).*

Rule 21: No petition, memorial, resolution, or other paper praying the abolition of slavery in the District of Columbia, or any State or Territory, or the slave trade between the States and the Territories of the United States, in which it now exists, shall be received by this House, or entertained in any way whatever.

Chapter 16

Equality before the Law

Charles Sumner

Abolitionist Charles Sumner (1811–1874) argued the country's first school integration case, Sarah C. Roberts v. The City of Boston, *in 1849. Sumner's associate in the case was Robert Morris, a black attorney. The court ruled that school segregation was neither unreasonable nor illegal. The Massachusetts legislature later passed a law banning school segregation, in 1855.*

In 1851, Sumner, a member of the Free Soil party who would later join the Republican party, won election to the U.S. Senate, where he served until his death.

The following selection is excerpted from Sumner's argument for school integration before the Supreme Court of Massachusetts, 4 December 1849. For the full text, see The Works of Charles Sumner *(Boston: Lee and Shepard, 1874), 2:327–76.*

May it please your Honors:—

Can any discrimination on account of race or color be made among children entitled to the benefit of our Common Schools under the Constitution and Laws of Massachusetts? This is the question which the Court is now to hear, to consider, and to decide.

Or, stating the question with more detail, and with more particular application to the facts of thc present case, are the Committee having superintendence of the Common Schools of Boston intrusted with *power,* under the Constitution and Laws of Massachusetts, to exclude colored children from the schools, and compel them to find education at separate schools, set apart for colored children only, at distances from their homes less convenient than schools open to white children? . . .

In opening this argument, I begin naturally with the fundamental proposition which, when once established, renders the conclusion irresistible. According to the Constitution of Massachusetts, *all men, without distinction of race or color, are equal before the law.* . . .

Equality under Constitution of Massachusetts and Declaration of Independence

. . . The Declaration of Independence . . . announces among self-evident truths, *"that all men are created equal;* that they are endowed by their Creator with certain unalienable rights; that among these are life, liberty, and the pursuit of happiness." The Constitution of Massachusetts repeats the same truth in a different form, saying, in its first article: *"All men are born free and equal,* and have certain natural essential, and unalienable rights, among which may be reckoned the right of enjoying and defending their lives and liberties." Another article explains what is meant by Equality, saying: "No man, nor corporation or association of men, have any other title to obtain advantages, or particular and exclusive privileges, distinct from those of the community, than what arises from the consideration of services rendered to the public; and this title being in nature neither hereditary, nor transmissible to children, or descendants, or relations by blood, the idea of a man being born a magistrate, lawgiver, or judge is absurd and unnatural." This language, in its natural signification, condemns every form of inequality in civil and political institutions. . . .

Obviously, men are not born equal in physical strength or in mental capacity, in beauty of form or health of body. Diversity or inequality in these respects is the law of creation. From this difference springs divine harmony. But this inequality is in no particular inconsistent with complete civil and political equality.

The equality declared by our fathers in 1776, and made the fundamental law of Massachusetts in 1780, was *Equality before the Law.* Its object was to efface all political or civil distinctions, and to abolish all institutions founded upon *birth.* "All men are *created* equal," says the Declaration of Independence. "All men are born free and equal," says the Massachusetts Bill of Rights. These are not vain words. Within the sphere of their influence, no person can be *created,* no person can be *born,* with civil or political privileges not enjoyed equally by all his fellow-citizens; nor can any institution be established, recognizing distinction of birth. Here is the Great Charter of every human being drawing vital breath upon this soil, whatever may be his condition, and whoever may be his parents. He may be poor, weak, humble, or black,—he may be of Caucasian, Jewish, Indian, or Ethiopian race,—he may be of French, German, English, or Irish extraction; but before the Constitution of Massachusetts all these distinctions disappear. He is not poor, weak, humble, or black; nor is he Caucasian, Jew, Indian, or Ethiopian; nor is he French, German, English, or Irish; he is a MAN, the equal of all his fellow-men. He is one of the children of the State, which, like an impartial parent, regards all its offspring with an equal care. . . .

Equality by Legislation of Massachusetts

The Legislature of Massachusetts, in entire harmony with the Constitution, has made no discrimination of race or color in the establishment of Common Schools. . . .

The provisions of the Law are entitled, *Of the Public Schools* [Revised Statutes, ch. 23], meaning our Common Schools. To these we must look to ascertain what, constitutes a Public School. . . .

If we examine the text of this statute, we shall find nothing to sustain the rule of exclusion which has been set up. The first section provides, that "in every town, containing fifty families or householders, there shall be kept in each year, at the charge of the town, by a teacher or teachers of competent ability and good morals, *one school* for the instruction of *children* in Orthography, Reading, Writing, English Grammar, Geography, Arithmetic, and Good Behavior, for the term of six months, or two or more such schools, for terms of time that shall together be equivalent to six months." The second, third, and fourth sections provide for the number of such schools in towns having respectively one hundred, one hundred and fifty, and five hundred families or householders. There is no language recognizing any discrimination of race or color. Thus, in every town, the schools, whether one or more, are "for the instruction of *children*" generally,—not children of any particular class or race or color, but children,—meaning the children of the town where the schools are. . . .

[T]here is but one Public School in Massachusetts. This is the Common School, equally free to all the inhabitants. There is nothing establishing an exclusive or separate school for any particular class, rich or poor, Catholic or Protestant, white or black. In the eye of the law there is but one class where all interests, opinions, conditions, and colors commingle in harmony,—excluding none. . . .

Separate Schools Inconsistent with Equality

It is easy to see that the exclusion of colored children from the Public Schools is a constant inconvenience to them and their parents, which white children and white parents are not obliged to bear. Here the facts are plain and unanswerable, showing a palpable violation of Equality. *The black and white are not equal before the law.* I am at a loss to understand how anybody can assert that they are.

Among the regulations of the Primary School Committee is one to this effect. "Scholars to go to the school nearest their residences. Applicants for admission to our schools (with the exception and provision referred to in the preceding rule) are especially entitled to enter the schools nearest to their places of residence." The exception here is "of those for whom special provision has been made" in separate schools,—that is, colored children.

In this rule—without the unfortunate exception—is part of the beauty so conspicuous in our Common Schools. It is the boast of England, that, through the multitude of courts, justice is brought to every man's door. It may also be the boast of our Common Schools, that, through the multitude of schools, education in Boston is brought to every *white* man's door. But it is not brought to every *black* man's door. He is obliged to go for it, to travel for it, to walk for it,—often a great distance. The facts in the present case are not so strong as those of other cases within my knowledge. But here the little child, only five years old, is compelled, if attending the nearest African School, to go a distance two thousand one hundred feet from her home, while the nearest Primary School is only nine hundred feet, and, in doing this, she passes by no less than five different Primary Schools, forming part of our Common Schools, and open to white children, all of which are closed to her. Surely this is not *Equality before the Law*. . . .

School Committee Have No Power to Discriminate on Account of Color

The Committee charged with the superintendence of the Common Schools of Boston have no power to make any discrimination on account of race or color.

It has been seen already that this power is inconsistent with the Declaration of Independence, with the Constitution and Laws of Massachusetts, and with adjudications of the Supreme Court. The stream cannot rise higher than the fountainhead; and if there be nothing in these elevated sources from which this power can spring, it must be considered a nullity. . . .

Separate School Not an Equivalent for Common School

But it is said that the School Committee, in thus classifying the children, have not violated any principle of Equality, inasmuch as they provide a school with competent instructors for colored children, where they have advantages equal to those provided for white children. It is argued, that, in excluding colored children from Common Schools open to white children, the Committee furnish an *equivalent*.

Here there are several answers. I shall touch them briefly, as they are included in what has been already said.

1. The separate school for colored children is not one of the schools established by the law relating to Public Schools. It is not a Common School. As such it has no legal existence, and therefore cannot be a *legal equivalent*. . . .

2. The second is that in point of fact the separate school is not an equivalent. We have already seen that it is the occasion of inconvenience to colored children, which would not arise, if they had access to the nearest Common School, besides compelling parents to pay an additional tax, and inflicting upon child and parent the stigma of Caste. Still further,—and this consideration cannot be neglected,—the matters taught in the two schools may be precisely the same, but a school exclusively devoted to one class must differ essentially in spirit and character from that Common School known to the law, where all classes meet together in Equality. It is a mockery to call it an equivalent.

3. But there is yet another answer. Admitting that it is an equivalent, still the colored children cannot be compelled to take it. Their rights are found in Equality before the Law; nor can they be called to renounce one jot of this. They have an equal right with white children to the Common Schools. A separate school, though well endowed, would not secure to them that precise Equality which they

would enjoy in the Common Schools. The Jews in Rome are confined to a particular district called the Ghetto, and in Frankfort [Germany] to a district known as the Jewish Quarter. It is possible that their accommodations are as good as they would be able to occupy, if left free to choose throughout Rome and Frankfort; but this compulsory segregation from the mass of citizens is of itself an *inequality* which we condemn. It is a vestige of ancient intolerance directed against a despised people. It is of the same character with the separate schools in Boston. . . .

Evils of Separate Schools

But it is said that these separate schools are for the benefit of both colors, and of the Public Schools. In similar spirit Slavery is sometimes said to be for the benefit of master and slave, and of the country where it exists. There is a mistake in the one case as great as in the other. This is clear. Nothing unjust, nothing ungenerous, can be for the benefit of any person or any thing. From some seeming selfish superiority, or from the gratified vanity of class, short-sighted mortals may hope to draw permanent good; but even-handed justice rebukes these efforts and redresses the wrong. The whites themselves are injured by the separation. Who can doubt this? With the Law as their monitor, they are taught to regard a portion of the human family, children of God, created in his image, coequals in his love, as a separate and degraded class; they are taught practically to deny that grand revelation of Christianity, the Brotherhood of Man. Hearts, while yet tender with childhood, are hardened, and ever afterward testify to this legalized uncharitableness. Nursed in the sentiments of Caste, receiving it with the earliest food of knowledge, they are unable to eradicate it from their natures, and then weakly and impiously charge upon our Heavenly Father the prejudice derived from an unchristian school. Their characters are debased, and they become less fit for the duties of citizenship. . . .

Who can say that this does not injure the blacks? Theirs, in its best estate, is an unhappy lot. A despised class, blasted by prejudice and shut out from various opportunities, they feel this proscription from the Common Schools as a peculiar brand. Beyond this, it deprives them of those healthful, animating influences which would come from participation in the studies of their white brethren. It adds to their discouragements. It widens their separation from the community, and postpones that great day of reconciliation which is yet to come.

The whole system of Common Schools suffers also. It is a narrow perception of their high aim which teaches that they are merely to furnish an equal amount of knowledge to all, and therefore, provided all be taught, it is of little consequence where and in what company. The law contemplates not only that all shall be taught, but that *all* shall be taught *together*. They are not only to receive equal quantities of knowledge, but all are to receive it in the same way. All are to approach the same common fountain together; nor can there be any exclusive source for individual or class. The school is the little world where the child is trained for the larger world of life. It is the microcosm preparatory to the macrocosm, and therefore it must cherish and develop the virtues and the sympathies needed in the larger world. And since, according to our institutions, all classes, without distinction of color, meet in the performance of civil duties, so should they all, without distinction of color, meet in the school, beginning there those relations of Equality which the Constitution and Laws promise to all. . . .

In the Caste Schools of Boston the prejudice of color seeks its final refuge. It is for you to drive it forth. You do well, when you rebuke and correct individual offences; but it is a higher office to rebuke and correct a vicious institution. Each individual is limited in influence; but an institution has the influence of numbers organized by law. The charity of one man may counteract or remedy the uncharitableness of another; but no individual can counteract or remedy the uncharitableness of an organized injury. Against it private benevolence is powerless. It is a monster to be hunted down by the public and the constituted authorities. And such is the institution of Caste in the Common Schools of Boston, which now awaits a just condemnation from a just Court.

Chapter 17

Free Blacks and the Fugitive Slave Act

Martin Delany

The Fugitive Slave Act of 1793 was expanded in 1850, increasing the jeopardy not only of runaway slaves but of free blacks as well.

Pioneer black nationalist Martin R. Delany (1812–1885) was born as a free black in Charlestown, Virginia (now West Virginia). Delany was one of the first blacks admitted to Harvard Medical School, and he cofounded the abolitionist newspaper the North Star *with Frederick Douglass. "I thank God for making me a man simply," Douglass said, "but Delany always thanks Him for making him a black man." "The black and colored races are four-sixths of all the population of the world," Delany wrote, "and these people are fast tending to a common cause with each other. The white races are but one third of the population of the globe . . . and it cannot much longer continue that two thirds will passively submit to the universal domination of this one third."*

Delany investigated various emigration schemes, including a free black republic in Nicaragua. In 1859 he explored sections of Africa. During the Civil War, his oldest son, Toussaint L'Ouverture—named after the black liberator of Haiti—fought as a member of the famous 54th Massachusetts Volunteers. In later years, Delany shifted his colonization interests to Liberia. He died in Ohio.

The following selection is excerpted from The Condition, Elevation, Emigration, and Destiny of the Colored People of the United States Politically Considered *(Philadelphia, 1852).*

The most prominent provisions of the Constitution of the United States, and those which form the fundamental basis of personal security, are they which provide, that every person shall be secure in their person and property: that no person may be deprived of liberty without due process of law, and that for crime or misdemeanor that there may be no process of law that shall work corruption of blood. By corruption of blood is meant, that process, by which a person is *degraded* and deprived of rights common to the enfranchised citizen—of the rights of an elector, and of eligibility to the office of a representative of the people; in a word, that no person nor their posterity, may ever be debased beneath the level of the recognised basis of American citizenship. This debasement and degradation is "corruption of blood;" politically understood—a legal acknowledgement of inferiority of birth.

Heretofore, it ever has been denied, that the United States recognised or knew any difference between the people—that the Constitution makes no distinction, but includes in its provisions, all the people alike. This is not true, and certainly is blind absurdity in us at least, who have suffered the dread consequences of this delusion, not now to see it.

By the provisions of this [Fugitive Slave] bill, the colored people of the United States are positively degraded beneath the level of the whites—are made liable at any time, in any place, and under all circumstances, to be arrested—and upon the claim of any white person, without the privilege, even of making a defence, sent into endless bondage. Let no visionary nonsense about *habeas corpus*, or a *fair trial*, deceive us; there are no such rights granted in this bill, and except where the commissioner is too ignorant to understand when reading it, or too stupid to enforce it when he does understand, there is no earthly chance—no hope under heaven for the colored person who is brought before one of these officers of the law. Any leniency that may be expected, must proceed from the whims or caprice of the magistrate—in fact, it is optional with them; and our rights and liberty entirely at their disposal.

We are slaves in the midst of freedom, waiting patiently, and unconcernedly—indifferently, and stupidly, for masters to come and lay claim to us, trusting to their generosity, whether or not they will own us and carry us into endless bondage.

The slave is more secure than we; he knows who holds the heel upon his bosom—we know not the wretch who may grasp us by the throat. His master may be a man of some conscientious scruples; ours may be unmerciful. Good or bad, mild or harsh, easy or hard, lenient or severe, saint or satan—whenever that master demands any one of us—even our affectionate wives and darling little children, *we must go into slavery*—there is *no alternative*. The *will* of the man who sits in judgment on our liberty, is the law. To him is given *all power* to say, whether or not we have a right to enjoy freedom. This is the power over the slave in the South—this is now extended to the North. The will of the man who sits in judgment over us is the law; because it is explicitly provided that the *decision* of the commissioner shall be final, from which there can be no appeal.

The freed man of the South is even more secure than the freeborn of the North; because such persons usually have their records in the slave states, bringing their "papers" with them; and the slaveholders will be faithful to their own acts. The Northern freeman knows no records; he despises the "papers."

Depend upon no promised protection of citizens in any quarter. Their own property and liberty are jeopardised, and they will not sacrifice them for us. This we may not expect them to do.

Besides, there are no people who ever lived, love their country and obey their laws as the Americans.

Their country is their Heaven—their Laws their Scriptures—and the decrees of their Magistrates obeyed as the fiat of God. It is the most consummate delusion and misdirected confidence to depend upon them for protection and for a moment suppose even our children safe while walking in the streets among them.

A people capable of originating and sustaining such a law as this, are not the people to whom we are willing to entrust our liberty at discretion.

What can we do?—What shall we do? This is the great and important question:—Shall we submit to be dragged like brutes before heartless men, and sent into degradation and bondage?—Shall we fly, or shall we resist? Ponder well and reflect.

A learned jurist in the United States, (Chief Justice John Gibson of Pennsylvania,) lays down this as a fundamental right in the United States: that "Every man's house is his castle, and he has the right to defend it unto the taking of life, against any attempt to enter it against his will, except for crime," by well authenticated process.

But we have no such right. It was not intended for us, any more than any other provision of the law, intended for the protection of Americans. The policy is against us—it is useless to contend against it.

This is the law of the land and must be obeyed; and we candidly advise that it is useless for us to contend against it. To suppose its repeal, is to anticipate an overthrow of the Confederate Union; and we must be allowed an expression of opinion, when we say, that candidly we believe, the existence of the Fugitive Slave Law *necessary* to the continuance of the National Compact. This Law is the foundation, of the Compromise—remove it, and the consequences are easily determined. We say necessary to the continuance of the National Compact: certainly we will not be understood as meaning that the enactment of such a Law was *really* necessary, or as favoring in the least this political monstrosity of the THIRTY-FIRST CONGRESS of the UNITED STATES of AMERICA—surely not at all; but we speak logically and politically, leaving morality and right out of the question—taking our position on the acknowledged popular basis of American Policy; arguing from premise to conclusion. We must abandon all vague theory, and look at *facts* as they really are[,] viewing ourselves in our true political position in the body politic. To imagine ourselves to be included in the body politic, except by express legislation, is at war with common sense, and contrary to fact. Legislation, the administration of the laws of the country, and the exercise of rights by the people, all prove to the contrary. We are politically, not of them, but aliens to the laws and political privileges of the country. These are truths—fixed facts, that quaint theory and exhausted moralising, are impregnable to, and fall harmlessly before.

It is useless to talk about our rights in individual States: we can have no rights there as citizens, not recognised in our common country; as the citizens of one State, are entitled to all the rights and privileges of an American citizen in all the States—the nullity of the one necessarily implying the nullity of the other. These provisions then do not include the colored people of the United States; since there is no power left in them, whereby they may protect us as their own citizens. Our descent, by the laws of the country, stamps us with inferiority—upon us has this law worked *corruption of blood*. We are in the hands of the General Government, and no State can rescue us. The Army and Navy stand at the service of our enslavers, the whole force of which, may at any moment—even in the dead of night, as has been done—when sunk in the depth of slumber, called out for the purpose of forcing our mothers, sisters, wives, and children, or ourselves, into hopeless servitude, there to weary out a miserable life, a relief from which, death would be hailed with joy. Heaven and earth—God and Humanity!—are not these sufficient to arouse the most worthless among mankind, of whatever descent, to a sense of their true position? These laws apply to us—shall we not be aroused?

Chapter 18

The Fugitive Slave Law

Harriet Jacobs

Harriet Jacobs (1813?–1897) was born into slavery in North Carolina and escaped to the North in 1842. In 1861, under the pseudonym "Linda Brent" she published a book about her life as a slave. In the 1880s she helped organize the National Association of Colored Women.

The following selection is excerpted from Incidents in the Life of a Slave Girl *(1861).*

I was alone again. It was necessary for me to be earning money, and I preferred that it should be among those who knew me. On my return from Rochester, I called at the house of Mr. Bruce, to see Mary, the darling little babe that had thawed my heart, when it was freezing into a cheerless distrust of all my fellow-beings. She was growing a tall girl now, but I loved her always. Mr. Bruce had married again, and it was proposed that I should become nurse to a new infant. I had but one hesitation, and that was my feeling of insecurity in New York, now greatly increased by the passage of the Fugitive Slave Law. However, I resolved to try the experiment. I was again fortunate in my employer. The new Mrs. Bruce was an American, brought up under aristocratic influences, and still living in the midst of them; but if she had any prejudice against color, I was never made aware of it; and as for the system of slavery, she had a most hearty dislike of it. No sophistry of Southerners could blind her to its enormity. She was a person of excellent principles and a noble heart. To me, from that hour to the present, she has been a true and sympathizing friend. Blessings be with her and hers!

About the time that I reentered the Bruce family, an event occurred of disastrous import to the colored people. The slave Hamlin, the first fugitive that came under the new law, was given up by the bloodhounds of the north to the bloodhounds of the south. It was the beginning of a reign of terror to the colored population. The great city rushed on in its whirl of excitement, taking no note of the "short and simple annals of the poor." But while fashionables were listening to the thrilling voice of Jenny Lind in Metropolitan Hall, the thrilling voices of poor hunted colored people went up, in an agony of supplication, to the Lord, from Zion's church. Many families, who had lived in the city for twenty years, fled from it now. Many a poor washerwoman, who, by hard labor, had made herself a comfortable home, was obliged to sacrifice her furniture, bid a hurried farewell to friends, and seek her fortune among strangers in Canada. Many a wife discovered a secret she had never known before—that her husband was a fugitive, and must leave her to insure his own safety. Worse still, many a husband discovered that his wife had fled from slavery years ago, and as "the child follows the condition of its mother," the children of his love were liable to be seized and carried into slavery. Every where, in those humble homes, there was consternation and anguish. But what cared the legislators of the "dominant race" for the blood they were crushing out of trampled hearts?

When my brother William spent his last evening with me, before he went to California, we talked nearly all the time of the distress brought on our oppressed people by the passage of this iniquitous law; and never had I seen him manifest such bitterness of spirit, such stern hostility to our oppressors. He was himself free from the operation of the law; for he did not run from any Slaveholding State, being brought into the Free States by his master. But I was subject to it; and so were hundreds of intelligent and industrious people all around us. I seldom ventured into the streets; and when it was necessary to do an errand for Mrs. Bruce, or any of the family, I went as much as possible through back streets and by-ways. What a disgrace to a city calling itself free, that inhabitants, guiltless of offence, and seeking to perform their duties conscientiously, should be condemned to live in such incessant fear, and have nowhere to turn for protection! This state of things, of course, gave rise to many impromptu vigilance committees. Every colored person, and every friend of their prosecuted race, kept their eyes wide open. Every evening I examined the newspapers carefully, to see what Southerners had put up at the hotels. I did this for my own sake, thinking my young mistress and her husband might be among the list; I wished also to give information to others, if necessary; for if many were "running to and fro," I resolved that "knowledge should be increased."

This brings up one of my Southern reminiscences, which I will here briefly relate. I was somewhat acquainted with a slave named Luke, who belonged to a wealthy man in our vicinity. His master died, leaving a son and daughter heirs to his large fortune. In the division of the slaves, Luke was included in the son's portion. This young man became a prey to the vices growing out of the "patriarchal institution," and when he went to the north, to complete his education, he carried his vices with him. He was brought home, deprived of the use of his limbs, by excessive dissipation. Luke was appointed to wait upon his bed-ridden master, whose despotic habits were greatly increased by exasperation at his own helplessness. He kept a cowhide beside him, and, for the most trivial occurrence, he would order his attendant to bare his back, and kneel beside the couch, while he whipped him till his strength was exhausted. Some days he was not allowed to wear anything but his shirt, in order to be in readiness to be flogged. A day seldom passed without his receiving more or less blows. If the slightest resistance was offered, the town constable was sent for to execute the punishment, and Luke learned from experience how much more the constable's strong arm was to be dreaded than the comparatively feeble one of his master. The arm of his tyrant grew weaker, and was finally palsied; and then the constable's services were in constant requisition. The fact that he was entirely dependent on Luke's care, and was obliged to be tended like an infant, instead of inspiring any gratitude or compassion towards his poor slave, seemed only to increase his irritability and cruelty. As he lay there on his bed, a mere degraded wreck of manhood, he took into his head the strangest freaks of despotism; and if Luke hesitated to submit to his orders, the constable was immediately sent for. Some of these freaks were of a nature too filthy to be repeated. When I fled from the house of bondage, I left poor Luke still chained to the bedside of this cruel and disgusting wretch.

One day, when I had been requested to do an errand for Mrs. Bruce, I was hurrying through back streets, as usual, when I saw a young man approaching, whose face was familiar to me. As he came nearer, I recognized Luke, I always rejoiced to see or hear of any one who had escaped from the black pit; but, remembering this poor fellow's extreme hardships, I was peculiarly glad to see him on Northern soil, though I no longer called it *free* soil. I well remembered what a desolate feeling it was to be alone among strangers, and I went up to him and greeted him cordially. At first, he did not know me; but when I mentioned my name, he remembered all about me. I told him of the Fugitive Slave Law, and asked him if he did not know that New York was a city of kidnappers.

He replied, "De risk ain't so bad for me, as 'tis fur you. 'Cause I runned away from de speculator, and you runned away from the massa. Dem speculators vont spen dar money to come here fur a runaway, if dey ain't sartin sure to put dar hans right on him. An I tell you I's tuk good car 'bout dat. I had too hard times down dar, to let 'em ketch dis nigger."

He then told me of the advice he had received, and the plans he had laid. I asked if he had money enough to take him to Canada. "'Pend upon it, I hab," he replied. "I tuk car fur dat. I'd bin workin all my days fur dem cussed whites, an got no pay but kicks and cuffs. So I tought dis nigger had a right to money nuff to bring him to de Free States. Massa Henry he lib till ebery body vish him dead; an ven he did die, I knowed de debbil would hab him, an vouldn't vant him to bring his money 'long too. So I tuk some of his bills, and put 'em in de pocket of his old trousers. An ven he was buried, dis nigger ask fur dem ole trousers, an dey gub 'em to me." With a low, chuckling laugh, he added, "You see I didn't steal it; dey gub it to me. I tell you, I had mighty hard time to keep de speculator from findin it; but he didn't git it."

This is a fair specimen of how moral sense is educated by slavery. When a man has his wages stolen from him, year after year, and the laws sanction and enforce the theft, how can he be expected to have more regard to honesty than has the man who robs him? I have become somewhat enlightened, but I confess that I agree with poor, ignorant, much-abused Luke, in thinking he had a *right* to that money, as a portion of his unpaid wages. He went to Canada forthwith, and I have not since heard from him.

All that winter I lived in a state of anxiety. When I took the children out to breathe the air, I closely observed the countenances of all I met. I dreaded the approach of summer, when snakes and slaveholders make their appearance. I was, in fact, a slave in New York, as subject to slave laws as I had been in a Slave State. Strange incongruity in a State called free!

Spring returned, and I received warning from the south that Dr. Flint knew of my return to my old place, and was making preparations to have me caught. I learned afterwards that my dress, and that of Mrs. Bruce's children had been described to him by some of the Northern tools, which slaveholders employ for their base purposes, and then indulge in sneers at their cupidity and mean servility.

I immediately informed Mrs. Bruce of my danger, and she took prompt measures for my safety. My place as nurse could not be supplied immediately, and this generous, sympathizing lady proposed that I should carry her baby away. It was a comfort to me to have the child with me; for the heart is reluctant to be torn away from every object it loves. But how few mothers would have consented to have one of their own babes become a fugitive, for the sake of a poor, hunted nurse, on whom the legislators of the country had let loose the bloodhounds! When I spoke of the sacrifice she was making, in depriving herself of her dear baby, she replied, "It is better for you to have baby with you, Linda; for it they get on your track, they will be obliged to bring the child to me; and then, if there is a possibility of saving you, you shall be saved."

This lady had a very wealthy relative, a benevolent gentleman in many respects, but aristocratic and pro-slavery. He remonstrated with her for harboring a fugitive slave; told her she was violating the laws of her country; and asked her if she was aware of the penalty. She replied, "I am very well aware of it. It is imprisonment and one thousand dollars fine. Shame on my country that it is so! I am ready to incur the penalty. I will go to the state's prison, rather than have any poor victim torn from *my* house, to be carried back to slavery."

The noble heart! The brave heart! The tears are in my eyes while I write of her. May the God of the helpless reward her for her sympathy with my persecuted people!

I was sent into New England, where I was sheltered by the wife of a senator, whom I shall always hold in grateful remembrance. This honorable gentleman would not have voted for the Fugitive State Law, as did the senator in "Uncle Tom's Cabin"; on the contrary, he was strongly opposed to it; but he was enough under its influence to be afraid of having me remain in his house many hours. So I was sent into the country, where I remained a month with the baby. When it was supposed that Dr. Flint's emissaries had lost track of me, and given up the pursuit for the present, I returned to New York.

Chapter 19

What to the Slave Is the Fourth of July?

Frederick Douglass

Frederick Douglass (1817?–1895), the foremost black leader of the nineteenth century, was born into slavery in Maryland. After escaping in 1838, he settled in Massachusetts, where he became a lecturer for the Massachusetts Antislavery Society and an early advocate of woman suffrage. He published Narrative of the Life of Frederick Douglass, *an autobiography about his life under slavery, in various editions beginning in 1845. In 1847, Douglass founded and edited the* North Star, *a weekly abolitionist newspaper that continued publication until 1864. Its masthead declared: "Right is of no sex—Truth is of no color—God is the Father of us all, and we are all Brethren." For biographies, see William McFeely,* Frederick Douglass *(1991) and David Blight,* Frederick Douglass' Civil War *(1989).*

The following selection is excerpted from his speech "The Meaning of July Fourth for the Negro," delivered 4 July 1852 in Rochester, New York. For the full text, see The Life and Writings of Frederick Douglass, *vol. 2, ed. Philip Foner (New York: International Publishers, 1950).*

Fellow–Citizens, pardon me, and allow me to ask, why am I called upon to speak here to-day? What have I, or those I represent, to do with your national independence? Are the great principles of political freedom and of natural justice, embodied in that Declaration of Independence, extended to us? And am I, therefore, called upon to bring our humble offering to the national altar, and to confess the benefits and express devout gratitude for the blessings resulting from your independence to us?

Would to God, both for your sakes and ours, that an affirmative answer could be truthfully returned to these questions! Then would my task be light, and my burden easy and delightful. For *who* is there so cold, that a nation's sympathy could not warm him? Who so obdurate and dead to the claims of gratitude, that would not thankfully acknowledge such priceless benefits? Who so stolid and selfish, that would not give his voice to swell the hallelujahs of a nation's jubilee, when the chains of servitude had been torn from his limbs? I am not that man. . . .

I say it with a sad sense of the disparity between us. I am not included within the pale of this glorious anniversary! Your high independence only reveals the immeasurable distance between us. The blessings in which you this day rejoice are not enjoyed in common. The rich inheritance of justice, liberty, prosperity, and independence, bequeathed by your fathers is shared by you, not by me. The sunlight that brought life and healing to you has brought stripes and death to me. This Fourth of July is *yours, not mine. You* may rejoice, *I* must mourn. To drag a man in fetters into the grand illuminated temple of liberty, and call upon him to join you in joyous anthems, were inhuman mockery and sacrilegious irony. Do you mean, citizens, to mock me, by asking me to speak to-day? . . .

Fellow-citizens, above your national, tumultuous joy, I hear the mournful wail of millions, whose chains, heavy and grievous yesterday, are to-day rendered more intolerable by the jubilant shouts that reach them. If I do forget, if I do not remember those bleeding children of sorrow this day, "may my right hand forget her cunning, and may my tongue cleave to the roof of my mouth!" To forget them, to pass lightly over their wrongs, and to chime in with the popular theme, would be treason most scandalous and shocking, and would make me a reproach before God and the world. My subject, then, fellow-citizens, is American Slavery. I shall see this day and its popular characteristics from the slave's point of view. Standing there, identified with the American bondman, making his wrongs mine, I do not hesitate to declare, with all my soul, that the character and conduct of this nation never looked blacker to me than on this Fourth of July! Whether we turn to the declarations of the past, or to the professions of the present, the conduct of the nation seems equally hideous and revolting. America is false to the past, false to the present, and solemnly binds herself to be false to the future. Standing with God and the crushed and bleeding slave on this occasion, I will, in the name of humanity, which is outraged, in the name of liberty, which is fettered, in the name of the Constitution and the Bible, which are disregarded and trampled upon, dare to call in question and to denounce, with all the emphasis I can command, everything that serves to perpetuate slavery—the great sin and shame of America! "I will not equivocate; I will not excuse"; I will use the severest language I can command, and yet not one word shall escape me that any man, whose judgement is not blinded by prejudice, or who is not at heart a slave holder, shall not confess to be right and just.

But I fancy I hear some of my audience say it is just in this circumstance that you and your brother abolitionists fail to make a favorable impression on the public mind. Would you argue more, and denounce less; would you persuade more and rebuke less; your cause would be much more likely to succeed. But, I submit, where all is plain there is nothing to be argued. What point in the anti-slavery creed would you have me argue? On what branch of the subject do the people of this country need light? Must I undertake to prove that the slave is a man? That point is conceded already. Nobody doubts it. The slave holders themselves acknowledge it in the enactment of laws for their government. They acknowledge it when they punish disobedience on the part of the slave. There are seventy-two crimes in the State of Virginia, which, if committed by a black man (no matter how ignorant he be), subject him to the punishment of death; while only two of these same crimes will subject a white man to like punishment. What is this but the acknowledgment that the slave is a moral, intellectual, and responsible being? The manhood of the slave is conceded. It is admitted in the fact that Southern statute books are covered with enactments, forbidding, under severe fines and penalties, the teaching of the slave to read and write. When you can point to any such laws in reference to the beasts of the field, then I may consent to argue the manhood of the slave. When the dogs in your streets, when the fowls of the air, when the cattle on your hills, when the fish of the sea, and the reptiles that crawl, shall be unable to distinguish the slave from a brute, *then* I can argue with you that the slave is a man!

For the present, it is enough to affirm the equal manhood of the Negro race. Is it not astonishing that, while we are plowing, planting, and reaping, using all kinds of mechanical tools, erecting houses, constructing bridges, building ships, working in metals of brass, iron, copper, silver, and gold; that, while we are reading, writing, and ciphering, acting as clerks, merchants, and secretaries, having among us lawyers, doctors, ministers, poets, authors, editors, orators, and teachers; that, while we are engaged in all the enterprises common to other men—digging gold in California, capturing the whale in the Pacific, feeding sheep and cattle on the hill-side, living, moving, acting, thinking, planning, living in families as husbands, wives, and children, and above all, confessing and worshipping the Christian God, and looking hopefully for life and immortality beyond the grave—we are called upon to prove that we are men!

Would you have me argue that man is entitled to liberty? That he is the rightful owner of his own body? You have already declared it. Must I argue the wrongfulness of slavery? Is that a question for Republicans? Is it to be settled by the rules of logic and argumentation, as a matter beset with great difficulty, involving a doubtful application of the principle of justice, hard to be understood? How should I look to-day in the presence of Americans, dividing and subdividing a discourse, to show that men have a natural right to freedom, speaking of it relatively and positively, negatively and affirmatively? To do so would be to make myself ridiculous, and to offer an insult to your understanding. There is not a man beneath the canopy of heaven who does not know that slavery is wrong *for him.*

What, am I to argue that it is wrong to make men brutes, to rob them of their liberty, to work them without wages, to keep them ignorant of their relations to their fellow men, to beat them with sticks, to flay their flesh with the lash, to load their limbs with irons, to hunt them with dogs, to sell them at auction, to sunder their families, to knock out their teeth, to burn their flesh, to starve them into obedience and submission to their masters? Must I argue that a system thus marked with blood and stained with pollution is *wrong*? No! I will not. I have better employment for my time and strength than such arguments would imply.

What, then, remains to be argued? Is it that slavery is not divine; that God did not establish it; that our doctors of divinity are mistaken? There is blasphemy in the thought. That which is inhuman cannot be divine. *Who* can reason on such a proposition? They that can, may; I cannot. The time for such argument is past.

At a time like this, scorching irony, not convincing argument, is needed. O! had I the ability, and could reach the nation's ear, I would to-day pour out a fiery stream of biting ridicule, blasting reproach, withering sarcasm, and stern rebuke. For it is not light that is needed, but fire; it is not the gentle shower, but thunder. We need the storm, the whirlwind, and the earthquake. The feeling of the nation must be quickened; the conscience of the nation must be roused; the propriety of the nation must be startled; the hypocrisy of the nation must be exposed; and its crimes against God and man must be denounced.

What, to the American slave, is your Fourth of July? I answer, a day that reveals to him more than all other days in the year, the gross injustice and cruelty to which he is the constant victim. To him your celebration is a sham; your boasted liberty, an unholy license; your national greatness, swelling vanity; your sounds of rejoicing are empty and heartless; your denunciation of tyrants, brass-fronted impudence; your shouts of liberty and equality, hollow mockery; your prayers and hymns, your sermons and thanksgivings, with all your religious parade and solemnity, are to him mere bombast, fraud, deception, impiety, and hypocrisy—a thin veil to cover up crimes which would disgrace a nation of savages. There is not a nation of the earth guilty of practices more shocking and bloody than are the people of these United States, at this very hour.

Go where you may, search where you will, roam through all the monarchies and despotisms of the Old World, travel through South America, search out every abuse, and when you have found the last, lay your facts by the side of the everyday practices of this nation, and you will say with me that, for revolting barbarity and shameless hypocrisy, America reigns without a rival.

Chapter 20

Dred Scott v. Sandford (1857)

In the 1850s, the Supreme Court was composed of five southerners (including the Chief Justice) from slaveholding families, two "doughfaces" (northerners with proslavery sympathies), and two other northerners. Seven judges had been appointed by Democratic presidents who were themselves southern slave owners.

In the 1830s Dred Scott, a black slave, lived for two years with his owner in the free state of Illinois and then moved to the Wisconsin Territory (an area where slavery was forbidden under the Missouri Compromise). Scott was later sent to Missouri, where he sued for his freedom. In Dred Scott v. Sandford, *a partisan 7–2 decision that aggravated already heated sectional differences, the Supreme Court ruled that Scott had not been made free by his previous residence. Chief Justice Roger Taney argued that a black man could not be a citizen of the United States, and therefore Scott had no status to sue; that Congress could not abolish slavery in the territories, and thus the Missouri Compromise was invalid; and that slaves were property protected under the Constitution. Perhaps most infamously, Taney stated that a black man "had no rights which the white man was bound to respect."*

The following selection is excerpted from Dred Scott v. Sandford *(1857).*

Mr. Chief Justice Roger Taney delivered the opinion of the court:

The question is simply this: Can a negro, whose ancestors were imported into this country and sold as slaves, become a member of the political community formed and brought into existence by the Constitution of the United States, and as such become entitled to all the rights, and privileges, and immunities, guaranteed by that instrument to the citizen? One of which rights is the privilege of suing in a court of the United States. . . .

The words "people of the United States" and "citizens" are synonymous terms. . . . The question before us is, whether the class of persons described in the plea in abatement compose a portion of this people, and are constituent members of this sovereignty? We think they are not, and that they are not included, and were not intended to be included, under the word "citizens" in the Constitution, and can therefore claim none of the rights and privileges which that instrument provides for and secures to citizens of the United States. On the contrary, they were at that time considered as a subordinate and inferior class of beings, who had been subjugated by the dominant race, and whether emancipated or not, yet remained subject to their authority, and had no rights or privileges but such as those who held the power and the Government might choose to grant them. . . .

The question then arises, whether the provisions of the Constitution, in relation to the personal rights and privileges to which the citizen of a State should be entitled, embraced the negro African race, at that time in this country, or who might afterwards be imported, who had then or should afterwards be made free in any State; and to put it in the power of a single State to make him a citizen of the United States, and endue him with the full rights of citizenship in every other State without consent? Does the Constitution of the United States act upon him whenever he shall be made free under the laws of a State, and raised there to the rank of a citizen, and immediately clothe him with all the privileges of a citizen in every other State, and in its own courts?

The court thinks the affirmative of these propositions cannot be maintained. And if it cannot, the plaintiff in error could not be a citizen of the State of Missouri, within the meaning of the Constitution of the United States, and consequently, was not entitled to sue in its courts. . . .

In the opinion of the court, the legislation and histories of the times, and the language used in the Declaration of Independence, show, that neither the class of persons who had been imported as slaves, nor their descendants, whether they had become free or not, were then acknowledged as a part of the people, nor intended to be included in the general words used in that memorable instrument.

It is difficult at this day to realize the state of public opinion in relation to that unfortunate race, which prevailed in the civilized and enlightened portions of the world at the time of the Declaration of Independence, and when the Constitution of the United States was framed and adopted. But the public history of every European nation displays it, in a manner too plain to be mistaken.

They had for more than a century before been regarded as beings of an inferior order; and altogether unfit to associate with the white race, either in social or political relations; and so far inferior, that they had no rights which the white man was bound to respect; and that the negro might justly and lawfully be reduced to slavery for his benefit. He was bought and sold, and treated as an ordinary article of merchandise and traffic, whenever a profit could be made by it. This opinion was at that time fixed and universal in the civilized portion of the white race. It was regarded as an axiom in morals as well as in politics, which no one thought of disputing, or supposed to be open to dispute; and men in every grade and position in society daily and habitually acted upon it in their private pursuits, as well as in matters of public concern, without doubting for a moment the correctness of this opinion.

And in no nation was this opinion more firmly fixed or more uniformly acted upon than by the English government and the English people. They not only seized them on the coast of Africa, and sold them or held them in slavery for their own use; but they took them as ordinary articles of merchandise to every county where they could make a profit on them, and were far more extensively engaged in this commerce than any other nation in the world. . . .

[Colonial Maryland and Massachusetts law] show that a perpetual and impassable barrier was intended to be erected between the white race and the one which they had reduced to slavery, and governed as subjects with absolute and despotic power, and which they then looked upon as so far below them in the scale of created beings, that intermarriages between white persons and negroes or mulattoes were regarded as unnatural and immoral, and punished as crimes, not only in the parties, but in the person who joined them in marriage. And no distinction in this respect was made between the free negro or mulatto and the slave, but his stigma, of the deepest degradation, was fixed upon the whole race. . . .

The language of the Declaration of Independence is equally conclusive. . . .

It . . . proceeds to say: "We hold these truths to be self-evident: that all men are created equal; that they are endowed by their Creator with certain inalienable rights; that among them is life, liberty and pursuit of happiness; that to secure these rights, governments are instituted, deriving their just powers from the consent of the governed."

The general words above quoted would seem to embrace the whole human family, and if they were used in a similar instrument at this day, would be so understood. But it is too clear for dispute, that the enslaved African race were not intended to be included, and formed no part of the people who framed and adopted this Declaration; for if the language, as understood in that day, would embrace them, the conduct of the distinguished men who framed the Declaration of Independence would have been utterly and flagrantly inconsistent with the principles they asserted; and instead of the sympathy of mankind, to which they so confidently appealed, they would have deserved and received universal rebuke and reprobation.

Yet the men who framed this Declaration were great men—high in literary acquirements—high in their sense of honor, and incapable of asserting principles inconsistent with those on which they were acting. . . .

This state of public opinion had undergone no change when the Constitution was adopted, as is equally evident from its provisions and language. . . .

[T]here are two clauses in the Constitution which point directly and specifically to the negro race as a separate class of persons, and show clearly that they were not regarded as a portion of the people or citizens of the government then formed.

One of these clauses reserves to each of the thirteen States the right to import slaves until the year 1808, if it thinks proper. . . . And by the other provision the States pledge themselves to each other to maintain the right of property of the master, by delivering up to him any slave who may have escaped from his service, and be found within their respective territories. . . .

No one of that race had ever migrated to the United States voluntarily; all of them had been brought here as articles of merchandise. . . .

No one, we presume, supposes that any change in public opinion or feeling, in relation to this unfortunate race, in the civilized nations of Europe or in this country, should induce the court to give to the words of the Constitution a more liberal construction in their favor than they were intended to bear when the instrument was framed and adopted. Such an argument would be altogether inadmissible in any tribunal called on to interpret it. If any of its provisions are deemed unjust, there is a mode prescribed in the instrument itself by which it may be amended; but while it remains unaltered, it must be construed now as it was understood at the time of its adoption. . . .

[U]pon a full and careful consideration of the subject, the court is of the opinion that, upon the facts stated in the plea in abatement, Dred Scott was not a citizen of Missouri within the meaning of the Constitution of the United States, and not entitled as such to sue in its courts; and, consequently, that the Circuit Court had no jurisdiction of the case, and that the judgment on the pleas in abatement is erroneous. . . .

The Act of Congress, upon which the plaintiff relies, declares that slavery and involuntary servitude, except as punishment for crime, shall be forever prohibited in all that part of the territory ceded by France, under the name of Louisiana, which lies north of thirty-six degrees thirty minutes north latitude and not included within the limits of Missouri. And the difficulty which meets us at the threshold of this part of the inquiry is whether Congress was authorized to pass this law under any of the powers granted to it by the Constitution; for, if the authority is not given by that instrument, it is the duty of this Court to declare it void and inoperative and incapable of conferring freedom upon anyone who is held as a slave under the laws of any of the States. . . .

We do not mean . . . to question the power of Congress in this respect. The power to expand the territory of the United States by the admission of new States is plainly given. . . .

But the power of Congress over the person or property of a citizen can never be a mere discretionary power under our Constitution and form of government. The powers of the government and the rights and privileges of the citizen are regulated and plainly defined by the Constitution itself. . . .

These powers, and others, in relation to rights of person, which it is not necessary here to enumerate, are in express and positive terms, denied to the general government; and the rights of private property have been guarded with equal care. Thus the rights of property are united with the rights of person and placed on the same ground by the Fifth Amendment to the Constitution, which provides that no person shall be deprived of life, liberty and property without due process of law. And an Act of Congress which deprives a citizen of the United States of his liberty and property, without due process of law, merely because he came himself or brought his property into a particular territory of the United States, and who had committed no offense against the law, could hardly be dignified with the name of due process of law. . . .

[The government] has no power over the person or property of a citizen but what the citizens of the United States have granted. And no laws or usages of other nations, or reasoning of statesmen or jurists upon the relations of master and slave, can enlarge the powers of the government or take from the citizens the right they have reserved. And if the Constitution recognizes the right of property of the master in a slave, and makes no distinction between that property owned by a citizen, no tribunal, acting under the authority of the United States, whether it be legislative, executive, or judicial, has a right to draw such a distinction or deny to it the benefit of the provisions and guaranties which have been provided for the protection of private property against the encroachments of the government.

Now, as we have already said in an earlier part of this opinion, upon a different point, the right of property in a slave is distinctly and expressly affirmed in the Constitution. The right to traffic in it, like an ordinary article of merchandise and property, was guaranteed to the citizens of the United States, in every State that might desire it. . . .

Upon these considerations it is the opinion of the court that the Act of Congress which prohibited a citizen from holding and owning property of this kind in the territory of the United States north of the line therein mentioned is not warranted by the Constitution and is therefore void; and that neither Dred Scott himself, nor any of his family, were made free by being carried into this territory; even if they had been carried there by the owner with the intention of becoming a permanent resident.

Chapter 21

Illinois No Longer a Free State

Chicago Tribune

The Chicago Tribune *published the following editorial condemning the Supreme Court after it ruled against Dred Scott. Three years later the* Tribune *would play a major role in urging the selection of Abraham Lincoln at the 1860 Republican National Convention, held in Chicago.*

The following selection is reprinted from the Chicago Tribune, *16 March 1857, 2.*

Is Illinois a Free State? She was one up to March 6th, 1857. On that day the five Slaveholders and one doughface[1] of the United States Supreme Court, constituting a majority of the National Tribunal, solemnly decided:

First—That black men, whose ancestors came from Africa, were not and could not be citizens of the United States.

Second—That black men *had no rights* which white men were bound to respect.

Third—That black men, whose ancestors were brought to this country as slaves, are *property,* exactly the same as oxen or sheep.

Fourth—That the Constitution of the United States recognizes *slaves as property,* and makes no difference whatever between them and horses, wagons, and any other kind of property.

From these premises the court laid down the law that a Slave-holder has the *same right* to take and hold Slaves in any Territory, that he has to take and hold horses; and that he cannot be deprived of the right to hold Slaves in the Territories, any more than of the right to hold his horses and farming utensils.

We may reply that it is a bad law; that it is a false interpretation of the Constitution; that it does not represent the judicial or legal opinion of the nation. So has [Supreme Court] Judges [John] McLean and [Benjamin] Curtis replied; but the five Slave-holders and one doughface have overruled their opinion, as well as every other man's, and settled the law. It is the final action of the National Judiciary, established by the founders of the Republic, to interpret the Constitution.

The court has only *applied* its decision to the Territories, but if the new doctrine applies to Territories it must apply with equal force to the States. No State has the constitutional or legal right to prevent the citizens of another State from bringing their horses, cows or furniture within its jurisdiction, and having brought them from holding or using them; and it is by virtue of the *Constitution* that the emigrant from one State into another possesses these rights of property. Now, if the Constitution of the United States recognizes slaves as property, differing in no respect, as the Supreme Court declares, from any other property, then no State Court, Legislature or State Constitution can deprive the owner of such slave property of the full use and enjoyment of it in any State, into which he may see proper to emigrate with his negroes.

Under this decision, [Sen. Stephen] Douglas may bring his plantation negroes, in North Carolina and Mississippi, into Illinois, and set them to farming his lands in this State, with the Editor of the Chicago *Times* for his overseer, and no law of the State of Illinois can interfere to prevent him. We really can see nothing in the law, as interpreted by [Supreme Court Chief Justice] Taney & Co., to prevent open[ing] a slave pen and an auction block for the sale of black men, women and children, right here in Chicago. . . . Slavery is now national. Freedom has no local habitation nor abiding place, save in the hearts of Freemen. Illinois, in law, *has ceased to be a free state!*

EDITORS' NOTE

1. "Doughfaces" were northerners with proslavery sentiments. The *Tribune* apparently makes a mistake on the count—there were two "doughface" Justices (Samuel Nelson and Robert Grier) who joined the five southern Justices for a 7–2 majority.

Chapter 22

Literacy, Slavery, and Religion

Janet Duitsman Cornelius

Janet Duitsman Cornelius is adjunct professor of history at Eastern Illinois University.

The following selection is reprinted from When I Can Read My Title Clear: Literacy, Slavery and Religion in the Antebellum South *(Columbia: University of South Carolina Press, 1991), 1–6, footnotes deleted. Reprinted with permission of University of South Carolina Press.*

> The frequent hearing of my mistress reading the Bible aloud . . . awakened my curiosity in respect to this *mystery* of reading, and roused in me the desire to learn. Up to this time I had known nothing whatever of this wonderful art, and my ignorance and inexperience of what it could do for me, as well as my confidence in my mistress, emboldened me to ask her to teach me to read. . . . In an incredibly short time, by her kind assistance, I had mastered the alphabet and could spell words of three or four letters. . . . [My master] forbade her to give me any further instruction . . . [but] the determination which he expressed to keep me in ignorance only rendered me the more resolute to seek intelligence. In learning to read, therefore, I am not sure that I do not owe quite as much to the opposition of my master as to the kindly assistance of my amiable mistress.
>
> —Frederick Douglass

Frederick Douglass' moving description of how and why he learned to read while he was a slave is one of the best known and most popular sections of his famous autobiography. The compelling stories of people who were forbidden to learn to read and write and who risked punishment and death to learn forced nineteenth century readers to become aware of the cruelties of enslavement of human beings. Narratives written by escaped slaves in the antebellum United States almost always included "a record of the barriers raised against slave literacy and the overwhelming difficulties encountered in learning to read and write."

What did literacy mean to black people in slavery? Survival, according to Vincent P. Franklin, who points out that "education and literacy were greatly valued among Afro-Americans enslaved in the United States because they say in their day-to-day experiences—from one generation to the next—that knowledge and information helped one to survive in a hostile environment." Literacy was a mechanism for forming identity, the freedom to become a person, according to James Olney. Olney finds significance in Douglass' conclusion to his narrative, which he ended with the words, "I subscribe myself . . . Frederick Douglass." According to Olney, "in that lettered utterance is assertion of identity and in identity is freedom—freedom from slavery, freedom from ignorance, freedom from non-being, freedom even from time," since writing endures beyond a moment or even beyond a lifetime.

Literacy also reinforced an image of self-worth: Lucius Holsey, who tried desperately to learn to read while an enslaved houseboy, "felt that constitutionally he was created the equal of any person here on earth and that, given a chance, he could rise to the height of any man," and that books were the path to proving himself as a human being. Milly Green's daughter recalled that Milly "was so proud of every scrap of book larnin' she could pick up" that she learned to read and write and that "atter de war was over she got to be a school teacher."

When African-Americans fought to gain literacy, they expressed a desire for freedom and self-determination which had deep roots in modern culture. The movement towards universal literacy and written culture is one of the most important democratic developments in the modern world. While scholars of literacy recognize literacy's usefulness as a medium of social control and industrial training, the majority still agree that the basic result of literacy has been and is one of liberation. As Roger Chartier explains in his study of the beginning of universal written culture in the Renaissance, "personal communion with a read or written text liberated the individual from the old mediators, freed him or her from the control of the group, and made it possible to cultivate an inner life." The ability to read and write gave people the power to relate in new ways to one another and to authority. According to Harvey Graff, few in the modern world would question "the value of literacy for achieving fulfilling, productive, expanding, and participating lives of freedom."

For enslaved African-Americans, literacy was more than a path to individual freedom—it was a communal act, a political demonstration of resistance to oppression and of self-determination for the black community. Through literacy the slave could obtain skills valuable in the white world, thereby defeating those whites who withheld the skills, and could use those skills for special privileges or to gain freedom. Scholars of literacy have charted the impact a few literate people can make in a culture of illiterates; they serve as mediators and translators into a wider world for those who do not read. This ability to disperse knowledge from the larger world was a crucial act of resistance during slavery. Word of abolition movements, the writings of escaped slave Frederick Douglass, and John Brown's execution quickly spread through the slave quarters because they were passed on by those enslaved African-Americans who could read.

Literacy was also linked with freedom during slavery because it facilitated the African-American's creation of a liberating religious consciousness within the slave community. To be able to read the Bible was the first ambition of the converted illiterate Christian since, according to evangelical Protestantism, the individual should search the Scriptures in order to be saved. But the African-American used the Bible in an additional way, creating with its imagery a new reality from the slave experience. The ability to read the Bible, therefore, gave the reader the special mastery and control over this "sacred text" essential to leadership in the black church. African-Americans who could read were designated preachers by their own people as well as by whites; they were respected by black people as religious authorities because they held the key to the Bible without having to depend on whites to interpret Scriptures to them.

Traditional "Bible literacy" in the Western world emphasized the reception of the Word from authorities, so religious motives for learning to read are often considered passive, not liberating. For enslaved African-Americans, on the other hand, there was a "close relationship between religion and resistance." The African world view makes no distinction between the secular and the religious; spirituality is at the core of existence. Therefore it was through the black church, "the new religion of oppressed people," that resistance was fashioned. According to Margaret Creel, the religion shaped by enslaved African-Americans "offered a politic for collective consciousness and group conformation within an African-Christian synthesis." The African-American collective religious faith was a "progressive force and shield against white psychological and cultural domination." Their faith provided African-Americans with a will to create and the courage to persevere, helping them to remain spiritually free in spite of physical bondage. Former slaves recalled their determination to learn to read the Bible as an act of rebellion against white oppression.

Though some used their reading and writing skills to escape from slavery, few of the slaves who acquired literacy had illusions that literacy would immediately transform their lives. Their goals were more specific: slaves who learned to read and write could use literacy to gain advantages for themselves and mediate for their fellow slaves. Towards these ends, slaves used ingenuity and patience and risked discovery, death, and dismemberment to learn to read and write.

Slaves also learned to read and write because whites taught them. Slaves maneuvered whites into teaching them, so whites were often casual, even unwitting, instructors, not realizing the impact of the power they were giving slaves. Other whites taught purposefully, for practical reasons; they could use literate slaves for their own needs. Others, influenced by the belief that literacy was an essential component of human progress, taught slaves in the conviction that all people should learn to read. The primary motivation for whites who intentionally taught slaves to read in defiance of law and custom, though, was traditional "Bible literacy," a compelling motive but one with inherent contradictions. Christian belief that all should read the Bible influenced some whites; though the majority of

Southerners were indifferent to the withholding of literacy for African-Americans, a handful of white missionaries, evangelists, and lay Christians in the South insisted that slaves should be taught to read the Scriptures. They disregarded or protested any laws to the contrary and contributed to the number of slaves who could read by the end of the Civil War. They not only taught slaves, but stirred the consciences of less missionary-minded Southerners to allow their slaves to learn. They also trained black leaders and, when possible, protected black schools and Sunday schools against mob fears of an enlightened slave population.

These whites were a small percentage of the southern population, but they were missionaries; as Max Warren says, the missionary movement was and has remained a minority movement within the churches in its enthusiasm and unworldliness. This small group devoted time to a largely unpopular cause. Some of them believed in the inferiority (perfectible) of the African, but not in his separate creation. They saw African-Americans as fellow human beings with souls to be saved. While some claimed that they could convert slaves by oral instruction only, in order to make their mission acceptable to the dominant white population, they privately believed that all Christians should read the Bible, and they tacitly or openly violated the law to teach them.

White teachers of slaves clung unrealistically to the concept that they could control the slaves' access to the written word and the uses slaves made of literacy. More of the white teachers taught reading alone than reading and writing both— for obvious practical reasons, since slaves could write passes and run away, but also because writing was a skill which had not been traditionally allowed to the poorer classes. However, their providing slaves with even restricted literacy made these slaveowners, missionaries, and other reformers seem foolishly idealistic to the majority of southern whites, who were reluctant to allow slaves the measure of equality implied by literacy and who feared any skill which could give slaves more autonomy. . . . [T]his reluctance . . . which dates back to the ambivalence with which European colonists refused to accept African laborers as fellow humans and to share with them the full benefits of Christianity, including the right to read the Bible. Fears of slave revolts, the uses literate slaves made of their skills to protest their condition, and the supposition that literacy would remove the slave from total owner control undermined projects for slave education.

Reserving literacy for a privileged class is common in many cultures. In traditional India, for example, those who usurped the knowledge of Holy Writ reserved to Brahmans were punished by having hot oil poured into their mouths and into their ears. In traditional Tibet reading was taught by monks and possession of books was a sign of status. Medieval Europe similarly guarded the word. As late as the sixteenth century Henry VIII barred "all women other than gentle and noble women, together with artificers, journeymen, husbandmen, labourers, and serving men of and under the degree of yeomen" from reading the Bible in English. However, white Southerners in the late eighteenth and early nineteenth century were in a unique position: they sought to prevent enslaved African-Americans from learning to read just as mass literacy was being vigorously promoted in England and in the northern United States as a positive good, necessary for training the citizens of a republic and for accustoming the population to industrial routine. Their defensiveness at being out of step made white Southerners increasingly adamant against literacy for their own enslaved working population.

Underlying this slaveowner defensiveness was the fear of a literate black population. Despite the protestations of the small group who would teach slaves that "Bible literacy" would uphold the social order, the majority of white Southerners knew better: they knew that knowledge was a two-edged sword which "could defend the social fabric or cut it to shreds." White Southerners were aware of the possibility that slaves who could read the Bible could also read David Walker's *Appeal* or *Freedom's Journal*. In fact, the Bible itself was dangerous, as proven by Walker, Nat Turner, and others who used its messages of liberation to appeal for slave revolution. Opposition to those who would teach slaves never ceased in the antebellum period and advocates of slave literacy were confronted with the contradictions of their position.

Chapter 23

Who Freed the Slaves?

Ira Berlin

Ira Berlin, professor of history at the University of Maryland at College Park, is the former director of the Freedmen and Southern Society Project, a documentary history of emancipation. He is the author of Slaves without Masters: The Free Black in the Antebellum South *(1975) and* Many Thousands Gone: The First Two Centuries of Slavery in North America *(1998), co-author of* Slaves No More *(1992), and co-editor of* Slavery and Freedom in the Age of the American Revolution *(1983),* Freedom: A Documentary History of Emancipation, 1861–1867 *(1983–), and* Remembering Slavery: African Americans Talk about Their Personal Experience of Slavery and Emancipation *(1998).*

The following selection is reprinted from "Emancipation and Its Meaning in American Life," Reconstruction 2, *no. 3 (1994): 41–44. Reprinted with permission of the author.*

On January 1, 1863, Abraham Lincoln promulgated his Emancipation Proclamation. A document whose grand title promised so much but whose bland words delivered so little, the Emancipation Proclamation was an enigma from the first. Contemporaries were unsure whether to condemn it as a failure of idealism or applaud it as a triumph of *realpolitik,* and the American people have remained similarly divided ever since. Few officially sponsored commemorations currently mark the day slaves once called "The Great Jubilee," and, of late, black Americans have taken to celebrating their liberation on Juneteenth, a previously little-known marker of the arrival of the Union army in Texas and the liquidation of slavery in the most distant corner of the Confederacy. Unlike our other icons—the Declaration of Independence and the Constitution, for example—the Emancipation Proclamation is not on regular display at the National Archives. Its exhibition earlier this year on the occasion of the 130th anniversary of its issuance was a moment of some note. The exhibit sent thousands of Americans into the streets, where they waited in long lines on frigid January days to see Lincoln's handiwork. At the end of the five-day exhibit, some 30,000 had filed past the Proclamation. As visitors left the Archives' great rotunda, the minions of Dan Rather, Bryant Gumble, and Tom Brokaw waited with microphones in hand. Before national television audiences, visitors declared themselves deeply moved by the great document. One told a reporter from the *Washington Post* that it had changed his life forever.

Such interest in a document whose faded words cannot be easily seen, let alone deciphered, and whose intricate logic cannot be easily unraveled, let alone comprehended, raises important questions about the role of history in the way Americans think about their racial past and present. It appears that the very inaccessibility of the Emancipation Proclamation makes Lincoln's pronouncement a focal point for conflicting notions about America's racial destiny. For many people, both black and white, the Proclamation bespeaks the distance the American people have travelled from the nightmarish reality of slavery—"a distant humiliation too painful to speak of." For others, it suggests the distance that has yet to be traversed—"we have to build on the changes that started with our ancestors 130 years ago." But, however they viewed the Proclamation, the visitors used Lincoln's edict as the occasion to call for rapprochement between black and white in a racially divided city, in a racially divided nation. Dismissing the notion that Lincoln embodied—rather than transcended—American racism ("The greatest honky of them all," Julius Lester once declared), the men and women who paraded before the Proclamation saw the document as a balm. It was as if Lincoln—or his words—could reach out across the ages and heal the wound. Mrs. Loretta Carter Hanes, a suburban Washington school teacher whose insistent requests to see the Proclamation had initiated the exhibit, told reporters of her hopes that the display would inaugurate another new birth of freedom.

The public presentation of the Proclamation also brought historians out in force. Meeting in Washington, the American Historical Association—with more than usual forethought—convened a panel entitled "Black, White, and Lincoln." Professor James M. McPherson of Princeton University delivered the lead paper entitled "Who Freed the Slaves?"

For historians, the issues involved in McPherson's question—and by implication Lincoln's proclamation—took on even greater weight because they represented a larger debate between those who looked to the top of the social order for cues in understanding the past and those who looked to the bottom. It was an old controversy that had previously appeared in the guise of a contest between social history and political history. Although the categories themselves had lost much of their luster in the post-structuralist age, the politically-charged debate over the very essence of the historical process had lost none of its bite—at least for scholars.

The question of who freed the slaves thus not only encompassed the specific issue of responsibility for emancipation in the American South, but also resonated loudly in contemporary controversies about the role of "Great White Men" in our history books and the canon of "Great Literature" in our curriculum. McPherson's paper and the discussion that followed reverberated with sharp condemnations and stout defenses of "great white males." Lines between scholars who gave "workers, immigrants, [and] women," their due and those who refused to acknowledge the "so-called 'non-elite'" were drawn taut. "Elitist history" was celebrated and denounced.

The debate among historians, although often parochial and self-absorbed, was not without its redeeming features. For like the concerns articulated by the visitors to the National Archives, it too addressed conflicting notions about the role of high authority, on the one hand, and the actions of ordinary men and women, on the other, in shaping American society. Both the citizens who queued up outside the Archives and the scholars who debated the issue within the confines of the American Historical Association's meeting found deep resonance in the exhibition of the Emancipation Proclamation. It gave both reason to consider the struggle for a politics (and a history) that is both appreciative of ordinary people and respectful of rightful authority in a democratic society.

The debate over origins of emancipation in the American South can be parsed in such a way as to divide historians into two camps, those who understand emancipation as the slaves' struggle to free themselves and those who see The Great Emancipator's hand at work. McPherson made precisely such a division. While acknowledging the role of the slaves in their own liberation, McPherson came down heavily on the side of Lincoln as the author of emancipation. He characterized the critics of Lincoln's preeminence—advocates of what he repeatedly called the "self-emancipation thesis"—as scholarly populists whose stock in trade was a celebration of the "so-called 'non-elite.'" Such scholars, McPherson implied, denied the historical role of "white males"—perhaps all regularly constituted authority—in a misguided celebration of the masses. Among those so denominated by McPherson were Robert Engs, Vincent Harding, and myself and my colleagues on the Freedmen and Southern Society Project at the University of Maryland. While other scholars were implicated, the Freedmen and Southern Society Project—"the largest scholarly enterprise on the history of emancipation"—was held responsible for elevating the "self-emancipation thesis" into what McPherson called a new orthodoxy. If such be the case, I—and I am sure the other members of the Project—am honored by the unanimity with which the Project's work has been accepted by a profession that rarely agrees on anything. However, McPherson's representation of the Project's position does no justice to the arguments made in *Freedom: A Documentary History of Emancipation.* Indeed, it is more in the nature of a caricature than a characterization.

Lincoln's proclamation, as its critics have noted, freed not a single slave who was not already entitled to freedom under legislation passed by Congress that previous year. It applied only to the slaves in territories then beyond the reach of federal authority. It specifically exempted Tennessee and Union-occupied portions of Louisiana and Virginia, and it left slavery in the loyal border states—Delaware, Maryland, Kentucky, and Missouri—untouched. Indeed, as an engine of emancipation, the Proclamation went no further than the Second Confiscation Act of July 1862, which freed all slaves who entered Union lines professing that their owners were disloyal, as well as those slaves who fell under federal control as Union troops occupied Confederate territory. Moreover, at its fullest, the Emancipation Proclamation rested upon the President's power as commander-in-chief and was subject to constitutional challenge. Even Lincoln recognized the limitations of his ill-defined wartime authority, and, as his commitment to emancipation grew firmer in 1863 and 1864, he pressed for passage of a constitutional amendment to affirm slavery's destruction.

What then was the point of the Proclamation? It spoke in muffled tones that heralded not the dawn of universal liberty but the compromised and piecemeal arrival of an undefined freedom. Indeed, the Proclamation's flat prose, ridiculed as having the moral grandeur of a bill of lading, suggests that the true authorship of African-American freedom lies elsewhere—not at the top of American society but at the bottom. McPherson is correct in noting that the editors of the Freedmen and Southern Society Project seized this insight and expanded it in *Freedom*.

From the first guns at Fort Sumter, the strongest advocates of emancipation were the slaves themselves. Lacking political standing or public voice, forbidden access to the weapons of war, slaves nevertheless tossed aside the grand pronouncements of Lincoln and other Union leaders that the sectional conflict was only a war for national unity. Instead, they moved directly to put their own freedom—and that of their posterity—atop the national agenda. Steadily, as opportunities arose, slaves risked all for freedom. By abandoning their owners, coming uninvited into Union lines, and offering their assistance as laborers, pioneers, guides, and spies, slaves forced federal soldiers at the lowest level to recognize their importance to the Union's success. That understanding travelled quickly up the chain of command. In time, it became evident even to the most obtuse federal commanders that every slave who crossed into Union lines was a double gain: one subtracted from the Confederacy and one added to the Union. The slaves' resolute determination to secure their liberty converted many white Americans to the view that the security of the Union depended upon the destruction of slavery. Eventually, this belief tipped the balance in favor of freedom, even among those who had little interest in the question of slavery and no love for black people.

Once the connection between the war and freedom had been made, slaves understood that a Union victory was imperative, and they did what they could to secure it. They threw their full weight behind the federal cause, and "tabooed" those few in their ranks who shunned the effort. More than 135,000 slave men became Union soldiers. Even deep in the Confederacy, where escape to federal lines was impossible, slaves did what they could to undermine the Confederacy and strengthen the Union—from aiding escaped northern prisoners of war to praying for northern military success. With their loyalty, their labor and their lives, slaves provided crucial information, muscle, and blood in support of the federal war effort. No one was more responsible for smashing the shackles of slavery than the slaves themselves.

But, as the slaves realized, they could not free themselves. Nowhere in the four volumes of *Freedom* do the editors of the Freedmen and Southern Society Project claim they did. Nowhere do the editors use the term of "self-emancipation." Slaves could—and they did—put the issue of freedom on the wartime agenda; they could—and they did—make certain that the question of their liberation did not disappear in the complex welter of the war; they could—and they did—insure that there was no retreat from the commitment to emancipation once the issue was drawn. In short, they did what was in their power to do with the weapons they had. They could not vote, pass laws, issue field orders, or promulgate great proclamations. That was the realm of citizens, legislators, military officers, and the president. However, the actions of the slaves made it possible for citizens, legislators, military officers, and the president to act. Thus, in many ways, slaves set others in motion. Slaves were the prime movers in the emancipation drama, not the sole movers. It does no disservice to Lincoln—or to anyone else—to say that his claim to greatness rests upon his willingness to act when the moment was right.

Lincoln, as McPherson emphasizes, was no friend of slavery. He believed, as he said many times, that "if slavery is not wrong, nothing is wrong." But, as president, Lincoln also believed he had a constitutional obligation not to interfere with slavery where it existed. Shortly before his inauguration, he offered to support a proposed constitutional amendment that would have prohibited any subsequent amendment authorizing Congress "to abolish or interfere . . . with the domestic institutions of any state, including slavery." As wartime leader, he feared the disaffection of the loyal slave states, which he understood to be critical to the success of the Union. Lincoln also doubted whether white and black could live as equals in American society and thought it best for black people to remove themselves physically from the United States. Like many white Americans from Thomas Jefferson to Henry Clay, Lincoln favored the colonization of former slaves in Africa or elsewhere. At his insistence, the congressional legislation providing for the emancipation of slaves in the District of Columbia in April 1862 included an appropriation to aid the removal of liberated slaves who wished to leave the United States. Through the end of 1862, Lincoln continually connected emancipation in the border states to the colonization of slaves somewhere beyond the borders of the United States.

Where others led on emancipation, Lincoln followed. Lincoln responded slowly to demands for emancipation as they worked their way up the military chain of command and as they echoed in northern public opinion. He revoked the field emancipations of Union generals John C. Frémont in August 1861 and David Hunter in May 1862, who invoked martial law to liberate slaves in Missouri and South Carolina, respectively. Through the first year and a half of the war, Lincoln—preoccupied with the loyalty of the slaveholding states within the Union and hopeful for the support of Whiggish slaveholders within the Confederacy—remained respectful of the rights of the master.

As pressure for emancipation grew in the spring of 1862, Lincoln continued to urge gradual, compensated emancipation. The compensation would be to slaveholders for property lost, not to slaves for labor stolen. In late September 1862, even while announcing that we would proclaim emancipation on January 1 if the rebellious states did not return to the Union, he continued to call for gradual, compensated emancipation in the border states and compensation for loyal slaveholders elsewhere. The preliminary emancipation proclamation also reiterated his support for colonizing freed slaves "upon this continent or elsewhere." As black laborers became essential to the Union war effort and as demands to enlist black men in the federal army mounted, the pressure for emancipation became inexorable. On January 1, 1863, Lincoln fulfilled his promise to free all slaves in the states still in rebellion. Had another Republican been in Lincoln's place, that person doubtless would have done the same. Without question, some would have acted more expeditiously and with greater bravado. Without question, some would have acted more cautiously with lesser resolve. In the end, Lincoln did what needed to be done. Others might be left behind; Lincoln would not.

Thus, when Lincoln finally acted, he moved with confidence and determination. He stripped the final Emancipation Proclamation of any reference to compensation for former slaveholders or colonization for former slaves. He added provisions that allowed for the service of black men in the Union army and navy. The Proclamation opened the door to the eventual enlistment of nearly 190,000 black men—most of them former slaves. Military enlistment became the surest solvent of slavery, extending to places the Emancipation Proclamation did not reach, especially the loyal slave states. Once slave men entered the Union army, they were free and they made it clear they expected their families to be free too. In March 1865, Congress confirmed this understanding and provided for the freedom of the immediate families of all black soldiers. Lincoln's actions, however tardy, gave force to all that the slaves had risked. The Emancipation Proclamation transformed the war in ways only the President could. After January 1, 1863, the Union army was an army of liberation and Lincoln was its commander.

Lincoln understood the importance of his role, both politically and morally—just as the slaves had understood theirs. Having determined to free the slaves, Lincoln declared he would not take back the Emancipation Proclamation even when military failure and political reverses threatened that policy. He praised the role of black soldiers in preserving the Union and liquidating chattel bondage. The growing presence of black men in Union ranks deepened Lincoln's commitment to emancipation. Lincoln later suggested that black soldiers might have the vote, perhaps his greatest concession to racial equality. To secure the freedom that his Proclamation had promised, Lincoln promoted passage of the Thirteenth Amendment, although he did not live to see its ratification.

The Emancipation Proclamation's place in the drama of emancipation is thus secure—as is Lincoln's. To deny it is to ignore the intense struggle by which freedom arrived. It is to ignore the Union soldiers who sheltered slaves, the abolitionists who stumped for emancipation, and the thousands of men and women who—like Lincoln—changed their minds as slaves made the case for universal liberty. Reducing the Emancipation Proclamation to a nullity and Lincoln to a cipher denies human agency as fully as writing the slaves out of the struggle for freedom.

Both Lincoln and the slaves played their appointed parts in the drama of emancipation. From a historian's perspective, denying their complementary roles limits understanding of the complex interaction of human agency and events which resulted in slavery's demise. The Freedmen and Southern Society Project has sought to restore the fullness of the history of emancipation by expanding the terrain upon which it should be understood, emphasizing—and documenting—the *process* by which freedom arrived. While the editors argue that the slaves were in fact the prime movers of emancipation, nowhere do they deny Lincoln's centrality to the events that culminated in universal freedom. In fact, rather than single out slaves or exclude Lincoln (as the term "self-emancipation" implies), the editors argue for the significance of others as well: white Union soldiers—few of them racial egalitarians—who saw firsthand how slavery weakened the Union cause; their families and friends in the North—eager for federal victory—who learned from these soldiers the strength the Confederate regime drew from bonded labor; the northern men and women—most of them with no connection to the abolition movement—who acted upon such news to petition Congress; and the congress-men and senators who eventually moved in favor of freedom. This roster, of course, does not include all those involved in the social and political process that ended slavery in the American South. It omits the slaveholders, no bit players in the drama. Taken as a whole, however, the Project's work does suggest something of the complexity of emancipation and the limitation of seeing slavery's end as the product of any one individual—or element—in the social order.

Emphasizing that emancipation was not the work of one hand underscores the force of contingency—the crooked course by which universal freedom arrived. It captures the ebb and flow of events which, at times, placed Lincoln among the op-ponents of emancipation and then propelled him to the forefront of freedom's friends. It emphasizes the clash of wills that is the essence of politics—whether it involves enfranchised legislators or voteless slaves. Politics, perforce, necessitates an on-the-ground struggle among different interests, not the unfolding of a single idea or perspective—whether that of an individual or an age. Lincoln, no less than the meanest slave, acted upon changing possibilities as he understood them. The very same events—secession and war—that gave the slaves' actions new meaning also gave Lincoln's actions new meaning. To think that Lincoln could have antici-pated these changes—or, more strangely still, somehow embodied them—imbues him with power over the course of events that no human being has ever enjoyed. Lincoln was part of history, not above it. Whatever he believed about slavery, in 1861 Lincoln did not see the war as an instrument of emancipation. The slaves did. Lincoln's commitment to emancipation changed with time because it had to. The slaves' commitment to universal freedom did not waver because it could not.

Complexity—contrary to McPherson—is not ambivalence or ambiguity. To tell the whole story—to follow that crooked course—does not diminish the clarity of an argument or mystify it into a maze of "nuances, paradox, or irony." Telling the entire tale is not a form of obscuration. If done right, it clarifies precisely because it consolidates the mass of competing claims under a single head. Elegance or sim-plicity of argument is useful only when it encompasses all of the evidence, not when it excludes or narrows it.

In a season when constituted authority once again tries to find the voice of the people and when the people are testing the measure of their leaders, it is well to recall the relationship of both to securing freedom's greatest victory. In this sense, slaves were right in celebrating January 1, 1863, as the Day of Jubilee. As Laretta Hanes noted 130 years later, "It meant so much to people because it was a ray of light, the hope of a new day coming. And it gave them courage." Indeed, the Emancipation Proclamation reminds us all—both those viewing its faded pages and those who studied it—that real changes derive from the actions of the people and requires the imprimatur of constituted authority. The Emancipation Proclamation teaches that "social" history is no less political than "political" history—for it too rests upon the bending of wills, which is the essence of politics—and that no political process is determined by a single individual. If the Emancipation Proclamation speaks to the central role of constituted authority—in this case Abraham Lincoln—in making history, it speaks no less loudly to the role of ordinary men and women, seizing the moment to make the world according to their own understanding of justice and human decency. The connection between the two should not be forgotten as we try to rebuild American politics—and try to write a history worthy of that politics.

2

Reconstruction

The alphabet is an abolitionist: Under slavery it was a criminal offense to teach blacks how to read. During Reconstruction African Americans led the way in building schools and establishing public education in the South. (Photo courtesy of the New-York Historical Society.)

Chapter 24

Introduction:
The Second American Revolution

Jonathan Birnbaum and Clarence Taylor

What exactly had the slaves won with their freedom? Slavery originated in the Americas as the solution to the labor problem. What role would free black labor play after emancipation? What rights would black workers have? Southern whites certainly had no problem recognizing this as the central question. "I am not an enemy to the negro," claimed Ku Klux Klan leader Nathan Bedford Forrest, a former Confederate general. "We want him here among us; he is the only laboring class we have."[1]

What would the post–Civil War South look like? After the end of slavery and the devastation of war, how would or should—since it was subject to debate—the South rebuild, reconstruct? The end of the war represented a revolutionary opportunity. Would the South move forward or fall back? Most significantly, what would be the status of the former slaves? What was the nature of their freedom? Did blacks and whites agree on the definition? If blacks were free, should they have the vote? If the vote was given to black men, should it also be extended to women? If blacks had legal equality, should they also have civil equality?

What would happen to the old plantations? Should members of the former Confederacy be treated as traitors; should they be jailed, fined, or lose their right to vote or run for elected office? Should the freedmen be given reparations for their former enslavement? Or should reparations be paid to the former slave owners for their loss of "property"? Should equality include an economic dimension, such as guarantees of land—"forty acres and a mule"—and access to credit?

The answers to these questions may seem inevitable to modern readers, but they were far from obvious to people at the time. Winning the war was not a final victory for black equality, only an opportunity; the struggle would continue to be fought during Reconstruction. The elevation of Tennessee's unsympathetic Andrew Johnson to the presidency, after the assassination of President Lincoln, would not make that struggle any easier (see chapter 37).

The three great institutional cornerstones of Reconstruction, as W. E. B. Du Bois noted in his earliest writing on the subject, were the black church (see chapter 27), black schools (see chapter 26), and the Freedmen's Bureau, a crucial, if often faltering form of federal support.[2]

Churches and schools were bustling centers of black self-activity. During the earliest years of Reconstruction, the Freedmen's Bureau was already reporting that black "churches and schools are going up in every direction." These improvements benefited whites as well as blacks. As Du Bois noted,

> The first great mass movement for public education at the expense of the state, in the South, came from Negroes. Many leaders before the war had advocated general education, but few had been listened to. Schools for indigents and paupers were supported, here and there, and more or less spasmodically. Some states had elaborate plans, but they were not carried out. Public education for all at public expense, was, in the South, a Negro idea.[3]

Paternalistic white missionary societies sent teachers to help educate the freedmen, but blacks didn't need to be taught the value of education. Blacks had been fighting for literacy since slavery (see chapter 22). During the earliest days of Reconstruction, before any state laws had been passed, it was "the former slaves themselves who played the central role in building, financing and operating . . . schools," wrote Herbert Gutman (see chapter 26).

During Segregation, the Reconstruction era was caricatured in textbooks and popular entertainment (as it had been earlier in southern white newspapers) as a tragic mistake, a period of carpetbaggers, scalawags, and black misrule (see chapter 36).[4] This notion was so widespread that historian Jesse Lemisch found himself asking, in a 1961 article, "Who Won the Civil War, Anyway?"[5]

Reconstruction represented a revolutionary opportunity to resolve the country's founding contradiction: the claim of equality in a land dependent upon black slavery. A war was fought and laws, acts, and constitutional amendments were written to resolve that contradiction. The country's abandonment of those laws—symbolized by the Compromise of 1877 (withdrawing Union troops from the South) and ratified by *Plessy v. Ferguson* (see chapter 39)—would postpone the civil rights project and eventually require a Second Reconstruction.

NOTES

1. *Report of the Joint Select Committee to Inquire into the Condition of Affairs in the Late Insurrectionary States,* 13 vols. (Washington, D.C., 1872), 13:34.

2. W. E. B. Du Bois, "Reconstruction and Its Benefits," *American Historical Review,* July 1910, 781.

3. W. E. B. Du Bois, "Founding the Public School," in *Black Reconstruction in America* (New York: Atheneum, 1935), 638.

4. For the most thorough debunking of the carpetbagger myth, see Richard Current, *Those Terrible Carpetbaggers* (New York: Oxford, 1988).

5. Jesse Lemisch, "Who Won the Civil War, Anyway?" *The Nation,* 8 April 1961, 300–302.

Chapter 25

The Second American Revolution

Eric Foner

Eric Foner, professor of history at Columbia University, has served as president of both the Organization of American Historians (1993–1994) and the American Historical Association (2000). He is the author of many works, including Reconstruction: America's Unfinished Revolution, 1863–1877 *(1988),* Nothing but Freedom: Emancipation and Its Legacy *(1983), "Blacks and the U.S. Constitution,"* New Left Review *(September–October 1990),* Freedom's Lawmakers: A Directory of Black Officeholders during Reconstruction *(2d ed., 1996), and* The Story of American Freedom *(1998). He is also the editor of* America's Black Past *(1970) and* The New American History *(2d ed., 1997), and co-editor of* The Reader's Companion to American History *(1991).*

The following selection is reprinted by permission from "The Second American Revolution," In These Times, *16–22 September 1987, 12–13.*

For other selections by Foner, see chapters 143 and 171.

The Civil War and Reconstruction produced not simply three constitutional amendments—the 13th, 14th and 15th—but a new American constitution. As a result of the greatest crisis in our country's history, it was amended first to abolish slavery, then to establish a national citizenship whose rights, enforced by the federal government, were to be enjoyed equally by blacks and whites, and finally, to enfranchise the nation's black male population.

These were revolutionary changes for a nation whose economy up to 1860 rested in considerable measure on slave labor, whose Constitution included clauses that protected the stability of slavery and the political power of slaveholders and whose laws, from the beginning, were grounded in racism.

The principles engrafted onto the Constitution in the amendments of the era are now so much a part of our political thinking (especially on the left) that it may be difficult to recognize how utterly unprecedented they were before the Civil War. Apart from a few abolitionists, virtually no white Americans before 1860 believed in equality before the law irrespective of race. And on the eve of the Civil War no state accorded blacks the same rights as whites.

Even outside the slave states the majority of blacks could not vote, testify in court against whites or attend public schools. A few Northern states even prohibited blacks by law from entering their territory. In the 1857 *Dred Scott* decision the Supreme Court announced that no black person could be a U.S. citizen (a plausible interpretation of the original Constitution and the subsequent practices of the state and federal governments).

Nor did most Americans before the Civil War look to the federal government to protect citizens' rights. The greatest threats to liberty, most believed, arose not from the abuse of local authority, but from a too-powerful national state. The Bill of Rights reflected this assumption, for it prohibited Congress, but not the states, from abridging citizens' fundamental rights. Nor did any real concept of national citizenship exist before 1860.

Recurring Debate

Indeed, the principles enshrined in the Civil War amendments were so unprecedented that the passionate political debate they inspired has continued to our own time. Only last year [1986] Attorney General Edwin Meese chastised the Supreme Court for a series of decisions based on the legal doctrine of "incorporation"— that is, that the 14th Amendment requires the states to respect the prohibitions on abuse of power that the Bill of Rights had originally applied to the federal government.

The justices, Meese argued, had strayed from the "original intent" of the amendment's framers. Meese, in turn, was chastised by Justice William Brennan for attempting to reverse decades of constitutional interpretation.

Neither an assessment of the recent debate nor a broader appreciation of how the Civil War amendments changed the Constitution can be arrived at without a careful look at the crisis of the 1860s. Two developments during the Civil War were crucial to placing the issue of black citizenship on the national agenda. One was the disintegration of slavery—a process initiated by blacks who abandoned their owners' plantations to head for the lines of the Union Army and given political sanction in the Emancipation Proclamation.

The second was the massive enrollment of blacks into the Union armed forces. By the end of the war, some 200,000 black men had served in the Army and Navy. The "logical result" of black military service, one senator observed in 1864, was that "the black man is henceforth to assume a new status among us."

At the same time, the exigencies of war created a profound alteration in the nature of American government. The need to mobilize the North's resources for modern war produced what one Republican called "a new government," with a greatly expanded income, bureaucracy and set of responsibilities.

And the war inspired a broad nationalism, embraced above all by anti-slavery reformers, black and white, and Radical Republicans in Congress. With emancipation, these men and women believed, the federal government had become not a threat to local autonomy and individual liberty, but the "custodian of freedom."

The amendments of the 1860s reflected the intersection of these two Civil War products—the idea of equality before the law and the newly empowered national state. The 13th, adopted by Congress in January 1865 and ratified the following December, not only abolished slavery throughout the Union (including the loyal border slave states to which the Emancipation Proclamation had not applied), but empowered Congress to enforce abolition with "appropriate legislation."

End as Beginning

"The one question of the age is settled," declared an anti-slavery Congressman, but the amendment closed one question only to open a host of others. Many Republicans envisioned a slaveless nation as one with "one law impartial over all." The amendment, they believed, authorized Congress to eliminate various kinds of discrimination against blacks as "badges of slavery" that must be swept away along with the South's "peculiar institution."

Most forthright in calling for further action on behalf of blacks' rights were the Radical Republicans, led in the House by Thaddeus Stevens of Pennsylvania and in the Senate by Charles Sumner of Massachusetts. The Union's victory in the Civil War, they believed, offered a golden opportunity to purge the nation of "the demon of caste," and to create what Stevens called a "perfect republic" based upon the principle of equality before the law.

Some Radicals, like Stevens, went even further, proposing that the national government confiscate lands belonging to the planter class and distribute them among the former slaves. Most Republicans were unwilling to go this far, but they did insist that blacks should enjoy the same opportunity as whites to compete for advancement in the economic marketplace.

When Congress reconvened in December 1865 the Radicals represented only a minority among Republicans. But events quickly pushed the more numerous moderates in their direction. Lincoln had been succeeded in office by Andrew Johnson of Tennessee. During the summer and fall of 1865, Johnson had initiated his own program of Reconstruction, which in effect placed the old planter class back in control of Southern affairs.

Southern public life was restricted entirely to whites, and the new state governments sought to establish a labor system as close to slavery as possible. Blacks were required by law to sign yearly labor contracts; refusal to do so, or attempting to leave work before a contract expired, meant arrest, a prison term or being leased out to anyone who would pay the culprit's fine. No such regulation applied to white citizens.

These laws, known as the Black Codes, seemed to the North to make a mockery of emancipation. In response, Congress in the spring of 1866 enacted the Civil Rights Act, which became law over Johnson's veto.

This measure defined all persons born in the U.S. (except Indians) as national citizens, and spelled out rights they were to enjoy equally without regard to race—including making contracts, bringing lawsuits, owning property and receiving equal treatment before the courts. No state could deprive an individual of these basic rights; if it did so, state officials would be held accountable in federal court.

In constitutional terms, the Civil Rights Act of 1866 represented the first attempt to give meaning to the 13th Amendment, to define the consequences of emancipation. If states could deny blacks the right to choose their employment, seek better jobs and enforce payment of wages, noted one Congressman, "then I demand to know, of what practical value is the amendment abolishing slavery?" But beyond these specific rights, Republicans also rejected the entire idea of laws differentiating between blacks and whites in access to the courts and penalties for breaches of the law.

Striking Departure

As the first statutory definition of American citizenship, the Civil Rights Act embodied a profound change in federal-state relations. Republican leader James G. Blaine later remarked, before the Civil War only "the wildest fancy of a distempered brain" could have envisioned a law of Congress requiring states to accord blacks "all the civil rights pertaining to a white man." Moreover, the bill invalidated many Northern laws discriminating against blacks. The underlying assumption—that the federal government possessed the power to define and protect citizens' rights—was a striking departure in American law.

One purpose of the 14th Amendment, approved by Congress in June 1866, was to prevent a future Congress from repealing the guarantees in the Civil Rights Act. But the amendment's purposes were broader than this. Its heart was the first section, which declared all persons born or naturalized in the U.S. both national and state citizens, and prohibited the states from abridging their "privileges or immunities," depriving any person of life, liberty or property without "due process of law," or denying them "equal protection of the laws."

For more than a century, politicians, judges, lawyers and scholars have debated the meaning of these elusive terms. The problem of ascertaining the amendment's "original intent" is compounded by the fact that its language was a compromise with which no one seemed "entirely satisfied." Yet despite many drafts, deletions and changes, its central principle remained constant: a national guarantee of equality before the law.

This was now so widely accepted in Republican circles, and had already been so fully discussed, that compared with now-forgotten clauses concerning representation in Congress, the Confederate debt and the disqualification of certain Confederates from office, the first section inspired relatively little debate. One congressman declared it to be "so just that no member of this House can seriously object to it."

Unlike the Civil Rights Act, which listed numerous specific rights a state could not abridge, the 14th Amendment used only broad language. Unlike a statute, it was intended as a statement of principle. Both Radical and moderate Republicans understood phrases like "privileges or immunities" and "equal protection of the laws" as subject to changing interpretation. They preferred to allow Congress and the federal courts maximum flexibility in combating the multitude of injustices confronting Southern blacks.

Indeed, it is ironic that an attorney general who prides himself on abiding by "original intent" chastises the federal courts for their judicial activism in interpreting the amendment. For Congress intentionally chose to rely on the federal courts for civil-rights enforcement. The alternative would have been either abandoning the freedmen, maintaining a standing army indefinitely in the South or establishing some kind of national police force to oversee Southern affairs.

It is equally apparent that, as Michigan's Sen. Jacob Howard declared, the amendment was intended to prohibit the states from infringing upon liberties guaranteed in the Bill of Rights. Republicans wished to force the states to respect such key provisions as freedom of speech, the right to bear arms, trial by impartial jury and protection against cruel and unusual punishment. In fact, the amendment was deemed necessary, in part, precisely because every one of these rights was being systematically violated in the South in 1866.

The Right to Vote

Transcending boundaries of race and region, the 14th Amendment changed and broadened the definition of freedom for all Americans, for its language challenged legal discrimination throughout the nation. Nonetheless, many reformers were deeply disappointed in the amendment. Republicans in 1866 were divided on the question of black suffrage. The amendment merely threatened to reduce Southern representation in Congress if blacks continued to be denied the franchise.

And, in its representation clause, the amendment for the first time introduced the word "male" into the Constitution. Suffrage restrictions that reduced the number of male voters would cost a state representation; women could continue to be barred from voting without penalty. The result was a split between advocates of blacks' rights and women's rights.

Both ideologically and politically, 19th-century feminism had been tied to abolition. During the war the organized women's movement had put aside the suffrage issue to join in the crusade for the Union and emancipation. Now leaders like Elizabeth Cady Stanton and Susan B. Anthony insisted that if the Constitution were to be changed, the claims of women must not be ignored.

To Radicals and abolitionists who insisted that this was "the Negro's hour," feminists defined it instead as the hour for change—an opportunity that must be seized or another generation might pass "ere the constitutional door will again be opened." In response Radicals, even those sympathetic to the idea of women's suffrage, insisted that tying the issues of black rights and women's suffrage would doom both. A Civil War had not been fought over the status of women, nor had 30 years of prior agitation awakened public consciousness on the issue.

Repudiated by the Southern states and President Johnson, the 14th Amendment became the centerpiece of the political campaign of 1866. When Republicans swept the fall elections, they moved not only to ensure the amendment's ratification, but granted the right to vote to black men in the South and mandated the formation of new Southern governments resting on manhood suffrage. Under this policy of Radical Reconstruction, interracial democracy flourished for several years throughout the South, and blacks probably exercised more genuine power than at any time in our history, before or since.

In 1869 Congress approved the last of the postwar amendments, the 15th, which prohibited the federal or state governments from depriving individuals of the vote on racial grounds. By allowing states to continue to bar women from the polls, it further angered feminist leaders. Moreover, its language left open the possibility of poll taxes, literacy tests and other ostensibly nonracial requirements which could, and would, be used to disfranchise the vast majority of Southern black men.

With the end of Reconstruction in 1877, the egalitarian impulse embodied in the amendments of the 1860s faded from national life. The three amendments remained parts of the Constitution, but as far as blacks were concerned they increasingly became dead letters.

Even in the early 1870s the Supreme Court had begun to restrict the rights protected under the 14th Amendment. After 1877 the federal courts employed their expanded powers primarily to protect corporations from local regulation (on the grounds that corporations were "persons" who could not be deprived of their property rights by state agencies). By 1896, in *Plessy vs. Ferguson*, the court found racial segregation mandated by state law perfectly compatible with the doctrine of equality before the law.

In the 20th century, the court slowly used the 14th Amendment to strike down state laws abridging freedom of speech and other provisions of the Bill of Rights. But only in our own time did a great mass movement and a socially conscious Supreme Court again breathe life into racial egalitarianism, and a broad view of national responsibility for citizens' rights that form the essence of the postwar amendments. If anything, the history of these amendments underscores how fragile individual rights can be, even when protected by the letter of the Constitution.

Chapter 26

Schools for Freedom

Herbert Gutman

Herbert Gutman (1928–1985) was often described as the country's leading labor and social historian. He wrote Slavery and the Numbers Game *(1975),* Work, Culture and Society in Industrializing America *(1976),* The Black Family in Slavery and Freedom, 1750–1925 *(1976), and* Power and Culture: Essays on the American Working Class *(1987). Gutman co-founded the American Social History Project (www.ashp.cuny.edu), which has produced* Who Built America? *a two-volume history of the United States, and other history materials.*

The following selection is excerpted from "Schools for Freedom: The Post-Emancipation Origins of Afro-American Education," a chapter originally intended for inclusion in Herb Gutman's The Black Family in Slavery and Freedom. *Reprinted with permission of Judith Gutman. A forty-page version, edited by Ira Berlin, was published in* Power and Culture. *The complete manuscript is on file with the Herbert G. Gutman Papers at the New York Public Library.*

"The principle of schools, of education," said James T. White, a black delegate to the 1868 Arkansas Constitutional Convention, "is intended to elevate our families." The role former slaves and other blacks such as White (an Indiana-born minister and Union Army veteran) played in bringing schools to their children offers a rare insight into the values of the black community as it emerged from slavery. Blacks voluntarily paid school tuition, purchased schoolbooks, hired, fed, boarded, and protected teachers, constructed and maintained school buildings, and engaged in other costly (and sometimes dangerous) activities to provide education for their children. To expect such sustained efforts from men and women fresh to freedom, poor by any material standard, and entirely without political power is, perhaps, much to ask. But evidence disclosing such efforts is indeed abundant.

The former slaves themselves, not the schools per se, remain the center of this study. Historians of American (and particularly Southern) education have reconstructed in close detail the work of Northern white schoolteachers and missionaries in the postbellum South. While making it clear that articulate freedmen and freedwomen enthusiastically welcomed education for their children, the existing literature—even by "revisionist" historians of the Reconstruction—emphasizes the energy sympathetic Northern whites expended in helping freedpeople establish schools. In actual fact, the former slaves themselves played the central role in building, financing, and operating these schools, a fact that adds to our understanding of the family sensibilities and parental concerns of these men and women. It also indicates some of the ways in which reciprocal obligations operated beyond the immediate family and bound together former slaves living in rural and urban communities.

Postwar educational efforts by blacks built on a firm base of educational activism during slavery. Scattered but nevertheless convincing evidence reveals that secret slaves schools had existed in a number of antebellum Southern cities. . . .

The efforts of blacks to educate themselves expanded greatly during the Civil War, especially in locales that fell to the Union Army. "One of the first acts of the Negroes, when they found themselves free," observed the American Freedmen's Inquiry Commission, "was to establish schools at their own expense." A pay school—the first school for wartime runaways—was opened in Alexandria, Virginia, on September 1, 1861, by two black women. Later that month, one of them joined Mrs. Mary Smith Peake, the daughter of an English father and a free black woman who had taught at an antebellum Hampton, Virginia school (and had her black stepfather among her pupils), to start a second contraband[1] school at Fortress Monroes, Virginia. White teachers did not work with the Alexandria contrabands until October 1862. By that time, blacks managed three other schools. Before the war's end, at least sixteen other black men and women taught or directed Alexandria schools for runaway slaves. By April 1863, about 2,000 former slaves had congregated in Alexandria and 400 children attended their schools. "The first demand of these fugitives when they come into the place," observed a *New York Evening Post* correspondent, "is that their children may go to school." "Another surprising fact," he went on, "is that the poor negro women had rather toil, earn and pay one dollar per month for their children's education, than to permit them to enter a charity school." The contraband blacks also built, by voluntary labor, a school worth about $500, and later enlarged and improved it, making it "well lathed and plastered."

But there was more to establishing a school than bricks and mortar. At the start, a dispute over whether white or black teachers should be "the superintendents" threatened this Alexandria school's future. The blacks called a meeting. "I wish you could have been at that meeting," reported North Carolina fugitive slave Harriet Jacobs, who had come to Virginia to teach. "Most of the people were slaves until quite recently, but they talked sensibly and . . . put the question to a vote in quite parliamentary style. The result was a decision that the colored teachers should have charge of the school." The school opened in January 1864 with 75 pupils; two months later, it had 225, and the following August it was "the largest school and schoolhouse in the city." Once it had opened, blacks maintained their support. "My table in the school room," an early Hampton teacher reported, "is loaded, morning and noon, with oranges, lemons, apples, figs, candies, and other sweet things too numerous to mention." Such gift-giving was common in many parts of the South.

Wartime Virginia and Maryland refugees also crowded Georgetown and the District of Columbia, and these places soon had their complement of black-run schools. William Slade, the president of the District's black Social, Civil, and Industrial Association, told the American Freedmen's Inquiry Commission in 1863 that District blacks paid tuition to support 14,000 children at twenty different schools. . . .

Schools grew with the arrival of the federal army. Norfolk [Virginia]'s first black schools met in the city's black churches in April 1863. Indeed, so many Norfolk blacks wanted schooling that after the first week white teachers hired fifteen "colored assistants." In January 1864, the Norfolk and Portsmouth schools together counted 2,600 pupils drawn from a contraband population of about 19,000. A careful survey in December 1864 revealed that about two-thirds of the contraband children between the ages of six and fourteen attended day schools in the military districts south and north of the James River. . . .

North Carolina contrabands knew their first school in the spring of 1862, taught by a white man in the New Bern African Methodist Episcopal Church. Army officers also gave a Baptist missionary two Beaufort churches in which to teach. He found them "very filthy and sadly out of repair," but Beaufort blacks soon agreed to raise funds for their improvement. . . .

In *Rehearsal for Reconstruction,* Willie Lee Rose fully described the schooling given South Carolina Sea Island blacks by Yankee missionaries and schoolteachers. Sea Island blacks contributed mightily to that effort. A White Boston Baptist clergyman started Beaufort's first school in early January 1862. "Both teachers and pupils are negroes," said one report. . . .

Beaufort was the only town of size on the Sea Islands, but schools also flourished in rural areas, some maintained by Northern benevolent societies like the National Freedmen's Relief Association (which had established twenty-two schools by 1864) and others by the blacks themselves. A former slave woman named Hettie (she had "stolen a knowledge of letters from time to time") began a day school in March 1863 and kept up her work after the Edisto blacks became war refugees on St. Helena's Island. Even before that time, white missionary-teachers arrived at the Smith plantation to find that "the children were all assembled by Cuffy, and he was teaching them when we went in." . . .

In other places, Sea Island parents shared in the supervision of the schools. Northern teachers encouraged St. Helena's blacks to form visiting committees to help manage that island's school. . . .

Farther west, blacks exhibited the same concern for wartime schooling. When Union Army recruiters first arrived in Nashville, Tennessee, they found that blacks had started "without any assistance" schools in which more than 800 children "received instruction from teachers paid by their parents—the slaves but just emancipated." A *New York Times* correspondent found it "a remarkable fact" that the blacks "at once" had "opened schools for themselves." A Nashville bookseller remarked that he had "sold more spelling books in a short time than he has done for years." The first school had opened in the fall of 1862 in the First Colored Baptist Church. Its teacher was Daniel Wadkins, an antebellum free black whose school for free black children had twice been close by worried whites in the 1850s. . . .

Former slaves also played an important role in wartime education in the Department of the Tennessee, a military district that included western Tennessee, northern Louisiana, and all of Arkansas and Mississippi. One National Freedmen's Relief Association official, noting the zeal for schooling among the blacks in Vicksburg, Mississippi, promised them a free school "instead of compelling the blacks to pay *sixty cents per month*." "They will starve, and freeze themselves in order to attend school, so highly do they value the privilege of learning to read, write and reckon . . . ," he added. Army officers initially withheld support, but finally offered two vacant lots without secure title, causing the blacks to construct movable school buildings. "The colored people," reported missionary Joseph Warren, "have subscribed liberally to aid in building these houses, and are giving personal attention to the business."

Blacks also established schools deep in the hinterland of the Mississippi Valley. . . .

Overall, Northern whites taught most Mississippi Valley black children in 1863 and 1864. But their parents, by paying tuition and giving help in numerous other ways, had played an indispensable part in the process. . . .

Between April 1865 and the advent of Radical Reconstruction two years later, educational opportunities for blacks expanded dramatically throughout the South, thanks in part to the newly established Freedmen's Bureau. But as during the war, initiative often rested with the blacks themselves. . . .

The general public and private policies that affected the education of blacks deserve brief notice. Except for Florida, where the legislature imposed a special education tax on blacks, no Southern state made provision to educate the former slaves. In establishing the Freedmen's Bureau, Congress did not include funds for education in 1865; not until the summer of 1866 did the federal government authorize the bureau to spend half a million dollars for the rental, construction, and repair of schoolhouses. Some additional money for the education of former slaves came from funds appropriated by several Northern states to purchase black substitutes in the South and thereby fill draft quotas. Bureau policies and a shortage of funds obliged the former slaves to take the initiative in establishing schools, and in this they were encouraged by the Northern benevolent societies. The New England Freedmen's Aid Society, for example, only offered funds to blacks who erected, repaired, and cared for schools, furnished board for teachers, and paid small tuition fees. Edward Everett Hale explained the guiding assumptions shared by many who managed these benevolent societies: "The policy . . . has not been to make these people beggars. 'Aide-toi et Dieu t'aidera' is their motto. The black people know they must support themselves, as they have always done." Hale admitted that such policies assured "suffering" but went on: "Where is there not suffering in this world? We have never said that the black man's life should be raised above suffering. We have said that he should be free to choose between inevitable hardships. This promise we perform."

In fact, blacks did not wait for state authorization, the advent of the bureau, or the advice of Northern societies to establish schools in 1865 and 1866. In the late fall of 1865, John W. Alvord, superintendent of education for the Freedmen's Bureau, toured the South. Everywhere he traveled, he informed General O. O. Howard, the bureau commissioner, he found "a class of schools got up and taught by colored people, rude and imperfect, but still groups of persons, old and young, *trying* to learn." They lacked "the patience to wait for the coming of a white teacher." Alvord estimated that the South knew "at least five hundred" such schools, many of them never before visited "by any white man." "In the absence of other teaching," he said, "they were determined to be self-taught." Alvord supplemented this official report with an even more enthusiastic statement to the *Freedman's Journal,* the monthly periodical of the American Tract Society. "All our party have been surprised by this unusual fact," he said of the black teacher and schools started by blacks. "A cellar, a shed, a private room, perhaps an old school-house, is the place," he went on, "and, in the midst of a group of thirty or forty children, an old negro in spectacles, or two or three young men surrounded by a hundred or more, themselves only in the rudiments of a spelling-book, and yet with a passion to teach what they *do* know; or a colored woman, who as a family servant had some privileges, and with a woman's compassion for her race—*these* are the institutions and the agencies." Schools taught by whites had ended in the summer, but some black teachers continued through the difficult season. "In truth," Alvord added, "these spontaneous efforts of the colored people would start up everywhere if books could be sent them." . . .

Official Freedmen's Bureau reports for 1866 and early 1867 fill in the Virginia picture. The bureau took notice of 136 teachers in January 1866 and 225 twelve months later. By March 1867, the number had risen to 278 (81 of them blacks). . . .

Local bureau officials filled in precise details. From Westmoreland and Richmond counties came words that "churches and schools are going up in every direction." "Colored preachers are exhorting their race to push forward the work of education," said a bureau officer. "Freedmen throng my office daily for papers or something to read. We want a few teachers." . . .

The detailed letters of two white Quaker teachers in Danville, Eunice Congdon and George Dixon, allow us to examine with greater precision the ways Virginia blacks sustained schools for their children and protected white teachers. Eunice Congdon and another white woman teacher arrived in Danville to teach early in the fall of 1865. Their early experiences were disheartening. "The first few days," Miss Congdon reported in October, "we tried boarding ourselves, getting our food cooked as best we could, and eating it off a trunk." Soon, a Union Army surgeon let them eat in the officers' mess, but charged them five dollars a week. Their funds quickly ran out, and the teachers lacked money to pay the carpenters who were building school benches. For a time, they ran classes in an army hospital. After promised money from Philadelphia Friends arrived, the school managed better. Yet throughout, the blacks played an active role. "I think the people will see to furnishing wood," wrote Miss Congdon. "We are going to suggest that they take up a contribution now and then among themselves to buy kerosene for the night school." By early February 1866, the Danville teachers had enrolled 299 day-school pupils and employed "a young colored girl to assist" in "the lowest division."

The Danville school taught more than reading and writing. In 1866, blacks crowded densely into it to hear the Civil Rights Bill of 1866 read and discussed. Miss Congdon called the discussion "rich and significant beyond description." Another time, the Northern teachers distributed seeds to Danville blacks. And when some black men formed a voluntary association called "The Mechanics' Society for Mutual Aid," they met in the schoolhouse and their president asked Miss Congdon to "send North and for him the book containing the names of the different *trades*, coming under the head of mechanics." Such community efforts suggest that schools had become more than mere educational institutions. And for that reason, among others, they provoked bitter opposition.

Opposition by whites to the Danville school increased after the Union Army withdrew from the town. The school remained there, however, owing to the courage displayed by Eunice Congdon, George Dixon, and Danville blacks. When Congdon fell ill, Dixon, who was then teaching English in Greensboro, North Carolina, came to help. Soon after his arrival, a white man attacked Eunice Congdon. "He attempted to 'finish' me," she reported. Dixon offered additional details, claiming that "a rebel" had awakened Congdon at one o'clock at night, "seizing both her arms and grasping them tightly." She asked who it was, and "the fellow muttered something which she did not understand." Congdon shouted, and a black servant overheard the commotion and hastened for Dixon, causing the intruder to flee through a window. A Union Army officer later learned that the man had planned to kill Miss Congdon, plunder the place, and then "set fire to the buildings." Threats against Miss Congdon were overheard in the streets. "A white woman," Dixon insisted, "told a colored child she need not go to school on Monday morning, because Miss Eunice would be dead." Danville blacks protected the teacher and the school. Dixon explained: "The colored men are kind in coming to keep a watch in the dead of night, but we are fearful of their coming in collision with the citizens, and blood being shed, as they will bring firearms with them and feel very desperate." "The colored people are our friends," Congdon confirmed. "They guard us every night." After Dixon arranged with a black carpenter to make school repairs and had bricks brought from an army arsenal to build a fireplace and flue, he left Danville. But before he left, he arranged "for a colored man to sleep in the house during my absence." Miss Congdon herself left Danville after the school year ended. "The first day school," she explained, "will be continued by four colored men whom we have initiated." More than this, other blacks promised to protect school property and records. When the Danville school closed for the summer, it had a full enrollment: 237 children had registered for its day classes. . . .

Blacks throughout the South voluntarily built and sustained schools in ways similar to those in Virginia, South Carolina, Louisiana and Georgia. Although their work cannot be detailed here, John Alvord's published semiannual reports allow a brief summary of that work before 1868. His reports contain serious flaws but nevertheless retain general value. In the fall of 1865, school attendance, as a percentage of all children eligible to attend, ranged from 43 percent in New York State to 93 percent in Boston. That same fall, 41 percent of eligible white children and 75 percent of eligible black children attended District of Columbia schools. An equally high percentage of black children attended the Memphis (72 percent) and Virginia (82 percent) schools. In the three years following the war, General O. O. Howard estimated that nearly one-third of black children over the entire South had some formal education. Not all of these former slaves and free blacks studied with Yankee schoolmarms. In December 1866, 37 percent of teachers in the South known to the Bureau were blacks. The percentage increased to over 40 in June 1867, and was even higher a year later. The bureau noted in June 1868 that 2,291 men and women were teaching blacks, and that 990 (43 percent) of them were blacks.

In the fall of 1866, moreover, blacks sustained in full or in part the operation of at least half of the Arkansas, Florida, Georgia, Kentucky, Louisiana, Maryland, and Texas schools. In five states (Alabama, North Carolina, South Carolina, Tennessee and Virginia), between 25 percent and 49 percent of the schools received financial support from resident blacks. . . .

Innumerable obstacles, which should not be minimized, hampered the voluntary efforts made by former slaves to educate their children before the start of Radical Reconstruction and the coming of free public education to the South. But neither should these difficulties be emphasized so as to divert our attention from the extraordinary energy and social purpose revealed by these men and women. Theirs was a magnificent effort. We study it in detail because of what it tells about important and little-understood historical processes. In examining how men and women fresh to freedom built and sustained schools, we find much more than simply a desire for schooling. It is inconceivable, for example, that former Memphis slaves would have paid more than $5,000 in tuition between November 1864 and June 1865 without preexisting notions of parental responsibility and kin obligation. Yet it is erroneous to find in their quest for education "proof" that the former slaves held "middle class" values. The ways in which former slaves built and sustained schools, for example, were quite alien to the "middle class." Yankee shopkeepers and successful artisans favored education, but did not move buildings ten miles and then reconstruct them as schoolhouses. Ohio and Indiana farmers paid school taxes, but did not stand guard over teachers threatened with violence. Former slaves did. The freedpeople's early postemancipation craving for and defense of schooling for themselves, and especially for their children, rested in good part on values and aspirations known among them as slaves. "The daily job of living did not end with enslavement," the anthropologist Sidney Mintz comments, "and the slaves could and did create viable patterns of life, for which their pasts were pool of available symbolic and material resources." That was true for the blacks after emancipation, too.

NOTE

1. In May 1861, fugitive slaves entering Union lines were denominated "contraband of war" by General Benjamin F. Butler, who gave them refuge but had no power to grant them legal freedom. The name stuck and became a generic term for former slaves, even after the passage of the Confiscation Act of 1862 and announcement of the Emancipation Proclamation legally freed those who reached federal lines.

Chapter 27

The Southern Black Church

Clarence Taylor and Jonathan Birnbaum

Among the most important institutions to emerge during Reconstruction was the independent black church. W. E. B. Du Bois described it as one of the three pillars of Reconstruction (along with schools and the Freedmen's Bureau).[1]

In the antebellum South, most blacks had been affiliated with white-controlled, biracial Protestant churches, but the Civil War led to the separation of white and black churches. This is not surprising, given the white churches' attitude toward and treatment of their black congregants. The few white churches that were willing to allow black membership demanded that blacks continue to sit in segregated seating in galleries or the back of the church—a requirement hardly acceptable after the arrival of freedom. In South Carolina, for instance, before the war forty-two thousand blacks belonged to biracial Methodist churches, but by the end of the war that number had dropped to six hundred.[2] In 1866—less than a year after the end of the war—South Carolina, Georgia, and Florida black Baptist churches had already set up their own association, and by 1880 the group had expanded throughout the South. Other Protestant denominations followed suit. At the turn of the century, Du Bois wrote, "There may be in the South a black man belonging to a white church today. But if so, he must be very old and very feeble."[3]

Independent of white influence, many of these churches became natural focal points for black political activity. The church served as the origin of thousands of later independent fraternal and mutual-aid societies. Black churches provided voter registration for blacks and meeting halls for the Republican Party and the Union League—an organization, joined by almost every southern black voter, that emphasized political and economic education (e.g., how to conduct strikes, contract for crops, sue employers). A North Carolina minister active in the league, who "describ[ed] himself as 'a poor Colord man'—proposed that the organization 'stand as gardians' for freedmen who 'don't know how to make a bargain . . . and see that they get the money.'"[4] The league also sponsored church and school building, fundraising for the sick, and, at some branches, self-defense organizations. Ministers routinely opened and led meetings.

Ministers were major actors in the politics of Reconstruction. "A man in this State cannot do his whole duty as a minister," said African Methodist Episcopal minister Charles H. Pearce, "except as he looks out for the political interests of his people."[5] The black clergy was based in the most independent black institution in the community, so it was no coincidence that African Americans selected a large number of clergy as their elected representatives. Black ministers, including William Gray, James Lynch (later elected to Congress), Hiram Revels, and Thomas Stringer, were elected to the Mississippi state legislature. More than thirty of the blacks who served in the South Carolina State legislature were ministers, according to historian Thomas Holt. The church, he writes "provided a flexible and sustaining employment, and opportunity for developing leadership qualities, and a pattern of public contacts with a potential political constituency."[6] According to Eric Foner, "Over 100 black ministers . . . [were] elected to legislative seats during Reconstruction."[7]

Given their prominent political roles, ministers were also natural targets for the Ku Klux Klan. All the activities the church excelled at—from community building to political mobilization—were seen as threats by the Klan, and ministers were frequent victims of Klan violence (see chapter 34).

Despite the repression of the Segregation era that followed, black churches survived, eventually providing an important base for a Second Reconstruction.

NOTES

1. W. E. B. Du Bois, "Reconstruction and Its Benefits," *American Historical Review,* July 1910, 781.

2. Eric Foner, "Reconstruction," *The Readers' Companion to American History,* ed. Eric Foner and John A. Garraty (New York: Houghton Mifflin, 1991), 921.

3. W. E. B. Du Bois, quoted in Benjamin Quarles, *The Negro in the Making of America,* rev. ed. (New York: Touchstone, 1987), 190.

4. Eric Foner, *Reconstruction: America's Unfinished Revolution, 1863–1877* (New York: Harper & Row, 1988), 285.

5. Ibid., 93.

6. Thomas Holt, *Black over White: Negro Political Leadership in South Carolina Reconstruction* (Urbana: University of Illinois Press), 229–41, 90.

7. Foner, *Reconstruction,* 93.

Chapter 28

Forty Acres and a Mule: Special Field Order No. 15

General William Tecumseh Sherman

The former slaves had very clear ideas about what freedom should have meant. Freedom meant more than the vote or the mere absence of chattel slavery. Freedom meant "placing us where we could reap the fruit of our own labor. . . to have land, and turn it and till it by our own labor," explained Garrison Frazier, a Baptist minister and former slave, at a meeting between General William Tecumseh Sherman and twenty leaders of Savannah, Georgia's black community on 12 January 1865. A few days later, Sherman issued Special Field Order No. 15, granting each former slave family forty acres of land outside Charleston. He later directed the army to assist the freedmen by loaning mules. Eric Foner speculates that this is the origin of the phrase "forty acres and a mule." About 40,000 freedmen took advantage of the offer. Generals O. O. Howard (after whom Washington, D.C.'s Howard University is named) and Rufus Saxton later expanded this program to other areas, until President Andrew Johnson commanded Howard to rescind the order. Most of the land was eventually returned to its previous Confederate owners, ending the opportunity of most blacks to have the freedom that economic independence would provide—and largely restricting the terms of debate during Reconstruction to the terms of employment.

The following selection is reprinted from "Special Field Order No. 15," 16 January 1865. The text is from Memoirs of General William T. Sherman *(New York: D. Appleton, 1886).*

1. The islands from Charleston south, the abandoned rice-fields along the rivers for thirty miles back from the sea, and the country bordering the St. John's River, Florida, are reserved and set apart for the settlement of the negroes now made free by the acts of war and the [Emancipation] proclamation of the President of the United States.

2. At Beaufort, Hilton Head, Savannah, Fernandina, St. Augustine, and Jacksonville, the blacks may remain in their chosen or accustomed vocations; but on the islands, and in the settlements hereafter to be established no white person whatever, unless military officers and soldiers detailed for duty, will be permitted

to reside; and the sole and exclusive management of affairs will be left to the freed people themselves, subject only to the United States military authority, and the acts of Congress. By the laws of war, and orders of the President of the United States, the negro is free, and must be dealt with as such. He cannot be subjected to conscription, or forced military service, save by the written orders of the highest military authority of the [War] department, under such regulations as the President or Congress may prescribe. Domestic servants, blacksmiths, carpenters, and other mechanics, will be free to select their own work and residence, but the young and able bodied negroes must be encouraged to enlist as soldiers in the service of the United States, to contribute their share toward maintaining their own freedom, and securing their rights as citizens of the United States.

Negroes so enlisted will be organized into companies, battalions, and regiments, under the orders of the United States military authorities, and will be paid, fed, and clothed, according to law. The bounties paid on enlistment may, with the consent of the recruit, go to assist his family and settlement in procuring agricultural implements, seed, tools, boots, clothing, and other articles necessary for their livelihood.

3. Whenever three respectable negroes, heads of families, shall desire to settle on land, and shall have selected for that purpose an island or a locality clearly defined within the limits above designated, the Inspector of Settlements and Plantations will himself, or by such subordinate officer as he may appoint, give them a license to settle such island or district, and afford them such assistance as he can to enable them to establish a peaceable agricultural settlement. The three parties named will subdivide the land, under the supervision of the inspector, among themselves, and such others as may choose to settle near them, so that each family shall have a plot of not more than forty acres of tillable ground, and, when it borders on some water channel, with not more than eight hundred feet water-front, in the possession of which land the military authorities will afford them protection until such time as they can protect themselves, or until Congress shall regulate their title. The quartermaster may, on the requisition of the inspector of Settlements and Plantations, place at the disposal of the inspector one or more of the captured steamers to ply between the settlements and one or more of the commercial points heretofore named, in order to afford the settlers the opportunity to supply their necessary wants, and to sell the products of their land and labor.

4. Whenever a negro has enlisted in the military service of the United States, he may locate his family in any one of the settlements at pleasure, and acquire a homestead, and all other rights and privileges of a settler, as though present in person. In like manner, negroes may settle their families and engage on board the gunboats, or in fishing, or in the navigation of the inland waters, without losing any claim to land or other advantages derived from this system. But no one, unless an actual settler as above defined, or unless absent on Government service, will be entitled to claim any right to land or property in any settlement by virtue of these orders.

5. In order to carry out this system of settlement, a general officer will be detailed as Inspector of Settlements and Plantations, whose duty it shall be to visit

the settlements, to regulate their police and general arrangement, and who will furnish personally to each head of a family, subject to the approval of the President of the United States, a possessory title in writing, giving as near as possible the description of boundaries; and who shall adjust all claims or conflicts that may arise under the same, subject to the like approval, treating such titles altogether as possessory. The same general officer will also be charged with the enlistment and organization of the negro recruits, and protecting their interests while absent from their settlements; and will be governed by the rules and regulations prescribed by the War Department for such purposes.

6. Brigadier-General R. Saxton is hereby appointed Inspector of Settlements and Plantations, and will at once enter on the performance of his duties. No change is intended or desired in the settlement now on Beaufort Island, nor will any rights to property heretofore acquired be affected thereby.

By order of Major-General W[illiam] T[ecumseh] Sherman
L. M. Datton, Assistant Adjutant-General

Chapter 29

A Proposal for Reconstruction

Thaddeus Stevens

Thaddeus Stevens (1792–1868), a strong advocate of public education, abolition-ism, and black civil rights, served as a Representative from Pennsylvania in the U.S. Congress from 1849–1853 and 1859–1868. Stevens was a key figure in the passage of Reconstruction legislation, including the Civil Rights Act of 1866, the Fourteenth Amendment, and the Reconstruction Act of 1867. Stevens advocated much stronger legislation, especially land reform—dividing up plantations for for-mer slaves—but his plans were considered too radical for most Republicans.

When Stevens died, he was buried in an integrated cemetery. A century later, in 1977, President Jimmy Carter, the former governor of Georgia, symbolically in-sisted on enrolling his daughter Amy in a Washington, D.C., public school—the Thaddeus Stevens School.

The following selection is excerpted from "Reconstruction. Speech of the Hon. Thaddeus Stevens delivered in the City of Lancaster, September 7, 1865," The Se-lected Papers of Thaddeus Stevens, *ed. Beverly Wilson Palmer (Pittsburgh: Uni-versity of Pittsburgh Press, 1998), 2:12–27.*

For more on Stevens, see Eric Foner, "Thaddeus Stevens, Confiscation, and Re-construction," in Politics and Ideology in the Age of the Civil War *(1980).*

Fellow Citizens:

In compliance with your request, I have come to give my views of the present con-dition of the Rebel States—of the proper mode of reorganizing the Government, and the future prospects of the Republic. During the whole progress of the war, I never for a moment felt doubt or despondency. I knew that the loyal North would conquer the Rebel despots who sought to destroy freedom. But since that traitor-ous confederation has been subdued, and we have entered upon the work of "re-construction" or "restoration," I cannot deny that my heart has become sad at the gloomy prospects before us.

Four years of bloody and expensive war, waged against the United States by eleven States, under a government called the "Confederate States of America," to which they acknowledged allegiance, have overthrown all governments within those States which could be acknowledged as legitimate by the Union. The armies of the Confederate States having been conquered and subdued, and their territory possessed by the United States, it becomes necessary to establish governments therein, which shall be republican in form and principles, and form a more "perfect Union" with the parent Government. It is desirable that such a course should be pursued as to exclude from those governments every vestige of human bondage, and render the same forever impossible in this nation; and to take care that no principles of self-destruction shall be incorporated therein. In effecting this, it is to be hoped that no provision of the Constitution will be infringed, and no principle of the law of nations disregarded. Especially must we take care that in rebuking this unjust and treasonable war, the authorities of the union shall indulge in no acts of usurpation which may tend to impair the stability and permanency of the nation. Within these limitations, we hold it to be the duty of the Government to inflict condign [well-deserved] punishment on the rebel belligerents, and so weaken their hands that they can never again endanger the Union; and so reform their municipal institutions as to make them republican in spirit as well as in name.

We especially insist that the property of the chief rebels should be seized and appropriated to the payment of the National debt, caused by the unjust and wicked war which they instigated.

How can such punishments be inflicted and such forfeitures produced without doing violence to established principles?

Two positions have been suggested.

First—To treat those States as never having been out of the Union, because the Constitution forbids secession, and therefore, a fact forbidden by law could not exist.

Second—To accept the position to which they placed themselves as severed from the Union; an independent government *de facto,* and an alien enemy to be dealt with according to the laws of War. . . .

South Carolina, the leader and embodiment of the rebellion, in the month of January, 1861, passed the following resolution by the unanimous vote of her Legislature:

"Resolved, That the separation of South Carolina from the Federal Union *is final,* and she has no further interests in the Constitution of the United States; and that the only appropriate negotiations between her and the Federal Government are as to their mutual relations as *foreign* States."

The convention that formed the Government of the Confederate States, and all the eleven states that composed it, adopted the same declaration, and pledged their lives and fortunes to support it. . . .

[A]ll writers agree that the victor may inflict punishment upon the vanquished enemy, even to the taking of his life, liberty, or the confiscation of all his property; but that this extreme right is never exercised except upon a cruel, barbarous, obstinate, or dangerous foe who has waged an unjust war. . . .

[W]e propose to confiscate all the estate of every rebel belligerent whose estate was worth $10,000, or whose land exceeded two hundred acres in quantity. Policy if not justice would require that the poor, the ignorant, and the coerced should be forgiven. They followed the example and teachings of their wealthy and intelligent neighbors. The rebellion would never have originated with them. Fortunately those who would thus escape form a large majority of the people, though possessing but a small portion of the wealth. The proportion of those exempt compared with the punished would be I believe about nine tenths.

There are about [four] millions of freedmen in the South.[1] The number of acres of land is 465,000,000. Of this, those who own above two hundred acres each number about 70,000 persons, holding, in the aggregate, (together with the States,) about 394,000,000 acres, leaving for all the others below 200 each, about 71,000,000 of acres. By thus forfeiting the estates of the leading rebels, the government would have 394,000,000 of acres, beside their town property, and yet nine-tenths of the people would remain untouched. Divide this land into convenient farms. Give, if you please, forty acres to each adult male freedman. Suppose there are one million of them. That would require 40,000,000 of acres, which, deducted from 394,000,000, leaves three hundred and fifty-four millions of acres for sale. Divide it into suitable farms, and sell it to the highest bidders. I think it, including town property, would average at least ten dollars per acre. That would produce $3,540,000,000—three billions five hundred and forty millions of dollars.

Let that be applied as follows to wit:

1. Invest $300,000,000 in six per cent government bonds, and add the interest semi-annually to the pensions of those who have become entitled by this villainous war.
2. Appropriate $200,000,000 to pay the damages done to loyal men, North and South, by the rebellion.
3. Pay the residue, being $3,040,000,000 towards the payment of the National debt.

What loyal man can object to this? Look around you, and every where behold your neighbors, some with an arm, some with a leg, some with an eye, carried away by rebel bullets. Others horribly mutilated in every form. And yet numerous others wearing the weeds which mark the death of those on whom they leaned for support. Contemplate these monuments of rebel perfidy, and of patriotic suffering, and then say if too much is asked for our valiant soldiers. . . .

The only argument of the Restorationists is, that the States could not and did not go out of the Union because the Constitution forbids it. By the same reasoning you could prove that no crime ever existed. No man ever committed murder for the law forbids it! He is a shallow reasoner who could make theory overrule fact!

If "Restoration," as it is now properly christened, is to prevail over "Reconstruction," will some learned pundit of that school inform me in what condition Slavery and the Slave laws are? I assert that upon that theory not a Slave has been liberated, not a Slave law has been abrogated, but on the "Restoration" the whole Slave code is in legal force. Slavery was protected by our Constitution in every State in the Union where it existed. While they remained under that protection no power in the Federal Government could abolish Slavery. If, however, the

Confederate States were admitted to be what they claimed, an independent belligerent *de facto,* then the war broke all treaties, compacts and ties between the parties, and slavery was left to its rights under the law of nations. These rights were none; for the law declares that "Man can hold no property in man."[2] Then the laws of war enabled us to declare every bondman free, so long as we held them in military possession. And the conqueror, through Congress, may declare them forever emancipated. But if the States are "States in the Union," then when war ceases they resume their positions with all their privileges untouched. There can be no "mutilated" restoration. That would be the work of Congress alone, and would be "Reconstruction."

While I hear it said everywhere that slavery is dead, I cannot learn who killed it. No thoughtful man has pretended that Lincoln's proclamation, so noble in sentiment, liberated a single slave. It expressly excluded from its operation all those within our lines. No slave within any part of the rebel States in our possession, or in Tennessee, but only those beyond our limits and beyond our power were declared free. . . .

[I]t is said, by those who have more sympathy with rebel wives and children than for the widows and orphans of loyal men, that this stripping the rebels of their estates and driving them to exile or to honest labor, would be harsh and severe upon innocent women and children. It may be so; but that is the result of the necessary laws of war. But it is revolutionary, say they. This plan would, no doubt, work a radical reorganization in Southern institutions, habits and manners. It is intended to revolutionize their principles and feelings. This may startle feeble minds and shake weak nerves. So do all great improvements in the political and moral world. It requires a heavy impetus to drive forward a sluggish people. When it was first proposed to free the slaves and arm the blacks, did not half the nation tremble? The prim conservatives, the snobs, and the male waiting-maids in Congress, were in hysterics.

The whole fabric of southern society *must* be changed, and never can it be done if this opportunity is lost. Without this, this Government can never be, as it never has been, a true republic. Heretofore, it had more the features of aristocracy than of democracy. The Southern States have been despotisms, not governments of the people. It is impossible that any practical equality of rights can exist where a few thousand men monopolize the whole landed property. The larger the number of small proprietors the more safe and stable the government. As the landed interest must govern, the more it is subdivided and held by independent owners, the better. What would be the condition of the State of New York if it were not for her independent yeomanry? . . . If the South is ever to be made a safe republic, let her lands be cultivated by the toil of the owners or the free labor of intelligent citizens. This must be done even though it drive her nobility into exile. If they go, all the better. It will be hard to persuade the owner of ten thousand acres of land, who drives a coach and four [horses], that he is not degraded by sitting at the same table, or in the same pew, with the embrowned and hard-handed farmer who has himself cultivated his own thriving homestead of 150 acres. This subdivision of the lands will yield ten bales of cotton to one that is made now, and he who produced it will own it and *feel himself a man.*

. . . I may say a word more of these persistent apologists of the South. For, when the virus of Slavery has once entered the veins of the slaveholder, no subsequent effort seems capable of wholly eradicating it. They are a family of considerable power, some merit, of admirable audacity and execrable selfishness. . . .

We have a duty to perform which our fathers were incapable of, which will be required at our hands by God and our Country. When our ancestors found a "more perfect Union" necessary, they found it impossible to agree upon a Constitution without tolerating, nay, guaranteeing, Slavery. They were obliged to acquiesce, trusting to time to work a speedy cure, in which they were disappointed. *They* had some excuse, some justification. But we can have none if we do not thoroughly eradicate Slavery and render it forever impossible in this republic. The Slave power made war upon the nation. They declared the "more perfect Union" dissolved—solemnly declared themselves a foreign nation, alien to this republic; for four years were in fact what they claimed to be. We accepted the war which they tendered and treated them as a government capable of making war. We have conquered them, and as a conquered enemy we can give them laws; can abolish all their municipal institutions and form new ones. If we do not make those institutions fit to last through generations of freemen, a heavy curse will be on us. . . .

If a majority of Congress can be found wise and firm enough to declare the Confederate States a conquered enemy, Reconstruction will be easy and legitimate; and the friends of freedom will long rule in the Councils of the Nation. If Restoration prevails the prospect is gloomy, and new "lords will make new laws." The Union party will be overwhelmed. The Copperhead party[3] has become extinct with Secession. But with Secession it will revive. Under "Restoration" every rebel State will send rebels to Congress; and they, with their allies in the North, will control Congress, and occupy the White House. Then restoration of laws and ancient Constitutions will be sure to follow, our public debt will be repudiated, or the rebel National debt will be added to ours, and the people be crushed beneath heavy burdens.

Let us forget all parties, and build on the broad platform of "reconstructing" the government out of the conquered territory converted into new and free States, and admitted into the Union by the sovereign power of Congress, with another plank—"THE PROPERTY OF THE REBELS SHALL PAY OUR NATIONAL DEBT, *and indemnify freed-men and loyal sufferers*—and that under no circumstances will we suffer the National debt to be repudiated, or the interest scaled below the contract rates; nor permit any part of the rebel debt to be assumed by the nation."

Let all who approve of these principles rally with us. Let all others go with Copperheads and rebels. Those will be the opposing parties. Young men, this duty devolves on you. Would to God, if only for that, that I were still in the prime of life, that I might aid you to fight through this last and greatest battle of freedom!

EDITORS' NOTES

1. Stevens's text here mistakenly indicates six million freedpeople. Elsewhere he cites the correct number—four million.

2. Stevens is quoting Sir Robert Joseph Phillimore, an English jurist, author of *Commentaries upon International Law* (1854–1861).

3. Copperheads were northerners—usually Democrats—who opposed the Civil War, advocating a negotiated settlement with the South.

Chapter 30

Woman's Rights

Sojourner Truth

Abolitionist and woman's rights activist Sojourner Truth (1797?–1883) was born into slavery in New York State. She escaped in 1826, one year before emancipation became mandatory throughout the state. She moved to New York City and became involved in religious revivalism before beginning her career as an abolitionist and changing her slave name, Isabella, to Sojourner Truth. She became a popular lecturer on abolition and woman's rights. She dictated and published an autobiography, The Narrative of Sojourner Truth, *in 1850. For biographies, see Carleton Mabee,* Sojourner Truth *(1993) and Nell Painter,* Sojourner Truth *(1996).*

The following selection is excerpted from "Annual Meeting of the Equal Rights Association," National Anti-Slavery Standard, *1 June 1867, 3.*

My friends, I am rejoiced that you are glad, but I don't know how you will feel when I get through. I come from another field—the country of the slave. They have got their rights—so much good luck: now what is to be done about it? I feel that I have got as much responsibility as anybody else. I have got as good rights as anybody. There is a great stir about colored men getting their rights, but not a word about the colored women; and if colored men get their rights, and not colored women get theirs, there will be a bad time about it. So I am for keeping the thing going while things are stirring; because if we wait till it is still, it will take a great while to get it going again. White women are a great deal smarter, and know more than colored women, while colored women do not know scarcely anything. They go out washing, which is about as high as a colored woman gets, and their men go about idle, strutting up and down; and when the women come home, they ask for their money and take it all, and then scold because there is no food. I want you to consider on that, chil'n. I want women to have their rights. In the Courts women have no right, no voice; nobody speaks for them. I wish woman to have her voice there among the pettifoggers. If it is not a fit place for women, it is unfit for men to be there. I am above eighty years old; it is about time for me to be going. But I suppose I am kept here because something remains for me to do; I suppose I am yet to help break the chain. I have done a great deal of work—as much as a man, but did not get so much pay. I used to work in the field and bind grain, keeping up with the cradler; but men never doing no more, got twice as much pay. So with the German women. They work in the field and do as much work, but do not get the pay. We do as much, we eat as much, we want as much. I suppose I am about the only colored woman that goes about to speak for the rights of the colored woman. I want to keep the thing stirring, now that the ice is broken. What we want is a little money. You men know that you get as much again as women when you write, or for what you do. When we get our rights, we shall not have to come to you for money, for then we shall have money enough of our own. It is a good consolation to know that when we have got this we shall not be coming to you any more. You have been having our right so long, that you think, like a slaveholder, that you own us. I know that it is hard for one who has held the reins for so long to give up; it cuts like a knife. It will feel all better when it closes up again. I have been in Washington about three years, seeing about those colored people. Now colored men have a right to vote; and what I want is to have colored women have the right to vote. There ought to be equal rights more than ever, since colored people have got their freedom. . . .

Well, children—I know it is hard for men to give up entirely. They must run in the old track. I was amused how men speaks up for one another. They cannot bear that a woman should say anything about the man, but they will stand here and take up the time in man's cause. But we are going, tremble or no tremble. Men is trying to help us. I know that all—the spirit they have got; and they cannot help us much until some of the spirit is taken out of them that belongs among the women. Men have got their rights, and women has not got their rights. That is the trouble. When woman gets her rights man will be right. How beautiful that will be. Then it will be peace on earth and good will to men. But it cannot be that until it be right. . . . It will come. . . . Yes, it will come quickly. It must come. And now when the waters is troubled, and now is the time to step into the pool. There is a great deal now with the minds, and now is the time to start forth. I was going to say that it was said to me some time ago that "a woman was not fit to have any rule. Do you want women to rule? They ain't fit. Don't you know that a woman had seven devils in her, and do you suppose that a man should put her to rule in the government?" "Seven devils is of no account" said I "just behold, the man had a legion." They never thought about that. A man had a legion and the devils didn't know where to go. That was the trouble. . . . I want to see, before I leave here—I want to see equality. I want to see women have their rights, and then will be no more war. All the fighting has been for selfishness. They wanted something more than their own, or to hold something that was not their own; but when we have woman's rights, there is nothing to fight for. I have got all I want, and you have got all you want, and what do you fight for? All the battles that have ever been was for selfishness—for a right that belonged to some one else, or fighting for his own right. The great fight was to keep the rights of the poor colored people. That made a great battle. And now I hope that this will be the last battle that will be in the world. Fighting for rights. And there never will be a fight without it is a fight for rights. See how beautiful it is! It covers the whole ground. We ought to have it all finished up now. Let us finish it up so that there be no more fighting. I have faith in God, and there is truth in humanity. Be strong women! blush not! tremble not!

I know men will get up and brat, brat, brat, brat about something which does not amount to anything except talk. We want to carry the point to one particular thing, and that is woman's rights, for nobody has any business with a right that belongs to her. I can make use of my own right. I want the same use of the same right. Do you want it? Then get it. If men had not taken something that did not belong to them they would not fear. But they tremble! They dodge! We will have nothing owned by anybody. . . . Men speak great lies, and it has made a great sore, but it will soon heal up. For I know when men, good men, discuss sometimes, that they say something or another and then take it half back. You must make a little allowance. . . . It is hard for them to get out of it. Now we will help you out, if you want to get out. I want you to keep a good faith and good courage. And I am going round after I get my business settled and get more equality. People in the North, I am going round to lecture on human rights. I will shake every place I go to.

Chapter 31

Woman Suffrage

Charlotte Rollin

Charlotte "Lottie" Rollin (1849–?) and her four sisters were born into a free black family in Charleston, South Carolina. Lottie, together with her sisters, attended a Catholic school for "colored people" before being sent north for secondary education. After the family moved to Columbia, the sisters were culturally and politically prominent in Reconstruction-era state politics. Rollin joined the American Woman Suffrage Association and was elected secretary of the state affiliate, the South Carolina Woman's Rights Association, in 1870.

The following selection, Rollin's speech to the Woman's Rights Convention in Columbia on 20 December 1870, is excerpted from Elizabeth Cady Stanton et al., eds. History of Woman Suffrage *(1876–1885), 3:828.*

It had been so universally the custom to treat the idea of woman suffrage with ridicule and merriment that it becomes necessary in submitting the subject for earnest deliberation that we assure the gentlemen present that our claim is made honestly and seriously. We ask suffrage not as a favor, not as a privilege, but as a right based on the ground that we are human beings, and as such, entitled to all human rights. While we concede that woman's ennobling influence should be confined chiefly to home and society, we claim that public opinion has had a tendency to limit woman's sphere to too small a circle, and until woman has had right of representation this will last, and other rights will be held by an insecure tenure.

Chapter 32

Black Women during Reconstruction

Frances Ellen Watkins Harper

Writer Frances Ellen Watkins Harper (1825–1911) was born to free parents in Maryland. Her parents died when she was three years old, and she was raised by relatives. Harper attended Baltimore's William Watkins Academy for Negro Youth, founded by her uncle. In her mid-twenties she moved to Ohio and became the first female teacher at Union Seminary (later renamed Wilberforce University). Along with her career as a novelist, poet, and essayist, Harper was a member of the Underground Railroad, an abolitionist and temperance lecturer, a founder of both the American Woman Suffrage Association and the National Association of Colored Women, and member of the African Methodist Episcopal Church. Harper's best-known novel was Iola Leroy *(1892).*

The following selection, emphasizing uplift and the most successful efforts of black women during Reconstruction, is excerpted from "Coloured Women of America," Englishwoman's Review, *15 January 1878, 10–15.*

The women as a class are quite equal to the men in energy and executive ability. In fact I find by close observation, that the mothers are the levers which move in education. The men talk about it, especially about election time, if they want an office for self or their candidate, but the women work most for it. They labour in many ways to support the family while the children attend school. They make great sacrifices to spare their own children during school hours. I know of girls from sixteen to twenty-two who iron till midnight that they may come to school in the day. Some of our scholars, aged about nineteen, living about thirty miles off, rented land, ploughed, planted, and then sold their cotton, in order to come to us. A woman near me, urged her husband to go in debt 500 dollars for a home, as the titles to the land they had built on were insecure, and she said to me, "We have five years to pay it in, and I shall begin to-day to do it, if life is spared. I will make a hundred dollars at washing, for I have done it." Yet they have seven little children to feed, clothe, and educate. In the field the women receive the same wages as the men, and are often preferred, clearing land, hoeing, or picking cotton, with equal ability.

In different departments of business, coloured women have not only been enabled to keep the wolf from the door, but also to acquire property, and in some cases the coloured woman is the mainstay of the family, and when work fails the men in large cities, the money which the wife can obtain by washing, ironing, and other services, often keeps pauperism at bay. I do not suppose, considering the state of her industrial lore and her limited advantages, that there is among the poorer classes a more helpful woman than the coloured woman as a labourer. When I was in Mississippi, I stopped with Mr. Montgomery, a former slave of Jefferson Davis's brother. His wife was a woman capable of taking on her hands 130 acres of land, and raising one hundred and seven bales of cotton by the force which she could organise. Since then I have received a very interesting letter from her daughter, who for years has held the position of Assistant Post-mistress. In her letter she says: "There are many women around me who would serve as models of executiveness anywhere. They do double duty, a man's share in the field, and a woman's part at home. they do any kind of field work, even ploughing, and at home the cooking, washing, milking, and gardening. But these have husbands; let me tell you of some widows and unaided women:—

"1st. Mrs. Hill, a widow, has rented, cultivated, and solely managed a farm of five acres for five years. She makes her garden, raises poultry, and cultivates enough corn and cotton to live comfortably, and keep a surplus in the bank. She saves something every year, and this is much, considering the low price of cotton and unfavourable seasons.

"2nd. Another woman, whose husband died in the service during the war, cultivated one acre, making vegetables for sale, besides a little cotton. She raises poultry, spins thread, and knits hose for a living. She supports herself comfortably, never having to ask credit or to borrow.

"[3rd.] Mrs. Jane Brown and Mrs. Halsey formed a partnership about ten years ago, leased nine acres and a horse, and have cultivated the land all that time, just the same as men would have done. They have saved considerable money from year to year, and are living independently. They have never had any expenses for labour, making and gathering the crops themselves.

"4th. Mrs. Henry by farming and peddling cakes, has the last seven years laid up seven hundred dollars. She is an invalid, and unable to work at all times. Since then she has been engaged in planting sweet potatoes and raising poultry and hogs. Last year she succeeded in raising 250 hogs, but lost two thirds by disease. She furnished eggs and chickens enough for family use, and sold a surplus of chickens, say fifty dozen chickens. On nine acres she made 600 bushels of sweet potatoes. The present year she has planted ten acres of potatoes. She has 100 hogs, thirty dozen chickens, a small lot of ducks and turkeys, and also a few sheep and goats. She has also a large garden under her supervision, which is planted in cabbages. She has two women and a boy to assist. Miss Montgomery, a coloured lady, says: 'I have constantly been engaged in bookkeeping for eight years, and for ten years as assistant post-mistress, doing all the work of the office. Now instead of bookkeeping, I manage a school of 133 pupils, and I have an assistant, and I am still attending to the post-office.' Of her sister she says, she is a better and swifter worker than herself; that she generally sews, but that last year she made 100 dozen jars of preserved fruit for sale. An acquaintance of mine, who lives in South

Carolina, and has been engaged in mission work, reports that, in supporting the family, women are the mainstay; that two-thirds of the truck gardening is done by them in South Carolina; that in the city they are more industrious than the men; that when the men lose their work through their political affiliations, the women stand by them, and say, 'stand by your principles.' And I have been informed by the same person that a number of women have homes of their own, bought by their hard earnings since freedom. Mr. Stewart, who was employed in the Freedmen's bank, says he has seen scores of coloured women in the South working and managing plantations of from twenty to 100 acres. . . ."

In higher walks of life too, the coloured women have made progress. The principal of the Coloured High School in Philadelphia was born a slave in the District of Columbia; but in early life she was taken North, and she resolved to get knowledge. When about fifteen years old, she obtained a situation as a house servant, with the privilege of going other day to receive instruction. Poverty was in her way, but instead of making it a stumbling block, she converted it into a stepping stone. She lived in one place about six years, and received seven dollars a month. A coloured lady presented her with a scholarship, and she entered Oberlin as a pupil. When she was sufficiently advanced, Oberlin was brave enough to accord her a place as a teacher in the preparatory department of the college, a position she has held for many years, graduating almost every year a number of pupils, a part of whom are scattered abroad as teachers in different parts of the country. Nearly all the coloured teachers in Washington are girls and women, a large percentage of whom were educated in the [D]istrict of Columbia. Nor is it only in the ranks of teachers that coloured women are content to remain. Some years since, two coloured women were studying in the Law School of Howard University. One of them, Miss Charlotte Ray, a member of this body, has since graduated, being, I believe, the first coloured woman in the country who has ever gained the distinction of being a graduated lawyer. Others have gone into medicine and have been practising in different States of the Union. In the Woman's Medical College of Pennsylvania, two coloured women were last year pursuing their studies as Matriculants, while a young woman, the daughter of a former fugitive slave, has held the position of an assistant resident physician in one of the hospitals. Miss Cole, of Philadelphia, held for some time the position of physician in the State Orphan Asylum in South Carolina. . . .

The coloured women have not been backward in promoting charities for their own sex and race. "One of the most efficient helpers is Mrs. Madison, who, although living in a humble and unpretending home, had succeeded in getting up a home for aged coloured women. By organized effort, coloured women have been enabled to help each other in sickness, and provide respectable funerals for the dead. . . . There are also, in several States, homes for aged coloured women: the largest I know of being in Philadelphia. This home was in a measure built by Stephen and Harriet Smith, coloured citizens of the State of Pennsylvania. Into this home men are also admitted. The City of Philadelphia has also another home for the homeless, which, besides giving them a temporary shelter, provides a permanent home for a number of aged coloured women. In looking over the statistics of miscellaneous charities, out of a list of fifty-seven charitable institutions, I see only nine in which there is any record of coloured inmates. Out of twenty-six Industrial Schools, I counted four. Out of a list of one hundred and fifty-seven orphan asylums, miscellaneous charities, and industrial schools, I find fifteen asylums in which there is some mention of coloured inmates. More than half the reform schools in 1874, had admitted coloured girls. The coloured women of Philadelphia have formed a Christian Relief Association, which has opened sewing schools for coloured girls, and which has been enabled, year after year, to lend a hand to some of the more needy of their race, and it also has, I understand, sustained an employment office for some time.

Chapter 33

Southern Discomfort

Whitelaw Reid

Whitelaw Reid (1837–1912) was a radical Republican journalist who wrote for various Ohio newspapers during the Civil War. After the war ended, he was one of the first northern journalists to extensively tour the South and report on conditions. At age thirty-one he was appointed managing editor of the New York Tribune. *In later years Reid's politics grew more conservative, perhaps, in part, reflecting his postwar investment in three cotton plantations.*

The following selection is excerpted from After the War: A Tour of the Southern States, 1865–1866 *(New York: Moore, Wilstach & Baldwin, 1866).*

From Montgomery I went down the River to Selma, Alabama. . . . Selma is the center of the rich cotton-growing belt of Alabama, and the lands there are probably unequaled by any to the eastward, and by only Mississippi and Red River lands to the west. . . .

[T]he [white] people had many complaints of [black] insubordination, so great that they were in actual fear for the lives of their families! Some of the newspapers thought "the scenes of bloodshed and massacre of St. Domingo[1] would be re-enacted in their midst, before the close of the year." "We speak advisedly," continued one frightened editor, "we have authentic information of the speeches and conversations of the blacks, sufficient to convince us of their purpose. They make no secret of their movement. Tell us not that we are alarmists. After due investigation and reflection upon this matter, we have determined to talk plainly, without fear or favor, and if our voice of warning is not heeded, we, at least, will have the consoling reflection that we have performed our duty."

All this silly talk was, doubtless, utterly without foundation. Negroes neglected to touch their hats to overseers or former masters whom they disliked; and straightway it was announced that they were growing too saucy for human endurance. They held meetings and sung songs about their freedom, whereupon it was conjectured that they were plotting for a rising against the whites. They refused to be beaten; and, behold, the grossest insubordination was existing among the negroes.

Carl Shurz gave an instance in point:

One of our military commanders was recently visited by a doctor living in one of the south-eastern counties of Georgia. The doctor looked very much disturbed.

"General," says he, "the negroes in my county are in a terrible state of insub-ordination, and we may look for an outbreak every moment. I come to implore your aid."

The General, already accustomed to such alarming reports, takes the matter with great coolness. "Doctor, I have heard of such things before. Is not your imagination a little excited? What reason should the negroes have to resort to violence?"

"General, you do not appreciate the dangers of the situation we are placed in. Our lives are not safe. It is impossible to put up with the demonstrations of insub-ordination on the part of the negroes. If they do not cease, I shall have to remove my family into the city. If we are not protected, we can not stay in the country. I would rather up my crop to the negroes than the lives of my wife and children."

"Now, Doctor, please go into particulars, and tell me what has happened."

"Well, General, formerly the slaves were obliged to retire to their cabins before nine o'clock in the evening. After that hour nobody was permitted outside. Now, when their work is done, they roam about just as they please, and when I tell them to go to their quarters, they do not mind me. Negroes from neighboring planta-tions will sometimes come to visit them, and they have a sort of meeting, and then they are cutting up sometimes until ten or eleven. You see, General, this is alarm-ing, and you must acknowledge that we are not safe."

"Well, Doctor, what are they doing when they have that sort of a meeting? Tell me all you know."

"Why, General, they are talking together, sometimes in whispers and sometimes loudly. They are having their conspiracies, I suppose. And then they are going on to sing and dance, and make a noise."

"Ah, now, Doctor," says the imperturbable General, "you see this is their year of jubilee. They must celebrate their freedom in some way. What harm is there in singing or dancing? Our Northern laborers sing and dance when they please, and nobody thinks anything of it; we rather enjoy it with them."

"Yes, that is all well enough, General; but these are negroes, who ought to be subordinate, and when I tell them to go to their quarters, and they don't do it, we can't put up with it."

"By the way, Doctor, have you made a contract with the negroes on your plantation."

"Yes."

"Do they work well?"

"Pretty well, so far. My crops are in pretty good condition."

"Do they steal much?"

"They steal some, but not very much."

"Well, then, Doctor, what have you to complain about?"

"O, General," says the Doctor, dolefully, "you do not appreciate the dangers of our situation."

"Now, Doctor, to cut the matter short, has a single act of violence been perpe-trated in your neighborhood by a negro against a white man?"

"Yes, sir; and I will tell you of one that has happened right in my family. I have a negro girl, eighteen years old, whom I raised. For ten years she has been waiting upon my old mother-in-law, who lives with me. A few days ago the old lady was dissatisfied about something, and told the girl that she felt like giving her a whipping. Now, what do you think? the negro girl actually informed my old mother-in-law that she would not submit to a whipping, but would resist. My old father-in-law then got mad, and threatened her; and she told him the same thing. Now, this is an intolerable state of things."

EDITORS' NOTE

1. Reid refers to events during the revolutionary overthrow of slavery in Haiti. For a history, see C. L. R. James, *The Black Jacobins: Toussaint L'Ouverture and the San Domingo Revolution* (New York: Random House, 1963).

Chapter 34

The Ku Klux Klan Conspiracy

Eugene Lawrence

The first Ku Klux Klan was founded in Tennessee in 1866. Originally formed as a fraternal organization, it soon switched its objectives to the enforcement of white supremacy. In 1867, delegates from several states named Nathan Bedford Forrest—the Confederate general whose troops had murdered surrendering black soldiers during the Fort Pillow Massacre—as the organization's first Grand Wizard. A number of similar groups, under various names, operated throughout the former Confederacy, terrorizing blacks and white Republicans. Southern states passed anti-Klan legislation that proved generally ineffective. Eventually, the federal government passed legislation and intervened with troops. In 1872, a joint congressional committee produced a thirteen-volume report on Klan activities in the South. With declining interest in the North, southern Democrats re-established white supremacist rule, ignoring Reconstruction amendments, disenfranchising blacks, and ending Reconstruction.

Journalist Eugene Lawrence frequently wrote about Klan activity for Harper's Weekly.

The following selection is excerpted from "The Ku-Klux Conspiracy," Harper's Weekly, *19 October 1872, 805–6.*

The Congressional reports on the Ku-Klux conspiracy show the real causes of the decline in the value of every kind of property in the Southern States, and the dangers that threaten the future of their industry and trade. The Democratic party has fallen under the control of a murderous faction: its more intelligent and prudent members have not sufficient courage to free themselves from the tyranny of robbers and assassins; the colored population and the white. Republicans, the industrious and the honest, in many parts of the South are disfranchised by intimidation and open violence; the governments of several States are plain usurpations; a minority of lawless men rule over the powerless majority, and once more threaten rebellion, defy the national government, and bring ruin upon their fellow-citizens. The Ku-Klux conspiracy has extended its mysterious links through every Southern State: it has usually flourished before and after every election with a sudden vigor, and has then sunk into obscurity until the hour for new efforts arrived; its measures are always the same, whether in Texas or Missouri; its members ride around at night in strange disguises; their victims are white and colored Republicans, their wives and children, honest workingmen, teachers, and active Baptist or Methodist ministers; sometimes United States officials or State judges and Senators have fallen before their rifles; sometimes the clergyman has been shot in his pulpit or the lawyer in his court-house; but oftener they are content to rob and burn the negro cabin, to seam the backs of its unlucky tenants with pitiless lashes, or leave the husband and the father bleeding and dying in the midst of his horror-stricken family. The pitiless cruelty of these Southern Democrats—for the chief object of the Ku-Klux assassins is always to insure the election of the Democratic officials—surpasses the barbarity of the savage. . . .

In Alabama the rage of the Democratic politicians seems chiefly turned against school-teachers, Methodist and Baptist preachers, and white Republicans who strive to elevate the colored race. The Ku-Klux labors have proved successful: a Democratic Governor has been elected (Lindsay), who denies the existence of any Ku-Klux conspiracy, and will see nothing of the brutal system of intimidation by which he has won an office; the State is ominously quiet. Governor Lindsay boasts of his power over the colored voters; the Democratic politicians assert that they are fast winning the negroes to their side—by what means who can fail to see? and that it can not be by any known train of argument is shown from the open assertion of leading Democrats that, had they the power, they would take from the colored population the right to vote at all.

The measures employed by the Democrats to recruit their party from the Republican side is best shown in the testimony of the Rev. Mr. Lakin, and his narrative of the fearful deeds of the Ku-Klux in Alabama is sustained and made probable by the long series of their similar crimes in every Southern State. Mr. Lakin was sent to Alabama by Bishop Clark, of Ohio, to renew the Methodist Episcopal Church in that State. He seems to have been unusually successful. He traveled over nearly all the counties of the State. He numbered seventy ministers or teachers among his assistants; he was presiding elder of his district, and was gladly welcomed in many humble cottages on the mountains, and in every negro cabin. He was chosen president of the State university. But in 1868 the Ku-Klux were awakened by the approaching election, and by the cheering words of their friends in the North, of Seymour, Buckalew, Kernan, and Wood; they drove the Rev. Mr. Lakin from the university; they threatened death to every Republican student. In the *Independent Monitor,* of Tuscaloosa, Alabama, appeared a leading article warning the new president to leave the State at once, and a cut was given, in which the Rev. Mr. Lakin was represented as hanging from the limb of a tree. It was also suggested that the end of "negroism" was near, and that there was room on the same limb for every "Grant negro." The Ku-Klux now renewed their terrible career, nor have we space even to allude to the details of their frightful deeds. Judge Thurlow was shot at Hunstville, where the disguised assassins had ridden in openly and in "line of battle;" Judge Charlton, another active Republican, was pursued and shot; a band of Ku-Klux rode into the town of Eutaw, in irresistible strength, seized a Mr. Boyd in his room at the hotel, and murdered him. The Rev. Mr. Lakin was threatened, shot at, and finally driven to take refuge in the mountains. The fate of many of his assistant preachers revives the image of the persecutions of Decius or Diocletian. A Mr. Sullivan was barbarously whipped; the Rev. J. A. M'Cutchen, a presiding elder, was driven from Demopolis; the Rev. James Buchanan, and the Rev. John W. Tailly, another presiding elder, were expelled by force; the Rev. Jesse Kingston was shot in his pulpit; the Rev. James Dorman whipped; Dean Reynolds whipped and left nearly dead, with both arms broken; a colored preacher and his son were murdered on the public road; the Rev. Mr. Taylor severely beaten; six churches were burned in one district; school-houses were every where destroyed, and the teachers, male or female, driven away or infamously ill treated; while in many a negro cabin disguised assassins murdered the unoffending inmates, and spread terror beyond conception in all the colored population of Alabama. Such were the means by which Alabama was converted to Democracy, and by which Mr. [Horace] Greeley and his associates must hope to gain the Southern vote.

The Ku-Klux sprang up almost at the same moment through all the Southern States. It terrified and subdued Louisiana; it swept over Texas; mounted and disguised ruffians rode through Mississippi in 1871, breaking up the colored schools, and driving away preachers and teachers; they covered Western Tennessee; they murdered, whipped, and tormented in North Carolina. In Georgia, we are told by Mr. Stearnes, whole counties of colored voters are disfranchised by the terrors of their fearful orgies. Not even the Congressional Committee [investigating the Klan] has been able to pierce the depths of this widespread conspiracy.

Chapter 35

Black Workers and Republicans in the South

David Montgomery

Labor historian David Montgomery is professor of history at Yale University and past president of the Organization of American Historians (1999–2000). His books include Beyond Equality: Labor and Radical Republicans, 1862–1872 *(1967),* Workers Control in America: Studies in the History of Work, Technology, and Labor Struggles *(1979), and* The Fall of the House of Labor: The Workplace, the State, and American Labor Activism, 1865–1925 *(1987).*

The following selection is reprinted from Citizen Worker: The Experience of Workers in the United States with Democracy and the Free Market during the Nineteenth Century *(New York: Cambridge University Press, 1993), 117–29, footnotes deleted. Reprinted with the permission of Cambridge University Press.*

The relationship of wage labor to democratic government, which had taken three-quarters of a century to crystallize in the North, was resolved with ferocious haste in the southern states after the Civil War. The collapse of slavery was followed in late 1865 by the enactment of state master-and-servant laws, augmented by new vagrancy statutes, in special codes regulating black labor. . . . [These] Black Codes were quickly overturned. The process by which they were abolished—and rights of citizenship secured—allied African Americans in the South to the Republican Party. In fact, no other group of working people in the history of the United States has ever linked its aspirations so tightly or with such unanimity to a political party. Nevertheless, the Republicans never became *their* party, in the sense of a party whose program and leadership were determined by black constituents.

Without a doubt the most widespread desire of former slaves was to settle on land of their own. Drafters of a petition to President [Andrew] Johnson from Edisto Island, South Carolina, expressed their indignation at the thought of being driven once again into their masters' fields: "Man that have stud upon the feal of battle & have shot there master & sons now Going to ask ether one for bread or for shelter or Comfortable for his wife & children sunch a thing the u st should not aught to Expect a man."

It was equally clear, however, that the land was not redistributed to its tillers. The petition just quoted came from the region covered by General William Tecumseh Sherman's famous Field Order No. 15 [see chapter 28—*Eds.*], the only large-scale effort to settle freed people on small plots carved from plantations that had been abandoned by their owners during the war. The occasion for the petition was President Andrew Johnson's restoration of those lands to pardoned former owners. General Oliver O. Howard of the Freedmen's Bureau was dispatched to inform the sea islanders in the presence of their former masters that only those few who could produce clear titles to the land they worked would be allowed to retain their plots. At a meeting in Edisto Island's Old Stone Church a committee of black men caucused and then responded that they wished to buy or lease the lands, but would not submit to employment by their former owners. The assembly, wrote a northern reporter, "endorses by sullen silence, or bursting sobs and groans."

Although many black military veterans used mustering-out pay to purchase land, even soldiers realistically feared that their discharges and their pay would arrive too late. "Run Right out of Slavery into Soldiery & we hadent nothing atoll & our wives & mothers most all of them is aperishing all about where we leave them," wrote such a soldier to his commander early in 1866. "Property & all the lands that would be sold cheap will be gone & we will have a Hard struggle to get along in the US."

Even though the depression of the 1870s threw vast tracts of southern land into state hands through tax defaults, most of that acreage made its way back to former owners, and only South Carolina and Mississippi systematically used such lands to homestead black families. By 1890, when the U.S. census first clearly distinguished patterns of land ownership and tenancy, only 14 percent of South Carolina's black farmers and 16 percent of those in Mississippi owned the land they worked. Virtually all their farms were outside the plantation regions of the states.

In practice, therefore, the labor question was fought out not over ownership of the land, but over the terms of contract. Plantations remained intact, even though many were bought by new owners or were leased out to some white person with operating capital, who then hired black workers. The federal Bureau of Refugees, Freedmen and Abandoned Lands often required former slaves to contract for a full crop year, especially in Louisiana, where many sugar planters had gone over to the Union side before the war's end. The bureau also created precedents beneficial to field hands, however, because it adjudicated black workers' grievances, and it insisted that workers' claims to wages took precedence over landlords' claims for rent or merchants' claims for credit advances. The bureau's assistant commissioner for Arkansas went so far as to have the 1869 crop seized by the army in order to insure that workers received their full contracted share from the sale. Although historians are far from agreed among themselves as to the role of the bureau—Professor Leon Litwack called it the "planter's guard"—the fact remains that land-owners themselves were overwhelmingly hostile to its "interference."

Worse even than the bureau, from the planters' perspective, was the presence of black soldiers. One white Mississippian explained why:

> The Negro Soldiery here are constantly telling our negroes, that for the next year, The Government will give them lands, provisions, Stock & all things necessary to carry on business for themselves,—& are constantly advising them not to make contracts with white persons, for the next year.—Strange to say the negroes believe such stories in spite of facts to the contrary told them by their ~~masters~~ [sic] employers.

The Black Codes, which were passed by every former Confederate state between late 1865 and the early months of 1866, resolved these ambiguities by openly reinstituting the law of master and servant for African Americans. All black men and women were obliged to contract by the middle of January to work for wages for the remainder of the year. Those who wished to pursue artisanal or commercial occupations were required to seek annual licenses from district courts. Civil officers were obliged to "arrest and carry back to his or her legal employer any freedman, free negro, or mulatto who shall have quit the service of his or her employer before the expiration of his or her term of service without good cause." Juries of freeholders were to assign deserters to their former employers or to new ones.

No provisions of the codes caused more distress in black households than those authorizing courts to bind out orphans or those under eighteen "whose parents have not the means or who refuse to provide for and support" them, with preference in assignment to be given "the former owner of said minors." From Maryland to Mississippi black women were engaged in efforts to reclaim their own children.

The practical significance of the Black Codes was revealed in a letter from twelve black soldiers in Mississippi to their commanding officer. It said:

> the Law in regard to the freedman is that they all have to have a written contract[.] judge jones mayor of this place is enforcing of the law[.] He says they have no right to rent a house nor land nor reside in town with[out] a white man to stand fer thim[.] He makes all men pay Two Dollars of Licience and he will not give Licence without a written contract[.] both women and men have to submit or go to Jail[.]
>
> His debuty is taking people all the time[.] men that is traverling is stoped and put in jail or Forced to contract[.] if this is the Law of the United States we will submit but if it is not we are willing to take our musket and surve three years Longer.

. . . [A]lmost a year before that letter was written, General Daniel Sickles had nullified South Carolina's code and proclaimed his own elaborate rules of contract and vagrancy based on the principle that "all laws shall be applicable alike to all inhabitants." The following April, Congress enshrined that doctrine in the Civil Rights Act, which made it a crime for any person to deprive another individual of equal rights to make and enforce contracts. When that act in turn was folded into the Fourteenth Amendment to the Constitution later in the year, the right of all men to contract for employment at will obtained the sanction of national law. Political economist Arthur Latham Perry summed up the ideals of the new order: "Society is one vast hive of buyers and sellers, every man bringing something to the market and carrying something off. . . . You do something for me, and I will do something for you, is the fundamental law of society."

Just what exertions were to be exchanged for what reward on southern plantations, however, could only be decided by sharp and sometimes bloody confrontations that in turn shaped the relationship of field hands to the Republican Party. Planters' efforts to graft the payment of money wages onto systems of gang labor inherited from slavery ran afoul of two obstacles. They had little cash to advance before sale of the year's crop, and once the driver's whip was withdrawn, gang labor maximized workers' solidarities. Planters did learn quickly to dismiss old and infirm former slaves. Even the South Carolina Black Code departed from the customs of slavery on this score, by requiring each black family to maintain its own "old and helpless members." Planters also learned to lay off laborers when work was slack. An army surgeon traveling in coastal South Carolina in June 1866 met "several troops" of freed people "who had just been discharged from plantations and were looking for work they knew not where." After the season's final thinning and weeding, the crop had been "laid by," and there was little work to do until harvest time, when hands could be hired to pick cotton by the pound. Resident workers fought this practice by greeting day laborers with great hostility so as to drive them off and compel the planters to hire and keep year round hands.

Workers' quest for stable employment did not, however, make them amenable to the contractual terms the planters wanted. Some form of wage masquerading as a share of the crop became commonplace as early as the 1866 season, because share payment did not oblige the employer to turn any money over to the worker until the crop was in, and the practice also gave the worker an interest in the size of the harvest. Always at issue, however, was the question of whose labor the planter had hired with that share, that of one person or that of an entire family. No issue generated more frequent personal quarrels than the refusal of married women to go to the fields. Moreover, intensive cultivation of the cash crop was best encouraged by placing many croppers on small lots; this maximized the return to the planter at the expense of the worker's standard of living. Battles over the number of families working a plantation could not be separated from disputes over the size of garden plots and the grazing area for livestock to which workers were entitled, or indeed from controversies over whether things other than cotton raised on the plantation belonged to the planter or to the worker. For that matter, to whom did the cotton itself belong before it was ginned and sold? Had the sharecropper any "interest" in the crop other than his year's pay? A major undertaking of the Ku Klux Klan was to intimidate workers from selling "what was not theirs."

In short, even on the resuscitated plantation the laborer sought to rent land by paying its owner a portion of the crop, while the employer sought to hire labor time in exchange for that same share. A Georgia freedwoman recounted a similar battle over household obligations when she returned to the plantation where she had formerly been a slave:

> my old Missus asked me if I came back to behave myself & do her work & I told her no that I came back to do my own work. I went to my own house & in the morning my old master came to me & asked me if I wouldn't go and milk the cows: I told him that my Missus had driven me off—well said he you go and do it—then my Mistress came out again & asked me if I came back to work for her like a "*nigger*"—I told her no that I was free & she said be off then & called me a stinking bitch. I afterwards wove 40 yds. of dress goods for her that she promised to pay me for; but she never paid me a cent for it . . . except give me a meal of victuals.

Masters' claims to all the workers' time were thus countered by freed people's readiness to do specified tasks in exchange for money payment or a share of the crop, plus a home and earth to be used at their own discretion. This encounter was especially damaging to rice planters, whose slaves had spent much of their time in ditching and water control work, which was to the rice worker what dead work was to the coal miner—arduous and uncompensated. Such controversies put an end to rice cultivation in some coastal areas and encouraged workers there to form land-buying associations to acquire portions of former rice estates. Elsewhere, they induced sugar planters to institute straightforward day labor and persuaded cotton growers to divide estates into family sharecropping units.

Workers quickly learned to pledge each other not to work for less than the terms to which they had agreed among themselves. Backed by sanctions of ostracism and even violence against nonconformists, former slaves increased the share of the crop offered workers from one-fourth, or the one-third specified by the Freedmen's Bureau, to one-half. Their most effective instrument was the paramilitary club, which brought men and women from various plantations together, often on Saturday market days. In response to planters' claims that six days' labor were owed, and to Black Code prohibitions against the bearing of arms by African Americans, the freed people appealed to U.S. military authorities that theirs were patriotic gatherings, defending the United States and often drilled by black army veterans. After the Reconstruction Acts of 1867 these armed contingents openly affiliated with the Union Leagues and became the most effective agencies for mobilizing Republican votes in the countryside.

To put it another way: The enfranchisement of black voters by the 1867 Reconstruction Acts grafted the new state Republican parties directly onto existing networks of solidarity, which rural laborers had fashioned in daily struggles around the terms under which they would work for wages. In urban areas (especially Richmond and New Orleans) mutual aid societies and black trade unions played similar roles. Nevertheless, the black field workers neither created nor led state Republican parties. Like the Reconstruction Acts, the Republican Party had been created in the North, and had been invented for purposes different from those of the field hands. Consequently, the Republican Party simultaneously politicized and restrained the action on the plantation.

In preparation for elections of delegates to state constitutional conventions required by the Reconstruction Acts, and in the subsequent balloting for state officials, Republican activists toured the southern countryside. Among them were more than eighty "colored itinerant lecturers," financed by the party's Congressional Committee. They were welcomed by Union League clubs, which were made up not only of black field and household workers, but often of beleaguered local white loyalists as well. Local economic grievances blended with state and national governmental issues in the clubs' discussions. In fact, it can be said that the distinction between economic and political questions, which was then so finely drawn by white trade unionists, made no sense in African-American organizations. Although the support lent by the Republicans to the everyday struggles of rural black workers was substantial, the party never defined its policies in terms of those struggles. Moreover, former slaves representing constituencies of rural men and women never occupied major executive offices, and they appeared in significant numbers in the state legislatures only in the final years of Republican rule in states where that regime lasted past 1872: Mississippi, South Carolina, Louisiana, Alabama, and Florida.

The new states bore little resemblance to the clientelistic politics of the slave owners, which had tightly circumscribed the role of government. South Carolina's Republicans created tax-supported universal education, built asylums to shelter the aged and poor, subsidized railroad construction, protected tenants and homesteaders against eviction, outlawed payment in scrip that could be redeemed only at plantation stores, allowed election of judges, and ended imprisonment for debt. They incorporated Union League contingents into the state militia, ended the leasing of convict laborers to private employers, and inhibited mob attacks against African-American property owners. Through their power in important legislative committees, leading black Republicans ultimately won control of South Carolina's land commission and used that body to shift estates forfeited to the government during the depression of the 1870s to black smallholders.

Perhaps most important of all, when disputes over work and crops led planters to charge their workers with contract violation, idleness, or theft, sheriffs and justices of the peace often lent a sympathetic ear to the former slaves. The complaint of a planter that "justice is generally administered solely in the interest of the laborer," was echoed by the editorial lament of the *Southern Argus* of Selma, Alabama: "There is a vagrant law on our statute books . . . but it is a dead letter because those who are charged with its enforcement are indebted to the vagrant vote for their offices."

To be sure, the first priority of southern Republicans, just like that of their northern mentors, was capitalist economic development. Nevertheless, the southern parties lacked the organic links to local economic elites that secured party hegemony and guided policy in the North. Quite the contrary, the vanquished elites of the South considered the new regimes illegitimate—unworthy of obedience and certainly unworthy of their taxes. In desperate need of revenues and of experienced and locally prestigious personnel, southern Republicans initially featured white candidates and extended patronage to any established political personality who would accept it. The speedy and violent removal of Republicans from power in Virginia, North Carolina, Tennessee, and Georgia showed the futility of this policy and encouraged African Americans to assert themselves more openly in party circles. Black workers from Richmond, Philadelphia, and Baltimore initiated their own National Labor Congress in 1869. It chastised the Republicans for their timidity on land redistribution, stimulated both urban and rural trade unionism, and demanded the establishment of state labor bureaus to provide wage-earners the active protection of government. A leading figure in the movement was Warwick Reed, a one-time slave, tobacco worker, and captain of a black militia unit, who was elected vice-president for Virginia by the nation's overwhelmingly white Industrial Congress in 1874.

Although prominent black Republicans seized the occasion to demand a greater role in their party's affairs, they also expressed anxiety over the strikes and political demands of their constituents. The *New Orleans Tribune,* voice of the historic free black elite, counseled striking black dockers in 1867 "not to jeopardize the future by rushing into some unreasonable excitement." When a South Carolina black labor convention with three hundred delegates petitioned the state legislature for land distribution, a legal nine-hour day, and labor commissioners in each county to oversee the claims of rural workers, the legislature rejected the proposals after heated debate. A white Republican from the Piedmont proclaimed, "Nobody has ever been able to legislate in regard to labor." He concluded, "The law of supply and demand must regulate the matter." William Whipper, a northern-born black lawyer and outspoken champion of civil rights who owned a rice plantation himself, agreed. He rejected the implication "that the people as a class are not able to take care of themselves." As if in confirmation of his view, Whipper was taken to court by his own workers for failing to pay them.

An acid test of the party's commitments arose when workers on rice plantations along the Combahee River struck against illegal scrip payment in the midst of the decisive election campaign of 1876. Although some prominent Republicans called for forceful suppression of picketing, the local militia was largely made up of strikers, and the aggressive challenge to activities in support of the strike came from an armed band of white vigilantes. The famous black congressman Robert Smalls personally intervened to separate the antagonists, and he persuaded the planters to agree to the strikers' demands that they obey the law requiring money wages. Ten arrested strikers were taken before a black trial judge in nearby Beaufort; he set them all free, to the applause of the crowd in the streets.

By the end of that year, however, the hopes of black men and women throughout the rural South had been crushed. It was not the laissez-faire inclinations of the Republicans that administered the devastating blow, but the triumph of the Democratic "Redeemers." The intellectual, political, and religious leaders of the white South had quite properly envisaged themselves before, during, and after the Civil War as the true guardians of classical republicanism in North America. The "citizen with us," planter-historian William Henry Trescott of South Carolina had written, "belongs . . . to a privileged class." He was a man of action who might be unequal in wealth or influence to other citizens but who shared with them recognized mastery over slaves, women, and children, and whose claim to participation in the polity was predicated on that mastery. As Stephanie McCurry has argued, racial, gender, and class hierarchies were inexorably intertwined in the belief held by defenders of the slave republic that "the restriction of political rights to a privileged few" was the region's "distinctive and superior characteristic." Although the conditions of all subordinate groups could stand improvement, the eminent political writer Louisa Susana McCord had written in 1852, "Here, as in all other improvements, the good must be brought about by working with, not against—by seconding, not opposing—Nature's laws." To defy the differences in entitlements and obligations that God and nature had bestowed on each social rank would turn society into a "wrangling dog kennel," she added. "Wo to the world which seeks its rulers where it should find drudges! Wo to the drudge who would exalt himself into the ruler!"

Although southern conservatives after the war had no choice but to concede that slavery was dead, the paramilitary organizations that they mobilized against the Republican state regimes openly fought to rescue the beleaguered "natural" hierarchies of race, gender, class, and property. Senator Thomas Bayard of Delaware defended the Ku Klux Klan as "a protective arm of natural society necessary to offset the influence of blacks whose own pretensions of power were artificially and unnaturally propped up by a standing army." Local black political leaders were the foremost target of killings and beatings, but not the only ones. The Klan assaulted both African Americans and white women who exhibited offensive independence, and it attacked with special venom and regularity when the two types of offenders were in some way linked, for example when black men bought or rented land from white widows. It also acted both as a labor organization for whites (fixing terms of employment or rental and driving off black competitors), and as an agency to discipline black workers. As one Georgia witness testified to Congress about the "class of people who have the old rebellious spirit in them still":

> If the negro is in their employ, they will protect him, unless they have any difficulty with him, and then they will report him to the Ku-Klux. . . . Just about the time they got done laying by their crops, the Ku-Klux would be brought in upon them, and they would be run off, so that they could take their crops.

Paramilitary and electoral activity were intertwined as inseparably in the conservatives' effort to restore historic "rulers" and "drudges" to their proper stations as they were in the uses made by former slaves of the Union Leagues, militia, and Republican Party. "Old men in the Tax Unions and young men in the Rifle Clubs," was the battle cry of South Carolina's Redeemers in 1876. The victors shattered Republican political organizations, wreaking especially bloody vengeance on party activists and on Union Leagues. They effectively suppressed the counter-pressures of workers' solidarities in all districts but those where the African-American population was most dense. They placed local sheriffs and judges directly under the authority of the white-supremacist state governments. And they festooned the statute books with legislation regulating in detail the issues of everyday confrontation between planters and workers: vagrancy, enticement, and criminal surety laws; laws restricting hunting rights and enclosing unimproved lands; laws declaring thefts of livestock or sales of standing crops to be felonies; laws giving the landlord or merchant-creditor first lien on the crop; and laws for leasing out to labor the thousands of African Americans sentenced under the new statutes. "The lords of the soil," concluded defeated Republican Albion Tourgee, "are the lords of the labor still."

Disfranchisement followed. "It is certain," the *Memphis Daily Avalanche* predicted in 1889, "that many years will elapse before the bulk of the Negroes will reawaken to an interest in elections, if relegated to their proper sphere, the corn and cotton fields."

Southern black workers were driven from the political arena while legislation clamped tight judicially enforced controls on their terms of contract. The states had imposed labor discipline on a free market system. State courts and many local sheriffs outdid the legislatures. Although statute law in every state limited the enforcement of crop liens to advances made to the worker against the current year's crop, courts in Alabama and Mississippi allowed the accumulation of lien indebtedness from year to year, while those of Georgia and North Carolina allowed creditors to seize personal tools and possessions if the crop proved insufficient to cover the debt. Arkansas's judges even approved confiscation of a sharecropper's sewing machine. In effect, distress judgments, which had disappeared from the North early in the century, had returned to the South. So did specific enforcement of contracts. Mississippi's legislature enacted laws in 1900 and 1906 making a tenant who left his landlord during a crop year subject to imprisonment for fraud. A coal miner from the Birmingham region described less formal sanctions faced by newly recruited miners who attempted to quit their jobs:

> lo! and behold! [The mine superintendent] touches the button, and smooth and smiling 'Squire Wingo appears as the heavy villain in this almost every-day transaction, and they (the transports) are placed under arrest, remanded to the mines, and are worked, guarded the same as convicts, until the Sloss Iron & Steel Company . . . have been sufficiently compensated for the trouble and expense of increasing the population of Alabama.

Although the southern Republican Party continued to battle the worse excesses of the new regime, such as the unrestrained exploitation of convict labor and the shrinking budgets of public schools, and to enjoy the active support of those black men who could still vote, it had been reduced to little more than an agency for distribution of federal offices, except perhaps in North Carolina, Virginia, and the Appalachian Mountain region. Black plantation laborers asked of their party above all else that it persuade Congress to protect those in the South who wished to exercise their rights of citizenship, while millenarian dreams inspired Exodusters along the lower Mississippi to flock to the riverbanks in hopes of finding a boat that would let them escape to Kansas.

The Democrats won and retained control of the South by proclaiming themselves the one legitimate "white man's party." Their ability to overawe rebellious political movements after the 1870s with the warning that any break in the ranks of white voters threatened to restore "Negro rule" provided a heavy ballast for property and for white supremacy that would guide the course of the national Democratic Party until the 1940s. Editor Patrick Ford of the *Irish World,* who worshipped at the shrine of Thomas Jefferson, protested in 1876 that if one asked a "Regular Democrat," "*What is a Democrat?* The instant answer from him would be: *A man who hates niggers!* . . . Never before was common sense so impudently outraged. Never before were words so recklessly twisted from their true meaning. Never!"

Chapter 36

The Reconstruction Myth

Peyton McCrary

Peyton McCrary is a historian with the Civil Rights Division of the Department of Justice in Washington, D.C. He taught at the university level for twenty years and was a visiting professor at Swarthmore College in 1998–1999. McCrary is the author of Abraham Lincoln and Reconstruction: The Louisiana Experiment *(1978). For the past eighteen years he has been publishing work on the problem of minority vote dilution in the South.*

The following selection is reprinted from Encyclopedia of Southern Culture, *edited by William Ferris and Charles Reagan Wilson. Copyright © 1989 by the University of North Carolina Press. Used by permission of the publisher.*

When historians christened the civil rights struggle of the 1960s "the Second Reconstruction," it came as no surprise to anyone. Ever since Rutherford B. Hayes pulled the last federal troops from the southern states in 1877, the specter of renewed national intervention on behalf of racial equality had been the fundamental myth of southern politician culture. The events of the Reconstruction period (usually seen as 1865–77), dramatic enough in their own right, took on demonic proportions in the imaginations of southern white conservatives who saw control by the "white supremacy Democrats" as the only road to salvation for this society. It took these "Redeemers" another quarter century to codify and institutionalize segregation and disfranchisement following the defeat of the Populist party—whose political revolt, according to Democratic campaign rhetoric, threatened to return the South to "the evils of Reconstruction." For yet another seven decades every proposal to alter the southern caste system or one-party rule promoted conservative Democrats to parade the great Reconstruction myth before their constituents or on the floor of Congress.

The Republican effort to reconstruct southern society and politics in the 1860s was, to be sure, a radical innovation in the American political tradition. The abolition of slavery during the Civil War was a revolutionary alteration of the southern economic system. In order to preserve a meaningful freedom for the former slaves, the Republican party favored a postwar policy of civil equality for blacks coupled with the establishment of a Freedmen's Bureau that would supervise the establishment of a free labor system in the South. In the political realm, Republicans found it necessary to enfranchise the freedmen after the war in order to prevent the former Confederates from dominating the new civil governments through the Democratic party. The votes of the freedmen, together with the support of a minority of southern whites, gave the Republicans an electoral majority in each state for at least a few years. This brief phase of Republican control in the South, together with the message of egalitarian federal laws and constitutional amendments, was what conservative whites meant by the term *Reconstruction.*

Reconstruction's mythic cast of characters includes the "carpetbaggers," whom southern whites portrayed as greedy interlopers exploiting the South; the "scalawags," who were traitorous native southern whites collaborating with the Yankees; the freedmen, who were sometimes seen as violent and depraved in the myth but mostly seemed ignorant and lost; and the former Confederates, who were the heroes of the story, all honorable, decent people with the South's best interests in mind.

Southern Democrats were willing to use any means necessary to end Republican control of their states, including political violence. Initially through secret organizations such as the Ku Klux Klan and later more openly, as with Wade Hampton's "Red Shirts" in South Carolina, the Democrats resorted to beatings, assassinations, and armed bands of horsemen at the polls to "redeem" the South from "Negro rule." They justified these extreme methods on the grounds the Reconstruction threatened the fundamental stability of their society: economic control by "the better sort," the social elevation of all whites, and the protection of white women from sexual aggression by blacks were at stake.

During the next two decades violence was occasionally used to discourage black political efforts, but the use of large-scale electoral corruption—against both black and white opponents—was a much more common Democratic tactic. Electoral corruption and violence escalated during the 1890s, when the People's party bolted the Democratic party. White conservatives justified both violence and corruption as necessary to prevent a return to black officeholding and Republican rule. By the turn of the century a growing number of northerners (even within the Republican party) had come to agree with the southern view. Ignoring the Fourteenth and Fifteenth Amendments—the "Reconstruction amendments"—the Supreme Court refused to overturn disfranchisement and accepted segregation as constitutional under the separate-but-equal formula.

During the Progressive era the southern view of Reconstruction became enshrined in the popular culture of the nation. Thomas Dixon's *The Clansman* (1905) was a fictional embodiment of the Reconstruction myth, and William A. Dunning's *Reconstruction, Political and Economic, 1865–1877* (1907) was the best example of a series of historical monographs portraying white suffering in the era. In 1915 Woodrow Wilson held an enthusiastic showing of D. W. Griffith's new film, *Birth of a Nation,* at the White House. The president applauded its cinematic tribute to the great Reconstruction myth, complete with the stereotypical rescue of a white damsel from the hands of a black rapist by the heroic Ku Klux Klan. Two decades later *Gone with the Wind* provided a celluloid update of the myth that survives into the age of the VCR.

Whenever the Congress considered a federal antilynching bill in the years between the two world wars, southern Democrats warned of a return to Reconstruction. The same refrain greeted certain New Deal programs, Franklin D. Roosevelt's Fair Employment Practices Commission, and Harry Truman's desegregation of the armed forces. As the Supreme Court began to strike down the white primary, segregated institutions of higher education, and restrictive covenants in the late 1940s, southern conservatives grew concerned that the justices might actually decide to interpret the Reconstruction amendments literally. In *Brown v. Board of Education,* which decided the school desegregation cases in 1954, the Court looked seriously at the intent of the framers of the Fourteenth Amendment—ignoring the myth, for once, in favor of serious historical analysis—but concluded that the issue was irrelevant to its unanimous opinion outlawing segregation. In their denunciation of the *Brown* decision, the [White] Citizens' Councils of the Deep South resuscitated the white-supremacy views of the 19th century and warned of the perils of a new Reconstruction.

The myth was not just the shibboleth of the far right. When John F. Kennedy published his *Profiles in Courage* in 1956, he pictured the first Reconstruction as a tragic mistake. Even after he gained the presidency, Kennedy held to the southern view and initially resisted federal intervention on the side of civil rights because he did not want to ignore what he regarded as the lessons of history concerning federal intervention in the South. Displaying an intellectual curiosity rare among chief executives, however, Kennedy actually invited historian David Donald to the White House to lead an after-dinner discussion of what modern historians were saying about the Reconstruction era. Whether this discussion had any impact on the president's thinking is undocumented, but he proceeded to put the federal government behind the enforcement of civil rights in the South to a degree unprecedented since the 1870s.

For white southerners who had grown up believing in the Reconstruction myth, the prospect was terrifying and infuriating. To refer to federal intervention as a Second Reconstruction was, in their eyes, to condemn such an idea out of hand. They characterized northern whites who came south as Freedom Riders, voter registration workers, or demonstrators on picket lines as latter-day abolitionists or carpetbaggers. Southern whites who criticized segregation, disfranchisement, or the jailing of civil rights workers were scalawags. A rejuvenated Ku Klux Klan engaged in savage beatings, bombings, and assassinations, only to be acquitted by all-white juries.

The Second Reconstruction was, however, far more successful than the first. This time federal intervention included systematic enforcement of civil rights legislation by the U.S. Justice Department, the Health, Education, and Welfare Department, and the courts. This time southern blacks used civil disobedience, manipulated opinion, obtained effective legal representation through public-interest law firms, and created their own heroes in mythic proportions.

By 1970, when a series of political leaders below the Mason-Dixon line were proclaiming a "New South" that turned its back on racial prejudice, a great change had taken place in the region's political culture. Racial prejudice was still alive and well, of course, but for the most part public discussion of the race question was couched in euphemisms and code words of the sort familiar outside of Dixie. No longer could white politicians expect to be taken seriously if they yelled about the evils of Reconstruction. The Second Reconstruction had arrived—and white southerners had learned to live with it. Some, including historians of that first experiment in racial equality, even came to relish being called scalawags.

Chapter 37

The Impeachment of President Andrew Johnson

Joshua Zeitz

After the assassination of President Abraham Lincoln, Vice President Andrew Johnson assumed the presidency. In 1868 he was impeached. The 1999 impeachment trial of President Bill Clinton encouraged renewed interest in Johnson's trial.

The following selection is reprinted by permission from "Impeach Johnson!" New Republic, *18 January 1999, 13–15.*

The story of Andrew Johnson's 1868 impeachment has become a veritable political fable: Persecuted by a Congress run by Radical Republicans who simply didn't like his attitude toward Reconstruction, Johnson was brought to trial for violating a law that was patently unconstitutional. Only because a few brave Republican senators broke ranks and voted for acquittal did the constitutional system, and the Republic, survive.

It is a good yarn, and one we've been hearing a lot about these days, now that the second-ever presidential impeachment trial is at hand. The *New York Times* recounted the affair this way: "After the Civil War, the Radical Republicans in control of Congress were able to override Johnson's vetoes and undermine the policy of leniency toward the defeated South begun under Abraham Lincoln, Johnson's slain predecessor." It then went on to conclude that the episode does "not bode well for high-minded nonpartisanship" in the case of Bill Clinton. Writing in the *New Yorker,* Jeffrey Toobin has called the events of 1868 a constitutional "fiasco" that marked "the low point in impeachment history."

But this conception of history lacks one key element: accuracy. Far from a martyr, Andrew Johnson remains the one president in American history who most clearly deserved impeachment and, quite probably, conviction. Johnson openly defied the will of Congress and trampled on the rights of American citizens. Although his trial turned on weak and highly technical charges, it was triggered by his pattern of defiant and, arguably, treasonous conduct—behavior that was clearly what the Founders had in mind when they established impeachment as a remedy for presidential wrongdoing. All of which is relevant today in the following way: Understood properly, Andrew Johnson's trespasses make the modern-day offenses of President Clinton seem trivial by comparison.

Our contemporary understanding of Johnson's impeachment traces back to the early twentieth century, when Columbia University's William Dunning lent academic respectability to a popular version of Reconstruction history pioneered by segregationist Southern Democrats and slavery apologists. Dunning wrote from the point of view of the defeated South and painted the Radical Republicans as villains. His interpretation served the ideological purposes of a majority-white country eager to put the divisions of the nineteenth century behind it, and it thus came to saturate public memory until the very dawn of the civil rights era. Indeed, its indirect influence is visible even in John F. Kennedy's 1955 book *Profiles in Courage,* which taught a generation of Americans to admire Edmund G. Ross, the Kansas Republican senator who cast the vote that acquitted Johnson.

But the real story of Johnson's impeachment should impart much different lessons. It all began in the summer of 1865. With Congress out of session until December, the president summarily invited several former Confederate states to rejoin the Union. He did so despite their recent election of onetime secessionists and Confederate officials to state and federal offices. He also overlooked their passage of "black codes" restricting the movement, property rights, and individual liberties of former slaves. It was an extraordinary seizure of power: Only weeks following the conclusion of a four-year civil war and the first assassination of an American president, Johnson acted unilaterally to readmit rebel states to the Union and to draw back into public office men who had committed high treason against the United States—men who were still unreconciled to the abolition of slavery.

Congress refused to acknowledge this brief period of "Presidential Reconstruction." The Republican majority instead passed a series of laws and a constitutional amendment guaranteeing former slaves fundamental personal and economic liberties, all over Johnson's veto or opposition. But the president still would not relent. Instead, he counteracted a vital provision of the Freedmen's Bureau Act by returning to former slaveholders abandoned lands that the Union Army had seized and subsequently doled out to former slaves; he also violated the Test Oath Act by appointing to office persons who could not swear a mandatory oath that they had not served the Confederacy.

In 1867, Congress passed (again over Johnson's veto) an act dividing the South into military districts and placing the former Confederate states under martial law pending their adoption of suitable constitutions guaranteeing civil liberties to former slaves. The president proceeded to spend the better part of 1867 defying the Military Reconstruction Act. Although the law empowered him to remove recalcitrant Southern officeholders, Johnson refused, claiming that he could not constitutionally warrant the use of the military for such purposes. Johnson also forbade the Army to try violations of federal law in its courts or to prohibit activities that were not in specific violation of federal or local statutes. In effect, he canceled out the very notion of martial law and refused to execute statutes enacted over his veto.

Johnson aggravated these acts with rhetorical offenses that threatened not just decorum but constitutional stability. On one occasion, he indicated his willingness to "oppose" those laws that he deemed "unconstitutional," with full knowledge that such "executive resistance . . . would likely produce violent collision between respective adherents to the two branches of government." Speaking to a crowd in Cleveland during his disastrous "swing around the circle" campaign tour of late 1866, Johnson was heckled by cries of "hang Jeff Davis!" To this he responded: "Why not hang Thad Stevens [leader of the House Republicans] and Wendell Phillips [a noted Boston abolitionist]? I can tell you, my countrymen, I have been fighting traitors in the South, and . . . I am prepared to fight traitors at the North, God being willing with your help."

Radical Republicans like Thaddeus Stevens saw all of this for what it was: a systematic effort to thwart the properly expressed will of Congress and to lend aid and comfort to unrepentant enemies of the Union. Yet, throughout 1867, the House refused his repeated calls to impeach Johnson; most members rejected his argument that presidential actions need not be manifestly illegal to be impeachable. Then, the president supplied radicals with just the legal pretense they needed to sway their more cautious colleagues. The event that triggered Johnson's indictment by the lower chamber was his violation in 1868 of the Tenure of Office Act, a law that required the president to seek Senate approval before removing Cabinet officials. When Johnson fired War Secretary Edwin Stanton despite congressional objections, the House drew up and passed eleven impeachment articles, nine of which focused on his violation of this statute. Only one article, the tenth, came close to addressing Stevens's concerns, and it did so only indirectly, focusing on Johnson's "certain intemperate, inflammatory and scandalous harangues" and "loud threats and bitter menaces as well against Congress."

Unfortunately, since none of the articles charged Johnson with his more serious constitutional offenses, what followed was a trial full of legal hairsplitting. The president's attorneys argued technicalities—for instance, that the Tenure of Office Act didn't really apply to Stanton since he was a Lincoln administration holdover, and the act referred only to appointees of the current chief executive. (They also argued, rightly, that the law was itself unconstitutional, although they had difficulty explaining why Johnson had initially complied with its provisions, asserting its unconstitutionality only after he failed to obtain the Senate's consent in Stanton's dismissal.) Forced to make its judgment exclusively on these grounds, the Senate failed to convict, by the narrowest of margins.

The question, of course, is whether Johnson deserved to be impeached for his other, more serious acts. And here the case seems rather compelling. While it's true the Republican Congress may not have been acting within its own constitutional authority all of the time, the fact remains that Johnson was colluding with enemies of the Union to block the federal government's right as victor to dictate the terms of peace; he was inciting violence against Congress; he was usurping the Supreme Court's powers of judicial review; and he was failing to take care that the laws be faithfully executed. Perhaps most important, he was trampling upon the individual rights of newly freed slaves.

Intellectually honest people can disagree whether the verdict ultimately served the nation's long-term interests. But two things seem clear. First, by comparison to Johnson's actions, Bill Clinton's offenses are fairly negligible—hardly the kind of constitutionally threatening acts for which impeachment ought to be reserved. Second, the current impeachment debacle demonstrates just how far the party of Lincoln has declined since the days it contemplated removing a president over the weighty issues of slavery, civil rights, and insurrection, rather than over the legal definition of sexual relations.

3

Segregation

Separate Worlds: The 1907 graduating class
of Spelman College in Atlanta. (Photo courtesy of Spelman College Archives.)

Chapter 38

Introduction: Separate and Unequal

Jonathan Birnbaum and Clarence Taylor

The central question of Reconstruction had been the meaning of freedom for the former slaves—the role and rights of free black labor. What did the counterrevolution, the overthrow of Reconstruction by the former Confederates, win? More than anything else, control over black labor.

Southern white Democrats presented themselves as "Redeemers"; they were, they said, redeeming self-government for the South. But Redemption was nothing more than a euphemism, a code word for white supremacy. The Democrats regaining governmental and economic mastery "redeemed" control over black labor. The southern economy depended upon black labor. As a white representative of the Athens, Georgia, Chamber of Commerce put it, "The negro is our only and best form for domestic and general labor" (see chapter 47). Slavery was the name of the previous system of social control; the new system would be called Segregation.

The government sanctioned the suppression of black civil rights at every level. Local governments in the South were involved in everything from Jim Crow to the atrocities of the Ku Klux Klan. State governments passed Jim Crow laws in the South (and tolerated discrimination patterns in the North). The federal government failed to enforce the Reconstruction-era amendments to the Constitution, beginning with the withdrawal of federal troops from the South in 1877 and culminating with *Plessy v. Ferguson,* the 1896 Supreme Court decision ratifying the federal government's endorsement of segregation. This was followed by federally sponsored racist propaganda during World War I, the suppression of blacks during the first Red Scare, and the infamous failure for the next fifty years to intervene in the South over the issues of lynching or disenfranchisement.

The system constructed to contain black civil rights did more than control black labor; it also limited white labor, women, and progressive reform in general. One of the South's control mechanisms was lynching. "At the same time as it enforced white supremacy," historian Nancy MacLean writes, "lynching also served to remind white women of their prescribed asexual, subordinate, and dependent roles in Southern society" (chapter 47). The repression of blacks was apiece with the repression in the broader society, not just within the South but nationally. Segregationists in Congress effectively postponed not only national civil rights legislation, but also New Deal labor reform (especially in agriculture) and women's rights.

In 1895, one year before *Plessy v. Ferguson,* Booker T. Washington, the most influential black leader of the period, gave a speech in Atlanta (see chapter 49)—dubbed "The Atlanta Compromise" by his critics—that called on blacks to abandon the struggle for civil rights: "The wisest among my race understand that the agitation of questions of social equality is the extremest folly, and that progress in the enjoyment of all the privileges that will come to us must be the result of severe and constant struggle rather than of artificial forcing."

Washington's surrender inspired opposition, first editorially and then organizationally. Ida B. Wells, W. E. B. Du Bois, William Monroe Trotter, and others attacked Washington for attempting to silence opposing views. By the time one hundred forty thousand black veterans returned from World War I, a new civil rights movement had arisen. In response came new private and local, state, and federal government mechanisms to subvert and contain that movement.

The Repression of Free Blacks

Chapter 39

Plessy v. Ferguson (1896)

Eight months after Booker T. Washington's "Atlanta Compromise" (see chapter 49), the Supreme Court, in Plessy v. Ferguson, *declared separate but equal the law of the land—providing legal justification for the six decades of Jim Crow segregation that followed.*

"[H]ad the majority of the Plessy Court realized . . . that their decision was wrong," wrote Judge A. Leon Higginbotham, "our nation might never have needed a Brown v. Board of Education, Missouri ex rel. Gaines v. Canada, Sweatt v. Painter, *or* McLaurin v. Oklahoma State Regents *in the field of education, because state-imposed segregation would not have been sanctioned by federal law. There also might have been no need for some of the other significant civil-rights cases that were initiated solely because the Supreme Court had held in* Plessy *that states could treat African Americans differently from how they treated the majority white population or any of the other major ethnic, religious, or national origin groups in this country. Even though many other racist forces were operating within American society—including the explicitly racist pronouncements by United States presidents, congressmen, and state governmental officials—the historical oppression of African Americans in the United States would have been far less pervasive had, in the Supreme Court, the 1896 views of Justice John Harlan prevailed."*[1]

The following selections are excerpts from the ruling and the dissent in Plessy v. Ferguson *(1896).*

Justice [Henry Billings] Brown delivered the opinion of the Court:

This case turns upon the constitutionality of an act of the General Assembly of the State of Louisiana, passed in 1890, providing for separate railway carriages for the white and colored races. . . .

The information filed in the criminal District Court charged in substance that [Homer] Plessy, being a passenger between two stations within the State of Louisiana, was assigned by officers of the company to the coach used for the [black] race to which he belonged, but he insisted upon going into a coach used by the [white] race to which he did not belong. Neither in the information nor plea was his particular race or color averred.

The constitutionality of this act is attacked upon the ground that it conflicts both with the Thirteenth Amendment of the Constitution, abolishing slavery, and the Fourteenth Amendment, which prohibits certain restrictive legislation on the part of the States. . . .

A statute which implies merely a legal distinction between the white and colored races—a distinction which is founded in the color of the two races, and which must always exist so long as white men are distinguished from the other race by color—has no tendency to destroy the legal equality of the two races, or reestablish a state of involuntary servitude. Indeed, we do not understand that the Thirteenth Amendment is strenuously relied upon by the plaintiff in error in this connection. . . .

By the Fourteenth Amendment, all persons born or naturalized in the United States, and subject to the jurisdiction thereof, are made citizens of the United States and of the State wherein they reside; and the States are forbidden from making or enforcing any law which shall abridge the privileges or immunities of citizens of the United States, or shall deprive any person of life, liberty, or property without due process of law, or deny to any person within their jurisdiction the equal protection of the laws. . . .

The object of the amendment was undoubtedly to enforce the absolute equality of the two races before the law, but in the nature of things it could not have been intended to abolish distinctions based upon color, or to enforce social, as distinguished from political, equality, or a commingling of the two races upon terms unsatisfactory to either. Laws permitting, and even requiring, their separation in places where they are liable to be brought into contact do not necessarily imply the inferiority of either race to the other, and have been generally, if not universally, recognized as within the competency of the state legislatures in the exercise of their police power. The most common instance of this is connected with the establishment of separate schools for white and colored children, which has been held to be a valid exercise of the legislative power even by courts of states where the political rights of the colored race have been longest and most earnestly enforced. . . .

So far, then, as a conflict with the Fourteenth Amendment is concerned, the case reduces itself to the question whether the statute of Louisiana is a reasonable regulation, and with respect to this there must necessarily be a large discretion on the part of the legislature. In determining the question of reasonableness it is at liberty to act with reference to the established usages, customs, and traditions of the people, and with a view to the promotion of their comfort, and the preservation of the public peace and good order. Gauged by this standard, we cannot say that a law which authorizes or even requires the separation of the two races in public conveyances is unreasonable or more obnoxious to the Fourteenth Amendment than the acts of Congress requiring separate schools for colored children in the District of Columbia, the constitutionality of which does not seem to have been questioned, or the corresponding acts of state legislatures.

We consider the underlying fallacy of the plaintiff's argument to consist in the assumption that the enforced separation of the two races stamps the colored race with a badge of inferiority. If this be so, it is not by reason of anything found in the act, but solely the colored race chooses to put that construction upon it. The argument necessarily assumes that if, as has been more than once the case, and is not unlikely to be so again, the colored race should become the dominant power in the state legislature, and should enact a law in precisely similar terms, it would thereby relegate the white race to an inferior position. We imagine that the white race, at least, would not acquiesce in this assumption. The argument also assumes that social prejudices may be overcome by legislation and that equal rights cannot be secured to the Negro except by an enforced commingling of the two races. We cannot accept this proposition. If the two races are to meet upon terms of social equality, it must be the result of natural affinities, a mutual appreciation of each other's merits, and a voluntary consent of individuals. . . . Legislation is powerless to eradicate racial instincts or to abolish distinctions based upon physical differences, and the attempt to do so can only result in accentuating the difficulties of the present situation. If the civil and political rights of both races be equal, one cannot be inferior to the other civilly or politically. If one race be inferior to the other socially, the Constitution of the United States cannot put them upon the same plane.

The judgment of the court below is therefore, Affirmed.

Judge John Marshall Harlan's dissent:

. . . However apparent the injustice of such legislation may be, we have only to consider whether it is consistent with the Constitution of the United States. . . .

The Thirteenth Amendment does not permit the withholding or the deprivation of any right necessarily inhering in freedom. It not only struck down the institution of slavery as previously existing in the United States, but it prevents the imposition of any burdens or disabilities that constitute badges of slavery or servitude. It decreed universal civil freedom in this country. This court has so adjudged. But that amendment having been found inadequate to the protection of the rights of those who had been in slavery, it was followed by the Fourteenth Amendment, which added greatly to the dignity and glory of American citizenship, and to the security of personal liberty, by declaring that "all persons born or naturalized in the United States and subject to the jurisdiction thereof, are citizens of the United States and of the State wherein they reside," and that "no State shall make or enforce any law which shall abridge the privileges or immunities of citizens of the United States; nor shall any State deprive any person of life, liberty or property without due process of law, nor deny to any person within its jurisdiction the equal protection of the laws." These two amendments, if enforced according to their true intent and meaning, will protect all the civil rights that pertain to freedom and citizenship. Finally, and to the end that no citizen should be denied, on account of his race, the privilege of participating in the political control of his country, it was declared by the Fifteenth Amendment that "the right of citizens of the United States to vote shall not be denied or abridged by the United States or by any State on account of race, color or previous condition of servitude."

These notable additions to the fundamental law were welcomed by the friends of liberty throughout the world. They removed the race line from our governmental systems. They had, as this court has said, a common purpose, namely, to secure "to a race recently emancipated, a race that through many generations have been held in slavery, all the civil rights that the superior race enjoy." They declared, in legal effect, this court has further said, "that the law in the States shall be the same for the black as for the white; that all persons, whether colored or white, shall stand equal before the laws of the States, and, in regard to the colored race, for whose protection the amendment was primarily designed, that no discrimination shall be made against them by law because of their color." . . .

Every one knows that the statute in question had its origin in the purpose, not so much to exclude white persons from railroad cars occupied by blacks, as to exclude colored people from coaches occupied by or assigned to white persons. Railroad corporations of Louisiana did not make discrimination among whites in the matter of accommodation for travellers. The thing to accomplish was, under the guise of giving equal accommodation for white and blacks, to compel the latter to keep to themselves while travelling in railroad passenger coaches. No one would be so wanting in candor as to assert the contrary. The fundamental objection, therefore, to the statute is that it interferes with the personal freedom of citizens. "Personal liberty," it has been well said, "consists in the power of locomotion, of changing situations, or removing one's person to whatsoever places one's own inclination may direct, without imprisonment or restraint, unless by due course of law." 1 Bl. Com. 134. If a white man and a black man choose to occupy the same public conveyance on a public highway, it is their right to do so, and no government, proceeding alone on grounds of race, can prevent it without infringing the personal liberty of each. . . .

The white race deems itself to be the dominant race in this country. And so it is, in prestige, in achievements, in education, in wealth and in power. So, I doubt not, it will continue to be for all time, if it remains true to its great heritage and holds fast to the principles of constitutional liberty. But in view of the Constitution, in the eye of the law, there is in this country no superior, dominant, ruling class of citizens. There is no caste here. Our Constitution is color-blind, and neither knows nor tolerates classes among citizens. In respect of civil rights, all citizens are equal before the law. The humblest is the peer of the most powerful. The law regards man as man, and takes no account of his surroundings or of his color when his civil rights as guaranteed by the supreme law of the land are involved. It is, therefore, to be regretted that this high tribunal, the final expositor of the fundamental law of the land, has reached the conclusion that it is competent for a State to regulate the enjoyment by citizens of their civil rights solely upon the basis of race.

In my opinion, the judgment this day rendered will, in time, prove to be quite as pernicious as the decision made by this tribunal in the *Dred Scott* case. It was adjudged in that case that the descendants of Africans who were imported into this country and sold as slaves were not included nor intended to be included under the word "citizens" in the Constitution, and could not claim any of the rights and privileges which that instrument provided for and secured to citizens of the United States; that at the time of the adoption of the Constitution they were "considered as a subordinate and inferior class of beings, who had been subjugated by the dominant race, and, whether emancipated or not, yet remained subject to their authority, and had no rights or privileges but such as those who held the power and the government might choose to grant them." 19 How. 393, 404. The recent amendments of the Constitution, it was supposed, had eradicated these principles from our institutions. But it seems that we have yet, in some of the States, a dominant race—a superior class of citizens, which assumes to regulate the enjoyment of civil rights, common to all citizens, upon the basis of race. The present decision, it may well be apprehended, will not only stimulate aggressions, more or less brutal and irritating, upon the admitted rights of colored citizens, but will encourage the belief that it is possible, by means of state enactments, to defeat the beneficent purposes which the people of the United States had in view when they adopted the recent amendments of the Constitution, by one of which the blacks of this country were made citizens of the United States and of the States in which they respectively reside, and whose privileges and immunities, as citizens, the States are forbidden to abridge. Sixty millions of whites are in no danger from the presence here of eight millions of blacks. The destinies of the two races, in this country, are indissolubly linked together, and the interests of both require that the common government of all shall not permit the seeds of race hate to be planted under the sanction of law. What can more certainly arouse race hate, what more certainly create and perpetuate a feeling of distrust between these races, than state enactments, which, in fact, proceed on the ground that colored citizens are so inferior and degraded that they cannot be allowed to sit in public coaches occupied by white citizens? That, as all will admit, is the real meaning of such legislation as was enacted in Louisiana. . . .

I am of opinion that the statute of Louisiana is inconsistent with the personal liberty of citizens, white and black, in that State, and hostile to both the spirit and letter of the Constitution of the United States. If laws of like character should be enacted in the several States of the Union, the effect would be in the highest degree mischievous. Slavery, as an institution tolerated by law would, it is true, have disappeared from our country, but there would remain a power in the States, by sinister legislation, to interfere with the full enjoyment of the blessings of freedom; to regulate civil rights, common to all citizens, upon the basis of race; and to place in a condition of legal inferiority a large body of American citizens, now constituting a part of the political community called the People of the United States, for whom, and by whom through representatives, our government is administered. Such a system is inconsistent with the guarantee given by the Constitution to each State of a republican form of government, and may be stricken down by Congressional action, or by the courts in the discharge of their solemn duty to maintain the supreme law of the land, anything in the constitution or laws of any State to the contrary notwithstanding.

For the reasons stated, I am constrained to withhold my assent from the opinion and judgment of the majority.

EDITORS' NOTE

1. A. Leon Higginbotham, "The Supreme Court's Legitimization of Racism: *Plessy v. Ferguson,*" in *Shades of Freedom* (New York: Oxford University Press, 1996), 118.

Chapter 40

Newspapers on *Plessy v. Ferguson*

Although we now look back on Plessy v. Ferguson *as a landmark blight on American jurisprudence, in 1896, after years of growing neglect of black rights in the North, the court's decision "aroused the barest indifference," according to historian Michael Kammen. A sampling from those few newspapers that bothered to comment follows. The New Orleans* Daily Picayune *offers an early example of Red-baiting to discredit the struggle for black civil rights.*

"Equality, but Not Socialism," New Orleans
Daily Picayune, *19 May 1896*

The Louisiana law which requires that the railways operating trains within the limits of the State shall furnish separate but equal facilities for white and negro passengers was passed upon by the Supreme Court of the United States, and was yesterday declared to be constitutional. . . .

As there are similar laws in all the States which abut on Louisiana, and, indeed, in most of the Southern States, this regulation for the separation of the races will operate continuously on all lines of Southern railway. Equality of rights does not mean community of rights. The laws must recognize and uphold this distinction; otherwise, if all rights were common as well as equal, there would be practically no such thing as private property, private life, or social distinctions, but all would belong to everybody who might choose to use it.

This would be absolute socialism, in which the individual would be extinguished in the vast mass of human beings, a condition repugnant to every principle of enlightened democracy.

"Editorial Notes," Independent,
New York, 21 May 1896

We cannot argue law with the Supreme Court of the United States, but we can argue morals. That court has decided that the Louisiana Jim Crow law is not unconstitutional, which requires railroad companies to provide separate coaches for whites and Negroes. But the law is a crime before God, no matter whether it does or does not contradict the Constitution of the United States. The Constitution is

not as broad as the Golden Rule, and the justices of the court have narrower jurisdiction than God has; nay, a narrower jurisdiction than any man's conscience.

"A Damnable Outrage," Parsons (Kansas) Weekly Blade *(a black-owned newspaper), 30 May 1896*

The Democratic majority of the Supreme Court of the United States has wantonly
disgraced . . . the highest tribunal of this the land that has proclaimed it the world
over that "all men are created equal" by declaring . . . the "Jim Crow" car laws of
the South to [be] constitutional. When such an august body stoops so low, then it
is time to put an end to the existence of infernal, infamous bodies. If such an act as
the Louisiana "Jim Crow" car law can be declared constitutional then it is time to
make null and void all that tail end of the Constitution; for it is certain that under
such circumstances it is of no earthly use. Justice Harlan was the only one on the
bench with grit enough in him to utter a protest against this damnable outrage
upon a race that for more than 275 years labored [in] the yoke of bondage.

Chapter 41

How Disenfranchisement Was Accomplished

Frances Fox Piven and Richard A. Cloward

Frances Fox Piven, professor of political science at the City University of New York, and Richard Cloward, professor of social work at Columbia University, helped found both the National Welfare Rights Organization and the Human Service Employees' Registration and Voter Education Campaign (Human SERVE).

Piven and Cloward are the authors of many works, including Regulating the Poor: The Functions of Public Welfare *(1971),* Poor People's Movements: Why They Succeed, How They Fail *(1977),* The New Class War *(1982), and* The Breaking of the American Social Compact *(1998).*

The following selection is excerpted from Why Americans Don't Vote *(New York: Pantheon, 1988), 78–85. Reprinted with permission of the authors.*

For other selections by Piven and Cloward, see chapters 84 and 134.

Disenfranchisement was part of the broader effort by the southern planter class to erect a system of political, economic, and social coercion over blacks that would permit the reestablishment of a quasi-feudal labor system. Experience showed that black enfranchisement interfered with this objective. As late as the turn of the century, blacks were still able to elect representatives to state and local office over much of the South, impeding the uses of the apparatus of state and local government to reestablish the caste labor system. Moreover, black voters could strike alliances with dissident electoral movements, as they had with northern-backed Republicans after the Civil War. Later, as the radical farmers' movement grew and opened new opportunities for insurgent black-white alliances, the pressure for disenfranchisement grew, and was extended to poor whites as well.

From the period of Reconstruction, black voting rights had been countered by reigning Democratic parties and their Bourbon allies with an extraordinary repertoire of inventive techniques ranging from trickery and fraud to outright violence.[1] And although fraud, trickery, and violence went far toward reducing black voter turnout, it apparently did not go far enough. While black voting appears to have fallen, particularly after federal troops were withdrawn in 1877, the evidence is that moderate levels of black participation were maintained, keeping southern Republican parties alive and providing significant potential support for populism in the 1890s.[2] Furthermore, fraud, trickery, and force had their limitations; they were inherently unstable, for their effective deployment depended on vigilant local organization, and they also made the Southern Democracy vulnerable to a national outcry and federal intervention, a danger that persisted long after Reconstruction.[3] "The prospect of federal enforcement of suffrage rights provoked anger, frustration and fear," according to [historian Richard] Bensel:

> The primary purpose . . . was to secure Republican control of the national government by recapturing marginal areas in the South. Electoral reform simultaneously released the Bourbons from the twin threats of federal intervention and agrarian class-based radicalism.[4]

Finally, there is some evidence that southern elites simply preferred legal methods of disenfranchisement to other and more irregular techniques.[5]

The southern solution to the problems posed by the black franchise was to attach conditions to the right to vote that did not mention blacks, and so ostensibly would not violate the Fifteenth Amendment, but which blacks would not fulfill. These disenfranchising devices were not created all at once. Rather, the campaign occurred in waves. As federal troops withdrew and the interest of northern reformers in the freedmen waned, the southern states gradually evolved the arrangements that would eventually strip some three-quarters of the population, black and white, of the right to vote.

> Each state became in effect a laboratory for testing one device or another. Indeed, the cross-fertilization and coordination between the movements to restrict the suffrage in the Southern states amounted to a public conspiracy.[6]

Some of the methods were already available. Georgia retained on the books an optional poll tax from the time when the payment of taxes was a common condition for the exercise of the suffrage. In 1877, the state simply moved to make its poll tax mandatory and far more onerous,[7] and turnout dropped precipitously.[8] Shortly afterward, in 1882, South Carolina adopted an "eight-box" law, followed by Florida in 1889, a device that required the voter to deposit separate ballots in each of the boxes marked for different candidates, making it virtually impossible for the illiterate to navigate the balloting process.

> In South Carolina, the requirement that, with eight or more ballot boxes before him, the voter must select the proper one for each ballot, in order to insure its being counted, furnished an effective means of neutralizing the ignorant black vote; for though the negroes, unable to read the lettering on the boxes, might acquire, by proper coaching, the power to discriminate among them by their relative positions, a moment's work by whites in transposing the boxes, would render useless an hour's laborious instruction.[9]

The introduction of officially printed ballots, organized by office rather than by party, was similarly confusing to the uneducated. These arrangements anticipated the straightforward literacy tests that were to come later. Meanwhile, the South developed voter registration procedures that were distinctive for the discretion that they granted local election officers in deciding whether potential voters were in fact qualified. These procedures were particularly useful in purging the electorate of blacks and poor whites in anticipation of constitutional conventions where more sweeping disenfranchising laws could then be enacted.[10]

As Populist dissidence mounted in the late 1880s, the southern disenfranchisement movement accelerated. Mississippi was another pioneer, introducing both a $2.00 poll tax and a literacy test in its constitutional convention of 1890, arrangements that drove voter participation down to 17 percent by 1900.[11] Florida and Tennessee followed quickly after, and then, in 1894, Arkansas fell in line. [Historian J. Morgan] Kousser offers persuasive evidence of the impact of these disenfranchising measures in simultaneously depressing turnout and reducing support for oppositional Republican or Populist parties in the states that adopted them during the early 1890s, when southern electoral challenges peaked.[12]

The momentum of the disenfranchising campaign accelerated again after 1896, as the earlier measures proved their effectiveness, and as the resistance offered by southern Populists and their poor white constituencies dissipated. The fact that national Republican leaders seemed to lose interest in protecting the electoral base of southern Republicanism once the party's national dominance was assured by the 1896 sweep of the North probably encouraged the disenfranchisers. The rising wave of race-baiting after [William Jennings] Bryan's defeat also helped pave the way by appealing to the racism of poor whites in an effort to win their support in completing the legal system of disenfranchisement.

Accordingly, after 1896, the remaining southern states followed the path laid out by Mississippi, introducing poll tax laws where none yet existed, or making existing poll tax measures more restrictive by raising the amount of the tax or by making it retroactive. In Texas, a poll tax had first been proposed in 1875, on the ostensible grounds that it would eliminate "irresponsible voters." But Texas was the birthplace and organizing center of the Farmers' Alliance, and it was not until 1902, when the Populists had disappeared, that a constitutional amendment establishing the poll tax was approved, this time frankly presented as a white-supremacy measure.[13] By 1904, turnout in Texas had plunged to 30 percent from its peak level of 80 percent twenty years earlier.

After the debacle of 1896, the southern states also acted rapidly to add literacy test barriers to poll tax barriers. To overcome the opposition of the poor and illiterate whites who would also be disenfranchised by these measures, complicated loopholes were introduced that could in principle refranchise some of those who were being disenfranchised. Thus "good character" clauses were added that permitted voter registrars to make exceptions, or clauses permitted registrars to accept "understanding" of some portion of the state constitution as a substitute for literacy, or grandfather and "fighting grandfather" clauses permitted exceptions to be made for those whose grandfathers had voted, or whose grandfathers had fought for the Confederacy. But these gestures to overcome the opposition of poor whites were usually allowed to lapse. In any case, the loopholes did not work and were probably not intended to work. Most poor whites were unwilling to risk the humiliation of failing the new voter tests.[14]

No one disputes that the southern system "worked." In the 1880s and 1890s, turnout in the South had regularly exceeded 60 percent, and sometimes reached

85 percent.[15] [Kevin] Phillips and [Paul] Blackman provide some dramatic examples of the change. In Arkansas, turnout dropped from over two-thirds to just over one-third between 1884 and 1904; in Mississippi, from almost 80 percent in 1876 to less than 17 percent in 1900; and in South Carolina participation plummeted from 83.7 percent in 1880 to 18 percent in 1900.[16] As the system of legal barriers was put in place, the black vote dwindled and then disappeared, and white turnout shrank as well. In Kousser's words, "The security of the black belt and the Democratic party had been purchased at the cost of abandoning popular government."[17]

Scholarly debate over the causes of turnout decline in the South turns on a rather narrow dispute having to do with the *relative weight* of force and fraud on the one hand, and legal barriers on the other hand. On the larger points, there is in fact no dispute: millions of blacks and poor whites were disenfranchised, and legal barriers mattered in that process. The boldness of the disenfranchising movement in the South makes the motives of the disenfranchisers and their techniques clear.

NOTES

1. For an overview, see C. Vann Woodward, *Burden of Southern History* (Baton Rouge: Lousiana State University, 1968). The techniques pioneered during Reconstruction to obstruct black voting have been described by John Hope Franklin, *From Slavery to Freedom* (New York: Vintage, 3rd ed., 1969), esp. chapter 18. The definitive work on the use of force in deterring blacks from voting is of course V. O. Key, *Southern Politics in State and Nation* (New York: Alfred A. Knopf, 1949, 1984), chapters 25–28.

2. J. Morgan Kousser, *The Shaping of Southern Politics: Suffrage Restrictions and the Establishment of the One-Party South* (New Haven: Yale University Press, 1974), 17–18, 28, and 78.

3. Kousser, 46–47.

4. Richard Franklin Bensel, *Sectionalism and American Political Development, 1880–1980* (Madison: University of Wisconsin Press, 1984), 76 and 81. For a description of the heated congressional battles over legislative proposals for federal intervention in southern elections before 1896, see Bensel, 73–88. The last effort to impose federal supervision, known as the "Force Bill," did not die in the Congress until [Grover] Cleveland's re-election in 1892.

5. Kousser, 263. Rusk and Stucker disagree with Kousser on this point, speculating that had informal methods of disenfranchisement been successful, the southern states would have avoided implementing laws that were susceptible to constitutional challenge. See Jerrold D. Rusk and John J. Stucker, "The Effect of Election Laws on Voter Participation," in Joel H. Sibley, et al., eds., *The History of American Electoral Behavior* (Princeton: Princeton University Press, 1978), 39.

6. Kousser, 39.

7. Rusk and Stucker, 211.

8. Kousser, 67 and table 3.2.

9. William A. Dunning, "The Undoing of Reconstruction," *Atlantic Monthly*, 1901, 443. Dunning also reports a remarkable instance of gerrymandering. "In Mississippi appeared the 'shoestring district,' three hundred miles long and about twenty wide, including

within its boundaries nearly all of the densest black communities of the state." Also, see Kousser, 50.

10. Joseph P. Harris, *Registration of Voters in the United States* (Washington, D.C.: Brookings, 1929), 157, and Kousser, 48–49.

11. See Kevin Phillips and Paul Blackman, *Electoral Reform and Voter Participation* (Stanford, Calif.: American Enterprise Institute and Hoover Institution, 1975), 8.

12. Kousser, 41 and table 1.5.

13. Archie P. McDonald, *The Texas Experience* (College Station: Texas A&M University Press, n.d.), 112–13.

14. A witness cited by William C. Pendleton [*Political History of Appalachian Virginia* (Dayton, Va.: Shenandoah Press, 1927), 459] offered this description of how poor whites reacted: "It was painful and pitiful to see the horror and dread visible on the faces of the illiterate poor white men who were waiting to take their turn before the inquisition. . . . This was horrible to behold, but it was still more horrible to see the marks of humiliation and despair that were stamped on the faces of honest but poor white men who had been refused registration and who had been robbed of their citizenship without cause. We saw them as they came from the presence of the registrars with bowed heads and agonized faces; and when they spoke, in many instances, there was a tear in the voice of the humiliated citizen." Of course this was only one of the ways in which poor southern whites were victimized by their own racism.

15. Kousser, 236.

16. Phillips and Blackman, 8.

17. Kousser, 103.

Chapter 42

Lynching

Ida B. Wells-Barnett

Journalist Ida B. Wells-Barnett (1862–1931), a leading civil rights, anti-lynching, and women's suffrage activist, was born in Mississippi during the Civil War. After the death of her parents in an 1878 yellow fever epidemic she raised her siblings and worked as a teacher, first in Virginia and then outside Memphis.

In 1887, she was ejected from a train for taking a seat in a whites-only car. With the help of a black lawyer, Wells sued the railroad company. She won the judgment but lost on appeal. In 1891, as editor of Free Speech, *a Memphis-based black newspaper, she published scathing articles about the lynching of three black men. When her office was destroyed and her life threatened, she moved to New York, where she continued her work as a columnist for the* New York Age. *Wells later moved to Chicago and wrote for the* Chicago Conservator, *the city's first black newspaper. In 1895 she married the paper's founder, the attorney Ferdinand Lee Barnett.*

Wells lectured across the United States, England, and Scotland against lynching; co-authored and distributed twenty thousand pamphlets protesting the absence of blacks at the 1893 Columbian Exposition; revived the Afro-American League as the more radical Afro-American Council; and founded numerous female and reform organizations, including the first black women's political club, which helped win the election of the first black alderman in Chicago. Her book on lynching, A Red Record *(1895), asserted, "'Equality before the law,' must become a fact as well as a theory before America is truly the 'land of the free and the home of the brave.'" She was an early opponent of Booker T. Washington and a founder of the National Association for the Advancement of Colored People (NAACP). U.S. Military Intelligence declared her "one of the most dangerous Negro agitators in the country."*

Wells's autobiography, edited by her daughter Alfreda M. Duster, was published posthumously as Crusade for Justice: The Autobiography of Ida B. Wells *(1970). For biographies, see Linda O. McMurry,* To Keep the Waters Troubled *(1999) and Paula Giddings,* The Life and Times of Ida B. Wells-Barnett *(forthcoming).*

The following selection is reprinted from the records of the founding convention of the NAACP, Proceedings of the National Negro Conference, 1909 *(New York: Arno Press, 1969).*

The lynching record for a quarter of a century merits the thoughtful study of the American people. It presents three salient facts:

First: Lynching is color-line murder.

Second: Crimes against women is the excuse, not the cause.

Third: It is a national crime and requires a national remedy.

Proof that lynching follows the color line is to be found in the statistics which have been kept for the past twenty-five years. During the few years preceding this period and while frontier lynch law existed, the executions showed a majority of white victims. Later, however, as law courts and authorized judiciary extended into the far West, lynch law rapidly abated, and its white victims became few and far between.

Just as the lynch-law regime came to a close in the West, a new mob movement started in the South. This was wholly political, its purpose being to suppress the colored vote by intimidation and murder. Thousands of assassins banded together under the name of Ku Klux Klans, "Midnight Raiders," "Knights of the Golden Circle," et cetera, et cetera, spread a reign of terror, by beating, shooting and killing colored people by the thousands. In a few years, the purpose was accomplished, and the black vote was suppressed. But mob murder continued.

From 1882, in which year fifty-two were lynched, down to the present, lynching has been along the color line. Mob murder increased yearly until in 1892 more than two hundred victims were lynched and statistics show that 3,284 men, women and children have been put to death in this quarter of a century. During the last ten years from 1899 to 1908 inclusive the number lynched was 959. Of this number 102 were white, while the colored victims numbered 857. No other nation, civilized or savage, burns its criminals; only under the Stars and Stripes is the human holocaust possible. Twenty-eight human beings burned at the stake, one of them a woman and two of them children, is the awful indictment against American civilization—the gruesome tribute which the nation pays to the color line.

Why is mob murder permitted by a Christian nation? What is the cause of this awful slaughter? This question is answered almost daily—always the same shameless falsehood that "Negroes are lynched to protect womanhood." Standing before a Chautauqua assemblage, John Temple Graves, at once champion of lynching and apologist for lynchers, said: "The mob stands today as the most potential bulwark between the women of the South and such a carnival of crime as would infuriate the world and precipitate the annihilation of the Negro race." This is the never-varying answer of lynchers and their apologists. All know that it is untrue. The cowardly lyncher revels in murder, then seeks to shield himself from public execration by claiming devotion to woman. But truth is mighty and the lynching record discloses the hypocrisy of the lyncher as well as his crime.

The Springfield, Illinois, mob [in 1908] rioted for two days [see chapter 44—Eds.], the militia of the entire state was called out, two men were lynched, hundreds of people driven from their homes, all because a white woman said a Negro assaulted her. A mad mob went to the jail, tried to lynch the victim of her charge and, not being able to find him, proceeded to pillage and burn the town and to lynch two innocent men. Later, after the police had found that the woman's charge was false, she published a retraction, the indictment was dismissed and the intended victim discharged. But the lynched victims were dead. Hundreds were homeless and Illinois was disgraced.

As a final and complete refutation of the charge that lynching is occasioned by crimes against women, a partial record of lynchings is cited; 285 persons were lynched for causes as follows:

Unknown cause, 92; no cause, 10; race prejudice, 49; miscegenation, 7; informing, 12; making threats, 11; keeping saloon, 3; practicing fraud, 5; practicing voodooism, 2; bad reputation, 8; unpopularity, 3; mistaken identity, 5; using improper language, 3; violation of contract, 1; writing insulting letter, 2; eloping, 2; poisoning horse, 1; poisoning well, 2; by white caps, 9; vigilantes, 14; Indians, 1; moonshining, 1; refusing evidence, 2; political causes, 5; disputing, 1; disobeying quarantine regulations, 2; slapping a child, 1; turning state's evidence, 3; protecting a Negro, 1; to prevent giving evidence, 1; knowledge of larceny, 1; writing letter to white woman, 1; asking white woman to marry, 1; jilting girl, 1; having smallpox, 1; concealing criminal, 2; threatening political exposure, 1; self-defense, 6; cruelty, 1; insulting language to woman, 5; quarreling with white man, 2; colonizing Negroes, 1; throwing stones, 1; quarreling, 1; gambling, 1.

Is there a remedy, or will the nation confess that it cannot protect its protectors at home as well as abroad? Various remedies have been suggested to abolish the lynching infamy, but year after year, the butchery of men, women and children continues in spite of plea and protest. Education is suggested as a preventive, but it is as grave a crime to murder an ignorant man as it is a scholar. True, few educated men have been lynched, but the hue and cry once started stops at no bounds, as was clearly shown by the lynchings in Atlanta, and in Springfield, Illinois.

Agitation, though helpful, will not alone stop the crime. Year after year statistics are published, meetings are held, resolutions are adopted and yet lynchings go on. Public sentiment does measurably decrease the sway of mob law, but the irresponsible bloodthirsty criminals who swept through the streets of Springfield, beating an inoffensive law-abiding citizen to death in one part of the town, and in another torturing and shooting to death a man who for threescore years had made a reputation for honesty, integrity and sobriety, had raised a family and had accumulated property, were not deterred from their heinous crimes by either education or agitation.

The only certain remedy is an appeal to law. Lawbreakers must be made to know that human life is sacred and that every citizen of this country is first a citizen of the United States and secondly a citizen of the state in which he belongs. This nation must assert itself and defend its federal citizenship at home as well as abroad. The strong arm of the government must reach across state lines whenever unbridled lawlessness defies state laws and must give to the individual citizen under the Stars and Stripes the same measure of protection which it gives to him when he travels in foreign lands.

Federal protection of American citizenship is the remedy for lynching. Foreigners are rarely lynched in America. If, by mistake, one is lynched, the national government quickly pays the damages. The recent agitation in California against the Japanese compelled this nation to recognize that federal power must yet assert itself to protect the nation from the treason of sovereign States. Thousands of American citizens have been put to death and no President has yet raised his hand in effective protest, but a simple insult to a native of Japan was quite sufficient to stir the government at Washington to prevent the threatened wrong. If the government has power to protect a foreigner from insult, certainly it has power to save a citizen's life.

The practical remedy has been more than once suggested in Congress. Senator [Jacob] Gallinger, of New Hampshire, in a resolution introduced in Congress called for an investigation "with the view of ascertaining whether there is a remedy for lynching which Congress may apply." The Senate Committee has under consideration a bill drawn by A. E. Pillsbury, formerly Attorney General of Massachusetts, providing for federal prosecution of lynchers in cases where the state fails to protect citizens or foreigners. Both of these resolutions indicate that the attention of the nation has been called to this phase of the lynching question.

As a final word, it would be a beginning in the right direction if this conference can see its way clear to establish a bureau for the investigation and publication of the details of every lynching, so that the public could know that an influential body of citizens has made it a duty to give the widest publicity to the facts in each case; that it will make an effort to secure expressions of opinion all over the country against lynching for the sake of the country's fair name; and lastly, but by no means least, to try to influence the daily papers of the country to refuse to become accessory to mobs either before or after the fact. Several of the greatest riots and most brutal burnt offerings of the mobs have been suggested and incited by the daily papers of the offending community. If the newspaper which suggests lynching in its accounts of an alleged crime, could be held legally as well as morally responsible for reporting that "threats of lynching were heard"; or, "it is feared that if the guilty one is caught, he will be lynched"; or, "there were cries of 'lynch him,' and the only reason the threat was not carried out was because no leader appeared," a long step toward a remedy will have been taken.

In a multitude of counsel there is wisdom. Upon the grave question presented by the slaughter of innocent men, women and children there should be an honest, courageous conference of patriotic, law-abiding citizens anxious to punish crime promptly, impartially and by due process of law, also to make life, liberty and property secure against mob rule.

Time was when lynching appeared to be sectional, but now it is national—a blight upon our nation, mocking our laws and disgracing our Christianity. "With malice toward none but with charity for all" let us undertake the work of making the "law of the land" effective and supreme upon every foot of American soil—a shield to the innocent; and to the guilty, punishment swift and sure.

Chapter 43

The Atlanta Massacre

"An Educated Negro"

The following report is reprinted from the Independent, *4 October 1906, 799–800. The editor of the New York–based* Independent *described the anonymous author as "an educated negro, a life-long resident of Georgia, in whom, were it safe to print his name, our readers would have every confidence."*

Atlanta, Ga., has again demonstrated that it is not a civilized community. Last Saturday the Atlanta *News,* hard pressed for existence in competition with two other afternoon papers, felt called upon to print sensational charges of assault upon white women by negroes. Not one of these charges has yet been proved, but the mere report was enough to call together all the white "toughs" in the city as soon as they had drawn their week's wages, and to give them license to set upon innocent and unsuspecting blacks wherever found and butcher them upon the spot.

The cause of all this violence, by careful inquiry, I have traced to four sources—one remote and three immediate.

The remote cause is the contest between Hoke Smith and Clark Howell for Governor, in which both men openly declared that negroes have no rights save those granted thru sufferance by the white people. The three immediate causes are: (1) There was circulated by the Atlanta newspapers—*The News* and *The Georgian* especially—the report that five assaults had occurred in one week and an additional one on Saturday—*not one of which charges has been proved.* (2) There is a sharp struggle for existence among three evening papers, which feel called upon to use any measures whatsoever to attract readers among a population that can be best attracted by abuse of the negro. (3) There is an increasing number of educated and prosperous negroes, whose business and whose success are an eyesore to some of the whites, who can in no peaceable way prevent that progress, as the facts here will show.

The facts about the most aggravating case of assault I have found to be as follows: A negro whose purpose was unknown was seen in the yard of a white woman; she drove him away with abusive language without asking him about his mission; the negro again returned and the woman again began to call him vile names and to scream and to cry that the negro was attempting to assault her. A mob at once assembled, and before they had well got together all the evening papers—*The News* and *The Georgian* especially—were circulating "extras" under the glaring headlines, "Another Assault." Then separate and extra editions of *The News* appeared hourly until dark, saying, "Another Assault." It seemed only necessary for a white woman to see a negro meeting her in the same street or looking at her on her front porch to make her cry out, "Assault!"

That is the evidence that drove the editors mad and made them advocate the gathering of a mob to murder peaceable negroes. It is coming out little by little that the whole affair was planned. A negro lad, the driver of a laundry wagon, told me that his employer said to him Saturday morning, "Well, Sammie, we are going to kill all the niggers tonight." The most horrible exhibition of savagery was in the treatment of negro passengers on the street cars as often as they came into the public square—negro men, women and children were beaten unmercifully. Even the negro barbers were dragged out of their shops while they were shaving white men, beaten and their shops demolished. One of the finest shops in the whole country had the glass front smashed because the owner was colored. It is believed that this violence upon the barbers was done by white barbers who were members of the mob and who have been unable to cope successfully in Atlanta in competition with negro barbers. They used the mob as a cover to destroy their competitors.

A hardware store and a pawnshop were broken into by the mob, and all revolvers and ammunition taken, but none of the stores would sell weapons to negroes. A negro fled thru a fruit house kept by Greeks, and when the Greeks attempted to defend their store against the mob, it was straightway demolished and the fruit taken. A stable owner, with revolver in hand, defied the mob to break open his door to take his horses to chase negroes to the suburbs. This only shows what one policeman might have done.

Where were the policemen? That is what all negroes asked at first, but when the bluecoats began to halt them on back streets, arrest them upon State charges for carrying concealed weapons, it became plain that the policemen were not interested in quelling the mob. When one was seen in a crowd he made no effort to use his club or his gun to rescue a prisoner. One of the newspapers confesses that on Peachtree street, in the heart of the city, where the mob gathered, "only one policeman could be seen, and, of course, he could do nothing with such a mob."

Where are the conservative, good white people? That is not a question any one will ask when he knows that *ten* of the leading white pulpits in Atlanta were vacant because the pastors of moral courage have either been driven away or will not come to stifle their conscience in such service. On Sunday morning only one pastor stood up *positively* for law and order, according to statements published in the Atlanta *Constitution,* and that one was a Catholic bishop. All the others said it was what you might expect.

What will be the outcome of all this? That is more a question for the white people North and South than it is for negroes. It certainly is not going to make the lawless element of whites, who are very much in the majority in Georgia, disposed to hate the negro less when he beats them in competition, as in the case of the barbers; it certainly is not going to frighten the negroes who are actually bad, and it certainly is not going to make the great majority of negroes, who are honest, law-abiding folk, assume the responsibility of chasing down every one of their number who is merely accused by some malicious, frightened white woman, any more than a report of theft is going to make the honest bankers of New York close their doors to hunt down absconding cashiers because they happen to be of the same race. All that Christian piety in humble homes, all that honest labor and forbearance, and all that teaching and preaching can do has been done by the better element of negroes to help their fellows; and if the white people of the south are going to expect negroes to co-operate in catching negroes accused of crime, or actual criminals, when experience proves every day that such persons have no hope in the world of a fair trial, then the white people are doomed to disappointment.

Chapter 44

The Race War in the North

William English Walling

In 1908, an anti-black riot in Springfield, Illinois—the home of Abraham Lincoln, "the Great Emancipator"—sharply demonstrated that race was not simply a southern problem but a national one.

Socialist William English Walling (1877–1936), the grandson of 1880 Democratic vice-presidential candidate William English, was a muckraking journalist and labor reformer. His article on the Springfield riot is usually credited with having led to the formation of the National Association for the Advancement of Colored People (NAACP).

The following selection is reprinted from "The Race War in the North," Independent, 3 September 1908, 529–34.

"Lincoln freed you, we'll show you where you belong," was one of the cries with which the Springfield mob set about to drive the negroes from town. The mob was composed of several thousand of Springfield's white citizens, while other thousands, including many women and children, and even prosperous business men in automobiles, calmly looked on, and the rioters proceeded hour after hour and on two days in succession to make deadly assaults on every negro they could lay their hands on, to sack and plunder their houses and stores, and to burn and murder on favorable occasion.

The American people have been fairly well informed by their newspapers of the action of that mob; they have also been told of certain alleged political and criminal conditions in Springfield and of the two crimes in particular which are offered by the mob itself as sufficient explanation why six thousand peaceful and innocent negroes should be driven by the fear of their lives from a town where some of them have lived honorably for half a hundred years. We have been assured by more cautious and indirect defenders of Springfield's populace that there was an exceptionally criminal element among the negroes encouraged by the bosses of both political parties. And now, after a few days of discussion, we are satisfied with these explanations, and demand only the punishment of those who took the most active part in the destruction of life and property. Assuming that there were exceptionally provocative causes for complaint against the negroes, we have closed our eyes to the whole awful and menacing truth—that a large part of the white population of Lincoln's home, supported largely by the farmers and miners of the neighboring towns, have initiated a permanent warfare with the negro race.

We do not need to be informed at great length of the character of this warfare. It is in all respects like that of the South, on which it is modeled. Its significance is threefold. First, that it has occurred in an important and historical Northern town; then, that the negroes, constituting scarcely more than a tenth of the population, in this case, could not possibly endanger the "supremacy" of the whites, and, finally, that the public opinion of the North, notwithstanding the fanatical, blind and almost insane hatred of the negro so clearly shown by the mob, is satisfied that there were "mitigating circumstances," not for the mob violence, which, it is agreed, should be punished to the full extent of the law, but for the race hatred, which is really the cause of it all. If these outrages had happened thirty years ago, when the memories of Lincoln, Garrison and Wendell Phillips were still fresh, what would not have happened in the North? Is there any doubt that the whole country would have been aflame, that all flimsy explanations and "mitigating circumstances" would have been thrown aside, and that the people of Springfield would have had to prove to the nation why they proposed to drive the negroes out, to hold a whole race responsible for a handful of criminals, and to force it to inferior place on the social scale?

For the underlying motive of the mob and of that large portion of Springfield's population that has long said that "something was bound to happen," and now approves of the riot and proposes to complete its purposes by using other means to drive as many as possible of the remaining two-thirds of the negroes out of town, was confessedly to teach the negroes their place and to warn them that too many could not obtain shelter under the favorable traditions of Lincoln's home town. I talked to many of them the day after the massacre and found no difference of opinion on the question. "Why, the niggers came to think they were as good as we are!" was the final justification offered, not once, but a dozen times.

On the morning after the first riot I was in Chicago and took the night train for Springfield, where I have often visited and am almost at home. On arriving in the town I found that the rioting had been continued thruout the night, and was even feared for the coming evening, in spite of the presence of nearly the whole militia of the State. Altho we visited the Mayor, military headquarters, the leading newspaper, and some prominent citizens, my wife and I gave most of our attention to the hospital, the negro quarters and the jail.

We at once discovered, to our amazement, that Springfield had no shame. She stood for the action of the mob. She hoped the rest of the negroes might flee. She threatened that the movement to drive them out would continue. I do not speak of the leading citizens, but of the masses of the people, of workingmen in the shops, the storekeepers in the stores, the drivers, the men on the street, the wounded in the hospitals and even the notorious "Joan of Arc" of the mob, Kate Howard, who had just been released from arrest on $4,000 bail. [She has since committed suicide.—*Editor of the Independent.*] The *Illinois State Journal of Springfield* expressed the prevailing feeling even on its editorial page:

While all good citizens deplore the consequences of this outburst of the mob spirit, many even of these consider the outburst was *inevitable,* at some time, from existing conditions, needing only an overt act, such as that of Thursday night, to bring it from latent existence into active operation. The implication is clear that conditions, not the populace, were to blame and that many good citizens could find no other remedy than that applied by the mob. It was not the fact of the whites' hatred toward the negroes, but of the negroes' own misconduct, general inferiority or unfitness for free institutions that were at fault.

On Sunday, August 16th, the day after the second lynching, a leading white minister recommended the Southern disfranchisement scheme as a remedy for *negro* (!) lawlessness, while all four ministers who were quoted in the press proposed swift "justice" for *the negroes,* rather than recommending true Christianity, democracy and brotherhood to the whites. Even the Governor's statement of the situation, strong as it was on the whole, was tainted in one place with a concession to Springfield opinion. He said that Burton, the first negro lynched, was killed after he had incensed the crowd by firing into it to protect his home from incendiaries. But when Burton's home was attacked there had already been considerable shooting between the blacks and whites. Moreover, according to his daughters, men had entered the house and threatened him with an axe and other weapons, while his firing of buckshot at random into a mob is by no means necessarily a murderous procedure. The Governor made, then, an understatement of the character of the mob, suggesting that the negroes had lost their heads and were accepting the mob's challenge to war. It is probable that Burton was defending not his home, but his life.

Besides suggestions in high places of the negro's brutality, criminality and unfitness for the ballot we heard in lower ranks all the opinions that pervade the South—that the negro does not need much education, that his present education even has been a mistake, that white cannot live in the same community with negroes except where the latter have been taught their inferiority, that lynching is the only way to teach them, etc. In fact, this went so far that we were led to suspect the existence of a Southern element in the town, and this is indeed the case. Many of the older citizens are from Kentucky or the southern part of Illinois. Moreover, many of the street railway employees are from the South. It was a street railway man's wife that was assaulted the night before the riots, and they were street railway employees, among others, that led the mob to the jail. Even the famous Kate Howard had received her inspiration, she told us, from the South. While traveling with her brother in Texas and Arkansas she had observed enviously that enforced separation of the races in cars and public places helped to teach the negro where he belonged. Returning home she had noticed the growing boycott of negroes in Springfield stores and restaurants, participated in the alarm that "no white women was safe," etc., and in the demand for negro blood. A woman of evident physical courage, she held that it was time for the population to act up to their professions, and by the cry of "cowards" is said to have goaded the mob into some of the worst of its deeds. She exhibited to us proudly the buckshot wounds in her fleshy arms (probably Burton's), and said she relied confidently on her fellow citizens to keep her from punishment.

This was the feeling also of the half hundred whites in the hospital. It was, in fact, only three days after the first disturbance when they fully realized that the lenient public opinion of Springfield was not the public opinion of Illinois or the North, that the rioters began to tremble. Still this did not prevent them later from insulting the militia, repeatedly firing at their outposts and almost openly organizing a political and business boycott to drive the remaining negroes out. Negro employers continue to receive threatening letters and are dismissing employees every day, while the stores, even the groceries, so fear to sell the negroes goods that the State has been compelled to intervene and purchase $10,000 worth in their behalf.

The menace is that if this thing continues it will offer *automatic rewards* to the riotous elements and negro haters in Springfield, make the reign of terror permanent there, and offer every temptation to similar white elements in other towns to imitate Springfield's example.

If the new Political League succeeds in permanently driving every negro from office; if the white laborers get the negro laborers' jobs; if masters of negro servants are able to keep them under the discipline of terror as I saw them doing at Springfield; if white shopkeepers and saloonkeepers get their colored rivals' trade; if the farmers of neighboring towns establish permanently their right to drive poor people out of their community, instead of offering them reasonable alms; if white miners can force their negro fellow-workers out and get their positions by closing the mines, then every community indulging in an outburst of race hatred will be assured of a great and certain financial reward, and all the lies, ignorance and brutality on which race hatred is based will spread over the land. For the action of these dozen farming and four coal mining communities near Springfield shows how rapidly the thing can spread. In the little town of Buffalo, fifteen miles away, for instance, they have just posted this sign in front of the interurban station:

All niggers are warned out of town by Monday, 12 m. sharp.

Buffalo Sharp Shooters.

Part of the Springfield press, far from discouraging this new effort to drive the negroes out, a far more serious attack on our colored brothers than the mob violence, either fails to condemn it in the only possible way, a complete denial of the whole hypocritical case against the negro, or indirectly approves it. An evening paper printed this on the third day after the outbreak:

NEGRO FAMILY
  LEAVES CITY
    WHEN ORDERED

The first negro family routed from Springfield by a mob was the Harvey family residing at 1144 North Seventh street, who were told Sunday morning to 'hike,' and carried out the orders yesterday afternoon. The family proved themselves obnoxious in many ways. They were the one negro family in the block and their presence was distasteful to all other citizens in that vicinity.

The tone of this notice is that of a jubilant threat. As the family left town only the day after, not on account of the mob, but the standing menace, the use of the word "first" is significant.

We have not mentioned the negro crimes which are alleged to have caused the disorders, as we are of the opinion that they could scarcely in any case have had much real connection either with the mob violence or the far more important race conflict that is still spreading geographically and growing in intensity from day to day.

The first crime is called a murder, resulting from an assault on a woman. An unknown negro was discovered at night in the room of two young white girls. The father and mother and two sons were also at home, however, and there is every probability that it was no assault but a common burglary. The father attacked the negro, was terribly cut up, and died. A few hours later a negro was found sleeping not very far away, and the press claimed that there was every evidence that he was the criminal. However, Judge Creighton, a man respected by the whole community, saw cause to postpone the case, and it was this short delay of six weeks that was used by the enemies of the negro in Springfield to suggest that the negroes' political influence was thwarting the "swift justice" of the law.

The *State Journal,* ignoring the common sense of the situation, stated editorially that Ballard, the victim, "had given his life in defense of his child," and added significantly: "This tragedy was not enacted in the black belt of Mississippi or of Georgia," and further, twelve lines below,

> Concerning him (the negro) and the questions which arise from his presence in the community, it is well to preserve silence at the present time. The state of the public mind is such that comment can only add fuel to the feeling that has burst forth with general knowledge of the crime.

The writer has been rather cautious, but has he not succeeded in suggesting clearly enough to readers of the character we have mentioned (1) that the deed was to be connected in some way with the race question; (2) that the public mind as it was, and events have since shown the world clearly what the writer must have known at that time, was justified; and (3) in directing their attention to the South as a basis of comparison?

Then what was the second crime, which occurred six weeks later, early in the morning of August 15th? This was an assault by a negro on a white woman in her home. There is little doubt of the nature of the crime intended. But in this case there was far more doubt of the identity of the negro arrested for the crime, who was of a relatively good character. However, the victim's portrait was printed and circulated among the crowd, first, as an incentive to lynch the suspected negro, then as a pretext for driving the negroes out.

As we do not lay much emphasis on these or the previous crimes of Springfield negroes, which were in no way in excess of those of the corresponding social elements of the white population, so we do not lay much stress on the frenzied, morbid violence of the mob. Mob psychology is the same everywhere. It can begin on a little thing. But Springfield had many mobs; they lasted two days and they initiated a state of affairs far worse than any of the immediate effects of their violence.

Either the spirit of the abolitionists, of Lincoln and of [the murdered abolitionist publisher Elijah] Lovejoy must be revived and we must come to treat the negro on a plane of absolute political and social equality, or [Mississippi senator J. K.] Vardaman and [South Carolina senator Ben] Tillman will soon have transferred the race war to the North.

Already Vardaman boasts "that such sad experiences as Springfield is undergoing will doubtless cause the people of the North to look with more toleration upon the methods employed by the Southern people."

The day these methods become general in the North every hope of political democracy will be dead, other weaker races and classes will be persecuted in the North as in the South, public education will undergo an eclipse, and American civilization will await either a rapid degeneration or another profounder and more revolutionary civil war, which shall obliterate not only the remains of slavery but all the other obstacles to a free democratic evolution that have grown up in its wake.

Yet who realizes the seriousness of the situation, and what large and powerful body of citizens is ready to come to their aid?

Chapter 45

Jim Crow and the Limits of Freedom, 1890–1940

Neil R. McMillen

Neil R. McMillen, professor of history at the University of Southern Mississippi, is the author of The Citizens' Council: Organized Resistance to the Second Reconstruction, 1954–64 *(1971) and editor of* Remaking Dixie: The Impact of World War II on the American South *(1997).*

The following selection is excerpted from Dark Journey: Black Mississippians in the Age of Jim Crow. *Copyright © 1989 by the Board of Trustees of the University of Illinois. Used with the permission of the University of Illinois Press. Footnotes deleted.*

In Mississippi the color line was drawn in the attitudes and habits of its people, black and white, well before it was sanctioned by law. By 1885, three years before the state enacted its first Jim Crow statute, the practice of racial discrimination was so firmly fixed that the Jackson *New Mississippian* dismissed the integrationist arguments of Louisiana novelist George Washington Cable as "obnoxious sentiment" agreeable only to Yankee "negrophilists." . . .

In this favoring climate, white supremacy in Mississippi reached its logical extreme, sometimes through the force of statute, more often by dint of custom. Beginning in 1888 with a separate coach law, "an act to promote the comfort of passengers on railroad trains," the state mandated "equal but separate accommodations" in sleeping cars (1888), railroad waiting rooms (1888), and trolleys (1904). After 1906 cities of more than 3,000 were directed to maintain three rest rooms in train depots, one each for white men and women and one for "colored." Taxi drivers were forbidden in 1922 to carry both races at one time. A separate bus bill failed during World War II, largely for economic reasons. But state lawmakers kept up with changing mass-transit patterns by requiring black passengers in 1940 to sit behind white passengers on motor buses. On all conveyances black nurses in the company of their mistresses or white children were usually seated in white compartments. The object of these laws, whites insisted, was to prevent "friction, disorder, and general unhappiness." Without them, one white editor asserted in

1910, Mississippi would be the scene of "more race clashes and dead niggers than have been heard of since [R]econstruction."

Blacks and whites apparently never attended the same schools in Mississippi. In 1878, biracial education was proscribed by statute and in 1890 it was made unconstitutional. In the latter year, polling places, already effectively closed to blacks by force and fraud, were formally reserved for whites by ostensibly legal means. It was, of course, unlawful for the two races to intermarry or otherwise cohabit; state law also required the specification of race on all bills for divorce. Black and white patients were kept apart by law in hospitals, public or private, and were prevented even from using the same entrances to state health care facilities. Black and white nurses could tend only the sick of their own race; black nurses employed by public institutions were required to work under white supervision. An annex to the state asylum was reserved for black lunatics. Blacks and whites could not be lawfully incarcerated in the same jail cells, and they could not be confined or worked together in the penitentiary system.

In 1940, the state senate narrowly rejected a Jim Crow textbook measure that would have required the exclusion of all reference to voting, elections, and democracy in civic books used by black public school children. Two decades earlier, however, the legislature had outlawed the advocacy of social equality. Under a law of 1920, anyone found "guilty of printing, publishing or circulating printed, typewritten or written matter urging or presenting for public accept[ance] or general information, arguments or suggestions in favor of social equality or of intermarriage" was subject to a fine of not more than $500, imprisonment of not more than six months, or both.

Beyond these formal provisions for the recognition of caste, however, racial segregation in Mississippi was largely a matter of custom. Service establishments—including barber shops and beauty parlors, and such places of public amusement and public accommodation as hotels, lodging houses, restaurants, theaters, saloons, and billiard halls—did not fall under the purview of state law until 1956, when proprietors during Mississippi's period of "massive resistance" to federal civil rights law were authorized to "choose or select" their patrons. Nor did municipal ordinances fill this gap in the legal code. During the civil rights era after World War II, some communities attempted to curtail direct-action campaigns for voter registration and desegregation by formally requiring segregated waiting rooms and toilet facilities or by proscribing such activities as parading, demonstrating, picketing, praying, singing, or orating on public streets and sidewalks. Prior to the 1950s, however, municipal law largely ignored the color line. Some towns and cities before World War I indirectly legislated against blacks through curfew and vagrancy laws that, though officially color-blind, were applied primarily to blacks. But throughout the Jim Crow years municipal laws regulating interracial contact were limited almost exclusively to cemeteries and jails. Excepting these measures and the occasional provision of the construction of a white library or for the repair of a racially separate school building, the pre–civil rights era ordinances of Mississippi's towns and cities did not address racial issues.

Thus, while the state's canon of racial exclusion or separation could hardly have been more complete, it was in substantial part informal. In Mississippi, as elsewhere in the region, there was a pronounced movement after 1890 from a system of de facto to one of de jure segregation. Perhaps more than any other state, Mississippi, as Joel Williamson has written, was "thoroughly and deeply Radicalized" by turn-of-the-century Negrophobia: "To be a Mississippian . . . was ipso facto to be a Radical [Negrophobe] or else to be alone in one's racial views." Yet this radical distemper was never fully institutionalized and the process of formally transcribing custom into law was fitfully pursued and never finished. Indeed, Mississippi seems to have had *fewer* Jim Crow laws during the entire segregation period than most southern states.

The explanation for this apparent paradox—the relative exiguity of legal apparatus in the most racially restrictive state—can be found in the confidence of the dominant race. Having defined the limits of freedom early, almost at the moment of emancipation, white Mississippians capitalized on increasing northern indifference late in the nineteenth century by closing some remaining loopholes in their social code with laws requiring segregation in public transportation, health care facilities, and state institutions. But little additional legislation was required, for there was no need legally to enjoin the unthinkable. Where deeply ingrained social habit prohibited interracial dining and drinking, law was superfluous. Where popular convention and white sensibilities governed virtually every phase of interracial contact, there was little cause legally to separate black from white. Quite simply, in places of public accommodation, at funerals or weddings, in courtrooms, tent shows, theaters, and other places of public assembly—indeed wherever the two races came together—the forces of social habit and white opinion were in themselves usually sufficient to ensure that the races knew their places and occupied them with neither a statute nor a white or "colored" sign to direct the way. "White supremacy," as one black Natchezian has written, "was based on oral or traditional discrimination without legal sanction. Negroes accepted these traditions as a way of life and as a method of survival." Indeed, so powerful was the force of custom that even the legal pretense of equality in separation was unnecessary.

Let there be no confusion, however. Because blacks normally lived within the letter of the racial canon, it does not follow that they were comfortable in subordination or that they accepted white dominance as either natural or just. . . . [T]he black Mississippians' response to the tightening noose of white racism was anything but docile. When it was feasible—and sometimes when it was not—they resisted white injustices and asserted their civil and political rights. To a degree even they sometimes underestimated, they managed to modify in small but psychologically meaningful ways the terms of their subordination. In the end, however, their possibilities were severely circumscribed. Fettered by a social system based on black disfranchisement and economic dependence and, ultimately, on the force of white arms, they could condition their circumstance but not fundamentally alter it. A few chose virtual suicide through open defiance; a great many left the state in search of personal dignity and material betterment. Those who remained accepted white-imposed limits on black freedom because they had no practical alternative.

More often than not Jim Crow custom required exclusion, not merely separation. Most recreational facilities, public and private, denied admission to blacks. Roller rinks, bowling alleys, swimming pools, and tennis courts opened only to whites. Dr. Theodore Roosevelt Mason Howard of Mound Bayou built the state's first swimming pool for blacks during World War II; until then, he believed, Delta field hands had no public places to go after sundown except black churches, schools, and "jook joints." Cinemas normally maintained Jim Crow ticket windows and entrances, and seated blacks only in "buzzard roosts" or "nigger galleries." Municipal libraries with but a few exceptions were for whites only. Except for those facilities kept by educational institutions, the Carnegie Negro Library in Meridian was the state's only black library until after World War I. In Clarksdale, where black patrons had once been segregated in a small basement room of Carnegie Public Library, a "colored branch" was opened in 1930, in large part through black fund-raising efforts. After World War II, Jackson, Oxford, and other communities followed suit with black branch libraries of their own.

Black motorists apparently bought gasoline wherever it was sold, but few service stations maintained "colored" rest rooms, and none seem to have kept them clean. Inconvenience, humiliation, and uncertainty nearly always accompanied the black traveler. Overnight lodgers throughout the Jim Crow period depended largely on the hospitality of their race or the chance discovery of a Negro rooming house. According to the U.S. Department of Commerce, only Columbus, Laurel, McComb, Meridian, and Yazoo City had black-operated hotels by 1938. Early in the automobile age white opinion and the local constabulary in some communities arbitrarily denied black motorists access to the public streets. Many towns informally restricted parking to whites on principal thoroughfares; for a time following World War I, Jackson's Capitol Street, portions of Greenwood, the entire city of Laurel, and doubtless all or parts of many other communities were known to be open only to white motor traffic. In the Delta, custom forbade black drivers to overtake vehicles driven by whites on unpaved roads. "Its against the law for a Negro to pass a white man," a black Holmes Countian reported in 1940, "because the black man might stir up dust that would get on the white folks."

. . . To avoid trouble with the dominant race they had to know that what one community or one individual permitted, others might proscribe. Because Jim Crow could be a stickler for minutia, even the young learned to attend carefully to the variety of local and personal white customs. "Every town had its own mores, its own unwritten restrictions," a black educator remembered of the period before World War II. "The trick was to find out from local [black] people what the 'rules' were."

The "niggertown" slums that dotted the landscapes of most Mississippi cities and towns were also the consequence of white social pressure and black poverty, not of law. . . .

Whatever their location, black housing districts . . . were instantly recognizable. Hortense Powdermaker's description of Indianola in 1939 could be applied to nearly any town or city in the state: "The most striking physical feature of the community is the segregation of Negro and white dwellings, and the contrast

between the two sections." Black homes were nearly always found in the least desirable sections, across or along the tracks in any community served by a railroad,
in low-lying areas, along flood-prone rivers and drainage ditches, abutting cemeteries and jails, adjacent to or within the local version of a tenderloin or industrial
district. Public services were minimal, reflective of the Negro's inability to vote.
Street paving and lighting, sidewalks, sewage and water systems, and other such
amenities as a pre–World War II Mississippi community might afford were reserved with few exceptions for white residential areas. . . .

The Etiquette of Race

The black Mississippians' "place," as whites defined it, was always more behavioral than spatial in nature. . . . The point of caste was made most characteristically in the everyday courtesies whites routinely withheld from blacks. In Mississippi, as elsewhere in the South, good manners were emphasized from birth and
even close friends often addressed each other formally. Black Mississippians, on
the other hand, were generally called—even by much younger whites—only by
their first names, nicknames, or simply "boy" and "girl." A favored person, particularly when old, might be called "auntie" or "uncle," "sister" or "elder"; a
well-regarded lawyer "esquire," a physician "doctor," a half-educated one-room
school teacher "professor." For a decade or two following Reconstruction, the
leading men of the race, particularly such political figures as John Roy Lynch or
James Hill, were actually addressed in some newspapers as "Mr." After 1890,
however, conventional terms of respect were rarely extended. Until the practice
was stopped by federal authorities, postal officials in at least one Delta town ef-
faced "Mr." and "Mrs." on envelopes thought to be addressed to blacks. In 1909,
African Methodist Episcopal Bishop Edward Wilkinson Lampton and his family
were forced to flee Greenville for the North after the clergyman's daughter impru-
dently insisted that a local telephone operator address her as "Miss." . . .

White men, however chivalrous toward white women, neither tipped nor removed their hats for black women, and of course shook black hands only in exceptional circumstances. Blacks on the other hand were expected to show deference at every turn: to wait in nearly any line until all whites were served; to approach a white home only by the back door; to yield the right of way to whites
when walking or driving; to show respect even to the poor whites they privately
mocked as "peckerwoods." As blacks sometimes joked among themselves, white
sensitivities were so easily roiled in the timber districts of the Piney Woods that
heedful black customers ordered "Mr. Prince Albert" tobacco.

The racial code also prohibited all forms of interracial activity that might imply
equality: eating or drinking, card playing, a social chat in a white family's parlor
or front porch. In rural areas, prudent blacks did not smoke cigars in white company, wear dress clothes on weekdays, drive large or expensive cars, or otherwise
carry an air of prosperity. Indeed, any deviation from the Sambo style could result
in trouble. "There was a day when the average Negro householder was afraid to

paint his house and fix up his premises because of the attitude of some white man," conservative Piney Woods schoolmaster Laurence Jones observed. Not every sign of black ambition was perceived as "being uppity," Jones added, "but the fact remains that a Negro did not always feel as safe in a neat cottage with attractive surroundings as he did in a tumbling-down shack." As late as the 1930s, affluent black Natchezians commonly took the precaution of concealing their wealth by depositing savings in several banks and, occasionally, even in northern institutions. Virtually everywhere in the state, the most educated and articulate blacks knew when they could afford to be themselves and when they could not.

Nor was it enough merely to observe the letter of the social ritual. Lest they appear "sassy" or "sullen," the black anthropologist Allison Davis has written, blacks had to show ready acquiescence by inflection and gesture, to appear by every outward sign to be "willingly and cheerfully" humble. "Whites are not satisfied if Negroes are cool, reserved, and self-possessed though polite," John Dollard discovered in Sunflower County; "they must be actively obliging and submissive." Few blacks risked seeming "biggity," a black Lawrence Countian remembered of the early post–World War II years. "At that time in Mississippi it was tough enough being black; to be known as a smart nigger would have been unbearable." "The white man is the boss," another black Mississippian observed. "You got to talk to him like he is the boss."

Above all, black Mississippians were expected to avoid controversy with the dominant race. It was a breach of caste to contradict any white; an angry exchange, even when provoked, was a foolhardy act; a flash of black rage could be as dangerous as physical assault. Some subjects, in fact were simply too sensitive for interracial discourse. Richard Wright's catalog of forbidden topics is incomplete but suggestive: "American white women; the Ku Klux Klan; France; and how Negro soldiers fared while there; French women; [the black boxer] Jack Johnson; the entire northern part of the United States; the Civil War; Abraham Lincoln; U.S. Grant; General Sherman; Catholics; the Pope; Jews; the Republican party; slavery; social equality; Communism; Socialism; the 13th, 14th, and 15th Amendments to the Constitution; or any topic calling for positive knowledge or manly self-assertion on the part of the Negro."

By his own account, Wright never cultivated what black Mississippians called a "white folks' manner." While a Jackson teenager, he remembered in his autobiography, a classmate instructed him in the mid-1920s on the ways of survival: "Dick, look, you're black, black, *black,* see? . . . White people make it their business to watch niggers. . . . And they pass the word around. . . . When you're in front of white people, *think* before you act, *think* before you speak. Your way of doing things is all right among *our* people, but not for *white* people. They won't stand for it." Try as he did, the future novelist found it "utterly impossible . . . to calculate, to scheme, to act, to plot all the time." Although he marveled at how skillfully the young people of his generation "acted out" their assigned roles, he could not play the part himself. "I would remember to dissemble for short periods, then I would forget and act straight and human again, not with the desire to harm anybody, but merely forgetting the artificial status of race and class."

Wright's path carried him out of Mississippi, first to Memphis in 1925 and then, in 1927, to Chicago. Those who stayed behind necessarily learned more accommodative behavior, usually at a very young age. No doubt black children quite unconsciously discovered the social utility of deference by observing their elders. Yet a substantial body of social science literature—and the testimony of the people themselves—demonstrates that the black community left little to chance, that the black child was usually given "specific training . . . within his own family to enable him to adjust to . . . white demands." By most accounts, black children in Mississippi were fully "adjusted" by as early as five or six years of age and no later than ten or twelve. "Being black is part of the air you breath," observed Charles Evers (who in 1969 became the first black mayor of Fayette): "Our mothers began telling us about being black from the day we were born. The white folks weren't any better than we were, Momma said, but they sure thought they were. . . . We got it hammered into us to watch our step, to stay in our place, or to get off the street when a white woman passed." The form and content of their training, of course, were as varied as the families that provided them. Some children, like some adults, no doubt internalized their subservient roles and accepted caste degradations and the master-servant relationship as somehow natural. Yet a great many more rejected the white world view. Evers, once again, remembered with admiration the disingenuousness of his Uncle Mark Thomas who "used a lot of psychology on white people." He "yes *sirred* and no *sirred*"; "he played them for fools, and he got almost anything he wanted. He wasn't a *Tom*, but he played it real cool." James Farmer, on the other hand, looked back in anger, remembering the humiliation of deference. Of a childhood spent, in part, in Holly Springs, Farmer vividly recalled "the complexity and absurdity of southern caste" and his own anguish at "my father's accommodation to a system that made him less than a man." Though he recognized even then that the elder Farmer was a "highly complex man" who projected several "distinct faces," the ten-year-old son nevertheless resented his father's "compromising if not subservient" behavior and he vowed "I'll never do that when I grow up. They'll have to kill me." "Scared or not," he thought, "I'd never kowtow to meanness."

The "white folks' manner"—whether of the Sambo type so common to rural blacks or the more refined forms of deference adopted by the educated black middle class—was not to be taken at face value. Although he personally found "The 'Massa' style of politeness in negroes" distasteful, Thomas Pearce Bailey recognized it for what it was. "Most negroes are naturally astute in dealing with the white man. . . . I doubt whether the negro that always has the word 'Boss' on his lips is either especially polite or especially humble; rather he is habituated to servile words, or else cunning enough to know they serve as a convenient mask."

Black Mississippians rarely spoke so plainly to whites, but among themselves or to trusted outsiders they could be brutally candid. "I know just how to get along with them," a Cleveland day laborer told a black sociologist on the eve of World War II. "I can make them think they own the world. It is nothing but a lot of jive that I hand them." But for his poverty, he said, he'd find a more hospitable place to live and "all the white folks could kiss where the sun don't shine." "Mississippi is awful," a Bolivar County woman told the same researcher, "All the important things Negroes can't do." Such resentment could, of course, explode into violence. . . . [U]nduly imperious whites sometimes learned that the obliging comment and the passive demeanor of the field hand and the domestic servant could melt away in a moment of passion.

The best strategy, most blacks agreed, was to minimize contacts with whites wherever possible and to appear obedient when necessary. "I stayed out [of] the way," reported Phil Larkin, a Laurel sawmill hand. "When you were told to get off the streets, you would get off the streets." For themselves, pretended servility was widely regarded as a loathsome but necessary act; for their children, many parents found it increasingly unacceptable after World War I. After sending her son to a northern school, a Greenville mother explained her reluctance to see him return: "For him to accept the same abuses to which we, his parents, are accustomed, would make him much less than the man we would have him to be." In the same ambivalent spirit, other blacks looked to the visits of their northern relatives with a mixture of anticipation and dread, longing to see them but fearing they could not make the required behavioral adjustments.

All told, this was a social code of forbidding complexity. Largely unwritten and subject to widely varying individual and local interpretations, it was nevertheless enforced in uncounted and often trivial ways. Yet it was anything but irrational, and its purpose must not be underestimated. If violence was the "instrument in reserve"—social ritual regulated day-to-day race relations. Within the context of a biracial social order based on white dominance, it served much the same function as "good manners" in any society. For the most part, the code assured white control without the need for more extreme forms of coercion.

Finally, it seems useful to remember that the black journey through Jim Crow Mississippi was not one of unrelieved darkness and that even within the cramped boundaries of the social code there was often room for the civility that seemed second nature to the southern region. Whatever they may have lacked in theoretical idealism for the black race in general, not a few whites, irrespective of wealth or breeding, were capable of practical acts of great decency to its individual members. "Personal relationships, the solving touch of human nature," as journalist Ray Stannard Baker discovered at the turn of the century, "play havoc with political theories and generalities. Mankind develops not by rules but by exceptions to rules." Indeed, race relations in Mississippi, as elsewhere in the South, were too fraught with paradox and contradiction to be easily described. Individually, whites and blacks sometimes defined the rules of caste, forming deep attachments and lifelong friendships that served both races well. Linked by a web of feeling and mutual dependency spun by generations of intimate association, whites and blacks often managed to behave as individuals with a warmth and deeply felt concern that went beyond mere paternalism and seemed curiously out of place in a society dominated by race. Although whites generally read more into these acts of interracial humanity than did blacks, the personal affections and the frequent courtesies were nonetheless genuine and they form a small but important part of a very complex story.

The Instrument in Reserve

If the tenor of everyday race relations was generally even, the threat of physical aggression was nevertheless ever present. When violence shattered the racial calm, some whites deplored it and many attributed its "excesses" to ungovernable redneck passions. But white Mississippians of every class seemed to regard coercive acts against erring black individuals as object lessons of universal benefit to the subordinate race. A judicious flogging here—and, in extreme circumstances, an isolated lynching there—allayed white anxieties by reaffirming the color line and striking fear into black hearts.

Considerations of the utility of black fear seemed to recur in white conversation. In moments of agitation, white exchanges, as Dollard learned in the 1930s, turned easily, almost naturally, to stories of "the 'what I did with that uppity nigger' type." Some of this was loose talk, a kind of racial one-upmanship that should not be taken at face value. Yet the confidence and frequency with which white Mississippians described retributive racial violence, even to outsiders, suggest not only its pervasiveness but its general acceptability as an instrument of white control.

White violence and the racial fears that engendered it were telling refutations of the standard myths of white supremacy. For if the Afro-American had been by nature the "servile and contented darky" who, as whites endlessly assured themselves, cared little for citizenship and nothing at all for suffrage and social equality, force would not have been a requirement of white dominance and, indeed, the color line would have borne less watching. As it was, however, whites were forever monitoring the behavior of both races, watching for the telltale transgressions that betrayed the "nigger lover" and the "uppity nigger." Representative examples abound, but three should suffice.

In 1891 an "impudent" sleeping-car porter was dragged from a train near the town of Lake and flogged for having "sassed" a white telegrapher. The Vicksburg *Evening Post* reported that white vigilantes "did not want to shoot him," so he was merely "badly disfigured." In 1906, a northern white missionary was assaulted and run out of Columbus when he was caught walking "arm-in-arm in close conversation" with a local black, an offense "not often witnessed" in Mississippi. The Columbus *Commercial* thought the transgressor's primary assailant did "JUST WHAT ANY OTHER GOOD CITIZEN SHOULD HAVE DONE." In 1934, a white mob near Pelahatchee beat to death seventy-year-old Henry Bedford, a black tenant farmer. He was said to have "talked disrespectfully" to his landlord.

Chapter 46

Blacks and the First Red Scare

Theodore Kornweibel, Jr.

Theodore Kornweibel, Jr., professor of African American history at San Diego State University, is the author of No Crystal Stair: Black Life and the Messenger, 1917–1928 *(1976).*

The following selection is excerpted from Seeing Red: Federal Campaigns against Black Militancy, 1919–1925 *(Bloomington: Indiana University Press, 1998), footnotes deleted. Reprinted by permission of Indiana University Press.*

Although federal officials did not entirely succeed, they played an important role aborting the most militant period of African American history prior to the modern civil rights era.

. . . American political intelligence . . . came of age during World War I and the postwar Red Scare. Federal agents monitored the activities of thousands of left-wing suspects, as well as others who defied conventional liberal-conservative labels. Many of them were black, and the federal government's crusade to suppress their militancy has never been told in its entirety. From 1918 into the early twenties, any African Americans who spoke out forcefully for the race—editors, union organizers, civil rights advocates, radical political activists, and Pan-Africanists— were likely to be investigated by a network of federal intelligence agencies. The "crime" which justified such surveillance was almost always the ideas they expressed. Agents of the federal government watched these individuals, tapped their phones, rifled their offices, opened their mail, infiltrated their organizations, intimidated their audiences, and caused them to suffer the prospect of prosecution, all because their beliefs were anathema. These abuses were only compounded by the fact that most federal investigators were "ill-equipped to discern between reform and revolution, defined discontent as subversion and filled their files with a miscellaneous melange of truth, half-truth, and trivia."

The federal government's political intelligence system which took shape during and after the war became a permanent establishment. Despite the fact that the Bureau of Investigation (renamed the FBI in 1935) was ordered by Attorney General Harlan Fiske Stone to cease political spying in 1924, it never did so. Nor did the army or State Department halt their intelligence activities during the interwar

years. World War II added new urgency and additional targets to the domestic intelligence system, which then moved unchecked into the Cold War era.

From the perspective of African American history, the same continuity can be
charted. Black suspects were an important target during the first Red Scare. "Radicals" continued to be monitored in the twenties and thirties. During World War II
outspoken African Americans narrowly avoided federal repression. The most significant continuity from 1919 to modern times was the twin fear that black militancy was communist-inspired, and that it was particularly directed toward
achieving "social equality," even intermarriage, with whites.

J. Edgar Hoover's role in this process cannot be overestimated. In spear-heading
the Bureau of Investigation's anti-radical crusade in 1919, he fixated on the belief
that racial militants were seeking to break down social barriers separating blacks
from whites, and that they were inspired by communists or were the pawns of
communists. These notions became imbedded in the FBI and its director. Hoover's
hostility toward Dr. Martin Luther King, Jr., and the civil rights movement of the
1960s was shaped by the fears which Hoover conjured up in 1919 and which he
helped cement into the Bureau's institutional memory. . . .

When Attorney General A. Mitchell Palmer, in late 1919, submitted to the Senate a lengthy report on the *Investigation Activities of the Department of Justice,*
he warned that America stood at Armageddon: Bolshevists, anarchists, and sedi-
tionists were besieging the nation. As part of their diabolical plans, "practically all
of the radical organizations in this country have looked upon the Negroes as particularly fertile ground for the spreading of their doctrines. These radical organizations have endeavored to enlist Negroes on their side, and in many respects have
been successful." As a consequence, "the Negro is 'seeing red.'"

Palmer's phrase carried a double meaning. As he (and Hoover and other intelligence bureaucrats) saw it, black rage had been unleashed, and not only in the previous summer's riots: "Defiance and insolently race-centered condemnation of the
white race is to be met with in every issue of the more radical publications." But in
fact militant blacks weren't anti-white; they were either expressing a Pan-Africanism which celebrated blackness, or expressing their hatred of lynching and mob
violence. Palmer and others in like position lost touch with reality on this score.
The second meaning implied even greater danger: there was said to exist "a well-
concerted movement among a certain class of Negro leaders of thought and action
to constitute themselves a determined and persistent source of radical opposition
to the Government and to the established rule of law and order," who proclaimed
"an outspoken advocacy of the Bolsheviki or Soviet doctrines." What the federal
intelligence establishment had done was use the "red" label to delegitimize blacks'
desires for peace, security, and liberation from the racial status quo. The Bolshevik
revolution was scarcely two years old, and guardians of every American orthodoxy—racial, political, economic—had already learned the power and usefulness
of red baiting.

There is a great irony here: Palmer, Hoover, and their peers, like bulls facing a
toreador, were also "seeing red." They raged against a black militancy whose
main weapon was rhetoric; they conjured up a communist bogeyman to avoid ac-

knowledging that blacks had genuine grievances against the racial status quo; they claimed that blacks would be happy and contented if not for the evil machinations of aliens and their subversive doctrines. On matters of race, the federal intelligence agencies served their country poorly. . . .

Overarching all other issues, in the months following the Armistice, was the fear that communism would spread across Europe and then invade the shores of America. As President Wilson sailed for Europe in March for a second round of peace negotiations, Germany was rocked by a general strike as part of an unsuccessful Bolshevik revolt. Commenting to his private physician on board the U.S.S. George Washington, President Wilson confided the fear that black soldiers returning from Europe would be "our greatest medium in conveying bolshevism to America." His apprehension was not unique. During the war many whites had believed that African Americans were less than wholeheartedly patriotic and were particular targets of enemy subversion, easily duped into acts of disloyalty. After 1918 these images evolved into fears that "the Negro is seeing Red." Federal intelligence targeted radicalism and militancy among blacks at the same time as native whites and foreigners suffered the same sort of attacks. Especially singled out were black periodicals.

A vibrant tradition of militant racial journalism was well established by World War I. William Monroe Trotter's *Boston Guardian,* founded in 1901, challenged the conservative strategies of Booker T. Washington. Robert Abbott's *Chicago Defender,* from its birth in 1905, excelled in condemning lynching and other examples of racism and, after 1915, exhorted blacks to leave the hated South for new freedoms and economic opportunities in northern cities. The National Association for the Advancement of Colored People, established in 1909, quickly found a militant voice in the *Crisis,* begun and edited by the well-known scholar and anti-Bookerite W. E. B. Du Bois. An even more militant "New Crowd Negro journalism" was born during the war, beginning with the socialist and anti-war *Messenger* in 1917, edited by transplanted southerners A. Philip Randolph and Chandler Owen. The following year witnessed the birth of Marcus Garvey's nationalist weekly *Negro World* and three monthlies: Cyril Briggs's *Crusader*; William Bridges's *Challenge*; and Hubert Harrison's *Negro Voice.* By the end of the war it was clear to observers of black journalism that African Americans, in many northern and some southern cities, were more insistent on change than ever before. The new militancy could neither be missed nor ignored.

Racial leadership, too, had evolved and matured in the two decades since Booker T. Washington's ascendancy to national influence. Du Bois's short-lived Niagara Movement helped crystalize opposition to Washington's advocacy of accommodation and conciliation toward white southerners. Its intention to revive the voice of protest against injustice and to fight for civil rights was adopted by the new NAACP. With Washington's death in 1915, new leadership styles and approaches to racial issues could more easily be tried. As hundreds of thousands of African Americans streamed out of the South to find wartime jobs in booming northern urban centers, would-be leaders like Garvey, Randolph, Owen, and Harrison mounted street-corner soapboxes to proclaim militant messages and

promote socialism, black nationalism, and other novel "isms." The New Crowd
Negro was born, intent on arousing the silent masses and challenging the ways
whites had defined civil rights and race relations for half a century. The democratic idealism of Woodrow Wilson's wartime rhetoric only increased the sense of
urgency and demand. By the end of the war America's white majority would be
confronted with demands for change as far reaching as those voiced during the
civil rights era two generations later. . . .

During the Red Scare following World War I, the *Crisis* advocated full civil
rights with the *Messenger* going even further, demanding complete social equality.
Neither goal was acceptable to Hoover in 1919, because each would destroy the
assumptions and power relationships on which white Americans organized their
present and planned their future. Both, he believed, would also weaken the nation
and leave it vulnerable to foreign ideologies and subversion. Nothing seemed fundamentally different to Hoover in the 1960s as King and others posed the most
militant threat ever to white supremacy, even though their weapon was nonviolence. Full civic and social equality for African Americans was as unthinkable then
as it had been two generations before. The Bureau's response to legitimate black
aspirations changed little if at all in fifty years; the federal intelligence community's hostility to black freedom had been engraved in stone in 1919 and 1920.

Chapter 47

The Second Klan

Nancy MacLean

Nancy MacLean is professor of history at Northwestern University. She is currently researching a social and cultural history of affirmative action.

The following selection is excerpted from Behind the Mask of Chivalry *by Nancy MacLean. Copyright © 1994 by Nancy MacLean. Used by permission of Oxford University Press, Inc. Footnotes deleted.*

The subordination of African Americans . . . undergirded the entire Southern economy: "the negro," as a representative of the Athens Chamber of Commerce put it, "is our only and best form of domestic and general labor." While Klansmen rarely spoke of this reliance openly—to have done so would have been to recognize black contributions to America—in practice they sought in numerous ways to ensure that blacks would remain a cheap, unorganized labor supply. Like its Reconstruction predecessor, the Klan of the 1920s may thus have posed its mission more often as the defense of white culture than as the restraint of black labor. But those familiar with the South understood that the distinction was academic: the purpose of the former was to safeguard the latter. "The races in the South may be divided into two classes," as an Athens mayor observed hyperbolically in 1923: "the Employer and the Employee." And, in fact, the second Klan, like the first, aspired to control black workers. When [Imperial Wizard William] Simmons asserted of his predecessors after Emancipation, "it's all rot about the K.K. swinging [lynching] niggers—niggers were loafing and K.K. made 'em go to work," the potential uses of his own organization could not have been lost on his listeners.

The anti-labor animus of the Klan's commitment to white supremacy appeared most clearly in other forums, however: namely, in the racial themes that pervaded the order's anti-communism and anti-Catholicism. Indeed, one key aspect of the threat Klansmen saw in communism was the unprecedented commitment of its white followers to black rights. The Klan thus denounced "Bolshevist agitation" for interracial trade unionism and pointed with alarm to the Communist Party's overtures to African Americans. Klansmen believed that communism would mean the end of racial hierarchy. The "worst" offense of Communist union organizers in North Carolina, in the view of the *Kourier,* was their advocacy of "negro equality."

Similarly, the Klan denounced the Catholic church for furthering "social equality." Klansmen attacked the church, in particular, for its recruitment and training of black priests to serve interracial congregations. The doctrine of the equality of believers and the practice of integrated congregations had the potential, in Klan eyes, to upend the social order. A Mississippi female Klan supporter thus summoned the specter of slave rebellions to depict the dangers of blacks' converting to Catholicism. The result would be the "horrors of Haiti and San Domingo": black men "yearning for the fertile fields and fair women of their masters." More generally, the Klan charged the Catholic church with being "after the negro as one of its major steps in dominating the American republic," an appeal to time-honored republican fears of those with no stake in society being used as an entering wedge for despots.

The Klan's varied attacks on African Americans, Jews, and immigrants in fact converged on a common core goal: securing the power of the white petite bourgeoisie in the face of challenges stemming from modern industrial capitalism. The Klan sought to deny political rights to those whom it perceived as threats to that power. Indeed, one purpose of Klan racialism was to convince people that only a small, select group was "fit" for self-government. Imperial Wizard Simmons insisted, for example, that the supposed inability of Africans and most Asians to control their own affairs mandated carrying "the 'white man's burden'" well into the future. More generally, he described universal suffrage as "a very dangerous political doctrine." The ballot was not a right, but "a privilege," and neither blacks nor immigrants deserved it. And while they were hardly the primary target of such assertions, poorer whites were not immune. Simmons himself insinuated that both property and literacy qualifications should apply to all voters.

His successor candidly announced that genuine democracy would impede the Klan's goals. "The Nordic can easily survive and rule," Evans explained, "if he holds for himself the advantages" secured by his forefathers. His supremacy would be lost, however, "if he surrenders those advantages" to immigrants and their children. The "Klansman's Creed" thus declared, "I believe my rights in this country are superior to those of foreigners." African Americans and immigrants were thus the most immediate and aggrieved victims of what by the Klan's own admission was a wider attack on democracy conducted in defense of property and privilege. In this way, class perspectives, motives, and goals were at the nerve center of the Klan's racialism. Racism enabled Klansmen to reconcile conflicting impulses: on one hand, their regard for white popular sovereignty and their commitment to private property; on the other hand, their discomfort with growing economic concentration and their fear of genuine democracy in a society with a massive, lately quite militant, working class. Yet the Klan's construction of "race" was also shaped profoundly by gender-specific perspectives and motives.

Sexual themes saturated the Klan's racial agitation. So obsessively that it appeared intentional, Klansmen used bodily imagery to discuss race. Such terms as "proper blending of blood," "insoluble and indigestible" races, "mongrel population," "body politic," "pure and undefiled" blood, "racial pollution," and the like infested Klan lexicon. But more important to the order's appeal were its oft-repeated allegations that men of other so-called races coveted native-born white women in various and distinctive ways. In effect, Klansmen turned conflicts between classes and ethnic groups into rivalry over which men might possess which women. . . .

Unquestionably, the evocation of sexual danger did shore up the white elite. But such interpretations fail to clear up the real enigma; why subordinate whites fell for the sleight of hand. That is, how could such rhetoric rally the whites who seemingly stood to gain little? Because other kinds of power were also at stake. The charge of rape, as historian Jacquelyn Dowd Hall astutely observed, derived its power from the fact that it "was embedded . . . in the heart not only of American racism, but of [white] American attitudes toward women as well." At the same time as it enforced white supremacy, lynching also served to remind white women of their prescribed asexual, subordinate, and dependent roles in Southern society. To counterpoise economic concerns and sexual anxieties is thus to create a false dichotomy.

Yet the evidence suggests that the prominence of sexual themes in the Klan's racism also had another important source. Male dominance and white supremacy shared common material roots in this setting. The key to the merging of economics and sexuality in Klan racism was the order's fealty to a vision of white petty-producer households in which women and youth were dominated by adult men. The Klan's racialism was thus grounded in the same domestic and social arrangements that its male supremacy and sexual conservatism issued from. Old traditions persisted in modified form in the way the male household head's control over the labor power and sexuality of his dependents helped ensure economic viability for contemporary farm and mill households. For all its irrational aspects, then, fear of female autonomy had a rational basis in the labor and service requirements of household survival. So, too, did control over women buttress racial hierarchy. Since racial affiliation was traced through the lineage of the mother, policing the borders of white society required the regulation of white women's sexuality. Not surprisingly, then, sexual relations between white women and black men became "the strongest taboo of the system." . . .

Yet, whereas the Klan used vigilantism to buttress rigidly demarcated gender roles among whites, it almost never attacked blacks for intraracial morals offenses. The only morals allegations it appears the Klan flogged blacks for were interracial infractions, such as selling moonshine to whites or having sex or marrying across the color line. Since one function of the Klan's conservative moral code was to solidify white supremacy by constituting "respectable" whites as a cohesive community distinct from blacks, the order's lack of interest in regulating morality within the black community made sense.

Indeed, the Klan worked diligently to deny blacks access to white models of gender. Klansmen made no pretense of offering even nominal protection to black women; they, like immigrant women, were by definition beyond the pale of the Klan's vaunted chivalry. Like black men, they, too, could be intimidated, kicked, beaten, or whipped; not even old age or pregnancy would shield them. The order also tried to deprive black men of the very signs of masculinity it encouraged white men to display. Thus, Klansmen were liable to attack black men for standing up for their rights as citizens, for amassing property, for protecting their kinfolk, or for defending their homes.

Indeed, most Klan attacks on African Americans stemmed from their assertions of their own rights or defense of those of other blacks. Efforts to register and vote by Southern blacks particularly irked the Klan. It employed parades and vigilante violence to "intimidate" prospective black voters and "make them more amenable to influence," in the euphemistic words of one former Klan leader. S. S. Mincey, a seventy-year-old black Republican leader in south central Georgia, was thus kidnapped and flogged to death in 1930 for his political activities; others received threats because of their protests against segregation or their participation in the NAACP.

Resistance to laboring on whites' terms—referred to by the Klan as "failure to work"—could also result in persecution. Still other African Americans suffered Klan vengeance for offering economic competition to whites or having achieved success on their own. The order set fire to black businesses and drove their owners from Waycross, Georgia, in 1922; it whipped black farm owners in other parts of the state to make them sell their property at a loss. In Springfield, Missouri, local Klansmen threatened a black physician on the grounds that he was performing abortions on white women, a baseless charge to camouflage their real complaint: the man's wife was a leading NAACP activist, and together the couple had "accumulated good property."

Finally, no matter how upright their morals, whites who defied the Klan's injunctions to class harmony might also suffer its wrath. As early as 1918, local Klan chapters burned crosses, kidnapped and beat or flogged union leaders, and ran activists out of town to prevent labor organizing and strikes. By 1923, an informed journalist could conclude that "the Klan is nearly everywhere and always an enemy of organized labor." Its record led even the politically timorous American Federation of Labor to adopt resolutions condemning the activities of masked organizations and the Ku Klux Klan specifically.

But if the argument so far advanced is true—if vigilante violence was Klan thought in action—then one must wonder why more evidence of such activities is not easily accessible. After all, it might be argued, even the hundreds of episodes reported in the national press seem few compared to the numbers enrolled in the Klan. Some recent studies have argued essentially this point: the Klan of this era, the authors say, was not particularly violent. Indeed, they explicitly distinguish it on these grounds from the Klans built during Reconstruction and the civil rights movement.

The problems with such arguments are many. First of all, they display the same fallacious emphasis on quantification that led a few historians in the early 1970s to play down the extent and significance of whipping as a means of control by slaveholders in the antebellum South. As Herbert Gutman pointed out in a biting critique of such efforts, not every slave had to be whipped regularly for the owners to make their will felt. Similarly, an episode of Klan flogging affected, not just the individual victim, but every member of the community who learned of it. Evoking this violence as they did, even warnings could instill sufficient terror to make people change their behavior. More generally, though, the problem with attempts to characterize the second Klan as nonviolent is their epistemological innocence: their assumption that, if evidence of violence does not appear in the usual sources—newspapers in particular—then it must not have occurred. Such interpretations have also tended to accept Klan leaders' public proclamations against "lawlessness."

Klan leaders did, after all, repeatedly deny that their movement engaged in extralegal activity, and the historian cannot simply ignore these disavowals. But to accept them at face value would be naive and dangerous. The same men, after all, regularly denied—sometimes in the same breath—that the Reconstruction-era Klan was violent or that their own organization was racist or anti-Semitic. The occasions of such denials were also important. They usually came after the public revelation of some vigilante activity attributed to the Klan. As part of an effort to evade prosecution, the disavowals were obviously self-interested.

A close reading of the wording of the denials suggests further cause for skepticism. Klan speakers and publications often purposefully qualified their affirmations of respect for the law. A guide to organizing Klan chapters spoke of how the Klan's investigating committee should aid law enforcement personnel "in the *proper* performance to their legal duties." The Klan's Constitution bound members "to protect and defend the [U.S.] Constitution . . . and all laws passed in *conformity thereto,* and to protect the States and the people thereof from *all invasion of their rights from any sources whatsoever.*" In other words, some laws were constitutional, therefore worthy of defense; others, it would seem, could be defied in the name of the people. Which was which, presumably, was up to the Klan.

Here the exclusivity of the Klan's vision of American citizenship played a critical enabling role. For the movement did not believe that anyone other than native-born, Protestant white people had the right to a say in American law-making; blacks, Jews, and Catholics had no place in public affairs. This is what Klan leaders meant when they said their movement had only "one purpose": "to put the Government of the United States into the hands of none but American citizens." Laws passed in the interests of other groups could thus be represented as necessarily illegitimate, while regulation of the activities of such "aliens" by true citizens was by definition lawful. African Americans were particularly vulnerable in this line of reasoning because the assumption that they were outsiders to American democracy and unworthy of due process of law was so ingrained in the dominant culture. Philosophically, then, Klansmen would have had little difficulty justifying vigilantism as law-abiding conduct.

In practical terms, their organization was also well suited to supporting and protecting such activities. Why don masks and robes if there was nothing to hide? "It is not logical," as one former member observed, "to believe that if the intent and purpose is good and for the general welfare, the members will be ashamed, or afraid, to be known." The order's commitment to strict confidentiality could also serve clandestine ends. Members were warned to keep quiet, especially about "Secret Work." "Just remember," concluded one such counsel, "even a sucker would not get caught if he kept his mouth shut." Nothing was left to chance. Members were tutored in "complete obligation," "secrecy and obedience," and "loyalty." As one manual for organizers bluntly put the code: "he who violates the standard ought to be made to pay the price." The warnings were not idle. When Klan secrets leaked in Athens, the organization saw the danger as sufficiently serious that it hired a private investigator to find out how and by whom. Those who violated their oath of loyalty to the Klan could suffer expulsion, social ostracism, and sometimes violence or even the threat of assassination.

Some evidence exists, moreover, that top Klan leaders actively fostered vigilante activities. Former Klan members reported that officials from the Imperial Palace—Simmons and [fellow Imperial Wizard Hiram] Evans included—tutored regional warlords in the how-tos of "rough stuff." For their part, members of the Simmons block, once deposed, charged that their former organization took upon itself "the purpose of regulating men and women at the whipping post, blackmail, murder, and arson." The testimony of disgruntled members should of course be handled with care. Still, the charges were remarkable both for their unanimity—despite coming from widely scattered parts of the country—and for their singularity. It is difficult to imagine the same things being said of any other contemporary organization, no matter how much it had disappointed its members.

Similarities in the methods employed by Klan floggers in different areas lend further credibility to accusations that the practice was institutionalized. The commonest pattern was for the Klan to discover the offending behavior either through its own "intelligence"-gathering apparatus or through a complaint made by a third party. The case would then be turned over [to] the chapter Klokann, or "investigating committee" head. If this body found the accused guilty, the first "corrective" act was usually a warning designed to intimidate": a note, a night-time visit, or a cross-burning or parade at their home. If the offenders failed to oblige, a group of Klansmen, often robed and wearing black masks—known internally as "the wrecking crew"—would abduct them from their homes under the cover of night. After taking them to a secluded site, usually a spot outside city limits, Klansmen would flog their victims with as many as fifty lashes with a thick leather strap.

Scattered evidence also suggests, however, that not all Klan members had access to knowledge of these activities. Some Atlanta-area members said that they had belonged for several years before they became aware of the local "secret committee" that carried out flogging operations. The Exalted Cyclops was fully aware of its activities, however; he appointed its chief—sometimes a different one for each action—and passed on complaints for action. The members of the committee were known only to its head—who drafted them—and the Exalted Cyclops.

On the rare occasions when Klan members were indicted or their methods exposed, Klan leaders followed what seemed a prefabricated script. As soon as arrests were made, national and state Klan officials set to work to thwart prosecution with public denials of culpability and efforts to suppress testimony and destroy evidence. While publicly condemning extralegal violence, the Klan quickly hired lawyers for its accused members. Its representatives also tried to intimidate witnesses, and sometimes journalists and even judges as well. The Imperial Office also sent its own "investigators" to stymie inquiry in the guise of aiding it. If a case did reach trial, Klan officials instructed subpoenaed members to lie on the stand—as they themselves did to the press—and tried to ensure juries stacked with their fellows. Here honor worked as insulation; historically, the rule of honor had helped to solidify military bodies against civilian interference. If none of these subterfuges succeeded, the Klan might protect itself with the specious claim that the local "secret" committees acted autonomously, without the formal authorization of the parent order.

These methods almost never failed. So efficacious were they that the governor of Oklahoma found he had to declare martial law and institute military tribunals in order to successfully prosecute Klan vigilantism. But he soon found himself impeached by the Klan-dominated state legislature. Not until 1987, in fact, was the Ku Klux Klan as a body ever successfully held accountable for the violence its members perpetrated in service to its goals.

Seen in this light, the relative lack of documentation of Klan vigilantism is much less puzzling. Indeed, the gaps in the record appear rather as yet another illustration of the Klan's remarkable power. That power included the capacity to shape—and distort—the historical record by keeping victims silent and journalists and courts at bay. Indeed, the Klan seems to have practiced violence most commonly where its members could get away with it—and, thus, where evidence of it would be least likely to survive.

Klan leaders were not stupid; they took care to prevent haphazard violence. To have engaged in vigilantism wherever they had members would have been to invite destruction of their movement. After all, there were parts of the country where its chapters could not even assemble publicly without risking counterattack. In many areas of the Northeast, for example, Catholics in particular mobilized fierce counter-demonstrations against the Klan. In such areas, Klan violence would have invited physical reprisal. Such people also cast ballots and sat on juries. Klans in areas in which Catholics, African Americans, or Jews were a significant part of the electorate, or where white non-members became aroused, might find themselves facing hostile courts or being subjected to restrictive laws, such as the anti-mask legislation proposed in several states and passed in a few. In short, where Klansmen and their sympathizers were in a minority, to have antagonized opponents would have invited bad publicity, prosecution, political battles, and possible retaliation.

A successful campaign of terror required conditions found in a different kind of setting: a restricted electorate, compliant politicians, a cowed press, and the active complicity of law enforcement officials. This environment was most common in the South. Hence it is not surprising that Southern Klans practiced the lion's share of vigilantism. They did it because they could. In the South, particularly in small towns and rural areas, the potential gains from vigilantism outweighed the costs. The groups who most barred the Klan's way in other areas of the country lacked power here: immigrants, because of their small numbers; workers, because of the Southern ruling class's fierce opposition to labor organization; and blacks, because of the coercive apparatus of Jim Crow. The only force left with any power to oppose the Klan, then, was the small fraction of the Southern elite that disdained it, men and women not notable for stiff resistance to injustice.

Operating in such an environment, many Southern public officials, perhaps most, gave tacit endorsement to Klan vigilantism, especially in the unsettled years immediately following the war. As a result, those responsible were seldom indicted and almost never convicted. In Georgia and Alabama, for example, governors Clifford Walker and Bibb Graves conspired from their executive offices to avert legal punishment for their fellow Klan members. Walker commuted the sentence of one of the only Georgia Klansmen indicted for vigilante activity. For his part, Walker's predecessor, Thomas Hardwick, assigned to the investigation of one flogging a sheriff and a police chief the victim had already identified as among his assailants.

Some evidence in fact suggests that the Klan enrolled or enlisted the support of law enforcement officials—police, prosecutors, justices of the peace, and judges—before initiating vigilante activity, presumably to stave off indictments. Such men, after all, had a history in the South at least of habitual violence against blacks who asserted their rights. Their off-duty practices were but one end of a continuum of repression; "extralegal force supplements and supports the legal action if it is considered uncertain or inadequate." Imperial Wizard Simmons even stated once, in defending the Klan from charges of vigilantism against blacks, that "there is never a stand taken unless an officer of the law supervise[s] K.K." In cases that did come to light, time after time it surfaced also that police or other law enforcement personnel had either participated in the violence, suggested that the Klan undertake it, belonged to the order, or condoned its activities more indirectly. Even Southern police who did not actually belong themselves were unlikely to disapprove of Klan violence. "They liked them," one Atlanta non-member on the police force recalled of his fellow officers' attitudes to the Klan; "they didn't have nothing against the Ku Klux." Some victims, having recognized law enforcement officials among their assailants, understandably believed prosecution futile.

It was. Since particularly in less populous rural counties, native-born white property-holders (those likeliest to sympathize with the Klan even if they did not belong) generally staffed the juries, the chances of conviction were scant in any case. Moreover, the few indicted Klansmen could look forward, in some states, to having fellow members decide their appeals in state supreme courts. "Experience seems to indicate," observed the Commission on Interracial Cooperation in 1927, "that in most American communities the members of lynching or flogging bands need have little or no fear of prosecution."

The rarity of prosecution resulted also from the vulnerability of the victims singled out by Klan floggers. Black residents especially appeared convinced that efforts to seek legal redress locally might only bring worse trouble upon them. Some would appeal to national organizations in Washington, D.C., without even bothering to try to obtain relief from local authorities. Their dismal appraisal of the prospects for redress through ordinary channels was well-founded in a state like

Georgia, where addressing a black female witness with the respectful title of "Miss" could land a black man in jail for contempt of court.

While black victims of the Klan had no hope of justice, most white victims had little more. Indeed, "through fear or shame," few of the Klan's white victims reported to legal authorities. "It is not considered an honor to be whipped by masked men," as one sardonic Georgian put it in 1927. A North Carolinian opponent of the Klan later explained that much of its support derived from a public consensus that "generally speaking the [white] people that they punished had a whole lot lacking in their character and they deserved some punishment." According to him, non-Klan white residents would point to people "leading these immoral lives, and they've been doing it for ten years and the children out there are suffering and nothing's being done about it. So the Klan did something about it; they put the whip to them." Neighbors like these were unlikely to indict or convict.

The most instructive illustration, however, of the factors conspiring to limit the documentary record of Klan violence comes from the case of a multiple lynching in Aiken, South Carolina. As a lynching, it was unusual as an episode of Klan vigilantism in the 1920s, which most commonly involved intimidation or violence short of murder. Yet, as a case of uncommon crime that would seem difficult to cover up, its resolution speaks eloquently about how less noteworthy incidents would be handled. The case was that of the Lowmans, a black family who lived in the countryside outside Aiken. In the spring of 1926, a sheriff and his deputies came to the Lowman home to arrest one of the sons on suspicion—later proved baseless—of selling whiskey. Finding him missing, the sheriff hit the young man's sister, Bertha, in the mouth; when Mrs. Lowman came to her daughter's rescue, he shot her through the heart. Hearing the shots, Lowman men ran in from the fields. A scuffle and weapon fire ensued, in which the sheriff was killed. The bullet most likely came from the gun of one of his own deputies, but the three Lowman siblings were arrested all the same. A "farcical" trial in a courtroom packed with armed Klan members resulted in death sentences for the two brothers and life imprisonment for their sister. Outraged, a black lawyer from Columbia, South Carolina, appealed the case to the State Supreme Court and won them a retrial. One of the brothers was acquitted as a result. Upon hearing of the acquittal, a mob began to gather in Aiken. Knowing what was coming, white men and women from as far as ninety miles away began to converge on the site. The mob marched on the jail and carried the prisoners outside town to the site where the crowd, now numbering almost a thousand, had gathered. There, Bertha Lowman "begged so piteously for her life that members of the mob had a hard time killing her." But they did. The mob leaders freed Bertha and her brothers and told them to run—only to fire dozens of shots into their backs when they did, to the glee of the crowd.

No one was indicted for the willful murder of Clarence, Damon, and Bertha Lowman. The coroner's jury charged the crime to "parties unknown." The governor paid lip service to the need to apprehend the guilty parties, but did nothing. Investigating for the NAACP, Walter White found out why. The dead sheriff and the deputies who first visited the Lowman home were all Klansmen. So was the new sheriff, who handed over his prisoners over to the mob without any struggle, and the Aiken attorney—and newly elected state representative—at whose office the murder was planned. The mob itself was organized, led, and staffed by the Klan—although it tried to enlist non-members so as to be able to maintain later, if need be, that the lynching "was not a Klan affair." White supplied the governor with the names, addresses, and occupations of the killers in the mob, all of whom belonged to the Klan. Fourteen of the twenty-four men were some kind of law enforcement personnel. Among the spectators at the lynching were the president and vice-president of one local manufacturing company, superintendents from three plants, and an overseer from another—along with three of the governor's own cousins. Not surprisingly, in these circumstances, the lynchers were never prosecuted. That fact alone should convince us of the dangers of uncritical reliance on public sources in writing the history of the Klan. If Walter White had not investigated, historians today would never have heard of the Lowman case, much less known of the leading part the Klan played in it. The official record would have had us conclude that the culprits were "parties unknown." Rarely does a story so vividly illustrate the maxim that history is written by the victors.

In short, the decision about whether to use violence was for the Klan a tactical one, one answered in the affirmative most often south of the Mason-Dixon line. Yet, even in areas where it seemed too risky to try at the moment, the possibility of violence at some later date loomed. For Klan culture generated a propensity to vigilantism like an acorn does an oak; all the seed needed to grow was nourishment from good soil. Vigilante violence was the concentrated expression of that culture, of the brutal determination to maintain inherited hierarchies of race, class, and gender that Klansmen sought to conceal with a mask of chivalry. "The only reason that men are not tarred and feathered, whipped and driven from their homes and deprived of their constitutional rights in Ohio," observed one astute contemporary, "is because the klan is not strong enough. When it is," he predicted, "those things will come."

The Black and Progressive Response

Chapter 48

Black Workers from Reconstruction to the Great Depression

Nell Irvin Painter

Nell Irvin Painter, professor of history and director of African American Studies at Princeton University, is the author of Exodusters: Black Migration to Kansas after Reconstruction *(1977),* Standing at Armageddon: The United States, 1877–1919 *(1987), and* Sojourner Truth: A Life, A Symbol *(1996), and editor of* The Narrative of Hosea Hudson: His Life as a Black Communist in the Deep South *(1979).*

The following selection is reprinted from Working for Democracy: American Workers from the Revolution to the Present, *ed. Paul Buhle and Alan Dawley. Copyright © 1985 by the Board of Trustees of the University of Illinois. Used with the permission of the University of Illinois Press.*

For another selection by Painter, see chapter 132.

Black workers' relationship to unions and labor politics is closely tied to black participation in politics, their minority status in nearly all occupations, and the race prejudice of white workers. Between 1865 and 1941 the record is pretty dismal. Until the late 1930s, when hundreds of thousands of Negroes had migrated from the South to the North, where they could vote and exercise political power, and when the new unions of the Congress of Industrial Organizations (CIO) began including them, black workers lacked effective voices in their workplaces and in the political arena.

The era of exclusion may now have passed forever from the labor scene. As long as Afro-Americans wield enough political clout to insure fair employment practices, labor will not easily return to the racist practices of the past. Yet as long as unemployment remains disproportionate, jobless black workers, particularly young people, provide a labor pool that threatens the achievements of organized labor in wages, work safety, and job security. It is possible that an anti-union administration in Washington may buy the allegiance of Negroes with low-paying non-union jobs, reopening a racial breach in the workforce that would be detrimental to all of labor.

After Slavery

A. Philip Randolph, the most prominent black unionist, noted that "the labor movement cannot afford to be split along any lines." That sentiment has been honored in words, at least, by nearly every federation of labor—if not by individual locals and unions or on the shop floor—from the time of the earliest post–Civil War labor organizations.

Between 1866 and the early 1870s the National Labor Union gave occasional lip service to the idea of organizing Negroes, but partisan politics and racial antipathy frustrated any meaningful action. Meanwhile, blacks organized their own union, the Colored National Labor Union, which lasted from 1869 to 1874 in the Washington area. This organization exemplified much that has typified black political activity from before the Civil War to the present time, for though nearly every Negro, male and female, works for a living, black leaders are not noted for their working-class demeanor. If anything, outstanding blacks have tended more to resemble gentlemen than workingmen.

Accordingly, many of the figures prominent in the Colored National Labor Union were not workers but race spokesmen, journalists and politicians such as Frederick Douglass, Henry Highland Garnet, and John Mercer Langston. But each of these men had worked hard as a youngster, and they shared a concern for the working-class interests of blacks that only a union could address. They also agreed that the Republican party best represented their interests as a race.

In the South, where most blacks lived until the 1960s, the Republican party in the late 1860s and early 1870s was the party of working people. In a region where the great majority farmed, land tenure and credit practices were prime concerns. To the extent that either party represented working-class interests in the heyday of black voting (1867–76), the Republican party stood for its constituency of newly enfranchised blacks. In the best conditions, as in Louisiana or South Carolina, Republicans in southern legislatures championed free public schools, land reform, and exemption laws (which placed personal property beyond the reach of foreclosure when a crop did not pay the landowner's or shopkeeper's share or rent). This identification of the Republican party with black interests outlived racial and economic realities, moving one black journalist to note, in 1918, the absurdity of "a race of tenants and workers accepting political leaders selected by landlords, bankers and big capitalists."

The Knights of Labor

The great labor movement of the late nineteenth century was the Knights of Labor. Begun in the late 1860s in Pennsylvania, it peaked in 1886 with more than 700,000 members. Taking the entire American working class, skilled and unskilled, as its constituency, the Knights hoped eventually to replace the wage system with a cooperative commonwealth encompassing all Americans regardless of sex or color. In the interim, however, the Knights' power translated into a wave of strikes that crested in 1886, the year of labor's great upheaval.

The most extensive of the year's 1,400 strikes spread across Texas, Kansas, Nebraska, Missouri, and Arkansas as the Knights of Labor struck the [Jay] Gould railroad system in what came to be known as the Great Southwestern Strike. The grievances of black workers lay at its center. The strike, which was ultimately lost, aimed to secure recognition of the Knights and to raise the wages of unskilled, poorly paid sectionmen, many of whom were black. Unlike the newly organized American Federation of Labor (AFL), the Knights of Labor embraced unskilled workers. At that time some 60,000 Knights were black, and black women made up several local assemblies—laundresses, domestic workers, and especially tobacco workers around Richmond, Virginia.

In 1886 the Knights of Labor was strong enough in Richmond to host the union's largest annual convention. But Richmond's southern mores provoked an incident that centered on a well-known Negro Knight, Frank Ferrell of New York City's outspoken District Assembly 49. When a Richmond hotelkeeper drew the color line against Ferrell, his white brothers joined him in lodgings in the Negro section of town. And in the convention's opening sessions Ferrell introduced Terence Powderly, the Grand Master Workman, with a ringing denunciation of racial discrimination.

The outcome pleased black workers but alienated southern white Knights, whose idea of appropriate union activity inclined less toward social reform than toward the pure and simple unionism of the AFL. As the Knights declined in the following years, the AFL shunned wider reforms for the most part and stuck to narrow, achievable aims.

This is not to say that in its early years the AFL did not speak and act occasionally to discourage racial proscription in its affiliated unions. When in the late 1880s the International Association of Machinists barred black workers, the AFL encouraged the organization of a rival union. Throughout the 1880s and most of the 1890s, the Federation spoke bravely of a union movement of all American workers regardless of color. In action, however, it was far less vigorous.

The People's Party

Spurned by the two major parties, many workers and farmers took part in the People's party, which grew out of a coalition of unions and farmers' alliances of the South and West. At the organizing meeting for the third party in 1891, Terence Powderly of the Knights of Labor and Ignatius Donnelly of the western Farmers' Alliance denounced sectionalism and the color line in politics. The People's party, they promised, would unite the producers of the South and West, farmers and workmen, black and white. Although the white southern Farmers' Alliance was militant on farm issues, it held back from the third-party movement because of the race issue. They had not objected to a separate Colored Farmers' Alliance so long as it did not show any great independence of action, but in the late 1880s and early 1890s the Colored Alliance offended the racial attitudes of white Alliancemen.

In 1889 in Mississippi, Colored Alliancemen boycotted white merchants who overcharged, a tactic Alliancemen had often used to good effect. But when the governor sent in the militia and several black Alliancemen were killed, their white counterparts kept silent. When the Colored Alliance supported the Lodge federal elections bill of 1890, which would have safeguarded black suffrage, white Alliancemen opposed the Colored Alliance. Finally, the Color Alliance organized a strike of agricultural workers (cotton pickers) in 1891—which the white Alliancemen broke, in their role of employers. There was to be no cooperation of southern producers across the color line in the late nineteenth century.

The most potent enemy of third-party politics in the South was the whites' fear of black political power, even when exercised in the interest of producer unity. There were some exceptions, such as Leonidas L. Polk of North Carolina and Tom Watson of Georgia, but for most southern whites the conviction that government was the preserve of white men overrode any sentiments of interracial class solidarity, on the land or in the shop.

American Separation of Labor

By the turn of the century, racial exclusion and segregation were becoming law, not just custom. By 1910 all southern states had virtually eliminated black voting through grandfather clauses or poll taxes. The pure and simple craft unionism of the AFL no longer challenged the color line in its unions or political parties. Racial exclusion was the rule in both places in the early twentieth century.

With the exception of the mineworkers' and longshoremen's unions, the left-led unions, and the unique Brotherhood of Sleeping Car Porters, black workers and organized labor were mutually exclusive until the rise of the CIO in the mid-1930s. In East St. Louis in 1917 and in Chicago in 1919, the combination of strikes and racially split workforces sparked anti-black pogroms. Although violent upheavals on the order of Chicago and East St. Louis were unusual, such conditions occurred time and again in industrial centers: unions excluded blacks, factories ordinarily did not employ blacks, but when white workers went out on strike, black workers—sometimes brought in from the South—got jobs as strikebreakers. To many white union men, a black man was naturally a scab.

Afro-Americans were divided and understandably ambivalent about organized labor in the nineteenth and early twentieth centuries. Reformers associated with white philanthropists, such as Booker T. Washington of Tuskegee Institute, played down the importance of unionization. But younger blacks recognized that Negroes needed unions as much as any other working-class group and that this natural leaning was frustrated only by racism in the labor movement. A. Philip Randolph, editor of the New York *Messenger,* called the AFL the "American Separation of Labor" and labeled it "the most wicked machine for the propagation of race prejudice in the country."

In fact, the AFL seemed bent on living up to Randolph's characterization in the first third of this century. When W. E. B. Du Bois and other blacks in the Niagara movement called for entry of blacks into unions in 1905, the AFL was not listening. During the vicious campaign waged by the railroad brotherhoods to oust Negroes from skilled jobs in that industry, the AFL registered no protest. And when the National Association for the Advancement of Colored People called for the formation of an interracial labor commission in the mid-1920s, Samuel Gompers and the Federation made no response.

Exceptions occurred only where blacks constituted a significant proportion of the workforce, as among longshoremen in coastal ports and in the industries clustered around Birmingham, Alabama, where half the miners and 65 percent of the iron- and steelworkers were Negroes. There an integrated labor movement flourished between 1894 and 1904. Operators broke both a series of strikes and the interracial unions by importing white workers from the North. But for a time at least, Birmingham's workers realized their full strength through interracial organization.

The only predominantly white AFL union with significant Negro membership was the United Mine Workers, formed in 1890, from the beginning a partially industrial union. In 1902 the mineworkers represented 20,000 Negro miners, or half the total blacks in the AFL. The UMW organized black miners in Ohio, Kentucky, West Virginia, Pennsylvania, and Alabama. It was fortunate both for the industrial union movement and for Afro-American workers that the impetus for the CIO came largely from the UMW, where blacks came closest to sharing equally in the union. The miners compiled a record for organizing black workers that was approached only by the small and marginal organizations on the left: the Industrial Workers of the World, the Western Federation of Miners (later the Mine, Mill and Smelter Workers Union), and the unions associated with the Communist party—the Trade Union Educational League, the Trade Union Unity League, and the American Negro Labor Congress.

The Brotherhood

This country's only predominantly black union was organized in 1925, when a group of Pullman porters approached the socialist journalist A. Philip Randolph. They belonged to a company union that they felt did not adequately represent them. Other porters had attempted to organize in 1900, 1912, and 1924, but without lasting success.

The Brotherhood of Sleeping Car Porters struggled for four years before receiving any recognition from the AFL and for a dozen years before being recognized by the Pullman Company. The Hotel and Restaurant Employees Alliance blocked the Brotherhood's application for affiliation with the AFL in 1926 on the grounds that the porters were more waiters than railroad workers. Yet the hotel and restaurant workers had made no attempt to organize the Pullman porters; indeed, their constitution barred black members. The hotel workers preferred to organize segregated auxiliaries for the porters. In 1928 the AFL accepted the Brotherhood as a group of affiliated locals and granted full international status in 1936.

In 1937 the Pullman Company recognized the Brotherhood in the first agreement ever signed between a Negro union and a major employer. The agreement provided for higher wages and the abolition of unpaid work and excessive working hours. Between 1926 and 1937 the company had denied the Brotherhood recognition by firing porters active in the union and replacing them with Filipino workers, and by contending that porters were not railroad workers and hence unaffected by the Railway Labor Act of 1926, which provided for union representation.

For Afro-Americans the Brotherhood was more than simply a union of Pullman porters. It stood for black labor in general. A. Philip Randolph, head of the union, came to be known as Mr. Black Labor, the most prominent spokesman for black workers within or without his or other unions. Black people of all sorts respected Randolph and the Brotherhood as the appropriate representative of the race.

Serious opposition came, rather, from the left. Radical criticism had begun as soon as the Brotherhood applied for affiliation with the AFL, when the American Negro Labor Congress criticized Randolph for selling out and forsaking "militant struggle in the interest of the workers for the policy of class collaboration with the bosses." The opposition of the ANLC, which never reached large numbers of black workers, was not as painful for Randolph as his break with the much larger National Negro Congress in 1940.

Randolph had been anti-Communist for decades when, as president of the National Negro Congress, he criticized the Soviet Union in a speech. The Congress voted him out of office and elected a former YMCA secretary who was closer to Communist party policies. This move, in connection with several other NNC actions that accorded closely with Communist party positions, made many blacks see the Congress as less of a black organization and more of an appendage of the Communist party. Randolph regretted his ouster from a national Afro-American organization, but the action did not prevent him from influencing federal employment policies.

Fair Employment Practices

The oldest grievance of black workers in this country has been exclusion from employment. When the United States geared up for defense production in 1940, black workers were routinely refused employment, even when they possessed valuable skills. The federal government awarded the contracts and paid the bills, but it did not enforce clauses that barred racial discrimination in war work. The existence of such clauses testified to the political clout of northern blacks, who, unlike their peers in southern states, could vote. Responding to a groundswell of black opinion, Randolph and the Brotherhood formed the March on Washington movement to bring 100,000 Negroes to the capital in 1941 to protest discrimination in war work and the armed forces: "We loyal American citizens demand the right to work and fight for our country," said the call to action.

Faced with this threat of mass action, President Franklin D. Roosevelt signed Executive Order 8802, one of the most important victories in the black struggle for equality. It banned racial discrimination in defense industries and government employment, but not in the armed forces, which remained segregated until the mid-1950s.

Organized black labor, embodied in Randolph and the Brotherhood of Sleeping Car Porters, spearheaded the movement for fair employment that opened industrial jobs to blacks. Access to remunerative employment was the vital first step of blacks out of a netherland of poverty and into the American mainstream. By the end of World War II black workers were positioned to take their rightful places in organized labor and to pressure for legislation that furthered their own working-class interests. The New Deal coalition of blacks, liberals, and organized labor produced the legislative underpinnings of the civil rights revolution and the social welfare programs of the Great Society that have so benefited workers and poor people in this country regardless of race.

Chapter 49

The Atlanta Address

Booker T. Washington

Educator Booker T. Washington (1856–1915), born into slavery in Virginia, was the co-founder of the Tuskegee Institute, a black school in Tuskegee, Alabama. During the formation of the Jim Crow South, his pedagogy emphasized industrial rather than classical education for blacks, and his public politics encouraged accommodation. Washington's successful fundraising efforts and his distribution of those funds to supporters (particularly in the black press) made him the most influential black man in the country during the early years of Segregation.

Ida B. Wells, W. E. B. Du Bois (see chapter 50), and William Monroe Trotter were among Washington's sharpest critics. Opposition to Jim Crow and Washington's strategy of accommodation led to the Niagara Movement and the founding of the NAACP. Du Bois claimed that the Niagara Movement received little attention because Washington had bought off the black press.

Washington's writings include his bestselling autobiography, Up from Slavery *(1901). For his collected works, see* The Booker T. Washington Papers, *ed. Louis Harlan (1972–).*

The following selection, the text of his most famous speech, the "Atlanta Address"—later referred to as the "Atlanta Compromise" by Du Bois and other critics—emphasizes his policy of accommodation. It was delivered 18 September 1895 (seven months after the death of Frederick Douglass), at the opening of the Cotton States Exposition in Atlanta.

One third of the population of the south is of the Negro race. No enterprise seeking the material, civil, or moral welfare of this section can disregard this element of our population and reach the highest success. I but convey to you, Mr. President and Directors, the sentiment of the masses of my race when I say that in no way have the value and manhood of the American Negro been more fittingly and generously recognized than by the managers of this magnificent Exposition at every stage of its progress. It is a recognition that will do more to cement the friendship of the two races than any occurrence since the dawn of freedom.

Not only this, but the opportunity here afforded will awaken among us a new era of industrial progress. Ignorant and inexperienced, it is not strange that in the first years of our new life we began at the top instead of at the bottom; that a seat in Congress or the State Legislature was more sought than real estate or industrial skill; that the political convention or stump speaking had more attraction than starting a dairy farm or truck garden.

A ship lost at sea for many days suddenly sighted a friendly vessel. From the mast of the unfortunate vessel was seen a signal: "Water, water; we die of thirst!" The answer from the friendly vessel at once came back: "Cast down your bucket where you are." A second time the signal, "Water, water; send us water!" ran up from the distressed vessel, and was answered: "Cast down your bucket where you are." The captain of the distressed vessel, at last heeding the injunction, cast down his bucket, and it came up full of fresh, sparkling water from the mouth of the Amazon River. To those of my race who depend upon bettering their condition in a foreign land, or who underestimate the importance of cultivating friendly relations with the Southern white man, who is his next door neighbor, I would say: "Cast down your bucket where you are"—cast it down in making friends in every manly way of the people of all races by whom we are surrounded.

Cast it down in agriculture, mechanics, in commerce, in domestic service, and in the professions. And in this connection it is well to bear in mind that whatever other sins the South may be called to bear, when it comes to business, pure and simple, it is in the South that the Negro is given a man's chance in the commercial world, and in nothing is this Exposition more eloquent than in emphasizing this chance. Our greatest danger is that in the great leap from slavery to freedom we may overlook the fact that the masses of us are to live by the productions of our hands, and fail to keep in mind that we shall prosper in proportion as we learn to dignify and glorify common labor, and put brains and skill into the common occupations of life; shall prosper in proportion as we learn to draw the line between the superficial and the substantial, the ornamental gewgaws of life and the useful. No race can prosper till it learns that there is as much dignity in tilling a field as in writing a poem. It is at the bottom of life we must begin, and not at the top. Nor should we permit our grievances to overshadow our opportunities.

To those of the white race who look to the incoming of those of foreign birth and strange tongue and habits for the prosperity of the South, were I permitted I would repeat what I say to my own race, "Cast down your bucket where you are." Cast it down among the 8,000,000 Negroes whose habits you know, whose fidelity and love you have tested in days when to have proved treacherous meant the ruin of your firesides. Cast down your bucket among these people who have, without strikes and labor wars, tilled your fields, cleared your forests, builded your railroads and cities, and brought forth treasures from the bowels of the earth, and helped make possible this magnificent representation of the progress of the South. Casting down your bucket among my people, helping and encouraging them as you are doing on these grounds, and, with education of head, hand and heart, you will find that they will buy your surplus land, make blossom the waste places in your fields, and run your factories. While doing this, you can be sure in the future, as in the past, that you and your families will be surrounded by the most patient, faithful, law-abiding, and unresentful people that the world has seen. As we have proved our loyalty to you in the past, in nursing your children, watching by the sick bed of your mothers and fathers, and often following them with tear-dimmed eyes to their graves, so in the future, in our humble way, we shall stand by you with a devotion that no foreigner can approach, ready to lay down our lives, if need be, in defense of yours, interlacing our industrial, commercial, civil, and religious life with yours in a way that shall make the interests of both races one. In all things that are purely social we can be as separate as the fingers, yet one as the hand in all things essential to mutual progress.

There is no defense or security for any of us except in the highest intelligence and development of all. If anywhere there are efforts tending to curtail the fullest growth of the Negro, let these efforts be turned into stimulating, encouraging, and making him the most useful and intelligent citizen. Effort or means so invested will pay a thousand per cent interest. These efforts will be twice blessed—blessing him that gives and him that takes.

There is no escape through law of man or God from the inevitable:

> The laws of changeless justice bind
>   Oppressor with oppressed;
> And Close as sin and suffering joined
>   We march to fate abreast.

Nearly sixteen millions of hands will aid you in pulling the load upwards, or they will pull against you the load downwards. We shall constitute one-third and more of the ignorance and crime of the South, or one-third its intelligence and progress; we shall contribute one-third to the business and industrial prosperity of the South, or we shall prove a veritable body of death, stagnating, depressing, retarding every effort to advance the body politic.

Gentlemen of the Exposition, as we present to you our humble effort at an exhibition of our progress, you must not expect overmuch. Starting thirty years ago with ownership here and there in a few quilts and pumpkins and chickens (gathered from miscellaneous sources), remember the path that has led from these to the invention and production of agricultural implements, buggies, steam engines, newspapers, books, statuary, carving, paintings, the management of drug stores and banks has not been trodden without contact with thorns and thistles. While we take pride in what we exhibit as a result of our independent efforts, we do not for a moment forget that our part in this exhibition would fall short of your expectations but for the constant help that has come to our educational life, not only from the Southern States, but especially from Northern philanthropists, who have made their gifts a constant stream of blessing and encouragement.

The wisest among my race understand that the agitation of questions of social equality is the extremest folly, and that progress in the enjoyment of all the privileges that will come to us must be the result of severe and constant struggle rather than of artificial forcing. No race that has anything to contribute to the markets of the world is long in any degree ostracized. It is important and right that all privileges of the law be ours, but it is vastly more important that we be prepared for the exercise of those privileges. The opportunity to earn a dollar in a factory just now is worth infinitely more than the opportunity to spend a dollar in an opera house.

In conclusion, may I repeat that nothing in thirty years has given us more hope and encouragement, and drawn us so near to you of the white race, as this opportunity offered by the Exposition; and here bending, as it were, over the altar that represents the results of the struggles of your race and mine, both starting practically empty-handed three decades ago, I pledge that, in your effort to work out the great and intricate problem which God has laid at the doors of the South, you shall have at all times the patient, sympathetic help of my race; only this be constantly in mind that, while from representations in these buildings of the products of field, of forest, of mine, of factory, letters, and art, much good will come, yet far above and beyond material benefits will be the higher good, that let us pray God will come, in a blotting out of sectional differences and racial animosities and suspicions, in a determination to administer absolute justice, in a willing obedience among all classes to the mandates of law. This coupled with our material prosperity, will bring into our beloved South a new heaven and a new earth.

Chapter 50

Of Mr. Booker T. Washington and Others

W. E. B. Du Bois

W. E. B. Du Bois (1868–1963) was a founder of Pan-Africanism, the Niagara Movement, and the National Association for the Advancement of Colored People (NAACP). He edited the NAACP's journal, the Crisis, *from 1910 to 1932. His voluminous writings as scholar, novelist, and political activist include* The Suppression of the African Slave Trade *(1896),* The Philadelphia Negro *(1899),* The Souls of Black Folk *(1903),* Black Reconstruction in America, 1860–1880 *(1935), and* The World and Africa *(1947).*

For a more complete listing of his work, see Herbert Aptheker's Annotated Bibliography of the Writings of W. E. B. Du Bois *(1973). For biographies, see Manning Marable,* W. E. B. Du Bois: Black Radical Democrat *(1986), Arnold Rampersad,* The Art and Imagination of W. E. B. Du Bois *(1976), and David Levering Lewis,* W. E. B. Du Bois, *2 vols., in progress (1993–).*

The following selection is excerpted from "Of Mr. Booker T. Washington and Others," in The Souls of Black Folks *(New York: McClurg, 1903).*

For other selections by Du Bois, see chapters 54 and 61.

Easily the most striking thing in the history of the American Negro since 1876 is the ascendancy of Mr. Booker T. Washington. It began at the time when war memories and ideals were rapidly passing; a day of astonishing commercial development was dawning; a sense of doubt and hesitation overtook the freedmen's sons,—then it was that his leading began. Mr. Washington came, with a single definite programme, at the psychological moment when the nation was a little ashamed of having bestowed so much sentiment on Negroes, and was concentrating its energies on Dollars. His programme of industrial education, conciliation of the South, and submission and silence as to civil and political rights, was not wholly original; the Free Negroes from 1830 up to war-time had striven to build industrial schools, and the American Missionary Association had from the first taught various trades; and [Joseph Charles] Price and others had sought a way of honorable alliance with the best of the Southerners. But Mr. Washington first indissolubly linked these things; he put enthusiasm, unlimited energy, and perfect faith into this programme, and changed it from a by-path into a veritable Way of Life. And the Tale of the methods by which he did this is a fascinating study of human life.

It startled the nation to hear a Negro advocating such a programme after many decades of bitter complaint; it startled and won the applause of the South, it interested and won the admiration of the North; and after a confused murmur of protest, it silenced if it did not convert the Negroes themselves.

To gain the sympathy and cooperation of the various elements comprising the white South was Mr. Washington's first task; and this, at the time Tuskegee was founded, seemed, for a black man, well-nigh impossible. And yet ten years later it was done in the word spoken at Atlanta: "In all things purely social we can be as separate as the five fingers, and yet one as the hand in all things essential to mutual progress." This "Atlanta Compromise" is by all odds the most notable in Mr. Washington's career. The South interpreted it in different ways: the radicals received it as a complete surrender of the demand for civil and political equality; the conservatives, as a generously conceived working basis for mutual understanding. So both approved it, and to-day its author is certainly the most distinguished Southerner since Jefferson Davis, and the one with the largest personal following.

Next to this achievement comes Mr. Washington's work in gaining place and consideration in the North. Others less shrewd and tactful had formerly essayed to sit on these two stools and had fallen between them; but as Mr. Washington knew the heart of the South from birth and training, so by singular insight he intuitively grasped the spirit of the age which was dominating the North. And so thoroughly did he learn the speech and thought of triumphant commercialism, and the ideals of material prosperity, that the picture of a lone black boy poring over a French grammar amid the weeds and dirt of a neglected home soon seemed to him the acme of absurdities. One wonders what Socrates and St. Francis of Assisi would say to this.

And yet this very singleness of vision and thorough oneness with his age is a mark of the successful man. It is as though Nature must needs make men narrow in order to give them force. So Mr. Washington's cult has gained unquestioning followers, his work has wonderfully prospered, his friends are legion, and his enemies are confounded. To-day he stands as the one recognized spokesman of his ten million fellows, and one of the most notable figures in a nation of seventy millions. One hesitates, therefore, to criticise a life which, beginning with so little, has done so much. And yet the time is come when one may speak in all sincerity and utter courtesy of the mistakes and shortcomings of Mr. Washington's career, as well as of his triumphs, without being thought captious or envious, and without forgetting that it is easier to do ill than well in the world.

The criticism that has hitherto met Mr. Washington has not always been of this broad character. In the South especially has he had to walk warily to avoid the harshest judgements,—and naturally so, for he is dealing with the one subject of deepest sensitiveness to that section. Twice—once when at the Chicago celebration of the Spanish-American War he alluded to the color-prejudice that is "eating away the vitals of the South," and once when he dined with President [Theodore] Roosevelt—has the resulting Southern criticism been violent enough to threaten seriously his popularity. In the North the feeling has several times forced itself into words, that Mr. Washington's counsels of submission overlooked certain elements of true manhood, and his educational programme was unnecessarily narrow. Usually, however, such criticism has not found open expression, although, too, the spiritual sons of the Abolitionists have not been prepared to acknowledge that the schools founded before Tuskegee, by men of broad ideals and self-sacrificing spirit, were wholly failures or worthy of ridicule. While, then, criticism has not failed to follow Mr. Washington, yet the prevailing public opinion of the land has been but too willing to deliver the solution of a wearisome problem into his hands, and say, "If that is all you and your race ask, take it."

Among his own people, however, Mr. Washington has encountered the strongest and most lasting opposition, amounting at times to bitterness, and even to-day continuing strong and insistent even though largely silenced in outward expression by the public opinion of the nation. Some of this opposition is, of course, mere envy; the disappointment of displaced demagogues and the spite of narrow minds. But aside from this, there is among educated and thoughtful colored men in all parts of the land a feeling of deep regret, sorrow, and apprehension at the wide currency and ascendancy which some of Mr. Washington's theories have gained. These same men admire his sincerity of purpose, and are willing to forgive much to honest endeavor which is doing something worth the doing. They cooperate with Mr. Washington as far as they conscientiously can; and, indeed, it is no ordinary tribute to this man's tact and power that, steering as he must between so many diverse interests and opinions, he so largely retains the respect of all.

But the hushing of the criticism of honest opponents is a dangerous thing. It leads some of the best of the critics to unfortunate silence and paralysis of effort, and others to burst into speech so passionately and intemperately as to lose listeners. Honest and earnest criticism from those whose interests are most nearly touched,—criticism of writers by readers, of government by those governed, of leaders by those led,—this is the soul of democracy and the safeguard of modern society. If the best of the American Negroes receive by outer pressure a leader whom they had not recognized before, manifestly there is here a certain palpable gain. Yet there is also irreparable loss,—a loss of that peculiarly valuable education which a group receives when by search and criticism it finds and commissions its own leaders. The way in which this is done is at once the most elementary and the nicest problem of social growth. History is but the record of such group-leadership; and yet how infinitely changeful is its type and character! And of all types and kinds, what can be more instructive than the leadership of a group within a group?—that curious double movement where real progress may be negative and actual advance be relative retrogression. All this is the social student's inspiration and despair.

Now in the past the American Negro has had instructive experience in the choosing of group leaders, founding thus a peculiar dynasty which in the light of present conditions is worth while studying. When sticks and stones and beasts form the sole environment of a people, their attitude is largely one of determined opposition to and conquest of natural forces. But when to earth and brute is added an environment of men and ideas, then the attitude of the imprisoned group may take three main forms,—a feeling of revolt and revenge; an attempt to adjust all thought and action to the will of the greater group; or, finally, a determined effort at self-realization and self-development despite environing opinion. The influence of all of these attitudes at various times can be traced in the history of the American Negro, and in the evolution of his successive leaders. . . .

Then came the Revolution of 1876, the suppression of the Negro votes, the changing and shifting of ideals, and the seeking of new lights in the great night. [Frederick] Douglass, in his old age, still bravely stood for the ideals of his early manhood,—ultimate assimilation *through* self-assertion, and on no other terms. For a time [Joseph Charles] Price arose as a new leader, destined, it seemed, not to give up, but to restate the old ideals in a form less repugnant to the white South. But he passed away in his prime. Then came the new leader. Nearly all the former ones had become leaders by the silent suffrage of their fellows, had sought to lead their own people alone, and were usually, save Douglass, little known outside their race. But Booker T. Washington arose as essentially the leader not of one race but of two,—a compromiser between the South, the North, and the Negro. Naturally the Negroes resented, at first bitterly, signs of compromise which surrendered their civil and political rights, even though this was to be exchanged for larger chances of economic development. The rich and dominating North, however, was not only weary of the race problem, but was investing largely in Southern enterprises, and welcomed any method of peaceful cooperation. Thus, by national opinion, the Negroes began to recognize Mr. Washington's leadership; and the voice of criticism was hushed.

Mr. Washington represents in Negro thought the old attitude of adjustment and submission; but adjustment at such a peculiar time as to make his programme unique. This is an age of unusual economic development, and Mr. Washington's programme naturally takes an economic cast, becoming a gospel of Work and Money to such an extent as apparently almost completely to overshadow the higher aims of life. Moreover, this is an age when the more advanced races are coming in closer contact with the less developed races, and the race-feeling is therefore intensified; and Mr. Washington's programme practically accepts the alleged inferiority of the Negro races. Again, in our own land, the reaction from the sentiment of war time has given impetus to race prejudice against Negroes, and Mr. Washington withdraws many of the high demands of Negroes as men and American citizens. In other periods of intensified prejudice all the Negro's tendency to self-assertion has been called forth; at this period a policy of submission is advocated. In the history of nearly all other races and peoples the doctrine preached at such crisis has been that manly self-respect is worth more than lands and houses, and that a people who voluntarily surrender such respect, or cease striving for it, are not worth civilizing.

In answer to this, it has been claimed that the Negro can survive only through submission. Mr. Washington distinctly asks that black people give up, at least for the present, three things,—

First, Political power,

Second, insistence on civil rights,

Third, higher education of Negro youth,—

and concentrate all their energies on industrial education, the accumulation of wealth, and the conciliation of the south. This policy has been courageously and insistently advocated for over fifteen years, and has been triumphant for perhaps ten years. As a result of this tender of the palm-branch, what has been the return? In these years there have occurred:

1. The disfranchisement of the Negro.
2. The legal creation of a distinct status of civil inferiority for the Negro.
3. The steady withdrawal of aid from institutions for the higher training of the Negro.

These movements are not, to be sure, direct results of Mr. Washington's teachings; but his propaganda has, without a shadow of doubt, helped their speedier accomplishment. The question then comes: Is it possible, and probable, that nine millions of men can make effective progress in economic lines if they are deprived of political rights, made a servile caste, and allowed only the most meagre chance for developing their exceptional men? If history and reason give any distinct answer to these questions, it is an emphatic *No*. And Mr. Washington thus faces the triple paradox of his career:

1. He is striving nobly to make Negro artisans business men and property-owners; but it is utterly impossible, under modern competitive methods, for workingmen and property-owners to defend their rights and exist without the right of suffrage.
2. He insists on thrift and self-respect, but at the same time counsels a silent submission to civic inferiority such as is bound to sap the manhood of any race in the long run.
3. He advocates common-school and industrial training, and depreciates institutions of higher learning; but neither the Negro common-schools, nor Tuskegee itself, could remain open a day were it not for teachers trained in Negro colleges, or trained by their graduates. . . .

It would be unjust to Mr. Washington not to acknowledge that in several instances he has opposed movements in the South which were unjust to the Negro; he sent memorials to the Louisiana and Alabama constitutional conventions, he has spoken against lynching, and in other ways has openly or silently set his influence against sinister schemes and unfortunate happenings. Notwithstanding this, it is equally true to assert that on the whole the distinct impression left by Mr. Washington's propaganda is, first, that the South is justified in its present attitude toward the Negro because of the Negro's degradation; secondly, that the prime cause of the Negro's failure to rise more quickly is his wrong education in the past; and, thirdly, that his future rise depends primarily on his own efforts. Each of these propositions is a dangerous half-truth. The supplementary truths must never be lost sight of: first, slavery and race-prejudice are potent if not sufficient causes of the Negro's position; second, industrial and common-school training were necessarily slow in planting because they had to await the black teachers trained by higher institutions,—it being extremely doubtful if any essentially different development was possible, and certainly a Tuskegee was unthinkable before 1880; and, third, while it is a great truth to say that the Negro must strive and strive mightily to help himself, it is equally true that unless his striving be not simply seconded, but rather aroused and encouraged, by the initiative of the richer and wiser environing group, he cannot hope for great success.

In his failure to realize and impress this last point, Mr. Washington is especially to be criticised. His doctrine has tended to make the whites, North and South, shift the burden of the Negro problem to the Negro's shoulders and stand aside as critical and rather pessimistic spectators; when in fact the burden belongs to the nation, and the hands of none of us are clean if we bend not our energies to righting these great wrongs. . . .

The black men of America have a duty to perform, a duty stern and delicate,— a forward movement to oppose a part of the work of their greatest leader. So far as Mr. Washington preaches Thrift, Patience, and Industrial Training for the masses, we must hold up his hands and strive with him, rejoicing in his honors and glorying in the strength of this Joshua called of God and of man to lead the headless host. But so far as Mr. Washington apologizes for injustice, North or South, does not rightly value the privilege and duty of voting, belittles the emasculating effects of caste distinctions, and opposes the higher training and ambition of our brighter minds,—so far as he, the South, or the Nation, does this,—we must unceasingly and firmly oppose them. By every civilized and peaceful method we must strive for the rights which the world accords to men, clinging unwaveringly to those great words which the sons of the Fathers would fain forget: "We hold these truths to be self-evident: That all men are created equal; that they are endowed by their Creator with certain unalienable rights; that among these are life, liberty, and the pursuit of happiness."

Report of the 1900 Pan-African Conference

Pan-Africanism is a movement promoting cooperation among and independence for people of African descent, linking civil rights struggles in the African diaspora with national liberation struggles in Africa. In 1900, the first Pan-African Conference was held in London.

The following selection is reprinted from the Report of the Pan-African Conference, held on the 23rd, 24th, and 25th July 1900 at Westminster Town Hall *(London, 1900), 10–12.*

In the metropolis of the modern world, in this the closing year of the nineteenth century, there has been assembled a congress of men and women of African blood, to deliberate solemnly upon the present situation and outlook of the darker races of mankind. The problem of the twentieth century is the problem of the colour line, the question as to how far differences of race, which show themselves chiefly in the colour of the skin and the texture of the hair, are going to be made, hereafter, the basis of denying to over half the world the right of sharing to their utmost ability the opportunities and privileges of modern civilisation.

To be sure, the darker races are to-day the least advanced in culture according to European standards. This has not, however, always been the case in the past, and certainly the world's history, both ancient and modern, has given many instances of no despicable ability and capacity among the blackest races of men.

In any case, the modern world must need remember that in this age, when the ends of the world are being brought so near together, the millions of black men in Africa, America, and the Islands of the Sea, not to speak of the brown and yellow myriads elsewhere, are bound to have great influence upon the world in the future, by reason of sheer numbers and physical contact. If now the world of culture bends itself towards giving Negroes and other dark men the largest and broadest opportunity for education and self-development, then this contact and influence is bound to have a beneficial effect upon the world and hasten human progress. But if, by reason of carelessness, prejudice, greed and injustice, the black world is to be exploited and ravished and degraded, the results must be deplorable, if not fatal, not simply to them, but to the high ideals of justice, freedom, and culture which a thousand years of Christian civilisation have held before Europe.

And now, therefore, to these ideals of civilisation, to the broader humanity of the followers of the Prince of Peace, we, the men and women of Africa in world congress assembled, do now solemnly appeal:—

Let the world take no backward step in that slow but sure progress which has successively refused to let the spirit of class, of caste, of privilege, or of birth, debar from like liberty and the pursuit of happiness a striving human soul.

Let not mere colour or race be a feature of distinction drawn between white and black men, regardless of worth or ability.

Let not the natives of Africa be sacrificed to the greed of gold, their liberties taken away, their family life debauched, their just aspirations repressed, and avenues of advancement and culture taken from them.

Let not the cloak of Christian missionary enterprise be allowed in the future, as so often in the past, to hide the ruthless economic exploitation and political downfall of less developed nations, whose chief fault has been reliance on the plighted faith of the Christian church.

Let the British nation, the first modern champion of Negro freedom, hasten to crown the work of [William] Wilberforce, and [Thomas] Clarkson, and [Thomas] Buxton, and [Alfred] Sharpe, Bishop [John] Colenso, and [David] Livingstone, and give, as soon as practicable, the rights of responsible government to the black colonies of Africa and the West Indies.

Let not the spirit of [William Lloyd] Garrison, [Wendell] Phillips, and [Frederick] Douglass wholly die out in America: may the conscience of a great nation rise and rebuke all dishonesty and unrighteous oppression toward the American Negro, and grant to him the right of franchise, security of person and property, and generous recognition of the great work he has accomplished in a generation toward raising nine millions of human beings from slavery to manhood.

Let the German Empire, and the French Republic, true to their great past, remember that the true worth of colonies lies in their prosperity and progress, and that justice, impartial alike to black and white, is the first element of prosperity.

Let the Congo Free State become a great central Negro State of the world, and let its prosperity be counted not simply in cash and commerce, but in the happiness and true advancement of its black people.

Let the nations of the World respect the integrity and independence of the free Negro States of Abyssinia, Liberia, [Haiti], etc., and let the inhabitants of these States, the independent tribes of Africa, the Negroes of the West Indies and America, and the black subjects of all nations take courage, strive ceaselessly, and fight bravely, that they may prove to the world their incontestable right to be counted among the great brotherhood of mankind.

Thus we appeal with boldness and confidence to the Great Powers of the civilised world, trusting in the wide spirit of humanity, and the deep sense of justice of our age, for a generous recognition of the righteousness of our cause.

ALEXANDER WALTERS (Bishop),
President, Pan-African Association.

HENRY B. BROWN,
Vice-President.

H. SYLVESTER WILLIAMS,
General Secretary.

W. E. BURGHARDT DU BOIS,
Chairman Committee on Address.

Chapter 52

The Niagara Movement
Declaration of Principles

The Niagara Movement, an organization of African Americans opposed to the ac-comodationist politics of Booker T. Washington, met at a hotel in Buffalo, New York (near Niagara Falls), in July 1905. The hotel's race prejudice forced them to shift the meeting across the border to Ontario, Canada. Central organizers included W. E. B. Du Bois, William Monroe Trotter, Frederick McGhee, and Charles Bentley. Booker T. Washington successfully pressured many black newspapers to ignore the new group, hampering its fundraising and future. Much of the Niagara Movement's platform was later adopted by the NAACP.

The following selection is reprinted from "The Niagara Movement Declaration of Principles" (1905).

Progress: The members of the conference, known as the Niagara Movement, assembled in annual meeting at Buffalo, July 11th, 12th and 13th, 1905, congratulate the Negro-Americans on certain undoubted evidences of progress in the last decade, particularly the increase of intelligence, the buying of property, the checking of crime, the uplift in home life, the advance in literature and art, and the demonstration of constructive and executive ability in the conduct of great religious, economic and educational institutions.

Suffrage: At the same time, we believe that this class of American citizens should protest emphatically and continually against the curtailment of their political rights. We believe in manhood suffrage; we believe that no man is so good, intelligent or wealthy as to be entrusted wholly with the welfare of his neighbor.

Civil Liberty: We believe also in protest against the curtailment of our civil rights. All American citizens have the right to equal treatment in places of public entertainment according to their behavior and deserts.

Economic Opportunity: We especially complain against the denial of equal opportunities to us in economic life; in the rural districts of the South this amounts to peonage and virtual slavery; all over the South it tends to crush labor and small business enterprises; and everywhere American prejudice, helped often by iniquitous laws, is making it more difficult for Negro-Americans to earn a decent living.

Education: Common school education should be free to all American children and compulsory. High school training should be adequately provided for all, and college training should be the monopoly of no class or race in any section of our common country. We believe that, in defense of our own institutions, the United States should aid common school education, particularly in the South, and we especially recommend concerted agitation to this end. We urge an increase in public high school facilities in the South, where the Negro-Americans are almost wholly without such provisions. We favor well-equipped trade and technical schools for the training of artisans, and the need of adequate and liberal endowment for a few institutions of higher education must be patent to sincere well-wishers of the race.

Courts: We demand upright judges in courts, juries selected without discrimination on account of color and the same measure of punishment and the same efforts at reformation for black as for white offenders. We need orphanages and farm schools for dependent children, juvenile reformatories for delinquents, and the abolition of the dehumanizing convict-lease system.

Public Opinion: We note with alarm the evident retrogression in this land of sound public opinion on the subject of manhood rights, republican government and human brotherhood, and we pray God that this nation will not degenerate into a mob of boasters and oppressors, but rather will return to the faith of the [Founding] fathers, that all men were created free and equal, with certain unalienable rights.

Health: We plead for health—for an opportunity to live in decent houses and localities, for a chance to rear our children in physical and moral cleanliness.

Employers and Labor Unions: We hold up for public execration the conduct of two opposite classes of men: The practice among employers of importing ignorant Negro-American laborers in emergencies, and then affording them neither protection nor permanent employment; and the practice of labor unions in proscribing and boycotting and oppressing thousands of their fellow-toilers, simply because they are black. These methods have accentuated and will accentuate the war of labor and capital, and they are disgraceful to both sides.

Protest: We refuse to allow the impression to remain that the Negro-American assents to inferiority, is submissive under oppression and apologetic before insults. Through helplessness we may submit, but the voice of protest of ten million Americans must never cease to assail the ears of their fellows, so long as America is unjust.

Color-Line: Any discrimination based simply on race or color is barbarous, we care not how hallowed it be by custom, expediency or prejudice. Differences made on account of ignorance, immorality, or disease are legitimate methods of fighting evil, and against them we have no word of protest; but discriminations based simply and solely on physical peculiarities, place of birth, color of skin, are relics of that unreasoning human savagery of which the world is and ought to be thoroughly ashamed.

"Jim Crow" Cars: We protest against the "Jim Crow" [railroad and street] car, since its effect is and must be to make us pay first-class fare for third-class accommodations, render us open to insults and discomfort and to crucify wantonly our manhood, womanhood and self-respect.

Soldiers: We regret that this nation has never seen fit adequately to reward the black soldiers who, in its five wars, have defended their country with their blood, and yet have been systematically denied the promotions which their abilities deserve. And we regard as unjust, the exclusion of black boys from the military and naval training schools.

War Amendments: We urge upon Congress the enactment of appropriate legislation for securing the proper enforcement of those articles of freedom, the thirteenth, fourteenth and fifteenth amendments of the Constitution of the United States.

Oppression: We repudiate the monstrous doctrine that the oppressor should be the sole authority as to the rights of the oppressed. The Negro race in America stolen, ravished and degraded, struggling up through difficulties and oppression, needs sympathy and receives criticism, needs help and is given hindrance, needs protection and is given mob-violence, needs justice and is given charity, needs leadership and is given cowardice and apology, needs bread and is given a stone. This nation will never stand justified before God until these things are changed.

The Church: Especially are we surprised and astonished at the recent attitude of the church of Christ—of an increase of a desire to bow to racial prejudice, to narrow the bounds of human brotherhood, and to segregate black men to some outer sanctuary. This is wrong, unchristian and disgraceful to the twentieth century civilization.

Agitation: Of the above grievances we do not hesitate to complain, and to complain loudly and insistently. To ignore, overlook, or apologize for these wrongs is to prove ourselves unworthy of freedom. Persistent manly agitation is the way to liberty, and toward this goal the Niagara Movement has started and asks the cooperation of all men of all races.

Help: At the same time we want to acknowledge with deep thankfulness the help of our fellowmen from the Abolitionist down to those who today still stand for equal opportunity and who have given and still give of their wealth and of their poverty for our advancement.

Duties: And while we are demanding and ought to demand, and will continue to demand the rights enumerated above, God forbid that we should ever forget to urge corresponding duties upon our people:

The duty to vote.

The duty to respect the rights of others.

The duty to work.

The duty to obey the laws.

The duty to be clean and orderly.

The duty to send our children to school.

The duty to respect ourselves, even as we respect others.

This statement, complaint and prayer we submit to the American people, and Almighty God.

Chapter 53

The Task for the Future

NAACP

The National Association for the Advancement of Colored People (NAACP) was founded in 1909.

The following selection is reprinted from "The Task for the Future—A Program for 1919," Report of the NAACP for the Years 1917 and 1918 *(New York, 1919), 76–80.*

First and foremost among the objectives for 1919 must be the strengthening of the Association's organization and resources. Its general program must be adapted to specific ends. Its chief aims have many times been stated:

1. A vote for every Negro man and woman on the same terms as for white men and women.
2. An equal chance to acquire the kind of an education that will enable the Negro everywhere wisely to use this vote.
3. A fair trial in the courts for all crimes of which he is accused, by judges in whose election he has participated without discrimination because of race.
4. A right to sit upon the jury which passes judgment upon him.
5. Defense against lynching and burning at the hands of mobs.
6. Equal service on railroad and other public carriers. This to mean sleeping car service, dining car service, Pullman service, at the same cost and upon the same terms as other passengers.
7. Equal right to the use of public parks, libraries and other community services for which he is taxed.
8. An equal chance for a livelihood in public and private employment.
9. The abolition of color-hyphenation and the substitution of "straight Americanism."

If it were not a painful fact that more than four-fifths of the colored people of the country are denied the above named elementary rights, it would seem an absurdity that an organization is necessary to demand for American citizens the exercise of such rights. One would think, if he were from Mars, or if he knew America only by reading the speeches of her leading statesmen, that all that would be needful would be to apply to the courts of the land and to the legislatures. Has not slavery been abolished? Are not all men equal before the law? Were not the Fourteenth and Fifteenth Amendments passed by the Congress of the United States and adopted by the states? Is not the Negro a man and a citizen?

When the fundamental rights of citizens are so wantonly denied and that denial justified and defended as it is by the lawmakers and dominant forces of so large a number of our states, it can be realized that the fight for the Negro's citizenship rights means a fundamental battle for real things, for life and liberty.

This fight is the Negro's fight. "Who would be free, himself must strike the blow." But, it is no less the white man's fight. The common citizenship rights of no group of people, to say nothing of nearly 12,000,000 of them, can be denied with impunity to the State and the social order which denies them. This fact should be plain to the dullest mind among us, with the upheavals of Europe before our very eyes. Whoso loves America and cherishes her institutions, owes it to himself and his country to join hands with the members of the National Association for the Advancement of Colored People to "Americanize" America and make the kind of democracy we Americans believe in to be the kind of democracy we shall have in fact, as well as in theory.

The Association seeks to overthrow race prejudice but its objective may better be described as a fight against *caste.* Those who seek to separate the Negro from the rest of Americans are intent upon establishing a caste system in America and making of all black men an *inferior caste.* As America could not exist "half slave and half free" so it cannot exist with an upper caste of whites and a lower caste of Negroes. Let no one be deceived by those who would contend that they strive only to maintain the purity of the white race" and that they wish to separate the races but to do no injustice to the black man. The appeal is to history which affords no example of any group or element of the population of any nation which was separated from the rest and at the same time treated with justice and consideration. Ask the Jew who was compelled to live in the proscribed Ghetto whether being held separate he was afforded the common rights of citizenship and the "equal protection of the laws?" To raise the question is to find the answer "leaping to the eyes," as the French say.

Nor should any one be led astray by the tiresome talk about "social equality." Social equality is a private question which may well be left to individual decision. But the prejudices of individuals cannot be accepted as the controlling policy of a state. The National Association for the Advancement of Colored People is concerned primarily with *public equality.* America is a nation—not a private club. The privileges no less than the duties of citizenship belong of right to no *separate class* of the people but to all the people, and to them as *individuals.* The Constitution and the laws are for the protection of the minority and of the unpopular, no less than for the favorites of fortune, or they are of no meaning as American instruments of government.

Such a right as has been outlined is worthy of the support of all Americans. The forces which seek to deny, and do deny, to the Negro his citizenship birthright, are powerful and entrenched. They hold the public offices. They administer the law. They say who may, and who may not vote, in large measure. They control and edit, in many sections, the influential organs of public opinion. They dominate. To dislodge them by legal and constitutional means as the N.A.A.C.P. proposes to endeavor to dislodge them, requires a strong organization and ample funds. These two things attained, victory is but a question of time, since justice will not forever be denied.

The lines along which the Association can best work are fairly clear. Its fight is of the brain and the soul and to the brain and the soul of America. *It seeks to reach the conscience of America.* America is a large and busy nation. It has many things to think of besides the Negro's welfare. In Congress and state legislatures and before the bar of public opinion, the Association must energetically and adequately defend the Negro's right to fair and equal treatment. To command the interest and hold the attention of the American people for *justice to the Negro* requires money to print and circulate literature which states the facts of the situation. And the appeal must be on the basis of the facts. It is easy to talk in general terms and abstractly. The presentation of concrete data necessitates ample funds.

Lynching must be stopped. Many Americans do not believe that such horrible things happen as do happen when Negroes are lynched and burned at the stake. Lynching can be stopped when we can reach the hearts and consciences of the American people. Again, money is needed.

Legal work must be done. Defenseless Negroes are every day denied the "equal protection of the laws" because there is not money enough in the Association's treasury to defend them, either as individuals or as a race.

Legislation must be watched. Good laws must be promoted wherever that be possible and bad laws opposed and defeated, wherever possible. Once more, money is essential.

The public must be kept informed. This means a regular press service under the supervision of a trained newspaperman who knows the difference between news and gossip, on the one hand, and mere opinion on the other. That colored people are contributing their fair share to the well-being of America must be made known. The war has made familiar the heroic deeds of the colored soldier. The colored civilian has been, and is now, contributing equally to America's welfare. If men have proven to be heroes in warfare, they must have had virtues in peace time. That law-abiding colored people are denied the commonest citizenship rights, must be brought home to all Americans who love fair play. Once again, money is needed.

The facts must be gathered and assembled. This requires effort. Facts are not gotten out of one's imagination Their gathering and interpretation is skilled work. Research workers of a practical experience are needed. Field investigations, in which domain the Association has already made some notable contributions, are essential to good work. More money.

The country must be thoroughly organized. The Association's nearly 200 branches are a good beginning. A field staff is essential to the upbuilding of this important branch development. A very large percentage of the branch members are colored people. As a race they have less means, and less experience in public organization, than white people. But, they are developing rapidly habits of efficiency in organization. Money, again is needed.

But, not money alone is needed. Men and women are vital to success. Public opinion is the main force upon which the Association relies for a *victory of justice*.

Chapter 54

Returning Soldiers

W. E. B. Du Bois

President Woodrow Wilson declared that World War I had to be fought to make the world safe for democracy, but when it was over, black soldiers returned to a "democracy" that still countenanced lynching and disenfranchisement.

During the war, Du Bois and the NAACP had encouraged blacks to demonstrate their patriotism and join the war effort. When the conflict ended, Du Bois wrote a blistering editorial—one of his most famous—criticizing the country in whose name the black veterans had fought, as part of a special May 1919 issue of the Crisis, entitled "Documents of the War." The Postmaster General thought the issue so inflammatory that he briefly stopped its distribution, until the government determined that it had no legal grounds for suppression. Afterwards, Du Bois found himself visited by FBI agents. His friend and literary executor, historian Herbert Aptheker, writes that the agents "ask[ed] him 'what he was up to.' Du Bois replied that he was trying to get the Constitution of the United States enforced; he added to the men from the Justice Department; 'what are you up to?'"[1]

The following selection is reprinted from "Returning Soldiers," Crisis, May 1919, 13–14.

We are returning from war! THE CRISIS and tens of thousands of black men were drafted into a great struggle. For bleeding France and what she means and has meant and will mean to us and humanity and against the threat of German race arrogance, we fought gladly and to the last drop of blood; for America and her highest ideals, we fought in far-off hope; for the dominant southern oligarchy entrenched in Washington, we fought in bitter resignation. For the America that represents and gloats in lynching, disfranchisement, caste, brutality and devilish insult—for this, in the hateful upturning and mixing of things, we were forced by vindictive fate to fight also.

But today we return! We return from the slavery of uniform which the world's madness demanded us to don to the freedom of civil garb. We stand again to look America squarely in the face and call a spade a spade. We sing: This country of ours, despite all its better souls have done and dreamed, is yet a shameful land.

It *lynches*.

And lynching is barbarism of a degree of contemptible nastiness unparalleled in human history. Yet for fifty years we have lynched two Negroes a week, and we have kept this up right through the war.

It *disfranchises* its own citizens.

Disfranchisement is the deliberate theft and robbery of the only protection of poor against rich and black against white. The land that disfranchises its citizens and calls itself a democracy lies and knows it lies.

It encourages *ignorance*.

It has never really tried to educate the Negro. A dominant minority does not want Negroes educated. It wants servants, dogs, whores and monkeys. And when this land allows a reactionary group by its stolen political power to force as many black folk into these categories as it possibly can, it cries in contemptible hypocrisy: "They threaten us with degeneracy; they cannot be educated."

It *steals* from us.

It organizes industry to cheat us. It cheats us out of our land; it cheats us out of our labor. It confiscates our savings. It reduces our wages. It raises our rent. It steals our profit. It taxes us without representation. It keeps us consistently and universally poor, and then feeds us on charity and derides our poverty.

It *insults* us.

It has organized a nation-wide and latterly a world-wide propaganda of deliberate and continuous insult and defamation of black blood wherever found. It decrees that it shall not be possible in travel nor residence, work nor play, education nor instruction for a black man to exist without tacit or open acknowledgment of his inferiority to the dirtiest white dog. And it looks upon any attempt to question or even discuss this dogma as arrogance, unwarranted assumption and treason.

This is the country to which we Soldiers of Democracy return. This is the fatherland for which we fought! But it is *our* fatherland. It was right for us to fight. The faults of *our* country are *our* faults. Under similar circumstances, we would fight again. But by the God of Heaven, we are cowards and jackasses if now that war is over, we do not marshal every ounce of our brain and brawn to fight a sterner, longer, more unbending battle against the forces of hell in our own land.

We *return*.

We *return from fighting*.

We *return fighting*.

Make way for Democracy! We saved it in France, and by the Great Jehovah, we will save it in the United States of America, or know the reason why.

EDITORS' NOTE

1. Herbert Aptheker, ed., *Documentary History of the Negro People* (Secaucus, N.J.: Citadel Press, 1973), 3:271n.

Chapter 55

Lynching a Domestic Question?

The Messenger

The victorious Allies had made great promises during World War I about democracy and self-determination. When the conflict ended, various peoples appealed to the Paris Peace Conference—white European ethnic groups demanding independence, Jews asking for a national homeland, Africans and Arabs calling for an end to European control. The editors of the Messenger *suggested that African Americans should join these groups. If the local, state, and national governments of the United States would not end lynching, then blacks should appeal to the higher court of world opinion at the Peace Conference.*

In later years, the NAACP's Walter White and Malcolm X would make similar suggestions about presenting to the United Nations evidence of a pattern of human rights violations in the United States. U.S. administrations, concerned about national prestige, did not take such criticisms lightly. It was partly in response to such actions that the government attempted to marginalize the influence of the black left during the first and second Red Scares and COINTELPRO.

This was not the first time African Americans had presented their case to a foreign audience; they had also appealed to the international community over the issue of slavery.

The Messenger *(1917–1928), which declared itself "the only radical Negro magazine in America," was edited by A. Philip Randolph and Chandler Owen.*

The following selection is a reprint of the editorial "Lynching a Domestic Question," Messenger, *July 1919.*

For other editorials from the Messenger, *see chapters 60 and 62. For another article by Randolph, see chapter 72.*

That the above title is not our opinion hardly needs to be stated by men who are internationalists, yet this is the type of chaff which men like James W. Johnson and Fred R. Moore of the *New York Age* handed out about the time the Peace Conference was beginning. The *Crisis* and nearly all the other Negro publications repeated this owl-like phrase with little or no knowledge of its meaning. Neither the Jews or the Irish have stood by any such foolhardy program. The Irish were so persistent in presenting their program that they sent a committee abroad and on June 6th by vote of 60 to 1, the Senate went on record in favor of giving Ireland's claims to independence a hearing before the Peace Conference. The only person who voted against it was John Sharp Williams of Mississippi and no one could expect John Sharp Williams to have any leanings toward independence and democracy for anybody, since his environment is the slave environment of Mississippi. International attention has also been drawn to the Jewish people's pogroms or lynchings. Everywhere it has had a good effect, just as the Abolitionists were able to bring more power to bear against slavery in Europe than could be secured in America. The editors of the MESSENGER have no difficulty in explaining the principle. It is simply this: The beneficiary of a system or institution can never be relied upon voluntarily to overthrow that institution or system. The country, which is responsible for the oppressions of Negroes, for mob violence and lynching, is not going to overthrow that wicked institution from which it benefits. No, lynching is not a domestic question, except in the rather domestic minds of Negro leaders, whose information is highly localized and highly domestic. The problems of the Negroes should be presented to every nation in the world, and this sham democracy, about which Americans prate, should be exposed for what it is,—a sham, a mockery, a rape on decency and a travesty on common sense. When lynching gets to be an international question, it will be the beginning of the end. The sooner the better. On with the dance!

Chapter 56

Address to President Wilson

William Monroe Trotter

President Woodrow Wilson is said to have described D. W. Griffith's Birth of a Nation, *a film presenting the Ku Klux Klan as the heroic savior of the South, as "like writing history with lightning." Whether this story is true or not, it does seem to capture his views on race. Wilson allowed the expansion of segregation in federal employment, and he called for the surveillance of legal black organizations and publications (see chapter 46).*

In 1913, Wilson met with a black delegation led by the crusading journalist William Monroe Trotter. The Chicago Defender *headlined its story on the meeting: "Afro-Americans Do Not Cringe: President of U.S. Becomes Incensed."*

Trotter (1872–1934) founded the Boston Guardian, *which he edited for thirty years. He was a fierce critic of Booker T. Washington, leading to his role as a founder of the Niagara Movement in 1905. Two years earlier, he had been arrested for heckling Washington. In 1906, he attacked President Theodore Roosevelt for discharging three companies of black soldiers in Brownsville, Texas. In 1910, he organized protests that led to the closing of Thomas Dixon's racist play* The Clansman *in Boston.*

After World War I, when the State Department denied him a passport, Trotter disguised himself to cross the Atlantic and attend meetings with groups petitioning the Peace Conference in Paris. In his later years, he enlisted support for the Scottsboro defendants. He ended his career as a strong supporter of Franklin D. Roosevelt.

The following selection is reprinted from "William Monroe Trotter's Address to President," Chicago Defender, *21 November 1914.*

One year ago we presented a national petition, signed by Afro-Americans in thirty-eight states, protesting against the segregation of employe[e]s of the national government whose ancestry could be traced in whole or in part to Africa, as instituted under your administration in the treasury and post office departments. We then appealed to you to undo this race segregation in accord with your duty as president and with your pre-election pledges. We stated that there could be no freedom, no respect from others, and no equality of citizenship under segregation for races, especially when applied to but one of the many racial elements in the government employ. For such placement of employe[e]s means a charge by the government of physical indecency or infection, or of being a lower order of beings or a subjection to the prejudices of other citizens, which constitutes inferiority of status. We protested such segregation as to working positions, eating tables, dressing rooms, rest rooms, lockers and especially public toilets in government buildings. We stated that such segregation was a public humiliation and degradation, entirely unmerited and far-reaching in its injurious effects, a gratuitous blow against ever-loyal citizens and against those many of whom aided and supported your elevation to the presidency of our common country.

At that time you stated you would investigate conditions for yourself. Now, after the lapse of a year, we have come back, having found that all the forms of segregation of government employe[e]s of African extraction are still practiced in the treasury and department buildings, and to a certain extent have spread into other government buildings.

Under the treasury department, in the bureau of engraving and printing, there is segregation not only in dressing rooms but in working positions, Afro-American employe[e]s being herded at separate tables, in eating, and in toilets. In the navy department there is herding at desks and separation in lavatories; in the post office department there is separation in work for Afro-American women in the alcove of the eighth floor, of Afro-American men in rooms on the seventh floor, with forbidding even of entrance into an adjoining room occupied by white clerks on the seventh floor, and of Afro-American men in separate rooms just instituted on the sixth floor, with separate lavatories for Afro-American men on the eighth floor; in the main treasury building in separate lavatories in the basement; in the interior department separate lavatories, which were specifically pointed out to you at our first hearing; in the state and other departments in separate lavatories; in marine hospital service building in separate lavatories, though there is but one Afro-American clerk to use it; in the war department in separate lavatories; in the post office department building separate lavatories; in the sewing and bindery divisions of the government printing office on the fifth floor there is herding at working positions of Afro-American women and separation in lavatories, and new segregation instituted by the division chief since our first audience with you. This lavatory segregation is the most degrading, most insulting of all. Afro-American employe[e]s who use the regular public lavatories on the floors where they work are cautioned and are then warned by superior officers against insubordination.

We have come by vote of this league to set before you this definite continuance of race segregation and to renew the protest and to ask you to abolish segregation of Afro-American employe[e]s in the executive department.

Because we cannot believe you capable of any disregard of your pledges we have been sent by the alarmed American citizens of color. They realize that if they can be segregated and thus humiliated by the national government at the national capital the beginning is made for the spread of that persecution and prosecution which makes property and life itself insecure in the South, the foundation of the whole fabric of their citizenship is unsettled.

They have made plain enough to you their opposition to segregation last year by a national anti-segregation petition, this year by a protest registered at the polls, voting against every Democratic candidate save those outspoken against segregation. The only Democrat elected governor in the eastern states was Governor [David] Welsh of Massachusetts, who appealed to you by letter to stop segregation. Thus have the Afro-Americans shown how they detest segregation.

In fact, so intense is their resentment that the movement to divide this solid race vote and make peace with the national Democracy, so suspiciously revived when you ran for the presidency, and which some of our families for two generations have been risking all to promote, bids fair to be undone.

Only two years ago you were heralded as perhaps the second Lincoln, and now the Afro-American leaders who supported you are hounded as false leaders and traitors to their race. What a change segregation has wrought!

You said that your "Colored fellow citizens could depend upon you for everything which would assist in advancing the interests of their race in the United States." Consider that pledge in the face of the continued color segregation! Fellow citizenship means congregation. Segregation destroys fellowship and citizenship. Consider that any passerby on the streets of the national capital, whether he be black or white, can enter and use the public lavatories in government buildings, while citizens of color who do the work of the government are excluded.

As equal citizens and by virtue of your public promises we are entitled at your hands to freedom from discrimination, restriction, imputation and insult in government employ. Have you a "new freedom" for white Americans and a new slavery for your "Afro-American fellow citizens"? God forbid!

We have been delegated to ask you to issue an executive order against any and all segregation of government employe[e]s because of race and color, and to ask whether you will do so. We await your reply, that we may give it to the waiting citizens of the United States of African extraction.

Chapter 57

The Higher Education of Women

Anna Julia Cooper

Educator Anna Julia Cooper (1858?–1964) was born into slavery in North Car-olina. Throughout her career she was a strong proponent of education for women and the elevation of black women for racial uplift.

After the Civil War, Cooper graduated from St. Augustine's Normal School, founded as a teacher training school for the former slaves. She continued there as a teacher before attending Oberlin College, where she earned both bachelor's and master's degrees. She went on to teach and serve as a principal at Washington Colored High School in Washington, D.C.

In 1892, Cooper co-founded the Colored Woman's League. She also partici-pated in the founding conference of the National Conference of Colored Women and the 1900 meeting of the Pan-African Conference. In 1925, she earned a Ph.D. in French from the University of Paris. Five years later, she founded Frelinghuysen University, an evening college for the working black residents of Washington, D.C.

The following selection is excerpted from A Voice from the South *(1892).*

In the very first year of our century, the year 1801, there appeared in Paris a book by Silvain Marechal, entitled "Shall Woman Learn the Alphabet." The book pro-poses a law prohibiting the alphabet to women, and quotes authorities weighty and various, to prove that the woman who knows the alphabet has already lost part of her womanliness. The author declares that woman can use the alphabet only as Moliere predicted they would, in spelling out the verb *amo* [love], that they have no occasion to peruse Ovid's *Ars Amoris,* since that is already the ground and limit of their intuitive furnishing; that Madame Guion would have been far more adorable had she remained a beautiful ignoramus as nature made her; that Ruth, Naomi, the Spartan woman, the Amazons, Penelope, Andromache, Lucretia, Joan of Arc, Petrarch's Laura, the daughters of Charlemagne, could not spell their names; while Sappho, Aspasia, Madame de Maintenon, and Madame de Stael could read altogether too well for their good; finally, that if women were once permitted to read Sophocles and work with logarithms, or to nibble at any side of the apple of knowledge, there would be an end forever to their sewing on buttons and embroidering slippers.

Please remember this book was published at the *beginning* of the Nineteenth Century. At the end of its first third, (in the year 1833) one solitary college in America [Oberlin College] decided to admit women within its sacred precincts, and organized what was called a "Ladies' Course" as well as the regular B.A. or Gentlemen's course.

It was felt to be an experiment—a rather dangerous experiment—and was adopted with fear and trembling by the good fathers, who looked as if they had been caught secretly mixing explosive compounds and were guiltily expecting every moment to see the foundations under them shaken and rent and their fair superstructure shattered into fragments.

But the girls came, and there was no upheaval. They performed their tasks modestly and intelligently. Once in a while one or two were found choosing the gentlemen's course. Still no collapse; and the dear, careful, scrupulous, frightened old professors were just getting their hearts out of their throats and preparing to draw one good free breath, when they found they would have to change the names of those courses; for there were as many ladies in the gentlemen's course as in the ladies', and a distinctively Ladies' Course, inferior in scope and aim to the regular classical course, did not and could not exist.

Other colleges gradually fell into line, and to-day there are one hundred and ninety-eight colleges for women, and two hundred and seven coeducational colleges and universities in the United States alone offering the degree of B.A. to women, and sending out yearly into the arteries of this nation a warm, rich flood of strong, brave, active, energetic, well-equipped, thoughtful women—women quick to see and eager to help the needs of this needy world—women who can think as well as feel, and who feel none the less because they think—women who are none the less tender and true for the parchment scroll they bear in their hands—women who have given a deeper, richer, nobler and grander meaning to the word "womanly" than any one-sided masculine definition could ever have suggested or inspired—women whom the world has long waited for in pain and anguish till there should be at last added to its forces and allowed to permeate its thought the complement of that masculine influence which has dominated it for fourteen centuries.

Since the idea of order and subordination succumbed to barbarian brawn and brutality in the fifth century, the civilized world has been like a child brought up by his father. It has needed the great mother heart to teach it to be pitiful, to love mercy, to succor the weak and care for the lowly. . . .

I ask the men and women who are teachers and co-workers for the highest interests of the race, that they give the girls a chance! We might as well expect to grow trees from leaves as hope to build up a civilization or a manhood without taking into consideration our women and the home life made by them, which must be the root and ground of the whole matter. Let us insist then on special encouragement for the education of our women and special care in their training. Let our girls feel that we expect something more of them than that they merely look pretty and appear well in society. Teach them that there is a race with special needs which they and only they can help; that the world needs and is already asking for their trained, efficient forces. Finally, if there is an ambitious girl with pluck and brain to take the higher education, encourage her to make the most of it. Let there be the same flourish of trumpets and clapping of hands as when a boy announces his determination to enter the lists; and then, as you know that she is physically the weaker of the two, don't stand from under and leave her to buffet the waves alone. Let her know that your heart is following her, that your hand, though she sees it not, is ready to support her. To be plain, I mean let money be raised and scholarships be founded in our colleges and universities for self-supporting, worthy young women, to offset and balance the aid that can always be found for boys who will take theology.

The earnest well trained Christian young woman, as a teacher, as a home-maker, as wife, mother, or silent influence even, is as potent a missionary agency among our people as is the theologian; and I claim that at the present stage of our development in the South she is even more important and necessary.

Let us then, here and now, recognize this force and resolve to make the most of it—not the boys less, but the girls more.

Chapter 58

Black Women and the Right to Vote

Darlene Clark Hine and Christie Anne Farnham

Darlene Clark Hine, professor of history at Michigan State University, is the au-thor of Black Victory: The Rise and Fall of the White Primary in Texas *(1979),* Black Women in White: Racial Conflict and Cooperation in the Nursing Profes-sion, 1890–1950 *(1989), and* Hine Sight: Black Women and the Re-Construction of American History *(1994), co-author of* A Shining Thread of Hope: The History of Black Women in America *(1998), editor of* The State of Afro-American History *(1986),* Black Women in United States History *(16 vols., 1990), and co-editor of* Black Women in America: An Historical Encyclopedia *(1993).*

Christie Anne Farnham, professor of history at Iowa State University, is the au-thor of The Education of the Southern Belle: Higher Education in the Antebellum South *(1994), founder of the* Journal of Women's History, *and editor of* Women of the American South *(1997).*

The following selection is excerpted with permission from "Black Women's Culture of Resistance and the Right to Vote," in Women of the American South: A Multicultural Reader, *ed. Christie Anne Farnham (New York: New York Univer-sity Press, 1997), 207–16, footnotes deleted.*

For another selection co-authored by Hine, see chapter 68.

Antebellum black women activists, like Sojourner Truth, Maria Stewart, Harriet Forten Purvis, Margaretta Forten, Sarah Remond, and Mary Ann Shadd Cary were northerners. Most black women lived in the South, where they were en-slaved; the few who were "free" were perforce constrained by southern society's conflation of suffrage with abolition. One "free" black woman, however, became a renowned activist by moving north. Frances Ellen Watkins Harper, poet, novel-ist, and journalist, was a free black born in Baltimore who moved to Ohio to teach at Union Seminary, the precursor of Wilberforce. An active agent of the Under-ground Railroad that helped escaping slaves, after the war she became a promi-nent black clubwoman, a national board member of the Woman's Christian Tem-perance Union, and a founder of the American Woman Suffrage Association in the post–Civil War period. After emancipation a new generation of black women ac-tivists emerged to continue the fight for suffrage and women's rights. Although not as well known as their northern counterparts, black southern women like

Charlotte Rollin and her sisters Frances, Louisa, and Kate of Charleston, South Carolina, and Adella Hunt Logan of Tuskegee, Alabama, exhibited astute political engagement and consciousness. Still others were southerners who had fled the South, like anti-lynching crusader Ida Wells-Barnett, who moved to Chicago after whites destroyed her Memphis newspaper and threatened her life.

The black women's club movement of the late nineteenth century was launched by the first generation born after slavery. As leaders, these educated, middle-class women swung their personal and organizational support to the suffrage cause. Northern women like Gertrude Bustill Mossell of Philadelphia, Josephine St. Pierre Ruffin of Boston, and Fannie Barrier Williams of Chicago had achieved positions of leadership in their communities. However, southern black women suffragists faced a daunting situation: the South was moving away from suffrage in its hate-filled and frequently violent campaign to disfranchise black men and nullify the Fifteenth Amendment to the U.S. Constitution. Southern legislators revised state constitutions to incorporate such strategems as poll taxes and literacy tests to remove black men from the voter rolls. They segregated society by statute and reinforced it with lynch law. Yet somehow, some southern black women found space, largely within educational communities and large urban areas, especially in the Upper South, to raise their voices to support the suffrage cause.

Whether in the North or South, these women consistently subscribed to universal suffrage—not suffrage restricted to the educated—and to the idea that black women needed the vote for protection and in order to exercise power in their own interest and for the good of their communities. This rationale implicitly aimed at changing racial and gender hierarchies in the United States. Within black communities the struggle for woman suffrage drew its meaning from racialized conceptions of gender and class. Nannie Helen Burroughs, founder of the National Training School for Women and Girls in Washington, D.C. and catalyst for the establishment of the Women's Convention Auxiliary of the National Baptist Convention (then the largest black women's organization in the United States), called the ballot "a weapon of moral defense." She explained, "When she [a black woman] appears in court in defense of her virtue, she is looked upon with amused contempt. She needs the ballot to reckon with men who place no value upon her virtue."

Black women activists fought the contemporary stereotype that painted all women of the race as unchaste. Like white women, they believed in a woman's culture that was morally superior to that found in the public sphere, and they employed this sometimes essentialist notion of woman's nature in their arguments for the franchise. "Racial uplift" was a key component of the black women's club movement. Anna Julia Cooper, a North Carolina native who was an educator, author, scholar, feminist, lecturer, and force in the black women's club movement, epitomized this view when she wrote that African American women were "the fundamental agency under God in the regeneration . . . of the race, as well as the groundwork and starting point of its progress upward."

The suffrage movement is instructive of women's way of struggle. The Nineteenth Amendment marked the achievement of a bloodless revolution, but it occurred only after long decades of agitation and conflict. Unraveling this process of social change exposes the ways sex, race, and class differences impeded women's efforts but also simultaneously motivated suffragists from time to time to build new boundary-crossing coalitions. It also reveals the strength of the antisuffrage forces and the compromises made in order to win the vote. Similarities and parallels between the modern Civil Rights Movement and the first wave of feminism abound. The unity among women, like that among black Americans, was fragile. Women and other excluded groups were unable to sustain a coherent movement that joined all races, religions, classes, and sexual identities equally. A closer look at the suffrage movement exposes these fissures.

The fight for the Fifteenth Amendment to give the vote to black men split the women suffragists in the late 1860s into two major umbrella organizations, each with its own leaders and ideological orientations: the National Woman Suffrage Association (NWSA) under Elizabeth Cady Stanton and Susan B. Anthony and the American Woman Suffrage Association (AWSA) lead by Lucy Stone, Henry Blackwell, and other northeasterners. The NWSA resented the fact that the Fifteenth Amendment gave the vote to former male slaves but not to women; therefore, they advocated a constitutional amendment for woman suffrage. The AWSA supported the Fifteenth Amendment out of political expediency and advocated state and local campaigns to achieve the vote for women.

Black women were members of both groups, although fewer were attracted to the NWSA, which was a more radical organization that explored a range of other issues, like "free love." Some AWSA members were black southerners, like Charlotte Rollin of Charleston, who was an ex-officio member of their executive committee at the 1872 meeting in New York City. She had spoken in support of universal suffrage on the floor of the South Carolina House of Representatives in 1869 [see chapter 31—Eds.] and had chaired the founding meeting of the interracial South Carolina Woman's Rights Association in 1870. Journalist Mary Ann Cary attended the NWSA convention in Washington in 1871 while she was a student at Howard University Law School. In 1876 she wrote to the NWSA on behalf of ninety-four black women from the District of Columbia, requesting that their names be included in an autograph book as signers of the NWSA's "Woman's Declaration of Rights."

Black women were caught in the middle. Unable to disaggregate themselves, they fought for woman suffrage and black enfranchisement sequentially and simultaneously. Such complexity of struggle was necessary. As the suffrage movement gained momentum at the turn of the century, black women confronted the racism of white suffragists while simultaneously encouraging black men to support women's quest for the vote. Black women had to straddle the racial and gender divide; to avoid slipping between the cracks they had to carve a distinct path that reflected their compounded identity as black women. Thus, black women engaged in the suffrage movement variously from the positions of African American, woman, and black woman.

Black men were aware of black women's double agency. In the March 1921 issue of *The Crisis*, editor W. E. B. Du Bois, an ardent supporter of woman suffrage, confessed that "a larger opportunity for the Negro during the past half-century has been carried on by colored women, although they have not always received the credit for it." In his 1903 book *The Souls of Black Folk,* he described the classic dilemma of double consciousness: "One ever feels his twoness—an American, a Negro; two souls, two thoughts, two unreconciled strivings; two warring ideals in one dark body, whose dogged strength alone keeps it from being torn asunder." The difference between his male perspective on double consciousness and that of black women was that what he saw as a dilemma or weakness was for black women a source of strength and power. It is now clear that black women never enjoyed the luxury of a mere twoness. Indeed, multiple and compounded identities and consciousnesses became critical holdings in their arsenal of weapons to gain suffrage, black freedom, and personal empowerment. This very multiplicity, however, rendered black women enigmatic, on the one hand, and fostered their legendary perseverance, on the other.

Part of that perseverance was demonstrated in their commitment to woman suffrage despite the racism of white suffragists. Younger suffragists brought about the reunification of suffrage organizations in 1890 (National American Woman Suffrage Association or NAWSA), and the leadership began a campaign to recruit the South. Historically, woman suffrage and abolition had been connected, making it unacceptable to white southerners. Using a strategy first developed by Henry Blackwell, NAWSA turned away from universal suffrage in favor of literacy qualifications, excluded southern blacks from their organization, and argued that giving women the vote would restore white supremacy by enlarging the white voter base, making it impossible for blacks to gain a majority. Educational qualifications that would give most white women the vote would render the black women's vote too small to matter, as a consequence of their lower educational rates. In this way white supremacy could be maintained without dependence on the state constitutional changes and segregation laws then being put into place, which white southerners feared might be overridden at the federal level. Marjorie Spruill Wheeler suggests that "Though historians usually focus on the race issue as a prime obstacle to the suffragists' success, there is considerable evidence to indicate that the race issue was, in fact, a major causative factor in the emergence in the 1890s of the woman suffrage movement in the South." It is, indeed, one of the ironies of history that racism was part of a move toward gender equality.

White southern suffragists born before 1865 and residing in states with large black populations, like Georgia's Rebecca Latimer Felton and Mississippi's Belle Kearney, were the most uncompromising racist suffragists. But even the national leadership moved in this direction. Frustrated by the large numbers of illiterate immigrant men arriving in the North who could vote by virtue of their sex, while native-born, educated women remained excluded, white suffragists moved from advocating universal suffrage to championing educational qualifications. Of the late nineteenth-century national leaders, Susan B. Anthony remained the least racist, but younger leaders like Carrie Chapman Catt shared many of the racist assumptions of the times that were widely held in the North as well as the South.

Seeking to organize the South, the NAWSA held its 1895 convention in Atlanta. Anthony asked Frederick Douglass to stay away so as not to offend southern whites. Douglass, the most famous black American in the nation and a prominent woman suffragist, had seconded Elizabeth Cady Stanton's proposal for the ballot at the Seneca Falls Convention of 1848, which launched the woman's rights movement. The NAWSA continued to court white southern support by holding its 1903 convention in New Orleans. At this meeting, the board endorsed the right of individual states to set forth their own positions on suffrage—a policy reinforcing white supremacy by opening the door for whites-only provisions that would not have been acceptable to the North in a federal amendment. While in New Orleans Anthony visited the Phillis Wheatley Club, whose president, Sylvanie Williams, did not hesitate to point out in her welcome speech the discrimination black women experienced in the suffrage movement.

Persisting in the face of such racist appeals was difficult, but many clubs, temperance unions, church auxiliaries, sororities, and educational groups began to add woman suffrage to their concerns. Activists like Cooper, Minnie Crosthwait, registrar at Fisk, and Lugenia Burns Hope of Atlanta University advocated woman suffrage in their speeches and writings. Memphis-born Mary Church Terrell, founder and first president of the National Association of Colored Women, was one of the leading black women activists [see chapter 59—Eds.]. Speaking before the 1890 National Woman Suffrage Association convention in Washington, D.C., she argued that "a White Woman has only one handicap to overcome—a great one, true, her sex; a colored woman faces two—her sex and her race. A colored man has only one—that of race." Organizations devoted exclusively to attaining the vote appeared in such cities as Memphis, Washington, Charleston, and St. Louis. Mary Ann Cary, for example, founded the Colored Women's Progressive Franchise Association in Washington in 1880. Adella Hunt Logan, teacher and later wife of a Tuskegee Institute administrator, was a life member of the NAWSA and published articles in the Woman's Journal and The Crisis, yet she was deliberately excluded from suffrage conventions in the South even though she was active in the Alabama Federation of Colored Women's Clubs and the Southern Federation of Colored Women's Clubs, and headed the department of suffrage for the NACW.

By the end of the century the Republican Party had abandoned its support of ballots for black men, Congress had refused to challenge the dubious constitutionality of southern stratagems, and the Supreme Court had permitted white supremacy to become legally entrenched in southern society. White southern suffragists' attempts to get woman suffrage into state constitutions also had been a failure. Southern politicians thought that the same kind of violence used against black male voters could not be widely used against black females, and they did not want to have to face black women's persistence. Demagogues like J. K. Vardaman, a senator from Mississippi, insisted, "The negro woman will be more offensive, more difficult to handle at the polls than the negro man." South Carolina senator "Pitchfork" Ben Tillman argued, "Experience has taught us that negro women are much more aggressive in asserting the 'rights of the race' than the negro men are."

The NAWSA's southern strategy had failed, and the fledgling white suffrage societies in the South died or became inactive. The argument that enfranchising women would solve the "Negro problem" not only lost saliency but now appeared to be an argument threatening white dominance.

By 1910, however, the southern suffrage campaign had entered a new phase. With white supremacy solidly ensconced, proponents now argued that there was no connection between the issues of woman suffrage and race. Instead, it was the Progressive movement that influenced strategy. Continued industrialization and urbanization had altered life for American women, increasing the size of the middle class and the number of college-educated women. The move into club work by women of both races, in part a consequence of these changes, led to the view even among antisuffragists that women had a role to play in public life in areas that were an extension of their domestic responsibilities, like education and sanitation. In the North, Progressives thought that woman suffrage would enhance their prospects for legislative success. In the South a major opponent of suffrage was the textile industry, which feared women's objections to child labor.

Catt's secret "winning plan" emphasized intensive lobbying of congressmen, pushing for referenda in states likely to pass woman suffrage and avoiding such fights where they were likely to fail (which included all southern states), and keeping the issue of black woman suffrage in the background. Alice Paul, who broke from the NAWSA to form the National Woman's Party, used pickets and hunger strikes and a policy of holding the party in power responsible for failure to pass a suffrage amendment; but she too sought to keep black women out of the spotlight. In the NWP's 1913 parade in front of the White House, Wells-Barnett was told not to march with the white suffragists from Chicago, for fear of offending white southerners. This failure to publicly support black woman suffrage made their cause vulnerable to various attempts to change the language of the Anthony amendment (as the woman suffrage proposal was known) to exclude black women. Strong objections by the NACW and the National Association for the Advancement of Colored People, coupled with the realization in the North that the votes of black men would be significant in any ratification battle, prevented the success of this "states' rights" strategy.

The Anthony amendment had been continuously before Congress since 1878, but it received little support until the second decade of the twentieth century. Finally, in 1919 the necessary two-thirds vote was attained. Before becoming part of the Constitution, however, the amendment needed the approval of thirty-six states. Texas became the ninth state in the Union and the first in the South to ratify the amendment, followed by Arkansas and Kentucky; however, Alabama, Georgia, South Carolina, Virginia, Maryland, Mississippi, Louisiana, and Delaware opposed it. Of the five states yet to take action, Connecticut, Vermont, and Florida failed to call special legislative sessions to address the issue, and North Carolina, which did so, did not pass the amendment. Attention then turned to Tennessee. The antis mounted a strong campaign, melting away support for the amendment, which finally passed by only one vote. The Nineteenth Amendment was added to the Constitution on August 26, 1920, ending a campaign that had begun in 1848. Eventually all of the southern states ratified; but some, clinging to the antebellum view of women as ladies too angelic and pure to be sullied by the evils of the political world, were incredibly slow to do so: Maryland (1941), Virginia (1952), Alabama (1953), Florida (1969), South Carolina (1969), Georgia (1970), Louisiana (1970), North Carolina (1971), and, finally, Mississippi (1984).

Initially, large numbers of black women registered throughout the South, especially in Georgia and Louisiana. They founded "colored women voters' leagues" to provide instructions to both men and women on how to qualify for registration. Southern whites, however, feared that black voters would bring back the two-party system by voting Republican, the party of Lincoln and Reconstruction. The example of Jacksonville, Florida, demonstrated the reality of such a threat. The NAWSA had changed its name to the League of Women Voters when success seemed assured. The Jacksonville branch, however, became the Duval County League of Democratic Women Voters when black women registered and voted in greater numbers than the white women. In fact, there is fragmentary evidence from cities where black women were not prevented from voting that they voted in greater proportions than white women and in about the same proportion as black men.

Despite such interest in the ballot, the white registrars and politicians soon perfected ways to largely eliminate black women's vote, all the while explaining low voter turnout as a manifestation of black apathy. Columbia, South Carolina, for example, kept black women from the voter rolls by requiring them to have paid taxes on property valued at three hundred dollars and pass a literacy test judged by white registrars. No such requirements were made for white women. The NAACP testified before Congress in 1920 concerning such abuses, but to no avail. The League of Women Voters again compromised its principles for the sake of retaining white southerners: it permitted African American women to speak about these abuses before its 1921 convention in Cleveland but took no action. The NWP's record was no better. *The Crisis* reported that "Miss Paul was indifferent" to an appeal from a delegation to the annual convention of sixty black women from fourteen states, whose statement declared that "Five million women in the United States cannot be denied their rights without all the women of the United States feeling the effect of that denial. No women are free until all are free." But Paul insisted that black women's inability to enjoy the franchise was a "racial" and not a feminist issue.

At this pivotal juncture the hopes of bridging the rift between black and white women vanished. Realizing that woman suffrage had failed to usher in a new era for African Americans, black women shifted their allegiance and altered their consciousness. By the mid-1930s black women became "race women." Burning from the dismissal of white suffragists, they reconcentrated activities and attention on dismantling American apartheid and white supremacy. From a high of two hundred thousand members, by 1930 the membership of the older NACW had dropped to approximately fifty thousand. Clearly, the always separate and distinct black women's culture needed revitalization in the Depression and World War II decades. By the 1930s, leading black political women had arrived at the conclusion that one massive political organization should be created through which they could make their collective voices heard. It is within this context that Mary McLeod Bethune founded the National Council of Negro Women in 1935.

In an initial press release, Bethune declared the purpose of the NCNW to be the development of "competent and courageous leadership among Negro women and [to] effect their integration and that of all Negro people into the political, economic, education, cultural, and social life of their communities and the nation." During the next twenty years black women's political consciousness and agency were mobilized to an impressive degree. As black women fought racial discrimination, Bethune confided to fellow clubwoman Mary Church Terrell that she intended for the NCNW to "insure greater cooperation among women in varied lines of endeavor." She thought it was time for "Negro women [to] . . . do some thinking on public questions." By the mid-1940s the NCNW had become the largest black women's organization in America, numbering eight hundred thousand members.

In Montgomery, Alabama, under the leadership of an English professor at Alabama State, black women organized the Women's Political Council. Jo Ann Robinson and her colleagues were the women who started the Montgomery Bus Boycott and in so doing laid the basis for the retirement of Jim Crow's strange career. The boycott ignited the modern Civil Rights Movement. Historian Sara Evans, commenting on the centrality of black women in the Movement, wrote, "In addition to their warmth and courage in taking in civil rights workers, these black women also furnished the backbone of leadership in local movements. Volunteers wrote home of 'Mama' doggedly attempting to register again and again or of a rural woman attending a precinct meeting. [And when] . . . no one showed up . . . with a neighbor as a witness, she called the meeting to order, elected herself a delegate and wrote up the minutes.

Black women opened the floodgates of protest that drenched the country for the next two decades, resulting in the passage of the Twenty-fourth Amendment to the U.S. Constitution in 1964, outlawing poll taxes, and the passage of the Voting Rights Act of 1965. That African Americans now enjoy the franchise is a testament to the effectiveness of black women's quiet persistence and, most important, the significance of the compounded identities and multiple consciousness of generations of resourceful black women.

Chapter 59

Woman Suffrage and the Fifteenth Amendment

Mary Church Terrell

Mary Church Terrell (1863–1954), founder and president of the National Association of Colored Women (NACW), was born into an elite, free black family in Memphis, Tennessee. She devoted her life to race and gender equality. Terrell graduated from Oberlin College in 1884 and later taught at Wilberforce University and then M Street High School in Washington, D.C., before founding the NACW in 1896.

The following selection is reprinted from "Woman Suffrage and the Fifteenth Amendment," Terrell's contribution to a symposium on votes for women in the Crisis, *August 1915.*

Even if I believed that women should be denied the right of suffrage, wild horses could not drag such an admission from my pen or my lips, for this reason: precisely the same arguments used to prove that the ballot be withheld from women are advanced to prove that colored men should not be allowed to vote. The reasons for repealing the Fifteenth Amendment differ but little from the arguments advanced by those who oppose the enfranchisement of women. Consequently, nothing could be more inconsistent than that colored people should use their influence against granting the ballot to women, if they believe that colored men should enjoy this right which citizenship confers.

What could be more absurd and ridiculous than that one group of individuals who are trying to throw off the yoke of oppression themselves, so as to get relief from conditions which handicap and injure them, should favor laws and customs which impede the progress of another unfortunate group and hinder them in every conceivable way. For the sake of consistency, therefore, if my sense of justice were not developed at all, and I could not reason intelligently, as a colored woman I should not tell my dearest friend that I opposed woman suffrage.

But how can any one who is able to use reason, and who believes in dealing out justice to all God's creatures, think it is right to withhold from one-half the human race rights and privileges freely accorded to the other half, which is neither more deserving nor more capable of exercising them?

For two thousand years mankind has been breaking down the various barriers which interposed themselves between human beings and their perfect freedom to exercise all the faculties with which they were divinely endowed. Even in monarchies old fetters which formerly restricted freedom, dwarfed the intellect and doomed certain individuals to narrow circumscribed spheres, because of the mere accident of birth are being loosed and broken one by one. In view of such wisdom and experience the political subjection of women in the United States can be likened only to a relic of barbarism, or to a spot upon the sun, or to an octopus holding this republic in its hideous grasp, so that further progress to the best form of government is impossible and that precious ideal its founders promised it would be seems nothing more tangible than a mirage.

Chapter 60

Woman Suffrage and the Negro

The Messenger

The Messenger *(1917–1928) was a black monthly magazine edited by then-social-ists A. Philip Randolph and Chandler Owen.*

The following selection is reprinted from the editorial "Woman Suffrage and the Negro," Messenger, *November 1917.*

For other editorials from the Messenger, *see chapters 55 and 62. For another selection by Randolph, see chapter 72.*

Woman suffrage is coming!

Some women want it, and some women don't want it.

Women are taxpayers, producers and consumers just the same as men are, and they are justly entitled to vote.

The sentimental and puritanical objections advanced by the squeamish moral-ists won't stand. Sex is no bar to woman's participating in the industrial world and it should be none to her participating in the political world.

Negro men should realize their responsibility and duty in the coming election on the question of woman suffrage. Remember that if the right to vote benefits the Negro man, the right to vote will also benefit the Negro woman.

If white women ought to have the right to vote, then colored women ought to have the right to vote. If it will be beneficial to one, it will be beneficial to the other. Colored Women are taxpayers, producers and consumers and they have a right to express their sentiment as regards the school systems, sanitation, the high cost of living, war and everything else which affects the general public. Of course, there are some colored women who will speak against woman suffrage, just as there are some white women who will speak for it. There were some Negro slaves who were opposed to freedom. Such kinks in the mind of the common people are not unusual.

Of course, when they are seen among the aristocracy, the reason is not difficult to see. Throughout history the few have attempted to keep the many in economic and political slavery.

But the great sweep of democracy moves on. The artificial standards of sex or race should not stand against it.

All peoples, regardless of race, creed or sex will be drawn into the vortex of world democracy.

Just as there could not be any union while some men were slaves and some men were free, there can be no democracy while white men vote and white women, colored women and colored men in the South don't vote.

Mr. Negro Voter, do your "bit."

Chapter 61

The Great Migration

W. E. B. Du Bois

Until World War I, the overwhelming majority of African Americans still lived in the rural South. Beginning with the northern labor shortage caused by the war, the twentieth century saw a major migration of blacks from the rural south to northern cities that transformed American labor and politics. About 500,000 blacks moved to northern cities during the war. This grassroots process continued through the 1970s, eventually resulting in the transfer of more than 6 million blacks. Historians now refer to this internal population shift as the Great Migration.

The following selection is excerpted from W. E. B. Du Bois, "The Economics of the Negro Problem," in The American Labor Year Book, 1917–18, *ed. Alexander Trachtenberg (New York, 1918), 180–82.*

For more details, see James Grossman, Land of Hope: Chicago, Black Southerners, and the Great Migration *(1989) and Joe Trotter, ed.,* The Great Migration in Historical Perspective *(1991).*

Since 1910, the most significant economic development among Negroes has been a large migration from the South. This has been estimated to have involved at least 250,000 and is still going on.

As to the reasons of the migration, undoubtedly the immediate cause was economic, and the movement began because of floods in middle Alabama and Mississippi and because the latest devastation of the boll weevil came in these same districts.

A second economic cause was the cutting off of immigration from Europe to the North and consequently widespread demand for common labor. The U.S. Department of Labor writes: "A representative of this department has made an investigation in regard thereto, but a report has not been printed for general distribution. It may be stated, however, that most of the help imported from the South has been employed by railroad companies, packinghouses, foundries, factories, automobile plants in northern states as far west as Nebraska. At the present time, the U.S. Employment Service is not cooperating in the direction of Negro help to the North."

The third reason has been outbreaks of mob violence in northern and southwestern Georgia and in western South Carolina.

These have been the three immediate causes, but back of them is, undoubtedly, the general dissatisfaction with the conditions in the South.

A colored man of Sumter, S.C., says: "The immediate occasion of the migration is, of course, the opportunity in the North, now at last open to us, for industrial betterment. The real causes are the conditions which we have had to bear because there was no escape."

These conditions he sums up as the destruction of the Negro's political rights, the curtailment of his civil rights, the lack of the protection of life, liberty and property, low wages, the Jim Crow [railroad and street] car, residential and labor segregation laws and poor educational facilities.

The full economic result of this migration and its extent in the future cannot be forecast at the present writing, but the chances are that the demand for labor caused by the European war will result in a large rearrangement of Negro laborers and accelerate all tendencies in the distribution of that labor along lines already noted.

Figures like these are beginning to place the so-called Negro problem beyond the realm of mere opinion and prejudice. Here we see a social evolution working itself out before our eyes. The mass of the freedmen are changing rapidly the economic basis of their social development. They have not given up their close connection with the soil, but they are changing its character tremendously, so that today a fourth of them are peasant proprietors. They are forcing themselves into the trades despite the long opposition of white labor unions. As small businessmen, purveying principally to their own group, they are gaining a foothold in trade. As more or less skilled employees, they form a considerable part of our transportation system and they are rapidly developing a professional class which serves its own group and also serves the nation at large.

Many indications of the effect of this new development are seen in the peculiar incidence of racial prejudice. We hear today less argument about Negro education and more about sumptuary laws to control Negro expenditure, freedom of movement and initiative and residence. Politically handicapped as the colored man is, he is learning to wield economic power, which shows that his political rights cannot long be held back. And finally, in the division of his occupations, there is evidence of forethought and calculation within the group which foreshadows greater cooperation for the future.

Since the above was written, there has been a series of important economic happenings involving the American Negro which ought to be noted.

Severe floods and the cotton boll weevil reduced Negro tenants in many parts of the lower South to great distress during the winter following the declaration of war [i.e., America's entrance into World War I—*Eds.*]. They sold their cotton at a low figure or had none to sell. When the price of cotton rose, the plantation owners reaped the benefit and immediately began plans for the next season, calculating on labor at an unusually low price.

Meantime, a great foreign immigration of common laborers was cut off by the war, and there arose in the North an unusual demand for common labor. The Negroes began to migrate. In eighteen months 250,000 left the South and moved into the North. They were chiefly attracted by wages which were from 50 to 200 percent above what they had been used to receiving. And they saw also a chance to escape the lynching and discrimination of the South.

Every effort was made by the South to retain them. They were arrested wholesale, labor agents were taxed $500 to $1,000 or more for licenses, and the daily press of the South began to take on a more conciliatory tone. A slow rise in wages has begun. The migration of Negroes, however, continues, since the demand continues. It is probable that not for a generation after the close of the war will there be any great immigration to the United States from Europe. In that case, the American Negro will have a chance to establish himself in large numbers in the North. We may look for migration of two or even three million.

To offset this, the labor unions have used every effort. The argument was that these blacks kept down the rate of wages. Undoubtedly they did keep wages from rising as high as they otherwise would have, but if Negroes had been received into the unions and trained into the philosophy of the labor cause (which for obvious reasons most of them did not know), they would have made as staunch union men as any. They are not working for low wages because they prefer to, but because they have to. Nine-tenths of the unions, however, are closed absolutely against them, either by constitutional provision or by action of the local unions. It is probable, therefore, that the friction will go on in the North. East St. Louis has already been echoed at Chester, Pa., and in other industrial centers.

Thus . . . industrial slavery, murder, riot and unbelievable cruelty have met the Negro—and this not at the hands of the employers but at the hands of his fellow laborers who have in reality common cause with him.

Chapter 62

Migration and Political Power

The Messenger

The Messenger *(1917–1928) was a black monthly magazine edited by then-socialists A. Philip Randolph and Chandler Owen.*

The following selection is reprinted from the editorial "Migration and Political Power," Messenger, *July 1919.*

For other editorials from the Messenger, *see chapters 55 and 60. For another selection by Randolph, see chapter 72.*

The Negroes have come from the South in large numbers and they are still coming. Before the movement is stopped it is not improbable that from three to four million Negroes may come into the North, East and West.

Let them come!

As they leave the chief "land of the lynching bee and the home of the slave" they secure better industrial opportunities, education for their children and political power. From states in which they were disfranchised they go into states where they have a man's right to vote—the right to be freedmen in fact.

With better industrial opportunity the Negroes secure wealth. They have something to fight about.

With better educational opportunity the Negroes secure information. They then have light to see how to fight—a lamp for guidance.

With the possession of the ballot the Negroes have political power—ammunition. They then have something to fight with.

Men don't fight very strongly unless they have something to fight about, and they don't fight very effectively unless they have something to fight with. As the Negro migrates North and West he secures political power to help himself in his new abode and at the same time to strike a blow for his less favored brothers in wicked "old Dixie."

Chapter 63

The Objectives of the
Universal Negro Improvement Association

Marcus Garvey

Jamaican-born black nationalist Marcus Garvey (1887–1940) began the "back to Africa movement," also known as Garveyism. He argued that equality could only be achieved through economic and political independence. Combining economic nationalism with Pan-Africanism, he founded the Universal Negro Improvement Association (UNIA) in 1911, a mass organization that at its peak may have had a million members in the United States, the Caribbean, and Africa. In 1916, he moved to the United States, setting up a branch of UNIA headquartered in Harlem and a weekly newspaper, the Negro World.

Selling stock by mail, Garvey formed the Black Star Line in 1919, an international shipping company that encouraged trade and transportation between Africa and the Americas. Three years later it suspended operation, as did most of UNIA's other businesses. At the instigation of the FBI, the Justice Department indicted him for mail fraud. In 1927, he was deported after serving a five-year jail term.

For Garvey's writings, see Robert Hill, ed., The Marcus Garvey and Universal Negro Improvement Association Papers *(10 vols. projected, 1983–). For biographies, see Judith Stein,* The World of Marcus Garvey: Race and Class in Modern Society *(1986) and Rupert Lewis,* Marcus Garvey *(1988).*

The following selection is excerpted from "Aims and Objects of Movement for Solution of Negro Problem," Philosophy and Opinions of Marcus Garvey, *ed. Amy Jacques-Garvey (New York: Universal Publishing House, 1926), 2:37–43.*

Generally the public is kept misinformed of the truth surrounding new movements of reform. Very seldom, if ever, reformers get the truth told about them and their movements. Because of this natural attitude, the Universal Negro Improvement Association has been greatly handicapped in its work, causing thereby one of the most liberal and helpful human movements of the twentieth century to be held up to ridicule by those who take pride in poking fun at anything not already successfully established.

The white man of America has become the natural leader of the world. He, because of his exalted position, is called upon to help in all human efforts. From nations to individuals the appeal is made to him for aid in all things affecting humanity, so, naturally, there can be no great mass movement or change without first acquainting the leader on whose sympathy and advice the world moves.

It is because of this, and more so because of a desire to be Christian friends with the white race, why I explain the aims and objects of the Universal Negro Improvement Association.

The Universal Negro Improvement Association is an organization among Negroes that is seeking to improve the condition of the race, with the view of establishing a nation in Africa where Negroes will be given the opportunity to develop by themselves, without creating the hatred and animosity that now exist in countries of the white race through Negroes rivaling them for the highest and best positions in government, politics, society and industry. The organization believes in the rights of all men, yellow, white and black. To us, the white race has a right to the peaceful possession and occupation of countries of its own and in like manner the yellow and black races have their rights. It is only by an honest and liberal consideration of such rights can the world be blessed with the peace that is sought by Christian teachers and leaders.

The Spiritual Brotherhood of Man

The following preamble to the constitution of the organization speaks for itself:

> The Universal Negro Improvement Association and African Communities' League is a social, friendly, humanitarian, charitable, educational, institutional, constructive, and expansive society, and is founded by persons, desiring to the utmost to work for the general uplift of the Negro peoples of the world. And the members pledge themselves to do all in their power to conserve the rights of their noble race and to respect the rights of all mankind, believing always in the Brotherhood of Man and the Fatherhood of God. The motto of the organization is: One God! One Aim! One Destiny! Therefore, let justice be done to all mankind, realizing that if the strong oppresses the weak confusion and discontent will ever mark the path of man, but with love, faith and charity toward all the reign of peace and plenty will be heralded into the world and the generation of men shall be called Blessed.

The declared objects of the association are:

> To establish a Universal Confraternity among the race; to promote the spirit of pride and love; to reclaim the fallen; to administer to and assist the needy; to assist in civilizing the backward tribes of Africa; to assist in the development of Independent Negro Nations and Communities; to establish a central nation for the race; to establish Commissaries or Agencies in the principal countries and cities of the world for the representation of all Negroes; to promote a conscientious Spiritual worship among the native tribes of Africa; to establish Universities, Colleges, Academies and Schools for the racial education and culture of the people; to work for better conditions among Negroes everywhere.

Supplying a Long Felt Want

The organization of the Universal Negro Improvement Association has supplied among Negroes a long-felt want. Hitherto the other Negro movements in America, with the exception of the Tuskegee effort of Booker T. Washington, sought to teach the Negro to aspire to social equality with the whites, meaning thereby the right to intermarry and fraternize in every social way. This has been the source of much trouble and still some Negro organizations continue to preach this dangerous "race destroying doctrine" added to a program of political agitation and aggression. The Universal Negro Improvement Association on the other hand believes in and teaches the pride and purity of race. We believe that the white race should uphold its racial pride and perpetuate itself, and that the black race should do likewise. We believe that there is room enough in the world for the various race groups to grow and develop by themselves without seeking to destroy the Creator's plan by the constant introduction of mongrel types.

The unfortunate condition of slavery as imposed upon the Negro, and which caused the mongrelization of the race, should not be legalized and continued now to the harm and detriment of both races.

The time has really come to give the Negro a chance to develop himself to a moral-standard-man, and it is for such an opportunity that the Universal Negro Improvement Association seeks in the creation of an African nation for Negroes, where the greatest latitude would be given to work out this racial ideal.

There are hundreds of thousands of colored people in America who desire race amalgamation and miscegenation as a solution of the race problem. These people are, therefore, opposed to the race pride ideas of black and white; but the thoughtful of both races will naturally ignore the ravings of such persons and honestly work for the solution of a problem that has been forced upon us.

Liberal white America and race loving Negroes are bound to think at this time and thus evolve a program or plan by which there can be a fair and amicable settlement of the question.

We cannot put off the consideration of the matter, for time is pressing on our hands. The educated Negro is making rightful constitutional demands. The great white majority will never grant them, and thus we march on to danger if we do not now stop and adjust the matter.

The time is opportune to regulate the relationship between both races. Let the Negro have a country of his own. Help him to return to his original home, Africa, and there give him the opportunity to climb from the lowest to the highest positions in a state of his own. If not, then the nation will have to hearken to the demand of the aggressive, "social equality" organization, known as the National Association for the Advancement of Colored People, of which W. E. B. Du Bois is leader, which declares vehemently for social and political equality, viz.: Negroes and whites in the same hotels, homes, residential districts, public and private places, a Negro as president, members of the Cabinet, Governors of States, Mayors of cities, and leaders of society in the United States. In this agitation, Du Bois is ably supported by the "Chicago Defender," a colored newspaper published in

Chicago. This paper advocates Negroes in the Cabinet and Senate. All these, as everybody knows, are the Negroes' constitutional rights, but reason dictates that the masses of the white race will never stand by the ascendency of an opposite minority group to the favored positions in a government, society and industry that exist by the will of the majority, hence the demand of the Du Bois group of colored lead, ultimately, to further disturbances in riots, lynching and mob rule. The only logical solution therefore, is to supply the Negro with opportunities and environments of his own, and there point him to the fullness of his ambition.

Negroes Who Seek Social Equality

The Negro who seeks the White House in America could find ample play for his ambition in Africa. The Negro who seeks the office of Secretary of State in America would have a fair chance of demonstrating his diplomacy in Africa. The Negro who seeks a seat in the Senate or of being governor of a State in America, would be provided with a glorious chance for statesmanship in Africa.

The Negro has a claim on American white sympathy that can not be denied. The Negro has labored for 300 years in contributing to America's greatness. White America will not be unmindful, therefore, of this consideration, but will treat him kindly. Yet all human beings have a limit to their humanity. The humanity of white America, we realize, will seek self-protection and self-preservation, and that is why the thoughtful and reasonable Negro sees no hope in America for satisfying the aggressive program of the National Association for the Advancement of Colored People, but advances the reasonable plan of the Universal Negro Improvement Association, that of creating in Africa a nation and government for the Negro race.

This plan when properly undertaken and prosecuted will solve the race problem in America in fifty years. Africa affords a wonderful opportunity at the present time for colonization by the Negroes of the Western world. There is Liberia, already established as an independent Negro government. Let white America assist Afro-Americans to go there and help develop the country. Then, there are the late German colonies; let white sentiment force England and France to turn them over to the American and West Indian Negroes who fought for the Allies in the World's War [World War I]. Then, France, England and Belgium owe America billions of dollars which they claim they cannot afford to repay immediately. Let them compromise by turning over Sierra Leone and the Ivory Coast on the West Coast of Africa and add them to Liberia and help make Liberia a state worthy of her history.

The Negroes of Africa and America are one in blood. They have sprung from the same common stock. They can work and live together and thus make their own racial contribution to the world.

Will deep thinking and liberal white America help? It is a considerate duty.

It is true that a large number of self-seeking colored agitators and so-called political leaders, who hanker after social equality and fight for the impossible in politics and governments, will rave, but remember that the slave-holder raved, but the North said, "Let the slaves go free"; the British Parliament raved when the Colonists said, "We want a free and American nation"; the Monarchists of France raved when the people declared for a more liberal form of government.

The masses of Negroes think differently from the self-appointed leaders of the race. The majority of Negro leaders are selfish, self-appointed and not elected by the people. The people desire freedom in a land of their own, while the colored politician desires office and social equality for himself in America, and that is why we are asking white America to help the masses to realize their objective. . . .

Help the Negro to Return Home

Surely the time has come for the Negro to look homeward. He has won civilization and Christianity at the price of slavery. The Negro who is thoughtful and serviceable, feels that God intended him to give to his brothers still in darkness, the light of his civilization. The very light element of Negroes do not want to go back to Africa. They believe that in time, through miscegenation, the American race will be of their type. This is a fallacy and in that respect the agitation of the mulatto leader Dr. W. E. B. Du Bois and the National Association for the Advancement of Colored People is dangerous to both races.

The off-colored people, being children of the Negro race, should combine to reestablish the purity of their own race, rather than seek to perpetuate the abuse of both races. That is to say, all elements of the Negro race should be encouraged to get together and form themselves into a healthy whole, rather than seeking to lose their identities through miscegenation and social intercourse with the white race. These statements are made because we desire an honest solution of the problem and no flattery or deception will bring that about.

Let the white and Negro people settle down in all seriousness and in true sympathy and solve the problem. When that is done, a new day of peace and good will will be ushered in.

The natural opponents among Negroes to a program of this kind are that lazy element who believe always in following the line of least resistance, being of themselves void of initiative and the pioneering spirit to do for themselves. The professional Negro leader and the class who are agitating for social equality feel that it is too much work for them to settle down and build up a civilization of their own. They feel it is easier to seize on to the civilization of the white man and under the guise of constitutional rights fight for those things that the white man has created. Natural reason suggests that the white man will not yield them, hence such leaders are but fools for their pains. Teach the Negro to do for himself, help him the best way possible in that direction; but to encourage him into the belief that he is going to possess himself of the things that others have fought and died for, is to build up in his mind false hopes never to be realized. As for instance, Dr. W. E. B. Du Bois, who has been educated by white charity, is a brilliant scholar, but he is not a hard worker. He prefers to use his higher intellectual abilities to fight for a place among white men in society, industry and in politics, rather than use that ability to work and create for his own race that which the race could be able to take credit for. He would not think of repeating for his race the work of the Pilgrim Fathers or the Colonists who laid the foundation of America, but he prefers to fight and agitate for the privilege of dancing with a white lady at a ball at the Biltmore or at the Astoria hotels in New York. That kind of leadership will destroy the Negro in America and against which the Universal Negro Improvement Association is fighting.

The Universal Negro Improvement Association is composed of all shades of Negroes—blacks, mulattoes and yellows, who are all working honestly for the purification of their race, and for sympathetic adjustment of the race problem.

Chapter 64

The Garvey Milieu

Alan Dawley

Alan Dawley, professor of history at the College of New Jersey, is the author of Class and Community: The Industrial Revolution in Lynn *(1976) and co-editor of* Working for Democracy: American Workers from the Revolution to the Present *(1985).*

As the country at large wrestled with the impact of emerging social forces on inherited liberal state structures, the South made a significant contribution in unashamedly restating such hierarchical values as employer absolutism, white supremacy, and women's subordination. These values played important roles in rationalizing the newly emerging forms of authority—corporate managerial prerogatives, racial segregation, and privileged access for men to the highest positions of pay and power. If the reactionary politics of the 1920s were crucial in securing a new form of social hierarchy against opposing egalitarian potentials, then, surely, the ruling values of the South played a major part.

Northerners who normally gagged on openly hierarchical values made an exception for white supremacy. As hundreds of thousands of southern black migrants poured into the North, the question inevitably arose how they would be inducted into northern life. Would northern states imitate their southern counterparts by enacting Jim Crow statutes? Would they, instead, treat the new arrivals as just another group of immigrants left to fend for themselves in the pluralist marketplace? If Washington stood foursquare behind *de jure* segregation in Dixie, would it do the same in the liberal North?

One thing was clear. The rapid expansion of the black population required abandonment of the exclusionary practices common in the nineteenth century, when a number of northern states had excluded African-Americans from legal residence and full citizenship; when manufacturers had all but excluded African-Americans from employment, quite the reverse of their southern counterparts; and when most trade unions, including the railway brotherhoods and the machinists, had prohibited black members by constitution or initiation rites. Now as the tide of migrants to the North rose ever higher, outright exclusion became untenable. It was equally clear that Afro-Americans were not going to be treated as just another ethnic group. First of all, they were the most thoroughly dispossessed of the migrants to northern cities. Almost none accumulated significant business capital, and relatively few could afford home ownership. In northern cities such as Chicago, the foreign born were four times more likely than black families to own a home. In terms of both individual and intergenerational mobility, the evidence is overwhelming that whatever differences existed among European-Americans, all fared better than African-Americans. None of the Polonias and Little Italies that dotted the urban landscape were as impermeable as the emerging racial ghettos of South Chicago and Harlem. Whereas a shift in the relative position of, say, Poles and Norwegians affected little else, a shift in the color line affected the entire social order. In short, the Afro-American experience was unique.

All this suggests that race carried far more weight than ethnicity did, not because of genes or skin color but because it stood as a fundamental element of social hierarchy in the supposedly egalitarian North. De facto segregation made the black ghetto a basic part of every major northern city. Although the driving forces behind the creation of the ghetto were economic and cultural, the role of the state cannot be gain-said. Authorities refrained from prosecuting white rioters, overlooked employment discrimination, sanctioned restrictive covenants and other practices that led to segregated housing, and tolerated the second-class schools, hospitals, and services that became the standing outrage of everyday life. Insofar as all this underwrote the job ceiling, inferior schooling, and the whole cycle of poverty, northern municipal and state governments became the official guarantors of inequality.

Segregation may have set the limiting conditions, but it did not determine what Afro-Americans would do with them. They determined that for themselves, and for a time the leading force in the black community was Marcus Garvey and his Universal Negro Improvement Association (UNIA). From his Harlem base, the charismatic Jamaican immigrant spread his message throughout the country— "Up, you mighty race, you can accomplish what you will." He captured hope, not despair, and his identification with Africa was not an escapist fantasy, but a search for historical identity to instill race price. Unlike intellectuals, who never got outside isolated circles of pan-African agitation, Garvey bridged the gap between the Afro-Caribbean elite and the native black masses, and he did it while rejecting the typical prejudice within the black community in favor of light skin. Just as national leaders in other ethnic groups reacted to Anglo-Saxon scorn with prideful presentations of their own national cultures, so Garvey turned white civilization inside out with the aim of constructing a great black civilization.

Like other forms of ethnic consciousness, Garvey's racial nationalism came on strong with the fragmentation of working-class protest after the defeat of the great strikes [of 1919]. It swelled in the face of frustration both for socialists such as A. Philip Randolph, who ran into the same Red Scare brick wall as his white comrades, and for liberals such as Du Bois, who fell victim to the same reversal of hope as his fellow progressives. With trade unions in decline and the NAACP at a plateau, as many as 2 million flocked to the UNIA at its peak from 1920 to 1922, making it the biggest mass organization in Afro-American history outside the churches and fraternal/sororal organizations.

In its economic doctrines, the UNIA combined capitalism and nationalism, personal wealth and racial progress. It sought to pool the meager resources of sharecroppers, beauticians, and schoolteachers in investment schemes such as the Black Star Line, an international shipping company. Garvey's agents sold shares by the thousands in what was billed as the UNIA "navy." What distinguished this venture from the numbers racket, proliferating in the ghettos at the same time, was the fact that the line's ship, the *Yarmouth*, actually made voyages in the hope that, one day, the venture would be the sea bridge to Liberia. As a poor person's investment trust, it sought to address the material privation of the black community through the values of family capitalism. In his twin message of race pride and individual accumulation, Garvey was in perfect accord with the restoration of race consciousness and old-fashioned proprietary values in the culture at large. He was right in step with the prevailing idea that "the business of America is business," and, in fact, he supported Calvin Coolidge in 1924.

But the same factors that created the UNIA made it impossible for it to succeed. Garvey's numerous critics included the socialist editors of *The Messenger,* who wrote: "Negroes are the easy marks of the sharpers, having as it were some vague idea that they can make millions like Ford, Rockefeller, and Morgan by buying stocks." Du Bois in this state of his protean career was less averse to black capitalism, but as an implacable opponent of segregation he saw Garvey's racial separatism as merely white supremacy turned upside down. Garvey himself gave his critics fatal ammunition by praising the separatist message of the KKK after meeting with one of its leaders.

Deeply embroiled in controversy within the black community, Garvey was unable to forge a unified defense against the federal government's attempt to put him behind bars. Military intelligence and the Bureau of Investigation had already put him under surveillance during the war [World War I], and the growth of Garvey's following convinced J. Edgar Hoover and his bureau boss, William Burns, that it was time to rein in this "dangerous agitator." Disguising their political motives, they secured a criminal indictment against Garvey, who went on trial for mail fraud in May 1923. Instead of building a politically principled defense, Garvey fell into the government's trap by proclaiming his innocence and blaming his associates, which only gave credence to charges against the organization he ran. The trial itself had heavy racial and class overtones: Judge Julian Mack was an elite jurist of German-Jewish ancestry who had contributed to the NAACP but who could not comprehend Garvey's street-wise self-help schemes as anything but personal greed. Garvey actually lived quite modestly for all his public pomp, but he let fly anti-Semitic remarks about his Jewish persecutors, along with diatribes against Du Bois. Through this haze of class and racial prejudice, no one focused clearly on the political purpose of the trial, which was accomplished by Garvey's conviction, jailing, and, in 1927, his deportation to Jamaica.

This effort by the oppressed to cope with their predicament embraced fundamental values of their oppressors. There is nothing unusual in that phenomenon. What is surprising is Garvey's faith in a judicial system that was determined to convict him regardless of his innocence. He spoke favorably of American justice even as he portrayed himself as the victim of a conspiracy; apparently because he believed in universal standards of justice so compelling that even white men might adhere to them. In the same light, Garvey appealed to the universal aspiration for liberation, to which all who opposed racism and colonialism could adhere. That higher appeal set him off from his many venal contemporaries, including the high-placed merchants of greed in [President Warren] Harding's Ohio gang, and plain racketeers such as Al Capone, to whom there was no social movement, only the law of the strong and weak; and no universal yearning for freedom, only the desire for money and power. But an important ambiguity remains in the Garvey movement: at times, it gave vent to the same kind of intolerance that helped create it. Hate turned back hate. And that ambiguity was passed along to Garvey's closest successor, the Nation of Islam and its successive leaders W. D. Fard, Elijah Muhammed, and Louis Farrakhan.

Black nationalism was not just a reaction to white supremacy. It gave expression to authentic impulses within the Afro-American community—esteem, discipline, organization, self-improvement—and it inspired national anticolonial movements in Africa and cultural revival in the Caribbean. But it was inescapably paired with its opposite, because the myth of white supremacy was a fundamental ruling structure of American life. The pretense of a common Caucasian community could unite the elite and, more important in a democratic culture, bond otherwise social inferiors to their superiors. By contrast, the fictions of Nordic superiority or Anglo-Saxon "good blood," besides their mutual exclusions and inner confusions, could not embrace the majority of the country. Anti-Semitism served that purpose, but white racism served it best.

For that reason, black nationalism was the most significant and most tenacious of the ethnic nationalisms embedded in American culture. Irish nationalism lost its sting with Irish independence; Polish-American, Greek-American, and all the other American-immigrant cultures were rapidly becoming what the moderate Americanizers hoped—colorful ethnic variations on a central theme, fully compatible with mass culture and dominant marketplace values. Only African-American culture posed an indigestible alternative, because even when it did not adopt nationalist forms, it refused assent to the ruling structures of white supremacy. Locked in a fateful embrace, the opposing myths of black nationalism and white supremacy were doomed forever in a dance of death. Transcendence would have to come from other aspects of Afro-American culture—the tradition of freedom going back through Reconstruction to emancipation; but that was not reborn until the civil rights movement of the 1950s and 1960s. In the meantime, racism performed its labors of division and thereby denied progressive and radical social movements the necessary social base from which to compel a hearing for social justice.

Chapter 65

The Scottsboro Case

Robin D. G. Kelley

Robin D. G. Kelley, professor of history and Africana studies at New York University, is the author of Hammer and Hoe: Alabama Communists during the Great Depression *(1990),* Race Rebels: Culture, Politics and the Black Working Class *(1994), and* Yo Mama's Disfunktional! Fighting the Culture Wars in Urban America *(1997), and co-editor of* Imagining Home: Class, Culture, and Nationalism in the African Diaspora *(1994) and* The Young Oxford History of African Americans *(11 vols., 1995–1997).*

The following selection is a reprint of "Scottsboro" by Robin Kelley, from Encyclopedia of the American Left, *2d ed., ed. Mari Jo Buhle, Paul Buhle, and Dan Georgakas. Copyright © 1998 by Oxford University Press, Inc. Used by permission of Oxford University Press, Inc.*

For another selection by Kelley, see chapter 174.

The International Labor Defense's (ILD) involvement in the Scottsboro case, more than any other event, crystallized black support for the Communist Party in the 1930s. Accused of raping two white women (Ruby Bates and Victoria Price) on a freight train near Paint Rock, Alabama, nine young black men (Charlie Weems, Ozie Powell, Clarence Norris, Olen Montgomery, Willie Roberson, Haywood Patterson, Andy and Roy Wright, Eugene Williams), ages thirteen to twenty-one, were arrested on March 25, 1931, tried without adequate counsel, and hastily convicted on the basis of shallow evidence. All but Roy Wright were sentenced to death. Already in the midst of a mass antilynching campaign begun a year earlier, the ILD gained the confidence of the defendants and their parents, initiated a legal and political campaign for their freedom, and in the process waged a vicious battle for control over the case with the NAACP, who accused the Communists of using the young men for propaganda purposes.

The Scottsboro case was not simply an isolated instance of injustice, the Communists argued, but represented a common manifestation of national oppression and class rule in the South. Maintaining that a fair and impartial trial was impossible, the Party and its auxiliaries publicized the case widely in order to apply mass pressure on the Alabama justice system. Protests erupted throughout the country and as far away as Paris, Moscow, and South Africa, and the governor of Alabama was bombarded with telegrams, postcards, and letters demanding the immediate release of the "Scottsboro Boys." Through Scottsboro and other related cases, black and white Communists gained entrance into churches, lodges, and clubs in the African-American community, and eventually the ILD was regarded by some as a welcome addition to the panoply of "racial defense" organizations. Moreover, although the "Scottsboro Boys" apparently never directly identified with the Party's goals, they became cultural symbols on the Left, the subject of poems, songs, plays, and short stories that were published, circulated, and performed throughout the world.

The ILD waged a more conventional struggle in the courts as well. Its lawyers secured a new trial on appeal by arguing that the defendants were denied the right of counsel. For the new Scottsboro trials, which opened on March 27, 1933, the ILD had retained renowned criminal lawyer Samuel Leibowitz. More significant, a month before the trail date Ruby Bates repudiated the rape charge. Yet, despite new evidence and a brilliant defense, the all-white jury still found the Scottsboro defendants guilty—a verdict that seemed to buttress the Communists' interpretation of justice under capitalism and augmented the ILD's popularity in the black community. In fact, pressure from black militants and some sympathetic clergy and middle-class spokesmen compelled the virulently anticommunist NAACP secretary, Walter White, to develop a working relationship with the ILD in the spring of 1933. Several months later, however, in an unprecedented decision, Alabama circuit Judge James E. Horton overturned the March 1933 verdict and ordered a new trial.

Following a number of incredibly foolish legal and ethical mistakes (including an attempt to bribe Victoria Price), star lawyer Samuel Leibowitz bolted the ILD, which began to lose its prestige in the mid-1930s. With support of conservative black leaders, white liberals, and clergymen, Leibowitz founded the American Scottsboro Committee (ASC) in 1934. However, hostilities between the two bodies were slightly mitigated a year later when the ILD turned to the coalition-building politics of the Popular Front. In a tenuous alliance the ILD, ASC, NAACP, and ACLU formed the Scottsboro Defense Committee, which opted for a more reformist, legally oriented campaign in lieu of mass tactics. After failing to win the defendants' release in a 1936 trial, the SDC agreed to a strange plea bargain in 1937 whereby four defendants were released and the remaining five endured lengthy prison sentences—the last defendant was not freed until 1950.

Although the ILD did not win the defendants' unconditional release, its campaign to "Free the Scottsboro Boys" had tremendous legal and political implications during the early 1930s. For example, in one of the ILD's many appeals, a 1935 U.S. Supreme Court ruled that the defendant's constitutional rights were violated because blacks were systematically excluded from the jury rolls—a landmark opinion that spurred a battle to include African Americans on the jury rolls. Moreover, the realization that limited mass interracial action was possible challenged traditional liberalism and the politics of racial accommodation; the most scorned tactics of "mass pressure" would eventually be a precedent for civil rights activity two decades later.

Chapter 66

Women and Lynching

Jacquelyn Dowd Hall

Jacquelyn Dowd Hall, professor of history and director of Southern Oral History at the University of North Carolina, is the author of Revolt against Chivalry: Jesse Daniel Ames and the Women's Campaign against Lynching *(1979) and the co-author of* Like a Family: The Making of a Southern Cotton Mill World *(1987).*

The following selection is reprinted from "Women and Lynching," Southern Exposure, *Winter 1977. Reprinted with permission of* Southern Exposure.

> Southern trees bear a strange fruit,
> Blood on the leaves and blood at the root,
> Black bodies swinging in the Southern breeze,
> Strange fruit hanging from the poplar trees.
> —Billie Holiday

On May 3, 1930, a Sherman, Texas mob dragged George Hughes from a second floor cell and hanged him from a tree. Hughes was accused of raping his employer's wife. But the story told in the black community, and whispered in the white, was both chilling and familiar: an altercation over wages between a black laborer and a white farmer had erupted in ritual murder. The complicity of a moderate governor, the burning of the courthouse, reprisals against the black community—all brought the Sherman lynching unusual notoriety. But Hughes' death typified a long and deeply rooted tradition of extralegal racial violence.

Unlike other incidents in this bloody record, the Sherman lynching called forth a significant white response. In 1892, a black Memphis woman, Ida B. Wells Barnett, had initiated a one-woman anti-lynching campaign; after 1910, the NAACP carried on the struggle. But the first sign of the impact of this black-led movement on Southern whites came in 1930 when a Texas suffragist named Jessie Daniel Ames, moved by the Hughes lynching, launched a white women's campaign against lynching. Over the next 14 years, members of the Atlanta-based Association of Southern Women for the Prevention of Lynching sought to curb mob murder by disassociating the image of the Southern lady from its connotations of female vulnerability and retaliatory violence. They declared:

Lynching is an indefensible crime. Women dare no longer allow themselves to be the cloak behind which those bent upon personal revenge and savagery commit acts of violence and lawlessness in the name of women. We repudiate this disgraceful claim for all time.

Unlike most suffrage leaders, Jessie Daniel Ames brought the skills and consciousness acquired in the women's movement to bear on the struggle for racial justice. The historic link between abolitionism and women's rights had been broken by the late nineteenth century, when an organized women's movement emerged in the former slave states. Ames herself had registered no dissent against co-workers who argued that woman suffrage would help ensure social control by the white middle class. But as the Ku Klux Klan rose to power in the 1920s, she saw her efforts to mobilize enfranchised women behind progressive reforms undercut by racism and by her constituency's refusal to recognize the plight of those doubly oppressed by sex and race. As she shifted from women's rights to the interracial movement, she sought to connect women's opposition to violence with their strivings toward autonomy and social efficacy. In this sense, she led a revolt against chivalry which was part of a long process of both sexual and racial emancipation.

Two interlocking networks of organized women converged in the creation of the Anti-Lynching Association. From evangelical women's missionary societies, Ames drew the movement's language and assumptions. From such secular organizations as the League of Women Voters and the Joint Legislative Council, she acquired the campaign's pragmatic, issue-oriented style. Active, policy-making membership consisted at any one time of no more than 300 women. But the Association's claim to represent the viewpoint of the educated, middle-class white women of the South depended on the 109 women's groups which endorsed the anti-lynching campaign and on the 44,000 individuals who signed anti-lynching pledges.

Ames' commitment to grass-roots organizing, forged in the suffrage movement, found expression in the Association's central strategy: By "working through Baptist and Methodist missionary societies, organizations which go into the smallest communities when no other organizations will be found there," she hoped to reach the "wives and daughters of the man who lynched." Once won to the cause, rural church women could, in their role as moral guardians of the home and the community, act as a restraining force on male violence.

The social analysis of the Anti-Lynching Association began with its perception of the link between racial violence and attitudes toward women. Lynching was encouraged by the conviction that only such extreme sanctions stood between white women and the sexual aggression of black men. This "Southern rape complex," the Association argued, had no basis in fact. On the contrary, white women were often exploited and defamed in order to obscure the economic greed and sexual transgressions of white men. Rape and rumors of rape served as a kind of folk pornography in the Bible Belt. As stories spread, the victim was described in minute and progressively embellished detail: a public fantasy which implied a group participation in the rape of the woman almost as cathartic as the lynching of the alleged attacker. Indeed, the fear of rape, like the fear of lynching, functioned to keep a subordinate group in a state of anxiety and fear; both were ritual enactments of everyday power relationships.

Beginning with a rejection of this spurious protection, Association leaders developed an increasingly sophisticated analysis of racial violence. At the annual meeting of 1934, the Association adopted a resolution which Jessie Daniel Ames regarded as a landmark in Association thought:

> We declare as our deliberate conclusion that the crime of lynching is a logical result in every community that pursues the policy of humiliation and degradation of a part of its citizenship because of accident of birth; that exploits and intimidates the weaker element . . . for economic gain; that refuses equal educational opportunity to one portion of its children; that segregates arbitrarily a whole race. . . . and finally that denies a voice in the control of government to any fit and proper citizen because of race.

"The women," Ames proudly reported, "traced lynching directly to its roots in white supremacy."

Although the Association maintained its single-issue focus on lynching, its participants also confronted the explosive issue of interracial sex. They glimpsed the ways in which guilt over miscegenation, fear of sexual inadequacy, and economic tensions were translated into covert hostility toward white women, sexual exploitation of black women, and murderous rage against black men. Their response was to demand a single standard of morality: only when white men ceased to believe that "white women are their property and so are Negro women," would the racial war in the South over access to women come to an end. Only then would lynching cease and social reconstruction begin.

By World War II, the anti-lynching movement had succeeded in focusing the attention of an outraged world on the most spectacular form of racial oppression. The black migration to the North, emergence of an indigenous Southern liberalism, the interracial organizing drives of the CIO all contributed to the decline of extralegal violence. This successful struggle against terrorism made possible the emergence of the post–World War II civil-rights movement in the South. Only with the diffusion of massive repression, of overwhelming force, could the next phase of the black freedom movement begin: the direct-action assault on segregation in the Deep South.

On February 21, 1972, Jessie Daniel Ames died in a hospital in Austin, Texas. The civil-rights movement had long since bypassed the limits of her generation's vision of interracial cooperation and orderly legal processes. Ames had not become part of the folklore of Southern struggle. But, with the rebirth of feminism from the crucible of the civil-rights movement, her career has come to be seen in a more favorable light. On February 12, 1972, as Ames lay dying, Congresswoman Bella Abzug of New York addressed a Southern Women's Political Caucus in Nashville. Exhorting her audience to use the political power of organized women to affect the issues of the day, she could find no closer analogy for such a movement than the Association of Southern Women for the Prevention of Lynching. Jessie Daniel Ames would have wanted no better tribute.

Chapter 67

Blacks and the New Deal

Harvard Sitkoff

Harvard Sitkoff, professor of history at the University of New Hampshire, is the author of A New Deal for Blacks: The Emergence of Civil Rights as a National Issue *(1978), "Harry Truman and the Election of 1948: The Coming of Age of Civil Rights in American Politics,"* Journal of Southern History *(November 1971), and* The Struggle for Black Equality *(2d rev. ed., 1992), and the editor of* Fifty Years Later: The New Deal Evaluated *(1985).*

"Negroes" by Harvard Sitkoff. Reprinted with permission of G. K. Hall & Co., an imprint of Simon & Schuster Macmillan, from Franklin D. Roosevelt: Life and Times, an Encyclopedic View, *Otis L. Graham, Jr., and Meghan Robinson Wander, Editors. Copyright © 1985 by G. K. Hall & Co.*

For another selection by Sitkoff, see chapter 80.

No ethnic group anticipated the inauguration of Franklin Delano Roosevelt with less hope for a new deal than Afro-Americans; and none had less leverage on the president-elect. Despite an unemployment rate hovering around 50 percent, over two-thirds of the Negroes voting in 1932 went Republican, an even higher proportion than had voted for Herbert Hoover in 1928. The Democrats, for most blacks, remained the party that had opposed emancipation and Reconstruction and still defended racial discrimination, disfranchisement, segregation, and white supremacy. Roosevelt, in addition, had never done anything to champion the Negroes' cause. Indeed, his political career had been a model of deference to the white South on racial issues. His need to work harmoniously with a largely white southern-controlled Congress and white southern-staffed federal bureaucracy clearly augured for a continuation of racial neglect. Powerful party traditions of states' rights and decentralization further undermined the hopefulness of Negroes. Those who would administer the relief and recovery projects at the local level would likely be the very planters and politicians, industrialists and union leaders, who stood to gain the most by maintaining the oppression of blacks. The powerlessness of blacks in a political system dispensing assistance on the basis of the strength of the groups demanding it also dampened the expectations of the largely poor and unorganized black community. And the very ubiquity of the worst depression in American history made it even more unlikely that Roosevelt would act to remedy the plight of blacks. Hard times defined his mandate. None of his advisers considered jeopardizing economic reconstruction for some racial reform that would surely arouse a storm of political opposition.

The consequences of these conditions, reflecting three centuries of Negro poverty and powerlessness, were starkly revealed in the initial New Deal treatment of Afro-Americans. The indifference, if not racial hostility, of the National Recovery Administration (NRA) quickly earned it the black epithet "Negro Run Around." Heavily weighted in favor of large-scale, modernized business enterprises and unionized workers, the NRA codes forced many disadvantaged black entrepreneurs to close shop and permitted either lower wage scales for unorganized Negroes or the displacement of black workers by white employees. The Agricultural Adjustment Administration (AAA) practically invited discrimination by allowing white large landowners to dominate the county committees. The nearly 400,000 Negro sharecroppers and more than 300,000 black tenant farmers almost never received the proportionate share of crop reduction payments they were entitled to, and the AAA acquiesced in the wholesale eviction of tenants whose labor was no longer needed.

The latitude given local authorities similarly resulted in much discrimination and segregation in the Civilian Conservation Corps (CCC). Not until 1936 did the number of Negroes reach 10 percent of the total enrollment. Black enrollees always remained below the percentage of unemployed young Negroes in the nation; and they were largely confined to segregated CCC units and kept out of the training programs that could lead to their advancement. Those who had traditionally oppressed southern blacks also controlled the local administration of the Tennessee Valley Authority, and they too succeeded in maintaining living and working conditions that adhered to the customs of racial exclusion, discrimination, and segregation. The New Deal's early capitulation to racial prejudice was also manifest in the refusal to admit Negroes in the subsistence homestead program, the encouragement of residential segregation by the Federal Housing Administration, and the toleration of discrimination by state and local officials in the selection and payment of relief recipients for the Federal Emergency Relief Administration and the Civil Works Administration.

After 1934, however, counterforces gradually pushed Roosevelt and the New Deal toward a more equitable treatment of Negroes. Most important, a host of racial advancement and protest organizations campaigned for Negro rights on a scale, and with an intensity, unknown in previous decades. Simultaneously, a marked upsurge in the number of Negroes who registered and voted, especially in the states richest in electoral votes, developed a relatively sizable and volatile bloc that national politicians could no longer ignore. In addition, the radical Left and the labor movement, intellectuals and southern liberals, all for their own reasons, began to campaign for racial justice and equality and to demand racial reforms in the New Deal. Their efforts were augmented by the pressure for racial change within the Roosevelt administration emanating from people sympathetic to the Negro's cause such as Will Alexander, Harry Hopkins, Harold Ickes, Aubrey Williams, and particularly, Eleanor Roosevelt.

President Roosevelt could neither ignore the growing force for Negro rights nor disregard the strength of those arrayed against any change in the racial status quo. He did what he could in ways that would not cost him much politically. Always the fox and never the lion on racial issues, Roosevelt nevertheless took steps to ensure Negroes a far fairer and fuller share of New Deal benefits after 1934 and began to act in ways that had the unintended consequence of laying the groundwork for the Second Reconstruction. Largely because of the efforts of the Farm Security Administration, the National Youth Administration, the Public Works Administration, the United States Housing Administration, and the Works Progress Administration, the disparities between white and black in matters of employment, income, education, housing, and health narrowed significantly in the 1930s.

The New Deal also altered the participation of Negroes in government work. The number of blacks in federal jobs tripled during the thirties, more than doubling the proportion of Negro government employees in 1930. Moreover, the Roosevelt administration began to desegregate work facilities in federal agencies and departments, an unprecedented action, and to hire thousands of Negroes for managerial and professional positions. The President further broke prevailing customs of racial prejudice by appointing more than a hundred blacks to administrative posts in the New Deal. Those in Washington were popularly referred to as the Black Cabinet or the Black Brain Trust, and although they did not accomplish the transformation of the New Deal into a crusade for civil rights, they did succeed in making the federal government far more aware of black needs and in prodding other government officials to speak out for greater federal assistance to Negroes.

Additionally, Roosevelt's appointments to the Supreme Court championed the rights of minorities and formulated new constitutional guarantees to protect civil rights. With the exception of James Byrnes, Roosevelt's eight appointees played a key role in dismantling a century of law discriminating against blacks. Their decisions in the late 1930s and 1940s severely circumscribed the permissibility of private discrimination, left blacks less and less at the mercy of states' rights, and signaled the demise of the legality of the separate-but-equal doctrine.

Tentatively yet increasingly, Roosevelt also became more egalitarian in his gestures and rhetoric. By his well-publicized invitations to blacks to visit him in the White House, his conferences with civil rights leaders, his appearances before Negro audiences, and especially, his association with the campaigns for antilynching and anti–poll tax legislation, the president helped educate and inspire others. Two southern filibusters killed the chances for a federal act to prevent lynching, but lynchings did decline from a high of twenty-eight in 1933 to two in 1939. The pressure for federal legislation, moreover, persuaded several southern states to enact measures against both lynchings and the poll tax. As the head of his party, Roosevelt also charted a new racial course for the Democrats. In 1936, for the first time, the national party accredited Negroes as convention delegates; invited black reporters into the regular press box; selected Negroes to deliver an invocation, a welcome address, and a seconding speech for Roosevelt's nomination; and abolished the century-old rule, utilized by the white South as a veto, that required the Democratic nominee to win two-thirds of the delegates' votes in order to obtain the nomination. In 1940, Roosevelt insisted that the Democrats include a specific Negro plank in the party platform pledging to end racial discrimination in all government services and benefits. Such actions and the substantial assistance accorded Negroes by the New Deal led a majority of blacks to desert the Republican party for the first time in history in 1934; and in 1936 and 1940 more than two-thirds of the Negro vote went to Roosevelt.

"It is true that the millennium in race relations did not arrive under Roosevelt," the NAACP summed up the record. "But cynics and scoffers to the contrary, the great body of Negro citizens made progress." That swelled hope in the formerly disheartened. A belief that "we are on our way" took root in the Negro community. Despite the continuity of racism staining the New Deal, the beginnings of change helped transform despair and discouragement into a new Negro hopefulness that a better world could soon and surely be achieved.

Chapter 68

Mary McLeod Bethune and
the Black Cabinet

Darlene Clark Hine and Kathleen Thompson

Darlene Clark Hine is professor of history at Michigan State University. Kathleen Thompson is the co-editor of the Encyclopedia of Black Women in America *(1997).*

The following selection is excerpted by permission from A Shining Thread of Hope: The History of Black Women in America *(New York: Broadway Books, 1998), 250–52.*

For another selection co-authored by Hine, see chapter 58.

The most powerful black woman in American government to date never held an elected office. She was never even nominated to run. As with many other black women over the years, every position she held was one to which she was appointed. The black women's club movement was an unparalleled political training ground for its members. For Mary McLeod Bethune it was more than that. It was a power base. She used it, deliberately and with calculated effect, to gain the political influence she needed to accomplish great things for her people.

Bethune was born in South Carolina in 1875. After graduating from Scotia Seminary in North Carolina, she was rejected by the Presbyterian church's mission program because of her race. Instead, she became a teacher. In 1904, at the age of twenty-nine, she founded the Daytona Educational and Industrial Institute in Daytona, Florida. The school building was a rented house, and the student body consisted of four young women. Gradually, with the help of the community, it grew. Child-care advocate Lucy Miller Mitchell was a student at the school in those early years. "The colored families in that community supported Mrs. Bethune in many, perhaps unpretentious, ways," she remembered. "To help raise money, they would give chicken suppers. Many times, the money raised from these modest efforts helped to carry the grocery bills or to pay some of the teachers." Fourteen years later, Bethune's school was a four-year high school called the Daytona Normal and Industrial Institute. Among its missions was the training of African American teachers for Florida's public schools. In 1923, the Daytona

Institute merged with Cookman Institute, a nearby men's school, and became Bethune-Cookman College.

While she was developing her school, Bethune was also working in the club movement. In 1917, she became president of the Florida Fellowship of Colored Women's Clubs, a position she held until 1924 when she became president of the National Association of Colored Women (NACW). At that point, Bethune held the highest position an African American woman could expect to hold. She proceeded to use it. Her first important move involved the National Council of Women (NCW), a council of thirty-eight women's organizations, thirty-seven of which were white. As part of the NCW, the NACW was eligible to attend an international conference of women that took place every five years and was meeting in Washington, D.C., in 1925. Groups from thirty-five countries would be attending. Bethune had plans for this conference and she set to work.

She made sure that her chief lieutenants would be at the conference. She had demanded and been granted desegregated seating at all conference events. At the conference, when that policy was violated, she and the other members of the NACW walked out. The press was waiting, and Bethune was brilliant. She made a direct appeal to American patriotism. It was humiliating to the United States, she declared, for its citizens to practice and suffer from segregation in the presence of all these other countries. Bethune won the confrontation inside the conference, but more important, she won the first battle in her campaign to become the acknowledged representative of America's black women.

In 1927, Bethune traveled to nine European countries, representing African American women. She worked to establish a national headquarters for the NACW in Washington, D.C., with a paid secretary. If the NACW had not had a term limit, she might have remained there, in spite of the organization's drawbacks. And the NACW did have drawbacks, at least for Bethune's purposes. As historian Elaine M. Smith points out, "Although NACW had always taken a stand on some public questions directly affecting its membership, it had been basically a decentralized organization responding to local and state self-help projects—maintaining the [Frederick] Douglass home and establishing a $50,000 scholarship fund. Bethune had attempted to mold it into a unitary body that could forcefully and consistently project itself into a myriad of public issues as the authoritative voice of Black women."

When the Great Depression battered the country, the NACW became even more conservative, despite Bethune's best attempts. It was time for a change. On December 5, 1935, Bethune was one of thirty representatives of black women's *national* voluntary organizations who voted into being the National Council of Negro Women (NCNW). She was elected president of the new council. For her purposes, the national nature of the organizations was crucial, because each woman on the council headed a group that represented dozens or even hundreds of other groups. Counting the full membership of each organization, Mary McLeod Bethune now officially represented five hundred thousand women. When she spoke publicly, she spoke for all those women. Without ever running for public office, she had a constituency of half a million people.

During her work in the club movement, Bethune had become close friends with Eleanor Roosevelt, who brought her in to work with the federal government. The year after Bethune founded the NCNW, Franklin Roosevelt acknowledged her new status by appointing her to a post in the National Youth Administration (NYA). She and Eleanor Roosevelt persuaded the president that the NYA needed a Negro Division to assure that benefits would be distributed equally, and Bethune was appointed director of the Negro Division of the NYA. The highest position in the federal government ever held by a black woman, it gave her considerable status in the Roosevelt administration. This, added to the influence she already enjoyed as one of the First Lady's closest friends, made her the "race leader" of the Roosevelt years.

In her new role Bethune needed help, and so she organized the Federal Council on Negro Affairs, an informal networking group that came to be known as the "Black Cabinet." It included twenty-seven men and three women who were working within the alphabet-soup agencies. Bethune and her group were directly or indirectly responsible for, among other things, the admission of black women into the Women's Army Corps (WAC), the training of black pilots in the Civilian Pilot Training Program, and the creation of the Fair Employment Practices Commission. After Roosevelt's death, Bethune continued her active role in government under the presidency of Harry Truman. In spite of the fact that she was never elected to any office, she was probably the most powerful black woman ever to serve in the United States government. So far.

Chapter 69

Marian Anderson, Eleanor Roosevelt, and the D.A.R.

Elmer Anderson Carter

In 1939, when black opera star Marian Anderson was invited by Howard University to perform at Constitution Hall in Washington, D.C., she was banned by the Daughters of the American Revolution (DAR), the organization that controlled the building. The DAR had a "No Negroes" policy. Eleanor Roosevelt, in protest, publicly resigned her membership in the DAR.

Later, with the help of Secretary of the Interior Harold Ickes and the NAACP's Walter White, a crowd of 75,000 heard Anderson perform a free concert at the Lincoln Memorial.

Elmer Anderson Carter (d. 1973) was the editor of Opportunity, *the magazine of the National Urban League. He served as chair of the New York State Commission Against Discrimination and as Special Assistant on Intergroup Relations for Governor Nelson Rockefeller. Carter was the Republican party candidate for Manhattan Borough president in 1953.*

The following selection is excerpted by permission from "The Ladies of the D.A.R.," Opportunity, *March 1939, 67.*

The denial of Constitution Hall for the recital of Marian Anderson by the Daughters of the American Revolution is not surprising to those acquainted with the state of race relations in the nation's capital, nor can the later refusal of the Board of Education to make available a "white" public school auditorium be considered inconsistent with the philosophy by which racial segregation in education is justified.

Washington is one of the ranking cities in America in point of racial intolerance. Although some of the outward symbols of racial repression are absent, such as the Jim Crow car, in every other aspect of human relationship the stigma of inferiority and social ostracism is indelibly fastened on its Negro citizens. Racial segregation or discrimination is the accepted rule of conduct in governmental departments, in the theatres, in the hotels, in eating places, and in some public parks, as well as in the educational system; and whatever exceptions may exist serve only to make more conspicuous the general rule.

Insofar as racial segregation in the school system is either excused, defended or approved, it is difficult to see how its logical extension can be condemned. If a Negro girl is forbidden to enter a white high school for instruction, the Board of Education naturally can see no valid reason for permitting a Negro woman, even the world's greatest singer, to make use of one for a recital. The Board of Education, it is true, might on this occasion have exercised a little liberality but it cannot be fairly charged with inconsistency.

The ladies of the D.A.R., however, are guilty of shameful discourtesy. This is one of the inevitable concomitants of the adoption of theories of racial superiority and separatism. The ordinary inhibitions against violation of rules of common decency are smothered when the subject of their violation belongs to the proscribed group. Insult is habitually substituted for insight and incredible coarseness takes the place of that gentility which is supposed to be the mark of the well-born.

The resignation of Mrs. Eleanor R. Roosevelt from this organization under the circumstances is easily understood. Herself a gentlewoman inherently courteous to people no matter what their station or race or nationality, a true daughter of the American Revolution, she was repelled by an exhibition which is as crude as it is un-American.

Marian Anderson needs no sympathy. But our sympathy and pity go to the ladies of the D.A.R. who have given to America an exhibition of rudeness that has aroused universal contempt and scorn.

Chapter 70

Blacks and the CIO

Richard Thomas

Richard Thomas, professor of history at Michigan State University, is the author of The State of Black Detroit *(1987).*

The following selection is from Working for Democracy: American Workers from the Revolution to the Present, *ed. Paul Buhle and Alan Dawley. Copyright © 1985 by the Board of Trustees of the University of Illinois. Used with the permission of the University of Illinois Press.*

From its inception the American labor movement has been dogged by the persistent problem of racism within its ranks. Yet the movement has also scored impressive victories over class and racial oppression, because of the persistent challenge of black trade unionists. By insisting on the needs of all segments of the working class, black or white, employed or unemployed, the black challenge has been a catalyst for social justice within the labor movement.

This black challenge goes back to 1869, when the Colored National Labor Union convened to protest exclusion from the mainstream of the white trade union movement. Later on, gallant struggles for racial equality were waged in the Noble Order of the Knights of Labor (which was dubbed by some as "the black International") and the Industrial Workers of the World.

Such struggles made little headway in the American Federation of Labor under the reign of Samuel Gompers. On the other hand, the Congress of Industrial Organizations had to be sensitive to racial realities in the mass-production industries of steel, rubber, auto, mining and meatpacking, where there were large concentrations of black workers. It was at this point that the black challenge to labor had its greatest impact.

Before the CIO recruitment drive among black industrial workers, the most direct challenge to labor was strikebreaking. Contrary to many popular beliefs, before the CIO came on the labor scene, strikebreaking had become a conscious aspect of intraclass struggles against the white workers' racial dominance in the workplace. The CIO was able to divert this aspect of the black challenge to labor into a temporary class challenge to capitalists.

From the very beginning the CIO promised black workers a fair shake. During the 1936–37 organizing drives in steel and autos, the CIO organized on an integrated basis. In 1939 the Georgia Ku Klux Klan "declared war" on the textile workers' organizing committee because of its interracial program. Such actions prompted the NAACP to comment, "It has often been said that you can tell a man by the kind of enemies he makes. If this is true of organizations also, then the CIO is certainly an unparalleled blessing in our land." The CIO went on to earn more praise from black leaders and workers when it assigned leadership positions to black workers.

Some black leaders remained skeptical because of their past experiences with the AFL. Lester Granger, speaking for the National Urban League, cautioned black workers against "jubilantly rushing toward what they assume to be a new day for labor and a new organization to take the place of the AFL." But it was not long before the CIO won the endorsement of the National Negro Congress. The NNC was founded in 1936 (just a few months after the founding of the CIO) by more than 250 influential blacks, who called for a National Negro Congress made up of all black organizations "from old-line Republican to Communist" to address the urgent problems of black people. Organizing black industrial workers was considered to be one of the most pressing of these problems.

At the first session of the NNC held in Chicago, A. Philip Randolph told the delegates representing 585 organizations that their special mission was to "draw Negro workers into labor organizations and break down the color bar in the trade unions that now have it."

The pro-labor orientation of the NNC was crucial at a time when the CIO needed all the help it could get. The NNC not only endorsed the CIO but also, because of its strong Communist elements, provided the new industrial union with its most radical support.

As the CIO met the black challenge by fighting against the racism of both capitalists and workers, it became known among the black community as its best ally. During the Ford strike of 1941 many conservative local black leaders took Henry Ford's side against the UAW-CIO. But after Ford went down to defeat the UAW-CIO sided with black workers against white workers' attempts to prevent them from obtaining jobs in defense industries, the attitudes of these local black leaders changed drastically. By 1945 the black community, as one labor scholar has pointed out, "looked upon the CIO and the idea of labor solidarity as the black man's greatest hope for social and economic progress in the postwar period."

The honeymoon between black workers and the CIO soon ended, however. The persistent economic and social problems of black workers necessarily gave rise to new and more urgent challenges, many of which could not be effectively met by the CIO alone. The AFL was still very powerful and unrelenting in its racism. During their 1946 convention AFL members voted down resolutions to end segregated auxiliary locals. Meanwhile, the CIO was slowly losing its fighting spirit as it drifted into an "unholy alliance" with the AFL to discredit Communist-led unions.

Several years before their formal merger into the AFL-CIO, these two labor organizations competed with each other in driving out of the labor movement many of the very radicals who had worked hardest for black people. In fact, during

World War II left-wing unions did more than other unions in promoting racial equality. Such unions as the United Packing House Workers, the International Fur and Leather Workers Union, the Marine Cooks and Stewards, among others, laid the foundation for interracial labor solidarity. When the radical elements in these unions were purged, black workers were forced to struggle almost alone against persistent racism in the labor movement.

The first significant postwar challenge occurred in 1950 in the form of the National Negro Labor Conference. It arose in a period of great hardship for black workers. Most of the economic advances made by black industrial workers occurred between 1942 and 1945 and were largely lost during the postwar reconversion of war industries into peacetime production. Reconversion fell most heavily on black industrial workers because of their great concentration in unskilled war production jobs with the least possibility of reconversion to civilian production. In 1946 the Fair Employment Practices Commission's final report revealed that black workers were experiencing more unemployment than white workers in six of the seven war centers studied. The dire economic plight of black industrial workers was worsened by the government's failure to push for a strong permanent FEPC, without which black workers could not hope for much government protection.

As unemployment began steadily rising, many black workers began a descent into a permanent depression. On the heels of this job loss came a technological revolution that ate away at the heart of black employment—the unskilled and semi-skilled jobs. As northern black workers were struggling just to hold onto wartime gains, they were joined by tens of thousands of displaced southern black agricultural workers who were gradually being pushed northward by the impact of agricultural technology on the southern plantation economy. To compound hard times, organized labor in many ways was becoming part of the problem again, rather than part of the solution.

More than any other single segment of the American working class, black workers stood alone at this hour. Black middle-class organizations like the NAACP and the Urban League had no solutions to the problems of black workers. The promising National Negro Congress had lasted less than ten years, while the March on Washington Movement died during the post-war period.

But what about the labor movement and the promises of the CIO? Many white labor leaders believed they had met the major challenge of black workers by bringing them into the CIO on a nonracial basis and fighting for the rights of black workers to obtain jobs in the defense industries. These leaders failed to understand that the black working class had historically fought both a class and race struggle, and that to the black community the race struggle was much more compelling because it was being waged against both white capital and labor. The challenge facing leftists in the labor movement was to support black workers in both of these struggles. Unfortunately, even the most progressive segments failed to meet this challenge.

This challenge was voiced repeatedly at the National Labor Conference for Negro Rights held in Chicago in June 1950 (which led to the formation of the National Negro Labor Council a year later). The Communist party was among those initiating the NNLC and gave it active support throughout its existence. Black delegates from the AFL reported that the Federation was still discriminating against black workers. CIO black delegates accused it of retreating from its earlier position on the rights of black workers. All the delegates agreed that black workers were being discriminated against in apprenticeship training programs and that they were being barred from advancing into skilled and semi-skilled jobs by racist collective bargaining agreements.

Deciding the black workers had to take the lead in their own struggle, the Conference established a continuation committee composed of veteran black labor leaders. William R. Hood, recording secretary of Local 600, UAW-CIO, was made president of the committee; Cleveland Robinson, vice-president of the Distributive, Processing, and Office Workers Union (District 65), was made vice-president; and Coleman Young of the Amalgamated Clothing Workers staff, and by then a veteran labor leader in Detroit as well as former director of organization of the Wayne County CIO Council, was made executive secretary of the committee.

In less than a year this committee set up twenty-three Negro Labor Councils in major industrial cities, and these local NLCs immediately began combatting racial discrimination on all fronts. The NLC of Greater New York sprang into action a week after the national conference by calling a "Job Action Conference," which was attended by 250 trade unionists. They reported on problems in the building trades, printing, railroads, utilities, and other industries. The conference resulted in 250 jobs and a commitment from the public relations manager of Safeway stores promising that each qualified applicant would be given an equal opportunity for employment.

The NLC in Chicago began a drive against racial discrimination in the Woolworth and Scott stores, where blacks could shop but not work. The manager of Woolworth swore that he would not hire black saleswomen "until hell freezes over." But when the NLC set up picket lines around the stores, causing business to fall off by 85 percent, the stores gave up and hired black women. On the West Coast the NLC helped the Urban League in California's East Bay win a victory over the Key System Transit Lines, a local transport monopoly that had refused to hire black workers. The NLCs were equally effective in the South. The NLC led a successful struggle to force the Louisville Board of Education to prepare black workers for jobs that were to be opened by General Electric.

In 1952, during the NNLC's first campaign to have a "model FEPC clause" incorporated into every union contract, only the United Electrical Radio and Machine Workers Union (UE) did so. This union not only adapted the model clause as its official union policy but also set up a fair practices committee to take the lead in a "nationwide drive for the full rights of its black and women members." While left-wing trade unions, such as the Marine Cooks and Stewards and the International Longshoremen's and Warehousemen's Unions, offered their wholehearted support of the NLCs, other unions such as the UAW engaged in "red-baiting."

In Detroit one of the most successful NLCs, under the leadership of William R. Hood of Local 600, was a constant worry to the UAW leadership. The NLC and

Walter Reuther did not see eye to eye on the former's petition drive for a local FEPC ordinance. Reuther, along with seven other international officers, ordered all auto workers who had signed the petition to withdraw their names, calling the people behind the drive "irresponsible" and "Communist-inspired" because they had not consulted with the UAW-CIO.

But the conflict between black workers in the Detroit NLC and the UAW leadership went deeper than the clash over the FEPC drive. For several years black workers had been challenging the UAW's all-white male leadership to push more vigorously for the upgrading of black workers as well as the inclusion of blacks on the UAW's major policy making body, the International Executive Board. The UAW's failure to meet this challenge led black workers to continue their own independent struggles against the racism of both capitalists and labor.

Led by the Detroit NLC, black NLCs around the nation held a conference in October 1951 to set up a National Negro Labor Council (NNLC). Several white labor leaders of the AFL and the CIO accused the convention of "dual unionism." Organizers denied the charge and defined the NNLC's objective as building a new organization to encourage black workers to join unions and encourage unions to organize black workers. The delegates also informed their white trade union critics that "that day has ended when white trade union leaders or white leaders in any organization may presume to tell Negroes on what basis they shall come together to fight for their rights. . . . We ask your cooperation—but we do not ask your permission!"

The convention adopted two major tasks for itself: to defeat racial discrimination in industry, and to eliminate racism in the trade union movement and use it as a base from which trade unions and progressive white allies could struggle for the economic liberation of blacks. No sooner had the goals been stated than the newly formed organization was attacked by white CIO leaders, led by James B. Carey, as a tool of the Soviet Union. Such attacks masked the fears and unwillingness of many white labor leaders adequately to assess independent black working-class organizations. The red-baiting and "dual unionism" accusations helped pave the way for the House Committee on Un-American Activities (HUAC) to harass the NNLC. Such harassment, along with other adverse pressures, forced the demise of the NNLC in 1956.

Racism within the ranks of labor remained an issue, particularly after the merger of the AFL-CIO in 1955. Many black trade unionists saw the merger as a signal of organized labor's declining interest and commitment to the struggle against racism. Notwithstanding the vague promises of equality put into the new organization's constitution, black workers were well aware of the lack of enforcement that rendered such promises meaningless. The AFL-CIO constitution provided sanctions against affiliates dominated by "Communists" while providing little or no sanction against affiliates dominated by racists. It was clear that such a challenge—namely, to provide protection for nonwhite workers against union racism—was not to be taken seriously. No wonder, then, that five years later, in 1960, the NAACP's labor secretary, Herbert Hill, revealed that many AFL-CIO affiliates were yet restricting black workers to segregated locals, that black auto and

steel workers were yet confined to unskilled jobs, and that several southern affiliates were working with the White Citizens' Councils.

By 1960 American labor still had a long way to go in meeting the black challenge. While prominent white labor leaders would march alongside blacks in the
great civil rights demonstrations in Detroit, Washington, and Selma and would endorse the principle of equality in theory, they would fail to mount a strong and
persistent struggle against racism within their own ranks. This failure to mount
such a struggle left a vacuum that would only be filled by independent black labor
organizations.

Chapter 71

The Harlem Bus Boycott of 1941

Dominic J. Capeci, Jr.

Dominic J. Capeci, Jr., professor of history at Southwest Missouri State University, is the author of The Harlem Riot of 1943 *(1977),* Race Relations in Wartime Detroit *(1984), and* The Lynching of Cleo Wright *(1998), co-author of* Layered Violence: The Detroit Rioters of 1943 *(1991), and editor of* Detroit in the "Good War": The World War II Letters of Mayor Edward Jeffries and Friends *(1996). He is currently completing a study on the aftermath of the 1943 Detroit riot and an intellectual biography of W. E. B. Du Bois.*

The following selection is excerpted from "From Harlem to Montgomery: The Bus Boycotts and Leadership of Adam Clayton Powell, Jr., and Martin Luther King, Jr.," Historian, *August 1979, 721, 723–29, footnotes deleted. Reprinted with permission of the author.*

While much has been written about Martin Luther King, Jr., and the Montgomery Bus Boycott of 1956,[1] historians have ignored Adam Clayton Powell, Jr., and the Harlem Bus Boycott of 1941. The two boycotts were marked by similar leadership and occurred in decades of despair but in periods of major socioeconomic change. Although it was much smaller in size and more local in impact, a study of the Harlem boycott yields important information on Powell's leadership before his political career and, more significantly, on earlier protest philosophies and tactics. . . .

The Harlem bus boycott of 1941 was prompted by black degradation, rising expectations, and a heritage of black protest. Throughout the 1930s, black New Yorkers subsisted on marginal economic levels. As late as 1940, 40 percent of the city's black population received relief or federal monies for temporary jobs. Moreover, most blacks were relegated to menial positions. In Harlem, the largest black community of over two hundred thousand persons, hope was generated, nevertheless, as black leaders and white officials—like Mayor Fiorello H. La Guardia—pressed for change and as World War II held out promise for greater black employment opportunities.

Blacks had a longstanding grievance against the Fifth Avenue Coach Company and the New York Omnibus Corporation. In 1935, the Mayor's Commission on Conditions in Harlem reported that the Coach Company was "fixed in its policy of the exclusion of Negroes from employment." At the time of the bus boycott six years later, the Coach Company and the Omnibus Corporation together employed only sixteen blacks, mostly as janitors, none as drivers or mechanics, out of a labor force of thirty-five hundred persons. Hence, on March 10, 1941, when the Transport Workers Union (TWU), under the leadership of Michael J. Quill, went on strike against the bus companies, black leaders moved quickly to the union's support. The National Negro Congress, for example, "wholeheartedly" supported the strike, which lasted for twelve days and halted the service of thirteen hundred buses.

Under Roger Straugh's leadership, the Harlem Labor Union (HLU) began picketing local bus stops before the TWU strike had ended, demanding the employment of black bus drivers and mechanics. The Greater New York Coordinating Committee for Employment led by Powell and the Manhattan Council of the National Negro Congress directed by Hope R. Stevens joined with HLU, to form the United Bus Strike Committee (UBSC). The formal boycott, however, did not begin until March 24, four days after TWU had agreed to arbitration and two days after bus service had resumed. Moreover, Powell emerged as the spokesman for the boycotters, providing, in Urban Leaguer Elmer A. Carter's estimation, "dynamic leadership."

Before the boycott began, Powell received a quid pro quo from Quill. In return for black support of the TWU strike, the boycott would receive union backing. Later, on March 24, Quill assured Powell that blacks employed by the bus companies would be considered for union membership so long as they had clean records and had never been scabs. That evening, over fifteen hundred persons gathered at the Abyssinian Baptist Church and agreed to boycott the buses until blacks were hired as drivers and mechanics.

Powell's tactics drew from the Jobs-for-Negroes movement, in which many members of the United Bus Strike Committee had participated. Picket lines surrounded Harlem's bus stops, soup kitchens fed volunteers, and black chauffeurs and mechanics were registered. An "emergency jitney service" of privately owned automobiles transported some boycotters, but the key to the boycott's success was New York City's subway system and taxi companies which provided efficient, relatively inexpensive alternative transportation. Before the boycott terminated, volunteers painted placards, donated approximately $500, and gave the use of their automobiles. The month-long campaign kept sixty thousand persons off the buses each day at a loss of $3,000 in daily fares. It also drew together five hundred persons from various backgrounds and both races, as bandleaders, ministers, postal clerks, housewives, beauticians, and nurses walked the picket line. Celebrities, like musician Duke Ellington, actively supported the boycott.

Well aware of the significance of the church in black society, Powell made the Abyssinian Baptist Church one of two boycott headquarters. It was the location of the first and second boycott rallies. It provided volunteers experienced in protest, communications, and physical resources and, of course, became the base of Powell's operations and the center of his power.

Powell stressed the philosophy of nonviolent direct action. Blacks were to use only peaceful, legal avenues of redress. By appealing to "the Grace of God" and "the power of the masses," Powell combined religious and political themes; this combination of righteousness and self-help would enable "a black boy . . . to roll a bus up Seventh Avenue." Picket lines, as well as Powell's rhetoric, however, implied militancy. Those flouting the boycott, he declared, should be converted, "one way or another." Three years after the boycott, Powell summarized his nonviolent, though strident, philosophy in *Marching Blacks*: "No blows, no violence, but the steady unrelenting pressure of an increasing horde of people who knew they were right" would bring change.

The boycott was threatened first by violence and then by a misleading newspaper story. Following a UBSC rally at the Abyssinian Baptist Church on March 31, individuals hurled objects at several buses along Lenox Avenue. Fifty patrolmen dispersed those responsible, some of whom had attended the rally. "FEAR ANOTHER HARLEM RIOT" screamed the *Age*'s headlines. Of more concern to Powell and others was the *Amsterdam News* story of April 5. It announced that the bus companies had agreed to employ over two hundred black drivers and mechanics, providing that TWU waive the seniority rights of more than three hundred former bus employees waiting to be rehired. Such an agreement had been discussed, but no final decision had been reached. UBSC leaders moved quickly to maintain the boycott. They labeled the story "a lie," reorganized pickets, distributed leaflets, asked ministers to inform their congregations of "the true facts," and planned a mass meeting.

Despite crisis, the boycott and negotiations continued. Once Ritchie agreed to hire blacks, the major obstacle was TWU seniority policies. On April 17, Powell informed five thousand persons at the Golden Gate Ballroom that an agreement was imminent. Signed twelve days later, the agreement waived the seniority rights of all except ninety-one TWU drivers furloughed by the bus companies; after these men were reinstated, one hundred black drivers were to be hired. The next seventy mechanics employed would also be black, and thereafter, blacks and whites would be taken on alternately until 17 percent of the companies' labor force—exclusive of clerical staff—were black. This quota represented the percentage of black residents in Manhattan. Black workers would be enrolled as TWU members, although the bus companies exercised "sole discretion as to the type of Negro employees to be hired." The agreement would not take precedence over prior management-labor commitments provided they were nondiscriminatory. Of course, all boycott activities would cease. Powell declared that the agreement was made possible by new TWU contracts providing shorter hours and by additional municipal franchises enabling the bus companies to employ three hundred more persons.

Several factors made the Harlem boycott successful. Powell's agreement with Quill prevented bus company officials from playing blacks against whites in the TWU strike and the bus boycott. Throughout the strike, Quill raised the possibility of the bus companies employing strikebreakers. Blacks traditionally had been exploited as scabs and some of the bus terminals were strategically located in Harlem. Indeed, at least one Harlem correspondent informed Mayor La Guardia that two thousand black men could "start the bus lines in 5, 10, or 20 hours." Powell's agreement significantly reduced the possibility of TWU's strike being broken by force, and reciprocally, it assured that the bus boycott would not fail because of traditional union opposition toward blacks.

Powell's agreement with Quill also held out the hope that blacks would support labor in the upcoming subway negotiations between La Guardia and TWU leaders. During the previous June, the municipal government had bought and unified the Brooklyn-Manhattan Transit Corporation and the Interborough Rapid Transit Company, which had been operated by TWU and the Brotherhood of Locomotive Engineers. When La Guardia contended that neither the right to strike nor a closed shop could be permitted among civil service employees, labor officials retorted that the mayor had reneged on his obligations and anticipated a precedent-breaking conflict with the municipal government when the original contract expired on June 20, 1941. TWU leaders believed that mayoral reference to the bus strike as "bull-headed, obstinate and stupid" was designed to weaken their position in the coming subway negotiations. Obviously, public opinion would be crucial in that dispute. Hence, some blacks, like the *Age* editor, saw TWU support for the bus boycott as a trade-off for black support in the forthcoming union battle with the mayor.

Changing opinions and the impact of World War II helped make the Powell-Quill agreement possible. The racial attitudes of TWU leaders had been improving since 1938 when the union unsuccessfully sent blacks to be employed as drivers at the World's Fair. By World War II, Powell understood how uncomfortable society was in opposing a totalitarian, racist Nazi regime while practicing racial discrimination. "America," he stated later, "could not defeat Hitler abroad without defeating Hitlerism at home." Of equal importance, TWU leadership could pare seniority lists by three hundred unemployed members and make room for black employees because defense orders stimulated the economy and selective service calls [the draft] reduced union ranks. According to the *Afro-American* editor, the difficulty in finding bus drivers and mechanics provided blacks with unforeseen opportunities.

The boycott assured those opportunities. By early May, seven black mechanics had been hired by the bus companies and ten blacks were expected to begin chauffeur training within a week. Six months later, forty-three blacks had been employed in various classifications, including mechanic's helpers. Finally, on February 1, 1942, after all the ninety-odd furloughed white operators had been given opportunity for reemployment, the first ten black drivers employed by the Coach Company and the Omnibus Corporation began their routes.

That victory was historical. It drew blacks, labor, and management together in a successful effort to break down discriminatory employment practices in privately owned bus companies, and indirectly, it accelerated a similar trend that had already begun in the municipally owned transportation systems under La Guardia's leadership. The boycott also held out promise for "Negro-labor solidarity." Moreover, it effectively utilized the tactics and philosophies of the Jobs-for-Negroes movement, focused on the concept of equal opportunity, established the idea of a quota system, and provided safeguards for protecting blacks in their newly won jobs. All these elements were also attempted in the 1930s and 1960s, indicating the continuum in black protest that links militant means with traditional ends and nonviolent direct action tactics with greater participation in larger society. By exploiting both TWU ambitions and war manpower exigencies, Powell, Straugh, and Stevens created numerous jobs for black workers. But it was Powell who played the leading role, as he had done for the past decade, speaking out and organizing protests that brought approximately seventeen hundred jobs to Harlem. Exactly because of that record, blacks enthusiastically supported his successful candidacy for City Council in November 1941. His delivery of tangible gains merits mention, for as councilman and, later, congressman he had the reputation for imparting only catharsis to his constituents. Finally, Powell's boycott sparked other protests; numerous blacks agreed with the editor of the *Pittsburgh Courier,* who said, "If this can be done in New York, it can be done in other cities." Indeed, in May the National Association for the Advancement of Colored People launched a nationwide picket campaign against defense industries that held government contracts but refused to hire blacks; Powell journeyed to Chicago to help the Negro Labor Relations League launch a jobs campaign; and the Colored Clerks Circle of St. Louis prepared to boycott a local cleaning company. Official entry of the United States into World War II prevented the emergence of what might have been widespread black protest akin to that of the 1950s and 1960s.

EDITORS' NOTE

1. The Montgomery Bus Boycott began in December 1955 and lasted 381 days. For details, see chapter 94.

Chapter 72

The March on Washington Movement

A. Philip Randolph

A. Philip Randolph (1889–1979) was the leading black figure in the American labor movement. In 1917, he co-founded the Messenger, *a black monthly magazine, and in 1925 he became the general organizer of the Brotherhood of Sleeping Car Porters. Influenced by socialist and labor thinkers, he believed progress was most likely to come from the black working class rather than the black elite—the "talented tenth," in W. E. B. Du Bois's phrase. Although his politics became more conservative in later years, Randolph always emphasized the importance of the working class and economic goals in the struggle for civil rights.*

In 1941, Randolph planned a national march on Washington. After Roosevelt agreed to set up the Fair Employment Practices Committee to monitor employment in federal jobs, Randolph canceled the march but continued organizing. His efforts, wrote one black newspaper, "demonstrated to the Doubting Thomases among us that only mass action can pry open the doors that have been erected against America's black minority."[1] In 1963, Randolph originated the March on Washington, which featured Martin Luther King, Jr., and the Student Nonviolent Coordinating Committee's John Lewis among its speakers.

The following selection is reprinted from "Why We March," Survey Graphic, *November 1942, 488–89.*

Though I have found no Negroes who want to see the United Nations [the Allies opposing the Axis of Germany, Japan, and Italy] lose this war, I have found many who, before the war ends, want to see the stuffing knocked out of white supremacy and of empire over subject peoples. American Negroes, involved as we are in the general issues of the conflict, are confronted not with a choice but with the challenge both to win democracy for ourselves at home and to help win the war for democracy the world over.

There is no escape from the horns of this dilemma. There ought not to be escape. For if the war for democracy is not won abroad, the fight for democracy cannot be won at home. If this war cannot be won for the white peoples, it will not be won for the darker races.

Conversely, if freedom and equality are not vouchsafed the peoples of color, the war for democracy will not be won. Unless this double-barreled thesis is accepted and applied, the darker races will never wholeheartedly fight for the victory of the United Nations. That is why those familiar with the thinking of the American Negro have sensed his lack of enthusiasm, whether among the educated or uneducated, rich or poor, professional or non-professional, religious or secular, rural or urban, north, south, east or west.

That is why questions are being raised by Negroes in church, labor union and fraternal society; in poolroom, barbershop, schoolroom, hospital, hair-dressing parlor; on college campus, railroad, and bus. One can hear such questions asked as these: What have Negroes to fight for? What's the difference between Hitler and that "cracker" [Senator Herman] Talmadge of Georgia? Why has a man got to be Jim-Crowed to die for democracy? If you haven't got democracy yourself, how can you carry it to somebody else?

What are the reasons for this state of mind? This answer is: discrimination, segregation, Jim Crow. Witness the navy, the army, the air corps; and also government services at Washington. In many parts of the South, Negroes in Uncle Sam's uniform are being put upon, mobbed, sometimes even shot down by civilian and military police, and on occasion lynched. Vested political interest in race prejudice are so deeply entrenched that to them winning the war against Hitler is secondary to preventing Negroes from winning democracy for themselves. This is worth many divisions to Hitler and Hirohito. While labor, business, and farm are subjected to ceilings and floors and not allowed to carry on as usual, these interests trade in the dangerous business of race hate as usual.

When the defense program began and billions of the taxpayers' money were appropriated for guns, ships, tanks and bombs, Negroes presented themselves for work only to be given the cold shoulder. North as well as South, and despite their qualifications, Negroes were denied skilled employment. Not until their wrath and indignation took the form of a proposed march on Washington, scheduled for July 1, 1941, did things begin to move in the form of defense jobs for Negroes. The march was postponed by the timely issuance (June 25, 1941) of the famous Executive Order No. 8802 by President Roosevelt [see chapter 73—*Eds.*]. But this order and the President's Committee on Fair Employment Practice, established thereunder, have as yet only scratched the surface by way of eliminating discriminations on account of race or color in war industry. Both management and labor unions in too many places and too many ways are still drawing the color line.

It is to meet this situation squarely with direct action that the March on Washington Movement launched its present program of protest mass meetings. Twenty thousand were in attendance at Madison Square Garden, June 16; sixteen thousand in the Coliseum in Chicago, June 26; nine thousand in the City Auditorium of St. Louis, August 14. Meetings of such magnitude were unprecedented among Negroes. The vast throngs were drawn from all walks and levels of Negro life—businessmen, teachers, laundry workers, Pullman porters, waiters, and red caps; preachers, crapshooters, and social workers; jitterbugs and Ph.D.'s. They came and sat in silence, thinking, applauding only when they considered the truth was told, when they felt strongly that something was going to be done about it.

The March on Washington Movement is essentially a movement of the people. It is all Negro and pro-Negro, but not for that reason anti-white or anti-Semitic, or anti-Catholic, or anti-foreign, or anti-labor. Its major weapon is the non-violent demonstration of Negro mass power. Negro leadership has united back of its drive for jobs and justice. "Whether Negroes should march on Washington, and if so, when?" will be the focus of a forthcoming national conference. For the plan of a protest march has not been abandoned. Its purpose would be to demonstrate that American Negroes are in deadly earnest, and all out for their full rights. No power on earth can cause them today to abandon their fight to wipe out every vestige of second class citizenship and the dual standards that plague them.

A community is democratic only when the humblest and weakest person can enjoy the highest civil, economic, and social rights that the biggest and most powerful possess. To trample on these rights of both Negroes and poor whites is such a commonplace in the South that it takes readily to anti-social, anti-labor, anti-Semitic and anti-Catholic propaganda. It was because of laxness in enforcing the Weimar constitution in republican Germany that Nazism made headway. Oppression of the Negroes in the United States, like suppression of the Jews in Germany, may open the way for a fascist dictatorship.

By fighting for their rights now, American Negroes are helping to make America a moral and spiritual arsenal of democracy. Their fight against the poll tax, against lynch law, segregation, and Jim Crow, their fight for economic, political, and social equality, thus becomes part of the global war for freedom.

Program of the March on Washington Movement

1. We demand, in the interest of national unity, the abrogation of every law which makes a distinction in treatment between citizens based on religion, creed, color, or national origin. This means an end to Jim Crow in education, in housing, in transportation and in every other social, economic, and political privilege; and especially, we demand, in the capital of the nation, an end to all segregation in public places and in public institutions.
2. We demand legislation to enforce the Fifth and Fourteenth Amendments guaranteeing that no person shall be deprived of life, liberty or property without due process of law, so that the full weight of the national government may be used for the protection of life and thereby may end the disgrace of lynching.
3. We demand the enforcement of the Fourteenth and Fifteenth Amendments and the enactment of the Pepper Poll Tax bill so that all barriers in the exercise of the suffrage are eliminated.
4. We demand the abolition of segregation and discrimination in the army, navy, marine corps, air corps, and all other branches of national defense.
5. We demand an end to discrimination in jobs and job training. Further, we demand that the F.E.P.C. be made a permanent administrative agency of the

U.S. Government and it be given power to enforce its decisions based on its findings.

6. We demand that federal funds be withheld from any agency which practices discrimination in the use of such funds.

7. We demand colored and minority group representation on all administrative agencies so that these groups may have recognition of their democratic right to participate in formulating policies.

8. We demand representation for the colored and minority racial groups on all missions, political and technical, which will be sent to the peace conference so that the interest of all people everywhere may be fully recognized and justly provided for in the post-war settlement.

EDITORS' NOTE

1. Quoted in Jervis Anderson, *A. Philip Randolph* (New York: Harcourt Brace Jovanovich, 1973), 260.

Chapter 73

Executive Order 8802: Establishing the FEPC

Franklin D. Roosevelt

In 1941 A. Philip Randolph threatened to sponsor a national march on Washington (see chapter 72). In exchange for President Roosevelt's agreement to appoint a Fair Employment Practices Committee, Randolph postponed the march.

The following selection is a reprint of "Executive Order 8802," 25 June 1941.

Reaffirming Policy of Full Participation in the Defense Program by All Persons, Regardless of Race, Creed, Color, or National Origin, and Directing Certain Action in Furtherance of Said Policy

Whereas it is the policy of the United States to encourage full participation in the national defense program by all citizens of the United States, regardless of race, creed, color, or national origin, in the firm belief that the democratic way of life within the Nation can be defended successfully only with the help and support of all groups within its borders; and

Whereas there is evidence that available and needed workers have been barred from employment in industries engaged in defense production solely because of considerations of race, creed, color, or national origin, to the detriment of workers' morale and of national unity:

Now, therefore, by virtue of the authority vested in me by the Constitution and the statutes, and as a prerequisite to the successful conduct of our national defense production effort, I do hereby reaffirm the policy of the United States that there shall be no discrimination in the employment of workers in defense industries or government because of race, creed, color, or national origin, and I do hereby declare that it is the duty of employers and of labor organizations, in furtherance of said policy and of this order, to provide for the full and equitable participation of all workers in defense industries, without discrimination because of race, creed, color, or national origin;

And it is hereby ordered as follows:

1. All departments and agencies of the Government of the United States concerned with vocational and training programs for defense production shall take special measures appropriate to assure that such programs are administered without discrimination because of race, creed, color, or national origin;

2. All contracting agencies of the Government of the United States shall include in all defense contracts hereafter negotiated by them a provision obligating the contractor not to discriminate against any worker because of race, creed, color, or national origin;

3. There is established in the Office of Production Management a Committee on Fair Employment Practice, which shall consist of a chairman and four other members to be appointed by the President. The Chairman and members of the Committee shall serve as such without compensation but shall be entitled to actual and necessary transportation, subsistence and other expenses incidental to performance of their duties. The Committee shall receive and investigate complaints of discrimination in violation of the provisions of this order and shall take appropriate steps to redress grievances which it finds to be valid. The Committee shall also recommend to the several departments and agencies of the Government of the United States and to the President all measures which may be deemed by it necessary or proper to effectuate the provisions of this order.

FRANKLIN D. ROOSEVELT

The White House
June 25, 1941

Chapter 74

The Sharecroppers' Tale

Paul Buhle

Paul Buhle, a founding editor of the journal Radical America, *is professor of American Civilization at Brown University and director of the Oral History of the American Left at Tamiment Library, New York University.*

Among his many works, Buhle is the author of Marxism in the USA: From 1870 to the Present Day *(1987),* C. L. R. James: The Artist as Revolutionary *(1988), and* Taking Care of Business: Samuel Gompers, George Meany, Lane Kirkland, and the Tragedy of American Labor *(1999), and co-editor of* Working for Democracy: American Workers from the Revolution to the Present *(1985),* The Immigrant Left in the United States *(1996), and* Encyclopedia of the American Left *(2d ed., 1999).*

The following selection, originally entitled "Telling the Sharecroppers' Tale," is reprinted from the Guardian, *18 January 1989, 10–11. Reprinted with permission of the author.*

On January 10, 1939, 1,700 sharecropping families of southeastern Missouri moved out to the highways, where they camped in bitterly cold weather. Newspaper shots appeared across the country showing men, women, and children in makeshift tents of blankets and quilts, huddling around open fires.

Much of the U.S. was still in the Depression, with ample quantities of suffering for dramatic presentation. But something made these families unique: Blacks and whites rallied together, in the rural South, as if they had never imagined doing anything else, undeterred by racist terror—beatings, lynchings or humiliation.

Scholars would later call it the first act of the civil rights movement, in the sense of mass sit-ins by Southerners showing that the public space was theirs, too. A more exact characterization might place the tenant farmers' action as the link connecting the Populism of the 1890s and the multiracial radicalism of the 1960s.

Here hangs a tale which one of the best storytelling radicals of the century still unravels at every opportunity. At age 82, H. L. Mitchell is a tall, scraggy, pugnacious cuss likely to tell a joke when the audience expects sentimentalism. "Mitch," as young radicals of three generations have familiarly called him, has been touring campuses for a quarter-century and selling institutions the Southern Tenant Farmers Union's (STFU) microfilmed papers, while he talks about agrarian history and puts in a pitch for socialism today. To me, he's the damnedest down-home American agitator since Oklahoma's socialist-humorist Oscar Ameringer (whose 1930s paper, the *American Guardian,* gave the *Guardian* its name) died in 1942.

Only a Marxist with a big sense of humor could have done what Mitch has done and lived to tell the story so well. A new pictorial biography of him and his movement, "*Roll the Union On,*" and a 60-minute documentary film, "Our Land Too," expand Mitchell's stage and give us a good look at what he has been talking about.

Sharecropping = Slavery

It all goes back to small-town Tennessee of 1917 where Mitchell, an 11-year-old newsboy, rode a special excursion train to see a Black man lynched. The stench of the fumes and the sheer horror of the scene made a lasting impression upon him. The young man, a local Casanova and erstwhile bootlegger turned dry-cleaner, embraced the socialist cause and made his corner of a tiny Arkansas town a "Red Square" for the Norman Thomas campaign of 1932.

Mitchell and his Southern comrades turned naturally toward the social trauma of the region, the displacement of perhaps a half-million sharecroppers by the New Deal acreage restriction program in the cotton fields. President Franklin Roosevelt, concerned to retain his Dixiecrat allies and none too keen on racial equality himself, had allowed Southern planters to use federal land payments as a means of getting rid of sharecroppers so as to pocket all the money themselves. In response, Mitchell, along with a small number of other whites and Blacks, founded the STFU in 1934.

It was a brave—many said a foolhardy—thing to do. Interracial activity, whether political, intellectual or cultural, had been virtually unknown since Reconstruction. A tenants' union threatened the pocketbooks of the region's kingmakers. Local Ku Kluxers, sheriffs and plantation owners' thugs singled out STFU members and leaders for beating and death threats. Still, the little circle of militants registered progress. By calling for strikes in the mid-1930s against a further reduction of payment for crops, they won widespread loyalty and gathered up to 30,000 members who could pay some dues.

Mitchell and his fellow unionists meanwhile pulled off a major public relations success. Outside money flowed in from the left-wing Garland Fund, itself temporarily buoyed by the Soviet Union's repayment of a 1920s loan—probably the only serious "Moscow Gold" that the U.S. left ever received. Mayor Fiorello La Guardia declared Sharecroppers Week in New York City and actress Tallulah Bankhead (descendant of Southern planters) among others made public appeals. Meanwhile, *The Sharecroppers' Voice* appeared in Memphis and the Southern movement grew stronger.

Film footage of the union's early days, interracial crowds of farmers singing "We Shall Not Be Moved" and signing up for the union, must be seen in order to feel some of the intensity these events must have had for the participants. Narrator

Eddie Albert walks us through the story with clips and contemporary interviews of old timers, carefully refraining from dramatizing something which already has vast inherent drama. The contemporary newsreels offer a surprisingly sympathetic portrait of the STFU in action (sometimes reenacted, as when a union organizer and a woman reporter enter an Arkansas plantation district and are suddenly surrounded by white men with clubs).

Interviewers capture the poignancy in recollections not only of Mitchell, but also of other remarkable people like John Handcox, Black STFU vice president who wrote, for the sharecroppers, the famous CIO song, "Roll the Union On" (with its melody based upon a hymn).

We sense something enormous beginning to take place. From a historical viewpoint, sharecropping had been the method of keeping ex-slaves, along with millions of whites, in social bondage much like slavery. By 1938, the STFU had become a dangerous symbol of the region's (perhaps also the nation's) social contradictions suddenly adding up to radical change. As the movement spread to Oklahoma, the Tribal Council Chief of the Choctaws (by that time mostly tenant farmers) sent Mitchell a message: "The white man talks well. . . . When the white man and the Black man are ready to take back the land, just let us know, and we shall get our guns and come, too."

It didn't happen that way. Theodore Rosengarten's wonderful oral history of Alabama Communist sharecropper, Ned Cobb, *All God's Dangers* (1974) tells part of the reason why. Early in the 1930s, Black Communists in Alabama armed for self-defense and squared off with authorities in a series of shootouts. The Share Croppers' Union (SCU) succeeded in becoming the largest Communist-led movement of the 1930s South. But it failed to recruit significant white membership or (until near the end of its short life) to come up from a virtual underground existence into a real agricultural labor union. The conditions for organizing were just too tough.

Economically, the rural South was on the verge of a mechanization which would drastically reduce the agricultural worker's leverage, and virtually eradicate sharecropping. The sinking price of commodities in the Depression robbed the tenants still further of resources needed to fight. Politically, the New Deal's detente with planters meant no large-scale federal commitment to serious change. (The FBI was too busy tracking Communists to become involved in human rights.) As in Reconstruction, the U.S. lacked the will and Black Southerners the means to effect the needed democratic revolution.

1700 Families Camp Out

Organized labor also failed the tenant farmer. Not even the industrial union movement at its most militant and democratic could fit such agricultural workers into existing categories or make the necessary changes in the categories. Unlike industrial workers, sharecroppers did not always work for wages, and they could not come up with regular dues payments. Their organizations, STFU or SCU, were more like social movements than union institutions. Success for the tenant farmer demanded a sort of continuing civil rights crusade, where religious and community people could mix freely in a structure created for the problems immediately at hand.

Thus, the CIO's United Cannery, Agricultural, Packing and Allied Workers of America, which absorbed the STFU and part of the SCU, was better suited for other types of agricultural laborers, who worked on land they had never owned. With personal and political differences overcoming the hope for unity. Mitchell pulled a much-weakened STFU out of the CIO.

Mitchell then created what he called "Washington's smallest lobby," a ceaseless little corner of agitation in Congress and in the administration. So long as the sympathetic Eleanor Roosevelt remained in the White House, he got a fair hearing. President Harry Truman, who as Senator refused to help Missouri's tenant farmers, would close the door on labor crusading. But in 1939, Mitchell's contacts turned out to be very valuable.

In New York on union business, Mitchell read in the *New York Times* about the action of the Missouri tenant farmers. He tells this part of the story best. Mitchell recognized faces from the *Times* photo, because their leaders were STFU (and at least in one prominent case, former SCU) members. They had already learned some of the needed skills for mass mobilization, and with other local people, they acted magnificently to dramatize their plight.

In an interview with Washington University graduate student Jeff Sutter, Mitchell described what happened: "The strike occurred because of a thing we had been advocating for a long time. All the participants in the government program plowing up the cotton and reducing the acreage should be paid in proportion to their share and get checks from the government. We finally got that.

"What happened then, the plantation owners decided this is a way to get rid of all sharecroppers, pay them 75 cents or $1 a day during the time they were needed on the farm and make them pay rent on the houses, which had never happened before. . . . At least 1700 families in southeast Missouri moved onto the highways south of Sikestown down almost to the Arkansas line. They camped out."

When he saw the *Times* photo, Mitchell "called the president of the union, E. L. Butler. He hadn't even read it in the local papers; he didn't know a damned thing about it either. He said he'd go up there immediately. I told him I'd go to Washington and see what I could get done down there. . . . I met Mrs. Roosevelt and she got the President to order the governor of Missouri to send out the National Guard to provide tents.

"But before they could get there, the local authorities had moved them off the highways, where they could be seen, dumped them out in the open fields. One of the worst examples was a rather larger group, mostly Blacks, who were put on the spot between the levees and the Mississippi River, in what they called the spillways. They had guards on the gates going in and out. People didn't even have food, the water was just rainwater that happened to be in the spillway.

"They finally sent two men—at least one might get to St. Louis. They started out, with enough money to buy food on the way and busfare. The next morning, a small plane circled the camp, everybody got excited, but the leader of the group, who was a Black, a sergeant during World War I, said, 'Look fellas, spread out, maybe they want to bomb us, kill us all.' Then they dropped something off this plane. They found a big sack of bread, [which had] been sent by Martin Lichner, a secretary of the Socialist Party [in St. Louis] . . . and a note attached that help was on the way [and that] your friends arrived safely, both of them."

Tenant Farmers Strike

Eleanor Roosevelt's appeal for the sharecroppers, in her weekly magazine column, netted them $5000 ("that's like $50,000 today!" Mitchell chirps). The STFU brought tons of food and supplies to two relief headquarters. Mitchell and others successfully proposed to Congress the building of 10 labor villages, with nominal rent and access to rural employment, for the displaced tenants. That this was the best they could get illustrated the dilemma of the farm labor movement. Even at its best, it could only hold back the onslaught of deteriorating conditions.

Two years later, in 1941, remaining tenant farmers in southeast Missouri staged a dramatic strike against wage reductions, once more marked by Black and white unity and by the presence of Mitchell's friend, Pan-Africanist Marxist C.L.R. James, who spoke widely and wrote a pamphlet about the strike. Mitchell then worked to get tenant farmers out of the rural South, into the new war jobs and communities where they could gain living wages and an education.

The rest of the story is less dramatic, but just as important. *Roll the Union On* tells it one way, and "Our Land Too" tells it another. Mitchell maneuvered the STFU into the American Federation of Labor, where it lasted out the worst of the cold war years, and eventually into the Amalgamated Meatcutters Union. Along the way, he helped launch the farmworkers' organizing of the 1960s and then turned his attention to Southern fishers and sugar cane workers.

With the agribusiness transformation of the South, the exodus of small farmers and tenants alike accelerated, and the struggle permanently changed character. What did not change was the crusading spirit and the interracial quality. Chicanos in particular, active in hard-pressed southwest agricultural struggles for decades, now stepped into the publicity spotlight. When the United Farm Workers became the shining hope of an otherwise mostly sluggish and conservative U.S. labor movement, Mitchell's task had in a sense been completed.

But not in Mitchell's own mind. Back in the late 19th century, former slave and abolitionist agitator Harriet Tubman survived by hawking photos of herself, selling the image (as she used to say) to keep the substance alive. Mitchell is, despite a near-lifetime of pitifully small wages, in no danger of starvation. Nor is he an egotist who wants everyone to recognize his personal importance. Mitch wants his listeners, especially young people, to understand the importance of the agrarian story and the racial dimensions which made to the heart of U.S. society's (and the left's) real dilemma. He has probably worked harder than any veteran of a social movement—the Veterans of the Abraham Lincoln Brigade possibly excepted—to tirelessly document its history, by gathering the materials and encouraging the interviews that will help future scholars.

Is the 1939 strike "just history"? Not to Mitch, who sees in it a lesson about homelessness that the U.S. needs today.

Chapter 75

The "Double V" Campaign

Edgar T. Rouzeau

When the United States entered World War II, many African Americans questioned why they should be asked to fight fascism abroad when they still confronted racism at home. In 1942, the Pittsburgh Courier *began a campaign advocating a double victory for democracy—at home and abroad. "The Double V Campaign," as it was immediately dubbed, was adopted nationally throughout the African American community.*

After writing this article, Edgar Rouzeau, the editor and manager of the Courier's *New York office, became the first black journalist accredited to report from the front lines. He was later joined by seven other correspondents from the* Courier.

The Pittsburgh Courier *was founded in 1910. During the late 1920s, H. L. Mencken declared it the "best colored newspaper published." In the early 1930s, when the* Courier *criticized the popular radio show* Amos 'n' Andy *for its use of racial stereotypes, the paper's petition drive to have the show dropped raised about 600,000 signatures.*

By the end of World War II, the Courier *had more than 350,000 subscribers. In 1966, after years of declining circulation, the* Courier *was acquired by Sengstacke Publications, publisher of another important black newspaper, the* Chicago Defender. *In 1998, in honor of its reporting from 1940 to 1960, the* Pittsburgh Courier *received the George Polk Career Award in Journalism from the Long Island University Journalism Department.*

The following selection is reprinted from the first article on the Double V Campaign, "Black America Wars on Double Front for High Stakes," Pittsburgh Courier, *7 February 1942, 1. Reprinted with permission of the* Chicago Daily Defender.

Yes, Black America also has a stake for which to fight. The only difference, as between ours and that for which the white man throws his dice, is that ours has far more meaning to the progress of civilization, and proportionately is far more difficult of attainment.

As the white man sees this war, the present day convulsion of the world is simply the result of a clash of ideologies. But if this is so, how then did Black America become embroiled? We did not have a share in the formulation of these ideologies. Exploited, delimited, segregated and humiliated as we were, our opinion was not sought.

Had to Choose Quickly

And what are these ideologies? On the one hand—the Fascism of Italy, the National Socialism [Nazism] of Germany and the imperialism of Japan. On the other hand—the lily white democratic ideology of America and Great Britain plus the luke-warm enigma which stands for Russian Communism.

Our involvement is unexplainable only to the extent that we did not have a hand in the shaping of these ideologies. But we were trapped between these formidable and opposing blocs like the proverbial nut between the nut-cracker. Involvement was inescapable. As a matter-of-fact, common sense dictated that we choose quickly on one side or the other in order to avoid disaster.

Unquestioned Loyalty

That choice has been made, but not without misgivings, and not on grounds that a foreigner might suppose. Our choice is final and irrevocable and our legions are on the march. Black America has taken up arms for the duration on the side of white democracy. Throughout the length and breadth of these United States, in cities, villages and whistle stops, our youths are surrendering the things they love best, turning from loved ones to face the unknown, and for a cause in which their faith is all but shaken.

The adventure on which they are setting forth may end either in death or life-long mutilation. It will certainly result in hardships, untold sufferings and privation. And it would not be worth it if our stake was not so big and precious.

Has High Stakes

Where white America must fight on foreign soil for the salvation of these United States and for the preservation of "democracy," Black Americans must fight and die on these same battlefields, not merely for the salvation of America, not merely to secure the same degree of democracy for Black Americans that white Americans have long enjoyed, but to establish precedent for a world-wide principle of free association among men of all races, creeds and colors. That's the black man's stake.

Reduced to its very essence, this means that Black America must fight two wars and win in both. There is the convulsive war abroad. There is the bloodless war at home. The first must be fought with the destructive weapons of science. The other must be fought with the pen, in the classrooms and on the speaking platforms. Even in a democracy, freedom is not a bequest but a fruit of conquest. Ignorance brought us enslavement, both physical and mental. We must exercise intelligence to extricate ourselves. Remember, intelligence and freedom are boon companions.

We Lose All in Defeat

There is only this last consideration. If the United States is a loser in World War II, then Black America may not emerge victorious in its war at home. Although we have not enjoyed our full share of democracy in "democratic America" our chances of enjoying any democracy at all in a totalitarian America would be far more doubtful. Our two wars are inextricably intertwined. And this being true, we must believe sufficiently in our cause at home if we are to contribute our utmost toward a successful war effort abroad.

The suffering and privation may be great, but the rewards loom even greater. They are well worth any amount of blood we may be asked to spill, any amount of tears and sweat we may be asked to shed. If we are not equal to the sacrifice, we might as well rest our pens, padlock the classrooms and return to our old slave-masters. We will not have been worthy of democracy.

Chapter 76

Nazi and Dixie Nordics

Langston Hughes

*Poet Langston Hughes (1902–1967) was a central figure in the Harlem Renais-
sance. His verse regularly appeared in magazines such as the NAACP's* Crisis, *the
National Urban League's* Opportunity, *and the* New Masses, *a radical literary
journal.*

For collections of his political writings, see Good Morning Revolution: Uncol-
lected Social Protest Writings by Langston Hughes *(1973) and* Langston Hughes
and the Chicago Defender: Essays on Race, Politics, and Culture, 1942–62 *(1995).
For a biography, see Arnold Rampersad's* The Life of Langston Hughes *(2 vols.,
1986, 1988).*

The following selection is reprinted from "Nazi and Dixie Nordics," Chicago
Defender, *10 March 1945. Reprinted with permission of the* Chicago Daily
Defender.

"I doubt if education will change them," said an American schoolman who speaks
German and has traveled much in Germany. We were talking of the Hitlerites.
"Nazi ideologies are too deeply engrained to change them with books."

"They are certainly fanatics," reports a soldier back from the European front,
who has seen Nazi prisoners.

"They have killed and tortured my people," said a Jewish American of German
background. "How to get that cruelty out of them will be a problem after the
war."

"The Germans are the victims of a mass psychosis," says an American sociologist. "It will take drastic measures to control them when peace comes."

These people were talking about Germans in Germany. To a Negro, they might
just as well have been speaking of white Southerners in Dixie. Our local Nordics
have a mass psychosis, too, when it comes to race. As the Hitlerites treat the Jews,
so they treat the Negroes, in varying degrees of viciousness ranging from the denial of educational opportunities to the denial of employment, from buses that
pass Negroes by to jailers who beat and torture Negro prisoners, from the denial
of the ballot to the denial of the right to live.

What to Do with Dixie?

Just as the allied administrators of a conquered Germany will be puzzled as to what to do about the Nazi character, so American Negro citizens are puzzled as to what to do about the Dixie character. When a whole people are accustomed to kicking another group of people around—in Germany the Jews, in America the Negroes—education seems a very weak and long-range remedy indeed, although it must certainly be a part of any solution.

Unconditional surrender and armed intervention will go a long way in controlling German behavior toward what few Jews are left there. But nobody is confronting our Southerners with Unconditional Decency as regards their Negro neighbors.

How are we going to get rid of the stupidities of Jim Crow in the South? What are we going to do with a people who want all the best things for themselves, just because they are white—the best seats on the buses, the best coaches on the trains, the best schools, the best jobs—just because they are white?

What are we going to do with folks who wish to continue to deny Negroes the ballot—as the Germans denied it to the Jews in Europe? Who wish to continue to segregate Negroes as the Nazis ghettoized Jews in Poland? Who wish to continue to force our Red Cross to mark Negro blood AA—*Afro-American*—as things Jewish are labeled *Yude* in Germany? What are we going to do with people like that here in America?

Our Own Bigots

Such people certainly do not believe in Americanism. They do not believe in democracy, they do not believe in law. They do not believe in social decency. They do not even believe in courtesy.

What are we going to do with the millions of white Americans of the South who pay our United States Constitution not the least mind when it comes to democratic treatment of their Negro fellow-citizens?

I think our Congress had well take up that problem, along with the problem of what to do about Nazi Germany. The two problems have much in common— Berlin and Birmingham. The Jewish people and the Negro people both know the meaning of Nordic supremacy. We have both looked into the eyes of terror.

Klansmen and Storm Troopers are brothers under the skin. The Grand Kleagle of the Klan has already stated to the press that there will be 5,000,000 Ku Kluxers ready to reorganize their Klaverns after the war. That will be quite dangerous for Negroes—but it will be much more dangerous to America as a whole, especially labor, Jews, Catholics, and the foreign born. We had better consider that problem now. It is just as important as what to do about Germany.

Democracy, like charity, really begins at home. With a mote in one's own eye, it is hard to remove the beam from another's. A general eye-cleaning from Dortmund to Dixie wouldn't do any harm. The whole English-speaking Caucasian world, from white Australia, to Jim Crow South Africa, needs its eyes opened. They are full of the dust of race prejudice. Our own American Southland is almost blind as a result.

Where can we find a specialist to treat eyes clouded by Nordic "superiority"? We intend to lead Germany, but it is not easy for the near-blind to lead the blind. We must do something about our own bigots, too, and soon!

Chapter 77

The Civil Rights Congress

Gerald Horne

Gerald Horne is professor of history and director of the Black Cultural Center and the Institute for African-American Research at the University of North Carolina. He received 305,000 votes in California as the Peace and Freedom party candidate for U.S. Senate in 1992. His books include Black and Red: W. E. B. Du Bois and the Afro-American Response to the Cold War, 1944–1963 *(1985),* Reversing Discrimination: The Case for Affirmative Action *(1992),* Black Liberation–Red Scare: Ben Davis and the Communist Party *(1994),* Testaments of Courage: Selections from Men's Slave Narratives *(1995),* Powell v. Alabama: The Scottsboro Boys and American Justice *(1997), and* Race Woman: The Lives of Shirley Graham Du Bois *(2000).*

The following selection is a reprint of "Civil Rights Congress" by Gerald Horne, from Encyclopedia of the American Left, *2d ed., ed. Mari Jo Buhle, Paul Buhle, and Dan Georgakas. Copyright © 1998 by Oxford University Press, Inc. Used by permission of Oxford University Press, Inc.*

It was called the most successful "Communist front" of all time. Dashiell Hammett, author of *The Thin Man* and longtime companion of Lillian Hellman, went to jail because of his association with it. Paul Robeson was stoned at Peekskill as he raised money for it. What stirred such passion was the Civil Rights Congress (CRC), which during its existence from 1946 to 1956 fought for and established a number of civil rights and liberties rulings that expanded the rights of all in the United States.

CRC was formed in the early postwar period when the impending Cold War and McCarthyism could be sensed but had not yet been established. It was formed as a result of a merger among the International Labor Defense (which was catapulted to prominence as a result of its vigorous defense of the Scottsboro Nine [see chapter 65—*Eds.*] and Angelo Herndon, among others), the National Negro Congress (an early effort to form a "Black United Front" among Afro-Americans), and the National Federation for Constitutional Liberties. Early on they developed a specialty in fighting "black" and "red" cases.

One of the CRC's earliest black cases was that of Willie McGee, a Mississippi truckdriver whose white lover accused him of rape after her husband discovered their affair. In their attempt to save McGee's life, CRC launched a national and international campaign that made his name a household word. They helped to publicize the fact that rape of white women had been used historically as a reason to lynch or execute black men. A significant percentage of their cases had this theme, including the Martinsville Seven—another one of their more significant cases. Even in their declining days, they were still able to mobilize masses around the case of black teenager Emmett Till, the Chicago resident who was lynched on an ill-fated trip to Mississippi in 1955 after allegedly "getting fresh" with a white woman. The flip side of this emphasis was their defense of Rose Lee Ingram, the black female sharecropper from Georgia who was assaulted by her white land-lord, whom she then fatally dispatched. This emphasis touched a raw nerve in the national consciousness among blacks and whites, as CRC linked sensitive ques-tions of race, sex and exploitation.

Long before Montgomery, CRC was "softening up" the racists in the Deep South for the subsequent onslaught led by Rev. Martin Luther King, Jr. In the early 1950s they led "Freedom Rides" to Virginia to save the Martinsville Seven. But their success in bringing domestic racism to the international arena may have been their most significant contribution. In the postwar period Jim Crow was be-coming an aching Achilles heel in the execution of U.S. foreign policy. How could hearts and minds be won in an increasingly "colored" world when people of color were being subjected to such pernicious discrimination here? CRC seized upon this contradiction when it published the landmark study We Charge Genocide, which detailed the heinous crimes committed against Afro-Americans and was filed at the United Nations. Reprinted in many languages and many thousands of copies, this work was an international embarrassment for the U.S. government and was a factor in bringing down the walls of Jim Crow.

Still, as dramatic and riveting as their "black" cases were, perhaps more con-troversial were their "red" cases. CRC was the major organization fighting the Smith Act frame-ups, the McCarran Act, the Communist Control Act, the House Un-American Activities Committee, and the panoply of laws and institutions formed to enforce a Cold War consensus. Their opinion was that defense of the Communist Party was the first line in the defense of civil liberties generally. Hence, they were avid in their defense of the CP leadership, which ultimately in-volved imprisonment for scores of activists on the grounds of "teaching and advo-cating" Marxism-Leninism—not seeking to overthrow the government, as is com-monly misunderstood. Despite this gargantuan labor, a number of Communists in CRC felt that not enough attention was paid to these cases or to repression of the labor movement, as evidenced by the passage of the Taft-Hartley Act. Others felt that the battle for Afro-American equality was the cutting edge in the battle for democracy generally, thus justifying this emphasis. The fact that the beginning of the end for HUAC came when they brought their traveling road-show to Atlanta and encountered a united civil rights leadership does lend some credence to the last notion.

The practical and theoretical battles were conducted within an organization that at its zenith may have had 10,000 members, during a time when progressive organizations were not proliferating. The CRC's strongest chapters were in such critically important cities as New York, Detroit, Seattle, the San Francisco Bay Area, and Los Angeles. Though it was derided as a "Communist front," a number of the Party's internal weaknesses did not unduly influence CRC negatively. For example, during a time when the CP was conducting a vigorous campaign to uproot white chauvinism that was later deemed by the leadership to have been conducted improperly, the brunt of the deleterious impact managed to escape CRC despite—or perhaps because of—their own vigorous campaigns on behalf of McGee, Ingram et al.

CRC had titanic clashes with both the ACLU and the NAACP. "Free speech" for racism and the Ku Klux Klan was a bone of contention with the ACLU, though that organization's ingrained anticommunism certainly played a role in their conflicts. CRC's conflicts with the NAACP were more complex. That group was avowedly "anti-imperialist" and experienced tremendous growth during those days of lessened anticommunism, 1941–45. This was the time when black Communist Ben Davis was elected to the New York City Council from Harlem with the support of NAACP executive secretary Roy Wilkins; but the alliance was not able to withstand the blows of the Cold War. Nevertheless, just as Booker T. Washington publicly disdained battles against aspects of Jim Crow while secretly funding them, the NAACP maintained forms of cooperation with CRC while hewing to the official line publicly. This was aided by the contradictions of Jim Crow itself; Wilkins lived across the hall from CRC leader William Patterson in a segregated Harlem apartment building, 409 Edgecombe Avenue.

The U.S. government, a major target of CRC broadsides, was a major factor in bringing on their dissolution. The Subversive Activities Control Board, in particular, forced the liquidation not only of CRC but also the Council on African Affairs (the premier organization pushing decolonization and antiapartheid) and other Left-led organizations. Yet, there was significant continuity between CRC and the post-Montgomery movement, as many who had honed their skills fighting for McGee went on to press for the Civil Rights Act of 1964, the Voting Rights Act of 1965, and counsel the Black Panther Party. This was CRC's ultimate legacy.

4

The Second Reconstruction

Founding mothers of the modern civil rights movement: Septima Clark (left) and Rosa Parks at the Highlander Folk School in Tennessee. (Photo courtesy of Highlander Research and Education Center.)

Chapter 78

Introduction:
The Modern Civil Rights Movement

Jonathan Birnbaum and Clarence Taylor

The United States was born with great promise. "All men are created equal," trumpeted the Declaration of Independence. But after the Revolution slavery continued, endorsed and formally supported not only at the state and local level but by the national Constitution.

The grave contradiction of a country claiming freedom as its core principle while enslaving millions was finally resolved through a bloody civil war that cost 600,000 lives. Now, at last, the United States would fulfill its promise of freedom and equality for all its people. The Reconstruction–era amendments of the Constitution underlined that. But that promise was brought low by the repression, disenfranchisement, and compromise that were formalized as Segregation. The country's promise of civil rights for all its citizens was a dream deferred once again.

During Segregation, blacks and a small group of whites[1] laid the groundwork for reviving that promise. A central foundation for that project was the NAACP's long, painstaking series of court cases culminating in *Brown v. Board of Education.*

In 1787, the year the Constitution was composed in Philadelphia, a group of black citizens led by the Rev. Prince Hall petitioned the Massachusetts state legislature for equal educational facilities (see chapter 6). In 1827, a black woman calling herself "Matilda" wrote a letter to *Freedom's Journal* requesting that black women not be forgotten when it came to education (see chapter 9). In 1849, Sarah Roberts challenged Boston's legal right to force black students to attend separate schools (see chapter 16). Throughout slavery, blacks sought to learn how to read and write. Slave owners, always fearing potential danger, passed laws against educating blacks (see chapter 22). "The alphabet is an abolitionist. If you would keep a people enslaved, refuse to teach them to read," said *Harper's Weekly*. Black "schools are going up in every direction," reported an agent of the Freedmen's Bureau during Reconstruction (see chapter 26). It is altogether fitting that the black struggle for civil rights would culminate in *Brown*—a victory for black education.

But contrary to the textbooks, that one court case was not the origin of the modern civil rights movement. And, sadly, one court case did not conclude the struggle. For one thing, the Supreme Court did not require immediate compliance (see chapter 81). "All deliberate speed" was all that was required, which resulted in further compromise and delay.

Southern senators and representatives condemned *Brown* with the "Southern Manifesto" (see chapter 148). Throughout the South there was massive, state-endorsed resistance, including a grand assault on the NAACP, crushing the group's activity and membership. A single court ruling would not decide the struggle. As Melissa Fay Green writes, "[C]ivil rights was not a one time event . . . it had to be fought for in every little community."[2]

The NAACP's legal work continued, but the focus of the struggle shifted from the courts to a social movement–centered strategy of nonviolent direct action throughout the South and, eventually, the nation. Mainstays in that struggle were local black labor leaders, such as Montgomery, Alabama's E. D. Nixon, and black women such as Jo Ann Robinson, Septima Clark, Rosa Parks, Fannie Lou Hamer, and Ella Baker. Meanwhile, the movement's public leadership face shifted to the black churches and black male ministers. One of the few traditional black institutions that survived Segregation was the church, as historian Herb Gutman noted. "[T]he church was transformed by what happened in the civil rights movement. . . . [A]n everyday institution became the basis for an oppositional movement."[3]

The rank and file of that movement was overwhelmingly working class, which is not surprising, since Segregation's primary intent was to control black labor. Throughout Segregation—and even during most of the modern civil rights movement—Red Scare tactics against blacks, labor, and the left played a pivotal role in undermining and delaying the struggle for civil rights. Ellen Schrecker, a historian specializing in this era, writes:

> As we assess the consequences of McCarthyism's assault on the left, we encounter a world of things that did not happen: reforms that were never implemented, unions that were never organized, movements that never started. . . . And questions that were never asked. . . .
>
> [A] case can be made that the anticommunist crusade, besides isolating an important group of activists, deflected the civil rights movement from pressing for economic, as well as legal and political, change. . . .
>
> Within the South, McCarthyism eliminated options and narrowed the struggle for black equality. Again it is a question of lost opportunities. For a brief moment in the late forties, there was the possibility that the region's organized black workers and its more liberal whites might have been able to build an interracial civil rights movement with a strong grassroots based in the African American community. . . .
>
> Middle-class whites who might have worked for integration in the South were also silenced during the McCarthy years. . . .
>
> Anticommunism proved invaluable to white supremacists during the 1940s and 1950s. It provided them a more up-to-date and respectable cover than mere racism and hooked them into a national network of rightwing activists. At the same time it reinforced their traditional contention that outside agitators were behind the move for civil rights.[4]

The impact of these Red Scare tactics continued into the 1960s. On July 22, 1964, rising to speak in opposition to the passage of the 1964 Civil Rights Act, with a text clearly courtesy of the FBI, Mississippi Senator James Eastland condemned "Communist infiltration of the so-called civil rights movement."[5] The senator, who had "killed all but one of 121 civil rights measures over the past decade,"[6] concluded his extraordinary rant by questioning the recent disappearance of three civil rights workers. "The people of my State do not know what happened to the three individuals who are missing in Neshoba County, Miss.," Eastland asserted,

> any more than my colleagues in this Chamber [the Senate] know. . . . [R]acial agitators in both the North and the South proclaim that the missing ones have been the victims of persecution and racial violence. . . . [B]ut many people in our State assert that there is just as much evidence, as of today, that they are voluntarily missing as there is that they have been abducted. No one wants to charge that a hoax has been perpetrated . . . but as time goes on and the search continues, if some evidence of a crime is not produced, I think the people of America will be justified in considering other alternatives, as more valid solutions to the mystery, instead of accepting as true the accusation of the agitators that heinous crime has been committed.[7]

Forty-four days after their disappearance, civil rights workers Michael Schwerner, James Chaney, and Andrew Goodman were found shot and buried in an earthen dam.[8] Eastland did not amend his remarks.

The tactics of the emerging civil rights movement—ranging from boycotts to nonviolent civil disobedience—had their antecedents in tactics employed during previous periods in both the North and the South. Although Martin Luther King usually credited Boston University and India's Mohandas Gandhi for teaching him about nonviolence, the more immediate credit went to older black labor activists such as Bayard Rustin, who, as King acknowledged, instructed him on the practical applications of this principle. And while much was made of Gandhi and India's struggle for independence from Britain as the basis for such a strategy, the real roots, as Gandhi himself acknowledged, lay in a much older *American* tradition—from seventeenth-century Quaker dissenters to nineteenth-century abolitionists—a tradition "developed as much by American women as by men."[9]

The following section discusses the shift from the NAACP's legal strategy to one of direct action; the shift from labor to religious leadership in the direct action campaign; the struggle in the North; Black Power; electoral politics; current examples of discrimination, and affirmative action.

NOTES

1. See John Egerton, *Speak Now against the Day: The Generation before the Civil Rights Movement in the South* (New York: Knopf, 1994), Charles M. Payne, *I've Got the Light of Freedom: The Organizing Tradition and the Mississippi Freedom Struggle* (Berkeley: University of California Press, 1995), and John Dittmer, *Local People: The Struggle for Civil Rights in Mississippi* (Champaign: University of Illinois Press, 1995).

2. Melissa Fay Green, *Praying for Sheetrock* (Reading, Mass: Addison-Wesley, 1991).

3. "An Unpublished Interview with Herbert Gutman on U.S. Labor History," *Socialism*

and Democracy (Spring/Summer 1990), 64.

4. Ellen Schrecker, *Many Are the Crimes: McCarthyism and America* (New York: Little, Brown, 1998), 369, 389, 390, and 391. Also see chapter 87 below.

5. Senator James Eastland, "Communist Infiltration into the So-Called Civil Rights Movement," *Congressional Record,* 22 July 1964, 16593.

6. Taylor Branch, *Pillar of Fire: America in the King Years 1963–65* (New York: Simon and Schuster, 1998), 267.

7. Eastland, "Communist Infiltration," 16596.

8. Seth Cagin and Philip Dray, *We Are Not Afraid: The Story of Goodman, Schwerner and Chaney and the Civil Rights Campaign for Mississippi* (New York: Macmillan, 1988).

9. Gerda Lerner, "Nonviolent Resistance: The History of an Idea," in *Why History Matters* (New York: Oxford University Press, 1997).

The Legal Strategy

Chapter 79

Charles Hamilton Houston and the NAACP Legal Strategy

Patricia Sullivan

Patricia Sullivan is a visiting professor at the W. E. B. Du Bois Institute at Harvard University.

The following selection is excerpted from Days of Hope: Race and Democracy in the New Deal Era *by Patricia Sullivan. Copyright © 1996 by the University of North Carolina Press. Used by permission of the publisher.*

"At the heart of the dark labyrinth of America's complex problems is the crisis in the South," wrote University of Virginia student Palmer Weber in 1938. Weber commended Franklin Roosevelt's successful effort to focus national attention on the region with the widely noted *Report on the Economic Conditions of the South.* Southerners themselves had finally become conscious "of the inherited shackles of tenancy, disease and illiteracy." Such general social problems, he noted, had become "accepted subjects of discussion," and this was a significant development. "But," Weber continued, "the black thread in the crisis ridden pattern of [the region's] social culture has not yet been examined. Neither Mr. Roosevelt nor the Southern New Dealers have publicly considered the social significance of the Southern Negro."

As illustrated by Lowell Mellett's decision to exclude blacks from participating in the report of the National Emergency Council (NEC), the Roosevelt administration carefully avoided any suggestion that it aimed to upset the racial status quo in the South. But Roosevelt's attempt to purge southern obstructionists in the 1938 primary elections and bring the South into line with the national Democratic Party implicitly challenged the political foundation of white supremacy. Roosevelt's ill-fated intervention supported the political aspirations of disfranchised groups who had mobilized in response to the Depression and the New Deal. It resulted in the founding of the Southern Conference for Human Welfare (SCHW), a biracial coalition dedicated to ending voter restrictions in the South and completing the liberal realignment of the Democratic Party.

By 1938 a loose political network had developed around the labor movement, local branches of the National Association for the Advancement of Colored People (NAACP), voter leagues, Communist Party initiatives, and New Deal programs.

During the 1930s a small number of individuals from widely different backgrounds gave form and direction to the democratic activism that developed outside of the insular structure of southern politics. Palmer Weber, Charles Houston, and Lucy Randolph Mason serve as useful examples of the range of leadership that emerged. Palmer Weber, a native of Smithfield, Virginia, was a radical student organizer at the University of Virginia before joining southern New Dealers in Washington in 1940 and the SCHW's legislative fight to abolish the poll tax. Charles Hamilton Houston, a brilliant legal mind and strategist, traveled tens of thousands of miles throughout the South, building the NAACP's southern-based campaign to equalize education and secure voting rights. Lucy Randolph Mason, whose Virginia lineage stretched back to George Mason, a signer of the Declaration of Independence, became the leading public representative of the Congress of Industrial Organizations (CIO) in the South and worked as a union publicist and voting-rights proponent. . . .

Charles Hamilton Houston . . . navigated the possibilities created by the economic dislocation and shifting political alliances of the Depression years. As chief legal counsel for the NAACP, he was uniquely able to recognize openings in the South's caste-bound society. Starting in 1934, Houston began traveling extensively in the South, observing and documenting conditions in black communities, becoming familiar with local leadership and organizations, and encouraging the renewed political interest and activism evident in the early 1930s. "The work of the next decade," Houston wrote NAACP Executive Secretary Walter White in 1934, "will have to be concentrated in the South."

Charles Houston was slightly older than the New Deal generation of black activists. He was born in Washington, D.C., in 1895 and . . . was part of Washington's black middle class. The grandson of runaway slaves, Houston inherited a strong sense of racial pride and benefited from William and Katherine Houston's commitment to provide their only son with the best education possible. From Dunbar High School, he went on to Amherst College, where, during his first year, he was the only person of African descent at the college. "The alienation born of racism," wrote biographer Genna Rae McNeil, became "a catalyst for Charles's . . . personal self-reliance." He graduated Phi Beta Kappa in 1915 and delivered a commencement address on the life of [the African-American poet] Paul Laurence Dunbar, despite protests from faculty members unfamiliar with the subject.

Formal education was interrupted by service in World War I, an experience that fundamentally shaped Houston's personal expectations and goals. The daily indignities heaped on black soldiers in the segregated armed forces were compounded by his experience as a judge-advocate, during which he witnessed the blatant disregard of fairness and justice when black soldiers were the subjects of prosecution. Houston wrote, "I made up my mind that I would never get caught again without knowing something about my rights; that if luck was with me, and I got through this war, I would study law and use my time fighting for men who could not strike back." In the fall of 1919, Houston enrolled in Harvard Law School and became the first person of his race elected to the editorial board of the *Harvard Law Review*. During his second year, he organized a student luncheon at Harvard for

Marcus Garvey, who, Houston later explained, "made a permanent contribution in teaching the simple dignity of being black." After obtaining an LL.B. and a doctorate in law from Harvard, he received a Harvard-sponsored scholarship to support a year of study in comparative law at the University of Madrid. Spain afforded Houston an experience of racial egalitarianism that "colored [his] entire life on the race question."

With the normal channels of political participation closed to black Americans, Charles Houston envisioned a unique and critical role for black lawyers. As early as 1922, Houston proposed that there must be a black lawyer in every community, preferably trained at black institutions by black teachers. Applying the innovative theory of social jurisprudence advanced at Harvard by Roscoe Pound, Felix Frankfurter, and others, Houston explained that through the creative exploration and application of the Constitution, the black lawyer could achieve reforms that were unattainable through traditional political channels. Houston applied his vision as a member of the Howard University Law School faculty (1924–35), where he was appointed vice-dean in 1929. He transformed the school from a nonaccredited night school into a full-time, accredited program and created a laboratory for the development of civil rights law. The rigorous course he implemented reflected his conception of social engineering and the responsibilities of black leadership. The black lawyer, Houston maintained, should "be trained as a social engineer and group interpreter." He added, "Due to the Negro's social and political condition . . . the Negro lawyer must be prepared to anticipate, guide and interpret his group's advancement." Houston educated a generation of black civil rights lawyers, many from the South, who would implement the NAACP's protracted assault on the legal foundation of white supremacy.

By enhancing the power of the federal government, the economic crisis of the Depression and the advent of the New Deal reinforced Houston's emphasis on national citizenship. He was alert to the vastly expanded range of possibilities for political education and action, possibilities created by the social dislocation and government experimentation of the 1930s. Houston investigated the racial application of New Deal programs and publicized cases of discrimination, lobbied the Roosevelt administration for fair treatment, testified before Congress on the racial implications of a wide array of legislation, and played a leading role in the fight for antilynching legislation.

The development of racially progressive political views among white liberals won Houston's attention. Speaking to groups like the Virginia Commission on Interracial Cooperation and the YWCA, he cautioned them not to act "out of any sentimental interest in the Negro." It was in the self-interest of white liberals to confront the race problem, which, he warned, could "yet be the decisive factor in the success or failure of the New Deal." Their goal, Houston advised, should be to "free white America from the senseless phobias and contemptuous arrogance towards all peoples of the non-nordic stock." He acknowledged the magnitude of the task but suggested that they strive to make their "own generation open its eyes" and realize when it was "cutting off its nose to spite its face." He noted, "The South is doing [this] when it squeezes Negro wages and as a consequence cuts down his consuming power in the community." And he urged them to "save young America from the blight of race prejudice." . . .

The early years of the New Deal coincided with Houston's deepening involvement in the NAACP. As the association's legal counsel and trusted adviser to Executive Secretary Walter White, Houston played a critical role in the NAACP's development during these years. By the early 1930s, the NAACP was in the process of completing a major transition, at least at the national level, away from the predominantly white-led organization founded in 1909 and toward an expanding role for black leadership and a greater reliance on black membership. But the New York–based organization continued to maintain a narrow legal focus, tended to rely on prominent white constitutional lawyers for its major cases, and remained remote from the lives and experiences of the majority of black Americans, especially those living in the South. The brief flurry of branch activity in the South after World War I failed to reach much beyond the professional classes and receded by the late 1920s. The NAACP meeting in Oklahoma in 1934 marked the first time a national convention had been held in the South since the Atlanta meeting of 1921. Speaking to the national convention in 1933 and 1934, Houston joined a chorus of voices in urging a major revision of association policy and priorities to meet the crisis of the Depression. "Take the Association home to the people in 1934," he implored the Oklahoma gathering.

A case in the 1930s exposed the inadequacy of the NAACP's approach to the South. When news of the arrest of nine young black men charged with raping two white women near Scottsboro, Alabama, reached New York in the spring of 1931, Walter White had no local contacts to call on for a direct report. The nearest NAACP branch, in Chattanooga, had collapsed in 1930. White followed the case in the press, which relied primarily on southern newspapers, and the NAACP remained aloof. Meanwhile, when Charles Dirba, assistant secretary of the International Labor Defense (ILD) and a member of the Communist Party's Central Committee, read about the arrest, he telegraphed Lowell Wakefield, a party organizer in Birmingham, whom he urged to conduct a careful investigation of the case. Wakefield and Douglas McKenzie, a black organizer for the League of Struggle for Negro Rights, attended the trials in Scottsboro. Dependent on a weak and ineffectual team of defense lawyers, the young men were quickly tried and sentenced to death, amid a mob atmosphere. The ILD immediately acted to secure representation for the appeal of the case and publicized the "legal lynching" of the Scottsboro defendants. The ILD won the acclaim of much of the black press and its readership, which chided the NAACP's belated efforts to wrest control of the case from a group that had acted boldly and decisively. . . .

Throughout the 1930s, Charles Houston referred to the Scottsboro case as a pivotal event in the development of black protest. The ILD's "uncompromising resistance to southern prejudice," he explained, "set a new standard for agitation for equality." As a symbol of "the whole position of oppression of the Negro people in America," the Scottsboro case "fused all the elements of the Negro people into a common resistance more than any other issue within a generation." Whereas most black people had tended to "stay away" from black people in trouble—"with the idea of not letting trouble spread to themselves"—they joined in the fight for the "Scottsboro Boys" because they "were made to feel that even without the ordinary weapons of democracy . . . [they] still had the force . . . with which they themselves could bring to bear pressures and affect the result of the trial and arbitrations." Furthermore, he explained, "The Communists have made it impossible for any aspirant to Negro leadership to advocate less than full economic, political and social equality and expect to retain the respect and confidence of the group."

For Houston, ideological disputes about the Communist Party assumptions and goals were of little consequence. What mattered were the patterns of interaction that developed between Communist Party organizers and black people in Alabama. Unlike traditional civil rights and interracial groups, which maintained a paternalistic approach to the "masses," Communists worked among the sharecroppers and unemployed, "offering them full and complete brotherhood, without regard to race, creed or previous condition of servitude." Consequently, they were "the first to fire the masses with a sense of their raw, potential power, and the first to openly preach the doctrine of mass resistance and mass struggle: Unite and Fight!" Through their organizing efforts, Communists turned the attention of blacks to the issue of class and emphasized its relation to racial oppression.

Although Houston concentrated his organizing efforts within the black community, he viewed this as a part of a broader effort to build class-based alliances among southern blacks and whites. "The white and black miners in the Birmingham district have presented the ultimate solution," he observed in 1934, "by forming together in one common union to fight shoulder to shoulder for their common interest." That same year, Houston told the annual convention of the NAACP that permanent black progress against injustice and discrimination in the South would depend on whether or not blacks could form an alliance with poor whites, because the separation of the two races was impeding the progress of both. "Together they can win against the forces which are seeking to exploit them and keep them down. Separately they will lose and the other fellow will continue to win."

Houston never doubted that the NAACP had a unique role to play as potentially the most effective black organization in the country, but the role would require a major reorganization and reorientation of the association's program. By the time Houston assumed responsibility for the NAACP's legal campaign against racial discrimination in education in 1934, he was prepared to mediate between the national office and its potential southern constituency. Houston was an astute student of the region and its people, having traveled through the South extensively, always on multipurpose trips. A month-long trip late in 1934 was typical. He visited eleven towns in Georgia, the Carolinas, and Virginia, several of them more than once. He spoke at thirteen black colleges, recruited applicants for Howard University Law School, consulted with black lawyers in each state, spoke in churches, attended the district conference of the African Methodist Episcopal (AME) Zion Church in Rock Hill, South Carolina, and met with teachers groups, NAACP branches, and the North Carolina statewide conference of the Tobacco

Workers Union. On the same trip, he investigated school facilities, rural conditions, and the administration of federal relief and jobs and, with the assistance of Edward Lovett, began to document his findings with photographs and films. All the while, he deliberately cultivated support for the NAACP's program and sought out individuals "of force, vision . . . [and] keenness" who had the capacity to "be effective on the race issue in the South."

Houston's efforts to expand the base of NAACP activity in the South were equaled by his steady drive to place the southern situation at the center of national NAACP deliberations. He pressed for a reorganization of the association's structure so that the southern membership could participate in defining the national program. In supporting the nomination of Roscoe Dunjee, editor of the *Oklahoma Black Dispatch,* to the NAACP national board, Houston advised White: "Dunjee is a man of the people, and knows the Southwest situation." Certainly, he added, White needed someone on the board who could vocalize "the aspirations of that section." . . .

Under Houston's direction, the NAACP's legal campaign against racial discrimination in education stimulated the revival and expansion of NAACP branch activity. Beginning with a protracted challenge to the most blatant inequities in public education, namely the denial of graduate and professional educational opportunities to black students and the racial basis of teachers' salaries, Houston and his associates crafted a strategy that steadily eroded the legal foundations of segregation. Houston's insistence on working with all-black counsel had particular resonance in southern courtrooms. Here, often for the first time, black people witnessed one of their race functioning in a context of total equality, calling white state officials to account in full public view. Such trial scenes were reenacted in pool halls and barbershops. By 1938, Houston noted, hopefully, that the fight for graduate and professional education was "generating spontaneously out of the group itself"; every case had "been fought by Negro lawyers who practically donated their services."

Houston's efforts in the South, an associate recalled, were fueled by his confidence in the capacity "within the black community and the Negro race to bring about change." The legal campaign was a slow and deliberate process, which sought to establish roots in local communities. In endless rounds of meetings with small and large groups, throughout the South, Houston and Thurgood Marshall, his protégé and former student, explained the mechanics of the legal fight, its political significance, and its relationship to broader community concerns. They routinely encouraged people to pay their poll tax, persist in the effort to register and vote, and organize political clubs, explaining that legal victories must be backed up by organized pressure and support. Often they found people fearful of initiating litigation or political action and, in some cases, apathetic about the need for struggle. "This means we have to . . . slow down," Houston would say, "until we have developed a sustaining mass interest behind the programs. . . . The social and public factors must be developed at least along with and if possible before the actual litigation commences." . . .

The election . . . marked the culmination of a three-year effort on the part of the Roosevelt administration to fully engage the tentative allegiance of black voters, who had been steadily drifting away from the party of Lincoln. The battle for the northern black vote emerged as a major feature of the 1936 campaign. For the first time, the black vote was a part of the political reporting in the national press, and both parties pursued an aggressive advertising campaign in the black press. Although the Roosevelt administration failed to endorse any racially sensitive policies, such as antilynching legislation, it presided over a national convention that, for the first time, opened its doors to the equal participation of black reporters and the handful of black delegates in attendance, drawing a howl of protest from Senator E. D. Smith and the South Carolina delegation. Mary McLeod Bethune and other members of the "Black Cabinet" [see chapter 68—*Eds.*] took part in a sophisticated campaign aimed at black voters; the campaign included an extravagant, multicity celebration of the seventy-third anniversary of the Emancipation Proclamation. These appeals only reinforced the bonds woven by New Deal relief and jobs, ensuring Roosevelt's sweep of the black vote. "The amazing switch of this great group of voters," wrote political analyst Frank R. Kent, "is the real political sensation of the time."

The successful wooing of the northern black vote dominated the rhetoric of southern conservatives as they swelled the ranks of the anti–New Deal coalition. "Acceptance of the Negro on terms of political equality," stormed Senator Smith, had "humiliated the South." But the black vote was still tightly confined by law and custom in the South. It was the new labor movement, working in tandem with the Roosevelt administration and congressional supporters, that immediately threatened to penetrate the "Solid South" and undermine the economic and racial status quo. During 1937 and 1938, the CIO sponsored its first southern organizing drive, providing critical reinforcement to efforts that had taken root among industrial workers and sharecroppers earlier in the decade and generating a reaction that further exposed the police repression, violence, and political disfranchisement that pervaded southern society. . . .

The end of 1938 found the New Deal in retreat on Capitol Hill, with southern conservative Democrats leading the charge. That same year, the Supreme Court, now dominated by Roosevelt appointees, ruled that Lloyd L. Gaines be admitted to the University of Missouri Law School, giving the NAACP its first legal victory in the campaign for equal education. Paul Murray, whose application to the University of North Carolina had been rejected solely on racial grounds, observed that *Gaines* was the "first major breach in the solid wall of segregated education since *Plessy*." It was "the beginning of the end." Black southerners, in increasing numbers, continued to petition state Democratic parties for admission to the primary elections; the NAACP would soon prepare to take another challenge to the Supreme Court in its twenty-year legal battle against the all-white primary. In 1939, the SCHW launched a movement to abolish the poll tax. Its lobbying campaign for federal anti–poll tax legislation made the right to vote a national issue.

Although the legislative phase of the New Deal may have ended by 1938, its political consequences for the South, for African Americans, and for the Democratic Party was just beginning to be realized. Palmer Weber and Charles Houston were among those who maintained that the fate of New Deal reform would depend largely on what happened in the South. "The economic wage slavery and social suppression cursing the South today stood between the progressive forces of the New Deal and the recovery and reform they sought," observed Houston. Weber concurred. Perhaps, he wrote hopefully in November 1938, "as the tides of liberalism run deeper; the value of racial cooperation will come to be understood—even in the far South."

Chapter 80

The NAACP and *Brown*

Harvard Sitkoff

Harvard Sitkoff is professor of history at the University of New Hampshire.

The following selection is excerpted from The Struggle for Black Equality, 1954–1992 *(New York: Farrar Straus & Giroux, 1993). Reprinted with permission of Farrar, Straus & Giroux.*

For another selection by Sitkoff, see chapter 67.

White supremacists . . . played on the obsessive American fear of Communism to discredit the civil-rights cause. They equated challenges to the racial status quo with un-Americanism, and missed no opportunity to link the black struggle with Communist ideology and subversion. In the heyday of red-baiting after World War II, these tactics worked. Most civil-rights groups avoided direct action. Their leadership opted for a conservative posture to avoid even a hint of radicalism. When a small interracial band of pacifists and socialists from the Congress of Racial Equality and the Fellowship of Reconciliation journeyed throughout the upper South to test compliance of a Supreme Court ruling against segregation in interstate travel, the Negro press barely reported the news, and other civil-rights organizations shunned the 1947 Journey of Reconciliation. The following year they opposed A. Philip Randolph's call for civil disobedience to protest Jim Crow in the armed forces. With undue haste, the civil-rights leadership condemned the pro-Soviet remarks of Paul Robeson, a controversial black singer and actor, and disassociated themselves from the Marxist stance of W. E. B. Du Bois. The fear of McCarthyism so inhibited blacks that they failed to use the Korean War as a lever for racial reform, as they had World War II. At mid-century, direct action had ceased being a tactic in the quest for racial justice.

That suited the NAACP hierarchy. Never entirely at ease with the black mass actions during the New Deal and early war years, the NAACP became less a protest organization and more an agency of litigation and lobbying after World War II. No longer fearing that competition from more combative black groups would overshadow the NAACP, its branches in the South concentrated on voter registration, while those in the North endeavored to secure fair-employment and fair-housing ordinances. By 1953, twelve states and thirty cities had adopted fair-employment laws of varying effectiveness. Median black-family income rose from

$1,624 to $2,338 between 1947 and 1952. As a percentage of median white-family income, black earnings jumped from 41 percent in 1940 to 51 percent in 1949, and to 57 percent in 1952. That year, nearly 40 percent of blacks were engaged in professional, white-collar, skilled, and semi-skilled work, double the proportion of 1940. The life expectancy of blacks increased from 53.1 years in 1940 to 61.7 years in 1953, compared to 64.2 and 69.6 for whites, and the proportion of black families owning their homes went from 25 percent to 30 percent in the forties. Meanwhile, the proportion of blacks aged five to nineteen enrolled in school leaped from 60 percent in 1930 to 68.4 percent in 1940, to 74.8 percent in 1950. That figure still lagged behind the 79.3 percent of whites in school, but the gap had narrowed dramatically. And the number of blacks in college had soared from about 27,000 in 1930 to over 113,000 in 1950.

Such gains apparently justified the NAACP's approach and secured its hegemony in race relations. The national office and legal staff at midcentury marshaled all their resources for a courtroom assault on de jure school segregation. Many blacks believed integrated education to be the main route to racial equality. No other African-American protest group put forth an alternative strategy of social change. By 1954, all the hopes of blacks rested on the success of the NAACP litigation. It had become an article of faith that a Supreme Court decision ruling school segregation unconstitutional would cause the quick death of Jim Crow in America.

The first major crack in the edifice of school segregation had come in 1938, when the NAACP won a Supreme Court ruling which held that an out-of-state scholarship to a black Missourian wishing to study law at the University of Missouri denied that student the equal protection of the laws guaranteed by the Constitution. The Court declared that Missouri could not exclude blacks from its law school when it offered African-Americans only out-of-state tuition grants as an alternative. Hoping to make segregation so prohibitively expensive that the South would dismantle its biracial system because of the financial burden, the NAACP launched a series of suits seeking complete equality in facilities governed by the separate-but-equal rule. Then, emboldened by the strides made by blacks during the Second World War, the NAACP's Legal Defense and Education Fund, led by Thurgood Marshall and based on a foundation of scores of courageous African-American plaintiffs, shifted from skirmishes on the inequality of separate facilities to a direct attack on segregation itself. Marshall hoped his strategy would force the Court to overrule *Plessy*, the 1896 opinion that declared segregation no infringement on civil rights if the states provided blacks with separate accommodations equal to those given to whites. Marshall's work resulted first in three unanimous decisions on a single day in 1950 which demolished the separate-but-equal facade. The high court struck down Jim Crow on railway dining cars in the South; it ruled that if a state chose not to establish an equal and separate school for blacks, then it could not segregate blacks within the white school; and, lastly, the tribunal so emphasized the importance of "intangible factors" in determining the equality of separate schools that separate-but-equal no longer seemed possible. Although the Supreme Court held that it was not necessary to reexamine Plessy to grant relief to the three black plaintiffs, the 1950 decisions made the end of segregated schooling for students at all levels a near-certainty.

Working closely with the grassroots leadership of the local chapters, Marshall began to coordinate a series of lawsuits in 1950 charging segregated education with being discriminatory per se, even if the facilities were equal. In Clarendon County, South Carolina, the NAACP sued in the name of several black schoolchildren, and in Prince Edward County, Virginia, they represented black high-school students. In New Castle County, Delaware, and in the District of Columbia, Marshall filed suits on behalf of both elementary and high-school black students. And in Topeka, Kansas, the NAACP argued the case of Oliver Brown, who sought to enjoin enforcement of a state law that permitted cities to maintain segregated schools, which forced his eight-year-old daughter, Linda, to travel a mile by bus to reach a black school even though she lived only three blocks from an all-white elementary school. Risking their jobs and lives, the plaintiffs persisted, and on December 9, 1952, the Supreme Court heard oral argument on all five cases, combined and docketed under the name of the petitioner listed first—Oliver Brown. Unexpectedly, the NAACP was aided by the Truman Administration, which, in its last days, filed a brief as a friend of the Court arguing against the constitutionality of segregation.

The Supreme Court initially divided on the question of overturning *Plessy.* After several months of discussion, two justices changed their mind, creating a slim majority in favor of the NAACP's contention. Now the question became whether the justices in the minority could be likewise persuaded. To that end, the Court voted for a reargument. It asked the litigants to prepare answers to questions pertaining to the intentions of the framers of the Fourteenth Amendment, the power of the Court to abolish segregation in the schools, and, if the tribunal did have such a right and chose to exercise it, whether the Supreme Court could permit gradual desegregation or did it have to order an instant end to segregation. While the lawyers revised their briefs, Chief Justice Fred Vinson died suddenly in the summer of 1953. The new President, Dwight D. Eisenhower, appointed California Governor Earl Warren to fill the vacant post. Vinson had sought to avoid ruling on *Plessy,* and in all likelihood, two other justices would have voted with him, resulting in either a further postponement on the constitutionality of school segregation or a seriously split decision.

Following the reargument, which began on December 7 and lasted for three days, the nation waited for what commentators predicted would be a historic decision. But for half a year the Court remained silent. Behind closed doors, the bickering and bargaining continued. A clear majority of the justices wanted to void segregation in the schools and to reverse *Plessy.* Two justices held out, and Warren kept postponing the decision, hoping he could gain their concurrence. Above all, the Chief Justice wanted the Court's ruling to be unanimous. Anything less on a social issue so sensitive, on a political question so explosive, would destroy the chance for full compliance by Southern whites. So, patiently, Warren beseeched and compromised. Finally, early in May, the two dissenters gave the Chief Justice their assent.

By Monday, May 17, 1954, the Supreme Court ruling on school segregation had been so overdue that many forgot its imminence. The morning's newspapers gave no hint that a decision would be announced. Most journalists in Washington speculated on the consequences of a French loss of Dien Bien Phu in Vietnam, on the outcome of the Army-McCarthy hearings, and on the chances for more rain. Even those reporters seated in the ornate chamber of the Supreme Court did not anticipate that the segregation decision would be announced when the Court convened at noon.

After forty minutes of routine business, the Chief Justice leaned forward and began to read: "I have for announcement the judgment and opinion of the Court in No. 1—*Oliver Brown et al. v. Board of Education of Topeka.*" Warren traced the paths that led the cases to the Supreme Court and reviewed the history of the Fourteenth Amendment, finding it "inconclusive" in relation to school segregation because public education, particularly in the South, had barely developed in the 1860s. "Today," the Chief Justice continued, "education is perhaps the most important function of state and local governments." Since it is the key to opportunity and advancement in American life, public education "is a right which must be made available to all on equal terms." On this premise, he came to the nub of the matter: "Does segregation of children in public schools solely on the basis of race, even though the physical facilities and other 'tangible' factors may be equal, deprive the children of the minority group of equal educational opportunities?"

Warren paused. "We believe that it does." Buttressed by a footnote citing several contemporary studies on the psychological effects of segregation, the former governor contended that the separation of black children "from others of similar age and qualifications solely because of their race generates a feeling of inferiority as to their status in the community that may affect their hearts and minds in a way unlikely ever to be undone." He ended in a rising voice. "We conclude that in the field of public education the doctrine of 'separate but equal' has no place. Separate educational facilities are inherently unequal. Therefore, we hold that the plaintiffs and others similarly situated for whom the actions have been brought are, by reason of the segregation complained of, deprived of the equal protection of the laws guaranteed by the Fourteenth Amendment."

Blacks shouted hosannas as they heard the news. They hailed Marshall, the black lawyer who had used the white man's laws before an all-white Supreme Court to win a verdict voiding segregation. Their jubilant leaders vied in choosing superlatives to laud the decision. *Brown* would be the precedent for declaring unconstitutional any state-imposed or enforced segregation. African-Americans in pursuit of full citizenship rights now had not only morality on their side but the law as well. Surely, most rhapsodized, a new day in race relations had dawned. *Brown* promised a truly equal education for black children in integrated classrooms throughout the nation. More, it offered the real beginning of a multiracial society. Robert Williams of North Carolina, who would later urge African-Americans to get guns to assert their due, remembered: "My inner emotions must have been approximate to the Negro slaves' when they first heard about the Emancipation Proclamation. . . . I felt that at last the government was willing to assert itself on behalf of first-class citizenship, even for Negroes. I experienced a sense of loyalty that I had never felt before. I was sure that this was the beginning of a new era of American democracy." *Brown* heightened the aspirations and expectations of African-Americans as nothing before had. It *proved* that the Southern segregation system could be challenged and defeated. It *proved* that change was possible. Nearly a century after their professed freedom had been stalled, compromised, and stolen, blacks confidently anticipated being free and equal at last.

Little in the next year shook this faith. Few Dixie politicians rushed to echo Mississippi Senator James O. Eastland that the South "will not abide by nor obey this legislative decision by a political court." Most educators foresaw scant difficulty in putting the court ruling into effect. According to a *New York Times* survey of school officials, none thought "that the threats to abandon the public school system would be carried out. . . . No one expected any violence or any real crisis to develop." Several hundred school districts in the border states (Delaware, Kentucky, Maryland, Missouri, Oklahoma, and West Virginia) and in states with local option on segregation (Arizona, Kansas, New Mexico, and Wyoming) quickly and peacefully integrated their classrooms, as did the District of Columbia at President Eisenhower's direction.

Then, on May 31, 1955, the momentum stopped. Just fifty-four weeks after the Supreme Court had taken a giant stride toward the demise of Jim Crow, it stepped backward. Its implementation decision on the *Brown* ruling rejected the NAACP's plea to order instant and total school desegregation. The justices, instead, adopted the "go slow" approach advocated by the Justice Department and by the attorneys general of the Southern states. The Court assigned the responsibility for drawing up plans for desegregation to local school authorities and left it to local federal judges to determine the pace of desegregation, requiring only that a "prompt and reasonable start toward full compliance" be made and that desegregation proceed "with all deliberate speed." Acknowledging the potential for difficulties, the Supreme Court refused to set a deadline and authorized delays when necessary. For the first time, the Supreme Court had vindicated a constitutional right and then deferred its exercise.

However much the Warren Court foresaw the endless round of further litigation and obstruction this invited, circumstances dictated the decision for gradualism. It was the price of unanimity in *Brown v. Board of Education,* the compromise needed to keep two justices from dissenting. Warren deeply believed that a divided Court on so sensitive an issue "would have been catastrophic," that only a unanimous desegregation decision stood a chance of public support.

He accepted gradualism to allay the fears of those justices who worried that the Court's inability to enforce a momentous ruling would discredit the judicial process. The compromise also reflected the unpopularity of *Brown* in the South. Public-opinion polls showed more than 80 percent of white Southerners opposed to school desegregation, and the Supreme Court hoped to head off resistance to the law of the land by permitting the change to be piecemeal. To order immediate school desegregation, the Court reckoned, would force most Southern politicians to take up the cudgels of defiance to federal authority, an action only a tiny minority had taken to date. The Justices sought to contain the rebellion, since they could not count on the other branches of the federal government.

No help would come from the White House. President Dwight D. Eisenhower refused to endorse or support the *Brown* ruling. Covetous of the votes of white Southerners and wedded to a restrictive view of Presidential authority, Eisenhower stated that he would express neither "approbation nor disapproval" of *Brown v. Board of Education.* He lumped together those who demanded compliance with the Court decision and those who obstructed it, publicly denouncing "extremists on both sides." To one of his aides, Eisenhower emphasized: "I am convinced that the Supreme Court decision set back progress in the South at least fifteen years. . . . It's all very well to talk about school integration—if you remember you may also be talking about social *dis*integration. Feelings are deep on this. . . . And the fellow who tries to tell me that you can do these things by force is just plain nuts."

Eisenhower preferred change as a result of education, rather than coercion. But he would not educate. The President rejected pleas that he tour the South seeking compliance, or call a conference of Southern moderates, or appeal on television to the national for understanding. He simply did not favor school desegregation, much as he had never approved desegregation of the armed forces. Eisenhower regretted he had ever appointed Earl Warren to the Supreme Court, calling it "the biggest damfool mistake I ever made." And the titular head of the Democratic Party, Adlai Stevenson, barely differed on this issue from his GOP rival. Stevenson asked that the white South be "given time and patience," rejected the idea of using federal troops to enforce court-ordered desegregation, and opposed all proposals that would bar federal aid to schools maintaining segregation.

To be sure, no danger existed in the mid-fifties that Congress would legislate to speed desegregation. A conservative coalition of Midwestern Republicans and Southern Democrats controlled both the House of Representatives and the Senate, guarding against any infringement on states' rights. Not content merely to stonewall any move to support *Brown,* Southern congressmen mobilized in 1956 to fight against what Senator Richard Russell of Georgia termed "a flagrant abuse of judicial power" and what Virginia Senator Harry Byrd called "the most serious blow that has been struck against the rights of the states." On March 12, 1956, 101 members of Congress from the South signed a "Declaration of Constitutional Principles" asking their states to refuse to obey the desegregation order. Labeling *Brown* "unwarranted" and "contrary to the Constitution," the Southern manifesto [see chapter 148—*Eds.*] proclaimed that the Supreme Court possessed no power to demand an end to segregation, that only a state, and not the federal government, can decide whether a school should be segregated or not, and that the states would be in the right in opposing the Court's order.

The manifesto, along with Eisenhower's silence and the Supreme Court's paradoxical "deliberate speed" ruling, ushered in an era of massive resistance to the law of the land in the eleven states of the Old Confederacy. Defiance of the Court and the Constitution became the touchstone of Southern loyalty, the necessary proof of one's concern for the security of the white race. With the overwhelming support of the South's white press and pulpit, segregationist politicians resurrected

John C. Calhoun's notions of "interposition" and "nullification" to thwart federal authority.

White supremacists first resorted to stalling, doing nothing until confronted with the federal-court injunction. This forced black parents and NAACP attorneys to initiate individual desegregation suits in the more than two thousand Southern school districts. Usually, the black plaintiffs faced economic intimidation by the local white power structure; often they risked physical harm; always, they encountered repeated postponements due to crowded court dockets and motions for delay by school authorities. After years of harassment to the plaintiffs, mounting legal costs to the NAACP, lost jobs, mortgages foreclosed, loans denied, and incalculable psychological damage to blacks due to threats and fear, school authorities would finally come up with a plan for the most limited, token desegregation.

Then black schoolchildren had to face the horrors of racist resistance. In one school district after another, segregationists forced young African-Americans to walk a gauntlet of hate, fear, and ignorance, to pass by rock-throwing mobs and pickets shrieking "Nigger! Nigger! Nigger!" They pressured white teachers to ignore or persecute the black students, and encouraged white children to torment and threaten their new black classmates. "'If you come back to school, I'll cut your guts out!' could be heard in the halls," recalled a Tennessee high-school teacher. "Eggs smashed on their books, ink smeared on their clothes, in the lockers, knives flourished in their presence, nails tossed in their faces and spiked in their seats. Vulgar words constantly whispered in their ears." The harassment proved too much for some blacks. They re-enrolled their children in segregated schools; they moved to other towns and states. But more and more blacks endured the hatred and persisted in their struggle for dignity and equality.

To frustrate such black courage, segregationists pressed for new laws to obstruct integration. "As long as we can legislate, we can segregate," said one white supremacist, and the Southern states rushed pell-mell to enact more than 450 laws and resolutions to prevent or limit school desegregation. Some acts required schools faced with desegregation orders to cease operation; others revoked the license of any teacher who taught mixed classes; still more amended compulsory-attendance laws, so that no child could be required to enroll in an integrated school, and provided for state payments of private-academy tuition, so that districts could abolish their public-school system rather than desegregate.

Of all the legislative tactics of massive resistance, none proved more successful than the pupil-placement law. Theoretically, it guaranteed each child "freedom of choice" in the selection of a school. Local authorities could not consider race in assigning pupils to particular schools. But they could accept or reject transfer applications on such criteria as, in the Georgia law, "the psychological qualification of the pupil," "the psychological effect upon the pupil of attendance at a particular school," and "the morals, conduct, health and personal standards of the pupil." Invariably, school boards assigned black and white children to different schools. In 1958, moreover, the Supreme Court upheld the constitutionality of the pupil-placement laws, which were nondiscriminatory at face value but which actually maintained school systems as rigidly segregated as those which the justices had struck down four years earlier.

To frustrate blacks further, most of the Southern states also passed measures to hound and harass the NAACP, which had almost singlehandedly carried the campaign for school desegregation. Various laws required the NAACP to make public its membership lists, made membership a cause for dismissal of public-school teachers and state employees, charged the association with committing "barratry" (the persistent instigation of lawsuits), and made it a crime for organizations to cause trouble by attacking local segregation ordinances. By 1958 the NAACP had lost 246 branches in the South, and the South's percentage of the NAACP's total membership had dropped from nearly 50 percent to just about 25 percent. In time, the Supreme Court struck down all the anti-NAACP laws, but for several years the association was forced to divert energy, money, and talent away from the desegregation battle to the fight for its own survival.

Chapter 81

Brown v. Board of Education (1954)

Brown v. Board of Education overturned Plessy v. Ferguson (see chapter 39) and its doctrine of separate but equal. "The Supreme Court has finally reconciled the Constitution with the preamble of the Declaration of Independence," historian Arthur Schlesinger, Sr., told the New York Times. One year later that optimism was undercut when the court announced that its decision only needed to be applied with "all deliberate speed," rather than insisting on immediate implementation.

The following selection is reprinted from the Supreme Court's ruling in Brown v. Board of Education I (1954), footnotes deleted. It is followed by the Court's enforcement decree, known as Brown v. Board of Education II (1955).

Brown v. Board of Education I

Mr. Chief Justice Warren delivered the opinion of the Court.

These cases come to us from the States of Kansas, South Carolina, Virginia, and Delaware. They are premised on different facts and different local conditions, but a common legal question justifies their consideration together in this consolidated opinion.

In each of the cases, minors of the Negro race, through their legal representatives, seek the aid of the courts in obtaining admission to the public schools of their community on a non-segregated basis. In each instance, they have been denied admission to schools attended by white children under laws requiring or permitting segregation according to race. This segregation was alleged to deprive the plaintiffs of the equal protection of the laws under the Fourteenth Amendment. In each of the cases other than the Delaware case, a three-judge federal district court denied relief to the plaintiffs on the so-called "separate but equal" doctrine announced by this Court in *Plessy v. Ferguson*, 163 U.S. 537. . . . Under that doctrine, equality of treatment is accorded when the races are provided substantially equal facilities, even though these facilities be separate. In the Delaware case, the Supreme Court of Delaware adhered to that doctrine, but ordered that the plaintiffs be admitted to the white schools because of their superiority to the Negro schools.

The plaintiffs contend that segregated public schools are not "equal" and cannot be made "equal," and that hence they are deprived of the equal protection of the laws. Because of the obvious importance of the question presented, the Court took jurisdiction. Argument was heard in the 1952 Term, and reargument was heard this Term on certain questions propounded by the Court.

Reargument was largely devoted to the circumstances surrounding the adoption of the Fourteenth Amendment in 1868. It covered exhaustively consideration of the Amendment in Congress, ratification by the states, then existing practices in racial segregation, and the views of proponents and opponents of the Amendment. This discussion and our own investigation convince us that, although these sources cast some light, it is not enough to resolve the problem with which we are faced. At best, they are inconclusive. The most avid proponents of the post-War Amendments undoubtedly intended them to remove all legal distinctions among "all persons born or naturalized in the United States." Their opponents, just as certainly, were antagonistic to both the letter and the spirit of the Amendments and wished them to have the most limited effect. What others in Congress and the state legislatures had in mind cannot be determined with any degree of certainty.

An additional reason for the inconclusive nature of the Amendment's history, with respect to segregated schools, is the status of public education at that time. In the South, the movement toward free common schools, supported by general taxation, had not yet taken hold. Education of white children was largely in the hands of private groups. Education of Negroes was almost nonexistent, and practically all of the race were illiterate. In fact, any education of Negroes was forbidden by law in some states. Today, in contrast, many Negroes have achieved outstanding success in the arts and sciences as well as in the business and professional world. It is true that public school education at the time of the Amendment had advanced further in the North, but the effect of the Amendment on Northern States was generally ignored in the congressional debates. Even in the North, the conditions of public education did not approximate those existing today. The curriculum was usually rudimentary; ungraded schools were common in rural areas; the school term was but three months a year in many states; and compulsory school attendance was virtually unknown. As a consequence, it is not surprising that there should be so little in the history of the Fourteenth Amendment relating to its intended effect on public education.

In the first cases in this Court construing the Fourteenth Amendment, decided shortly after its adoption, the Court interpreted it as proscribing all state-imposed discriminations against the Negro race. The doctrine of "separate but equal" did not make its appearance in this Court until 1896 in the case of *Plessy v. Ferguson, supra,* involving not education but transportation. American courts have since labored with the doctrine for over half a century. In this Court, there have been six cases involving the "separate but equal" doctrine in the field of public education. In *Cumming v. County Board of Education,* 175 U.S. 528, and *Gong Lum v. Rice,* 275 U.S. 78, the validity of the doctrine itself was not challenged. In more recent cases, all on the graduate school level, inequality was found in that specific benefits enjoyed by white students were denied to Negro students of the same educational qualifications. *Missouri ex rel. Gaines v. Canada,* 305 U.S. 337; *Sipuel v. Oklahoma,* 332 U.S. 631; *Sweatt v. Painter,* 339 U.S. 629; *McLaurin v. Oklahoma State Regents,* 339 U.S. 637. In none of these cases was it necessary to re-examine the doctrine to grant relief to the Negro plaintiff. And in *Sweatt v. Painter supra*, the Court expressly reserved decision on the question whether *Plessy v. Ferguson* should be held inapplicable to public education.

In the instant cases, that question is directly presented. Here, unlike *Sweatt v. Painter*, there are findings below that the Negro and white schools involved have been equalized, or are being equalized, with respect to buildings, curricula, qualifications and salaries of teachers, and other "tangible" factors. Our decision, therefore, cannot turn on merely a comparison of these tangible factors in the Negro and white schools involved in each of the cases. We must look instead to the effect of segregation itself on public education.

In approaching this problem, we cannot turn the clock back to 1868 when the Amendment was adopted, or even to 1896 when *Plessy v. Ferguson* was written. We must consider public education in the light of its full development and its present place in American life throughout the Nation. Only in this way can it be determined if segregation in public schools deprives these plaintiffs of the equal protection of the laws.

Today, education is perhaps the most important function of state and local governments. Compulsory school attendance laws and the great expenditures for education both demonstrate our recognition of the importance of education to our democratic society. It is required in the performance of our most basic public responsibilities, even service in the armed forces. It is the very foundation of good citizenship. Today it is a principal instrument in awakening the child to cultural values, in preparing him for later professional training, and in helping him to adjust normally to his environment. In these days, it is doubtful that any child may reasonably be expected to succeed in life if he is denied the opportunity of an education. Such an opportunity, where the state has undertaken to provide it, is a right which must be made available to all on equal terms.

We come then to the question presented: Does segregation of children in public schools solely on the basis of race, even though the physical facilities and other "tangible" factors may be equal, deprive the children of the minority group of equal education opportunities? We believe that it does.

In *Sweatt v. Painter, supra*, in finding that a segregated law school for Negroes could not provide them equal educational opportunities, this Court relied in large part on "those qualities which are incapable of objective measurement but which make for greatness in a law school." In *McLaurin v. Oklahoma State Regents, supra*, the Court, in requiring that a Negro admitted to a white graduate school be treated like all other students, again resorted to intangible considerations: ". . . his ability to study, to engage in discussions and exchange views with other students, and, in general, to learn his profession." Such considerations apply with added force to children in grade and high schools. To separate them from others of similar age and qualifications solely because of their race generates a feeling of inferiority as to their status in the community that may affect their hearts and minds in a way unlikely ever to be undone. The effect of this separation on their educational opportunities was well stated by a finding in the Kansas case by a court which nevertheless felt compelled to rule against the Negro plaintiffs:

> Segregation of white and colored children in public schools has a detrimental effect upon the colored children. The impact is greater when it has the sanction of the law; for the policy of separating the races is usually interpreted as denoting the inferiority of the negro group. A sense of inferiority affects the motivation of the child to learn. Segregation with the sanction of law, therefore, has a tendency to [retard] the educational and mental development of negro children and to deprive them of some of the benefits they would receive in a racial[ly] integrated school system.

Whatever may have been the extent of psychological knowledge at the time of *Plessy v. Ferguson,* this finding is amply supported by modern authority. Any language in *Plessy v. Ferguson* contrary to this finding is rejected. We conclude that in the field of public education the doctrine of "separate but equal" has no place. Separate educational facilities are inherently unequal. Therefore, we hold that the plaintiffs and others similarly situated for whom the actions have been brought are, by reason of the segregation complained of, deprived of the equal protection of the laws guaranteed by the Fourteenth Amendment. This disposition makes unnecessary any discussion whether such segregation also violates the Due Process Clause of the Fourteenth Amendment.

Because these are class actions, because of the wide applicability of this decision, and because of the great variety of local conditions, the formulation of decrees in these cases presents problems of considerable complexity. On reargument, the consideration of appropriate relief was necessarily subordinated to the primary question—the constitutionality of segregation in public education. We have now announced that such segregation is a denial of the equal protection of the laws. In order that we may have the full assistance of the parties in formulating decrees, the cases will be restored to the docket, and the parties are requested to present further argument on Questions 4 and 5 previously propounded by the Court for the reargument of this Term. The Attorney General of the United States is again invited to participate. The Attorneys General of the states requiring or permitting segregation in public education will also be permitted to appear as amici curiae upon request to do so by September 15, 1954, and submission of briefs by October 1, 1954.

It is so ordered.

Brown v. Board of Education II: Enforcement Decree

Mr. Chief Justice Warren delivered the opinion of the Court.

These cases were decided on May 17, 1954. The opinions of that date declaring the fundamental principle that racial discrimination in public education is unconstitutional, are incorporated herein by reference. All provisions of federal, state, or local law requiring or permitting such discrimination must yield to this principle. There remains for consideration the manner in which relief is to be accorded.

Because these cases arose under different local conditions and their disposition will involve a variety of local problems we requested further argument on the question of relief. In view of the nationwide importance of the decision, we invited the Attorney General of the United States and the Attorneys General of all states requiring or permitting racial discrimination in public education to present their views on that question. The parties, the United States, and the States of Florida, North Carolina, Arkansas, Oklahoma, Maryland, and Texas filed briefs and participated in the oral argument.

These presentations were informative and helpful to the Court in its consideration of the complexities arising from the transition to a system of public education freed of racial discrimination. The presentations also demonstrated that substantial steps to eliminate racial discrimination in public schools have already been taken, not only in some of the communities in which these cases arose, but in some of the states appearing as amici curiae, and in other states as well. Substantial progress has been made in the District of Columbia and in the communities in Kansas and Delaware involved in this litigation. The defendants in the cases coming to us from South Carolina and Virginia are awaiting the decision of this Court concerning relief.

Full implementation of these constitutional principles may require solution of varied local school problems. School authorities have the primary responsibility for elucidating, assessing, and solving these problems; courts will have to consider whether the action of school authorities constitutes good faith implementation of the governing constitutional principles. Because of their proximity to local conditions and the possible need for further bearings, the courts which originally heard these cases can best perform this judicial appraisal. Accordingly, we believe it appropriate to remand the cases to those courts.

In fashioning and effectuating the decrees, the courts will be guided by equitable principles. Traditionally, equity has been characterized by a practical flexibility in shaping its remedies and by a facility for adjusting and reconciling public and private needs. These cases call for the exercise of these traditional attributes of equity power. At stake is the personal interest of the plaintiffs in admission to public schools as soon as practicable on a nondiscriminatory basis. To effectuate this interest may call for elimination of a variety of obstacles in making the transition to school systems operated in accordance with the constitutional principles set forth in our May 17, 1954, decision. Courts of equity may properly take into account the public interest in the elimination of such obstacles in a systematic and effective manner. But it should go without saying that the vitality of these constitutional principles cannot be allowed to yield simply because of disagreement with them.

While giving weight to these public and private considerations, the courts will require that the defendants make a prompt and reasonable start toward full compliance with our May 17, 1954, ruling. Once such a start has been made, the courts may find that additional time is necessary to carry out the ruling in an effective manner. The burden rests upon the defendants to establish that such time is necessary in the public interest and is consistent with good faith compliance at the earliest practicable date. To that end, the courts may consider problems related to administration, arising from the physical condition of the school plant, the school transportation system, personnel, revision of school districts and attendance areas into compact units to achieve a system of determining admission to the public schools on a nonracial basis, and revision of local laws and regulations which may be necessary in solving the foregoing problems. They will also consider the adequacy of any plans the defendants may propose to meet these problems and to effectuate a transition to a racially nondiscriminatory school system. During this period of transition, the courts will retain jurisdiction of these cases.

The judgments below, except that in the Delaware case, are accordingly reversed and the cases are remanded to the District Courts to take such proceedings and enter such orders and decrees consistent with this opinion as are necessary and proper to admit to public schools on a racially nondiscriminatory basis with all deliberate speed the parties to these cases. The judgment in the Delaware case ordering the immediate admission of the plaintiffs to schools previously attended only by white children—is affirmed on the basis of the principles stated in our May 17, 1954, opinion, but the case is remanded to the Supreme Court of Delaware for such further proceedings as that Court may deem necessary in light of this opinion.

It is so ordered.

Chapter 82

Mississippi Murders

Myrlie Evers with William Peters

Myrlie Evers's husband, Medgar (1925–1963), the Mississippi field secretary for the NAACP, was murdered outside their home on 12 June 1963—just hours after President John F. Kennedy's television address on civil rights (see chapter 103). According to an FBI informant, Byron De La Beckwith (a member of the White Citizens' Council) bragged at a 1965 Ku Klux Klan meeting that "killing that nigger gave me no more inner discomfort than our wives endure when they give birth to our children." Thirty years later, in 1994, after two previous trials had failed to reach a decision, Beckwith was finally convicted of murder and sentenced to life in prison.

Myrlie Evers-Williams is on the Board of Directors and Executive Committee of the NAACP. She served as chair from 1995 to 1998. She is the author (with Melinda Blau) of Watch Me Fly: What I Learned on the Way to Becoming the Woman I Was Meant to Be *(1999).*

The following selection is excerpted from For Us, the Living *(New York: Doubleday, 1967). Copyright © 1967 by Mrs. Medgar Evers and William Peters. Reprinted by permission of Curtis Brown, Ltd.*

The sixty-year-old farmer had been threatened with death if he did not slow down on his political activities, but, according to his family, he had ignored the threats.

Though the murder had taken place at ten o'clock on a Saturday morning, a time when the court house square was normally jammed with people, officials claimed no witnesses could be found. Then a white farmer, Noah Smith, was charged with the murder in a warrant filed by a courageous district attorney. Eventually two more white men were arrested, but when the grand jury met in September, it failed to return an indictment.

Even before that predictable end, almost as though the state of Mississippi had officially declared an open season on Negroes, murderers struck again. This time the victim was a fourteen-year-old Negro boy from Chicago, Emmett Till, visiting his uncle in the Mississippi Delta. The purported reason for the killing, widely disseminated by the press, was that Till had asked for a date with a married white woman seven years his senior.

There were, of course, embellishments on this theme, though no one ever charged the youth with more than a lewd suggestion or a "wolf whistle." But

because of the overtones of sex, by which Mississippi often justifies its use of violence against male Negroes, it could have been just another Mississippi lynching.
It wasn't. This one somehow struck a spark of indignation that ignited protests
around the world. Kidnapped forcibly in the middle of the night, pistol-whipped,
stripped naked, shot through the head with a .45-caliber Colt automatic, barb-
wired to a seventy-four-pound cotton gin fan, and dumped into twenty feet of
water in the Tallahatchie River, young Emmett Till became in death what he could
never have been in life: a rallying cry and a cause.

Two white men were arrested for the sadistic murder: J. W. Milam, thirty-six,
and his half-brother, Roy Bryant, twenty-four. Both were identified as the men
who took young Till at gun-point from his uncle's home. Both admitted having
taken him but only for the purpose of frightening him. Indicted and tried for murder in Sumner, Mississippi, they were acquitted by an all-white jury that deliber-
ated one hour and seven minutes. Two months later a grand jury in Greenwood
refused even to indict them for the abduction both had publicly admitted. Two
months after that, in case anyone was still in doubt, reporter William Bradford
Huie, in an article in *Look,* quoted both men on the exact details of the murder
they now calmly described. Acquitted once, they could not, of course, be tried
again.

These were sensational climaxes to a sensational murder, but, even before they
were reached, the Till case attracted the kind of world and national attention
Medgar had brooded about those many months before when he speculated privately about a Mississippi Mau Mau. For weeks before the murder trial, newsmen
from all over the country probed the psyche of the Delta, interviewing whites and
Negroes, turning up some of the conditions of the benighted area. Angry and frustrated over this particularly vicious killing, Medgar made it his mission to see that
word of it was spread as widely and accurately as possible. Publicizing the crime
and the subsequent defeat of justice became a major NAACP effort.

Those were weeks of frenzied activity, weeks of special danger, for Medgar
made many trips to the Delta, investigating, questioning, searching out witnesses
before they could be frightened into silence. There were wild night drives to Memphis, where witnesses were put on planes for safer places until their presence
would be needed at the trial. And, more than once, there were chases along the
long, straight, unlighted highways that led from the Delta back to Jackson.

Medgar was by this time well known throughout the state, and his car was
often sighted by police and sheriff's men minutes after he entered a Delta county.
Frequently he was followed throughout his trips around the Delta. He had already
begun to make it a practice to return to Jackson each night if possible, as much
for the safety of the people he would otherwise have stayed with as for himself.
Several times, when he started back after dark, he had to jam the accelerator to
the floorboard to "shake the car's tail," as he put it, in the faces of anonymous
pursuers.

Medgar never pretended he wasn't frightened at such experiences, though he
often concealed the details from me. Usually I found out later, when the subject
came up at the office with someone else or when a friend who had been with him

let the secret drop. There was no hiding the extra precautions he sometimes took. When Emmet Till's body was found, Medgar and Amzie Moore, an NAACP leader from Cleveland, Mississippi, set off from our house one morning with Ruby Hurley, down from Birmingham, to investigate. All of them were dressed in overalls and beat-up shoes, with Mrs. Hurley wearing a red bandanna over her head. To complete the disguise, Amzie had borrowed a car with license plates from a Delta county. Watching them leave, knowing the tension and hate that gripped the Delta, I lived through the day in a daze of fear until their safe return that night.

While Medgar worked in the Delta, I was swamped at the office with telephone calls from the press, from friends, from unknown Negroes who wanted to know what was happening. I had to buy and read six or seven newspapers a day, clipping every word about the Till case for our own files and for the national office in New York. If Medgar's name had been mentioned in one of the papers, I could anticipate a spate of obscene and abusive telephone calls.

Looking back, I know that from that time on I never lost the fear that Medgar himself would be killed. It was like a physical presence inside me, now subdued, now alive and aching, a parasite of terror that woke to remind me of its existence whenever things were particularly bad. Medgar would leave the house for one of his trips to the Delta, and I could feel my stomach contract in cold fear that I would never see him again. When he was home, when he spent a whole day in the office, it was like a reprieve, for I somehow had the absurd idea that nothing could happen to him if we were together. It was about this time that I began trying to live each day for itself, to count as special blessings those days when I knew he was in no special danger. It is a philosophy more easily preached than practiced, but I made a thousand conscious attempts to live it in the years that followed, knowing that the only alternative was some kind of breakdown.

I never completely understood what it was that made the murder of Emmett Till so different from the ones that had preceded it. In part, I suppose it was his youth. Medgar was convinced that the existence of our office in Jackson and the enormous efforts of the NAACP to get out the news made a tremendous difference. Whatever the answer, it was the murder of this fourteen-year-old out-of-state visitor that touched off the world-wide clamor and cast the glare of a world spotlight on Mississippi's racism. Ironically, the deaths of George Lee and Lamar Smith, both directly connected with the struggle for civil rights, had caused nothing like the public attention attracted by the Till case.

And perhaps that was the explanation. George Lee and Lamar Smith had been murdered for doing what everyone knew Negroes were murdered for doing. Neither murder had the shock effect of the brutal slaying of a fourteen-year-old boy who had certainly done nothing more than act fresh. The Till case, in a way, was the story in microcosm of every Negro in Mississippi. For it was the proof that even youth was no defense against the ultimate terror, that lynching was still the final means by which white supremacy would be upheld, that whites could still murder Negroes with impunity, and that the upper- and middle-class white people of the state would uphold such killings through their police and newspapers and courts of law. It was the proof that Mississippi had no intention of changing its ways, that no Negro's life was really safe, and that the federal government was either powerless, as it claimed, or simply unwilling to step in to erase this blot on the nation's reputation for decency and justice. It was the proof, if proof were needed, that there would be no real change in Mississippi until the rest of the country decided that change there must be and then forced it.

It was toward that end that the NAACP published in November 1955 an eight-page booklet that infuriated Mississippi's politicians. Titled, *M is for Mississippi and Murder,* every word of it was true. It began with a section called "Backdrop for Murder," which recounted recent news stories originating in Mississippi.

One, from an AP dispatch dated September 9, 1954, read in part: "White men who want to keep segregation in force are banding into 'citizens councils' throughout Mississippi, several legislators said today.

"The peaceful approach was emphasized by several leaders in Washington County. . . . But some other legislators from the Delta and other 'black counties' where Negroes outnumber whites predicted bloodshed. . . .

"One said 'a few killings' would be the best thing for the state just before the people vote on a proposed constitutional amendment empowering the Legislature to abolish public schools.

"The 'few killings' would make certain that the people would approve the amendment and 'would save a lot of bloodshed later on,' he added."

A reporter for the Memphis *Press-Scimitar* wrote from a Citizens Council rally on August 12, 1955, quoting Senator Eastland: "On May 17 the Constitution of the United States was destroyed. . . . You are not required to obey any court which passes out such a ruling. In fact, you are obligated to defy it."

In a speech at Greenville, John C. Satterfield, president of the Mississippi Bar Association and a member of the board of governors of the American Bar Association, listed three methods of continuing segregation. Though he said it was "abhorrent," one of them was "the gun and torch."

Frederick Sullens, editor of the Jackson *Daily News,* was quoted in a speech before the American Society of Newspaper Editors in Washington, D.C.: "Mississippi will not obey the decision. If an effort is made to send Negroes to school with white children, there will be bloodshed. The stains of that bloodshed will be on the Supreme Court steps."

In a front-page editorial in Mr. Sullens' paper, Dr. A. H. McCoy, state president of the NAACP, was described as "insolent, arrogant and hot-headed." The editorial continued, "The fanatical mouthings of McCoy have reached the limit. If not suppressed by his own race, he will become the white man's problem."

An editorial in the Yazoo *Herald,* at the height of tension over the Till case read: "Through the furor over the Emmett Till case we hope someone gets this over to the nine ninnies who comprise the present U.S. Supreme Court. Some of the young Negro's blood is on their hands also."

Finally the booklet cited a New York *Herald Tribune* story by Homer Bigart, quoting Robert P. Patterson, executive secretary of the Mississippi Citizens Councils: "Sir, this is not the United States. This is Sunflower County, Mississippi."

Summarizing the new stories, the NAACP booklet said: "In this climate of opinion which derides the courts and the rule of law, which harps on violence, sometimes nakedly and sometimes through the device of repeated disavowal, three persons were murdered in Mississippi between May 7 and August 28, 1955." It then recounted details of the murders of George Lee, Lamar Smith, and Emmett Till.

Medgar had just received copies of the booklet from New York when an urgent call came from Belzoni with word of yet another shooting. His heart sank as he heard the name: Gus Courts, the Negro grocer who had been president of the NAACP branch when George Lee was murdered in Belzoni less than seven months earlier. Within an hour, Medgar had alerted the press, the national office, Ruby Hurley in Birmingham, and the state officers in Mississippi. Before daybreak he was off to Mound Bayou, where Courts lay critically wounded in the hospital.

Gus Courts' story was simple and straightforward, and though he was in serious condition, he was conscious and able to tell it. Medgar made sure it was related in detail to the press. "I'd known for a long time it was coming, and I'd tried to get prepared in my mind for it," Courts told one reporter. "But that's a hard thing to do when you know they're going to try to slip up and steal your life in the night and not out in the bright."

Courts was sixty-five and in pain, but he knew the importance of telling his story. "They shot me because I wanted to vote," he said simply. "They said I was agitating to put Negroes in the white schools, but that ain't so. I was just advocating for the vote. I felt I ought to have my rights."

Courts told the long story of his attempts to vote, of the complaint he and George Lee had filed with the Justice Department two years before when Sheriff Ike Shelton refused to take their poll taxes. He told how he had finally become one of not quite a hundred Negroes in Humphreys County who were registered to vote. "About twenty of us went to vote in the July primary in 1954," he said, "but instead of giving us ballots they gave us questionnaires. We were supposed to answer questions like 'Do you believe in integration?'"

None of them got to vote, Courts said. No Negro had voted in Humphreys County since Reconstruction. And after the White Citizens Council put the screws on them, most of the registered Negroes took their names off the registration list. "Finally it got down to eight or nine of us," Courts told the reporter. "Since that was so few I guess some white folks figured it wouldn't hurt to shoot that eight or nine. But I made up my mind to stick on the list."

Courts said that when he had finally registered, "one of the council members brought the list around. He said, 'If you don't take your name off you're going to be put out of your store.' Three days later the landlord said, 'I've got another use for the building,' so I had to move."

Labor Days

Chapter 83

Labor, Radicals, and the Civil Rights Movement

Robert Korstad and Nelson Lichtenstein

Robert Korstad, professor of public policy studies and history at Duke University, is director of "Behind the Veil," an oral history project documenting African American life in the Jim Crow South. He is the author of Dreaming of a Time: The School of Public Health, The University of North Carolina at Chapel Hill *(1990), and co-author of* Like a Family: The Making of a Southern Cotton Mill World *(1987). Nelson Lichtenstein, professor of history at the Catholic University of America, is the author of* Labor's War at Home: The CIO in World War II *(1982) and* Walter Reuther: The Most Dangerous Man in Detroit *(1995), and editor of* Industrial Democracy in America *(1996).*

The following selection is reprinted from "Labor, Radicals, and the Early Civil Rights Movement," Journal of American History, *December 1988, 786–811, footnotes deleted. Reprinted by permission of the authors and the* Journal of American History.

Most historians would agree that the modern civil rights movement did not begin with the Supreme Court's decision in *Brown v. Board of Education.* Yet all too often the movement's history has been written as if events before the mid-1950s constituted a kind of prehistory, important only insofar as they laid the legal and political foundation for the spectacular advances that came later. Those were the "forgotten years of the Negro Revolution," wrote one historian; they were the "seed time of racial and legal metamorphosis," according to another. But such a periodization profoundly underestimates the tempo and misjudges the social dynamic of the freedom struggle.

The civil rights era began, dramatically and decisively, in the early 1940s when the social structure of black America took on an increasingly urban, proletarian character. A predominantly southern rural and small town population was soon transformed into one of the most urban of all major ethnic groups. More than two million blacks migrated to northern and western industrial areas during the 1940s, while another million moved from farm to city within the South. Northern black voters doubled their numbers between 1940 and 1948, and in the eleven states of the Old South black registration more than quadrupled, reaching over one million by 1952. Likewise, membership in the National Association for the Advancement of Colored People (NAACP) soared, growing from 50,000 in 355 branches in 1940 to almost 450,000 in 1,073 branches six years later.

The half million black workers who joined unions affiliated with the Congress of Industrial Organizations (CIO) were in the vanguard of efforts to transform race relations. The NAACP and the Urban League had become more friendly toward labor in the Depression era, but their legal and social work orientation had not prepared them to act effectively in the workplaces and working-class neighborhoods where black Americans fought their most decisive struggles of the late 1930s and 1940s. By the early forties it was commonplace for sympathetic observers to assert the centrality of mass unionization in the civil rights struggle. A Rosenwald Fund study concluded, not without misgivings, that "the characteristic movements among Negroes are now for the first time becoming proletarian"; while a *Crisis* reporter found the CIO a "lamp of democracy" throughout the old Confederate states. "The South has not known such a force since the historic Union Leagues in the great days of the Reconstruction era."

This movement gained much of its dynamic character from the relationship that arose between unionized blacks and the federal government and proved somewhat similar to the creative tension that linked the church-based civil rights movement and the state almost two decades later. In the 1950s the *Brown* decision legitimated much of the subsequent social struggle, but it remained essentially a dead letter until given political force by a growing protest movement. In like manner, the rise of industrial unions and the evolution of late New Deal labor legislation offered working-class blacks an economic and political standard by which they could legitimate their demands and stimulate a popular struggle. The "one man, one vote" policy implemented in thousands of National Labor Relations Board (NLRB) elections, the industrial "citizenship" that union contracts offered once-marginal elements of the working class, and the patriotic egalitarianism of the government's wartime propaganda—all generated a rights consciousness that gave working-class black militancy a moral justification in some ways as powerful as that evoked by the Baptist spirituality of Martin Luther King, Jr., a generation later. During the war the Fair Employment Practices Committee (FEPC) held little direct authority, but like the Civil Rights Commission of the late 1950s, it served to expose racist conditions and spur on black activism wherever it undertook its well-publicized investigations. And just as a disruptive and independent civil rights movement in the 1960s could pressure the federal government to enforce its own laws and move against local elites, so too did the mobilization of the black working class in the 1940s make civil rights an issue that could not be ignored by union officers, white executives, or government officials.

This essay explores two examples of the workplace-oriented civil rights militancy that arose in the 1940s—one in the South and one in the North. It analyzes the unionization of predominantly black tobacco workers in Winston-Salem, North Carolina, and the ferment in the United Auto Workers in Detroit, Michigan, that made that city a center of black working-class activism in the North.

Similar movements took root among newly organized workers in the cotton compress mills of Memphis, the tobacco factories of Richmond and Charleston, the steel mills of Pittsburgh and Birmingham, the stockyards and farm equipment factories of Chicago and Louisville, and the shipyards of Baltimore and Oakland.

Winston-Salem in the War

Winston-Salem had been a center of tobacco processing since the 1880s, and the R. J. Reynolds Tobacco Company dominated the life of the city's eighty thousand citizens. By the 1940s whites held most of the higher paying machine-tending jobs, but blacks formed the majority of the work force, concentrated in the preparation departments where they cleaned, stemmed, and conditioned the tobacco. The jobs were physically demanding, the air was hot and dusty, and in departments with machinery, the noise was deafening. Most black workers made only a few cents above minimum wage, and benefits were few. Black women workers experienced frequent verbal and occasional sexual abuse. Reynolds maintained a determined opposition to trade unionism, and two unsuccessful American Federation of Labor (AFL) efforts to organize segregated locals had soured most black workers on trade unionism.

But in 1943 a CIO organizing effort succeeded. Led by the United Cannery, Agricultural, Packing and Allied Workers of America (UCAPAWA), a new union drive championed black dignity and self-organization, employing several young black organizers who had gotten their start in the interracial Southern Tenant Farmers Union. Their discreet two-year organizing campaign made a dramatic breakthrough when black women in one of the stemmeries stopped work on June 17. A severe labor shortage, chronic wage grievances, and a recent speedup gave the women both the resources and the incentive to transform a departmental sitdown into a festive, plant-wide strike. The UCAPAWA quickly signed up about eight thousand black workers, organized a committee to negotiate with the company, and asked the NLRB to hold an election.

The effort to win union recognition at Reynolds sparked a spirited debate about who constituted the legitimate leadership of the black community in Winston-Salem. Midway through the campaign, six local black business and professional men—a college professor, an undertaker, a dentist, a store owner, and two ministers—dubbed "colored leaders" by the *Winston-Salem Journal,* wrote a long letter to the editor urging workers to reject the "followers of John L. Lewis and William Green" and to remain loyal to Reynolds. In the absence of any formal leadership, elected or otherwise, representatives of Winston-Salem's small black middle class had served as spokesmen, brokering with the white elite for small concessions in a tightly segregated society. The fight for collective bargaining, they argued, had to remain secondary to the more important goal of racial betterment, which could only be achieved by "good will, friendly understanding, and mutual respect and co-operation between the races." Partly because of their own vulnerability to economic pressure, such traditional black leaders judged unions, like other institutions, by their ability to deliver jobs and maintain a precarious racial equilibrium.

The union campaign at Reynolds transformed the expectations tobacco workers held of the old community leadership. Reynolds workers responded to calls for moderation from "college-trained people" with indignation. "Our leaders," complained Mabel Jessup, "always look clean and refreshed at the end of the hottest day, because they work in very pleasant environments. . . . All I ask of our leaders is that they obtain a job in one of the factories as a laborer and work two weeks. Then write what they think." W. L. Griffin felt betrayed. "I have attended church regularly for the past thirty years," he wrote, "and unity and co-operation have been taught and preached from the pulpits of the various Negro churches. Now that the laboring class of people are about to unite and co-operate on a wholesale scale for the purpose of collective bargaining, these same leaders seem to disagree with that which they have taught their people." Others rejected the influence of people who "have always told us what the white people want, but somehow or other are particularly silent on what we want." "We feel we are the leaders instead of you," asserted a group of union members.

Reynolds, the only major tobacco manufacturer in the country not under a union contract, followed tried and true methods to break the union. Management used lower-level supervisors to intimidate unionists and supported a "no union" movement among white workers, whose organizers were given freedom to roam the company's workshops and warehouses. That group, the R. J. Reynolds Employees Association, sought a place on the NLRB ballot in order to delay the increasingly certain CIO victory. Meanwhile, the white business community organized an Emergency Citizens Committee to help defeat the CIO. In a well-publicized resolution, the committee blamed the recent strikes on "self-seeking representatives of the CIO" and warned that continued subversion of existing race relations would "likely lead to riots and bloodshed."

In earlier times, this combination of anti-union forces would probably have derailed the organizing effort. But during World War II, black workers had allies who helped shift the balance of power. The NLRB closely supervised each stage of the election process and denied the company's request to divide the work force into two bargaining units, which would have weakened the position of black workers. When local judges sought to delay the election, government attorneys removed the case to federal court. In December 1943 an NLRB election gave the CIO a resounding victory. But continued federal assistance, from the United States Conciliation Service and the National War Labor Board, was still needed to secure Reynolds workers a union contract in 1944.

That first agreement resembled hundreds of other wartime labor-management contracts, but in the context of Winston-Salem's traditional system of race relations it had radical implications, because it generated a new set of shop floor rights embodied in the seniority, grievance, and wage adjustment procedures. The contract did not attack factory segregation—for the most part white workers continued to control the better-paying jobs—but it did call forth a new corps of black leaders to defend the rights Reynolds workers had recently won. The one hundred or so elected shop stewards were the "most important people in the plant," remembered union activist Velma Hopkins. They were the "natural leaders," people who had "taken up money for flowers if someone died or would talk to the foreman [even] before the union." Now the union structure reinforced the capabilities of such workers: "We had training classes for the shop stewards: What to do, how to do it. We went over the contract thoroughly." The shop stewards transformed the traditional paternalism of Reynolds management into an explicit system of benefits and responsibilities. They made the collective bargaining agreement a bill of rights.

The growing self-confidence of black women, who constituted roughly half of the total work force, proved particularly subversive of existing social relations. To the white men who ran the Reynolds plants, nothing could have been more disturbing than the demand that they negotiate on the basis of equality with people whom they regarded as deeply inferior—by virtue of their sex as well as their class and race. When union leaders like Theodosia Simpson, Velma Hopkins, and Moranda Smith sat down at the bargaining table with company executives, social stereotypes naturally came under assault, but the challenge proved equally dramatic on the shop floor. For example Ruby Jones, the daughter of a railway fireman, became one of the most outspoken shop stewards. Perplexed by her newfound aggressiveness, a foreman demanded, "Ruby, what do you want?" "I want your respect," she replied, "that's all I ask."

By the summer of 1944, Local 22 of the reorganized and renamed Food, Tobacco, Agricultural and Allied Workers (FTA) had become the center of an alternative social world that linked black workers together regardless of job, neighborhood, or church affiliation. The union hall, only a few blocks from the Reynolds Building, housed a constant round of meetings, plays, and musical entertainments, as well as classes in labor history, black history, and current events. Local 22 sponsored softball teams, checker tournaments, sewing circles, and swimming clubs. Its vigorous educational program and well-stocked library introduced many black workers (and a few whites) to a larger radical culture few had glimpsed before. "You know, at that little library the [the city of Winston-Salem] had for us, you couldn't find any books on Negro history," remembered Viola Brown. "They didn't have books by [Herbert] Aptheker, [W. E. B.] Du Bois, or Frederick Douglass. But we had them at *our* library."

The Communist party was the key political grouping in FTA and in Local 22. FTA president Donald Henderson had long been associated with the party, and many organizers who passed through Winston-Salem shared his political sympathies. By 1947 party organizers had recruited about 150 Winston-Salem blacks, almost all tobacco workers. Most of these workers saw the party as both a militant civil rights organization, which in the 1930s had defended such black victims of white southern racism as the Scottsboro boys and Angelo Herndon, and as a cosmopolitan group, introducing members to the larger world of politics and ideas. The white North Carolina Communist leader Junius Scales recalled that the "top leaders [of Local 22] . . . just soaked up all the educational efforts that were directed at them. The Party's program had an explanation of events locally, nationally, and worldwide which substantiated everything they had felt instinc-tively. . . . It really meant business on racism." The party was an integrated institu-tion in which the social conventions of the segregated South were self-consciously violated, but it also accommodated itself to the culture of the black community. In Winston-Salem, therefore, the party met regularly in a black church and started the meetings with a hymn and a prayer.

The Communist party's relative success in Winston-Salem was replicated in other black industrial districts. In the South a clear majority of the party's new re-cruits were black, and in northern states like Illinois and Michigan the proportion ranged from 25 to 40 percent. The party's relative success among American blacks was not based on its programmatic consistency: during the late 1940s the NAACP and other critics pointed out that the wartime party had denounced civil rights struggles when they challenged the Roosevelt administration or its conduct of the war effort, but that the party grew more militant once Soviet-American relations cooled. However, the party never abandoned its assault on Jim Crow and unlike the NAACP, which directed much of its energy toward the courts and Congress, the Communists or their front groups more often organized around social or po-litical issues subject to locally initiated protests, petitions, and pickets. Moreover, the party adopted what today would be called an affirmative action policy that recognized the special disabilities under which black workers functioned, in the party as well as in the larger community. Although there were elements of to-kenism and manipulation in the implementation of that policy, the party's unique effort to develop black leaders gave the Communists a special standing among po-litically active blacks.

Tobacco industry trade unionism revitalized black political activism in Win-ston-Salem. Until the coming of the CIO, NAACP attacks on racial discrimination seemed radical, and few blacks risked associating with the organization. A 1942 membership drive did increase branch size from 11 to 100, but most new members came from the traditional black middle class: mainly teachers and municipal bus drivers. The Winston-Salem NAACP became a mass organization only after Local 22 conducted its own campaign for the city branch. As tobacco workers poured in, the local NAACP reached a membership of 1,991 by 1946, making it the largest unit in North Carolina.

Unionists also attacked the policies that had disenfranchised Winston-Salem blacks for more than two generations. As part of the CIO Political Action Com-mittee's voter registration and mobilization drive, Local 22 inaugurated citizen-ship classes, political rallies, and citywide mass meetings. Union activists chal-lenged the power of registrars to judge the qualifications of black applicants and insisted that black veterans vote without further tests. The activists encouraged the city's blacks to participate in electoral politics. "Politics is food, clothes, and housing," declared the committee that registered some seven hundred new black voters in the months before the 1944 elections. After a visit to Winston-Salem in 1944, a *Pittsburgh Courier* correspondent wrote, "I was aware of a growing soli-darity and intelligent mass action that will mean the dawn of a New Day in the South. One cannot visit Winston-Salem and mingle with the thousands of workers without sensing a revolution in thought and action. If there is a 'New' Negro, he is to be found in the ranks of the labor movement."

Organization and political power gave the black community greater leverage at city hall and at the county courthouse. NAACP and union officials regularly took part in municipal government debate on social services for the black community, minority representation on the police and fire departments, and low-cost public housing. In 1944 and 1946 newly enfranchised blacks helped reelect Congressman John Folger, a New Deal supporter, against strong conservative opposition. In 1947, after black registration had increased some tenfold in the previous three years, a minister, Kenneth Williams, won a seat on the Board of Aldermen, becoming the first black city official in the twentieth-century South to be elected against a white opponent.

Civil Rights Militancy in Detroit

The social dynamic that had begun to revolutionize Winston-Salem played itself out on a far larger scale in Detroit, making that city a center of civil rights militancy in the war years. Newly organized black auto workers pushed forward the frontier of racial equality on the shop floor, in the political arena, and within the powerful, million-member United Auto Workers. Despite increasing racism among white workers, union goals and civil rights aims largely paralleled each other in the 1940s.

In 1940 about 4 percent of all auto workers were black; the proportion more than doubled during the war and rose to about one-fifth of the auto work force in 1960. Although proportionally less numerous than in Winston-Salem, blacks were nevertheless central to the labor process in many of Detroit's key manufacturing facilities. Excluded from assembly operations and skilled work, blacks dominated the difficult and unhealthy, but absolutely essential work in foundry, paint shop, and wet sanding operations.

Ford Motor Company's great River Rouge complex contained the largest concentration of black workers in the country. More than half of its nine thousand black workers labored in the foundry, but Henry Ford's peculiar brand of interwar paternalism had enabled blacks to secure some jobs in virtually every Ford department. The company therefore proved a mecca for black workers. Those who worked there proudly announced, "I work for Henry Ford," and wore their plant badges on the lapels of their Sunday coats. Ford reinforced his hold on the loyalty of Detroit's black working class by establishing what amounted to a separate personnel department that recruited new workers on the recommendation of an influential black minister. That policy, which continued until the early 1940s, strengthened the pro-company, anti-union attitude of most churchmen and reinforced the hostility shown the early CIO by leaders of the Detroit Urban League and the local NAACP branch.

UAW leaders recognized that unless black workers were recruited to the union they might undermine efforts to consolidate UAW power in key manufacturing facilities. The danger became clear during the racially divisive 1939 Chrysler Corporation strike when management tried to start a back-to-work movement spearheaded by black workers, and it proved even more apparent during the 1940–41 Ford organizing drive, when black workers hesitated to join the union. During the April 1941 Ford strike, several hundred scabbed inside the plant. In response, UAW leaders made a concerted effort to win over elements of the local black bourgeoisie who were not directly dependent on Ford's patronage network. The ensuing conflict within the Detroit NAACP chapter was only resolved in favor of the UAW after Ford's unionization. Thereafter black workers, whose participation in union activities had lagged well behind those of most whites, became among the most steadfast UAW members. The UAW itself provided an alternative focus of power, both cooperating with and challenging the black church and the NAACP as the most effective and legitimate spokesman for the black community.

Many talented, politically sophisticated black officers and staffers emerged in the UAW during the mid-1940s, although never in numbers approaching their proportion of union membership. Blacks were a majority in almost every foundry and in most paint shops, so locals that represented manufacturing facilities usually adopted the United Mine Workers formula of including a black on the election slate as one of the top four officers. Locals with a large black membership also elected blacks to the annual UAW convention, where the one hundred and fifty to two hundred black delegates in attendance represented about 7 or 8 percent of the total voting roll. And almost a score of blacks also secured appointment as highly visible UAW international representatives during the early 1940s.

Ford's River Rouge complex overshadowed all other Detroit area production facilities as a center of black political power. Although most blacks had probably voted against the UAW in the NLRB elections of May 1941, the unionization process, particularly radical in its reorganization of shop floor social relations at the Rouge, helped transform the consciousness of these industrial workers. With several hundred shop committeemen in the vanguard, workers intimidated many foremen, challenged top management, and broke the company spy system. "We noticed a very definite change in attitude of the working man," recalled one supervisor. "It was terrible for a while . . . the bosses were just people to look down on after the union came in." For the next decade, Rouge Local 600 proved a center of civil rights militancy and a training ground for black leaders. The Rouge foundry sent more than a score of black delegates to every UAW convention, provided at least half of all black staffers hired by the UAW, and customarily supplied Local 600 with one of its top officers. Foundryman Shelton Tappes, a 1936 migrant from Alabama, helped negotiate a then-unique anti-discrimination clause into the first UAW-Ford contract and went on to serve as recording secretary of the sixty thousand-member local in the mid-1940s.

The Rouge was also a center of Communist party strength in Detroit. The radical tradition there had remained unbroken since World War I when the Industrial Workers of the World and other radical union groups had briefly flourished. Skilled workers from Northern Europe had provided most members during the difficult interwar years, but after 1941 the party recruited heavily among blacks, and at its peak in the late 1940s it enrolled 450 workers, almost half from the foundry. The Rouge was one of the few workplaces in the country where Communists, black or white, could proclaim their political allegiance without immediate persecution. As late as 1948 Nelson Davis, the black Communist elected vice-president of the nine thousand-man Rouge foundry unit within Local 600, sold several hundred subscriptions to the *Daily Worker* every year. But even here, Communist influence among black workers rested on the party's identification with the civil rights issues; indeed many blacks saw the party's foundry department "club" as little more than a militant race organization.

With almost one hundred thousand black workers organized in the Detroit area, black union activists played a central role in the civil rights struggle. They demanded the hiring and promotion of black workers in metropolitan war plants, poured into the Detroit NAACP chapter, and mobilized thousands to defend black occupancy of the Sojourner Truth Homes, a federally funded project that became a violent center of conflict between white neighborhood groups and the housing-starved black community. In those efforts black activists encountered enormous resistance not only from plant management and the Detroit political elite but also from white workers, midlevel union leaders under direct pressure from white constituents, and conservatives in the black community. But as in the civil rights movement of the early 1960s, black militants held the political initiative, so that powerful white elites—the top office holders in the UAW, company personnel officers, and the government officials who staffed the War Labor Board and War Manpower Commission—had to yield before this new wave of civil militancy.

As in Winston-Salem, mass unionization transformed the character of the black community's traditional race advancement organizations. Under pressure from Local 600 leaders like Tappes, Horace Sheffield (his rival for leadership of the foundry), and the pro-union minister Charles Hill, the NAACP and the Urban League became more militant and activist. Black community leadership still came largely from traditional strata: lawyers, ministers, doctors, and teachers, but the union upsurge reshaped the protest agenda and opened the door to new forms of mass struggle. The NAACP itself underwent a remarkable transformation. In the successful effort to keep the Sojourner Truth housing project open to blacks, NAACP officials had for the first time worked closely with the UAW militants who organized the demonstrations and protests that forestalled city or federal capitulation to the white neighborhood groups that fought black occupancy. That mobilization in turn energized the local NAACP, as almost twenty thousand new members joined, making the Detroit branch by far the largest in the nation. Black workers poured in from the region's recently unionized foundries, tire plants, and converted auto/aircraft facilities, and from city government, streetcar lines, restaurants, and retail stores.

By 1943 the Detroit NAACP was one of the most working-class chapters in the country. Its new labor committee, the largest and most active group in the branch, served as a forum for black workers to air their grievances and as a pressure group, urging companies and the government to advance black job rights. With UAW support, the labor committee sponsored an April 1943 march and rally that brought ten thousand to Cadillac Square to demand that managers open war industry jobs to thousands of still-unemployed black women in the region. Although the NAACP old guard repulsed a direct electoral challenge from UAW members and their sympathizers, the chapter added two unionists to its executive board and backed protest campaigns largely shaped by UAW militants: mass rallies, picket lines, and big lobbying delegations to city hall, Lansing, and Washington. By the end of the war the ministerial leadership of the black community was in eclipse. Horace White, a Congregational minister admitted: "The CIO has usurped moral leadership in the [Negro] community."

On the shop floor, black workers sought to break out of traditional job ghettos in the foundry and janitorial service, precipitating a series of explosive "hate" strikes as white workers walked off the job to stop the integration of black workers into formerly all-white departments. The strikes were almost always failures, however, not only because federal officials and UAW leaders quickly mobilized to cut them off but also because they failed to intimidate most black workers. During the war there were probably as many demonstrations and protest strikes led by black workers as racially inspired white walkouts. For example, at Packard, scene of one of the most infamous hate strikes of the war, black workers eventually triumphed over white recalcitrance. A racialist personnel manager, a divided union leadership, and a heavily southern work force heightened racial tensions and precipitated several white stoppages that culminated in June 1943 when more than twenty-five thousand whites quit work to prevent the transfer of three blacks into an all-white department. But black workers were also active. Under the leadership of foundryman Christopher Alston, a Young Communist League member, they had earlier shut down the foundry to demand that union leaders take more forceful action against recalcitrant whites; and in the months after the big wildcat hate strike, those same blacks conducted strikes and protests that kept the attention of federal officials and local union leaders focused on their problems. Their militancy paid off; by the end of 1943 about five hundred blacks had moved out of the Packard foundry and into heretofore all-white production jobs.

Although newly assertive second-generation Poles and Hungarians had come to see their jobs and neighborhoods as under attack from the equally militant black community, top UAW officials championed civil rights during the war. In the aftermath of the great Detroit race riot of 1943, in which the police and roving bands of whites killed twenty-five blacks, the UAW stood out as the only predominantly white institution to defend the black community and denounce police brutality. During the hate strikes, UAW leaders often sought the protection of a War Labor Board back-to-work order in order to deflect white rank-and-file anger onto the government and away from themselves. But officials like UAW Vice-president Walter Reuther made it clear that "the UAW-CIO would tell any worker that refused to work with a colored worker that he could leave the plant because he did not belong there."

Intraunion competition for black political support encouraged white UAW officials to put civil rights issues high on their agenda. During the 1940s black staffers and local union activists participated in an informal caucus that agitated for more black representatives in the union hierarchy and more effort to upgrade black workers in the auto shops. Initially chaired by Shelton Tappes of Local 600, the group was reorganized and strengthened by George Crockett, an FEPC lawyer the UAW hired to head its own Fair Employment Practices Committee in 1944. The overwhelming majority of UAW blacks, however, backed the caucus led by Secretary-Treasurer George Addes and Vice-president Richard Frankensteen, in which Communists played an influential role. The Addes-Frankensteen caucus endorsed the symbolically crucial demand for a Negro seat on the UAW executive board and generally supported black-white slates in local union elections. The other major UAW faction was led by Walter Reuther and a coterie of ex-socialists and Catholics, whose own internal union support came from workers in the General Motors plants (Flint and Western Michigan), in the South, and in the aircraft fabricating facilities of the East and Midwest. Support for Reuther's faction was particularly strong among the more assimilated Catholics and Appalachian whites in northern industry. Reuther denounced proposals for a black executive board seat as "reverse Jim Crow," but his group also advocated civil rights, not so much because they expected to win black political support, but because the rapid growth of a quasi-autonomous black movement had made militancy on civil rights the sine qua non of serious political leadership in the UAW.

A Moment of Opportunity

By the mid-1940s, civil rights issues had reached a level of national political salience that they would not regain for another fifteen years. Once the domain of Afro-American protest groups, leftist clergymen, and Communist-led unions and front organizations, civil rights advocacy was becoming a defining characteristic of urban liberalism. Thus ten states established fair employment practice commissions between 1945 and 1950, and four major cities—Chicago, Milwaukee, Minneapolis and Philadelphia—enacted tough laws against job bias. Backed by the CIO, the Americans for Democratic Action spearheaded a successful effort to strengthen the Democratic party's civil rights plank at the 1948 convention.

In the South the labor movement seemed on the verge of a major breakthrough. *Fortune* magazine predicted that the CIO's "Operation Dixie" would soon organize key southern industries like textiles. Black workers proved exceptionally responsive to such union campaigns, especially in industries like lumber, furniture, and tobacco, where they were sometimes a majority of the work force. Between 1944 and 1946 the CIO's political action apparatus helped elect liberal congressmen and senators in a few southern states, while organizations that promoted interracial cooperation, such as the Southern Conference for Human Welfare and Highlander Folk School, experienced their most rapid growth and greatest effectiveness in 1946 and 1947.

The opportune moment soon passed. Thereafter, a decade-long decline in working-class black activism destroyed the organizational coherence and ideological clan of the labor-based civil rights movement. That defeat has been largely obscured by the brilliant legal victories won by civil rights lawyers in the 1940s and 1950s, and by the reemergence of a new mass movement in the next decade. But in Winston-Salem, Detroit, and other industrial regions, the time had passed when unionized black labor was in the vanguard of the freedom struggle. Three elements contributed to the decline. First, the employer offensive of the late 1940s put all labor on the defensive. Conservatives used the Communist issue to attack New Deal and Fair Deal reforms, a strategy that isolated Communist-oriented black leaders and helped destroy what was left of the Popular Front. The employers' campaign proved particularly effective against many recently organized CIO locals and disproportionate numbers of black members. Meanwhile, mechanization and decentralization of the most labor intensive and heavily black production facilities sapped the self-confidence of the black working class and contributed to high rates of urban unemployment in the years after the Korean War.

Second, the most characteristic institutions of American liberalism, including the unions, race advancement organizations, and liberal advocacy organizations, adopted a legal-administrative, if not a bureaucratic, approach to winning citizenship rights for blacks. The major legislative goal of the union-backed Leadership Conference on Civil Rights in the 1950s was revision of Senate Rule 22, to limit the use of the filibuster that had long blocked passage of a national FEPC and other civil rights legislation. The UAW and other big unions cooperated with the NAACP in the effort, but the work was slow and frustrating and the struggle far removed from the shop floor or the drugstore lunch counter.

Finally, the routinization of the postwar industrial relations system precluded efforts by black workers to mobilize a constituency independent of the leadership. Focusing on incremental collective bargaining gains and committed to social change only if it was well controlled, the big unions became less responsive to the particular interests of their black members. By 1960 blacks had formed oppositional movements in several old CIO unions, but they now encountered resistance to their demands not only from much of the white rank and file but also from union leaders who presided over institutions that had accommodated themselves to much of the industrial status quo.

Postwar Reaction: Winston-Salem

Like most labor intensive southern employers, R. J. Reynolds never reached an accommodation with union labor, although it signed contracts with Local 22 in 1945 and 1946. Minimum wage laws and collective bargaining agreements had greatly increased costs of production, especially in the stemmeries, and the black women employed there were the heart and soul of the union. Soon after the war, the company began a mechanization campaign that eliminated several predominantly black departments. When the factories closed for Christmas in 1945 new stemming machines installed in one plant displaced over seven hundred black women. The union proposed a "share the work plan," but the company was determined to cut its work force and change its racial composition by recruiting white workers from surrounding counties. The black proportion of the manufacturing labor force in Winston-Salem dropped from 44 to 36 percent between 1940 and 1960.

The technological offensive undermined union strength, but by itself Reynolds could not destroy Local 22. When contract negotiations began in 1947, the company rejected union demands for a wage increase patterned after those won in steel, auto, and rubber earlier in the spring. Somewhat reluctantly, Local 22 called a strike on May 1. Black workers and virtually all of the Negro community solidly backed the union, which held out for thirty-eight days until a compromise settlement was reached. But, in a pattern replicated throughout industrial America in those years, Communist influence within the union became the key issue around which management and its allies mounted their attack. The *Winston-Salem Journal* soon denounced Local 22 as "captured . . . lock, stock and barrel" by the Communist party, warning readers that the strike would lead to "open rioting." This exposé brought Local 22 officers under the scrutiny of the House Committee on Un-American Activities (HUAC), which held a highly publicized hearing on the Winston-Salem situation in the summer of 1947.

Communist party members contributed to the volatility of the situation. In the late 1940s, Local 22 found itself politically vulnerable when foreign policy resolutions passed by the shop stewards' council followed Communist party pronouncements. The party's insistence on the promotion of blacks into public leadership positions sometimes put workers with little formal education into union leadership jobs they could not handle. Moreover, the party's obsession with "white chauvinism" backfired. After the 1947 strike, Local 22 made a concerted effort to recruit white workers. Some young veterans joined the local, although the union allowed most to pay their dues secretly. The party objected, remembered North Carolina leader Junius Scales, "'If they got any guts,' they would say, 'let them stand up and fight,' not realizing, as many black workers and union leaders realized, that for a white worker to just *belong* to a predominantly black union at that time was an act of great courage."

With its work force increasingly polarized along racial and political lines, Reynolds renewed its offensive in the spring of 1948. Black workers remained remarkably loyal to the union leadership, but the anticommunist campaign had turned most white employees against the union and eroded support among blacks not directly involved in the conflict. The company refused to negotiate with Local 22 on the grounds that the union had not complied with the new Taft-Hartley Act. The law required union officers to sign an affidavit swearing they were not members of the Communist party before a union could be certified as a bargaining agent by the NLRB. Initially, all the CIO internationals had refused to sign the affidavits, but by 1948 only Communist-oriented unions such as FTA still held out. When Reynolds proved intransigent, there was little the union could do. FTA had no standing with the NLRB, and it was too weak to win another strike.

At the same time, Local 22 began to feel repercussions from the conflict within the CIO over the status of unions, like the FTA, that had rejected the Marshall Plan and endorsed Henry Wallace's Progressive party presidential campaign in

1948. A rival CIO union, the United Transport Service Employees (UTSE), sent organizers into Winston-Salem to persuade black workers to abandon Local 22. In a March 1950 NLRB election, which the FTA requested after complying with the Taft-Hartley Act, UTSE joined Local 22 on the ballot. The FTA local retained solid support among its black constituency, who faithfully paid dues to their stewards even after the contract had expired and in the face of condemnation of their union—from the company, the CIO, and HUAC. Even the black community leader Alderman Williams asked workers to vote against the union and "send the Communists away for good." Yet Local 22 captured a plurality of all the votes cast, and in a runoff two weeks later it won outright. But when the NLRB accepted the ballots of lower-level white supervisors, the scales again tipped against the local.

Local 22 disappeared from Winston-Salem's political and economic life, and a far more accommodative black community leadership filled the void left by the union's defeat. Beginning in the mid-1940s, a coalition of middle-class blacks and white business moderates had sought to counter the growing union influence within the black community. They requested a study of local race relations by the National Urban League's Community Relations Project (CRP). Largely financed by Hanes Hosiery president James G. Hanes, the CRP study appeared in late 1947 and called for improved health, education and recreational facilities, but it made no mention of workplace issues. The Urban League foresaw a cautious, "step by step approach" and proposed that an advisory committee drawn from the black middle class discuss community issues with their white counterparts and help city officials and white philanthropists channel welfare services to the black community. The *Winston-Salem Journal* called the CRP's recommendations a "blueprint for better community relations" but one that would not alter "the framework of race relations."

The Urban League's program helped make Winston-Salem a model of racial moderation. Blacks continued to register and vote in relatively high numbers and to select a single black alderman. The city high school was integrated without incident in 1957, while Winston-Salem desegregated its libraries, golf course, coliseum, and the police and fire departments. But the dynamic and democratic quality of the black struggle in Winston-Salem would never be recaptured. NAACP membership declined to less than five hundred in the early 1950s, and the decision making once again moved behind closed doors. When a grievance arose from the black community, a group of ministers met quietly with Hanes; a few phone calls by the white industrialist led to desegregation of the privately owned bus company in 1958.

A similar story unfolded in the plants of the R. J. Reynolds Tobacco Company. After the destruction of Local 22, the company blacklisted several leading union activists, yet Reynolds continued to abide by many of the wage standards, benefit provisions, and seniority policies negotiated during the union era. The company reorganized its personnel department; rationalized procedures for hiring, firing, and evaluating employees; and upgraded its supervisory force by weeding out old-timers and replacing them with college-educated foremen. To forestall union activity, Reynolds kept its wages slightly ahead of the rates paid by its unionized competitors.

In February 1960, when sit-ins began at segregated Winston-Salem lunch counters, the voices of black protest were again heard in the city's streets. But the generation of blacks who had sustained Local 22 played little role in the new mobilization. College and high school students predominated on the picket lines and in the new protest organizations that confronted white paternalism and challenged the black community's ministerial leadership. NAACP membership rose once again; more radical blacks organized a chapter of the Congress of Racial Equality (CORE). Public segregation soon collapsed.

The subsequent trajectory of the freedom struggle in Winston-Salem was typical of that in many black communities. Heightened racial tensions set the stage for a 1967 riot and a burst of radicalism, followed by the demobilization of the protest movement and years of trench warfare in the city council. The political career of Larry Little, the son of Reynolds workers who had been members of Local 22, highlighted the contrasts between the two generations of black activists. Little moved from leadership of the North Carolina Black Panther party in 1969 to city alderman in 1977, but despite the radicalism of his rhetoric, crucial issues of economic security and workplace democracy were not restored to the political agenda in Winston-Salem. Because black activists of his generation confronted the city's white elite without the organized backing of a lively, mass institution like Local 22, their challenge proved more episodic and less effective than that of the previous generation.

The Limits of Liberalism in Postwar Detroit

A similar demobilization took place in Detroit after the war. There the union, as well as the companies, helped undermine the independent working-class base black activists had built in the six years since UAW organization of the Ford Motor Company. Racial issues were not of primary importance in the factional conflict of 1946 and 1947 that brought Walter Reuther to the presidency of the UAW. The victory of his caucus was based both on rank-and-file endorsement of Reuther's bold social vision, especially as exemplified in the General Motors strike of 1945–46, and in the Reuther group's anticommunism, which struck an increasingly responsive chord after passage of the Taft-Hartley Act. Nevertheless, the Reuther victory greatly diminished black influence and independence within the UAW and the liberal-labor community in which the union played such an important role. Reuther was as racially egalitarian as his opponents, but the political logic of his bitterly contested victory—he won less than 10 percent of black delegate votes in 1946—meant that Reuther owed no organizational debt to the growing proportion of union members who were black.

When the Reuther group consolidated their control of the union in 1947, there was a large turnover in the Negro UAW staff. Blacks with ties to the opposition, such as John Conyers, Sr., and William Hardin, two of the first black staffers, and

the articulate lawyer, George Crockett, the de facto leader of the UAW's black caucus, were ousted from their posts. The young dynamo, Coleman Young, lost his
job with the Wayne County CIO council. Tappes was hired as a UAW international representative in the early 1950s, but only after he had broken with the
Communists and lost his base of support in the Rouge plant.

During the 1950s and 1960s, the Reuther group understood that civil rights
was a litmus test of labor liberalism. Reuther sat on the board of directors of the
NAACP, and the UAW probably contributed more funds to that organization than
all other trade unions combined. The UAW also proved a ready source of emergency funds for the Montgomery Improvement Association, the Southern Christian Leadership Conference (SCLC), and Students for a Democratic Society's early
community organizing activities. Reuther was outraged that the AFL-CIO did not
endorse the 1963 March on Washington; his union had provided much of the
early funding, and he would be the most prominent white to speak at the interracial gathering.

Reuther also maintained a high profile on civil rights issues within the UAW. As
president, he appointed himself co-director of the union's Fair Employment Practices Department and used the FEPD post to denounce racial discrimination and
identify himself with postwar civil rights issues. Reuther pushed for a fair employment practices bill in Michigan and led the successful UAW effort to integrate the
American Bowling Congress. During the crucial months after he had won the
UAW presidency, but before his caucus had consolidated control of the union,
such activism helped defuse black opposition; when Reuther was reelected in 1947
he won about half of all black delegate votes.

Despite this public, and well-publicized appearance, the emergence of a more
stable postwar brand of unionism undermined civil rights activism in the UAW. As
in many unions, the Reuther regime sought to eliminate or to coopt potentially
dissident centers of political power. Local 600 was such a center of opposition,
where black unionists still within the Communist orbit continued to play an influential, if somewhat muted, role well into the 1950s. Immediately after the 1952
HUAC hearings in Detroit, which publicized the continuing presence of Communists in Local 600, the UAW International Executive Board put the huge local
under its direct administration. Six months later, tens of thousands of Rouge
workers reelected their old officers, but the influence and independence of the
giant local nevertheless waned in the next few years. Leaders of the UAW defused
much of the local's oppositional character by appointing many of its key leaders,
including Tappes and Sheffield, to the national union staff.

Equally important, Ford's postwar automation and decentralization slashed the
Rouge work force in half, eliminating the predominantly black production
foundry. The same phenomenon was taking place in many of Detroit's other high
unionized production facilities, so that by the late 1960s a ring of relatively small
and mainly white manufacturing facilities surrounded Detroit's million plus black
population. Meanwhile, high levels of black unemployment became a permanent
feature of the urban landscape after the 1957–1958 recession. Not unexpectedly,
the size and social influence of the unionized black working class ceased to grow,

though this stagnation was masked by the militance of inner-city minority youth late in the 1960s.

The UAW's Fair Employment Practices Department also defused civil rights activism in the union. After 1946 the department was led by William Oliver, a black foundryman from Ford's Highland Park factory. Unlike the politicized blacks from the Rouge, Oliver had no large reservoir of political support in the UAW, nor did he attempt to build one. During Oliver's tenure, the FEPD had a dual role; it represented the UAW to the national civil rights community, the NAACP, the Urban League, and the more liberal federal agencies and congressmen; and it processed discrimination complaints as they percolated up from black workers in the locals. Rather than serving as an organizing center for UAW blacks, the FEPD bureaucratized the union's civil rights activities. "We are a fire station" admitted Tappes, who served in the department during the 1950s and 1960s, "and when the bell rings we run to put out the fire."

A UAW retreat from civil rights militancy also became evident in politics. From 1937 to 1949, the UAW sought to reshape Detroit's formally "nonpartisan" electoral politics along interracial class lines. Thus in 1945 and 1949 Richard Frankensteen and George Edwards, both former UAW leaders, fought mayoral campaigns that helped move integrated housing and police brutality to the center of local political debate. Both were defeated by conservative incumbents, but their labor-oriented campaigns nevertheless provided a focus around which civil rights forces could mobilize. However, after the CIO's "bitterest political defeat in the motor city," in 1949, the UAW ceased to expend its political capital in what many of its leaders now considered fruitless campaigns to take over city hall. The UAW continued to back the liberal governor G. Mennen Williams, but in the city proper the union made peace with conservatives like Albert Cobo and Louis Miriani, who had built much of their political base on segregationist homeowner movements.

Neither the Communist party nor the NAACP was able to fill the void opened up by the UAW default. In the early 1950s many erstwhile leaders of the union's black caucus joined the Detroit Negro Labor Council (NLC), a Communist front organization. But the NLC faced relentless pressure from the NAACP, HUAC, and the UAW, which denounced the council as a "Communist-dominated, dual unionist organization which has as its sole objective the disruption and wrecking of the American labor movement." Both the UAW and the NAACP made exclusion of Communists from civil rights coalition work a high priority in the early 1950s, and the NCL dissolved in 1956. The NAACP, of course, maintained a cordial relationship with the UAW, but it also declined in postwar Detroit. After reaching a wartime peak of twenty-four thousand in 1944, membership dropped to six thousand in 1950, when there was much discussion of the need to "rehabilitate" what had once been the organization's largest unit. In the early 1950s national NAACP membership also fell to less than half its wartime level.

When civil rights reemerged as a major issue in union and city politics in the late 1950s, the Reuther leadership often found its interests counterposed to the forces mobilized by the freedom movement of that era. By 1960 Detroit's population was about 30 percent black, and upwards of a quarter of all auto workers were Mexican or black. At the Rouge plant between 50 and 60 percent of production workers were nonwhite.

Reuther's mode of civil rights advocacy seemed increasingly inadequate as the feats and conflicts of the early Cold War era receded. Two issues seemed particularly egregious. First, black participation in UAW skilled trades apprenticeship programs stood at minuscule levels, 1 percent or less. Second, no black sat on the UAW executive board, although blacks had been demanding that symbolically important post in UAW convention debates since the early 1940s. Failure to make progress on those problems genuinely embarrassed white UAW leaders, but Reuther and his colleagues were trapped by the regime over which they presided. Reuther hesitated to take on the militant and well-organized skilled trades, then in the midst of a long-simmering craft rebellion against the UAW's industrial unionism. Nor could a black be easily placed on the UAW executive board. In no UAW region did blacks command a majority of all workers; moreover Reuther loyalists held all existing posts. Creating a new executive board slot seemed the only alternative, but that would dilute the power of existing board members and flatly repudiate Reuther's longstanding opposition to a specifically black seat on the executive board.

In this context, and in the immediate aftermath of the Montgomery bus boycott, an independent black protest movement reemerged in Detroit politics with the founding of the Trade Union Leadership Council (TULC) in 1957. Initially TULC was little more than a caucus of UAW black staffers, but under the leadership of Horace Sheffield the organization challenged Reutherite hegemony. Despite the UAW's good reputation, Sheffield explained in 1960, a black-led organization was needed because "the liberal white trade unionists had long been 'mothballed' . . . by the extensive growth of 'business unionism.'" TULC opened a new chapter in Detroit politics in the 1961 mayoralty race. The incumbent mayor, Miriani, had the support of virtually all elements of the Detroit power structure, including the UAW, but he was hated by most blacks and not a few whites because of his defense of Detroit's increasingly brutal and racist police department. Sheffield used the mayoral campaign of Jerome Cavanagh, a young liberal lawyer, to establish his own network among Detroit's black trade union officials and make the TULC a mass organization of over seven thousand members in 1962 and 1963. Thereafter, a number of black activists whose political roots went back to the anti-Reuther forces of the 1940s won elective office, sometimes over bitter UAW protest. They included John Conyers, Jr., who took Detroit's second black congressional seat in 1964, George Crockett, who won election as Recorders Court judge in 1966 and later went on to Congress, and Coleman Young, who became mayor in 1973.

TULC proved less successful in remolding UAW politics. The organization's mushroom growth, combined with the growth of the civil rights movement, forced the UAW to put a black on its executive board in 1962. But for this position the Reuther leadership chose none of the blacks prominently associated with TULC militancy, but instead the relatively little known Nelson Jack Edwards, a black staff representative. Although black appointments to the UAW staff increased markedly in the 1960s, TULC failed to generate a mass movement among rank-and-file black workers. TULC represented the generation of black activists politicized in the 1940s, but many had spent the intervening years on union staffs or in local office so they no longer enjoyed an organic link with the younger black militants who were flooding into Detroit's auto shops.

When the Dodge Revolutionary Union Movement (DRUM) and other black insurgencies [see chapter 128—*Eds.*] swept through the auto industry in the late 1960s, the new generation had come to see UAW liberalism as indistinguishable from corporate conservatism. They were mistaken, but in 1968, that year of great expectations and smashed hopes, such distinctions seemed beside the point. Many TULC veterans found DRUM's wholesale condemnation of the UAW irresponsible, while the young militants thought their elders merely a reformist wing of Reuther's union leadership. A reported exchange conveys DRUM members' impatience with TULC veterans' loyalty to the union. Shelton Tappes is said to have told a group of black Chrysler workers who had been fired for staging an outlaw strike and were picketing Solidarity House, the UAW's official home: "If the TULC had done what it was organized for there wouldn't be any such development as DRUM." And one of the young pickets reportedly answered, "And if Reuther and the other bureaucrats had done what the *union* was organized for, there wouldn't have been any need for TULC."

Conclusion

E. P. Thompson once asserted that most social movements have a life cycle of about six years. And unless they make a decisive political impact in that time, that "window of opportunity," they will have little effect on the larger political structures they hope to transform. For the black freedom struggle the mid-1940s offered such a time of opportunity, when a high-wage, high-employment economy, rapid unionization, and a pervasive federal presence gave the black working class remarkable self-confidence, which established the framework for the growth of an autonomous labor-oriented civil rights movements. The narrowing of public discourse in the early Cold War era contributed largely to the defeat and diffusion of that movement. The rise of anticommunism shattered the Popular Front coalition on civil rights, while the retreat and containment of the union movement deprived black activists of the political and social space necessary to carry on an independent struggle.

The disintegration of the black movement in the late 1940s ensured that when the civil rights struggle of the 1960s emerged it would have a different social character and an alternative political agenda, which eventually proved inadequate to the immense social problems that lay before it. Like the movement of the 1940s, the protests of the 1960s mobilized a black community that was overwhelmingly working-class. However, the key institutions of the new movement were not the trade unions, but the black church and independent protest organizations. Its community orientations and stirring championship of democratic values gave the modern civil rights movement a transcendent moral power that enabled a handful of organizers from groups like the Student Nonviolent Coordinating Committee, SCLC, and CORE to mobilize tens of thousands of Americans in a series of dramatic and crucial struggles. Yet even as this Second Reconstruction abolished legal segregation and discrimination, many movement activists, including Martin Luther King, Jr., recognized the limits of their accomplishments. After 1965 they sought to raise issues of economic equality and working-class empowerment to the moral high ground earlier occupied by the assault against de jure segregation. In retrospect, we can see how greatly they were handicapped by their inability to seize the opportunities a very different sort of civil rights movement found and lost twenty years before.

Chapter 84

Migration and Electoral Politics

Frances Fox Piven and Richard A. Cloward

The first wave of the Great Migration of southern blacks to northern cities began during World War I (see chapters 61 and 62). A second wave, from the 1940s to the 1960s, was triggered by new technologies that displaced agricultural workers. This population shift led to accompanying changes in electoral politics.

Frances Fox Piven is professor of political science at the City University of New York. Richard Cloward is professor of social work at Columbia University.

The following selection is excerpted from Poor People's Movements *by Richard A. Cloward and Frances Fox Piven. Copyright © 1977 by Frances Fox Piven and Richard A. Cloward. Reprinted by permission of Pantheon Books, a division of Random House, Inc.*

For other selections by Piven and Cloward, see chapters 41 and 134.

By 1940 blacks began leaving the South in great numbers. Year by year the impact of this demographic revolution on the northern electoral system was immense, for blacks were concentrating in the northern cities of the most populous, industrialized states. In other words they were concentrated in the electoral strongholds of the Democratic Party. And as their voting numbers swelled, leaders in the northern wing of the party began to acknowledge that concessions to blacks would have to be made.

The race issue emerged in the election of 1948. It probably would not have emerged so early as a presidential campaign issue were it not for the formation of the Progressive Party led by Henry Wallace [vice president during Roosevelt's third term, 1941–1944]: Wallace directed his appeals to northern liberals and to blacks. Clark Clifford, [President Harry] Truman's chief campaign strategist, was worried about the president's strength among blacks, and not just because of Wallace. The Republicans were also making symbolic appeals to the black voter. Thus Clifford warned Truman that

> the Republicans were doing everything they could to win back this electorate. He predicted that the Republicans would "offer an FEPC, an anti–poll tax bill, and an anti-lynching bill" in the next Congressional session. To counter, the president had to push for whatever action he felt necessary "to protect the rights of minority groups." Although the South might not like this action, it was the "lesser of two evils."[1]

At the same time, Clifford advised Truman that "as always, the South can be considered safely Democratic. And in formulating national policy, it can be safely ignored."[2]

Accordingly Truman gave the appearance of championing civil rights. "Although he went much further than any previous President . . . he failed to match rhetoric with concrete efforts . . ."[3] Thus Truman called for a broad range of civil rights measures in an address to Congress on January 7, and on February 2, he delivered a special civil rights message to Congress which outlined a ten-point program, including outlawing the poll tax, establishing a permanent FEPC [Fair Employment Practices Committee], and making lynching a federal crime. But having promised to issue executive orders abolishing segregation in the armed forces and discrimination in federal employment—actions which were within his immediate power—he did neither (not, at least, until after the unanticipated and turbulent events of the nominating convention in the summer).

The nominating convention scuttled Truman's essentially rhetorical civil rights strategy. Liberal leaders intent on securing a strong civil rights plank despite Truman's opposition were joined by influential northern machine leaders who believed Truman would lose the election. They "were less concerned with Southern diehards bolting than with solidifying the Negro vote behind their local and state candidates. Henry Wallace was making a powerful appeal to this constituency in major cities. Any spectacular demonstration of the Democrats as resolute defenders of Negro interests that would head off the Wallace threat was to be welcomed."[4] Consequently a strong civil rights plank was pushed through on the floor of the convention, leading Alabama and Mississippi to walk out. The Dixiecrat forces, drawing upon dissident elements throughout the South, convened two days later in Birmingham to form a States' Rights Party with Senator J. Strom Thurmond of South Carolina as its presidential nominee. With these events Truman was pushed all the more to the left on the race question, and he immediately issued the executive orders he had promised months earlier. "Thus a border-state politician intent on pursuing an ambiguous racial policy had the torch of civil rights unexpectedly thrust into his hands."[5] In the ensuing election, Truman won (with the aid of the black vote) despite the loss of four Deep South states—Louisiana, South Carolina, Alabama, and Mississippi—to the States' Rights Party.

The militancy of southern leaders in 1948 reflected the continuing, though rapidly diminishing, political and economic stakes in the exploitation of blacks, especially in the Deep South. Moreover the hoisting of the States' Rights banner afforded southern leaders an opportunity to mobilize opposition to the offensive social and economic policies of the New Deal and the Fair Deal. [Samuel] Lubell refers to this as "a double insurgency: an economic revolt aimed at checking government spending and the power of labor unions, and a racial reaction designed to counter the influence of Negro voting in the North."[6]

Thus it cannot be said that the cause of securing civil rights legislation was immediately advanced by these events. Southern defections in the election of 1948 foreshadowed the possible dissolution of that regional base, and so concessions to the South—namely, maintaining the racial status quo—became the order of the day, as [Adlai] Stevenson's posture in campaigning for the Democratic nomination in 1952 revealed. In one speech prior to the convention Stevenson declared that "I reject as contemptible the reckless assertions that the South is a prison in which half the people are prisoners and the other half are wardens."[7] During the nominating convention he expressed great concern that the fight over civil rights "might drive the South out of the party—the party needed unity."[8] With his acquiescence, the delegation from Illinois voted to seat the Dixiecrat delegations without a [party] "loyalty pledge," a position which antagonized many northern advocates of civil rights. By reason of his personal convictions and his concern that the South had to be kept within the framework of the Democratic Party, Stevenson emerged as a compromise candidate, defeating [Estes] Kefauver and [Averell] Harriman after several ballots. He then named Senator John Sparkman of Alabama as his running mate.

Throughout the campaign Stevenson continued to appease the South, and gave relatively little attention to the black vote in the northern cities.[9] "He repeatedly indicated concern about losing the South,"[10] and time and again he asserted that the responsibility for dealing with the race problem properly resided with the states:

> He fell back on an old proposal that the federal FEPC relinquish jurisdiction to states that had FEPC's of their own. What about the filibuster? "I suppose the President might properly be concerned with the rules of the Senate. . . . I should certainly want to study it. . . . I am told that it has disadvantages as well as advantages. There are other considerations involved in unlimited and free debate that must not be overlooked in our anxiety to advance in one field alone."[11]

As it happens, this policy of conciliation did not stem the tide of defections in the subsequent election because an entirely different force was also at work. To be sure, the Dixiecrat states, where race was the preeminent issue, returned to the Democratic ranks, although South Carolina and Louisiana did so by very slim majorities. But in the Outer South the Republicans made big gains; Virginia, Florida, Tennessee, and Texas delivered their electoral votes to Eisenhower. Republican strength in the Outer South was especially noticeable among the growing white middle classes in the cities, while Democratic strength tended to be concentrated among whites in the declining small towns and rural areas of the Deep South.[12]

The election of 1952 thus revealed the political effects of a second form of economic change that was sweeping the South: industrial modernization. This modernizing trend was casting up a new white middle class in the cities and suburbs (especially in the states of the Outer South) whose political sympathies inclined toward the Republican Party. These changes in the class structure became apparent in the election of 1952, which "marked a turning point in Republican fortunes, the beginnings of a southern Republicanism that would contest elections, first at the presidential level, then at the state and local levels, evolving gradually into a credible opposition party everywhere except the inner core of the Deep South— and even there sporadically."[13]

In other words, the rupture between the northern and southern wings of the Democratic party which occurred in 1948 was no transient phenomenon. Both agricultural and industrial modernization were contributing to a deep and widening fissure. Each of these economic forces was eroding the Democratic Party's base in the South in a different way. Indeed some political analysts even reached the conclusion at the time that the Democratic Party might not survive. Lubell was one:

> The most heavily Democratic districts in the North . . . are becoming those which are poorest economically and which have the largest Negro populations—two characteristics which tend to pull the representatives of these districts back to the old appeals of the New Deal. If this trend continues, as seems likely, the Congressmen from these districts will find themselves in sharpening conflict with the Southern districts, both with the anti-Negro sentiments, so strong in the rural South, and the economic conservatism of the rising middle-class elements in the Southern cities. . . . The underlying tensions between these two wings of "sure" Democratic seats are sufficiently intense so that the cracking apart of the Democratic party must be rated a possibility.[14]

In this prediction, of course, Lubell was wrong. His mistake was partly in failing to take account of the large stakes the dominant leadership of the South, its congressional delegation, had in the Democratic party. From the start of party splintering in 1948 the southern congressional delegation kept its distance from third-party adventurism. "Continued agitation for an independent political movement came primarily from the [White] Citizens' Councils and aging Dixiecrat forces" at the state and local level.[15] As a result of its longevity in Congress the southern delegation enjoyed tremendous power in national affairs; it had a large claim on federal patronage, and had a decisive impact on the allocation of billions of dollars in defense funds for the construction of military, space, and industrial complexes, many of which came to be located in the South. Nor were shifts in party identification free of risks to electoral incumbency itself. The mystique of the Democratic Party still held sway below the Mason-Dixon line despite the racial tensions of the times. Consequently southern congressional leaders confined themselves to encouraging presidential Republicanism, unpledged electors, and other stratagems to threaten the national Democratic Party, but they did not bolt. In effect they defined the limits of the southern white resistance movement and thereby weakened it. But within these limits they helped the North-South fissure grow.

Because of this fissure, blacks did not benefit much at this stage from their growing voting numbers in the North. Black loyalty to the Democratic Party was not in doubt; in fact it had been intensifying. Referring to the trends in black voting with migration to the North, Lubell observed that "as their numbers have increased so has their Democratic party loyalty. . . . Truman got a heavier proportion of the Negro vote than did Roosevelt, while Stevenson [in the election of 1952] did even better among the Negroes than Truman."[16] The firm allegiance of black voters thus encouraged Democratic strategists to decide that it was defections among southern voters which constituted the main problem of the party. For this reason the civil rights issue continued to be sacrificed to the goal of regional unity. It was the South, in short, that initially benefitted from electoral instability. But that was to change, for if the South was becoming antagonized and restive over the race issue, so too were blacks.

NOTES

1. Allen Yarnell, *Democrats and Progressives: The 1948 Election as a Test of Postwar Liberalism* (Berkeley: University of California Press, 1974), 44. There is considerable dispute among analysts of the election of the 1948 over the question of whether Truman's rhetorical position on civil rights during the campaign was owed to the Wallace threat, or to the threat that the Republicans would capture votes among blacks. Among those who make a strong case that Wallace was the primary force are [Barton] Bernstein, [William] Berman and [Philip H.] Vaughn. By contrast, Yarnell reaches the conclusion that the Republicans were the much greater threat (see especially 35, 44 and 69). For the purposes of our analysis, this dispute is not crucial. What is crucial is that the civil rights question was gradually emerging as an electoral issue.

2. Bert Cochran, *Harry Truman and the Crisis Presidency* (New York: Funk and Wagnalls, 1974), 230.

3. S. M. Hartmann, *Truman and the 80th Congress* (Columbia: University of Missouri Press, 1971), 150–51.

4. Cochran, 230.

5. Cochran, 231.

6. Samuel Lubell, White and Black (New York: Harper Colophon, 1966), 186.

7. Cochran, *Adlai Stevenson: Patrician among Politicians* (New York: Funk and Wagnalls, 1969), 222.

8. John Bartlow Martin, *Adlai Stevenson of Illinois* (Garden City: Doubleday, 1976), 589.

9. Cochran, 1969, 221–22.

10. Martin, 597.

11. Martin, 611.

12. Lubell, 179 ff.

13. George Brown Tindall, *The Disruption of the Solid South* (Athens: University of Georgia Press, 1972), 49.

14. Lubell, 215–16.

15. Numan V. Bartley, *The Rise of Massive Resistance* (Baton Rouge: Louisiana University Press, 1969), 290.

16. Lubell, 214.

Chapter 85

To Secure These Rights

The President's Committee on Civil Rights

In 1946, a black delegation led by Walter White, director of the NAACP, met with President Harry S. Truman to discuss discrimination against blacks in the United States. Spurred by the meeting and electoral considerations (see chapters 84 and 87), Truman responded by appointing a President's Committee on Civil Rights, which produced a report the following year.

The following selection is excerpted from To Secure These Rights: The Report of the President's Committee on Civil Rights *(Washington, D.C.: U.S. Government Printing Office, 1947).*

Our American heritage of freedom and equality has given us prestige among the nations of the world and a strong feeling of national pride at home. There is much reason for that pride. But pride is no substitute for steady and honest performance, and the record shows that at varying times in American history the gulf between ideals and practice has been wide. . . .

The Crime of Lynching

In 1946 at least six persons in the United States were lynched by mobs. Three of them had not been charged, either by the police or anyone else, with an offense. . . . All were Negroes. . . .

While available statistics show that, decade by decade, lynchings have decreased, this Committee has found that in the year 1947 lynching remains one of the most serious threats to the civil rights of Americans. It is still possible for a mob to abduct and murder a person in some sections of the country with almost certain assurance of escaping punishment for the crime. The decade from 1936 through 1946 saw at least 43 lynchings. No person received the death penalty, and the majority of guilty persons were not even prosecuted.

The communities in which lynchings occur tend to condone the crime. Punishment of lynchers is not accepted as the responsibility of state or local governments in these communities. Frequently, state officials participate in the crime, actively or passively. Federal efforts to punish the crime are resisted. Condonation of lynching is indicated by the failure of some local law enforcement officials to make adequate efforts to break up a mob. It is further shown by failure in most cases to make any real effort to apprehend or try those guilty. If the federal government enters a case, local officials sometimes actively resist the federal investigation. Local citizens often combine to impede the effort to apprehend the criminals by convenient "loss of memory"; grand juries refuse to indict; trial juries acquit in the face of overwhelming proof of guilt. . . .

Police Brutality

We have reported the failure of some public officials to fulfill their most elementary duty—the protection of persons against mob violence. We must also report more widespread and varied forms of official misconduct. These include violent physical attacks by police officers on members of minority groups, the use of third degree methods to extort confessions, and brutality against prisoners. . . .

In various localities, scattered throughout the country, unprofessional or undisciplined police, while avoiding brutality, fail to recognize and to safeguard the civil rights of the citizenry. . . . At times this appears in unwarranted arrests, unduly prolonged detention before arraignment, and the abuse of the search and seizure power. Cases involving these breaches of civil rights constantly come before the courts. . . .

Where lawless police forces exist, their activities may impair the civil rights of any citizen. In one place the brunt of illegal police activity may fall on suspected vagrants, in another on union organizers, and in another on unpopular racial or religious minorities, such as Negroes, Mexicans, or Jehovah's Witnesses. . . .

Much of the illegal official action which has been brought to the attention of the Committee is centered in the South. There is evidence of lawless police action against whites and Negroes alike, but the dominant pattern is that of race prejudice. . . .

The files of the Department abound with evidence of illegal official action in southern states. In one case, the victim was arrested on a charge of stealing a tire, taken to the courthouse, beaten by three officers with a blackjack until his head was a bloody pulp, and then dragged unconscious through the streets to the jail where he was thrown, dying, onto the floor. In another case, a constable arrested a Negro, against whom he bore a personal grudge, beat him brutally with a bullwhip and then forced his victim, in spite of his protestations of being unable to swim, to jump into a river where he drowned. In a third case, there was evidence that officers arrested a Negro maid on the charge of stealing jewelry from her employer, took her to jail and severely beat and whipped her in an unsuccessful effort to extort a confession. All of these cases occurred within the last five years.

There are other cases in the files of the Department of Justice of officers who seem to be "trigger-happy" where weak or poor persons are concerned. In a number of instances, Negroes have been shot, supposedly in self-defense, under circumstances indicating, at best, unsatisfactory police work in the handling of criminals, and, at worst, a callous willingness to kill. . . .

The total picture—adding the connivance of some police officials in lynchings to their record of brutality against Negroes in other situations—is, in the opinion of this Committee, a serious reflection of American justice. We know that Americans everywhere deplore this violence. We recognize further that there are many law enforcement officers in the South and the North who do not commit violent acts against Negroes or other friendless culprits. We are convinced, however, that the incidence of police brutality against Negroes is disturbingly high.

Administration of Justice

In addition to the treatment experienced by the weak and friendless person at the hands of police officers, he sometimes finds that the judicial process itself does not give him full and equal justice. This may appear in unfair and perfunctory trials, or in fines and prison sentences that are heavier than those imposed on other members of the community guilty of the same offenses. . . .

The United States Supreme Court in a number of recent decisions has censured state courts for accepting evidence procured by third-degree methods, for failing to provide accused persons with adequate legal counsel, and for excluding Negroes from jury lists. . . .

The different standards of justice which we have allowed to exist in our country have had further repercussions. In certain states, the white population can threaten and do violence to the minority members with little or no fear of legal reprisal. Minority groups are sometimes convinced that they cannot expect fair treatment from the legal machinery. . . .

The Right to Vote

The right of all qualified citizens to vote is today considered axiomatic by most Americans. . . . In theory the aim has been achieved, but in fact there are many backwaters in our political life where the right to vote is not assured to every qualified citizen. . . .

The denial of the suffrage on account of race is the most serious present interference with the right to vote. . . .

As legal devices for disfranchising the Negro have been held unconstitutional, new methods have been improvised to take their place. Intimidation and the threat of intimidation have always loomed behind these legal devices to make sure that the desired result is achieved. . . .

The Right to Bear Arms

Underlying the theory of compulsory wartime military service in a democratic state is the principle that every citizen, regardless of his station in life, must assist in defense of the nation when its security is threatened. Despite the discrimination which they encounter in so many fields, minority group members have time and again met this responsibility. Moreover, since equality in military service assumes great importance as a symbol of democratic goals, minorities have regarded it not only as a duty but as a right.

Yet the record shows that the members of several minorities, fighting and dying for the survival of the nation in which they met bitter prejudice, found that there was discrimination against them even as they fell in battle. Prejudice in any area is an ugly, undemocratic phenomenon; in the armed services, where all men run the risk of death, it is particularly repugnant.

The Right to Employment

A man's right to an equal chance to utilize fully his skills and knowledge is essential. The meaning of a job goes far beyond the paycheck. . . .

In private business, in government, and in labor unions, the war years saw a marked advance both in hiring policies and in the removal of on-the-job discriminatory practices. Several factors contributed to this progress. The short labor market, the sense of unity among the people, and the leadership provided by the government all helped bring about a lessening of unfair employment practices. Yet we did not eliminate discrimination in employment. The Final Report of the federal Fair Employment Practice Committee, established in 1941 by President Roosevelt to eliminate discrimination in both government and private employment related to the war effort, make this clear.

Four out of five cases which arose during the life of the Committee, concerned Negroes. However, many other minorities have suffered from discriminatory employment practices. The FEPC reports show that eight percent of the Committee's docket involved complaints of discrimination because of creed, and 70 percent of these concerned Jews. . . .

Discriminatory hiring practices.—Discrimination is most acutely felt by minority group members in their inability to get a job suited to their qualifications. Exclusion of Negroes, Jews, or Mexicans in the process of hiring is effected in various ways—by newspaper advertisements requesting only whites or gentiles to apply, by registration or application blanks on which a space is reserved for "race" or "religion," by discriminatory job orders placed with employment agencies, or by the arbitrary policy of a company official in charge of hiring. . . .

Discrimination in hiring has forced many minority workers into low-paying and often menial jobs such as common laborer and domestic servant. . . .

On-the-job discrimination.—If he can get hired, the minority worker often finds that he is being paid less than other workers. This wage discrimination is sharply evident in studies made of individual cities and is especially exaggerated in the South. . . . [Wage] differences are not caused solely by the relegation of the

Negroes to lower types of work, but reflect wage discriminations between whites and Negroes for the same type of work. . . .

Nor can the disparity be blamed entirely on differences in education and training. The 1940 census reveals that the median annual income of Negro high school graduates was only $775 as compared with $1,454 for the white high school graduate; that the median Negro college graduate received $1,074 while his white counterpart was earning $2,046; that while 23.3 percent of white high school graduates had wages or salary incomes over $2,000, but four percent of Negro graduates achieved that level. . . .

The Right to Education

The United States has made remarkable progress toward the goal of universal education for its people. . . . Yet we have not finally eliminated prejudice and discrimination from the operation of either our pubic or our private schools and colleges. We have failed to provide Negroes and, to a lesser extent, other minority group members with equality of educational opportunities in our public institutions, particularly in the elementary and secondary school levels. We have allowed discrimination in the operation of many of our private institutions of higher education, particularly in the North with respect to Jewish students.

Discrimination in public schools.—The failure to give Negroes equal education opportunities is naturally most acute in the South, where approximately 10 million Negroes live. . . .

[I]t is the South's segregated school system which most directly discriminates against the Negro. This segregation is found today in 17 southern states and the District of Columbia. Poverty-stricken though it was after the close of the Civil War, the South chose to maintain two sets of public schools, one for the whites and one for the Negroes. With respect to education, as well as to other public services, the Committee believes that the "separate but equal" rule has not been obeyed in practice. There is a marked difference in quality between the educational opportunities offered white children and Negro children in the separate schools. Whatever test is used—expenditure per pupil, teachers' salaries, the number of pupils per teacher, transportation of students, adequacy of school buildings and educational equipment, length of school term, extent of curriculum—Negro students are invariably at a disadvantage. Opportunities for Negroes in public institutions of higher education in the South—particularly at the professional graduate school level—are severely limited. . . .

In the North, segregation in education is not formal, and in some states is prohibited. Nevertheless, the existence of residential restrictions in many northern cities has had discriminatory effects on Negro education. In Chicago, for example, the schools which are most crowded and employ double shift schedules are practically all in Negro neighborhoods. . . .

The Right to Housing

. . . Discrimination in housing results primarily from business practices. These practices may arise from special interests of business groups, such as the profits to be derived from confining minorities to slum areas, or they may reflect community prejudice. One of the most common practices is the policy of landlords and real estate agents to prevent Negroes from renting outside of designated areas. Again, it is "good business" to develop exclusive "restricted" suburban developments which are barred to all but white gentiles. When Negro veterans seek "GI" loans in order to build homes, they are likely to find that credit from private banks, without whose services there is no possibility of taking advantage of the GI Bill of Rights, is less freely available to members of their race. Private builders show a tendency not to construct new homes except for white occupancy. These interlocking business customs and devices form the core of our discriminatory policy. But community prejudice also finds expression in open public agitation against construction of public housing projects for Negroes, and by violence against Negroes who seek to occupy public housing projects or to build in "white" sections. . . .

The Climate of Opinion

. . . The achievement of full civil rights in law may do as much to end prejudice as the end of prejudice may do to achieve full civil rights. The fewer the opportunities there are to use inequality in the law as a reinforcement of prejudice, the sooner prejudice will vanish. . . .

The Time Is Now

Twice before in American history the nation has found it necessary to review the state of its civil rights. The first time was during the 15 years between 1776 and 1791, from the drafting of the Declaration of Independence through the Articles of Confederation experiment to the writing of the Constitution and the Bill of Rights. It was then that the distinctively American heritage was finally distilled from earlier views of liberty. The second time was when the Union was temporarily sundered over the question of whether it could exist "half-slave" and "half-free."

It is our profound conviction that we have come to a time for a third re-examination of the situation, and a sustained drive ahead. Our reasons for believing this are those of conscience, of self-interest, and of survival in a threatening world. Or to put it another way, we have a moral reason, an economic reason, and an international reason for believing that the time for action is now.

Chapter 86

Executive Order 9981: Barring Segregation in the Armed Forces

Harry S. Truman

Executive Order 9981, 26 July 1948, reprinted from "Executive Orders," Title 3 Code of Federal Regulations, 1943–1948 (Washington, D.C.: Government Printing Office, 1957), 722.

Whereas it is essential that there be maintained in the armed services of the United States the highest standards of democracy, with equality of treatment and opportunity for all those who serve in our country's defense:

Now, therefore, by virtue of the authority vested in me as President of the United States, by the Constitution and the statutes of the United States, and as Commander in Chief of the armed services, it is hereby ordered as follows:

1. It is hereby declared to be the policy of the President that there shall be equality of treatment and opportunity for all persons in the armed services without regard to race, color, religion or national origin. This policy shall be put into effect as rapidly as possible, having due regard to the time required to effectuate any necessary changes without impairing efficiency or morale.

2. There shall be created in the National Military Establishment an advisory committee to be known as the President's Committee on Equality of Treatment and Opportunity in the Armed Services, which shall be composed of seven members to be designated by the President.

3. The Committee is authorized on behalf of the president to examine into the rules, procedures and practices of the armed services in order to determine in what respect such rules, procedures and practices may be altered or improved with a view to carrying out the policy of this order. The Committee shall confer and advise with the Secretary of Defense, the Secretary of the Army, the Secretary of the Navy, and the Secretary of the Air Force, and shall make such recommendations to the President and to said Secretaries as in the judgment of the Committee will effectuate the policy hereof.

4. All executive departments and agencies of the Federal Government are authorized and directed to cooperate with the Committee in its work, and to furnish

the Committee such information or the services of such persons as the Committee may require in the performance of its duties.

5. When requested by the Committee to do so, persons in the armed services or in any of the executive departments and agencies of the Federal Government shall testify before the Committee and shall make available for the use of the Committee such documents and other information as the Committee may require.

6. The Committee shall continue to exist until such time as the President shall terminate its existence by Executive Order.

Chapter 87

The Second Red Scare: The Cold War in Black America

Manning Marable

Manning Marable, professor of history and director of the Institute for African American Studies at Columbia University, is the author of How Capitalism Under-developed Black America *(1983),* W. E. B. Du Bois: Black Radical Democrat *(1986), "The Racial Contours of the Constitution,"* Howard Law Journal *(1987),* Beyond Black and White: Transforming African American Politics *(1995),* Speaking Truth to Power: Essays on Race, Resistance, and Radicalism *(1996), and* Black Leadership *(1998).*

The following selection is excerpted from Race, Reform and Rebellion: The Second Reconstruction in Black America, 1945–1990, 2d ed. *(Jackson: University Press of Mississippi, 1991), 18–32, footnotes deleted. Reprinted by permission of the author.*

For more selections by Marable, see chapters 130 and 172.

The democratic upsurge of black people which characterized the late 1950s could have happened ten years earlier. With the notable exception of the *Brown* decision of 17 May 1954, which ordered the desegregation of public schools, most of the important Supreme Court decisions that aided civil rights proponents had been passed some years before. In May 1946, for example, the high court ruled that state laws requiring segregation on interstate buses were unconstitutional. In *Smith v. Allwright,* delivered 3 April 1944, by an eight to one margin, the Supreme Court ended the use of the all-white primary election. By the spring of 1946, there were 75,000 black registered voters in Texas and 100,000 black voters in Georgia. Yet the sit-ins, the non-violent street demonstrations, did not yet occur; the facade of white supremacy was crumbling, yet for almost ten years there was no overt and mass movement which challenged racism in the streets. This interim decade, between World War II and the Montgomery County, Alabama, bus boycott of December 1955, has also generally been ignored by black social historians. I think that the answer to the question, Why were mass popular protests for desegregation relatively weak or nonexistent in the period 1945–54?, is precisely the answer to the second question: Why have historians of the black movement done so little research on the post-war period? The impact of the Cold War, the anti-communist purges and near-totalitarian social environment, had a devastating effect upon the cause of blacks' civil rights and civil liberties. As this chapter will illustrate, the paranoid mood of anti-communist America made it difficult for any other reasonable reform movement to exist. The sterile legacy of anti-communism, felt even today, has so influenced many American historians that they are not even able to comment on the facts before them.

By the end of 1946, the Soviet Union and the United States had reached a clear breaking point in their relations. From the Soviets' perspective, the Americans were ungrateful for their preeminent role in the anti-fascist war effort, and lacked any critical understanding of their domestic and foreign requirements needed to restore peace and economic order. The Soviets had lost 20 million men and women in World War II. During the summer of 1946, the worst drought of the twentieth century dried up all the crops in the Ukraine and Volga lands, and millions were on the verge of starvation. Urban consumption declined to only 40 percent of 1940 totals. "In the coal-mines of the Donetz Basin men were still pumping water out of the shafts. . . . The steel mills, rattling with wear and tear, turned out only 12 million tons of ingot, a fraction of the American output. Engineering plants were worked by adolescent semi-skilled labour. People were dressed in rags; many were barefoot." The Soviet Union was simply in no condition to fight another war, but it did feel that its national interests had to be preserved. The Americans were driven by other motives. For many political conservatives and emigrants from Eastern Europe, World War II had been "the wrong war against the wrong enemy," writes social historian David Caute. "These groups were joined after 1944 by others initially favorable to the war but subsequently appalled by the spread of Soviet communism in Eastern Europe and by the reduction of [these] nations to satellite status. Here Catholic indignation ran high." Anti-communist liberals in both major political parties "soon developed a determination to halt Soviet encroachment by every available means and to deal roughly with elements at home—communists, fellow travelers, progressives—who foolishly or wickedly adopted the Soviet point of view." American corporate interests were concerned about expanding investments abroad and reducing or eliminating all pro-labor legislation sponsored by the New Deal at home. The anti-communist campaign permitted them to do both, as well as to flush suspected leftists out of positions of trade union authority. A great many post-war politicians, such as Wisconsin Senator Joe McCarthy and California Senator Richard M. Nixon, simply "recognized a good thing when they saw it, [and] cynically manipulated public hysteria for their own political purposes," [writes historian Richard Pollenberg].

Noted playwright Lillian Hellman accurately describes the post-war "Red Scare" period as a "Scoundrel Time":

> It was not the first time in history that the confusions of honest people were picked up in space by cheap baddies who, hearing a few bars of popular notes, made them into an opera of public disorder, staged and sung, as much of the congressional testimony shows, in the wards of an insane asylum. A theme is always necessary, a plain, simple, unadorned theme to confuse the ignorant. The anti-Red theme was easily

chosen . . . not alone because we were frightened of socialism, but chiefly, I think, to destroy the remains of Roosevelt and his sometimes advanced work. The McCarthy group . . . chose the anti-Red scare with perhaps more cynicism than Hitler picked anti-Semitism.

In March 1947, Truman asked Congress to spend $400 million in economic aid and military hardware to halt leftist movements in Turkey and Greece. In the following years, five million investigations of public employees suspected of communist sympathies were held. Trade unions were pressured to purge all communists and anti-racist activists with leftist credentials. By July 1947, union leader Philip Murray ordered the CIO executive committee, "If communism is an issue in your unions, throw it to hell out, and throw its advocates out along with it." The CIO convention of 1949 expelled the 50,000-member United Electrical, Radio, and Machine Workers union for being dominated by leftists; within months, eleven progressive unions with nearly one million members were purged from the CIO. In 1949, 15 states passed "anti-subversion laws." "Writing or speaking subversive words" in Michigan was a crime punishable by a life sentence in prison. In 1952, Tennessee mandated the death penalty for the espousal of revolutionary Marxist ideas. That same year, Massachusetts required a three-year term in the state prison for anyone who allowed a Communist Party meeting to be held in their homes. Georgia, Indiana, Pennsylvania and Washington outlawed the Communist Party. The U.S. Attorney General, Tom Clark of Texas, warned all Americans in January 1948: "Those who do not believe in the ideology of the United States, shall not be allowed to stay in the United States."

"The wealthiest, most secure nation in the world was sweat-drenched in fear," Caute writes. "Federal, state and municipal employees worried about their pasts, their student indiscretions, their slenderest associations. . . . Some hastened to save their own skin by denouncing a colleague. In schools, universities, town halls and local professional associations, a continuous, pious mumbling of oaths was heard—the liturgy of fear." For black Americans, the "Scoundrel Time" was refracted through the prism of race, and was viewed in the light of their own particular class interests. For many black industrial and rural agricultural workers, the communists were the most dedicated proponents of racial equality and desegregation. In the 1930s, they had organized a vigorous defense of the Scottsboro Nine [see chapter 65—Eds.], a group of young black men unjustly convicted of rape in Alabama. The Party had sponsored Unemployed Councils, and provided the major force to desegregate American labor unions. For the aspiring black middle class, the image of the Communist Party was entirely different. Many black preachers had often denounced Marxism because of its philosophical atheism. Black entrepreneurs were dedicated to the free enterprise system, and sought to enrich themselves through the existing economic order. Many black leaders had condemned the Party during World War II for urging blacks to maintain labor's "no strike" pledges. [Philip] Foner notes, "It was to be exceedingly difficult for the communists to overcome the resentment among blacks created by the Party's wartime policies. The communists never completely erased the feeling in sections of the black community that they had placed the Soviet Union's survival above the battle for black equality." In general, black middle-class leaders attempted to divorce themselves from the communists as the reactionary trend was building across the country.

The most prominent black leaders were affected in different ways by the outbreak of the domestic Cold War. [A. Philip] Randolph was the doyen of the black labor movement. During World War I, he and his radical associate Chandler Owen had edited the militantly socialist journal the *Messenger*, and were known throughout Harlem as the "Lenin and Trotsky" of the black movement. During the Red Summer of 1919, President Woodrow Wilson had denounced Randolph as "the most dangerous Negro in America." During the mid-1920s Randolph had organized the Brotherhood of Sleeping Car Porters, and began to moderate his leftist views considerably. His fierce struggle with the Communist Party over the leadership of the National Negro Congress from 1935 and 1939 left a bitter anti-communist bias in his entire political outlook. During the war, he had continued to urge black workers to adopt a "strategy and maneuver (of) mass civil disobedience and non-cooperation" to fight racism. But Randolph opposed, certainly from this point onward, any co-operation or "united front" activity with the communists. In 1947, he organized the Committee Against Jim Crow in Military Service and Training, and threatened the Senate Armed Services Committee that he would direct a massive civil disobedience effort if the U.S. armed forces were not promptly desegregated. But in the post-war years, Randolph deliberately eschewed any political or organizational links with revolutionary Marxists. In his speeches and writings, he denounced the domestic communist "conspiracy" at every opportunity. By clearly separating the interests of black labor from the radical left, he believed that he could gain the political support of many anti-communist liberals and the Truman Administration. As Randolph declared before a congressional committee in 1948, racial segregation "is the greatest single propaganda and political weapon in the hands of Russia and international communism today."

Although elected to Congress only in 1944, Adam Clayton Powell, Jr., quickly emerged as the most influential black public official for the next two decades. Almost twenty years younger than Randolph, Powell had acquired his reputation as a dedicated militant during the Great Depression. As the son of the leader of one of the largest black churches in the nation, Harlem's Abyssinian Baptist Church, Powell led a series of popular boycotts which called for black jobs and greater welfare and social services. A charismatic speaker whose entire "way of life" was "an act of rebellion," Powell had at first no reservations about joining with the communists who defended the interests of black poor and working people. The practical contributions of the Party were praised by Powell in a 1945 statement: "There is no group in America, including the Christian church, that practices racial brotherhood one-tenth as much as the Communist Party." Once in Congress, Powell led the fight against anti-communism. In early 1947, when two congressional contempt citations were passed against communists who refused to divulge information to the House Un-American Activities Committee (HUAC) by votes of 370 to 1 and 357 to 2, only Powell and progressive New York Congressman Vito Marcantonio voted against the majority. Powell recognized that every defender of racial segregation in Congress was also a devout proponent of anticommunist legislation, and that the Negro had no other alternative except to champion the civil liberties of the left in order to protect the black community's own interests. This advanced perspective, which would prove to be correct in later years, found little support among the black middle class, despite Powell's continued personal popularity. Within Congress itself, Powell was contemptuously dismissed as a political pariah for fifteen years.

Since 1930, the leader of the NAACP had been Walter White. Under his direction the organization had grown in numbers and political influence. During the 1920s, he had written a provocative investigative report on lynchings in the South. As an assistant secretary to James Weldon Johnson he had served tirelessly, and with Johnson's retirement White slowly moved the NAACP to the right. Internally, co-workers who resisted any of White's initiatives were soon fired. In [W. E. B.] Du Bois's words, White was absolutely self-centered and egotistical to the point that he was almost unconscious of it. He seemed really to believe that his personal interests and the interest of the race and organization were identical. This led to curious complications because to attain his objects he was often absolutely unscrupulous. In 1933–34, White feuded with Du Bois over the NAACP's lack of coherent economic policy for blacks to deal with the Great Depression. In despair and outrage, Du Bois resigned as editor of the NAACP journal, the *Crisis,* in June 1934, after 24 years of service. Du Bois returned to the NAACP after an absence of ten years as research director, but with the outbreak of the Cold War, White pressured the board to fire him within three years because of Du Bois's "radical thought" and progressive activities in international peace and Pan-Africanist movements. White's bitter relationship with Du Bois was manifested in his opposition to the entire American left generally. From the beginning of his tenure at the NAACP, he had fought any influence of communists or independent radicals in the organization. He supported the early "witch-hunts" to exclude communists from all levels of the federal government. When in late 1947, a poll of the NAACP national office revealed that 70 percent of the staff intended to support former vice president Henry Wallace on the Progressive Party ticket in opposition to Truman, White warned Du Bois and other Wallace advocates not to take part in any electoral campaign. Simultaneously, White was already "making a nationwide drive for Truman, by letter, newspaper articles, telegrams and public speech." Like Randolph, White attempted to identify the struggle for black equality with the anti-communist impulse.

The most prominent black supporters of progressive and leftist politics were Du Bois and the famous cultural artist-activist Paul Robeson. Du Bois had been an independent socialist since 1904, but had experienced a series of volatile confrontations with revolutionary Marxists. In the wake of the Bolshevik Revolution, he denounced the entire concept of the "dictatorship of the proletariat," and told the readers of the *Crisis* that he was "not prepared to dogmatize with Marx and Lenin." As late as 1944, Du Bois had written that "the program of the American

Communist Party was suicidal." Yet after extensive travels in the Soviet Union in 1926, 1936 and 1949, Du Bois's view on matters shifted considerably. He concluded that the Soviets' anti-imperialist positions promoting the necessity for African political independence from European colonial rule were genuinely progressive; he was impressed with the Soviet Union's extensive domestic educational, social and technological gains. By the late 1940s, he believed that the black liberation movement in America had to incorporate a socialist perspective, and that blacks had to be in the forefront in promoting peaceful co-existence with the Soviet bloc. Robeson was politically closer to the communist movement for a greater period of time. In the late 1930s, he supported the progressive government of Spain against the Nazi-backed Spanish fascists in that country's bloody civil war. He recognized earlier than Du Bois that the rise in domestic anti-communism would become a force to stifle progressive change and the civil rights of blacks. In early 1949, in a controversial address in Paris, he declared that U.S. policies toward Africa were "similar to that of Hitler and Goebbels." The Soviet Union "has raised our people to full human dignity." These and other statements led to Robeson's wide public censure. His noted career as a Shakespearean actor and singer, which was described by American critics as the most gifted of his generation before 1945, crashed in short order. To muffle Robeson's impact, HUAC quickly called black baseball player Jackie Robinson before the committee to denounce him. Robeson had been a "famous ex-athlete and a great singer and actor," Robinson admitted, but his subversive statements gave support to the communist cause. "We can win the fight [against segregation] without the Communists and we don't want their help."

As the presidential election of 1948 approached, the Truman Administration recognized that the Negro electorate would play an unusually decisive role in the campaign. More than Roosevelt, Truman privately viewed the blacks' goals of social and political equality with great contempt. But the administration's aggressively anti-communist polemics could not create a sufficient electoral bloc among white voters which would guarantee victory that November. Democratic party disaffections grew on the left and right, with Wallace's Progressive Party and the southern-based States' Rights Party, which nominated hard-line segregationist Strom Thurmond of South Carolina. The Republicans renominated popular New York governor Thomas Dewey as their standard-bearer, a politician who had run a very creditable race against Roosevelt in 1944. Presidential advisers informed Truman that he might even win the popular vote, but without critical black support in the industrial Northeast, the Midwest, and California, he would lose the electoral college count to Dewey—or, as in 1800 and 1824, a disastrous stalemate could occur and the House of Representatives might have to select a president in 1949. Thus, for the first time since 1876, it seemed apparent that blacks would decide the national election. Truman immediately responded to blacks' interests by publicly calling for new civil rights legislation. He promised to promote fair employment procedures and to press federal contractors aggressively to comply with desegregation guidelines. On 26 July 1949, the president issued an executive order to the effect "that there shall be equality of treatment and opportunity for all persons in the armed forces without regard to race, color, religion or national origin." Randolph promptly suspended the Committee Against Jim Crow in Military Service and Training's plans for a proposed boycott. White and his NAACP supporters exhorted blacks to reject the Wallace campaign, and urged them to vote for Truman in the interests of civil rights. White's efforts were a triumph for Cold War liberalism. In Harlem, Truman received 90,000 votes to Wallace's 21,000 votes, even though the Progressive Party's anti-racist platform was far superior to that of Truman's. In Pittsburgh, only 2,000 blacks cast ballots for Wallace. In California, Ohio and Illinois, black voters provided the decisive electoral edge for Truman over Dewey. Overall, Truman carried about two-thirds of the black vote, and with that margin he won the election. True to his campaign promises, in 1949 Truman continued to promote modest biracial reform efforts at the federal level, while at the same time escalating the Cold War at home. Truman's victory silenced and isolated black progressives for many years, and committed the NAACP and most middle-class black leaders to an alliance with Democratic presidents who did not usually share black workers' interests, except in ways which would promote their own needs at a given moment. Accommodation, anti-communism, and tacit allegiance to white liberals and labor bureaucrats became the principal tenets of black middle-class politics for the next decade.

Without much public fanfare or notice, a series of new political formations created by blacks and liberal whites began to emerge at this time. Blacks in South Carolina formed the Progressive Democratic Party to challenge the whites-only state Democratic Party. By May 1944, the Progressive Democrats had organized chapters in 39 of the state's 46 counties, and had begun an independent electoral strategy to expand the number of registered black voters in South Carolina. That same year, the biracial Southern Regional Council was formed in Atlanta, a coalition of clergy and professionals who supported the gradual but steady abolition of Jim Crow. The most important new biracial group, however, was the Congress of Racial Equality (CORE), established in 1942 by the pacifist Fellowship of Reconciliation, directed by A. J. Muste. Of CORE's 50 charter members, at least a dozen were black, including a Howard University divinity school graduate, James Farmer. The black youth secretary for the Fellowship of Reconciliation, social democrat and pacifist Bayard Rustin, gave political purpose and direction to the young formation. One of CORE's first actions was a confrontation with barbers at the University of Chicago who in November 1942 refused to cut Rustin's hair. From these modest beginnings, CORE developed into a civil rights group which emphasized non-violent direct action, rather than the litigation and moral suasion techniques of Walter White and the NAACP. Unlike the older organization, it was democratic, and most funds raised by chapters remained at the local level. By 1947, there were 13 CORE chapters, mostly in Ohio, New York, Illinois, Kansas, and Minnesota. CORE chapters staged a series of non-violent boycotts to desegregate lunch counters and schools in a series of northern and midwest cities. White Methodist student leader George Houser and Rustin developed a plan for CORE to test desegregation laws on interstate buses in the upper South during the late autumn of 1946. Perhaps hearing about the proposed "Journeys of Reconciliation," NAACP leaders, including attorney Thurgood Marshall, warned that: "A disobedience movement on the part of Negroes and their white allies, if employed in the South, would result in wholesale slaughter with no good achieved." Walter White, true to form, refused to provide any financial support for the effort. On 9 April 1947, a small party of 8 blacks and 8 whites left Washington, D.C. determined to sit in whites-only sections of the buses. In the journeys, CORE members were repeatedly arrested and intimidated by southern police, bus drivers, and the local courts. Rustin and other activists were sentenced to serve 30 days on North Carolina's jail gang. The Journeys of Reconciliation failed to overturn the South's racial codes, but in the process they established a pattern of civil rights protest which would be revived with greater effectiveness as the Freedom Ride movement in the 1960s.

By the early 1950s, the progress towards civil rights began to slow down perceptibly. The number of registered black southern voters reached 1.2 million by 1952. Yet "in the lower South, apart from a very few cities," C. Vann Woodward writes, "little change in Negro voting or office-holding could be detected. By one means or another, including intimidation and terror, Negroes were effectively prevented from registering even when they had the courage to try." On 2 June 1946, a black army veteran, Etoy Fletcher, was flogged publicly in Brandon, Mississippi for attempting to register. Senator Theodore Bilbo of Mississippi boasted that only 1,500 out of 500,000 black potential voters were registered in his state. "The best way to keep a nigger away from a white primary is to see him the night before," Bilbo declared. The *Jackson Daily News* (Mississippi) warned the state's few registered black voters: "Don't attempt to participate in the Democratic primary anywhere in Mississippi. . . . Staying away from the polls will be the best way to prevent unhealthy and unhappy results." Southern registrars employed Kafkaesque tests to determine whether blacks were "literate" enough to vote. One white registrar in Forest County, Mississippi, asked black potential voters this question: "How many bubbles are in a bar of soap?" As one Alabama political leader explained, the vote of even one black person in the deep South was an intolerable threat to the entire structure of Jim Crow. "If it was necessary to eliminate the Negro in 1901, because of certain inherent characteristics, it is even more necessary now because some intellectual progress makes the Negro more dangerous to our political structure now than in 1901. The Negro has the same disposition to live without working that his ancestors had in the jungle 10,000 years ago." Most of these racist politicians were still leading figures in the national Democratic Party, and were represented in powerful posts in the Truman Administration.

Truman himself was virtually silent from 1946–53 as white racist vigilante groups proliferated. As the black population in Los Angeles County, California, reached 200,000 by 1946, the Ku Klux Klan began to appear on the West Coast. Klan organizations were formed throughout the South, and were reported active in Pennsylvania and New Jersey. In New York the state attorney general estimated that there were 1,000 Klansmen in his state alone in the late 1940s. In the face of growing racist opposition, the NAACP counseled continued reliance upon the Truman Administration, legal challenges to segregation laws, and a general policy which spurned direct action. The failure and tragedy of this conservative approach to social change was in its parochial vision and tacit acceptance of the Cold War politics. By refusing to work with Marxists, the NAACP lost the most principled anti-racist organizers and activists. Instead of confronting the racists politically, with the commitment of a Robeson or a Du Bois, they accepted the prevailing xenophobia of the times, and in the end undercut their own efforts to desegregate society. The anti-communist impulse even affected CORE, to its detriment. A few CORE chapters, in Columbus, Ohio, and Chicago, encouraged Marxist participation in the early 1940s. In 1949, however, when Trotskyists joined the San Francisco chapter, the national office voided its affiliation. In 1948 Houser and CORE's executive committee drafted a "Statement on Communism," which was passed unanimously by its convention that year. CORE denounced any ties with "Communist-controlled" groups, and CORE members were ordered not to co-operate or work, with so-called communist-front organizations. As CORE's historians noted, this action did not prevent "conservatives and racists from continuing to attack CORE as Communist-controlled. Despite its vigorous anti-communist position, CORE suffered considerably from the McCarthyite hysteria of the period. The Red Scare, by labeling radical reform groups subversive, seriously impeded CORE's growth." By 1954, CORE had all but ceased to exist as an organization.

As the Cold War intensified, the repression of black progressives increased. Aided by local and state police, a gang of whites disrupted a concert given by Paul Robeson in Peekskill, New York in 1948. HUAC witnesses declared that Robeson was "the black Stalin among Negroes." In August 1950, the U.S. government revoked his passport for eight years. Officials prevented Robeson entering Canada in 1952, although no passport was necessary to visit that country. Du Bois ran for the U.S. Senate in New York in the autumn of 1950 on the progressive American Labor Party ticket, and denounced the anti-communist policies of both major parties. Despite wide public censure, he received 206,000 votes, and polled 15 percent of Harlem's ballots. The Truman Administration finally moved to eliminate Du Bois's still considerable prestige within the black community. On 8 February 1951, Du Bois was indicted for allegedly serving as an "agent of a foreign principal" in his anti-war work with the Peace Information Center in New York. The 82-year-old black man was handcuffed, fingerprinted, and portrayed in the national media as a common criminal. Before his trial, the New York *Herald-Tribune* convicted him in a prominent editorial: "The Du Bois outfit was set up to promote a tricky appeal of Soviet origin, poisonous in its surface innocence, which made it appear that a signature against the use of atomic weapons would forthwith insure world peace. It was, in short, an attempt to disarm America and yet ignore every form of Communist aggression." An international committee was formed to defend Du Bois and his colleagues at the Peace Information Center. Threatened with a fine of $100,000 and a five-year jail term, Du Bois continued to denounce the Truman Administration while out on bail. In November 1951, a federal judge dismissed all charges against Du Bois, when the government failed to introduce a single piece of evidence that implied that he was a communist agent.

Despite Du Bois's acquittal, the government had accomplished its primary objectives. Du Bois's voluminous writings on Negro sociology, history and politics were removed from thousands of libraries and universities. The State Department illegally withheld his passport for seven years. Black public opinion moved even further to the right. One leading black newspaper which had carried Du Bois's essays for decades, the *Chicago Defender*, declared that "it is a supreme tragedy that he should have become embroiled in activities that have been exposed as subversive in the twilight of his years." The oldest Negro fraternity, which Du Bois had helped to found in 1906, Alpha Phi Alpha, did not rally to his defense. Only one of thirty Alpha Phi Alpha chapters expressed public support for Du Bois. Virtually every black college president except Charles S. Johnson of Fisk University, Du Bois's *alma mater*, said nothing about the case. The NAACP was especially conspicuous in its moral cowardice. White told NAACP board members that the government had definite proof which would convict Du Bois. The NAACP Legal Defense lawyers made no overtures to provide assistance. The central office contacted NAACP local chapters with strongly worded advice about "not touching" Du Bois's case. Black schoolteachers' groups and the black National Baptist Convention took no action. The entire ordeal left Du Bois in bitter doubt about the political future of the Negro middle class:

> The reaction of Negroes [to the case] revealed a distinct cleavage not hitherto clear in American Negro opinion. The intelligentsia, the successful business and professional men, were . . . either silent or actually antagonistic. The reasons were clear; many believed that the government had actual proof of subversive activities on our part; until the very end they awaited their disclosure. [These blacks] had become American in their acception of exploitation as defensible, and in their imitation of American "conspicuous expenditure." They proposed to make money and spend it as pleased them. They had beautiful homes, large and expensive cars and fur coats. They hated "communism" and "socialism" as much as any white American.

On many black college campuses, the Red Scare was reflected in a growing exclusion of radical views from classroom discourse. Any faculty member who had a history of militant activism, either in the Communist Party or in other suspicious groups, could be fired. Two examples from Fisk University can be cited. Giovanni Rossi Lomanitz had been an active Party member in the early 1940s, working in the Federation of Architects, Engineers, Chemists and Technicians. A former associate of J. Robert Oppenheimer, Lomanitz taught at Cornell and in the late 1940s began an appointment at Fisk. In 1949 HUAC subpoenaed Lomanitz, and before the committee he refused to testify against himself, citing the Fifth Amendment. In twenty-four hours, despite the support of faculty and students, president Charles S. Johnson dismissed Lomanitz without due process. Five years later, Fisk mathematics professor Lee Lorch was summoned before HUAC. Lorch pointedly denied being a member of the Communist Party during his tenure at Fisk, and refused to answer questions about his alleged Party membership before 1941 by evoking the First Amendment. Johnson issued a public statement that Lorch's position before HUAC "is for all practical purposes tantamount to admission of membership in the Communist Party." Out of a faculty of 70, 48 urged Fisk's Board of Trustees to retain him, as did 22 student leaders and 150 alumni. Fisk instead ended Lorch's contract, as of June 1955.

A number of black former activists agreed to become informers against the communists. In the federal trial of twelve leading Party officials, which included two blacks, New York City councilman Benjamin J. Davis and Henry Winston, staged in New York City during July and August 1948, one of the government's black witnesses was an autoworker, William Cummings. Cummings joined the Party in 1943 for the FBI in Toledo, Ohio, and told the jury that communists "taught militants that one day the streets would run with blood." The defendants received sentences ranging from three to five years in federal prisons, and were ordered to pay fines of $5,000 each. Some of the Party's oldest black recruits turned into agents for the government. William O. Nowell, born in a southern sharecropper's family, joined the Party in the late 1920s. Trained in the Soviet Union, he rose as a Party leader in Detroit's trade union struggles. When he was expelled from the Party in 1936, he promptly worked as an agent in Henry Ford's "goon squad," threatening and beating other autoworkers. From 1948 until 1954, Nowell became a "professional anti-communist," testifying in approximately 40 trials and hearings. Manning Johnson entered the Party in 1930, and quickly climbed to its national committee in the ten years before his departure. Johnson repeatedly perjured himself at numerous trials, later claiming with pride that he would lie "a thousand times" to protect "the security of the government." The U.S. Justice Department paid Johnson $4,500 a year for his services. Ex-communist Leonard Patterson received $3,800 a year for two years, testifying against his former comrades before HUAC and in the courts. North Carolina black attorney Clayton Clontz joined the Party after the war, and covertly informed the FBI on its activities from August 1948 until February 1953. In the trial of one communist, Clontz made the astonishing claim that he was told that Soviet troops would land in the U.S. if America "declared war on [U.S.] communists in the revolution."

The purge of communists and radicals from organized labor in 1947–50 was the principal reason for the decline in the AFL-CIO's commitment to the struggle against racial segregation. In the wake of the NAACP's stampede to the right, a left of center space on the political spectrum was open, and militant black workers took advantage of the opportunity. In June 1950, nearly 1,000 delegates met in Chicago at the National Labor Conference for Negro Rights. Robeson gave a moving plenary address which condemned the Cold War and supported detente with the Soviet bloc countries. Black delegates from AFL unions noted that the federation still maintained all-white unions, and black veterans of the CIO argued that their organization had all but abandoned the struggle for Negro rights. The Chicago conference established a steering committee for the coordination of future work, which included Coleman Young, a Detroit leader of the Amalgamated Clothing Workers, UAW activist William R. Hood, and Cleveland Robinson, vice president of the Distributive, Processing, and Office Workers Union. In 1950 and 1951, the committee helped to develop 23 Negro Labor Councils, each fighting to end segregated facilities at the workplace, expanding black job opportunities, and attacking racism in the workplace, expanding black job opportunities, and attacking racism in the unions. The militant Detroit Council, led by Hood, inspired the call for the creation of a new black progressive labor organization. In October 1951, the National Negro Labor Council was formed in Cincinnati, Ohio. The delegates at the convention represented unions expelled from the CIO for retaining communists, as well as members of both the AFL and CIO. Hood emerged as the president, and Young was elected executive secretary. Almost immediately, the National Negro Labor Council came under direct attack. CIO leaders denounced Hood, Young and other black labor activists as the "tool(s) of the Soviet Union." Lester Granger of the National Urban League criticized the council as "subversive." In its brief history, the organization pressured to desegregate jobs in major U.S. firms; organized campaigns to increase black workers' salaries and to upgrade their job ranks; led pickets against hotels and companies practicing Jim Crow; and challenged the unions to advance more black workers into leadership positions. The pressure against the [Council's] pickets and protest activities was enormous. By December 1954, HUAC denounced the "pro-communist ideology" of the organization. It is true that communists participated in the National Negro Labor Council, but in no way were the desegregationist programs it carried out dictated or even directly influenced by the Party. By 1956, however, due to political pressures from the U.S. government, corporations and white labor leaders, the National Negro Labor Council had disappeared.

Besides Robeson, Du Bois, and the militant workers of the National Negro Labor Council, few examples or models of black resistance existed, except in the Communist Party. Black communist leader Henry Winston was confined during his 1948 trial in a poorly ventilated, closet-like cell. Despite two heart attacks, and following this, the judge's denial that he be seen by his family doctor, Winston's will to fight remained strong. At the April 1952 trial of black communists Pettis Perry and Claudia Jones, Perry described himself "as a victim of a frame-up so enormous as to resemble the Reichstag Fire trial" of 1933. Secretary of the Party's Negro Commission, Perry defiantly asked the court, "How could a Negro get justice from a white jury?" A native West Indian Marxist, Jones "delivered a long indictment of America's treatment of black people." Convicted, Perry received three years and a $5,000 fine; Jones, one year and one day in jail, and a $2,000 fine. Claude Lightfoot, secretary of the Illinois party, was arrested in June 1954, and had to stay in jail four months until $30,000 bail money could be collected. Convicted in January 1955, the black World War II veteran was given five years and a $5,000 fine. Prison life for these black revolutionaries was difficult physically, but their resistance remained uncompromised. Claudia Jones's acute asthmatic and cardiac conditions were made worse by having to work at a prison loom. In ten months she was sent to a hospital, and she died not long after her release. Prison doctors refused to treat Winston's eyesight, and as a result he became blind. Confronted with segregated accommodation in the federal prison at Terre Haute, Indiana, Benjamin Davis filed a suit against prison officials. Despite being placed on "round-the-clock administrative segregation," Davis refused to be defeated.

The black middle class's almost complete capitulation to anti-communism not only liquidated the moderately progressive impulse of the New Deal years and 1945–46; it made the Negroes unwitting accomplices of a Cold War domestic policy which was, directly, both racist and politically reactionary. When paranoid librarians took Du Bois's works off their shelves, they did not stop there—banned literature often included black publications such as the *Negro Digest* and the NAACP's *Crisis,* as well as the *New Republic, The Nation,* and other white-oriented liberal journals friendly to desegregation causes. When Robeson was blacklisted along with Lillian Hellman, director Dalton Trumbo and the "Hollywood Ten," did blacks think their feeble voices praising American patriotism would save black actors and artists? The wife of Adam Clayton Powell, Hazel Scott, a talented singer and pianist, could not obtain employment for years. Black television actor William Marshall, stage performer Canada Lee, and others were victimized by blacklists. When Randolph defended anti-communism at home, did he not recognize that in doing so he became a tool for American interests and power abroad? In 1952, Randolph traveled with socialist leader Norman Thomas to Asia under the auspices of the Congress for Cultural Freedom. Speaking in Japan and Burma, he denounced Russia's "slavery" and emphasized the progress made in U.S. race relations. In 1967, it was revealed that the Congress for Cultural Freedom was a subsidized front for the U.S. Central Intelligence Agency (CIA). Historian Christopher Lasch's criticisms of Thomas could be made with equal vigor of Randolph: "He does not see that he was being used [for different purposes] from the ones he thought he was advancing. He thought he was working for democratic reform . . . whereas the CIA valued him as a showpiece, an anti-Communist who happened to be a Socialist." By serving as the "left wing of McCarthyism," Randolph, White and other Negro leaders retarded the black movement for a decade or more.

Chapter 88

Remembering Jackie Robinson

Peter Dreier

Peter Dreier, professor of politics and director of the Public Policy Program at Occidental College, is a frequent contributor to newspapers and journals on public policy issues.

The following selection, "Remembering Jackie Robinson," is reprinted from Tikkun Magazine, a Bi-monthly Jewish Critique of Politics, Culture, and Society, March 1997. Information and subscriptions are available from Tikkun, 26 Fell Street, San Francisco, CA 94102.

For other selections by Dreier, see chapters 177 and 181.

Nineteen ninety-seven marks the 50th anniversary of Jackie Robinson's courageous triumph over baseball's apartheid system. When Robinson took the field for the Brooklyn Dodgers on April 15, 1947, he was the first black player in modern baseball.

To commemorate this milestone, Major League Baseball will honor Robinson by sewing patches on all players' uniforms. This year will see a proliferation of books, TV movies, and conferences about Robinson, who has not received the respect he deserves. Today, many Americans under 30, including some African American superstars, can't even identify Robinson, much less appreciate his accomplishment.

Many consider Robinson (1919–1972) America's greatest all-around athlete. The grandson of a slave and son of a sharecropper, he was a four-sport athlete at UCLA, played professional football and then briefly in baseball's Negro Leagues. He spent his major league career (1947 to 1956) with the Brooklyn Dodgers, was chosen Rookie of the Year in 1947 and Most Valuable Player in 1949. An outstanding baserunner with a .311 lifetime batting average, he led the Dodgers to six pennants and was elected to the Hall of Fame.

Like baseball, America is more racially integrated than it was in Robinson's day. We've seen the dismantling of legal segregation, growth of the black middle class, and a virtual end to the overt daily terror imposed on blacks. Without discounting the persistence of segregated neighborhoods, black poverty, and racial bigotry, the progress is undeniable.

Even so, American race relations seems to have reached an ideological impasse. The dominant race relations metaphors of Robinson's era—integration, the melting pot, and assimilation—were unambiguous. Progressives believed in a color-blind society. It was easy to answer, which side are you on? Today's disputes over multiculturalism, affirmative action, and racial preferences, and even (in the views of some black educators and playwright August Wilson) self-segregation make the political landscape more confusing.

Robinson's legacy is caught in contemporary culture wars. He was often criticized by 1960s black nationalists for being an Uncle Tom or a symbolic token. Some of their heirs now view baseball's integration with ambivalence for its role in destroying the Negro Leagues. And a writer in the conservative *National Review* last year used Robinson's success to argue against government policies like affirmative action, claiming it was a "triumph of the competitive market" and the "[b]aseball owners finally realized that the more they cared about the color of people's money, the less they could afford to care about the color of their skin."

In reality, black Americans welcomed baseball's integration as much as they welcomed the end of separate drinking fountains. The demise of the Negro Leagues was a small price to pay to defeat Jim Crow. And contrary to the conservative view, the dismantling of baseball's color line was a triumph of social protest in the pre-King era, not of enlightened capitalists. As historian Jules Tygiel explains in *Baseball's Great Experiment,* the Negro press, civil rights groups, and progressive whites waged a sustained campaign to integrate baseball that involved demonstrations, boycotts, political maneuvering, and other forms of pressure that would gain greater currency the following decade. Martin Luther King once told Dodgers pitcher Don Newcombe, "You'll never know what you and Jackie and Roy [Campanella] did to make it possible to do my job."

Dodger general manager Branch Rickey selected Robinson to break the sport's color barrier as much for his personal characteristics as for his baseball skill. He could have chosen other Negro League players with greater talent or name recognition, but he wanted someone who today we call a "role model." He knew that if the "experiment" failed, the cause of baseball integration would be set back for many years. Robinson was well-educated and articulate, born in the segregated deep South, but raised among whites in Southern California.

Rickey knew that Robinson had a hot temper and strong political views. As an Army officer in World War II, Robinson was courtmartialed (although later acquitted) for resisting bus segregation at Ft. Hood, Texas. Rickey calculated that Robinson could handle the emotional pressure while helping the Dodgers on the field. Robinson promised Rickey he wouldn't respond to the inevitable verbal barbs and even physical abuse.

Rickey could not count on the other owners or most players to support his plan. But the Robinson experiment succeeded—on the field and at the box office. The Dodgers soon hired other blacks who helped turn the 1950s club into one of baseball's greatest teams. But as late as 1953, only six of the then-16 major league teams had black players. It wasn't until 1959 that the last hold out, the Boston Red Sox, hired a black player. Today Black and Latino players are well represented. The Cleveland Indians hired the first black manager, Frank Robinson, in 1975; today there are four.

Robinson's achievement did more than change the way baseball is played and who plays it. His actions on and off the diamond helped pave the way for America to confront its racial hypocrisy. The dignity with which Robinson handled his encounters with racism among fellow players and fans drew public attention to the issue, stirred the consciences of many white Americans, and gave black Americans a tremendous boost of pride and self-confidence.

By hiring Robinson, the Dodgers earned the loyalty not only of blacks but also among many white Americans—most fiercely American Jews—who believed that integrating our national pastime was a critical steppingstone to tearing down many other obstacles to equal opportunity.

After Robinson had established himself as a superstar, Rickey gave him the green light to unleash his temper. On the field, he fought constantly with umpires and opposing players. Off the field, he was outspoken—in speeches, interviews, and his newspaper column—against racial injustice. He viewed his sports celebrity as a platform from which to challenge American racism. Many sportswriters and most other players—including some of his fellow black players, content simply to be playing in the majors—considered Robinson too angry and vocal.

Until his death, Robinson continued speaking out. He was one of the NAACP's best fundraisers, but resigned in 1967, criticizing the organization for its failure to involve "younger, more progressive voices." He pushed major league baseball to hire blacks as managers and executives and even refused an invitation to an Old Timers game, "until I see genuine interest in breaking the barriers that deny access to managerial and front office positions."

When Robinson retired from baseball, no team offered him a position as a manager, coach or executive. He joined the business world and became an advocate for integrating corporate America. His initial faith in free enterprise led Robinson into several controversial political alliances, including a 1960 endorsement of Richard Nixon—a stance he later regretted.

Baseball has changed dramatically since Robinson's day. Then, baseball had little competition from other sports for fan loyalty. Subject to the feudal reserve clause, players remained with the same teams for years, binding them to local fans. Most players' salaries were not much higher than those of average workers; indeed, players lived in the same neighborhoods as their fans. Sportswriters rarely probed players' personal lives or potential scandals, allowing athletes to become All-American heroes. Today, the public is angry with both spoiled million-dollar players and greedy owners. Teams are no longer family businesses, but owned by corporate conglomerates. Baseball is now beset by strikes and footloose teams threatening to move unless cities build tax-funded megastadiums.

The celebration of Robinson's achievement comes as Americans, disenchanted with the current corporatization of baseball, are awash in baseball nostalgia. His saga offers America a chance to remind disillusioned fans about a time when baseball occupied the nation's moral high ground and helped move the country closer to its ideals. But Robinson's legacy is also to remind us of the unfinished agenda of the civil rights revolution.

Chapter 89

Paul Robeson and the House Un-American Activities Committee

The Red Scare and its advocates, such as the House Un-American Activities Committee (HUAC), narrowed political debate, silencing alternatives offered by the left, postponing the civil rights movement, and severing its links to anti-colonial struggles.

Paul Robeson (1898–1976), the son of a former slave, was born in Princeton, N.J. He was the third black student to attend Rutgers, the state university, where he set records in football and was twice voted All-American. Robeson was also a baseball and track and field star, a debater, class valedictorian, and a Phi Beta Kappa member. His senior thesis on the unenforced Fourteenth Amendment was entitled "The Sleeping Giant." Finding racial barriers in the field of law after graduating from Columbia University, Robeson went on to a blazingly successful international career as a singer and actor. In the 1940s he was one of the most prominent and popular performers in the United States. Politically outspoken, Robeson was a strong supporter of labor, civil rights, and other progressive, domestic, and international causes. Despite his enormous fame, Robeson's career and reputation were largely erased by McCarthyism. He is almost unknown today.

Robeson's autobiography was entitled Here I Stand *(1958). For a collection of his speeches and writings, see* Paul Robeson Speaks *(1978).*

The following selection is excerpted from Hearings before the Committee on Un-American Activities, House of Representatives, 84th Congress, Second Session, June 12, 1956. *For the full text of Robeson's testimony, see* Paul Robeson Speaks, *ed. Philip Foner (New York: Citadel, 1978).*

For more on Robeson, see Martin Duberman, Paul Robeson: A Biography *(1989) and Jeffrey C. Stewart, ed.,* Paul Robeson: Artist and Citizen *(1998).*

A Subcommittee of the Committee on Un-American Activities convened at 10 A.M., in the caucus room of the Old House Office Building, the Honorable Francis E. Walter (Chairman) presiding.

Committee members present: Representatives Francis E. Walter of Pennsylvania, Clyde Doyle of California, Bernard W. Kearney of New York, and Gordon H. Scherer of Ohio.

Staff members present: Richard Arens, Director, and Donald T. Appell, Investigator.

The Chairman: The Committee will be in order. This morning the Committee resumes its series of hearings on the vital issue of the use of American passports as travel documents in furtherance of the objectives of the Communist conspiracy. . . .

Mr. Arens: Paul Robeson, will you please come forward? Please identify yourself by name, residence and occupation.

Mr. Robeson: My name is Paul Robeson. I live at 16 Jumel Terrace, New York City, and I am an actor and singer by occupation, and law on the side now and then. . . .

Mr. Arens: Are you now a member of the Communist Party?

Mr. Robeson: Oh please, please, please.

Mr. Scherer: Please answer, will you, Mr. Robeson?

Mr. Robeson: What is the Communist Party? What do you mean by that?

Mr. Scherer: I ask that you direct the witness to answer the question.

Mr. Robeson: What do you mean by the Communist Party? As far as I know it is a legal party like the Republican Party and the Democratic Party. Do you mean—which, belonging to a party of Communists or belonging to a party of people who have sacrificed for my people and for all Americans and workers, that they can live in dignity? Do you mean that party?

Mr. Arens: Are you now a member of the Communist Party?

Mr. Robeson: Would you like to come to the ballot box when I vote and take out the ballot and see? . . .

Mr. Robeson: To whom am I talking . . . ?

The Chairman: You are speaking to the chairman of this committee.

Mr. Robeson: Mr. Walter?

The Chairman: Yes.

Mr. Robeson: The Pennsylvania Walter?

The Chairman: That is right.

Mr. Robeson: Representative of the steelworkers?

The Chairman: That is right.

Mr. Robeson: Of the coal mining workers and not United States Steel, by any chance? A great patriot.

The Chairman: That is right.

Mr. Robeson: You are the author of all of the bills that are going to keep all kinds of decent people out of the country.

The Chairman: No, only your kind.

Mr. Robeson: Colored people like myself, from the West Indies and all kinds, and just the Teutonic Anglo-Saxon stock that you would let come in.

The Chairman: We are trying to make it easier to get rid of your kind, too.

Mr. Robeson: You do not want any colored people to come in?

The Chairman: Proceed. . . .

Mr. Robeson: Could I say that . . . the reason I am here today, you know, from the mouth of the State Department itself, is because I should not be allowed to travel because I have struggled for years for the independence of the colonial peoples of Africa, and for many years I have so labored and I can say modestly that my name is very much honored in South Africa and all over Africa in my struggles for their independence. That is the kind of independence like Sukarno got in Indonesia. Unless we are double-talking, then these efforts in the interest of Africa would be in the same context. The other reason that I am here today is again from the State Department and from the court record of the Court of Appeals, that when I am abroad I speak out against the injustices against the Negro people of this land. I sent a message to the Bandung Conference and so forth. That is why I am here. This is the basis and I am not being tried for whether I am a Communist, I am being tried for fighting for the rights of my people who are still second-class citizens in this United States of America. My mother was born in your State, Mr. Walter, and my mother was a Quaker, and my ancestors in the time of Washington baked bread for George Washington's troops when they crossed the Delaware, and my own father was a slave. I stand here struggling for the rights of my people to be full citizens in this country and they are not. They are not in Mississippi and they are not in Montgomery, Ala. and they are not in Washington, and they are nowhere, and that is why I am here today. You want to shut up every Negro who has the courage to stand up and fight for the rights of his people, for the rights of workers and I have been on many a picket line for the steelworkers too. And that is why I am here today.

The Chairman: Now just a minute.

Mr. Robeson: All of this is nonsense.

The Chairman: You ought to read Jackie Robinson's testimony.

Mr. Robeson: I know Jackie Robinson, and I am sure that in his heart he would take back a lot of what he said about any reference to me. I was one of the last people, Mr. Walter, to speak to [the Commissioner of Baseball] Judge [Kenesaw Mountain] Landis, to see that Jackie Robinson had a chance to play baseball. Get the pictures and get the record. I was taken by Landis by the hand, and I addressed the combined owners of the American and National Leagues, pleading for Robinson to be able to play baseball like I played professional football. . . .

Mr. Robeson: I would say that in Russia I felt for the first time like a full human being, and no colored prejudice like in Mississippi and no colored prejudice like in Washington and it was the first time I felt like a human being, where I did not feel the pressure of color as I feel in this committee today.

Mr. Scherer: Why do you not stay in Russia?

Mr. Robeson: Because my father was a slave, and my people died to build this country, and I am going to stay here and have a part of it just like you. And no Fascist-minded people will drive me from it. Is that clear? I am for peace with the Soviet Union and I am for peace with China, and I am not for peace or friendship with the Fascist Franco, and I am not for peace with Fascist Nazi Germans, and I am for peace with decent people in the world.

Mr. Scherer: The reason you are here is because you are promoting the Communist cause in this country

Mr. Robeson: I am here because I am opposing the neo-Facist cause which I see arising in these committees. You are like the [18th Century] Alien [and] Sedition Act, and [Thomas] Jefferson could be sitting here, and Frederick Douglass could be sitting here and Eugene Debs could be here.

The Chairman: Are you going to answer the questions?

Mr. Robeson: I am answering them.

The Chairman: What is your answer to this question?

Mr. Robeson: I have answered the question. . . .

The Chairman: Now, what prejudice are you talking about? You were graduated from Rutgers and you were graduated from the University of Pennsylvania. I remember seeing you play football at Lehigh.

Mr. Robeson: We beat Lehigh.

The Chairman: And we had a lot of trouble with you.

Mr. Robeson: That is right. DeWysocki was playing in my team.

The Chairman: There was no prejudice against you. Why did you not send your son to Rutgers?

Mr. Robeson: Just a moment. It all depends a great deal. This is something that I challenge very deeply, and very sincerely, the fact that the success of a few Negroes, including myself or Jackie Robinson can make up—and here is a study from Columbia University—for $700 a year for thousands of Negro families in the South. My father was a slave, and I have cousins who are sharecroppers and I do not see my success in terms of myself. That is the reason, my own success has not meant what it should mean. I have sacrificed literally hundreds of thousands, if not millions, of dollars for what I believe in. . . .

The Chairman: Now I would invite your attention, if you please, to the *Daily Worker* of June 29, 1949, with reference to a get-together with you and [New York City Councilman and Communist Party member] Ben Davis. Do you know Ben Davis?

Mr. Robeson: One of my dearest friends, one of the finest Americans you can imagine, born of a fine family, who went to Amherst [College] and was a great man.

The Chairman: The answer is "Yes"?

Mr. Robeson: And a very great friend and nothing could make me prouder than to know him.

The Chairman: That answers the question.

Mr. Arens: Did I understand you to laud his patriotism?

Mr. Robeson: I say that he is as patriotic an American as there can be, and you gentlemen belong with the Alien and Sedition Acts, and you are the nonpatriots, and you are the un-Americans and you ought to be ashamed of yourselves.

The Chairman: Just a minute, the hearing is now adjourned.

Mr. Robeson: I should think it would be.

The Chairman: I have endured all of this that I can.

Mr. Robeson: Can I read my statement?

The Chairman: No, you cannot read it. The meeting is adjourned.

Mr. Robeson: I think it should be and you should adjourn this forever, that is what I would say.

The Chairman: We will convene at 2 o'clock this afternoon.

Mr. Friedman: Will the statement be accepted for the record without being read?

The Chairman: No, it will not.

Chapter 90

The Highlander School

Myles Horton

Myles Horton (1905–1990) was the founder and director of the Highlander Folk School, a radical adult education center that has played a major role in the labor and civil rights movements since 1932. Horton is the author (with Judith Kohl and Herbert Kohl) of The Long Haul: An Autobiography *(1990) and co-author with Paulo Freire of* We Make the Road by Walking: Conversations on Education and Social Change *(1990).*

The following selection, originally entitled "Thou Shall Not Teach," is excerpted from It Happened Here: Recollections of Political Repression in America, *ed. Bud Schultz and Ruth Schultz (Berkeley: University of California Press, 1989), 23–24, 27, 28–33. Copyright © 1989 The Regents of the University of California.*

I grew up in a religious background, like most people in the South. And poor. We were living in the country, sharecropping. I had to start work away from home when I was fifteen. I wanted to do something in the way of education, and I assumed I could get a job in the mountains in some kind of college or high school. I wanted my teaching to have to do with helping people live a more creative life. I also wanted to help people deal with economic problems, because it was such a poor area.

There were no examples or models of the education I had in mind. After I spent about five years trying to find them, including visiting schools in this country and other countries, I decided that the best thing to do was to think through the principles I believed in, set up a school that would enable me to teach that way, and then get a job teaching in it. That's how the Highlander Folk School came about, in 1932.

Highlander was located in Grundy County, one of the eleven poorest counties in the United States. We used education as a way of organizing. We made it clear that we weren't bringing people together to tell them what to do. We had confidence in their ability to share their experiences and learn from each other and learn to trust their own judgment. That's pretty much what Highlander has always done. And we did organize. We had eighty percent of the adult population in that county in unions of one kind or another—women, men, everybody. . . .

By the time the CIO was formed, Highlander had more contacts in the South than anybody else. They asked us for organizers, and we recommended people for most of their key jobs. When the CIO organized unions, they sent their members to Highlander for training, because that's where they got their ideas and they liked our way of working. Pretty soon Highlander became the educational center of the CIO in the South. . . .

During the McCarthy period, the Senate Internal Security Subcommittee, which was run by Senator James Eastland, was investigating those of us who were working with Blacks. They were trying to harass us and make charges of communism to scare Black people away so they wouldn't associate with us. When I was called before the committee in 1954, they wanted me to name names of people who had been at Highlander and who had been associated with me in various activities. I refused to do that. I told them I'd be glad to answer any questions about myself, because I never had any problem talking about what I believe. In fact, I spent my life talking about what I believe. But I wouldn't talk about anybody else.

I'd learned from my good friend [civil libertarian] Alexander Meiklejohn that when this country was born, all power was vested in the people. They had taken power away from the British and had it in their hands. The people had to decide what to do with that power. So they decided to delegate some of it to a federal government and some to state governments. But there was one power that they never delegated to the state or federal government. That was the power of freedom of speech and of petition. They said, "We'll keep that to ourselves. That's something we're not going to let anybody handle."

So I said to the Eastland Committee, "I still have that, I have that power that was never delegated to you or anybody else, and I am going to exercise it. If the freedom to speak means anything, it means the freedom not to speak. Because if you can make me speak, if you can tell me what to say, then I have no freedom. That's the power over which your committee has no jurisdiction. It's just up to me and my conscience."

Eastland got furious: "I'm going to cite you for contempt if you don't answer the questions." And I said, "I don't see that that will be much of a problem, senator. I'm willing to testify that I'm in contempt of this committee. I'm in contempt of you and everything you stand for." And he said, "Throw him out!" I was picked up by a couple of federal marshals and thrown down on the marble steps of the court of justice.

We had come to the conclusion that we couldn't make much headway working toward democracy without dealing with the problem of racism. Out of that kind of thinking another Highlander program grew. Most of the people who became leaders of the Student Nonviolent Coordinating Committee attended Highlander workshops. We also developed the Citizenship School Program, which spread all over the South. It finally became the official program of the Southern Christian Leadership Conference.

We had the same experience with the civil rights movement we had with the CIO. People who had already been to Highlander became leaders of the civil rights movement, so Highlander was kind of on the inside. Rosa Parks started things off in Montgomery by refusing to get off her seat on the bus. That wasn't just one of those fluke things. For a Black person to violate the law and custom, to carry out an act of civil disobedience, takes a lot of thinking and courage. It isn't just something somebody does incidentally.

A Black labor organizer in Montgomery, E. D. Nixon, a Pullman porter, immediately took that situation and organized it. It took what Rosa Parks and E. D. Nixon did to lay the basis for the great bus boycott in Montgomery. Then Martin Luther King, Jr., joined in and became the leader everyone knows about.

Fortunately, the Communist issue was never a big issue in the civil rights movement. It was an issue for some northern supporters, liberals, but not in the South, not with SNCC, and not with the Southern Christian Leadership Conference. King would just not allow it. He knew it could be the most divisive thing that could happen to the movement.

But the opposition tried. The governor of Georgia appropriated money to send an undercover photographer, a man named Ed Friend, to take pictures of Highlander's twenty-fifth anniversary in 1957. He took a whole lot of them. These were pictures of Blacks and whites swimming together, Blacks and whites dancing together, eating together, meeting together, and so on. They put one of those pictures on billboards all over the South, captioned "Highlander, A Communist Training School." The John Birch Society and the Governor's Committee of the State of Georgia put them out. They claimed that they spent over a million dollars on billboards. The picture had Martin Luther King, Jr., Rosa Parks, Aubrey Williams, and Septima Clark and me and other people in the front row. And Pete Seeger's elbow. Pete said he came within an elbow's distance of being in the famous picture.

That picture was used all over the South to discredit King and the civil rights movement. FBI Director J. Edgar Hoover said that King was connected to Highlander, and Highlander was Communist, therefore King was Communist. When the local FBI office in Atlanta told him Highlander wasn't Communist, Hoover said, "Well, King is Communist, and that proves Highlander is Communist." You could have it either way.

In Tennessee, the opposition tried to close Highlander down at a committee hearing of the state legislature in Nashville. Ed Friend, the Georgia governor's undercover photographer, was at the hearing. He made some interesting statements. He said that integration is communism and it's against our way of life. He said that he could prove it, and he showed all those pictures he took at our twenty-fifth anniversary. I said, "They are good pictures, and we're very proud of them." I offered to buy them from him.

At the same hearing, they tried to prove that Highlander was Communist through guilt by association. They said such and such a person was accused of being a Communist, and they wrote his name on the blackboard. Somebody else was accused, and they put that name up. All the names of the people who were activists in the South and trying to bring about racial equality and organize labor unions were put on the blackboard. Then they wrote Highlander in the middle, and they drew lines from Highlander to all these people. They'd ask me these questions: "Do you know these people? Did you help organize this?" I answered yes to all their questions, Highlander was involved with everybody on that list, one way or another.

"Now," they said, "we have proof that some of these people are Communists. Look at this drawing. Doesn't it prove that Highlander is Communist?" And I said, "Well, it only proves that you can write names on a blackboard and draw lines between them." They were fit to be tied.

Later on, they used more sophisticated ways of trying to do Highlander in. It started with a raid on Highlander while I was at a conference in Europe, but that didn't keep them from charging me with walking around the lake at Highlander that night with my one arm around a Black woman and a bottle of beer in my hand. The fact that I had a passport showing that I was out of the country at that time didn't cut any ice with the court. Well, if you think that's being framed, I was arrested once for drunken driving when I wasn't drunk and I wasn't driving.

The night of the raid in July 1959 was the night that one of the verses of "We Shall Overcome" was born. A group of young people, a youth choir from Reverend Seay's church in Montgomery, was at Highlander. He thought it would be good for them to know there were white people that they could deal with as equals. Suddenly, raiders came in with flashlights. They must have been vigilantes and some police officers, but they weren't in uniform. They demanded the lights be turned on, but they couldn't get anybody at Highlander to do it. They were furious, you know, running around with flashlights. In the meantime, the kids started to sing "We Shall Overcome." It made them feel good. The raiders yelled, "Shut up and turn on the lights!" Then some kid said, "We're not afraid." Then they started singing, "We are not afraid. We are not afraid." That's when that verse was born, the night of the raid.

Recently, we had some visitors at Highlander from Ireland. They said the Irish were singing "We Shall Overcome" there. The verse "We are not afraid" was used more than any other because the Irish were trying to say they were not afraid of the British army. And that came out of those kids at Highlander the night of the raid. So there was both civil disobedience history and music history made that night.

Three staff members at Highlander were arrested and charged with serving liquor and drinking. It was a church group. Mrs. Septima Clark, who was arrested, is a great Methodist leader who doesn't drink. And Guy Carawan is a folk singer who doesn't drink. The other guy who was arrested didn't drink either. They arrested three people who didn't drink on the charge of serving liquor. The raid was to set up the legal situation so they could void our charter and confiscate our property. The people who opposed us had to have a technical way of getting a case against us into the courts.

It took two years to get the prosecution witnesses to memorize their stories, and even then they got mixed up at the trial. They didn't have a single witness, not one witness, who wasn't forced to testify because their sons were in prison or they were facing charges themselves or their husbands were up on charges. They promised these people to let their kids out of reform school, to drop charges against them, and to pay them if they testified. And even though a lot of them got their testimony mixed up, the judge and jury didn't object.

Finally, through a series of clever plans that were evidently agreed on in advance by the state supreme court and the district judges, they were able to get a conviction on technicalities with which they could void our charter and confiscate our property. Which they did. Highlander was found guilty of selling beer without a license.

The judge said that if there are three people in a room and one goes out and gets three bottles of beer and brings them back, and the other two give him a quarter apiece, legally he's selling beer and he has to have a license. He used that as an example. He said that Highlander did that. People at Highlander did do that when union workshops were in session. They did it because they didn't want to go in town to a white-only bar and leave the Blacks behind. Well, that was one of the technicalities on which we were charged and convicted.

The other technicality was that I had set up Highlander so I could use it for personal gain. The jury agreed that I hadn't used it for personal gain yet, but I was going to and had set it up in such a way that "when the melon got big," I was "going to cut the melon." So I was convicted of going to cut the melon when the melon got big—that I was going to do something, not that I *did* anything.

What really bothered them was that Highlander was integrated. Integration was against the Tennessee law until just a few years ago. We violated that law for forty-six years. That was the basis for confiscating the property, the basis for lawsuits, for everything else. But we just kept on violating it as an act of civil disobedience. We had no intention of stopping. After they confiscated our property, we reorganized, set up a new school, and kept violating the same law. We violated it until the state repealed it.

Chapter 91

If the Negro Wins, Labor Wins

Martin Luther King, Jr.

Martin Luther King, Jr. (1929–1968), the son and maternal grandson of Baptist ministers, was born in Atlanta, Georgia. He studied for the ministry at Crozer Theological Seminary and received his Ph.D. in theology from Boston University. Soon after taking on his first pulpit, he achieved national prominence, at age 26, as a result of his role in the Montgomery Bus Boycott (see chapter 94) and his strong advocacy of nonviolent civil disobedience. In 1957 King co-founded the Southern Christian Leadership Conference (SCLC), which organized throughout the South and eventually expanded into the North. In 1964 he was awarded the Nobel Peace Prize. He later became an outspoken critic of the War in Vietnam. Through much of his career he was under surveillance by the FBI. At the end of his life King called for an Economic Bill of Rights and a Poor People's Campaign (see chapter 119). He was in Memphis to support city sanitation workers striking for union recognition, when he was assassinated on 4 April 1968.

King's books include Stride toward Freedom *(1958),* Why We Can't Wait *(1964), and* Where Do We Go from Here? *(1967). For his complete writings, see Clayborne Carson, ed.,* The Papers of Martin Luther King, Jr. *(in progress, 1992–). The best one-volume collection is James Washington, ed.,* A Testament of Hope *(1986). For biographical studies, see Taylor Branch,* America in the King Years *(3 vols., in progress, 1988–), David Garrow,* Bearing the Cross *(1986), and Adam Fairclough,* To Redeem the Soul of America *(1987).*

The following selection is reprinted from Martin Luther King, "If the Negro Wins, Labor Wins," 11 December 1961. Reprinted by arrangement with The Heirs to the Estate of Martin Luther King, Jr., c/o Writers House, Inc. as agent for the proprietor. Copyright © 1961 by Martin Luther King, Jr., copyright renewed 1989 The Estate of Martin Luther King, Jr.

For other selections by King, see chapters 95, 102, and 106.

Martin Luther King presented the following address to a meeting of the AFL-CIO in Bal Harbour, Florida, in 1961.

Less than a century ago the laborer had no rights, little or no respect, and led a life which was socially submerged and barren.

He was hired and fired by economic despots whose power over him decreed his life or death. The children of workers had no childhood and no future. They, too, worked for pennies an hour and by the time they reached their teens they were worn-out old men, devoid of spirit, devoid of hope and devoid of self-respect. Jack London described a child worker in these words: "He did not walk like a man. He did not look like a man. He was a travesty of the human. It was a twisted and stunted and nameless piece of life that shambled like a sickly ape, arms loose-hanging, stoop-shouldered, narrow-chested, grotesque and terrible."

American industry organized misery into sweatshops and proclaimed the right of capital to act without restraints and without conscience.

Victor Hugo, literary genius of that day, commented bitterly that there was always more misery in the lower classes than there was humanity in the upper classes. The inspiring answer to this intolerable and dehumanizing existence was economic organization through trade unions. The worker became determined not to wait for charitable impulses to grow in his employer. He constructed the means by which a fairer sharing of the fruits of his toil had to be given to him or the wheels of industry, which he alone turned, would halt and wealth for no one would be available.

History Remembers

This revolution within industry was fought mercilessly by those who blindly believed their right to uncontrolled profits was a law of the universe, and that without the maintenance of the old order catastrophe faced the nation.

History is a great teacher. Now, every one knows that the labor movement did not diminish the strength of the nation but enlarged it. By raising the living standards of millions, labor miraculously created a market for industry and lifted the whole nation to undreamed levels of production. Those who today attack labor forget these simple truths, but history remembers them.

Labor's next monumental struggle emerged in the thirties when it wrote into federal law the right freely to organize and bargain collectively. It was now apparently emancipated. The days when workers were jailed for organizing, and when in the English Parliament Lord Macaulay had to debate against a bill decreeing the death penalty for anyone engaging in a strike, were grim but almost forgotten memories.

Yet, the Wagner Act, like any other legislation, tended merely to declare rights but did not deliver them. Labor had to bring the law to life by exercising its rights in practice over stubborn, tenacious opposition. It was warned to go slow, to be moderate, not to stir up strife. But labor knew it was always the right time to do right, and it spread its organization over the nation and achieved equality organizationally with capital. The day of economic democracy was born.

Negroes in the United States read this history of labor and find it mirrors their own experience. We are confronted by powerful forces telling us to rely on the good will and understanding of those who profit by exploiting us. They deplore our discontent, they resent our will to organize, so that we may guarantee that humanity will prevail and equality will be exacted. They are shocked that action organizations, sit-ins, civil disobedience, and protests are becoming our everyday tools, just as strikes, demonstrations and union organization became yours to insure that bargaining power genuinely existed on both sides of the table.

We want to rely upon the good will of those who oppose us. Indeed, we have brought forward the method of nonviolence to give an example of unilateral good will in an effort to evoke it in those who have not yet felt it in their hearts. But we know that if we are not simultaneously organizing our strength we will have no means to move forward. If we do not advance, the crushing burden of centuries of neglect and economic deprivation will destroy our will, our spirits and our hopes. In this way labor's historic tradition of moving forward to create vital people as consumers and citizens has become our own tradition, and for the same reasons.

This unity of purpose is not an historical coincidence. Negroes are almost entirely a working people. There are pitifully few Negro millionaires and few Negro employers. Our needs are identical with labor's needs: decent wages, fair working conditions, livable housing, old age security, health and welfare measures, conditions in which families can grow, have education for their children and respect in the community. That is why Negroes support labor's demands and fight laws which curb labor. That is why the labor-hater and labor-baiter is virtually always a twin-headed creature spewing anti-Negro epithets from one mouth and anti-labor propaganda from the other mouth.

The duality of interests of labor and Negroes makes any crisis which lacerates you a crisis from which we bleed. As we stand on the threshold of the second half of the twentieth century, a crisis confronts us both. Those who in the second half of the nineteenth century could not tolerate organized labor have had a rebirth of power and seek to regain the despotism of that era while retaining the wealth and privileges of the twentieth century. Whether it be the ultra-right wing in the form of [John] Birch societies or the alliance which former President Eisenhower denounced, the alliance between big military and big industry, or the coalition of southern dixiecrats and northern reactionaries, whatever the form, these menaces now threaten everything decent and fair in American life.

Their target is labor, liberals, and the Negro people, not scattered "reds" or even Justice Warren, former presidents Eisenhower and Truman and President Kennedy, who are in truth beyond the reach of their crude and vicious falsehoods.

Labor today faces a grave crisis, perhaps the most calamitous since it began its march from the shadows of want and insecurity. In the next ten to twenty years automation will grind jobs into dust as it grinds out unbelievable volumes of production. This period is made to order for those who would seek to drive labor into impotency by viciously attacking it at every point of weakness.

Labor's True Friends

Hard-core unemployment is now an ugly and unavoidable fact of life. Like malignant cancer, it has grown year by year and continues its spread. But automation can be used to generate an abundance of wealth for people or an abundance of poverty for millions as its human-like machines turn out human scrap along with machine scrap as a by-product of production. Our society, with its ability to perform miracles with machinery, has the capacity to make some miracles for men— if it values men as highly as it values machines.

To find a great design to solve a grave problem labor will have to intervene in the political life of the nation to chart a course which distributes the abundance to all instead of concentrating it among a few. The strength to carry through such a program requires that labor know its friends and collaborate as a friend. If all that I have said is sound, labor has no firmer friend than the twenty million Negroes whose lives will be deeply affected by the new patterns of production.

To say that we are friends would be an empty platitude if we fail to behave as friends and honestly look to weaknesses in our relationship. Unfortunately there are weaknesses. Labor has not adequately used its great power, its vision and resources to advance Negro rights. Undeniably it has done more than other forces in American society to this end. Aid from real friends in labor has often come when the flames of struggle heighten. But Negroes are a solid component within the labor movement and a reliable bulwark for labor's whole program, and should expect more from it exactly as a member of a family expects more from his relatives than he expects from his neighbors.

Labor, which made impatience for long-delayed justice for itself a vital motive force, cannot lack understanding of the Negro's impatience. It cannot speak, with the reactionaries' calm indifference, of progress around some obscure corner not yet possible even to see. There is a maxim in the law—justice too long delayed, is justice denied. When a Negro leader who has a reputation of purity and honesty which has benefited the whole labor movement criticizes it, his motives should not be reviled nor his earnestness rebuked. Instead, the possibility that he is revealing a weakness in the labor movement which it can ill afford, should receive thoughtful examination. A man who has dedicated his long and faultless life to the labor movement cannot be raising questions harmful to it any more than a lifelong devoted parent can become the enemy of his child. The report of a committee may smother with legal constructions a list of complaints and dispose of it for the day. But if it buries a far larger truth it has disposed of nothing and made justice more elusive.

Bias Exists in Unions

Discrimination does exist in the labor movement. It is true that organized labor has taken significant steps to remove the yoke of discrimination from its own body. But in spite of this, some unions, governed by the racist ethos, have contributed to the degraded economic status of the Negro. Negroes have been barred from membership in certain unions, and denied apprenticeship training and vocational education. In every section of the country one can find local unions existing as a serious and vicious obstacle when the Negro seeks jobs or upgrading in employment. Labor must honestly admit these shameful conditions, and design the battle plan which will defeat and eliminate them. In this way, labor would be unearthing the big truth and utilizing its strength against the bleakness of injustice in the spirit of its finest traditions.

How can labor rise to the heights of its potential statesmanship and cement its bonds with Negroes to their mutual advantage?

First: Labor should accept the logic of its special position with respect to Negroes and the struggle for equality. Although organized labor has taken actions to eliminate discrimination in its ranks, it has not raised high enough the standard for the general community. Your conduct should and can set an example for others, as you have done in other crusades for social justice. You should root out vigorously every manifestation of discrimination so that some internationals, central labor bodies or locals may not besmirch the positive accomplishments of labor. I am aware this is not easy nor popular—but the eight-hour day was not popular nor easy to achieve. Nor was outlawing anti-labor injunctions. But you accomplished all of these with a massive will and determination. Out of such struggle for democratic rights you won both economic gains and the respect of the country, and you will win both again if you make Negro rights a great crusade.

Second: The political strength you are going to need to prevent automation from becoming a Moloch, consuming jobs and contract gains, can be multiplied if you tap the vast reservoir of Negro political power. Negroes, given the vote, will vote liberal and labor because they need the same liberal legislation labor needs.

To give just an example of the importance of the Negro vote to labor, I might cite the arresting fact that the only state in the South which repealed the right-to-work law is Louisiana. This was achieved because the Negro vote in that state grew large enough to become a balance of power, and it went along with labor to wipe out anti-labor legislation. Thus, support to assist us in securing the vote can make the difference between success and defeat for us both. You have organizing experience we need and you have an apparatus unparalleled in the nation. You recognized five years ago a moral opportunity and responsibility when several of your leaders, including Mr. Meany, Mr. Dubinsky, Mr. Reuther and Mr. MacDonald and others, projected a two million dollar campaign to assist the struggling Negroes fighting bitterly in handicapped circumstances in the South. A ten-thousand dollar contribution was voted by the ILGWU to begin the drive, but for reasons unknown to me, the drive was never begun. The cost to us in lack of resources during these turbulent, violent years, is hard to describe. We are mindful that many unions thought of as immorally rich, in truth have problems in meeting the budget to properly service their members. So we do not ask that you tax your treasuries. Instead, we ask that you appeal to your members for one dollar apiece to make democracy real for millions of deprived American citizens. For this you have the experience, the organization and most of all, the understanding.

If you would do these two things now in this convention—resolve to deal effectively with discrimination and provide financial aid for our struggle in the South—this convention will have a glorious moral deed to add to an illustrious history.

The two most dynamic and cohesive liberal forces in the country are the labor movement and the Negro freedom movement. Together we can be architects of democracy in a South now rapidly industrializing. Together we can retool the political structure of the South, sending to Congress steadfast liberals who, joining with those from northern industrial states, will extend the frontiers of democracy for the whole nation. Together we can bring about the day when there will be no separate identification of Negroes and labor.

There is no intrinsic difference, as I have tried to demonstrate. Differences have been contrived by outsiders who seek to impose disunity by dividing brothers because the color of their skin has a different shade. I look forward confidently to the day when all who work for a living will be one with no thought to their separateness as Negroes, Jews, Italians or any other distinctions.

This will be the day when we shall bring into full realization the American dream—a dream yet unfilled. A dream of equality of opportunity, of privilege and property widely distributed; a dream of a land where men will not take necessities from the many to give luxuries to the few; a dream of a land where men will not argue that the color of a man's skin determines the content of his character; a dream of a nation where all our gifts and resources are held not for ourselves alone but as instruments of service for the rest of humanity; the dream of a country where every man will respect the dignity and worth of human personality—that is the dream.

We Shall Overcome

And as we struggle to make racial and economic justice a reality, let us maintain faith in the future. We will confront difficulties and frustrating moments in the struggle to make justice a reality, but we must believe somehow that these problems can be solved.

There is a little song that we sing in the movement taking place in the South. It goes like this, "We shall overcome. We shall overcome." Deep in my heart I do believe we shall overcome. And somehow all over America we must believe that we shall overcome and that these problems can be solved. They will be solved before the victory is won.

Some of us will have to get scarred up, but we shall overcome. Before the victory of justice is a reality, some may even face physical death. But if physical death is the price that some must pay to free their children and their brothers from a permanent life of psychological death, then nothing could be more moral. Before the victory is won more will have to go to jail. We must be willing to go to jail and transform the jails from dungeons of shame to havens of freedom and human dignity. Yes, before the victory is won, some will be misunderstood. Some will be dismissed as dangerous rabble-rousers and agitators. Some will be called reds and Communists merely because they believe in economic justice and the brotherhood of man. But we shall overcome.

Brotherhood of Man

I am convinced that we shall overcome because the arc of the universe is long but it bends toward justice. We shall overcome because Carlyle is right when he says, "No lie can live forever." We shall overcome because William Cullen Bryant is right when he says, "Truth crushed to earth will rise again." We shall overcome because James Russell Lowell was right when he proclaimed: "Truth forever on the scaffold, wrong forever on the throne, yet that scaffold sways the future."

And so if we will go out with this faith and with this determination to solve these problems, we will bring into being that new day and that new America. When that day comes, the fears of insecurity and the doubts clouding our future will be transformed into radiant confidence, into glowing excitement to reach creative goals and into an abiding moral balance where the brotherhood of man will be undergirded by a secure and expanding prosperity for all.

Yes, this will be the day when all of God's children, black men, and white men, Jews and Gentiles, Protestants and Catholics, will be able to join hands all over this nation and sing in the words of the old Negro spiritual: "Free At Last, Free At Last. Thank God Almighty, We Are Free At Last."

Chapter 92

CORE and the Pacifist Roots of Civil Rights

Milton Viorst

Milton Viorst, a contributing correspondent to the Washington Quarterly, *previously worked as a reporter for the* Bergen Record, Newark Star Ledger, *and* Washington Post *and as the Washington correspondent for the* New York Post *and as a staff writer for the* New Yorker. *Viorst has written several books on national and international politics.*

The following selection is excerpted from Fire in the Streets: America in the 1960s *(New York: Simon and Schuster, 1979), 133–39. Copyright © 1979 by Milton Viorst. Reprinted with the permission of The Wylie Agency, Inc.*

James Farmer became national director of CORE on February 1, 1961, a few days after Kennedy's inauguration. His selection represented a decision by CORE to embark on a militant direct action campaign. CORE had pioneered in the strategy of nonviolence in the 1940s, but throughout the decade of the 1950s little had been heard of the organization. During the Montgomery bus boycott King drew on CORE's experience, and during the sit-ins CORE came alive again with field counseling throughout the South. Now CORE, aroused by the times and challenged by SCLC, wanted to reassert its eminence. In choosing Farmer, CORE found a dynamic and eloquent leader with a long history in civil rights demonstrations. Farmer was impatient to get back into the battle.

Born in Texas in 1920, James Farmer was, like Martin Luther King, Jr., the son of a minister of the gospel. James Leonard Farmer, Sr., a Methodist, was no ordinary preacher, however. Long before blacks thought much about scholarship, the elder Farmer had acquired a doctorate of divinity at Boston University, where King acquired a doctorate many years later. An Old Testament scholar and a master of languages, Farmer's father would undoubtedly have held an esteemed pulpit, or a chair at a fine university, were he not black. Instead, he moved from one black college to another, culminating his career at Howard University in Washington, D.C. In a quiet college atmosphere, sheltered by books from a racist society that loomed beyond the walls, Jim Farmer grew up.

Farmer received his bachelor's degree from Wiley College in Marshall, Texas, and from there entered the divinity school at Howard to follow in his father's footsteps. But at Howard he found himself growing wary of the black church and was strongly influenced by critical interpretations by Max Weber and R. H. Tawney of Protestant orthodoxy. He wrote a thesis which held that the black clergy's function, intentional or not, was to preserve the dominant racial values of the society. Far from seeing black ministers as instruments of social change, Farmer ridiculed them for their dependence on segregation for their livelihood and status. As for the Methodist Church, in which he had been raised, it had recently been reorganized only to reaffirm its segregated structure, and Farmer felt deceived by it. In 1941, he received his degree in divinity from Howard but, to his father's dismay, he declined to be ordained.

I interviewed Farmer several times as he moved from job to job during the 1970s. Since the golden days of the civil rights movement, his career had had ups and downs, but he continued to work tirelessly for racial equality, in government and labor unions and foundations. Whenever I saw him, he was brimming with energy, and seemed still a bit disorganized, but he transmitted the restlessness of a young racehorse.

"Martin King and I saw the Church quite differently," Farmer said to me. "I must admit I was surprised at the extent to which the black church became involved in the civil rights battle, in Montgomery and after. I didn't realize how much the ministers had changed in the 1940s and 1950s, when I was out of contact with the South. During the Freedom Ride, CORE relied heavily on the black churches. But I can't take back the fact that I lost interest in the church very early. Faced with problems on this earth, I looked for answers in the secular world."

While he was still at Howard, Farmer's thinking had led him to the circle of Howard Thurman, a black professor of theology who was national vice-chairman of the Fellowship of Reconciliation. Since World War I, FOR had been a tiny flame that kept alive the radical ideals of Christian pacifism and racial equality. In 1940, A. J. Muste became FOR's chief executive, and brought with him Gandhian concepts of nonviolent direct action to apply to these ideals. Farmer became a part-time field organizer for FOR, and began to study Gandhi's lessons.

Meanwhile, World War II approached, and FOR's hope of finding "nonviolent alternatives" to the conflict faded. Most of FOR's members were conscientious objectors, despite their loathing for the racism of the Nazis, and many were to go to jail for their convictions. Farmer said he would have gone to prison himself, but for a black draft board in Washington which refused to prosecute him. Instead, at Muste's invitation, he went to Chicago to serve at FOR's headquarters as secretary for race relations. Serving with him on the staff was Bayard Rustin, FOR's secretary for youth.

Farmer said that, shortly after taking the job in Chicago, he sent Muste a memorandum proposing that FOR undertake a campaign against racial barriers, using Gandhi's techniques. Only the NAACP, working through the courts, had a civil rights program at that time. Not only was the NAACP's pace glacial, however, Farmer said, but its objectives, such as equal pay for black teachers in a segregated systems in the South, conveyed a reluctance to make a final break with the "separate but equal" doctrine. The NAACP did not take warmly to rivals in the field.

But Farmer said he thought the NAACP's methods were not working, and that it was time to experiment in nonviolent direct action.

In reply to Farmer's memo, Muste in 1940 authorized establishment of the Committee of Racial Equality, which was renamed the Congress of Racial Equality on becoming autonomous the following year. The name was chosen with the acronym CORE in mind, Farmer said, to present notice that the aim of its work was nothing less than the heart of racism. Administratively and financially, FOR was for many years the chief supporter of CORE. But because CORE rejected a permanent commitment to nonviolence, which Muste maintained and King would adopt many years later, Farmer said, it had to sever its official ties and establish an identity of its own.

"We dreamed of a mass movement," Farmer said, "and we did not think then that a revolution could be conducted by pacifists. For CORE, nonviolence was never more than a tactic. When a person participated in a CORE project, he was required to be nonviolent. But I agreed with Gandhi, and I quoted him as saying, 'I would rather have a man resist injustice with violence than fail to resist out of cowardice.' Nonviolence did not have to be the personal philosophy of a CORE member, and he could be quite violent in other circumstances if he chose."

CORE's first target in Chicago was a roller-skating rink which excluded blacks, several blocks from the Southside ghetto. He and an FOR band tried conscientiously to follow Gandhi's sequence of investigation, negotiation, publicity and finally, demonstration. But after the investigation, he said, the negotiation got nowhere, and the newspapers provided no publicity. For several months, however, CORE maintained picket lines at the rink, which brought business virtually to a halt, Farmer said, and at last management gave in.

It was an exhilarating moment for the members of the young organization, and America's first victory for Gandhian nonviolence. The second victory came in May 1943, when Chicago CORE conducted the first successful sit-in—still generally called, after labor movement tactics, a "sit-down"—against segregation at the Jack Spratt restaurant. By then, CORE chapters had been formed in at least seven Northern cities, and Farmer remembered that he was feeling extremely hopeful.

Farmer had nostalgia in his voice when he said, "We were young then, and we'd stay up all night planning and scheming. We really felt we were at the edge of a great wave."

Farmer was by now the national chairman of CORE but the members, as well as most of the leadership, were largely white. "The reaction of blacks when you said nonviolence in the 1940s and '50s," Farmer recalled, "was, you must be some kind of nut. Somebody's going to hit you and you're not going to hit back?" It was easier to find a few idealistic, well-educated whites and train them in nonviolence, he said, than to find blacks willing to go through the pain and humiliation of trying to integrate a restaurant. Farmer remembered that CORE by then had become not only three or four to one white, but increasingly elitist. It was also overwhelmingly Northern, having hardly penetrated the South at all.

Gradually, the early euphoria ebbed, Farmer said. The members tried Gandhi's techniques at swimming pools and theaters, as well as restaurants. They even made efforts to apply the method against segregated jobs and housing. But more often than not, encounters ended in defeat. The prospect of desegregating America restaurant by restaurant, theater by theater seemed hopeless. Momentum was absent, and what few victories CORE won gave no hint of the massive, nonviolent uprising of which its founders had dreamed.

"At one point, we wondered whether we had to give up the ghost," he said. "We weren't growing. We weren't getting any publicity. There seemed to be no interest in the black community. It was hard to keep the chapters alive." Finally, Farmer said, he and the others in CORE's tiny revolutionary band had to take nonrevolutionary jobs to earn a living.

CORE's most spectacular achievement during its early period was the Journey of Reconciliation in April 1947. Initiated by Bayard Rustin, it was conceived in response to the Supreme Court's *Irene Morgan* ruling that segregation on buses traveling interstate routes was unconstitutional. Rustin organized a contingent of eight blacks and eight whites to ride Greyhound and Trailways buses through Virginia, Kentucky and North Carolina to test the decision. They were, for the most part, highly disciplined, confirmed pacifists like himself. Before embarking on the trip, the volunteers received intensive training in responding nonviolently to the abuses they expected to receive from drivers, policemen and hostile crowds.

The NAACP opposed the Journey of Reconciliation, and Thurgood Marshall warned Southern blacks to keep their distance from the "well-meaning radical groups" that were headed their way. Nonetheless, the riders were warmly taken in by church and college groups, and even by NAACP chapters, along their route. The talks they gave to their hosts, and the considerable publicity received in the press, helped spread the name of CORE and the message of nonviolence.

In fact, the riders on the Journey of Reconciliation encountered relatively little abuse and virtually no violence. But their goals were modest. Since the Supreme Court, in the *Irene Morgan* decision, had not addressed itself to the issue of segregation within terminals, the volunteers tested desegregation only in the buses themselves. Furthermore, they limited their trip to the Upper South, knowing the greater dangers of the Deep South. Still, twelve arrests were made and, after all the appeals were exhausted, Rustin and two of his white companions served twenty-two days on a North Carolina road gang.

In his report on the Journey of Reconciliation to CORE and FOR, Rustin reaffirmed his belief that the NAACP's litigation strategy would leave segregation in the South untouched. "Without direct action on the part of groups and individuals," he wrote, "the Jim Crow pattern in the South cannot be broken." Rustin and his comrades were jailed for exercising a constitutional right, as defined by the *Irene Morgan* decision, and yet the federal government did nothing. It would take fourteen years and a major change in the social climate before blacks and whites were again willing to test their right to ride interstate buses through the South together—and some of them would be brutally beaten even then before the federal government came to their aid.

"In the 1940s, at every one of the annual CORE conventions," Jim Farmer said, "a motion would be made that we begin activities in the Deep South, try to start the nonviolent movement, with noncooperation and civil disobedience throughout the South. The motion was regularly defeated. As a matter of fact, I spoke against these motions on several occasions.

"My feeling in the 1940s was that there would have been lynchings, that we would have been killed right there on the spot. Even in the 1960s, Southern sheriffs were able to respond to nonviolent protest with police dogs and cattle prods, and in the 1940s, there was no supportive federal government to protect us, and no television to put it all on display before the country. We could very well have had a massacre."

Organizationally, CORE survived the 1940s and 1950s, but it had lost its earlier audacity. At the start of the 1960s, it was little known and without resources. Secular at its start, it had never expanded its Northern, predominantly white base, and it was ignored by Southern blacks. CORE was hardly in step in 1960 when the civil rights movement suddenly emerged from obscurity—church oriented, overwhelmingly Southern, popularly based, almost wholly black.

Yet what CORE had done through all these years was critical: it had kept alive the flame of an idea. The idea was of nonviolent direct action, which it had inherited from FOR, which in turn had acquired it from Gandhi. CORE had helped pass the idea on to King at Montgomery. Bayard Rustin was the most important figure in the transmission to King, but he was assisted by others who had continued to live with the heritage, including Farmer himself.

The Churches' Hour

Chapter 93

The Baton Rouge Bus Boycott

Aldon Morris

Popular histories of the civil rights movement often begin with the story of the Montgomery Bus Boycott, but Montgomery—despite its major role in the history of the movement—was neither the South's first bus boycott nor the origin of many of the tactics that have been claimed, as Aldon Morris, professor of sociology at Northwestern University, discusses.

The following selection is reprinted by permission of The Free Press, a Division of Simon & Schuster, from The Origins of the Civil Rights Movement: Black Communities Organizing for Change *by Aldon D. Morris. Copyright © 1984 by The Free Press.*

In Baton Rouge, the capital of Louisiana, the tripartite system of domination imposed on blacks was firmly in place in 1953. Under the Jim Crow system, every public bus had a "colored section" in the back and a "white section" in the front. If the white section filled up, blacks had to move farther toward the back, carrying with them the sign designating "colored." When blacks filled up the colored section, however, they had to stand even though seats in the white section were vacant. Most of the bus routes passed through the black community, which meant that the colored section was often full and the entire white section empty. In the heart of their own community, blacks had to stand over vacant seats designated for white passengers.

A Jim Crow bus was one of the few places in the South where blacks and whites were segregated under the same roof and in full view of each other. A segregated bus ride dramatized the painful humiliation of the Jim Crow system. White bus drivers often pulled away from a stop before blacks were seated, or even with a boarding black hanging half out of the bus. The Reverend T. J. Jemison, a black minister in Baton Rouge, recalls, "The Negro passenger had been molested and insulted and intimidated and all Negroes at that time were tired of segregation and mistreatment and injustice." Furthermore, the Baton Rouge bus company was overwhelmingly financed by blacks. Their fares accounted for at least two-thirds of the bus company's revenue. The practice of racial segregation on the bus was therefore an economically vulnerable enterprise.

In March of 1953 black leaders in Baton Rouge successfully petitioned the City

Council to pass an ordinance permitting blacks to be seated on a first-come-first-served basis. The only stipulation was that blacks had to sit from the rear to the front of the bus while whites sat from the front to the rear. The ordinance did not require that any seats be reserved for whites. When the ordinance went into effect on March 11 blacks began sitting in front seats previously reserved for white customers.

The bus drivers, all of whom were white, refused to accept Ordinance 222 and ordered blacks not to occupy front seats reserved for whites. When the City Council and black leaders informed the drivers that the new ordinance had to be obeyed, the drivers decided to go on strike. They demanded that the four front seats be reserved for whites and the four rear seats for blacks. As a result of the strike the Attorney General ruled that Ordinance 222 was illegal because it conflicted with Louisiana's segregation laws. When the buses began rolling after the four-day strike, blacks found that drivers were continuing to insist that they sit in the back.

The Mass Bus Boycott

In June 1953 the black community of Baton Rouge began a mass boycott against the segregated buses. The official leader of the boycott was the Reverend T. J. Jemison, pastor of Mt. Zion Baptist, one of the largest black churches in the city. When white drivers refused to allow blacks to sit in the front of the bus, Jemison and Raymond Scott made a radio appeal to blacks not to ride the buses. Reverend Jemison recounts that the boycott was 100 percent effective: "Nobody rode the bus during our strike. There were about eight people who didn't hear the call that night [on the radio] and they rode to work. But by afternoon there was nobody riding the bus. For ten days not a Negro rode the bus." A *New York Times* article in 1953 confirmed that at least 90 percent of the black passengers refused to ride the buses during the boycott.

The boycott galvanized the black community of Baton Rouge. Nightly mass meetings were held throughout the seven days of the boycott. They attracted such large numbers that Jemison's church, with a seating capacity of 1,000, proved to be too small. The meetings were therefore held in the auditorium of the local segregated public school, which normally seated about 1,200. On those hot June nights, 2,500 to 3,000 people would wedge themselves into the auditorium, and according to Jemison they stood around the walls, sat on window sills, and occupied all available space. Bumper-to-bumper traffic en route to the mass meetings tied up the town of Baton Rouge. Everyone was aware that this was an important development. The scale and vigor of the nightly activity left an indelible impression on whites as well as blacks.

Officials of the movement closed down the community's saloons after 6:00 P.M. The drunks and winos of the black community were not allowed to do their customary drinking out on the streets. But, Jemison recalls, "they didn't seem to mind too much because their new role was to open up the car doors of movement participants as they arrived." Even they sensed that they were taking part in an important drama. The movement's leadership set up their own "police department," and city policemen remained outside the black community during the boycott. According to Jemison, the movement's "police department" did an effective job patrolling the community and providing him with bodyguards.

The refusal to ride buses, of course, confronted the protesters with the problem of how to eat and pay rent if they had no transportation to and from work. The black community laboriously worked out a "free car lift" to solve this problem. Personal cars were used to pick up the black work force on corners just as the buses had done. They would then proceed down the regular bus routes discharging passengers at their destinations. The car lift was highly organized, with a dispatch center and drivers stationed across the city prepared to swing into action when instructed. The passengers were not charged fares. If fares had been charged, the whole operation could have been shut down for functioning without taxi licenses. Movement strategists had to be aware of all the legal catches and skilled at avoiding them.

A mass movement such as the Baton Rouge boycott requires a high degree of planning and organization. Communication networks had to be activated, someone had to decide on the movement's meeting place, money had to be raised and strategies formulated. The Baton Rouge mass bus boycott suggests that movements are the products of organizing efforts and preexisting institutions. To understand the dynamics of the Baton Rouge movement a discussion of leadership, organization and finance is necessary.

Leadership

The Reverend T. J. Jemison became the official leader and spokesman of the Baton Rouge movement. Reverend Jemison held a bachelor's and a master's degree from two black universities, Alabama State and Virginia Union, respectively. He had also done graduate work at New York University. As pastor of the largest and most respected church in the community, he was economically independent of the white community. This independence enabled Jemison to avoid many of the constraints facing the black leadership that functioned within the tripartite system of domination. Yet the severity of oppression of the black community made the masses distrustful of anyone claiming to be a leader. They knew that any leader would be subjected to pressure from whites to abandon the masses for personal gain. Jemison was not free from suspicion, but in several incidents prior to the boycott he had proved that his leadership was authentic.

One case involved the white owner of a candy store in the heart of the black community. When little black girls came in on their way to school to buy candy, the proprietor would take them behind a curtain and fondle them. No one would tackle this problem because the man was white. The owner was persuaded to close the store when Jemison threatened to have his business disrupted by some "young tough" blacks. In another incident, word circulated about a family comprising a mother, father, and nine children living in one 14-by-14 foot room. Jemison led a community effort to pool resources and buy the family a 60-by-90 foot lot on which a seven-room home was built. Jemison was relatively new in the community, and it was rumored that he had had the title to the property put in his name; after all, "people just don't do what he did." Immediately Jemison and his followers took out a full-page newspaper ad that showed the title in the family's name. Jemison later recalled that "from that point . . . they had confidence. There were other incidents, several of them. It was incidents like this that made people know that I was more or less for other people rather than for myself, and that I could be followed and that I could be trusted."

Jemison was also helped to become the leader of the Baton Rouge movement by his "newcomer" status. Contrary to popular belief among outsiders, a black community is usually well stocked with organized groups. This was true of Baton Rouge in the early 1950s. Many of its black inhabitants belonged to various churches, civic organizations, the NAACP, the Masons, lodges, and other groups. As in any organized social setting, various factions competed for cherished resources, prestige, and power. The longer a group or community leader has been in such a setting, the more likely he or she is to have made enemies or, more fundamentally, to be identified as representing a particular camp or special interest.

This is why the "newcomer" status was important for the Baton Rouge boycott leader. To cite Reverend Jemison:

> I didn't have any conflict from others. And I was new in the community, more or less. I didn't come until 'forty-nine. So I didn't have the deep-seated problems with others, having been on this side or that side. I was a middle-of-the-road man. This is the same thing that happened in Montgomery. You had different ones there that had been leaders in that community. But King had just come.

The lateness of Jemison's arrival thus enhanced his ability to unite the diverse segments of the community for sustained protest.

Finally, Jemison became well integrated into community activities and belonged to a number of organizations. As a minister he was clearly connected to the black masses and the black clergy network that stretched across Baton Rouge. This network gave him access to the resources and organized work forces of the church community. In addition to managing his own large church congregation, Reverend Jemison belonged to the Baton Rouge Community Group, a local civic organization. Significantly, he was a member of the local NAACP and had previously served as its president. Most activities aimed at changing the racial status quo in Baton Rouge had been conducted by the NAACP. One of the many contributions of the NAACP to the rise of the modern civil rights movement was the training it provided to the modern civil rights leaders, many of whom were high-ranking officers of the NAACP.

Organization

The Baton Rouge boycott movement was mobilized and directed through the local black churches and the United Defense League (UDL). The local churches provided the institutional link to the masses. Jemison's large congregation immediately agreed to support the boycott. Community support spread when Jemison called other ministers throughout the city and asked that their congregations join the boycott. It is not necessary for everyone to belong to a church for the entire community to become unified for protest. Individuals who did not belong were sure to have relatives, friends, co-workers or neighbors who did, and so the word got passed. Because churches were highly respected, any program initiated and backed by them had an excellent chance to gain mass support. Black church congregations all over Baton Rouge rallied behind the boycott of 1953. The churches supplied the manpower, finances, and communication networks that brought about the indispensable mass participation.

The UDL was a unique organization formed in June 1953 to direct the mass bus boycott. Churches were not ideal as the decision-making center of a mass movement; they were too numerous and were preoccupied with too many other functions unrelated to protest. Besides, the church had no control over significant secular groups or formal ties to their leadership. It proved necessary to form an organization that was church-related but also included other important organized groups in the community. After its success in Baton Rouge, this procedure of forming a church-related organization became the fundamental organizing principle of many later movements. Jemison recalled: "We started an organization and we called it the United Defense League. And the reason we called it United Defense League, all of the other organizations within the community—there were about five or six—came together and united. They didn't lose their individual identity. But for the overall purpose of the whole community we formed what we call a United Defense League." Thus the UDL became an organization of organizations.

Up to this point the boycott has been described as if it had one leader. That was not at all the case. The large number of ministers involved gave the movement a diverse leadership, because ministers were already leaders of their congregations. The UDL added to the leadership's depth by engaging the leadership skills of the entire community. It promoted creativity, discouraged jealousies and rivalries, eliminated needless duplication of effort, and maximized group cohesiveness. Measures to ensure solidarity were explicitly built into the UDL. Jemison explains:

> We brought all of them [leaders of the other community organizations] in, and recognized them as leaders, so that they would feel a part of the movement, and that it wasn't just my movement because there were many in the downtown power structure who would say to them that I was stealing their thunder, and they were all under me. But I tried to put them on the par, on the Board of Directors that would do the governing of this organization. And that was the one thing that kept us together. No matter how the power structure and splinter white groups tried to tear us apart, we were able to maintain a united front. . . . We were united.

Clearly, then, the organization of organizations, the UDL, prevented the white power structure from exploiting schisms within the movement. Being separate from yet related to the mass-based black church, it joined with the churches to supply the comprehensive framework through which the Baton Rouge movement was organized and directed.

Finance

Social protest has to be financed. Investigation of how the Baton Rouge movement was financed leads directly to the black church. Just before the boycott Jemison's congregation had given him $650 to cover expenses for a business trip. The Sunday before the boycott Jemison informed the congregation that he was canceling the trip because of the pending boycott. He then told the church committee, "I want you to let me use this $650 as the first gift towards the boycott." An experienced official of the church, Jemison knew his personal example would communicate the seriousness of the boycott and the absolute necessity of financing it to the congregation and other churchmen of the city.

The Mt. Zion Baptist Church Committee set the financing process in motion by allowing the $650 to go toward the boycott. "That $650 inspired those in the church to give," Jemison says. "That Sunday morning our church gave $1,500." Jemison immediately approached the rest of Baton Rouge's church community: "I called around to churches that I had a chance to reach and told them what I was going to do, and that Sunday we took in somewhere—I think it was around about $3,800. That was how we started financing it."

Passing the hat became a regular feature of the nightly mass meetings. The mass meetings were the pulse and lifeline of the movement—its information center; the occasion for inspiration, rejuvenation, and commitment by means of rousing sermons and unifying black spirituals; the opportunity for planning and strategy sessions; and the financial center. The entire car lift, including maintenance and such equipment as tires and batteries, was financed by money raised at the church-based mass meetings. Jemison remembers: "At night we would have mass meetings. And the people would give money for the cars, but they would be giving it in just a mass rally. And we would pay for the gas that they were using. Monthly. Weekly. We wouldn't let anybody individually pay for anything." Such financing enabled the movement to operate the car lift without a taxi license.

The movement's police department, which consisted of five bodyguards, was also financed with money collected at mass meetings, as were the countless ancillary goods and services required in any mass effort. In a summary of the movement's financial business, Jemison concluded: "The black citizens, mainly, and a few whites, contributed enough money to pay for all the tires, and batteries, and gas, and my bodyguards. And we owed nobody nothing. The black community paid for all that." Hence, the churches were more than symbolic extensions of the movement. They became the bedrock through which movement funds were raised and other valuable resources activated. The procedure for collecting funds that was developed for the explicit purpose of indigenously supporting black protest in Baton Rouge was to endure throughout the modern civil rights movement.

Victory and Impact

The boycott differed from past protests in Baton Rouge, which had been initiated by the NAACP and had attempted to work through the courts. The Baton Rouge boycott was a mass, church-based, direct-action movement guided by a new organization of organizations. The boycott leaders formed the new organization after deciding that the NAACP was incapable of directing a mass protest. The main tactic of the movement—economic boycott—effectively disrupted the economy of the bus company, causing it to lose $1,600 a day.

The demand of the black community was that blacks be allowed to occupy bus seats on a first-come-first-served basis, with no seats reserved for whites. To bring the effective mass bus boycott to a close the white power structure of Baton Rouge decided to work out a compromise with the movement leaders. The compromise stipulated that the two side front seats be reserved for whites while the long rear seat be reserved for blacks. All of the remaining seats were to be filled on a first-come-first-served basis.

On the sixth day of the boycott the Executive Council of the UDL met and considered the compromise. Reverend Jemison urged that the compromise be accepted on a temporary basis and that the legality of bus segregation itself could be determined through the courts. There was heated debate over the compromise, although it was finally accepted by a 5-to-3 vote. The movement leaders took the proposal to a mass meeting attended by 8,000 blacks. According to the *State Times* "a standing show of approval, or disapproval from the audience, at Jemison's request, showed a majority in favor of the group decision." However, some movement leaders and many of the rank-and-file were dissatisfied with the compromise, arguing that the force of the mass movement was capable of ending bus segregation. The *State Times* reported the response at the mass meeting: "An echoing ovation of voices shouting 'stay off, stay off' rose up from the Memorial Stadium after Jemison's statement. . . . Other shouts of 'walk, walk' were heard throughout the audience, when Jemison said, 'But some of you good people have to work'."

The boycott officially ended June 25, 1953, after Jemison informed the group that the free car lift would cease functioning. It appears that the Baton Rouge boycott could have functioned indefinitely, as did the subsequent Montgomery boycott, if the leaders had not accepted the compromise. In retrospect Reverend Jemison admitted: "My vision was not anywhere, at that particular time, other than to see that Negroes could sit down when they paid the same fare."

The limited victory in Baton Rouge was easier than in some later movements, because the white power structure did not stand solidly behind the striking bus drivers. That does not diminish its importance as a major victory against the Jim Crow system in Baton Rouge. It was not simply a victory of a black middle class desiring integration. Most higher-income blacks could avoid the humiliation of the buses by driving private cars. A victory for the entire community, it was the first evidence that the system of racial segregation could be challenged by mass action.

The impact of the mass bus boycott went beyond Baton Rouge. The news of it was disseminated through the black ministerial networks across the country. Jemison's access to those networks was solid. His father had been president of the 5-million-member National Baptist Congress for twelve years, and Jemison himself had been elected in 1953 as that body's National Secretary. In 1956, Rev. Jemison carried the blueprint of the Baton Rouge movement to the National Baptist Convention and made it available to activist clergy. Martin Luther King, Jr., and Ralph Abernathy, both ministers in Montgomery, Alabama, were well aware of the Baton Rouge movement and consulted closely with Reverend Jemison when the famous Montgomery boycott was launched in 1955. Similarly, the Reverend C. K. Steele, who became the leader of a mass bus boycott in Tallahassee, Florida, in 1956, was familiar with the Baton Rouge boycott and also consulted closely with Jemison. The Reverend A. L. David of New Orleans, who led a protest against bus segregation in that city in 1957, was well aware of the earlier protest in Baton Rouge. Small wonder that in organizational dynamics the later movements resembled the historic Baton Rouge movement, which provided a successful model.

The Baton Rouge boycott occurred before the famous 1954 school desegregation decision won by the NAACP and also predated the more celebrated 1955–56 Montgomery bus boycott. But it was the Baton Rouge movement, largely without assistance from outside elites, that opened the direct action phase of the modern civil rights movement. Its impact was temporarily overshadowed, however, by the 1954 Supreme Court decision in *Brown v. Board of Education of Topeka,* which thrust the NAACP into the limelight and crystallized the emerging massive resistance movement dedicated to systematically destroying the NAACP across the South.

Chapter 94

Rosa Parks and the Montgomery Bus Boycott

Herbert Kohl

The story of Rosa Parks and the Montgomery bus boycott is an example, writes educator Herbert Kohl, of "the misrepresentation of African American struggles for equality in school textbooks. It shows how the story of Rosa Parks, which is also the story of community-based struggle against segregation, has been turned into a tale of individual frustration, thereby defusing its political content."

Kohl is the author of many works, including Thirty-Six Children *(1967),* The Open Classroom *(1969),* Reading: How To *(1973),* On Teaching *(1976),* Growing Minds: On Becoming a Teacher *(1985), and* "I Won't Learn from You" and Other Thoughts on Creative Maladjustment *(1994).*

The following selection is reprinted by permission from "The Story of Rosa Parks and the Montgomery Bus Boycott Revisited," in Should We Burn Babar? *(New York: New Press, 1995), appendices deleted.*

Racism, and the direct confrontation between African American and European American people in the United States, is an issue that is usually considered too sensitive to be dealt with directly in the elementary school classroom. When confrontation between African Americans and European Americans occurs in children's literature, it is routinely described as a problem between individuals that can be worked out on a personal basis. In the few cases where racism is addressed as a social problem, there has to be a happy ending. This is most readily apparent in the biographical treatment of Rosa Parks, one of the two names that most children in the United States associate with the Civil Rights movement in the southern United States during the 1960s; the other is Martin Luther King Jr.

Over the past few years, during visits to schools, I've talked with children about the Civil Rights movement. One of the things I ask the children is what they know of Rosa Parks and her involvement in the Montgomery bus boycott. This focus developed after I observed a play about civil rights in a fourth-grade classroom in southern California several years ago. One scene in the play took place on a bus in Montgomery, Alabama. A tired Rosa Parks got on the bus and sat down. The child portraying Mrs. Parks was dressed in shabby clothes and carried two worn shopping bags. She sat down next to the driver, and other children got on the bus until all the seats in front were filled up. Then a boy got on and asked her to move.

She refused, and the bus driver told her he didn't want any trouble. Politely he asked her to move to the back of the bus. She refused again and the scene ended. In the next scene we see a crowd of students, African American and European American, carrying signs saying Don't Ride the Buses, We Shall Overcome, and Blacks and Whites Together. One of the students, playing Martin Luther King Jr., addressed the rest of the class, saying something to the effect that African American and European American people in Montgomery got angry because Rosa Parks was arrested for not moving to the back of the bus, and that they were boycotting the buses until all people could ride wherever they wanted. The play ended with a narrator pointing out that the bus problem in Montgomery was solved by people coming together to protest peacefully for justice.

Before talking to the children about their perceptions of Rosa Parks and her motivations, I had a moment to talk with the teacher about a major misrepresentation of facts in the play: there were no European Americans involved in boycotting the buses in Montgomery. The struggle was organized and maintained by the African American community, and to represent it as an interracial struggle was to take the power and credit away from that community. The teacher agreed that the play took some liberty with history but said that since his class was interracial, it was better for all the children to do the play as an integrated struggle. Otherwise, he said, the play might lead to racial strife in the classroom. I disagreed and pointed out that by showing the power of organized African Americans, it might lead all the children to recognize and appreciate the strength oppressed people can show when confronting their oppressors. In addition, the fact that European Americans joined the struggle later on could lead to very interesting discussions about social change and struggles for justice, and could be related to the current situation in South Africa and the resurgence of overt racism in the United States. He disagreed and ended our chat by telling me how hard it was to manage an integrated classroom.

I contented myself with asking the children about Rosa Parks. The girl who played Mrs. Parks, Anna, told me that she imagined "Rosa," as she called Mrs. Parks, to be a poor woman who did tiring and unpleasant work. She added that she imagined Rosa was on her way home to a large family that she had to take care of all by herself when she refused to move to the back of the bus. In other words, Rosa Parks was, in her mind, a poor, single parent with lots of children, and an unskilled worker. I asked her how she got that idea, and she replied that's just the kind of person she felt Rosa Parks must be. She added that nobody had ever told her that her view was wrong, so she never bothered to question it. Her teacher backed her up and claimed that she had made reasonable assumptions about Rosa Parks, ones that he felt were true to the way Rosa Parks was portrayed in the books they had in class. I couldn't argue with that last comment.

I changed the subject and asked Anna why Rosa Parks's arrest led to a boycott. She said she didn't know. Maybe Rosa had a friend who told everybody, or maybe it was in the newspaper. One of the other students suggested that her arrest was on TV and everybody came out to protest because they didn't think it was right to arrest someone just for not moving to the back of the bus. The boycott was, to them, some form of spontaneous action that involved no planning or strategy.

All the children admired Rosa Parks for not moving. Some said she must be a very stubborn person, others that she had to be so angry that she didn't care what happened to her. They agreed that it took a special person to be so courageous and wondered if they would be able to muster such courage. I got the impression that Mrs. Parks's exceptional courage might be an excuse for them to not act.

I decided to push the issue a bit and asked the class why Rosa Parks had to move to the back of the bus anyway. One of the African American children said it was segregated in the South back then, and African Americans and European Americans couldn't do things together. When I asked why there was segregation in those days there was absolute silence. I shifted a bit and asked if the African Americans and European Americans in their classroom could do things together. One of the boys answered, "In school they do, mostly." Since I was just a guest I left it at that. However, it was clear to me that issues of racial conflict were not explicitly discussed in this classroom, and that the play about the Montgomery bus boycott left the children with some vague sense of unity and victory, but with no sense of the risk and courage of the African American people who originated the struggle for civil rights in the United States or of the history and nature of segregation. I have no idea whether there was any racism manifest in the everyday lives of the children in that classroom, but wondered whether they or the teacher were at all prepared to deal with it if it erupted.

The children's visualization of Rosa Parks, whom they felt free to call by her first name, was particularly distressing. As well as poor, they imagined her to be without education or sophistication, a person who acted on impulse and emotion rather than intelligence and moral conviction. There was no sense of her as a community leader or as part of an organized struggle against oppression. I decided to find out how common this view was, and I have been astonished to find that those children's view of Rosa Parks is not at all different from that of most European American adults and almost all the school children I have questioned.

The image of "Rosa the Tired," and the story that goes with it, exists on the level of a national cultural icon in the United States. School textbooks and children's books are major perpetuators of this myth, but none of them I've seen quote sources for their distorted personal information about Mrs. Parks. Yet, most American children's first encounter with the Civil Rights movement comes through these writings. Dozens of children's books and textbooks I've looked at present the same version of Rosa Parks and the Montgomery bus boycott. This version can be reduced to the following generic story, which I fabricated and could be titled:

"Rosa Was Tired: The Story of the Montgomery Bus Boycott"

Rosa Parks was a poor seamstress. She lived in Montgomery, Alabama, during the 1950s. In those days there was still segregation in parts of the United States. That meant that African Americans and European Americans were not allowed to use the same public facilities such as restaurants or swimming pools. It also meant that whenever it was crowded on the city buses African Americans had to give up seats in front to European Americans and move to the back of the bus.

One day on her way home from work Rosa was tired and sat down in the front of the bus. As the bus got crowded she was asked to give up her seat to a European American man, and she refused. The bus driver told her she had to go to the back of the bus, and she still refused to move. It was a hot day, and she was tired and angry, and became very stubborn.

The driver called a policeman, who arrested Rosa.

When other African Americans in Montgomery heard this they became angry too, so they decided to refuse to ride the buses until everyone was allowed to ride together. They boycotted the buses.

The boycott, which was led by Martin Luther King Jr., succeeded. Now African Americans and European Americans can ride the buses together in Montgomery.

Rosa Parks was a very brave person.

This story seems innocent enough. Rosa Parks is treated with respect and dignity and the African American community is given credit for running the boycott and winning the struggle. It reflects the view of Mrs. Parks often found in adult literature as well as writings for children. For example, in the book by eminent psychiatrist Robert Coles, *The Moral Life of Children* (Boston: Houghton Mifflin, 1986), we find the following quote:

> We had come to know . . . a group of poor and poorly educated people, who, nevertheless, acquitted themselves impressively in pursuit of significant ethical objectives. I think of Rosa Parks, a seamstress, whose decision to sit where she pleased on a Montgomery, Alabama, bus in the middle 1950s preceded the emergence of the so-called Civil Rights movement and of Dr. King and Ralph Abernathy as leaders of it. (P. 25)

A more recent example of this can be found in Robert Fulghum's best-selling book, *It Was on Fire When I Lay Down on It* (Ivy Books, 1988).

> I write this on the first day of December in 1988, the anniversary of a moment when someone sat still and lit the fuse to social dynamite. On this day in 1955, a forty-two-year-old woman was on her way home from work. Getting on a public bus, she paid her fare and sat down on the first vacant seat. It was good to sit down—her feet were tired. As the bus filled with passengers, the driver turned and told her to give up her seat and move on back in the bus. She sat still. The driver got up and shouted, "MOVE IT!" She sat still. Passengers grumbled, cursed her, pushed at her. Still she sat. So the driver got off the bus, called the police, and they came to haul her off to jail and into history.
>
> Rosa Parks. Not an activist or a radical. Just a quiet, conservative, churchgoing woman with a nice family and a decent job as a seamstress. For all the eloquent phrases that have been turned about her place in the flow of history, she did not get on that bus looking for trouble or trying to make a statement. Going home was all she had in mind, like everybody else. She was anchored to her seat by her own dignity. Rosa Parks simply wasn't going to be a "nigger" for anybody anymore. And all she knew to do was to sit still. (Pp. 109–110)

And here's a current textbook version of the Montgomery bus boycott story written for elementary school children. It comes from the Heath Social Studies series for elementary school, *Exploring My World* by Jeff Passe and Evangeline Nicholas (Lexington, MA: 1991, D.C. Heath, reproduced on page 188 of the Teachers' Guide) and is similar in content to my generic tale:

> When Rosa Parks rode on a bus, she had to sit all the way in the back. Her city had a law. It said black people could not sit in the front of a bus.
>
> One day Rosa was tired. She sat in the front. The bus driver told her to move. She did not. He called the police. Rosa was put in jail.
>
> Some citizens tried to help. One of them was Martin Luther King Jr. The citizens decided to stop riding buses until the law was changed.
>
> Their plan worked. The law was changed. Soon, many other unfair laws were changed. Rosa Parks led the way!

The Teachers' Guide to this text informs teachers that "Mrs. Parks' single act brought about the desegregation of buses all over the country." In a lesson plan referring to Rosa Parks's being told to move to the back of the bus, it informs teachers to "tell children they will be reading about a woman who became angry when this happened to her. She decided she was not being treated fairly, and she was not going to put up with that kind of treatment anymore. Have children read to find out how the actions of Rosa Parks helped to change the way black people were treated." (p. 188)

This book was published in 1991 and is certainly still in use. It encourages presenting the Montgomery bus boycott as the single act of a person who was tired and angry. Intelligent and passionate opposition to racism is simply not part of the story. In the entire part of the guide dealing with the Montgomery bus boycott, there is no mention of racism at all. Instead the problem is unfairness, a more generic and softer form of abuse that avoids dealing with the fact that the great majority of White people in Montgomery were racist and capable of being violent and cruel to maintain segregation. Thus we have an adequate picture of neither the courage of Rosa Parks nor the intelligence and resolve of the African American community in the face of racism.

Research into the history of the Montgomery bus boycott, however, reveals some distressing characteristics of this generic story, which misrepresents an organized and carefully planned movement for social change as a spontaneous outburst based upon frustration and anger. The following annotations on "Rosa Was Tired" suggest that we need a new story, one more in line with the truth and directed at showing the organizational intelligence and determination of the African American community in Birmingham, as well as the role of the bus boycott in the larger struggle to desegregate Birmingham and the South.

The Annotated "Rosa Was Tired"

Rosa Parks was a seamstress who was poor. She lived in Montgomery, Alabama, during the 1950s.

Rosa Parks was one of the first women in Montgomery to join the NAACP and was its secretary for years. At the NAACP she worked with E. D. Nixon, vice president of the Brotherhood of Sleeping Car Porters, who was president of the Montgomery NAACP, and learned about union struggles from him. She also worked with the youth division of the NAACP, and she took a youth NAACP group to visit the Freedom Train when it came to Montgomery in 1954. The train, which carried the originals of the U.S. Constitution and the Declaration of Independence, was traveling around the United States promoting the virtues of democracy. Since its visit was a federal project, access to the exhibits could not legally be segregated. Mrs. Parks took advantage of that fact to visit the train. There, Rosa Parks and the members of the youth group mingled freely with European Americans from Montgomery who were also looking at the documents. This overt act of crossing the boundaries of segregation did not endear Rosa Parks to the Montgomery political and social establishment.

Her work as a seamstress in a large department store was secondary to her community work. As she says in an interview in *My Soul Is Rested* by Howard Raines (New York: Bantam, 1978, p. 35), she had "almost a life history of being rebellious against being mistreated because of my color." She was well known to all of the African American leaders in Montgomery for her opposition to segregation, her leadership abilities, and her moral strength. Since 1954 and the Supreme Court's *Brown v. Topeka Board of Education* decision, she had been working on the desegregation of the Montgomery schools. In addition, she was good friends with Clifford and Virginia Durr, European Americans who were well known opponents of segregation. She had also attended an interracial meeting at the Highlander Folk School in Tennessee a few months before the boycott. Highlander was known throughout the South as a radical education center that was overtly planning for the total desegregation of the South, and Rosa Parks was aware of that when she attended the meeting. At that meeting, which dealt with plans for school desegregation in the South, she indicated that she intended to become an active participant in other attempts to break down the barriers of segregation. Finally, Rosa Parks had the active support of her mother and her husband in her civil rights activities. To call Rosa Parks a poor, tired seamstress and not talk about her role as a community leader as well is to turn an organized struggle for freedom into a personal act of frustration. It is a thorough misrepresentation of the Civil Rights movement in Montgomery, Alabama, and an insult to Mrs. Parks as well. Here is a more appropriate way of beginning a children's version of the Montgomery bus boycott:

It was 1955. Everyone in the African American community in Montgomery, Alabama, knew Rosa Parks. She was a community leader, and people admired her courage. All throughout her life she had opposed prejudice, even if it got her into trouble.

In those days there was still segregation in parts of the United States. That meant that African Americans and European Americans were not allowed to use the same public facilities. . . .

The existence of legalized segregation in the South during the 1950s is integral to the story of the Montgomery bus boycott, yet it is an embarrassment to many school people and difficult to explain to children without accounting for the moral corruption of the majority of the European American community in the South. The sentence I composed is one way of avoiding direct confrontation with the moral issues of segregation. First it says, "In those days there was still segregation" as if segregation were no longer an issue. However, as recently as July 1, 1990, an article by Ron Rapoport of the *Los Angeles Daily News* (reprinted in the Santa Rosa, CA, *Press Democrat,* July 1, 1990) focused on the current segregation of private golf clubs in Birmingham and other parts of the United States. In the article he says:

> It certainly isn't a secret that Shoal Creek Country Club has no black members because, in the words of its founder, Hall Thompson, "that's just not done in Birmingham."
>
> There are lots of places where it's just not done and not just in the South, either. Many of the golf courses that host PGA (Professional Golfers Association) events are restricted and while it may not often become a public issue, that does not mean people are not aware of it.
>
> As for shame, well, that is a commodity that is in short supply as well.
>
> "The country club is our home," Thompson said, "and we pick and choose who we want."

To this day the club still has only one African American member, who has special status as a guest member. Ironically, in 1994 a young African American golfer won a tournament at the club while other African Americans demonstrated outside its gates, protesting the club's segregationist policies.

Locating segregation in the past is a way of avoiding dealing with its current manifestations and implying that racism is no longer a major problem in the United States. This is particularly pernicious at a time when overt racism is once again becoming a common phenomenon and when children have to be helped to understand and eliminate it.

Describing integration passively ("there was still segregation" instead of "European Americans segregated facilities so that African Americans couldn't use them") avoids the issue of activist racist activity on the part of some Whites. Since there was legalized segregation in Alabama, and Mrs. Parks was arrested for a violation of the Alabama state law that institutionalized segregation in public facilities, there must have been racists to have passed those laws. Yet they are absent from the narrative, which doesn't talk overtly about racism. The avoidance of direct discussion of what to do about individuals who are racist is all too characteristic of school programs and children's literature.

This avoidance of dealing directly with racism is also evident in the next sentence, which says that "African Americans and European Americans were not allowed to use the same public facilities." It puts African Americans and European Americans on the same footing, as if there were some symmetry and both were punished by the segregation laws. A more appropriate way of describing the situation would be:

> African American people were prevented by law from using the same public facilities as European Americans. In addition, the African American facilities were vastly inferior to the ones made available to European Americans.

Even this rewriting is too generous given the pervasive, brutal and absolute nature of segregation in the pre–civil rights South. Perhaps the best analogy that could be used here is apartheid, as legalized segregation in the South hardly differed from South Africa's policy of total separation of the races to ensure White dominance.

I've raised the question with a number of educators, both African American and European American, of how to expose children to the reality of segregation and racism. Most of the European American and a few of the African American educators felt that young children do not need to be exposed to the harsh and violent history of segregation in the United States. They worried about the effects such exposure would have on race relations in their classrooms, and especially about provoking rage on the part of African American students. The other educators felt that, given the resurgence of overt racism in the United States these days, allowing rage and anger to come out was the only way African American and European American children could work from the reality of difference and separation toward a common life. They felt that conflict was a positive thing that could be healing when confronted directly, and that avoiding the horrors of racism was just another way of perpetuating them. I agree with this second group and believe that some recasting of the third and fourth sentences of "Rosa Was Tired" is called for:

> In those days Alabama was legally segregated. That means that African American people were prevented by the state law from using the same swimming pools, schools, and other public facilities as European Americans. There also were separate entrances, toilets, and drinking fountains for African Americans and European Americans in places such as bus and train stations. The facilities African Americans were allowed to use were not only separate from the ones European Americans used but were also very inferior. The reason for this was racism, the belief that European Americans were superior to African Americans and that therefore European Americans deserved better facilities.

. . . Whenever it was crowded on the city buses African Americans had to give up seats in front to European Americans and move to the back of the bus.

Actually African Americans were never allowed to sit in the front of the bus in the South in those days. The front seats were *reserved* for European Americans. Between five and ten rows back the "Colored" section began. When the front of the bus filled up, African Americans seated in the "Colored" section had to give up their seats and move toward the back of the bus. Thus, for example, an elderly African American woman would have to give up her seat to a European American teenage male at the peril of being arrested. Consistent with the comments I've been making so far, and with the truth of the experience of segregation, this sentence should be expanded as follows:

In those days public buses were divided into two sections, one at the front for European Americans, which was supposed to be "for Whites only." From five to ten rows back the section for African Americans began. That part of the bus was called the "Colored" section.

Whenever it was crowded on the city buses African American people were forced to give up seats in the "Colored" section to European Americans and move to the back of the bus. For example, an elderly African American woman would have to give up her seat to a European American teenage male. If she refused she could be arrested for breaking the segregation laws.

One day on her way home from work Rosa was tired and sat down in the front of the bus.

Rosa Parks did not sit in the front of the bus. She sat in the front row of the "Colored" section. When the bus got crowded she refused to give up her seat in the "Colored" section to a European American. It is important to point this out, as it indicates quite clearly that it was not her intent, on that day, to break the segregation laws.

At this point the story lapses into the familiar and refers to Rosa Parks as "Rosa." The question of whether to use the first name for historical characters in a factual story is complicated. One argument in favor of doing so is that young children will more readily identify with characters who are presented in a personalized and familiar way. However, given that it was a sanctioned social practice in the South during the time of the story for European Americans to call African American adults by their first names as a way of reinforcing the African Americans' inferior status (African Americans could never call European Americans by their first names without breaking the social code of segregation), it seems unwise to use that practice in the story.

In addition, it's reasonable to assume that Rosa Parks was not any more tired on that one day than on other days. She worked at an exhausting full-time job and was also active full-time in the community. To emphasize her being tired is another way of saying that her defiance of segregation was an accidental result of her fatigue and consequent short temper on that particular day. However, rage is not a one-day thing, and Rosa Parks acted with full knowledge of what she was doing.

It is more respectful and historically accurate to make these changes:

December 1, 1955, on her way home from work, Rosa Parks took the bus as usual. She sat down in the front row of the "Colored" section.

As the bus got crowded she was asked to give up her seat to a European American man, and she refused. The bus driver told her she had to go to the back of the bus, and she still refused to move. It was a hot day, and she was tired and angry, and become very stubborn.

The driver called a policeman, who arrested Rosa.

Rosa Parks described her experiences with buses in her own words (*My Soul Is Rested*):

> I had problems with bus drivers over the years because I didn't see fit to pay my money into the front and then go around to the back. Sometimes bus drivers wouldn't permit me to get on the bus, and I had been evicted from the bus. But, as I say, there had been incidents over the years. One of the things that made this . . . (incident) . . . get so much publicity was the fact that the police were called in and I was placed under arrest. See, if I had just been evicted from the bus and he hadn't placed me under arrest or had any charges brought against me, it probably could have been just another incident. (P. 31)

More recently, in *Voices of Freedom* by Henry Hampton and Steve Fayer (New York: Bantam, 1990), she described her thoughts that day in the following way:

> Having to take a certain section [on a bus] because of your race was humiliating, but having to stand up because a particular driver wanted to keep a white person from having to stand was, to my mind, most inhumane.
>
> More than seventy-five, between eighty-five and I think ninety, percent of the patronage of the buses were black people, because more white people could own and drive their own cars than blacks. I happened to be the secretary of the Montgomery branch of the NAACP as well as the NAACP Youth Council adviser. Many cases did come to my attention that nothing came out of because the person that was abused would be too intimidated to sign an affidavit, or to make a statement. Over the years, I had had my own problems with the bus drivers. In fact, some did tell me not to ride their buses if I felt that I was too important to go to the back door to get on. One had evicted me from the bus in 1943, which did not cause anything more than just a passing glance.
>
> On December 1, 1955, I had finished my day's work as a tailor's assistant in the Montgomery Fair department store and I was on my way home. There was one vacant seat on the Cleveland Avenue bus, which I took, alongside a man and two women across the aisle. There were still a few vacant seats in the white section in the front, of course. We went to the next stop without being disturbed. On the third, the front seats were occupied and this one man, a white man, was standing. The driver asked us to stand up and let him have those seats, and when none of us moved at his first words, he said, "You all make it light on yourselves and let me have those seats." And the man who was sitting next to the window stood up, and I made room for him to pass by me. The two women across the aisle stood up and moved out. When the driver saw me still sitting, he asked if I was going to stand up and I said, "No, I'm not."
>
> And he said, "Well, if you don't stand up, I'm going to call the police and have you arrested."
>
> I said, "You may do that."
>
> He did get off the bus, and I still stayed where I was. Two policemen came on the bus. One of the policemen asked me if the bus driver had asked me to stand and I said yes.

He said, "Why don't you stand up?"
And I asked him, "Why do you push us around?"
He said, "I do not know, but the law is the law and you're under arrest." (Pp. 19, 20)

Mere anger and stubbornness could not account for the clear resolve with which Rosa Parks acted. Nor was she, as Robert Fulghum says in the selection from his book quoted at the beginning of this issue, "Not an activist or a radical. Just a quiet, conservative, churchgoing woman with a nice family and a decent job as a seamstress." She knew what she was doing, understood the consequences, and was prepared to confront segregation head on at whatever sacrifice she had to make. A more accurate account of the event, taking into consideration Rosa Parks's past history, might be:

As the bus got crowded the driver demanded that she give up her seat to a European American man, and move to the back of the bus. This was not the first time that this had happened to Rosa Parks. In the past she had refused to move, and the driver had simply put her off the bus. Mrs. Parks hated segregation, and along with many other African American people, refused to obey many of its unfair rules. On this day she refused to do what the bus driver demanded.

The bus driver commanded her once more to go to the back of the bus and she stayed in her seat, looking straight ahead and not moving an inch. He got angry at her and became very stubborn. He called a policeman, who arrested Mrs. Parks.

When other African Americans in Montgomery heard this they became angry too, so they decided to refuse to ride the buses until everyone was allowed to ride together. They boycotted the buses.

The connection between Rosa Parks's arrest and the boycott is a mystery in most accounts of what happened in Montgomery. Community support for the boycott is portrayed as being instantaneous and miraculously effective the very day after Mrs. Parks was arrested. Things don't happen that way, and it is an insult to the intelligence and courage of the African American community in Montgomery to turn their planned resistance to segregation into a spontaneous emotional response. The actual situation was more interesting and complex. Not only Rosa Parks had defied the bus segregation laws in the past: According to E. D. Nixon, in the three months preceding Mrs. Parks's arrest at least three other African American people had been arrested in Montgomery for refusing to give up their bus seats to European American people. In each case, Nixon and other people in leadership positions in the African American community in Montgomery investigated the background of the person arrested. They were looking for someone who had the respect of the community and the strength to deal with the racist police force as well as all the publicity that would result from being at the center of a bus boycott. This leads to the most important point left out in popularized accounts of the Montgomery bus boycott: the boycott had been planned and organized before Rosa Parks was arrested. It was an event waiting to take place, and that is why it could be mobilized so quickly. Rosa Parks's arrest brought it about because she was part of the African American leadership in Montgomery and was trusted not to cave in under the pressure everyone knew she would be exposed to, including threats to her life.

But the story goes back even farther than that. There was an African American women's organization in Montgomery called the Women's Political Council (WPC). It was headed those days by Jo Ann Gibson Robinson, who was a professor of English at Alabama State University in Montgomery, an all-African American university. In 1949 Ms. Gibson was put off a bus in Montgomery for refusing to move from her seat in the fifth row of an almost empty bus to the back of the bus. She and other women in Montgomery resolved to do something about bus segregation. As she says in her book *The Montgomery Bus Boycott and the Women Who Started It: The Memoir of Jo Ann Gibson Robinson* (Knoxville: University of Tennessee Press, 1987), "It was during the period of 1949–1955 that the Women's Political Council of Montgomery—founded in 1946 with Dr. Mary Burks as president and headed from 1950 on by me—prepared to stage a bus boycott when the time was ripe and the people were ready. The right time came in 1955." (p. 17)

This story of collective decision making, willed risk, and coordinated action is more dramatic than the story of an angry individual who sparked a demonstration; it has more to teach children who themselves may have to organize and act collectively against oppressive forces in the future. Here's one way to tell this complex story to young children:

Mrs. Parks was not the first African American person to be arrested in Montgomery for refusing to move to the back of the bus. In the months before her refusal, at least three other people were arrested for the same reason. In fact, African American leaders in Montgomery were planning to overcome segregation. One way they wanted to do this was to have every African American person boycott the buses. Since most of the bus riders in the city were African American, the buses would go broke if they refused to let African Americans and European Americans ride the buses as equals.

From 1949 right up to the day Mrs. Parks refused to move, the Women's Political Council of Montgomery prepared to stage a bus boycott because of how African Americans were treated on the bus. African American people in Montgomery were ready to support the boycott. They were just waiting for the time to be ripe. Nineteen fifty-five was the time.

However, none of the people who were arrested before Mrs. Parks was were leaders. She was a leader, and the day she was arrested the leadership called a meeting at the Dexter Avenue Baptist Church. They decided to begin their refusal to ride the buses the next morning. They knew Mrs. Parks had the courage to deal with the pressure of defying segregation and would not yield even if her life was threatened.

The next day the Montgomery bus boycott began.

The boycott, which was led by Martin Luther King Jr., succeeded. Now African Americans and European Americans can ride the buses together in Montgomery. Rosa Parks was a very brave person.

The boycott was planned by the WPC, E. D. Nixon, and others in Montgomery. Martin Luther King Jr. was a new member of the community. He had just taken over the Dexter Avenue Baptist Church, and when Nixon told him that Rosa Parks's arrest was just what everybody was waiting for to kick off a bus boycott and assault the institution of segregation, King was at first reluctant. However, the community people chose him to lead, and he accepted their call. The boycott lasted 381 inconvenient days, something not usually mentioned in children's books. It did succeed and was one of the events that sparked the entire Civil Rights movement. People who had been planning an overt attack on segregation for years took that victory as a sign that the time was ripe, even though the people involved in the Montgomery boycott did not themselves anticipate such results. Here's one possible way to convey this to children:

There was a young new minister in Montgomery those days. His name was Martin Luther King Jr. People in the community felt that he was a special person and asked him to lead the boycott. At first he wasn't sure. He worried about the violence that might result from the boycott. However, he quickly made up his mind that it was time to destroy segregation and accepted the people's call for him to be their leader.

The Montgomery bus boycott lasted 381 days. For over a year the African American people of Montgomery, Alabama, stayed off the buses. Some walked to work, others rode bicycles or shared car rides. It was very hard for them, but they knew that what they were doing was very important for all African American people in the South.

The boycott succeeded, and by the end of 1956 African Americans and European Americans could ride the buses in Montgomery as equals. However, the struggle for the complete elimination of segregation had just begun.

We all owe a great deal to the courage and intelligence of Rosa Parks and the entire African American community of Montgomery, Alabama. They took risks to make democracy work for all of us.

Concluding Thoughts

What remains, then, is to retitle the story. The revised version is still about Rosa Parks, but it is also about the African American people of Montgomery, Alabama. It takes the usual, individualized version of the Rosa Parks tale and puts it in the context of a coherent, community-based social struggle. This does not diminish Rosa Parks in any way. It places her, however, in the midst of a consciously planned movement for social change, and reminds me of the freedom song "We Shall Not Be Moved," for it was precisely Rosa Parks's and the community's refusal to be moved that made the boycott possible. For that reason the new title, "She Would Not Be Moved: The Story of Rosa Parks and the Montgomery Bus Boycott" makes sense.

As it turns out, my retelling of the story of Rosa Parks and the Montgomery bus boycott is not the only recent one. In 1990, thirty-five years after the event, we finally have a full, moving, and historically accurate 124-page retelling of the story written for young people. The book, *Rosa Parks: The Movement Organizes* by Kai Friese (Englewood Cliffs, NJ: Silver Burdett, 1990), is one of nine volumes in a series edited by the scholar Aldon Morris entitled *The History of the Civil Rights Movement*. Other volumes in the series, such as those about Ella Baker and Fannie Lou Hamer, also provide a fuller, more accurate look at people's struggles during the Civil Rights movement of the 1960s than has been available to young people until now. These volumes are gifts to all of us from a number of African American scholars who have reclaimed history from the distortions and omissions of years of irresponsible writing for children about the Civil Rights movement. They are models of how history and biography can directly confront racial conflict and illuminate social struggle. This is particularly true of the Rosa Parks volume, which takes us up to date in Mrs. Parks's life and informs us that she remained active over the years, working for social and economic justice in Congressman John Conyer's office in Detroit.

The book, which credits all the people involved in making the Montgomery boycott possible, provides a portrait of a community mobilized for justice. It also leaves us with a sense of the struggle that still needs to be waged to eliminate racism in the United States.

Rosa Parks has also written an autobiography (with Jim Haskins), which presents a more personal version of the story given here.

When the story of the Montgomery bus boycott is told merely as a tale of a single heroic person, it leaves children hanging. Not everyone is a hero or heroine. Of course, the idea that only special people can create change is useful if you want to prevent mass movements and keep change from happening. Not every child can be a Rosa Parks, but everyone can imagine her- or himself as a participant in the boycott. As a tale of a social movement and a community effort to overthrow injustice, the Rosa Parks story as I've tried to rewrite it and as Kai Friese has told it opens the possibility of every child identifying her- or himself as an activist, as someone who can help make justice happen. And it is that kind of empowerment that people in the United States desperately need.

Chapter 95

The Social Organization of Nonviolence

Martin Luther King, Jr.

The following selection is reprinted from Martin Luther King, Jr., "The Social Organization of Nonviolence," Liberation, October 1959. Reprinted by arrangement with The Heirs to the Estate of Martin Luther King, Jr., c/o Writers House, Inc. as agent for the proprietor. Copyright 1959 by Martin Luther King, Jr., copyright renewed 1986 The Estate of Martin Luther King, Jr.

For other selections by King, see chapters 91, 102, and 106.

Paradoxically, the struggle for civil rights has reached a stage of profound crisis, although its outward aspect is distinctly less turbulent and victories of token integration have been won in the hard-resistance areas of Virginia and Arkansas.

The crisis has its origin in a decision rendered by the Supreme Court more than a year ago which upheld the pupil placement law. Though little noticed then, this decision fundamentally weakened the historic 1954 ruling of the Court. It is imperceptibly becoming the basis of a de facto compromise between the powerful contending forces.

The 1954 decision required for effective implementation resolute federal action supported by mass action to undergird all necessary changes. It is obvious that federal action by the legislative and executive branches was half-hearted and inadequate. The activity of Negro forces, while heroic in some instances, and impressive in other sporadic situations, lacked consistency and militancy sufficient to fill the void left by government default. The segregationists were swift to seize these advantages, and unrestrained by moral or social conscience, defied the law boldly and brazenly.

The net effect of this social equation has led to the present situation, which is without clearcut victory for either side. Token integration is a developing pattern. This type of integration is merely an affirmation of a principle without the substance of change.

It is, like the Supreme Court decision, a pronouncement of justice, but by itself does not insure that the millions of Negro children will be educated in conditions of equality. This is not to say that it is without value. It has substantial importance. However, it fundamentally changes the outlook of the whole movement, for it raises the prospect of long, slow change without a predictable end. As we have seen in northern cities, token integration has become a pattern in many communities and remained frozen, even though environmental attitudes are substantially less hostile to full integration than in the South.

Three Views of Violence

This then is the danger. Full integration can easily become a distant or mythical goal—major integration may be long postponed, and in the quest for social calm a compromise firmly implanted in which the real goals are merely token integration for a long period to come.

The Negro was the tragic victim of another compromise in 1877, when his full equality was bargained away by the federal government and a condition somewhat above slave status but short of genuine citizenship became his social and political existence for nearly a century.

There is reason to believe that the Negro of 1959 will not accept supinely any such compromises in the contemporary struggle for integration. His struggle will continue, but the obstacles will determine its specific nature. It is axiomatic in social life that the imposition of frustrations leads to two kinds of reactions. One is the development of a wholesome social organization to resist with effective, firm measures any efforts to impede progress. The other is a confused, anger-motivated drive to strike back violently, to inflict damage. Primarily, it seeks to cause injury to retaliate for wrongful suffering. Secondarily, it seeks real progress, it is punitive—not radical or constructive.

The current calls for violence have their roots in this latter tendency. Here one must be clear that there are three different views on the subject of violence. One is the approach of pure nonviolence, which cannot readily or easily attract large masses, for it requires extraordinary discipline and courage. The second is violence exercised in self-defense, which all societies, from the most primitive to the most cultured and civilized, accept as moral and legal. The principle of self-defense, even involving weapons and bloodshed, has never been condemned, even by Gandhi, who sanctioned it for those unable to master pure nonviolence. The third is the advocacy of violence as a tool of advancement, organized as in warfare, deliberately and consciously. To this tendency many Negroes are being tempted today. There are incalculable perils in this approach. It is not the danger or sacrifice of physical being which is primary, though it cannot be contemplated without a sense of deep concern for human life. The greatest danger is that it will fail to attract Negroes to a real collective struggle, and will confuse the large uncommitted middle group, which as yet has not supported either side. Further, it will mislead Negroes into the belief that this is the only path and place them as a minority in a position where they confront a far larger adversary than it is possible to defeat in this form of combat. When the Negro uses force in self-defense he does not forfeit support—he may even win it, by the courage and self-respect it reflects. When he seeks to initiate violence he provokes questions about the necessity for it, and inevitably is blamed for its consequences. It is unfortunately true that however the

Negro acts, his struggle will not be free of violence initiated by his enemies, and he will need ample courage and willingness to sacrifice to defeat this manifestation of violence. But if he seeks it and organizes it, he cannot win. Does this leave the Negro without a positive method to advance? Mr. Robert Williams[1] would have us believe that there is no effective and practical alternative. He argues that we must be cringing and submissive or take up arms. To so place the issue distorts the whole problem. There are other meaningful alternatives.

The Negro people can organize socially to initiate many forms of struggle which can drive their enemies back without resort to futile and harmful violence. In the history of the movement for racial advancement, many creative forms have been developed—the mass boycott, sit-down protests and strikes, sit-ins—refusal to pay fines and bail for unjust arrests—mass marches—mass meetings—prayer pilgrimages, etc. Indeed, in Mr. Williams' own community of Monroe, North Carolina, a striking example of collective community action won a significant victory without use of arms or threats of violence. When the police incarcerated a Negro doctor unjustly, the aroused people of Monroe marched to the police station, crowded into its halls and corridors, and refused to leave until their colleague was released. Unable to arrest everyone, the authorities released the doctor and neither side attempted to unleash violence. This experience was related by the doctor who was the intended victim.

There is more power in socially organized masses on the march than there is in guns in the hands of a few desperate men. Our enemies would prefer to deal with a small armed group rather than with a huge, unarmed but resolute mass of people. However, it is necessary that the mass-action method be persistent and unyielding. Gandhi said the Indian people must "never let them rest," referring to the British. He urged them to keep protesting daily and weekly, in a variety of ways. This method inspired and organized the Indian masses and disorganized and demobilized the British. It educates its myriad participants, socially and morally. All history teaches us that like a turbulent ocean beating great cliffs into fragments of rock, the determined movement of people incessantly demanding their rights always disintegrates the old order.

It is this form of struggle—non-cooperation with evil through mass actions— "never letting them rest"—which offers the more effective road for those who have been tempted and goaded to violence. It needs the bold and the brave because it is not free of danger. It faces the vicious and evil enemies squarely. It requires dedicated people, because it is a backbreaking task to arouse, to organize, and to educate tens of thousands for disciplined, sustained action. From this form of struggle more emerges that is permanent and damaging to the enemy than from a few acts of organized violence.

Our present urgent necessity is to cease our internal fighting and turn outward to the enemy—using every form of mass action yet known—create new forms— and resolve never to let them rest. This is the social lever which will force open the door to freedom. Our powerful weapons are the voices, the feet, and the bodies of dedicated, united people, moving without rest toward a just goal. Greater tyrants than southern segregationists have been subdued and defeated by this form of struggle. We have not yet used it, and it would be tragic if we spurn it because we have failed to perceive its dynamic strength and power.

Cashing In on War?

I am reluctant to inject a personal defense against charges by Mr. Williams that I am inconsistent in my struggle against war and too weak-kneed to protest nuclear war. Merely to set the record straight, may I state that repeatedly, in public addresses and in my writings, I have unequivocally declared my hatred for this most colossal of all evils and I have condemned any organizer of war, regardless of his rank or nationality. I have signed numerous statements with other Americans condemning nuclear testing and have authorized publication of my name in advertisements appearing in the largest-circulation newspapers in the country, without concern that it was then "unpopular" to so speak out.

EDITORS' NOTE

1. For a discussion of Williams, see Timothy B. Tyson, *Radio Free Dixie: Robert F. Williams and the Roots of Black Power* (Chapel Hill: University of North Carolina Press, 1999).

Chapter 96

SCLC and "The Beloved Community"

The following selection is excerpted from "This Is SCLC," a Southern Christian Leadership Conference pamphlet (n.d.).

Aims and Purposes of SCLC

The Southern Christian Leadership Conference has the basic aim of achieving full citizenship rights, equality, and the integration of the Negro in all aspects of American life. SCLC is a service agency to facilitate coordinated action of local community groups within the frame of their indigenous organizations and natural leadership. SCLC activity revolves around two main focal points: the use of nonviolent philosophy as a means of creative protest; and securing the right of the ballot for every citizen.

Philosophy of SCLC

The basic tenets of Hebraic-Christian tradition coupled with the Gandhian concept of *satyagraha*—truth force—is at the heart of SCLC's philosophy. Christian nonviolence actively resists evil in any form. It never seeks to humiliate the opponent, only to win him. Suffering is accepted without retaliation. Internal violence of the spirit is as much to be rejected as external physical violence. At the center of nonviolence is redemptive love. Creatively used, the philosophy of nonviolence can restore the broken community in America. SCLC is convinced that nonviolence is the most potent force available to an oppressed people in their struggle for freedom and dignity.

SCLC and Nonviolent Mass Direct Action

SCLC believes that the American dilemma in race relations can best and most quickly be resolved through the action of thousands of people, committed to the philosophy of nonviolence, who will physically identify themselves in a just and moral struggle. It is not enough to be intellectually dissatisfied with an evil system. The true nonviolent resister presents his physical body as an instrument to defeat the system. Through nonviolent mass direct action, the evil system is creatively dramatized in order that the conscience of the community may grapple with the rightness or wrongness of the issue at hand. . . .

SCLC and Voter Registration

The right of the ballot is basic to the exercise of full citizenship rights. All across the South, subtle and flagrant obstacles confront the Negro when he seeks to register and vote. Poll taxes, long form questionnaires, harassment, economic reprisal, and sometimes death, meet those who dare to seek this exercise of the ballot. In areas where there is little or no attempt to block the voting attempts of the Negro, apathy generally is deeply etched upon the habits of the community. SCLC, with its specialized staff, works on both fronts: aiding local communities through every means available to secure the right to vote (e.g. filing complaints with the Civil Rights Commission) and arousing interest through voter-registration workshops to point up the importance of the ballot. Periodically, SCLC, upon invitation, conducts a voter-registration drive to enhance a community's opportunity to free itself from economic and political servitude. SCLC believes that the most important step the Negro can take is that short walk to the voting booth.

SCLC and Civil Disobedience

SCLC sees civil disobedience as a natural consequence of nonviolence when the resister is confronted by unjust and immoral laws. This does not imply that SCLC advocates either anarchy or lawlessness. The Conference firmly believes that all people have a moral responsibility to obey laws that are just. It recognizes, however, that there also are unjust laws. From a purely moral point of view, an unjust law is one that is out of harmony with the moral law of the universe, or, as the religionist would say, out of harmony with the Law of God. More concretely, an unjust law is one in which the minority is compelled to observe a code which is not binding on the majority. An unjust law is one in which people are required to obey a code that they had no part in making because they were denied the right to vote. In the face of such obvious inequality, where difference is made legal, the nonviolent resister has no alternative but to disobey the unjust law. In disobeying such a law, he does so peacefully, openly and nonviolently. Most important, he *willingly* accepts the penalty for breaking the law. This distinguishes SCLC's position on civil disobedience from the "uncivil disobedience" of the racist opposition in the South. In the face of laws they consider unjust, they seek to defy, evade, and circumvent the law, BUT they are *unwilling* to accept the penalty for breaking the law. The end result of their defiance is anarchy and disrespect for the law. SCLC, on the other hand, believes that civil disobedience involves the highest respect for the law. He who openly disobeys a law that conscience tells him is unjust and willingly accepts the penalty is giving evidence that he so respects the law that he belongs in jail until it is changed. . . .

SCLC and Segregation

SCLC is firmly opposed to segregation in any form that it takes and pledges itself to work unrelentingly to rid every vestige of its scars from our nation through nonviolent means. Segregation is an evil and its presence in our nation has blighted our larger destiny as a leader in world affairs. Segregation does as much harm to the *segregator* as it does to the *segregated*. The *segregated* develops a false sense of inferiority and the *segregator* develops a false sense of superiority, both contrary to the American ideal of democracy. America must rid herself of segregation not alone because it is politically expedient, but because it is morally right!

SCLC and Constructive Program

SCLC's basic program fosters nonviolent resistance to all forms of racial injustice, including state and local laws and practices, even when this means going to jail; and imaginative, bold constructive action to end the demoralization caused by the legacy of slavery and segregation—inferior schools, slums, and second-class citizenship. Thus, the Conference works on two fronts. On the one hand, it resists continuously the system of segregation which is the basic cause of lagging standards; on the other hand, it works constructively to improve the standards themselves. There MUST be a balance between attacking the causes and healing the effects of segregation.

SCLC and the Beloved Community

The ultimate aim of SCLC is to foster and create the "beloved community" in America where brotherhood is a reality. It rejects any doctrine of black supremacy for this merely substitutes one kind of tyranny for another. The Conference does not foster moving the Negro from a position of disadvantage to one of advantage for this would thereby subvert justice. SCLC works for integration. Our ultimate goal is genuine intergroup and interpersonal living—*integration*. Only through nonviolence can reconciliation and the creation of the beloved community be effected. The international focus on America and her internal problems against the dread prospect of a hot war, demand our seeking this end.

Chapter 97

On King's Influences and Borrowings

Arnold Rampersad

In 1990 it was disclosed that portions of Martin Luther King, Jr.'s, Ph.D. dissertation were plagiarized, prompting discussion about his influences, originality and political contribution.

Arnold Rampersad, professor of English at Stanford University, is the author of The Art and Imagination of W. E. B. Du Bois *(1976) and* The Life of Langston Hughes *(2 vols., 1986, 1988), and co-author, with Arthur Ashe, of* Days of Grace: A Memoir *(1993).*

The following selection, Rampersad's review of Keith D. Miller's Voice of Deliverance: The Language of Martin Luther King, Jr., and Its Sources, *is reprinted from "The Fountain That Led to the Mountain," Newsday, 17 November 1991. Reprinted by permission of the author.*

For a roundtable discussion about the issues raised in this article, see Journal of American History, *June 1991, 11–123.*

Voice of Deliverance is an absorbing book, and one based squarely on a paradox. It proposes to identify the true originality of Martin Luther King Jr. as an orator by exposing the extent of his borrowing, or stealing, from the works of others. "It is time to give credit," [author Keith] Miller writes, "where credit is due." But far from seeking to destroy King, Miller admires him deeply and seeks to celebrate his achievement by illuminating it.

The idea of King as plagiarist is not news. Following discoveries in the King editorial project at Stanford University, Boston University recently recognized officially that portions of King's doctoral dissertation had been plagiarized. Undoubtedly, King knew the rules of academic scholarship, which are most severe with regard to dissertations.

The university faced a tricky decision: whether or not to revoke the degree it granted King. It decided not to do so. In a way, people who admire King face the same question. In light of the news of his plagiarism (not to mention other news), do we revoke the degree of moral authority we once awarded him? Do we look the other way?

Miller asks us to see the matter in an entirely different way. A university professor and the son of a retired Disciples of Christ minister who helped him track down sources, he brushes off the matter of the dissertation. The official portrait of King as a deep scholar of philosophy and theology (a portrait King did not discourage) was useful to his great social and political cause but was only a pose, in Miller's view. King accomplished what he did by quickly moving beyond scholarship, theology and philosophy.

On the other hand, passage after passage here proves that King lifted whole paragraphs and sections from the sermons of other ministers. These borrowings are a vital part of even major addresses and essays, such as his Nobel Prize lecture (1964), his "I Have a Dream" speech (1963) and his "Letter from Birmingham Jail" (1963).

The greatest revelation in this book, however, is not how much material King borrowed but from whom he borrowed. Miller's discoveries amount to a major re-evaluation of our current understanding of King as a thinker and a leader. "By attributing King's thought and language to his encounters with philosophers," he writes, "scholars have crafted a highly distorted image of King."

The author demolishes the notion that King went away from his home in Atlanta with few important opinions and ideas, and that his major beliefs were shaped by the writings of philosophers and theologians encountered at Crozer Theological Seminary, where he earned a bachelor's degree in divinity, and Boston University, where he took a Ph.D. Miller finds many white thinkers and writers who helped to shape King—but not those whites highlighted in accepted versions of King's education; and he also gives a different, much enlarged account of the roles of blacks in that education.

Rather than emphasize such figures as the theologians Reinhold Niebuhr and Paul Tillich, or the social gospeler Walter Rauschenbusch, Miller stresses that King's intellectual foundations were laid definitively at Ebenezer Baptist Church in Atlanta, where his father was pastor for 44 years. From King Sr., whom Miller—in defiance of scholarly opinion—flatly calls the greatest intellectual influence on his son, King learned the ideas and styles of the black folk preaching tradition based in the religion of the slaves. This instruction "proved far more important for King" than anything he learned at Morehouse College (where he earned his undergraduate degree), at Crozer or at Boston University.

Miller also traces the strong influence on King of other black ministers and preachers such as the scholarly Benjamin Mays of Morehouse, the spectacularly charismatic C. L. Franklin of Detroit and the mystical Howard Thurman and Mordecai Johnson of Howard University, who spurred King's first interest in Gandhi and nonviolence. For example, King's understanding of love, so critical to his religious and social views, derived not from Anders Nygren's "Agape and Eros," as King himself tried at times to suggest, but "from the black church." Even his faith in nonviolence, which defined the terms of his physical challenge to white supremacy in the South, reflected not unqualified devotion to the teachings of Gandhi, as is generally assumed, but King's highly selective modification of Gandhian principles and practices worked out in accordance with American and especially African American realities.

The central mystery posed by King, in Miller's analysis, is exactly how he found out "what no black person had ever discovered before": how to move so many whites to identify with the black desire for freedom and social justice, and how to attain the moral high ground in the rhetorical war between segregation and liberalism. "How did this process occur?" Miller asks. "What made King a superstar?"

Not surprisingly (except for the fact that scholars have looked elsewhere), King learned from whites, and from blacks attuned to whites, how to talk to whites. At Crozer Seminary, King's most important step *"by far"* (Miller's emphasis) was his immersion in the work of certain nationally popular and influential preachers, mainly white, including J. Wallace Hamilton and Harry E. Fosdick, whose weekly radio ministry attracted as many as 2 million listeners. These men were aware of philosophy and theology but were first and foremost preachers committed to moving sinners to Christ. By opening himself to the language and ideas of their sermons and then alchemizing them into his own, King was able to refine the rhetorical techniques and the thinking that would carry him to the heights of leadership.

By this point, there was little or no real deception.

"In his public discourse, no matter how much he borrowed," Miller says, King "invariably sounded exactly like himself. And he seemed—and was—absolutely sincere."

Like Hamilton and Fosdick, King's characteristic public utterance was preacherly, not theological or philosophical. This assertion is diminishing only if one takes King too solemnly as an intellectual.

And footnoting didn't matter to King, who "rejected ambivalent white attitudes toward borrowing."

Seminary professors warned against using other people's material, but the collections of sermons were there on the library shelves, and the typical hardworking minister was obliged to use them.

Moreover, the tradition of folk preaching, not unlike high literary and artistic traditions of earlier times, valued imitation and resented a puzzling originality. Congregations responded far more warmly to familiar quotations than to the new or the arcane.

What was true for whites was even more true for blacks, Miller argues. The black folk-pulpit supplied King "with the rhetorical assumption that language is common treasure—not private property—and with a well-established practice of borrowing and voice merging that he adapted to print."

In an appendix, Miller lists 35 "Key Figures" who shaped King's language and thought. He thinks there might be others, but his collations and comparisons prove most of his points about influence.

Voice of Deliverance is an important, vigorously researched and convincing book that gets close to the heart of the phenomenon that was Martin Luther King Jr.

Chapter 98

Women and Community Leadership

Ella Baker

Ella Baker (1903–1986) was a central—though, as a woman, often slighted—figure in African-American politics. She worked as a Harlem organizer during the Depression, as an NAACP organizer in the 1940s, and as interim director of the Southern Christian Leadership Conference (SCLC) and co-founder of the Student Nonviolent Coordinating Committee (SNCC). For a biography, see Joanne Grant, Ella Baker (1998).

Interviewer Gerda Lerner, emeritus professor of history at the University of Wisconsin and past president of the Organization of American Historians (1981–1982), is the author of many works, including The Grimke Sisters from South Carolina: Rebels against Slavery *(1967),* The Majority Finds Its Past: Placing Women in History *(1979), and* The Creation of Patriarchy *(1986).*

The following selection is an interview of Baker taped by Gerda Lerner and reproduced by permission from Gerda Lerner, Black Women in White America *(New York: Pantheon Books, 1972), 346–52.*

In my organizational work, I have never thought in terms of my "making a contribution." I just thought of myself as functioning where there was a need. And if I have made a contribution I think it may be that I had some influence on a large number of people.

As assistant field secretary of the branches of the NAACP, much of my work was in the South. At that time the NAACP was the leader on the cutting edge of social change. I remember when NAACP membership in the South was the basis for getting beaten up or even killed.

I used to leave New York about the 15th of February and travel through the South for four to five months. I would go to, say, Birmingham, Alabama and help to organize membership campaigns. And in the process of helping to organize membership campaigns, there was opportunity for developing community reaction. You would go into areas where people were not yet organized in the NAACP and try to get them more involved. Maybe you would start with some simple thing like the fact that they had no street lights, or the fact that in the given area somebody had been arrested or had been jailed in a manner that was considered illegal and unfair, and the like. You would deal with whatever the local problem was, and on the basis of the needs of the people you would try to organize them in the NAACP.

Black people who were living in the South were constantly living with violence. Part of the job was to help them to understand what that violence was and how they in an organized fashion could help to stem it. The major job was getting people to understand that they had something within their power that they could use, and it could only be used if they understood what was happening and how group action could counter violence even when it was perpetrated by the police or, in some instances, the state. My basic sense of it has always been to get people to understand that in the long run they themselves are the only protection they have against violence or injustice. If they only had ten members in the NAACP at a given point, those ten members could be in touch with twenty-five members in the next little town, with fifty in the next and throughout the state as a result of the organization of state conferences, and they, of course, could be linked up with the national. People have to be made to understand that they cannot look for salvation anywhere but to themselves.

I left the NAACP and then worked at fundraising with the National Urban League Service Fund and with several national health organizations. However, I continued my work with the NAACP on the local level. I became the advisor for the Youth Council. Then I served as President of the New York branch at a point where it had sunk to a low level in membership and otherwise. And in the process of serving as President we tried to bring the NAACP back, as I called it, to the people. We moved the branch out of an office building and located it where it would be more visible to the Harlem community. We started developing an active branch. It became one of the largest branches. I was President for a couple of years. It was strictly volunteer work which lasted until four o'clock in the morning, sometimes.

When the 1954 Supreme Court decision on school desegregation came, I was serving as chairman of the Educational Committee of the New York branch. We began to deal with the problems of *de facto* segregation, and the results of the *de facto* segregation which were evidenced largely in the achievement levels of black children, going down instead of going up after they entered public school. We had called the first committee meeting and Kenneth Clark became the chairman of that committee. During that period, I served on the Mayor's Commission on School Integration, with the subdivision on zoning. In the summer of 1957, I gave time to organizing what we called Parents in Action for Quality Education.

I've never believed that the people who control things really were willing and able to pay the price of integration. From a practical standpoint, anyone who looked at the Harlem area knew that the potential for integration per se was basically impossible unless there were some radically innovative things done. And those innovative things would not be acceptable to those who ran the school system, nor to communities, nor even to the people who call themselves supporters of integration. I did a good deal of speaking, and I went to Queens, I went to the upper West side, and the people very eagerly said they wanted school integration. But when you raised the question of whether they would permit or would welcome Blacks to live in the same houses with them, which was the only practical way at that stage to achieve integration, they squirmed. Integration certainly had to be pushed concurrently with changing the quality of education that the black children were getting, and changing the attitudes of the educational establishment toward the black community.

I don't think we achieved too much with the committee except to pinpoint certain issues and to have survived some very sharp confrontations with the Superintendent and others on the Board of Education. But out of it came increased fervor on the part of the black communities to make some changes. One of the gratifying things to me is the fact that even as late as this year I have met people who were in that group and who have been continuously active in the struggle for quality education in the black communities ever since.

There certainly has been progress in the direction of the capacity of people to face this issue. And to me, when people themselves know what they are looking for and recognize that they can exercise some influence by action, that's progress.

Come 1957, I went down South a couple of times in connection with the formation of the Southern Christian Leadership Conference. At the end of '57 there was the need for someone to go down to set up the office of SCLC in Atlanta and to coordinate what it considered its first South-wide project, which was the holding of simultaneous meetings on February 12th in twenty different cities. I went down with the idea of not spending more than six weeks there, giving myself a month to get the thing going, and then two weeks to clean it up. I stayed with SCLC for two and a half years, because they didn't have anybody. My official capacity was varied. When I first went down, I didn't insist on a title, which is nothing new or unusual for me; it didn't bother me. I was just there in person. And then they were looking for a minister, a man, and I helped to find a minister and a man, and he stayed a while, and when he came I decided that since I was doing what I was doing, he was the director and I became, I think, co-director. And then there was nobody, and of course there was no money in those days, so I kept on until the summer of 1960. And prior to that, of course, the sit-ins had started, and I was able to get the SCLC to at least sponsor the conference in Raleigh. We had hoped to call together about 100 or 125 of the young leaders who had emerged in the sit-ins in the South. But of course the sit-ins had been so dynamic in the field that when we got to the meeting we had two hundred and some people, including some from the North. And out of that conference of the Easter weekend of 1960, which I coordinated and organized, we had a committee that came out of it, and out of that committee SNCC was born.

And after SNCC came into existence, of course, it opened up a new era of struggle. I felt the urge to stay close by. Because if I had done anything anywhere, it had been largely in the role of supporting things, and in the background of things that needed to be done for the organizations that were supposedly out front. So I felt if I had done it for the elders, I could do it for young people.

I had no difficulty relating to the young people. I spoke their language in terms of the meaning of what they had to say. I didn't change my speech pattern and they didn't have to change their speech pattern. But we were able to communicate.

I never had any income or paid relationship with SNCC. In order to be available to do things with SNCC, I first found a two-year project with the Southern Region of the National Student YWCA in a special Human Relations Program. Then I took up a relationship with the Southern Conference Educational Fund (SCEF). I still am on their staff in a consultative role, and I stayed in Atlanta until the summer of '64, spring and summer of '64. I was asked to come up and help organize the challenge of the Mississippi Freedom Democratic Party at the Democratic Convention. So offices were set up in Washington and I functioned there until after the convention, closed up the office, and then moved back to New York from Atlanta.

There are those, some of the young people especially, who have said to me that if I had not been a woman I would have been well known in certain places, and perhaps held certain kinds of positions.

I have always felt it was a handicap for oppressed peoples to depend so largely upon a leader, because unfortunately in our culture, the charismatic leader usually becomes a leader because he has found a spot in the public limelight. It usually means he has been touted through the public media, which means that the media made him and the media may undo him. There is also the danger in our culture that, because a person is called upon to give public statements and is acclaimed by the establishment, such a person gets to the point of believing that he is the movement. Such people get so involved with playing the game of being important that they exhaust themselves and their time, and they don't do the work of actually organizing people.

For myself, circumstances frequently dictated what had to be done as I saw it. For example, I had no plans to go down and set up the office of SCLC. But it seemed unless something were done whatever impetus had been gained would be lost, and nobody else was available who was willing or able to do it. So I went because to me it was more important to see what was a potential for all of us than it was to do what I might have done for myself. I knew from the beginning that as a woman, an older woman, in a group of ministers who are accustomed to having women largely as supporters, there was no place for me to have come into a leadership role. The competition wasn't worth it.

The movement of the '50's and '60's was carried largely by women, since it came out of church groups. It was sort of second nature to women to play a supportive role. How many made a conscious decision on the basis of the larger goals, how many on the basis of habit pattern, I don't know. But it's true that the numbers of women who carried the movement is much larger than that of men. Black women have had to carry this role, and I think the younger women are insisting on an equal footing.

I don't advocate anybody following the pattern I followed, unless they find themselves in a situation where they think that the larger goals will be short-changed if they don't. From the standpoint of the historical pattern of the society, which seems to assume that this is the best role for women, I think that certainly the young people who are challenging this ought to be challenging it, and it ought to be changed. But I also think you have to have a certain sense of your own value, and a sense of security on your part, to be able to forgo the glamor of what the leadership role offers. From the standpoint of my work and my own self-concepts, I don't think I have thought of myself largely as a woman. I thought of myself as an individual with a certain amount of sense of the need to participate in the movement. I have always thought what is needed is the development of people who are interested not in being leaders as much as in developing leadership among other people. Every time I see a young person who has come through the system to a stage where he could profit from the system and identify with it, but who identifies more with the struggle of black people who have not had his chance, every time I find such a person I take a new hope. I feel a new life as a result of it.

Chapter 99

The Student Nonviolent Coordinating Committee

Howard Zinn

Historian and playwright Howard Zinn has taught at Spelman College and Boston University. His books include The Southern Mystique *(1964),* SNCC: The New Abolitionists *(1964),* The Politics of History *(1970),* A People's History of the United States *(2d ed., 1995),* Declarations of Independence: Cross-Examining American Ideology *(1990),* The Zinn Reader: Writings on Disobedience and Democracy *(1997), and the memoir* You Can't Be Neutral on a Moving Train *(1994).*

Zinn's most recent play is Marx in Soho: A Play on History *(1999). An earlier work,* Emma, *based on the life of the anarchist Emma Goldman, has been performed in Boston, New York, London, and Tokyo.*

The following selection is reprinted from "Student Nonviolent Coordinating Committee" by Howard Zinn, from Encyclopedia of the American Left, *2d ed., ed. Mari Jo Buhle, Paul Buhle, and Dan Georgakas. Copyright © 1998 by Oxford University Press, Inc. Used by permission of Oxford University Press, Inc.*

For other selections by Zinn, see chapters 108 and 187.

SNCC—pronounced snick—was formed in the spring of 1960 by mostly black college students who were involved in the lunch counter sit-ins then sweeping the South. They met in Raleigh, North Carolina, at the initiative of Ella Baker, a middle-aged black woman, a veteran of NAACP struggles since the 1930s, who from this time would give intellectual guidance and spiritual inspiration to the young people in SNCC.

Advocating nonviolent direct action, SNCC quickly became the militant thrusting point of the civil rights movement. Using a tiny office in Atlanta as headquarters and paid ten dollars a week, several dozen SNCC "field secretaries" moved out into the Deep South, embedded themselves in the black communities, lived in ramshackle "Freedom Houses," gained the confidence of local blacks, enlisted the aid of local youngsters, and began the dangerous work of challenging racial segregation in every form.

They reorganized the "Freedom Rides" in the spring of 1961, after the Congress of Racial Equality encountered bus-burnings and brutal beatings, and ended up beaten themselves, and jailed. They organized local people to demonstrate against segregation in Albany, Georgia, to register voters in Selma, Alabama, and Hattiesburg, Mississippi, and all over the Deep South. In the summer of 1964, they invited more than 1,000 northern students to come to Mississippi to help with voter registration, teach in "Freedom Schools," and bring racism to national attention. That summer, three SNCC people (two white, one black) were murdered in Neshoba County, Mississippi, and that August, black Mississippians were rebuffed by the Democratic Party at its national convention, which agreed to recognize only the white voting delegation.

SNCC, based on its own bitter experience with federal inaction in the face of white violence, was certainly the most angry and the most independent of civil rights groups in the South. Speaking to the huge biracial March on Washington in the summer of 1963, SNCC leader John Lewis, in the face of censorship by other black leaders, insisted on criticizing the Kennedy administration for its failure to defend black rights.

It would be wrong, in understanding SNCC, to ignore the heritage of older American radical movements. A few of its field secretaries, educated in the North, had some contact with radical ideas. Ella Baker came out of the Left struggles of the thirties and forties, and was also influenced by the socialist, anti-imperialist thinking of W. E. B. Du Bois. There was also some impact from the Southern radical tradition: the Southern Conference Education Fund, and the Highlander Folk School. But SNCC was not consciously ideological; its militancy, its spontaneous radicalism, was shaped mostly by its immediate experience in the southern struggle, its closeness to the black poor, its perception that the government, national as well as local, was tied to powerful political and economic interests, and could not be trusted.

When the southern movement had achieved its immediate aims—the right to vote, the end of legal segregation, a new black consciousness, and a new white perception of blacks as refusing to accept the old order—it lost direction and momentum. It was up against the stone wall of the American system. The recognition that racism, while legally eliminated, was deeply embedded in the institutions of the country, especially in those economic arrangements that created a class of poor, and that this class would be largely black, led to more bitterness, more militancy. The cry of "Black Power," arising in 1965–66, meant different things to different people but signaled the frustration of a movement that was at once victorious and unfulfilled.

In this climate, SNCC quickly disintegrated, its people scattered and uncertain, some joining new groups, other still battling, though isolated. But it had affected the thinking of countless people, black and white, and played a pioneering role in creating the climate of the sixties. Its hostility to government (SNCC people were among the first draft resisters), its early raising of the issue (by young SNCC women in the Atlanta office) of sexual equality, its suspicion of centralized authority, and its closeness to grass-roots feelings, all prefigured the great movements of the sixties, against the Vietnam War, for gender equality, and the independent radicalism that came to be called the New Left.

Chapter 100

SNCC Statement of Purpose

James M. Lawson, Jr.

James M. Lawson, Jr., is a member of SCLC and was a founding member of SNCC. In 1958, while studying for the ministry at Vanderbilt University, he began conducting nonviolence workshops in the South. He recently retired as pastor of the Holman United Methodist Church in Los Angeles.

The following selection is reprinted from "SNCC Statement of Purpose," 14 May 1960. Reprinted by permission of the author.

We affirm the philosophical or religious ideal of nonviolence as the foundation of our purpose, the pre-supposition of our faith, and the manner of our action. Nonviolence as it grows from Judaic-Christian traditions seeks a social order of justice permeated by love. Integration of human endeavor represents the crucial first step towards such a society.

Through nonviolence, courage displaces fear; love transforms hate. Acceptance dissipates prejudice; hope ends despair. Peace dominates war; faith reconciles doubt. Mutual regard cancels enmity. Justice for all overthrows injustice. The redemptive community supersedes systems of gross social immorality.

Love is the central motif of nonviolence. Love is the force by which God binds man to himself and man to man. Such love goes to the extreme; it remains loving and forgiving even in the midst of hostility. It matches the capacity of evil to inflict suffering with an even more enduring capacity to absorb evil, all the while persisting in love.

By appealing to conscience and standing on the moral nature of human existence, nonviolence nurtures the atmosphere in which reconciliation and justice become actual possibilities.

Chapter 101

Suppose Not Negroes but Men of Property Were Being Beaten in Mississippi

I. F. Stone

Investigative journalist I. F. Stone (1907–1989) was the writer, editor, and publisher of I. F. Stone's Weekly *(1953–1971). He began his newspaper career at age fourteen, when he founded a monthly, the* Progress. *He went on to write for the* Nation, PM, *the* New York Post, *the* Daily Compass, *and other newspapers and magazines. In the 1950s, out of work and under attack from Red-baiters, he founded the* Weekly. *When he ceased publication the newsletter had a circulation of 70,000.*

After retiring from the Weekly, *Stone was a frequent contributor to the* New York Review of Books *and the* Nation. *His books include* The Court Disposes *(1937),* Business as Usual *(1941),* The Hidden History of the Korean War *(1952),* The Truman Era *(1953),* The Haunted Fifties *(1964),* In a Time of Torment *(1967),* The Killings at Kent State *(1971), and* The Trial of Socrates *(1988).*

The following selection is reprinted from "Suppose Not Negroes but Men of Property Were Being Beaten in Mississippi?" I. F. Stone's Weekly, 29 April 1963. Reprinted by permission of Jeremy J. Stone.

For another selection by Stone, see chapter 119.

Of course we don't mean it seriously. We're merely putting it forward as a classroom exercise in jurisprudence. But let us suppose it was not the rights of Negroes but the rights of property which were menaced in Mississippi. Let us suppose that, thanks to a sudden disappearance of racism, poor whites and Negroes had suddenly united and elected their own men to the state government, replacing even the sheriffs and the police officers. And suppose that these new law-enforcement officers began to harass, to beat, to shoot and occasionally to kill men of property on one excuse or another—failure to pay minimum wages on the plantations, or failure to provide fair accounting in mills and stores. Suppose that when property owners tried to demonstrate police dogs were set upon them. Suppose that when they tried to appeal to the Civil Rights Commission in Washington, the Mississippi legislature passed special laws (like Sections 2155.4, 2155.5 and 2155.6 enacted in 1960) making it a crime punishable by five years in jail to make false statements to any Federal investigator, providing that in such prosecutions the two-witness rule for perjury would be suspended and one witness would be enough for conviction, and applying this sanction even to immaterial statements (that is, any inconsequential slip of the tongue). Suppose the Attorney General had timidly refused to allow the Civil Rights Commission to hold public hearings in Mississippi lest this disturb the atmosphere! Suppose bombs had been thrown, not into some poor N.A.A.C.P. or C.O.R.E. office, but into (forgive the expression) A BANK. Suppose the Civil Rights Commission in desperation had then called on the President and the Congress to suspend all Federal aid to Mississippi until it agreed to safeguard fundamental rights guaranteed by the Federal Constitution. Q.: Would this suggestion evoke a shush-shush of legalistic horror from the liberal pundits of the great newspapers? Or would the U.S. Army take over Mississippi tomorrow?

Chapter 102

Letter from Birmingham City Jail

Martin Luther King, Jr.

The direct action campaign in Birmingham, Alabama, brought national publicity and federal government attention, leading to concessions from what King described as "probably the most thoroughly segregated city in the United States." According to SCLC historian Adam Fairclough, the campaign also encouraged the Kennedy administration to submit to Congress the bill passed under the Johnson administration as the 1964 Civil Rights Act.

While King was in jail, 12–20 April 1963, for violating a court injunction by leading a protest march in Birmingham, he wrote his now classic response to a published statement by eight Alabama clergymen criticizing the use of direct action as "unwise and untimely." An edited version of King's answer, described by him as more polished, was later published, with the abbreviated title "Letter from Birmingham Jail," in King's Why We Can't Wait *(1964).*

The following selection is reprinted from Martin Luther King, Jr., "Letter from Birmingham City Jail," 16 April 1963. Reprinted by arrangement with The Heirs to the Estate of Martin Luther King, Jr., c/o Writers House, Inc. as agent for the proprietor. Copyright 1963 by Martin Luther King, Jr., copyright renewed 1991 The Estate of Martin Luther King, Jr.

For other selections by King, see chapters 91, 95, and 106.

My dear Fellow Clergymen:

While confined here in the Birmingham city jail, I came across your recent statement calling our present activities "unwise and untimely." Seldom, if ever, do I pause to answer criticism of my work and ideas. If I sought to answer all of the criticisms that cross my desk, my secretaries would be engaged in little else in the course of the day, and I would have no time for constructive work. But since I feel that you are men of genuine good will and your criticisms are sincerely set forth, I would like to answer your statement in what I hope will be patient and reasonable terms.

I think I should give the reason for my being in Birmingham, since you have been influenced by the argument of "outsiders coming in." I have the honor of serving as president of the Southern Christian Leadership Conference, an organization operating in every southern state, with headquarters in Atlanta, Georgia.

We have some eighty-five affiliated organizations all across the South—one being the Alabama Christian Movement for Human Rights. Whenever necessary and possible we share staff, educational and financial resources with our affiliates. Several months ago our affiliate here in Birmingham invited us to be on call to engage in a nonviolent direct-action program if such were deemed necessary. We readily consented and when the hour came we lived up to our promises. So I am here, along with several members of my staff, because we were invited here. I am here because I have basic organizational ties here.

Beyond this, I am in Birmingham because injustice is here. Just as the eighth century prophets left their little villages and carried their "thus saith the Lord" far beyond the boundaries of their hometowns; and just as the Apostle Paul left his little village of Tarsus and carried the gospel of Jesus Christ to practically every hamlet and city of the Graeco-Roman world, I too am compelled to carry the gospel of freedom beyond my particular hometown. Like Paul, I must constantly respond to the Macedonian call for aid.

Moreover, I am cognizant of the interrelatedness of all communities and states. I cannot sit idly by in Atlanta and not be concerned about what happens in Birmingham. Injustice anywhere is a threat to justice everywhere. We are caught in an inescapable network of mutuality, tied in a single garment of destiny. Whatever affects one directly affects all indirectly. Never again can we afford to live with the narrow, provincial "outside agitator" idea. Anyone who lives in the United States can never be considered an outsider anywhere in this country.

You deplore the demonstrations that are presently taking place in Birmingham. But I am sorry your statement did not express a similar concern for the conditions that brought the demonstrations into being. I am sure that each of you would want to go beyond the superficial social analyst who looks merely at effects, and does not grapple with underlying causes. I would not hesitate to say that it is unfortunate that so-called demonstrations are taking place in Birmingham at this time, but I would say in more emphatic terms that it is even more unfortunate that the white power structure of this city left the Negro community with no other alternative.

In any nonviolent campaign there are four basic steps: (1) collection of the facts to determine whether injustices are alive, (2) negotiation, (3) self-purification, and (4) direct action. We have gone through all of these steps in Birmingham. There can be no gainsaying of the fact that racial injustice engulfs this community.

Birmingham is probably the most thoroughly segregated city in the United States. Its ugly record of police brutality is known in every section of this country. Its unjust treatment of Negroes in the courts is a notorious reality. There have been more unsolved bombings of Negro homes and churches in Birmingham than in any city in this nation. These are the hard, brutal and unbelievable facts. On the basis of these conditions Negro leaders sought to negotiate with the city fathers. But the political leaders consistently refused to engage in good faith negotiation.

Then came the opportunity last September to talk with some of the leaders of the economic community. In these negotiating sessions certain promises were made by the merchants—such as the promise to remove the humiliating racial signs from the stores. On the basis of these promises Rev. Shuttlesworth and the leaders of the Alabama Christian Movement for Human Rights agreed to call a moratorium on any type of demonstrations. As the weeks and months unfolded we realized that we were the victims of a broken promise. The signs remained. Like so many experiences of the past we were confronted with blasted hopes, and the dark shadow of a deep disappointment settled upon us. So we had no alternative except that of preparing for direct action, whereby we would present our very bodies as a means of laying our case before the conscience of the local and national community. We were not unmindful of the difficulties involved. So we decided to go through a process of self-purification. We started having workshops on nonviolence and repeatedly asked ourselves the questions, "Are you able to accept blows without retaliating?" "Are you able to endure the ordeals of jail?" We decided to set our direct-action program around the Easter season, realizing that with the exception of Christmas, this was the largest shopping period of the year. Knowing that a strong economic withdrawal program would be the by-product of direct action, we felt that this was the best time to bring pressure to bear on the merchants for the needed changes. Then it occurred to us that the March election was ahead and so we speedily decided to postpone action until after election day. When we discovered that Mr. Connor was in the run-off, we decided again to postpone action so that the demonstrations could not be used to cloud the issues. At this time we agreed to begin our nonviolent witness the day after the run-off.

This reveals that we did not move irresponsibly into direct action. We too wanted to see Mr. Connor defeated; so we went through postponement after postponement to aid in this community need. After this we felt that direct action could be delayed no longer.

You may well ask, "Why direct action? Why sit-ins, marches, etc.? Isn't negotiation a better path?" You are exactly right in your call for negotiation. Indeed, this is the purpose of direct action. Nonviolent direct action seeks to create such a crisis and establish such creative tension that a community that has constantly refused to negotiate is forced to confront the issue. It seeks so to dramatize the issue that it can no longer be ignored. I just referred to the creation of tension as a part of the work of the nonviolent resister. This may sound rather shocking. But I must confess that I am not afraid of the word tension. I have earnestly worked and preached against violent tension, but there is a type of constructive, nonviolent tension that is necessary for growth. Just as Socrates felt that it was necessary to create a tension in the mind so that individuals could rise from the bondage of myths and half-truths to the unfettered realm of creative analysis and objective appraisal, we must see the need of having nonviolent gadflies to create the kind of tension in society that will help men to rise from the dark depths of prejudice and racism to the majestic heights of understanding and brotherhood. So the purpose of the direct action is to create a situation so crisis-packed that it will inevitably open the door to negotiation. We, therefore, concur with you in your call for negotiation. Too long has our beloved Southland been bogged down in the tragic attempt to live in monologue rather than dialogue.

One of the basic points in your statement is that our acts are untimely. Some have asked, "Why didn't you give the new administration time to act?" The only answer that I can give to this inquiry is that the new administration must be prodded about as much as the outgoing one before it acts. We will be sadly mistaken if we feel that the election of Mr. Boutwell will bring the millennium to Birmingham. While Mr. Boutwell is much more articulate and gentle than Mr. Connor, they are both segregationists, dedicated to the task of maintaining the status quo. The hope I see in Mr. Boutwell is that he will be reasonable enough to see the futility of massive resistance to desegregation. But he will not see this without pressure from the devotees of civil rights. My friends, I must say to you that we have not made a single gain in civil rights without determined legal and nonviolent pressure. History is the long and tragic story of the fact that privileged groups seldom give up their privileges voluntarily. Individuals may see the moral light and voluntarily give up their unjust posture; but as Reinhold Niebuhr has reminded us, groups are more immoral than individuals.

We know through painful experience that freedom is never voluntarily given by the oppressor; it must be demanded by the oppressed. Frankly, I have never yet engaged in a direct action movement that was "well-timed," according to the timetable of those who have not suffered unduly from the disease of segregation. For years now I have heard the word "Wait!" It rings in the ear of every Negro with a piercing familiarity. This "Wait" has almost always meant "Never." It has been a tranquilizing thalidomide, relieving the emotional stress for a moment, only to give birth to an ill-formed infant of frustration. We must come to see with the distinguished jurist of yesterday that "justice too long delayed is justice denied." We have waited for more than 340 years for our constitutional and God-given rights. The nations of Asia and Africa are moving with jetlike speed toward the goal of political independence, and we still creep at horse and buggy pace toward the gaining of a cup of coffee at a lunch counter. I guess it is easy for those who have never felt the stinging darts of segregation to say, "Wait." But when you have seen vicious mobs lynch your mothers and fathers at will and drown your sisters and brothers at whim; when you have seen hate-filled policemen curse, kick, brutalize and even kill your black brothers and sisters with impunity; when you see the vast majority of your twenty million Negro brothers smothering in an airtight cage of poverty in the midst of an affluent society; when you suddenly find your tongue twisted and your speech stammering as you seek to explain to your six-year-old daughter why she can't go to the public amusement park that has just been advertised on television, and see tears welling up in her little eyes when she is told that Funtown is closed to colored children, and see the depressing clouds of inferiority beginning to form in her little mental sky, and see her begin to distort her little personality by unconsciously developing a bitterness toward white people; when you have to concoct an answer for a five-year-old son asking in agonizing pathos: "Daddy, why do white people treat colored people so mean?"; when you take a cross-country drive and find it necessary to sleep night after night in the uncomfortable corners of your automobile because no motel will accept you; when you are humiliated day in and day out by nagging signs reading "white" and "colored"; when your first name becomes "nigger" and your middle name becomes "boy" (however old you are) and your last name becomes "John," and when your wife and mother are never given the respected title "Mrs."; when you are harried by day and haunted by night by the fact that you are a Negro, living constantly at tiptoe stance never quite knowing what to expect next, and plagued with inner fears and outer resentments; when you are forever fighting a degenerating sense of "nobodiness"; then you will understand why we find it difficult to wait. There comes a time when the cup of endurance runs over, and men are no longer willing to be plunged into an abyss of injustice where they experience the blackness of corroding despair. I hope, sirs, you can understand our legitimate and unavoidable impatience.

You express a great deal of anxiety over our willingness to break laws. This is certainly a legitimate concern. Since we so diligently urge people to obey the Supreme Court's decision of 1954 outlawing segregation in the public schools, it is rather strange and paradoxical to find us consciously breaking laws. One may well ask, "How can you advocate breaking some laws and obeying others?" The answer is found in the fact that there are two types of laws: there are *just* and there are *unjust* laws. I would agree with St. Augustine that "An unjust law is no law at all."

Now what is the difference between the two? How does one determine when a law is just or unjust? A just law is a man-made code that squares with the moral law or the law of God. An unjust law is a code that is out of harmony with the moral law. To put it in the terms of St. Thomas Aquinas, an unjust law is a human law that is not rooted in eternal law and natural law. Any law that uplifts human personality is just. Any law that degrades human personality is unjust. All segregation statutes are unjust because segregation distorts the soul and damages the personality. It gives the segregator a false sense of superiority, and the segregated a false sense of inferiority. To use the words of Martin Buber, the great Jewish philosopher, segregation substitutes an "I-it" relationship for an "I-thou" relationship and ends up relegating persons to the status of things. So segregation is not only politically, economically and sociologically unsound, but it is morally wrong and sinful. Paul Tillich has said that sin is separation. Isn't segregation an existential expression of man's tragic separation, an expression of his awful estrangement, his terrible sinfulness? So I can urge men to disobey segregation ordinances because they are morally wrong.

Let us turn to a more concrete example of just and unjust laws. An unjust law is a code that a majority group inflicts on a minority that is not binding on itself. This is difference made legal. On the other hand a just law is a code that a majority compels a minority to follow that it is willing to follow itself. This is sameness made legal.

Let me give another explanation. An unjust law is a code inflicted upon a minority which that minority had no part in enacting or creating because they did not have the unhampered right to vote. Who can say that the legislature of Alabama which set up the segregation laws was democratically elected? Throughout the state of Alabama all types of conniving methods are used to prevent Negroes from becoming registered voters and there are some counties without a single Negro registered to vote despite the fact that the Negro constitutes a majority of the population. Can any law set up in such a state be considered democratically structured?

These are just a few examples of unjust and just laws. There are some instances when a law is just on its face and unjust in its application. For instance, I was arrested Friday on a charge of parading without a permit. Now there is nothing wrong with an ordinance which requires a permit for a parade, but when the ordinance is used to preserve segregation and to deny citizens the First Amendment privilege of peaceful assembly and peaceful protest, then it becomes unjust.

I hope you can see the distinction I am trying to point out. In no sense do I advocate evading or defying the law as the rabid segregationist would do. This would lead to anarchy. One who breaks an unjust law must do it *openly, lovingly* (not hatefully as the white mothers did in New Orleans when they were seen on television screaming, "nigger, nigger, nigger"), and with a willingness to accept the penalty. I submit that an individual who breaks a law that conscience tells him is unjust, and willingly accepts the penalty by staying in jail to arouse the conscience of the community over its injustice, is in reality expressing the very highest respect for law.

Of course, there is nothing new about this kind of civil disobedience. It was seen sublimely in the refusal of Shadrach, Meshach, and Abednego to obey the laws of Nebuchadnezzar because a higher moral law was involved. It was practiced superbly by the early Christians who were willing to face hungry lions and the excruciating pain of chopping blocks, before submitting to certain unjust laws of the Roman Empire. To a degree academic freedom is a reality today because Socrates practiced civil disobedience.

We can never forget that everything Hitler did in Germany was "legal" and everything the Hungarian freedom fighters did in Hungary was "illegal." It was "illegal" to aid and comfort a Jew in Hitler's Germany. But I am sure that if I had lived in Germany during that time I would have aided and comforted my Jewish brothers even though it was illegal. If I lived in a Communist country today where certain principles dear to the Christian faith are suppressed, I believe I would openly advocate disobeying these anti-religious laws. I must make two honest confessions to you, my Christian and Jewish brothers. First, I must confess that over the last few years I have been gravely disappointed with the white moderate. I have almost reached the regrettable conclusion that the Negro's great stumbling block in the stride toward freedom is not the White Citizen's Counciler or the Ku Klux Klanner, but the white moderate who is more devoted to "order" than to justice; who prefers a negative peace which is the absence of tension to a positive peace which is the presence of justice; who constantly says, "I agree with you in the goal you seek, but I can't agree with your methods of direct action"; who paternalistically believes that he can set the timetable for another man's freedom; who lives by the myth of time and who constantly advises the Negro to wait until a "more convenient season." Shallow understanding from people of good will is more frustrating than absolute misunderstanding from people of ill will. Lukewarm acceptance is much more bewildering than outright rejection.

I had hoped that the white moderate would understand that law and order exist for the purpose of establishing justice, and that when they fail to do this they become dangerously structured dams that block the flow of social progress. I had hoped that the white moderate would understand that the present tension of the South is merely a necessary phase of the transition from an obnoxious negative peace, where the Negro passively accepted his unjust plight, to a substance-filled positive peace, where all men will respect the dignity and worth of human personality. Actually, we who engage in nonviolent direct action are not the creators of tension. We merely bring to the surface the hidden tension that is already alive. We bring it out in the open where it can be seen and dealt with. Like a boil that can never be cured so long as it is covered up but must be opened with all its pus-flowing ugliness to the natural medicines of air and light, injustice must likewise be exposed, with all of the tension its exposing creates, to the light of human conscience and the air of national opinion before it can be cured.

In your statement you asserted that our actions, even though peaceful, must be condemned because they precipitate violence. But can this assertion be logically made? Isn't this like condemning the robbed man because his possession of money precipitated the evil act of robbery? Isn't this like condemning Socrates because his unswerving commitment to truth and his philosophical delvings precipitated the misguided popular mind to make him drink the hemlock? Isn't this like condemning Jesus because His unique God-consciousness and never-ceasing devotion to His will precipitated the evil act of crucifixion? We must come to see, as federal courts have consistently affirmed, that it is immoral to urge an individual to withdraw his efforts to gain his basic constitutional rights because the quest precipitates violence. Society must protect the robbed and punish the robber.

I had also hoped that the white moderate would reject the myth of time. I received a letter this morning from a white brother in Texas which said: "All Christians know that the colored people will receive equal rights eventually, but it is possible that you are in too great of a religious hurry. It has taken Christianity almost two thousand years to accomplish what it has. The teachings of Christ take time to come to earth." All that is said here grows out of a tragic misconception of time. It is the strangely irrational notion that there is something in the very flow of time that will inevitably cure all ills. Actually time is neutral. It can be used either destructively or constructively. I am coming to feel that the people of ill will have used time much more effectively than have the people of good will. We will have to repent in this generation not merely for the vitriolic words and actions of the bad people, but for the appalling silence of the good people. We must come to see that human progress never rolls in on wheels of inevitability. It comes through the tireless efforts and persistent work of men willing to be co-workers with God, and without this hard work time itself becomes an ally of the forces of social stagnation. We must use time creatively, and forever realize that the time is always ripe to do right. Now is the time to make real the promise of democracy, and transform our pending national elegy into a creative psalm of brotherhood. Now is the time to lift our national policy from the quicksand of racial injustice to the solid rock of human dignity.

You spoke of our activity in Birmingham as extreme. At first I was rather disappointed that fellow clergymen would see my nonviolent efforts as those of an extremist. I started thinking about the fact that I stand in the middle of two opposing forces in the Negro community. One is a force of complacency made up of Negroes who, as a result of long years of oppression, have been so completely drained of self-respect and a sense of "somebodiness" that they have adjusted to segregation, and, of a few Negroes in the middle class who, because of a degree of academic and economic security, and because at points they profit by segregation, have unconsciously become insensitive to the problems of the masses. The other force is one of bitterness and hatred, and comes perilously close to advocating violence. It is expressed in the various black nationalist groups that are springing up over the nation, the largest and best known being Elijah Muhammad's Muslim movement. This movement is nourished by the contemporary frustration over the continued existence of racial discrimination. It is made up of people who have lost faith in America, who have absolutely repudiated Christianity, and who have concluded that the white man is an incurable "devil." I have tried to stand between these two forces, saying that we need not follow the "do-nothingism" of the complacent or the hatred and despair of the black nationalist. There is the more excellent way of love and nonviolent protest. I am grateful to God that, through the Negro church, the dimension of nonviolence became an integral part of our struggle. If this philosophy had not emerged, I am convinced that by now many streets of the South would be flowing with floods of blood. And I am further convinced that if our white brothers dismiss as "rabble-rousers" and "outside agitators" those of us who are working through the channels of nonviolent direct action and refuse to support our nonviolent efforts, millions of Negroes, out of frustration and despair, will seek solace and security in black nationalist ideologies, a development that will lead inevitably to a frightening racial nightmare.

Oppressed people cannot remain oppressed forever. The urge for freedom will eventually come. This is what happened to the American Negro. Something within has reminded him of his birthright of freedom; something without has reminded him he can gain it. Consciously and unconsciously, he has been swept in by what the Germans call the Zeitgeist, and with his black brothers of Africa, and his brown and yellow brothers of Asia, South America, and the Caribbean, he is moving with a sense of cosmic urgency toward the promised land of racial justice. Recognizing this vital urge that has engulfed the Negro community, one should readily understand public demonstrations. The Negro has many pent-up resentments and latent frustrations. He has to get them out. So let him march sometime; let him have his prayer pilgrimages to the city hall; understand why he must have sit-ins and freedom rides. If his repressed emotions do not come out in these nonviolent ways, they will come out in ominous expressions of violence. This is not a threat; it is a fact of history. So I have not said to my people "get rid of your discontent." But I have tried to say that this normal and healthy discontent can be channelized through the creative outlet of nonviolent direct action. Now this approach is being dismissed as extremist. I must admit I was initially disappointed in being so categorized.

But as I continued to think about the matter I gradually gained a measure of satisfaction from being considered an extremist. Was not Jesus an extremist in love—"Love your enemies, bless them that curse you, pray for them that despitefully use you." Was not Amos an extremist for justice—"Let justice roll down like waters and righteousness like a mighty stream." Was not Paul an extremist for the gospel of Jesus Christ—"I bear in my body the marks of the Lord Jesus." Was not Martin Luther an extremist—"Here I stand; I can do none other so help me God." Was not John Bunyan an extremist—"I will stay in jail to the end of my days before I make a butchery of my conscience." Was not Abraham Lincoln an extremist—"This nation cannot survive half slave and half free." Was not Thomas Jefferson an extremist—"We hold these truths to be self-evident, that all men are created equal." So the question is not whether we will be extremist, but what kind of extremist will we be. Will we be extremists for hate or extremists for love? Will we be extremists for the preservation of injustice—or will be extremists for the cause of justice? In that dramatic scene on Calvary's hill, three men were crucified. We must not forget that all three were crucified for the same crime—the crime of extremism. Two were extremists for immorality, and thus fell below their environment. The other, Jesus Christ, was an extremist for love, truth, and goodness, and thereby rose above his environment. So, after all, maybe the South, the nation, and the world are in dire need of creative extremists.

I had hoped that the white moderate would see this. Maybe I was too optimistic. Maybe I expected too much. I guess I should have realized that few members of a race that oppressed another race can understand or appreciate the deep groans and passionate yearnings of those that have been oppressed, and still fewer have the vision to see that injustice must be rooted out by strong, persistent, and determined action. I am thankful, however, that some of our white brothers have grasped the meaning of this social revolution and committed themselves to it. They are still all too small in quantity, but they are big in quality. Some like Ralph McGill, Lillian Smith, Harry Golden, and James Dabbs have written about our struggle in eloquent, prophetic and understanding terms. Others have marched with us down nameless streets of the South. They have languished in filthy, roach-infested jails, suffering the abuse and brutality of policemen who see them as "dirty nigger-lovers." They, unlike so many of their moderate brothers and sisters, have recognized the urgency of the moment and sensed the need for powerful "action" antidotes to combat the disease of segregation.

Let me rush on to mention my other major disappointment. I have been so greatly disappointed with the white church and its leadership. Of course, there are some notable exceptions. I am not unmindful of the fact that each of you has taken some significant stands on this issue. I commend you, Rev. Stallings, for your Christian stance on this past Sunday, in welcoming Negroes to your worship service on a non-segregated basis. I commend the Catholic leaders of this state for integrating Springhill College several years ago.

But despite these notable exceptions I must honestly reiterate that I have been disappointed with the church. I do not say that as one of the negative critics who can always find something wrong with the church. I say it as a minister of the gospel, who loves the church; who was nurtured in its bosom; who has been sustained by its spiritual blessings and who will remain true to it as long as the cord of life shall lengthen.

I had the strange feeling when I was suddenly catapulted into the leadership of the bus protest in Montgomery several years ago that we would have the support of the white church. I felt that white ministers, priests and rabbis of the South would be some of our strongest allies. Instead, some have been outright opponents, refusing to understand the freedom movement and misrepresenting its leaders; all too many others have been more cautious than courageous and have remained silent behind the anesthetizing security of the stained-glass windows.

In spite of my shattered dreams of the past, I came to Birmingham with the hope that the white religious leadership of this community would see the justice of our cause, and with deep moral concern, serve as the channel through which our just grievances would get to the power structure. I had hoped that each of you would understand. But again I have been disappointed. I have heard numerous religious leaders of the South admonish their worshippers to comply with a desegregation decision because it is the *law,* but I have longed to hear white ministers say, "Follow this decree because integration is morally *right* and the Negro is your brother." In the midst of blatant injustices inflicted upon the Negro, I have watched white churches stand on the sideline and merely mouth pious irrelevancies and sanctimonious trivialities. In the midst of a mighty struggle to rid our nation of racial and economic injustice, I have heard many ministers say, "Those are social issues with which the gospel has no real concern," and I have watched so many churches commit themselves to a completely otherworldly religion which made a strange distinction between body and soul, the sacred and the secular.

So here we are moving toward the exit of the twentieth century with a religious community largely adjusted to the status quo, standing as a taillight behind other community agencies rather than a headlight leading men to higher levels of justice.

I have traveled the length and breadth of Alabama, Mississippi, and all the other southern states. On sweltering summer days and crisp autumn mornings I have looked at her beautiful churches with their lofty spires pointing heavenward. I have beheld the impressive outlay of her massive religious education buildings. Over and over again I have found myself asking: "What kind of people worship here? Who is their God? Where were their voices when the lips of Governor Barnett dripped with words of interposition and nullification? Where were they when Governor Wallace gave a clarion call for defiance and hatred? Where were their voices of support when tired, bruised and weary Negro men and women decided to rise from the dark dungeons of complacency to the bright hills of creative protest?"

Yes, these questions are still in my mind. In deep disappointment, I have wept over the laxity of the church. But be assured that my tears have been tears of love. There can be no deep disappointment where there is not deep love. Yes, I love the church; I love her sacred walls. How could I do otherwise? I am in the rather unique position of being the son, the grandson, and the great-grandson of preachers. Yes, I see the church as the body of Christ. But, oh! How we have blemished and scarred that body through social neglect and fear of being nonconformists.

There was a time when the church was very powerful. It was during that period when the early Christians rejoiced when they were deemed worthy to suffer for what they believed. In those days the church was not merely a thermometer that recorded the ideas and principles of popular opinion; it was a thermostat that transformed the mores of society. Wherever the early Christians entered a town the power structure got disturbed and immediately sought to convict them for being "disturbers of the peace" and "outside agitators." But they went on with the conviction that they were "a colony of heaven," and had to obey God rather than man. They were small in number but big in commitment. They were too God-intoxicated to be "astronomically intimidated." They brought an end to such ancient evils as infanticide and gladiatorial contests.

Things are different now. The contemporary church is often a weak, ineffectual voice with an uncertain sound. It is so often the arch-supporter of the status quo. Far from being disturbed by the presence of the church, the power structure of the average community is consoled by the church's silent and often vocal sanction of things as they are.

But the judgment of God is upon the church as never before. If the church of today does not recapture the sacrificial spirit of the early church, it will lose its authentic ring, forfeit the loyalty of millions, and be dismissed as an irrelevant social club with no meaning for the twentieth century. I am meeting young people every day whose disappointment with the church has risen to outright disgust.

Maybe again, I have been too optimistic. Is organized religion too inextricably bound to the status quo to save our nation and the world? Maybe I must turn my faith to the inner spiritual church, the church within the church, as the true *ecclesia* and the hope of the world. But again I am thankful to God that some noble souls from the ranks of organized religion have broken loose from the paralyzing chains of conformity and joined us as active partners in the struggle for freedom. They have left their secure congregations and walked the streets of Albany, Georgia, with us. They have gone through the highways of the South on tortuous rides for freedom. Yes, they have gone to jail with us. Some have been kicked out of their churches, and lost support of their bishops and fellow ministers. But they have gone with the faith that right defeated is stronger than evil triumphant. These men have been the leaven in the lump of the race. Their witness has been the spiritual salt that has preserved the true meaning of the gospel in these troubled times. They have carved a tunnel of hope through the dark mountain of disappointment.

I hope the church as a whole will meet the challenge of this decisive hour. But even if the church does not come to the aid of justice, I have no despair about the future. I have no fear about the outcome of our struggle in Birmingham, even if our motives are presently misunderstood. We will reach the goal of freedom in Birmingham and all over the nation, because the goal of America is freedom. Abuse and scorned though we may be, our destiny is tied up the destiny of America. Before the Pilgrims landed at Plymouth, we were here. Before the pen of Jefferson etched across the pages of history the majestic words of the Declaration of Independence, we were here. For more than two centuries our foreparents labored in this country without wages; they made cotton king; and they built the homes of their masters in the midst of brutal injustice and shameful humiliation—and yet out of a bottomless vitality they continued to thrive and develop. If the inexpressible cruelties of slavery could not stop us, the opposition we now face will surely fail. We will win our freedom because the sacred heritage of our nation and the eternal will of God are embodied in our echoing demands.

I must close now. But before closing I am impelled to mention one other point in your statement that has troubled me profoundly. You warmly commended the Birmingham police force for keeping "order" and "preventing violence." I don't believe you would have so warmly commended the police force if you had seen its angry violent dogs literally biting six unarmed, nonviolent Negroes. I don't believe you would so quickly commend the policemen if you would observe their ugly and inhuman treatment of Negroes here in the city jail; if you would watch them push and curse old Negro women and young Negro girls; if you would see them slap and kick Negro men and young boys; if you will observe them, as they did on two occasions, refuse to give us food because we wanted to sing our grace together. I'm sorry I can't join you in your praise of the Birmingham police department.

It is true they have been rather disciplined in their public handling of the demonstrators. In this sense they have been rather publicly "nonviolent." But for what purpose? To preserve the evil system of segregation. Over the last few years I have consistently preached that nonviolence demands that the means we use must be as pure as the ends we seek. So I have tried to make it clear that it is wrong to use immoral means to attain moral ends. But now I must affirm that it is just as wrong, or even more so, to use moral means to preserve immoral ends. Maybe Mr. Connor and his policemen have been rather publicly nonviolent, as Chief Pritchett was in Albany, Georgia, but they have used the moral means of nonviolence to maintain the immoral end of flagrant racial injustice. T. S. Eliot has said that there is no greater treason than to do the right deed for the wrong reason.

I wish you had commended the Negro sit-inners and demonstrators of Birmingham for their sublime courage, their willingness to suffer and their amazing discipline in the midst of the most inhuman provocation. One day the South will recognize its real heroes. They will be the James Merediths, courageously and with a majestic sense of purpose facing jeering and hostile mobs and the agonizing loneliness that characterizes the life of the pioneer. They will be old, oppressed, battered Negro women, symbolized in a seventy-two-year-old woman of Montgomery, Alabama, who rose up with a sense of dignity and with her people decided not to ride segregated buses, and responded to one who inquired about her tiredness with ungrammatical profundity: "My feet is tired, but my soul is rested." They will be the young high school and college students, young ministers of the gospel and a host of their elders courageously and nonviolently sitting-in at lunch counters and willingly going to jail for conscience' sake. One day the South will know that when these disinherited children of God sat down at lunch counters they were in reality standing up for the best in the American dream and the most sacred values in our Judeo-Christian heritage, and thusly, carrying our whole nation back to those great wells of democracy which were dug deep by the Founding Fathers in the formulation of the Constitution and the Declaration of Independence.

Never before have I written a letter this long (or should I say book?). I'm afraid that it is much too long to take your precious time. I can assure you that it would have been much shorter if I had been writing from a comfortable desk, but what else is there to do when you are alone for days in the dull monotony of a narrow jail cell other than write long letters, think strange thoughts, and pray long prayers?

If I have said anything in this letter that is an overstatement of the truth and is indicative of an unreasonable impatience, I beg you to forgive me. If I have said anything that is an understatement of the truth and is indicative of my having a patience that makes me patient with anything less than brotherhood, I beg God to forgive me.

I hope this letter finds you strong in the faith. I also hope that circumstances will soon make it possible for me to meet each of you, not as an integrationist or a civil rights leader but as a fellow clergyman and a Christian brother. Let us all hope that the dark clouds of racial prejudice will soon pass away and the deep fog of misunderstanding will be lifted from our fear-drenched communities and in some not too distant tomorrow the radiant stars of love and brotherhood will shine over our great nation with all of their scintillating beauty.

Yours for the cause of Peace and Brotherhood,

Martin Luther King, Jr.

Chapter 103

Television Address on Civil Rights

John F. Kennedy

On 11 June 1963, a few weeks after the Birmingham demonstrations, Governor George Wallace stood in the doorway at the University of Alabama to block two black students from registering for classes. President Kennedy sent in the National Guard and later spoke to the nation on national television. Shortly after the address, NAACP field secretary Medgar Evers was murdered outside his home in Mississippi (see chapter 82).

The following selection is excerpted from "Radio and Television Report to the American People on Civil Rights," June 11, 1963," Public Papers of the Presidents of the United States, John F. Kennedy, 1963 *(Washington, D.C., 1964), 468–71.*

This afternoon, following a series of threats and defiant statements, the presence of Alabama National Guardsmen was required on the campus of the University of Alabama to carry out the final and unequivocal order of the United States District Court of the Northern District of Alabama. That order called for the admission of two clearly qualified young Alabama residents who happened to have been born Negro.

That they were admitted peacefully on the campus is due in good measure to the conduct of the students of the University of Alabama who met their responsibilities in a constructive way.

I hope that every American, regardless of where he lives, will stop and examine his conscience about this and other related incidents. This Nation was founded by men of many nations and backgrounds. It was founded on the principle that all men are created equal, and that the rights of every man are diminished when the rights of one man are threatened.

Today we are committed to a worldwide struggle to promote and protect the rights of all who wish to be free. And when Americans are sent to Viet-Nam or West Berlin we do not ask for whites only. It ought to be possible, therefore, for American students of any color to attend any public institution they select without having to be backed up by troops.

It ought to be possible for American consumers of any color to receive equal service in places of public accommodation, such as hotels and restaurants and theaters and retail stores, without being forced to resort to demonstrations in the street, and it ought to be possible for American citizens of any color to register and to vote in a free election without interference or fear of reprisal.

It ought to be possible, in short, for every American to enjoy the privileges of being American without regard to his race or his color. In short, every American ought to have the right to be treated as he would wish to be treated, as one would wish his children to be treated. But this is not the case.

The Negro baby born in America today, regardless of the section of the Nation in which he is born, has about one-half as much chance of completing high school as a white baby, born in the same place, on the same day . . . twice as much chance of becoming unemployed . . . a life expectancy which is seven years shorter, and the prospects of earning only half as much.

This is not a sectional issue. Difficulties over segregation and discrimination exist in every city in every State of the Union, producing in many cities a rising tide of discontent that threatens the public safety. Nor is this a partisan issue. In a time of domestic crisis, men of good will and generosity should be able to unite regardless of party or politics. This is not even a legal or legislative issue alone. It is better to settle these matters in the courts than on the streets, and new laws are needed at every level. But law alone cannot make men see right.

We are confronted primarily with a moral issue. It is as old as the scriptures and is as clear as the American Constitution.

The heart of the question is whether all Americans are to be afforded equal rights and equal opportunities, whether we are going to treat our fellow Americans as we want to be treated. If an American, because his skin is dark, cannot eat lunch in a restaurant open to the public; if he cannot send his children to the best public school available, if he cannot vote for the public officials who represent him, if, in short, he cannot enjoy the full and free life which all of us want, then who among us would be content to have the color of his skin changed and stand in his place? Who among us would then be content with the counsels of patience and delay.

One hundred years of delay have passed since President Lincoln freed the slaves, yet their heirs, their grandsons, are not fully free. They are not yet freed from the bonds of injustice. They are not yet freed from social and economic injustice. And this Nation, for all its hopes and all its boasts, will not be fully free until all its citizens are free.

We preach freedom around the world, and we mean it. And we cherish our freedom here at home. But are we to say to the world, and more importantly to each other, that this is the land of the free, except for the Negroes; that we have no second-class citizens except Negroes; that we have no class or cast[e] system, no ghettoes, no master race except with respect to Negroes?

Now the time has come for this Nation to fulfill its promise. The events in Birmingham and elsewhere have so increased the cries for equality that no city or state or legislative body can prudently choose to ignore them.

The fires of frustration and discord are burning in every city, North and South, where legal remedies are not at hand. Redress is sought in the streets in demonstrations, parades and protests, which create tensions and threaten violence and threaten lives.

We face, therefore, a moral crisis as a country and as a people. It cannot be met by repressive police action. It cannot be left to increased demonstrations in the streets. It cannot be quieted by token moves or talk. It is a time to act in the Congress, in your State and local legislative body and, above all, in all of our daily lives.

It is not enough to pin the blame on others, to say this is a problem of one section of the country or another, or deplore the fact[s] that we face. A great change is at hand, and our task, our obligation is to make that revolution, that change, peaceful and constructive for all.

Those who do nothing are inviting shame as well as violence. Those who act boldly are recognizing right as well as reality.

Next week I shall ask the Congress of the United States to act, to make a commitment it has not fully made in this century to the proposition that race has no place in American life or law. . . .

I am, therefore, asking the Congress to enact legislation giving all Americans the right to be served in facilities which are open to the public—hotels, restaurants, theaters, retail stores, and similar establishments. . . .

I am also asking Congress to authorize the Federal Government to participate more fully in lawsuits designed to end segregation in public education. . . .

Other features will also be requested, including greater protection for the right to vote. But legislation, I repeat, cannot solve this problem alone. It must be solved in the homes of every American in every community across our country. . . .

We have a right to expect that the Negro community will be responsible, will uphold the law. But they have a right to expect that the law will be fair, that the Constitution will be color blind, as Justice Harlan said at the turn of the century.

This is what we are talking about and this is a matter which concerns this country and what it stands for, and in meeting it I ask the support of all our citizens.

Chapter 104

What Really Happened at the March on Washington?

Nicolaus Mills

Nicolaus Mills, professor of American Studies at Sarah Lawrence College, is the author of Like a Holy Crusade: Mississippi, 1964 *(1993) and* The Triumph of Meanness: America's War against Its Better Self *(1997), and editor of* Busing U.S.A. *(1979),* Culture in an Age of Money: The Legacy of the 1980s in America *(1990),* Debating Affirmative Action *(1994), and* Arguing Immigration *(1994).*

The following selection is reprinted from "Heard and Unheard Speeches: What Really Happened at the March on Washington," Dissent, *Summer 1988. Reprinted by permission of the author and* Dissent.

For another selection by Mills, see chapter 107.

It was not the speech Martin Luther King planned to give. He wanted his contribution to the March on Washington to be brief, "sort of a *Gettysburg Address.*" He would, he knew, be following a long list of speakers. A fiery sermon would not do. Not for this audience. The aim of the march was to pressure Congress into passing President Kennedy's Civil Rights Bill. Demonstration, not civil disobedience, the march sponsors had agreed, would be the order of the day. It was crucial to make sure the crowd that had come to Washington stayed calm and did nothing to offend the congressmen on whom final passage of civil rights legislation depended. In an earlier meeting with the leaders of the march, the President himself had warned against "the wrong kind of demonstration at the wrong time."

Once King took the microphone and looked out at the two hundred thousand people gathered around the Reflecting Pool of the Lincoln Memorial, he knew, however, that neither he nor any of the march sponsors had imagined a gathering on this scale. Downtown Washington was deserted, but everywhere King looked there were people. They were even perched in the trees that bordered the Reflecting Pool. The marchers had begun assembling at the Washington Monument in early dawn. By 10:30 there were fifty thousand, and by noon the number had doubled. Opening the program, A. Philip Randolph, the seventy-four-year-old director of the march, announced, "We are gathered here in the largest demonstration in the history of this nation." King, too, was awed. As he waited for the applause that greeted him to die down, his movements were stiff, almost jerky. He started out reading his prepared speech, and only after he had gotten through most of it did he begin to speak extemporaneously.

It was a decision that made all the difference in the world. Until his "I have a dream" peroration, there was little in King's speech that moved his audience. He had tried too hard to write an updated *Gettysburg Address*. What emerged from his prepared text was not moral passion but historical self-consciousness. It was a speech so dominated by carefully worked out metaphors that it left little room for spontaneity. In Lincolnesque fashion King began, "Five score years ago, a great American, in whose symbolic shadow we stand today, signed the Emancipation Proclamation." Next came an even more elaborate historical reference—to the promissory note the Founding Fathers signed when they wrote the Declaration of Independence and the Constitution. "It is obvious today that America had defaulted on this promissory note, insofar as citizens of color are concerned." King declared, "Instead of honoring this sacred obligation, America has given the Negro people a bad check, a check which has come back marked 'insufficient funds'."

"But we refuse to believe that the bank of justice is bankrupt," King continued. "*Now* is the time to make real the promises of democracy. *Now* is the time to rise from the dark and desolate valley of segregation to the sunlit path of racial justice." Then, after a litany of all that was wrong with black life in America, King moved on to another appeal for action. "We cannot be satisfied as long as the Negro in Mississippi cannot vote and the Negro in New York believes he has nothing for which to vote," he insisted.

Once King began to speak of his dream, however, what he had to say became an altogether different story. "I'd used it many times before, that thing about 'I have a dream'," King would modestly acknowledge. But in the context of the March on Washington, there was nothing "used" about King's peroration. It transformed his words so that his speech no longer had a clear-cut beginning, middle, and end. It became a dialogue between him and the crowd. King offered a dream. The crowd answered back with applause. King responded with a new dream. It was no longer just civil rights that King was talking about now. It was civil religion—the nation's destiny as the carrying out of God's will. As King began to speak about his dream, God's purposes, American history, and the fate of the nation's black population became inseparable. His "I have a dream" image was the Bible made political, the southern revivalist tradition linked to the idea of equality.

King would cite the Declaration of Independence, then picture the sons of former slaves and the sons of former slave owners sitting down together at the table of brotherhood. He would quote Isaiah—"Every valley shall be exalted and every hill and mountain shall be made low"—and imagine freedom ringing from "every hill and molehill in Mississippi." He would call for the day when "all God's children will be able to sing with new meaning, 'My country 'tis of thee, sweet land of liberty,'" and he would end by envisioning a future in which the entire nation would "join hands and sing in the words of the old Negro spiritual, 'Free at last. Free at last. Thank God, Almighty, we are free at last.'"

King's vision took the country from its beginnings to the present, and as he repeated his "I have a dream" litany (four times in the first paragraph in which he used it, eight times in all), the momentum of what he was saying began to build. Each dream stood on its own, yet melted into the others. And as the process repeated itself, the hope King was expressing became more tenable.

In the next day's *New York Times,* columnist James Reston summed up King's speech by comparing his words to those of Roger Williams, Sam Adams, Henry Thoreau, William Lloyd Garrison, and Eugene Debs. "Each time the dream was a promise out of our ancient articles of faith: phrases from the Constitution, lines from the great anthem of the nation, guarantees from the Bill of Rights, all ending with the vision that they might one day all come true," Reston wrote. It was the kind of front-page analysis political speeches rarely receive in this country, but King had created a context in which Reston's praise did not seem extravagant. By the time King finished, there wasn't a base he had failed to touch. Built on repetition, his speech grew stronger as it was replayed on television in homes across the country. One did not have to be in the crowd at the Lincoln Memorial to identify with the hope it expressed.

King's success at the March on Washington was especially crucial for the civil rights movement. Plans for the march had been in the works since 1962, when A. Philip Randolph, the founder and president of the Brotherhood of Sleeping Car Porters, proposed a "mass descent" on Washington that would draw public attention to the economic plight of blacks in America and the need for more civil rights legislation. But by early 1963 it seemed unlikely that there would be a march. Randolph could not get other civil rights leaders to agree that the time was right. Only in June, when Martin Luther King concluded that the civil rights demonstrations he had been conducting in Birmingham against Public Safety Commissioner Eugene "Bull" Connor and the city's merchants needed to be followed by protests on a national level, did prospects for holding the march revive. Even then, the civil rights leadership was divided over how the march should be conducted and who should foot the bill for it. The problem of paying for the march was removed when Stephen Currier, president of the liberal Taconic Foundation, proposed the establishment of the Council for United Civil Rights Leadership (CUCRL), which would serve as a clearinghouse for dividing the larger contributions that Currier himself promised to solicit on behalf of the march.

But not until June 24 was the date for the march set, and even at that point infighting continued. The NAACP's Roy Wilkins objected to Bayard Rustin, who had spent time in prison for refusing to serve in the army and had an arrest record for homosexuality, being named director of the march (Rustin was instead given the title of deputy director). The leadership of the Student Nonviolent Coordinating Committee (SNCC) was unhappy with the decision of the march sponsors to forbid civil disobedience.

King's speech did not make such internal differences vanish, but it did deflect public attention from what divided the march's black leaders, who, in addition to Randolph and King, included Roy Wilkins of the NAACP, John Lewis of SNCC, James Farmer of CORE, and Whitney J. Young, Jr. of the National Urban League.

King's vision of a civil rights movement rooted in a belief in American justice forced the public and the media to think about the reasons for the march. After King finished speaking, it was easy for Bayard Rustin to step to the podium and get the crowd to roar its approval of the goals of the march. The nation was put in the same position. In the face of King's dream, it seemed petty to dwell on any divisions among the march's six black sponsors.

King's speech also furthered the kind of biracial coalition the established civil rights movement believed was needed in order to get Congress to act. In addition to the black sponsors of the march, there were four key white sponsors: Walter Reuther, president of the United Automobile Workers; Matthew Ahmann, director of the National Catholic Conference for Interracial Justice; Rabbi Joachim Prinz, president of the American Jewish Congress; and the Reverend Eugene Carson Blake, the chief executive officer of the United Presbyterian Church. King's speech not only said they were welcome; it said that in a country where racial justice was both a religious and secular concern the kinds of organizations these men belonged to had an obligation to participate in the civil rights movement.

Finally, King's triumph at the march on Washington was crucial for the Kennedy administration. The relationship between King and Kennedy had become extremely complicated by 1963. During the 1960 presidential campaign Kennedy had publicly intervened to have King released from a Georgia jail, and in 1963, when King was in jail in Alabama, Kennedy had acted again, this time calling Coretta King to assure her the FBI had ascertained that her husband was safe. The calls earned Kennedy the gratitude of the King family as well as a great many black votes. But the calls did not make King look the other way when the Kennedy administration sought to keep "order" in the South rather than support black protest. In early June, King made headlines when he described the President's record on civil rights as "inadequate" and charged him with not living up to his campaign promises.

Only reluctantly did the President commit himself to supporting the March on Washington. It was not until June 22, after plans to hold a march sometime in August were announced, that the President asked the leaders of the march to the White House. At that meeting he did everything in his power, short of asking them to call off the march, to discourage them from going ahead with it. "It seemed to me a great mistake to announce a march on Washington before the [Civil Rights] bill was even in committee," the President told the march leaders. "Now we are in a new phase, the legislative phase, and results are essential. . . . we have, first, to oppose demonstrations which will lead to violence, and, second, give Congress a fair chance to work it will." Three weeks then went by before the President gave his formal blessing to the march, and in doing so, he made sure that the press understood that in his mind it was "not a march on the capital" but "a peaceful assembly calling for a redress of grievances."

The President was gambling. By coming out ahead of time in favor of the march, he wanted to make sure that its target was the southern senators opposing his Civil Rights Bill rather than his own record on civil rights. The national reaction to King's "I have a dream" speech redeemed that strategy. The optimism of

King's speech, its equation of civil rights and Americanism, was tailor-made to the kind of political image the Kennedy administration wanted to project. The order maintained by marchers added to that image. At the end of the day, the President no longer had to worry that he had made a mistake in supporting the march. He could share in the march's triumph by inviting its leaders to the White House and announcing, "This nation can properly be proud of the demonstration that has occurred here today. The leaders of the organizations sponsoring the march and all who have participated in it deserve our appreciation for the detailed preparations that made it possible and for the orderly manner in which it has been conducted."

As he listened to the speeches and watched the marchers (three-fourths of whom, a Bureau of Social Science Research survey would reveal, held white-collar jobs) Malcolm X, then at the height of his influence as a black nationalist, was horrified. The organization that so impressed reporters—eighty thousand pre-made lunches, one thousand five hundred volunteer marshals, printed picket signs—struck Malcolm as proof of how thoroughly the march leaders had caved in to white demands. "Who ever heard of angry revolutionaries swinging their bare feet together with their oppressor in lily pad pools, with gospels and guitars and 'I have a dream' speeches?" Malcolm would write in his *Autobiography.* "There wasn't a single logistics aspect uncontrolled. The marchers had been instructed to bring no signs—signs were provided. They had been told to sing one song: 'We Shall Overcome.' They had been told *how* to arrive, *when, where* to arrive, where to assemble, when to *start* marching, the *route* to march."

Malcolm X was not the only black leader with doubts about the march. For very different reasons, John Lewis, the new chairman of SNCC, also had doubts. At twenty-five, the youngest of the march sponsors, Lewis was initially ignored by most of the press and the other march leaders. The Sunday before the march, the *New York Times Magazine* carried a symposium on what black leaders wanted, but neither Lewis nor SNCC was asked to participate, and when the time came to divide the money that had been raised for the civil rights organizations sponsoring the march, SNCC found itself shortchanged. While the NAACP and Urban League received $125,000 each and King's Southern Christian Leadership Conference (SCLC) $50,000, SNCC, whose field secretaries in Mississippi were risking their lives daily, got only $15,000.

What was most troubling to Lewis about the march was not, however, its logistics or the financial treatment of SNCC. What bothered Lewis most were the compromises the march sponsors were prepared to make in order to maintain unity and gain the support of the Kennedy administration. The constituency that John Lewis spoke for was, as far as he was concerned, already on the front lines in the South. In addressing the March on Washington, Lewis saw his task as one of shattering illusions and setting the record straight. It was all that was missing from the March on Washington that preoccupied Lewis. "We march today for jobs and freedom, but we have nothing to be proud of," Lewis declared in his opening sentences. "For hundreds and thousands of our brothers are not here. They have no money for their transportation, for they are receiving starvation wages or no wages at all. While we stand here, there are sharecroppers in the Delta of Mississippi who are out in the fields working for less than three dollars a day for twelve hours of work."

Few at the march and still fewer watching on television were prepared for Lewis's anger. But as he warmed up and got further into his speech, Lewis made no attempt to close the distance he had staked out in his opening paragraph. In contrast to King, who would wait for applause before going on to a new idea, Lewis moved at his own pace, barely pausing to catch his breath between paragraphs. The Kennedy administration and the moderate tone of the march were his next targets. "It is true that we support the present civil rights bill in Congress. We support it with great reservations, however. Unless Title Three is put in this bill, there is nothing to protect young children and old women from police dogs and fire houses, their penalty for engaging in peaceful demonstrations," Lewis declared. "As it stands now the voting section of this bill will not help thousands of black people who want to vote." Blacks in America are at the end of their patience, Lewis warned. It was now up to the federal government to intervene on their behalf or face the consequences. "To those who have said be patient and wait, we must say that we cannot be patient, we do not want to be free gradually. We want our freedom and we want it now," Lewis insisted. Then in a far more militant reference to the Founding Fathers than King's gentle one, Lewis went on to conclude, "All of us must get in this great social revolution sweeping our nation. Get in and stay in the streets of every city, every village, and every hamlet of this nation until true freedom comes, until the unfinished revolution of 1776 is complete."

Lewis's most powerful criticisms were not, however, voiced in the speech he gave at the Lincoln Memorial but in the speech he intended to deliver but was forced to change. An advance copy of the speech had been read by Attorney General Robert Kennedy and his assistant for civil rights, Burke Marshall. They then passed on the speech to Patrick Cardinal O'Boyle, the Catholic prelate scheduled to give the march invocation. O'Boyle's negative reaction to the speech was the same as Kennedy's, and he threatened to withdraw from the march unless Lewis's militant language was changed. When news of Cardinal O'Boyle's objections reached Bayard Rustin on Tuesday, he called a meeting of the march sponsors and that night met with Lewis in an effort to get him to change his text. Lewis refused, and early Wednesday morning, with the start of the march just hours away, the dispute continued. O'Boyle's objections put Rustin in a difficult position. The specific deletions that the cardinal wanted, as David Garrow notes in *Bearing the Cross*, had been drafted by Tom Kahn, Rustin's aide. But to lose O'Boyle's support at this juncture would be to lose the kind of unity the march was designed to achieve. O'Boyle warned that, if the changes in Lewis's speech were not made, he and the other religious leaders would leave the march. Finally, with the march program only minutes away, Lewis agreed to change his speech. In a small room just behind the statue of Lincoln, Lewis and SNCC staffers James Forman and Courtland Cox worked out a new speech designed to meet the cardinal's demands.

Lewis's decision to change his speech did not, however, persuade him that his original draft had been a mistake. The militancy of what he had planned to say had not been imposed on him by Tom Kahn. Lewis was among the SNCC leaders who wanted demonstrations at the Justice Department to be included in the march plans, and he believed then, as he would observe twenty-five years later, "The speech was very much in keeping with American ideals." Nothing in the original speech would have been a surprise to anyone who knew the commitment Lewis had made to the civil rights movement, beginning with the Nashville sit-ins of 1960. But there was an unmistakable difference in Lewis's two speeches. At the March on Washington Lewis was struggling not only to keep a lid on his emotions but to express himself in language that fell short of what he wanted to say.

It was a different story with the uncensored speech. There Lewis spoke for a SNCC that was skeptical of the Kennedys and believed, as James Forman would later write, that the administration wanted the march "to take the steam out of the black anger then rising in the South." At the march Lewis had softened his doubts about the president's Civil Rights Bill, first announcing that SNCC supported the bill, then announcing that it had reservations. In his original speech, on the other hand, Lewis felt no need for such qualification. "In good conscience we cannot support, wholeheartedly, the administration's civil rights bill, for it is too little, and too late," he declared. "There is not one thing in the bill that will protect our people from police brutality."

By the end of the 1960s, it would be de rigueur for any black leader who wanted to be seen as militant to attack liberal civil rights legislation, but there was nothing contrived about the anger in Lewis's undelivered speech. His was not the kind of put-on protest that Tom Wolfe would later characterize as "mau-mauing" the white man. In style and substance the passages that so upset Cardinal O'Boyle matched Lewis's politics. It was General Sherman in Georgia, not Abraham Lincoln at Gettysburg, "The Battle Hymn of the Republic," rather than soothing black spirituals, that Lewis wanted his Washington audience to go away thinking about. As his original text made clear in the bluntest possible language, Lewis believed that the real problem for blacks in the South was not southern politicians so much as the American political system itself. "This nation is still a place of cheap political leaders who build their careers on immoral compromises and ally themselves with open forms of political, economic, and social exploitation. What political leader here can stand up and say, 'My party is the party of principles'?" Lewis asked. The party of Kennedy, he pointed out, was also the party of Mississippi Senator James Eastland. Although the two men seemed like opposites, their conduct was often similar. The President, Lewis argued, had not merely proposed an inadequate civil rights bill, he was doing his best to slow the pace of black protest. "Mr. Kennedy is trying to take the revolution out of the street and put it into the courts," Lewis charged. "I want to know, which side is the Federal Government on?"

There was, however, no turning back the forces that the civil rights revolution had unleashed, Lewis insisted, and in the conclusion of his speech, the part that most offended Cardinal O'Boyle, Lewis predicted what blacks would and should do: "Listen Mr. Kennedy, listen Mr. Congressman, listen fellow citizens, the black masses are on the march for jobs and freedom, and we must say to the politicians that there won't be a 'cooling-off' period." In his final paragraph Lewis assumed the voice of a modern Jeremiah, predicting that the civil rights revolution of the 1960s would conquer the South much as the Civil War had. By comparison with King's language, Lewis's language here was spare, a march tune rather than a hymn. But Lewis, too, could use metaphor and there was no mistaking the threat in his deliberately repetitive syntax ("We will"/"We shall" each key sentence began). "The time will come when we will not confine our marching to Washington," Lewis proclaimed. "We will march through the South, through the heart of Dixie, the way Sherman did. We shall pursue our own 'scorched earth' policy and burn Jim Crow to the ground—non-violently. We shall fragment the South into a thousand pieces and put them back together in the image of democracy. We will make the action of the past few months look petty."

John Lewis would later insist that the militant role he played at the March on Washington worked to SNCC's benefit. In his year-end report to SNCC, Lewis would look back on the march and observe, "Since that time I find that people are asking questions about SNCC. What is SNCC's program? What is SNCC doing? Who is SNCC? And usually when they do find out, they want in some way or another to become identified with SNCC. For this we can thank our good brethren Archbishop O'Boyle, Messrs. Wilkins, King, Young, and Randolph." In 1963, Lewis's view was shared by few outside SNCC. In less than a year, it would be clear, however, that, although the drama of the March on Washington belonged to Martin Luther King, its prophetic voice belonged to John Lewis.

In signaling SNCC's break with the conventional liberalism of the early 1960s, Lewis had forecast both the strategy and the tone of the next stage of civil rights activity in the South. The compromises the March on Washington's black sponsors had made in order to win over the media and the Kennedy administration would no longer be the way of the future. A new era was at hand, one in which blacks like Lewis would continue to work with whites, but now in coalitions they determined, not on the liberal assumptions of "We're all in this together."

By the following June there would be a new cutting edge to the civil rights movement. It would not be supplied by the lawyers of the NAACP or the ministers of SCLC but by a generation of young SNCC field secretaries, most of them in their twenties, most of them unknown to the public. For the next two years, until Lewis was replaced by Stokely Carmichael as SNCC chairman, they would lead the civil rights movement through its most productive period. The result would be the Civil Rights Act of 1964, the Voting Rights Act of 1965, and most dramatic of all, the Mississippi Summer Project, in which a SNCC-led volunteer army, composed primarily of northern college students, would show that even the most racially feared state in the Deep South could be challenged.

Chapter 105

Which Side Is the Federal Government On?

John Lewis

Representative John Lewis (D–GA), former national chair of the Student Nonviolent Coordinating Committee, has been the Representative for the Fifth U.S. Congressional District of Georgia since 1987. He is a member of both the Congressional Black Caucus and the Progressive Caucus, and is the author (with Michael D'Orso) of Walking with the Wind: A Memoir of the Movement *(1998).*

Lewis addressed the 1963 March on Washington as a representative of SNCC. Responding to concerns from organizers, his speech was toned down at the last minute. In his 1998 autobiography, Lewis wrote, "My speech, although it was adjusted and changed, did what SNCC and I needed it to do. In its tone, it established and conveyed our firm and angry position on the hard issues of the day. As for content, it specified those issues and put them directly in the face of the government. It may have been less fierce than the original draft, but it still hit hard. It still had sting."

The following selection is the original version of Lewis's speech. Reprinted by permission from the author.

We march today for jobs and freedom, but we have nothing to be proud of. For hundreds and thousands of our brothers are not here. They have no money for their transportation, for they are receiving starvation wages . . . or no wages, at all.

In good conscience, we cannot support, wholeheartedly, the administration's civil rights bill, for it is too little, and too late. There's not one thing in the bill that will protect our people from police brutality.

This bill will not protect young children and old women from police dogs and fire hoses, for engaging in peaceful demonstrations. This bill will not protect the citizens in Danville, Virginia, who must live in constant fear in a police state. This bill will not protect the hundreds of people who have been arrested on trumped-up charges. What about the three young men in Americus, Georgia, who face the death penalty for engaging in peaceful protest?

The voting section of this bill will not help thousands of black citizens who want to vote. It will not help the citizens of Mississippi, of Alabama, and Georgia, who are qualified to vote, but lack a 6th Grade education. "One man, one vote," is the African cry. It is ours, too. (It must be ours.)

People have been forced to leave their homes because they dared to exercise their right to register to vote. What is in the bill that will protect the homeless and starving people of this nation? What is there in this bill to insure the equality of a maid who earns $5 a week in the home of a family whose income is $100,000 a year?

For the first time in 100 years this nation is being awakened to the fact the segregation is evil and that it must be destroyed in all forms. Your presence today proves that you have been aroused to the point of action.

We are now involved in a serious revolution. This nation is still a place of cheap political leaders who build their careers on immoral compromises and ally themselves with open forms of political, economic and social exploitation. What political leader here can stand up and say "My party is the party of principles"? The party of Kennedy is also the party of Eastland. The party of Javits is also the party of Goldwater. Where is *our* party?

In some parts of the South we work in the fields from sun-up to sun-down for $12 a week. In Albany, Georgia, nine of our leaders have been indicted not by Dixiecrats but by the Federal Government for peaceful protest. But what did the Federal Government do when Albany's Deputy Sheriff beat Attorney C. B. King and left him half-dead? What did the Federal Government do when local police officials kicked and assaulted the pregnant wife of Slater King, and she lost her baby?

It seems to me that the Albany indictment is part of a conspiracy on the part of the Federal Government and local politicians in the interest of expediency.

I want to know, which side is the Federal Government on?

The revolution is at hand, and we must free ourselves of the chains of political and economic slavery. The non-violent revolution is saying, "We will not wait for the courts to act, for we have been waiting for hundreds of years. We will not wait for the President, the Justice Department, nor Congress, but we will take matters into our own hands and create a source of power, outside of any national structure that could and would assure us a victory." To those who have said, "Be Patient and Wait," we must say that, "Patience is a dirty and nasty word." We cannot be patient, we do not want to be free gradually, we want our freedom, and we want it now. We cannot depend on any political party, for both the Democrats and the Republicans have betrayed the basic principles of the Declaration of Independence.

We all recognize the fact that if any radical social, political and economic changes are to take place in our society, the people, the masses, must bring them about. In the struggle we must seek more than mere civil rights; we must work for the community of love, peace and true brotherhood. Our minds, souls, and hearts cannot rest until freedom and justice exist for *all the people.*

The revolution is a serious one. Mr. Kennedy is trying to take the revolution out of the street and put it into the courts. Listen, Mr. Kennedy, listen Mr. Congressman, listen fellow citizens, the black masses are on the march for jobs and freedom, and we must say to the politicians that there won't be a "cooling-off" period.

All of us must get in the revolution. Get in and stay in the streets of every city, every village and every hamlet of this nation, until true Freedom comes, until the revolution is complete. In the Delta of Mississippi, in southwest Georgia, in Alabama, Harlem, Chicago, Detroit, Philadelphia and all over this nation. The black masses are on the march!

We won't stop now. All of the forces of Eastland, Barnett, Wallace and Thurmond won't stop this revolution. The time will come when we will not confine our marching to Washington. We will march through the South through the Heart of Dixie, the way Sherman did. We shall pursue our own "scorched earth" policy and burn Jim Crow to the ground—non-violently. We shall fragment the South into a thousand pieces and put them back together in the image of democracy. We will make the action of the past few months look petty. And I say to you, WAKE UP AMERICA!!!

Chapter 106

I Have a Dream

Martin Luther King, Jr.

The final speaker at the 1963 national march on Washington was Martin Luther King, Jr. Just before he addressed the enormous crowd assembled around the Lincoln Memorial, singer Mahalia Jackson leaned over to him and whispered, "Tell them about the dream, Martin."

The following selection is reprinted from Martin Luther King, Jr., "I Have a Dream," 28 August 1963. Reprinted by arrangement with The Heirs to the Estate of Martin Luther King, Jr., c/o Writers House, Inc. as agent for the proprietor. Copyright 1963 by Martin Luther King, Jr., copyright renewed 1991 The Estate of Martin Luther King, Jr.

For other selections by King, see chapters 91, 95, and 102.

I am happy to join with you today in what will go down in history as the greatest demonstration for freedom in the history of our nation.

Fivescore years ago, a great American, in whose symbolic shadow we stand today, signed the Emancipation Proclamation. This momentous decree came as a great beacon of hope to millions of Negro slaves, who had been seared in the flames of withering injustice. It came as a joyous daybreak to end the long night of their captivity.

But one hundred years later, the Negro still is not free; one hundred years later, the life of the Negro is still sadly crippled by the manacles of segregation and the chains of discrimination; one hundred years later, the Negro lives on a lonely island of poverty in the midst of a vast ocean of material prosperity; one hundred years later, the Negro is still languished in the corners of American society and finds himself in exile in his own land.

So we've come here today to dramatize a shameful condition. In a sense we've come to our nation's capital to cash a check. When the architects of our republic wrote the magnificent words of the Constitution and the Declaration of Independence, they were signing a promissory note to which every American was to fall heir. This note was the promise that all men, yes, black men as well as white men, would be guaranteed the unalienable rights of life, liberty, and the pursuit of happiness.

It is obvious today that America has defaulted on this promissory note in so far as her citizens of color are concerned. Instead of honoring this sacred obligation,

America has given the Negro people a bad check; a check which has come back marked "insufficient funds." We refuse to believe that the bank of justice is bankrupt. We refuse to believe that there are insufficient funds in the great vaults of opportunity of this nation. And so we've come to cash this check, a check that will give us upon demand the riches of freedom and the security of justice.

We have also come to his hallowed spot to remind America of the fierce urgency of now. This is no time to engage in the luxury of cooling off or to take the tranquilizing drug of gradualism. Now is the time to make real the promises of democracy; now is the time to rise from the dark and desolate valley of segregation to the sunlit path of racial justice; now is the time to lift our nation from the quicksands of racial injustice to the solid rock of brotherhood; now is the time to make justice a reality to all of God's children. It would be fatal for the nation to overlook the urgency of the moment. This sweltering summer of the Negro's legitimate discontent will not pass until there is an invigorating autumn of freedom and equality.

Nineteen sixty-three is not an end, but a beginning. And those who hope that the Negro needed to blow off steam and will now be content, will have a rude awakening if the nation returns to business as usual.

There will be neither rest nor tranquility in America until the Negro is granted his citizenship rights. The whirlwinds of revolt will continue to shake the foundations of our nation until the bright day of justice emerges.

But there is something that I must say to my people who stand on the warm threshold which leads into the palace of justice. In the process of gaining our rightful place we must not be guilty of wrongful deeds.

Let us not seek to satisfy our thirst for freedom by drinking from the cup of bitterness and hatred. We must forever conduct our struggle on the high plane of dignity and discipline. We must not allow our creative protest to degenerate into physical violence. Again and again we must rise to the majestic heights of meeting physical force with soul force.

The marvelous new militancy which has engulfed the Negro community must not lead us to a distrust of all white people, for many of our white brothers, as evidenced by their presence here today, have come to realize that their destiny is tied up with our destiny and they have come to realize that their freedom is inextricably bound to our freedom. This offense we share mounted to storm the battlements of injustice must be carried forth by a biracial army. We cannot walk alone.

And as we walk, we must make the pledge that we shall always march ahead. We cannot turn back. There are those who are asking the devotees of civil rights, "When will you be satisfied?" We can never be satisfied as long as the Negro is the victim of the unspeakable horrors of police brutality.

We can never be satisfied as long as our bodies, heavy with the fatigue of travel, cannot gain lodging in the motels of the highways and the hotels of the cities. We cannot be satisfied as long as the Negro's basic mobility is from a smaller ghetto to a larger one.

We can never be satisfied as long as our children are stripped of their selfhood and robbed of their dignity by signs stating "for white only." We cannot be satisfied as long as the Negro in Mississippi cannot vote and a Negro in New York believes he has nothing for which to vote. No, we are not satisfied, and we will not be satisfied until justice rolls down like waters and righteousness like a mighty stream.

I am not unmindful that some of you have come here out of excessive trials and tribulations. Some of you have come fresh from narrow jail cells. Some of you have come from areas where your quest for freedom left you battered by storms of persecutions and staggered by the winds of police brutality. You have been the veterans of creative suffering. Continue to work with the faith that unearned suffering is redemptive.

Go back to Mississippi; go back to Alabama; go back to South Carolina; go back to Georgia; go back to Louisiana; go back to the slums and ghettos of the northern cities, knowing that somehow this situation can and will be changed. Let us not wallow in the valley of despair.

So I say to you, my friends, that even though we must face the difficulties of today and tomorrow, I still have a dream. It is a dream deeply rooted in the American dream that one day this nation will rise up and live out the true meaning of its creed—we hold these truths to be self-evident, that all men are created equal.

I have a dream that one day on the red hills of Georgia, the sons of former slaves and sons of former slave-owners will be able to sit down together at the table of brotherhood.

I have a dream that one day, even the state of Mississippi, a state sweltering with the heat of injustice, sweltering with the heat of oppression, will be transformed into an oasis of freedom and justice.

I have a dream my four little children will one day live in a nation where they will not be judged by the color of their skin but by content of their character. I have a dream today!

I have a dream that one day, down in Alabama, with its vicious racists, with its governor having his lips dripping with the words of interposition and nullification, that one day, right down there in Alabama, little black boys and black girls will be able to join hands with little white boys and white girls as sisters and brothers. I have a dream today!

I have a dream that one day every valley shall be exalted, every hill and mountain shall be made low, the rough places shall be made plain, and the crooked places shall be made straight and the glory of the Lord will be revealed and all flesh shall see it together.

This is our hope. This is the faith that I go back to the South with.

With this faith we will be able to hew out of the mountain of despair a stone of hope. With this faith we will be able to transform the jangling discords of our nation into a beautiful symphony of brotherhood.

With this faith we will be able to work together, to pray together, to struggle together, to go to jail together, to stand up for freedom together, knowing that we will be free one day. This will be the day when all of God's children will be able to sing with new meaning—"my country 'tis of thee; sweet land of liberty; of thee I sing; land where my fathers died, land of the pilgrim's pride, from every mountain side, let freedom ring"—and if America is to be a great nation, this must become true.

So let freedom ring from the prodigious hilltops of New Hampshire.

Let freedom ring from the mighty mountains of New York.

Let freedom ring from the heightening Alleghenies of Pennsylvania.

Let freedom ring from the snow-capped Rockies of Colorado.

Let freedom ring from the curvaceous slopes of California.

But not only that.

Let freedom ring from Stone Mountain of Georgia.

Let freedom ring from Lookout Mountain of Tennessee.

Let freedom ring from every hill and molehill of Mississippi, from every mountainside, let freedom ring.

And when this happens, when we allow freedom to ring, when we let it ring from every village and hamlet, from every state and city, we will be able to speed up that day when all of God's children—black men and white men, Jews and Gentiles, Protestants and Catholics—will be able to join hands and to sing in the words of the old Negro spiritual, "Free at last! Free at last! Thank God Almighty, we are free at last!"

Chapter 107

Movie Myths about Mississippi Summer

Nicolaus Mills

Nicolaus Mills is professor of American Studies at Sarah Lawrence College.

The following selection, originally entitled "The Right Place but the Wrong He-roes," is reprinted from Newsday, *20 January 1989. Copyright © 1989 Nicolaus Mills. Reprinted with the permission of the author.*

For another selection by Mills, see chapter 104.

Twenty-five years ago, the idea behind the Mississippi Summer Project of 1964 was as simple as it was daring: A thousand volunteers, most of them northern college students, would come to Mississippi for the summer. Under the direction of a civil rights coalition led by the Student Nonviolent Coordinating Committee, the volunteers would work on voter registration, start Freedom Schools and help build a political party open to all races. The Summer Project would show, its organizers believed, that the segregationist laws keeping more than 90 percent of Mississippi's eligible blacks from voting could be overcome.

It was a dream that would take more than a summer to accomplish. In the eyes of most white Mississippians, the Summer Project was an invasion. Participants were looked on as the enemy. Before the summer was up, 37 black churches were burned, 80 volunteers beaten and scores arrested. But the worst violence occurred on June 21, as the Summer Project was just starting. On that night, three young civil rights workers—a black Mississippian, James Chaney, and two white New Yorkers, Michael Schwerner and Andrew Goodman—were shot as they were driving back from visiting a black church that had been burned to the ground.

"I am mindful that only yesterday in Philadelphia, Mississippi, young people seeking to secure the right to vote were brutalized and murdered," Martin Luther King would observe in his 1964 Nobel Peace Prize acceptance speech. As a nation, we have not, however, been mindful of the tragedy of Chaney, Schwerner and Goodman. When we think of the 1960s, we prefer to remember the Camelot days of the Kennedy administration or the "right stuff" of the astronauts.

Now, as a result of a controversial new film, Alan Parker's *Mississippi Burning*, Chaney, Schwerner and Goodman and the Mississippi Summer Project are news again. It is a welcome change, but the movie raises a question: What really happened in Mississippi in the summer of 1964?

In Parker's film, which he has acknowledged is a fictionalized version of Mississippi in 1964, we don't get a historical answer. *Mississippi Burning* begins with the murder of the three civil rights workers, then turns into a made-up account of how two FBI agents cracked the case. The heart of the movie is the relationship of the two agents. Ward (played by Willem Dafoe) is a young idealist who believes that the best way to solve the murders is by following FBI procedure. Anderson (played by Gene Hackman) is an ex-Mississippi sheriff who believes that only by bending the law can the killers be caught. Anderson eventually persuades Ward to see Mississippi his way, and what brings the film to its conclusion are the steps Anderson takes to terrorize the murderers of the three civil rights workers into turning on each other.

The result is a first-rate thriller that demonstrates why there was a need for the Summer Project. But the film poses a terrible danger if we allow its references to actual events to make us see it as a docudrama that tells the story of the civil rights movement in Mississippi that summer. For what the film suggests, if we take it as representative of that period in American history, is that the FBI was a central force in the civil rights movement and that Mississippi blacks were basically passive witnesses to the most important struggle of their lives.

Nothing could be further from the truth.

In the summer of 1964, the FBI discovered where the bodies of Chaney, Schwerner and Goodman were buried—by offering a $30,000 reward. Later, by infiltrating the Ku Klux Klan, the FBI helped bring about the conviction, on civil rights charges only, of eight of the men responsible for the murders, including the deputy of Neshoba County. But for most of J. Edgar Hoover's years as director, the FBI was hostile to the civil rights movement. In June, 1964, the FBI did not even have an office in Mississippi.

The real Mississippi heroes of 1964 were neither the FBI nor the Kennedy administration nor the civil rights establishment. They were the young SNCC field secretaries who, after years of working alone, organized the Summer Project. They were the northern college students who answered the call to come South. Above all, they were the black families of Mississippi who at the risk of their jobs and lives opened their houses to the civil rights movement.

There is, however, little point in trying to say who was more heroic. Both groups needed the other. In 1964, there was no way, as the project's organizers acknowledged, that Mississippi blacks could have mounted massive political protest without terrible bloodshed. But there was also no way that white volunteers, most of whom had never been in the Deep South before, could have ever survived the summer without the protection offered by the black community.

The year ended with fewer than 1,700 new black voters making it onto Mississippi voter rolls. It would take the 1965 Voting Rights Act for major political change to occur. But what the summer established was the willingness of blacks and whites to put their lives on the line to challenge American racism at its worst. Never again would Mississippi officials have credibility when they said the state's blacks didn't vote because they were happy with their lot. The Summer Project brought the terror of Mississippi political life into the open, and the terror could not survive the exposure.

Twenty-five years later, there is no need to turn these men and women into super-heroes. But there is a need to see them in context, to make sure what they achieved is not filtered back to us primarily as a white experience or a police story.

What makes the summer of 1964 so meaningful for us today, when racial progress seems to have stalled, is the picture it presents of ordinary Americans—black and white—acting together in extraordinary ways, giving themselves to a cause without lending themselves to fanaticism. We cannot afford to lose that picture or the memory of it that prompted John Lewis—currently a Georgia congressman, in 1964 chairman of SNCC—to write of that Mississippi summer: "Most of all, there was an all-pervading sense that one was involved in a movement larger than oneself, almost like a Holy Crusade, an idea whose time had come."

Chapter 108

Freedom Schools

Howard Zinn

Historian and playwright Howard Zinn has taught at Spelman College and Boston University.

The following selection, originally entitled "Schools in Context: The Mississippi Idea," is reprinted with permission from the 23 November 1964 issue of the Nation *magazine.*

For other selections by Zinn, see chapters 99 and 187.

For more on Freedom Schools, see Florence Howe, "Mississippi's Freedom Schools," Harvard Educational Review *(Spring 1965) and "Mississippi Freedom Schools,"* Radical Teacher 40 *(Fall 1991).*

The idea, and the term "freedom school," were first brought before the civil rights movement by a slender Howard University student named Charles Cobb, who several years ago interrupted his studies to plunge into the Mississippi Delta as a field secretary for the Student Nonviolent Coordinating Committee. Cobb pursued his scheme with quiet, slow persistence, and when plans were laid last fall for a big "Mississippi Summer," with 1,000 or more volunteers to arrive in the state, Freedom Schools were on the agenda. Bob Moses, director of the Mississippi project, has a Masters degree from Harvard. He gave the idea close attention, and when Northern students were recruited during the spring many of them were told to be ready to teach.

The man who took charge of the summer Freedom School project for COFO (the Council of Federated Organizations: a union of SNCC, CORE and other civil rights groups in Mississippi) was Staughton Lynd, a young historian whose field, some might have noted warningly, is the American Revolution. He had spent three years in north Georgia in a rural cooperative community, and then three more years at Spelman College, a Negro women's college in Atlanta. He had just resigned from Spelman in protest against restrictions on the academic freedom of both students and faculty, and was then immediately hired by Yale University. From the orientation session at Oxford, Ohio, in early June to the end of August, Lynd was a dynamo of an administrator, driving into the remotest rural regions of Mississippi to keep the schools going.

At Oxford, the Freedom School teachers were warned about difficulties: "You'll arrive in Ruleville, in the Delta. It will be 100 degrees, and you'll be sweaty and dirty. You won't be able to bathe often or sleep well or eat good food. The first day of school, there may be four teachers and three students. And the local Negro minister will phone to say you can't use his church basement after all, because his life has been threatened. And the curriculum we've drawn up—Negro history and American government—may be something you know only a little about yourself. Well, you'll knock on doors all day in the hot sun to find students. You'll meet on someone's lawn under a tree. You'll tear up the curriculum and teach what you know."

They were also told to be prepared for violence, injury, even death. But they hardly expected it so soon. The first batch of teachers had just left the orientation session for Mississippi when word came that one of the summer volunteers (Andrew Goodman), a white community center director (Mickey Schwerner) and a local Meridian Negro youth (James Chaney) were missing. A publicity stunt, said Mississippi officials. But the SNCC veterans of Mississippi disagreed. "Man, those guys are dead," Jim Forman said.

The summer volunteers got into cars and into buses, and moved into Mississippi. Two hundred Freedom School teachers spread out over the state, from Biloxi in the Gulf Coast up into Ruleville in the Delta, and farther north to Holly Springs, covering twenty-five communities. Day by day, more and more Negro kids came around to the schools, and the expected enrollment of 1,000 rose to 1,500 then to 2,000.

One of the Jackson Freedom Schools opened in early August in a church basement just a short walk from the state COFO office on Lynch Street. Its combination of disorder and inspiration was very much like that of the other schools in the state. The "faculty" was more experienced than most: a young high school teacher of English from Vermont acted as "coordinator"—a combination of principal, janitor, recreation supervisor, and father confessor. Another youthful junior high school teacher of mathematics was from Brooklyn; there was one college professor of history who had taught for a number of years in a Southern Negro college; also, an enthusiastic young woman named Jimmy Miller, whose husband, Warren Miller, had written in *The Cool World* about young Harlem Negro kids. The teachers lived in spare rooms, or spare corners of rooms, in Negro houses of the neighborhood.

Two days before the school was set to open, in close to 100 degree heat, the teachers canvassed the neighborhood for students. Each asked one of the Negro youngsters hanging around the COFO office to go along with him, so as to establish from the start that these were friendly visitors walking up on the porches, knocking on the doors, asking: "Do y'all know about the Freedom School starting on Wednesday over at Pratt Memorial Church?" No, they mostly didn't, and so the information passed across the threshold: "It's for teen-age boys and girls, to learn about Negro history, and the Constitution, and the civil rights movement, and mathematics, and maybe French and Spanish, the way they don't get learning in the regular school." Kids on bicycles stopped, and one friend told another, and the word was passed on.

No one paid attention to details like age requirements, so that at the opening of school, sixty kids showed up, from six to nineteen; Jimmy Miller marched the six to ten children off to a corner, to read with them, and teach them freedom songs, and sound out French words whose English equivalents they had not yet discovered, and painstakingly correct their spelling.

With the older ones, fourteen to nineteen, any idea of going in an organized way through an outline of Negro history or American government was soon dropped. Beyond a core of seven or eight who came faithfully every morning at nine and stayed until mid-afternoon, there were a dozen others who came and went as they liked. So the history professor started each day from where the mood struck him, from some point on which he thought the students' recognition might be fastened just long enough to pull them onward. One day, it was an editorial in the morning's *Clarion-Ledger,* charging that civil rights workers were teaching people to break the law. "What do you think about that editorial? Is it true? If you could write a letter to the editor about it, what would you say? . . . Here's paper and pencil, go ahead. We'll pick out one or two and *really* send them to the editor." This was not education for grades, not writing for teacher's approval, but for an immediate use; it was a learning surrounded with urgency. And the students responded with seriousness, picking apart the issues: Are we for the law? Is there a higher law? When is civil disobedience justified? Then the teacher explored with them the differences between statutory law, constitutional law, "natural" law.

On another day the teacher told his students about the annual fair he had visited the previous afternoon. It was held in Neshoba County where the bodies of the three murdered civil rights workers had just been discovered. A strain of tension and fear pervaded the crowds that day at the fair. Gov. Paul Johnson had said: "It is not Mississippi's obligation to enforce federal statutes." A representative of the John Birch Society had said: "I am for the Constitution, for freedom, for the open Bible." The students were asked: Do you disagree? Aren't you for the Constitution? For freedom? The discussion became heated. Distinctions were drawn, and became more and more refined, all by the students themselves, the teacher just listening: "Which Constitution does he mean, U.S. or Mississippi? . . . Maybe we're for different parts of the U.S. Constitution . . . Well, maybe we're for the same part, but we *interpret* it differently." . . .

The Jackson Freedom Schools faced only mild harassment. Early in the session, while canvassing for more students, two teachers—one a slim, blonde Skidmore undergraduate—were picked up by the police, held for several hours, then discharged. Violence spluttered around the COFO office in Jackson one ugly Saturday night: a young man building book shelves for a Freedom School bookmobile on the street across from the office was clubbed to the ground by a white man who fled in a car; a dance hall where teachers and students were spending the evening was sprayed with bullets by a passing car, and a Negro boy was wounded; crosses were burned. But by Mississippi standards, Jackson was peaceful.

In the rural areas of the state, the danger was greater. A church used as a Freedom School in the little town of Fluckstadt was burned to the ground (when the teachers arrived on the scene, fifteen youngsters were waiting under a tree for class to begin). A Northern doctor who spent the summer in Mississippi with the movement told of the two white girls who lived along in a hilltop house out in the country, 30 miles from Canton, and held a Freedom School there. In McComb, so dangerous that the Justice Department pleaded with the Mississippi project not to send anyone in there, a Freedom School was started by a Washington, D.C., speech teacher, a young Negro named Ralph Featherstone. Two days after the first contingent arrived, a bomb exploded in the midst of sleeping SNCC workers. But 100 children came regularly to attend the McComb Freedom School.

Violence took the headlines, but behind it a phenomenal thing was happening to Mississippi: 2,000 young people were having experiences that would—for some in a small way, for some drastically—change their lives.

The kind of teaching that was done in the Freedom Schools was, despite its departure from orthodoxy—or, more likely, because of it—just about the best kind there is. For the teachers were selected not by any mechanical set of requirements but on the basis of general intelligence, enthusiasm and the kind of social conscience that would drive them to spend a hot summer in Mississippi without pay. They taught, not out of textbooks, but out of life, trying to link the daily headlines with the best and deepest of man's intellectual tradition.

Their object was not to cram a prescribed amount of factual material into young minds, but to give them that first look into new worlds which would, some day if not immediately, lead them to books and people and ideas not found in the everyday lives of Mississippi Negroes. They didn't always succeed, but even their failures were warmed by the affection that sprang up everywhere between teachers and students, both aware that they talked with one another inside a common cradle of concern. . . .

In these classes, discussions of democracy, of the philosophy of nonviolence, were hardly academic. In one Jackson school the class met to elect delegates to a convention of all the Jackson Freedom Schools. An older fellow named Jimmy, age 24, had been hanging around the class for the past few days. He spoke breezily of having recently spent three years in jail for a knifing. The teacher suggested that Jimmy sit up at the desk and chair the meeting. He laughed and complied, "OK, now, I'll choose the delegates," he announced. There were objections from all over the room: "We've got to *elect* them!"

"What kind of resolutions are we going to propose to the convention?" a girl asked. One was suggested: "If any kid is treated brutally in school in Jackson, all the kids in the Jackson schools walk out; we'll have a chairman in each school; we won't act just on say-so; we'll get written affidavits and witnesses before we take action. It's something like a student union."

The teacher was curious: "Do students get beaten up in your schools?" A girl answered: her principal had beaten a boy until he bled.

Jimmy then told how he'd been beaten by a teacher when he was younger. And how he and some friends had then found the teacher alone and taken revenge.

"We had a nice understanding after that." He hesitated. "But I don't know what I'd do now. You know this nonviolence we're talking about. If it happened now I might beat him. Or I might just laugh and go away. I was young then and full of hate. At that time, I see something I want. I take it. Now, I *ask*. It's the movement I guess . . . I want my son to come up different."

Role playing was used very often in the Freedom Schools. "Kids that age are natural actors," a teacher explained. "And it puts them in other people's shoes. We don't want to win easy arguments over straw foes. They have got to be tough thinkers, tough arguers." The teacher listed on the blackboard [1964 Republican presidential nominee] Barry Goldwater's reasons for voting against the civil rights bill: (1) It is unconstitutional. (2) No law will end prejudice ("We cannot pass a law that will make you like me or me like you."). (3) It can't be enforced. (4) It violates the idea of States' rights. The class went over the arguments, with one boy portraying Goldwater, and defending his point powerfully, another trying to break them down.

Outside on the street, in front of the building, an energetic, redheaded teacher was pointing to a blackboard propped up in the sun, the kids sitting in rows in the shade of the building. "OK, we can build any kind of community we want now. What will the rules be?" This was a hortatory kind of teaching, but a kind the schools fostered: constantly talking with students not just about what is, but about what *should be.* . . .

One teacher spent a whole hour with his students discussing the word "skeptical." He told them: This is a Freedom School and we should mean what we say. We should feel free to think as we want, question whomever we like, whether it's our parents, our ministers, our teachers, yes, me, right here. Don't take my word for things. Check up on them. Be *skeptical*." For these youngsters it was a new way of looking at the classroom. They told how in their high school in Jackson the rooms were wired so that at the flick of a switch the principal could listen in on any class in the school. Teachers were afraid to discuss controversial subjects. . . .

Without a strict curriculum to follow, the schools capitalized on the unexpected. A class held out in the sun would take advantage of passers-by, draw them into discussion. One day, three Negro women came by who'd just been trying to register to vote and had been rebuffed. The teacher beckoned: "Come over here and tell my students what happened." And so the children learned about the registration procedure, about voting, about what to tell their parents about going down to register. One of the middle-aged women, her anger still fresh, told them they must become educated if they wanted to change things. . . .

The road from study to action was short. Those who attended the schools began to come to mass rallies, to canvass for registration of voters, to question things around them for the first time. In Shaw County, "out in the rural," when the regular school began its session in August (Negro schools in the Delta open in August so that the children will be available for cotton picking in the fall), white Freedom School teachers were turned away from the regular school cafeteria, where some students had invited them to a lunch. The students then boycotted the school and flocked in large numbers to the local Freedom School.

The Freedom Schools' challenge to the social structure of Mississippi was obvious from the start. Its challenge to American education as a whole is more subtle. There is, to begin with, the provocative suggestion that an entire school system can be created in any community outside the official order, and critical of its suppositions. But beyond that, other questions were posed by the Mississippi experiment of last summer.

Can we, somehow, bring teachers and students together, not through the artificial sieve of certification and examination but on the basis of their common attraction to an exciting social goal? Can we solve the old educational problem of teaching children crucial values, while avoiding a blanket imposition of the teacher's ideas? Can this be done by honestly accepting as an educational goal that we want better human beings in the rising generation than we had in the last, and that this requires a forthright declaration that the educational process cherishes equality, justice, compassion and world brotherhood? Is it not possible to create a hunger for those goals through the fiercest argument about whether or not they are worthwhile? And cannot the schools have a running, no-ideas-barred exchange of views about alternative ways to those goals?

Is there, in the floating, prosperous, nervous American social order of the Sixties, a national equivalent to the excitement of the civil rights movement, one strong enough in its pull to create a motivation for learning that even the enticements of monetary success cannot match? Would it be possible to declare boldly that the aim of the schools is to find solutions for poverty, for injustice, for race and national hatred, and to turn all educational efforts into a national striving for those solutions?

Perhaps people can begin, here and there (not waiting for the government, but leading it) to set up other pilot ventures, imperfect but suggestive, like the one last summer in Mississippi. Education can, and should be dangerous.

Chapter 109

The Mississippi Freedom Democratic Party

Southern Exposure

Reprinted by permission from "The Mississippi Freedom Party," Southern Exposure, Spring 1981.

One of the many leaders of the struggle in Mississippi was Fannie Lou Hamer. A black Mississippian, she resided in Ruleville, in Sunflower County, her entire life. She worked at a plantation for 18 years before being fired for her activities in the Freedom Movement. At that time, she became a SNCC field secretary. In 1964, she ran for Congress and was vice-chairperson of the Mississippi Freedom Democratic Party delegation to the Democratic National Convention in Atlantic City.

The regular Mississippi State Democratic Convention was held on July 28, and resolved: "We believe the Southern white man is the truest friend the Negro ever had; we believe in separation of the races in all phases of life."

A week later, 300 people from all over Mississippi attended the Mississippi Freedom Democratic Party's state convention in Jackson. Unlike the regular state party, the MFDP pledged their support to the national party, and because of their loyalty, they were convinced they would be allowed to represent Mississippi at the Democratic National Convention. They elected 68 delegates and alternates from their number to travel to Atlantic City, with Aaron Henry as chairperson of the delegation and Fannie Lou Hamer as vice-chairperson.

The MFDP delegates arrived in Atlantic City on Friday, August 21. They immediately began the task of contacting members of the Credentials Committee, urging them to vote to unseat the regular delegation, but it became clear early in the Committee proceedings that this would be a difficult task. Many MFDP supporters felt that if the issue could get on the floor of the convention, where the national television audience could hear the debate and see how their delegations voted, there would be enough pressure to seat the MFDP.

The turning point of the convention was the MFDP testimony before the Credentials Committee on Saturday afternoon. Mrs. Fannie Lou Hamer gave the most moving testimony. She recounted her experiences in attempting to register and of being beaten in Winona, Mississippi, in 1963.

The strength of the MFDP created conflicts for [President] Lyndon Johnson, who virtually controlled the convention but feared a walkout by the entire South if the

Freedom Delegation were seated. He assigned Hubert Humphrey, a leader of the liberal wing of the Democratic Party, the job of defeating the Freedom Delegation.

Besides putting intense pressure on members of the Credentials Committee to reject the MFDP cause, the president offered a compromise: the MFDP could have two at-large seats, with the delegates selected by the president, and a pledge from the National Democratic Party never to seat a lily-white delegation again, beginning in 1968. The regular Mississippi delegation would be seated after taking a [party] loyalty oath.

Tuesday was the crucial day. With the Credentials Committee scheduled to meet at two p.m., the MFDP caucused at 10 a.m. Bob Moses asked the delegation if they would accept the seating of just two delegates. Led by Fannie Lou Hamer, they voted almost unanimously to reject the compromise, although Aaron Henry, who would have been one of the delegates, supported it.

Though the compromise was portrayed by much of the press as a symbolic victory for the MFDP, the Freedom delegation, representing thousands of disfranchised black Mississippians, felt the acceptance of two at-large seats, occupied by hand-picked delegates, represented useless token desegregation. The Freedom Party delegates came to Atlantic City asking to be part of the national Democratic Party. Their challenge rested on the legal and moral grounds of exclusion, that they were forcibly restrained from taking part in the Democratic Party in their own state. The fact that the regular delegation from Mississippi would be allowed to occupy the Mississippi section and cast a full state vote was a total rejection of the MFDP's demands, not a compromise.

In discussing the president's compromise, Ed King, who would have been the other hand-picked delegate, said he told Humphrey, at the convention, "I'm sure Mrs. Hamer has to be part of it." According to King, Humphrey replied, "The president has said that he will not let that illiterate woman on the floor of the Democratic convention."

Hamer, who died in 1977, gave her view of some of the events at the convention and in Mississippi during an interview conducted by Anne Romaine in 1966.

Fannie Lou Hamer:

When we went to Atlantic City, we didn't go there for publicity, we went there because we believed that America was what it said it was, "the land of the free." And I thought with all of my heart that the people would have been unseated in Atlantic City. And I believed that, because if the Constitution of this United States means something to all of us, then I knew they would unseat them. So we went to Atlantic City with all of this hope. I never will forget the experience. One day I was going in the hall and Roy Wilkins [then executive secretary of the NAACP] said, "Mrs. Hamer, you people have put your point across. You don't know anything, you're ignorant, you don't know anything about politics. I've been in the business over 20 years. You people have put your point across, now why don't you pack up and go home?" That was blow number one.

And then I talked at one time with [Humphrey] who is now the vice-president of the United States. [After all] that we had been hearing about Hubert Humphrey and his stand for civil rights, I was delighted even to have a chance to talk with this man. But here sat a little round-eyed man with his eyes full of tears, when our attorney at the time, Joseph Rauh, said if we didn't stop pushing like we was pushing them and fighting to come to the floor, that Mr. Humphrey wouldn't be nominated that night for vice-president of the United States. I was amazed, and I said, "Well, Mr. Humphrey, do you mean to tell me that your position is more important to you than 400,000 black lives?" And I didn't try to force nobody else to say it, but I told him I wouldn't stoop to no two votes at large.

This was blows to me, really blows, and I left there full of tears. You see, for year after year, for the past 300 years, all that we have ever got was a compromise, you know. They said 100 years ago we were free, but today people are being beaten, people are being shot down, people are still begging for the same chance that they were begging for 100 years ago. In fact, it's worse now than it was 100 years ago.

I was very close to Dr. Henry, and I remember one time he met me in the hall and he said, "Mrs. Hamer, we going to have to listen to some of them that know much more about politics than we know. And we going to have to listen to them." And I said, "Tell me what leaders you talking about." And he said, "You know we got great leaders." I said, "That's right, because all those people from SNCC are some of the greatest leaders I ever seen. But now don't go telling me about anybody that ain't been in Mississippi two weeks and don't know nothing about the problem, because they're not leading us." And that's the truth.

The reason I respect SNCC now is [that] it was the only organization that did the hard work that had to be done in Mississippi. I went to them one time because I got so upset, I might be just, you know, just too full out. So I went to Bob [Moses], I went to Jim Forman, I went to Ella Baker, and I said, "Why don't you tell me something. I believe I'm right, but I might be wrong. I respect you, and I will respect your decision. Whatever you say, if you think I'm wrong, even though I felt like I was right, I would have done it."

They told me, I'll never forget this, everyone would say almost the same thing, they'd say, "Now look, Mrs. Hamer, you're the people living in Mississippi, and you people know what you've experienced in Mississippi, we don't have to tell you nothing, you make your own decision." See, we'd never been allowed to do that before. Cause you see, if we are free people as Negroes, if we are free, then I don't think you're supposed to tell me how much of my freedom I'm supposed to have. Because we're human beings, too. You see there just is a difference in our colors.

In Mississippi, there's no more time for white people choosing the leader, handpicking the leader that's going to lead me, cause we ain't going to follow. They might kill us, but you ain't going to pick this white owl over there for me, when I know everything she going to say when she get in front of that white man, "Yes sir, yes sir." We're getting sick of this. We want somebody that's going to say, "Well, now this is wrong, let's talk about something this way." And that's what we been fussing about.

A few of the Mississippi delegation favored the compromise and wanted me to convince the others, but I said, "I'm not making a decision for the 68 delegates. I won't do it." So, you see, after they talked to these people and we didn't know nothing about it, then they had the press outside waiting [to write] that they was going to accept the compromise. They had them out there. You know, I said, "I'm just going to get up and say what I feel." People come in to talk that day that we hadn't never seen before. "I think you people is making a moral victory." I said, "What do you mean, moral victory, we ain't getting nothing." What kind of moral victory was that, that we'd done sit up there, and they'd seen us on television? We come on back home and go right up on the first tree that we get to because, you know, that's what they were going to do to us. What had we gained?

I said, "I don't see how all of these people are stepping on the bandwagon now that didn't come way up there from Mississippi, 68 delegates subject to being killed on our way back, to compromise no more than we'd gotten here. They only gave us two votes at large cause they knowed we wouldn't have nothing." I said, "We just didn't come here for just that."

This was what was going to happen. I was standing between Dr. Henry and Reverend Edwin King, so they wasn't going to hear nothing but what me and Henry and Reverend King said. If Henry had said compromise, the country would have thought today we had compromised. But that's one time they weren't going to hear that word, not out of Henry.

I've never carried no weapon, but I would have bit him so hard, he wouldn't have known what had happened.

Ever since then, so many rumors have got out about me that you would think I was King Kong. A lot of people say I advocate violence. I've never been violent, you know, never in my life. But if I know I'm right you don't stop me. Now you might kill me but you will not stop me from saying I am right. Now they thought they had us sewed up, bag sewed up, but I told it everywhere. You can kill a man, but you can't kill ideas. Cause that idea's going to be transferred from one generation till after while, if it's not too late for all of us, we'll be free.

Chapter 110

Testimony before the
1964 DNC Credentials Committee

Fannie Lou Hamer

Excerpted from "Testimony of Fannie Lou Hamer before the Credentials Committee of the Democratic National Convention," 22 August 1964, in Atlantic City, New Jersey.

For biographies of Hamer, see Kay Mills, This Little Light of Mine *(1993) and Chana Kai Lee,* For Freedom's Sake *(1999).*

Mr. Chairman, and the Credentials Committee, my name is Mrs. Fannie Lou Hamer, and I live at 626 East Lafayette Street, Ruleville, Mississippi, Sunflower County, the home of Senator James O. Eastland, and Senator [John] Stennis.

It was the 31st of August in 1962 that 18 of us traveled 26 miles to the county courthouse in Indianola to try to register to try to become first-class citizens. We was met in Indianola by Mississippi men, Highway Patrolmen and they only allowed two of us in to take the literacy test at the time. After we had taken the test and started back to Ruleville, we was held up by the City Police and the State Highway Patrolmen and carried back to Indianola, where the bus driver was charged that day with driving a bus the wrong color.

After we paid the fine among us, we continued on to Ruleville, and Reverend Jeff Sunny carried me the four miles in the rural area where I had worked as a time-keeper and sharecropper for 18 years. I was met there by my children, who told me the plantation owner was angry because I had gone down to try to register.

After they told me, my husband came, and said the plantation owner was raising cain because I had tried to register, and before he quit talking the plantation owner came, and said, "Fannie Lou, do you know—did Pap tell you what I said?" And I said, "Yes sir." He said, "I mean that. . . . If you don't go down and withdraw . . . you might have to go because we are not ready for that in Mississippi."

And I addressed him and told him and said, "I didn't try to register for you. I tried to register for myself." I had to leave that same night.

On the 10th of September, 1962, 16 bullets was fired into the home of Mr. and Mrs. Robert Tucker for me. That same night two girls were shot in Ruleville, Mississippi. Also Mr. Joe McDonald's house was shot in.

And in June, the 9th, 1963, I had attended a voter registration workshop, was returning back to Mississippi. Ten of us was traveling by the Continental Trailways bus. When we got to Winona, Mississippi, which is Montgomery County, four of the people got off to use the washroom. . . . The four people that had gone to use the restaurant was ordered out. . . . One of the ladies said, "It was a state highway patrolman and a chief of police ordered us out." . . . I saw when they began to get the four people in a highway patrolman's car. I stepped off the bus to see what was happening and somebody screamed from the car that the four workers was in and said, "Get that one there," and when I went to get in the car, when the man told me I was under arrest, he kicked me.

I was carried to the county jail, and put in the booking room. They left some of the people in the booking room and began to place us in cells. I was placed in a cell with a young woman called Miss Euvester Simpson. After I was placed in the cell I began to hear sounds of licks and screams. I could hear the sounds of licks and horrible screams, and I could hear somebody say, "Can you say, yes sir, nigger? Can you say yes, sir?"

And they would say horrible names. She would say, "Yes, I can say yes, sir."

"So say it."

She says, "I don't know you well enough."

They beat her, I don't know how long, and after a while she began to pray and asked God to have mercy on those people.

And it wasn't too long before three white men came to my cell. One of these men was a State Highway Patrolman and he asked me where I was from, and I told him Ruleville. He said, "We are going to check this."

And they left my cell and it wasn't too long before they came back. He said, "You are from Ruleville all right," and he used a curse word, and he said, "We are going to make you wish you was dead."

I was carried out of that cell into another cell where they had two Negro prisoners. The State Highway Patrolman ordered the first Negro to take the blackjack. The first Negro prisoner ordered me, by orders from the State Highway Patrolman, for me to lay down on a bunk bed on my face, and I laid on my face. The first Negro began to beat, and I was beat by the first Negro until he was exhausted, and I was holding my hands behind at this time on my left side because I suffered polio when I was six years old. After the first Negro had beat until he was exhausted the state Highway Patrolman ordered the second Negro to take the blackjack.

The second Negro began to beat and I began to work my feet, and the State Highway Patrolman ordered the first Negro who had beat to set on my feet to keep me from working my feet. I began to scream and one white man got up and began to beat me in my head and tell me to hush.

One white man—my dress had worked up high, he walked over and pulled my dress down and he pulled my dress back, back up.

I was in jail when Medgar Evers was murdered [see chapter 82—*Eds.*].

All of this on account we want to register, to become first-class citizens, and if the Freedom Democratic Party is not seated now, I question America, is this America, the land of the free and the home of the brave where we have to sleep with our telephones off the hooks because our lives be threatened daily because we want to live as decent human beings, in America?

Thank you.

Chapter 111

Civil Rights and Black Protest Music

Bernice Johnson Reagon

Bernice Johnson Reagon, the lead singer of Sweet Honey in the Rock and one of the original Freedom Singers, is a curator at the Smithsonian Natural Museum of American History and professor of history at American University. She is the author of "We'll Understand It By and By": Pioneering African American Gospel Composers (1993).

The following selection, originally entitled "In Our Hands: Thoughts on Black Music," is reprinted from Sing Out! *January 1976, 1–2, 5. Copyright © 1976 Sing Out! Corporation. Used by permission. All rights reserved.*

In the early 1960's, I was in college at Albany State [College in Georgia]. My major interests were music and biology. In music I was a contralto soloist with the choir, studying Italian arias and German leider. The Black music I sang was of three types:

1) Spirituals sung by the college choir. These were arranged by such people as Nathaniel Dett and William Dawson and had major injections of European musical harmony and composition. 2) Rhythm 'n Blues, music done by and for Blacks in social settings. This included the music of bands at proms, juke boxes, and football game songs. 3) Church music; gospel was a major part of Black church music by the time I was in college. I was a soloist with the gospel choir.

Prior to the gospel choir, introduced in my church when I was 12, was many years experience with unaccompanied music—Black choral singing, hymns, lined out by strong song leaders with full, powerful, richly ornate congregational responses. These hymns were offset by upbeat, clapping call-and-response songs.

I saw people in church sing and pray until they shouted. I knew *that* music as a part of a cultural expression that was powerful enough to take people from their conscious selves to a place where the physical and intellectual being worked in harmony with the spirit. I enjoyed and needed that experience. The music of the church was an integral part of the cultural world into which I was born.

Outside of church, I saw music as good, powerful sounds you made or listened to. Rhythm and blues—you danced to; music of the college choir—you clapped after the number was finished.

The Civil Rights Movement changed my view of music. It was after my first march. I began to sing a song and in the course of singing changed the song so that it made sense for that particular moment. Although I was not consciously aware of it, this was one of my earliest experiences with how my music was supposed to *function*. This music was to be integrative of and consistent with everything I was doing at that time; it was to be tied to activities that went beyond artistic affairs such as concerts, dances, and church meetings.

The next level of awareness came while in jail. I had grown up in a rural area outside the city limits, riding a bus to public school or driving to college. My life had been a pretty consistent, balanced blend of church, school, and proper upbringing. I was aware of a Black educated class that taught me in high school and college, of taxi cabs I never rode in, and of people who used buses I never boarded. I went to school with their children.

In jail with me were all these people. All ages. In my section were women from about 13 to 80 years old. Ministers' wives and teachers and teachers' wives who had only nodded at me or clapped at a concert or spoken to my mother. A few people from my classes. A large number of people who rode the segregated city buses. One or two women who had been drinking along the two-block stretch of Little Harlem as the march went by. Very quickly, clashes arose: around age, who would have authority, what was proper behavior?

The Albany Movement was already a singing movement and we took the songs to jail. There the songs I had sung because they made me feel good or because they said what I thought about a specific issue did something. I would start a song and everybody would join in. After the song, the differences among us would not be as great. Somehow, making a song required an expression of that which was common to us all. The songs did not feel like the same songs I had sung in college. This music was like an instrument, like holding a tool in your hand.

I found that although I was younger than many of the women in my section of the jail, I was asked to take on leadership roles. First as a song leader and then in most other matters concerning the group, especially in discussions, or when speaking with prison officials.

I fell in love with that kind of music. I saw that to define music as something you listen to, something that pleases you, is very different from defining it as an instrument with which you can drive a point. In both instances, you can have the same song. But using it as an instrument makes it a different kind of music.

The next level of awareness occurred during the first mass meeting after my release from jail. I was asked to lead the song that I had changed after the first march. When I opened my mouth and began to sing, there was a force and power within myself I had never heard before. Somehow this music—music I could use as an instrument to do things with, music that was mine to shape and change so that it made the statement I needed to make—released a kind of power and required a level of concentrated energy I did not know I had. I liked the feeling.

For several years, I worked with the Movement eventually doing Civil Rights songs with the Freedom Singers. The Freedom Singers used the songs, interspersed with narrative, to convey the story of the Civil Rights Movement's struggles. The songs were more powerful than spoken conversation. They became a major way of making people who were not on the scene feel the intensity of what was happening in the south. Hopefully, they would move people to take a stand, to organize support groups or participate in the various projects.

The Georgia Sea Island Singers, whom I first heard at the Newport Festival, were a major link. Bessie Jones, coming from within 20 miles of Albany, Georgia, had a repertoire and song-leading style I recognized from the churches I had grown up in. She, along with John Davis, would talk about songs that Black people had sung as slaves and what those songs meant in terms of their struggle to be free. The songs did not sound like the spirituals I had sung in college choirs; they sounded like the songs I had grown up with in church. There I had been told the songs had to do with worship of Jesus Christ.

The next few years I spent focusing on three components: 1) The music I had found in the Civil Rights Movement. 2) Songs of the Georgia Sea Island Singers and other traditional groups, and the ways in which those songs were linked to the struggles of Black peoples at earlier times. 3) Songs of the church that now sounded like those traditional songs, and came close to having, for many people, the same kind of freeing power.

There was another experience that helped to shape my present day use of music. After getting out of jail, the mother of the church my father pastored was at the mass meeting. She prayed, a prayer I had heard hundreds of times. I had focused on its sound, tune, rhythm, chant, whether the moans came at the proper pace and intensity. That morning I heard every word that she said. She did not have to change one word of a prayer she had been praying for much of her Christian life for me to know she was addressing the issues we were facing at that moment. More than her personal prayer, it felt like an analysis of the Albany, Georgia Black community.

My collection, study, and creation of Black music had been, to a large extent, about freeing the sounds and the words and the messages from casings in which they have been put, about hearing clearly what the music has to say about Black people and their struggle.

When I first began to search, I looked for what was then being called folk music, rather than for other Black forms, such as jazz, rhythm and blues, or gospel. It slowly dawned on me that during the Movement we had used all those forms. When we were relaxing in the office, we made up songs using popular rhythm and blues tunes, songs based in rhythm and blues also came out of jails, especially from the sit-in movement and the march to Selma, Alabama. "Oh Wallace, You Never Can Jail Us All" is an example from Selma. "You Better Leave Segregation Alone" came out of the Nashville Freedom Rides and was based on a bit by Little Willie John, "You Better Leave My Kitten Alone." Gospel choirs became the major musical vehicle in the urban center of Birmingham, with the choir led by Carlton Reese. There was also a gospel choir in the Chicago work [when King and SCLC went North], as well as an instrumental ensemble led by Ben Branch.

Jazz had not been a strong part of my musical life. I began to hear it as I traveled north. Thelonious Monk and Charlie Mingus played on the first SNCC benefit at Carnegie Hall. I heard of and then heard Coltrane. Then I began to pick up the pieces that had been laid by Charlie Parker and Coleman Hawkins and whole lifetimes of music. This music had no words. But, it had power, intensity and movement under various degrees of pressure; it had vocal texture and color. I could feel that the music knew how it felt to be Black and Angry. Black and Down, Black and Loved, Black and Fighting.

I now believe that Black music exists in every place where Black people run, every corner where they live, every level on which they struggle. We have been there a long while, in many situations. It takes all that we have created to sing our song. I believe that Black musicians/artists have a responsibility to be conscious of their world and to let their consciousness be heard in their songs.

And we need it all—blues, gospel, ballads, children's games, dance, rhythms, jazz, lovesongs, topical songs—doing what it has always done. We need Black music that functions in relation to the people and community who provide the nurturing compost that makes its creation and continuation possible.

Chapter 112

From Protest to Politics

Bayard Rustin

What is the best way of consolidating the advances of the civil rights movement? asked Bayard Rustin. In 1965, he argued that it meant building alliances with the liberal wing of the Democratic party.

Civil rights leader Bayard Rustin (1910–1987) was an early adviser to Martin Luther King, Jr. He was a member of the pacifist Fellowship of Reconciliation (FOR), an organizer of FOR's 1947 Freedom Ride, a youth organizer for the canceled 1941 March on Washington, and the deputy director of the 1963 March on Washington. His books include Down the Line: The Collected Writings of Bayard Rustin *(1971) and* Strategies for Freedom *(1976).*

Reprinted from Commentary, *February 1965, by permission; all rights reserved.*

The decade spanned by the 1954 Supreme Court decision on school desegregation and the Civil Rights Act of 1964 will undoubtedly be recorded as the period in which the legal foundations of racism in America were destroyed. To be sure, pockets of resistance remain; but it would be hard to quarrel with the assertion that the elaborate legal structure of segregation and discrimination, particularly in relation to public accommodations, has virtually collapsed. On the other hand, without making light of the human sacrifices involved in the direct-action tactics (sit-ins, freedom rides, and the rest) that were so instrumental to this achievement, we must recognize that in desegregating public accommodations, we affected institutions which are relatively peripheral both to the American socio-economic order and to the fundamental conditions of life of the Negro people. In a highly industrialized, 20th-century civilization, we hit Jim Crow precisely where it was most anachronistic, dispensable, and vulnerable—in hotels, lunch counters, terminals, libraries, swimming pools, and the like. For in these forms, Jim Crow does impede the flow of commerce in the broadest sense: it is a nuisance in a society on the move (and on the make). Not surprisingly, therefore, it was the most mobility-conscious and relatively liberated groups in the Negro community—lower-middle-class college students—who launched the attack that brought down this imposing but hollow structure.

The term "classical" appears especially apt for this phase of the civil rights movement. But in the few years that have passed since the first flush of sit-ins, several developments have taken place that have complicated matters enormously. One is the shifting focus of the movement in the South, symbolized by Birmingham; another is the spread of the revolution to the North; and the third, common to the other two, is the expansion of the movement's base in the Negro community. To attempt to disentangle these three strands is to do violence to reality. David Danzig's perceptive article, "The Meaning of Negro Strategy" (*Commentary* magazine, February 1964), correctly saw in the Birmingham events the victory of the concept of collective struggle over individual achievement as the road to Negro freedom. And Birmingham remains the unmatched symbol of grass-roots protest involving all strata of the black community. It was also in this most industrialized of Southern cities that the single-issue demands of the movement's classical stage gave way to the "package deal." No longer were Negroes satisfied with integrating lunch counters. They now sought advances in employment, housing, school integration, police protection, and so forth.

Thus, the movement in the South began to attack areas of discrimination which were not so remote from the Northern experience as were Jim Crow lunch counters. At the same time, the interrelationship of these apparently distinct areas became increasingly evident. What is the value of winning access to public accommodations for those who lack money to use them? The minute the movement faced this question, it was compelled to expand its vision beyond race relations to economic relations, including the role of education in modern society. And what also became clear is that all these interrelated problems, by their very nature, are not soluble by private, voluntary efforts but require government action—or politics. Already Southern demonstrators had recognized that the most effective way to strike at the police brutality they suffered from was by getting rid of the local sheriff—and that meant political action, which in turn meant, and still means, political action within the Democratic party where the only meaningful primary contests in the South are fought.

And so, in Mississippi, thanks largely to the leadership of Bob Moses, a turn toward political action has been taken. More than voter registration is involved here. A conscious bid for *political power* is being made, and in the course of that effort a tactical shift is being effected: direct-action techniques are being subordinated to a strategy calling for the building of community institutions or power bases. Clearly, the implications of this shift reach far beyond Mississippi. What began as a protest movement is being challenged to translate itself into a political movement. Is this the right course? And if it is, can the transformation be accomplished?

The very decade which has witnessed the decline of legal Jim Crow has also seen the rise of *de facto* segregation in our most fundamental socio-economic institutions. More Negroes are unemployed today than in 1954, and the unemployment gap between the races is wider. The median income of Negroes has dropped from 57 per cent to 54 per cent of that of whites. A higher percentage of Negro workers is now concentrated in jobs vulnerable to automation than was the case ten years ago. More Negroes attend *de facto* segregated schools today than when the Supreme Court handed down its famous decision; while school integration proceeds at a snail's pace in the South, the number of Northern schools with an excessive proportion of minority youth proliferates. And behind this is the continuing growth of racial slums, spreading over our central cities and trapping Negro youth in a milieu which, whatever its legal definition, sows an unimaginable demoralization. Again, legal niceties aside, a resident of a racial ghetto lives in segregated housing, and more Negroes fall into this category than ever before.

These are the facts of life which generate frustration in the Negro community and challenge the civil rights movement. At issue, after all, is not *civil rights,* strictly speaking, but social and economic conditions. Last summer's riots were not race riots; they were outbursts of class aggression in a society where class and color definitions are converging disastrously. How can the (perhaps misnamed) civil rights movement deal with this problem?

Before trying to answer, let me first insist that the task of the movement is vastly complicated by the failure of many whites of good will to understand the nature of our problem. There is a widespread assumption that the removal of artificial racial barriers should result in the automatic integration of the Negro into all aspects of American life. This myth is fostered by facile analogies with the experience of various ethnic immigrant groups, particularly the Jews. But the analogies with the Jews do not hold for three simple but profound reasons. First, Jews have a long history as a literate people, a resource which has afforded them opportunities to advance in the academic and professional worlds, to achieve intellectual status even in the midst of economic hardship, and to evolve sustaining value systems in the context of ghetto life. Negroes, for the greater part of their presence in this country, were forbidden by law to read or write. Second, Jews have a long history of family stability, the importance of which in terms of aspiration and self-image is obvious. The Negro family structure was totally destroyed by slavery and with it the possibility of cultural transmission (the right of Negroes to marry and rear children is barely a century old). Third, Jews are white and have the *option* of relinquishing their cultural-religious identity, intermarrying, passing, etc. Negroes, or at least the overwhelming majority of them, do not have this option. There is also a fourth, vulgar reason. If the Jewish and Negro communities are not comparable in terms of education, family structure, and color, it is also true that their respective economic roles bear little resemblance.

This matter of economic role brings us to the greater problem—the fact that we are moving into an era in which the natural functioning of the market does not by itself ensure every man with will and ambition a place in the productive process. The immigrant who came to this country during the late 19th and early 20th centuries entered a society which was expanding territorially and/or economically. It was then possible to start at the bottom, as an unskilled or semi-skilled worker, and move up the ladder, acquiring new skills along the way. Especially was this true when industrial unionism was burgeoning, giving new dignity and higher wages to organized workers. Today the situation has changed. We are not expanding territorially, the western frontier is settled, labor organizing has leveled off, our rate of economic growth has been stagnant for a decade. And we are in the midst of a technological revolution which is altering the fundamental structure of the labor force, destroying unskilled and semi-skilled jobs—jobs in which Negroes are disproportionately concentrated.

Whatever the pace of this technological revolution may be, the *direction* is clear: the lower rungs of the economic ladder are being lopped off. This means that an individual will no longer be able to start at the bottom and work his way up; he will have to start in the middle or on top, and hold on tight. It will not even be enough to have certain specific skills, for many skilled jobs are also vulnerable to automation. A broad educational background, permitting vocational adaptability and flexibility, seems more imperative than ever. We live in a society where, as Secretary of Labor Willard Wirtz puts it, machines have the equivalent of a high school diploma. Yet the average educational attainment of American Negroes is 8.2 years.

Negroes, of course, are not the only people being affected by these developments. It is reported that there are now 50 per cent fewer unskilled and semi-skilled jobs than there are high school dropouts. Almost one-third of the 26 million young people entering the labor market in the 1960s will be dropouts. But the percentage of Negro dropouts nationally is 57 per cent, and in New York City, among Negroes 25 years of age or over, it is 68 per cent. They are without a future.

To what extent can the kind of self-help campaign recently prescribed by Eric Hoffer in the *New York Times Magazine* cope with such a situation? I would advise those who think that self-help is the answer to familiarize themselves with the long history of such efforts in the Negro community, and to consider why so many foundered on the shoals of ghetto life. It goes without saying that any effort to combat demoralization and apathy is desirable, but we must understand that demoralization in the Negro community is largely a common-sense response to an objective reality. Negro youths have no need of statistics to perceive, fairly accurately, what their odds are in American society. Indeed, from the point of view of motivation, some of the healthiest Negro youngsters I know are juvenile delinquents: vigorously pursuing the American Dream of material acquisition and status, yet finding the conventional means of attaining it blocked off, they do not yield to defeatism but resort to illegal (and often ingenious) methods. They are not alien to American culture. They are, in Gunnar Myrdal's phrase, "exaggerated Americans." To want a Cadillac is not un-American: to push a cart in the garment center is. If Negroes are to be persuaded that the conventional path (school, work, etc.) is superior, we had better provide evidence which is now sorely lacking. It is a double cruelty to harangue Negro youth about education and training when we do not know what jobs will be available to them. When a Negro youth can reasonably foresee a future free of slums, when the prospect of gainful employment is realistic, we will see motivation and self-help in abundant enough quantities.

Meanwhile, there is an ironic similarity between the self-help advocated by many liberals and the doctrines of the Black Muslims. Professional sociologists, psychiatrists, and social workers have expressed amazement at the Muslims' success in transforming prostitutes and dope addicts into respectable citizens. But every prostitute the Muslims convert to a model of Calvinist virtue is replaced by the ghetto with two more. Dedicated as they are to maintenance of the ghetto, the

Muslims are powerless to affect substantial moral reform. So too with every other group or program which is not aimed at the destruction of slums, their causes and effects. Self-help efforts, directly or indirectly, must be geared to mobilizing people into power units capable of effecting social change. That is, their goal must be genuine self-help, not merely self-improvement. Obviously, where self-improvement activities succeed in imparting to their participants a feeling of some control over their environment, those involved may find their appetites for change whetted; they may move into the political arena.

Let me sum up what I have thus far been trying to say: the civil rights movement is evolving from a protest movement into a full-fledged *social movement*—an evolution calling its very name into question. It is now concerned not merely with removing the barriers to full *opportunity* but with achieving the fact of *equality*. From sit-ins and freedom rides we have gone into rent strikes, boycotts, community organization, and political action. As a consequence of this natural evolution, the Negro today finds himself stymied by obstacles of far greater magnitude than the legal barriers he was attacking before: automation, urban decay, *de facto* school segregation. These are problems which, while conditioned by Jim Crow, do not vanish upon its demise. They are more deeply rooted in our socio-economic order; they are the result of the total society's failure to meet not only the Negro's needs, but human needs generally.

These propositions have won increasing recognition and acceptance, but with a curious twist. They have formed the common premise of two apparently contradictory lines of thought which simultaneously nourish and antagonize each other. On the one hand, there is the reasoning of the *New York Times* moderate who says the problems are so enormous and complicated that Negro militancy is a futile irritation, and that the need is for "intelligent moderation." Thus, during the first New York school boycott, the *Times* editorialized that Negro demands, while abstractly just, would necessitate massive reforms, the funds for which could not realistically be anticipated; therefore the just demands were also foolish demands and would only antagonize white people. Moderates of this stripe are often correct in perceiving the difficulty or impossibility of racial progress in the context of present social and economic policies. But they accept the context as fixed. They ignore (or perhaps see all too well) the potentialities inherent in linking Negro demands to broader pressures for radical revision of existing policies. They apparently see nothing strange in the fact that in the last twenty-five years we have spent nearly a trillion dollars fighting or preparing for wars, yet throw up our hands before the need for overhauling our schools, cleaning the slums, and really abolishing poverty. My quarrel with these moderates is that they do not even envision radical changes; their admonitions of moderation are, for all practical purposes, admonitions to the Negro to adjust to the status quo, and are therefore immoral.

The more effectively the moderates argue their case, the more they convince Negroes that American society will not or cannot be reorganized for full racial equality. Michael Harrington has said that a successful war on poverty might well require the expenditure of a $100 billion. Where, the Negro wonders, are the forces now in motion to compel such a commitment? If the voices of the moderates were raised in an insistence upon a reallocation of national resources at levels that could not be confused with tokenism (that is, if the moderates stopped being moderates), Negroes would have greater grounds for hope. Meanwhile, the Negro movement cannot escape a sense of isolation.

It is precisely this sense of isolation that gives rise to the second line of thought I want to examine—the tendency within the civil rights movement which, despite its militancy, pursues what I call a "no-win" policy. Sharing with many moderates a recognition of the magnitude of the obstacles to freedom, spokesmen for this tendency survey the American scene and find no forces prepared to move toward radical solutions. From this they conclude that the only viable strategy is shock; above all, the hypocrisy of white liberals must be exposed. These spokesmen are often described as the radicals of the movement, but they are really its moralists. They seek to change white hearts—by traumatizing them. Frequently abetted by white self-flagellants, they may gleefully applaud (though not really agreeing with) Malcolm X because, while they admit he has no program, they think he can frighten white people into doing the right thing. To believe this, of course, you must be convinced, even if unconsciously, that at the core of the white man's heart lies a buried affection for Negroes—a proposition one may be permitted to doubt. But in any case, hearts are not relevant to the issue; neither racial affinities nor racial hostilities are rooted there. It is institutions—social, political, and economic institutions—which are the ultimate molders of collective sentiments. Let these institutions be reconstructed *today,* and let the ineluctable gradualism of history govern the formation of a new psychology.

My quarrel with the "no-win" tendency in the civil rights movement (and the reason I have so designated it) parallels my quarrel with the moderates outside the movement. As the latter lack the vision or will for fundamental change, the former lack a realistic strategy for achieving it. For such a strategy they substitute militancy. But militancy is a matter of posture and volume and not of effect.

I believe that the Negro's struggle for equality in America is essentially revolutionary. While most Negroes—in their hearts—unquestionably seek only to enjoy the fruits of American society as it now exists, their quest cannot *objectively* be satisfied within the framework of existing political and economic relations. The young Negro who would demonstrate his way into the labor market may be motivated by a thoroughly bourgeois ambition and thoroughly "capitalist" considerations, but he will end up having to favor a great expansion of the public sector of the economy. At any rate, that is the position the movement will be forced to take as it looks at the number of jobs being generated by the private economy, and if it is to remain true to the masses of Negroes.

The revolutionary character of the Negro's struggle is manifest in the fact that this struggle may have done more to democratize life for whites than for Negroes. Clearly, it was the sit-in movement of young Southern Negroes which, as it galvanized white students, banished the ugliest features of McCarthyism from the American campus and resurrected political debate. It was not until Negroes assaulted *de facto* school segregation in the urban centers that the issue of quality education for *all* children stirred into motion. Finally, it seems reasonably clear that the civil rights movement, directly and through the resurgence of social conscience it kindled, did more to initiate the war on poverty than any other single force.

It will be—it has been—argued that these by-products of the Negro struggle are not revolutionary. But the term revolutionary, as I am using it, does not connote violence; it refers to the qualitative transformation of fundamental institutions, more or less rapidly, to the point where the social and economic structure which they comprised can no longer be said to be the same. The Negro struggle has hardly run its course; and it will not stop moving until it has been utterly defeated or won substantial equality. But I fail to see how the movement can be victorious in the absence of radical programs for full employment, abolition of slums, the reconstruction of our educational system, new definitions of work and leisure. Adding up the cost of such programs, we can only conclude that we are talking about a refashioning of our political economy. It has been estimated, for example, that the price of replacing New York City's slums with public housing would be $17 billion. Again, a multi-billion dollar federal public-works program, dwarfing the currently proposed $2 billion program, is required to reabsorb unskilled and semi-skilled workers into the labor market—and this must be done if Negro workers in these categories are to be employed. "Preferential treatment" cannot help them.

I am not trying here to delineate a total program, only to suggest the scope of economic reforms which are most immediately related to the plight of the Negro community. One could speculate on their political implications—whether, for example, they do not indicate the obsolescence of state government and the superiority of regional structures as viable units of planning. Such speculations aside, it is clear that Negro needs cannot be satisfied unless we go beyond what has so far been placed on the agenda. How are these radical objectives to be achieved? The answer is simple, deceptively so: *through political power.*

There is a strong moralistic strain in the civil rights movement which would remind us that power corrupts, forgetting that the absence of power also corrupts. But this is not the view I want to debate here, for it is waning. Our problem is posed by those who accept the need for political power but do not understand the nature of the object and therefore lack sound strategies for achieving it; they tend to confuse political institutions with lunch counters.

A handful of Negroes, acting alone, could integrate a lunch counter by strategically locating their bodies so as *directly* to interrupt the operation of the proprietor's will; their numbers were relatively unimportant. In politics, however, such a confrontation is difficult because the interests involved are merely *represented*. In the execution of a political decision a direct confrontation may ensue (as when federal marshals escorted James Meredith into the University of Mississippi—to turn from an example of non-violent coercion to one of force backed up with the threat of violence). But in arriving at a political decision, numbers and organizations are crucial, especially for the economically disenfranchised. (Needless to say, I am assuming that the forms of political democracy exist in American, however imperfectly, that they are valued, and that elitist or putschist conceptions of exercising power are beyond the pale of discussion for the civil rights movement.)

Neither that movement nor the country's twenty million black people can win political power alone. We need allies. The future of the Negro struggle depends on whether the contradictions of this society can be resolved by a coalition of progressive forces which becomes the *effective* political majority in the United States. I speak of the coalition which staged the March on Washington, passed the Civil Rights Act, and laid the basis for the Johnson landslide—Negroes, trade unionists, liberals, and religious groups.

There are those who argue that a coalition strategy would force the Negro to surrender his political independence to white liberals, that he would be neutralized, deprived of his cutting edge, absorbed into the Establishment. Some who take this position urged last year that votes be withheld from the Johnson-Humphrey ticket as a demonstration of the Negro's political power. Curiously enough, these people who sought to demonstrate power through the non-exercise of it, also point to the Negro "swing vote" in crucial urban areas as the source of the Negro's independent political power. But here they are closer to being right: the urban Negro vote will grow in importance in the coming years. If there is anything positive in the spread of the ghetto, it is the potential political power base thus created, and to realize this potential is one of the most challenging and urgent tasks before the civil rights movement. If the movement can wrest leadership of the ghetto vote from the machines, it will have acquired an organized constituency such as other major groups in our society now have.

But we must also remember that the effectiveness of a swing vote depends solely on "other" votes. It derives its power from them. In that sense, it can never be "independent," but must opt for one candidate or the other, even if by default. Thus coalitions are inescapable, however tentative they may be. And this is the case in all but those few situations in which Negroes running on an independent ticket might conceivably win. "Independence," in other words, is not a value in itself. The issue is which coalition to join and how to make it responsive to your program. Necessarily there will be compromise. But the difference between expediency and morality in politics is the difference between selling out a principle and making smaller concessions to win larger ones. The leader who shrinks from this task reveals not his purity but his lack of political sense.

The task of molding a political movement out of the March on Washington coalition is not simple, but no alternatives have been advanced. We need to choose our allies on the basis of common political objectives. It has become fashionable in some no-win Negro circles to decry the white liberal as the main enemy (his hypocrisy is what sustains racism); by virtue of this reverse recitation of the reactionary's litany (liberalism leads to socialism, which leads to Communism) the Negro is left in majestic isolation, except for a tiny band of fervent white initiates. But the objective fact is that *Eastland and Goldwater* are the main enemies—they and the opponents of civil rights, of the war on poverty, of Medicare, of social security, of federal aid to education, of unions, and so forth. The labor movement, despite its obvious faults, has been the largest single organized force in this country pushing for progressive social legislation. And where the Negro-based liberal axis is weak, as in the farm belt, it was the religious groups that were must influential in rallying support for the Civil Rights Bill.

The durability of the coalition was interestingly tested during the election. I do not believe that the Johnson landslide proved the "white backlash" to be a myth. It proved, rather, that economic interests are more fundamental than prejudice: the backlashers decided that loss of social security was, after all, too high a price to pay for a slap at the Negro. This lesson was a valuable first step in re-educating such people, and it must be kept alive, for the civil rights movement will be advanced only to the degree that social and economic welfare gets to be inextricably entangled with civil rights.

The 1964 elections marked a turning point in American politics. The Democratic landslide was not merely the result of a negative reaction to Goldwaterism; it was also the expression of a majority liberal consensus. The near unanimity with which Negro voters joined in that expression was, I am convinced, a vindication of the July 25th statement by Negro leaders calling for a strategic turn toward political action and a temporary curtailment of mass demonstrations. Despite the controversy surrounding the statement, the instinctive response it met with in the community is suggested by the fact the demonstrations were down 75 per cent as compared with the same period in 1963. But should so high a percentage of Negro voters have gone to Johnson, or should they have held back to narrow his margin of victory and thus give greater visibility to our swing vote? How has our loyalty changed things? Certainly the Negro vote had higher visibility in 1960, when a switch of only 7 per cent from the Republican column of 1956 elected President Kennedy. But the slimness of Kennedy's victory—of his "mandate"—dictated a go-slow approach on civil rights, at least until the Birmingham upheaval.

Although Johnson's popular majority was so large that he could have won without such overwhelming Negro support, that support was important from several angles. Beyond adding to Johnson's total national margin, it was specifically responsible for his victories in Virginia, Florida, Tennessee, and Arkansas. Goldwater took only those states where fewer than 45 per cent of eligible Negroes were registered. That Johnson would have won those states had Negro voting rights been enforced is a lesson not likely to be lost on a man who would have been happy with a unanimous electoral college. In any case, the 1.6 million Southern Negroes who voted have had a shattering impact on the Southern political party structure, as illustrated in the changed composition of the Southern congressional delegation. The "backlash" gave the Republicans five House seats in Alabama, one in Georgia, and one in Mississippi. But on the Democratic side, seven segregationists were defeated while all nine Southerners who voted for the Civil Rights Act were re-elected. It may be premature to predict a Southern Democratic party of Negroes and white moderates and a Republican Party of refugee racists and economic conservatives, but there certainly is a strong tendency toward such a realignment; and an additional 3.6 million Negroes of voting age in the eleven Southern states are still to be heard from. Even the *tendency* toward disintegration of the Democratic party's racist wing defines a new context for Presidential and liberal strategy in the congressional battles ahead. Thus the Negro vote (North as well as South), while not *decisive* in the Presidential race, was enormously effective. It was a dramatic element of a historic mandate which contains vast possibilities and dangers that will fundamentally affect the future course of the civil rights movement.

The liberal congressional sweep raises hope for an assault on the seniority system, Rule Twenty-two, and other citadels of Dixiecrat-Republican power. The overwhelming of this conservative coalition should also mean progress on much bottlenecked legislation of profound interest to the movement (e.g., bills by Senators [Joseph] Clark and [Gaylord] Nelson on planning, manpower, and employment). Moreover, the irrelevance of the South to Johnson's victory gives the President more freedom to act than his predecessor had and more leverage to the movement to pressure for executive action in Mississippi and other racist strongholds.

None of this *guarantees* vigorous executive or legislative action, for the other side of the Johnson landslide is that it has a Gaullist quality. Goldwater's capture of the Republican party forced into the Democratic camp many disparate elements which do not belong there, Big Business being the major example. Johnson, who wants to be President "of all people," may try to keep his new coalition together by sticking close to the political center. But if he decides to do this, it is unlikely that even his political genius will be able to hold together a coalition so inherently unstable and rife with contradictions. It must come apart. Should it do so while Johnson is pursuing a centrist course, then the mandate will have been wastefully dissipated. However, if the mandate is seized upon to set fundamental changes in motion, then the basis can be laid for a new mandate, a new coalition including hitherto inert and dispossessed strata of the population.

Here is where the cutting edge of the civil rights movement can be applied. We must see to it that the reorganization of the "consensus party" proceeds along lines which will make it an effective vehicle for social reconstruction, a role it cannot play so long as it furnishes Southern racism with its national political power. (One of Barry Goldwater's few attractive ideas was that the Dixiecrats belong with him in the same party.) And nowhere has the civil rights movement's political cutting edge been more magnificently demonstrated than at Atlantic City, where the Mississippi Freedom Democratic Party not only secured recognition as a bona fide component of the national party, but in the process routed the representatives of the most rabid racists—the white Mississippi and Alabama delegations. While I still believe that the FDP made a tactical error in spurning the compromise, there is no question that they launched a political revolution whose logic is the displacement of Dixiecrat power. They launched that revolution within a major political institution and as part of a coalitional effort.

The role of the civil rights movement in the reorganization of American political life is programmatic as well as strategic. We are challenged now to broaden our social vision, to develop functional programs with concrete objectives. We need to propose alternatives to technological unemployment, urban decay, and the rest. We need to be calling for public works and training, for national economic planning, for federal aid to education, for attractive public housing—all this on a sufficiently massive scale to make a difference. We need to protest the notion that our integration into American life, so long delayed, must now proceed in an atmosphere of competitive scarcity instead of in the security of abundance which technology makes possible. We cannot claim to have answers to all the complex problems of modern society. That is too much to ask of a movement still battling barbarism in Mississippi. But we can agitate the right questions by probing at the contradictions which still stand in the way of the "Great Society." The questions having been asked, motion must begin in the larger society, for there is a limit to what Negroes can do alone.

Chapter 113

The Selma Movement and the Voting Rights Act of 1965

Steven F. Lawson

Steven F. Lawson, professor of history at Rutgers University, is the author of Black Ballots: Voting Rights in the South, 1944–1969 *(1976) and* In Pursuit of Power: Southern Blacks and Electoral Politics, 1965–1982 *(1985), and co-editor of* Debating the Civil Rights Movement *(1999).*

The following selection is excerpted from his book Running for Freedom: Civil Rights and Black Politics in America *(New York: McGraw Hill, 1991), 105, 107–16. Reprinted with permission of The McGraw-Hill Companies.*

The distance between Oslo, Norway, and Selma, Alabama, spanned more than an ocean and thousands of miles. For African-Americans it represented the difference between dignity and degradation. The Winner of the 1964 Nobel Peace Prize, Dr. Martin Luther King, Jr., returned to the United States after obtaining his prestigious award in Oslo and journeyed to Selma in hope of eliminating the gap between the honorific treatment he had received abroad and the lack of respect blacks were accorded at home. Specifically, he sought to do something about the continuing denial of their right to vote. Throughout the former Confederate states, approximately 57 percent of eligible blacks remained off the suffrage rolls; in Alabama, the figure was a more shocking 77 percent; and in Dallas County, where Selma was the county seat, only 335 blacks out of a total population of 15,000 were registered. With this in mind, on January 2, 1965, Dr. King told an audience gathered at Selma's Brown Chapel AME Church what was at stake in the demonstrations the SCLC was about to launch. "When we get the right to vote," he predicted, "we will send to the statehouse not men who will stand in the doorways of universities to keep Negroes out, but men who will uphold the cause of justice." . . .

The unofficial capital of the Alabama black belt, Selma had served as an arsenal and naval foundry for the Confederacy. In 1865, Union forces torched the town, and memories of the Civil War and Reconstruction still burned in the minds of local whites. This section of the state had backed the Dixiecrat challenge in 1948, and the attitude of many white officials toward blacks was summed up by James

A. Hare, a Dallas County judge. "Your Negro," he asserted, "is a mixture of African types like the Congolite who has a long heel and the blue-gummed Ebo whose I.Q. is about 50 or 55." James G. Clark, the Dallas County sheriff, practiced the "Bull" Connor brand of law enforcement, showed little patience for civil rights protesters, and seemed genuinely to enjoy roughing them up. Sporting a green helmet adorned with an eagle and a Confederate flag and dressing in the style of the World War II general George S. Patton, Clark led his deputies in poking demonstrators with electric cattle prods, beating them with clubs, and dispersing them with tear gas.

This stronghold of segregation and police-state tactics offered an inviting setting for King and the SCLC to wage a major assault against political disfranchisement. From his previous encounter with Connor in Birmingham, the Nobel laureate had learned that the application of nonviolent pressure would provoke intemperate, racist lawmen to commit acts of brutality. The SCLC's strategy depended on blacks behaving with restraint in the face of such vicious attacks and on television cameras and journalists recording the confrontation so as to prick the conscience of an outraged nation. Injuries and fatalities would very likely accompany this struggle, but King was seeking drama, not bloodshed. By carefully stage managing events at Selma, by combining disruption with prudence he hoped to appeal to the larger audience of the public and the more specific one of the President and lawmakers in Washington D.C.

King's troops marched along the trail blazed by SNCC and local black activists in Selma. In 1963, two SNCC field-workers had established a beachhead in the town and conducted a voter registration drive that led to the formation of the Dallas County Voters League (DCVL). This indigenous association was headed by Reverend Frederick Reese. A high school teacher and Baptist clergyman, Reese felt strongly that black educators should take an active role in the freedom struggle. Dependent on white school boards and county administrators for their livelihood, many teachers had refrained from becoming actively involved in the movement. Reese believed that his colleagues had both a personal and professional obligation to seek to become registered voters and challenge those who tried to thwart them; otherwise, they could not properly fulfill their responsibility of instructing their pupils in exercising the duties of citizenship.

Amelia P. Boynton joined Reese as a prime mover behind the creation of the Voters League. The widow of the county's black agricultural extension agent, Mrs. Boynton was an independent businesswomen who operated an employment and insurance agency in Selma. Along with her husband, she had actively taken part in civil rights efforts and was especially concerned with efforts to increase black voter registration. Herself an enrolled voter, Boynton was well aware of the discriminatory treatment most blacks suffered. She knew of one official who could barely pronounce the words "constitutionality" and "interrogatory" on a literacy test administered to a black teacher. After the applicant interrupted the clerk to read the words correctly, "the registrar turned with red anger" and flunked her. Boynton had originally invited SNCC into the county to aid the DCVL in mobilizing blacks against such injustices.

Spearheaded by Reverend Reese and Mrs. Boynton, the league sponsored voter registration workshops to encourage blacks to enroll. In the autumn of 1963, together with SNCC, it held a "Freedom Day" rally at the county courthouse that spurred more than 300 blacks to make an attempt to sign up to vote. Instead, the applicants met resistance from the board of registrars and from Sheriff Clark and his deputies, who tried to prevent the would-be enrollees from receiving food and water as they stood for hours waiting on line to enroll. Throughout the following year, SNCC continued to organize voter registration drives in Dallas County but met with scant success.

At the same time, the federal government tackled the registration problem in its usual fashion. Justice Department lawyers had filed suits to restrain Clark from interfering with voter registration activities, and in November 1963, they won a ruling barring county registrars from using the literacy test to discriminate against black applicants. However, this decree failed to deter officials from engaging in biased practices against prospective black voters, and additional legal action to stop them proved unsuccessful. To make matters worse, a local judge issued an injunction blocking the Voters League from conducting mass meetings. By 1965, after several years of frustrating litigation, less than 400 Dallas County blacks had managed to register to vote. Acknowledging this failure, Attorney General Nicholas Katzenbach complained of "the inadequacy of the judicial process to deal effectively and expeditiously with a problem so deep-seated and so complex."

The inability of the federal courts to remedy unfair registration practices was matched by the unwillingness of the executive branch to protect suffrage workers from harassment. Adhering to the policy of his predecessors, [President Lyndon] Johnson refused to deploy federal marshals to Dallas County to safeguard voter registration workers from the menace of Sheriff Clark and his deputies. The chief executive preferred to leave law enforcement under the control of local authorities, barring a total breakdown of public order. In a similar manner, the Justice Department refused to instruct FBI agents to offer relief when they saw the constitutional rights of suffragists under attack. For example, on Freedom Day, October 7, 1963, the FBI merely observed and took notes as peaceful protesters were pushed around and arrested by Sheriff Clark and his men on the steps of the U.S. courthouse. Observing this scene firsthand exasperated Howard Zinn. "For all the good the federal officials did," the historian and adviser to SNCC bitterly commented, "[Alabama Governor] George Wallace might have been President of the United States."

Despite the racist intimidation and the failure of the national government to check it, blacks in Selma refused to retreat. SNCC had helped galvanize the community behind the struggle for political empowerment and set in motion forces for liberation that could not be easily turned back. SNCC's executive secretary, James Forman, celebrated Freedom Day as "the day when a century of Southern fear and terror . . . had not been able to stop the forward thrust of a people determined . . . to be free." Nevertheless, SNCC's efforts had sputtered, and local black leaders called in civil rights reinforcements. Their immediate goal was to secure help in registering residents of their own and surrounding counties; nonetheless, in late

1964, when the Dallas County Voters League invited King and the SCLC to Selma, it opened the way for the enfranchisement of the majority of blacks throughout the South.

The second day of the new year brought King to Selma to shape the kind of crisis that would force the federal government to crack white southern interference with black voting. During January and February 1965, the SCLC mobilized blacks in a march to the courthouse, where they would petition to register. At first, a moderate white faction in Selma, represented by the city's director of public safety, Wilson Baker, kept Sheriff Clark and his troops in line. This group, which had taken over political control of the city, believed that brutal suppression of black protest would generate unfavorable publicity and endanger new opportunities for business and civic development. "[T]he social, economic, and industrial complexion of this community," the editor of Selma's newspaper commented, "has suddenly and simultaneously arrived at a point from which there can be no turning aside." Restraint more than racial reform was uppermost on their minds, as Baker declared in referring to the demonstrators: "If we can only get the bastards out of town without getting them arrested, we'll have 'em whipped." Patience, however, was a virtue Clark did not possess, and he soon ordered the arrest of scores of peaceful black protesters.

His tough posture did not deter Selma's blacks; it only united them further. When usually cautious middle-class African-American teachers joined Reverend Reese on a march to the courthouse, they raised black solidarity to a new height. Though the educators did not wind up in jail, on February 1, Martin Luther King, Jr., did. Imprisoned for four days, King directed his aides from his cell to pressure President Johnson "to intervene in some way." Upon his release, he met personally with the chief executive and received assurances that a voting rights bill was in preparation.

Meanwhile, the SCLC attempted to hasten delivery of this promised congressional legislation. In mid-February a night march in neighboring Perry County resulted in the first fatality of the Selma suffrage campaign. In conjunction with the Perry County Civic League, the SCLC had convened a mass meeting and attempted to conduct a peaceful rally, only to come under siege from city, county, and state police. While trying to shield his mother from a beating by a state trooper, twenty-six-year-old Jimmie Lee Jackson was shot in the stomach and later died. Several reporters, including Richard Valeriani of the National Broadcasting Company, were also injured in the melee, thereby ensuring that this police riot received unfavorable publicity from the national media. A series of protests continued throughout the month, and King pledged, "We are going to bring a voting bill into being in the streets of Selma."

In the aftermath of Jackson's shooting, the SCLC began to conceive of dramatically expanding the demonstrations into a march from Selma to Montgomery, fifty miles away. Following the murder, blacks in Perry County discussed the possibility of carrying Jackson's body to Montgomery and depositing it on the steps of the state capitol. "We had to do something," Albert Turner, one of the local leaders recalled, "to point out to the nation the evils of the system." After Jackson's burial, the SCLC picked up on the idea and planned a mass march from Selma to Montgomery to begin on Sunday, March 7. With King having returned to Atlanta that day, one of his aides, Hosea Williams, and the chairman of SNCC, John Lewis, led 600 protesters over the Edmund Pettus Bridge toward the capital city. Before they could get across, however, state troopers and Clark's posse charged into the procession, lobbed tear gas canisters, and clubbed and chased the marchers back to town. Mrs. Boynton, who had previously been roughed up by the sheriff, was knocked unconscious in the assault. "The horses . . . were more humane than the troopers; they stepped over their fallen victims," she wryly remarked.

This display of raw aggression finally provided the SCLC with the provocative incident it needed to mobilize public opinion and secure federal intervention. Television cameras vividly recorded the events of "Bloody Sunday," and the American Broadcasting Company interrupted its network premier showing of the film *Judgment at Nuremburg,* the story of the Nazi war trials, to present footage of the Fascist-style behavior here at home.

Throughout this period, King and other civil rights leaders held several meetings with the President and urged him to introduce legislation immediately to outlaw literacy requirements for voter registration and to authorize the assignment of federal registrars. Johnson intended to support a suffrage measure, but he had several options from which to choose, including taking the slow route of a constitutional amendment. The escalating racial conflict in Selma prompted the chief executive to scuttle any proposal that did not move swiftly to dismantle discriminatory registration barriers. A growing coalition of lawmakers in both political parties called for quick congressional action, and outside of Dixie, civil rights sympathizers held a wave of protests in support of the Selma marchers. In the nation's capital hundreds of marchers demanded that Washington come to the aid of the suffragists, and a contingent from SNCC dramatically mounted a sit-in at the Justice Department to push it in the same direction. Meanwhile, the demonstrations in Alabama and the national outcry they engendered pushed President Johnson to accelerate his legislative timetable, dictated the selection of the most potent legislative option, and created the favorable political climate to guarantee its passage.

Even before the President had an opportunity to move forward, King and his followers precipitated a new crisis. They rescheduled the pilgrimage to Montgomery for March 9, despite the issuance of a federal court decree postponing it. King had not violated a federal judicial order before, but in this instance he was ready to proceed to show that racist violence could not be used to derail the civil rights movement. President Johnson sent to Selma his personal emissary, LeRoy Collins, former governor of Florida and director of the federal Community Relations Service, who carried on negotiations separately with the marchers and the state police and successfully defused the crisis. Accordingly, the protesters walked to the end of the bridge, knelt in prayer, and turned back, while the troopers calmly monitored the situation. This peaceful resolution did not prevent a group of whites from killing one of the returning marchers, the Reverend James Reeb, a white minister from Boston. Brutally beaten while he walked the streets of Selma, Reeb soon died of his wounds. After federal Judge Frank M. Johnson lifted his ban, the parade finally began on March 21, two weeks after Bloody Sunday. By that time Governor George C. Wallace refused to furnish protection for the marchers, forcing Johnson to federalize the Alabama National Guard for that purpose. Their presence generally deterred violence but could not prevent one further slaying of a white civil rights volunteer, Mrs. Viola Liuzzo of Detroit, as she rode in her car with a black companion en route to Montgomery to pick up returning marchers. The deaths of Liuzzo and Reeb especially shocked northern whites, including the President.

In the meantime, this renewed round of demonstrations produced the long-awaited presidential proposal on voting rights. On March 15, in a magnificent address to a joint session of Congress televised to an audience of 70 million Americans, Johnson praised the Selma demonstrators as freedom fighters and admonished Congress to allow "no delay, no hesitation, no compromise with" passage of remedial legislation to aid their cause. In one eloquent and memorable moment, he adopted the language of the civil rights movement and promised, "We shall overcome." Two days later, the administration measure reached the halls of Congress.

The Selma struggle had developed along two different fronts. Local movement leaders in Dallas County desired above all to unclog the registration process in their community. As its top priority, the DCVL hoped to place blacks on the voter lists and welcomed any action that brought significant modifications in biased registration procedures. When a federal judge instructed the enrollment board to cease administering literacy tests and to start processing black applicants at a speedier rate, the Voters League considered it a substantial step toward reaching its major goal. In contrast, the SCLC looked beyond the immediate arena and focused on obtaining national legislation to enfranchise blacks throughout the region. King and his aides argued "that if Selma Negroes gained [the right to vote] under special court order or through community agreement . . . this would not satisfy SCLC." Nevertheless, the grassroots goal and the broader civil rights aim remained intertwined in support of extending the ballot; only the tactics differed. In the end, the voting rights bill, forged as a result of the Selma campaign, gave each side what it desired.

Johnson's suffrage plan took the forceful approach recommended by civil rights proponents. Instead of a constitutional amendment, the chief executive asked Congress simply to pass legislation that suspended literacy tests, authorized the attorney general to dispatch federal registrars and observers to recalcitrant counties, and empowered the Justice Department to clear in advance changes in state electoral rules that might unfairly burden black voters. Johnson's lawyers had designed these provisions to enforce suffrage expansion through the administrative machinery of the executive branch rather than by the judiciary, where equal voting rights had been stalled for so long. Consequently, the measure contained an automatic triggering mechanism devised to snare only those states and localities that employed a literacy test and in which less than a majority of those eligible had registered to vote or had voted in the presidential election of 1964. As a result of this formula, Alabama, Georgia, Louisiana, Mississippi, South Carolina, Virginia, and sections of North Carolina would come under federal supervision.

Introduced in March, the voting rights bill encountered relatively little difficulty in Congress, and by early August it had become law. The final version followed closely the outline of Johnson's recommendation and also adopted a provision allowing the affected jurisdictions to escape coverage once they proved to the federal district court in Washington, D.C., that they had not employed a discriminatory test or device for the previous five years. In addition, the lawmakers issued a finding that the poll tax infringed upon the right to vote, and they directed that attorney general to initiate litigation, which resulted the following year in the removal of the levy in the four southern states that still required it in non-federal elections. (The Twenty-fourth Amendment, ratified in 1964, had eliminated the franchise fee in all national elections.)

This landmark legislation emerged in such powerful shape for a variety of reasons. The President displayed a strong commitment to the bill and exercised firm leadership in guiding it through the legislature. His aides worked diligently to round up key votes and keep supporters in line at critical moments. Johnson helped win over to his position the Senate Republican leader, Everett Dirksen of Illinois, which guaranteed bipartisan backing for the administration's version of the measure. The President's task was made easier because of the favorable climate of opinion created by Reverend King's handling of the Selma episode. Southern whites found it increasingly difficult to defend the brutal opposition to black suffrage in Alabama, and their congressional representatives failed to mount their customary fierce challenge to the legislation. A Gallup Poll taken during the march to Montgomery reported that 76 percent of the nation favored a voting rights bill; in the South a surprising 49 percent of the sample indicated approval compared with 37 percent in opposition. Democratic Representative Hale Boggs of Louisiana summed up the sentiment of forty of his colleagues from the South who voted for the legislation: "I . . . support this bill because I believe the fundamental right to vote must be a part of this great experiment in human progress under freedom which is America."

The Voting Rights Act resulted in the reenfranchisement of the majority of southern blacks. Within four years after its passage, approximately three-fifths of southern black adults had registered to vote. The most striking gains occurred in the deep South, where resistance to the suffrage had been most harsh. In Mississippi, black registration leaped from 6.7 percent in 1964 to 59.4 in 1968. Similarly, black enrollment in Alabama jumped from 23 percent to 53 percent. In Dallas County, the scene of the Selma demonstrations, the number of registered blacks soared from less than 1,000 to over 8,500 within months after the suffrage law took effect.

The combination of federal power and grassroots activism helped generate the stunning rise in black political participation.

Chapter 114

Address on Voting Rights

Lyndon Johnson

The following selection is excerpted from President Lyndon Johnson's evening address on voting rights to a joint session of Congress, "Special Message to the Congress: The American Promise. March 15, 1965," Public Papers of the Presidents of the United States, Lyndon B. Johnson, 1965 (Washington, D.C., 1966), 1:281–87.

For another selection by Johnson, see chapter 117.

I speak tonight for the dignity of man and the destiny of democracy.

I urge every member of both parties, Americans of all religions and of all colors, from every section of this country, to join me in the cause.

At times history and fate meet at a single time in a single place to shape a turning point in man's unending search for freedom. So it was at Lexington and Concord. So it was a century ago at Appomattox. So it was last week in Selma, Alabama.

There, long-suffering men and women peacefully protested the denial of their rights as Americans. Many were brutally assaulted. One good man, a man of God, was killed.

There is no cause for pride in what has happened in Selma. There is no cause for self-satisfaction in the long denial of equal rights of millions of Americans. But there is cause for hope and for faith in our democracy in what is happening here tonight.

For the cries of pain and the hymns and protests of oppressed people, have summoned into convocation all the majesty of this great Government—the Government of the greatest Nation on earth.

Our mission is at once the oldest and the most basic of this country: to right wrong, to do justice, to serve man.

In our time we have come to live with the moments of great crisis. . . . But rarely in any time does an issue lay bare the secret heart of America itself. Rarely are we met with a challenge, not to our growth or abundance, our welfare or our security, but rather to the values and the purposes and the meaning of our beloved Nation.

The issue of equal rights for American Negroes is such an issue. And should we defeat every enemy, and should we double our wealth and conquer the stars and still be unequal to this issue, then we will have failed as a people and as a nation.

For with a country as with a person, "What is a man profited, if he shall gain the whole world, and lose his own soul?"

There is no Negro problem. There is no Southern problem. There is no Northern problem. There is only an American problem. And we are met here tonight as Americans—not as Democrats or Republicans—we are met here as Americans to solve that problem.

This was the first nation in the history of the world to be founded with a purpose. The great phrases of that purpose still sound in every American heart, North and South: "All men are created equal"—"government by consent of the governed"—"give me liberty or give me death." Those are not just clever words. Those are not just empty theories. In their name Americans have fought and died for two centuries, and tonight around the world they stand there as guardians of our liberty, risking their lives.

Those words are a promise to every citizen that he shall share in the dignity of man. This dignity cannot be found in a man's possessions. It cannot be found in his power or in his position. It really rests on his right to be treated as a man equal in opportunity to all others. It says that he shall share in freedom, he shall choose his leaders, educate his children, provide for his family according to his ability and his merits as a human being.

To apply any other test—to deny a man his hopes because of his color or race, or his religion, or the place of his birth—is not only to do injustice, it is to deny America and to dishonor the dead who gave their lives for American freedom.

Our fathers believed that if this noble view of the rights of man was to flourish, it must be rooted in democracy. The most basic right of all was the right to choose your own leaders. The history of this country in large measure is the history of expansion of that right to all of our people.

Many of the issues of civil rights are very complex and most difficult. But about this there can and should be no argument. Every American citizen must have an equal right to vote. There is no reason which can excuse the denial of that right. There is no duty which weighs more heavily on us than the duty we have to ensure that right.

Yet the harsh fact is that in many places in this country men and women are kept from voting simply because they are Negroes.

Every device of which human ingenuity is capable has been used to deny this right. The Negro citizen may go to register only to be told that the day is wrong, or the hour is late, or the official in charge is absent. And if he persists and if he manages to present himself to the registrar, he may be disqualified because he did not spell out his middle name or because he abbreviated a word on the application.

And if he manages to fill out an application he is given a test. The registrar is the sole judge of whether he passes this test. He may be asked to recite the entire Constitution, or explain the most complex provisions of State laws. And even a college degree cannot be used to prove that he can read and write.

For the fact is that the only way to pass these barriers is to show a white skin.

Experience has clearly shown that the existing process of law cannot overcome systematic and ingenious discrimination. No law that we now have on the books—and I have helped to put three of them there—can ensure the right to vote when local officials are determined to deny it.

In such a case our duty must be clear to all of us. The Constitution says that no person shall be kept from voting because of his race or his color. We have all sworn an oath before God to support and to defend that Constitution. We must now act in obedience to that oath.

Wednesday I will send to Congress a law designed to eliminate illegal barriers to the right to vote.

The broad principle of that bill will be in the hands of the Democratic and Republican leaders tomorrow. After they have reviewed it, it will come here formally as a bill. . . .

This bill will strike down restrictions to voting in all elections—Federal, State, and local—which have been used to deny Negroes the right to vote.

This bill will establish a simple, uniform standard which cannot be used, however ingenious the effort, to flout our Constitution.

It will provide for citizens to be registered by officials of the United States Government if the state officials refuse to register them.

It will eliminate tedious, unnecessary lawsuits which delay the right to vote.

Finally, this legislation will ensure that properly registered individuals are not prohibited from voting.

I will welcome the suggestions from all of the Members of Congress—I have no doubt that I will get some—on ways and means to strengthen this law and to make it effective. But experience has plainly shown that this is the only path to carry out the command of the Constitution.

To those who seek to avoid action by their National Government in their own communities, who want to and who seek to maintain purely local control over elections, the answer is simple:

Open your polling places to all your people.

Allow men and women to register and vote whatever the color of their skin.

Extend the rights of citizenship to every citizen of this land.

There is no constitutional issue here. The command of the Constitution is plain.

There is no moral issue. It is wrong—deadly wrong—to deny any of your fellow Americans the right to vote in this country.

There is no issue of States rights or national rights. There is only the struggle for human rights.

I have not the slightest doubt what will be your answer.

The last time a President sent a civil rights bill to the Congress it contained a provision to protect voting rights in Federal elections. That civil rights bill was passed after 8 long months of debate. And when that bill came to my desk from the Congress for my signature, the heart of the voting provision had been eliminated.

This time, on this issue, there must be no delay, no hesitation and no compromise with our purpose. . . .

But even if we pass this bill, the battle will not be over. What happened in Selma is part of a far larger movement which reaches into every section and state of America. It is the effort of American Negroes to secure for themselves the full blessings of American life.

Their cause must be our cause too. Because it is not just Negroes, but really it is all of us, who must overcome the crippling legacy of bigotry and injustice.

And we shall overcome.

As a man whose roots go deeply into Southern soil I know how agonizing racial feelings are. I know how difficult it is to reshape the attitudes and the structure of our society. . . .

It was more than a hundred years ago that Abraham Lincoln, the great President of another party, signed the Emancipation Proclamation, but emancipation is a proclamation and not a fact.

A century has passed, more than a hundred years, since equality was promised. And yet the Negro is not equal.

A century has passed since the day of promise. And the promise is unkept.

The time of justice has now come. I tell you that I believe sincerely that no force can hold it back. It is right in the eyes of man and God that it should come. And when it does, I think that day will brighten the lives of every American.

For Negroes are not the only victims. How many white children have gone uneducated, how many white families have lived in stark poverty, how many white lives have been scarred by fear because we wasted our energy and our substance to maintain the barrier of hatred and terror?

So I say to all of you here and to all in the Nation tonight, that those who appeal to you to hold on to the past do so at the cost of denying you your future.

This great, rich, restless country can offer opportunity and education and hope to all: black and white, North and South, sharecropper and city dweller. These are the enemies: poverty, ignorance, disease. They are the enemies and not our fellow man, not our neighbor. And these enemies too, poverty, disease and ignorance, we shall overcome. . . .

This is one Nation. What happens in Selma or in Cincinnati is a matter of legitimate concern to every American. But let each of us look within our own hearts and our own communities, and let each of us put our shoulder to the wheel to root out injustice wherever it exists. . . .

The real hero of this struggle is the American Negro. His actions and protests, his courage to risk safety and even to risk his life, have awakened the conscience of this Nation. His demonstrations have been designed to call attention to injustice, designed to provoke change, designed to stir reform.

He has called upon us to make good the promise of America. And who among us can say that we would have made the same progress were it not for his persistent bravery, and his faith in American democracy. . . .

The bill that I am presenting to you will be known as a civil rights bill. But, in a larger sense, most of the program I am recommending is a civil rights program. Its object is to open the city of hope to all people of all races.

Because all Americans just must have the right to vote. And we are going to give them that right.

All Americans must have the privileges of citizenship regardless of race. And they are going to have those privileges of citizenship regardless of race.

But I would like to caution you and remind you that to exercise these privileges takes much more than just legal right. It requires a trained mind and a healthy body. It requires a decent home, and the chance to find a job, and the opportunity to escape from the clutches of poverty.

Of course, people cannot contribute to the Nation if they are never taught to read or write, if their bodies are stunted from hunger, if their sickness goes untended, if their life is spent in hopeless poverty just drawing a welfare check.

So we want to open the gates to opportunity. But we are also going to give all our people, black and white, the help that they need to walk through those gates. . . .

This is the richest and most powerful country which ever occupied this globe. The might of past empires is little compared to ours. But I do not want to be the President who built empires, or sought grandeur, or extended dominion.

I want to be the President who educated young children to the wonders of their world. I want to be the President who helped to feed the hungry and to prepare them to be taxpayers instead of taxeaters.

I want to be the President who helped the poor to find their own way and who protected the right of every citizen to vote in every election.

I want to be the President who helped to end hatred among his fellow men and who prompted love among the people of all races and all regions and all parties. I want to be the President who helped to end war among the brothers of this earth. . . .

I want this to be the Congress, Republicans and Democrats alike, which did all those things for all these people. . . .

God will not favor everything that we do. It is rather our duty to divine His will. But I cannot help believing that He truly understands and that He really favors the undertaking that we begin here tonight.

Economic Justice
The North Has Problems Too

Chapter 115

Report of the National Advisory Commission on Civil Disorders

Kerner Commission

Riots shook the Watts section of Los Angeles in 1965 as well as other cities over the following two years, resulting in deaths and extensive property damage. In 1967, President Johnson appointed the National Advisory Commission on Civil Disorders—better known as the Kerner Commission, after its chair, Governor Otto Kerner of Illinois—to investigate.

The summer of 1967 again brought racial disorders to American cities, and with them shock, fear and bewilderment to the nation.

The worst came during a two-week period in July, first in Newark and then in Detroit. Each set of a chain reaction in neighboring communities.

On July 28, 1967, the President of the United States established this Commission and directed us to answer three basic questions:

What happened?

Why did it happen?

What can be done to prevent it from happening again?

To respond to these questions, we have undertaken a broad range of studies and investigations. We have visited the riot cities; we have heard many witnesses; we have sought the counsel of experts across the country.

This is our basic conclusion: Our nation is moving toward two societies, one black, one white—separate and unequal.

Reaction to last summer's disorders has quickened the movement and deepened the division. Discrimination and segregation have long permeated much of American life; they now threaten the future of every American.

This deepening racial division is not inevitable. The movement apart can be reversed. Choice is still possible. Our principal task is to define that choice and to press for a national resolution.

To pursue our present course will involve the continuing polarization of the American community and, ultimately, the destruction of basic democratic values.

The alternative is not blind regression or capitulation to lawlessness. It is the realization of common opportunities for all within a single society.

This alternative will require a commitment to national action—compassionate, massive and sustained, backed by the resources of the most powerful and the richest nation on this earth. From every American it will require new attitudes, new understanding, and, above all, new will.

The vital needs of the nation must be met: hard choices must be made, and, if necessary, new taxes enacted.

Violence cannot build a better society. Disruption and disorder nourish repression, not justice. They strike at the freedom of every citizen. The community cannot—it will not—tolerate coercion and mob rule.

Violence and destruction must be ended—in the streets of the ghetto and in the lives of people.

Segregation and poverty have created in the racial ghetto a destructive environment totally unknown to most white Americans.

What white Americans have never fully understood—but what the Negro can never forget—is that white society is deeply implicated in the ghetto. White institutions created it, white institutions maintain it, and white society condones it.

It is time now to turn with all the purpose at our command to the major unfinished business of this nation. It is time to adopt strategies for action that will produce quick and visible progress. It is time to make good the promises of American democracy to all citizens—urban and rural, white and black, Spanish-surname, American Indian, and every minority group.

Our recommendations embrace three basic principles:

- To mount programs on a scale equal to the dimension of the problems;
- To aim these programs for high impact in the immediate future in order to close the gap between promise and performance;
- To undertake new initiatives and experiments that can change the system of failure and frustration that now dominates the ghetto and weakens our society.

These programs will require unprecedented levels of funding and performance, but they neither probe deeper nor demand more than the problems which called them forth. There can be no higher priority for national action and no higher claim on the nation's conscience.

Chapter 116

The Watts Uprising

Gerald Horne

Gerald Horne is professor of history and director of the Black Cultural Center and the Institute for African-American Research at the University of North Carolina.

The following selection is excerpted from Fire This Time: The Watts Uprising *and the 1960s (Charlottesville: University Press of Virginia, 1995). Reprinted with permission of the University Press of Virginia. Footnotes deleted.*

For another selection by Horne, see chapter 77.

At least 34 people died in Los Angeles during the Watts Uprising of August 1965; 1,000 more were injured, and 4,000 arrested. Property damage was estimated at $200 million in the 46.5-square-mile zone (larger than Manhattan or San Francisco) where approximately 35,000 adults "active as rioters" and 72,000 "close spectators" swarmed. On hand to oppose them were 16,000 National Guard, Los Angeles Police Department, highway patrol, and other law enforcement officers; fewer personnel were used by the United States that same year to subdue the Dominican Republic.

Within the larger area of conflict, the twenty-square-mile district of Watts-Willowbrook was devastated. In its eastern portion lived one-sixth of Los Angeles County's black population of little more than one-half million (the county included the city and other territory); two-thirds of the adult residents had less than a high school education and one in eight was illiterate. Income levels were lower than any other section of the county except for the skid row district of downtown LA. Though most of those killed were black, most of the property damage was suffered by a ruling elite and middle class who were predominantly white.

In the area bordered by Washington Boulevard to the north, Rosecrans Avenue to the south, Alameda Street to the east, and Crenshaw Boulevard to the west, 261 buildings were damaged or destroyed by fire, along with almost all of the latter's contents. The epicenter of destruction was on 103rd Street. In one three-block area 41 buildings occupied primarily by food, liquor, furniture, and clothing stores were demolished. Few homes, churches, or libraries were damaged, a fact that supports the contention that the Watts Uprising was no mindless riot but rather a conscious, though inchoate, insurrection.

In the period before the Red Scare, Los Angeles possessed one of the stronger left and progressive movements in the nation; this left was based predominantly in the working class—trade unions—and the black community, working class and middle class alike; the middle class did not exercise the hegemony in black political life that it came to later. The repression of the left created an ideological vacuum that would later be filled by black nationalism and this nationalism exploded in Watts in August 1965. This nationalism eventually had at least three strands: the Nation of Islam, "cultural nationalists," and the Black Panther party; the first two assumed primacy during the 1960s while the latter—which had ties to the reviled left—disappeared. . . .

The creation and subsequent filling of this vacuum defines the meaning of the Watts Revolt of 1965 and, indeed, the meaning of the 1960s. By the time the 1960s arrived, it was clear that Jim Crow not only had to go but was going. However, the civil rights movement had its most dramatic and substantive impact in the Deep South, not Los Angeles. For many black Angelenos it was disorienting to hear talk of a revolution in race relations but to see little evidence of it in their lives. Moreover, by 1965 militant and multiracial confrontation of police brutality and other ills was disappearing; in such an environment it became easier to imagine that a monolithic Euro-American populace stood opposed to the faintest hint of black progress.

Unions, hampered by Red Scare restrictions, such as the Taft-Hartley bill, found it difficult to organize or embrace the black migrants flooding into Southern California. Thus excluded, these migrants turned in growing numbers to the Nation of Islam, attracted by its doctrine of self-sufficiency and "do for self." Blacks were faced with a paradox: at the same time they were undergoing a proletarianization process in their move from the fields of Texas and Louisiana to the factories of Los Angeles, unions and working-class ideology were declining while the fundamentally middle-class ideology of NOI was ascending. This "Nation of Shopkeepers" ideology not only created illusions about the economic destiny of blacks, it also served to reinforce the passive acceptance of the decline of unions. Gangs, with their dream of emulating other racial and ethnic groups by constructing illicit commercial empires, played a similar ideological role. Significantly, both gangs and the NOI recruited heavily in prisons, where the Civil Rights Congress previously had chalked up some of its more important victories; with the decline of unions and working-class organizations there was a concomitant growth in the ranks of the "lumpen proletariat" and its own distinct ideology.

Part of the appeal of the NOI was its relentless pursuit of a middle-class ideal in the oppositional garb of Islam; its promise to "clean up" the perceived rough edges of the incoming black migrants paralleled what the National Urban League was attempting. Though the community that both purported to represent was predominantly working class, both organizations stressed the donning of the middle-class uniform of suit and tie as a route to respectability. The National Association for the Advancement of Colored People was firmly in the grips of a more traditional middle-class leadership, exemplified by the light-skinned banker H. Claude Hudson. As working-class organizations declined, gangs flourished by stressing racial, religious, and family ties.

Eventually the rise of gangs influenced the nascent Black Panther party and the NOI, as well as music, dress, language, cinema, and other areas of peculiar relevance to Los Angeles. This influence was transmitted via the BPP to the predominantly white Students for a Democratic Society, the Weathermen or "Weatherpeople," and others.

The rise in influence of gangs brought with it a brand of black nationalism that hurt black women. Nationalism generally can have negative consequences for women, and the black nationalism developing in LA was no exception. Part of the "liberation" proclaimed by many male black nationalists in LA was the "right" to emulate the patriarchy of the Euro-American community. Moreover, the influence of gangs and the lumpen proletariat with their penchant for settling disputes through violence and their devaluing of women through prostitution complicated male-female relations in the black community. The subjugation of black women served to negate many of the positive aspects of black nationalism, such as pride in being black. Still, these gangs filled a socioeconomic vacuum left by the decline of unions and a love and caring vacuum left by the weakening of family structure.

The black nationalism that ultimately detonated in Watts was not just a reaction against white racism; it was also a reaction against the historic and stereotypical notion that blacks were the "female" of the races: subordinated, subordinate, dominated, timid. Through black nationalism a slice of race cum gender privilege could be reclaimed by means of a sometimes brutal masculinity that, after all, was normative among other races and ethnicities in the sprawling city of Los Angeles.

That black nationalism was ignited in Los Angeles should not have been surprising given the atmosphere of what might be called "compounded racism." Not only was the city torn by the simple biracial polarity that existed in most of the country, it was also home to other groups—principally Mexican Americans and Asian-Americans—who often carried negative ideas about the darker skinned. Moreover, many black Angelenos had roots in Louisiana, where conflicts between lighter- and darker-skinned blacks had a lengthy history. In an environment where class consciousness had been suppressed, color consciousness was enhanced, providing fertile soil for the growth of black nationalism.

Black nationalism, in part, represented an attempt to create a bond between darker- and lighter-skinned blacks and to curb tensions that had developed because, among other reasons, employers of whatever hue often favored the latter over the former. Similarly, societal norms infected by white supremacy dictated to darker women and men that through skin lighteners and hair straighteners they should mimic their lighter counterparts. To be sure, black nationalism did not simply arise in Southern California in 1965; it was a phenomenon that had waxed and waned in the United States since at least the nineteenth century, just as Islam was no stranger to Africans in the Americas. What was relatively new about this black nationalism was its potent antiwhite character and, to a lesser extent, its muscular nature. The Nation of Islam was born in the early 1930s, but at that time there was a left movement to provide a multiracial and militant alternative; thus, the NOI's ranks were thin. As the left weakened, however, the NOI began to grow: by 1965 the NOI probably had as many members and influenced as many as the Civil Rights Congress at its zenith. The rise of the NOI in LA made for a contradictory and confused black nationalism. The theology of this sect maintained that blacks were Asiatic at a time when black nationalism to many meant an identification with Africa along with pride in nappy hair and dark skin. The NOI's identification with Asia was at times the cause of some ambivalence among its adherents.

Nationalism was not monolithic. Aside from the NOI, there were "cultural nationalists," often artists and intellectuals influenced by the transatlantic currents of Negritude, as well as anti-imperialists who identified with armed struggle in Africa, Asia and Latin America but did not want to fight for their government in Vietnam or Santo Domingo—or Watts.

The Black Panther party, which bloomed in the ashes of Watts, had ties to the diminished left. Its internationalism was an enhanced reflection of what its members had experienced in a California that diverged sharply from the national pattern of simple biracial polarity. However, the socioeconomic decline of South LA and related factors created conditions favorable for the flourishing of gangs and a culture that left a deep and damaging imprint on everything it touched, including the BPP. Concomitantly, COINTELPRO [see chapter 153—*Eds.*] targeted the BPP, and this hastened its demise.

There is a link that joins the apparently conflicting agendas of the middle-class ideology of the NOI, "cultural nationalists," the NAACP leadership—and the gangs. The NOI, the cultural nationalists, and some of the gangs clamored for blacks to control businesses in black communities. This was a touchy issue since to some it implied a form of "ethnic cleansing" in South LA; it was made more sensitive by the left's lengthy campaign for Negro self-determination with its inference of black control of institutions in the black community. When the goal of black control moved toward realization, those who were positioned to benefit were many black entrepreneurs close to the NAACP leadership and the Sons of Watts, an organization viewed by many as a glorified gang.

Working-class blacks did benefit in the aftermath of the revolt. Many received government jobs and joined public-sector unions. However, they rarely asserted themselves with the kind of working-class ideology that was expressed in South Africa, for example, by the mostly black Congress of South African Trade Unions. The right wing's constant emphasis on reducing the size of government ensured that these black workers would face constant insecurity.

The NAACP was affected profoundly by the Red Scare. It was forced to oust from organizational influence black and nonblack leftists alike. Those whites who fought racism militantly were branded Red or Pink and purged. Frank Barnes, the militant president of the Santa Monica branch, was suspended from his post office job on loyalty charges after organizing a picket line for jobs at a local Sears Roebuck store. In the charges, filed pursuant to Executive Order 9835, it was alleged that he had been and was at that time "affiliated or sympathetic with an organization, association, movement, group, or combination of persons designated by the Attorney General as subversive." Barnes was also a fervent advocate of internal democracy in the centralized NAACP, and shortly thereafter he was ousted from the presidency; removing him from influence set the stage for the NAACP in LA to be dominated by middle-class professionals often distant from the concerns of working-class black Angelenos. By 1965 the NAACP would hesitate to collaborate with Communist union leaders like John Howard Lawson or Emil Freed or even a union leader who simply ran afoul of the Red Scare, such as Frank Barnes.

The triumph of the middle class in the NAACP ultimately was harmful for South LA. As black migrants flowed into Southern California after World War II, they were associated with the dislocation their arrival was said to bring. More blacks meant more opportunities for antiblack racism and more competition for scarce housing and employment. Many of the new arrivals in Watts particularly were scorned for their alleged untidiness, viewed as a relic of their rural backgrounds. Unlike many in the middle class, they did not wear suits and ties daily because their employment did not require it or allow it. Unlike those bourgeois leaders at the apex of the NAACP leadership, they did not have deep roots in Southern California. Year-of-arrival consciousness became a substitute for class consciousness.

By the time of the Watts conflagration of 1965, the NAACP was scorned and deemed out of touch with the black masses. That this leadership tended to be lighter skinned than the majority of the community they purported to represent became an issue of no small significance in August 1965. Similarly, the black Christian church had failed to attend to the temporal needs of many of its parishioners. Taken together, the perceived failures of these two venerable institutions created an opening for the Nation of Islam with its militant rhetoric about presumed oppressors.

The triumph of the middle class in the NAACP underscored the vitality of the California Dream. Those with attractive homes, well-tailored suits, larger cars, and hefty bank accounts were thought to be better people and happier; this description did not apply to many in South LA. The events of 11–18 August 1965 assumed the form of a "food riot," an eruption of commodity fetishism, and a potlatch of destruction among those denied the dream. The organizational channels through which the marginalized traditionally had expressed their anger had been eroded.

In the resulting void along with nationalism, year-of-arrival consciousness, and the like arose generational conflict. Justifiably the youth of 1965 asked what the older generation had done to combat Jim Crow; many of the youth did not recall or were made to forget the militance of W. E. B. Du Bois and Ben Davis [a New York City councilman and a leading Communist Party official], not to mention Pettis Perry [the leading black Communist in Southern California before the Red Scare]. Thus, the answers they received were incomplete, unsatisfying, unimpressive. The younger generation concluded that there had been an excess of middle-class prudence and the time had come for militance. Unfortunately, this laudable response was colored by the ascending influence of gangs, whose often violent bravado could have benefited from a dash of prudence.

Although the case of *Brown v. Board of Education* in 1954 and the Montgomery bus boycott of 1955 precipitated a new conversation on a race, South LA was not disposed to participate in it. The sacrifices of black youth, from Emmett Till to the Student Nonviolent Coordinating Committee, earned them a distinct place at the table along with the NOI, cultural nationalists, gangs, the BPP, and the NAACP; to many of the youth, all appeared attractive except the last. Simultaneously, the attack on Aid to Families with Dependent Children—i.e., welfare—was not just an attack on women, it was an attack on youth.

Hence, the meaning of what happened in the 1960s cannot be divorced from what had happened in the 1950s, most notably, the Red Scare. Those forces arising in the 1960s were marked indelibly by what happened in the previous decade. Ironically, this meant that those activists who arose in the 1960s not only were obligated by the prevailing consensus to keep apart from figures like Ben Davis, John Howard Lawson, Pettis Perry, and Frank Barnes, they often were unaware of their existence.

The decline of the left also set the stage for the rise of ultraright forces bent on eviscerating the public sector; it was the government—city, state, and federal—that sought to hamstring racial discrimination via legislation and regulation, and the weakening of this sector had a negative impact on blacks. Government was the chief employer in LA; in it blacks—City Councilman Tom Bradley for one—were placed at the highest levels, as they were not generally in the private sector. The attack on government was, in effect, an attack on blacks.

The Watts Uprising was a milestone marking the previous era from what was to come. For blacks it marked the rise of black nationalism, as blacks revolted against police brutality. But what began as a black revolt against the police quickly became a police revolt against blacks. This latter revolt was a milestone too, one marking the onset of a "white backlash" that would propel Ronald Reagan into the governor's mansion in Sacramento and then the White House. White backlash proved to be more potent than what had given it impetus, black nationalism. This too was the meaning of the 1960s.

Chapter 117

The Great Society

Lyndon Johnson

The following selection is excerpted from President Lyndon Johnson's speech at the University of Michigan in Ann Arbor, 22 May 1964, Public Papers of the Presidents of the United States, Lyndon B. Johnson, 1964 (Washington, D.C., 1963–64), 1:704–7.

For another selection by Johnson, see chapter 114.

I have come today from the turmoil of your Capital to the tranquillity of your campus to speak about the future of your country.

The purpose of protecting the life of our Nation and preserving the liberty of our citizens is to pursue the happiness of our people. Our success in that pursuit is the test of our success as a Nation.

For a century we labored to settle and to subdue a continent. For half a century we called upon unbounded invention and untiring industry to create an order of plenty for all of our people.

The challenge of the next half century is whether we have the wisdom to use that wealth to enrich and elevate our national life, and to advance the quality of our American civilization.

Your imagination, your initiative, and your indignation will determine whether we build a society where progress is the servant of our needs, or a society where old values and new visions are buried under unbridled growth. For in your time we have the opportunity to move not only toward the rich society and the powerful society, but upward to the Great Society.

The Great Society rests on abundance and liberty for all. It demands an end to poverty and racial injustice, to which we are totally committed in out time. But that is just the beginning.

The Great Society is a place where every child can find knowledge to enrich his mind and to enlarge his talents. It is a place where leisure is a welcome chance to build and reflect, not a feared cause of boredom and restlessness. It is a place where the city of man serves not only the needs of the body and the demands of commerce but the desire for beauty and the hunger for community.

It is a place where man can renew contact with nature. It is a place which honors creation for its own sake and for what it adds to the understanding of the race.

It is a place where men are more concerned with the quality of their goals than the quantity of their goods.

But most of all, the Great Society is not a safe harbor, a resting place, a final objective, a finished work. It is a challenge constantly renewed, beckoning us toward a destiny where the meaning of our lives matches the marvelous products of our labor.

So I want to talk to you today about three places where we begin to build the Great Society—in our cities, in our countryside, and in our classrooms.

Many of you will live to see the day, perhaps 50 years from now, when there will be 400 million Americans—four-fifths of them in urban areas. In the remainder of this century urban population will double, city land will double, and we will have to build homes, highways, and facilities equal to all those built since this country was first settled. So in the next 40 years we must re-build the entire urban United States.

Aristotle said: "Men come together in cities in order to live, but they remain together in order to live the good life." It is harder and harder to live the good life in American cities today.

The catalog of ills is long: there is the decay of the centers and the despoiling of the suburbs. There is not enough housing for our people or transportation for our traffic. Open land is vanishing and old landmarks are violated.

Worst of all expansion is eroding the precious and time honored values of community with neighbors and communion with nature. The loss of these values breeds loneliness and boredom and indifference.

Our society will never be great until our cities are great. Today the frontier of imagination and innovation is inside those cities and not beyond their borders.

New experiments are already going on. It will be the task of your generation to make the American city a place where future generations will come, not only to live but to live the good life.

I understand that if I stayed here tonight I would see that Michigan students are really doing their best to live the good life.

This is the place where the Peace Corps was started. It is inspiring to see how all of you, while you are in this country, are trying so hard to live at the level of the people.

A second place where we begin to build the Great Society is in our countryside. We have always prided ourselves on being not only America the strong and America the free, but America the beautiful. Today that beauty is in danger. The water we drink, the food we eat, the very air that we breathe, are threatened with pollution. Our parks are overcrowded, our seashores overburdened. Green fields and dense forests are disappearing.

A few years ago we were greatly concerned about the "Ugly American." Today we must act to prevent an ugly America.

For once the battle is lost, once our natural splendor is destroyed, it can never be recaptured. And once man can no longer walk with beauty or wonder at nature his spirit will wither and his sustenance be wasted.

A third place to build the Great Society is in the classrooms of America. There your children's lives will be shaped. Our society will not be great until every young mind is set free to scan the farthest reaches of thought and imagination. We are still far from that goal. . . .

Each year more than 100,000 high school graduates, with proved ability, do not enter college because they cannot afford it. And if we cannot educate today's youth, what will we do in 1970 when elementary school enrollment will be 5 million greater than 1960? And high school enrollment will rise by 5 million. College enrollment will increase by more than 3 million.

In many places, classrooms are overcrowded and curricula are outdated. Most of our qualified teachers are underpaid, and many of our paid teachers are unqualified. So we must give every child a place to sit and a teacher to learn from. Poverty must not be a bar to learning, and learning must offer an escape from poverty.

But more classrooms and more teachers are not enough. We must seek an educational system which grows in excellence as it grows in size. This means better training for our teachers. It means preparing youth to enjoy their hours of leisure as well as their hours of labor. It means exploring new techniques of teaching, to find new ways to stimulate the love of learning and the capacity for creation.

These are three of the central issues of the Great Society. While our Government has many programs directed at those issues, I do not pretend that we have the full answer to those problems.

But I do promise this: We are going to assemble the best thought and the broadest knowledge from all over the world to find those answers for America. I intend to establish working groups to prepare a series of White House conferences and meetings—on the cities, on natural beauty, on the quality of education, and on other emerging challenges. And from these meetings and from this inspiration and from these studies we will begin to set our course toward the Great Society.

The solution to these problems does not rest on a massive program in Washington, nor can it rely solely on the strained resources of local authority. They require us to create new concepts of cooperation, a creative federalism, between the National Capital and the leaders of local communities.

Woodrow Wilson once wrote: "Every man sent out from his university should be a man of his Nation as well as a man of his time."

Within your lifetime powerful forces, already loosed, will take us toward a way of life beyond the realm of our experience, almost beyond the bounds of our imagination.

For better or for worse, your generation has been appointed by history to deal with those problems and to lead America toward a new age. You have the chance never before afforded to any people in any age. You can help build a society where the demands of morality, and the needs of the spirit, can be realized in the life of the Nation.

So, will you join in the battle to give every citizen the full equality which God enjoins and the law requires, whatever his belief, or race, or the color of his skin?

Will you join in the battle to give every citizen an escape from the crushing weight of poverty?

Will you join in the battle to make it possible for all nations to live in enduring peace—as neighbors and not as mortal enemies?

Will you join in the battle to build the Great Society, to prove that our material progress is only the foundation on which we will build a richer life of mind and spirit?

There are those timid souls who say this battle cannot be won; that we are condemned to a soulless wealth. I do not agree. We have the power to shape the civilization that we want. But we need your will, your labor, your hearts, if we are to build that kind of society.

Those who came to this land sought to build more than just a new country. They sought a new world. So I have come here today to your campus to say that you can make their vision our reality. So let us from this moment begin our work so that in the future men will look back and say: It was then, after a long and weary way, that man turned the exploits of his genius to the full enrichment of his life.

Thank you. Good-bye.

Chapter 118

The SCLC and Chicago

Adam Fairclough

"When the Reverend Martin Luther King Jr. took his civil rights crusade to Chicago early in 1966 more blacks lived in Cook County, Illinois, than in any other county in the nation," writes historian Roger Biles in his biography of then mayor Richard J. Daley. "Not only did more blacks reside in Chicago than in the entire state of Mississippi, but more blacks occupied the city's larger public housing projects than populated Selma, Alabama—the 1965 site of King's greatest victory."

Adam Fairclough, professor of history at the University of Leeds, is the author of Race and Democracy: The Civil Rights Struggle in Louisiana, 1915–1972 *(1995) and* Martin Luther King, Jr. *(1995).*

The following selection is excerpted by permission from To Redeem the Soul of America: The Southern Christian Leadership Conference and Martin Luther King, Jr. *(Athens: University of Georgia Press, 1987), footnotes deleted.*

As an exemplar of Northern racism, Chicago could hardly be bettered. Intense and often violent hostility to blacks has long been a hallmark of the nation's second city. In the early years of the century the Great Migration of blacks from the Southern countryside intensified white antagonism and led to the riot of 1919, a four-day spasm which left thirty-eight people dead. Blacks were already concentrated in the South Side of Chicago and largely excluded from the rest of the city. The riot reinforced this pattern and, in the words of historian Allan Spear, "destroyed whatever hope remained for a peacefully integrated city." Segregation did not have the force of statute—it did not need to. The Chicago Real Estate Board (CREB), which excluded blacks, fostered and perpetuated a dual housing market that made segregation a social and economic reality. In 1921 the CREB adopted the "restrictive covenant," a model sales contract which prohibited the buyer from selling or renting to blacks. By the 1940s such covenants applied to four-fifths of all white-owned residential property.

During the postwar decades, segregation increased rather than diminished. Despite a 1948 ruling by the Supreme Court which outlawed the restrictive covenant, the city's real estate brokers, lending institutions, and white property owners found ways of continuing to exclude blacks from white areas. Outright violence provided a final sanction against unwanted black neighbors. Attempts by blacks to live outside clearly defined black areas triggered arson, bombings, and at least a dozen riots between 1945 and 1964. The laxity of the authorities in quelling these outbursts confirmed the prevalent belief that Chicago's "color line" had the tacit support of city hall. As the black population swelled from 250,000 in 1940 to almost a million twenty years later, the South Side ghetto expanded and a second enclave came into being on the West Side, adjacent to the downtown Loop. White out-migration—between 1932 and 1960 Chicago experienced a net decline in its white population of 424,000—exacerbated the pattern of residential segregation. With the exception of a few neighborhoods, white and black lived in separate and exclusive zones, the one out of choice, the other out of necessity. True, about 10 percent of Cook County's blacks lived outside Chicago proper, but the vast majority of them resided "in the ghettos of . . . satellite cities, such as Evanston, or in all-Negro suburbs." Yet the Democratic administration of Mayor Daley, which had governed Chicago since 1955, insisted that blacks lived in separate areas "because of cultural, social and other ties," not because of discrimination. There were no "ghettos" in Chicago, Daley claimed.

The Urban League, usually the most cautious and conservative civil rights organization, had taken the lead in attempting to puncture this official complacency. Edwin C. Berry reconstructed the Chicago Urban League after a disastrous schism in 1955. Dissatisfied with its traditional role as a "glorified employment agency," Berry set out to expose and document the reality of racial discrimination. In 1956 he called Chicago the most segregated city in the United States and, gathering together a talented research staff, proceeded to supply chapter and verse. The South, he contended, was less a geographic region than a "state of mind, much of which has moved to Chicago." More than any other individual, "Bill" Berry paved the way for the black protest movement of the 1960s. When SCLC came to Chicago, he became a key adviser.

But the structure of the Urban League, with its organic ties to white business, made it impossible for Berry to undertake the kind of "dynamic community organizing efforts" which he had promised. Neighborhood groups like The Woodlawn Organization (TWO), on the other hand, had a more popular orientation. The Woodlawn Organization was a creation of the Industrial Areas Foundation, Saul Alinsky's vehicle for the promotion of democratic self-help associations in poor and working-class areas. Founded in 1961, and embracing a ghetto neighborhood south of the University of Chicago, TWO was a federation of about eighty local groups, including churches and businessmen's clubs. Once set up, TWO spurred black voter registration, organized rent strikes, fought the university's "urban renewal" schemes, and agitated for better schools. Charles Silberman of *Fortune* magazine praised TWO for its emphasis on self-help and community involvement, holding it up as a model for black advancement in the ghettos of the North.

Thanks largely to the efforts of TWO and the Urban League, segregation in the public schools became the focus of black discontent, the famous 1954 decision of the Supreme Court in *Brown v. Board of Education* had applied only to schools which had been segregated by law; segregated schools in the North, the Court assumed, merely reflected patterns of residence. But the Urban League claimed that the Chicago Board of Education actively fostered segregation, creating a double standard of education. . . .

The controversy over segregated schools spawned the Committee for Integrated Education, which gave way in 1963 to the CCCO [the Coordinating Council of Community Organizations], a coalition of about forty organizations, both black and white. The CCCO organized two, one-day school boycotts, which enjoyed wide support from black parents. The city refused, however, to accede to the CCCO's main demand: the dismissal of Benjamin C. Willis, the superintendent of schools. Willis denied the charge of segregation and adamantly refused to transfer black children from overcrowded ghetto schools to underused "white" schools. The issue came to a head in 1965, when the board of education renewed Willis' contract. On June 10 the CCCO began to stage protest marches; during the following month the police arrested about seven hundred demonstrators, most of whom had been picketing the home of Mayor Daley. The American Civil Liberties Union challenged the arrests on the grounds of the First Amendment. Nevertheless, the protests soon declined from an initial peak of six hundred marchers a day to fewer than one hundred. The CCCO wanted SCLC to put fire into the campaign. . . .

King hoped that [SCLC associate] James Bevel could devise an effective strategy for the campaign. During the last three months of 1965, Bevel and his team of fourteen established themselves on the West Side and surveyed their surroundings. What they found appalled them. . . . This blight, Bevel reasoned, was not simply a by-product of inadvertent neglect, lingering prejudice, and mass migration. The ghetto persisted because powerful outside interests had an economic stake in it. By confining blacks to limited areas, the real estate interests boosted prices and interest rates within the ghetto and slums. Merchants made minimal investments, charged premium prices, and then carried off their profits to the suburbs. The building unions excluded blacks so as to increase the wages and job security of their white members. The Democratic machine condoned and buttressed these parasitic arrangements. . . .

As he evolved his analysis, his ideas on how to approach the problem underwent a transformation. When he arrived in Chicago, Bevel had been anxious to reach out to the white population, enlisting the support of students, businessmen, suburban housewives, and all people of goodwill. He had wanted to indoctrinate blacks in nonviolence so that they could "communicate love to white people." As they began their work, however, Bevel and his staff were forced to de-emphasize interracialism and nonviolence as a *philosophy*. Apart from deep racism in the white population, the reciprocal antiwhite sentiments of many ghetto blacks, particularly the young, made a movement of "black and white together" problematic. . . .

By the end of 1965 Bevel was thinking in terms of a "grassroots movement" of the black poor that could act independently of, and even in opposition to, the white majority. To raise the political consciousness of the masses and wean them away from Daley's machine, he proposed to organize slum-dwellers into self-governing associations. . . . [H]e argued that tenant unions could provide a starting point for this type of organization. . . . To this end, Bevel began organizing in the East Garfield Park district of the West Side, starting with an area of seven thousand people.

As Bevel's team labored on the West Side, Jesse Jackson was laying the groundwork for Operation Breadbasket. Jackson actually wore two hats. Recruited during the Selma campaign, he returned to Chicago to liaise between the CCCO and SCLC. In October he received a Ford Foundation grant to work as a community organizer in Kenwood-Oakland, a South Side neighborhood which had been "annexed" by the ghetto after the Second World War. Conditions there, as reported by Jackson, were as bad as anything to be found on the West Side. Working through churches, parent-teacher associations, and other local groups, Jackson tried to involve residents in the Kenwood-Oakland Community Organization, which he founded and led himself. Jackson's second, more important task was to enlist the support of Chicago's black ministers. SCLC needed churches for meeting places and organizing centers. It also wanted to establish Operation Breadbasket so that ministers could instigate consumer boycotts—or use the threat of such boycotts—to force white employers to hire more blacks. Jackson, not yet ordained himself, won the backing of Clay Evans, pastor of the Fellowship Baptist Church and president of the Baptist Ministers Conference. When King outlined the Operation Breadbasket concept to a meeting at Jubilee Temple on February 11, more than three hundred preachers heard him. Under Jackson's direction, Operation Breadbasket began to take root.

It was a mark of his swift rise in SCLC's hierarchy that Jackson met King at Chicago O'Hare International Airport when the latter arrived on January 5 to attend a two-day conference with the CCCO leadership. The agenda of this conclave showed the SCLC still had to find living quarters for King, Andrew Young, and Bernard Lee, and that a structure for the SCLC-CCCO alliance had yet to be devised. King decided to rent an apartment in the heart of the West Side ghetto. A precise resolution of the second question had to wait, but it was agreed that King and Albert Raby, the convener of the CCCO, should act as co-chairmen of a Chicago Freedom Movement. King undertook to increase SCLC's Chicago staff from fourteen to fifty and to spend at least two days a week in the city.

At a press conference on January 7, King defined the campaign as a "multifaceted assault" on the evils of the city slum. Acknowledging his debt to Bevel, he argued that the problem was "simply a matter of economic exploitation." He promised a three-stage campaign. The first was to be an effort to combat the "somnolence of despair" in the ghettos by uniting the poor in "Unions to End Slums." In stage two, beginning on March 1, the movement would employ probing demonstrations to "reveal the agents of exploitation" and mold "community consensus . . . around specific targets." By May, the movement's "non-violent army" should be ready to launch a "massive action," with the help and support of "the major religious groups, the trade union movement and various elements of the liberal community." The campaign demanded a positive response from city, state, and federal governments. SCLC had always used local situations to dramatize the need for national solutions. "Our work will be aimed at Washington,"

King stated. SCLC expected, at the very least, a significant expansion of the War on Poverty and the passage by Congress of "open-housing" legislation. . . .

With no prospect of taking on additional workers, SCLC found its staffing levels hopelessly inadequate. With never more than fifty staff members in the city, Chicago overwhelmed SCLC's resources. The West Side contained three hundred thousand blacks and Puerto Ricans; the black population of the entire city stood at approximately a million. Bevel complained that the CCCO furnished little help. . . .

The recruitment of black youths, who had provided much of SCLC's demonstration manpower in the South, posed an especially difficult challenge. . . . The gangs were disdainful of the church, antagonistic towards whites, and contemptuous of the word "nonviolence." . . .

SCLC claimed a large measure of success for its work with the Chicago gangs. In an early report from the West Side, Bevel wrote that "a real transformation seemed to be taking place in the lives of some of the boys." In May, he claimed that three thousand gang members were being trained in nonviolence and would soon be ready to "close down Chicago." A month later, SCLC organized a gang "convention" at the palatial Palmer House, where King urged the youths to stop fighting among themselves and start working with the Chicago Freedom Movement. "From that period on," Orange remembered, "we worked with these guys." Some became King's unofficial bodyguards; others served as marshals on demonstrations. "We saw some of the most violent individuals accepting nonviolent discipline," King related in 1967. . . . But others were skeptical about these claims. "King's aides have failed in their stated attempt to make movement workers out the Blackstone Rangers," wrote Judy Coburn in *New Republic*. To be sure, a few gang members joined SCLC's crusade, but most remained cynically aloof and continued their own internecine vendettas. Even those attracted to King found it difficult to accept SCLC's emphasis on interracialism and nonviolence. "As he preached nonviolence to them" Coretta King recalled, "many of them still said, 'We believe in violence.'" . . .

King's attempts to dramatize slum conditions were imaginative but unproductive. On January 26, under the glare of popping flashbulbs, he moved into a squalid Lawndale apartment. But as local journalist Mike Royko cynically and accurately commented, "Chicagoans already knew about slums. Whites were indifferent and Negroes didn't have to be reminded where they lived." . . .

King genuinely believed that by drawing attention to slum conditions SCLC might instill a greater sensitivity in the city government towards the problems of Chicago's black poor. But Mayor Daley's politicking, although shrewd, betrayed a lack of concern which he found exasperating and depressing. . . .

Social justice, King had come to believe, demanded nothing less than a drastic redistribution of wealth in favor of the poor, yet Daley's shallow responses reminded him that there was still no disposition on the part of government to even consider such a policy. Writing in *Nation,* he attributed the stiffening of white resistance to the civil rights movement to the fact that blacks were now attacking "financial privilege." During his visit to Europe in late March, King praised

America's "amazing capacity to accept changes," but blamed "powerful forces . . . who make high profits at the Negro's expense" for the persistence of the ghetto. His brief stay in Sweden, which again impressed him with its absence of poverty, accentuated King's growing doubts about the American economic order and increased his attraction to Scandinavian-style democratic socialism. . . .

Faced with intransigence from the realtors and malign neglect from city hall, SCLC went ahead with demonstrations in Chicago's white neighborhoods. On July 27 the CFM adopted an "Open City Action Report," which proposed to test racial toleration in ten areas. The first test consisted of an all-night vigil outside a real estate office in Gage Park, in the southwestern part of the city. The protest came to a premature end when two hundred jeering whites drove the pickets away. The next day, July 30, the first march proper took place, when an integrated group of 250 returned to Gage Park. Local whites shouted abuse and hurled bottles. When a seventy-car convoy disgorged the marchers again the next day, a furious white crowd wrecked two dozen vehicles and injured sixty people. Al Raby and Jesse Jackson were both struck by missiles.

King and Raby criticized the police for being "either unwilling or unable to disperse the riotous mobs." Thereafter the police were present in larger numbers, and they made a determined effort to keep the white crowds at bay. The sight of the white policemen protecting the marchers, however, drove the local populace to a higher pitch of fury. On August 2, 140 policemen battled a thousand whites in Belmont-Cragin, an area northwest of Lawndale. When Bevel led 350 marchers back there the following day, the size of the white crowd had doubled. The police line held. On August 5, King led a march through Gage Park in person. At first he seemed nonchalant about the white onlookers, who numbered between four and five thousand. The presence of 1,000 policemen did not, however, prevent the 800 marchers from being pelted with "rocks, bottles, cherry bombs and eggs—some dropped by residents perched in trees." The violence disturbed King and frightened him, although he did not show it at the time. After a rock struck his head, causing him to fall to his knees, he joked, "It hurts, but it's not an injury." . . .

The forays into Chicago's white neighborhoods continued for three more weeks. On August 7, Bevel and Raby took fifteen hundred protesters—the largest demonstration so far—back to Belmont-Cragin. Rain and a thousand policemen kept the white crowd fairly subdued.

On August 8, Jesse Jackson dropped a bombshell: the CFM had scheduled simultaneous marches for two days hence, one in Bogan, the other in Cicero. Bogan was an area of Irish, Italian, and Eastern European immigrants and their descendants; like all such Chicago neighborhoods, it wanted to remain "white." Cicero's reputation was more sinister. A suburb of seventy thousand people, it had become notorious in the late 1920s and 1930s as the Mafia's main base in Cook County. It also had the dubious distinction of having stopped any blacks from living there. In 1952, Gov. Adlai Stevenson called out the National Guard in order to quell a riot against Negro "intruders." According to Don Rose, the CFM's publicity director, Jackson "seriously overstepped his authority" in announcing the Cicero march.

King, in Mississippi at the time, apparently had no intention of marching through Cicero so soon, if at all. "We were batting the threat around for leverage, never saying anything definite about it," Rose later explained.

Sanctioned by King or not, Jackson's announcement sent shock waves through city and county halls. The sheriff of Cook County, Richard B. Ogilvie, warned that the white reaction in Cicero could "make Gage Park look like a tea-party"; he promised to use "every possible legal means" to prevent the march. The prospect of a Cicero bloodbath also horrified many of the CFM's white sympathizers, evoking anxious demands that the marches should stop. The weightiest voice belonged to Archbishop Cody, who warned on August 10 that further demonstrations "will very likely [result in] serious injury to many persons and perhaps even loss of life." The leaders of the CFM, he added, had a "serious moral obligation" to consider a halt to the marches; "with a heavy heart," he urged them to do so. Another key CFM supporter, Robert Johnson of the United Auto Workers, also changed his mind. In March, he had vowed that "the UAW is in this thing all the way." But on August 11, Johnson joined other labor leaders in meeting Daley and then endorsing Cody's plea. . . .

The *Chicago Tribune* fulminated against he CFM's tactics. "Causing violence to achieve political ends is criminal syndicalism," it asserted. "If the marchers keep up their sabotage it will be time to indict the whole lot of them." The *Tribune*'s angry editorials provided one yardstick of the marches' effectiveness. Provocative or not, they placed Daley in a quandary. With the police attempting to protect the marchers, his administration was receiving the blame for what most whites perceived as a black invasion. And with the autumn elections approaching, the Republicans stood to benefit from the "backlash." "Every time we march," Bevel exulted, "Daley loses 10,000 votes—from the whites." Moreover, with the CFM staging multiple marches, and with a Cicero march in the offing, there was a real possibility that the white crowds might swamp the police and inflict serious casualties. Andy Young hinted that SCLC was prepared to bring about martial law. As Mike Royko later put it, "King had Daley reeling. . . . Another 1919 was getting closer all the time."

Desperate to stop the marches, Daley agreed to a "summit conference" with the CFM and other interested parties, to be held on August 17, at St. James's Episcopal Church. . . .

One thing became clear immediately after the talking began: Daley would agree to virtually anything in order to secure a cancellation of the marches. The CFM realized, however, that commitments by Daley had little value in the absence of hard-and-fast commitments from CREB: CREB was the main obstacle to open housing and bore the brunt of the CFM's arguments. Yet CREB appeared immovable. Its spokesmen, Ross Beatty and Arthur Mohl, denied any responsibility for housing discrimination and disclaimed any duty to fight it. . . .

King would have none of this. Restaurant and hotel owners across the South had used these arguments to hold out against desegregation. Yet when the Civil Rights Act came into being, they adapted to the change and suffered no loss of clientele. King dismissed the claim that realtors merely reflected the attitudes of their clients as a sophistry. He pointed out that the industry had spent $5 million to kill California's fair housing law, and was presently lobbying Congress to defeat the civil rights bill. The real estate industry was hardly neutral: it had helped to *create* discriminatory attitudes. . . .

The session ended with both sides accepting [chairman Ben] Heineman's proposal for the appointment of a subcommittee, and then agreeing to meet again on August 26 to consider the committee's draft. . . .

When the negotiators met again on August 26, both sides accepted the ten-point agreement drafted by Bishop Montgomery's subcommittee. King and Raby complained about the injunction; they also expressed concern about the implementation of the pact. Nevertheless, they undertook to end the marches. Speaking to reporters afterwards, King hailed the agreement as "far-reaching and creative." *Newsweek* described it as "a solid vindication of Southern-style protest in a Northern city."

But the "Summit Agreement" was riddled with loopholes. The *Chicago Tribune,* which had recently described King, Bevel and Raby as "paid professional agitators," immediately detected the two most obvious weaknesses. First, there was no timetable for implementation; second, CREB still refused to drop its legal action against Chicago's fair housing ordinance. . . .

All in all, the Summit Agreement amounted to little more than various pledges of nondiscrimination.

In a report to SCLC's administrative committee, King optimistically detected "some evidence that the pact's good faith will be upheld." He nevertheless gave his approval to a crash program of voter registration in Chicago so that "slum dwellers can begin to break the grip of machine politics." Hosea Williams arrived in mid-December, with fifteen members of his Southern staff, brimming with confidence that he could "change things politically" in the city. But the drive failed miserably. After two months SCLC had contacted an infinitesimal fraction of the 150,000 unregistered blacks in Chicago. How many it actually persuaded to register is unclear: Williams claimed 32,000; the city, which refused to open neighborhood registration centers, put the figure at 320. This poor showing was partly the result of inadequate funding, but it also reflected the reluctance of the CCCO to mount an all-out attack on the Democratic machine. . . .

In April 1967 Daley was reelected to a fourth four-year term. He received a 73 percent plurality, winning more than four-fifths of the black vote. SCLC had not only failed to defeat Daley, it had not even come close. With his political base more secure than ever, Daley ignored King and the CCCO and forgot about the Summit Agreement. The campaign for open housing had failed as completely as the drive for integrated schools. As the CCCO fell apart, Raby resigned as its convener and chief spokesman. "When the next riots hit," he warned, "the whites had better not look to me to cool things. That was what the Chicago Freedom Movement was trying to do, but the Mayor wasn't listening." . . .

SCLC had lived with talk of a "white backlash" for three years and had always dismissed the notion that direct action did anything more than expose prejudice that was already there. To the white trade union and religious leaders who backed the CCCO, however, the hostility and anger which the open-housing marches evoked were dangerous new forces. After the riots in Gage Park and elsewhere, they began to ask whether the marches might not be reinforcing white prejudices. If King had turned down the Summit Agreement and persisted with the marches, his white support, already eroding, would have crumbled. Young later castigated Cody and the other religious leaders for their "insipid moral neutrality," which, he believed, caused them to betray the movement:

> They were really trying to be neutral and serve as arbitrators in what was a moral issue that they had to take sides on. They tried to be a mediator between the movement and the Mayor, as though there were wrongs on both sides. And they were just really naive. . . . When we tried to raise the issue of the injunction with the Mayor, it was the Federation of Churches representative who got up and interceded and tried to block it. He . . . suggested that the court should decide on it. He never realized that to take an injunction case on up to the Supreme Court would cost from $25,000–$50,000. And, of course, they never suggested that they should contribute towards that.

After Chicago, Young had little faith in the church as a vehicle for social reform.

There was another, quite straightforward, reason why King accepted the pact: he trusted the other signatories to keep their part of the bargain. In doing so, he made two crucial errors. First, promises by the mayor and the religious leaders cut little ice with the real estate interests: King went against his own dictum that the political power structure follows the economic power structure, not vice versa. As C. T. Vivian argued, SCLC confronted Daley rather than the real estate board; the Summit Agreement was a "deal with everybody but those who made the decisions." Second, King badly underestimated the mendacity and duplicity of his opponents. Vivian thought SCLC let Daley off the hook by stopping the marches too soon: "We should have *forced* that thing into Cicero . . . even if it meant some of our skulls being cracked, because that's our line." Later, analyzing the city's failure to live up to the agreement, King arrived at the same conclusion. "I look back over," he told his staff, "and wish we'd gone to Cicero."

SCLC discovered in Chicago that discrimination was a far more insidious and tenacious enemy than segregation. It also found itself progressively more isolated as the administration turned its back, as too many blacks stayed cynically aloof, and as white liberals joined the anti-war movement or swelled the conservative chorus in calling for an end to demonstrations. Now, as the Chicago campaign sputtered to its dispiriting conclusion, SCLC found itself confronting a new, altogether different, and in some ways more dangerous, challenge—one that came from within the civil rights movement itself. In June 1966 the ideological tensions which had already stretched black unity almost to the breaking point finally split the movement asunder. In addition to fighting white racism, SCLC had to fend off an attack upon its fundamental principles. That attack came in the form of a deceptively simple slogan consisting of two words and an exclamation mark: "Black Power!"

Chapter 119

Resurrection City and the
Poor People's Campaign

I. F. Stone

In October 1967 Martin Luther King, Jr., proposed plans for a Poor People's Campaign, a march of several thousand people to Washington, D.C., where they would construct a shantytown and threaten mass civil disobedience until the federal government dealt with poverty by enacting economic reforms. The campaign represented a concerted attempt by SCLC to address broad economic issues with a class-based, cross-racial alliance of poor blacks, whites, Hispanics, and Native Americans. The FBI, under orders from J. Edgar Hoover, immediately responded with an extensive national effort to disrupt the march.

In April, reflecting SCLC's growing emphasis on economic justice, King postponed his organizing efforts for the campaign to support striking sanitation workers in Memphis. On 3 April he addressed a rally. "Like anybody, I would like to live a long life," he said. "Longevity has its place. But I'm not concerned about that now. I just want to do God's will. And He's allowed me to go up to the mountain top. And I've looked over. And I've seen the Promised Land. I may not get there with you. But I want you to know tonight that we as a people will get to the Promised Land. So I'm happy tonight. I'm not worried about anything. I'm not fearing any man. 'Mine eyes have seen the glory of the coming of the Lord.'" The next day he was assassinated.

Four weeks later, with planning in chaos, the first marchers commemorated King's murder by leaving from Memphis—by mule train, bus, and car—with SCLC's new leader, Ralph Abernathy. When they arrived in Washington, D.C., Coretta Scott King and Robert Kennedy addressed a support rally and Abernathy named their ramshackle collection of tents and sheds constructed within sight of the White House and Capitol "Resurrection City." Along with incomplete planning, the campaign was beset with wholesale depression following the assassination, almost constant poor weather, up to 3,000 residents occupying an area designed for 1,500, in-fighting over strategy, a deaf ear from the White House, and the continuous work of the FBI to undermine the campaigners' efforts. Three weeks after their arrival, Robert Kennedy was assassinated in California after winning the state's Democratic presidential primary. By late June, SCLC was forced to leave.

"Having agreed that Congress [was] unlikely to be affected by the sight of a few thousand poor people," Calvin Trillin wrote, "commentators tend[ed] to

blame the Poor People's Campaign for a futile demonstration rather than blame Congress for being unresponsive to the needs of the poor."[1] *Investigative journalist I. F. Stone (1907–1989), the writer, editor, and publisher of I. F. Stone's Weekly (1953–1971), was one of the few journalists who did not consider the campaign a complete disaster.*

The following selection is excerpted from two stories from I. F. Stone's Weekly: "The Fire Has Only Just Begun," 15 April 1968, and "Billions for Missiles and Pennies for Poverty," 8 July 1968. Reprinted by permission of Jeremy J. Stone.

For another selection by Stone, see chapter 101.

For further discussion of the FBI's efforts to discredit King and subvert the Poor People's Campaign, see Gerald D. McKnight, The Last Crusade *(1998).*

April 15, 1968—The assassination of Dr. Martin Luther King, Jr., was the occasion for one of those massive outpourings of hypocrisy characteristic of the human race. He stood in that line of saints which goes back from Gandhi to Jesus; his violent end, like theirs, reflects the hostility of mankind to those who annoy it by trying hard to pull it one more painful step further up the ladder from ape to angel.

The President and the Washington establishment had been working desperately up until the very moment of Dr. King's killing to keep him and his Poor People's March out of the capital; his death, at first, promised to let them rest in peace. The masses they sang were not so much of requiem as of thanksgiving that the nation's No. 1 Agitator had been laid to rest at last. . . .

Dr. King was a victim of white racism. Its record encourages such murders. Dr. King was only the most eminent in a long series of civil rights victims. The killers are rarely caught, even more rarely convicted; the penalties are light. The complicity, in this case, may go further. It is strange that the killer was so easily able to escape when the motel in which he was killed was ringed with police; some came within a few moments from the very direction of the fatal shot. Violent anti-Negro organizations like the Klan have their cells in many police forces. The Memphis police had shown their hatred in the indiscriminate violence with which they broke up Dr. King's march a week earlier. The Attorney General should be pressed to include the Memphis police in his investigation of the slaying.

Though Dr. King was the greatest Southerner of our time, few Southern political leaders expressed any sorrow over his passing. Most, like [Senator John] Stennis of Mississippi, ventured no more than antiseptic and ambivalent condemnation of *all* violence. In the House on April 8 the few Southerners who spoke deplored the riots more than the killing. The one exception was Representative Bob Eckhardt of Texas, who dared call Dr. King "my black brother." Privately many white Southerners rejoiced, and their influence was reflected in the scandalous failure to declare a holiday in the District [of Columbia] the day Dr. King was buried. Though stores closed, government offices were open and Negro mailmen delivered the mail as usual. This is still, despite its black majority, a Southern-ruled town; it shuts down on Washington's birthday, but not Lincoln's.

The most powerful of the District's absentee rulers, Senator Robert C. Byrd (D–W. Va.), went so far as to imply in a Senate speech April 5, that Dr. King was to blame for his own death. Byrd said those who organize mass demonstrations may "in the end . . . become themselves the victims of the forces that they set in motion." While Dr. King "usually spoke of nonviolence," Byrd went on smugly, "violence all too often attended his action and, at the last, he himself met a violent end." This should make Byrd the South's favorite criminologist.

Byrd is the Senator to whom the blacks of Washington must come for school and welfare money. As chairman of the Senate Appropriations subcommittee on the District of Columbia budget, Byrd wields far more power than the city's figurehead Negro "Mayor." He has used this key position to block liberalization of welfare rules not only in the District but in the country, since the federal government can hardly apply elsewhere rules more liberal than those he will allow in the District. Byrd has become the national pillar of the "man in the house" rule. This, as the report of the Commission on Civil Disorders protested, makes it necessary for the unemployed father to "abandon his family or see them go hungry." In this sense not a few of the child looters in our gutted ghettoes can trace their delinquency straight back to Robert C. Byrd.

For whites who live like myself in almost lily-white Northwest Washington on the very edge of suburbia, the ghetto disorders might have taken place in a distant country, viewed on TV like Vietnam (which it begins to resemble), or as a tourist attraction on a visit in the bright spring sunshine before curfew to the sullen and ruined ghetto business districts. It was not until five days after the trouble started that two young soldiers turned up for the first time to guard our own neighboring shopping center—"as a precautionary measure," they explained—and tape appeared on its liquor-store windows. Even sympathetic and radical whites found themselves insulated from what was going on not just by the military cordons but even more by an indiscriminate black hostility. Even some liberal and leftist families with children moved out of integrated neighborhoods on the edge of the ghetto in apprehension. These were our first refugees from black power.

Nothing could be more deceptive than the nationwide mourning. Beneath the surface nothing has changed, except perhaps for the worst. The President has called off his address to a joint session indefinitely. His Senate Majority Leader, [Mike] Mansfield, warns the Congress not to be "impetuous" in reacting to the disorders. How fortunate we should be if all our dangers were as remote as this one! The new civil rights bill, if it passes, is more than likely to bring new evils in its anti-riot provisions than reform in housing.

In Washington, as in most cities hit by black violence, the police and the troops have been on their best behavior to the point where business spokesmen are complaining that there has been too much leniency in dealing with looters. For once, to the Administration's credit, lives have been put ahead of property. Had police and soldiers begun to shoot, the killings would have become a massacre and the riots a black revolution. As it is, in Washington at least, the black community has been grateful for the protection afforded it. But this leniency is unlikely to survive when and if white rather than black areas begin to go up in smoke. There is little time left for the big multi-billion-dollar program which alone can rehabilitate the hopeless and bitter generation of blacks that racial discrimination and the slums have bred. Whites still think they can escape the problem by moving to the suburbs, and as long as they think so, nothing will be done. There are already 55,000 troops in our 110 scarred cities—more than we had in Vietnam three years ago. Already the police talk of guerrilla war. If it comes, a half million troops will not be enough to contain it. A looting suspect told one reporter at a police station here, "We're going to burn this whole place. It might take years but we'll do it." This is the agony of a lost race speaking. If we cannot respond with swift compassion, this is the beginning of our decline and fall.

July 8, 1968—The day the poor were driven out of Resurrection City was the day the Senate voted to approve an anti-missile system. Monday, June 24 deserves to go down in history for its symbolic significance. Congress turned a flinty banker's face to the poor but took the first step toward the deployment of an ABM (anti-ballistic missile) network which could cost more than their most utopian demands. The first installment for Sentinel, the "thin" one, is $5 billion. The total cost of the big one the military-industrial complex wants can easily run to $50 billion. Even that is only the beginning. For the ABM will set off a new spiral in the arms race, as each side builds more missiles to overwhelm the other's anti-missiles, and then more anti-missiles to counter the new missiles. "And at the end of it all," as [Senator Gaylord] Nelson of Wisconsin told the Senate that day, the U.S. and the Soviet Union "will be right back where we started, except out of pocket $50 to $100 billion."

While the chief lobbyist of the poor, the Reverend Ralph David Abernathy [the new leader of SCLC], went to jail, the lobbyists of the military-industrial complex celebrated their biggest victory. The ABM will prove to be our most wasteful handout. But the lobbyists who sold this bill of goods did not have to live in the shanties or confront the police lines on their way to the Capitol. The clients of the welfare state ought to get acquainted with the clients of the warfare state. The decision to go ahead with the ABM, the *Congressional Quarterly* said in a special study May 24 of the military-industrial complex, will benefit more than 15,000 companies including such major defense contractors as General Electric, General Dynamics and Thiokol-Chemical. One brokerage firm told its customers last summer that the day Congress approved the ABM was "the day they will shake the money tree for electronic companies." In the last quarter of 1967, after Johnson overruled [Defense Secretary Robert] McNamara and approved the Sentinel, seventy-five mutual investment funds "sold $90 million in other stock holdings [the *Congressional Quarterly* report says] and invested the proceeds in electronics."

The ABM is the latest breakthrough in the arms race, and it is time to recognize the arms race for what it is—the socialism of the rich. It is the welfare system which supports some of our richest corporations. The physicist Ralph Lapp, who did so much to arouse the country to the fallout danger in the campaign against nuclear testing, has provided the best overall view of what the ABM and the arms race really means in his new book, *The Weapons Culture*. The spokesmen for the poor should use it as ammunition. Dr. Lapp observed that the so-called free enter-prise system "has been distorted into a kind of 'defense socialism,' in which the welfare of the country is permanently tied to the continued growth of military technology and the continued stockpiling of military hardware." Dr. Lapp esti-mates that since World War II the U.S. has spent about one trillion dollars—1,000 billions or 1,000,000 millions—on armament! The program has fallen like manna on the country-club set and—with the related space program—created a whole new generation of millionaires. We could have cleaned up every slum and solved every racial and social problem with a fraction of the money, thought and energy which went into military hardware, most of it already junked as obsolete.[2]

Solidarity Day brought a vast throng to Washington and half a dozen Establish-ment phonies hastened to address it from the Lincoln Memorial. But no occa-sional upsurge of benevolent feeling, much less spurious oratorical generalities about poverty, is going to change the allocation of resources between those who grow rich on weaponry and those who decay on welfare. The swift liquidation of Resurrection City once the visitors had departed was the reflection of a more per-manent solidarity among those who fatten on the waste of national income. Those poor shanties the police destroyed were the first signs, we hope, of a widening and continued struggle against the inhumanity and the irrationality of our spending policy. During the House debate June 26 which ended with sharp cuts in the wel-fare budget, a typical Iowa Republican opponent of the poverty program said the country did not have "money to throw away . . . on this type of luxury" while a tightwad on the Democratic side ([Daniel] Flood of Pennsylvania) cried, "What do you want? Diamonds? What are you going to use for money? Cigar store cou-pons?" But when it comes to the war machine and the space program the billions flow freely.

[Representative Edith] Green of Oregon protested that this same Congress had voted $4 billion for the space program. "That means," she said, "we are willing to spend more dollars for outer space than we are willing to spend in total amount of tax dollars for the education of fifty million boys and girls in our elementary and secondary schools." But education, unlike the race for the moon, does not rain dollars on Houston, Texas. "It makes me heart-sick," Mrs. Green cried, "to see my nation spending in one day in Vietnam more than the total amount of increase I am requesting that affects two million teachers and the quality of education for fifty million boys and girls." It is not only the blacks nor only the poor who suffer from the huge allocations to the war and space machines. It is the quality of Amer-ican life. Urban blight and pollution could be ended permanently for what that war in Vietnam has cost us. Abernathy's little army has been fighting a battle for all of us.

Resurrection City is supposed to have been a mess. I found it inspiring. It re-minded me of the Jewish displaced persons' camps I visited in Germany after the war [World War II]. There was the same squalor and the same bad smells, but also the same hope and the same will to rebuild from the ashes of adversity. To orga-nize the hopeless, to give them fresh spirit, to set them marching was truly resur-rection. If much went wrong, that was to be expected; what was miraculous was that so much could be accomplished with the supposed dregs of society. Disorganization is hardly a novelty in Washington; you can find it everywhere from Capitol Hill to the Pentagon. The striking thing about Resurrection City is that there was so much genuine non-racialism. The organizers have been given very little credit for bridging a gap everyone deplores. The Reverend Ralph David Abernathy is not the first man of God to be ridiculed and jailed. The wry humor of the poor he led was summed up for me by that touching sign on one of the mule wagons. "Don't Laugh Folks," it said, "Jesus Was A Poor Man." It would be tragic if their voices were so easily smothered.

The skewed vision which afflicts the respectable in our society was beautifully summed up in the outburst of concern for the twenty-three skinny mules that finally made it to Washington. The first edition of the *Washington Daily News* June 28 carried across its front page a picture of a mule in clover with a caption saying that the mules had been moved to pasture land in Columbia, Maryland, "where the meadows go for $8,000 an acre and their next-door neighbors are $15,000 show horses and $20,000 stallions. 'They're going to be treated better than any mules in the history of muledom,' one bountiful lady says." What of the poor hungry human mules who balked at their heavy burdens?

When the Vietnamese war causes inflation, the poor bear the burden in the shape of higher living costs; they eat less. When higher taxes are imposed and the budget cut to save the dollar from inflation, the poor pay again in the shape of fewer jobs and reduced welfare. And now that there is hope the Vietnam war may be ending and more funds available to help them, the Under Secretary of the Treasury [Joseph Barr] tells a Town Hall audience in Los Angeles June 25 that he doubts the end of the war will bring any sizable reduction in the military budget. Mr. Barr estimated that "a cessation of hostilities would result in great pressures to rebuild stock in military supplies and equipment to a more acceptable level." He informs us that "We have been fighting this war on a very, very lean [only $80 billion!] budget." How dare the poor be so obstreperous when the Pentagon is so hungry?

EDITORS' NOTES

1. Calvin Trillin, "U.S. Journal: Resurrection City," *New Yorker,* 15 June 1968, 71.
2. The United States and the Soviet Union signed an anti-ballistic missile (ABM) treaty in 1972. President Reagan, in apparent violation of the treaty, renewed spending on a new system, commonly referred to as "Star Wars," in 1983. Since then, the United States has spent $88.4 billion on ballistic missile research.

The United States spent more than $14.9 trillion (adjusted for FY2000) on its military during the Cold War (1946–1991), according to Chris Hellman, a senior analyst with the Center for Defense Information in Washington, D.C. From 1993 to 1999, the United States spent an additional $2.4 trillion.

Chapter 120

The Welfare Rights Movement

James MacGregor Burns and Stewart Burns

James MacGregor Burns is the author of many works, including Roosevelt *(2 vols., 1956, 1970) and* The American Experiment *(3 vols., 1982–1989). Stewart Burns is the author of* Social Movements of the 1960s: Searching for Democracy *(1990) and editor of* Daybreak of Freedom: The Montgomery Bus Boycott *(1997).*

The following selection is excerpted from A People's Charter: The Pursuit of Rights in America. *Copyright © 1991 by James MacGregor Burns and Stewart Burns. Reprinted by permission of Alfred A. Knopf, Inc.*

King's death knocked the wind out of the Poor People's Campaign, which was already running aground. The army of the poor descended on Washington in mid-May and put up a tent shantytown of canvas and plywood. Soon heavy rains conspired with human disorganization to make inhospitable the flooded, muddy "Resurrection City" and it had to be abandoned. The poor, who always seemed to lose, had been routed once again.

Other activists embarked on a different strategy to end poverty in the world's wealthiest nation. In fall 1965, social work scholar Richard Cloward and political scientist Frances Fox Piven circulated a working paper among civil rights and antipoverty organizers later published in the *Nation*. Responding to the black movement's search for new directions, they proposed organizing a mass movement of welfare recipients, who were mainly women. Given that for every existing recipient, another was eligible, several million of the poor could be recruited to the welfare rolls. And given that welfare agencies typically refused to grant clients the full benefits to which they were entitled, Cloward and Piven pointed to a huge untapped potential for expanded payments. If these were the immediate objectives, their longer-term goal was to disrupt the welfare system and foster such a grave bureaucratic, fiscal, and electoral crisis that Washington would be compelled to guarantee an unconditional, livable income for all citizens.

Without any leadership the urban poor already had been sweeping into welfare centers in much larger numbers, which resulted in a near quadrupling of clients during the 1960s. The freedom movement had taught poor people that they had rights as citizens, even economic rights, while at the same time activists and antipoverty lawyers were inducing bureaucrats to loosen eligibility requirements.

"Accompanying the rise in expectation," [historian James] Patterson observes, "was a broadened, if unforseen, definition of the rights of citizenship" to include economic and social needs, a redefinition explained partly by improvements in education and mass communication. Simultaneously the idea of economic rights had begun to take hold in academic and policy circles. Liberal economist Robert Theobald argued for the poor's "entitlements," stating that "we all need to adopt the concept of an absolute constitutional right to an income" from the federal government sufficient to enable every citizen to live with dignity. Thirteen hundred economists petitioned Congress for a national system of income guarantees and supplements.

Many activists dismissed the Cloward-Piven strategy, either because they did not think the welfare poor could be organized or because they felt that economic solutions required the creation of jobs, not the perpetuation of dependence. One experienced organizer, however, took hold of these ideas as the answer to his political frustration. George Wiley, great-grandson of slaves, had grown up in Rhode Island, conquered one racial barrier after another, including becoming the first black to earn a Ph.D. in chemistry from Cornell, and in the early 1960s had blossomed as a prominent research chemist at Syracuse University. But civil rights activism inexorably took over his life, as he worked first as a local CORE leader, then with James Farmer as CORE's associate director. He came to realize that neither CORE nor any other existing rights group was prepared to build the grassroots movement of poor people he dreamed of.

"A lot of us who have come out of the civil rights movement have been quite frustrated," Wiley reflected, "about finding significant handles for bringing about some substantial change in the living conditions of people in the northern ghettoes. . . . For millions—particularly people who can't work, the aged or female heads of households—just encouraging them to assert their rights is a very attractive thing. . . . The potential here is enormous for getting the people involved in demanding rights as human beings from a system that doesn't treat them as human beings."

As a first step, in June 1966 Wiley's new Poverty/Rights Action Center coordinated protests for specific "welfare rights" in twenty-five cities. Marching 150 miles from Cleveland to Ohio's state capital to present grievances to the governor, several hundred welfare women sang:

> We feed our children bread and beans
> While rich folks ride in limousines.
> After all, we're human beings,
> Marching down Columbus Road.

Responding to such expressions of need, Wiley created the National Welfare Rights Organization to represent the lowest stratum of the American citizenry—impoverished urban women of color. Not merely an extension of the civil rights movement, welfare rights was a distinct "social protest of women who were poor," historian Guida West discovered. NWRO was led jointly by Wiley and a national board of dynamic, no-nonsense black welfare mothers including chair

Johnnie Tillmon from Los Angeles; the shared leadership was animated by creative tension. Calling for concrete reforms grounded in principles of adequate income, dignity, justice, and democracy, NWRO set forth its goal: "Jobs or income now! Decent jobs with adequate wages for those who can work; adequate income for those who can not work."

Local groups multiplied in 1967 and 1968. With the help of resources from the national office such as "how-to" welfare rights handbooks, they carried out the "street strategy" of creative direct action. Most effective were "basic need" campaigns to secure special grants for winter clothing, furniture, and school lunches. NWRO organizing spread throughout the country, even among poor whites in Appalachia and the South, but it proved most successful in New York and Massachusetts. In New York City, the [New York] Times reported that demonstrators were invading and camping out en masse in welfare centers, breaking down administrative procedures, wreaking havoc on "the mountains of paperwork," and throwing welfare services into "a state of crisis and near-chaos." More often than not they won their demands.

In Washington, Wiley skillfully lobbied Congress and the welfare bureaucrats for reform. He and Columbia University law professor Edward Sparer fashioned a legal strategy using antipoverty lawyers and class-action suits that liberalized policies and led to several Supreme Court decisions that nullified provisions denying recipients certain procedural rights. But as the explosion of welfare clients and funding reached crisis proportions—linked by the media to urban riots—a public backlash set in. The Democratic Congress enacted punitive restrictions, many states cut welfare benefits, New York and Massachusetts abolished special grant programs and the Nixon era's more conservative Supreme Court, led by Chief Justice Warren Burger, limited welfare clients' right to privacy. Eventually the attack on the welfare poor, combined with NWRO's internal divisions and its shift from direct action to lobbying, brought about its collapse in the early 1970s. Yet in the long run, the movement's success in expanding access, obtaining fairer treatment, and educating the public helped to solidify the legitimacy of welfare entitlements and to give greater dignity and self-respect to those who claimed them.

Reverend Andrew Young, SCLC's executive director during the 1960s, later credited welfare rights organizing with pushing the civil rights movement toward economic goals. Why did he think it took so long? "Religion was the language the South understood," Young explained, "and there was an almost calculated avoidance of any economic questions. . . . In SCLC we were working with college students, with independent business people. The civil rights movement, up until 1968, anyway, was really a middle-class movement. There were middle-class goals, middle-class aspirations, middle-class membership, and even though a lot of poor people went to jail . . . it was still essentially a middle-class operation." . . .

To end poverty and to "guarantee the right to a decent life to all Americans," as NWRO leader Beulah Sanders put it, the implementation of economic rights would have required going beyond incremental gains facilitated by economic growth—the traditional liberal approach—to actual redistribution of the American economic pie. But democratic redistribution of wealth by the government has remained a taboo in American political culture, especially in eras of economic downturn.

Still, the structural constraints of the "system" have not been all that has stood in the way of achieving economic and social rights. Movement leaders often accepted the inevitability of such constraints when in fact more options and leeway were available. In most rights campaigns, leaders had a fairly comprehensive vision of what their followers were entitled to, but at some point they decided, or reluctantly agreed, to divide rights claims into categories (legal, civil, political, social, economic), to set priorities among them, and to choose short-term political expediency over longer-term linkages of rights that would likely bring less immediate payoff. Though they frequently assumed that winning rights near at hand would lead to securing others, rarely did gaining one type of right automatically open the door to the claiming of another more remote or elusive. More radical factions sometimes tried to broaden the focus, particularly to integrate political with economic and social demands, but the mainstream leaders normally chose a less risky course. This politics of compartmentalization and deferral has entailed major social costs.

The tendency to compartmentalize rights claims resulted from several interconnected factors: the sway of liberal ideology that separated politics from society and the economy; the fragmentation of the political system with its divided powers and checks and balances; the government's openness to assimilating reform if gradual and piecemeal; the pull of American pragmatism; and the strategic priority of social movements to maximize the constituency of support by reducing goals to the lowest common denominator. Activists' lifelong conditioning to the limits of the political realm was continually reaffirmed by the experience of politics as "the art of the possible" with its incentives and rewards for playing by the rules. A vicious circle revolved: the more that reformers, over time, accepted apparent political limits in order to make incremental progress, the less pressure was put on the state to carry out substantive reform that pushed beyond those limits. And the more impoverished was the historical achievement of real reform, the more utopian seemed the activists who still sought it.

Black Power

Chapter 121

We Must Have Justice

Elijah Muhammad

The black nationalist Nation of Islam (NOI)—also known as the Black Muslims—was founded by Wallace D. Fard, who disappeared in 1934. His associate, Elijah Muhammad (1897–1975), took over the leadership in the 1930s and transformed the group into a national organization. NOI advocated the divinity of Fard, black racial superiority, and a separatist agenda.

Elijah Muhammad's son Wallace D. Muhammad (now known as Imam Warith D. Muhammed) converted to orthodox Islam in the 1960s and maintained ties with Malcolm X even after Malcolm split with NOI. After Elijah Muhammad's death, his son moved the group into the Islamic mainstream, renaming it the Muslim American Society. Several splinter groups of NOI continue, the most prominent under the leadership of Louis Farrakhan.

For biographies of Elijah Muhammad, see Claude Andrew Clegg, An Original Man *(1977) and Karl Evanzz,* The Messenger *(1999).*

The following selection is reprinted from an address given by Elijah Muhammad on 21 June 1963.

This is the question of today among the black people of America: Shall we have or get justice? The answer is yes; if you seek it from the right source and the right source is from Allah, truth and self.

Everything except the above three has failed us in the way of justice.

Let us then, all [leaders] meet together and see how best we can get justice for our people without selling their birthrights for a "mess of porridge," as Jacob did Esau.

We want justice for the so-called Negroes regardless of the price. We are fast learning that nonviolence is not respected. Church services, praying and singing glory hallelujah are not regarded any more than singing the blues.

It was pitiful to look at college students headed by a college leader, Mr. Martin Luther King, on TV singing and praying to the devils to allow him and his followers to share in with them [whites], respect the Negroes, and be able to dine and have everything in common together, while the devils were shaking their heads saying no, no.

One poor brother leading the others said to the devil, "Why not? Why not? Am I not a human being?"

The police and his dogs were sicked upon the whole group of beggars, and the poor people were driven off without the respect of dogs. Shall we have justice? Since everything fails but Allah, truth and self, unite on the side of Allah and truth and come follow me and you will get justice, money, good homes, and friendship in all walks of life, and some of the earth that we can call our own, separated from people that have brought us to disgrace and shame.

We are falling on our knees praying to a merciless enemy, begging and pleading with blood and tears streaming down our bodies, without the slightest sympathy from the universally known murderers. The so-called Negroes have been fooled in the knowledge of the American white race. The average so-called Negro thinks he is dealing with a people that are of the God of righteousness, but they have just become rich and wicked.

The so-called Negroes must remember the poorer the whites are, the more wicked they are when it comes to the so-called Negroes. The entire black nation must know that God has revealed this race of people to be the true race of devils, and there is no righteousness in them. Nature did not give them any righteousness, says Allah to me.

They know to do good but cannot. Their religious teachings mean nothing in the way of being righteous people. A few here and there wish to go all right, but they are outnumbered a thousand to one.

Now, let us go from them and build a nation ourselves that God and the nations of the earth will respect. Your loving to live and become one of the race of devils, who have proven to you for four hundred years that they do not want you for anything but to enslave you in their behalf, is outright foolish and ignorant. Do not you want your own black nation to see you in a better light of understanding?

The government wants to enforce integration, and will be successful after some bloodshed, wherein, the so-called Negro will lose the most blood. The government is and will do anything to keep the blind, deaf and dumb Negroes from going over to Allah and the Islamic nation [the Black Muslims].

What future will we, the twenty million blacks in America, have in a forced integration? Seeking equal employment and equal recognition would only be temporary, but some of this earth that you can call your own where you can build your own employment would be permanent!

This is the desire of God for us. He did it for Israel, and made a triple job of it in Belshazzar. To give you some of this earth is the purpose of His coming.

Chapter 122

The Ballot or the Bullet

Malcolm X

Malcolm X (1925–1965) was born as Malcolm Little. His parents were members of the Garvey movement (see chapters 63 and 64). While serving time in prison for burglary, he joined the Nation of Islam and changed his name to Malcolm X. After his release he went on to become the chief spokesperson for NOI. Malcolm later modified some of his views, criticized NOI leader Elijah Muhammad, and in 1964 formed two new groups, the Muslim Mosque, Inc., and the Organization of Afro-American Unity. In the 4 December 1964 issue of NOI's Muhammad Speaks, *Louis Farrakhan (then known as Louis X) wrote: "Only those who wish to be led to hell, or to their doom, will follow Malcolm. The die is set, and Malcolm shall not escape. . . . Such a man as Malcolm deserves to die."*

On 21 February 1965, Malcolm X was assassinated while speaking at the Audubon Ballroom in Harlem. Three members of NOI were convicted of the murder. One confessed, insisting that the others were innocent. Questions remain about the role of the FBI and the New York Police Department in inciting and allowing the murder to take place.

Malcolm X was the author (with Alex Haley) of The Autobiography of Malcolm X *(1965). Collections of his speeches include* Malcolm X Speaks *(1965),* By Any Means Necessary *(1970), and* February 1965 *(1992).*

The following selection is reprinted from "The Ballot or the Bullet," a speech delivered in Cleveland on 3 April 1964 after his break with NOI. Copyright © 1965, 1989 by Betty Shabazz and Pathfinder Press. Reprinted by permission.

Mr. Moderator, Brother [Louis] Lomax, brothers and sisters, friends and enemies: I just can't believe everyone in here is a friend and I don't want to leave anybody out. The question tonight, as I understand it, is "The Negro Revolt, and Where Do We Go from Here?" or "What Next?" In my little humble way of understanding it, it points toward either the ballot or the bullet.

Before we try and explain what is meant by the ballot or the bullet, I would like to clarify something concerning myself. I'm still a Muslim, my religion is still Islam. That's my personal belief. Just as Adam Clayton Powell is a Christian minister who heads the Abyssinian Baptist Church in New York, but at the same time takes part in the political struggles to try and bring about rights to the black people in the country; and Dr. Martin Luther King is a Christian minister down in Atlanta, Georgia, who heads another organization fighting for the civil rights of black people in this country; and Rev. [Milton] Galamison, I guess you've heard of him, is another Christian minister in New York who has been deeply involved in the school boycotts to eliminate segregated education;[1] well, I myself am a minister, not a Christian minister, but a Muslim minister; and I believe in action on all fronts by whatever means necessary.

Although I'm still a Muslim, I'm not here tonight to discuss my religion. I'm not here to try and change your religion. I'm not here to argue or discuss anything that we differ about, because it's time for us to submerge our differences and realize that it is best for us to first see that we have the same problem, a common problem—a problem that will make you catch hell whether you're a Baptist, or a Methodist, or a Muslim, or a nationalist. Whether you're educated or illiterate, whether you live on the boulevard or in the alley, you're going to catch hell just like I am. We're all in the same boat and we all are going to catch the same hell from the same man. He just happens to be a white man. All of us have suffered here, in this country, political oppression at the hands of the white man, economic exploitation at the hands of the white man, and social degradation at the hands of the white man.

Now in speaking like this, it doesn't mean that we're anti-white, but it does mean we're anti-exploitation, we're anti-degradation, we're anti-oppression. And if the white man doesn't want us to be anti-him, let him stop oppressing and exploiting and degrading us. Whether we are Christians or Muslims or nationalists or agnostics or atheists, we must first learn to forget our differences. If we have differences, let us differ in the closet; when we come out in front, let us not have anything to argue about until we get finished arguing with the man. If the late President Kennedy could get together with Khrushchev and exchange some wheat, we certainly have more in common with each other than Kennedy and Khrushchev had with each other.

If we don't do something real soon, I think you'll have to agree that we're going to be forced either to use the ballot or the bullet. It's one or the other in 1964. It isn't that time is running out—time has run out! 1964 threatens to be the most explosive year America has ever witnessed. The most explosive year. Why? It's also a political year. It's year when all of the white politicians will be back in the so-called Negro community jiving you and me for some votes. The year when all of the white political crooks will be right back in your and my community with their false promises, building up our hopes for a let down, with their trickery and their treachery, with their false promises which they don't intend to keep. As they nourish these dissatisfactions, it can only lead to one thing, an explosion; and now we have the type of black man on the scene in America today—I'm sorry, Brother Lomax—who just doesn't intend to turn the other cheek any longer.

Don't let anybody tell you anything about the odds are against you. If they draft you, they send you to Korea and make you face 800 million Chinese. If you can be brave over there, you can be brave right here. These odds aren't as great as those odds. And if you fight here, you will at least know what you're fighting for.

I'm not a politician, not even a student of politics; in fact, I'm not a student of much of anything. I'm not a Democrat, I'm not a Republican, and I don't even consider myself an American. If you and I were Americans, there'd be no problem. Those Hunkies that just got off the boat, they're already Americans; Polacks are already Americans; the Italian refugees are already Americans. Everything that came out of Europe, every blue-eyed thing, is already American. And as long as you and I have been over here, we aren't Americans yet.

Well, I am one who doesn't believe in deluding myself. I'm not going to sit at your table and watch you eat, with nothing on my plate, and call myself a diner. Sitting at the table doesn't make you a diner, unless you eat some of what's on the plate. Being here in America doesn't make you an American. Being born here in America doesn't make you an American. Why, if birth made you American, you wouldn't need any legislation, you wouldn't need any amendments to the Constitution, you wouldn't be faced with civil-rights filibustering in Washington, D.C., right now. They don't have to pass civil-rights legislation to make a Polack an American.

No, I'm not an American. I'm one of the 22 million black people who are the victims of Americanism. One of the 22 million black people who are the victims of democracy, nothing but disguised hypocrisy. So, I'm not standing here speaking to you as an American, or a patriot, or a flag-saluter, or a flag-waver—no, not I. I'm speaking as a victim of this American system. And I see America through the eyes of the victim. I don't see any American dream; I see an American nightmare.

These 22 million victims are waking up. Their eyes are coming open. They're beginning to see what they used to only look at. They're becoming politically mature. They are realizing that there are new political trends from coast to coast. As they see these new political trends, it's possible for them to see that every time there's an election the races are so close that they have to have a recount. They had to recount in Massachusetts to see who was going to be governor, it was so close. It was the same way in Rhode Island, in Minnesota, and in many other parts of the country. And the same with Kennedy and Nixon when they ran for president. It was so close they had to count all over again. Well, what does this mean? It means that when white people are evenly divided, and black people have a bloc of votes of their own, it is left up to them to determine who's going to sit in the White House and who's going to be in the dog house.

It was the black man's vote that put the present administration in Washington D.C. Your vote, your dumb vote, your ignorant vote, your wasted vote put in an administration in Washington D.C., that has seen fit to pass every kind of legislation imaginable, saving you until last, then filibustering on top of that. And your and my leaders have the audacity to run around clapping their hands and talk about how much progress we're making. And what a good president we have. If he [Lyndon Johnson] wasn't good in Texas, he sure can't be good in Washington, D.C. Because Texas is a lynch state. It is in the same breath as Mississippi, no different; only they lynch you in Texas with a Texas accent and lynch you in Mississippi with a Mississippi accent. And these Negro leaders have the audacity to go and have some coffee in the White House with a Texan, a Southern cracker—that's all he is—and then come out and tell you and me that he's going to be better for us because, since he's from the South, he knows how to deal with the Southerners. What kind of logic is that? Let Eastland be president, he's from the South too. He should be better able to deal with them than Johnson.

In this present administration they have in the House of Representatives 257 Democrats to only 177 Republicans. They control two-thirds of the House vote. Why can't they pass something that will help you and me? In the Senate, there are 67 senators who are of the Democratic Party. Only 33 of them are Republicans. Why, the Democrats have got the government sewed up, and you're the one who sewed it up for them. And what have they given you for it? Four years in office, and just now getting around to some civil-rights legislation. Just now, after everything else is gone, out of the way, they're going to sit down now and play with you all summer long—the same old giant con game that they call filibuster. All those are in cahoots together. Don't you ever think they're not in cahoots together, for the man that is heading the civil-rights filibuster is a man from Georgia named Richard Russell. When Johnson became president, the first man he asked for when he got back to Washington, D.C., was "Dicky"—that's how tight they are. That's his boy, that's his pal, that's his buddy. But they're playing the same old con game. One of them makes believe he's for you, and he's got it fixed where the other one is so tight against you, he never has to keep his promise.

So it's time in 1964 to wake up. And when you see them coming up with that kind of conspiracy, let them know your eyes are open. And let them know you got something else that's wide open too. It's got to be the ballot or the bullet. The ballot or the bullet. If you're afraid to use an expression like that, you should get out of the country, you should get back in the cotton patch, you should get back in the alley. They get all the Negro vote, and after they get it, the Negro gets nothing in return. All they did when they got to Washington was give a few big Negroes big jobs. Those big Negroes didn't need big jobs, they already had jobs. That's camouflage, that's trickery, that's treachery, window-dressing. I'm not trying to knock out the Democrats for the Republicans, we'll get to them in a minute. But it's true—you put the Democrats first and the Democrats put you last.

Look at it the way it is. What alibis do they use, since they control Congress and Senate? What alibi do they use when you and I ask, "Well, when are you going to keep your promise?" They blame the Dixiecrats. What is a Dixiecrat? A Democrat. A Dixiecrat is nothing but a Democrat in disguise. The titular head of the Democrats is also the head of the Dixiecrats, because the Dixiecrats are part of the Democratic Party. The Democrats have never kicked the Dixiecrats out of the party. The Dixiecrats bolted themselves once [in 1948], but the Democrats didn't put them out. Imagine, these lowdown Southern segregationists put the Northern Democrats down. But the Northern Democrats have never put the Dixiecrats down. No, look at that thing the way it is. They have got a con game going on, a political con game, and you and I are in the middle. It's time for you and me to wake up and start looking at it like it is, and trying to understand it like it is; and then we can deal with it like it is.

The Dixiecrats in Washington, D.C., control the key committees that run the government. The only reason the Dixiecrats control these committees is because they have seniority. The only reason they have seniority is because they come from states where Negroes can't vote. This is not even a government that's based on democracy. It is not a government that is made up of representatives of the people. Half of the people in the South can't even vote. Eastland is not even supposed to be in Washington. Half of the senators and congressmen who occupy these key positions in Washington, D.C., are there illegally, are there unconstitutionally.

I was in Washington, D.C., a week ago Thursday, when they were debating whether or not they should let the bill come onto the floor. And in the back room where the Senate meets, there's a huge map of the United States, and on that map it shows that the Southern section of the country, the states that are most heavily concentrated with Negroes, are the ones that have senators and congressmen standing up filibustering and doing all other kinds of trickery to keep the Negro from being able to vote. This is pitiful. But it's not pitiful for us any longer; it's actually pitiful for the white man, because soon now, as the Negro awakens a little more and sees the vise that he's in, sees the bag that he's in, sees the real game that he's in, then the Negro's going to develop a new tactic.

These senators and congressmen actually violate the constitutional amendments that guarantee the people of that particular state or county the right to vote. And the Constitution itself has within it the machinery to expel any representative from a state where the voting rights of the people are violated. You don't even need new legislation, because they will be replaced by black representatives from counties and districts where the black man is in the majority, not in the minority.

If the black man in these Southern states had his full voting rights, the key Dixiecrats in Washington, D.C., which means the key Democrats in Washington, D.C., would lose their seats. The Democratic Party itself would lose its power. It would cease to be powerful as a party. When you see the amount of power that would be lost by the Democratic Party if it were to lose the Dixiecrat wing, or branch, or element, you can see where it's against the interests of the Democrats to give voting rights to Negroes in states where the Democrats have been in complete power and authority ever since the Civil War. You just can't belong to that party without analyzing it.

I say again, I'm not anti-Democrat, I'm not anti-Republican, I'm not anti-anything. I'm just questioning their sincerity, and some of the strategy that they've been using on our people by promising them promises that they don't intend to keep. When you keep the Democrats in power, you're keeping the Dixiecrats in power. I doubt that my good Brother Lomax will deny that. A vote for a Democrat is a vote for a Dixiecrat. That's why, in 1964, it's time now for you and me to become more politically mature and realize what the ballot is for; what we're supposed to get when we cast a ballot; and that if we don't cast a ballot, it's going to end up in a situation where we're going to have to cast a bullet. It's either a ballot or a bullet.

In the North, they do it a different way. They have a system that's known as gerrymandering, whatever that means. It means when Negroes become too heavily concentrated in a certain area, and begin to gain too much political power, the white man comes along and changes the district lines. You may say, "Why do you keep saying white man?" Because it's the white man who does it. I haven't ever seen any Negro changing any lines. They don't let him get near the line. It's the white man who does this. And usually, it's the white man who grins at you the most, and pats you on the back, and is supposed to be your friend. He may be friendly, but he is not your friend.

So, what I'm trying to impress upon you, in essence, is this: You and I in America are faced not with a segregationist conspiracy, we're faced with a government conspiracy. Everyone who's filibustering is a senator—that's the government. Everyone who's finagling in Washington, D.C., is a congressman—that's the government. You don't have anybody putting blocks in your path but people who are part of the government. The same government that you go abroad to fight for and die for is the government that is in a conspiracy to deprive you of decent housing, deprive you of decent education. You don't need to go to the employer alone, it is the government itself, the government of America, that is responsible for the oppression and exploitation and degradation of black people in this country. And you should drop it in their lap. This government has failed the Negro. This so-called democracy has failed the Negro. And all these white liberals have definitely failed the Negro.

So, where do we go from here? First, we need some friends. We need some new allies. The entire civil-rights struggle needs a new interpretation, a broader interpretation. We need to look at this civil-rights thing from another angle—from the inside as well as from the outside. To those of us whose philosophy is black nationalism, the only way you can get involved in the civil-rights struggle is give it a new interpretation. That old interpretation excluded us. It kept us out. So, we're giving a new interpretation to the civil-rights struggle, an interpretation that will enable us to come into it, take part in it. And these handkerchief-heads who have been dillydallying and pussyfooting and compromising—we don't intend to let them pussyfoot and dillydally and compromise any longer.

How can you thank a man for giving you what's already yours? How then can you thank him for giving you only part of what's already yours? You haven't even made progress, if what's being given to you, you should have had already. That's not progress. And I love my Brother Lomax, the way he pointed out we're right back where we were in 1954. We're not even as far up as we were in 1954. We're behind where we were in 1954. There's more segregation now than there was in 1954. There's more racial animosity, more racial hatred, more racial violence today in 1964, than there was in 1954. Where is the progress?

And now you're facing a situation where the young Negro's coming up. They don't want to hear that "turn-the-other-cheek" stuff, no. In Jacksonville, those were teenagers, they were throwing Molotov cocktails. Negroes have never done that before. But it shows you there's a new deal coming in. There's new thinking coming in. There's new strategy coming in. It'll be Molotov cocktails this month, hand grenades next month, and something else next month. It'll be ballots, or it'll be bullets. It'll be liberty, or it will be death. The only difference about this kind of death—it'll be reciprocal. You know what is meant by "reciprocal"? That's one of Brother Lomax's words, I stole it from him. I don't usually deal with those big words because I don't usually deal with big people. I deal with small people. I find you can get a whole lot of small people and whip hell out of a whole lot of big people. They haven't got anything to lose, and they've got everything to gain. And they'll let you know in a minute: "It takes two to tango; when I go, you go."

The black nationalists, those whose philosophy is black nationalism, in bringing about this new interpretation of the entire meaning of civil rights, look upon it as meaning, as Brother Lomax has pointed out, equality of opportunity. Well, we're justified in seeking civil rights, if it means equality of opportunity, because all we're doing there is trying to collect for our investment. Our mothers and fathers invested sweat and blood. Three hundred and ten years we worked in this country without a dime in return. You let the white man walk around here talking about how rich this country is, but you never stop to think how it got rich so quick. It got rich because you made it rich.

You take the people who are in this audience right now. They're poor, we're all poor as individuals. Our weekly salary individually amounts to hardly anything. But if you take the salary of everyone in here collectively it'll fill up a whole lot of baskets. It's a lot of wealth. If you can collect the wages of just these people right here for a year, you'll be rich—richer than rich. When you look at it like that, think how rich Uncle Sam had to become, not with this handful, but millions of black people. Your and my mother and father, who didn't work an eight-hour shift, but worked from "can't see" in the morning until "can't see" at night, and worked for nothing, making the white man rich, making Uncle Sam rich.

This is our investment. This is our contribution—our blood. Not only did we give of our free labor, we gave of our blood. Every time he had a call to arms, we were the first ones in uniform. We died on every battlefield the white man had. We have made a greater sacrifice than anybody who's standing up in America today. We have made a greater contribution and have collected less. Civil rights, for those of us whose philosophy is black nationalism, means: "Give it to us now. Don't wait for next year. Give it to us yesterday, and that's not fast enough."

I might stop right here to point out one thing. Whenever you're going after something that belongs to you, anyone who's depriving you of the right to have it is a criminal. Understand that. Whenever you are going after something that is yours, you are within your legal rights to lay claim to it. And anyone who puts forth any effort to deprive you of that which is yours, is breaking the law, is a criminal. And this was pointed out by the Supreme Court decision. It outlawed segregation. Which means segregation is against the law. Which means a segregationist is breaking the law. A segregationist is a criminal. You can't label him as anything other than that. And when you demonstrate against segregation, the law is on your side. The Supreme Court is on your side.

Now, who is it that opposes you in carrying out the law? The police department itself. With police dogs and clubs. Whenever you demonstrate against segregation, whether it is segregated education, segregated housing, or anything else, the law is on your side, and anyone who stands in the way is not the law any longer. They are breaking the law, they are not representatives of the law. Any time you demonstrate against segregation and a man has the audacity to put a police dog on you, kill that dog, kill him, I'm telling you, kill that dog. I say it, if they put me in jail tomorrow, kill—that—dog. Then you'll put a stop to it. Now, if these white people in here don't want to see that kind of action, get down and tell the mayor to tell the police department to pull the dogs in. That's all you have to do. If you don't do it, someone else will.

If you don't take this kind of stand, your little children will grow up and look at you and think "shame." If you don't take an uncompromising stand—I don't mean go out and get violent; but at the same time you should never be nonviolent unless you run into some nonviolence. I'm nonviolent with those who are nonviolent with me. But when you drop that violence on me, then you've made me go insane, and I'm not responsible for what I do. And that's the way every Negro should get. Any time you know you're within the law, within your legal rights, within your moral rights, in accord with justice, then die for what you believe in. But don't die alone. Let your dying be reciprocal. This is what is meant by equality. What's good for the goose is good for the gander.

When we begin to get in this area, we need new friends, we need new allies. We need to expand the civil-rights struggle to a higher level—to the level of human rights. Whenever you are in a civil-rights struggle, whether you know it or not, you are confining yourself to the jurisdiction of Uncle Sam. No one from the outside world can speak out in our behalf as long as your struggle is a civil-rights struggle. Civil rights comes within the domestic affairs of this country. All of our African brothers and our Asian brothers and our Latin-American brothers cannot open their mouths and interfere in the domestic affairs of the United States and as long as it's civil rights, this comes under the jurisdiction of Uncle Sam.

But the United Nations has what's known as the charter of human rights, it has a committee that deals in human rights. You may wonder why all of the atrocities that have been committed in Africa and in Hungary and in Asia and in Latin America are brought before the U.N., and the Negro problem is never brought before the U.N. This is part of the conspiracy. This old, tricky, blue-eyed liberal who is supposed to be subsidizing our struggle, and supposed to be acting in the capacity of an adviser, never tells you anything about human rights. They keep you barking up the civil-rights tree, you don't even know there's a human-rights tree on the same floor.

When you expand the civil-rights struggle to the level of human rights, you can then take the case of the black man in this country before the nation in the U.N. You can take it before the General Assembly. You can take Uncle Sam before a world court. But the only level you can do it on is the level of human rights. Civil rights keeps you under his restrictions, under his jurisdiction. Civil rights keeps you in his pocket. Civil rights means you're asking Uncle Sam to treat you right. Human rights are something you were born with. Human rights are your God-given rights. Human rights are the rights that are recognized by all nations of this earth. And any time any one violates your human rights, you can take them to the world court. Uncle Sam's hands are dripping with blood, dripping with the blood of the black man in this country. He's the earth's number-one hypocrite. He has the audacity—yes, he has—imagine him posing as the leader of the free world.

The free world!—and you over here singing "We Shall Overcome." Expand the civil-rights struggle to the level of human rights, take it into the United Nations, where our African brothers can throw their weight on our side, where our Asian brothers can throw their weight on our side, and where 800 million Chinamen are sitting there waiting to throw their weight on our side.

Let the world know how bloody his hands are. Let the world know the hypocrisy that's practiced over here. Let it be the ballot or the bullet. Let him know that it must be the ballot or the bullet.

When you take your case to Washington, D.C., you're taking it to the criminal who's responsible; it's like running from the wolf to the fox. They're all in cahoots together. They all work political chicanery and make you look like a chump before the eyes of the world. Here you are walking around in America, getting ready to be drafted and sent abroad, like a tin soldier, and when you get over there, people ask you what you are fighting for, and you have to stick your tongue in your cheek. No, take Uncle Sam to court, take him before the world.

By ballot I only mean freedom. Don't you know—I disagree with Lomax on this issue—that the ballot is more important than the dollar? Can I prove it? Yes. Look in the U.N. There are poor nations in the U.N.: yet those poor nations can get together with their voting power and keep the rich nations from making a move. They have one nation—one vote, everyone has an equal vote. And when those brothers in Asia, and Africa and the darker parts of the earth get together, their voting power is sufficient to hold Sam in check. Or Russia in check. Or some other section of the earth in check. So, the ballot is most important.

Right now, in this country, if you and I, 22 million African-Americans—that's what we are—Africans who are in America. You're nothing but Africans. Nothing but Africans. In fact, you'd get farther calling yourself African instead of Negro. Africans don't catch hell. You're the only one catching hell. They don't have to pass civil-rights bills for Africans. An African can go anywhere he wants right now. All you've got to do is tie your head up. That's right, go anywhere you want. Just stop being a Negro. Change your name to Hoogagagooba. That'll show you how silly the white man is. You're dealing with a silly man. A friend of mine who's very dark put a turban on his head and went into a restaurant in Atlanta before they called themselves desegregated. He went into a white restaurant, he sat down, they served him, and he said, "What would happen if a Negro came in here?" And there he's sitting, black as night, but because he had his head wrapped up the waitress looked back at him and says, "Why, there wouldn't no nigger dare come in here."

So, you're dealing with a man whose bias and prejudice are making him lose his mind, his intelligence, every day. He's frightened. He looks around and sees what's taking place on this earth, and he sees that the pendulum of time is swinging in your direction. The dark people are waking up. They're losing their fear of the white man. No place where he's fighting right now is he winning. Everywhere he's fighting, he's fighting someone your and my complexion. And they're beating him. He can't win any more. He's won his last battle. He failed to win the Korean War. He couldn't win it. He had to sign a truce. That's a loss. Any time Uncle Sam, with all his machinery for warfare, is held to a draw by some rice-eaters, he's lost the battle. He had to sign a truce. America's not supposed to sign a truce. She's supposed to be bad. But she's not bad any more. She's bad as long as she can use her hydrogen bomb, but she can't use hers for fear Russia might use hers. Russia can't use hers, for fear that Sam might use his. So, both of them are weaponless. They can't use the weapon because each weapon nullifies the other's. So the only place where action can take place is on the ground. And the white man can't win another war fighting on the ground. Those days are over. The black man knows it, the brown man knows it, the red man knows it, and the yellow man knows it. So they engage him in guerrilla warfare. That's not his style. You've got to have heart to be a guerrilla warrior, and he hasn't go any heart. I'm telling you now.

I just want to give you a little briefing on guerrilla warfare because, before you know it, before you know it—It takes heart to be a guerrilla warrior because you are on your own. In conventional warfare you have tanks and a whole lot of other people with you to back you up, planes over your head and all that kind of stuff. But a guerrilla is on his own. All you have is a rifle, some sneakers and a bowl of rice, and that's all you need—and a lot of heart. The Japanese on some of those islands in the Pacific, when the American soldiers landed, one Japanese sometimes could hold the whole army off. He'd just wait until the sun went down, and when the sun came up they were all equal. He would take his little blade and slip from bush to bush, and from American to American. The white soldiers couldn't cope with that. Whenever you see a white soldier that fought in the Pacific, he has the shakes, he has a nervous condition, because they scared him to death.

The same thing happened to the French up in French Indochina. People who just a few years previous were rice farmers got together and ran the heavily-mechanized French army out of Indochina. You don't need it—modern warfare today won't work. This is the day of the guerrilla. They did the same thing in Algeria. Algerians, who were nothing but Bedouins, took a rifle and sneaked off to the hills, and de Gaulle and all of his highfalutin' war machinery couldn't defeat those guerrillas. Nowhere on this earth does the white man win in a guerrilla warfare. It's not his speed. Just as guerrilla warfare is prevailing in Asia and in parts of Africa and in parts of Latin America, you've got to be mighty naive, or you've got to play the black man cheap, if you don't think some day he's going to wake up and find that it's got to be the ballot or the bullet.

I would like to say, in closing, a few things concerning the Muslim Mosque, Inc., which we established recently in New York City. It's true we're Muslims and our religion is Islam, but we don't mix our religion with our politics and our economics and our social and civil activities—not any more. We keep our religion in our mosque. After our religious services are over, then as Muslims we become involved in political action, economic action and social and civil action. We become involved with anybody, anywhere, any time and in any manner that's designed to eliminate the evils, the political, economic and social evils that are afflicting the people of our community.

The political philosophy of black nationalism means that the black man should control the politics and the politicians in his own community; no more. The black man in the black community; no more. The black man in the black community has to be reeducated into the science of politics so he will know what politics is supposed to bring him in return. Don't be throwing out any ballots. A ballot is like a bullet. You don't throw your ballots until you see a target, and if that target is not within your reach, keep your ballot in your pocket. The political philosophy of black nationalism is being taught in the Christian church. It's being taught in the NAACP. It's being taught in CORE meetings. It's being taught in SNCC meetings. It's being taught in Muslim meetings. It's being taught where nothing but atheists and agnostics come together. It's being taught everywhere. Black people are fed up with the dillydallying, pussyfooting, compromising approach that we've been using toward getting our freedom. We want freedom now, but we're not going to get it saying "We Shall Overcome." We've got to fight until we overcome.

The economic philosophy of black nationalism is pure and simple. It only means that we should control the economy of our community. Why should white people be running all the stores in our community? Why should white people be running the banks of our community? Why should the economy of our community be in the hands of the white man? Why? If a black man can't move his store into a white community, you tell me why a white man should move his store into a black community. The philosophy of black nationalism involves a re-education program in the black community in regards to economics. Our people have to be made to see that any time you take your dollar out of your community and spend it in a community where you don't live, the community where you live will get poorer and poorer, and the community where you spend your money will get richer and richer. Then you wonder why where you live is always a ghetto or a slum area. And where you and I are concerned, not only do we lose it when we spend it out of the community, but the white man has got all our stores in the community tied up; so that though we spend it in the community, at sundown the man who runs the store takes it over across town somewhere. He's got us in a vise.

So the economic philosophy of black nationalism means in every church, in ever civic organization, in every fraternal order, it's time now for our people to become conscious of the importance of controlling the economy of our community. If we own the stores, if we operate the businesses, if we try and establish some industry in our own community, then we're developing to the position where we are creating employment for our own kind. Once you gain control of the economy of your own community, then you don't have to picket and boycott and beg some cracker downtown for a job in his business.

The social philosophy of black nationalism only means that we have to get together and remove the evils, the vices, alcoholism, drug addiction, and other evils that are destroying the moral fiber of our community. We ourselves have to lift the level of our community, the standard of our community to a higher level, make our own society beautiful so that we will be satisfied in our own social circles and won't be running around here trying to knock our way into a social circle where we're not wanted.

So I say, in spreading a gospel such as black nationalism, it is not designed to make the black man re-evaluate the white man—you know him already—but to make the black man re-evaluate himself. Don't change the white man's mind—you can't change his mind, and that whole thing about appealing to the moral conscience of America—America's conscience is bankrupt. She lost all conscience a long time ago. Uncle Sam has no conscience. They don't know what morals are. They don't try and eliminate an evil because it's evil, or because it's illegal, or because it's immoral; the eliminate it only when it threatens their existence. So you're wasting your time appealing to the moral conscience of a bankrupt man like Uncle Sam. If he had a conscience, he'd straighten this thing out with no more pressure being put upon him. So it is not necessary to change the white man's mind. We have to change our own mind. You can't change his mind about us. We've got to change our own minds about each other. We have to see each other with new eyes. We have to see each other as brothers and sisters. We have to come together with warmth so we can develop unity and harmony that's necessary to get this problem solved ourselves. How can we do this? How can we avoid jealousy? How can we avoid the suspicion and the divisions that exist in the community? I'll tell you how.

I have watched how Billy Graham comes into a city, spreading what he calls the gospel of Christ, which is only white nationalism. That's what he is. Billy Graham is a white nationalist; I'm a black nationalist. But since it's the natural tendency for leaders to be jealous and look upon a powerful figure like Graham with suspicion and envy, how is it possible for him to come into a city and get all the cooperation of the church leaders? Don't think because they're church leaders that they don't have weaknesses that make them envious and jealous—no, everybody's got it. It's not an accident that when they want to choose a cardinal [for Pope] over there in Rome, they get in a closet so you can't hear them cussing and fighting and carrying on.

Billy Graham comes in preaching the gospel of Christ, he evangelizes the gospel, he stirs everybody up, but he never tries to start a church. If he came in trying to start a church, all the churches would be against him. So, he just comes in talking about Christ and tells everybody who gets Christ to go to any church were Christ is; and in this way the church cooperates with him. So we're going to take a page from his book.

Our gospel is black nationalism. We're not trying to threaten the existence of any organization, but we're spreading the gospel of black nationalism. Anywhere there's a church that is also preaching and practicing the gospel of black nationalism, join the church. If the NAACP is preaching and practicing the gospel of black nationalism, join the NAACP. If CORE is spreading and practicing the gospel of black nationalism, join CORE. Join any organization that has a gospel that's for the uplift of the black man. And when you get into it and see them pussyfooting or compromising, pull out of it because that's not black nationalism. We'll find another one.

And in this manner, the organizations will increase in number and in quantity and quality, and by August, it is then our intention to have a black nationalist convention which will consist of delegates from all over the country who are interested in the political, economic and social philosophy of black nationalism. After these delegates convene, we will hold a seminar, we will hold discussions, we will listen to everyone. We want to hear some new ideas and new solutions and new answers. And at that time, if we see fit then to form a black nationalist party, we'll form a black nationalist party. If it's necessary to form a black nationalist army, we'll form a black nationalist army. It'll be the ballot or the bullet. It'll be liberty or it'll be death.

It's time for you and me to stop sitting in this country, letting some cracker senators, Northern crackers and Southern crackers, sit there in Washington D.C., and come to a conclusion in their mind that you and I are supposed to have civil rights. There's no white man going to tell me anything about *my* rights. Brothers and sisters, always remember, if it doesn't take senators and congressmen and presidential proclamations to give freedom to the white man, it is not necessary for legislation or proclamation or Supreme Court decisions to give freedom to the black man. You let that white man know, if this is a country of freedom, let it be a country of freedom; and if it's not a country of freedom, change it.

We will work with anybody, anywhere, at any time, who is genuinely interested in tackling the problem head-on, nonviolently as long as the enemy is nonviolent, but violent when the enemy gets violent. We'll work with you on the voter-registration drive, we'll work with you on school boycotts—I don't believe in any kind of integration; I'm not even worried about it because I know you're not going to get it anyway; you're not going to get it because you're afraid to die; you've got to be ready to die if you try to force yourself on the white man, because he'll get just as violent as those crackers in Mississippi, right here in Cleveland. But we will still work with you on the school boycotts because we're against a segregated school system. A segregated school system produced children who, when they graduate, graduate with crippled minds. But this does not mean that a school is segregated because it's all black. A segregated school means a school that is controlled by people who have no real interest in it whatsoever.

Let me explain what I mean. A segregated district or community is a community in which people live, but outsiders control the politics and the economy of the community. It's the all-Negro section that's a segregated community. Why? The white man controls his own school, his own bank, his own economy, his own politics, his own everything, his own community—but he also controls yours. When you're under someone else's control, you're segregated. They'll always give you the lowest or the worst that there is to offer, but it doesn't mean you're segregated just because you have your own. You've got to *control* your own. Just like the white man has control of his, you need to control yours.

You know the best way to get rid of segregation? The white man is more afraid of separation than he is of integration. Segregation means that he puts you away from him, but not far enough for you to be out of his jurisdiction; separation means you're gone. And the white man will integrate faster than he'll let you separate. So we will work with you against the segregated school system because it's criminal, because it is absolutely destructive, in every way imaginable, to the minds of the children who have to be exposed to that type of crippling education.

Last but not least, I must say this concerning the great controversy over rifles and shotguns. The only thing that I've ever said is that in areas where the government has proven itself either unwilling or unable to defend the lives and the property of Negroes, it's time for Negroes to defend themselves. Article number two of the constitutional amendments provides you and me the right to own a rifle or a shotgun. It is constitutionally legal to own a shotgun or a rifle. This doesn't mean you're going to get a rifle and form battalions and go out looking for white folks, although you'd be within your rights—I mean, you'd be justified; but that would be illegal and we don't do anything illegal. If the white man doesn't want the black man buying rifles and shotguns, then let the government do its job. That's all. And don't let the white man come to you and ask you what you think about what Malcolm says—why, you old Uncle Tom. He would never ask you if he thought you were going to say, "Amen!" No, he is making a Tom out of you.

So this doesn't mean forming rifle clubs and going out looking for people, but it is time, in 1964, if you are a man, to let that man know. If he's not going to do his job in running the government and providing you and me with the protection that our taxes are supposed to be for, since he spends all those billions for his defense budget, he certainly can't begrudge you and me spending $12 or $15 for a single-shot, or double-action. I hope you understand. Don't go out shooting people, but any time, brothers and sisters, and especially the men in this audience—some of you wearing Congressional Medals of Honor, with shoulders this wide, chests this big, muscles that big—any time you and I sit around and read where they bomb a church and murder in cold blood, not some grownups, but four little girls while they were praying to the same god the white man taught them to pray to, and you and I see the government go down and can't find who did it.

Why, this man—he can find Eichmann hiding down in Argentina somewhere. Let two or three American soldiers, who are minding somebody else's business way over in South Vietnam, get killed, and he'll send battleships, sticking his nose in their business. He wanted to send troops to Cuba and make them have what he calls free elections—this old cracker who doesn't have free elections in his own country. No, if you never see me another time in your life, if I die in the morning, I'll die saying one thing: the ballot or the bullet, the ballot or the bullet.

If a Negro in 1964 has to sit around and wait for some cracker senator to filibuster when it comes to the rights of black people, why, you and I should hang our heads in shame. You talk about a march on Washington in 1963, you haven't seen anything. There's some more going down in '64. And this time they're not going like they went last year. They're not going singing "We Shall Overcome." They're not going with white friends. They're not going with placards already painted for them. They're not going with round-trip tickets. They're going with one-way tickets.

And if they don't want that non-nonviolent army going down there, tell them to bring the filibuster to a halt. The black nationalists aren't going to wait. Lyndon B. Johnson is the head of the Democratic Party. If he's for civil rights, let him go into the Senate next week and declare himself. Let him go in there right now and declare himself. Let him go in there and denounce the Southern branch of his party. Let him go in there right now and take a moral stand—right now, not later. Tell him, don't wait until election time. If he waits too long, brothers and sisters, he will be responsible for letting a condition develop in this country which will create a climate that will bring seeds up out of the ground with vegetation on the end of them looking like something these people never dreamed of. In 1964, it's the ballot or the bullet. Thank you.

EDITORS' NOTE

1. See Clarence Taylor, *Knocking at Our Own Door: Milton A. Galamison and the Struggle to Integrate New York City Schools* (New York: Columbia University Press, 1997).

Chapter 123

Malcolm and Martin: A Common Solution

Clayborne Carson

Clayborne Carson, professor of history at Stanford University and director of the Martin Luther King, Jr., Papers at Stanford, is the author of In Struggle: SNCC and the Black Awakening of the 1960s *(1981) and the editor of* The Autobiography of Martin Luther King, Jr. *(1998).*

The following selection, originally titled "A 'Common Solution,'" is reprinted from Emerge: Black America's News Magazine, *February 1998, 44–52. Reprinted with permission of* Emerge.

For another selection co-authored by Carson, see chapter 126.

Three decades after their deaths, Malcolm X and Dr. Martin Luther King Jr. still symbolize opposing ideological positions that divide African-Americans. Their clashes set the tone for internecine battles that have continued to disrupt Black communities. Which path to social justice is correct? By any means necessary? Or nonviolence? Integration or separation? Spike Lee raised the issue of the contrast between the two men at the end of his great film, *Do the Right Thing*. A photograph of the two looms silently on the screen.

But was the split between them inevitable? How incompatible were their ideas, really? Were they in some ways complementary? Must African-Americans choose between their ideological legacies? Or is it possible that Malcolm and Martin would have resolved their differences had they not been assassinated? Does their unresolved discord represent a missed opportunity that has hobbled African-American political life?

Why, now, years after their deaths, are these questions relevant? As we enter the next millennium, with so many of our people still impoverished, and the basic notion of African-American equality still a debatable one in the United States, there remains much to be learned from the relationship of these two extraordinary men.

There has been much speculation about what Malcolm or Martin would have done had they lived longer, but until recently, we could only wonder about what kind of relationship they had when alive. Although the two men met only briefly, there is considerable evidence regarding their attitudes toward each other and, more significantly, about how those attitudes changed over time.

On July 31, 1963, less than a month before the March on Washington for Jobs and Freedom, Malcolm X invited Martin Luther King Jr. and other national civil rights leaders to speak at a Muslim rally in Harlem. In his letter, Malcolm warned that the nation's racial crisis might "erupt into an uncontrollable explosion" and insisted that racial unity was urgently needed.

"If capitalistic Kennedy and communistic Khrushchev can find something in common on which to form a United Front despite their tremendous ideological differences, it is a disgrace for Negro leaders not to be able to submerge our 'minor' differences in order to seek a common solution to a common problem posed by a Common Enemy," Malcolm argued.

Although as the minister of the Nation of Islam, Malcolm assured the civil rights leaders that he would "moderate the meeting and guarantee order and courtesy for all speakers," none of the invited leaders accepted his invitation. NAACP leader Roy Wilkins cited a previous speaking commitment in his response, even as he expressed appreciation for Malcolm's assurance of civility: "I am afraid I cannot say the same for some outdoor rallies held in New York City in Harlem and elsewhere in which the Muslims were not the sponsors and not responsible for order."

Martin [Luther] King did not respond to Malcolm's invitation. In the midst of preparations for the Washington march, his staff may not have even brought the invitation to his attention. Although Malcolm had begun writing to Martin in 1957, he received only perfunctory replies from the civil rights leader's office. Early in 1958, Nation of Islam leader Elijah Muhammad attended one of Martin's speeches in Chicago. The two talked afterward, but Martin's staff turned down a subsequent invitation for Martin to appear at a Muslim rally in Hyde Park. His secretary, Maude Ballou, also rejected Malcolm's 1960 invitation to a Muslim "education rally," claiming that it arrived too late. During the early 1960s, Malcolm tried to attract Martin's attention by occasional visits or telephone calls to the SCLC headquarters, but he was only able to talk to office staff.

To what extent did these rebuffs add to the intensity of Malcolm's criticisms of Martin's nonviolent approach? Although some of the differences between the two men were surely based on deeply held religious and political convictions, there also were common aspects of their personalities that might have enabled them to resolve their differences. Both were sons of politically active Baptist ministers who saw religion as a tool for social transformation; both were well informed about the relationship between the African-American freedom struggle and Third World liberation movements; both were men of integrity and courage.

Yet, Martin also was a privileged insider within the largest African-American denomination, while Malcolm was a member of a small Islamic group that was isolated from the Black religious mainstream. Malcolm was not invited to the March on Washington, and he may have been bitter over being ignored by King and excluded from the inner circles of national Black leadership.

Soon after the march, Malcolm delivered one of his strongest speeches against national civil rights leaders who he said had allowed themselves to be "used against the Negro revolution." In his "Message to the Grass Roots" speech deliv-

ered Nov. 10, 1963, in Detroit, he charged that the march's White financial backers had manipulated Black leaders, thereby transforming a potentially militant
mass protest into a "picnic, a circus." While suggesting that White supporters of
the march should get Academy Awards because "they acted like they really loved
Negroes and fooled a whole lot of Negroes," Malcolm sardonically noted that the
Black leaders also deserved awards "for best supporting cast."

Given Malcolm's verbal hostility and his advocacy of racial separatism, it was
not surprising that Martin rejected the occasional overtures from his fiercest Black
critic. He may have thought that he had little to gain and much to lose from any
association with the Nation of Islam. A summer 1963 national survey of African-
Americans by *Newsweek* magazine found that 88 percent had positive opinions
regarding Martin Luther King, while only 15 percent thought positively about
Muhammad (Malcolm was not even listed on the survey form). Nevertheless,
Martin could not ignore Malcolm's increasing popularity, especially among
young, politically active Black people.

Firmly convinced that nonviolent direct action was the only effective tactic
available to discontented Blacks, Martin struggled to understand why some alienated African-Americans were attracted to Black nationalist rhetoric. "Malcolm
was clearly a product of the hate and violence invested in the Negro's blighted existence in this nation," he observed. "He, like so many of our number, was a victim of the despair inevitably deriving from the conditions of oppression, poverty
and injustice which engulf the masses of our race. In his youth, there was no hope,
no preaching, teaching or movements of nonviolence. He was too young for the
Garvey Movement, and too poor to be a Communist—for the Communists geared
their work to Negro intellectuals and labor without realizing that the masses of
Negroes were unrelated to either—and yet he possessed a native intelligence and
drive which demanded an outlet and means of expression."

Although Martin saw Malcolm as "very articulate" and conceded that he had
"some of the answers," he condemned "the demagogic oratory" of "extremist
leaders who preach revolution" yet were "invariably unwilling to lead what they
know would certainly end in bloody, chaotic and total defeat." He strongly disagreed with Malcolm's rhetorical militancy, which he saw as far less useful for
African-Americans than nonviolent direct action. Reflecting on their differences,
Martin said, "I have often wished that he would talk less of violence, because violence is not going to solve our problem. And in his litany of articulating the despair of the Negro without offering any positive, creative alternative, I feel that
Malcolm has done himself and our people a great disservice. Fiery, demagogic oratory in the black ghettos, urging Negroes to arm themselves and prepare to engage in violence, as he has done, can reap nothing but grief."

Martin was also disturbed by the personal nature of some of Malcolm's verbal
assaults. Suspecting that Malcolm may have been responsible for an egg-throwing
incident he endured in Harlem, Martin was dismayed that some Black nationalists
"transferred their bitterness toward the white man to me," seeing him as "soft" or
"a sort of polished Uncle Tom." For Martin, such criticisms were hypocritical, because nonviolent activists were at least confronting Southern racists rather than

simply engaging them in verbal combat. "They don't see that there's a great deal of difference between nonresistance to evil and nonviolent resistance."

Despite the wide ideological gulf that existed between the two men in 1964, the mass protests of that year had set in motion forces that neither one could control or even fully understand. While King was being pushed toward greater militancy by an upsurge of grass-roots protest activity throughout the South, including campaigns by the Student Nonviolent Coordinating Committee (SNCC), Malcolm was becoming increasingly dissatisfied with Elijah Muhammad's policy of nonengagement, which prevented members of the Nation of Islam from participating in politics and protest. In his autobiography, Malcolm acknowledged his disappointment over the failure of the Nation of Islam to become involved in the escalating freedom struggle of the early 1960s: "I felt that, wherever black people committed themselves, in the Little Rocks and the Birminghams and other places, militantly disciplined Muslims should also be there for all the world to see, and respect, and discuss. It could be heard increasingly in the Negro communities: 'Those Muslims *talk* tough, but they never *do* anything, unless somebody bothers Muslims.'"

Moreover, Malcolm knew that the Nation of Islam's apolitical stance obscured Elijah Muhammad's willingness to make political accommodations with reactionary, racist Whites when it served his purposes. In January 1961, Muhammad had sent Malcolm to Atlanta to meet with Ku Klux Klan officials to obtain the White supremacist group's support for the Nation's plan to create a separate Black state. This meeting, which remained a well-kept secret until Malcolm's break with the Nation, and Muhammad's long-term relationship with Nazi leader George Lincoln Rockwell, were certainly factors that caused Malcolm to become increasingly skeptical of Muhammad's motives and integrity.

By the end of 1963, Elijah Muhammad reacted to Malcolm's increasing popularity, independence and outspokenness by suspending his most effective recruiter. The pretext for the suspension was Malcolm's statement that the assassination of President John F. Kennedy was a case of "chickens coming home to roost." Actually, the split between the two men derived from Malcolm's determination to follow a course that paralleled King's—that is, to combine religious leadership and political action.

By the time Malcolm returned from his pilgrimage to Mecca in the spring of 1964, he was prepared to break with the Nation of Islam and to begin building ties to the more militant elements within the Southern freedom struggle. Although his principal objective was to forge an alliance with grass-roots leaders and youthful activists in SNCC, he also sought to repair the damage caused by his earlier criticisms of Martin and other national civil rights leaders. "I've forgotten everything bad that the other leaders have said about me," he said soon after forming the Organization of Afro-American Unity (OAAU), "and I pray they can also forget the many bad things I've said about them."

When Martin was facing White mob violence in St. Augustine, Fla., in 1964, Malcolm sent a telegram to offer assistance: "If the federal government will not send troops to your aid, just say the word and we will immediately dispatch some of our brothers there to organize self defense units among our people and the [Ku

Klux Klan] will then receive a taste of its own medicine. The day of turning the other cheek to those brute beasts is over."

Eventually, Malcolm succeeded in his effort to meet with his main ideological adversary. On March 26, 1964, Martin emerged from a news conference at the U.S. Capitol to discover Malcolm X waiting for him. As photographers gathered around, the two men shook hands. Malcolm orchestrated the impromptu meeting, grinning broadly at the clearly surprised Martin while remarking, "Now you're going to get investigated." This passing encounter did not result in any concerted efforts to bridge the gulf between the two men, for Malcolm was more concerned about the vicious infighting in his own camp, while King's attention was focused on the pending civil rights legislation.

Later in 1964, Malcolm was able to meet with a number of SNCC workers, including its chairman, John Lewis, and Mississippi organizer Fannie Lou Hamer. He saw the OAAU as a potential bridge between the revitalized Black nationalist movement and the Black freedom struggle. At a time when many veteran civil rights activists were looking to Malcolm for guidance in mobilizing discontented urban Blacks, he was looking to the Southern struggle for inspiration in his effort to politicize the moribund Black nationalist movement.

In early February 1965, Malcolm continued his overtures to the Southern struggle by going to Selma, Ala., during a major voting rights campaign. SNCC workers arranged his appearances in order to encourage Black students to join their efforts, and Malcolm's fiery speeches served their purposes even as his words disturbed SCLC representatives. Martin, who was in jail at the time, heard that Malcolm said "some pretty passionate things against me," but he also learned that Malcolm's demeanor was more cordial during a private meeting with Coretta King. "He spoke at length to my wife Coretta about his personal struggles and expressed an interest in working more closely with the nonviolent movement," Martin recalled. "He thought he could help me more by attacking me than praising me. He thought it would make it easier for me in the long run. He said, 'If the white people realize what the alternative is, perhaps they will be more willing to hear Dr. King.'"

Just a few weeks after the visit to Selma, on Feb. 21, Malcolm X was assassinated. His death ended any chance that he would be able to discuss with King his goal of forging "a common solution to a common problem." Martin called the assassination "shocking and tragic."

He sent a telegram to Malcolm's widow, Betty Shabazz: "While we did not always see eye to eye on methods to solve the race problem, I always had a deep affection for Malcolm and felt that he had a great ability to put his finger on the existence and root of the problem," Martin wrote. "He was an eloquent spokesman for his point of view and no one can honestly doubt that Malcolm had a great concern for the problems that we face as a race."

Martin regretted that Malcolm did not have the chance to develop his growing "interest in politics as a way of dealing with the problems of the Negro." Unfortunately, Martin lamented, "history would not have it so. A man who lived under the torment of knowledge of the rape of his grandmother and murder of his father under the conditions of the present social order, does not readily accept that social order or seek to integrate into it."

Martin saw Malcolm's murder as a symptom of the kind of conflict that was not only undermining African-American political life but also newly independent African nations, such as the Congo. "The American Negro cannot afford to destroy its leadership," Martin observed. "Certainly we will continue to disagree, but we must disagree without becoming violently disagreeable. We will still suffer the temptation to bitterness, but we must learn that hate is too great a burden for a people moving on toward their date with destiny. Men of talent are too scarce to be destroyed by envy, greed and tribal rivalry before they reach their full maturity." He asserted that Malcolm's murder deprived "the world of a potentially great leader."

Martin would witness the destructive internal conflicts that disrupted African-American political life in the years after Malcolm's assassination. More than Martin could have known in 1965, Malcolm's death signaled the beginning of bitter battles among proponents of the ideological alternatives the two men represented.

FBI director J. Edgar Hoover was among the White leaders who sought to exploit the ideological differences symbolized by the two leaders. Hoover saw Malcolm and Martin as among the potential messiahs who might have been able, in the words of his infamous 1968 memorandum expanding the Bureau's Counterintelligence Program [see chapter 153—Eds.], to "unify, and electrify" the militant Black movement. Rather than recognizing the points of convergence in the ideas of Martin and Malcolm, most Black leaders of the era after King's death in 1968 saw them as irreconcilable options. Black people were advised to choose between Martin and Malcolm, rather than affirming that each offered a partial answer to the problems of race.

Unlike many of their followers, the two men understood at the end of their lives that their basic messages were compatible rather than contradictory. Both saw the building of strong, Black-controlled institutions in African-American communities did not contradict the goal of achieving equal rights within the American political system; indeed, the achievement of the one goal would contribute to the achievement of the other. Perhaps the most important consequence of their tragic deaths was that they were unavailable to serve as elder statesmen for the African-American freedom struggle during the period of ideological uncertainty after the passage of historic civil rights legislation.

Had they lived, Malcolm and Martin might have advised their followers that the differences between the two were not as significant as was their common sense of dedication to the struggle for racial advancement. Malcolm came to realize that nonviolent tactics could be used militantly and were essential aspects of any mass struggle. Indeed, he was himself a peaceful man who never adopted a strategy of violence. Martin, for his part, remained philosophically committed to the ideals of Gandhian nonviolence, but he increasingly recognized that mass militancy driven by positive racial consciousness was essential for African-American progress. "I am not sad that black Americans are rebelling," he remarked in his last published essay. "Without this magnificent ferment among Negroes, the old evasions and procrastinations would have continued indefinitely."

Malcolm and Martin understood the African-American dilemma from different perspectives rooted in their different experiences. Each leader was a visionary, yet the ideas of each were still evolving until their lives were cut short by assassination; neither fully comprehended, for example, the leadership potential of women. They were great leaders, but they were also products of a historical period of tremendous mass struggles.

Malcolm experienced the enduring problems of poverty, despair and powerlessness that we have yet to overcome. He insisted that Blacks address these problems by strengthening the institutions in their communities and by acquiring a strong sense of positive racial identity. He continues to have special significance for African-Americans at the bottom of the U.S. social order, because he was once there and felt the bitterness and frustration of those who remain there. He continues to inspire and enlighten Black people who experience the American nightmare rather than the American dream.

Martin also understood the importance of racial pride, even if he took such pride for granted. He recognized that African-Americans would never be free until they signed their own emancipation proclamation "with the pen and ink of assertive selfhood," but he also saw that the destiny of African Americans was inextricably linked to that of all people and that any freedom struggle should have reconciliation as its ultimate goal. His message can enlighten us in these times when racial and ethnic conflicts have engulfed many nations and may yet engulf this one. He knew that nonviolent struggles seeking reconciliation and redemption do not offer the same excitement and emotional satisfaction as revenge and retaliation; yet he also understood that, despite our differences, we are inextricably bound together in a network of interdependence on our increasingly endangered planet.

Chapter 124

What We Want

Stokely Carmichael

Black power advocate Stokely Carmichael (1941–1998)—later known as Kwame Ture—joined CORE in 1960. After graduating from Howard University, he joined SNCC, serving as its Mississippi Project director in 1964 and working on the 1965 Selma Campaign before becoming chair of the organization in 1966. In May 1966, Carmichael electrified a crowd in Greenville, Mississippi, when he said, "The only way we are gonna stop white men from whippin' us is to take over. We been saying 'freedom' for six years and we ain't got nothin'. What we gonna start saying now is 'black power.'" Carmichael's advocacy of black power, which shifted SNCC's focus from peaceful integration to black liberation, led to the expulsion of whites from the organization.

Many have criticized Carmichael's advocacy of black power as undermining SNCC and the civil rights movement. Stanley Crouch, for instance, writes, "The organization [SNCC] became a shambles as white support was driven out. Stokely Carmichael and Rap Brown devoted their efforts to inflammatory rabble rousing, encouraging the anarchy of urban 'revolts.'" Other writers, such as Salim Muwakkil, have argued, "[T]he subject of black power that Stokely Carmichael broached that summer of 1966 had little to do with inflicting harm on white America. It had everything to do with liberating the sense of agency that white supremacy had buried deep in the African-American psyche."

The Black Panther Party named Carmichael its honorary prime minister in 1967. In 1969, he resigned from the party, condemning its dogmatism and alliance with white groups. Later that year, with his politics shifting from a U.S. civil rights focus to a Pan-African socialist perspective, Carmichael moved to Guinea in West Africa.

The following selection is reprinted with permission from "What We Want," New York Review of Books, 22 September 1966, 5.

One of the tragedies of the struggle against racism is that up to now there has been no national organization which could speak to the growing militancy of young black people in the urban ghetto. There has been only a civil rights movement, whose tone of voice was adapted to an audience of liberal whites. It served as a sort of buffer zone between them and angry young blacks. None of its so-called leaders could go into a rioting community and be listened to. In a sense, I blame ourselves—together with the mass media—for what has happened in Watts, Harlem, Chicago, Cleveland, Omaha. Each time the people in those cities saw Martin Luther King get slapped, they became angry; when they saw four little black girls bombed to death [in a Birmingham church], they were angrier; and when nothing happened, they were steaming. We had nothing to offer that they could see, except to go out and be beaten again. We helped to build their frustration.

For too many years, black Americans marched and had their heads broken and got shot. They were saying to the country, "Look, you guys are supposed to be nice guys and we are only going to do what we are supposed to do—why do you beat us up, why don't you give us what we ask, why don't you straighten yourselves out?" After years of this, we are at almost the same point—because we demonstrated from a position of weakness. We cannot be expected any longer to march and have our heads broken in order to say to whites: come on, you're nice guys. For you are not nice guys. We have found you out.

An organization which claims to speak for the needs of a community—as does the Student Nonviolent Coordinating Committee—must speak in the tone of that community, not as somebody else's buffer zone. This is the significance of black power as a slogan. For once, black people are going to use the words they want to use—not just the words whites want to hear. And they will do this no matter how often the press tries to stop the use of the slogan by equating it with racism or separatism.

An organization which claims to be working for the needs of a community—as SNCC does—must work to provide that community with a position of strength from which to make its voice heard. This is the significance of black power beyond the slogan.

Black power can be clearly defined for those who do not attach the fears of white America to their questions about it. We should begin with the basic fact that black Americans have two problems: they are poor and they are black. All other problems arise from this two-sided reality: lack of education, the so-called apathy of black men. Any program to end racism must address itself to that double reality.

Almost from its beginning, SNCC sought to address itself to both conditions with a program aimed at winning political power for impoverished Southern blacks. We had to begin with politics because black Americans are a propertyless people in a country where property is valued above all. We had to work for power, because this country does not function by morality, love, and nonviolence, but by power. Thus we determined to win political power, with the idea of moving on from there into activity that would have economic effects. With power, the masses could *make or participate in making* the decisions which govern their destinies, and thus create basic change in their day-to-day lives. . . .

Ultimately, the economic foundations of this country must be shaken if black people are to control their lives. The colonies of the United States—and this includes the black ghettoes within its borders, north and south—must be liberated. For a century, this nation has been like an octopus of exploitation, its tentacles stretching from Mississippi and Harlem to South America, the Middle East, southern Africa, and Vietnam; the form of exploitation varies from area to area but the essential result has been the same—a powerful few have been maintained and enriched at the expense of the poor and voiceless colored masses. This pattern must be broken. As its grip loosens here and there around the world, the hopes of black Americans become more realistic. For racism to die, a totally different America must be born. . . .

Whites will not see that I, for example, as a person oppressed because of my blackness, have common cause with other blacks who are oppressed because of blackness. This is not to say that there are no white people who see things as I do, but that it is black people I must speak to first. It must be the oppressed to whom SNCC addresses itself primarily, not to friends from the oppressing group. . . .

This does not mean we don't welcome help, or friends. But we want the right to decide whether anyone is, in fact, our friend. . . .

Black people do not want to "take over" this country. They don't want to "get whitey"; they just want to get him off their backs, as the saying goes. It was for example the exploitation by Jewish landlords and merchants which first created black resentment toward Jews—not Judaism. The white man is irrelevant to blacks, except as an oppressive force. Blacks want to be in his place, yes, but not in order to terrorize and lynch and starve him. They want to be in his place because that is where a decent life can be had.

But our vision is not merely of a society in which all black men have enough to buy the good things of life. When we urge that black money go into black pockets, we mean the communal pocket. We want to see money go back into the community and used to benefit it. We want to see the cooperative concept applied in business and banking. We want to see black ghetto residents demand that an exploiting store keeper sell them, at minimal cost, a building or a shop that they will own and improve, cooperatively; they can back their demand with a rent strike, or a boycott, and a community so unified behind them that no one else will move into the building or buy at the store. The society we seek to build among black people, then, is not a capitalist one. It is a society in which the spirit of community and humanistic love prevail. The word love is suspect; black expectations of what it might produce have been betrayed too often. But those were expectations of a response from the white community, which failed us. The love we seek to encourage is within the black community, the only American community where men call each other "brother" when they meet. We can build a community of love only where we have the ability and power to do so: among blacks.

As for white America, perhaps it can stop crying out against "black supremacy," "black nationalism," "racism in reverse," and begin facing reality. The reality is that this nation, from top to bottom, is racist; that racism is not primarily a problem of "human relations" but of an exploitation maintained—either actively or through silence—by the society as a whole. Camus and Sartre have asked, can a man condemn himself? Can whites, particularly liberal whites, condemn themselves? Can they stop blaming us, and blame their own system? Are they capable of the shame which might become a revolutionary emotion?

We have found that they usually cannot condemn themselves, and so we have done it. But the rebuilding of this society, if at all possible, is basically the responsibility of whites—not blacks. We won't fight to save the present society, in Vietnam or anywhere else. We are just going to work, in the way we see fit, and on goals we define, not for civil rights but for all our human rights.

Chapter 125

The Black Panther Party Ten-Point Program

Huey Newton

In the mid-1960s SNCC organizers and local black leaders in Lowndes County, Alabama, ran a black slate of candidates using the black panther as their symbol. That symbol was also adopted in Oakland, California, by Huey Newton and Bobby Seale when they formed the Black Panther Party in 1966. By 1969 it had chapters in most large cities in the United States.

The following selection, usually credited to Newton, is reprinted from "The Black Panther Ten-Point Program" (n.d.).

1. We want freedom. We want power to determine the destiny of our Black Community.
We believe that black people will not be free until we are able to determine our destiny.

2. We want full employment for our people.
We believe that the federal government is responsible and obligated to give every man employment or a guaranteed income. We believe that if the white American businessmen will not give full employment, then the means of production should be taken from the businessmen and placed in the community so that the people of the community can organize and employ all of its people and give a high standard of living.

3. We want an end to the robbery by the white man of our Black Community.
We believe that this racist government has robbed us and now we are demanding the overdue debt of forty acres and two mules. Forty acres and two mules was promised 100 years ago as restitution for slave labor and mass murder of black people. We will accept the payment in currency which will be distributed to our many communities. The Germans are now aiding the Jews in Israel for the genocide of the Jewish people. The Germans murdered six million Jews. The American racist has taken part in the slaughter of over fifty million black people; therefore, we feel that this is a modest demand that we make.

4. We want decent housing, fit for shelter of human beings.

We believe that if the white landlords will not give decent housing to our black community, then the housing and land should be made into cooperatives so that our community, with government aid, can build and make decent housing for its people.

5. We want education for our people that exposes the true nature of this decadent American society. We want education that teaches us our true history and our role in the present-day society.

We believe in an educational system that will give to our people a knowledge of self. If a man does not have knowledge of himself and his position in society and the world, then he has little chance to relate to anything else.

6. We want all black men to be exempt from military service.

We believe that Black people should not be forced to fight in the military service to defend a racist government that does not protect us. We will not fight and kill other people of color in the world who, like black people, are being victimized by the white racist government of America. We will protect ourselves from the force and violence of the racist police and the racist military, by whatever means necessary.

7. We want an immediate end to POLICE BRUTALITY and MURDER of black people.

We believe we can end police brutality in our black community by organizing black self-defense groups that are dedicated to defending our black community from racist police oppression and brutality. The Second Amendment to the Constitution of the United States gives a right to bear arms. We therefore believe that all black people should arm themselves for self-defense.

8. We want freedom for all black men held in federal, state, county and city prisons and jails.

We believe that all black people should be released from the many jails and prisons because they have not received a fair and impartial trial.

9. We want all black people when brought to trial to be tried in court by a jury of their peer group or people from their black communities, as defined by the Constitution of the United States.

We believe that the courts should follow the United States Constitution so that black people will receive fair trials. The 14th Amendment of the U.S. Constitution gives a man a right to be tried by his peer group. A peer is a person from a similar economic, social, religious, geographical, environmental, historical and racial background. To do this the court will be forced to select a jury from the black community from which the black defendant came. We have been, and are being tried by all-white juries that have no understanding of the "average reasoning man" of the black community.

10. We want land, bread, housing, education, clothing, justice and peace. And as our major political objective, a United Nations–supervised plebiscite to be held throughout the black colony in which only black colonial subjects will be allowed to participate, for the purpose of determining the will of black people as to their national destiny.

When in the course of human events, it becomes necessary for one people to dissolve the political bonds which have connected them with another, and to assume, among the powers of the earth, the separate and equal station to which the laws of nature and nature's God entitle them, a decent respect to the opinions of mankind required that they should declare the causes which impel them to the separation.

We hold these truths to be self-evident; that all men are created equal; that they are endowed by their Creator with certain unalienable rights; that among these are life, liberty and the pursuit of happiness. **That, to secure these rights, governments are instituted among men, deriving their just powers from the consent of the governed; that, whenever any form of government becomes destructive of these ends, it is the right of the people to alter or to abolish it, and to institute a new government, laying its foundation on such principles, and organizing its powers in such form, as to them shall seem most likely to effect their safety and happiness.** Prudence, indeed, will dictate that governments long established should not be changed for light and transient causes; and, accordingly, all experience hath shown, that mankind are more disposed to suffer, while evils are sufferable, than to right themselves by abolishing the forms to which they are accustomed. **But, when a long train of abuses and usurpations, pursuing invariably the same object, evinces a design to reduce them under absolute despotism, it is their right, it is their duty, to throw off such government, and to provide new guards for their future security.**

Chapter 126

The Black Panther Party

Clayborne Carson and David Malcolm Carson

Clayborne Carson is professor of history at Stanford University and director of the Martin Luther King, Jr., Papers at Stanford. David Malcolm Carson is an attorney involved with economic community development in the San Francisco Bay Area.

The following selection is a reprint of "Black Panthers" by Clayborne Carson and David Malcolm Carson, from Encyclopedia of the American Left, *2d ed., ed. Mari Jo Buhle, Paul Buhle, and Dan Georgakas. Copyright © 1998 by Oxford University Press, Inc. Used by permission of Oxford University Press, Inc.*

For another selection by Clayborne Carson, see chapter 123.

Founded in October 1966 by Huey Newton (1942–1989) and Bobby Seale (b. 1936), the Black Panther Party for Self-Defense became the most widely known black militant political organization of the late 1960s. The Black Panthers attracted widespread support among young urban blacks, who wore the group's distinctive black leather jackets and black berets and often openly displayed weapons. Also attracting the attention of local police and the FBI, the group declined as a result of deadly shootouts and destructive counterintelligence activities [see chapter 153—*Eds.*] that exacerbated disputes between Panthers and other black militant groups.

Newton was already a black militant activist in 1961 when he met Seale, a fellow student at Oakland's Merritt College. Both joined the Afro-American Association, a black cultural organization led by Donald Warden, but they became dissatisfied with Warden's procapitalist form of black nationalism. Their sentiments were more in accord with those of Malcolm X, especially after his 1964 break with Elijah Muhammad's Nation of Islam, and of Robert F. Williams, the then Cuban-based guerrilla warfare advocate. After affiliations with the Merritt's Soul Student Advisory Council and with the Williams-inspired Revolutionary Action Movement, Newton and Seale created the BPP in order to expand their political activity, which mainly involved "patrolling the pigs"—that is, monitoring police activities in black communities to ensure that civil rights were respected.

The BPP dropped "for Self-Defense" from its name in 1967, but the group remained a paramilitary organization held together by Newton's eclectic ideas, which were drawn from Marxist-Leninist and black nationalist writings and from the examples of revolutionary movements in Asia and Africa. Although Newton and Seale once gained funds and notoriety by selling books containing the quotations of Mao Tse-tung, the revolutionary tract that most influenced Panther leaders during the mid-1960s was Frantz Fanon's *Wretched of the Earth* (1965). The party's appeal among young blacks was based not on its unrefined ideology but on its willingness to challenge police power by asserting the right of armed self-defense for blacks. The explicit political goals of the Panthers were summarized in the last item of their ten-point Platform and Program: "We want land, bread, housing, education, clothing, justice, and peace. And as our major political objective, a United Nations–supervised plebiscite to be held throughout the black colony in which only black colonial subjects will be allowed to participate, for the purpose of determining the will of black people as to their national destiny."

On October 28, 1967, the development of the BPP was profoundly affected by Huey Newton's arrest on murder charges after an altercation with Oakland police that resulted in the death of one policeman and the wounding of another. With the party's principal leader in jail, the role of spokesmen increasingly fell to Seale and Eldridge Cleaver [1935–1998], a former prison activist and Malcolm X follower who became the Panthers' minister of information. Cleaver, a writer for the New Left journal *Ramparts* and a powerful public speaker, increasingly shaped public perceptions of the Panthers with his calls for black retribution and scathing verbal attacks against black counterrevolutionaries.

During February 1968, former SNCC leader Stokely Carmichael, who had been asked by Cleaver and Seale to appear at "Free Huey" rallies, challenged Cleaver's role as the dominant spokesman for the party. Carmichael's Pan-African perspective, emphasizing racial unity, contrasted sharply with the desire of other Panther leaders to emphasize class struggle and to attract white leftist support in the campaign to free Newton. Although Carmichael downplayed his policy criticisms of the party until he resigned as the Panther's prime minister in the summer of 1969, the ideological and personal tensions between Carmichael and other Panthers signaled the beginning of a period of often vicious infighting within the black militant community. A SNCC-Panther alliance announced at the February rallies broke apart by the following summer. After the Panthers branded Ron Karenga, the head of a Los Angeles–based group called US, a "pork-chop nationalist," escalating disputes between these two organizations culminated in January 1969 with a gun battle on the UCLA campus that left two Panthers dead.

Police raids and covert efforts of the FBI's counterintelligence program contributed to the tendency of Panther leaders to suspect the motives of black militants who did not fully agree with the party's strategy or tactics. In August 1967 the FBI targeted the Panthers when it launched its COINTELPRO operations designed to prevent "a coalition of militant black nationalist groups" and the emergence of a "black messiah" "who might unify and electrify these violence-prone elements." FBI-inspired misinformation, infiltration by informers, and numerous police assaults contributed to the Panther's siege mentality. On April 6, 1968, police attacked a house containing several Panthers, killing the seventeen-year-old treasurer of the party and wounding Cleaver, who was returned to prison as a parole violator. In September 1968 Newton was convicted of voluntary manslaughter and sentenced to from two to fifteen years in prison. The following December, two Chicago leaders of the party, Fred Hampton and Mark Clark, were killed in a police raid. By the end of the decade, according to the party's attorney, twenty-eight Panthers had been killed. At that time, Newton was still in jail (his conviction was reversed on appeal in 1970); Cleaver had left for exile in Algeria rather than return to prison; and many other Panthers elsewhere were facing long prison terms as a result of intense repression. In 1970 Connecticut authorities began an unsuccessful effort to convict Seale of the murder of a Panther in that state.

During the early 1970s, the BPP, weakened by external attacks, legal problems, and internal schisms, rapidly declined as a political force. After Newton was released from prison in 1970, he sought to revive the party by rejecting Cleaver's inflammatory rhetoric emphasizing immediate armed struggle. In place of police confrontations, Newton stressed community service, such as free-breakfast programs for children and, during the mid-1970s, participation in electoral politics. These efforts to regain support were negated, however, by published charges that Newton and other Panthers engaged in extortion and assaults directed against other blacks. By the mid-1970s, most Panther veterans, including Seale and Cleaver, had deserted or were expelled from the group, and Newton, faced with various criminal charges, fled to Cuba. Upon his return to the U.S., Newton remained a controversial figure. Although he completed a doctorate and remained politically active, he was also involved in the drug trade. He was shot to death in Oakland in the summer of 1989 in a drug-related incident.

Chapter 127

Women and the Black Panther Party

Angela G. Brown

Angela G. Brown, a Ph.D. student in the history department at Stanford University, is currently completing a dissertation on the Black Panther Party. Her senior honors thesis at Harvard University was "Servants of the People: A History of Women in the Black Panther Party."

The following selection is reprinted by permission from "Black Panther Party," in Darlene Clark Hine et al. eds., Black Women in America *(Bloomington: Indiana University Press, 1993).*

Throughout U.S. history Black women have always participated in political movements within their communities. Although their roles have not been highlighted by the media in the past, Black women have organized as well as participated in the daily functions of various organizations. The Black Panther Party (BPP) was no exception to this rule.

Huey P. Newton and Bobby Seale founded the Black Panther Party in Oakland, California on October 15, 1966. The organization was established by men and the predominantly male leadership was the focus of media coverage. Nevertheless, women played significant roles within the organization from 1967 until it ceased to function in the early 1980s. Female BPP members held party leadership positions at local levels as well as national levels, delivered speeches at rallies, and participated in the BPP community survival programs (free food, clothing, and health services, among other necessities).

Women who joined the Black Panther Party participated for a variety of reasons. Some women joined to develop their skills in political organization, other women joined to support spouses or significant others who were affiliated with the party, and still others joined to endorse the party's goals.

The three most prominent women at the top of the organization's hierarchy were Kathleen Neal Cleaver, Elaine Brown, and Ericka Huggins. Cleaver was the first woman to hold a national leadership position; she was communication secretary from 1967 to 1971. Elaine Brown held many positions in the BPP before she became the first and only female chairperson of the party, from 1974 to 1977. Ericka Huggins directed the BPP-initiated Oakland Community School from 1973 to 1981.

The community programs of the BPP, often directed and staffed by female members, included free breakfast for schoolchildren; free medical care, such as sickle cell anemia testing; free transportation to visit relatives in prison and for senior citizens; free shoes and clothing; political education classes; voter registration; petition campaigns for community control of police; and legal aid and advice, among other programs.

Although in doctrine the BPP internal structure allowed for no differential treatment on account of sex, once women joined the party they confronted gender-based discrimination and gender-specific tasks. From 1967 until the party folded, many women encountered sexism, and male chauvinism was an issue within the Panther community. A letter from Eldridge Cleaver to Ericka Huggins appeared on the July 5, 1969 issue of the *Black Panther* (the official party newspaper) addressing the issue: "Women are our other half, they're not our stronger half, they're not our weaker half, but they are our other half and that we sell ourselves out, we sell our children out and we sell our women out when we treat them in any other manner." Despite Cleaver's comments, sexism still continued in the BPP, and beginning in 1969, female members began to voice their displeasure with their treatment in the *Black Panther* and at BPP meetings. They also increased their participation in leadership roles and community activities.

Male chauvinism was not the only issue BPP women faced. Questions of female sexuality and motherhood plagued some women. They complained of being pressured into engaging in sexual activity. Reproduction and birth control were also issues. Many confronted the difficulties of rearing a child and being a full-time political activist. Moreover, mothers who were Panthers risked being incarcerated and separated from their children.

Two former female BPP members who experienced the hardships of being a mother and being a full-time political activist are Assata Shakur (formerly JoAnne Chesimard) and Akua Njere (formerly Deborah Johnson). Shakur became pregnant while incarcerated and was separated from her daughter immediately after birth. Shakur's mother raised the child while Shakur was incarcerated. Shakur was emotionally affected by the separation from her daughter and the possible negative effects that such a separation might have on their relationship.

Njere is the mother of the son of Fred Hampton, slain BPP Chairman of the Illinois chapter. Like Shakur, she was also contemplative about the relationship that would develop between her son and herself. For a short period after her son's birth, Njere's mother cared for Fred Hampton, Jr. Meanwhile, Njere attempted to continue full-time participation in the BPP. Njere soon decided that she needed more time to care for her son. Such constraints caused Njere to even consider leaving the Party to avoid jeopardizing her relationship with her son.

The pressures that female members of the BPP faced sometimes caused them to rescind their membership. Since police surveillance and harassment were equally problematic for women and men, female members faced both internal and external pressures. Nevertheless, there were female members who remained politically active in the party.

During its active reign the Black Panther Party leaders instituted many programs that had a lasting effect on Black society and society-at-large. Unquestionably, the female Panther members were an integral part of the creation of this legacy. From their involvement in the community service programs to their national leadership positions, the female Panther members maintained day-to-day functions of the party.

The decline of the BPP was the result of numerous activities and attitude clashes. The intensity of undercover FBI involvement and local police harassment helped to weaken and curtail public interest in the party's activities and members' involvement. The national leadership had also fallen apart over the course of ten years. Throughout this decline, however, large numbers of women sustained the organization's community programs until 1981, when the final Oakland-based program closed.

Chapter 128

Black Power and Labor

William L. Van Deburg

William L. Van Deburg, professor of Afro-American Studies at the University of Wisconsin at Madison, is the author of Slavery and Race in American Popular Culture *(1984) and* Black Camelot: African-American Culture Heroes in Their Times, 1960–1980 *(1997), and editor of* Modern Black Nationalism *(1997).*

The following selection is excerpted by permission from New Day in Babylon: The Black Power Movement and American Culture, 1965–1975 *(Chicago: University of Chicago Press, 1992), footnotes deleted. Copyright © 1992 by the University of Chicago Press.*

For more on DRUM, see JoAnn Wypijewski, "Pounding Out a DRUM Beat," New Left Review *234 (March/April 1999).*

> Dare to Fight! Dare to Win!
> Fight, Fail, Fight again, Fail again—Fight on to Victory!
> Long Live Black People in This Racist Land! Death to
> Their Enemies! Long Live the Heroic Black Workers Struggle!
> —Dodge Revolutionary Union Movement, 1968

During the Black Power era, black labor not only raised its gloved fist in protest, it threw down the gauntlet. Both the corporations for whom they worked and the unions which purportedly represented their interests felt the pressure to alter prevailing power relationships. As a result, the labor movement's traditional rallying song, "Solidarity," took on new meaning for all concerned.

New independent black unions and black caucuses within established unions expressed their members' concerns in dramatic fashion. In 1967, for example, 500 black workers at the Ford plant in Mahwah, New Jersey, shut down production for three days after a foreman called a production worker a "black bastard." Although the United Auto Workers Union (UAW) urged them to return to work, they stayed out until the foreman was removed from the plant. Following this wildcat strike, the United Black Brothers of Mahwah Ford was organized and began a campaign to eliminate all supervisors who were "diseased with racial bigotry." Early the next year in Chicago, members of the Concerned Transit Workers caucus challenged the leadership of their AFL-CIO-affiliated local. Although about 72 percent of the city's 6,800 bus drivers were Afro-Americans, all top officers and 22 of 26 executive board members of Amalgamated Transit Union's Division 241 were white. Feeling that "this is nothing different than the old plantation system," blacks focused their protest on a union rule allowing pensioners (a nearly all-white group) to vote in union elections. Frustrated in this reform attempt, they initiated a series of walkouts—one of which was timed to coincide with the 1968 Democratic National Convention. More than 140 drivers were suspended and 42 were fired for their disruptive actions. Elsewhere, militant workers leafletted at factory gates, picketed convention halls and disrupted production lines. Although specific issues differed depending upon whether one's affiliation was with the United Community Construction Workers of Boston, the Maryland Freedom Union, or the American Federation of Teachers Association, the black workers' grievances tended to center upon the issue of control. Despite token appointments as plant supervisors and union officeholders, they continued to perceive themselves as second-class citizens within the American workplace. A nondiscrimination clause in union contracts meant little, they said, if white union leaders and company officials neglected to press for its full implementation. Only increased black representation in positions of authority could guarantee that black laborers' concerns would be taken seriously—and even that possibility might vanish if blacks appointed to high posts were estranged from the tenets of Black Power. Without an infusion of this empowering ideology, the nation's factories would continue to resemble modern-day plantations with the second-line black leadership performing the role of house servants and the rank-and-file mired in a filed slaves' existence.

Nowhere was the Black Power sentiment more visible than in the auto industry. Job training initiatives spawned by the riots of the mid-sixties lured thousands of unemployed blacks into a new world of foundries, presses, and assembly lines. In some plants, African-Americans came to compose 60 to 75 percent of the work force. Most had little seniority and even fewer emotional ties to their employers. Before long, these young black workers began to challenge established patterns of industrial authority which earlier generations either had learned to live with or had concluded were impervious to change. The Dodge Revolutionary Union Movement (DRUM) and the League of Revolutionary Black Workers were born of this discontent.

Founded in May, 1968, in the aftermath of a wildcat strike at Chrysler's Assembly Plant (Dodge Main) in Hamtramck, Michigan, DRUM moved quickly to establish its priorities. "Our sole objective," its leaders asserted, "is to break the bonds of white racist control over the lives and destiny of black workers." These chains of exploitation were evident, they said, in the practice of assigning the easiest jobs to whites and speeding up production on the lines dominated by blacks. Discrimination was said to be rampant—in promotion decisions, in the skilled trades, and in the form of racial slurs heard daily throughout the plant. The UAW was perceived as being of little help in resolving these matters because it too was controlled by insensitive whites. The union not only had failed to address their grievances and continually upheld a "racist" seniority system which worked against the interests of young blacks, it also had dared add insult to injury by officially endorsing the annual Detroit Police Field Day.

Certainly, it didn't take a trained sociologist to conclude that the racial and power relationships at the Hamtramck assembly plant had become extremely volatile by the time of DRUM's founding. Said one white worker: "At Dodge Main, there's a young black work force being supervised by reactionary Polacks. Like, you've got a 63-year-old Pole bossing 25-year-old jitterbugs." A black worker agreed, noting somewhat more critically that "everywhere I look there sits some honky, looking down on me."

To remedy this untenable situation, DRUM proposed a series of major affirmative action appointments. After pointing out that 90 percent of the foremen, 99 percent of the general foremen, and all of the plant superintendents at Dodge Main were white, leaders demanded that some 60 blacks be promoted to these positions. DRUM also wanted all security guards, plant doctors, and half of the nursing staff to be recruited from the black community. It even demanded that "a black brother" be appointed head of Chrysler's board of directors.

Other tactics used in the quest for power were somewhat more confrontational. Displeased with UAW representation, DRUM urged black workers to cease paying union dues and, instead, channel the money into the Detroit black community "to aid in self-determination for black people." In an effort to ferret out enemies of all stripes, editors of the militants' weekly newspaper published a damning expose of "Uncle Toms" at Dodge Main. Soon thereafter, DRUM members dressed in greasy overalls and carrying picket signs disrupted a Detroit Urban League luncheon at which League officials had planned to present representatives from Chrysler, Ford, and General Motors with equal opportunity awards. On another occasion, when the organization began to run short of money, it held a combination rally and fund-raising raffle. To symbolize what was deemed the proper perspective on revolutionary change, the group awarded an M-1 rifle, a shotgun, and a bag of groceries as the top three prizes. Finally, to back up claims that "our line is the hard line," DRUM supporters set up picket lines at the entrance gates to Dodge Main in early July 1968. Seventy percent of the plant's black workers were persuaded to stay off the job. As a result of the three day walkout, Chrysler lost an estimated 1,900 units of production. Auto industry executives were put on notice that the volatile combination of unmet black grievances and Black Power ideology invariably sparked internal combustion.

DRUM served as an organizational model for militant associations of black workers such as FRUM (Ford Revolutionary Union Movement), GRUM (General Motors Revolutionary Union Movement), and HRUM (Harvester Revolutionary Union Movement) which formed at other plants. To sustain and give direction to these separate units, the League of Revolutionary Black Workers was established in 1969. Although the League served as an umbrella support organization for the individual workers' units, it was conceptualized on a much grander scale. Black laborers—"the vanguard of the liberation struggle"—would unite with black students, intellectuals, and community residents to "completely close down the American economic system."

To this end, the League organized demonstrations, mounted challenges to union elections, and helped develop revolutionary union movements in other cities and industries. Broadening DRUM's challenge to the establishment, League spokespersons urged the firing of Walter Reuther and the election of a black UAW president. They demanded the opening of skilled trades and apprenticeships to any black worker who applied, the use of UAW investment funds to finance black economic development programs, the shifting of all union strike funds to black financial institutions, and recognition of the League and its affiliates as the "official spokesman" for black workers at both the local and national levels.

Even as it directed these considerable demands to the UAW hierarchy, the League held white unionists at arm's length. It was said that white laborers also were exploited, but retention of white skin privilege diluted their militance. Time and again they had chosen to defend their position of privilege within the proletariat rather than enter into an alliance with militant blacks. This self-serving attitude not only impeded the development of class consciousness, but actually buttressed the prevailing system of racism and exploitation. Thus, according to the League, a multiracial workers' revolution was made unlikely by white racism. Someday, perhaps, whites could be accepted as allies, but first they would have to be radicalized by the black workers' example. The coming revolution against American "racism, capitalism, and imperialism" would be fought and won by black people, led by the black working class.

While the League believed that the best way to organize black America into a powerful force for liberation was first to organize the factories, it did not confine its activities—or concerns—to the workplace. League members, many of whom had been active in community organizing, employed a variety of mechanisms to take their message into the black community. They helped black residents to deal more effectively with their local units of government, supported activist candidates for public office, and spoke out on issues of broad concern—calling for an end to the Vietnam War and the reallocation of defense expenditures "to meet the pressing needs of the black and poor populations of America." Taking to heart novelist John Oliver Killens's notion that a truly liberated black labor movement would have its own Black Studies program, publishing house, and perhaps even a "Black Book-of-the-Month" club, the League established Black Star Press and Black Star Publishing. A book store was opened to market the League's publications. Its Black Star Productions film unit made *Finally Got the News,* a movie on the history of the League, and distributed films about Al Fatah and other revolutionary groups. By entering the cultural sphere in this manner, the League hoped to provide class conscious black laborers with "respite from the total alienation of work."

There was little relief, however, from the organizational problems which continually plagued the League and led to its decline as a force in the auto plants after 1970. Internal disagreements over the scope of the black workers' struggle dissipated group energies. Ideological disputes poisoned personal relationships, festering, and remaining unresolved. Unity of purpose and approach became difficult to maintain when nationalist-oriented members not only rejected alliances with non-black militants, but stated that neither Marx nor Lenin had anything to offer because they, too, were white.

External forces also contributed to the weakening of League influence. The UAW worked hard to meet the black workers' challenge. Even as it blasted the militants as "a handful of fanatics" and sternly warned union members against supporting any group that sought to divide the work force along racial lines, big labor made certain concessions to the League's demands. Having determined that the best way to deal with the Black Power threat was to address the question of representation, the union suddenly found places for a limited number of blacks on executive boards and in staff jobs. This UAW response coincided with a major slump in automobile sales during 1969–70. The impact of the subsequent industry-wide layoffs was felt most severely by young black workers with little seniority—the very group for whom the League's appeal was greatest. Together, the prescient actions of the union leadership and the effects of a slumping economy operated to reduce the attraction of militant ideology among black workers.

Industrial capitalism was not overthrown by the Black Power movement. It was, however, put on notice. The need for a more powerful black voice and a more substantive black presence in the boardrooms and executive suites of big labor and big business was made clear. The UAW leadership's response to the demand for increased participation in decision-making reveals that this most practical of "real world" associations knew exactly what was at issue when existing institutional relationships were challenged. In hindsight, it is apparent that they also were quite adept at determining what it would take to diffuse that challenge.

Nevertheless, to diffuse is not to destroy. The sentiment which propelled the rise of DRUM and the League of Revolutionary Black Workers continued to find expression in the battle against racism in Detroit's public schools; in the continuing effort to improve job opportunities and housing; and in the campaign to wrest control of the city's political life from the white power structure. The spirit of these militant workers also lived on in the various cultural productions which were employed to disseminate their urgent message. One of these, a bold, unpretentious ode in praise of DRUM, speaks of this tenacity:

> For hours and years with sweated tears
> Trying to break our chain . . .
> We broke our backs and died in packs
> To find our manhood slain . . .
> But now we stand for DRUM's at hand
> To lead our freedom fight,
> And now til then we'll unite like men
> For now we know our might. . . .

After the black insurgents declared that "the factories belong to the people and we workers are the people" neither the industrial "plantation" nor its operatives ever could be the same again.

Electoral and Street Politics

Chapter 129

The Nixon Administration and Civil Rights

William Clay

Nine black members of the House of Representatives who were critical of the Nixon administration formed the Congressional Black Caucus (CBC) in 1971. In April 1971, they met with Nixon to discuss their concerns, presenting a list of sixty recommendations, including stronger enforcement of civil rights laws, appointing more black federal judges, declaring drug addiction a national crisis and requiring programs for its eradication, cutting diplomatic and economic relations with South Africa, and withdrawing troops from Vietnam.

During the past thirty years, the CBC has regularly developed legislation (including alternative budgets), sponsored unofficial hearings and educational projects, and served as a model for other caucus groups. In the 1980s and 1990s, when Congress was particularly concerned with budget deficits, the CBC routinely offered socially oriented low-deficit and balanced-budget alternatives.

Representative William Clay (D–MO) has been the representative for the First U.S. Congressional District of Missouri since 1969. His speech assessing the Nixon administration's early record on civil rights articulates some of the concerns that led to the founding of the caucus. The following selection is excerpted from Representative William Clay, "Civil Rights Progress," Congressional Record, 23 July 1969, 20567–9.

I rise today with my colleague Louis Stokes, of Ohio, to vent the concern of black Americans that this administration is intent on letting years of hard-earned civil rights progress be compromised by embittered conservatives. Black people joined by white liberals are convinced that our only role over the next 3 years must be to conduct a holding action. It is not easy to accept this new kind of responsibility, for over the past 8 years we have learned to work for progress through legislation, through local, State, and national involvement in the issues, and through articulating the needs of people to an attentive audience.

I am not saying that our former audiences always responded as we would have had them respond—but they did listen and they did make strides toward equal educational, social, and economic opportunities for black people.

Now there is no audience except the people of this Nation. It is to them we must appeal for understanding of the conditions and deprivations which must be overcome through a national commitment. In this administration, the demands of the poor, of minorities—and of black people in particular—are falling on deaf, insensitive ears.

President Nixon started off on a sour note by telling us he did not appoint any black people to his Cabinet because he could not find any qualified black citizens. In this day and age, saying that is like saying, "Some of my best friends are black." . . .

Why should we not rise today, then, to exclaim that black people know, by now, what the President's views are on black people? Sometimes, we think we have been swept into a time machine, and it is right back to 1877 when Rutherford B. Hayes was President.

Consider the record: With the first week of the Nixon administration, title VI guidelines for school desegregation were "suspended" so as to provide five southern school districts—which had disregarded the law of the land since 1954—extra time to meet Federal standards.

Under Executive Order No. 11246—with rules and regulations promulgated thereunder—the Federal Government is obligated to do no business with companies which practice employment discrimination. In March, the Department of Defense awarded major contracts to three textile firms with established records of discriminatory practices. They were awarded in violation of regulations which require written assurances of future compliance with the Executive order.

The Federal contract compliance mechanism has the potential for affecting one-third of the jobs in this economy. If the Government resolves to enforce the law, thousands of minority group citizens could thereby gain access to jobs and dignity.

Before finally testifying on June 26, the Attorney General canceled five scheduled appearances before the House Judiciary Committee to present administration views on extension of the Voting Rights Act. The cancellations coincided with reports emanating from the Justice Department that the delays were precipitated by administration desires to dilute the effectiveness of the enforcement mechanisms provided in the present act. Unfortunately, the Attorney General's testimony proved these reports were accurate. I am gratified by the wisdom of the House Judiciary Committee which has reported the legislation to extend the Voting Rights Act without administration revisions.

The handling of the appointment of a new head of the EEOC [Equal Employment Opportunity Commission] added to the evidence that this administration will weaken enforcement on civil rights generally and mandates against job discrimination in particular. . . .

This administration has even recommended that the tax reform bill include a provision calling for foundations to lose their tax exempt status if they give any money to voter registration programs. Black people know that without the financial assistance of major foundations, we would not have registered black voters in the Southern States. Mr. [Charles] Evers would not now be mayor of Fayette, Miss., and Carl Stokes would not be mayor of Cleveland. . . .

My colleagues here know that the Economic Opportunity Act and its program is being dismantled with the precision of a surgeon's knife. All that is left is the office to administer to poverty. And to administer to poverty, the President chose a former Congressman who represented a district where the average income of his constituents was $9,300—a man who knows little about poverty, a man who voted against the original Economic Opportunity Act. This is how poverty is being administered in Washington. . . .

When Treasury Secretary David Kennedy first took office, he testified before a Senate committee to the effect that some increase in unemployment might be the price of controlling the inflationary spiral. In the past month, while consideration of the surtax was pending before the House, the administration spread the word that their anti-inflationary policies would soon be felt by the economy. Consequently, I am not surprised by the labor statistics report indicating an increase in black unemployment in poverty neighborhoods. Black people know that they are the last hired and the first fired.

The report shows that one out of every three black youths is unemployed, while only one of every eight white youths suffers joblessness. The kinds of employment and training needs of black youths and adults who are confined to the cores of our cities are simply not being addressed. There has been no response to their conditions. The black youth unemployment rate is merely an indication of harder times to come—when these youth become adult unemployment statistics.

Indications from this administration are that the commitment to the need for comprehensive youth training and all-around job preparation will be deferred. This Nation can put a man on the moon, but it cannot put black men on the job.

It is all downhill in the Nation's Capital—priorities are sadly confused while this President acts on his obvious decision to accommodate [conservatives] and southerners. Our hypocritical society continues.

In fiscal year 1968, this Government paid well over $1 billion in farm payments—and this figure does not include subsidy payments made in an amount less than $5,000 per farmer. . . .

Meanwhile, during this same period, the Government spent less than $300 million for its low-rent public housing programs and only $900 million in the Federal food program which includes school lunch and milk payments, commodity distribution, and food stamps.

It has been said before, but it deserves repetition—there is something basically wrong when a nation fails to feed its hungry while it pays its farmers not to produce food. . . .

Any discussion of a guaranteed income program for poor people in this Nation must be prefaced by a discussion of the guaranteed income program which now exists—not for poor people but for rich farmers.

Senator James O. Eastland, third ranking member of the Senate Agriculture Committee, received a subsidy of $116,978 last year for his plantation. At the same time, citizens of Mississippi suffer the most dire hardships of hunger. In the State of Mississippi a ceiling has been applied to payments for dependent children of $9.50 a month, or $114 for a full year. And yet Senator Eastland has consistently opposed the proposal to place a ceiling on farm subsidy payments. No comment on this situation is necessary; it speaks for itself. . . .

The Bureau of the Budget has made the most damaging recommendation of the past decade relating to support for education and libraries in America. The total allotted for all purposes for fiscal year 1970 to the Department of Health, Education, and Welfare is $3.2 billion, or about 1.5 percent of the total Federal budget. That means 98.5 percent of the total Federal budget [goes elsewhere]. Ask any American what service he would most desire his Government to provide and I believe most would say education. Our faith in education is truly one of the distinctions of this country. In America we have been taught that through education, anything is possible for our children. Men are more concerned than ever that their children be given a better start, a better job, a better and more secure life, and they are believers in education and training toward that end.

Now we have a government which upholds its responsibility for a common defense and ignores its responsibility for justice and domestic tranquillity. And in the Preamble to the Constitution the responsibility for establishing Justice and insuring domestic tranquillity comes first.

These misplaced priorities bring a severe blow to the pursuit of equal educational opportunity and quality. It is a sad commentary on this Nation's social conscience that defense spending should equal $80 billion while health, education, and welfare spending totals only $3.2 billion. . . .

Racism must be removed from this land. The Federal Government can accelerate or impede this progress by its own policies and practices. Presently, the incidents of discrimination by this Government are flagrant abuses of responsible leadership.

Chapter 130

The Gary Black Political Convention of 1972

Manning Marable

Manning Marable is professor of history and director of the Institute for African American Studies at Columbia University.

The following selection is reprinted from " 'In an Hour of Great Crisis': The Gary Black Political Convention of 1972," Guardian, 12 February 1992. Reprinted by permission of the author.

For other selections by Marable, see chapters 87 and 172.

> We come to Gary in an hour of great crisis and tremendous promise for Black America. While the white nation hovers on the brink of chaos, while its politicians offer no hope of real change, we stand on the edge of history and are faced with an amazing and frightening choice: We may choose . . . to slip back into the decadent white politics of American life, or we may press forward, moving relentlessly from Gary to the creation of our own black life. The choice is large, but the time is very short.
>
> —From the preamble document of the National Black Political Convention, Gary, Ind., March 10–11, 1972

Next month marks the 20th anniversary of perhaps the most significant mass political convention in African-American history, the 1972 National Black Political Convention.

The Gary convention drew almost 3,000 official delegates and between 5,000 and 6,000 additional observers and produced one of the most progressive and challenging documents ever written on behalf of the Black struggle for freedom.

Organized by three very different political leaders, Mayor Richard Hatcher of Gary, then–Black nationalist Amiri Baraka, and Rep. Charles Diggs of Detroit, the gathering attracted and—if only for a moment—unified a broader range of Black activists than has any subsequent event. And only the eloquence and power expressed in Martin Luther King Jr.'s memorable "Letter from Birmingham Jail," drafted nine years earlier, equals the language of the "Black Agenda," the Gary convention document.

Today, standing two decades removed from what many historians now refer to as the high point of the Black Power movement of the late 1960s and early 1970s, it is important to reconstruct the political environment, perceptions and personalities of that time. To answer the larger question of why and how the present-day Black struggle may be revived and renewed, it is necessary to relearn the contours of our own movement, its manifestoes and its mistakes.

Black nationalism, the ideology of which dominated the African-American political terrain between the Meredith march through Mississippi during the hot summer of 1966 and the resignation of Richard Nixon in the Watergate scandal eight years later, was at no point monolithic. Some Black Powerites, the "cultural nationalists," tended to emphasize the centrality of culture within their politics, identified themselves with Africa's heritage and traditions, and opposed coalitions with progressive white and working-class formations on narrowly racial grounds.

Other Black nationalists, in groups such as Detroit's League of Revolutionary Black Workers and the Black Panther Party, stressed the nexus of racism and capitalism, advocated coalitions with other oppressed peoples, and attacked U.S. imperialism abroad. Black middle-class politicians and entrepreneurs drew eclectically from the popularity of nationalism, promoting the slogans "Buy Black!" and "community controlled schools."

Nearly all of these elements had in common the conviction that the Black struggle had transcended its dependence on the liberal politics of integration personified by King and propounded by the Southern Christian Leadership Conference, the National Association for the Advancement of Colored People, the National Urban League and other moderate reformist groups. The goal of the struggle was no longer an integrated cup of coffee at a lunch counter in the South or the right to exercise one's electoral franchise without harassment. The challenge of the '70s was to create a "Black agenda," a comprehensive statement and program for action that could empower all elements of the African-American community.

Many hoped such an agenda would create the foundations for an independent Black political party, or perhaps an independent Black campaign for the presidency. It was a strategy that implied that race was the single most important variable or element in the political mobilization of African Americans. Since all shared a common racial identity, political unity could be achieved across partisan and ideological lines. As Baraka expressed it, the goal of Black activists was "to minimize the ideological difference for the sake of 'umoja mweusi,' Black unity."

The search for a higher level of unity was initiated by several leaders and formations. In Washington, the pivotal figure was Diggs, then chairperson of the newly established Congressional Black Caucus. In 1971, the CBC held a series of national hearings and forums on a wide variety of issues, including health care, education, mass communications, African foreign policy and racism within the military. From these hearings would emerge a "Black agenda" on public policy, which would be the basis of Black Congressional activism and a political yardstick to judge white candidates courting Black votes. At a CBC-sponsored meeting of

Black elected officials from local and state governments, Diggs initiated a call for a national Black political convention.

Almost immediately, some CBC members began to shift uneasily in their seats. A few had already made private deals to support pro-war candidate Hubert Humphrey for the Democratic presidential nomination in 1972. Others complained that Diggs had acted without a formal vote of support by caucus members. But the nationalist protest impetus from below forced these wavering officials and civil rights bureaucrats to embrace the "Black agenda" and the concept of a national political convention of Black activists.

A Catalyst for Unity

From the ranks of the nationalists, the concept of a broad-based unity gathering had tremendous appeal. At the preliminary meeting hosted by Hatcher in Northlake, Ill., on Sept. 24–25, 1971, almost every single element of the Black movement was represented. Participants included Reps. Walter Fauntroy, John Conyers, Barbara Jordan and Augustus Hawkins; arch–Black capitalist Roy Innis of the Congress of Racial Equality; Urban League leader Vernon Jordan; Andrew Young, the former lieutenant of King's who was soon to be elected to Congress from Atlanta; liberal Democrat Julian Bond; and nationalist Baraka. The decision was made to sponsor a national convention in Gary to serve as a catalyst for Black unity. Young agreed to raise funds for any subsequent meetings.

"Nationtime, Nationtime!"

The leadership of the NAACP and other traditional integrationists began to lobby aggressively against the Black convention mobilization. NAACP head Roy Wilkins denounced the goals and public policy statements of the convention's organizers even before the actual meeting took place. A volatile national gathering of community leaders, Pan-Africanist nationalists, local officials and socialists would be dangerous and unpredictable. A broad group of Black leaders was implicitly rejecting the integrationists' strategies of building coalitions with white liberals and national Democratic Party chieftains and championing racially integrated schools, affirmative action and civil rights legislation.

The new Black politics would be based instead on direct confrontation with white institutions and the advocacy of Black interests that could unite all socio-economic classes within the African-American community. Most of the newly elected Black municipal officials and mayors across the country, whose numbers swelled from barely 100 in 1964 to more than 1,400 by 1970, now spoke of "nation-time" and "Black empowerment," rather than "we shall overcome."

March 1972—and the ideas that met in Gary—marked the zenith of the nationalist movement of the mid-20th century. The thousands of activists who arrived for the convention were enthusiastic, militant and optimistic. Even the integrationist reformers who attended the gathering, including Coretta Scott King and Jesse Jackson, were swept up emotionally in the spirit of nationalist fervor. The politics of the participants was captured in one word, chanted by thousands: "Nationtime! Nationtime! Nationtime!"

In his keynote address, Hatcher attempted to frame the parameters for the new Black politics of unity. He argued that all aspects of the Black political struggle for empowerment had to be supported, from trade union organizing to the Black Panthers. The two-party system and both white capitalist political parties were committed to institutional racism. Therefore, African-Americans had to rely on the strategy of Black unity for collective advancement. "We shall no longer bargain away our support for petty jobs or symbolic offices," Hatcher warned. "If we are to support any political party, the price will now run high—very high."

Prefiguring the Rainbow

Hatcher called for the creation of a National Black Political Assembly, a formation that would initiate local assemblies in which community activists and Black elected officials would collaborate. Such a new party would include a decision-making process working "from the bottom up, not the top down."

The formation must advocate full employment, free college education with adequate stipends, decent housing and the abolition of the drug traffic in the Black community, he said. Prefiguring by more than a decade the rise of [Jesse] Jackson's Rainbow Coalition, Hatcher promised that the new Black politics would become a vanguard for other oppressed groups:

> And when, and if, we form a third political movement, we shall take with us Chicanos, Puerto Ricans, Orientals, a wonderful kaleidoscope of colors. And that is not all. We shall also take with us the best of white America. We shall take with us many a white youth nauseated by the corrupt values rotting the innards of this society; many a white intellectual . . . many of the white poor, and many of the white working class, too.

But there were glaring omissions in Hatcher's oration. He declared war on the two-party system, but was silent about the manner in which a transition to a new party structure would be implemented. He deplored the effects of capitalism without actually identifying the system by name; he called for major reforms in the structure of society but spoke largely in electoral terms. Nor did he urge other non-electoral avenues of protest such as boycotts, mass demonstrations and strikes. Would these new assemblies simply become vehicles to promote the electoral interests of Black politicians?

The most controversial resolutions passed by the convention concerned the issues of school desegregation and the Middle East. The nationalists had never accepted the integrationists' education strategy of eliminating all-Black schools and transporting Black children into the unfriendly outposts of the white suburbs. Instead, nationalists favored community-controlled schools with extensive parental input in decision-making, combined with what would later be termed Afrocentric curriculum. The Gary convention denounced school busing for the purpose of racial integration as a false solution to the educational problems of the Black community.

On Israel, the nationalists' sympathies were on the side of the Arab states, particularly after the June 1967 war, which culminated in the Israeli occupation of the Palestinian lands in the West Bank and Gaza Strip. The convention strongly condemned Israel as the aggressor in the region and questioned U.S. financial and political support for the Israeli regime.

Even before the convention's final session, the unity declared by middle-class politicians with the nationalist's agenda began to unravel. Baraka openly complained that District of Columbia Rep. Fauntroy, the chairperson of Gary's platform committee, was trying to "slip back and forth between the Congressional Black Caucus and the convention wearing both hats," attempting to moderate the language and content of the convention's resolutions. The CBC circulated press releases hours after the convention in an effort to avert charges that it condoned the anti-Israeli statements from the gathering. The Congressional Black Caucus reaffirmed its unyielding friendship for Israel: "As the Black elected representatives to the U.S. Congress, we reaffirm our position that we fully respect the right of the Jewish people to have their own state in their historical National Homeland. We vigorously oppose the efforts of any group that would seek to weaken or undermine Israel's right to existence."

Within months, most of the nation's Black elected officials had distanced themselves from Baraka. A few even denied that they had ever attended the Gary convention. Reps. William Clay and Fauntroy and Jesse Jackson endorsed the presidential candidacy of George McGovern; Charles Evers and Cleveland politician Arnold Pinckney backed Humphrey.

Despite these defections, the other participants of Gary committed themselves to building the National Black Political Assembly, a pre-party formation dedicated to the goals of the "Black Agenda." A triumvirate leadership functioned behind Baraka, Diggs and Hatcher for several years. At state and local levels, community-based Black nationalists created their own assemblies around an economic and social agenda of Black unity.

One such local activist was Ron Daniels in Youngstown, Ohio, who developed a strong political base for progressive nationalist politics and soon began to acquire national attention. Baraka exerted his ideological and political influence in dozens of assemblies through his own formation, the Congress of Afrikan People.

But despite the hopes and convictions expressed in the Gary resolutions, the quest for Black unity across ideological and class boundaries would prove to be elusive. By 1975, Hatcher and Diggs had removed themselves from the leadership. Baraka had renounced his cultural nationalist orientation and had converted the Congress of Afrikan People to a version of Marxism-Leninism influenced by Chinese Communism. In December 1975, the Assembly's new chairperson, Daniels, engineered a purge of Baraka and his leftist allies at a regional meeting in Dayton, Ohio. Daniels later justified the maneuver as the defeat of a "highly disruptive and sectarian force . . . which seemed bent on using the NBPA for its own purposes."

Only 1,000 people attended the National Black Political Convention held in Cincinnati in March 1976. Less than two years later, the National Black Assembly movement had only about 300 local and state activists and members.

But whatever the Gary convention failed to accomplish—including the creation of an effective progressive alternative to the Democratic Party—it was a moment of historical significance and political relevance for current struggles.

At Gary, a substantial segment of the national Black leadership was forced to recognize that fundamental empowerment was impossible within the existing economic and social structures of U.S. society. Gary set into motion the forces which would come together in the 1980's behind Jackson's presidential campaigns of 1984 and 1988. Most crucially, the vision of power articulated in the convention's preamble document still represents a challenge for all oppressed people:

> The choice is large, but the time is very short. . . . The crises we face as Black people are the crises of the entire society. They go deep, to the very bones and marrow, to the essential nature of America's economic, political and cultural systems. They are the natural end-product of a society built on the twin foundations of white racism and white capitalism.

Chapter 131

Police Violence and Riots

John Conyers, Jr.

Representative John Conyers, Jr. (D–MI), former chair of the House of Representatives' Government Operations Committee, has been the Representative for the First U.S. Congressional District of Michigan since 1965. He is a member of both the Congressional Black Caucus and the Progressive Caucus.

The following selection, "Police Violence and Riots," Black Scholar, *January/February 1981, 2–5 is reprinted by permission of* Black Scholar.

For another selection by Conyers, see chapter 139.

It is amazing that more than a decade after long hot summers of racial unrest, violence, and looting that social scientists still cannot agree—nor apparently understand—why blacks riot.

Many experts were called upon by the Kerner Commission when it investigated the causes of the 1960's riots. Those experts were bewildered when confronted with the paradoxical facts: in the years prior to and during the most devastating disturbances, significant political and economic gains had been achieved by black Americans. Educational attainment rose. Relative incomes rose. The number of black elected officials rose. Yet it was in those cities where the gains seemed greatest that the violence, looting, and rampages in the streets were most severe.

Detroit, a mecca for black dreams of economic mobility, is a clear example of this paradox. "Why should the jobless, the homeless, the hungry and tired, the frustrated and angry of Detroit riot?" the experts might have asked. "They receive higher incomes, have better housing, and more supermarkets to serve them than their less advantaged counterparts in the acknowledged racist South!" Nonetheless, riot they did. Forty-three persons died; 7,200 were arrested; the damage totaled an estimated $43 million.

In 1980, in a relatively prosperous city like Miami, the calm and tranquility was shaken by anxious days of anger and anarchy. There are any number of economically depressed areas in this country that did *not* erupt in violence and destruction. Did the material gains won during the War on Poverty eliminate the roots of riots? Did black economic progress avert future outbreaks of discontent and rage? The paradoxical facts of the 1960's remain with us in the 1980's.

The "J-Curve Theory" was once offered to explain this paradox. The theory explains that if after a long period of rising expectations, realization of these expectations lags behind, then the potential for civil violence increases. Some researchers have found that the facts do not support this theory. In fact, some have argued that there is no relationship between riots, on the one hand, and economic opportunities, racism, police brutality and other obvious correlates of urban violence, on the other. They go so far as to suggest that riots are merely random occurrences. Events like the senseless beatings and brutality by police officers in Miami are regarded as unimportant precipitating events.

Well, these scholars can't see what happens in a riot prone city. What I propose to the intellectual speculators is what might be called the "C-Curve Theory." What is it that we see in common among all of the riots, past or present?

We see a historical pattern of excessive use of force by police against minority communities. Not just a few isolated cases of subtle harassment, but repeated and sustained instances of clear brutality and beatings.

We see rage and frustration in the black community. A feeling of despair and hopelessness arises from the intolerable high levels of unemployment. There is a sense of outrage toward the Double Standard of criminal justice. There is a bitterness over the lack of significant political power.

The event that triggers the riot is frequently the same. A white policeman unmercifully and publicly beats a black person who is often innocent of any criminal act or the police, usually white, break up a meeting or a bar-scene without any reason. The rage and frustration erupts in the ghetto. The past pattern of police violence is not easily forgotten. People roam in the streets and loot and fight back because, even if they don't, they will end up trapped in a racist system of criminal justice.

This is so simple a theory, I do not see how others cannot see it. It reminds me of the story about the little boy who walked around with his hands over his eyes all day. When asked why he inconvenienced himself so, he responded that he wanted to learn how to "see" in the dark.

In preparation for hearings on the Miami riots, the House Subcommittee on Crime, which I chair, has accumulated considerable information on the causes of riots. We have heard from noted social theorists, community activists, black police organizations, legal scholars, and some victims of brutal beatings by the police.

What we have learned is that there is a lack of responsiveness in riot prone areas to minority people's needs. We have learned that there is an insensitivity on the part of the entire criminal justice system toward the residents of ghetto areas. We have learned that astronomically high levels of unemployment, especially among black teenagers, are linked to both crimes for profit and racial violence. And most importantly, we have learned that history repeats itself as we see again and again that police use of excessive force leads to riots.

A clear and undeniable conclusion emerges from our preliminary investigation. A very real division in economic resources—a very unequal distribution of wealth—means that while money incomes are rising for some, unemployment and poverty loom for many. The haves accumulate and the have-nots must watch with frustration.

On top of the economic inequality, there lies the unequal justice. When a black man shoots a police officer, he is quickly arrested, tried, convicted, and sentenced to life or death. When a white policeman shoots an innocent young black, it is called justifiable homicide: the most visible symbol in the black community of the oppression of the criminal justice system is back on the streets the next day. This leads to anger.

The anger is fueled by a sustained pattern of harassment, beatings and demeaning acts by the police. Police violence is a crime. The crime of police brutality probably contributes more to the increase of frustration, anger—and violent riots—in ghetto areas than any other single illegal act. In fact, police violence is the worst type of crime because it leads to the general breakdown of law, often carries official sanction, and is the trigger of massive racial violence that devastates whole communities.

The evidence from Miami provides convincing support for the theory of riots I have sketched. In February, 1980, the Metro police broke into the home of a black school teacher. It was a drug raid. The police beat the shocked resident until several of his ribs were broken. Because of a mix-up, the drug raid was made at the wrong house. An innocent black school teacher was viciously brutalized. Was this an isolated example of over-zealous anti-drug agents doing their job; a slip-up; a mistake? Or was this one of many recurring instances in a pattern of violence?

The *Miami Herald* began an extensive examination of police brutality in South Florida to answer these questions. They found that in an average week three brutality complaints are filed against police in the Miami area. Not all the police are found to use excessive force. In fact, only a handful of the officers accounted for most of the complaints. Yet those officers are rarely fired; few are found guilty of any wrong doing by the internal disciplinary system. This is incongruous because nearly a quarter of citizen's claims for damages in brutality cases are awarded by the Miami courts. The police department says that the accused officer is not guilty. The court says he is.

To make matters worse, so the *Miami Herald* found, the city and county were losing so many brutality cases and having to litigate so many claims that their liability insurance was almost cancelled. Hundreds of thousands of dollars were paid out of taxpayer's pockets to settle police brutality claims.

If you were an insurance agent, and your client cost you many times in settlements than he paid in premiums, and this sort of situation goes on year after year, would you believe that there was no pattern of culpability? There had been a persistent pattern of police violence and brutality in Miami. The black community knew it. The police knew it. Even the city's insurance company knew it.

Just as a pattern of police violence precedes a potential ghetto riot, so too does a general feeling of hopelessness. The frustrations and the rage I have mentioned are rooted deeply in (a) economic inequalities, (b) racism in the criminal justice system, and (c) a lack of political power.

Examples of the combined effects of political impotence and racism in the criminal justice system abound. The jury that acquitted the alleged murderers of the black Miami executive was all white. The state and federal judges are overwhelmingly white. The United States Attorney's offices are overwhelmingly white. The local prosecutors' offices are overwhelmingly white. The crimes that black men and women are convicted of—robbery, burglary, assault and larceny—are black crimes. The crimes that whites commit, but are not convicted of—fraud, price-fixing, Securities Exchange Commission violations—are euphemistically called white-collar crimes. In Miami alone, billions of dollars of trade is reportedly conducted annually in illegal transactions involving gambling, drugs, and prostitution. Relatively few arrests are made. Minorities are not believed to control, nor to receive the profit from these lucrative activities. Yet minorities are daily accused of the most unprofitable crimes, which ironically consume the largest fractions of prosecutors' time and energy.

Examples of the unequal distribution of economic resources are readily apparent. Labor market analysts in Miami have informed the Subcommittee on Crime that the levels of unemployment in Liberty City [a predominantly black section of Miami] are far higher than the officially reported rates. The United States Department of Labor estimates that the black teenage unemployment rate was about 35 per cent in May, 1980. Our sources say that the actual rate was almost twice that in Liberty City prior to the riots and that the idleness and bitterness caused by unemployment helped bring on the riot.

The evidence shows that basic economic injustices generate the frustration of those who riot. The evidence shows that unequal treatment in the criminal justice system and political powerlessness add to the anger of those who riot. The evidence shows that a pattern of police violence makes a city prone to a riot. And clearly, undeniably, and unequivocally, the evidence shows that police brutality precipitates riots.

So why haven't we learned the lesson of the sixties? Some cities like Detroit have. Effective minority hiring and promotion strategies, for example, have resulted in police departments with sensitive, attuned officers. Expansion of summer youth employment programs have resulted in jobs rather than idleness and hopelessness among youth. Election of black mayors and city councils and the appointment of black judges have brought hope and empowerment to many in our urban ghettos.

We can work together to help cities like Miami develop strategies to eliminate police violence. We can eliminate police violence. We can eliminate unjustified police shootings and the unnecessary use of deadly force. We can eliminate the brutality and senseless beating by a few of the men in blue. The result will not just be fewer riots. The result will be greater respect for the law and a criminal justice system based on fairness and yes, justice.

Chapter 132

Rodney King, Police Brutality, and Riots

Nell Irvin Painter

In 1991 a bystander videotaped Los Angeles police officers beating a black man, Rodney King. Riots erupted across the country after a jury found the officers innocent of any crime. In a later trial several of the officers were convicted of civil rights violations.

Nell Irvin Painter is professor of history at Princeton University.

The following selection is reprinted from "New Medium Brings Old Message to Uninitiated," In These Times, 13 May 1992, 7. Reprinted by permission of In These Times.

For another selection by Painter, see chapter 48.

Tragic and telegenic, the Rodney King beating began with and produced enough violence to shock viewers around the world.

Taken all together, the beating, the verdict and the riots may even have brought masses of Americans to consider the significance of class within race, a connection that the national politics of the '80s tend to erase. We may now come to realize that, even though poverty more and more wears a dark face, issues of race are no longer merely stories in black and white.

The politics of the '80s—characterized by evasion and with willful manipulation of negative racial stereotypes—aimed at obscuring historical relationships. National leaders severed the connection between centuries' worth of oppression and discrimination of the basis of race, on the one hand, and the remedy of affirmative action on the other. It is well past time that we read the past to realize that little in the Rodney King affair is new or mysterious.

An Old Story

The very accessibility of the images seemed to set this case apart from instances of police brutality that went before. But the only part that is new is that this time a cameraman happened to catch it on video. Black people, other people of color and the poor of all races have been familiar with police brutality for generations.

Police brutality is as old as time, as old as slave patrols, as old as the Pinkertons. In recent decades and with uneven success, victims have taken their cases to court. This time the evidence perfectly suited the medium of television, and an old story reached a wide audience. This time the amazement—at the beating, at the verdict—spread beyond the people who were beaten and those who were on their side. Thanks to that cameraman, a lot of Americans discovered the crime of police brutality for the first time.

Remembrance—of the long histories of officially sanctioned police brutality, of the urban disturbances that have followed in their wake and of earlier reports full of thoughtful remedies—further deepens the tragedy of the Rodney King affair. Trials of police who use too much force aren't very common, but they, too, have their history, as in Liberty City, Miami, in 1980, when police were acquitted of murdering an innocent black motorcyclist.

The history of urban riots that were anti-black dates much further back than this history of burning and looting in the '60s. Nonetheless, most Americans don't know or don't remember the New York City Draft Riots of 1863, the worst urban disturbance in U.S. history.[1] Although the Draft Riots began as a protest against conscription, more than 100 African-Americans, many of whom were children, died in the violence. The East St. Louis, Ill., riot of 1917 (which inspired Harlem Renaissance poet Claude McKay to write "If We Must Die") and the "Red Summer" of riots across the country in 1919 also produced one-sided death tolls of far more blacks than whites.[2] The pattern of white attack on non-white victims persisted into the '40s: In 1943, white mobs attacked Mexican-Americans in Los Angeles (the "zoot suit riots") and African-Americans in Detroit, although the casualties were not completely non-white.[3]

Only in the '60s was the connection firmly established between the word "riot" and black people. African-Americans took to the streets, setting fires and looting in New York in 1964, in Watts/Los Angeles in 1965, in Newark and Detroit in 1967, and in Washington, D.C., in 1968, as well as all across the country in the aftermath of the assassination of Martin Luther King Jr.

Grief and Frustration

The Los Angeles riot, "the war" of '92, seems most to resemble 1968's outbreak of grief and frustration. By the time tempers flared in Watts and Detroit and Washington, D.C., so many blacks had died—50? 60? more?—in the pursuit of basic civil rights that support for the non-violence associated with King was wearing awfully thin. Appeals for self-defense and for black power were mounting. In 1968, King had less and less company in his insistence on non-violent protest, but his pacifism did not protect him from murder. King's assassination was shocking and infuriating. If even Martin Luther King had fallen victim to murderous white supremacy, if even his life was worth naught, what was the worth of any black person's life in this country?

A generation later, the acquittal of Rodney King's assailants, captured on videotape in the act of administering a savage beating to a man handcuffed on the ground, seemed shocking and infuriating. Now television coverage has rewritten for the nation a question that people of color have asked themselves time and again in their own neighborhoods. The nation—along with the neighborhoods—wants to know: Why?

The inevitable inquiries, findings, recommendations and remedies have a history as old as the riots. The immediate causes of the disturbances of the '60s were nearly always police brutality or rumors of police brutality. The underlying causes—explained in report after report—also began to sound familiar: discrimination, poverty, unemployment, lack of governmental services.

The most eloquent of the reports, the Kerner Report of 1968, is still read and still current. But its roots lie in the 1947 report of President Harry S. Truman's Committee on Civil Rights. The report, titled "To Secure These Rights," began by indicting lynching and police brutality—practices that proved how little America respected the value of black life.

An inclusive report that touches on most of the themes that reappeared in the civil-rights movement of the '50s and '60s, "To Secure These Rights" [see chapter 85—Eds.] is well worth reading today, if only to remind us how long remedies have been recognized and agreed upon—and how long the political will has not been sufficient to sustain fundamental reform. Today's remedies will be familiar from 1947 and 1968, but because South-Central Los Angeles has changed over time, some answers must change also.

One great lesson of the '60s that came out of the civil-rights movement and the war on poverty was the importance of neighborhood based organizations led by local people. The Student Non-Violent Coordinating Committee of the early '60s and the Model Cities Project of the late '60s have both been spoken of disparagingly since their time. But in different ways, each managed to bring poor and working-class people of color to an appreciation of their power as citizens. This, in turn, stretched prevailing notions of democracy—that officeholders are supposed to speak as though they are college educated and as though they share an identity of interests with the rich and middle class.

Organization from the bottom up will be crucial in reform, and it will deliver an important lesson that we are perhaps ready to hear. South-Central Los Angeles, like many other inner cities in the U.S., is no longer a study of monoliths coded in black and white.

For better or worse, the '80s proved that black conservatives do, indeed, exist. Clarence Thomas, Anita Hill and their friends demolished completely easy equations of blackness with the liberal wing of the Democratic Party—with any wing of the Democratic Party. Working-class black people exhibit the same ideological heterogeneity.

The poor and working-class people who will need to organize toward the regeneration of their neighborhoods are also heterogeneous ethnically and racially. Effective organization, therefore, will need to reach out to people of many backgrounds. Allies from within and outside inner-city neighborhoods who want to be of help can't afford to remain racially or ethnically parochial. We are accustomed to using the language of race to talk about class, but recent experience shows that poverty and joblessness have more than a black face.

Rebuilding South-Central Los Angeles in these recession-ridden, postindustrial times will prove challenging in the extreme, but the path may already be discerned. It leads from one beaten black body to a rainbow coalition organized from the grass roots.

EDITORS' NOTES

1. For details, see Iver Bernstein, *The New York City Draft Riot* (New York: Oxford University Press, 1990.

2. In 1919, major race riots took place in dozens of areas across the country, including Chicago, Omaha, Knoxville, Charleston, Washington, D.C., and rural Arkansas. In Chicago, over five days, 38 persons were killed and 537 injured. Two years later, rioting whites may have killed more than 100 blacks in Tulsa. It was not until eighty years later that the Oklahoma legislature set up a commission to investigate the cover-up of this largely unknown event and decide on possible reparations. See Brent Staples, "Searching for Graves—and Justice—in Tulsa," *New York Times,* 20 March 1999.

3. In 1943 there were also race riots in New York City, Mobile, Alabama, and Beaumont, Texas. See Dominic J. Capeci, Jr., *The Harlem Riot of 1943* (Philadelphia: Temple: University Press, 1977).

Chapter 133

Black Power in the Age of Jackson

Andrew Kopkind

Jesse Jackson ran for the presidency in 1984 and 1988. The following excerpted article about the 1984 campaign assessed his prospects and his roots in the civil rights movement. Jackson went on to win primaries in South Carolina, Louisiana, and Washington, D.C.

Andrew Kopkind (1935–1994) was associate editor of the Nation. *He frequently wrote about civil rights, cold war liberalism, and the rise of the New Right. Along with his work for the* Nation, *he wrote for the* New Republic, Hard Times, Ramparts, Working Papers for a New Society, *the* New York Review of Books, *and the* Village Voice. *A collection of his articles was published posthumously as* The Thirty Years' War: Dispatches and Diversions of a Radical Journalist, 1965–1994 (1995).

The following selection, "Black Power in the Age of Jackson," is reprinted with permission from the 26 November 1983 issue of the Nation *magazine.*

Black power is an engine that drives the great vehicles of social change in America. The Civil War and the civil rights movement, slave revolts and student sit-ins, Marcus Garvey's separatism and Malcolm X's nationalism: black people's epic struggle for equality and quest for identity create both the pretext and the context for national upheaval and transformation. It is a radical dynamic that pertains to America's peculiar racial history, and in each generation it produces unique politics and unexpected leaders. Suddenly, in this electoral season, the politics are presidential and the leader is Jesse Jackson.

The national media plaster Jackson's face on magazine covers, pull him in front of television cameras and tuck him into the most conventional categories of presidential candidacy. Even the press that can't stand (or understand) his politics makes Jackson into some kind of hero; *Newsweek*'s cover story includes "a Jackson album" of snapshots, showing the candidate in historic poses from college football field to victory night after Chicago's mayoral election last winter. Not since John F. Kennedy burst into celebrity a quarter-century ago has a political upstart so captivated the press and captured attention, space and even *Time*: "He can be fascinating and frightening, inspiring and irritating, charismatic and controversial."

Such effusions are accompanied by detailed analyses, often with charts, of the mathematical probabilities for Jackson's strategy to succeed in the primaries. Then come discussions of Jackson's stated or implied positions on what pundits take to be issues in the election: missiles, motherhood and the Palestine Liberation Organization, for three. Finally, Jackson albums usually include an extended essay by the resident philosopher on every black child's dream of becoming President of the United States.

The level of muddle, misinformation, wrong thinking and barely disguised racism in all the hoopla is extraordinary, if predictable. In listing Jackson's "downside," commentators invariably call him "ambitious," "egotistical," "opportunistic" and "driven," as if such qualities were rare among presidential candidates. Who could be more ambitious then John Glenn, more opportunistic than Walter Mondale, more frightening than Ronald Reagan, more irritating than Gary Hart? But somehow (we *know* how) Jackson is fair game for taunts and teases from the press while lighter folks get off with more qualified criticisms.

By the same token, the Jackson campaign and the phenomenon of a black political power movement are consistently denigrated or trivialized. Many politicians see the surge of black activism as merely the latest minority bid for the spoils of office (and even that bespeaks a misreading of the history of ethnic politics); one leftish columnist said cynically, "The whole thing will end with Mondale making Jackson his Secretary of HUD, or something." I've heard it said that Jackson's purpose is to "keep the Democrats honest," an oxymoronic hope at best, or, along the same lines, to "revive the New Deal coalition," an improbably medical and political dream.

The cynics may have a point; they often do. The media may be able to frame the Jackson campaign in familiar terms of charisma, count and the delegate clout; those are the most comfortable cliches. Politicians may defang and defuse the frightening and explosive elements of the movement; that is their perogative. But black politics in the Age of Jackson has a vastly different center of gravity, historical message and meaning. "It's all about power," Stoney Cooks, a longtime associate of Atlanta Mayor Andrew Young, told me recently. It's also about race, about class, about enfranchisement and disenfranchisement, and about the mechanisms of change in the American epic; it is at the very heart of the upheaval. In the course of a few months everything has moved: the spirit is impatient, the mood is militant, the tempo is rising and the color is black.

The speed of change is unprecedented. At this time last year, black politicians were nearly invisible in white America. The decline of the old civil rights movement, the force of the white backlash to integration and affirmative action, and the rise of Reaganism had pushed black struggles into a memory hole. Only two years ago, Adam Clymer, a senior political analyst for *The New York Times*, surveyed the scene and discovered that "the political influence of blacks in America has fallen to its lowest level in two decades."

The gains blacks had made in employment, education and political office after passage of the various anti-discrimination acts of the 1960s proved to be limited, and by the end of the next decade many of the vectors of progress were reversed.

A report issued this year by the Center for the Study of Social Policy, a liberal think tank, showed that the median income for blacks was only 56 percent of that for whites—virtually the same as it was in 1960. Even worse, 45 percent of all adult black males were unemployed in 1982—almost twice as many as in 1960, also a year of economic downturn. Politically, black officeholders are still a token presence, even in Southern states with large black populations. There are no blacks among the eighty-two members of Congress from the seven states of the Deep South, where the Voting Rights Act of 1965 was targeted. As Jesse Jackson says repeatedly in his stump speeches, "Eighteen years after the Voting Rights Act, only 1 percent of elected officials are black. At that rate, it will take us 198 years to achieve parity."

Social relations between blacks and whites had been similarly stymied if they had not actually deteriorated, by the mid-1970s. Racist chic replaced radical chic (if the latter was ever anything more than a gonzo magazine headline); liberal guilt ebbed and liberal good will dissipated. Liberal malice, on the other hand, became socially legitimate and politically shrewd. New York's Mayor Ed Koch, who once marched for black equality in Dixie, runs from it like the plague in his own hometown, and there are other politicians like him. The elaborate coded vocabulary used to disguise their racist ethic fools none but the most gullible editorial writers. Black and white voters (and non-voters) know how to translate "death penalty, "victims' rights," "poverty pimps," "welfare cheats" and "special interests" when used in white political parlance. And they act accordingly on election day. All during the 1970s, whites voted for whites and many blacks didn't bother.

Things started changing a year ago. The black political movement arose from the cynicism, disillusionment and reaction of the last long years; indeed, the movement was fashioned by the despair of the decade following the demise of the civil rights campaigns. It appeared not only *after* that time of hopelessness, of rejection, of broken promises and false starts but *because* of the many failures. That is crucial for the movement, and for Jesse Jackson as well.

Both Jackson and the movement exploded into political prominence and media visibility during the Chicago mayoral campaign of Harold Washington. That contest became the pivotal event in the development of the new black consciousness, what Jackson calls the beginning of "a six-week drama around the [Washington] victory and a six-month trauma afterward." It was vastly different from other black electoral victories of the past fifteen years because it was won in direct opposition to—and at the expense of—white Democrats of the liberal persuasion.

Walter Mondale and Edward Kennedy, the diarchs of Democratic liberalism, came to Chicago to stump for Washington's opponents: Kennedy for incumbent Mayor Jane Byrne, Mondale for Richard M. Daley, son of the late cloutish mayor. They hardly took notice of Washington's presence or his point, which was that it was black people's "turn" to hold office. The white politicians simply assumed what all white Democrats have assumed since the New Deal: blacks would be satisfied with the leavings of liberal power—the trickle-down effects of welfare policies and expanded public employment programs. As it turned out, those assumptions were obsolete.

Mondale and Kennedy came to Chicago to beat Harold Washington, Jackson remarked to me one steamy morning late last summer in a van bouncing through a backwater Mississippi on a voter registration weekend. "You couldn't pay them to do that again. Things have changed."

What happened in Chicago was the beginning of the process Jackson called the "renegotiation" of the relationship between blacks and the Democratic Party. For half a century, the Democrats have in a sense contracted to provide for and protect blacks and others traditionally rejected by the American system. Blacks were to respond with votes, support, enthusiasm and, perhaps most important, moral legitimacy. "Black voting is always sort of a moral initiative," Jackson said in a speech not long ago.

As the contract has run its course through several renewals but no serious reconstructions, the Democrats have often tried to wriggle out of important clauses. Even the great New Dealer Franklin Roosevelt was lambasted by black leaders for his poor performance; many did not want to support his campaign for a third term. [John] Kennedy fudged on civil rights until the movement overtook him; organizers of the 1963 March on Washington were so suspicious of his motives and wary of his rhetoric that they rejected his request to speak at the Lincoln Memorial.

Lyndon Johnson wanted to be remembered for saying "We shall overcome" at a joint session of Congress, but before that, as he prepared for his nomination at the 1964 Democratic convention, he ordered the destruction of the most important independent black political movement of that era, the Mississippi Freedom Democratic Party. It's a long and sad tale, but the upshot is that Johnson and Hubert Humphrey demanded that blacks give up any hope of independent political standing and submit to the priorities, needs and strategies of white Democratic leaders if they wanted anti-poverty and civil rights benefits.

Most whites forgot the Freedom Democrats' challenge soon after the convention. But black activists and political workers—including everyone I met at the heart of the Jackson campaign—remember it vividly. For them, it is the landmark event in the development of black power consciousness and its political expression.

Everything Jesse Jackson is saying this year about blacks in politics—"We want our share," "It's our turn," "Blacks will no longer be the Harlem Globetrotters of the Democratic Party"—was first shouted, in many of the same words, by young black civil rights workers and militants in the wake of the liberal "betrayal" of the Freedom Democrats. I heard the basic Jackson speech in 1966 in Mississippi, when the first cries of "black power" went up in Lowndes Country, Alabama, where members of the Student Nonviolent Coordinating Committee settled down to start the Black Panther Party [see chapter 126—*Eds.*]; in Oakland, California, where other black youths were organizing a similar project in an urban ghetto.

In all those cases, black power politics was the specific response to Democratic failures to give organized blacks a share in the power and profits of political control. But as a slogan and an idea, black power is old hat. Why has it taken nearly two decades for it to find expression in mainstream politics?

Jackson told me that blacks had to develop a certain amount of "maturity" before they could assimilate black power concepts and act on them. That means, perhaps, that they had to hear Democratic promises, believe them and see them broken. In other words, they had to want the Great Society and see it destroyed by the Democrats' bureaucratic control in Washington and their war in Vietnam; they had to suffer the depredations of corporate conservatism under Nixon; they had to plead for a better deal from Carter and see that hope deferred by the exigencies of Democratic inflation-fighting and cold war–mongering, and they had to bear the brunt of Reaganism's ravages, unaided and hardly comforted by their Democratic protectors. It's no wonder that in Chicago, blacks refused en masse to follow Mondale and Kennedy and give their votes to the white establishment which had led them on and let them down so many times.

To follow the political logic of black power politics is easier than to chart its future. But to see what the result of renegotiation may mean, it is best to start with Jesse Jackson's concept of black voting as a moral initiative. That view is surely more than bluff and pride. Black political activity has a unique potential in the American electoral scheme as a strategy in the struggle for justice and equality. That is not to say black votes count for more than those of any other group, but the fact of racism and the history of black exclusion give black electoral movements a special spiritual force. A corollary to the formulation of moral initiative is Jackson's notion, which he explained to a New York audience recently, that "most other groups ride on the coattail of black strategy." That is not an altogether endearing insight: scores of self-perceived or self-constructed voting communities pretend to pre-eminence, not to mention political leadership. Whites of all stripes have historically ignored blacks and dismissed race as irrelevant or dangerous in political organization. Leftists sometimes call race mere "superstructure" over a class and economic fundament—an ideological maneuver that allows them to support whites against blacks in hopes of mobilizing the working-class racist vote for an economic "populist." Many liberals will plead "color blindness" at election time in order to preserve the myth of democratic equality. Most people, of course, simply shut race out of their mind when not actively expressing contempt or practicing violence against the nearest minority target. But because racism is a paradigm for every other ideology of exclusion, campaigns to combat it—black political campaigns—can provide an example for every other struggle in the system.

Jackson's "rainbow coalition" is an attempt to organize the political strength of all deprived and rejected constituencies around the moral force and political energy of the black movement. It is no gimmick, and although Jackson may throw the term around too breezily, he is serious about it. It is the essence of his campaign.

"The civil rights movement . . . laid the foundations, provided the climate and in many instances trained the initial organizers of the women's, gay, anti-nuclear, environmental and other movements in the seventies and eighties," he told the audience at the gay Human Rights Campaign Fund dinner in New York. "Discrimination, oppression and on occasion genocide have been used to force blacks, women and Native Americans into their proper place. All of us feel deprived in twentieth-century America, and America is still organized by cash—the cash system that is still dominated by white males."

The political demands of the rainbow coalition, implicit in its construction and explicit in Jackson's speeches, are extraordinary. They are racial, sexual, economic and ideological. What other major-party candidate in this century has talked about deprivation in a "cash system dominated by white males"? No wonder Jackson is scaring conventional politicians half to death.

Bruce Bolling, Boston's black city councilor, told a reporter last spring that Jackson "may be viewed as threatening. He's talking about a coalition of people on the outside, and in some quarters people might be anxious about that kind of direction."

It is enormously difficult to convince even a fraction of the "people on the outside" that their interests lie in political coalition, and even harder to talk them all into accepting black leadership—much less Jesse Jackson. And yet it makes perfect sense. The Democrats understand it, but their coalitions have always served the purposes of the white male cash system. Jackson's campaign would establish an opposition to that dominance.

For its part, the Democratic Party leadership seems to have given up on opposition. It has supported Reagan in his imperial invasions; it has grown silent in the face of the business recovery; it has adopted "neoliberal" prejudices against labor, the poor, social welfare and economic redistribution. It is left to Jesse Jackson to stake out opposition ground on America's intervention in Lebanon and the invasion of Grenada, for instance; on the nuclear arms race and corporate accountability and racial equity. It would hardly be an election campaign without him.

It should be said, although it hardly needs saying, that the contradictions in his candidacy and in the black political movement are heavy enough to bring the whole thing down at any time with just a little shoving. There will be plenty of that. Jackson's personality, background, faults and foibles will be excruciatingly exploited. He is so far out of the mold of the typical political candidate that almost everything he ever said or did, or says or does, can be used to invalidate his effort. Is the bookkeeping at PUSH (his Chicago-based organization, People United to Serve Humanity) messy? Did he say the wrong thing on abortion. Did he offend Jews, social democrats, environmentalists, lesbians? Probably. He makes a lot of mistakes, even in his own terms. But until now, at least, he had not been crafting a serious bid for the presidency, and he has not stopped along the way to think that everything can, and will be used against him.

Chapter 134

Race and the Democrats

Richard A. Cloward and Frances Fox Piven

Frances Fox Piven is professor of political science at the City University of New York. Richard A. Cloward is professor of social work at Columbia University.

The following selection, "Race and the Democrats," is reprinted with permission from the 9 December 1991 issue of the Nation *magazine.*

For other selections by Piven and Cloward, see chapters 41 and 84.

The current political wisdom, even among some on the left, is that blacks and liberals are to blame for the troubles of the Democratic Party. Supposedly, divisive demands for race-specific remedies for past discrimination advanced by blacks and their liberal allies antagonized the white working class, destroying the biracial and class-based coalition that championed progressive reform in America. By this account, it was wrongheaded to demand affirmative action or school integration or—most egregious of all—"welfare rights," because these policies highlighted race and exacerbated racial divisions. And it was nothing short of madness to advance these demands with the flamboyant and disruptive tactics that characterized the black movement.

There are three weaknesses in this argument, all fatal. The New Deal Democratic Party was not a working-class party; neither was it supported by a biracial coalition. And there was no way blacks could win concessions without alienating whites.

For a brief moment at the depth of the Depression, widespread panic and rising insurgency in the urban North prodded F.D.R. to adopt labor-oriented policies and rhetoric. But over the slightly longer run, it became clear that the party was hostage to its Southern wing. Constitutional arrangements were weighted toward the South in both the Electoral College and the Senate, and Congressional seniority arrangements delivered control of key committees to Southern one-party oligarchs.

Moreover, these oligarchs remained unchallenged, because constitutionally based governmental decentralization permitted states to use voter registration barriers to disfranchise blacks and most poor whites. As representatives of upper-strata whites, Southern Congressmen moved easily into alliances with Republicans, limiting Northern working-class power and preventing the New Deal coalition from becoming a labor party. Nor was there any possibility of a biracial party during the 1930s, since 80 percent of blacks lived in the South, where they were disfranchised.

The South extracted a high price for its fealty to the party (Roosevelt won as much as 85 percent of the Southern vote), mainly by blocking any national policies that would interfere with the low-wage and caste-bound Southern labor system. Southern Congressmen promoted right-to-work laws and other antilabor legislation, thus weakening the unions that had begun to serve as the mobilizing infrastructure of the Democratic Party. One consequence was that working-class voters could not control Democratic Presidents. Harry Truman may have vetoed the Taft-Hartley Act, but he invoked its strike-curbing provisions twelve times in the year after the veto override. No Democratic President has made a serious effort to repeal Section 14B of Taft-Hartley, which legalized state right-to-work laws.

The South was nothing less than triumphant in shaping the nation's social welfare policy. Most of the programs promoted by labor parties in Europe—income protections for the unemployed, the old and the poor; minimum wages; and so on—would have wreaked havoc on the Southern economic system, especially its labor system. Accordingly, after the worst years of the Depression, Southern Congressmen who controlled committees joined with Republicans to defeat more generous income support programs and gave states and localities authority over eligibility and benefit levels in many key programs. Nor did the New Deal party champion the low-cost housing and universal health care that later became common in Western Europe. And macroeconomic policy was not used to promote the low unemployment that strengthens workers in the marketplace.

Winning little through the state, organized labor increasingly turned to the workplace to win benefits—pension and health plans, for example. That explains why American workers showed less robust support than Europeans for both their government and their political party. It also explains a deep cleavage within the American working class. As better-organized workers won private-sector benefits, they came to resent paying taxes to finance benefits for others who were forced to rely on social welfare programs. Little wonder that working-class support for the Democrats began to slip before race became a central axis of political alignment.

As Northern working-class loyalties eroded, industrialization and urbanization in the South produced a new middle class with Republican preferences, weakening the Democratic Party all the more. But it was the eruption of the civil rights movement, and the support it won from Northern Democrats, that actually destroyed the old Southern oligarchy. As civil rights litigation and protests drove more whites into the Republican ranks, a Democratic Party desperate for new voting support was forced to enfranchise blacks. Moreover, Southern defections and rising black insurgency raised the price for black support in the North, where growing black numbers had become key to Democratic victories. The national party finally responded by expanding the social welfare programs initiated in the 1930s, and by legislating a battery of Great Society services, benefits, jobs and organizing resources. These inevitably provoked conflict with the white working class. Little wonder that white working-class voters on both sides of the Mason-Dixon line, their party allegiance in presidential contests already faltering, decided that the Democratic Party had deserted them, and so they deserted it.

None of this was lost on Republican strategists. The 1948 Dixiecrat revolt showed that Democratic troubles over race could be exploited; by the 1960s, some Republican strategists were trumpeting a new Republican majority that would begin with the realignment of white Southerners. When Republicans threw their support behind civil rights legislation they knew Southern whites would blame the Democrats. And as racial conflict flared in the North, Richard Nixon promoted affirmative action in the unionized construction trades with his "Philadelphia Plan," while his Justice Department pressed the courts for school busing plans. Later, with the overwhelming majority of Southern whites voting Republican in presidential contests and with Northern white working-class voters defecting in droves, Republicans adroitly shifted position by playing on white discontent over affirmative action and integration, as well as fear of crime and resentment of burgeoning means-tested welfare costs. In this more complicated sense, race is indeed—as the critics charge—a major reason the Democrats have been unable to win the presidency in a quarter-century, the post-Watergate election aside. Oddly, though, the critics have little to say about the Southern power brokers who crippled the Democratic Party's capacity to build a firm working-class base, or about the Republican power brokers who maneuvered to worsen racial divisions for partisan advantage.

Instead, it is blacks and liberals who are castigated for failing to devise a strategy that would avoid the shoals of racial conflict. Presumably, they should have crafted broader or universal demands so as to make possible an alliance with the white working class, divisive Republican stratagems notwithstanding. As a matter of historical fact, blacks and their allies did demand universalistic programs, and that was precisely the problem. They fought for integration in education, housing and jobs, as well as for the same political rights enjoyed by whites. And in response to those demands for a more universalistic society, many whites rose up in outrage and defected from the Democratic Party. The notion—virtually axiomatic among political and policy analysts—that universalistic demands avoid conflict is simply wrong.

Moreover, even as blacks made universalistic demands, what they often got instead were particularistic programs, even race-specific ones, designed by national Democratic politicians to avoid conflict with the white working class. Much of the Great Society legislation was fashioned to funnel services and benefits directly to black neighborhoods precisely to avoid arousing white ethnic resentments by challenging their control of municipal services and jobs. As it happened, that strategy was not entirely successful. When riots and other expressions of anger mounted in the ghettos, some of the Great Society programs became launching pads for protest, litigation and political mobilization against white domination in the big cities, which explains why critics who bemoan the resulting working-class rage and defections now define the "social engineering" of the Great Society as a disastrous policy error.

Nothing so incenses critics as the successful drives in the 1960s to gain more income for blacks through welfare. Blacks, they say, should have demanded full employment or universal income programs, such as children's allowances, instead. But this criticism fails to take account of the crippling policies inherited from the 1930s. Workers in the United States—struggling against both the business-dominated Republican Party and the Southern oligarchy—ended up with policies favoring low inflation rather than high employment, and with a system that rested on means-tested and work-conditioned rather than universal programs. Even so, agricultural workers were simply excluded from those programs. Consequently, when agricultural modernization in the South produced millions of unemployed after World War II, migrating blacks were not eligible for anything. They were not even eligible for welfare, which fended off applicants with state residence laws, employable-mother rules, suitable-home regulations, man-in-the-house provisions and bureaucratic rebuffs. Few benefits were given out until women began welfare rights protests in the mid-1960s.

We thought at the time that obtaining welfare benefits would be a gain for the mounting numbers of impoverished families in the big cities (and we have not changed our minds). Moreover, we thought rising welfare rolls, by producing fiscal strain and worsening racial tension, would prompt the national Democratic Party to federalize welfare in order to moderate this source of fiscal stress and internal conflict in its big-city coalitions. We were slightly off in this prediction: Congress instead relieved fiscal pressures at the local level by incorporating the old-age and disability categories into a new Supplemental Security Income program. Still, S.S.I. was the most significant reform of the means-tested programs since they were created by the Social Security Act of 1935.

In any case, critics seem to think that these impoverished women shouldn't have demanded welfare because white ethnics would be offended. They should have waited for the white working class to link arms in a fight for full employment or for universal income programs. But there was about as much chance of that happening as there was that Southern white workers would link arms with blacks in the struggle for desegregation and voting rights. The political truth is that blacks got what they got precisely because mass protest, by exacerbating divisions in the North/South and in big-city electoral coalitions, forced the Democratic Party to make voting-rights concessions intended to rebuild its strength in the South and social-program concessions intended to moderate conflict in the cities.

Chapter 135

Mississippi Abolishes Slavery

Reuters North American Wire Service

The following selection is reprinted from Reuters North American Wire Service's "Mississippi Votes to Abolish Slavery," 16 March 1995. Copyright © Reuters Limited 1995. Reprinted with permission.

Mississippi formally ratified the 13th Amendment to the U.S. Constitution Thursday, becoming the last state in the Union to approve the abolition of slavery.

Nearly 130 years after the 13th Amendment became law in the United States, the Mississippi House of Representatives voted unanimously and without discussion to approve the measure. The state Senate did likewise a month ago.

State officials said the bill now must be signed by the lieutenant governor and the House speaker. Mississippi Gov. Kirk Fordice's approval is not required.

"This does make a statement in terms of the progress this state has made and the direction it's taking," said state Sen. Hillman Frazier, a black Democrat from Jackson who authored the bill after discovering that Mississippi had not ratified the original amendment.

The Mississippi Legislature that rejected the 13th Amendment more than a century ago consisted of white lawmakers embittered by the Confederacy's defeat the previous year. They had demanded that former slave-owners receive compensation for slaves freed after the war.

The amendment abolishing slavery in the United States became law on Dec. 18, 1865, after being ratified by 27 of the 36 states which then existed.

Nine states, including Mississippi, Kentucky, Texas and Florida, either rejected the amendment or didn't act, in some cases because they had not yet been fully restored to the Union.

All of those states have since ratified the amendment, however. The last to do so before Mississippi was Kentucky, in 1976.

Of all Southern states, Mississippi has suffered most from a reputation for racial oppression.

It was among the last to abandon racial segregation laws in the 1960s and has been depicted in books, documentaries and Hollywood films as a hotbed of Ku Klux Klan activity.

Frazier said the latest initiative was helped along by press coverage, saying he has taken telephone calls from supporters around the world. "Once it received international attention, it had to pass or we would have looked silly," he said.

Chapter 136

Undercounting Minorities

Clarence Lusane

Clarence Lusane, a professor in the School of International Service at American University, is the author of Pipe Dream Blues: Racism and the War on Drugs *(1991),* African Americans at the Crossroads: The Restructuring of Black Leadership and the 1992 Elections *(1994), and* Race in the Global Era: African Americans at the Millennium *(1997).*

The following selection is reprinted from "Invisible Nation," Chicago Tribune, 3 September 1998. Copyright © 1998 Clarence Lusane. Reprinted with the permission of the author.

For another selection by Lusane, see chapter 152.

By fiat, there will be fewer African-Americans, Latinos, poor people, children and homeless people in the year 2000. That's the likely outcome of a recent decision by a three-judge panel to prevent the Census Bureau from using statistical sampling for the 2000 census.

On Aug. 24, the panel unanimously concluded, in response to a suit filed by congressional Republicans, that sampling violated the Census Act.

The census debate is deeply political. The results of the census decide how federal, state and local political districts are apportioned and how the political pie is sliced. The census determines funding for myriad federal programs, including energy assistance, child assistance and low-cost housing.

Traditionally, the census has undercounted the poor, children and people of color, thus depriving these groups of millions of dollars in federal aid. From 1940 to 1980, the census improved its methods. But the 1990 census, states the Census Bureau, was "the first in history to be less accurate than the previous one." The bureau admits it missed 5 percent of Hispanics, 4.4 percent of African-Americans, 3.1 percent of Asian Pacific Islanders and 12.2 percent of Native Americans on reservations. But it only missed 0.7 percent of non-Hispanic whites. An estimated 4 million people were double counted in the 1990 census in addition to the 8 million to 9 million who were missed.

To get a more accurate count, the Clinton administration supported a new method: statistical sampling. Instead of trying to count every head, the Census Bureau would use sophisticated statistical techniques to reduce cost, limit non-responsiveness and increase accuracy, particularly in the area of minority undercount. These same techniques are used to calculate the nation's unemployment rate and the gross national product.

Without sampling, the number of minority citizens enumerated in the 2000 census is likely to fall far short of the reality.

Part of the problem with head counting has to do with important demographic and social changes that make it more difficult to get an accurate reading of the black population.

Blacks are fleeing public housing. Some are being evicted. Others have to leave when their housing complexes are demolished. This is creating a nomadic subgroup of African-Americans that few have shown any willingness or capacity to track.

Many prisoners, especially African-Americans, are miscounted. Black prisoners are often warehoused in rural areas and counted in those populations rather than counted as part of urban enclaves where they usually live.

Children, disproportionately poor and of color, accounted for more than half of those not counted. The homeless and rural renters were also undercounted.

Despite these irregularities and problems, in 1996 the U.S. Supreme Court ruled in *Department of Commerce vs. New York* that the secretary of commerce did not have to adjust figures from the 1990 census. That decision meant that many communities across the nation did not receive their fair share of federal resources. In response, the Clinton administration proposed in 1997 that statistical sampling be employed in the 2000 census.

Since the poor and people of color tend to vote Democratic, the Republicans have opposed sampling. They have couched their arguments in constitutional terms, contending that "actual enumeration," as stated in Article 1 of the Constitution, means that the population must be counted one-by-one, and anything different from that is a constitutional violation. This assertion misinterprets the Constitution, which does not detail how the census enumeration is to occur. In any case, the United States has grown considerably and it has become impractical, if not impossible, to attempt to count the population one-by-one.

Carping by conservatives conflicts with the opinions of experts. A panel of scholars and researchers established by the National Academy of Sciences argued that not only should sampling occur, but that without it the 2000 census will be less accurate than the 1990 one.

An undercount of historic proportions appears upon the horizon for the 2000 census. Partisan bloodletting is once again drowning the hopes of inclusion for less privileged communities.[1]

EDITORS' NOTE

1. In January 1999, four months after the publication of this article, the Supreme Court ruled against the use of statistical sampling.

Chapter 137

The Color of Money

Public Campaign

Public Campaign is a nonprofit, nonpartisan organization working for compre-
hensive campaign finance reform. The following selection is reprinted from "'The
Color of Money': Groundbreaking Report Shows a World of Campaign Finance
as Separate and Unequal," 23 September 1998.
*   For a full copy of "The Color of Money" and more information on Public Cam-*
paign's Clean-Money proposals, see www.publicampaign.org or call 202/293-0222.

People of color are demonstrably absent from what has become one of the most
significant elements of the election process, namely campaign financing. This is
dramatically documented in a new study, "The Color of Money: Campaign Contributions and Race," released by Public Campaign today.

The analysis of who contributes to federal elections and who doesn't paints a
vivid and disturbing portrait of two societies: the vast majority of campaign contributions came from areas that are primarily white and wealthy, effectively disenfranchising most people of color.

"It should be the people and not the almighty dollar that speak on election day.
Public Campaign's report on the 'Color of Money' shows that now, more than
ever, there is a need to reform our system of campaign financing to ensure that one
person, one vote remains a fundamental principle of our democratic process," said
U.S. Representative John Lewis (D–GA).

"These data are enlightening. They remind us that the goal of achieving a truly
democratic system—where each political proposal will be judged on its merit and
the strength of ideas—will likely remain out of reach until we change the current
campaign finance system that now allows policy decisions to be shaped by the relative influence of political patrons who line up on opposite sides of an issue," said
U.S. Rep. Luis Gutierrez (D–IL).

"These findings are significant because in today's election process, those who
can afford to give the most money to campaigns are those who have the most influence over our government and our policies," said Ellen Miller, executive director of Public Campaign. "The world of campaign finance is as segregated as any
other area of American society. In this case, those who cannot afford to give
money are effectively shut out of the political process."

Using data from the 1990 census, together with data on contributions for the 1995–1996 federal election cycle, the report compares zip codes that are the leading sources of campaign money to zip codes where people of color reside for all 50 states. The report also takes a more in-depth look at the ten "top giving" cities (Washington, DC; New York City; Los Angeles; Chicago; Boston; Atlanta; Detroit; Houston; San Francisco; and Philadelphia). In state after state and city after city, maps showing where the bulk of campaign contributions come from compared to where people of color live are almost photo-negatives of each other.

The people who donate to campaigns (primarily white and wealthy) live in one set of neighborhoods, while those who cannot afford to contribute money—including most people of color—primarily live in another set of neighborhoods.

People of color represented in this report include African American, Latino, Asian American and Native American populations. While there are people of color who do participate in the campaign finance system, just as there are many white people who do not, the disparity between those who overwhelmingly comprise the donor class and people of color is too great to ignore.

The 100,000 residents of just one elite zip code in Manhattan (10021) gave nearly twice as much money as the 9.5 million residents of all the zip codes throughout the country in which people of color comprise well over half of the population (483 zip codes). For every $86.72 that New Yorkers living in this exclusive area contributed, 59 cents was contributed by people living in the 483 zip codes.

The 26 zip code areas nationwide that, together, provided the most money in the 1995–1996 election cycle contributed approximately the same amount as the nearly 2,500 zip codes in which over half the population is people of color ($67,088,583 compared to $66,359,620). Meanwhile, the combined population of the 2,500 zip codes in which there are a majority people of color is 60 times greater (41,393,028) than the combined population of the 26 elite zip codes (686,075).

In the Los Angeles area, the two per capita contributions we calculated provide one of the most dramatic comparisons between the city's highest contributing zip code (90067), and the adjacent 46 zips with majority-minority populations: 90067 residents gave an average of nearly $900 each, while those in the majority-minority areas gave 97 cents apiece.

In the context of today's election campaigns, money is a critical element in determining who runs and wins. In the 1996 elections, 92 percent of the House races and 88 percent of the Senate races were won by the candidate who spent the most money. According to the Center for Responsive Politics, it cost candidates $673,739 on average to win a House seat in that election and $4.7 million on average to win a Senate seat in that election.

As Public Campaign releases its report nationally, more than 20 states nationwide are holding their own events and releasing state data as part of a "National Week of Action" from September 21–27 focusing on the link between the historic struggle to win the right to vote and the current struggle to get private money out of politics. This kind of campaign finance reform is viewed by many as a crucial next step in the voting rights movement.

Campaign contribution data for the report includes individual campaign contributions (of $200 or more) to federal candidates, political parties and political action committees (PACs) for the 1995–1996 election cycle, and was obtained from the Center for Responsive Politics. The United States Census Bureau provided data for populations by zip code, including racial composition.[1]

EDITORS' NOTE

1. For a discussion of campaign finance reform, see chapter 182.

Discrimination
Ongoing Examples

Chapter 138

The Possessive Investment in Whiteness

George Lipsitz

George Lipsitz, professor of ethnic studies at the University of California, San Diego, is the author of Time Passages: Collective Memory and American Popular Culture *(1990)*, Rainbow at Midnight: Labor and Culture in the 1940s *(1994), and* A Life in the Struggle: Ivory Perry and the Culture of Opposition *(1995).*

The following selection is excerpted and reprinted from the introduction and chapter 2 of The Possessive Investment in Whiteness: How People Profit from Identity Politics *by George Lipsitz by permission of Temple University Press. Copyright © 1998 by Temple University. All Rights Reserved.*

For another selection by Lipsitz, see chapter 173.

[B]oth public policy and private prejudice have created a "possessive investment in whiteness" that is responsible for the racialized hierarchies of our society. I use the term "possessive investment" both literally and figuratively. Whiteness has a cash value: it accounts for advantages that come to individuals through profits made from housing secured in discriminatory markets, through the unequal educations allocated to children of different races, through insider networks that channel employment opportunities to the relatives and friends of those who have profited most from present and past racial discrimination, and especially through intergenerational transfers of inherited wealth that pass on the spoils of discrimination to succeeding generations. I argue that white Americans are encouraged to invest in whiteness to remain true to an identity that provides them with resources, power and opportunity. . . .

I hope it is clear that opposing whiteness is not the same as opposing white people. White supremacy is an equal opportunity employer; nonwhite people can become active agents of white supremacy as well as passive participants in its hierarchies and rewards. One way of becoming an insider is by participating in the exclusion of other outsiders. An individual might even secure a seat on the Supreme Court on this basis. On the other hand, if not every white supremacist is white, it follows that not all white people have to become complicit with white supremacy, that there is an element of choice in all of this. White people always have the option of becoming antiracist, although not enough have done so. We do not choose our color, but we do choose our commitments. We do not choose our parents, but we do choose our politics. Yet we do not make these decisions in a vacuum; they occur within a social structure that gives value to whiteness and offers rewards for racism. . . .

Because American society has not acknowledged the ways in which we have created a possessive investment in whiteness, the disadvantages of racial minorities may seem unrelated to the advantages given to whites. Minority disadvantages are said to stem from innate deficiencies, rather than from systematic disenfranchisement and discrimination. Especially since the passage of the 1964 and 1965 Civil Rights Acts, the dominant discourse in our society argues that the problems facing communities of color no longer stem primarily from discrimination but from the characteristics of those communities themselves, from unrestrained sexual behavior and childbirths out of wedlock, crime, welfare dependency, and a perverse sense of group identity and group entitlement that stands in the way of individual achievement and advancement.

In this regard, it is vital to look at the actual record of civil rights laws and their enforcement. Contrary to their stated intentions, civil rights laws have actually augmented the possessive investment in whiteness, not because civil rights legislation is by nature unwise or impractical, but because these particular laws were structured to be ineffective and largely unenforceable. The conservatives are not wrong when they attribute the problems facing aggrieved racial minorities to a crisis of values, rampant violations of law and order, and pernicious group politics. But by projecting these negative judgments onto minority individuals and groups, they evade the fact that the history of the past five decades demonstrates that the most fanatical group politics, the most flagrant violations of the law, and the vilest evasions of responsible and moral behavior have been enacted by whites. Massive white opposition to the implementation (rather than the mere articulation) of antidiscrimination statutes stands as a stunning indictment of the character of European Americans and shows how the racial problem in the United States remains at heart a white problem. At every stage over the past fifty years, whites have responded to civil rights laws with coordinated collective politics characterized by resistance, refusal, and renegotiation.

Fair Housing

In 1890, San Francisco's board of supervisors passed an ordinance mandating the removal of Chinese Americans from neighborhoods ripe for redevelopment close to downtown. The law ordered their resettlement in isolated industrial areas of the city filled with waste dumps and other environmental hazards. Although overturned by the courts, the San Francisco Segregation Ordinance of 1890 prefigured laws in other cities aimed mainly at preventing racial minorities (especially African Americans) from moving into houses on blocks where whites were the majority of the homeowners. All across the nation in the years immediately before World War I, city governments put the force of law behind residential segregation through racial zoning. When the Supreme Court declared these ordinances unconstitutional in 1917, real estate brokers, political leaders, and bankers turned to restrictive covenants and other private deed restrictions to prevent integration and consequently enhance the material rewards of whiteness.

Between 1924 and 1950 realtors throughout the United States subscribed to a national code that bound them to the view that "a realtor should never be instrumental in introducing into a neighborhood a character of property or occupancy, members of any race or nationality, or any individual whose presence will clearly be detrimental to property values in the neighborhood." Local codes were even more explicit in excluding "detrimental" groups from white neighborhoods.

Mob violence and vigilante action accompanied the legal sanctioning of segregation in many places. As evidenced in the important scholarship of Thomas Sugrue and Arnold Hirsch, northern whites especially succeeded in preserving racially exclusive neighborhoods during the 1940s and 1950s through mob actions that went largely unpunished by law enforcement authorities afraid to challenge crimes enacted on behalf of the possessive investment in whiteness. Most of the time violence was not needed to preserve segregation because restrictive covenants achieved the same ends through peaceful although still coercive means. As private agreements written into deed restrictions on the resale of property, restrictive covenants satisfied the courts and effectively constricted the housing market for groups subject to discrimination, while providing an artificially inflated equity for those practicing it. African American community organizations, who took the lead in opposing restrictive covenants in the courts, attained partial success in 1948 when the Supreme Court ruled in *Shelley v. Kraemer* that state courts who enforced these deed restrictions against the will of buyers and sellers violated the Constitution. Yet even while acknowledging the unfairness of restrictive covenants, the Court's decision provided justification, legitimation, and guidance for resisting racial desegregation. Although it prevented states from enforcing restrictive covenants on their own, it did not make it illegal for property owners to adhere to them voluntarily, and it did not ban the registration of restrictive covenants with local authorities. This meant that people denied the opportunity to buy a home (and thus accumulate assets) because of a restrictive covenant had to initiate legal action and bear the complete cost and burden of securing justice themselves.

When the courts ruled on behalf of minorities, white resistance grew into outright refusal. After the Supreme Court decision in *Shelley v. Kraemer,* the FHA persisted in its policy of recommending and even requiring restrictive covenants as a condition for receiving government-secured home loans. White home owners, realtors, and bankers realized that restrictive covenants could remain in force despite *Shelley v. Kraemer* and, more important, that the ruling did nothing to challenge the other major mechanisms for real estate discrimination, including redlining (denying loans to areas inhabited by racial minorities), steering (directing minority buyers solely to homes in minority neighborhoods), and block busting (playing on the white fear of a change in neighborhood racial balance to promote panic sales, getting whites to sell their homes for small amounts and then selling those same homes to minority buyers at extremely high prices).

In the wake of *Shelley v. Kraemer,* resistance and refusal to desegregate the private housing market helped preserve the possessive investment in whiteness for white home owners for the next twenty years. In the life of a nation, twenty years is not long, but in the lives of individuals, twenty years of rights denied can have devastating effects—inhibiting their accumulation of assets, depriving them of the increased equity that comes with home ownership, and devaluating the assets that they might have passed on to their children. Resistance and refusal preserved the possessive investment in whiteness and forced those excluded from its benefits to try to renegotiate the issue of residential segregation through other channels.

In the presidential election of 1960, African American voters in key northern cities provided the crucial margin that elected John F. Kennedy. Afraid to challenge the segregationists in his own party who held key positions in Congress, Kennedy attempted to respond to minority demands for fair housing by issuing his own executive orders, especially Order 11063 that required government agencies to oppose discrimination in federally supported housing. Once again, white resistance rather than compliance was the order of the day. Federal officials quickly realized that the president would not object if they simply did not communicate his order to local housing authorities. The FHA even refused to apply Executive Order 11063 to its own loans, even though that agency ran the largest federally supported housing program.

White resistance to Kennedy's executive order reflected and exacerbated popular support among whites for racial discrimination. In 1964, California voters overwhelmingly supported a referendum repealing that state's fair-housing law. California governor Edmund G. "Pat" Brown, who supported the open-housing law, later admitted he "was completely out of tune with the white citizens of the state who felt that the right to sell their property to whomever they wanted was a privileged right, a right of ownership, a constitutional right." These acts of resistance and refusal forced a renegotiation of the legal status of open-housing laws. The 1964 Civil Rights Act specifically exempted federal mortgage insurance programs from antidiscrimination requirements—a stipulation that virtually guaranteed the continuation of discrimination in home lending. When Lyndon Johnson asked Congress to pass a fair-housing bill in 1966, his request produced "some of the most vicious mail LBJ received on any subject," according to White House aide Joseph Califano (and Johnson certainly received more than his share of hate mail on a variety of subjects). Republican minority leader Everett Dirksen attacked the proposed 1966 bill with particular relish, claiming that white opposition to fair housing stemmed not from whites' racial prejudice but from blacks' bad behavior when they moved into white areas. The House of Representatives passed a bill that accomplished the opposite of what Johnson had requested, acknowledging the "right" of individuals to discriminate in selling their homes and to require their realtors to discriminate as well. Martin Luther King, Jr., and other civil rights leaders argued that the bill was not worth passing, and only a filibuster by its opponents in the Senate prevented it from becoming law.

The death of Dr. King in 1968—and the riots that erupted in its wake—forced another renegotiation of fair-housing issues twenty years after *Shelley v. Kraemer.*

When Congress finally passed a comprehensive fair-housing law, it actually encouraged white resistance through provisions that rendered it virtually unenforceable. Title VIII of the Fair Housing Act authorized the Department of Housing and Urban Development to investigate complaints made directly to the HUD secretary but forbade that agency to initiate investigations on its own. The act gave the HUD secretary only thirty days to process complaints and to decide if action was warranted, but even if the agency pursued cases, it had no enforcement power and could only encourage the party guilty of discrimination to accept "conference, conciliation, and persuasion." In rare instances, HUD could refer cases to the attorney general for legal action, but Title VIII authorized action by the Justice Department only when cases "raised an issue of general public importance" or revealed "a pattern or practice" of discrimination. Denial of an individual's constitutional rights was not considered serious enough for action in this realm. People faced with discrimination in the housing market were required to file suit within 180 days of the alleged discriminatory act or within 30 days of the end of mediation. This meant that people suffering from violations of their rights had to bring action on their own behalf, hire their own attorneys, pay their own legal fees and court costs, and bear the burden of proof to establish that "serious" acts of discrimination had indeed taken place. After all that, the act restricted punitive damages in clear-cut cases of discrimination to a maximum of $1,000.

Surely the contours of the 1968 Fair Housing Act make it unique in the annals of legal discourse. As Patricia Roberts Harris noted when she served as secretary of housing and urban development during the Carter administration, there are very few incidents of law breaking where authorities cannot punish the lawbreakers but instead may only ask if the law breaker wishes to talk about the matter with the victim. Despite its palpable weaknesses, however, the 1968 law provoked thousands of complaints about housing discrimination each year, which foundered on the opportunities for resistance and refusal built into the act itself. During the 1970s fewer than 30 percent of the complaints filed with HUD led to mediation, and close to 50 percent of those remained in noncompliance. A study conducted in 1980 demonstrated that only slightly more than one-third of the complaints to HUD led to voluntary consent agreements, and half of those were settled in favor of the party accused of discrimination. As of 1980, only five victims of discrimination have received damages in excess of $3,500. By 1986, the antidiscrimination mechanisms established in the 1968 law had led to decisions on only about four hundred fair-housing cases. Subsequent changes have strengthened aspects of the enforcement and punitive mechanisms of the law, but even today most experts estimate more than two million cases of housing discrimination occur every year without legal action being taken against them.

The process of resistance, refusal, and renegotiation that plagued fair-housing efforts from *Shelley v. Kraemer* through the 1968 Fair Housing Act was not an aberration; it has characterized every judicial, legislative, and executive effort on behalf of open housing for the past fifty years. For example, when plaintiffs filed suit in federal court charging racial discrimination by Chicago's public-housing authority in the 1960s, a federal judge initially skeptical of their claims eventually found the housing authority guilty in 1969. He ordered the city to construct seven hundred new units of public housing in white neighborhoods and to locate 75 percent of new public housing outside the inner-city ghetto. The Chicago Housing Authority resisted this order initially and, when finally faced with the necessity of compliance, responded by ceasing construction of all new public housing as a means of evading integration.

Similarly, the St. Louis suburb of Black Jack reincorporated and changed its zoning laws in 1970 in order to block construction of a low- and middle-income integrated housing development. Secretary of Housing and Urban Development George Romney filed a lawsuit against the municipality in federal court, as he was required to do by law, but Attorney General John Mitchell intervened in order to protect Black Jack's resistance to desegregation by ordering Romney to drop the suit. The executive branch put even more clout behind this resistance when President Nixon announced he would suspend enforcement of all civil rights laws for a year while his staff studied the situation. Over that year, hundreds of grants were approved by the government without seeing if they complied with federal civil rights laws. Nixon conceded that denying housing to people because of their race was wrong, but he added that he found it equally wrong for cities opposed to federally assisted (and therefore integrated) housing to "have it imposed from Washington by bureaucratic fiat." Nixon's tactic of affirming support for integration in the abstract while acting to undermine the mechanisms that made it possible in practice became a standard response among white politicians to desegregation demands during the civil rights and post–civil rights eras. These politicians soon discovered that their obstructionism made them tremendously popular among white voters.

White resistance manifested as refusal to abide by fair-housing laws continued to guide federal policy in the 1970s and 1980s. A survey conducted by HUD in the 1970s disclosed that black "testers" sent out to inquire about housing for rent or sale received less information than white testers on housing for sale 15 percent of the time, and they received less information than white testers about the availability of rental housing 27 percent of the time. As late as 1970, officials of the Federal Home Loan Bank Board redlined postal zip code areas where the black population was increasing. Training manuals designed for use by private appraisers in 1977 continued to describe desirable neighborhoods as "100 percent Caucasian" along with the phrase "without adverse effects from minorities." Yet federal and state officials remained virtually inactive in the enforcement of fair-housing laws.

Because white resistance and refusal has always led to renegotiation of the terms of open housing, every triumph by fair-housing advocates has turned out to be an empty victory. For example, opponents of the racially unequal consequences of urban renewal won a long-sought victory in 1970 with the passage of the Uniform Relocation Assistance and Real Property Acquisition Act, which mandated for the first time that local housing authorities replace the low-income units they destroy (most often occupied by racial minorities). Congress responded by eliminating the urban renewal program altogether, replacing it with community development block grants that emphasized luxury housing for upper-and middle-class home owners. In St. Louis, the city evicted five hundred families (almost all of them African American) from the Pershing Waterman Redevelopment area, gave $5.8 million in tax abatements to developers, demolished nine buildings at city expense, secured $1.4 million in federal block grant funds, and sold 106 parcels of land to the developers for $122 per parcel. Yet because the Pershing Redevelopment Company was a private enterprise, and because the funding came from block grants rather than urban renewal funds, none of the dislocated families received a single dollar in relocation assistance.

Similarly, Congress passed the Equal Credit Opportunity Act in 1974, which expressly prohibited discrimination in real estate lending, requiring banks to record the racial identities of applicants rejected and accepted for loans. When bankers refused to collect the required data, ten civil rights groups filed suit in 1976, asking the courts to order the comptroller of the currency, the Federal Deposit Insurance Corporation (FDIC), and the Home Loan Bank Board to obey the 1974 law. These agencies did sign a court order agreeing to collect the required materials, but the comptroller of the currency and the FDIC ceased keeping records based on race in 1981 when the court order expired. Home Loan Bank Board records revealed that blacks continued to face rejection rates several times higher than those encountered by white applicants. Having resisted the law initially, the federal agencies complied with the law for a short time when compelled to do so by a court order, then reverted to absolute refusal.

Advocates of fair housing attempted to renegotiate the issue with the passage of the 1975 Home Mortgage Disclosure Act and the 1977 Community Investment Act. These bills required lenders to identify which neighborhoods received their home-improvement and mortgage loans, and to demonstrate their willingness to supply capital to worthy borrowers in low-income areas. If enforced, these acts might have made a substantial difference, but the Reagan administration rendered them moot by ignoring the law. Reagan's appointee as director of the Justice Department's Civil Rights Division, William Bradford Reynolds, filed only two housing discrimination suits in his first twenty months in office, a distinct drop from the average of thirty-two cases a year filed during the Nixon and Ford presidencies or even the nineteen per year during the final two years of the Carter administration.

When the number of housing discrimination complaints filed with HUD doubled, the Reagan Justice Department neglected nearly every serious complaint and initiated frivolous suits against plans that maintained integrated housing and prevented block busting by regulating the racial balance in housing developments. For example, the administration took action aimed at invalidating deed restrictions in one of the few genuinely integrated areas of Houston, the Houston Oaks subdivision, because the original deeds contained restrictive covenants (which were neither enforced nor honored by the residents). The administration also used the Paperwork Reduction Act as an excuse to stop HUD from gathering data on the racial identities of participants in its housing programs. By refusing to gather data on true discrimination, the Reagan administration strengthened resistance to fair-housing laws to the point of encouraging outright refusal to obey them.

Precisely because of white resistance to desegregation, the subsidized housing program had the highest percentage of black recipients of any federal benefits program—38.5 percent in 1979. In 1980, language in an amendment to the Housing and Community Development Act would have allowed local housing authorities to address directly the urgent housing situation of racial minorities by designating housing for those in greatest need, but the Reagan administration came to power shortly afterwards and made the victory a hollow one by virtually eliminating all federal funding for subsidized housing—from $26.1 billion in 1981 to $2.1 billion in 1985. While cutting allocations for these programs aimed at providing simple subsistence and income maintenance for a primarily black clientele, the Reagan administration retained the home owner mortgage deduction, a federal housing policy more costly to the government but one that helps a primarily white clientele accumulate assets.

The 1988 Fair Housing Amendments Act, which addressed many important shortcomings in previous fair-housing legislation, came at a time when high housing prices kept many people of color out of the market. In addition, housing in the United States has become so hypersegregated, loan procedures so discriminatory, and enforcement of fair-housing laws so infrequent that federal law acknowledging the rights of all people to secure housing on a fair basis may have no effect on their ability to actually do so. Whites who became home owners under blatantly discriminatory circumstances condoned and protected by the judicial, legislative, and executive branches of government have also become more formidable competitors for housing, as value of their homes has increased as a result of appreciation and inflation. Median prices on new homes and on sales of existing homes increased by almost 230 percent between 1970 and 1985, while the consumer price index rose by 177 percent.

The possessive investment in whiteness generated by failure to enforce fair-housing legislation has concrete costs for people of color. Melvin Oliver and Tom Shapiro estimate that discrimination in the home loan industry alone costs black homeowners $10.5 billion in extra payments, and that every black home owner is deprived of nearly $4,000 as a result of the 54 percent higher rate they pay on home mortgages. The costs for those who cannot enter the housing market, and who consequently neither build equity nor qualify for the home owners' tax deduction, is, of course, much higher. The appreciated value of owner-occupied homes constitutes the single greatest source of wealth for white Americans. It is the factor most responsible for the disparity between blacks and whites in respect to wealth—a disparity between the two groups much greater than their differences in income. It is the basis for intergenerational transfers of wealth that enable white parents to give their children financial advantages over the children of other groups. Housing plays a crucial role in determining educational opportunities as well, because school funding based on property tax assessments in most localities gives better opportunities to white children than to children from minority communities. Opportunities for employment are also affected by housing choices, especially given the location of new places of employment in suburbs and reduced funding for public transportation. In addition, housing affects health conditions, with environmental and health hazards disproportionately located in minority communities.

Whiteness has a value in our society. Its value originates not in the wisdom of white home buyers or the improvements they have made on their property, but from the ways in which patterns of bad faith and nonenforcement of antidiscrimination laws have enabled the beneficiaries of past and present discrimination to protect their gains and pass them on to succeeding generations. These benefits stem directly from the pattern of resistance, refusal, and renegotiation that white individuals and their elected representatives have fashioned in response to antidiscrimination legislation. If these dynamics applied only to housing, they would be damaging enough, but the same process of resistance, refusal, and renegotiation has characterized the history of antidiscrimination legislation and court rulings in education and employment as well.

School Desegregation

Unequal opportunities for education play a crucial role in racializing life chances in the United States. Just as the 1948 *Shelley v. Kraemer* decision and the 1968 Fair Housing Act are often credited incorrectly with ending discrimination in housing, the Supreme Court's 1954 ruling in *Brown v. Board of Education* is widely acknowledged as the turning point in ending school segregation. Yet once again, mere articulation of antidiscrimination principles did not lead to their implementation. Like laws against discrimination in housing, official policies designed to end segregated education have been consistently undermined and defeated by white resistance and refusal.

The 1954 *Brown* case culminated sixteen years of school desegregation lawsuits filed by the NAACP and other civil rights and community groups. In that decision, the Court conceded that government bodies had played a crucial role in promoting and preserving racial differences by limiting black students to separate and therefore inherently unequal educations. Yet while ruling against de jure segregation in the abstract, the decision provided no means for dismantling the structures that crafted advantages for white students out of the disadvantages of students of color. The plaintiffs in *Brown* sought more for their children than physical proximity to whites; they pursued desegregation as a means of securing for black students the same educational resources and opportunities routinely provided to whites. The *Brown* decision helped frustrate their aims, however, because it outlawed only one technique of inequality—de jure segregation—without addressing the ways in which discrimination in housing, employment, and access to public services enabled whites to resegregate the schools by moving to suburban districts. In addition, as Cheryl I. Harris argues, by ordering implementation of its decision "with all deliberate speed," the Supreme Court in *Brown I* and *Brown II* allowed for more deliberation than speed. The Court allowed the white perpetrators of discrimination "to control, manage, postpone, and if necessary, thwart change." . . .

Failure to enforce civil rights laws banning discrimination in housing, education, and hiring, along with efforts to undermine affirmative action and other remedies designed to advance the cause of social justice, renders racism structural and institutional rather than private and personal. Whites may or may not be openly racist in their personal decisions or private interactions with others, but they nonetheless benefit systematically from the structural impediments to minority access to quality housing, schools, and jobs. Michael Omi makes a useful distinction between "referential" racism (the snarling, sneering, cross-burning displays of antipathy toward minorities) and "inferential" racism (a system of structured inequality that allows white people to remain self-satisfied and smug about their own innocence). Inferential racism allows whites to disown Louisiana politician David Duke or Los Angeles Police Department detective Mark Fuhrman as individual "racists" (although Duke has twice received the majority of white votes in statewide elections and Fuhrman appeared frequently on talk shows and placed a book on the best-seller list after escaping jail time for his acts of perjury in the O. J. Simpson case), while assuming that the houses they own, the schools they attend, and the jobs they hold come to them exclusively on the basis of individual merit.

Chapter 139

Discrimination and Racism Continue

John Conyers, Jr.

Representative John Conyers, Jr. (D–MI) has been the Representative for the First U.S. Congressional District of Michigan since 1965.

The following selection is reprinted from "We're Not There Yet: Assault on Affirmative Action Ignores the Fact That Discrimination and Racism Continue," Roll Call, *16 June 1997. Reprinted with permission of Roll Call, Inc.*

For another selection by Conyers, see chapter 131.

Over the last several years, we have witnessed a full-scale assault on affirmative action programs. In 1995, the Supreme Court, in *Adarand v. Pena,* held that consideration of race or ethnicity in federal affirmative action initiatives was subject to the highest level of judicial scrutiny and was only permitted if narrowly tailored to serve a compelling interest.

In California last fall, voters passed Proposition 209, banning affirmative action with regard to race, sex, or ethnicity in public employment, education, or contracting. Last year's Fifth Circuit decision in *Hopwood v. Texas* has been construed as preventing public colleges from taking race into account in admission criteria, while a similar limitation was imposed on the University of California system by its Board of Regents.

And in Congress, measures such as last year's Dole-Canady bill would prevent the federal government from using race or gender in any program or initiative, ending more than 30 years of bipartisan progress and cooperation concerning civil rights.

Current Evidence of Discrimination

The premise behind this unprecedented assault is that the need for affirmative action has lapsed as discrimination in our society has supposedly receded. However, a review of the evidence clearly indicates that discrimination continues to be persistent and widespread.

While the nature of racism and discrimination has changed—moving from a de jure form in the 1950s, when segregation was openly sanctioned, to the more subtle, de facto form of the 1990s, when discrimination is abhorred in theory but frequently practiced, often in disguise—the continual existence is undeniable, notwithstanding the speeches hailing a "colorblind" society. As retired Gen. Colin Powell stated regarding the California initiative, "My concern with Proposition 209 is that it essentially says we're there—that there's no longer any need to take [color and gender] into consideration. I don't think our rhetoric has yet matched our reality."

Employment

In November 1995, the bipartisan Glass Ceiling Commission found that 95 percent of top corporate jobs in America are held by white males, with African-Americans holding less than 1 percent of top management jobs and women holding 3 to 5 percent of senior-level positions. Black unemployment was also found to be twice that of white unemployment.

The commission also found that African-Americans and women continue to be paid less than their white counterparts for comparable work, with African-American women earning only 60 percent of the amount earned by white males. Tester programs have consistently shown that when black and white job candidates with identical resumes apply for the same job, the white candidates are overwhelmingly more successful in obtaining interviews and ultimately jobs.

Just this year, we learned of discriminatory conduct at Texaco Corporation, including tapes of top management officials referring to African-American workers as "black jelly beans."

We have also recently seen the likes of Donald Rochon, a black FBI agent who arrived at work each day to discover racial epithets and death threats posted on his desk. We discovered that federal agents from the Bureau of Alcohol, Tobacco & Firearms participate in the "Good Ol' Boys" weekend outings, which ritualize racism and deify the Ku Klux Klan. At the same time, we have seen a proliferation of serious and credible class action suits brought against the FBI, the ATF, the Immigration and Naturalization Service, and other agencies.

Housing

Tester programs by the Urban Institute and others confirm that whites are far more likely to be shown apartments and other rental units than similarly situated minorities. In addition, racial intolerance and violence has become all too commonplace in many communities.

For example, last year an African-American woman and her children were driven out of their new home in a white Philadelphia neighborhood. In addition to graffiti smeared over her home, racial epithets chanted outside her window, and the flying of the Confederate flag by one of her neighbors, the woman received a letter threatening the lives of her family if she did not move out, which she eventually did.

Education

For the first time since the decision in *Brown v. Board of Education,* our public schools are becoming increasingly segregated by race. A recent Harvard study found that from 1968 to 1994, there are "clear signs that . . . the nation is headed backwards to a greater segregation of black students" and that Latino students "now experience more isolation from whites and more concentration in high-poverty schools than any other group of students."

A 1995 report by the Southern Education Foundation found that not one of 12 states that formally administered segregated universities or colleges can demonstrate an "acceptable level of success in desegregating its higher education system."

Unequal access to education plays an important role in creating and perpetuating economic disparities. In 1993, less than 3 percent of college graduates were unemployed, but whereas 22.6 percent of whites had college degrees, only 12.2 percent of African-American and 9 percent of Hispanics did.

Justice

The situation is no different in our criminal justice system. It is not commonly known that white Americans account for more than half of the crack/cocaine use but only 4 percent of the federal prosecutions for the offense. Only 38 percent of crack users are black, but they represent nearly nine out of every ten prosecutions.

Studies of the Minnesota federal courts' practices found that black defendants awaiting trial on federal charges are held in jail at a far higher rate than whites.

Scores of African-Americans—including black police officers, prominent athletes and actors, and Members of Congress—have experienced the humiliation of being stopped for no other reason than the alleged traffic violation sometimes referred to as "driving while black." Maryland police statistics show that 73 percent of cars stopped and searched on I-95 between Baltimore and Delaware since January 1995 were operated by African-Americans, despite the fact that only 14 percent of those driving along that stretch were black.

Reactionary Responses

The responses to the perceived excesses of affirmative action remedies are tantamount to "throwing out the baby with the bath water." Eliminating the ability of admissions offices to take race into account in fostering a diverse student body has brought about a radical re-segregation of our public universities.

African-American admissions to UCLA's law school have dropped by 80 percent; UC Berkeley's has dropped by 75 percent. In the wake of *Hopwood*, the University of Texas Law School faces the specter of having no African-Americans in its first year class in 1997.

Although the constitutionality of Proposition 209 is still subject to appeal, it is not difficult to understand why the district court threw it out. The law targets minorities by making it almost impossible for harmed individuals and groups to obtain relief from insidious, persistent discrimination. And while other groups can seek recourse for wrongs through their state legislators, only minorities will be effectively barred from seeking any remedies for discrimination in the political process because of the state constitutional enshrinement.

If, for example, a state agency were to engage in widespread "pattern and practice" discrimination against Hispanic employees, it would be nearly impossible to obtain a group-wide remedy for those workers with Proposition 209 in place.

Last year's Dole-Canady bill is far to the right of the Reagan-Bush civil rights agenda. This draconian bill—expected to be reintroduced shortly—would have prevented the federal government from ever taking into account race or gender as a remedy to ongoing discrimination. The legislation goes well beyond *Adarand* by banning the use of goals and timetables, even where they are narrowly tailored to serve a compelling interest.

Even relief that was limited to the goal of bringing excluded minorities into a pool from which applicants would be selected without regard to race or gender—such as the successful outreach programs that have been used by the armed services—would be banned under the Dole-Canady bill.

It is for these reasons, among others, that Powell has strongly opposed efforts to end affirmative action, reminding us in that context that he "was not the first person who had the potential. I was the first person who came along after the government had secured our right to equal treatment and affirmative action so I could be measured by my performance and not by the color of my skin."

The Dole-Canady bill would also gut Executive Order 11246 encouraging federal contractors to remedy discrimination and promote diversity with goals. The executive order has enormous support in the business community and has brought the progress of diversity into the federal market place. Originally ordered by President Lyndon Johnson in 1965, this federal policy has won the support of every subsequent President, including Presidents Nixon, Ford, Reagan, and Bush.

Dole-Canady would also have ended every program designed to cure ongoing discrimination against women, including ending the Small Business Administration program helping women get even a modest share of federal contracts of which they have previously been locked out. Even worse, the bill would overturn decades of well-settled Title VII law concerning sex discrimination, and it would open the door to intentional discrimination against women in contracting.

As a matter of law, Dole-Canady would effectively prohibit the federal government from designing group remedies to respond to blatant and persistent racism. And because it goes so far as to block implementation of court-ordered or consensual remedies for the deprivation of constitutional rights, it would raise serious equal-protection and other constitutional issues.

Stop "Playing Race Card"

The reality is that we are a nation that was literally born into inequality. Almost 100 years later, it took a bloody civil war to finally end formal slavery. Women were not granted the right to vote until the ratification of the 19th Amendment in 1920 [see chapter 58—*Eds.*]. And it wasn't until the 1954 *Brown v. Board* decision that the absurd concept of separate but equal schools was discarded, with private discrimination continuing to be legal for another decade. So we shouldn't be at all surprised that racism and discrimination continue to be "our national curse."

The real question facing Congress today is which one of two directions will we take amid compelling evidence of ongoing bias. Since the advent of Republican control of the House, there has been virtually no scrutiny of the problem of discrimination, but rather only of the problems of remedying discrimination. Rather than moving us in the direction of fairness, integration, and equality—the direction which even Presidents Nixon, Ford, Reagan, and Bush often moved—the current GOP Congressional agenda seeks to move us in the direction of the *Hopwood* decision and Proposition 209.

Instead of continually scrutinizing perceived defects in remedies to discrimination, we need to examine the persistent, invidious, intractable, and often disguised nature of race and gender discrimination that is an undeniable fact in America today. In any one year, there are more than 90,000 discrimination-based complaints, and litigation can only respond to a small fraction of the abuses.

We need to ask ourselves if we are willing to backtrack to the pre-*Brown* era, when the races faced starkly different and unequal worlds. Just as the Jim Crow laws hastened an era of state-sanctioned segregation, today's assault on affirmative action could hearken a period of de facto segregation. Instead of "playing the race card," we need to work together as a nation to build upon our diversity and truly eradicate our legacy of discrimination.

Chapter 140

Education's "Savage Inequalities"

Steven Wishnia

Steven Wishnia, a senior editor for High Times, *has written for the* Nation, *the* Village Voice, *and* Musician *magazines. He is currently completing a collection of short stories.*

The following selection is reprinted from "Kozol: Kids Damned to 'Savage Inequalities,'" Guardian, *9 October 1991. Reprinted by permission of the author.*

In 1965, Jonathan Kozol was fired from his job as a fourth-grade teacher in Boston for "curriculum deviation"—reading poems by Langston Hughes and Robert Frost that weren't in the official syllabus.

Death at an Early Age, his book about his experiences in the city's ghetto schools, depicted an educational netherworld: classes held in a crumbling auditorium, with one child nearly decapitated when a jerry-rigged blackboard collapsed; ancient, racist textbooks; teachers who dismissed the children as hopelessly ignorant, and a frail, disturbed 8-year-old beaten in the basement almost weekly by teachers with bamboo whips.

Twenty-five years later, Kozol returned to U.S. schools to write a new book, *Savage Inequalities* (recently published by Crown) and discovered that things have gotten worse.

"We've not only failed to live up to *Brown*" (the Supreme Court's 1954 school desegregation decision), he says. "We're not even up to *Plessy,*" the Court's 1896 "separate but equal" ruling. "Our schools," he adds, "are more separate and more unequal."

Reagan's Malign Neglect

There is less overt racism in schools today, Kozol told the *Guardian* in an interview before a recent lecture at the State University of New York at Stony Brook. "Teachers tend to be far more sensitive to issues of cultural diversity," he said, and the increasing numbers of Black and Latino teachers and administrators have also helped sensitize white teachers. But racism has made a "terrifying resurgence" in the rest of the country, and the federal government "completely turned its back on poor people" in the '80s. Schools and children in them now have to contend with the devastating legacies of the Reagan era's malign neglect: crack, homelessness, pollution and lack of health care outside the schools, and all the ills brought on by fiscal starvation inside.

In East St. Louis, Ill., a 98 percent Black city so poor it had to eliminate municipal garbage collection, Kozol found schools with no toilet seats that had to close several times when raw sewage backed up into the halls. In Chicago, two sixth-grade girls fight over a crayon. Their school rations pencils, paper and crayons to keep from running out in the middle of the year. It sends students to a high school where more than three-quarters of the students drop out.

In the Bronx, he found a high school where the roof leaked so much that a waterfall rushed down the stairs every time it rained. Camden, N.J., schools had antique typewriters but no computers to teach word processing, no books for a ninth-grade writing class and seven badly ripped copies of *A Tale of Two Cities* for an 11th-grade English class of 10.

A 14-year-old East St. Louis girl commented that naming a junior high school after Dr. Martin Luther King, when the "school is full of sewer water and the doors are locked with chains," was "like a terrible joke on history."

"There is nothing I can say that is as damning as what the children say," Kozol told the Stony Brook audience Sept. 12.

Education for the Poor

The differences are drastic when compared with the suburban schools he also visited: in Princeton, N.J., where the high school had 200 IBM computers and a Dow Jones hookup to study stock transactions, and New Trier High School in the Chicago suburb of Winnetka, often cited as the best public high school in the United States.

There is little in *Savage Inequalities* that would shock anyone who's ever spent time in inner-city schools. Yet few solutions are on the agenda of politicians or the mainstream media, who usually blame parents, teachers or individual administrators for children's failure to learn.

Kozol doesn't believe that having large numbers of children with crack-addicted or alcoholic parents is a valid excuse for schools to fail. "The justification for public education is that regardless of what else is happening in a child's life, the school can make a difference," he says. If public schools can't, "they shouldn't exist. We should just close them up and not pretend that we're educating poor children."

Dual System Exists

There is a simple solution, he says: money. If New York City schools had the $15,000 per pupil that top-rated districts in affluent suburbs spend each year—instead of half that amount—class sizes could be cut by half.

"A teacher who is good with 40 kids is super-good with 20," he says. "A mediocre teacher who has an awful time with 40 kids might manage to do a pretty good job with 20."

If city schools had suburban-size classes of 18 children, he continues, there would be "no need to filter out the one or two boys who cause trouble. In a class of 35, the two or three boys who cause you trouble screw up the whole school day for everyone else" because the teacher doesn't have time to give them the attention, affection and discipline they need.

"I don't want to take 200 IBM computers from the kids in Princeton," he told the Stony Brook crowd. "I want to give the kids in Camden 200 Apples." He got the most applause when he urged abolishing the inequitable system of financing schools through local property taxes.

Most of the commonly suggested solutions to the schools' crisis—"magnet" and alternative schools, more choice for parents in picking schools and all-Black-male schools—are sidestepping this main issue, according to Kozol.

He reluctantly supports the all-Black-male schools proposed in Detroit, Milwaukee and Brooklyn, N.Y.: He's "philosophically opposed to any official sponsorship of segregation," but says that since many schools are all-Black already and the troublesome students who get shunted into their special-education classes are overwhelmingly male, why not revamp the curriculum, put in some resources, "make it something terrific and call it an African-American immersion school."

However, he says, the real issue is "why this Society permits segregated schools and why it permits them to be so unequal." The only truly integrated schools he found were in Jackson, Miss.—and the most segregated were in New York City. But he contends that if New York's schools had as much money as their suburban neighbors, white parents wouldn't send their kids to private schools, and segregated classes wouldn't be an issue.

Though he also says he is a "great believer" in alternative education, he has reservations about the public alternative schools springing up in several cities, like Central Park East Secondary School in New York's East Harlem. He lushly praises the East Harlem school's director, Deborah Meier, but doesn't think the experiment—a network of smaller, less impersonal schools specializing in different subjects—can be replicated successfully in other places.

Because parents have to make special efforts to get their kids into both alternative and selective "magnet schools," he says, they tend to "filter out the most needy children while serving as a magnet for the more fortunate." The most sophisticated parents—middle class, white or Black—can get their children into these schools, while poorer parents often don't know how to ask or can't get their kids in. This, he warns, means that poorer children are left in schools drained of the most active, outspoken parents and their kids—perpetuating the "dual system."

Bush Voted against Civil Rights

The same argument underlies Kozol's opposition to the Bush administration's push for "choice" between public and private schools in its "America 2000" report—except that the Bush plan isn't even inspired by good intentions, he says. The idea that free-market competition would force bad schools to improve is worthless without the money to buy adequate supplies and pay enough to attract good teachers, he argues. The "segregation academies" that opened in the South in the aftermath of the *Brown* decision also emphasized free choice, he adds—and it's not a coincidence that Bush voted against the 1964 civil rights bill as a member of Congress.

The report's "pretentious capitalizations"—it's full of references to "Choice" and "the New American School"—are a "symbol of the degree to which rhetoric overtakes reality" in the Bush plan, Kozol notes.

As for the right-wing attack on multicultural education and "political correctness," Kozol finds it "profoundly insulting when demagogic conservatives tell us we're diluting the curriculum by wanting to include a decent amount of non-Western material."

He envisions putting Third World liberation theorist Frantz Fanon alongside Alexander Hamilton and 19th century English philosopher John Stuart Mill in the political theory canon, but adds that multicultural readings shouldn't just be politically angry works. It's not merely "a good deed, to make us feel better," he argues; white kids would also benefit from reading classic Latin American, Chinese and Indian literature. "Half the people in the world live there," he says.

Outraged Innocence

"I was a victim of 'political correctness,'" he adds. "I never heard of Langston Hughes until some Black parents told me about him, and I majored in English and American literature at Harvard."

Kozol, who says he was apolitical before he started teaching, calls himself "an eternal optimist"—and retains the outraged innocence of '60s politics. "I persist in believing there are an awful lot of decent people in America," he says. "It's still worth making a straightforward ethical appeal."

"You know the argument you always hear for Head Start: 'We ought to do this because it's going to be cost-effective. If we help these kids it'll save us money later on'?" he continues. "I don't like that argument. It's true. It would be cost-effective. But I think we ought to do these things because they're decent."

Shopping While Black

Lena Williams

Last month, Cedric Holloway, a 20-year-old chef's helper, decided to invest $1,000 of his savings in a certificate of deposit or money-market account. Wearing a Syracuse University Orangemen cap, baggy jeans and a shirt, he went to a branch of the Great Western Bank in Tamarac, Fla., to investigate rates. After visiting three other banks, he returned to Great Western with more questions, then left again to go over the information.

As he sat in his car outside the bank reading brochures, he found himself surrounded by sheriff's deputies with their guns drawn. He was ordered out of the car, handcuffed and read his rights. Bank employees, thinking he might be planning a robbery, had called the police. After 45 minutes of questioning, the police accepted his explanation that he had been trying to put money into the bank.

While on a lecture tour in New York last year, Julianne Malveaux, a college professor and syndicated columnist, was approached by a salesclerk at Saks Fifth Avenue and accused of switching the tags on an expensive silk dress she was planning to buy. She said another salesclerk convinced her colleague that the store, not Ms. Malveaux, had switched the tags.

Mr. Holloway and Ms. Malveaux are black, their accusers are white, and the victims see these incidents not as isolated cases, but as part of a pattern of discrimination and humiliation that affects blacks in the marketplace. Businesses often say such scrutiny is used to protect not only their establishments, but also their customers. Thirty years have passed since the lunch counter sit-ins that led to civil-rights laws guaranteeing all people "full and equal enjoyment" of the goods, services, advantages and facilities of public accommodations. But black

Americans say segregation's legacy persists and such privileges are not universally available.

No official agency collects data on whether incidents like those Mr. Holloway and Ms. Malveaux experienced are on the rise. But in interviews, blacks of all ages, regions and economic levels tell similar stories of bad service, public humiliation and legal harassment when confronted by representatives of service industries that, the blacks say, do not acknowledge blacks' growing economic power, private resources and buying patterns.

Moreover, the discrimination is often far subtler than a face-to-face confrontation. This was illustrated earlier this month when a Hispanic woman making a purchase at a Cignal clothing store in Boston noticed that as a salesclerk was filling in information that had been stamped on the back of her personal check, there was a section marked "race"—and the clerk left it blank. When she received her canceled check, the "race" section had been filled in.

The woman, Jacqueline Perczek, who is not black, later officially objected to the practice. Within days, Cignal, a subsidiary of Merry-Go-Round Enterprises Inc., in Towson, Md., dropped its policy of classifying shoppers as "W" for white, "H" for Hispanic and "07," a company shorthand for black. Company officials said nothing about the practice was racist.

"The information was not utilized for any purpose—good, bad or indifferent," said Bruce Harrison, a lawyer for Cignal. He said the company wanted the data for identification if a check bounced.

Such practices have been termed "economic racism" by some. "Economic racism, in which money and social status are used as barriers, is more pervasive than the overt racism of the past," said Ms. Malveaux, an economist who is a professor of Afro-American studies at the University of California at Berkeley. "Increasingly, black consumers are being subjected to this newer, more subtle kind of racism that deprives them of their rights."

Considerable debate has occurred among blacks about how to handle such incidents. In one camp are those who advocate buying the merchandise or service at issue, if only to prove they can afford to. But other blacks say that puts money in the pockets of the offending whites. These blacks say a more effective response is to refuse to patronize places that do not openly welcome their business. But that response, blacks on the other side say, only confirms whites' doubts about whether blacks can afford the merchandise.

When she has been slighted in a store, Gertrude Barber, a Washington tax accountant, said, "What I do is let them run my credit card through that little machine and get the approval number. Then I tell them to tear up the sales and credit slips, give them a lecture on racial prejudice, then walk out the door leaving them holding pieces of paper."

Several stereotypes seem to underlie the discrimination, said Dr. Joe R. Feagin, a professor of sociology at the University of Florida who has studied discrimination in public places.

"Blacks are seen as shoplifters, as unclean, as disreputable poor," Dr. Feagin, who is white, wrote in the February issue of the *American Sociological Review.*

"No matter how affluent and influential, a black person cannot escape the stigma of being black even while relaxing or shopping."

This perception is rooted, in part, in statistics that show that a disproportionate number of blacks are below the poverty level or are charged with crimes and incarcerated. But the numbers do not reflect the growing number of blacks with disposable incomes and an inclination to spend.

According to the Census Bureau, of the 10,486,000 black American households, 264,000 had earnings of $50,000 to $54,999 in 1989, the latest year for which figures were available; 92,000 other households earned more than $70,000 that year, and 81,000 more than $100,000.

While other racial and ethnic groups and women are also targets of discrimination in public places, blacks say they feel the brunt of such discrimination more than any other group because their color immediately sets them apart.

The result has been an increasing impatience and rage among middle-class blacks. In the 1950's and 1960's, some blacks responded to white mistreatment in public accommodations with deference or resignation while others took part in demonstrations. But today, such incidents are more likely to provoke a verbal confrontation or a lawsuit.

"Black-white interaction today is being renegotiated," Dr. Feagin said. "Prior to societal desegregation, blacks were typically expected to respond to discriminating whites with great deference, stepping off sidewalks when whites went by. Since the 1960's, whites have encountered a majority of blacks who do not respond with deference when faced with discrimination. They may withdraw or deny, but they do not shuffle."

Mr. Holloway, the Florida chef's helper, for example, has filed a discrimination complaint against Great Western, seeking damages for false imprisonment. At the time, the bank branch representatives said robbers often came into a bank seeking information, then returned to rob it.

Kevin Hawkins, a spokesman at Great Western's headquarters in Beverly Hills, Calif., called the incident "a terrible error in judgment."

A similar incident last September in Wellesley, Mass., involving a professional basketball player, Dee Brown of the Boston Celtics, and his fiancee, Jill Edmondson, drew national attention. Mr. Brown was forced at gunpoint by police officers to lie on the sidewalk after a bank teller said he resembled a suspect in a robbery. The couple settled a complaint against the Wellesley police for $5,000.

The popular culture has also been increasingly used to prick the nation's conscience and bring the problem into the open. In recent months, episodes of television programs like "L.A. Law," "In Living Color" and "The Fresh Prince of Bel Air" have dealt with the issue.

Debbie Allen, the actress and producer-director of the television series "A Different World," said a white clerk at a Beverly Hills jewelry store not only refused to show her merchandise, but also "assumed because I was black, I couldn't afford anything in the store." Ms. Allen later produced a fictionalized account of the incident for the program.

By their nature, these incidents tend to affect blacks of some means, who are more likely to come into contact with whites in places where the presence of blacks is unusual. Many blacks said in interviews that they were convinced that the recession had heightened racial tensions, giving rise to confrontations and causing resentment among those whites who may think blacks have attained status or wealth because of preferential treatment.

"You have working-class whites doing poorly," said Ms. Malveaux, the Berkeley professor. "They see blacks doing well, and they don't process the statistics that show only a third of us are doing well, and it causes problems."

Veterans of civil-rights battles say this form of discrimination may be more difficult to defeat than the institutional racism of the past, in part because it is more subtle.

Some civil-rights advocates also say many middle-class blacks, the group most likely to prompt change, hesitate to complain.

Just as bothersome, those interviewed said, is that many blacks say they constantly have to defend claims of discrimination to whites who do not believe it is a continuing problem.

"As a white, I can corroborate their feelings," Dr. Feagin said. "Ninety-eight percent of whites have no idea what it's like to walk in black shoes. Even the most liberal white Americans think middle-class blacks pretty much have it made."

Most blacks interviewed said they often adjusted their everyday lives to try to avoid prejudicial treatment, either by wearing obvious symbols of class—fancy pens, briefcases, suits—or by sticking to restaurants, hotels and stores recommended by black friends and colleagues.

"I make a habit of dressing a certain way, usually a jacket and tie, when I go shopping in the city," said Lawrence Otis Graham, a 28-year-old New York lawyer.

"When I walk into a store, they don't see my Princeton undergraduate degree, my Harvard law degree, my associate law status," Mr. Graham added. "They see a black man. Credentials do not make your blackness invisible, no matter how impressive they may be."

But while such forms of discrimination may be mere annoyances, most blacks worry more about incidents that expose them to severe violations of their rights. Last year, while waiting for a flight at Stapleton International Airport in Denver, Daniel Lamaute, the owner of the Lamaute Financial Group, a financial consulting concern in Los Angeles, said he narrowly escaped arrest by two white police officers.

"They started pushing me toward the interrogation room, when another police officer came by and said, 'That's not the one I want,'" the 37-year-old Mr. Lamaute said.

He said he later learned through airport officials that well-dressed black pickpockets were mingling with travelers. Still he complained to officials and received apologies from the Mayor of Denver and the Governor of Colorado.

Apologies aside, these discriminatory acts create what Dr. Alvin Poussaint of Harvard University and other black psychologists describe as a feeling of "dis-ease."

"What it does to our collective psyche is that it makes sure you never forget that you are black and not welcomed," Dr. Poussaint said. "It is a constant reminder that you live in a society with stereotypes of blacks that you are not free from."

Chapter 142

Environmental Racism

Robert F. Kennedy, Jr., and Dennis Rivera

Robert F. Kennedy, Jr., is a lawyer for the Hudson Riverkeeper and the Natural Resources Defense Council. Dennis Rivera is president of Local 1199 of the Drug, Hospital, and Health Care Employees Union.

The following selection is reprinted from "Pollution's Chief Victims: The Poor," New York Times, 15 August 1992. Copyright © 1992 by The New York Times. Reprinted by permission.

For more on environmental racism, see Robert D. Bullard, ed., Confronting Environmental Racism *(1993) and Daniel J. Faber, ed.,* The Struggle for Ecological Democracy *(1998).*

It is a popular perception that environmental protection is the exclusive concern of the privileged. In fact, it is the poor and disfranchised who are at greatest risk from environmental abuse. Inexorably, society's wastes flow toward communities debilitated by social unrest, high illiteracy and unemployment, and low voter registration. They have become toxic dumping grounds while receiving few of the safeguards that prudence and decency demand but only political power can obtain. Examples abound across the nation.

- When well-connected Manhattan residents objected to proposals to put the North River sewage treatment plant at West 72d Street, obliging city officials moved the facility to west Harlem. The chronic stench of the poorly designed plant is one more demoralizing obstacle to revitalization of the neighborhood.
- New York State's largest medical-waste incinerator, originally proposed for suburban Rockland County, towers over a densely populated South Bronx neighborhood. Its emissions may include lead, cadmium, mercury, dibenzofurans and dioxin. New York City plans to construct seven additional incinerators in low-income neighborhoods that will produce 7,000 tons of poisonous gas a year.
- The Environmental Protection Agency said in a report this spring that three of every four toxic-waste dumps that fail to comply with the agency's regulations are in black or Hispanic neighborhoods.

The nation's largest toxic-waste dump is in Emelle, Ala., an utterly impoverished city that is 80 percent black. The highest concentration of such dumps is on Chicago's South Side. Half of the country's blacks and Hispanics live in neighborhoods with hazardous waste dumps.

- Two million tons of radioactive uranium has been dumped on Native American lands. Navajo teen-agers have sexual-organ cancer at 17 times the national average.
- Some 300,000 Hispanic farm laborers suffer each year from illnesses related to pesticides.
- Inner-city children in Los Angeles have 10 to 15 percent less lung efficiency than those in less smoggy cities. Pollution-related asthma is killing African-Americans at five times the rate it kills whites.
- Eight million children, principally poor and minority, have lead poisoning. They live in substandard housing that has peeling paint and lead pipes. Often they live near highways, incinerators or toxic waste sites. Forty-four percent of urban black children are at risk from lead poisoning.

What can the labor and environmental movements do about all this? Environmentalists must diversify their staffs and directors racially and culturally and support the growing environmental justice movement by sharing with it technical, legal, lobbying and financing resources.

Unions must continue to alert their members to environmental threats on the job and in their neighborhoods. Workers should help organize and lobby against dangerous facilities in poor communities and in favor of alternatives like recycling.

Together, we should work for laws that force the government and developers to provide communities with complete information about the dangers of new facilities. We can pressure Congress to reauthorize the Resource Conservation Recovery Act that will ban the production of toxic materials that cannot be reused or recycled.

We must fight to restore Federal programs, cut during the Reagan-Bush era, to rebuild sewage plants and water delivery systems, increase recycling, revitalize city parks and expand public transportation.

Society must recognize that economic and social injustice are a virulent form of pollution. As we endeavor to heal the wounds that afflict our planet, we must also heal the inequities that divide our nation.

Affirmative Action

Chapter 143

Affirmative Action and History

Eric Foner

Eric Foner, professor of history at Columbia University, serves on the editorial board of the Nation *magazine.*

The following selection, "Hiring Quotas for White Males Only: Affirmative Action and History," is reprinted with permission from the 26 June 1995 issue of the Nation *magazine.*

For other selections by Foner, see chapters 25 and 171.

Thirty-two years ago, I graduated from Columbia College. My class of 700 was all-male and virtually all-white. Most of us were young men of ability, yet had we been forced to compete for admission with women and racial minorities, fewer than half of us would have been at Columbia. None of us, to my knowledge, suffered debilitating self-doubt because we were the beneficiaries of affirmative action—that is, favored treatment on the basis of our race and gender.

Affirmative action has emerged as the latest "wedge issue" of American politics. The recent abrogation of California affirmative action programs by Governor Pete Wilson, and the Clinton Administration's halting efforts to re-evaluate federal policy, suggest the issue is now coming to a head. As a historian, I find the current debate dismaying not only because of the crass effort to set Americans against one another for partisan advantage but also because the entire discussion lacks a sense of history.

Opponents of affirmative action, for example, have tried to wrap themselves in the mantle of the civil rights movement, seizing upon the 1963 speech in which Martin Luther King Jr. looked forward to the time when his children would be judged not by the "color of their skin" but by the "content of their character." Rarely mentioned is that King came to be a strong supporter of affirmative action.

In his last book, *Where Do We Go From Here?*, a brooding meditation on America's long history of racism, King acknowledged that "special treatment" for blacks seemed to conflict with the ideal of opportunity based on individual merit. But, he continued, "a society that has done something special against the Negro for hundreds of years must now do something special for him."

Our country, King realized, has never operated on a colorblind basis. From the beginning of the Republic, membership in American society was defined in racial terms. The first naturalization law, enacted in 1790, restricted citizenship for those emigrating from abroad to "free white persons." Free blacks, even in the North, were barred from juries, public schools, government employment and the militia and regular army. Not until after the Civil War were blacks deemed worthy to be American citizens, while Asians were barred from naturalization until the 1940s.

White immigrants certainly faced discrimination. But they had access to the political power, jobs and residential neighborhoods denied to blacks. In the nineteenth century, the men among them enjoyed the right to vote even before they were naturalized. Until well into this century, however, the vast majority of black Americans were excluded from the suffrage except for a period immediately after the Civil War. White men, native and immigrant, could find well-paid craft and industrial jobs, while employers and unions limited nonwhites (and women) to unskilled and menial employment. The "American standard of living" was an entitlement of white men alone.

There is no point in dwelling morbidly on past injustices. But this record of unequal treatment cannot be dismissed as "vague or ancient wrongs" with no bearing on the present, as Republican strategist William Kristol recently claimed. Slavery may be gone and legal segregation dismantled, but the effects of past discrimination live on in seniority systems that preserve intact the results of a racially segmented job market, a black unemployment rate double that of whites and pervasive housing segregation.

Past racism is embedded in the two-tier, racially divided system of social insurance still on the books today. Because key Congressional committees in the 1930s were controlled by Southerners with all-white electorates, they did not allow the supposedly universal entitlement of Social Security to cover the largest categories of black workers—agricultural laborers and domestics. Social Security excluded 80 percent of employed black women, who were forced to depend for a safety net on the much less generous "welfare" system.

The notion that affirmative action stigmatizes its recipients reflects not just belief in advancement according to individual merit but the older idea that the "normal" American is white. There are firemen and black firemen, construction workers and black construction workers: Nonwhites (and women) who obtain such jobs are still widely viewed as interlopers, depriving white men of positions or promotions to which they are historically entitled.

I have yet to meet the white male in whom special favoritism (getting a job, for example, through relatives or an old boys' network, or because of racial discrimination by a union or employer) fostered doubt about his own abilities. In a society where belief in black inferiority is still widespread (witness the success of *The Bell Curve*), many whites and some blacks may question the abilities of beneficiaries of affirmative action. But this social "cost" hardly counterbalances the enormous social benefits affirmative action has produced.

Nonwhites (and even more so, white women) have made deep inroads into the lower middle class and into professions once reserved for white males. Columbia College now admits women and minority students. Would these and other opportunities have opened as widely and as quickly without the pressure of affirmative action programs? American history suggests they would not.

It is certainly true, as critics charge, that affirmative action's benefits have not spread to the poorest members of the black community. The children of Harlem, regrettably, are not in a position to take advantage of the spots Columbia has opened to blacks. But rather than simply ratifying the advantages of already affluent blacks, who traditionally advanced by servicing the segregated black community, affirmative action has helped to create a new black middle class, resting on professional and managerial positions within white society.

This new class is much more vulnerable than its white counterpart to the shifting fortunes of the economy and politics. Far more middle-class blacks than whites depend on public employment—positions now threatened by the downsizing of federal, state and municipal governments. The fact that other actions are needed to address the problems of the "underclass" hardly negates the proven value of affirmative action in expanding black access to the middle class and skilled working class.

There is no harm in rethinking the ways affirmative action is implemented—reexamining, for example, the expansion to numerous other groups of a program originally intended to deal with the legacy of slavery and segregation. In principle, there may well be merit in redefining disadvantage to include poor whites. The present cry for affirmative action based on class rather than race, however, seems as much an evasion as a serious effort to rethink public policy. Efforts to uplift the poor, while indispensable in a just society, are neither a substitute for nor incompatible with programs that address the legacy of the race-based discrimination to which blacks have historically been subjected. Without a robust class politics, moreover, class policies are unlikely to get very far. The present Congress may well dismantle affirmative action, but it hardly seems sympathetic to broad "color-blind" programs to assist the poor.

At a time of deindustrialization and stagnant real wages, many whites have come to blame affirmative action for declining economic prospects. Let us not delude ourselves, however, into thinking that eliminating affirmative action will produce a society in which rewards are based on merit. Despite our rhetoric, equal opportunity has never been the American way. For nearly all our history, affirmative action has been a prerogative of white men.

Chapter 144

The Great White Myth

Anna Quindlen

Novelist Anna Quindlen is a former columnist for the New York Times. *Two collections of her columns have been published,* Living Out Loud *(1988) and* Thinking Out Loud *(1994). Quindlen's novels include* Object Lessons *(1991),* One True Thing *(1994), and* Black and Blue *(1998).*

The following selection is reprinted from "The Great White Myth," New York Times, 15 January 1992. Copyright © 1992 by The New York Times. Reprinted by permission.

In a college classroom, a young white man rises and asks about the future. What, he wants to know, can it possibly hold for him when most of the jobs, most of the good positions, most of the spots in professional schools are being given to women and, most especially, to blacks?

The temptation to be short, sarcastic, incredulous in reply is powerful. But you have to remember that kids learn their lessons from adults. That's what the mother of two black children who were sprayed with white paint in the Bronx said last week about the assailants, teen-agers who called her son and daughter "nigger" and vowed they would turn them white. "Can you imagine what they are being taught at home?" she asked.

A nation of laws, we like to believe that when they are changed, attitudes will change along with them. This is naive. America continues to be a country whose people are obsessed with some spurious pecking order. Leaving, at the bottom, blacks to be taught at age 12 and 14 through the utter humiliation of having their faces cleaned with paint thinner that there are those who think that even white in a bottle is better than not white at all.

Each generation finds its own reasons to hate. The worried young white men I've met on college campuses in the last year have internalized the newest myth of American race relations, and it has made them bitter. It is called affirmative action, a.k.a. the systematic oppression of white men. All good things in life, they've learned, from college admission to executive position, are being given to black citizens. The verb is ubiquitous: given.

Never mind that you can walk through the offices of almost any big company and see a sea of white faces. Never mind that with all that has been written about preferential treatment for minority law students, only about 7,500 of the 127,000 students enrolled in law school last year were African-American. Never mind that only 3 percent of the doctors in this country are black.

Never mind that in the good old days preferential treatment was routinely given to brothers and sons of workers in certain lines of work. Perceptions of programs to educate and hire more black citizens as, in part, an antidote to decades of systematic exclusion have been inflated to enormous proportions in the public mind. Like hot air balloons they fill up the blue sky of the American landscape with the gaudy stripes of hyperbole. Listen and you will believe that the construction sites, the precinct houses, the investment banks are filled with African-Americans.

Unless you actually visit them.

The opponents of affirmative action programs say they are opposing the rank unfairness of preferential treatment. But there was no great hue and cry when colleges were candid about wanting to have geographic diversity, perhaps giving the kid from Montana an edge. There has been no national outcry when legacy applicants whose transcripts were supplemented by Dad's alumni status—and cash contributions to the college—were admitted over more qualified comers. We somehow only discovered that life was not fair when the beneficiaries happened to be black.

And so the chasm widens. The old myth was the black American incapable of prosperity. It was common knowledge that welfare was purely a benefits program for blacks; it was common knowledge although it was false. The percentage of whites on public assistance is almost identical to the percentage of blacks.

The new myth is that the world is full of black Americans prospering unfairly at white expense, and anecdotal evidence abounds. The stories about the incompetent black co-worker always leave out two things: the incompetent white co-workers and the talented black ones. They also leave out the tendency of so many managers to hire those who seem most like themselves when young.

"It seems like if you're a white male you don't have a chance," said another young man on a campus where a scant 5 percent of his classmates were black. What the kid really means is that he no longer has the edge, that the rules of a system that may have served his father well have changed. It is one of those good-old-days constructs to believe it was a system based purely on merit, but we know that's not true. It is a system that once favored him, and others like him. Now sometimes—just sometimes—it favors someone different.

Chapter 145

How the Press Frames Affirmative Action

Janine Jackson

Janine Jackson is the program director for Fairness & Accuracy in Reporting (FAIR). She is a frequent contributor to FAIR's bimonthly magazine, EXTRA!, and the co-editor of The FAIR Reader: An EXTRA! Review of Press and Politics *(1996). For more information on FAIR, see www.fair.org.*

The following selection is reprinted from "White Man's Burden: How the Press Frames Affirmative Action," Extra!, *September/October 1995. Reprinted with permission of* Extra!

"Quotas Quashed," crowed the front page of the June 13 *New York Post*. "High Court Sinks Most Affirmative Action Programs." Inside, *Post* writers described the *Adarand v. Pena* ruling, in which the Supreme Court tightened criteria for some race-conscious federal programs, as a "bombshell decision" that "dealt a crippling blow to affirmative action."

All the June 12 ruling really said was that federal programs must meet the same narrower requirements already established for the states. Some specific programs were challenged, but the court explicitly acknowledged the ongoing existence of racism and sexism and the continued need for remedies. The mainstream press has been less inclined than the court to acknowledge these realities.

Although most reporting has been more subtle than the *New York Post*'s, affirmative action coverage has, with a few exceptions, been marked by inaccurate and misleading language, the absorption of all policy issues into presidential politics and the tendency to portray what is, after all, a question of past and continuing discrimination against women and people of color as most importantly the concern of white men.

Terms of Debate

"Affirmative action" is the general term applied to a variety of federal, state and private sector programs aimed at achieving racial and gender diversity in the workforce and in education. Affirmative action is surrounded by misconceptions, which its opponents find easy to exploit. But rather than carefully examining—

and perhaps defusing—the issue, many in the press have further clouded and inflamed things with misapplied terminology.

The most obvious example is the word "quota." Quotas are illegal unless imposed by a court, as every relevant Supreme Court ruling since the 1978 *Bakke* case has made clear. Anyone who has been denied a job through an illegal quota can find a ready remedy in the court.

But this fact, reiterated in the Civil Rights Act of 1991 [see chapter 160—*Eds.*], hasn't stopped media outlets from using the hot-button term as shorthand for any and all affirmative action. Not only right-wing papers like the *Washington Times*, which referred in one news article (1/8/95) to "affirmative action (read: race-based quotas)," but outlets like the *New York Times* have made this error (7/21/95, 7/22/95).

Some pundits simply disavowed any attempt to correct the record, as when columnist John Leo wrote, "Everyone knows that 'goals and timetables' means 'quotas' but nobody is supposed to say so out loud" (*U.S. News & World Report*, 3/13/95).

No less misleading is the reference to "racial preferences." This term plays on the idea that affirmative action policies artificially promote some groups over others, without regard to qualifications.

In fact, most affirmative action programs rely on tools like aggressive recruitment and outreach plans to achieve diversity. When set-asides have been used, as with construction contracts, it is because there is proof that qualified applicants have been rejected on the basis of their race. As the law stands now, all federal and state affirmative action programs must establish a record of discrimination—in other words, that it is whites or men who have been receiving "preferences."

Media's frequent use of the term "racial preference" also obscures the fact that the policies aim at gender as well as racial equality. The *Washington Post* (2/23/95), for example, referred matter-of-factly to "the beneficiaries of affirmative action (commonly African-Americans)," although most studies, including one by the Labor Department in 1984, indicate that the primary beneficiaries have been white women (*Washington Post*, 5/31/95).

Crucial Language Choices

Despite the inaccuracy of the term, as *Washington Post* columnist Dorothy Gilliam pointed out (6/17/95), mainstream media regularly substitute "preferences" for affirmative action. *USA Today* (7/19/95) referred to "affirmative action, which provides preferences for minorities and women in hiring, contracting and college admissions." The *Sacramento Bee* (7/23/95) reported that Clinton "rejected calls . . . to dismantle affirmative action programs, arguing that racial preferences are fair and do not discriminate against white men."

But if there's one thing pollsters have shown, it's that the language used to talk about diversity programs is crucial. An April survey by Louis Harris and the Feminist Majority Foundation showed that white people make strong distinctions between the terms "affirmative action" and "preferential treatment." Fifty-five percent of whites think "preferential treatment" means "hiring minorities and women who are not otherwise qualified over qualified white men," and 47 percent equated it with "reverse discrimination—against white men."

But only 26 percent of whites accept the claim that "affirmative action" means "giving one race or one group an advantage they don't deserve"; 71 percent said that it was "making opportunities for everyone including women and minorities."

The authors of the so-called California Civil Rights Initiative [banning affirmative action] have based their whole campaign on this linguistic deception. The referendum bans the use of race or sex criteria for "either discriminating against or granting preferential treatment to" anyone doing business with the state.

Eighty-one percent of Californians surveyed in the Harris/Feminist Majority poll said they supported the referendum. But when asked if they would still support the measure if it would "outlaw all affirmative action programs for women and minorities"—which both opponents and proponents think it would—the 81 percent support drops to 29 percent, and opposition rises from 11 percent to 58 percent.

Based on results like these, pollster Harris concluded that "it is not only misleading to use 'affirmative action' and 'preferential treatment' interchangeably, but it is nothing less than deceitful as well."

His comments might have been directed at the press, whose misuses of such charged terms not only misrepresents the issue, but also give a deceptive accounting of public opinion. People may be opposed to "quotas" and "preferential treatment," while still favoring "affirmative action," which is reducible to neither.

But leading media seem bent on depicting the nation as hostile to affirmative action. A *Time* feature (3/20/95) asserted that "the public overwhelmingly wants to get rid of affirmative action." As "proof," it cited only an *L.A. Times* poll (2/21/95) in which 39 percent of respondents said that affirmative action "goes too far." If 39 percent is an overwhelming majority, then Walter Mondale was our 41st president.

The Real "Wedge Issue"

In their "fallout" coverage after the *Adarand v. Pena* ruling, the country's major dailies couldn't resist the urge to tell the story in terms of what it might mean for Bill Clinton or the Republicans. Comments from presidential contenders Sen. Bob Dole (R.-Kansas) and Sen. Phil Gramm (R.-Texas) got precedence in page-one stories, while the responses of, for example, the Congressional Black Caucus or civil rights leaders came further down or on back pages.

The June 13 front-page stories in the *New York Times, Washington Post* and *Los Angeles Times* also managed to omit any exploration of ongoing, present-day racism—the real "wedge issue," and the underlying problem that affirmative action programs, whatever their particular form, attempt to address.

Reporters would not have needed to search very hard for compelling evidence of continued racism. They might have pointed to a 1991 Urban Institute study that found white job-seekers were 50 percent more likely to be hired compared to identically qualified blacks. Or surveys that show that a majority of whites still cling to negative stereotypes about blacks.

Reporters could have cited many recent examples of corporate racism, like Denny's refusing to serve black customers in 1993, or the major [Washington] D.C.-area bank that was forced to pay $11 million after being caught "redlining"—denying mortgages to minority neighborhoods.

And on the very day (3/15/95) that Bob Dole claimed that "the American people sense all too clearly that the race-counting game has gone too far," the Glass Ceiling Commission initiated by his wife, Elizabeth Hanford Dole, released a report that revealed that 97 percent of top managers in the biggest U.S. companies are still white men, and that women and minorities are still disproportionately represented among the working poor. (John Leo dismissed the study as "a wonderful example of desperately rooting around for bad news"—*U.S. News and World Report*, 6/5/95.)

Such information would have undermined opponents' claims that affirmative action is no longer necessary and refocused attention on the ongoing problems of discrimination. But confronting the reality of racism and sexism—in other words, considering affirmative action from the point of view of those most directly affected—has not been mass media's favored approach.

No White Men Need Apply?

In the [1994] congressional election, many mainstream reporters found "angry white men" and their "swing vote" the single most interesting factor, while the non-voting millions of disgruntled black, Latino and working-class people elicited little interest or concern. Similarly, a number of pundits appear to believe that the most important thing about affirmative action is how white men feel about it.

This skewed focus was epitomized in the Feb. 13 *U.S. News & World Report*, whose cover asked the absurd question: "Does Affirmative Action Mean . . . NO WHITE MEN NEED APPLY?"

In the guise of explaining the "sound and fury" around the subject, *U.S. News'* Steven Roberts simply recounted many of the most prejudicial myths about affirmative action. The notion that what's at issue is "past racism" was flagged in the article's subhead, which defined the debate as "whether women and minorities still deserve favored treatment." As evidence that racial minorities are "no longer disadvantaged," Roberts states that "most of the young people applying for jobs and to colleges today were not even born when legal segregation ended"—the simplistic implication being that any prejudice that might impede minorities' advancement disappeared with [the defeat of] Jim Crow laws.

Then there's the idea that women and minorities are themselves affirmative action's staunchest enemies. Polls have repeatedly indicated these groups' support for the programs (for example, the Roper Center for Public Opinion Research, in *Public Perspective*, 6/7/95). But Roberts cites instead conservatives Thomas Sowell and

Linda Chavez (described as "a Hispanic activist," not as a former Reagan speech-writer), who claims, without evidence, that going to university on an affirmative action program is a "very disheartening experience" for young people.

Roberts also trots out the familiar accusation that the "civil rights lobby" has suppressed any discussion of the topic; an unidentified congress member claims, "The problem is political correctness—you can't talk openly." Later, however, we're told that *critics* of affirmative action "control the key committees and the congressional calendar."

Comparatively little consideration is given to the arguments of affirmative action's proponents. And Roberts can hardly contain his wink to the reader as he says that the job of these proponents is "to debunk the 'myth' that unqualified women and minorities are being hired in large numbers." If Roberts has proof that, in fact, "large numbers" of "unqualified" women and minorities *are* getting jobs they don't deserve, he doesn't provide it.

A vivid demonstration of *U.S. News'* confusion between unsupported rhetoric about "reverse discrimination" and the realities of racism is the graphic that accompanies the story. In the drawing, a ladder descends to earth, shaped like a large hand, the stars and stripes on the sleeve indicating that it depicts a "helping hand" from Uncle Sam. While black men and white and black women climb the proffered ladder, a white man is left grounded, separated from the "ladder of opportunity" by a gaping abyss.

The image of "the white man left behind" is repeated on the following pages, juxtaposed, ironically enough, with statistical charts indicating white men's continued dominance of the job market, and their utter outstripping of all other groups in terms of wages. Black men make, on average, 74 percent of what white men make; white women 70.8 percent. For black women, the figure is 63.7 percent; for Latino men and women, 64.8 percent and 53.9 percent, respectively. It's hard to believe that no one at *U.S. News* noticed the obvious contradiction between the illustration's message and the reality presented in the facts and figures.

Affirmative action is undoubtedly a politicized issue, with leading politicians vying to see who will come out most firmly against it, or, alternately, who can support it most restrainedly. But covering the issue primarily as "a hot topic on the presidential campaign trail," as *Time* did in its March 20 feature, often means that deeper questions about the effects of the policies on people's lives go unexplored.

Newsweek's Joe Klein subsumed the issue almost completely to party politics; his June 26 column warned Clinton that "race" itself "could wreck his presidency." Klein exhorts the president to "tell blacks that government can't cure racism" or "force integration." But what affirmative action proponent claims that the policies "cure racism"? And why should anti-discrimination policies' inability to "force integration" be an argument for their elimination?

Klein's motives are revealed when he explains why white people ought to care about opportunity for minorities: It's all those "alienated fatherless children creating havoc in the streets," he warns. "The chaos they cause could destroy this country." Naturally, the first thing Klein recommends whites do "for" blacks is to "spend more on policing."

Anti-Logic

Columnists like Joe Klein claim that they are vehemently opposed to affirmative action only because of their long-held beliefs in a "merit-based" society. Pundits who've never used the word "class" except pejoratively now claim that their problem with affirmative action is that it doesn't "fix class disparities." And columnists whose concern for the advancement of black people has been heretofore undetectable are now desperately troubled by the "stigma" affirmative action purportedly attaches to its beneficiaries.

Indeed, the mainstream press is overflowing with earnest calls for "color blindness" from the likes of *U.S. News'* John Leo (2/13/95) and the *Washington Times'* Wesley Pruden (2/28/95), disingenuously invoking the memory of Martin Luther King. But anyone who reads these columnists knows that while they're outraged by the tiny incidence of "reverse discrimination" (less than 3 percent of federal job discrimination complaints are made by white men), rampant examples of plain old discrimination scarcely register with them.

In a December 1994 column, for example, James J. Kilpatrick bemoaned "the racism in reverse that has done such fearful damage" to our society (*Baltimore Sun*, 12/9/94). This is the same James J. Kilpatrick who in the 1950s and '60s fiercely fought school desegregation and wrote, as recalled in Z magazine (5/95), that "in terms of values that last, and mean something, and excite universal admiration and respect, what has man gained from the history of the Negro race? The answer, alas, is 'virtually nothing.'" Why on earth should we credit calls for "equality" from people like this?

This anti-affirmative action pundits' disingenuousness is most glaringly obvious from their failure to support any concrete method of actually *achieving* the equality of opportunity they claim is their ideal. If the goal were really a "level playing field," would the elimination of anti-discrimination programs really be the first step—more important than substantial investment in public education, or health care, or urban infrastructure?

Yet pundits like *New Republic* managing editor Andrew Sullivan (*New York Times* op-ed, 7/23/95) throw in such recommendations—which would be monumental if intended seriously—at the end or in the margins of their diatribes against any form of anti-discrimination policy organized around race or gender.

At this argument's most perverse, support for affirmative action is actually equated with racism, as when James Pinkerton, in the "Column Right" section of the *Los Angeles Times* (1/19/95), argued that "those who . . . have emphasized racial categories at the expense of color-blindness must bear some responsibility for legitimizing the racially categorizing thinking that results. One such result is *The Bell Curve.*"

In other words, arguing that blacks and other minorities are systematically discriminated against is the same as saying that they're genetically inferior. Big Brother would be proud.

Chapter 146

Position Paper on Affirmative Action

National Employment Lawyers Association

The National Employment Lawyers Association (NELA), founded in 1985, repre-
sents employee rights. For further information, see www.nela.org.
   The following selection is reprinted by permission of the National Employment
Lawyers Association. Copyright © 1995 by the National Employment Lawyers
Association.

The National Employment Lawyers Association (NELA) expresses its strong sup-port for affirmative action as an important enforcement tool in the nation's con-tinuing effort to eliminate discrimination.[1] NELA's more than 2,300 members have represented hundreds of thousands of individuals seeking equal job opportu-nities. Based on that experience, we are acutely aware of the realities of the 1990's workplace. It is clear that the usual victims of employment discrimination con-tinue to be women and people of color.

We hear regularly from female and minority clients who have experienced di-rect discrimination based on their race, color or national origin. These individuals have experienced a broad range of discriminatory treatment—they have been de-nied access to positions for which they are well-qualified; subjected to sexually and racially hostile job settings where their self-esteem and sensibilities are as-saulted on a daily basis; held to higher standards of workplace performance or be-havior than white or male colleagues; channeled into marginal or dead-end jobs, despite their skills and training for advancement; and terminated or forced to re-sign because of discriminatory treatment by their employer.

Our experiences are not isolated: judges and juries yearly issue hundreds of decisions reflecting the unfortunate and persistent lack of equal employment op-portunity for women and people of color. Accordingly, we endorse the use of remedies and voluntary actions that take race, gender and national origin into account among the many necessary steps toward our national goal of equal opportunity.

What Affirmative Action Is—and Isn't

It is regrettable that the current debate has involved substantial misinformation about affirmative action and its social impact on American society. The United States Commission of Civil Rights has defined affirmative action as:

> . . . [A]ny measure, beyond simple termination of a discriminatory practice, adopted to correct or compensate for past discrimination or prevent discrimination from occurring in the future.[2]

Affirmative action does not mean quotas, reverse discrimination or hiring unqualified workers. Quotas and "reverse discrimination" are illegal. As to hiring, the courts have repeatedly held that affirmative action considerations do not come into play unless an individual is qualified for the position in the first instance.[3] Rather, affirmative action encompasses a wide range of actions intended to ensure the full participation of women and minorities in the workplace, and prevent discrimination in the future. An effective affirmative action policy focuses on individual potential, using hiring standards that correspond to the actual skills required rather than relying on non job-related and often biased selection methods.

In spite of the loud protests of affirmative action's opponents, reverse discrimination is extremely rare. EEOC records for fiscal 1994 indicate that charges of "reverse discrimination" constitute approximately 2 percent of all charges filed with the agency.[4] Moreover, a recent U.S. Department of Labor study of over 3,000 discrimination cases filed between 1990 and 1994 found that a high proportion of reverse discrimination claims brought by white men are factually unsupported.[5] Where a white or male is actually harmed by discrimination, of course, the courts can provide appropriate relief.

Discrimination Persists

Much of the debate regarding affirmative action is based on the misperception that discrimination no longer exists, or that if it does, simple legal prohibitions against discrimination will suffice. Nothing could be further from the truth. Notwithstanding the substantial gains achieved by women and people of color in the labor market, discrimination remains a stark reality. Discrimination claims have continued to increase dramatically, with thousands of cases filed each year in state and federal courts, and an even greater volume of complaints filed with the EEOC and state and local fair employment agencies.

The stories our clients tell us about continuing employment discrimination are confirmed by the statistics. Most recently, the bipartisan Glass Ceiling Commission issued its fact-finding report, finding an "enduring aptness to the 'glass ceiling' metaphor."[6] After extensive hearings and research, the Commission concluded that women and people of color rarely reach the highest levels of business and that even when they do, they receive lower compensation than comparable whites.[7] At Fortune 1000 Industrial and Fortune 500 companies, 97 percent of senior managers are white. In Fortune 2000 industrial and service companies, only five percent of senior managers are women, virtually all of them white. Of equal concern, very few women of color are even in the "pipeline" positions leading to the top jobs.[8]

The Commission also concluded that women and people of color face "three levels of artificial barriers to [their] advancement": societal barriers, including both "conscious and unconscious stereotyping, prejudice and bias"; governmental barriers, including "lack of vigorous and consistent monitoring and law enforcement"; and internal structural barriers, including "outreach and recruitment practices that do not seek out or reach or recruit minorities and women," "initial placement and clustering" in positions that are not on the "career track to the top," lack of mentoring, training and opportunities for career development, and use of different, often biased performance standards.[9]

The Glass Ceiling Commission focused on the nation's largest businesses. Other statistics demonstrate a similar pattern. For example, although white men constitute a minority of the total work force (47 percent) and of the college educated work force (48 percent), they dominate the top jobs in virtually every field.[10] White males comprise 91.7 percent of officers and 88.1 percent of directors.[11] White men hold over 90 percent of the top news media jobs.[12] White men constitute over 86 percent of partners in major law firms.[13] White men make up 85 percent of tenured college professors.[14] White men occupy over 80 percent of the management jobs in advertising, marketing and public relations.[15] The median weekly earnings of white males in 1992 were 33 percent higher than those of any other group in America.[16]

African Americans, who constitute 11 percent of the total workforce, made up less than 4 percent of the following occupations as of 1993: lawyers and judges (2.7 percent), dentists (1.9 percent), doctors (3.7 percent), industrial engineers (3.4 percent), engineers (3.7 percent), managers in marketing, advertising and public relations (3.1 percent).[17] Hispanics make up 7.9 percent of the labor force, yet they are all but invisible in corporate decision-making positions.[18] Similarly, Asian and Pacific Islander Americans are seriously underrepresented in executive level management jobs, even where they have all the credentials for higher paying positions.[19]

Recent studies using employment testers, conducted by the Fair Employment Council (FEC) of Greater Washington and the Urban Institute, further demonstrate the existence of ongoing discrimination. The FEC found, for example, that black job applicant testers were treated significantly worse than comparable whites in 24 percent of tests; in tests pairing Anglo and Latino applicants, the discrimination rate was 22 percent.[20] The Urban Institute in 1990 found that 20 percent of the time white applicants advanced further in the hiring process than equally qualified blacks. In only 7 percent of the tests conducted did the black tester advance further than the white tester.[21]

Women workers likewise continue to face workplace barriers. Seventy percent of the 57 million working women in the United States make less than $20,000, and 40 percent earn less than $10,000.[22] A recent study concluded that women continue to earn approximately 70 percent of the salaries earned by comparable men. While women are over half of the adult population[23] and nearly half of the workforce,[24] most continue to work in traditional jobs such as teachers, nurses and librarians. Women remain severely underrepresented in most non-traditional professional occupations as well as blue collar trades. For example, women constitute only 8.6 percent of all engineers; 3.9 percent of airplane pilots and navigators; less than 1 percent of carpenters; and just over 20 percent of doctors and lawyers. Even where women have moved into occupations and professions in significant numbers, they have not advanced to the same degree. Women make up 23 percent of lawyers, but only 11 percent of partners in law firms.[25] Women are 48 percent of journalists, but hold only 6 percent of the top jobs in journalism.[26] Women are 72 percent of elementary school teachers, but only 29 percent of school principals.[27]

Minority women have lagged particularly behind. They occupy a disproportionately high percentage of the lowest paid jobs—typists, clerks, nurse's aides, factory workers—and are often concentrated in the contingent workforce.[28] In 1993, for example, black women earned a median income of $19,816, compared to $22,023 for white women and $31,089 for white men. Hispanic women earned a median income of $16,758.[29] Even in sectors where women have made inroads into management, women of color continue to be underrepresented, underpaid and undervalued.

Affirmative Action Works—and It's Still Needed

The continuing reality of discrimination means that this is not the time to end affirmative action. In fact, many of the important gains made by women and people of color over the past 30 years have resulted from affirmative action. One 1984 study concluded that affirmative action had significantly reduced job segregation and improved occupational status and mobility for minorities and women.[30]

Numerous other studies conducted during the 1970s and 1980s underscore that minorities and women made substantially greater gains where affirmative action programs were in place.[31] For example, a 1983 Department of Labor review of more than 77,000 companies found that minority employment increased more than 20 percent and female employment more than 15 percent where companies were subject to federal affirmative action plans. Movement of women and people of color into formerly segregated job titles was also greater for such companies, such as, for example, banking. In 1970, 17.6 percent of bank officials and financial managers were women. After aggressive affirmative action enforcement efforts by the Department of Labor, that number more than doubled to 38 percent by 1981. One expert has concluded that "more than five million people of color and six million women are in higher occupational categories today than they would be if we still distributed people through the labor force the way we did in the sixties."[32]

A recent report issued by the Equal Employment Advisory Council (EEAC), an employer group, also evaluated the benefits of federally mandated affirmative action programs, noting that conscious attention to affirmative action also helps identify and eliminate discriminatory practices.[33] If an employer is not "attracting individuals from all segments of the community," EEAC concludes, it is not able to "develop fully the pool of available workers" or "compete effectively in a global marketplace."[34]

Conclusion

We are still a long way from a color-blind and gender-blind workplace. Our national and international future requires that we insist on using the most effective tools available to secure equal rights for all in the workplace. From our perspective as employment lawyers and civil rights advocates, we know that court decisions address only a fraction of the serious cases of discrimination. As long as there is discrimination based on race, national origin and gender, we must use remedies and undertake voluntary actions that take race, ethnicity and gender into account. We must acknowledge that such efforts have proven essential and remain so if we are to achieve this nation's promise of equal opportunity.

NOTES

1. This position paper is intended to address affirmative action arising in the workplace. Affirmative action in the context of government contracting programs involves different legal and policy considerations. The Supreme Court's recent decision in *Adarand Constructors, Inc. v. Pena,* No. 93-1841 (June 12, 1995), should not have a negative impact on employment discrimination cases.

2. U.S. Commission on Civil Rights, *Statement on Affirmative Action,* Clearinghouse Pub. 54 (October, 1977).

3. See, e.g., *Johnson v. Transportation Agency,* Santa Clara County, 480 U.S. 616 (1987).

4. U.S. Equal Employment Opportunity Commission, "Charge Statistics Reflecting Types of Reverse Discrimination FY 1987–1994."

5. "No 'Widespread Abuse' in Job Cases, Few Reverse Bias Claims, Study Says," *Daily Labor Report* (BNA), March 23, 1995, p. AA-1 (hereinafter "Reverse Discrimination Study").

6. "Good for Business: Making Full Use of the Nation's Human Capital," Fact-Finding Report of the Glass Ceiling Commission (U.S. Department of Labor, March 16, 1995) (Special BNA Supplement, hereafter "Glass Ceiling Report").

7. Glass Ceiling Report, Introduction by Secretary of Labor, pp. S2–3.

8. *Id.*

9. *Id.,* "Overview," pp. 5–6.

10. U.S. Department of Commerce, Census Bureau, *Statistical Abstract of the United States,* 1993, Tables No. 622 at 393 and 234 at 154 (hereinafter *Statistical Abstract*).

11. Mark Lowery, "The Way on Equal Opportunity," *Black Enterprise,* February 1995.

12. *Newsweek,* April 24, 1989; *Newsday,* August 1, 1994, quoting the American Society of Newspaper Editors.

13. *National Law Journal,* August 9, 1994.

14. *Statistical Abstract,* Table No. 637 at 407–10.

15. *Statistical Abstract,* Table No. 637 at 407–10.

16. *Statistical Abstract,* Table No. 671 at 426.

17. *Statistical Abstract,* Table No. 622 at 393, Table No. 637 at 407–10.

18. Glass Ceiling Report, p. 125.

19. Glass Ceiling Report, p. 106.

20. Bendick, et. al., "Measuring Employment Discrimination Through Controlled Experiments," *The Review of Black Political Economy,* Summer 1994.

21. Turner, et. al., *Opportunities Denied, Opportunities Diminished: Discrimination in Hiring* (Urban Institute Press, 1991).

22. U.S. Bureau of the Census, Current Population Reports, "Money Income of Households, Families, and Persons in the United States: 1992," Series P-60, No. 184.

23. *Statistical Abstract,* p. 13.

24. *Id.,* at 396.

25. Curan and Carson, American Bar Foundation, "The Lawyer Statistical Report" (1994).

26. "A Long Way to Go," *Newsweek,* April 24, 1989, at 74.

27. Commission on Professionals in Science and Technology, *Professional Women and Minorities: A Total Human Resource Compendium,* 142, table 5-11 (1994).

28. See *1994–1995 Profile of Working Women,* p. 1.

29. Institute for Women's Policy Research, "The Wage Gap: Women's and Men's Earnings," (1995).

30. Citizen's Commission on Civil Rights, *Affirmative Action to Open the Doors of Job Opportunity,* 123–29 (1984).

31. See, e.g., J. Leonard, *The Effectiveness of Equal Employment Law and Affirmative Action Regulation* (School of Business Administration, Univ. of California, Berkeley, 1985); J. Field, *Affirmative Action: A Fresh Look at the Record 22 Years after the Beginning* (Center for National Policy Review); J. O'Neill, *The Economic Progress of Black Men in America* (U.S. Commission on Civil Rights, 1986); *EEO Policies and Programs, Personnel Policies Forum Survey No. 141* (BNA, 1986); H. Hammerman, *A Decade of New Opportunity: Affirmative Action in the 1970s* (Potomac Institute, 1985).

32. Reverse Discrimination Study, supra, n. 4, quoting from A. W. Blumrosen, "How the Courts are Handling Reverse Discrimination Claims," Appendix A.

33. Special Memorandum, "Critical Issues in the Affirmative Action Debate: Executive Order 11246," EEAC, March 17, 1995 (hereafter "EEAC Report").

34. EEAC Report, pp. 4, 10.

5

Backlash Redux

A white high school student attacks a black attorney after a 1976 anti-busing meeting in Boston. Three months later the nation joined in celebrating the bicentennial of the Declaration of Independence and its promise that "all men are created equal." *Boston Herald* photographer Stanley Forman's picture earned a Pulitzer Prize in 1977. (Photo courtesy of Stanley Forman, copyright © 1976 Stanley Forman.)

Chapter 147

Introduction: Redemption II

Jonathan Birnbaum and Clarence Taylor

The successes of the modern civil rights movement have been subject to a gradual chipping away and even outright assault and dismantling for some time now. This Second Redemption—ending the modern civil rights period—was formalized with the 1980 election of Ronald Reagan, whose policies rolled back many advances of the previous period.

Of course, this new backlash period did not emerge from nowhere. It has deep roots. Even during periods of civil rights progress, there were always reactionary elements organizing. During Reconstruction, Democrats and the Klan actively sought to dismantle gains almost as soon as the Civil War ended. During the first stirrings of the Second Reconstruction—the modern civil rights movement—when President Truman endorsed civil rights planks for the 1948 Democratic platform, Senator Strom Thurmond jumped ship to head the segregationist States' Rights Party ticket (dubbed the Dixiecrats), winning four states (Alabama, Louisiana, Mississippi, and South Carolina) and more than a million votes.[1] And when the Supreme Court pronounced its decision in *Brown v. Board of Education* in 1954—the traditional textbook date for the start of the modern civil rights movement—most southern senators and representatives responded with the "Southern Manifesto" condemning the court's decision (see chapter 148). Eight years later, during the heyday of the civil rights movement, Senator Barry Goldwater, the Republican candidate for president, voted against the 1964 Civil Rights Act, inaugurating the party's shift to a "Southern Strategy" (see chapter 151). Goldwater's campaign included a television commercial that featured rioters and muggers, contrasted with patriotic children saluting the flag, presaging George Bush's 1988 race-coded Willie Horton commercials attacking Democratic candidate Michael Dukakis. A Goldwater aide confided to columnist Drew Pearson that it was intended to "obviously and frankly play on prejudices.[2]

This book is organized according to the major pendulum swings of reaction and progress that have characterized the United States's history on civil rights. Within these major periods there have always been oppositional forces organizing. In this case, those countertendencies amounted to a qualitatively different period by 1980.

This new assault on civil rights also coincided, not coincidentally, with major assaults on organized labor, feminists, environmentalists, and other progressive groups. According to former neoconservative Michael Lind:

The southernization of the right has always meant more than the "southern strategy" devised by Goldwater and Nixon and perfected by Reagan and Bush—a strategy for luring white southerners away from the Democratic coalition. It means the adoption, by the leaders and intellectuals of the American right, of a "culture-war" approach to politics that was perfected by southern conservative Democrats during the period of their one-party rule in the South from the end of Reconstruction until the civil rights revolution. It means, as well, the adoption by the Republican leadership of a "southern" rather than a "northern" vision of the future of American capitalism and American politics—a vision of the United States as a low-wage, low-tax, low-investment industrial society like the New South of 1875–1965, a kind of early-twentieth-century Mississippi or Alabama recreated on a continental scale.[3]

This Second Redemption has interesting parallels with the Redemption period of Segregation—a rollback of civil rights, attacks on the rights of women, pro-business tax cuts and subsidies, cutbacks in the funding of education and other social programs, and calls for teaching biblical morality in the classroom.[4]

This section begins with selections discussing the roots of this new backlash during the Second Reconstruction before shifting to a set of readings about the new period.

NOTES

1. Thurmond's presidential bid was a short-term failure, but it had long-term consequences. After the election, Thurmond briefly returned to the Senate as a Democrat before switching parties to join the Republicans in time to vote against the 1964 Civil Rights Act. More significantly, his campaign helped lead to the Republican Southern Strategy.

2. Samuel G. Freedman, "The First Days of the Loaded Political Image," *New York Times,* 1 September 1996, 30.

3. Michael Lind, *Up from Conservatism: Why the Right Is Wrong for America* (New York: Free Press, 1996), 123–24.

4. See Eric Foner, "Redemption II," *New York Times,* 7 November 1981.

The Roots of Backlash

Chapter 148

The Southern Manifesto

The Southern Manifesto, a segregationist response to the Supreme Court's decision in Brown v. Board of Education, *was signed by nineteen southern senators and eighty-two members of the House of Representatives. Only three senators from the eleven southern states that composed the old Confederacy refused to sign—Lyndon Johnson (D–TX), Estes Kefauver (D–TN), and Albert Gore, Sr. (D–TN).*

The following selection is reprinted from "Declaration of Constitutional Principles," Congressional Record, 12 March 1956.

The unwarranted decision of the Supreme Court in the public school cases is now bearing the fruit always produced when men substitute naked power for established law.

The Founding Fathers gave us a Constitution of checks and balances because they realized the inescapable lesson of history that no man or group of men can be safely entrusted with unlimited power. They framed this Constitution with its provisions for change by amendment in order to secure the fundamentals of government against the dangers of temporary popular passion or the personal predilections of public officeholders.

We regard the decision of the Supreme Court in the school cases as a clear abuse of judicial power. It climaxes a trend in the Federal judiciary undertaking to legislate, in derogation of the authority of Congress, and to encroach upon the reserved rights of the States and the people.

The original Constitution does not mention education. Neither does the 14th amendment nor any other amendment. The debates preceding the submission of the 14th amendment clearly show that there was no intent that it should affect the systems of education maintained by the States.

The very Congress which proposed the amendment subsequently provided for segregated schools in the District of Columbia.

When the amendment was adopted, in 1868, there were 37 States of the Union. Every one of the 26 States that had any substantial racial differences among its people either approved the operation of segregated schools already in existence or subsequently established such schools by action of the same lawmaking body which considered the 14th amendment.

As admitted by the Supreme Court in the public school case (*Brown v. Board of Education*), the doctrine of separate but equal schools "apparently originated in

Roberts v. City of Boston (1849), upholding school segregation against attack as being violative of a State constitutional guarantee of equality." This constitutional doctrine began in the North—not in the South, and it was followed not only in Massachusetts, but in Connecticut, New York, Illinois, Indiana, Michigan, Minnesota, New Jersey, Ohio, Pennsylvania, and other northern States until they, exercising their rights as States through the constitutional processes of local self-government, changed their school systems.

In the case of *Plessy v. Ferguson*, in 1896, the Supreme Court expressly declared that under the 14th amendment no person was denied any of his rights if the States provided separate but equal public facilities. This decision has been followed in many other cases. It is notable that the Supreme Court, speaking through Chief Justice Taft, a former President of the United States, unanimously declared, in 1927, in *Lum v. Rice*, that the "separate but equal" principle is "within the discretion of the State in regulating its public schools and does not conflict with the 14th amendment."

This interpretation, restated time and again, became a part of the life of the people of many of the States and confirmed their habits, customs, traditions, and way of life. It is founded on elemental humanity and commonsense, for parents should not be deprived by Government of the right to direct the lives of and education of their own children.

Though there has been no constitutional amendment or act of Congress changing this established legal principle almost a century old, the Supreme Court of the United States, with no legal basis for such action, undertook to exercise their naked judicial power and substituted their personal political and social ideas for the established law of the land.

This unwarranted exercise of power by the Court, contrary to the Constitution, is creating chaos and confusion in the States principally affected. It is destroying the amicable relations between the white and Negro races that have been created through 90 years of patient effort by the good people of both races. It has planted hatred and suspicion where there has been heretofore friendship and understanding.

Without regard to the consent of the governed, outside agitators are threatening immediate and revolutionary changes in our public-school systems. If done, this is certain to destroy the system of public education in some of the States.

With the gravest concern for the explosive and dangerous condition created by this decision and inflamed by outside meddlers:

We reaffirm our reliance on the Constitution as the fundamental law of the land.

We decry the Supreme Court's encroachments on rights reserved to the States and to the people, contrary to established law and to the Constitution.

We commend the motives of those States which have declared the intention to resist forced integration by any lawful means.

We appeal to the States and people who are not directly affected by these decisions to consider the constitutional principles involved against the time when they, too, on issues vital to them, may be the victims of judicial encroachment.

Even though we constitute a minority in the present Congress, we have full faith that a majority of the American people believe in the dual system of Government which has enabled us to achieve our greatness and will in time demand that the reserved rights of the States and of the people be made secure against judicial usurpation.

We pledge ourselves to use all lawful means to bring about a reversal of this decision which is contrary to the Constitution and to prevent the use of force in its implementation.

In this trying period, as we all seek to right this wrong, we appeal to our people not to be provoked by the agitators and troublemakers invading our States and to scrupulously refrain from disorders and lawless acts.

Signed by:

Members of the United States Senate:

Walter F. George; Richard B. Russell; John Stennis; Sam J. Ervin, Jr.; Strom Thurmond; Harry F. Byrd; A. Willis Robertson; John L. McClellan; Allen J. Ellender; Russell B. Long; Lister Hill; James O. Eastland; W. Kerr Scott; John Sparkman; Olin D. Johnston; Price Daniel; J. W. Fulbright; George A. Smathers; Spessard L. Holland.

Members of the United States House of Representatives:

Alabama: Frank W. Boykin; George M. Grant; George W. Andrews; Kenneth A. Roberts; Albert Rains; Armistead I. Selden, Jr.; Carl Elliott; Robert E. Jones; George Huddleston, Jr.

Arkansas: E. C. Gathings; Wilbur D. Mills; James W. Trimble; Oren Harris; Brooks Hays; W. F. Norrell.

Florida: Charles E. Bennett; Robert L. F. Sikes; A. S. Herlong, Jr.; Paul G. Rogers; James A. Haley; D. R. Matthews; William C. Cramer.

Georgia: Prince H. Preston; John L. Pilcher; E. L. Forrester; John James Flynt, Jr.; James C. Davis; Carl Vinson; Henderson Lanham; Iris F. Blitch; Phil M. Landrum; Paul Brown.

Louisiana: F. Edward Hebert; Hale Boggs; Edwin E. Willis; Overton Brooks; Otto E. Passman; James H. Morrison; T. Ashton Thompson; George S. Long.

Mississippi: Thomas G. Abernethy; Jamie L. Whitten; Frank E. Smith; John Bell Williams; Arthur Winstead; William M. Colmer.

North Carolina: Herbert C. Bonner; L. H. Fountain; Graham A. Barden; Carl T. Durham; F. Ertel Carlyle; Hugh Q. Alexander; Woodrow W. Jones; George A. Shuford; Charles R. Jonas.

South Carolina: L. Mendel Rivers; John J. Riley; W. J. Bryan Dorn; Robert T. Ashmore; James P. Richards; John L. McMillan.

Tennessee: James B. Frazier, Jr.; Tom Murray; Jere Cooper; Clifford Davis; Ross Bass; Joe L. Evins.

Texas: Wright Patman; John Dowdy; Walter Rogers; O. C. Fisher; Martin Dies.

Virginia: Edward J. Robeson, Jr.; Porter Hardy, Jr.; J. Vaughan Gary; Watkins M. Abbitt; William M. Tuck; Richard H. Poff; Burr P. Harrison; Howard W. Smith; W. Pat Jennings; Joel T. Broyhill.

Chapter 149

George Wallace and the Roots
of Modern Republicanism

Taylor Branch

Taylor Branch is the author of America in the King Years, *a trilogy about Martin Luther King and the civil rights movement. Volume 1,* Parting the Waters *(1988), covering the period from 1954 to 1963, was awarded the Pulitzer Prize. Volume 2,* Pillar of Fire *(1998), covers the period from 1963 to 1965. Branch is currently completing the final volume.*

The following selection, "The Democratic Father of Modern Republicanism," a review of Dan T. Carter's Politics of Rage, *is reprinted from the* Washington Monthly, *October 1995, 48–51. Reprinted with permission from the* Washington Monthly. *Copyright by The Washington Monthly Company, 1611 Connecticut Ave., N.W., Washington, D.C. 20009, (202) 462-0128.*

George Wallace is the most prophetic embarrassment in American political history. He is detective Mark Fuhrman raised to colossal stature. Suppose, if you can, that the snarling tribal enforcer from the O. J. Simpson trial were to capitalize miraculously on the crudest self-indictments of his own mouth, somehow recovering enough of his blow-dried professionalism to get elected governor of Idaho four or five times. Suppose further that Governor Fuhrman quickly eclipsed Ross Perot, Jesse Jackson, and Colin Powell to become the nation's leading maverick force and along the way tore up partisan alignments that had stabilized American politics for more than a century. Then, Fuhrman would become a blinding legend, up there in Wallace country.

In 1963, the year of his debut as the new governor of Alabama, George Wallace appeared to guarantee himself a contemptible obscurity with three decisive acts. By his "Segregation forever!" inaugural address in January, he proved himself flat wrong on the seminal question of his time. In June, by "standing in the schoolhouse door" to block the enrollment of the first two black students at the last legally segregated state university, Wallace got himself shoved aside as a loser by federalized units of his own National Guard. In September, by excusing and belittling a crime of terror so pure that it galvanized a shocked nation—the bombing death during church hours of four black girls dressed in Sunday-school white—Wallace stamped himself as the Klanish symbol of unspeakable hate.

Thus spectacularly revealed as backward, ineffectual, and genocidally cruel—some of his later supporters actually wore "I like Eich" buttons in tribute to executed Nazi war criminal Adolf Eichmann—Wallace promptly ran for president in 1964. Northern voters flocked to his shoestring campaign in numbers that amazed Wallace himself. In many respects, Wallace dominated the politics of the next two national elections, but respectable observers ever since have turned away from him as a haunting unmentionable. Brushing by what he called "a Southern populist of the meanest streak," Theodore White all but excluded Wallace from his book of reflections on postwar electoral politics.

Last year, in the first comprehensive biography, *George Wallace: American Populist,* former *Newsweek* correspondent Stephen Lesher interpreted Wallace as the harbinger of today's not-always-pretty national populist sentiments. Now comes Emory University historian Dan T. Carter with a second biography. A pleasure to read and an excellent, sweeping piece of work, *The Politics of Rage* is less forgiving of Wallace but no less certain that there is a profound lesson hidden in his career. Meanwhile, the old governor himself hangs on to life in retirement—crippled, incoherent, and repentant, apologizing tearfully to anyone ever damaged by his cries of "nigger." He is abandoned in the flesh even as writers ponder at last what it means that the zeitgeist is crawling to his door. [He died in 1998.—Eds.]

George Wallace was colorful on all sides, whether nasty, picaresque, evil, or downright funny, and his life brims with good stories for anyone who gets past the initial discomfort of race. From Carter's account we learn that in 1963, Wallace brought to his first appearance at Harvard a strangely bifocal speech, half a thoughtful treatise on *The Federalist Papers* and half a diatribe written by a Klan leader named Ace, author of the "Segregation forever!" address [see chapter 150—Eds.]. Having introduced Ace by the exploits of his Klavern, which included one infamous ritual castration of a black man plucked randomly off the street, Carter lets readers grow accustomed to Ace's dual role over the years as Wallace's chief speechwriter. In public, Wallace used Ace's words to charm many of the Harvard students with his sporting treatment of hecklers. In private, Ace planned Wallace's 1968 presidential campaign at a country club convention in Alabama, together with an assortment of tycoons, Holocaust-deniers, super-patriots, and the ideological ancestors of today's religious right from across the nation.

Carter has a fine eye for archival detail, and he does not overlook salient issues from the complexities of state government. In one of my favorite nuggets, he explains in passing how Wallace used Alabama's self-insurance system. For decades, the state had found it cheaper to self-insure than to buy commercial insurance against fire and other hazards to public buildings, especially rural schools. However, to quiet accusations of socialistic risk management, Alabama agreed to forfeit most of these market savings by making estimated payment to insurance companies in lieu of "lost" premiums. Wallace shrewdly turned this corporate kitty into a political one by selectively channeling payments to friendly companies, which often turned out to be the ones that shared retainers with politicians Wallace wanted to control. Rounded out and polished, this practice amounted to legal payola from the state treasury.

This story is one of countless tangents from the career of another obsessive politician who was lit up on stage but hollow everywhere else, using up three wives. The life of Wallace is absorbing because both Lesher and Carter claim for him an overarching legacy that applies outside Alabama and down through our time. This is the central question: how to define his influence. "If he did not create the conservative groundswell that transformed American politics in the eighties," writes Carter, "he anticipated many of its themes." As indicated by his pastiche of subtitles, Carter approximates a thesis from several different angles but does not state one baldly. He associates Wallace with a "new" conservativism that is reckless by temperament and hostile to authority. Wallace's "attacks on the federal government have become the gospel of modern conservatism," Carter incisively declares, but he does not spell out whether racial hatred has transformed a general theory of government, or vice versa.

On race, both Lesher and Carter gravitate to the dilemma of how much to forgive Wallace in his old age. Has he truly changed? Did he really mean all those horrible segregationist deeds, or was hatred merely the edge of an ambition that is being validated now by history? In politics, Carter senses the powerful, paradoxical effects of Wallace the diehard Democrat on Republican analysts such as Kevin Phillips. "In a recommendation of breathtaking cynicism," writes Carter, "Phillips urged his party [in 1969] to work vigorously to maintain and expand black voting rights in the South, not as a moral issue, but because it would hasten the transfer of whites—North *and* South—to the Republican Party."

In my own research, which has brushed over Wallace in his early years as governor, I have come across one strikingly succinct formulation of his original secret, written in 1964 by an awestruck Alabama reporter struggling to explain the success of Wallace's first speeches outside the South: "He gave every hearer a chance to transmute a latent hostility toward the Negro into a hostility toward big government. The technique was effective." All these phrases carried understated meaning—"every hearer," "latent hostility," "big government," "technique." The reporter recognized that Wallace's power began in rhetorical innovation. Without harping on racial epithets, as everyone expected him to do, Wallace talked all around race by touching on the related fears of domination, coining new expressions such as "forced busing" and "big government," which were anything but common clichés 30 years ago.

Writing about those early speeches, Lesher picks out many creations that have gained resonance, including Wallace's scornful references to "tax, tax, spend, spend" politicians, the "ultra-liberal controlled media," and of course, the "pointy-headed bureaucrats" from "central government" in Washington, who "can't even park their bicycles straight." Carter, for his part, opens a chapter with a quotation from Martin Luther King, Jr. that (I am sorry to say) had escaped me entirely. In 1963, across huge gaps of philosophy and pain, King appraised his nemesis as an "artful" fellow orator of fearful potential. "He just has four speeches," said King "but he works on them and hones them, so they are little, minor classics."

Two main obstacles block the understanding of Wallace as a new moon above the national tides, pioneering a kind of velvet racialism in political rhetoric. First is the lingering image of his inflammatory lynch talk. Subtlety of words is not the first characteristic that jumps to mind for a governor who once vowed not to be "out-niggered" on the campaign stump. For a historian of Carter's depth, moreover, there is an abiding awareness that Wallace performed treacherous cosmetic surgery just above exposed nerves and arteries of racial politics.

A reminder of bloodcurdling reality ruined the second Wallace campaign for president in 1968. When he tried to choose a moderate for his running mate as a third-party candidate, supporters revolted against ex-governor of Kentucky "Happy" Chandler, branding him an "out-and-out integrationist," who as baseball commissioner, had permitted Jackie Robinson to enter the major leagues. Shaken, Wallace substituted General Curtis LeMay at the last minute, but no amount of backroom coaching could keep the champion of strategic air power from waxing fond over nuclear weapons. "For once in his life, George Wallace was speechless," writes Carter in an entertaining account of the ruinous press conference at which LeMay volunteered that "the land crabs are a little bit hot" 10 years after bomb tests on Bikini Atoll.

The cleansing elevation above racial politics did not always go smoothly for Wallace, who lapsed again after being humiliated back home in a 1970 primary. His brother Gerald prescribed a fallback strategy for the runoff campaign against the incumbent governor—"We'll just throw the niggers around his neck"—and Wallace himself denounced Governor Albert Brewer as a "tool of black militants," in "spotted alliance" with do-gooders and liberal reporters. Wallace doctored photographs to show Brewer's daughters with black boyfriends, and hit the airwaves with the following announcement: "Suppose your wife is driving home at 11 o'clock at night. She is stopped by a highway patrolman. He turns out to be black. Think about it . . . Elect George C. Wallace." He squeezed out an ugly victory at some cost to his national dignity.

A second factor obscures the trajectory of Wallace's influence: He was the father of a new, whiteman's anti-government, anti-Washington Republican Party even though he still hated Republicans. From redneck to Republican and from raw to Reagan, he was a transitional figure for the partisan structure as well as the texture of American politics. To appreciate these sweeping changes, we must remember that when Wallace first ran for president in 1964, there were no Southern Republicans in the House of Representatives. Not one. Of 172 Republicans in the House, 138 supported the landmark civil rights bill that outlawed segregation that year. The GOP was still the party of Lincoln, but the first seven Southern Republicans were elected to the House that year, five of them Wallace supporters from Alabama. Now 30 years later, white Southern candidates are completing their evacuation of the Democratic Party. The congressional delegation from Georgia consists of eight white Republicans and three black Democrats—a lineup scarcely imaginable in the sixties.

George Wallace laid the groundwork for the partisan revolution by campaigning against *both* national parties as agents of federal tyranny. Republicans and Democrats were identical partners—"Tweedledum and Tweedledee," he called them—"seizing control" of local schools, businesses, and courts to carry out the integrationist agenda. Oddly enough, Wallace's scathing attacks mirrored the rhetoric of Malcolm X, who saw integration as a sham and not a "dime's worth" of difference between Democrats and Republicans. Wallace and Malcolm X ridiculed white liberals in almost identical language, gleefully describing the bulging private schools and panic bridges thrown up to new suburbs. By skewering the stiff compromise between the two parties, Wallace helped to make the word "liberal" a general epithet.

Carter is at his best in describing the contest between Wallace and Richard Nixon. After winning the White House in 1968, Nixon was consumed by political threats to his reelection. But not from Democrats. "My concern was about Wallace," he wrote privately. Unlike the rest of the world, which tried to dismiss Wallace after his second national failure, Nixon focused on the growing menace of a third-party candidate who, in spite of the LeMay fiasco, had won 58 electoral votes and carried only one less state than GOP nominee Barry Goldwater in 1964. The slightest improvement in the Wallace vote in 1968 would have elected Hubert Humphrey.

Therefore Nixon set out to destroy or seduce Wallace before 1972. Carter's account of the skullduggery is captivating and newsworthy; it reads like a real-life preview of Watergate—which it was. Nixon sent a clandestine $400,000 to finance Albert Brewer, Wallace's opponent in 1970. When Wallace won anyway, Nixon wrote "Need to Handle Wallace" at the top of his strategy pad for 1972. His minions spent all of 1971 trying to indict Wallace for something. In a transparent settlement, the Justice Department publicly dropped its corruption investigation of brother Gerald Wallace one day before Governor Wallace announced that he would run for president as a Democrat this time, not as an independent. Much to Nixon's relief, Wallace carved up the Democrats instead of him. His "non-racial" attacks on school busing paralyzed presidential rivals "like so many deer frozen by the bright lights of an oncoming car," says Carter. In the early Florida primary, Wallace placed far ahead of Humphrey, McGovern, Muskie, and eight other Democrats. He rolled up victories until May, winning Michigan and Maryland in the same week that Wallace himself was paralyzed by the bullets of a would-be assassin.

Nixon remained terrified of Wallace even as a paraplegic. His "greatest nightmare," writes Carter, was that Wallace would miss the Democratic primaries but recover enough to run as an independent again in the general election. Accordingly, the White House provided Wallace with comfort money in the hospital, and Nixon sent both Billy Graham and John Connolly to beg Wallace to stay out of the race. They succeeded. Two years later, on his own political deathbed, Nixon himself begged Wallace to speak up against impeachment. "Well Al, there goes the presidency," he sighed to Al Haig when Wallace refused.

Nixon knew that Wallace voters were becoming natural Republicans. With revenue sharing—his version of today's block grants—Nixon moved from Lincoln Republicanism toward a posture compatible with Wallace's version of state's rights. From his sickbed, Wallace watched the white South follow the path he had marked toward an anti-government ideology that the Republican party adopted. For more than a century, his Democrats had straddled a core identity that upheld both the common people and the segregated South. Now segregation was being lost, formally, and at the same time Wallace's racial alchemy was eating away at the party's distinctive bond with ordinary citizens. Today Wallace's legacy is clear. He enticed the children of FDR Democrats to think of government not as a savior, refuge, compact of fellow citizens—or even as their problem—but as the enemy.

Chapter 150

Segregation Forever

George Wallace

George Wallace (1919–1998) served four terms as governor of Alabama, winning elections in 1962, 1970, 1974, and 1982. He ran for the presidency as an independent in 1968, winning five states and 13 percent of the popular vote. He was shot while campaigning in the 1972 Democratic presidential primary.

Wallace first ran for governor in 1958, and lost. The winner, John Patterson, said the "primary reason I beat him was because he was considered soft on the race question at the time." The night of his defeat, Wallace vowed that "no son-of-a-bitch will ever out-nigger me again." In the 1962 campaign, after running a race-baiting campaign with Klan support, Wallace won his first term as governor. He was sworn in standing on the gold star that commemorates the spot where Jefferson Davis was sworn in as president of the Confederacy. His acceptance speech, excerpted below, was written by Ku Klux Klansman Asa Carter.

Wallace went on to become a national symbol for segregation. When a court ordered that two black students—James Hood and Vivian Malone—be admitted to the University of Alabama, Wallace personally stood in the schoolhouse door to block their entry, forcing the Justice Department to send in the Alabama National Guard to enforce the court decision.

Late in life, Wallace sought forgiveness for his past actions, but some question the sincerity of his apologies. According to a New York Times *editorial, "For the sake of expediency . . . [Wallace] transformed himself in the watershed year of 1963 into America's foremost racist. . . . He died in denial about the fact that the 'pragmatic' step he took to win the statehouse triggered a murder epidemic that took the lives of 10 people who were either demonstrating for civil rights or simply breathing in Alabama while being black."*

The following excerpt is reprinted from "The Inaugural Address of Governor George C. Wallace," 14 January 1963, Montgomery, Alabama.

Today I have stood, where once Jefferson Davis stood, and took an oath to my people. It is very appropriate then that from this Cradle of the Confederacy, this very Heart of the Great Anglo-Saxon Southland, that today we sound the drum for freedom as have our generations of forebears before us done, time and again down through history. Let us rise to the call of freedom-loving blood that is in us and send our answer to the tyranny that clanks its chains upon the South. In the name of the greatest people that have ever trod this earth I draw the line in the dust and toss the gauntlet before the feet of tyranny and I say, segregation now, segregation tomorrow, segregation forever. . . .

Let us send this message back to Washington by our representatives who are with us today, that from this day we are standing up, and the heel of tyranny does not fit the neck of an upright man . . . that we intend to take the offensive and carry our fight for freedom across this nation, wielding the balance of power we know we possess in the Southland . . . that WE, not the insipid bloc voters of some sections, will determine in the next election who shall sit in the White House of these United States . . . that from this day, from this hour, from this minute we give the word of a race of honor that we will tolerate their boot in our face no longer . . . and let those certain judges put that in their opium pipes of power and smoke it for what it is worth.

Hear me, Southerners! You sons and daughters who have moved north and west throughout this nation. We call upon you from your native soil to join with us in national support and vote. And we know wherever you are away from the hearths of the Southland that you will respond, for though you may live in the farthest reaches of this vast country, your heart has never left Dixieland. . . .

What I have said about segregation goes double this day. And what I have said to or about some federal judges goes TRIPLE this day. . . .

Not so long ago men stood in marvel and awe at the cities, the buildings, the schools, the autobahns that the government of Hitler's Germany had built. Just as centuries before they stood in wonder at Rome's building. But it could not stand, for the system that built it had rotted the souls of the builders and in turn rotted the foundation of what God meant that men should be. Today that same system on an international scale is sweeping the world. It is the "changing world" of which we are told. It is called "new" and "liberal." It is as old as the oldest dictator. It is degenerate and decadent. . . . [T]he international racism of the liberals seek to persecute the international white minority to the whim of the international colored majority so that we are footballed about according to the favor of the Afro-Asian bloc. . . .

It is this theory of international power politic that led a group of men on the Supreme Court for the first time in American history to issue an edict, based not on legal precedent, but upon a volume, the editor of which has said our Constitution is outdated and must be changed and the writers of which, some had admittedly belonged to as many as half a hundred communist-front organizations. It is this theory that led this same group of men to briefly bare the ungodly core of that philosophy in forbidding little school children to say a prayer. And we find the evidence of that ungodliness even in the removal of the words "in God we trust" from some of our dollars, which was placed there as like evidence by our founding fathers as the faith upon which this system of government was built. It is the spirit of power thirst that caused a President in Washington to take up Caesar's pen and with one stroke of it, make a law. A Law which the law making body of Congress refused to pass, a law that tells us that we can or cannot buy or sell our very homes, except by his conditions [anti-discrimination laws] and except at HIS discretion. It is the spirit of power thirst that led that same President to launch a full offensive of twenty-five thousand troops against a university—of all places—in his own country and against his own people, when this nation maintains only six thousand troops in the beleaguered city of Berlin. We have witnessed such acts of "might makes right" over the world as men yielded to the temptation to play God, but we have never before witnessed it in America. We reject such acts as free men. We do not defy, for there is nothing to defy, since as free men we do not recognize any government right to give freedom or deny freedom. No government erected by man has that right. As Thomas Jefferson has said, "The God who gave us life, gave us liberty at the same time; no King holds the right of liberty in his hands." Nor does any ruler in American government. . . .

This nation was never meant to be a unit of one, but a united of the many. That is the exact reason our freedom loving forefathers established the states, so as to divide the rights and powers among the many states, insuring that no central power could gain master government control. . . .

And so it was meant in our racial lives. Each race, within its own framework has the freedom to teach, to instruct, to develop, to ask for and receive deserved help from others of separate racial stations. This is the great freedom of our American founding fathers. But if we amalgamate into the one unit as advocated by the communist philosophers then the enrichment of our lives, the freedom for our development, is gone forever. We become, therefore, a mongrel unit of one under a single all powerful government, and we stand for everything and for nothing.

The true brotherhood of America, of respecting the separateness of others and uniting in effort has been so twisted and distorted from its original concept that there is small wonder that communism is winning the world.

We invite the negro citizens of Alabama to work with us from his separate racial station, as we will work with him, to develop, to grow in individual freedom and enrichment. . . .

But we warn those, of any group, who would follow the false doctrine of communistic amalgamation [integration] that we will not surrender our system of government, our freedom of race and religion, that freedom was won at a hard price and if it requires a hard price to retain it we are able and quite willing to pay it.

The liberals' theory that poverty, discrimination and lack of opportunity is the cause of communism is a false theory. If it were true the South would have been the biggest single communist bloc in the western hemisphere long ago. For after the great War Between the States [the Civil War], our people faced a desolate land of burned universities, destroyed crops and homes, with manpower depleted and crippled, and even the mule, which was required to work the land, was so scarce that whole communities shared one animal to make the spring plowing. There were no government hand-outs, no Marshall Plan aid, no coddling to make sure that our people would not suffer; instead the South was set upon by the vulturous carpetbagger and federal troops, all loyal Southerners were denied the vote at the point of bayonet, so that the infamous, illegal 14th Amendment might be passed.

There was no money no food and no hope of either. But our grandfathers bent their knee only in church and bowed their head only to God.

Not for one single instant did they ever consider the easy way of federal dictatorship and amalgamation in return for fat bellies. They fought . . .

And that is why today, I stand ashamed of the fat, well-fed whimperers who say that it is inevitable, that our cause is lost. I am ashamed of them and I am ashamed for them. They do not represent the people of the Southland.

And may we take note of one other fact, with all the trouble with communists that some sections of this country have there are not enough native communists in the South to fill up a telephone booth, and THAT is a matter of public FBI record.

We remind all within hearing of this Southland that a *Southerner*, Peyton Randolph, presided over the Continental Congress in our nation's beginning, that a *Southerner*, Thomas Jefferson, wrote the Declaration of Independence, that a *Southerner*, George Washington, is the Father of our Country, that a *Southerner*, James Madison, authored our Constitution, that a *Southerner*, George Mason, authored the Bill of Rights and it was a *Southerner* who said, "Give me liberty or give me death," Patrick Henry.

Southerners played a most magnificent part in erecting this great divinely inspired system of freedom and as God is our witness, Southerners will save it. . . .

My pledge to you to "Stand up for Alabama," is a stronger pledge today than it was the first day I made that pledge. I shall "Stand up for Alabama," as Governor of our State. You stand with me and we, together, can give courageous leadership to millions of people throughout this nation who look to the South for their hope in this fight to win and preserve our freedoms and liberties.

Chapter 151

The Southern Strategy

Dan T. Carter

Dan T. Carter, professor of history at Emory University, is the author of Scotts-
boro: A Tragedy of the American South *(1979),* When the War Was Over: The
Failure of Self-Reconstruction in the South *(1985), and* The Politics of Rage:
George Wallace, the Origins of the New Conservatism, and the Transformation of
American Politics *(1995), and the co-editor of* The Adaptable South *(1991).*

The following selection is excerpted by permission from From George Wallace
to Newt Gingrich: Race in the Conservative Counterrevolution, 1963–1994, *by
Dan T. Carter (Baton Rouge: Louisiana State University Press, 1996), 24–35,
footnotes deleted. Copyright © 1996 by Louisiana State University Press.*

For another selection by Carter, see chapter 178.

By the summer of 1968, almost eight years after his loss to John Kennedy and six
years after Pat Brown trounced him in his campaign for the California governor-
ship, Richard Nixon had nearly completed his own Long March to the presidency.
During those years of exile, American politics had been turned upside down. The
assassinations of John Kennedy and Martin Luther King, the race riots of the mid-
1960s, the escalation of the war in Vietnam, and the explosion of the antiwar
movement had created a whole new constellation of issues. In the first six months
of 1968, Eugene McCarthy had driven Lyndon Johnson from seeking a second
term, then Robert Kennedy had surged forward as the Democratic front-runner,
only to be gunned down in California. Hubert Humphrey had accepted the Democratic nomination at a convention spoiled by riots in Chicago's streets and bitter
divisiveness within his own party. Pollsters gave Nixon a twenty-point lead over
his Democratic opponent. Even before the debacle in Chicago, Nixon's acclama-
tion by a united Republican convention in Miami seemed more a coronation than
the opening round of a presidential campaign.

At his West Coast retreat at Mission Bay, California, Nixon and his staff spent
the week after the convention planning fund raising for the coming months and
surveying the issues they believed would dominate the coming race: the war in
Vietnam abroad; inflation and the growing spiral of civic disobedience and racial
conflict at home. . . .

In June of 1967, H. R. Haldeman had prepared a memorandum that laid out the critical role television would play in the reemergence of Nixon. Rallies and repeated exposure to opponents' supporters ("and paid troublemakers") were counterproductive. The time had come for political campaigning to "move out of the dark ages and into the brave new world of the omnipresent eye." . . .

Nixon's men knew the tools of their trade. Television would allow minimum uncontrolled exposure of the candidate and an opportunity for maximum manipulation of the electorate. As one of Nixon's media advisers told him even before his nomination: "Voters are basically lazy, basically uninterested in making an *effort* to understand what we're talking about. . . . Reason requires a high degree of discipline, of concentration. . . . The emotions are more easily roused, closer to the surface, more malleable. . . . It's the aura that surrounds the charismatic figure more than it is the figure itself, that draws the followers. Our task is to build that aura." . . .

Nixon had begun shaping his political strategy for 1968 after the Goldwater fiasco. Capturing the South was the linchpin of his plan. The notion that Goldwater had started the Southern Strategy was so much "bullshit," Nixon would later insist; it was Eisenhower who had campaigned in the South in 1952 and 1956, making dramatic inroads and drawing support from both the old Dixiecrats and an emerging middle-class constituency more in tune with traditional Republican economic conservatism than old-style racism. By 1964, however, the civil rights movement had galvanized angry whites within the region, nowhere more intensely than in the Deep South. Goldwater had been drawn to that constituency like a moth to a flame. As a result, Nixon later concluded, he "ran as a racist candidate . . . and he won the wrong [southern] states": Mississippi, Georgia, Alabama, Louisiana, and South Carolina. With that political shrewdness that seldom failed him, Nixon saw that Goldwater's decision to identify with what one aide called the "foam-at-the-mouth segregationists" weakened Republicans' appeals to moderates in the border states and in the North. That was one reason Nixon chose Spiro Agnew of Maryland as his running mate. Initially the Maryland governor was widely regarded as a moderate, but Nixon deployed him as a surrogate Wallace. The Deep South could be counted on to come home to the Republicans because the national Democratic Party—with its sensitivity to its black constituency—did not offer a viable alternative.

Harry Dent, a former aide to Strom Thurmond and one of the principal architects of the Southern Strategy, repeatedly insisted that neither that strategy nor the GOP candidate's generally conservative emphasis in 1968 was racist. And, in fact, he (like other members of the Nixon team) scrupulously avoided explicit references to race. The problem with the liberalism of the Democrats, Dent charged, was not that it was too pro-black; its real failure was that it had created an America in which the streets were "filled with radical dissenters, cities were literally burning down, crime seemed uncontrollable," and vast social programs were creating a class of the permanently dependent even as they bankrupted the middle class. The rising tide of economic and social conservatism clearly complemented opposition to federal activism, North and South. But it was disingenuous to argue (as did Dent and other practitioners of the Southern Strategy) that race was irrelevant; the political driving force of Nixon's policies toward the South was seldom simply an abstract notion about the "preservation of individual freedom."

In reality, almost every issue in the campaign was tightly interwoven with issues of race. In 1968 the American economy was drawing near the end of a remarkable quarter-century of sustained growth and rising wages across the income spectrum. Between 1947 and 1965, the purchasing power of middle-class and lower-middle-class workers rose an average of more than 2 percent per year. But that steady ascension had begun to slow in the late 1960s. Between 1965 and 1968, a combination of accelerating price increases and sharp hikes in payroll and income taxes led to a near stagnation in real wages for the average blue-collar and salaried white-collar worker. Family income remained stable and even rose slightly, but primarily because of the movement of women into the work force. Families were working harder in order to stay in place.

Higher taxes and the first wave of inflation generated by the Vietnam War also affected black and Hispanic Americans; nevertheless, nonwhites made remarkable economic as well as political gains through the 1960s. It would become an accepted truism that the Civil Rights Acts of the 1960s primarily benefited upwardly mobile and middle-class blacks. In reality, there were significant increases for working-class blacks as well. Between 1961 and 1968, total "aggregate" income for whites increased 56 percent, while the total for nonwhites went up 110 percent. Most of that increase stemmed from an upgrading in occupations as black Americans—particularly in the South—commanded higher-wage jobs. During these same years, the antipoverty and social welfare programs of the Kennedy and Johnson administrations transferred approximately $121 billion to individuals living below the poverty line; over 30 percent of those funds went to black Americans. Had that amount been retained by white Americans in low- and middle-income brackets, it would have added less than three-eighths of 1 percent to their actual disposable income. But that was not the public perception. The slowdown in the rate of economic growth surprised a white working class accustomed to a steadily rising standard of living. The poor—particularly the black poor—became increasingly appealing scapegoats.

Issues of race were interwoven with concerns over social disorder in American streets. At a Wallace rally or a Nixon appearance, the distinction between heckling protesters and street muggers seemed almost nonexistent. In the minds of many of Nixon's listeners—and in Nixon's mind, however often he denied it—race and disorder were always linked. And occasionally his facade slipped. On one occasion early in the campaign, he taped a television commercial attacking the decline of "law and order" in American cities. Viewing the finished product, an unguarded Nixon became more expansive with his staff. The commercial "hits it right on the nose," he said enthusiastically. "It's all about law and order and the damn Negro–Puerto Rican groups out there." Nixon did not have to mention race any more than did Ronald Reagan when he began one of his famous discourses on welfare queens using food stamps to buy porterhouse steaks; the audience was already primed to make that connection. (As longtime Nixon aide John Ehrlichman would later acknowledge, his boss genuinely believed that blacks could only "marginally benefit from Federal programs because blacks were genetically inferior to whites.")

For nearly a hundred years after the Civil War, the racial phobias of white southern Democrats had been used to maintain a solid Democratic South. To Nixon, it seemed poetic justice that the tables should be turned. The trick lay in sympathizing with and appealing to the fears of angry whites without appearing to become an extremist and driving away moderates—or, as Ehrlichman described the process, to present a position on crime, education, or public housing in such a way that a voter could "avoid admitting to himself that he was attracted by a racist appeal."

Such tactics were not reserved for southern whites. Measuring national attitudes on race is notoriously difficult; even the increasing sophistication of polling in the 1950s and 1960s often failed to distinguish between momentary responses to headline-grabbing racial incidents and long-term attitudinal changes. If the shape and dimensions of a white backlash were still unclear, however, it required no great political insight to detect the emergence of that white political undertow. The work of pollsters Louis Harris, George Gallup, the Roper Research Associates, and the University of Michigan Survey Research Center simply documented what dozens of contemporary reporters and political leaders sensed: the growing hostility to the gains made by the civil rights movement and the intention to resist further civil rights gains. The race riots of 1966 and 1967 and the increasing federal pressure to integrate northern schools and housing made it apparent that capital could be made among discontented white Democrats in the North as well as in the South. The task for Nixon was to move just to the right of a Democratic Party that had to be mindful of its black constituency. Complicating the process was the fact that the GOP candidate genuinely wanted to avoid a divisive presidential campaign. This desire did not stem from any concern over polarizing the American electorate; rather—in 1968, at least—Nixon had great ambitions for his presidency in domestic as well as foreign affairs. He believed a bitter campaign would make his task more difficult.

At least as early as 1966, Nixon had grasped the threat that George Wallace posed to his personal political future and to the fortunes of the Republican Party. On one of his many fund-raising tours—generating IOUs for the 1968 campaign—Nixon stopped off in South Carolina for a rally and benefit for Strom Thurmond and the state's emerging Republican Party. Thurmond's aide Harry Dent drove Nixon to the airport. His passenger made no attempt to be coy. "I'm running for the presidency," he announced. And while he had no illusions about the difficulties of getting the nomination and defeating Johnson (who he assumed would run for reelection), George Wallace was his greatest barrier to election. If Wallace should "take most of the South," Nixon would be "unable to win enough votes in the rest of the country to gain a clear majority." Either Johnson would win outright or the election would go into the Democrat-controlled House of Representatives. Wallace, Nixon concluded intensely, was the key to his chances for winning the presidency.

By late summer, 1968, Johnson was no longer a candidate. Polls showed Nixon leading a battered Humphrey by as many as twenty points. But, with memories of his cliffhanger defeat in 1960, Nixon was convinced that the race would be much closer.

He was right. Wallace climbed steadily in the polls to claim more than 20 percent of the electorate. Almost imperceptibly, disgruntled Democrats outside the South began to abandon their tentative allegiance to the GOP and to return to the party of their fathers. By the last week in September, Nixon still had a ten-point lead, but it was shrinking week by week. Wallace's strong position in the South revived the growing possibility that Humphrey might squeak through with a narrow victory, or—as Wallace had hoped—the election might be thrown into the House.

Capturing a majority of the southern electoral votes became a matter of survival for Nixon. He could not be certain whether Wallace helped or hurt him in the heartland states of the Midwest; one poll suggested that a majority of Wallace supporters outside the South would—if forced to choose—pick Humphrey over Nixon by a narrow margin. Another named Nixon as the second choice of the majority of northern Wallace voters. But the pollsters were consistent in their finding that the Republican was the second choice of 80 percent of Wallace voters in the South. How could he strip away these southern voters? That was proving more difficult than Nixon had imagined, particularly since he wanted to run a nondivisive campaign.

Nixon himself conceived the counterattack against the Alabama challenger, but maneuvers were directed by Harry Dent, who took charge of an ostensibly independent southern operation for the general election with the unlikely title "Thurmond Speaks for Nixon-Agnew." Dent coordinated strategy with the GOP campaign and in fact cleared every major decision through John Mitchell, although a wary Nixon never officially brought Dent on board his team.

Nowhere was Nixon's caution more evident than in his handling of the critical question of desegregation. In the mid- and late 1960s, southern school districts had resisted court-ordered desegregation with a variety of so-called freedom of choice plans, which placed the burden of desegregation upon black parents (since it seemed apparent that most whites would not choose to send their children to black schools). "Freedom of choice" became a popular rallying cry, suggesting grass-roots democracy—the right of parents to choose—and neutrality on the question of race. Of course, everyone knew that freedom of choice plans minimized comprehensive desegregation.

To southern Republicans, it was obvious that most white Americans—North and South—were increasingly opposed to the Johnson administration's attempts to bring about significant desegregation of the schools. By September, Nixon's running mate, Agnew, was in full-throated pursuit of the Democrats as the party of treason abroad and permissiveness at home, but neither he nor Nixon made more than the vaguest response to southern Republicans' pleas that the campaign commit itself to stopping (or dramatically slowing) the pace of desegregation in the South.

In mid-September, as he watched his southern base erode under attacks from Wallace, Nixon agreed to an interview with two Charlotte television newsmen. In a carefully planned trial balloon, the GOP nominee endorsed freedom of choice plans and attacked mandated desegregation plans. Placing "slum"—*i.e.,* predominantly black—children in schools in wealthier areas was counterproductive, he declared, because "they are two or three grades behind and all you do is destroy their ability to compete." Without explicitly endorsing freedom of choice plans, he made clear (he thought) his opposition to busing. But the shift in his position on this sensitive issue was so subtle it passed unnoticed by the press. A frustrated Dent wanted to use excerpts from the interview in televised advertisements to drive home Nixon's new stance, but the former vice-president, fearful of the political fallout, hesitated for more than three weeks. In the end, he decided to take the risk. On October 7, in an interview with UPI editors in Washington, he reiterated his opposition to "forced busing" and his support for freedom of choice plans. When Humphrey spoke to the same editors two days later and attacked freedom of choice plans as a "subterfuge for segregation," Dent moved into action and began to place regional ads comparing the two candidates' positions.

At the same time, Dent's careful polling in the South revealed Wallace's Achilles' heel: the fear of angry white southerners that a vote for the Alabama governor would allow Humphrey to win the election. Thurmond's aide put together a commercial in which country-music star Stuart Hamblen sang a sad song of southerners who were chasing a rabbit—George Wallace—while the real enemy of the South, Hubert Humphrey, waltzed into the White House. Dent and several southerners on the Republican team urged that the Nixon campaign buy up blocks of advertising on southern country-music stations, particularly slots on the Wally Fowler Gospel Hour and the popular shows hosted by Buck Owens, Ernest Tubb, and the Wilburn Brothers. Publicity director Harry Treleaven and the advertising wizards at Fuller, Smith and Ross recoiled in horror, but South Carolina textile industrialist Roger Milliken, whose long career as a union buster had given him a finely honed sense of his workers' *mentalité*, did not have to be persuaded. Within twenty-four hours, he and four fellow textile magnates raised sufficient money to enlist Roy Acuff, Tex Ritter, and Stuart Hamblen in Dent's down-home campaign.

Nixon himself took to the airwaves across the region to drive home his message the last week of the campaign. "There's been a lot of double-talk about the role of the South in the campaign of nineteen sixty-eight, and I think it's time for some straight talk," he declared. The people of the South—by which he meant most of the white people of the South—would vote three to one against Humphrey if given the option, he earnestly told his audience. Without mentioning Wallace by name, he warned that a "divided vote" would play into the hands of the Humphrey Democrats. "And so I say," he concluded, "don't play their game. Don't divide your vote. Vote for . . . the only team that can provide the new leadership that American needs, the Nixon-Agnew team. And I pledge to you we will restore law and order in this country."

The Nixon strategy worked, in part because the Wallace campaign had suffered a number of self-inflicted wounds, the greatest of which was the Alabamian's disastrous choice of retired Air Force general Curtis ("Bombs Away") LeMay as his running mate. Like a stuck phonograph needle, LeMay kept returning to his favorite subject: Americans' "irrational" fear of nuclear weapons (Hubert Humphrey began referring gleefully to the Wallace-LeMay ticket as "the Bombsey Twins"). By election day the Wallace candidacy—like most third-party movements—had faltered. Nevertheless, one of every eight voters supported him, and he showed surprising strength outside his own region. In addition to the five southern states he carried, Wallace polled from 8 to 15 percent of the vote in eighteen nonsouthern states. A statistically insignificant shift of votes in Tennessee and the two Carolinas and a 1 percent increase in the Democratic vote in Ohio and New Jersey would indeed have thrown the election into the House of Representatives.

It was a close call, and it did not bode well for the future majority Richard Nixon hoped to build. The most salient figures that emerged following the 1968 election came from pollsters Richard Scammon and Ben Wattenberg: four of every five Wallace voters in the South, and slightly more than three of every five in the North, would have voted for Nixon with Wallace out of the contest. Richard Nixon began to plan his reelection campaign in the first week after Inauguration Day. It is tempting to read history backwards, to strip away the awkward stops, starts, and detours of Nixon's policies as he sought to evolve a political strategy that would bring Wallace voters into the Republican Party yet would not make Nixon appear to capitulate to the darker side of the third-party movement. If there is one thing that is clear from the history of the Nixon years, it is the absence of any ideological dogmatism.

Chapter 152

The Nixon That Black Folks Knew

Clarence Lusane

Clarence Lusane is a professor in the School of International Service at American University.

The following selection, originally entitled "Paranoid, Criminal, and Reactionary: The Nixon That Black Folks Knew," is reprinted from Radical History Review *60 (Fall 1994), 167–69. Reprinted with permission of the author.*

For another selection by Lusane, see chapter 136.

When the history of Black America in the twentieth century is written, many names will arise as heroic figures who helped to shape and define the times. Among those names will be Martin [Luther King, Jr.], Malcolm [X], Fannie [Lou Hamer], W. E. B. [Du Bois], Angela [Davis], and Rosa [Parks]. To that list, be sure to add the name of Frank Wills. Perhaps it is part of the universal balance, the galactic cry for justice that it was an African American who tackled Richard Nixon's end run against democracy and helped launch the investigation that ultimately drove Nixon from office in disgrace.

While Nixon is being canonized and politically reconstructed in death, Wills has languished in poverty since he first discovered the Nixonoids breaking into the headquarters of the Democratic National Committee in 1972. While Nixon and the Watergate gang made millions in book deals and media contracts, Wills was forced to leave [Washington] D.C., where he could not find work even as a janitor.

I, for one, feel an eternal debt to brother Frank. During his fifty-year reign in public life, the real Nixon compiled a record of crimes against Black America that was unmatched by virtually any other President and few other political figures.

In the 1940s and 1950s as an aide to the red-baiting, morphine using, racist Senator Joseph McCarthy, and as President Eisenhower's Vice President, Nixon gleefully helped to persecute and pursue African-American activists including W. E. B. Du Bois, Harry Belafonte, Paul Robeson, black members of the Communist Party, U.S.A, and other radical groups. Martin Luther King, Jr. did not escape the charges of "communist" in that era, and even moderates, such as the NAACP's Roy Wilkins, were accused of being red sympathizers.

In 1968, Nixon captured the White House, employing what has become known as the "Southern Strategy." Nixon and the Republicans concluded that they could win the presidency by playing the race card and going after southern Whites with open racial appeals. Reagan and Bush would also use this strategy with success in 1980, 1984, and 1988. (Nixon failed with this strategy in 1960 against Kennedy.)

African Americans and people of color were Nixonized both globally and on the domestic front. After Nixon was elected, he continued the ungodly and destructive Vietnam War. From 1968 to 1973, 1,435 blacks died in the Vietnam war while thousands more were injured, as Nixon, Henry Kissinger, General [William] Westmoreland, and the Nixon posse lied to Congress and the nation and prolonged the war. Hundreds of thousands were killed and millions were made homeless in Southeast Asia because of Nixon's policies.

In South Africa, the Nixon administration sided with the apartheid government and charged the CIA with the task of helping the South Africans in their efforts to destroy the African National Congress.

On the domestic side, his effort to block the renewal of the Voting Rights Act in 1970 angered black political leaders. Nixon's opposition was a part of his promise to southern whites that if elected he would try to reverse Supreme Court decisions concerning civil rights. A number of black leaders and entertainers would later show up on Nixon's "enemies list," including Representative John Conyers and Bill Cosby.

Nixon's 1972 drug war and his law-and-order campaigns were overwhelmingly aimed at urban blacks. So was J. Edgar Hoover's and the FBI's COINTELPRO (Counterintelligence Program), which intensified under the Nixon regime against Black Power and civil rights movements. There were 295 operations against the black movement from 1965 to 1971; 233 of those were aimed at the Black Panther Party [see chapter 153—*Eds.*].

In 1971, the Congressional Black Caucus was formed and one of its first tasks was to develop a list of sixty demands that were presented to Nixon. His rejection of the list and earlier refusal to even meet with black members explains why, in January of that year, twelve of the thirteen black congressmen—Republican Senator Edward Brooke being the exception—boycotted Nixon's State of the Union address.

How the black community felt about Nixon was demonstrated in its response to the famous Sammy Davis, Jr. embrace of Nixon during his 1972 reelection bid. Davis was ostracized and labeled an Uncle Tom by many blacks. Pearl Bailey and James Brown were similarly castigated for supporting Nixon.

For all of his yah-yahs about black capitalism being equal to real "Black Power," Nixon's agenda for the black community amounted to more jails, less relief, and Republican rhetoric. His vile, evil, paranoid, hypocritical, disgraceful, insincere, unredemptive and criminal-minded career deserves a royal condemnation and certainly not the mourning, glorification, genuflecting, and rebirth that has been accorded in the wake of his demise.

Martin Luther King, Jr. speculated, at one point, that Nixon could be "the most dangerous man in America" for African Americans, given his apparent lack of support for black voting and civil rights. Fittingly, the Nixon Presidency came to a humiliating and shameful coda when the House Judiciary Committee—with two black members, Barbara Jordan and John Conyers, casting the deciding votes—recommended Nixon's impeachment, leading to his resignation shortly thereafter.

In honor of Frank Wills, bury Nixon and all that he stood for deep, tight, and permanent.

Chapter 153

The FBI, COINTELPRO,
and the Repression of Civil Rights

James W. Loewen

*"It is hard to exaggerate the truly sinister role played by [J. Edgar] Hoover and his
FBI, and thus the Justice Department, in the way the United States government responded to the organized efforts of black Americans to achieve equal treatment
under law," wrote former* New York Times *investigative journalist David Burnham. "The sheer scope of Hoover's efforts to shape the racial beliefs of generations of government officials who were personally involved in attacking black citizens and to undermine the federal response to these social upheavals can only be
described as malevolent."*[1]

*James W. Loewen taught sociology at the University of Vermont and Tougaloo
College. He is the co-author of* Mississippi: Conflict and Change *(1980).*

The following selection is reprinted from Lies My Teacher Told Me *(New York:
New Press, 1995), 224–30. Copyright © 1995 by James Loewen. Reprinted by
permission of The New Press.*

Between 1960 and 1968 the civil rights movement repeatedly appealed to the federal government for protection and for implementation of federal law, including
the Fourteenth Amendment and other laws passed during Reconstruction. Especially during the Kennedy administration, governmental response was woefully inadequate. In Mississippi, movement officers displayed this bitter rejoinder:

> THERE'S A STREET IN ITTA BENA CALLED FREEDOM.
> THERE'S A TOWN IN MISSISSIPPI CALLED LIBERTY.
> THERE'S A DEPARTMENT IN WASHINGTON CALLED JUSTICE.

The Federal Bureau of Investigation's response to the movement's call was especially important, since the FBI is the premier national law enforcement agency.
The bureau had a long and unfortunate history of antagonism toward African
Americans. J. Edgar Hoover and the agency that became the FBI got their start investigating alleged communists during the Woodrow Wilson administration [see
chapter 46—Eds.]. Although the last four years of that administration saw more
antiblack race riots than any other time in our history, Wilson had agents focus on

gathering intelligence on African Americans, not on white Americans who were violating blacks' civil rights. Hoover explained the antiblack race riot of 1919 in Washington, D.C., as due to "the numerous assaults committed by Negroes upon white women." In that year the agency institutionalized its surveillance of black organizations, not white organizations like the Ku Klux Klan. In the bureau's early years there were few black agents, but by the 1930s Hoover had weeded out all but two. By the early 1960s the FBI had not a single black officer, although Hoover tried to claim it did by counting his chauffeurs.[2] FBI agents in the South were mostly white Southerners who cared what their white Southern neighbors thought of them and were themselves white supremacists. And although this next complaint is reminiscent of the diner who protested that the soup was terrible and there wasn't enough of it, the bureau had far too few agents in the South. In Mississippi it had no office at all and relied for its initial reports on local sheriffs and police chiefs, often precisely the people from whom the civil rights movement sought protection.

Even in the 1960s Hoover remained an avowed white supremacist who thought the 1954 Supreme Court decision outlawing racial segregation in *Brown v. Board of Education* was a terrible error. He helped Kentucky prosecute a Caucasian civil rights leader, Carl Braden, for selling a house in a white neighborhood to a black family. In August 1963 Hoover initiated a campaign to destroy Martin Luther King, Jr., and the civil rights movement. With the approval of Attorney General Robert F. Kennedy, he tapped the telephones of King's conversations with and about women. The FBI then passed on the lurid details, including photographs, transcripts, and tapes, to Sen. Strom Thurmond and other white supremacists, reporters, labor leaders, foundation administrators, and, of course, the President. In 1964 a high FBI administrator sent a tape recording of King having sex, along with an anonymous note suggesting that King kill himself, to the office of King's organization, the Southern Christian Leadership Conference (SCLC). The FBI must have known that the incident might not actually persuade King to commit suicide; but the bureau's intention was apparently to get Coretta Scott King to divorce her husband or to blackmail King into abandoning the civil rights movement.[3] The FBI tried to sabotage receptions in King's honor when he traveled to Europe to claim the Nobel Peace Prize. Hoover called King "the most notorious liar in the country" and tried to prove that the SCLC was infested with communists. King wasn't the only target: Hoover also passed on disinformation about the Mississippi Summer Project; other civil rights organizations such as CORE and SNCC; and other civil rights leaders, including Jesse Jackson.[4]

At the same time the FBI refused to pass on to King information about death threats to him.[5] The FBI knew these threats were serious, for civil rights workers were indeed being killed. In Mississippi alone, civil rights workers endured more than a thousand arrests at the hands of local officials, thirty-five shooting incidents, and six murders. The FBI repeatedly claimed, however, that protecting civil rights workers from violence was not its job.[6] In 1962 SNCC sued Robert F. Kennedy and J. Edgar Hoover to force them to protect civil rights demonstrators. Desperate to get the federal government to enforce the law in the Deep South,

Mississippi civil rights workers Amzie Moore and Robert Moses hit upon the 1964 "Freedom Summer" idea: bring 1,000 northern college students, most of them white, to Mississippi to work among blacks for civil rights. Even this helped little: white supremacists bombed thirty homes and burned thirty-seven churches in the summer of 1964 alone.[7] After the national outcry prompted by the murders of James Chaney, Andrew Goodman, and Michael Schwerner in Philadelphia, Mississippi, however, the FBI finally opened an office in Jackson. Later that summer, at the 1964 Democratic national convention in Atlantic City, the FBI tapped the phones of the Mississippi Freedom Democratic party and Martin Luther King, Jr.; in so doing, the bureau was complying with a request from President Lyndon Johnson.[8]

Because I lived and did research in Mississippi, I have concentrated on acts of the federal government and the civil rights movement in that state, but the FBI's attack on black and interracial organizations was national in scope. For example, after Congress passed the 1964 Civil Rights Bill, a bowling alley in Orangeburg, South Carolina, refused to obey the law. Students from the nearby black state college demonstrated against the facility. State troopers fired on the demonstrators, killing three and wounding twenty-eight, many of them shot in the balls of their feet as they ran away and threw themselves on the ground to avoid the gunfire. The FBI responded not by helping to identify which officers fired in what became known as "the Orangeburg Massacre," but by falsifying information about the students to help the troopers with their defense.[9] In California, Chicago, and elsewhere in the North, the bureau tried to eliminate the breakfast programs of the Black Panther organization, spread false rumors about venereal disease and encounters with prostitutes to break up Panther marriages, helped escalate conflict between other black groups and the Panthers, and helped Chicago police raid the apartment of Panther leader Fred Hampton and kill him in his bed in 1969.[10] The FBI warned black leader Stokely Carmichael's mother of a fictitious Black Panther plot to murder her son, prompting Carmichael to flee the United States.[11] It is even possible that the FBI or the CIA was involved in the murder of Martin Luther King, Jr. "Raoul" in Montreal, who supplied King's convicted killer, James Earl Ray, with the alias "Eric Gault," was apparently a CIA agent. Certainly Ray, a country boy with no income, could never have traveled to Montreal, arranged a false identity, and flown to London without help. Despite or because of these incongruities, the FBI has never shown any interest in uncovering the conspiracy that killed King. Instead, shortly after King's death in 1968, the FBI twice broke into SNCC offices. Years later the bureau tried to prevent King's birthday from becoming a national holiday.[12]

The FBI investigated black faculty members at colleges and universities from Virginia to Montana to California. In 1970 Hoover approved the automatic investigation of "all black student unions and similar organizations organized to project the demands of black students." The institution at which I taught, Tougaloo College, was a special target: at one point agents in Jackson even proposed to "neutralize" the entire college, in part because its students had sponsored "out-of-state militant Negro speakers, voter-registration drives, and African cultural seminars and lectures

. . . [and] condemned various publicized injustices to the civil rights of Negroes in Mississippi." Obviously high crimes and misdemeanors![13]

The FBI's conduct and the federal leadership that tolerated it and sometimes requested it are part of the legacy of the 1960s, alongside such positive achievements as the 1964 Civil Rights Act and the 1965 Voting Rights Act. As Kenneth O'Reilly put it, "when the FBI stood against black people, so did the government."[14] How do American history textbooks treat this legacy? They simply leave out everything bad that the government ever did. They omit not only the FBI's campaign against the civil rights movement, but also its break-ins and undercover investigations of church groups, organizations promoting changes in U.S. policy in Latin America, and the U.S. Supreme Court.[15] Textbooks don't even want to say anything bad about *state* governments: all ten narrative textbooks in my sample include part of Martin Luther King's "I Have a Dream" speech, but nine of them censor out his negative comments about the governments of Alabama and Mississippi.

Not only do textbooks fail to blame the federal government for its opposition to the civil rights movement, many actually credit the government, almost single-handedly, for the advances made during the period. In so doing, textbooks follow what we might call the Hollywood approach to civil rights. To date Hollywood's main feature film on the movement is Alan Parker's *Mississippi Burning*. In that movie, the three civil rights workers get killed in the first five minutes; for the rest of its two hours the movie portrays not a single civil rights worker or black Mississippian over the age of twelve with whom the viewer could possibly identify. Instead, Parker concocts two fictional white FBI agents who play out the hoary "good cop/bad cop" formula and in the process double-handedly solve the murders. In reality—that is, in the real story on which the movie was based—supporters of the civil rights movement, including Michael Schwerner's widow, Rita, and every white northern friend the movement could muster, pressured Congress and the executive branch of the federal government to force the FBI to open a Mississippi office and make bringing the murders to justice a priority. Meanwhile, Hoover tapped Schwerner's father's telephone to see if he might be a communist! Everyone in eastern Mississippi knew for weeks who had committed the murder and that the Neshoba County deputy sheriff was involved. No innovative police work was required; the FBI finally apprehended the conspirators after bribing one of them with $30,000 to testify against the others.[16]

American history textbooks offer a Parkerlike analysis of the entire civil rights movement. Like the arrests of the Mississippi Klansmen, advances in civil rights are simply the result of good government. Federal initiative in itself "explains" such milestones as the Civil Rights Act of 1964 and the Voting Rights Act of 1965. John F. Kennedy proposed them, Lyndon Baines Johnson passed them through Congress, and thus we have them today. Or, in the immortal passive voice of *American History*, "Another civil rights measure, the Voting Rights Act, was passed." Several textbooks even reverse the time order, putting the bills first, the civil rights movement later.[17] [Of those studied,] only *American Adventures* and *Discovering American History* show the basic dynamics of the civil rights movement: African Americans, often with white allies, challenged an unjust law or practice in a nonviolent way, which then incited the whites to respond barbarically to defend "civilization," in turn appalling the nation and convincing some people to change the law or practice. Only the same two books celebrate the courage of the civil rights volunteers. And only *Discovering American History* tells how the movement directly challenged the mores of segregation, with the result that some civil rights workers were killed or beaten by white racists simply for holding hands as an interracial couple or eating together in a restaurant. No book educates students about the dynamics that in a democracy should characterize the interrelationship between the people and their government.[18] Thus no book tells how citizens can and in fact have forced the government to respond to them.

Instead, textbooks tell us about the outstanding leadership of John F. Kennedy on civil rights. *The Challenge of Freedom* provides a typical treatment:

> President Kennedy and his administration responded to the call for racial equality. In June 1963 the President asked for congressional action on far-reaching equal rights laws. Following the President's example, thousands of Americans became involved in the equal rights movement as well. In August 1963 more than 200,000 people took part in a march in Washington D.C.

This account reverses leader and led. In reality, Kennedy initially tried to stop the march and sent his vice-president to Norway to keep him away from it because he felt Lyndon Johnson was too pro–civil rights. Even Arthur Schlesinger, Jr., a Kennedy partisan, has dryly noted that "the best spirit of Kennedy was largely absent from the racial deliberations of his presidency."[19]

The damage is not localized to the unfounded boost textbooks give to Kennedy's reputation, however. When describing the attack on segregation that culminated in the 1954 Supreme Court decision, *Triumph of the American Nation* makes no mention that African Americans were the plaintiffs and attorneys in *Brown v. Board of Education* or that prior cases also brought by the NAACP prepared the way.[20] Today many black students think that desegregation was something the federal government imposed on the black community. They have no idea it was something the black community forced on the federal government.[21] Meanwhile, young white Americans can reasonably infer that the federal government has been nice enough to blacks. Crediting the federal government for actions instigated by African American students today, surely helps them feel that they "have never done anything," as Malcolm X put it.

Textbooks treat the environmental movement similarly, telling how "Congress passed" the laws setting up the Environmental Protection Agency while giving little or no mention to the environmental crusade. Students are again left to infer that the government typically does the right thing on its own. Many teachers don't help; a study of twelve randomly selected teachers of twelfth-grade American government courses found that about the only way the teachers suggested that individuals could influence local or national governments was through voting.[22]

Textbook authors seem to believe that Americans can be loyal to their government only so long as they believe it has never done anything bad. Textbooks therefore present a U.S. government that deserves students' allegiance, not their criticism. "We live in the greatest country in the world," wrote James F. Delong, an associate of the right-wing textbook critic Mel Gabler, in his critique of *American Adventures*. "Any book billing itself as a story of this country should certainly get that heritage and pride across." *American Adventures*, in conveying the basic dynamic of the civil rights movement, implies that the U.S. government was not doing all it should for the civil rights. Perhaps as a result, *Adventures* failed Delong's patriotism test: "I will not, I can not endorse it for use in our schools.[23]

The textbooks' sycophantic presentations of the federal government may help win adoptions, but they don't win students' attention. It is boring to read about all the good things the government did on its own, with no dramatic struggles. Moreover, most adult Americans no longer trust government as credulously as they did in the 1950s. Between about 1960 and 1974 revelation after revelation of misconduct and deceit in the federal executive branch shattered the trust of the American people, as confirmed in poll after opinion poll. Textbook authors, since they are unwilling to say bad things about the government, come across as the last innocents in America. Their trust is poignant. They present students with a benign government whose statements should be believed. This is hardly the opinion of their parents, who, according to opinion polls, remain deeply skeptical of what leaders in the federal government tell them. To encounter so little material in school about the bad things the government has done, especially when parents and the daily newspaper tell a different story, "makes all education suspect," according to Donald Barr.[24]

Nor can the textbook authors' servile approach to the government teach students to be effective citizens. Just as the [myth] of Columbus-the-wise [who believes the world is round] has as its flip side the archetype of the superstitious unruly crew, so the archetype of a wise and good government implies that the correct role for us citizens is to follow its leadership. Without pushing the point too far, it does seem that many twentieth-century nondemocratic states, from the Third Reich to the Central African Empire, have had citizens who gave their governments too much rather than too little allegiance. The United States, on the other hand, has been blessed with dissenters. Some of these dissenters have had to flee the country. Since 1776 Canada has provided a refuge for Americans who disagreed with policies of the U.S. government, from Tories who fled harassment during and after the Revolution, to free blacks who sought haven from the *Dred Scott* ruling, to young men of draftable age who opposed the Vietnam War. No textbook mentions this Canadian role, because no textbook portrays a U.S. government that might ever merit such principled opposition.[25]

Certainly many political scientists and historians in the United States suggest that governmental actions are a greater threat to democracy than citizen disloyalty. Many worry that the dominance of the executive branch has eroded the checks and balances built into the Constitution. Some analysts also believe that the might of the federal government vis-à-vis state governments has made a mockery of federalism. From the Woodrow Wilson administration until now, the federal executive has grown ever stronger and now looms as by far our nation's largest employer. In the last thirty years, the power of the CIA, the National Security Council, and other covert agencies has grown to become, in some eyes, a fearsome fourth branch of government. Threats to democracy abound when officials in the FBI, the CIA, the State Department, and other institutions of government determine not only our policies but also what the people and the Congress need to know about them.[26]

By downplaying covert and illegal acts by government, textbook authors narcotize students from thinking about such issues as the increasing dominance of the executive branch. By taking the government's side, textbooks encourage students to conclude that criticism is incompatible with citizenship. And by presenting government actions in a vacuum, rather than as responses to such institutions as multinational corporations and civil rights organizations, textbooks mystify the creative tension between the people and their leaders. All this encourages students to throw up their hands in the belief that the government determines everything anyway, so why bother, especially if its actions are usually so benign. Thus our American history textbooks minimize the potential power of the people and, despite their best patriotic efforts, take a stance that is overtly antidemocratic.

NOTES

1. Editors' note: David Burnham, "Uncivil Wrongs and Civil Rights," in *Above the Law: Secret Deals, Political Fixes, and other Misadventures of the U.S. Department of Justice* (New York: Scribner, 1996), 276.

2. Kenneth O'Reilly, *"Racial Matters": The FBI's Secret File on Black America* (New York: Free Press, 1989), 9, 12–13, 17, and 96–99; Charles Ameringer, *U.S. Foreign Intelligence* (Lexington, Mass.: D.C. Heath, 1990), 109.

3. O'Reilly, *"Racial Matters,"* 43, 126, 144, and 355; David J. Garrow, *The FBI and Martin Luther King, Jr.* (New York: Penguin, 1981), 125–26, 161–64; Taylor Branch, *Parting the Waters* (New York: Simon and Schuster, 1988), 861; Ameringer, *U.S. Foreign Intelligence*, 322–23; Frank J. Donner, *The Age of Surveillance* (New York: Alfred A. Knopf, 1980), 214–19; Athan Theoharis and John Stuart Cox, *The Boss* (Philadelphia: Temple University Press, 1988), 354–57. The media, in those days respecting a barrier between private and public lives, generally refused to use the material.

4. Ameringer, *U.S. Foreign Intelligence*, 323; Branch, *Parting the Waters*, 835–65; O'Reilly, *"Racial Matters,"* 140, 186; Garrow, *The FBI and Martin Luther King, Jr.*, 130–31; Donner, *The Age of Surveillance*, 217.

5. Branch, *Parting the Waters*, 692.

6. O'Reilly, *"Racial Matters,"* 357.

7. James W. Loewen and Charles Sallis, *Mississippi: Conflict and Change* (New York: Pantheon, 1980), 265–83.

8. O'Reilly, *"Racial Matters,"* 186.

9. Ibid., 256; Arlie Schardt, "Civil Rights: Too Much, Too Late," in Pat Watters and Stephen Gillers, *Investigating the FBI* (New York: Ballantine, 1973), 167–79.

10. Adam Hochschild, "His Life as a Panther," *New York Times Book Review*, January 31, 1993; O'Reilly, *"Racial Matters,"* 302–16; Donner, *The Age of Surveillance*, 220–32.

11. Donner, *The Age of Surveillance*, 220.

12. Ibid., 214–19; John Edginton and John Sergeant, "The Murder of Martin Luther

King, Jr.," *Covert Action Information Bulletin*, no. 34 (summer 1990): 21–27; Theoharis and Cox, *The Boss*, 439. See also Ameringer, *U.S. Foreign Intelligence*, 322; John Elliff, "Aspects of Federal Civil Rights Enforcement," in *Law in American History*, vol. 5 of *Perspectives in American History* (Cambridge: Harvard University Press, 1971), 643–47.

13. O'Reilly, *"Racial Matters,"* 336–37. Division administrators toned down the Jackson agents, reminding them to focus on the Tougaloo Political Action Committee, "since Tougaloo College, per se, is not a counterintelligence target." See also Donner, *The Age of Surveillance*, 219–20. Donner says the FBI forced the departure from Mississippi of Muhammad Kenyatta, a prominent black nationalist in Jackson. In internal memos, FBI agents took credit for setting up Kenyatta on the charge of attempting to steal a television set from Tougaloo College. Actually Kenyatta hastened his own departure by getting caught while doing just that.

14. O'Reilly, *"Racial Matters,"* 337.

15. Ross Gelbspan, *Break-ins, Death Threats, and the FBI* (Boston: South End Press, 1991).

16. Seth Cagin and Philip Dray, *We Are Not Afraid* (New York: Bantam Books, 1991), describes the murders and the FBI's reluctant but eventually effective police work.

17. One textbook, *The United States—A History of the Republic*, does draw a connection between the Selma march and the Voting Rights Act: "President Johnson pressed for further civil rights legislation after the Reverend James J. Reeb, a black civil rights worker, was shot during a voter registration campaign in Selma, Alabama." Reeb was a white Unitarian minister who had come to Selma to participate in the Selma-to-Montgomery march. *A History of the Republic* offers one of the fuller accounts of the civil rights movement, but other than this half-sentence about Reeb places the movement *after* the legislation it influenced.

18. In two vignette chapters on the Montgomery movement and Martin Luther King, Jr., *American Adventures* tells how the civil rights movement pressured Congress to pass the Civil Rights Act of 1964, but in its vignette chapter on Lyndon Johnson, *Adventures* gives the credit to LBJ and Robert Kennedy.

19. Arthur Schlesinger, Jr., quoted in Branch, *Parting the Waters*, 918–19.

20. *Triumph of the American Nation* does tell later of President Reagan's opposition to affirmative action, his support for tax breaks to segregated schools, and the decline of black income during his administration.

21. See Beverly Kraft, "Some Lack Knowledge about Evers," Jackson *Clarion Ledger*, January 20, 1994, 1A.

22. Patrick Ferguson, "Promoting Political Participation: Teachers' Attitudes and Instructional Practices" (San Francisco: American Educational Research Association, 1989).

23. Critique by James F. Delong (Hoover, Ala.: 1986, typescript, distributed by Mel Gabler's Educational Research Analysts, 1993).

24. Donald Barr, *Who Pushed Humpty Dumpty? Dilemmas in American Education Today* (New York: Atheneum, 1972), 308.

25. Michigan State Board of Education, *1982–1983 Michigan Social Studies Textbook Report* (Lansing, Mich.: Michigan State Board of Education, 1984).

26. Richard Rubenstein, *The Cunning of History* (New York: Harper, 1987), 80–82; Clarence Lusane, *Pipe Dream Blues* (Boston: South End Press, 1991), 4, 116–22, and 200–201.

Chapter 154

The Urban Fiscal Crisis and the Rebirth of Conservativism

William K. Tabb

William K. Tabb, professor of economics at Queens College and professor of sociology at the City University of New York, is the author of The Political Economy of the Black Ghetto *(1970) and* The Postwar Japanese System *(1995), editor of* Churches in Struggle: Liberation Theologies and Social Change in North America *(1986) and* The Future of Socialism *(1990), and co-editor of* Marxism and the Metropolis: New Perspectives in Urban Political Economy *(1978) and* Instability and Change in the World Economy *(1989).*

No crisis is ever as simple or as isolated an event as the headline writers suggest, and when the subject is as complex as the [1970s] New York City fiscal crisis, the search for explanations can carry us far indeed. New York City in the mid-1970s was the tip of the iceberg, the visible part of a far more enormous and dangerous phenomenon: the decline of the industrial northeast and the transformation of its cities to suit the purposes of the corporations and service industries. There is thus every reason to reconstruct the events and meaning of the near bankruptcy of the nation's largest city. Its crisis was both an augur and a cause of problems elsewhere. In a sense, federal policy toward New York, and toward older cities generally, revealed a crucial turn in U.S. politics, the extension of the benign neglect shown toward racial minorities and the poor since the beginning of the decade to a larger part of the population. It was an important step on the road to reducing government involvement in social issues and relying increasingly on the market. . . .

New York City illustrates the process by which, across the nation, the liberal 1960s turned into the neoconservative 1970s. In the 1960s, the issues in the nation's cities were poverty and discrimination, geographic exclusion and racial oppression. Federal monies were earmarked for low-income, inner-city neighborhoods; spending decisions were to be made after consultation with residents; neighborhood rebuilding and community self-determination were the stated goals.

The War on Poverty offered funding to local governments if they would follow federal guidelines for providing social services and job training. Such programs were a response both to the needs of the economy for workers in a period of relatively full employment and to black militancy.

By the end of the 1960s, however, developing stagflation and balance of payments problems led to a revision of the overall strategy and to the progressive dismantlement of existing programs. At the same time, massive funds were allocated for the reinforcement of repressive policies. With rising unemployment, retraining was no longer a corporate priority; reasserting control over urban spending priorities was. The Model Cities program was an early manifestation of this change in direction: the emphasis was on "saving the cities," but the idea of autonomous community mobilization was explicitly rejected and the power of local authorities restored. With President Nixon's revenue-sharing policy, initiated in 1972, the change of direction, in social and political terms, was complete. By the time of the Reagan administration, federally raised funds were being distributed to state governments, reformist federal agencies were being bypassed, social welfare expenditures were reduced, and political power was confirmed as the domain of local authorities and their real estate allies.

The relationship between technological change and the organization of production is complex. In the 1960s the civil rights movement got a push from the rapid mechanization of cotton production in the southern black belt. It became more cost efficient to dispose with hundreds of thousands of laborers, working for a few dollars a day, and to bring in machinery. The resulting black migration to the northern cities was rapid and painful for those involved. There were no federal programs of transitional assistance, no planning for the introduction of new technologies so that social distress would be minimized. Similarly, the movement of people and jobs out of the central cities has created urban fiscal problems because there has been no sensible planning, and no understanding of how federal highway subsidies, housing programs, and investment tax credits set up anti-central-city biases among private decision-makers.

To freedom riders and voter registration workers in the south, and to rent strike and welfare rights organizers in the north, the issues may have been civil rights and human needs, but the basic cause of the problem was the failure to develop sensible social controls over technology and policies assuring full employment. Activists may not have been aware that in ameliorating the worst abuses of the old form of juridical racism and custom, they were a modernizing force contributing to the rise of a "new south," which would rapidly become an area attractive to economic investment. Perhaps some liberal figures understood the benefits of the civil rights movement: wanting to modernize the seniority system in Congress (it inhibited a stronger executive), committed to the growth of multinational corporations, and looking for areas for expansion, they need not have engaged in conspiracy in order to ally with the activists.

Nor, a decade later, when downtown elites—bankers, developers, and their allies—found it increasingly difficult to urban-renew racial minorities and ethnic white working-class families out of central city land, did they conspire to bring about a fiscal crisis. The decisions as to where new industrial investment was to take place created the conditions for fiscal crisis; the downtown elites simply offered leadership in solving it in self-serving ways.

The policies put into practice in the 1960s may be described as redistributive liberalism, and in the 1970s as neoconservative reprivatization. The redistributive liberalism of the 1960s saw the basic system as sound, and government as a transforming agency that could solve such long-standing social problems as discrimination and poverty. As long as the economy was growing, it seemed both possible and desirable to take part of the growth dividend and redistribute it to those who had been left out of the affluent society: jobs could be created and public works programs instituted, while money could be invested in education so that the children of ghetto residents could be given equality of educational opportunity.

It turned out that "throwing money at the problem" did not solve it. However, before a debate over why this was so could develop, the economy moved into a period of crisis. Europe and Japan had not only recovered from the economic devastation of World War II, but were exporting more to the United States than they were buying from it. A worldwide dollar shortage became an embarrassing glut. President Nixon reversed the practice of post-war monetary economic accord: the dollar was not only devalued twice, but the United States went off the gold standard, moved away from free trade, and adopted wage-price controls.

The problems of the poor were no longer on center stage. The slow growth rate of the economy, inflation, and rising unemployment took the headlines and made governmental failure all too evident. As funds became scarce, existing programs were reviewed and found wanting. A neoconservative political philosophy gained the ascendancy, putting forward the old belief that the free market system could allocate resources far more efficiently and effectively than any government bureaucracy, that people's expectations as to what government should do for them had sapped the country's energy and lessened the will to work, and that taxes had risen to the point that they had become a disincentive to productive effort. The way to overcome the fiscal crisis was therefore to "reprivatize" the economy: services would be bought instead of received for "free" from the government (but paid for out of tax dollars); resource allocation would be left to the market, more and better housing would be built, neighborhoods would be improved, and services would be more efficiently and cheaply brought to local communities. The idea came to be accepted that it was not the government's place to help the oppressed and exploited, but rather to see that markets worked efficiently. The benefits of growth would then trickle down to the poor. Here was Calvin Coolidge-ism reborn.

But this approach has devastating side effects. Private capital does everything it can to undermine the financial ability of the local government to maintain service levels and to operate an equitable system of taxation; economic dislocation and social fragmentation are the result. The shift to reprivatization is accompanied by a shift to localism, to the benefit of the wealthy: schools and hospitals, golf courses and parks provided by local tax units ensure that the wealthy, while paying a lower proportion of their incomes in local taxes, can enjoy a high level of services, while lower income people can be excluded through high property costs, zoning laws, and racism. A family seeking a better life is thus forced to do this through upward mobility and relocation rather than class struggle and politics of redistribution. Democracy is used as a convenient cover for income segregation by political jurisdiction.

The firm belief that freedom of choice in the marketplace and democracy go together obscures this process. Cutting government services by letting local districts decide how to spend their money only intensifies the suffering of those who need government help. This is because reprivatization represents a redistribution of well being: the rich save money (lower taxes), but the poor suffer because they are not able to *buy* private education, garbage collection, or a library card. Second, the private provision of services may well be cheaper—the private garbage company may pay its workers less, may not provide hospitalization benefits, may not have a pension plan—but the workers receive less compensation. Third, if services are provided privately, the opportunity for citizens to vote a minimal level of amenities is eroded—not only do the poor get less at a greater cost, but they lose their ability to vote a higher level of service. Thus adequate mass transit, for instance, which cannot be purchased individually, becomes an impossible goal. Instead, everyone is forced to buy what he or she can, in this case probably a private car, thus adding to congestion and pollution. Reprivatization does something more: through the use of government subsidies, it guides market choices and removes the provision of services from direct government control. Job creation is encouraged by offering investment subsidies. Housing construction is stimulated by interest-rate subsidies and property tax abatements. This, then, is the long default—the effort to bring back the world of laissez-faire, in which social responsibility is reduced to private charity. And it is not unique to New York City: on the contrary, the shift to neoconservative reprivatization that is proceeding rapidly under the Reagan administration is, as we have said, merely the New York scenario writ large. . . .

In October of 1975, when he denied aid to New York City, President Ford said: "As for New York's much discussed welfare burden, the record shows more than one current welfare recipient in ten may be legally ineligible for welfare assistance." The inference was clear: people were cheating. And Secretary of the Treasury [William] Simon stated: "It bears noting that among cities over 1 million—all of which have larger underprivileged populations—only New York spends more than $20 per capita on welfare and related social services. Its figure is $315 per capita."

The figures do seem to indicate that the "explosion" of the relief rolls was a major factor in bringing on the city's fiscal crisis. Between 1960 and 1972, the number of city residents receiving some form of public assistance more than tripled (from 324,200 to 1,265,300). But while the figures may have been correct, the inference that New York was spendthrift, a welfare haven, was not.

In 1974, New York City's per capita expenditure for all forms of income maintenance was $158.94, 30.4 percent of which was raised through its own tax efforts. The second largest spender was Los Angeles County, which spent $24.85 per capita, while Chicago spent only $4.89 and Baltimore $1.23—because in each of these the county or state bore more of the cost. And if we look at the amount actually *paid* to recipients, New York was well within the range of other cities. Actual public assistance payments—$94 per capita per month in 1974—were lower than those in Chicago, Detroit, Philadelphia, or Milwaukee. Nor does New York have a particularly unusual *proportion* of its population on welfare. In February 1975, 12.6 percent of the population received welfare aid, while in Baltimore the figure was 16.8 percent, in St. Louis, 16.4 percent, in Boston, 17 percent, and in Washington, D.C., 14.9 percent.

And payments were hardly generous. By 1981 a welfare family of four in New York City was receiving only $258 a month for all living expenses except rent, or $2.15 a day per person for food, school supplies, clothes, carfare, phone, and everything else. An additional $116 a month in food stamps raised the per person income to $3.04 a day, but the monthly rental grants were limited to $218, and more than a third of the recipients had to put a portion of the money received for other items toward rent. The basic welfare grant has not been increased since 1974, and in 1981 it was worth $129 in 1974 dollars.

As to the alleged number of ineligibles—an issue that easily upsets rank-and-file taxpayers and wins points for conservative politicians—Mayor [Abe] Beame's Commissioner of Welfare estimated that most ineligibility is due to staff error and inefficiency rather than to client misrepresentation or fraud. The local agencies, drowning in cases, understaffed and underfunded, do not serve their clients adequately; the victims are, for the most part, the desperately needy. In fact, more recipients are harassed off welfare or have their cases closed by fiat than cheat the government, and in the mid-1970s most of the appeals brought against city agency action were reversed by the state, while a third were conceded by the city before reaching the appeal board. Thousands of other recipients did not, and do not, contest unfair decisions. Even the state's Department of Social Services readily admits that nearly a third of the families it has called ineligible for welfare are in fact eligible for some form of relief. It also recognizes that the department, by its own rules, underpays clients more than 18 percent of the time. The case for "cheating" by the welfare agencies themselves is far stronger than the reverse. In 1981 Martin Burdick, assistant deputy commissioner in the Human Resources Administration, reported on a recent citywide sample of case eligibility and benefit errors in the food stamp program. While errors were found to involve one-quarter of the funds spent on food stamps all over the city, over two-thirds of these were attributable to the agency, not to the clients.

Prior to the onset of the crisis, the number of persons receiving public assistance in New York City had fallen steadily. But not until Mayor [Ed] Koch was elected did welfare rolls begin to be cut systematically. Actions that had been presented as the result of bureaucratic foul-ups were now taken consciously—in order to drive people off welfare. Puerto Rican welfare recipients were treated with special insensitivity. In a major study of 105,000 welfare cases in 1975, the Office of Civil Rights of the Department of Health, Education, and Welfare found families had lost $4.3 million because of delays related to their inability to speak English, and an additional $1 million in related expenditures (hiring their own interpreters, extra child care, lost wages, etc.).

Koch selected as his administrators people who would carry out a war on the poor, especially the minority poor. His Director of Human Services told researchers that the number of people receiving welfare would be "what she wanted it to be," and indeed, by mid-1978 the rejection rate was almost twice that of 1976. In fiscal 1977–78, by limiting intake, rejecting applicants, and uncovering "ineligibles," the department had reduced the rolls by 40,000. However, when the Task Force on the New York City Crisis finally obtained an audit of a sample of rejected applicants, it found that a majority had been improperly rejected.

The attack on welfare recipients was not confined to New York: it was part of a national trend to penalize the poor for their poverty. As in New York, payments fell, rolls were carefully scrutinized, and cuts were made whenever possible. Yet surprisingly, given the media cliché that welfare recipients are lazy and refuse to work, most welfare recipients were shown to have some earnings, and to take jobs if they are available and it is economically rational to do so. Over the decade 1968–78, single-parent families increased nationally from 9 percent of all families with children to 16 percent among whites and between 33 to 50 percent among blacks. In 1978, the average income of female-headed families with a young child was $4,700; only 16 percent had incomes above $10,000. (In comparison, the average husband-wife family with a small child had an income of nearly $18,000.) Many of these female-headed families were forced to take Aid to Families with Dependent Children (AFDC), whose payments are below the government's own poverty line in most states. In Texas, for example, a family of four received $140 a month in 1980. Nationally, AFDC benefits fell by 20 percent between 1969 and 1981. Given the figures, it is not surprising that most recipients prefer to work. During a typical month almost 30 percent of heads of welfare families work and another 16 percent actively look for work. Over a year, almost half of all AFDC family heads work, and because other family members also work, about two-thirds of AFDC families have earnings from labor-market participation.

Addressing Congress on February 18, 1981, [President] Reagan spoke of the seven "safety net" programs that he would exempt from cuts—Social Security, Medicare, Supplemental Security Income, school lunch and breakfast programs, Head Start, and summer jobs for young people. Yet within six months, his administration had tried to cut Social Security benefits and to redefine ketchup as a vegetable (to lower the cost of school lunches). Budget director David Stockman presented the dismantlement of these programs as "reforms."

Not surprisingly, with the cut in federal aid and the reassignment of responsibility to local governments, social welfare spending of all sorts has declined, as states and cities have tried to hold the line on basic programs. In 1981, for instance, Arkansas Governor Frank White defended a 24 percent reduction to Aid to Families with Dependent Children (from $188 to $144 a month) by saying that 97 percent of adults getting this money could work if they wanted to. Yet two-thirds of the recipients of these funds nationwide are under ten years of age, and they would be the major victims of these policies. This, along with cuts in food stamps and other programs, would make the difficulty of substituting even more pronounced.

Chapter 155

Boston's Battle over Busing

Ronald P. Formisano

Ronald P. Formisano, professor of history at the University of Florida, is the author of The Transformation of Political Culture: Massachusetts Parties, 1790s–1840s *(1983) and co-editor of* Boston 1700–1980 *(1984).*

The following selection is excerpted from Boston against Busing: Race, Class, and Ethnicity in the 1960s and 1970s *by Ronald P. Formisano. Copyright © 1991 by the University of North Carolina Press. Used by permission of the publisher. Footnotes deleted.*

For discussion of an earlier attempt to integrate Boston schools, see chapter 16.

During the fall of 1974 shocking images of racial bigotry and violence emerged from Boston, that graceful, cosmopolitan city known for the excellence of its educational, cultural, and scientific institutions, a city once called "the Athens of America." As court-ordered desegregation of the public schools began, entailing extensive crosstown busing of both black and white pupils, racial conflict that had been escalating for over a decade overflowed into streets and schools.

In 1974 the tough, mostly Irish, working-class neighborhood of South Boston became as much a symbol of white racism as Selma, Alabama had been in 1964. Wild, raging mobs of white men and women confronted armies of police, while youths in their teens and younger hurled rocks, bottles, and racial epithets at buses carrying terrified black youngsters to school. Clashes with police erupted frequently and schools in other white neighborhoods became armed camps. The violence continued, arising alternately from whites and blacks, engulfing the innocent as well as the engaged: a black man stalked and beaten with hockey sticks; a white student carried out of Hyde Park High with a knife wound, then another stabbed by a black at South Boston High; a white man dragged from his car and beaten to death; a black lawyer beaten on the steps of City Hall by young white protesters and struck with the staff of an American flag used as a spear [see photo, p. 714—*Eds.*]. Some observers, recalling a dramatic outburst of Southern opposition to desegregation in 1957, now called Boston "the Little Rock of the North."

Organized resistance to desegregation, or what its opponents called "forced busing," ground on for three grim years. Opposition to the court orders became, in the words of the United States Civil Rights Commission, "the accepted community norm. Behavior in defiance of the constitutional process seemed to many—albeit erroneously—to be a legitimate exercise of individual rights." The intensity and duration of the antibusing resistance in Boston dwarfed that encountered in any other American city. The federal district court judge who decided the case in June 1974, W. Arthur Garrity, Jr., shepherded implementation for eleven years, issuing 415 orders and becoming more involved in the everyday school operations than any judge in the history of desegregation. For some of those who tried to keep the peace in Boston, comparisons to Belfast in Northern Ireland seemed more appropriate in conveying the sense of "hopelessness" and "protracted struggle leading to no solution."

Though a relative peace eventually prevailed in the schools (urban schools in the 1970s were hardly oases of tranquility), incidents of racial violence persisted at a high level and did not taper off until the 1980s. Although Boston's racial climate has improved steadily since former antibuser Raymond Flynn's election as mayor in 1983, many wounds fester. Remnants of the antibusing movement persisted into the 1980s, and Boston still wears the reputation, at least partly deserved, of being a racist city, a reputation which clings to it like a bad odor that all the winds of the Atlantic cannot blow away.

To label an entire city racist, however, clearly violates common sense, and to explain the antibusing movement I mean in part the organized groups, principally ROAR (Restore Our Alienated Rights), that were dominated mostly by antibusing's Mother Superior, Louise Day Hicks of South Boston. I refer also to the vast number of white Bostonians who were not ROAR members but who participated in protests of some kind. Eighty percent of white parents thought the court orders to be bad policy, and their responses varied greatly. Many moderates throughout the city agonized over the conflicting demands of conscience, duty, and the law and what they saw as potential danger to their children's welfare. The travail of many decent whites caught in a whipsaw of decent intention and negative experience is a story that has not been told.

Explanations of antibusing also err, I believe, in attaching too much importance to the role of individual leaders. Louise Hicks, for example, became synonymous with antibusing, beginning in 1963 when as chair of the school committee she contested the demands of the local National Association for the Advancement of Colored People (NAACP) for better schools for blacks. But consistent majorities on the school committee, with or without Hicks, pursued essentially the same policies for a dozen years.

Antibusing in Boston, especially its organized active expressions, can be seen as a case of reactionary populism, a type of grassroots social movement that has flared frequently in American history. From "regulators" in the eighteenth century, to nativists and agrarians in the nineteenth, to urban Progressives in the twentieth, these movements have been bundles of contradictory tendencies seeking greater democracy or opportunity, perhaps, while simultaneously expressing intolerance or denying the legitimacy of certain group interests. Our modern populisms especially seem to be inhibited, to be cramped by limited horizons, and they easily go sour from a lack of faith rooted in a sense of powerlessness. Yet many antibusers shared with other protesters of the 1970s at least the attempt to regain control over their lives.

Social scientists too often homogenize such internally diverse movements by stamping them as either liberal or conservative, radical or reactionary. Sometimes the labels are justified, but grassroots insurgencies often defy ready classification. Hence this description of Boston antibusing as reactionary populism, while an oxymoron, should not be seen as unusual. Indeed, in Canarsie, New York, in the early 1970s, white reaction to desegregation, according to Jonathan Rieder, "was a disorderly affair. Backlash contained democratic, populist, conspiratorial, racist, humanistic, pragmatic, and meritocratic impulses."

Reactionary populism is used here as a term of neither blame nor praise, but descriptively. Boston's antibusing movement was populist in that it sprang from the bottom half of the population, from working-, lower-middle- and middle-class city dwellers who felt their children, neighborhoods, and status to be threatened. Like many other citizens' movements of the 1970s, antibusing expressed rampant citizen alienation from impersonal government, drawing on an ingrained, deeply felt sense of injustice, unfairness, and deprivation of rights.

Several neighborhoods that became strongholds of antibusing tended to see the fight against the court orders of a suburban, "out-of-town, out-of-touch" judge as a continuation of wars waged in recent years against the depredations of highway construction, urban renewal, and airport expansion promoted by social engineers, bureaucrats, and above all, outsiders. Antibusing exuded the same anti-elitism and fierce class resentments that had erupted in these earlier struggles of neighborhood defense.

Yet while populist in many ways, Boston's antibusing movement was not reformist. It sought little more than a return to the status quo in the school system that existed before the court orders. It did not challenge established political and economic power, and militant activists too often expressed hostility, or at a minimum, insensitivity, to the just demands of black citizens for a full share of their rights. Fear of blacks, specifically of poor ghetto blacks, fed antibusers' feelings of being trodden on, while their outrage at injustice and feelings of powerlessness often fed their hostility to blacks.

. . . [M]any blacks in fact opposed the court orders and mandatory desegregation, and some resisted the implication of racial balancing of schools that black youngsters could not learn unless they were in a classroom with white youngsters. The black struggle for decent schools . . . in Boston sprang largely from the democratic interaction of a school committee elected at large and various of its constituents.

That democracy and segregation were linked was only one of the many ironies involved in Boston's trauma. Several other "jokes of history" derived from the impact of the 1960s. The white antibusers, for example, consciously and unconsciously imitated black civil rights activists. More generally, the antibusers were in many ways children of the 1960s. The enormous cultural and social upheavals of that decade, above all the loosening of public standards of conduct and the decline of authority, powerfully shaped organized antibusing. . . .

Sitting before their televisions and watching—usually with disdain—the protesters of the 1960s and 1970s, the antibusers had learned powerful lessons that they would seek to apply against school desegregation.

Of course the greatest irony of all was the activist antibusers' imitation of the black civil rights movement, which had served as midwife to most 1960s movements. Antibusers frequently staged demonstrations aimed at gaining media coverage and affecting public opinion in the way that they believed civil rights protesters had done a few years earlier. The antibusers usually failed to realize that the civil rights movement had gained widest public support during its nonviolent phase, whereas antibusing in 1974 quickly became associated with violence. Still, they wanted to see themselves portrayed with the sympathy the media had bestowed on the followers of Martin Luther King, Jr.; that is, as victims. By replaying the strategy of civil rights activists, they hoped that the media would legitimize their cause.

When antibusers compared themselves to black activists, they usually ended up seething with bitterness. "They were heroes and martyrs," they lamented, "but we are racists." Who regarded the antibusers as racists? The liberals, suburbanites, elite politicians, outsiders, and especially the media. For antibusers these groups not only overlapped, but "the liberal establishment" and the media were virtually the same thing: a hated enemy who presumed to judge them from the safety of their "lily-white" suburbs. The media doubly frustrated the antibusers by portraying them as racists and by refusing to anoint them with victim status, much less to bestow on them a mantle of morality. But the liberal media earlier had readily legitimized black demonstrators and hairy, unruly youth. For the antibusers, the contrast was infuriating.

Aside from the antibusers' conscious imitation of civil rights and antiwar movements, the 1960s affected them in other ways just as profoundly, though perhaps not as consciously. The decline of authority, or rather, of respect for authority, spread from the young and rebellious throughout much of the population. Traditional mores and values came under scathing questioning and attack from all quarters, not just from radicals, intellectuals, or those on the margins. Irreverence burst into the mainstream, and that most powerful domestic agent of change, television, reflected and promoted the decline of confidence in public and private institutions. Television was, both in its news and entertainment programs, perhaps only the most ubiquitous of debunking agents.

The antibusers of the 1970s sprang mainly from groups who in the 1950s had tended to be orderly, conformist, and self-conscious about their public demeanor. In the 1960s they were at first repelled by the outrageous behavior of black and antiwar protesters and shocked by deviant lifestyles. Richard M. Nixon had labeled them "the silent majority": decent, hard-working, reflexively patriotic, and trusting in authority. But they too lost respect, lost faith, and when pressed themselves, many turned to modes of action that a short time before had marked those whom they scorned and resented. It is hard to imagine ethnic neighborhoods mobilized in street protest during the 1950s—but then that comfortable, seemingly secure postwar world had suddenly changed.

The civil rights movement had done most to define the new era, acting as a generative force of this axial decade leading out of postwar triumphalism and self-congratulation. The black crusade had revealed a lie and a sickness at the core of

American society, and once self-doubt began it spread, especially among the young who now inhabited college campuses in record numbers. The civil rights movement went through several phases, however, changing from nonviolence and heroic suffering in the South to aggressive demands for "Black Power" in South and North. Legal victories in Congress in 1964-65 did not relieve the poverty and lack of opportunity that defined living conditions for many blacks, and a mounting sense of relative deprivation gave rise to massive urban riots in black ghettos in the mid- and late-1960s. Militant black separatists such as the Black Panthers used revolutionary rhetoric and went armed, further frightening many whites and provoking lethal responses from local police and the FBI.

Both separatist and integrationist black leaders exhorted blacks to nurture self-love, pride in their history, and a self-conscious African-American identity, and this helped to inspire similar upwellings from other inhabitants of America's cultural salad bowl. Those European groups who had been part of the great immigration of 1890–1924 and who had been intimidated by the ideology of the "Melting Pot" now began to emerge from the shadow cast by British-American dominance of the nation's identity. The cry of "Black is Beautiful" taught those of Irish, Polish, Italian, or Slavic background, among others, to look at their roots with new reverence. Many urban ethnics thus were caught up in a cultural chauvinism that often fed the backlash.

Several recent writers have argued that the ethnic revival of the 1960s came at a time when ethnicity was in fact fading—and was in part a product of that recession. Being "ethnic," like being African-American, was often an act of will. Ethnicity had changed from being "a taken-for-granted part of everyday life" to being "private and voluntary," from "the status of an irrevocable fact of birth to an ingredient of lifestyle." Yet even the forces that submerged ethnicity also contributed to raising barriers against blacks: the black influx into central cities, by arousing consciousness of race, helped make various white groups less conscious of their ethnic differences and diverted white antagonism to blacks.

On balance, "ideological ethnicity" reinforced the backlash by providing it with a rhetoric for resistance to desegregation. The ethnics of the "urban villages" of the North often felt most vulnerable to blacks in the latter's efforts to break out of the ghetto, and for the urban ethnics theirs was foremost a vulnerability of place. It was their schools and their blocks into which blacks would be coming.

Furthermore, not only did New England and Boston tend to be more ethnicity-aware than other parts of the country, but Boston's neighborhoods commonly swelled with a localist pride that made their residents highly conscious of turf. Within neighborhoods, pockets of ethnicity, class, and place flourished, often identified by parish, squares, corners, hills, and the like. These small worlds often reacted with instinctive hostility to any outsiders.

Besides the militant, organized antibusers, opposition to Judge Garrity's court orders and the plans of 1974–75 also involved many thousands of moderate whites who did not join ROAR, who disapproved of violence, and who rejected illegal activities, including school boycotts. Many moderates believed fully in integrated schools; some had been sending their children to schools that were integrated.

Hundreds and thousands of individual families grappled conscientiously with the fear, anxiety, and vicissitudes of sending their children to schools and streets they saw as dangerous, and which often were. The moderates' story has not been told.

The Boston Home and School Association (HSA) constituted one moderate group whose role has not been appreciated by earlier histories. The Boston HSA, similar to parent-teacher associations, has been viewed as militantly antibusing and as a creature of the Boston School Committee. But while local chapters were diverse, most citywide leaders were pragmatists.

As individual and group responses varied across the city, so did neighborhood expressions of antibusing. The sound and fury of South Boston and Charlestown captured media attention, but at the opposite end of the neighborhood spectrum from Southie was semisuburban, middle-class West Roxbury, where antibusing opinion was nearly as intense as in South Boston but where antibusing *action* found expression in a very different *style*. South Boston's militants tolerated no dissent from their hard line. They engaged in every form of protest but were best known for their collective actions: marches, motorcades, rallies, disruptions of traffic and meetings, and violent street clashes with police. By contrast, West Roxbury's style tended to be individualistic, pragmatic, and legalist, tolerant and permissive of different views, and cool to boycotts and street demonstrations.

A small minority of antibusers deliberately practiced terrorism against blacks and especially whites for at least three years. Their targeting of white moderates—most of whom strongly disagreed with the court orders but tried to comply—probably affected the course of desegregation more than the harassment of blacks. Antibusing vigilantes, based especially in South Boston, exercised a disproportionate influence because they were tough, because the moderates lacked leadership and also perceived the court orders as unfair, and because it takes only a few incidents of violence to intimidate one's neighbors. Of course racism added an ugly, frenetic charge of ferocity and violence to many antibusing protests. But as powerful as racism was, it formed only a part of the story.

Both the sweeping nature of the court remedy as well as the powerful resistance to it owed much to the Boston School Committee's long resistance to even the most limited attempts to implement desegregation. From 1963 to 1974 majorities of the five-member, elected school committee engaged routinely in blatant discriminatory practices, heedlessly letting evidence accumulate on the public record that would create iron-clad proof of their guilt. A series of politicians, playing upon and being tossed about by their constituents' fears, stepped forward as pied pipers of the white backlash.

These backlash entrepreneurs, joined by neighborhood populists cast up from the grassroots, *virtually created an antibusing movement before busing ever existed.* They also caused racial fear and hostility to be much worse than it would have been. The entrepreneurs' actions sometimes sprang in part from genuine concern for preserving neighborhoods. They arose, too, from the desire both to gain office for access to patronage and sometimes to try to ride antibusing to higher office. Whatever the motivation, the Boston School Committee ran a dual school system, and its leaders kept telling their constituents that busing would never come to Boston.

To an astonishing degree, many citizens of Boston simply could not believe that busing would actually happen. This mind-set, along with its offspring notion that busing could be stopped somehow by protest, arose in part from Boston's unique political culture in which many citizens believe that "everything is politics," that issues were negotiable, and that interest groups competed for tangible rewards while talk of principles and laws were mere camouflage. Thus the belief persisted, especially among working-class whites, as William A. Henry, III, said, "that busing was not a constitutional remedy for previous lawbreaking and political abuse, but was simply some sort of political maneuver that could be 'fixed' like a traffic ticket."

If the antibusing politicos had done the most to create an antibusing movement up to 1974, the judge and his advisers helped to sustain antibusing after 1974. Anyone who reads Garrity's decision in *Morgan v. Hennigan* will understand why he found the school committee guilty of segregative practices. But the judge then imposed on the city a desegregation plan with which he was barely familiar. Designed by officials working for the State Board of Education, which had been battling the school committee for years, the plan appeared to be punitive, particularly in its pairing of the antibusing hotbed of South Boston with the ghetto of Roxbury. When the school committee refused to review or revise the plan, it defaulted on the chance to eliminate some of its worst features. Implemented by a reluctant and sometimes subversive school administration, the plan's reality often became horrific for thousands of parents.

Of course the intensity of antibusing after 1974 depended on many other causes as well, including the hostility or neutrality to the court orders of most of the city's political and institutional leaders; the permissive attitude of the police and local courts to antibusers arrested for disorderly conduct; and the physical absence from the city of the economic and status elites, who from the safe distance of their suburban retreats were unable or unwilling to ameliorate the situation.

The civil rights movement, which came into being after World War II, generated powerful and contradictory responses among white Americans. The South reacted with massive resistance to the Supreme Court's 1954 decision in *Brown v. Topeka Board of Education*, which struck down the region's "separate but equal" system of segregated schools that had been established by state and local law. Many northern whites, meanwhile, became allies of the black civil rights struggle. Ironically, an Irish Catholic from Massachusetts, John F. Kennedy, placed the awesome moral weight of the presidency behind the black quest. The civil rights movement would peak after Kennedy's assassination with Congress's passage of the Civil Rights Act of 1964 and the Voting Rights Act of 1965. This legislation, sometimes called "The Second Reconstruction," sought to undo the caste system of the South. But civil rights agitation, a mostly southern phenomenon until the early 1960's, already had moved North. And some northern whites were reacting fearfully to black demands for equal opportunity. When spectacular urban riots exploded in black ghettos after 1964, whites would feel additionally threatened by demands for affirmative action to move blacks ahead at a faster pace to compensate for generations of discrimination.

White reactions in Massachusetts and Boston presented a microcosm of differing reactions in the nation. On the one hand, sympathetic whites mobilized a constituency of conscience to promote black aspirations, which in Boston had become fixated on improving the educational facilities available to black children. A coalition of liberal and cosmopolitan whites succeeded in gaining passage of a state Racial Imbalance Act in 1965 whose intent was to desegregate the state's schools, and particularly those of Boston. On the other hand, the Boston School Committee, dominated by Irish politicians and highly sensitive to aroused local groups, adamantly resisted demands for school reform. Indeed, Boston and Mrs. Hicks became symbols as early as 1963 of the "white backlash" that was perhaps the most significant northern white response to the civil rights movement.

The Boston ruled by Brahmin merchants and Yankee Protestants and famous for its abolitionists, feminists, Mugwumps, and exotic native radicals had long ago faded into history and folklore, its politics taken over by the Irish, who had grown from an often despised, exploited, and discriminated-against minority to a political majority. Political patronage was hardly invented by the Irish Americans, but they brought to politics a particularly intense ethos of interest-group politics and "spirit of patronage." Enjoying several advantages over other immigrant groups, they seldom practiced politics as a way of maximizing public good, but rather, in nonideological fashion, as a means to upward mobility by gaining status and patronage, and distributing jobs, favors, and contracts to kin and friends. Their ethic was personalist, particularist, and competitive.

Boston's political culture, in short, was predisposed to receive inhospitably a moralistic movement (civil rights) promoting a particular group (black) interest. In addition, a long history of Irish-black hostility dated back to before the Civil War, generated in part by Yankee reformers tending to be sympathetic to black slaves and freedpersons but hostile to Irish Catholic immigrants. Native Protestants often treated the poor Irish "Papists" as "niggers," and the Irish then vented their resentment against a class that they regarded as pariahs. The insecure among the Irish could reassure themselves by making sure that the blacks were kept below them. Blacks and Irish Catholics often have continued to regard one another with hostility across cultural barricades that are composed in part of perceptions and stereotypes, but also real differences, both cultural and material.

The Irish, with select allies from other ethnic groups, used the public schools less as an educational than as an employment system. Having earlier wrested control of the city and its patronage from the Yankees, the Irish assumed that politics was a street fight in which interest groups competed for the rewards of power by mobilizing voters, winning elections, and making deals. They were not inclined to give away anything to the black civil rights leaders who seemed to be seeking leverage by assuming for their group a special moral status based on white guilt. Yankees or Jews might have been susceptible to such an appeal—most Irish were not.

Thus when the Boston NAACP went to the school committee in the early 1960s, complaining of inferior schools and degrading teaching and demanding that school officials admit that de facto segregation (arising from residential patterns) existed in the schools, the committee balked at most black demands. So began a struggle that would last until 1974, during which time the school committee would rebuff all attempts to end its many practices that maintained or promoted segregation.

The close, powerful tie between democracy and segregation that existed in Boston's schools was nourished in large part by the committee, which had served for years as a stepping-stone for aspiring politicians. This point has been well recognized, but it has tended to obscure the fact that, for some politicians, election to the committee, because of its patronage power (it was nonpaid), was an end in itself.

If political culture, race, ethnicity, and place contributed to antibusing in Boston, so too did class. Judge Garrity always regarded *Morgan v. Hennigan* purely "as a race case." But various studies of the controversy have emphasized class and status resentments—as well as race—as powerful forces in antibusing. The role of class was connected to broad changes that took place in the distribution of blacks within the United States during the twentieth century. As blacks continued to migrate from South to North and into central cities after World War II, white movement to the suburbs from cities accelerated enormously. It was, in fact, the greatest exodus in United States history. It drained the white population out of the city limits and engorged the near and far suburbs.

In the 1950s Boston's suburbs grew from two to three million, spurred by the growth of electronic industries on Route 128 girdling Boston. By 1960 Boston's ratio of population in the central city to population in its adjoining metropolitan area was one of the lowest in the country (.27, compared, for example, to .46 for Philadelphia and .73 for New York). Of course, the suburbs were almost entirely white, while blacks, Hispanics, and later Asians were ringed into the central city by the suburban noose.

Thus metropolitan patterns of segregation created a situation throughout much of the nation and in Boston that called for *metropolitan* solutions to desegregation. In 1972 a federal district court judge tried to bring the city of Detroit, whose school population was overwhelmingly black, together with outer county districts to create viable school desegregation. But in 1974, as the outcry against busing among whites and in Congress reached a fever pitch, the Supreme Court, by a five to four split decision in *Milliken v. Bradley*, declared that no proof had been given that state or local governments had been responsible for the racial composition of the Detroit schools or for residential patterns in Detroit. For the majority, Justice Potter Stewart said that the concentration of blacks in Detroit was "caused by an unknown and perhaps unknowable factors such as immigration, birthrates, economic changes, or cumulative acts of private racial fears." In contrast, as Professor Thomas Pettigrew pointed out, there are many things in social science that are "unknown and perhaps unknowable," but the "tight, unremitting containment of urban blacks over the past half-century within the bowels of American cities is not one of them."

Indeed, the federal government did most to abet suburban residential apartheid. The government provided massive aid to the housing industry to localities, to banks, and to individual in the form of mortgage insurance and loans, and subsidized the suburbs further through highway programs. And rural towns insured their transformation into white enclaves with large-lot zoning, restrictions on multifamily dwellings, the waste of buildable land, and resistance to various social services. Of course bankers and realtors engaged in discriminatory lending and channeling practices as they had for decades. The government also subsidized the Route 128 high-tech boom, which created jobs where blacks (and the poor) did not live and were not likely to find housing. From 1958 to 1967 over 66,000 new jobs came into being in the Route 128 complex, while several thousand jobs were lost in Boston, just as the city was experiencing its largest black in-migration. Blacks did not live near the new jobs and lacked the means to get to them. The state Commission Against Discrimination belatedly labeled Route 128 "Boston's Road to Segregation."

Throughout the country the segregation of minorities was paralleled by a less complete but nevertheless pronounced clustering of less affluent whites in central cities. Some working-class whites chose to live in cities. Others were trapped by lack of resources. In either case, when the Supreme Court decided to prohibit metropolitan remedies for school segregation, it was insuring that desegregation remedies would involve mostly the black and white lower classes, while middle-, upper-middle-, and upper-class whites would be largely excluded. Further, once desegregation began those whites in the city with the most resources could more easily escape "the law of the land" by sending their children to private schools or moving out.

The results of the postwar migrations were exaggerated in Boston because it was so small in relation to its metropolitan area, in territory as well as population. The roots of this ran back to the late nineteenth century when Boston began to annex contiguous suburban towns even as many native Protestant whites began to move to those towns in search of rustic purity and to escape the burgeoning political power of the Irish. Ironically, the native middle class saw annexation in part as a way to keep the city government in their hands and away from the Irish while also tapping new sources of tax revenue. But in 1873 Brookline declined annexation and halted Boston's growth. Prosperous towns like Brookline had already provided themselves with waterworks, good schools, and other municipal services, and suburban and rural Yankees wished to keep separate from the city, from its high taxes, and the Irish. So Boston entered the twentieth century as one of the most geographically truncated cities in the country.

In 1970 some half a million persons lived in Boston, but another million and a half, perhaps 99 percent white, lived in the metropolitan area. They enjoyed the superior facilities of a cosmopolitan downtown, often held jobs in the city, but had no part in any of its attempts to deal with the burning national issue of racial discrimination.

Further, had more of the middle classes remained in Boston, they might have exerted a moderating influence on the city's school politics. But a large part of what remained of the Jewish middle class had been driven out after 1968 by a well-intentioned program to aid minorities and create integrated housing. In the wake of Martin Luther King's assassination, Mayor Kevin White had persuaded a consortium of Boston banks (BBURG, Boston Banks' Urban Renewal Group) to provide $27 million in mortgages to low-income black families. Unfortunately, realtors and bankers quickly exploited the program to make money and to turn a thriving Jewish neighborhood into a black ghetto. BBURG selected Mattapan, which ran through two Irish neighborhoods and was a thriving self-contained Jewish community, and "redlined" it—granting mortgages to blacks only within that corridor. BBURG expected less trouble from Jews than from the Irish or Italians, in part because of their reputation for liberalism. Real estate agents suddenly showed up on white doorsteps warning that blacks would be moving in by the hundreds and saying, "Your neighbor across the street is selling to a black. I thought maybe you'd be interested in selling." Some residents fought back with a biracial group that tried to put realtors out of business, but in three years Mattapan became 90 percent black, the ghetto had been merely enlarged, and more white middle-class moderates were driven out of the city.

In a different way the extensive system of Catholic parochial schools also removed a potentially calming element, since these families tended to be somewhat better off or aspired to be. Some one-third of all school-age youngsters went to Catholic schools, with their parents paying taxes for public schools as well as the extra fees that went to the church. The Catholic schools also figured prominently as havens for fleeing white families once busing began.

For a long time Boston's economy had been relatively stagnant, lacking growth industries and an expansive infrastructure. New workplaces almost always were built outside Boston, whether factories in the 1840s or laboratories in the 1950s. By 1970 the old city had been transformed primarily into a "postindustrial administrative and service center." The Irish had succeeded in politics but as a group depended heavily on jobs with government or with utilities such as the phone company, which enjoyed an unusually high degree of job security. This contributed to the Irish sense of anxiety when facing black demands for integration. Boston's economy, politics, and heritage of ethnic rivalry all made for a lack of generosity and openness among ethnic groups.

In 1970 Boston had become one of the costliest cities in which to live in the continental United States. At the same time the median family income ranked only twenty-fourth out of the largest thirty cities. Then in the early 1970s a national economic recession hit Boston with particular severity. The hard times brought by stagflation, a rare combination of both higher inflation and unemployment, made black-white relations, already tense along a number of fronts, even worse.

Meanwhile, school desegregation was just one way in which the white and predominantly Irish hold on public employment was being challenged. In a series of affirmative action suits and decisions beginning in 1970, blacks, Hispanics, and public agencies challenged the patronage and kinship networks of recruitment in the Police, Fire, and Public Works Departments. In November 1971, Federal District Judge Charles E. Wyzanski, Jr. found that police department exams from 1968–70 had discriminated unintentionally against minorities and had favored whites. Wyzanski's attempts to get the police to hire minorities turned into a protracted struggle over the next three years, even as women began to be added to the department during 1972–73.

It was not just that the Irish of Southie, Charlestown, or Dorchester heavily staffed these agencies but also that sons and nephews followed routinely in the steps of fathers and uncles. The Fire Department especially was "one big family," literally, up to 1974 when a U.S. district judge ruled its entrance exams discriminatory and ordered the firemen to bring minority representation up to levels comparable to the Boston population as a whole. In 1975 the United States Supreme Court declined to hear a challenge to the order by the firefighters' union, and after that the department hired one member of a racial minority for every white.

White workers in the construction industry, where the jobless rate climbed as high as 50 percent, similarly felt themselves under siege. Firstly, employers began hiring young, out-of-town, nonunion labor, stirring demonstrations in downtown Boston by angry hardhats. But by 1976 the competition for jobs between black and white workers took center stage and formed another part of the racial conflict that already centered in the schools. In 1974 the city, construction companies, and unions had agreed to aid minority workers by requiring 30 percent minority employees on construction jobs in inner-city areas of dominant minority residence. But soon the Third World Jobs Clearing House, a lobbying and hiring agency supported in large part by city funds, was demanding that the minority quota be raised to 50 percent. That spring, groups of mostly black workers began picketing jobs in ghetto areas, with violence breaking out at several places. A construction site in Dorchester suffered $4,000 worth of vandalism, and workers were forced to flee. Radical members of the Third World Association declared their intention of closing down more sites. The South Boston Marshalls, a vigilante group which provided security for antibusing parades, began to appear at construction yards in a show of solidarity with white workers.

In April union representatives complained of harassment to the city and then on May 7, 2,000 boisterous white construction workers marched on City Hall to protest job stoppages and demand that the city stop funding the Third World Jobs Clearing House. Union men insisted to reporters that their protest was not about race: "It's my job. I need a job. You been workin' 10–12 years, some guy comes along from this Third World and grabs your job. What the hell?" sputtered one union man. An unemployed white worker from South Boston complained, "Every time I try to join a carpenters, electrical or iron workers union they tell me they are only taking minorities. But if you don't have a union card you can't work and if you aren't black you can't get a union card." Third World spokesmen countered by asserting that companies should not be allowed to operate in the city if they were not hiring Boston residents (and many white hardhats lived outside the city): "Boston jobs for Boston people. We feel it is outrageous for suburbanites to come into Boston to work on construction sites when 12 percent of Boston residents are unemployed." The minority workers' agitation threatened white workers generally because they feared that their sons and nephews would not be able to use preferential apprenticing systems to get access to good jobs. This coincided with what they saw happening to their kids in the public schools, so they saw themselves doubly at risk.

Several writers have drawn a direct connection between unemployment and antibusing activity. Two neighborhoods with the most antibusing, South Boston and Charlestown, were indeed among areas with the highest levels of unemployment. Yet antibusing sentiment and action cut widely across the ranks of the unemployed and employed and raged in both prosperous and depressed neighborhoods. Still, the economic slump, added to Boston's long-term stagnation, certainly made matters worse. As the Mayor's Committee on Violence said in June 1976, too many Bostonians lacked money, work, decent housing, and hope. "They see neighbors with good-paying jobs sending their children to private schools. They see those with better jobs living in the suburbs, where, they believe, you don't have to fear opening your door or walking down the street. They also see that society and the establishment orders their children bused. Then, the whole focus of their grievances is directed toward that issue."

"Their children," indeed, were bused, if by that is meant Bostonians at the lower end of the economic scale. In 1972–73, for example, 76 percent of the city's public school students came from families with incomes low enough for them to get free or reduced-price lunches. During 1974–75 the pool of poor left behind grew larger as the more affluent families tended to be the first to leave the schools. In 1976, 61 percent of an estimated seventy-eight thousand pupils came from families at or below the federal poverty level.

As woeful as many Boston schools may have been by middle-class standards, the fact is that their localist, working-class clienteles cherished them, especially the neighborhood high schools. These old, often dilapidated but beloved buildings served less as educational institutions providing upward mobility and more as community socializing agents. For the working-class kids of Southie, Charlestown, or East Boston, high school days were often the best times of their lives, after which many moved on to unexciting, dreary jobs or became mothers and fathers soon after bringing their youth to a close well before middle-class youths who attended college. One Southie young woman told me that while growing up she was "just dying to go to Southie High," and "thought it would be the greatest thing in the world to go to the senior prom." The sports teams of these schools commanded deep affection and passionate loyalty. Young men grew into middle age wearing their high school letter sweaters or team jackets.

The desegregation planners, however, looked upon the Southie Highs of the world as at best anachronisms, and at worst as narrow, parochial places perpetuating distrust of outsiders, prejudice, ethnic and racial stereotypes, and outmoded and ineffective modes of education, trapping their students in a cycle of immobility. The planners (e.g., Board of Education employees, Judge Garrity's advisers) believed that it was right on both moral and utilitarian grounds to "take away" the Southie Highs from their communities. The planners assumed the superiority of their middle-class and cosmopolitan values to those of persons and groups they judged to be localist, uneducated, and, unlike themselves, bigoted.

Thus, Boston's desegregation controversy was very much a contest over whose values would prevail. Those trying to defend localist, ethnic, and communitarian values were at a distinct disadvantage because their efforts too often resulted in violence, too often soured into racial hatred, or sometimes had been prompted by it in the first place. This did not mean, however, that the self-righteous cosmopolitans seeking to change localist life-styles were necessarily morally superior.

Social scientists have conducted an extensive debate, often highly technical and arcane to the layman, to assess the role of racism in motivating protest against school desegregation. Some scholars maintain that racism in some form plays the major role in stimulating opposition to desegregation, while others argue that nonracial factors count more heavily. Researchers reemphasizing racism maintain that most whites oppose busing, especially two-way busing, because they calculate that the benefits are not justified by the costs. Although such studies of Boston have demoted racism as an explanatory factor, the relative importance of the causes of opposition to desegregation promise to remain "very much at issue."

The different findings arise in part as they normally do from different assumptions, methods, and cases chosen for study. They also spring from some fairly massive incongruities that have existed in national public opinion over the past two decades. Since World War II the American public has moved increasingly toward acceptance in principle of an integrated society. By 1970 support levels in the north for integrated schools were reaching 90 percent. But then something happened. As the busing controversy heated up, support for specific policies to implement school desegregation dropped sharply, and the decline seemed directly related to federal efforts to implement school desegregation. Meanwhile, racial isolation in the nation's schools, particularly in the northeast, actually increased. By 1986, as Harold Cruse put it, "despite the *Brown* decision . . . legal segregation has been almost universally replaced by *de facto* segregation in public schools; and in both South and North, most black and white schoolchildren are as 'separate' as in 1954, *if not more so.*"

It seems puzzling that "white Americans increasingly reject racial injustice in principle but are reluctant to accept the measures necessary to eliminate the injustice." They endorse school integration in the abstract, expect it to happen, and seem to be accepting contact with middle-class blacks in many social relationships. But when faced with potentially extensive contact with poor blacks, which arouses fears of schools and neighborhoods being "invaded" or "overrun" by the black underclass, then resistance skyrockets. Most Boston antibusers bitterly resented being tagged as racists, in part because they saw themselves as having attitudes very much resembling most Americans. They were right insofar as most whites shared their ambivalence and unwillingness to implement school integration through involuntary busing.

White Bostonians also found themselves wondering about a state of affairs in school desegregation that had evolved from a 1954 Supreme Court decision which said it was wrong to bus a black child in Topeka, Kansas past a white school in her neighborhood to an all-black school across town, to a federal court decision requiring their children to be bused past their neighborhood school—which in a few cases was integrated at least partially—to schools in black neighborhoods across town. . . .

In fact, the 1954 *Brown* decision had been freighted with ambiguities, including a tension between simply providing blacks with equal access to white schools and requiring that schools be balanced racially. Moreover, the 1964 Civil Rights Act explicitly mandated color blindness in its implementation, particularly in those sections that gave federal officials leverage by requiring nondiscrimination in schools receiving federal money. But a race-neutral approach disappeared as "the push for racial equity [came] to rely on racial information as a way of gauging, first, the pace of desegregation and, later, the effects of various measures on black advancement.

Boston's Catholics possessed additional reasons to be confused. The Roman Catholic Church historically opposed state intervention into the private affairs of families and nowhere had its objections been greater than in the area of childrens' education. Catholic doctrine defined the family as anterior "in idea and in fact to the gathering of men into a commonwealth." Though in recent years church teaching has swung behind state intervention to aid the poor and propertyless victimized by unjust or oppressive social structures, family rights in childrens' education had been vigorously defended by the hierarchy for over a hundred years in its efforts to get Catholics to provide parochial schooling. Catholic parents had been led to believe for generations that they held a "right in usage, if not a right in law, to control educational choices for their children."

Working class and Catholic Boston was not in the end "the Little Rock" but rather the "New Orleans of the North." In 1957 Governor Orval Faubus of Arkansas was seeking reelection to an unprecedented third term, and he manufactured the crisis at Central High School in Little Rock. Several schools in the state already had desegregated peacefully, but Faubus declared a state of emergency, sent in the National Guard to keep out black children, and roused segregationists throughout the region to descend on Little Rock and demonstrate. The Little Rock crisis resulted mostly from one man's ambition.

In 1960 a desegregation controversy in New Orleans, however, anticipated Boston's in several ways, just as the graceful, old tourist city itself more resembled Boston. The nation's second busiest port, it was a city of high culture as well as heterogeneous ethnic groups, home of liberal French Catholicism as well as rabid segregationism, a city with an aristocratic elite as well as a polyglot underclass.

Violence erupted in November 1960 when four black first-graders entered two previously all-white elementary schools. Whites by the thousands rioted through downtown, hurling rocks and bottles. For months a crowd of women (whom reporters called "the cheerleaders") gathered in front of the schools every day, forcing small black children to run a gauntlet of obscenity, spittle, and shoves, while harassing the few whites who ignored a school boycott.

New Orleans and Louisiana differed greatly, of course, from Boston and Massachusetts. Segregationism was avowed openly in Louisiana by major politicians. The mayor was allied with segregationists, while the state government and legislature uniformly expressed hostility to desegregation. But given the differences, consider the similarities: a federal court ordered desegregation after protracted resistance by a school board that continually acted as if the schools would never be integrated; the Catholic church at first advocated desegregation, then fell silent; a mayor with a "reform" reputation disappointed integrationists; no viable political parties existed, no political machinery by which desegregation could be promoted; an influential civic-business elite, based on old money and high status, toyed with politics only sporadically and shunned desegregation; and finally and most importantly, the schools chosen to be desegregated were in one of the city's poorest neighborhoods.

The choice of schools ironically illustrated the naïveté of those who think that controversial policy decisions can be done "scientifically" and "without politics." Moderate members of the school board used a computer program to select a tiny number of black children who would desegregate. Elaborate screening produced a handful of well-scrubbed black youngsters. Little care, however, was taken in the choice of the white schools. Since they needed to be schools with median grades low enough to admit the black children, two elementary schools in rundown, poor, white Ward 9 were selected. The ward housed an ethnic potpourri of working class and welfare families, many of whom lived in housing projects. The neighborhood was the most neglected in the city and, to make matters worse, abutted St. Bernard Parish, controlled by boss Leander Perez, a rich segregationist who hired pickets to protest and who made his own schools available as refuges for the boycotters.

The school board claimed "the machine did it," but in choosing schools the board ignored advice to use other sections of the city where black children already lived. They also refused offers of help from affluent white parents who volunteered to have their schools desegregated first. One sign carried by a protester in the Ninth Ward signaled the message thus delivered: "If you are poor, mix; if you are rich, forget about it; some law."

A year later, in 1961, desegregation went very differently in New Orleans. The elite of old families and rich businessmen called for peace; the mayor gave the police firm orders to disperse crowds; and the school board did not hide behind a computer but chose schools in the silk-stocking wards. Now violence subsided, and on its second try New Orleans peacefully began the desegregation of its schools. Thirteen years later Boston finally would begin its desegregation, unfortunately with many of the dynamics in action that made New Orleans' first attempt disastrous.

EDITORS' NOTE

In July 1999, the Boston School Committee, threatened with a lawsuit charging discrimination against white children, voted 5 to 2 to end mandatory busing. See Robert A. Jordan, "School Committee Vote an Ending That May Only Invite Resegregation," Boston Globe, 18 July 1999.

According to a report from the Civil Rights Project at the Harvard Graduate School of Education, "The [Clinton] Administration affirms its support for integrated schools but has no set of policies that would foster or support them, no research program to learn how to help them work better, no aggressive legal strategy to fight against segregation and no critical discussion of the impact of the current pro-segregation court decisions on the country and no plan to help stabilize integration in hundreds of racially changing suburban school districts. . . . This is the first Democratic administration in 40 years that has had no program for school integration. . . .

"After 12 years of intense and focused opposition to desegregation orders under Presidents Reagan and Bush and successful confirmation of hundreds of conservative federal judges, the law now is much closer to Reagan's vision than to that of the Warren and Burger Courts. Mandatory desegregation orders are being dissolved on a large scale and voluntary ones are being challenged in many courts. There has been no significant countervailing intellectual, political or legal force from the Clinton Administration that might reverse trends." Gary Orfield and John T. Yun, "Resegregation in American School" (The Civil Rights Project, Harvard University, June 1999; www.law.harvard.edu/civilrights/publications/resegregation99.html).

In September 1999, Charlotte, N.C., under court order from Federal District Court Judge Robert Potter, a Reagan appointee and former campaign worker for busing opponent Senator Jesse Helms (R–NC), joined Nashville, Oklahoma City, Denver, Wilmington, Del., and Cleveland, in ending court ordered busing.

Backlash

Chapter 156

The Tax Revolt

Alan Brinkley

Alan Brinkley, professor of history at Columbia University, is the author of Voices
of Protest: Huey Long, Father Coughlin and the Great Depression *(1982),* The
End of Reform: New Deal Liberalism in Recession and War *(1995), and* Liberalism and Its Discontents *(1998).*

The following selection is excerpted from The Unfinished Nation *(New York: Mc-
Graw Hill, 1997), 907. Reprinted with permission of The McGraw-Hill Companies.*

At least equally important to the success of the new right was a new and potent
conservative issue: the tax revolt. It had its public beginnings in 1978, when
Howard Jarvis, a conservative activist, launched a successful tax revolt in California with Proposition 13, a referendum question on the state ballot rolling back
property-tax rates. Similar antitax movements soon began in other states and
eventually spread to national politics.

For more than thirty years after the New Deal, Republican conservatives had
struggled to halt and even reverse the growth of the federal government. But during most of those years, as right-wing politicians from Robert Taft to Barry Goldwater discovered, attacking government programs did not succeed in attracting
majority support. Every federal program had a political constituency, and the
biggest and most expensive programs had the broadest support. Proposition 13
and similar initiatives gave members of the right a better way to undermine government than by attacking specific programs: attacking taxes. By separating the
issue of taxes from the issue of what taxes supported, the right found a way to
achieve the most controversial elements of its own agenda (eroding the government's ability to launch new ventures and even to sustain old ones) without openly
antagonizing the millions of voters who supported specific programs. Virtually no
one liked to pay taxes, and as the economy grew weaker and the relative burden
of paying taxes grew heavier, that resentment naturally rose. The right exploited
that resentment and, in the process, expanded its constituency far beyond anything it had known before. The 1980 presidential election propelled it to a historic
victory.

Chapter 157

Campus Racism and the Reagan Budget Cuts

Joseph S. Murphy

Political scientist Joseph S. Murphy (1933–1998) was the chancellor of the City University of New York from 1982 to 1990. Prior to that, he served as assistant office secretary in the Department of Health, Education, and Welfare in Washington (1966–1967); associate director of the Job Corps in the Office of Economic Opportunity in Washington (1967–1968); director of Peace Corps operations in Ethiopia (1968–1970); Vice Chancellor for Higher Education for the State of New Jersey (1970–1971); president of Queens College (1971–1977), and president of Bennington University (1977–1982). In later years, Murphy returned to teaching at the CUNY Graduate School and the university's worker education program.

The following selection is reprinted from "Racism and the Reagan Budget Cuts," a speech delivered at "Campus Bigotry: Modes of Response," a conference of the Anti-Defamation League, 8 April 1990. Reprinted with permission of Susan Crile.

There has not in recent years been a more appropriate time to talk about bigotry on campus—and everywhere else. It directly results from a set of public policies pursued through the 1980s and a failure of leadership at every level, possibly including our own. It is something to which attention must be paid.

And attention is being paid. Last Thursday, as I was working on these remarks, I had in front of me each of the major metropolitan newspapers. The headline in the *Daily News* was "Race Speech Is Protested," and the story dealt with the audience reaction at Long Island University to a speech by Professor Michael Levin of City College. The *Post* had a similar story headed "Outrage at LIU Over Speech by 'Racist'." *Newsday* broadened the coverage with a background piece headed "Educators See Rise in Campus Hate," and they ran a second news article about a member of the Columbia University soccer team who used an awards ceremony as the occasion to condemn his university for having too many Jews. The *Times* had an article that dealt indirectly with racial equity issues at one of the units of City University.

Now, racism anywhere and perpetrated against any group ought to concern all of us as citizens in a society that purports to adhere to democratic values. But I think that there are certain unique qualities embodied by the academy that make prejudice on campus particularly offensive and particularly problematic. We, of all institutions should be immune from those who, by definition, base their ideas and actions on ignorance. But we operate within a set of constraints that severely limit our ability to strike back. Nor can we compel any of our students to bring to campus an unbiased mind. We cannot do these things because our obligation as educators is to promote free interchange of ideas and to foster a climate where truth prevails not because error is ruled out of existence, but because it fails to meet commonly understood tests of intellectual merit.

Let no one here underestimate the complexity of that task. The question before us, about which men and women have argued for years, is this one: How can the university, committed as it is to debate aimed at discovering truth, work within its constraints to eliminate bigotry? How do we on the one hand protect everyone's right to say whatever he or she wishes, no matter how idiotic, and on the other hand make it clear that bigotry is antithetical to everything we stand for?

That is a hard subject. Had we defined the issue to encompass only *acts* of violence, the intellectual task would be easier. It would probably take us no more than a moment to agree that no university can countenance physical attacks on groups or on individuals because they are members of particular groups. It makes no difference whether the victims are black or Jewish or homosexual. It makes no difference whether the attackers act on the basis of some genuine or imagined historical grievance.

But having said that we have to turn to the harder issues. The real problem on most campuses is not the isolated act of violence, terrible as that is, but the set of underlying attitudes that breed such violence. Last Thursday may have been an atypically busy day on the bigotry front, but it is clear that the problem is a large and growing one.

According to *The Chronicle of Higher Education*, anti-Semitism on campus is at a ten-year high, beyond offensive jokes and slurs, to the circulation of catalogues promoting neo-Nazi literature. Assaults on women continue to increase, and so do attacks on people of unorthodox sexual orientation.

Why now? Why, in 1990, a full generation after the most comprehensive civil rights legislation was implemented—and twenty-five years after our society signaled its commitment to full access to the university for people of all racial and income groups? What has brought us to the point that we have to address issues of bigotry that should long since have been put behind us?

One answer is to say that intergroup conflict is the inevitable result of scarcity of resources. If there's not much room at the top, or not much wealth to be distributed at the middle or even at the bottom, then people will form into whatever tribal subgroups make sense and start attacking one another for the food or the jobs or the places in the university that do exist. By this analysis, if the problem is scarcity, the answer is abundance: To diminish bigotry, one need only make more wealth of whatever kind available to everyone and people won't see any need to continue fighting one another. Marxists, neo-Marxists, traditional socialists, left-of-center Democrats, even liberal Republicans can buy that hypothesis. It fits nicely into a standard analytical framework. It explains why eight years of Ronald Reagan and eight years of accelerated maldistribution of national wealth has led not just to bigotry on campus but to ethnic conflict in almost every major city in the country.

But Reaganism—which is really just shorthand for the ruthless plundering of our national treasure; the privatization of society—had to do with more than money, and it will take more than money, more than the Peace Dividend [money which might be shifted from Pentagon spending with the end of the Cold War—Eds.],[1] to solve the problems it created. In its purest form Reaganism not only produced but celebrated a denial of social idealism, the renunciation of the concept of community and the elevation of unbridled greed to the status of virtue. It proclaimed a privatist ideology that seeped through society and trickled down even as the wealth supposedly generated by supply-side economics did not. It invaded every institution and in the academy it worked to transform us from the community of scholars and students we aspired to be (even if we never achieved the ideal) to an arena in which individuals bid and competed and worked against each other for the private goal of a credential valued by the economic marketplace. The environment thereby created—and I do not hold us in the profession immune from criticism, since we acquiesced in much of this—was not just anti-communal but cold, indifferent, and antithetical to the concept of cooperation toward some larger shared purpose, goal or mission.

Of course this was more true at some places than at others. But on the whole, and even at some of the very expensive private schools, we went from the old, outmoded concept of *in loco parentis* [responsible "in place of the parents"] to the new and cheaper concept of "none of my business." So it is small wonder that students—who after all mirror the society from which they come—would seek to band together in small groups that give them some sense of identity and comfort. And it is small wonder as well that, absent strong direction or involvement or concern by the institutions themselves, some of these small groups—or disgruntled individuals—would turn against others perceived as different from themselves and with whom they have little contact.

More important than the analysis of why bigotry is increasing is the question of what we intend to do about it. We have heard today about some of the modes of response at The City University of New York and at other places. At CUNY we have been active on this issue for a long time: Our Board of Trustees set forth a commitment to "Pluralism and Diversity" as our official policy two years ago and we are working on implementing that commitment on a campus-by-campus basis. Obviously we need to continue and expand our efforts.

What I want to talk about are not specific programs, but some more fundamental operating principles that ought to guide us. I have six basic goals in mind—six things I think it is critical that we do:

First and most fundamentally, we have to make it clear that bias-related violence will never be tolerated, condoned, or excused—not because of past or present injustice, or because of the failure of the system to respond adequately through normal channels, or because someone somewhere believes that he or she must engage in violent behavior in order to be heard. The right to security of person must be inalienable in the community at large as well as in the university. If it is not, we have nothing that can honestly be called a community *or* a university.

Second—and on this point there may well be debate among this audience—we must protect orderly free speech even when it hurts; protect the right of every student and every faculty member to express whatever ideas they may have, however loathsome. *But note that our obligation to protect free speech in no way compromises our freedom to respond—or our obligation to do so.* The racist or anti-female or anti-Semitic remark made publicly that gets a quick and overpowering rebuttal does less harm than the suppressed comment that circulates away from the light of inspection.

Third, we ought to fulfill our role as educators and help our students see the distinction between bigotry and legitimate, if sharp and even hurtful, commentary. To the extent possible, we should remove from the classroom the chilling fear that the expression of controversial views will open the speaker to unwarranted charges of bigotry. But again, nothing in that compromises anyone else's right to respond on the points at issue.

Fourth, let us accept the wisdom of Adlai Stevenson's famous remark when he was spat upon in Dallas, and someone asked him if the people who did that should be sent to jail. "No," he said, "they should be sent to school." We ought to make sure that all of our students—and to the extent possible members of the community at large—have access to the kind of education that brings people above the level of bigotry. There may be a lot of bigots around with university degrees—but there are no well-educated bigots. The two things—the college degree and the college education—are not always synonymous, and we ought to guarantee that the curriculum we offer exposes students to the contribution of many cultures and to critical ideas and rational ways of analysis that work to overcome the influence of a largely close-minded society.

Fifth, we should recognize and help our students to recognize that we do indeed live in a pluralistic society. The old American metaphor of the melting pot has lost its power. The more compelling metaphor is the one of the salad bowl, with lots of ingredients not so much co-mingling as coexisting. This may not be what some of us were brought up to view as the American ideal, but it is the American reality. And on our campuses we serve a collection of distinct groups—some with overlapping memberships, but each with a clear identity. To ignore that fact is to engage in a fantasy.

So we have to foster a climate not just of respect for individuals, but of respect for groups and an understanding that there are indeed ethnic and social differences among people but that these differences in no way connote any kind of inferiority or superiority. The appropriate goal is not to banish subgroups from campus, but to get them to work constructively and cooperatively and to recognize that they are part of a larger whole.

Sixth and finally, we must promote what, for want of a better word, we might call "civility." That's the word that the Carnegie Foundation for the Advancement of Teaching uses in a report they have just put out on the loss of community on the

American campus, and for all of its strained gentility, the term does connote a concept all of us can understand. At the root of that concept is recognition of the right to exist in a climate of tolerance and mutual respect, the right to speak, the right to be heard, and the right to rebut what others say. There is nothing mutually contradictory between civility and legitimate intellectual conflict. They should coexist at every college and probably within every department. One of the basic functions of a university administration ought to be to assure that the conflict is waged in a climate where civility prevails.

The fact is that we live in a bigoted time. Intergroup cannibalism in a fierce battle for limited resources is the order of the day, and for at least the past five years every major conflict in our midst has degenerated into a field day for ethnic confrontation. That has happened in national politics and in most institutions of American society and we have not been immune. The academy, however, bears a special responsibility both for dealing with prejudice and for fostering full and unconstrained expression of controversial ideas. Our mandate is complex but it is essential that we try to fulfill it. If we in the university fail to confront bigotry in our midst, to rebut the bigot, and at the same time to hold true to the First Amendment values that underly our existence, then no other institution in this society in this decade will do better. And we chance the irreversible destruction of those fragile ties that make us worthy of being called a civilization.

EDITORS' NOTE

1. Walter Kaufman, a military policy consultant at the Brookings Institution, estimated that by the end of the 1990s the United States could be spending $140 billion less per year on its military budget than in 1990—thanks to the Peace Dividend. See Walter Kaufman, *Glasnost, Perestroika, and U.S. Defense Spending* (Washington, D.C.: Brookings Institution, 1990).

Chapter 158

The War against the Poor

Herbert J. Gans

Herbert J. Gans, professor of sociology at Columbia University, is the author of Deciding What's News *(1979),* More Equality *(1983),* Middle American Individualism: The Future of Liberal Democracy *(1988), and many other works.*

"The War against the Poor" is reprinted from Dissent, Fall 1992, 461–65. *Reprinted with permission of the author and* Dissent. *Gans's article was later expanded into a book,* The War against the Poor: The Underclass and Antipoverty Policy *(1995).*

While liberals have been talking about resuming the War on Poverty, elected officials are doing something very different: waging a war on the poor. Even the riot [in response to the Rodney King verdict] that took place in Los Angeles in early May [1992] did not interrupt that war, perhaps because the riot was a mixture of protest, looting and destruction.

The war on the poor was initiated by dramatic shifts in the domestic and world economy which have turned more and more unskilled and semiskilled workers into surplus labor. Private enterprise participated actively by shipping jobs overseas and by treating workers as expendable. Government has done its part as well, increasingly restricting the welfare state safety net to the middle class. Effective job-creation schemes, housing programs, educational and social services that serve the poor—and some of the working classes—are vanishing. Once people become poor, it becomes even harder for them to escape poverty.

Despite the willingness to help the poor expressed in public opinion polls, other more covert attitudes have created a political climate that makes the war on the poor possible. Politicians compete with each other over who can capture the most headlines with new ways to punish the poor. However, too many of their constituents see the poor not as people without jobs, but as miscreants who behave badly because they do not abide by middle class or mainstream moral values. Those judged "guilty" are dismissed as the "undeserving poor"—or the underclass in today's language—people who do not deserve to escape poverty.

True, *some* poor people are indeed guilty of immoral behavior—that is, murderers, street criminals, drug sellers, child abusers.

Then there are poor people whose anger at their condition expresses itself in the kind of nihilism that cannot be defined as political protest. Even so, most of those labeled "undeserving" are simply poor people who for a variety of reasons cannot live up to mainstream behavioral standards, like remaining childless in adolescence, finding and holding a job, and staying off welfare. This does not make them immoral. Because poor adolescents do not have jobs does not mean they are lazy. Because their ghetto "cool" may deter employers does not mean they are unwilling to work. Still, the concept of an underclass lumps them with those who are criminal or violent.

Why do Americans accept so many untruths about the poor, and remaining unwilling to accept the truth when it is available? The obvious answer is that some of the poor frighten or anger those who are better-off. But they also serve as a lightning rod—scapegoats—for some problems among the better-off. Street criminals rightly evoke fears about personal safety, but they, and the decidedly innocent poor, also generate widespread anger about the failure of government to reduce "urban" and other problems.

Among whites, the anger is intertwined with fears about blacks and "Hispanics," or the newest immigrants, reflecting the fear of the stranger and newcomer from which their own ancestors suffered when they arrived here. (Few remember that, at the start of the twentieth century, the "Hebrews" then arriving were sometimes described as a "criminal race"—as the Irish had been earlier in the nineteenth century.)

The hostility toward today's welfare recipients is a subtler but equally revealing index to the fears of the more fortunate. This fear reflects a historic belief that people who are not economically self-sufficient can hurt the economy, although actual expenditures for welfare have always been small. Welfare recipients are also assumed to be getting something for nothing, often by people who are not overly upset about corrupt governmental or corporate officials who get a great deal of money for nothing or very little.

Welfare recipients possibly provoke anger among those concerned about their own economic security, especially in a declining economy. Welfare recipients are seen as living the easy life while everyone else is working harder than ever—and thus become easy scapegoats, which does not happen to the successful, who often live easier lives.

The concern with poor unmarried mothers, especially adolescents, whose number and family size have in fact long been declining, epitomized adult fears about the high levels of sexual activity and the constant possibility of pregnancy among *all* adolescent girls. In addition, the notion of the "undeserving poor" has become a symbol for the general decline of mainstream moral standards, especially those celebrated as "traditional" in American society.

Ironically, however, the "undeserving poor" can be forced to uphold some of these very standards in exchange for welfare, much as some Skid Row homeless still get a night's dinner and housing in exchange for sitting through a religious service. The missionaries in this case are secular: social workers and bureaucrats. But the basic moralistic expectations remain the same, including the demand that the poor live up to values that their socioeconomic superiors preach but do not always practice. Thus, social workers can have live-in lovers without being married, but their clients on welfare cannot. Members of the more fortunate classes are generally free from moral judgements altogether; no one talks about an undeserving middle class or the undeserving rich.

The war on the poor is probably best ended by job-centered economic growth that creates decent public and private jobs. Once poor people have such jobs, they are almost automatically considered deserving, eligible for a variety of other programs to help them or their children escape poverty.

The most constructive way to supply such jobs would be an updated New Deal that repairs failing infrastructures, creates new public facilities (including new data bases), and allows the old ones to function better—for example, by drastically reducing class size in public schools. Equally important are ways of reviving private enterprise and finding new niches for it in the global economy. Without them, there will not be enough well-paying jobs in factories, laboratories, and offices—or taxes to pay for public programs. Such programs are already being proposed these days, by Bill Clinton and in the Congress, but mainly for working-class people who have been made jobless and are now joining the welfare rolls.

Last but not least is a new approach to income grants for those who cannot work or find work. The latest fashion is to put welfare recipients to work, which would be a good idea if even decent entry-level jobs for them could be found or created. (Alas, when taxpayers discover how much cheaper it is to pay welfare than to create jobs, that remedy may end as it has before.)

Also needed is a non-punitive, universal income grant program, which goes to all people who still end up as part of the labor surplus. If such a program copied the European principle of not letting the incomes of the poor fall below 60 to 70 percent of the median income—in the United States, welfare recipients get a fifth of the median on average—the recipients would remain integral members of society, who could be required to make sure their children would not become poor. (Such a solution would also cut down the crime rate.)

However, even minimal conventional anti-poverty programs are politically unpopular at the moment. The 1992 Democratic presidential candidates paid little attention to the poor during the primaries, except in passing, in New York City and then again after Los Angeles. The future of antipoverty programs looks no brighter than before.

The time may be ripe to look more closely at how nonpoor Americans feel about poverty, and try to reduce their unwarranted fear and anger toward the poor—with the hope that they would then be more positive about reviving antipoverty efforts.

The first priority for reducing anger is effective policies against drugs and street crime, though they alone cannot stem all the negative feelings. Probably the only truly effective solution is a prosperous economy in which the anger between all groups is lessened; and a more egalitarian society, in which the displacement of such anger on the poor is no longer necessary, and the remaining class conflicts can be fought fairly.

This ideal is today more utopian than ever, but it ought to be kept in mind. Every step toward it will help a little. Meanwhile, in order to bring back anti-poverty programs, liberals, along with the poor and others who speak for the poor, could also try something else: initiating an intellectual and cultural defense of the poor. In a "sound bite": to fight *class* bigotry along with the racial kind.

Anti-bigotry programs work slowly and not always effectively, but they are as American as apple pie. Class bigotry is itself still a novel idea, but nothing would be lost by mounting a defense of the poor and putting it on the public agenda. Ten such defenses strike me as especially urgent:

1. Poverty is not equivalent to moral failure. That moral undesirables exist among the poor cannot be denied, but there is no evidence that their proportion is greater than among the more fortunate. "Bums" can be found at all economic levels. However, more prosperous miscreants tend to be less visible; the alcoholic co-worker can doze off at his desk, but the poor drunk is apt to be found in the gutter. Abusive middle-class parents may remain invisible for years, until their children are badly hurt, but violent poor parents soon draw the attention of child-welfare workers and may lose their children to foster care.

Troubled middle-class people have access to experts who can demonstrate that moral diagnoses are not enough. The abusive mother was herself abused; the school dropout has a learning disability; the young person who will not work suffers from depression. Poor people, on the other hand, rarely have access to such experts or to clinical treatment. For the poor, the explanations are usually moral, and the treatment is punitive.

2. "Undeservingness" is an effect of poverty. Whatever else can be said about unmarried mothers on welfare, school dropouts, and people unwilling to take minimum-wage dead-end jobs, their behavior is almost always *poverty related*.

This is, of course, true of many street criminals and drug sellers. Middle-class people, after all, do not turn into muggers and street drug dealers any more than they become fifteen-year-old unmarried mothers.

People who have not been poor themselves do not understand how much of what the poor do is poverty-related. Poor young women often do not want to marry the fathers of their children because such men cannot perform as breadwinners and might cope with their economic failures by battering their wives. Although a great deal of publicity is given to school dropouts, not enough has been said about the peer pressure of the poor, and even working-class, neighborhoods that discourages doing well in school.

3. The responsibilities of the poor. Conservatives, often mute about the responsibilities of the rich, stress the responsibilities of the poor. However, poor people sometimes feel no need to be responsible to society until society treats them responsibly. Acting irresponsibly becomes an angry reaction to, even a form of power over that society. Those whose irresponsibility is criminal deserve punishment and the clearly lazy deserve to lose their benefits. But who would punish an unmarried mother who goes on welfare to obtain medical benefits that a job cannot supply? Is she not acting responsibly toward her child? And how well can we judge anyone's responsibility without first knowing what choices, responsible and irresponsible, were actually open? Being poor often means having little choice to begin with.

4. The drastic scarcity of work for the poor. Many Americans, including too many economists, have long assumed that there are always more jobs than workers, that the jobless are at fault. This is, however, a myth—one of many Ronald Reagan liked to promote when he was president. The facts are just the opposite. Decent jobs that are open to the poor, especially to blacks, were the first to disappear when our deindustrialization began. This helps to explain why so many poor men have dropped out of the labor force, and are no longer even counted as jobless.

Incidentally, the myth that the unemployed are unwilling to work is never attached to the rising number of working- and middle-class jobless. But, then, they are not yet poor enough to be considered undeserving.

5. Black troubles and misbehavior are caused more by poverty than by race. Because the proportion of blacks who are criminals, school dropouts, heads of single-parent families, or unmarried mothers is higher than among whites, blacks increasingly have to face the outrageous indignity of being considered genetically or culturally undesirable. The plain fact is that the higher rates of nearly all social problems among blacks are the effects of being poor—including poverty brought about by discrimination. When poor whites are compared with poor blacks, those with social problems are not so different, although black proportions remain higher. Even this difference can be attributed to income disparity. Black poverty has been worse in all respects and by all indicators ever since blacks were brought here as slaves.

6. Blacks should not be treated like recent immigrants. Black job keepers sometimes face the additional burden of being expected, both by employers and the general public, to compete for jobs with recently arrived immigrants. This expectation calls on people who have been in America for generations to accept the subminimum wages, long hours, poor working conditions, and employer intimidation that are the lot of many immigrants. Actually, employers prefer immigrants because they are more easily exploited or more deferential than native-born Americans. To make matters worse, blacks are then blamed for lacking an "immigrant work ethic."

7. Debunking the metaphors of undeservingness. Society's wordsmiths—academics, journalists, and pundits—like to find, and their audiences like to hear, buzzwords that caricature moral failings among the poor; but it should not be forgotten that these terms were invented by the fortunate. *Not only is there no identifiable underclass, but a class "under" society is a social impossibility.* Welfare "dependents" are in that condition mainly because the economy had declared them surplus labor, and because they must rely on politicians and officials who determine their welfare eligibility.

Such metaphors are never applied to the more affluent. There are no hard-core millionaires, and troubled middle-class people will never be labeled an under-middle class. Women who choose to be financially dependent on their husbands are not described as spouse-dependent, while professors who rely on university trustees for their income are not called tenure-dependent.

8. *The dangers of class stereotypes.* Underclass and other terms for the undeserving poor are class stereotypes, which reinforce class discrimination much as racial stereotypes support racial discrimination. The main similarities between class and racial stereotypes still need to be identified.

Stereotypes sometimes turn into everyday labels that are so taken for granted that they turn into self-fulfilling prophecies—and then cause particular havoc among the more vulnerable poor. For example, boys from poor single-parent families are apt to be punished harder for minor delinquencies simply because of the stereotype that they are growing up without parental or other male supervision. Once they, and other poor people, are labeled as undeserving, public officials who are supposed to supply them with services feel justified in not being as helpful as before—though depriving poor people of an emergency rent payment or food grant may be enough to push them closer to homelessness or street crime.

The recent display of interest in and appeals for affirmative action along class lines—even by conservatives like Dinesh D'Souza—suggests that the time may be ripe to recognize, and begin to fight, the widespread existence of class discrimination and prejudice. The confrontation has to take place not only in everyday life but also in the country's major institutions, politics, and courts. The Constitution that is now interpreted as barring racial discrimination can perhaps be interpreted to bar class discrimination as well.

9. *Blaming the poor reduces neither poverty nor poverty-related behavior.* Labeling the poor as undeserving does not attack the causes of street crime, improve the schools of poor children, or reduce adult joblessness. Such labels are only a way of expressing anger toward the poor. Blaming the victim solves nothing except to make the blamers feel better temporarily. Such labeling justifies political ideologies and interests that oppose solutions, and thus increases the likelihood that nothing will be done about poverty—or crime.

10. *Improving reporting and scholarship about the poor.* Most poverty news is about crime, not poverty. How many reporters ever ask whether economic hardship is part of the crime story? The government's monthly jobless rate is reported, but not the shortage of jobs open to the poor. Likewise, the percentage of people below the poverty rate is an annual news story, but the actual income of the poor, often less than half the poverty line, or about $6,000 a year, is not mentioned.

The "spins," both in government statistics and in journalism, carry over into scholarship. Millions were spent to find and measure an underclass, but there is little ethnographic research to discover why the poor must live as they do. Researchers on homelessness look at mental illness as a cause of homelessness; they do not study it as a possible *effect!*

There are also innumerable other studies of the homeless, but too few about the labor markets and employers, housing industry and landlords, and other factors that create homelessness in the first place.

The Americans who feel most threatened by the poor are people from the working class, whom journalists currently call the middle class. They are apt to live nearest the poor. They will suffer most, other than the poor themselves, from street crime, as well as from the fear that the poor could take over their neighborhoods and jobs. Indeed, as inexpensive housing and secure jobs requiring little education become more scarce, the people only slightly above the poor in income and economic security fear that their superior status will shrink drastically. Viewing the poor as undeserving helps to maintain and even widen that status gap.

No wonder, then, that in the current economic crisis, the journalists' middle class and its job problems are the big story, and the poor appear mainly as the underclass, with candidates ignoring poverty. The political climate being what it is, this may even be unavoidable. Indeed, if the winner's margin in the coming elections comes from that middle class, the candidate must initiate enough economic programs to put *its* jobless back to work and to solve its healthcare, housing, and other problems.

That winner should be bold enough to make room in the program for the poor as well. Poverty, racial polarization, crime, and related problems cannot be allowed to rise higher without further reducing morale, quality of life, and economic competitiveness. Otherwise, America will not be a decent, safe, or pleasant place to live, even for the affluent.

Chapter 159

David Duke and the Southern Strategy

Tom Turnipseed

Perennial political candidate David Duke, former Nazi and Imperial Wizard of the Louisiana Knights of the Ku Klux Klan, ran as the Republican candidate for president in 1988, senate in 1990, governor of Louisiana in 1991, and Congress in 1999.

Lawyer Tom Turnipseed began his political career as a supporter of George Wallace. Since then, he says, "I've seen the error of my ways." He's currently involved with anti-racist work and South Carolina state politics. His work with the Southern Poverty Law Center helped win a $37 million judgment against the Klan in 1998. That year he also ran as the Democratic party candidate for attorney general in South Carolina.

The following selection is reprinted with permission from "Deserving David Duke," Columbia, S.C., Point, 26 October 1990.

For more on Duke, see James Ridgeway, Blood in the Face: The Ku Klux Klan, Aryan Nations, Nazi Skinheads, and the Rise of a New White Culture *(1990).*

The Republican Party deserves David Duke despite desperate attempts by the Republican hierarchy to disavow the Louisiana bigot. In 1968 a racist Republican "Southern Strategy" was devised to co-opt George Wallace's appeal to white bigotry and has been the building block of Republicanism in the South and beyond for more than 20 years. So the "chickens have come home to roost" (as Wallace would say) when Duke, the former Nazi and Klan leader, received an astounding 44 percent of the vote in the [1990] U.S. Senate race in Louisiana.

The Republican street strategy in the small towns and cities of South Carolina and throughout the South has been to spread the word that "blacks are taking over the Democratic Party," and good white folks should vote Republican. White flight suburbs of the South have become bastions of "Republicanism" with Republican candidates receiving up to 75 percent to 80 percent of the vote. Many whites who identify with Democratic principles and have voted the Democratic ticket are now being "shamed" for being in the same party with blacks and made to feel that they are betraying the "great white race."

South Carolina, the first Confederate state to secede from the Union, was the pivotal point in modern political party realignment on the race issue. Although the national Democratic Party had been relatively progressive on the race issue since F.D.R., Southern Democrats fought civil rights in Congress and party platform debates. In 1948, Governor Strom Thurmond led a "Dixiecrat" revolt against the national Democratic civil rights platform as a third party, "States rights" presidential candidate. Later, in the U.S. Senate Thurmond set a national filibuster record by his marathon speech against a civil rights bill. South Carolina again led the South on matters of racism when Thurmond switched to the Republican Party in 1964 to embrace Barry Goldwater's anti–civil rights stance in the Presidential campaign.

Goldwater lost, but in 1968 when Wallace was riding a strong white backlash to the civil rights movement, "ol' Strom" persuaded Richard Nixon to adopt a "Southern Strategy" which let potential Wallace voters know Nixon was for law and order and opposed to busing and quotas. The "Southern Strategy" worked for Nixon and has worked ever since for Republicans as they use racial polarization to succeed in the South.

Reagan and Bush, guided by Lee Atwater, a Thurmond protégé from South Carolina, used fear of crime and blacks to polarize white voters toward their national conservative constituency by talking about ending busing, quotas and crime in the streets and running Willie Horton ads. . . .

Perhaps the most frightening use of racist politics is the Republican Justice Department's alleged use of selective prosecution and harassment of black elected officials. The Congressional Black Caucus devoted their annual weekend conference [in 1989] to [discussing] the harassment of African-American leaders. Since almost all black elected leaders are Democrats, they make tempting targets for a politically oriented Justice Department of a political organization that has positioned itself as the "white folk's party." . . .

The Republicans can try to duck and dodge David Duke, but because of past performance, they really do deserve each other. It's sad that the party of Abraham Lincoln has become the party of David Duke. But the greatest challenge for the Democrats is to find leadership proud of their party's diversity and strong enough to bring racial reconciliation to a country facing perilous economic and ecological problems.

Chapter 160

The Civil Rights Act of 1991

Richard O. Curry

Richard O. Curry (1931–1997) was professor of history at the University of Connecticut. He wrote A House Divided *(1964),* Radicalism, Racism, and Party Realignment *(1969), edited* The Abolitionists *(rev. ed., 1973),* Freedom at Risk: Secrecy, Censorship, and Repression in the 1980s *(1988), and co-edited* American Chameleon: Individualism in Trans-National Context *(1991).*

The following selection is excerpted from An Uncertain Future: Thought Control and Repression during the Reagan-Bush Era *(Los Angeles: First Amendment Foundation, 1992), 75–77, 79–80, footnotes deleted. Reprinted with permission of Patricia Curry.*

Employment Discrimination Cases

The Civil Rights Act of 1964 made employment discrimination illegal. Its terminology on this point was sufficiently vague, however, that it permitted many employers to use "neutral" screening devices (a euphemism for discriminatory practices) in hiring their work force. For example, height and weight qualifications denied most women opportunity to become law enforcement officers, and the requirement of a high school diploma denied many members of minority groups an opportunity to compete for assembly line jobs. The American workplace, therefore, was segregated by sex, race, or both. All that changed in 1971 when the Supreme Court delivered its landmark decision, *Griggs v. Duke Power, Inc.* As one commentator phrased it, *Griggs* "deserves more credit for integrating America's workplace than any other law case." What the Court did, in short, was to establish a "disparate impact" standard. If statistical analysis revealed that a disproportionate number of minorities or women were excluded from certain jobs, a company was required to demonstrate, in court, that the qualifications were not only work-related but a "business necessity." Other important cases, including *Albermarle Paper Co. v. Moody* (1975) and *Dothard v. Rawlinson* (1977), not only strengthened the *Griggs* precedent but accelerated the process of integration.

The Supreme Court's New Majority, when it came to power in 1989, lost little time in reversing *Griggs*. In *Ward's Cove Packing Co. v. Atonio*, the Court, by a 5–4 majority, shifted the burden of proof from employers to employees. The

Ward's Cove decision, in fact, was a mirror image of *Griggs*. Employees were now required to prove that job qualifications were not work-related and were not a result of "business necessity." Statistics could be introduced as evidence in court only if employees "could also identify specific acts that caused the statistical disparity."

In 1989, the [Supreme] Court also decided several other discrimination cases. In *Martin v. Wilks*, the Court, in another 5–4 decision, ruled that white firefighters in Birmingham, Alabama could challenge a court-approved affirmative action settlement in which the fire department was required to hire and promote blacks.

In a related case, *Jett v. Dallas Independent School District*, the Court ruled, once again by a 5–4 margin, that the Civil Rights Act of 1866 could no longer be used to bring damage suits against cities which, allegedly, were guilty of racial discrimination. The act itself, however, was not invalidated, but in *Patterson v. McLean Credit Union*, the Court ruled that the act applied only to hiring practices and not to on-the-job discrimination.

Attention must also be called to two other cases decided in 1989. In *Croson v. City of Richmond*, the Court invalidated a city of Richmond ordinance that channeled thirty percent of public work funds to minority-owned construction companies. The ordinance, the Court ruled, violated the rights of white contractors who were being denied equal protection under the law.

In light of the Supreme Court's decisions to reverse or narrow the application of established precedents in discrimination cases, it is difficult to explain the Court's ruling in *Hopkins v. Price Waterhouse*. In this case, which involved three different majority opinions, the Court declared that in cases involving individuals, rather than groups, employers were required to demonstrate that discrimination, based on race, sex, or age, was not involved in their decision not to hire or promote someone. [*New York Times* legal correspondent] Linda Greenhouse observes that the *Hopkins* decision obviously reflects a "sharply different approach" from that taken in *Ward's Cove*. But cases involving efforts by "individual plaintiffs trying to prove that they were singled out for discriminatory treatment" is a "category," Greenhouse concludes, "to which conservatives on and off the Court have remained fairly sympathetic."

The Civil Rights Act of 1991

The *Ward's Cove* decision, however, not only produced a public outcry from organizations dedicated to protecting the rights of minorities and women, but resulted in the creation of a bipartisan congressional coalition which passed the Civil Rights Act of 1990. Its primary objective was to restore the "disparate impact" standard repudiated by the New Majority in *Ward's Cove*. Unfortunately, the margin of victory was not sufficiently large to override President Bush's veto. The president repeatedly, but wrongly, denounced the act as a "quota bill."

In 1991, Congress tried again, and after a long and rancorous debate, passed the Civil Rights Act of 1991. This time, the President signed the act into law. Mr.

Bush, administration officials, and conservative Republicans expressed satisfaction with the elimination of a "quota system" which the bill had never contained. Only the unwary, the unprincipled, or the uninformed ever took that position in the first place. What the law did, among other things, was to restore the *Griggs* standard. Hiring criteria, the law stated, must have a "manifest relationship to the requirements for effective job performance."

Mr. Bush, however, had a variety of political reasons for signing the 1991 act which had not existed the year before. For one thing, it allowed the president and other conservative Republicans to differentiate their position on race from that of David Duke [see chapter 159—Eds.]. For another, the law allowed women, for the first time, to collect compensatory and punitive damages in sex bias cases. By claiming some of the credit for this provision, Mr. Bush hoped to minimize the political damage done, especially among women voters, by Professor Anita Hill's allegations of sexual harassment during Justice [Clarence] Thomas's confirmation hearings. Even so, the law, which contained no limits for monetary awards in cases involving racial discrimination, limited awards in sex bias cases to $300,000.

With congressional Democrats and the Bush administration both claiming victory, the President, two days before signing the Civil Rights Act of 1991, found himself engulfed in still another firestorm. White House counsel C. Boyden Gray, a close presidential adviser, circulated a draft of a proposed executive order, which stated that all executive-branch agencies should "terminate" programs giving preference in hiring to minorities and women. The proposed order also stated that federal advisory guidelines regarding compliance with anti-discrimination laws by businesses would be abolished.

Senator John Danforth, the chief Republican sponsor of the Civil Rights Act, informed White House Chief of Staff, John Sununu, that the proposed executive order "was a disaster." It would "rub a national wound raw." After protests by Danforth, other Republican members of Congress, and some agency heads, President Bush ordered the most controversial language deleted. Even so, Marlin Fitzwater, the President's press secretary, refused to disavow the substance of Gray's memorandum. After further review, Fitzwater said, the Bush administration might yet decide to curtail federal affirmative action programs and guidelines.

New York Governor Mario Cuomo remarked: "What this proves to you is that they're not playing from any set of rules or principles." But the next day, at the Rose Garden ceremony, President Bush, in signing the act into law, appeared unflappable. "For the past few years," he said, "the issue of civil rights legislation has divided Americans. No more." The President went on to say: "Today we celebrate a law that will fight the evil of discrimination, while also building bridges of harmony between Americans of all races, sexes, creeds and backgrounds."

The sound and fury has subsided, at least momentarily, and most commentators agree that the new law overturned a number of Supreme Court decisions including *Ward's Cove v. Atonio* and *Equal Employment Opportunity Commission v. American Arabian Oil Co.*, a case in which the Supreme Court ruled that anti-discrimination laws did not apply to American citizens who worked for American companies overseas. Other commentators, especially lawyers specializing in job discrimination cases, observed that the Civil Rights Act of 1991 contains so many confusing and ambiguous provisions that it will take years of litigation to determine precisely what some aspects of the law actually mean.

Steven A. Holmes, a reporter who writes on legal issues, discusses several important unresolved issues raised the act. First, "Is the law retroactive?" Does it apply to cases that were pending when the law was passed, or only to "new cases?" Second, the law permits "women, the disabled and members of religious minorities" to receive up to $300,000 in punitive and compensatory damages. But the law is not clear as to "whether it means $300,000 per lawsuit or $300,000 for each allegation." In addition, can "employers legally continue programs that favor women and minority members in hiring and promotion?" The law's language is both confusing and contradictory. Moreover, what is the law's impact on "affirmative action for state and local governments and school boards that base hiring and promotion on civil service tests?" Beyond this, Holmes points out that the effects of the law on voluntary affirmative action programs—that is, those that were not court ordered, are "particularly troubling." Although the law says that it protects programs that are "in accordance with the law," it fails "to define that phrase." Does it refer to past Supreme Court decisions that have upheld "the use of race or sex in hiring or promotions?" Or does it refer to the new law which "says the consideration of race or sex is now illegal?"

Thus, the Civil Rights Act of 1991, which has reversed the Supreme Court's New Majority on some issues, has apparently created the proverbial "can of worms" that, in the future, will provide the current members of the [Supreme] Court with sufficient latitude to interpret the law in new and perhaps unanticipated ways.

The law's ambiguities and contradictions even suggest that if the timing and political astuteness of White House counsel C. Boyden Gray are subject to question, the substance of the proposed executive order he drafted on terminating federal affirmative action programs for women and minority groups may not actually conflict with the Civil Rights Act of 1991. If Congress fails to clarify some of the law's provisions—as predictably it will in the short run—then the law becomes the province of the Federal courts, where it faces an uncertain future.

Chapter 161

How "Welfare" Became a Dirty Word

Linda Gordon

Linda Gordon, professor of history at the University of Wisconsin at Madison, is the author of Woman's Body, Woman's Right: Birth Control in America *(1976),* Heroes of Their Own Lives: The Politics and History of Family Violence, Boston 1880–1960 *(1988), and* Pitied but Not Entitled: Single Mothers and the History of Welfare *(1994), and editor of* Women, the State, and Welfare *(1990).*

The following selection is a revision of an article previously published in the Chronicle of Higher Education, *20 July 1994, B1–B2. Reprinted with permission of the author.*

For more on the racial politics of welfare, see Michael K. Brown, Race, Money, and the American Welfare State *(1999) and Jill Quadagno,* The Color of Welfare: How Racism Undermined the War on Poverty *(1994).*

In the last half-century, the American definition of "welfare" has been reversed. A term that once meant prosperity, good health, good spirits, and social respect now implies poverty, bad health, despondency and social disrespect. A word used to describe the health of the body politic now evokes images of disease, slums, depressed single mothers, neglected children, crime, despair.

Today, welfare particularly refers to one universally maligned government program, Aid to Families with Dependent Children (AFDC), when it once referred to a vision of the good life. As we watch Congress dismantle federally-funded entitlements, it may be useful to understand how the concept of welfare became so despised.

The term welfare could logically refer to all of a government's contributions to its citizens' well-being, including provision of streets and sidewalks, schools, parks, police and fire protection, utilities, regulation of food and drugs, pollution control, building inspections, prevention of child abuse, and safe-sex education.

Even if we were to label as welfare only those programs that provide cash to citizens, we could include tax deductions for home mortgages and business expenses, farm subsidies, Medicare, and the old-age pensions provided under the Social Security Act, among many other government benefits.

The negative connotations of welfare in the United States rest among the several programs originally included in the Social Security Act of 1935. The pejorative connotation attached to AFDC, a program of aid to children and single parents (almost all of whom are women), was not present when the program began. AFDC came to be viewed negatively only in the 1950s and 1960s.

The designers of the original statute did not intend to create a stratified system but rather were trying to meet different needs with different programs, all formulated under the influence of a major crisis—the Great Depression of the 1930s. The most influential drafters of the Social Security Act advocated social insurance. Seeking to prevent poverty and another depression by providing assistance to breadwinners as soon as their wages were interrupted—by unemployment, illness, or old age—they installed unemployment compensation and old-age insurance as the centerpieces of the law.

Those programs excluded the majority of Americans, although for different reasons. Blacks, who in the 1930s were still mainly agricultural and domestic workers, were effectively excluded at the insistence of Southern Democrats, who controlled crucial Congressional committees and wanted to maintain a low-wage labor force in the South. Black exclusion was the price, President Roosevelt believed, of getting the law through Congress. Most white women were excluded because the drafters assumed that the majority of them would continue to be non-employed housewives, collecting benefits as dependents on their husbands.

The program of AFDC was written by women heading the U.S. Children's Bureau, who wanted to provide for women and children who did not have a male wage earner to support them. The program was not intended to be inferior to the other Social Security programs, merely small and temporary, because its framers believed that the model of the family in which the male was the breadwinner and the female the housewife would be the standard. The framers of AFDC even believed that the causes of single motherhood—widowhood, divorce, and out-of-wedlock parenthood—would decline as economic disruption abated. Because they considered families headed by mothers to be exceptional, they designed the AFDC program very differently from the social-insurance programs:

• AFDC would be means-tested. To receive aid, an applicant would have to prove her poverty, not just initially but repeatedly, and she was required to open all her records to investigation. If she owned assets such as a house, she would be required to sell it, to impoverish herself, before she could collect a stipend, and she would lose benefits the moment she earned even a poverty wage. By contrast, a person could collect old-age or unemployment insurance (the "social insurance" programs) even if he were a millionaire.

• AFDC recipients would be morals-tested. To get assistance, an applicant would have to prove that her housekeeping, child-rearing, and sexual behavior were respectable, submitting to invasions of privacy—such as unannounced inspections of her home—that recipients of old-age and unemployment insurance escaped. The social-insurance programs were entirely automatic once you qualified; you could spend your entire pension on illegal drugs without a social worker ever inquiring about it.

• AFDC would be more a state than a federal program. With the states providing two-thirds of the money and federal matching grants providing the rest, the program was initially a federal contribution to existing state and local systems for aiding the poor. (Although the federal contribution now exceeds 50 percent in some states, the states still maintain discretion over many program rules.) The social-insurance programs, by contrast, had the cachet of newness, New Deal innovation, and exclusively federal administration, which separated them from the tradition of the dole to the poor. The current proposal, to remove the federal government entirely from setting any standards at all for aid to single parents and their children, will of course allow the states further to burden AFDC recipients with stigmatizing requirements.

• AFDC was financed by general tax revenues. Thus it appeared to be a burden on those who paid property and income taxes. By contrast, the social-insurance programs were financed by a separate payroll tax, labeled "contributions," from workers covered by them, as well as from employers. Using the term "contributions" enabled the benefits to be categorized as earned stipends or entitlements. In fact, Social Security contributions have always been mingled with general revenue, and what beneficiaries receive is not determined by what they have contributed.

• Eligibility for social-insurance benefits flowed through employment in a covered occupation. The kinds of jobs women and minority men were most likely to hold were not covered. And funding social insurance through places of employment continued a process already developing for over a century of redefining "work" to mean paid employment and to trivialize and render invisible the work that so many women did in caring for children, homes, husbands and other dependents.

This stratification created the meaning of welfare today. AFDC was stigmatized because of its differences from the other social programs, which were not usually called welfare. Originally intended to serve what in the 1930s seemed the most deserving of all needy groups—helpless mothers left alone with children by heartless men—AFDC became shameful, making its recipients undeserving by the very fact of providing for them.

The history of how these differences arose shows the deep-seated sex and race distinctions that were incorporated into the U.S. welfare state from its beginnings. Because women were considered mainly dependents, it seemed unobjectionable to design the women's welfare program to treat them as dependents of the state, while men had to be helped without eroding their dignity and head-of-household status. Because most members of minority groups were not considered full citizens, white lawmakers thought it acceptable to bar them from entitlements by excluding their jobs from coverage under the unemployment and old-age pension programs. Indeed, at first, members of minority groups were also effectively excluded from the AFDC program, because there was no federal control over racist local administrators.

Much has changed in the 60 years since the Social Security program was designed, and the changes have combined to increase the need for, and decrease the political support for, AFDC.

• As part of a groundswell of civil-rights agitation in the 1950s, black women began asserting that the right to receive welfare was one they were entitled to as citizens, just like the right to vote. The success of this claim not only increased the AFDC rolls, but also increased the proportion of blacks among AFDC recipients. Then, in the 1960s, a welfare-rights movement forced the courts to restrict the arbitrary power of states to invade recipients' privacy and cut off benefits summarily. Even more important, this activism created a more dignified image of the work of poor single mothers, reminding the public that mothering was not only work, but socially useful work. As the welfare-rights movement declined in the 1970s, however, the stigma attached to welfare intensified, strengthened now by racist animosity toward the growing number of welfare recipients from minority groups.

• The increasing number of mothers in the labor force, including middle- and upper-income women, gradually undermined the ideological basis of AFDC: the assumption that mothers should be helped to stay home with their children. This made the AFDC requirement that its beneficiaries not work for wages seem anachronistic. The recipients, not the program, were blamed.

• Increasing divorce rates left more women alone to raise their children. Despite the greater numbers who worked, many single mothers could not earn enough to support themselves and their children and pay for child care. AFDC rolls thus expanded.

• The drastic decline of industrial jobs during the last two decades not only raised unemployment rates, but also left more people chronically unemployed, underemployed, or employed only sporadically. This has meant that interruption of wages—the problem that unemployment compensation was originally designed to address—is no longer the chief cause of poverty in the United States. Many of today's unemployed are not eligible for unemployment compensation, and the parents among them turn to AFDC. The majority of AFDC recipients have been employed but are not entitled to unemployment benefits.

• Since World War II, the better jobs have carried private benefits such as health insurance, company pensions, and disability insurance—benefits that undercut support among many Americans for AFDC.

The problems of unemployment, underemployment, and employment in casual labor have helped deepen the division in our system for providing social benefits between the "middle class" (those with permanent jobs), which gets honorable, supposedly earned benefits, and the people who receive welfare. The stigma attached to welfare is self-reinforcing: The low status of its recipients stigmatizes the program, and the low status of the program stigmatizes its recipients.

The poorer and more maligned welfare recipients are, the more difficult it is for them to build political support for improving welfare. The further their benefits deteriorate, the deeper their indigence and hopelessness become. By contrast, the fact that Social Security old-age pensions were not originally classified as welfare has strengthened the lobbying power of organizations that represent older citizens, such as the American Association of Retired Persons. This has helped them maintain the level of their benefits and has reinforced their identity as citizens collecting earned entitlements.

No one likes welfare. But the idea being bandied about today that it could be abolished is misleading, a political dead end, and morally indefensible. Our goal should be to abolish poverty, not welfare. In a democracy, you can't simultaneously try to improve a public assistance program and malign its recipients, because you have to develop popular support for trying to help them.

The Clinton administration's original welfare-reform proposal, now occluded by the even more brutal conservative proposals, started today's wave of attacks on the poor. President Clinton's rhetoric about changing welfare so as to support the values of "work and responsibility" scapegoats poor and minority mothers by implying that their problems are caused by laziness and irresponsibility, when in fact the vast majority of AFDC recipient parents are struggling valiantly to raise their children well against great obstacles.

The Clinton proposal offered nothing to alter the political, economic, and social decline of welfare recipients. It did include some changes aimed at reducing poverty, such as its call for more child-support and its proposal for subsidized and community-service jobs. But since the proposal was supposed to be "revenue-neutral," insufficient money would have been available to enable these programs to make a difference. The consistent and extreme under-funding of welfare programs since the New Deal has been a major contributor to today's politically constructed anti-welfare "public opinion."

The illusion that we have a welfare state in place then allows conservatives to blame welfare for "producing" today's escalating social problems. In fact, the federal government has never given "welfare" a serious test, all the while continuing to maintain corporate welfare—what many today call the other AFDC, Aid to Financially Dependent Corporations—funded at many tens of times what is spent on the poor.

Chapter 162

Lazy Lies about Welfare

Derrick Z. Jackson

Derrick Z. Jackson is a columnist with the Boston Globe.

The following selection, "Lazy Lies about Welfare," is reprinted from the Boston Globe, *29 April 1998. Reprinted courtesy of the* Boston Globe.

For more on the media coverage of "welfare reform," see Laura Flanders and Janine Jackson, "Reforming Welfare Coverage," EXTRA!, May/June 1997. For more on the impact of "welfare reform," see Peter Edelman, "The Worst Thing Bill Clinton Has Done," Atlantic Monthly, March 1997; Karen Houppert, "You're Not Entitled! Welfare 'Reform' Is Leading to Government Lawlessness," Nation, 25 October 1999; and Sarah Karp, "Minorities Off Welfare Get Few Jobs," Chicago Reporter, January 2000.

Over the last month, influential newspapers have published in-depth accounts on how welfare reform is not getting recipients into jobs and especially into jobs that lift them out of poverty. Despite the claims of New York Mayor Rudolph Giuliani that slashing welfare rolls "is probably the best thing that we've done," *The New York Times* received so much resistance from Giuliani for statistics that Bill Keller, the *Times*'s managing editor, said:

"City Hall's message seems to be that the press—and the voters and taxpayers—should celebrate what the mayor decrees to be reforms but should not look beyond the press releases or check the record or ask difficult questions. That's a remarkably cynical view of the responsibilities of public office."

On this day Keller was right. In a larger sense the Giuliani-*Times* spat serves only to underscore a stark irony. Welfare reform might not have been born so callously had the media not been so lazy as to produce irresponsible, cynical coverage.

In New York, less than a third of the people cut from the rolls went to jobs. Work is being pushed on welfare mothers even though there are only enough licensed child-care slots in the city's neediest sections for one out of every three or four children.

There is clear evidence that New York's 33,000 workfare participants are nothing but cheap labor. They clean and maintain streets, parks, and buildings for between $5,000 to $12,000 in welfare benefits while Giuliani has slashed the people who used to do those jobs for $20,000 to $40,000 a year.

All of this was predicted by welfare advocates. They had studies to show there were nowhere near enough jobs in large urban areas to lift people out of poverty. They warned that recipients needed far more education, training, and child care. They produced data that showed there was not enough public transportation to get ex-recipients out to the suburbs, where the new jobs are.

The media ignored the advocates. They found it more colorful to cruise ghettos to cast moral judgment than stake out CEOs, many of whom seem to be paid to get rid of jobs in the United States and send them abroad. ABC's Diane Sawyer once demanded of teenage mothers, "Why should taxpayers pay for your mistake? . . . Answer their question." There is no such hounding of corporations, whose tax breaks amount to seven times more than welfare for the poor.

The majority of people impacted by welfare reform are women. But for 30 years, from Senator Daniel Patrick Moynihan's "welfare dependency" to President Reagan's "welfare queens" to Charles Murray's *Losing Ground* to President Clinton's declaration that the biggest problem in this nation is teenage pregnancy, nearly all the booming voices for "reform" have been privileged men.

In a three-month study period in 1994–95, when welfare reform dominated the news, Fairness and Accuracy in Reporting found that 71 percent of the sources in stories on cutting welfare were men. Only nine percent of the sources were researchers and advocates for women on welfare. When ABC, NBC, and CBS all featured welfare reform on the same Sunday morning on their meet-the-press shows, no woman on welfare debated George Will or Pete Wilson.

Studies have shown that the blacker you make the issue, the more negative white Americans think of it. The media aided anti-welfare sentiment by depicting the poor as black. African-Americans are 29 percent of the poor. In a 1996 study by Yale professor Martin Gilens, 65 percent of poor people on the networks were African-American. African-Americans were 62 percent of the poor portrayed in *Newsweek, Time,* and *U.S. News and World Report.*

While Murray, Newt Gingrich, Robert Rector of the Heritage Foundation, and many conservative governors saturated the senses with apocalyptic visions of teenage mothers who have babies to get a welfare check, there were no household names who were factual counterpoints. Real experts on welfare like Kathleen Mullen Harris, author of *Teen Mothers*, found no such correlation between welfare and pregnancy. [Statistics on] teen pregnancy look worse today mostly because married women are having far fewer babies.

Corporate welfare at $250 billion a year costs taxpayers seven times more than welfare for the poor, nearly the equivalent of the budget for the military. But the media do not spotlight tax breaks for the powerful with seven times the power. In the [Boston] *Globe*'s major-newspaper database, the phrase "welfare reform" appeared 14 times more often than the phrase "corporate welfare."

Informing the public of the failures of welfare reform is important. But reform might not have failed so badly had the press been a fount of balanced information at the outset instead of a collapsed dam against a cascade of stereotypes. The media can lecture Giuliani today about his responsibilities to the truth. Yesterday, newspapers and television helped spread the lies.

Chapter 163

Race and the "New Democrats"

Michael Omi and Howard Winant

Michael Omi is professor of ethnic studies at the University of California at Berkeley. Howard Winant is professor of sociology at Temple University.

The following selection is excerpted with permission from Racial Formation in the United States: From the 1960s to the 1990s, *rev. ed. (New York: Routledge, 1994). Footnotes deleted.*

> In the 1960s, the liberals were widely seen as having failed to deal with major questions of law enforcement, taxation, fiscal management and the role of government, as well as race. They were repudiated, and the Republicans moved into a 25-year period of executive hegemony.
>
> Twelve years of Reagan and Bush has not cured the problems, either. It hasn't given us morning in America. It's produced more columns of smoke rising from our inner cities.
>
> —Kevin Phillips

Introduction

The Los Angeles riot of 1992 marked the beginning of a new period in U.S. racial politics. It served as a dramatic reminder for much of the nation of the continuing economic marginality, social decay, and human despair of the inner cities. Thanks to amateur cameraman George Holliday's videotape of the beating of black motorist Rodney King, police coercion and harassment were revealed in details more graphic than mainstream America had witnessed in years.

Occurring as it did in the final stretch of an important presidential campaign, the L.A. riot threatened to recast the election into a debate about race, social inequality, and urban decay. These topics, though, were none of the leading contenders' strongest suit. A renewed debate on racial issues could easily have polarized the electorate. It could have revealed the fundamental lack of vision on racial issues plaguing the entire political spectrum. Political leaders—who had by and large determined that the road to victory and influence did not pass through the inner city—were unnerved by the riot. They scrambled to find appropriate individuals, groups, policies, and priorities to blame for the tragic events in L.A.

In early May 1992, toward the conclusion of his 38-hour tour of Los Angeles in the wake of the riot, [President] George Bush stated:

> Things aren't right in too many cities across our country, and we must not return to the status quo. Not here, not in any city where the system perpetuates failure and hatred and poverty and despair.

"The system" to which Bush referred was not the one which disenfranchised minority voters, shipped industrial jobs overseas, and systematically underfunded inner city schools and hospitals. Rather, he claimed, liberal social welfare policies were to blame for the riot. Not only had they consumed many billions of federal dollars, but even worse, they had fostered state dependency, nurtured irresponsible personal behavior, and facilitated the overall deterioration of inner city communities. In place of such programs, Bush called for "policies that foster personal responsibility."

Bush's remarks underscored the dramatic shift in racial "common sense" which had occurred over the past twenty-five years. In the wake of the urban riots of the 1960s, a range of liberal social programs were implemented to deal with the invidious effects of racial discrimination and poverty. In the wake of the L.A. riots, those same programs were being blamed for causing them. The nation had come full circle.

Centrist Democrats who were grouped around Bill Clinton wanted to address some of these issues, but in a manner which would not make their party vulnerable to charges of merely refashioning 1960s-style liberal initiatives. At stake was an important part of the electorate. In order to win the election and reinvigorate the once-powerful Democratic coalition, Bill Clinton believed he needed to attract white working-class voters—the "Reagan Democrats." His appeal was based on lessons learned from the right, lessons about race. Pragmatic liberals in the Democratic camp proposed a more activist social policy emphasizing greater state investment in job creation, education, and infrastructural development. But they conspicuously avoided discussing racial matters such as residential segregation or discrimination. The Democrats' approach, which harked back to [John] Kennedy's remark that "A rising tide lifts all boats," aspired to "universalistic" rather than "group-specific" reforms.

Thus the surprising shift in U.S. racial politics which took shape around 1992 was not the riot itself, nor was it the Republican analysis which placed the blame on the racially defined minority poor and the welfare policies which had supposedly taught them irresponsibility and dependency. The "surprise" was rather the Democratic retreat from race and the party's limited but real adoption of Republican racial politics, with their support for "universalism" and their rejection of "race-specific" policies. With their appeals firmly directed toward white suburban voters, and their emphasis on [criticizing] economic stagnation ("It's the economy, stupid," was the Clinton staff's famous motto) rather than social and racial inequality, the Democrats went on to retake the presidency.

. . . We are, of course, concerned with the racial dimensions of Clinton's victory in 1992 and of his self-definition as a "new Democrat." But these should be understood as aspects of a broader phenomenon: the emerging hegemony of the racial project of *neoliberalism*. This developing neoliberal project seeks to rearticulate the neoconservative and new right racial projects of the Reagan-Bush years in a centrist framework of moderate redistribution and cultural universalism. Neoliberals deliberately try to avoid racial themes, both because they fear the divisiveness and polarization which characterized the racial reaction, and because they mistrust the "identity politics" whose origins lie in the 1960s. They want to close the Pandora's box of race.

It is still too early fully to analyze the liberal project which, as of this writing (July 1993), is still slouching toward Washington to be born. Yet some of the basic contours of racial neoliberalism can already be discerned. It is to these that we now turn our attention.

Neoliberalism and Race

Although on balance Clinton's racial politics are still better than those of Bush, the price of his election was paid by racially defined minorities who were forced to accept relegation of their issues to the electoral—and presumably governmental—back burner. The Clinton political formula reflected not only the pragmatic politics of winning a presidential election in the aftermath of twelve years of Republican rule but also the judgment that racial politics were divisive. The U.S., many influential thinkers argued, had to abandon the "disuniting" tendencies of a "politics of difference" in favor of a unifying and universalistic politics of common culture and national identity.

The furor over "multiculturalism" and "political correctness," which erupted in the late-1980s/early-1990s, particularly embodied these concerns. It was a moral panic about the continuing disruptive effects of racial divisions (and polarization around gender and sexuality as well) in American society. It generated various best-sellers, attracted serious media attention, and even prompted a presidential scolding in an address at the University of Michigan. The multiculturalism and political correctness debates confronted proponents of identity politics, especially those based in the universities, with a difficult dilemma. These struggles permitted the reappropriation of "universalism" and the values of a supposedly "common culture" by the right; they induced not only many conservatives, but also liberals and ex-leftists, to enlist in the defense of "standards" and "values" which served as stalking horses for quite authoritarian politics.

Both as political strategy and as cultural initiative, the neoliberal racial project is consolidating as the new form of racial hegemony in the 1990s. In its *structural* dimension it is designed to rearticulate the neoconservative and new right racial politics of redistribution. Unlike the neoconservative project, the racial neoliberalism of the 1990s does not claim to be color-blind; indeed it argues that any effort to reduce overall inequality in employment, income, education, health care access, etc., will disproportionately benefit those concentrated at the bottom of the socioeconomic ladder, where racial discrimination has its most damaging effects.

In its *signifying* or representational dimension, the neoliberal project avoids (as far as possible) framing issues or identities racially. Neoliberals argue that addressing social policy or political discourse overtly to matters of race simply serves to distract, or even hinder, the kinds of reforms which could most directly benefit racially defined minorities. To focus too much attention on race tends to fuel demagogy and separatism, and thus exacerbates the very difficulties which much racial discourse has ostensibly been intended to solve. To speak of *racism* is hard to avoid. Better to address racism by ignoring race, at least publicly.

In his 1992 campaign, Bill Clinton was endorsed and advised by sociologist William Julius Wilson. Wilson argued that Clinton had assembled a "remarkable biracial coalition" by promoting programs which unite rather than divide racial minorities and whites. Clinton's strategy, Wilson declared, had destroyed the myth that blacks respond only to race-specific issues and that whites, particularly the poor and working class, will not support a candidate heavily favored by blacks:

> [I]f the message emphasizes issues and programs that concern the families of all racial and ethnic groups, whites will see their mutual interests and join in a coalition with minorities to elect a progressive candidate.

This belief flows from Wilson's analysis in *The Truly Disadvantaged* (1987). There he argued that the impersonal forces of the market economy explain more about the current impoverishment of the inner city African American poor than any analysis relying on notions of racial discrimination. While he does not dismiss the effects of historical racial discrimination, his conclusion is that capital is "color-blind," and that the large-scale demographic, economic, and political changes which have negatively affected the ghetto have little to do with race. In this situation, race-specific policies, whose origins lie in the civil rights movement's drive for integration, can do little for the African American "underclass." Programs based on equality of individual opportunity on the one hand, or organized in terms of group preferential treatment on the other, are equally ineffective. Wilson ends his book with a call for *universal* programs, rather than group-targeted ones, to halt the deterioration of inner city communities:

> The hidden agenda is to improve the life chances of groups such as the ghetto underclass by emphasizing programs in which the more advantaged groups of all races can positively relate.

Wilson's policy prescription of universal programs, though obviously important, remains at best partial, since significant evidence exists that the racial discrimination which civil rights era legislation was designed to outlaw remains ubiquitous. But as a recipe for electing a Democrat after twelve years of the Reagan and Bush administrations' manipulation of white racial fears, Wilson's formula surely proved useful to the Clinton forces. Indeed, Wilson's "hidden agenda" was undoubtedly more effective as campaign strategy than it ever would be as social policy.

Another key analysis shaping the Clinton campaign was that of Thomas and Mary Edsall. Their book *Chain Reaction* argued that race has become a powerful wedge issue, fracturing what had been, since the New Deal, the majoritarian economic interests of the poor, working, and lower-middle classes in the traditional liberal coalition. Since 1965, whites have found less and less reason to carry the burden of redressing social grievances. Working-class and middle-class whites were directly affected, the Edsalls claim, by school integration, affirmative action programs of various sorts, and higher taxes to fund group-specific programs. The result of all this has been massive defections from the Democratic Party and the consolidation of a conservative Republican majority.

The Edsalls documented dramatic new patterns of segregation which have emerged as whites have moved to the suburbs and abandoned the declining cities. As a result, urban areas have become reservations, with majority black and Latino populations and declining tax bases. Their local governments are less and less capable of addressing the basic needs of their citizens. The nation as a whole is moving steadily toward a politics that will be dominated by the suburban vote. The suburbs allow white middle-class voters to fulfill communitarian impulses by taxing themselves for direct services (e.g., schools, libraries, police), while both ignoring urban decay and remaining fiscally conservative about federal spending. Thus whites shield their tax dollars from going into programs to benefit racial minorities and the poor. The Edsalls argue:

> What all this suggests is that a politics of suburban hegemony will come to characterize presidential elections. With a majority of the electorate equipped to address its own needs through local government, not only will urban blacks become increasingly isolated by city-county boundaries, but support for the federal government, a primary driving force behind black advancement, is likely to diminish.

The "new Democrats" sought a way out of this pessimistic scenario by simultaneously advocating universalistic reforms and blunting the wedge issue of race. The call for more jobs, better education, and increased social investment, was especially well-suited for the benefits it offered to suburban, middle-class, white voters who have been battered—though not on the scale of inner city residents—by recession. To dismiss charges of catering to minorities, Clinton adopted the rhetoric of "personal responsibility" and "family values" which was so successfully utilized by the right. In order to win back white suburbanites, liberals too claimed the right to "blame the victim," to disparage the "dependence" of welfare mothers, and bemoan the disintegration of the family. In their use of racially coded language, the "new Democrats" chose to remain silent on any explicit discussion of race and its overall meaning for politics.

This shift is apparent in the Clinton-Gore campaign document *Putting People First*. In this book the Democratic candidates list a host of proposals and policy initiatives they supported, many in areas where racial justice and inequality are particularly sensitive issues. For example, they propose expanding the Head Start program, insuring a minimum income for all working households through tax rate adjustments, and addressing unemployment through public sector job creation. These ideas are presented, however, without any mention of their impact on specific racial groups, indeed with as little reference to race as possible. Beyond pledging to enforce existing civil rights laws and to oppose discrimination in such areas as immigration, *Putting People First* consistently downplays racial themes. It makes no mention of affirmative action, preferring to argue, along the lines suggested by Wilson, for universal programs. Thus Clinton and Gore make the familiar argument that "For too long we've been told about 'us' and 'them'. . . . But there can be no 'them' in America. There's only us . . ." (pp. 64–65), and pledge to

> fight for civil rights, not just by protecting individual liberties, but by providing *equal economic opportunity*; support new anti-poverty initiatives that move beyond the outdated answers of both major parties and instead reflect the values most Americans share: work, family, individual responsibility, community.

This is neoliberal racial coding at its finest. Very little of this formula would seem out of place in a Republican campaign document or neoconservative policy paper. And what are those outdated antipoverty initiatives, one wonders? Presumably, they include such items as affirmative action, minority set-asides, and support for school desegregation. In fact, the one clear statement about race in the civil rights section of *Putting People First* is a pledge to oppose racial quotas!

While on the campaign trail, Clinton very rarely brought up race in a direct way—and then often made his point at the expense of racial minorities, as in the case of his rebuke of rap artist Sister Souljah for supposedly making racist remarks. Here his underlying racial message was that blacks were as guilty of racism as whites, and that black racism needed to be confronted and challenged as vigorously as any other form. This was an important symbolic issue for many whites. It relieved them of the onus of being the sole "oppressors" of the nation, took attention away from the structural manifestations of racism, ignored the continuity of racial hegemony and white supremacy across the decades, and reduced the issue of racism to a matter of group prejudice. Such an intervention could only have been designed to demonstrate "new Democrat" Clinton's independence from the traditional party deference to civil rights issues and organizations. In 1992, for the first time in almost half a century, the Democratic Party platform made no specific pledge to address racial injustices and inequalities.

The Clinton administration seeks to establish a new consensus with respect to race, a framework based on universal reforms and a rejection of group-specific demands. In many respects this neoliberal agenda has rearticulated the right-wing racial logic which gained currency during the racial reaction of the 1970s and 1980s. It is in fact an effort to steal the racial "thunder on the right."

But in its quest to avoid the potentially divisive aspects of racial politics by rearticulation, by learning from the enemy, neoliberalism has quite deliberately fostered neglect of issues of race. It has, in effect, buried race as a significant dimension of its politics. It has attempted to close the Pandora's box first opened—in contemporary terms—during the 1960s. At best it advances a "hidden agenda" which seeks to improve the lot of racial minorities while avoiding race-baiting from the right. But such a perspective, although ostensibly premised on creating community and avoiding divisive political conflicts, misses the depth and degree to which competing definitions of race continue to structure and signify politics in the U.S.

What's Wrong with the Neoliberal Racial Project?

U.S. society is racially both more diverse and more complex today than at any previous time in its history. Racial theory must address this reality. . . . Racial policy and politics must address it as well. Does the emergent neoliberal racial project, the "new Democratic" strategy employed by Clinton in his successful run for the presidency, fill this bill? We think not.

In our view, the neoliberal racial project has two basic flaws. First, it continues to conceive race in narrowly bipolar terms: black-white, city-suburb, etc. It thus neglects the increasing complexity of racial politics and racial identity today. Second, neoliberalism seeks to downplay the continuing significance of race in American society; indeed it promotes a false universalism which can only serve to mask underlying racial conflicts. Let us address these two issues in turn.

Dichotomizing Race

The lessons of the Los Angeles riot are instructive as a starting point to criticize bipolar conceptions of race. Journalist Tim Rutten described the devastation in the immediate wake of the Rodney King verdict as

> the nation's first multi-ethnic urban riot, one that involved not simply the traditional antagonism of one race toward another, but the mutual hostility, indifference, and willingness to loot of several different racial and ethnic groups.

Indeed if only for a fleeting moment, the Los Angeles riot served to focus media attention on generally neglected racial/ethnic subjects—Koreans, Central Americans, Chicanos—who were both victims and victimizers.

Unfortunately, this perspective on the riot was not sustained and explored by the mass media. Nor, as we have seen, were these issues tackled by the presidential candidates. Naturally the neoconservative candidate—George Bush—focused his response to the riot on welfare bashing and denunciations of the irresponsibility of the rioters. But for reasons we have already described, it proved expedient for "new Democrat" Bill Clinton to do something quite similar, to avoid any explicit discussion of racial injustice, to emphasize the necessity of a growing economy to solve social ills, and to invoke the rhetoric of hard work and personal responsibility in his response to the riot. Neither grappled with the growing racial diversity of the nation, and the meaning of a situation in which a wide range of different "racialized" groups find themselves both in conflict and accommodation with one another.

Of course, the candidates were not the only ones guilty of making the facts of the riot fit the prevailing bipolar black/white model of race relations. But in doing so, they emphasized once more the condition and consciousness of the black "underclass," while paying little or no attention to the widespread and multiracial discontent which crystallized in the riot. Nor did they concern themselves with the devastation's victims: principally Korean storeowners, but also businesses of every racial and ethnic provenance. Nor did the candidates, or the mass media, seem to notice or care that more Latinos were arrested during the riot than were blacks, or that substantial numbers of whites were also engaged in looting and burning.

Racial dichotomizing—focusing analysis and discussion of race solely on black-white relationships—is endemic in the U.S. As much as the politicians or mainstream media, academic analyses reproduce this distorted model of race as a largely black/white dichotomy. A list of the most recent popular books on race, works by such noted authors as Andrew Hacker, Thomas and Mary Edsall, Derrick Bell, and Studs Terkel, includes not one work with a perspective broader than the bipolar, exclusively black-white view. Too often, today as in the past, when scholars and journalists talk about race relations, they mean relations between African Americans and whites.

There are several obvious problems with this situation. First, if the complex nature of race relations in the post–civil rights era is not analyzed and theorized, if it is not the subject of media attention, neither politicians nor ordinary citizens will be able to grasp emerging trends. Antagonisms and alliances *among* racially defined minority groups, differentiation *within* these groups, and the changing dynamics of white racial identity, to pick but a few central issues, are examples of the crucial developments which such approaches miss almost entirely.

Second, the dominant mode of biracial theorizing ignores the fact that a range of specific issues—involving access to education, patterns of residential segregation, and stratification in labor markets—cannot be adequately addressed by narrowly assessing the relative situations of whites and blacks. In his analysis of race and higher education, for example, Andrew Hacker covers Asian Americans at some length in order to address race-based admissions policies. But his research unfortunately does not lead him to consider that America, in this area as well as in many others, may be more than simply "two nations."

A third and related problem of this racially bipolar vision is that policies such as affirmative action, immigration, welfare, bilingual education, and community economic development have different consequences for different racially defined minority groups. The meaning of affirmative action for Latinos, for example, may be quite distinct from its meaning for Asian Americans. Even as it affects different ethnic groups within a single racial category—say, Cubans and Salvadorans within the overall boundaries described by the term "Latino"—the implications of a particular social policy may vary widely. Policies and politics which are framed in black-white terms miss the ways in which specific initiatives structure the possibilities of conflict or accommodation among different racial minority groups.

Fourth, employing an exclusively black-white model ignores many particularities of contemporary racial politics. For example it neglects the increasingly racial scapegoating of particular minorities who are seen as somehow responsible for U.S. cultural and economic decline. Examples here include Japan-bashing and anti-Asian violence, and rising anti-immigrant sentiment directed particularly toward Asians and Latinos.

Fifth and finally, bipolar racial discourse tends at best to marginalize and at worst to eliminate other positions and voices in the ongoing dialogue about race in the U.S. A recent example of this was the critical exchanges in the media over the Hughes brothers' film *Menace II Society* (1993). When called upon to assess the film's impact on target audiences, both white and black cultural commentators interpreted and debated the meaning of a crucial scene in which a Korean shopkeeper and his wife are shot and killed. No one, however, asked Korean Americans what they thought.

The enormous task for racial theory is to begin to address these issues and developments in a way which would decisively break with the bipolar model of race that has informed, indeed structured, not only popular and academic discourse but also political initiatives in the area of race.

Universalism and Its Discontents

We have already discussed Bill Clinton's avoidance, as far as possible, of racial issues while on the road to the White House. Was this merely a campaign tactic, or is Clinton committed to downplaying discussion of race in favor of a supposedly more universalistic position—the neoliberal discourse—whose primary target audience is the white and suburban middle class, the "Reagan democrats"? Although the final verdict is not in, the early money is on the latter hypothesis.

Clinton sent a key signal when he withdrew the nomination of law professor Lani Guinier as head of the Justice Department's Civil Rights Division. Although by no means a radical, Guinier was portrayed as such in the right-wing media campaign led by Clint Bolick, Litigation Director of the conservative Institute for Justice in Washington and close associate of Supreme Court Justice Clarence Thomas. Bolick dubbed Guinier a "quota queen" in a *Wall Street Journal* op-ed piece, and the racist label (redolent of Ronald Reagan's remarks about "welfare queens") spread across the battlefields of Washington and the pages of the press, while the administration hardly lifted a finger to correct the record or defend its nominees. After allowing Guinier to twist in the wind for more than a month, Clinton withdrew her nomination, stating that her ideas on race were contrary to his own. His vision of an inclusive society, he argued, conflicted with that of his nominee, whose writing supported different political mechanisms and rules for minorities. Incredibly, Clinton claimed he had been unaware of Guinier's views when he first selected her. Those views, however, were not particularly extreme. The most radical thing Guinier had advocated, in a series of law review articles on the limits of voting rights remedies for electoral discrimination, was extension of electoral formulas for increasing minority electoral influence. These schemes—proportional voting in particular—were already in place in various (mostly southern) localities, and had been endorsed by the Reagan-Bush

Justice Department and the Supreme Court. Guinier had also criticized some of the redistricting arrangements developed after 1990, deals in which leading civil rights organizations, black politicians, and Republicans had cooperated to gerrymander various (again southern) legislative districts in order to guarantee black "safe seats" and, not incidentally, conservative white majorities in adjacent jurisdictions.

Guinier's sin, it is clear in retrospect, was not her supposed radicalism, but her willingness, indeed her eagerness, to discuss the changing dimensions of race in contemporary U.S. politics. She sought an open and democratic dialogue, to be held in legislative, academic, journalistic, and judicial fora, on the meaning of race in the post–civil rights era. This flew in the face of Clinton's political strategy of downplaying race. Had Clinton been willing to support Guinier—whether or not he associated himself with all her views—there would have been a contentious but ultimately productive debate in the Senate about the new contours of race. This in itself would have been an important advance. As Harlon Dalton, a law professor at Yale, commented:

> Her Senate hearings would have been a conversation about what democracy looks like in a multicultural society in the 1990s, and I think that's a conversation we need to have. Instead, the Senate and President ran away from it.

Clinton's performance in the Guinier affair, and more broadly his claim that he supports a "single society," rather than a "we and they" orientation to race, place him firmly in the camp of racial universalism. It is but a small distance from Clinton's neoliberal position to the neoconservative "color blind" position—from which, indeed, it was fashioned. In contrast, Guinier's recognition that, in the post–civil rights era as previously, racial injustice still operates, that it has taken on new forms, and that it needs to be opposed if democracy is to advance, in our view located her in a far more realistic position. Guinier understood the flexibility of racial identities and politics, but also affirmed that racism still shapes the U.S. social structure in a widespread fashion. She resisted the idea of closing Pandora's box; in fact she denied the possibility of closing it, arguing that the racial dimensions of U.S. politics are too complex, too basic, and too subtle to be downplayed for long.

We predict that this conflict will continue to plague the "new Democrats," and that it will set clear limits on the neoliberal racial project which has been central to their resurgence. The universalist view of race does not recognize the instability inherent in racial politics and identity. It treats race as something we can "get beyond." Paradoxically, this position shares with racial essentialism—as displayed, for example, in both white and black racial nationalisms—the belief that race is something fixed and permanent. It conceives of the choices posed by racial politics in a rigid "either-or" scenario. One must either become "color blind" or adopt the particularism supposedly inherent in one's racial identity.

From a racial formation perspective, this rigidly dichotomous model is absurd. Racial difference and racial identity are unstable. They are continuously being disputed, transformed, and eroded. The true challenge for both racial theory and racial politics is to find ways of disrupting the relationship and presumed fixity of both the universalist and the particularist positions.

We have suggested that the neoliberal project, with its deliberate neglect of racial politics, will reveal its ineffectiveness fairly quickly in the Clinton era. But if that judgment is proved correct, what opposing view can we propose, what strategic orientation do we recommend for the current and immediate future of U.S. racial politics? Obviously it would be presumptuous to prescribe some sweeping alternative approach. We can offer no simple formulas, we recognize that it takes courage and insight to resist the various herd mentalities which characterize racial politics today. But despite the difficulties, we are firmly convinced that it is still quite possible to distinguish the main features of the racial formation processes, as well as of the racism, that characterize our time.

We conclude by suggesting three general precepts which can guide analysis of the present situation. We do this not in an effort to exhaust, but simply to orient, understanding and action in respect to race and racism today. Our three precepts are the following: 1. Old fashioned racism still exists; 2. The traditional victimology of racism is moribund; and 3. To oppose racism one must remain conscious of race.

Old-Fashioned Racism Still Exists

The legacy of the past—of conquest, slavery, racial dictatorship and exclusion—may no longer weigh like a nightmare on the brain of the living, but it still lingers like a hangover or a sleepless night that has left us badly out of sorts. Without question, there has been significant progress toward racial democracy in the years since 1965, yet it is implausible to believe that racism is a thing of the past. To assert such a position today requires either that one deny the ubiquitous evidence of everyday life—its continuing segregation, its racially assigned poverty and privilege, its bigotry, fear, and nihilism—or that one engage in wholesale victim-blaming, a procedure that merely updates the racial prejudices of days gone by. So David Wellman's argument that "racism is a structural relationship based on the subordination of one racial group by another," continues to reflect some basic realities. But only some, since today the multipolarity of racial identities (not just black and white, but also red, brown, and yellow), the cross-cutting divisions of race, gender, and sexuality, and the tangible if still limited effects of egalitarian struggles have greatly complicated this picture.

The Traditional Victimology of Racism Has Become Moribund

In the past white supremacy was so thorough that it located all non-whites in positions of comprehensive subordination. Racially defined minorities at one time lacked even victim status, which at least implies guilt or conflict among the victimizers. Under the heel of conquest, in the face of "Indian removal," and under the regime of slavery, racial minorities simply got what their oppressors felt they deserved. This is the meaning of genocide and racial dictatorship. Thus the achievement of victim status, beginning in earnest around the turn of the century, was a challenge to white supremacy in some ways as serious as the civil rights and egalitarian challenges of the post–World War II period.

Today, however, the legacy of this achievement continues as *victimology*: the essentializing attribution of minority misfortunes *tout court* to victimization by whites. The tenacity of this viewpoint is indicated by the difficulty minority groups encounter when one of their own strays from the fold, exposing conflicts and inequalities within the community itself. The more heavily committed one is to a view based on the status of one's group as victim, the more difficult it is to accept the possibility that one's group may also contain victimizers.

Today less than ever does minority status correlate with victim status, yet because old-fashioned racism and white supremacy are far from dead, this linkage is not yet dead either. It is, however, somewhat moribund, doubtful, suspect, particularly when it is afforded *prima facie*—and thus essentializing—validity.

To Oppose Racism One Must Notice Race

In the U.S., race is present in every institution, every relationship, every individual. This is the case not only for the way society is organized—spatially, culturally, in terms of stratification, etc.—but also for our perceptions and understandings of personal experience. Thus as we watch the videotape of Rodney King being beaten, compare real estate prices in different neighborhoods, select a radio channel to enjoy while we drive to work, size up a potential client, customer, neighbor, or teacher, stand in line at the unemployment office, or carry out a thousand other normal tasks, we are compelled to think racially, to use the racial categories and meaning systems into which we have been socialized. Despite exhortations both sincere and hypocritical, it is not possible or even desirable to be "color-blind."

So today more than ever, opposing racism requires that we notice race, not ignore it, that we afford it the recognition it deserves and the subtlety it embodies. By noticing race we can begin to challenge racism, with its ever-more-absurd reduction of human experience to an essence attributed to all without regard for historical or social context. By noticing race we can challenge the state, the institution of civil society, and ourselves as individuals to combat the legacy of inequality and injustice inherited from the past. By noticing race we can develop the political insight and mobilization necessary to make the U.S. a more racially just and egalitarian society.

Chapter 164

Defunding the Congressional Black Caucus

Julianne Malveaux

When the Republicans took over Congress after the 1994 interim elections, one of their first actions was to cut the funding for congressional caucuses.

Julianne Malveaux is the author of Sex, Lies, and Stereotypes: Perspective of a Mad Economist *(1994) and* Wall Street, Main Street, and the Side Street: The Mad Economist Takes a Stroll *(1999).*

The following selection is reprinted from "No Real Savings, Sanity in Cutting Congressional Black Caucus," Baltimore Sun, *13 December 1994. Reprinted with permission of the author.*

Some Republican Party plans to streamline Congress may improve government operations. Limiting committee chairmanships to six years, banning proxy voting and opening committee meetings to the public make sense. But the decision to eliminate legislative service organizations neither makes sense nor saves money. It is a sneak attack on the Congressional Black Caucus, and an ill-conceived and incendiary strategy in a time of strained race relations.

Money to fund the legislative service organizations comes from the office budget of each member of Congress. Dues range from a few hundred dollars to several thousand. The Republicans aren't suggesting that congressional office budgets be cut; their own high living would be imperiled if they did. Instead, they're making it harder for House members to work together to fund groups like the Congressional Black Caucus.

The caucuses are efficient working groups that deal with the collective concerns of their members, providing joint research and lobbying in cases where legislative interests converge. The 23-year-old Congressional Black Caucus has been a linchpin in the struggle for a progressive agenda, highlighting issues that presidents from Richard Nixon to Bill Clinton tried to ignore.

For years, their alternative budgets have pragmatically argued that social spending and deficit reduction can happen if we simply cut the military budget. The caucus isn't wandering in some isolated desert on the left: More than 100 members of the 102nd Congress supported the black caucus alternative.

Just like term limits, grounding the caucus may come back to haunt senior Republicans. The caucus was targeted because it is too liberal, too Democratic and, yes, too black. Other alliances will bite the dust because they are too Republican, too right wing, and too white.

To call the caucus too Democratic is to buy into the argument that all Democrats think alike. The group's ideological bent, though mostly liberal, ranges from the progressive politics of California Democrats Maxine Waters and Ron Dellums to the more pragmatic moderation of William Jefferson, D–La., and Eddie Bernice Johnson, D–Texas. The membership comes from both urban and rural districts; such members as Cleo Fields, D–La., and Cynthia McKinney, D–Ga., are at risk because of judicial rulings on racial gerrymandering.

While the caucus has been a vehicle for the discussion of progressive issues and the impact of legislation on the nation's 35 million African Americans, its voting records show that the membership is not single-minded when the roll is called. Despite an impassioned plea to reject the crime bill by Rep. William Clay, D–Mo., the caucus split 21 for and 16 against. The caucus split on the General Agreement on Tariffs and Trade, too, with most members supporting President Clinton despite their fear of job loss from the trade agreement.

But the same Republicans who champion market forces for everything from social services to school choice are now suppressing market demand for the black caucus. Why shouldn't members of Congress be allowed to spend their office budgets as they choose? Caucus members pool funds because working together is more efficient than working alone. If there were no market for caucus services, the group would disappear. But Republicans are afraid of the market of ideas, and so are trying to stifle one of their most vocal opponents.

Imagine the organized caucus response to the mean-spirited "Contract with America," the document that seems intent on defining America as white and middle class. The alternative budget of the caucus will only make more sense when Republicans start pushing for $190 billion in giveaways without telling taxpayers where the money is going to come from.

Numerically, the black caucus can't win a vote against the Republican congressional majority. But it can win the debate by making more sense. Also, they can articulate the concerns of the disenfranchised—black people, poor people and others who see the Republican contract as a threat, not a promise.

In attempting to eliminate the black caucus, Republicans are acting out of fear, not out of a desire for efficiency. The Gingrinch who stole Christmas is at it again, trying to snatch the dreams and effective representation of the millions represented by the black caucus.

Chapter 165

Vouchers, the Right, and the Race Card

Bob Peterson and Barbara Miner

Bob Peterson, an editor of the quarterly magazine Rethinking Schools, *was 1995–1996 Wisconsin Elementary Teacher of the Year. Barbara Miner is the managing editor of* Rethinking Schools *(www.rethinkingschools.org).*

The following selection is reprinted from "The Color of 'Choice': Behind the Milwaukee School Voucher Movement," ColorLines, *Spring 1999. Information available from ColorLines, 4096 Piedmont Ave. #319, Oakland, CA 94611; 510/653-3415; colorlines@arc.org.*

Conservatives use the rhetoric of "choice" to portray vouchers as a vehicle for levelling the educational playing field for communities of color.

Nothing could be further from the truth. Just ask Wisconsin State Representative Polly Williams (D–Milwaukee).

Williams, who is African American, became a national spokesperson for vouchers in 1990 when she spearheaded a much-publicized, but very limited, voucher initiative for low-income students in Milwaukee. But recently Williams told the *Boston Globe* that "I knew that once they [white Republicans and rightwing foundations] figured they didn't need me as a black cover, they would try to take control of vouchers and use them for their own selfish interest."

In the last eight years, Williams has seen how Republicans and other conservative power-brokers use the rhetoric of equal opportunity to mask their real goal of privatizing Milwaukee's public schools and removing schools from public oversight, predominantly to the benefit of white families with money and privilege.

Why the Right Loves Vouchers

Just about every group on the right loves vouchers, a system in which the government gives students a "voucher" that can be used to pay for their education at any private or public school that will accept them. The religious right sees vouchers as a way to batter down the separation between church and state and to make the public pay for fundamentalist religious schools. Free-marketeers see vouchers as a way to privatize public education—opening up a $600 billion market and removing education from the messy realm of democratic control. For the libertarians, vouchers are a way to dismantle the biggest and most important public institution in this country.

All love the fact that vouchers transfer money away from public schools into private schools. Private schools are not subject to hard-won anti-discrimination or accessibility laws, educational quality standards, separation of church and state mandates, or public safety and environmental safeguards. They are accountable only to their owners.

Take the case of Tenasha Taylor. Tenasha, an African American student at University School, a private high school in Milwaukee, criticized the school as racist in a speech assigned by her English teacher. The school suspended her and asked her not to return the following fall. Tenasha sued on the grounds of free speech. The court ruled against her, saying: "It is an elementary principle of constitutional law that the protections afforded by the Bill of Rights do not apply to private actors such as University School. Generally, restrictions on constitutional rights that would be protected at a public high school . . . need not be honored at a private high school."

Contrary to the claims of its supporters, privatization of schools through vouchers would greatly aggravate the existing problems of racial inequality and poor standards in the schools.

Milton Friedman and Vouchers

Conservative economist Milton Friedman, infamous for his free-market economic blueprints for the Chilean dictatorship of Augusto Pinochet, initiated the concept of vouchers in the 1950s. At the time, only white segregationists rallied to his support. They established the first publicly funded school vouchers in the United States in Virginia in 1956 for the explicit purpose of circumventing the historic *Brown* desegregation decision of that same year by helping white people attend private academies.

Eventually, the Virginia program and similar plans passed by segregationist Southern legislatures in the 1950s were ruled unconstitutional. But following the rightward drift of national politics in recent decades, vouchers were resurrected. This time, voucher supporters have tried to appeal not only to their traditional white conservative base, but to people of color who are, not surprisingly, also dissatisfied with public education. As voucher advocate Daniel McGroarty put it in a strategy paper for the Milton and Rose D. Friedman Foundation, limited voucher programs targeting poor families should be used as a "beachhead"—a way "to win and hold new ground in the long march to universal school choice."

The Milwaukee Proving Ground

The Milwaukee-based, rightwing Bradley Foundation and other well-heeled voucher advocates chose the Milwaukee public schools as the proving ground for this strategy.

In 1990, the Wisconsin state legislature passed a limited voucher program for Milwaukee that was tailored to gain support from minorities. The program allowed a few hundred low-income children in Milwaukee to use publicly funded vouchers to attend a specified handful of non-religious private schools. The principal argument for this program was that it would allow low-income African American students to attend good private schools. And, indeed, the program has been quite popular in black Milwaukee.

Having established this "beachhead," voucher proponents are now moving to implement their full agenda. Recently, the program was opened to religious schools and was expanded to include up to 15,000 students. In June 1998, the Wisconsin Supreme Court ruled that the expansion does not violate the separation of church and state and the U.S. Supreme Court refused to hear the appeal, thereby leaving it intact. The ink was barely dry on the Wisconsin Supreme Court decision when Milwaukee Mayor John Norquist called for an end to the income cap for those receiving vouchers, currently set at about $23,000 a year for a family of four.

Rep. Williams was characteristically blunt in responding to the mayor's proposal. "He just said what they were already doing in the back rooms," Williams told *The Tampa Tribune*. "He wants to attract white people back to the city [by saying] 'You don't have to go to Milwaukee public schools [with black children] because we have opened a way for you.'" Williams contends that the conservative movers and shakers behind the voucher movement have been using African Americans all along.

Indeed, in the first five years of the Milwaukee program, the majority of voucher students were African American. But now that religious schools are included, the figures are expected to change dramatically. According to the Milwaukee NAACP, a voucher opponent, in 1996 only 10 percent of the students in Catholic elementary schools in Milwaukee were African American, compared to 61 percent in the public schools.

The proposed elimination of income requirements will aggravate the racial and class inequities still further, allowing predominantly white middle and upper class families to use public money to pay for private schooling.

Further, the money for the Milwaukee voucher program is being taken out of the budget of the Milwaukee public schools, which are expected to lose $22 million in funding in 1998–99 because of the voucher program. Thus, this state-mandated voucher program takes significant money out of a district whose population is about 80 percent students of color and already spends thousands of dollars less per student than surrounding white suburban districts. In the Milwaukee public schools, 61 percent of students are African American, 12 percent are Latino, 5 percent Asian, 1 percent Native American, and 20 percent are white.

As NAACP president Kweisi Mfume has said, many of the "best [public school] students will be skimmed off—those whom private schools find desirable for their own reasons. Since families will have to make up additional costs [of the private schools], those in the upper- and middle-income brackets will be helped the most." And, conversely, students who are the most challenging to educate due to race, class, or disability will be left in defunded public schools. In short, the voucher system profoundly aggravates existing class and racial biases in education.

The Bradley Foundation's Hidden Agenda

It is impossible to understand the voucher movement without understanding some of the power-brokers that are calling the shots. Several conservative foundations are involved, but the most notable is the Milwaukee-based Bradley Foundation. With assets of $461 million, Bradley is the country's most powerful conservative foundation. In the last decade, the foundation has poured millions of dollars into voucher initiatives.

The Bradley Foundation also gave almost $1 million to Charles Murray to research and co-author *The Bell Curve*, which argues that the majority of African Americans are biologically inferior and that educational resources should be allocated to the intellectual elite. Not surprisingly, *The Bell Curve*'s main proposal for educational reform is vouchers.

Robert Lowe, co-editor of *Selling Out Our Schools: Vouchers, Markets, and the Future of Public Education*, argues, "The link between *The Bell Curve* and the Bradley Foundation strongly suggests that the interest of the foundation . . . is the diversion of resources spent on urban schools, whose students are largely deemed uneducable, to the allegedly worthy children of more affluent families."

Defend Public Education

Forty years ago white-dominated Southern state legislatures gave vouchers to white people so they could opt out of a desegregated school system. Today, the white-dominated state legislatures of Wisconsin and Ohio are essentially doing the same thing: using vouchers to let white families take their children out of integrated schools and abandon the notion that the government has a responsibility to provide all children with equal, quality education. A voucher program similar to Milwaukee's exists in Cleveland, and voucher plans have been proposed in at least 28 other states. In addition, corporate magnates such as Wal-Mart's John Walton have funded private voucher programs in a number of urban areas—programs unabashedly designed to build political pressure for publicly supported vouchers.

Voucher supporters have enacted laws which promote a lessening of our communities' responsibility to our children, aggravate racial and class inequalities, remove education from democratic control, and instead promote an individual "solution" to a social problem—the education of our children.

But vouchers are not a solution. Instead, advocates of equity and social justice must work to reform public schools and demand that they fulfill their responsibility to provide equal education to all children. There is no doubt that public schools must do a better job of giving students the skills they need to understand, maneuver in, and improve society. However, progressives must not be tricked into thinking that the only alternative is a system of private schools and for-profit endeavors. At issue is our very system of providing a free, public education to all children.

Chapter 166

The Prison Industrial Complex

Angela Davis

Angela Davis, professor of the history of consciousness at the University of California at Santa Cruz, is the author of Angela Davis: An Autobiography *(1974),* Women, Race, and Class *(1981),* Women, Culture, and Politics *(1988), and* Blues Legacies and Black Feminism: Gertrude "Ma" Rainey, Bessie Smith, and Billie Holiday *(1998). A past member of the Central Committee of the Communist Party, she is currently active with the Committees of Correspondence and other progressive groups.*

The following selection is reprinted from "Masked Racism: Reflections on the Prison Industrial Complex," ColorLines, Fall 1998. Information available from ColorLines, 4096 Piedmont Ave. #319, Oakland, CA 94611; 510/653-3415; colorlines@arc.org.

For more on discrimination in the criminal justice system, see David Cole, No Equal Justice *(1999), Marc Mauer,* Race to Incarcerate *(1999), and Christian Parenti,* Lockdown America *(1999).*

Imprisonment has become the response of first resort to far too many of the social problems that burden people who are ensconced in poverty. These problems often are veiled by being conveniently grouped together under the category "crime" and by the automatic attribution of criminal behavior to people of color. Homelessness, unemployment, drug addiction, mental illness, and illiteracy are only a few of the problems that disappear from public view when the human beings contending with them are relegated to cages.

Prisons thus perform a feat of magic. Or rather the people who continually vote in new prison bonds and tacitly assent to a proliferating network of prisons and jails have been tricked into believing in the magic of imprisonment. But prisons do not disappear problems, they disappear human beings. And the practice of disappearing vast numbers of people from poor, immigrant, and racially marginalized communities has literally become big business.

The seeming effortlessness of magic always conceals an enormous amount of behind-the-scenes work. When prisons disappear human beings in order to convey the illusion of solving social problems, penal infrastructures must be created to accommodate a rapidly swelling population of caged people. Goods and services must be provided to keep imprisoned populations alive. Sometimes these populations must be kept busy and at other times—particularly in repressive super-maximum prisons and in INS detention centers—they must be deprived of virtually all meaningful activity. Vast numbers of handcuffed and shackled people are moved across state borders as they are transferred from one state or federal prison to another.

All this work, which used to be the primary province of government, is now also performed by private corporations, whose links to government in the field of what is euphemistically called "corrections" resonate dangerously with the military industrial complex. The dividends that accrue from investment in the punishment industry, like those that accrue from investment in weapons production, only amount to social destruction. Taking into account the structural similarities and profitability of business-government linkages in the realms of military production and public punishment, the expanding penal system can now be characterized as a "prison industrial complex."

The Color of Imprisonment

Almost two million people are currently locked up in the immense network of U.S. prisons and jails. More than 70 percent of the imprisoned population are people of color. It is rarely acknowledged that the fastest growing group of prisoners are black women and that Native American prisoners are the largest group per capita. Approximately five million people—including those on probation and parole—are directly under the surveillance of the criminal justice system.

Three decades ago, the imprisoned population was approximately one-eighth its current size. While women still constitute a relatively small percentage of people behind bars, today the number of incarcerated women in California alone is almost twice what the nationwide women's prison population was in 1970. According to Elliott Currie, "[t]he prison has become a looming presence in our society to an extent unparalleled in our history—or that of any other industrial democracy. Short of major wars, mass incarceration has been the most thoroughly implemented government social program of our time."

To deliver up bodies destined for profitable punishment, the political economy of prisons relies on racialized assumptions of criminality—such as images of black welfare mothers reproducing criminal children—and on racist practices in arrest, conviction, and sentencing patterns. Colored bodies constitute the main human raw material in this vast experiment to disappear the major social problems of our time. Once the aura of magic is stripped away from the imprisonment solution, what is revealed is racism, class bias, and the parasitic seduction of capitalist profit. The prison industrial system materially and morally impoverishes its inhabitants and devours the social wealth needed to address the very problems that have led to spiraling numbers of prisoners.

As prisons take up more and more space on the social landscape, other government programs that have previously sought to respond to social needs—such as Temporary Assistance to Needy Families—are being squeezed out of existence.

The deterioration of public education, including prioritizing discipline and security over learning in public schools located in poor communities, is directly related to the prison "solution."

Profiting from Prisoners

As prisons proliferate in U.S. society, private capital has become enmeshed in the punishment industry. And precisely because of their profit potential, prisons are becoming increasingly important to the U.S. economy. If the notion of punishment as a source of potentially stupendous profits is disturbing by itself, then the strategic dependence on racist structures and ideologies to render mass punishment palatable and profitable is even more troubling.

Prison privatization is the most obvious instance of capital's current movement toward the prison industry. While government-run prisons are often in gross violation of international human rights standards, private prisons are even less accountable. In March of this year, the Corrections Corporation of America (CCA), the largest U.S. private prison company, claimed 54,944 beds in 68 facilities under contract or development in the U.S., Puerto Rico, the United Kingdom, and Australia. Following the global trend of subjecting more women to public punishment, CCA recently opened a women's prison outside Melbourne. The company recently identified California as its "new frontier."

Wackenhut Corrections Corporation (WCC), the second largest U.S. prison company, claimed contracts and awards to manage 46 facilities in North America, U.K., and Australia. It boasts a total of 30,424 beds as well as contracts for prisoner health care services, transportation, and security.

Currently, the stocks of both CCA and WCC are doing extremely well. Between 1996 and 1997, CCA's revenues increased by 58 percent, from $293 million to $462 million. Its net profit grew from $30.9 million to $53.9 million. WCC raised its revenues from $138 million in 1996 to $210 million in 1997. Unlike public correctional facilities, the vast profits of these private facilities rely on the employment of non-union labor.

The Prison Industrial Complex

But private prison companies are only the most visible component of the increasing corporatization of punishment. Government contracts to build prisons have bolstered the construction industry. The architectural community has identified prison design as a major new niche. Technology developed for the military by companies like Westinghouse is being marketed for use in law enforcement and punishment.

Moreover, corporations that appear to be far removed from the business of punishment are intimately involved in the expansion of the prison industrial complex. Prison construction bonds are one of the many sources of profitable investment for leading financiers such as Merrill Lynch. MCI charges prisoners and their families outrageous prices for the precious telephone calls which are often the only contact prisoners have with the free world.

Many corporations whose products we consume on a daily basis have learned that prison labor power can be as profitable as third world labor power exploited by U.S.-based global corporations. Both relegate formerly unionized workers to joblessness and many even wind up in prison. Some of the companies that use prison labor are IBM, Motorola, Compaq, Texas Instruments, Honeywell, Microsoft, and Boeing. But it is not only the hi-tech industries that reap the profits of prison labor. Nordstrom department stores sell jeans that are marketed as "Prison Blues" as well as t-shirts and jackets made in Oregon prisons. The advertising slogan for these clothes is "made on the inside to be worn on the outside." Maryland prisoners inspect glass bottles and jars used by Revlon and Pierre Cardin, and schools throughout the world buy graduation caps and gowns made by South Carolina prisoners.

"For private business," write Eve Goldberg and Linda Evans (a political prisoner inside the Federal Correctional Institution at Dublin, California), "prison labor is like a pot of gold. No strikes. No union organizing. No health benefits, unemployment insurance, or workers' compensation to pay. No language barriers, as in foreign countries. New leviathan prisons are being built on thousands of eerie acres of factories inside the walls. Prisoners do data entry for Chevron, make telephone reservations for TWA, raise hogs, shovel manure, make circuit boards, limousines, waterbeds, and lingerie for Victoria's Secret—all at a fraction of the cost of 'free labor.'"

Devouring the Social Wealth

Although prison labor—which ultimately is compensated at a rate far below the minimum wage—is hugely profitable for the private companies that use it, the penal system as a whole does not produce wealth. It devours the social wealth that could be used to subsidize housing for the homeless, to ameliorate public education for poor and racially marginalized communities, to open free drug rehabilitation programs for people who wish to kick their habits, to create a national health care system, to expand programs to combat HIV, to eradicate domestic abuse— and, in the process, to create well-paying jobs for the unemployed.

Since 1984 more than twenty new prisons have opened in California, while only one new campus was added to the California State University system and none to the University of California system. In 1996–97, higher education received only 8.7 percent of the State's General Fund while corrections received 9.6 percent. Now that affirmative action has been declared illegal in California, it is obvious that education is increasingly reserved for certain people, while prisons are reserved for others. Five times as many black men are presently in prison as in four-year colleges and universities. This new segregation has dangerous implications for the entire country.

By segregating people labeled as criminals, prison simultaneously fortifies and conceals the structural racism of the U.S. economy. Claims of low unemployment rates—even in black communities—make sense only if one assumes that the vast numbers of people in prison have really disappeared and thus have no legitimate claims to jobs. The numbers of black and Latino men currently incarcerated amount to two percent of the male labor force. According to criminologist David Downes, "[t]reating incarceration as a type of hidden unemployment may raise the jobless rate for men by about one-third, to 8 percent. The effect on the black labor force is greater still, raising the [black] male unemployment rate from 11 percent to 19 percent."

Hidden Agenda

Mass incarceration is not a solution to unemployment, nor is it a solution to the vast array of social problems that are hidden away in a rapidly growing network of prisons and jails. However, the great majority of people have been tricked into believing in the efficacy of imprisonment, even though the historical record clearly demonstrates that prisons do not work. Racism has undermined our ability to create a popular critical discourse to contest the ideological trickery that posits imprisonment as key to public safety. The focus of state policy is rapidly shifting from social welfare to social control.

Black, Latino, Native American, and many Asian youth are portrayed as the purveyors of violence, traffickers of drugs, and as envious of commodities that they have no right to possess. Young black and Latina women are represented as sexually promiscuous and as indiscriminately propagating babies and poverty. Criminality and deviance are racialized. Surveillance is thus focused on communities of color, immigrants, the unemployed, the undereducated, the homeless, and in general on those who have a diminishing claim to social resources. Their claim to social resources continues to diminish in large part because law enforcement and penal measures increasingly devour these resources. The prison industrial complex has thus created a vicious cycle of punishment which only further impoverishes those whose impoverishment is supposedly "solved" by imprisonment.

Therefore, as the emphasis of government policy shifts from social welfare to crime control, racism sinks more deeply into the economic and ideological structures of U.S. society. Meanwhile, conservative crusaders against affirmative action and bilingual education proclaim the end of racism, while their opponents suggest that racism's remnants can be dispelled through dialogue and conversation. But conversations about "race relations" will hardly dismantle a prison industrial complex that thrives on and nourishes the racism hidden within the deep structures of our society.

The emergence of a U.S. prison industrial complex within a context of cascading conservatism marks a new historical moment, whose dangers are unprecedented. But so are its opportunities. Considering the impressive number of grassroots projects that continue to resist the expansion of the punishment industry, it ought to be possible to bring these efforts together to create radical and nationally visible movements that can legitimize anti-capitalist critiques of the prison industrial complex. It ought to be possible to build movements in defense of prisoners' human rights and movements that persuasively argue that what we need is not new prisons, but new health care, housing, education, drug programs, jobs, and education. To safeguard a democratic future, it is possible and necessary to weave together the many and increasing strands of resistance to the prison industrial complex into a powerful movement for social transformation.

Chapter 167

Felony Disenfranchisement

Holly Sklar

Holly Sklar is the author of Chaos or Community? Seeking Solutions, Not Scapegoats for Bad Economics *(1995), co-author of* Poverty in the American Dream
(1983), Streets of Hope *(1994), and* Shifting Fortunes: The Perils of the Growing
American Wealth Gap *(1999), and editor of* Trilateralism *(1980). She is a frequent
contributor to* Z Magazine.

*The following selection is reprinted from "Many American Blacks Are Losing
the Right to Vote," Las Vegas Review-Journal, 4 February 1997. Reprinted with
permission of the author.*

*For more information on felony disenfranchisement, see "Losing the Vote: The
Impact of Felony Disenfranchisement Laws in the United States," an October
1998 report by the Sentencing Project (www.sentencingproject.org) and Human
Rights Watch (www.hrw.org).*

For another selection by Sklar, see chapter 182.

One out of seven black males of voting age has lost the right to vote because of
felony convictions.

While many of these individuals will regain their voting rights after imprisonment, parole or probation, "the cumulative impact of such large numbers of persons being disenfranchised from the electoral process clearly dilutes the political
power of the African-American community," says a report by the Sentencing Project, in Washington, D.C.

Virginia is one of 13 states that permanently disenfranchise most convicted
felons. It doesn't matter if felony offenders work and pay taxes and are model citizens for the rest of their lives. They can't exercise their democratic right to vote.

As reported by the National Criminal Justice Commission, a Virginia legislator
"explained that the criminal disenfranchisement law was passed with a view to
the elimination of every Negro voter." *The Richmond Times-Dispatch* reports that
blacks constitute 19 percent of Virginia's population, but 60 percent of its convicted felons.

The other 12 states that permanently take away the right to vote are Alabama,
Arizona, Delaware, Florida, Iowa, Kentucky, Maryland, Mississippi, Nevada, New
Mexico, Tennessee and Wyoming. Eighteen states disenfranchise felony offenders

while they are on probation or parole. All but four states take away the right to vote during incarceration.

The United States imprisons a greater percentage of its people than any other nation, and that percentage is growing rapidly. The Bureau of Justice Statistics reports, "At year-end 1985, 1 in every 320 United States residents were incarcerated. By year-end 1995 that ratio had increased to 1 in every 167."

Blacks are locked up at a rate nearly eight times that of whites. According to the Sentencing Project, on any given day one out of three black men in their 20s is in prison or jail, on probation or on parole. Many of them are nonviolent, low-level drug offenders who would not have been arrested at all, much less charged with felonies, if they were white.

Three out of four drug users are non-Hispanic whites, but blacks are much more likely to be arrested for drug offenses and receive longer sentences. As the Sentencing Project reports, blacks constitute 13 percent of all past-month drug users, but 35 percent of arrests for drug possession, 55 percent of convictions, and 74 percent of prison sentences.

"There's as much cocaine in the Sears Tower or in the stock exchange as there is in the black community," said Commander Charles Ramsey, supervisor of the Chicago Police Department's narcotics division. "But those guys are harder to catch."

Police chief John Dale of Albany, N.Y., said, "We're locking up kids who are scrambling for crumbs, not the people who make big money."

Many of them are scrambling for crumbs because they can't find jobs. The black unemployment rate is more than double that of whites.

Marijuana possession, not cocaine, is the leading cause of arrest for drug offenders. In numerous states, possessing, selling or growing even small amounts of marijuana can land you in prison for many more years than the average murderer—and the government can seize your home, farm and other assets.

By government count, about 23 million Americans, mostly white, have used marijuana, cocaine or some other illicit drug in the past year. Many of them would now be convicted felons if the war on drugs evenly targeted blacks and whites.

Let's remove racial bias from the criminal justice system and truly make our society safer. RAND research shows the long-term crime-reduction value of treatment and prevention. For example, $1 million invested in incentives for disadvantaged students to graduate from high school would result in a reduction of 258 crimes per year compared to 60 crimes a year through building and operating prisons. Crime prevention is the wiser course.

Chapter 168

Chain Gang Blues

Alex Lichtenstein

Alex Lichtenstein, professor of history at Florida International University, is the author of Twice the Work of Free Labor: The Political Economy of Convict Labor in the New South *(1995). He is currently finishing a book on race and labor in Miami during the 1940s.*

The following selection is reprinted from "Chain Gang Blues," Dissent, *Fall 1996, 7–10. Reprinted with permission of the author and* Dissent.

In the midst of the Great Depression the American public was treated to a sudden outpouring of revelations about the horrors of the South's most notorious penal institution, the chain gang. Even today, many people know the Warner Brothers 1932 hit film *I Am a Fugitive from a Chain Gang* starring Paul Muni. This Hollywood rendition of Robert E. Burns's serialized true adventure story *I Am a Fugitive from the Georgia Chain Gang!* (1932), cast instant national disgrace upon Georgia's penal system and made Burns a popular hero, a white everyman struggling against bureaucratic indifference and state-sanctioned cruelty.

Burns's story attained mass cultural appeal, but the depression-era left produced its own exposes of southern "justice" that achieved wide circulation as well. These accounts focused more appropriately on the plight of African-American prisoners, who made up the vast majority of those sent to the chain gang for petty crimes. In 1932 radical investigative reporter John Spivak talked his way into Georgia's convict camps, and then published a thinly fictionalized proletarian novel about the chain gang entitled *Georgia Nigger*. Spivak's "novel" came replete with photographs documenting the shocking tortures he had observed, and the book was serialized by the Communist party in the *Daily Worker*. By the mid-thirties the International Labor Defense (ILD) pledged itself to defend anyone who escaped from a southern chain gang, white or black. The National Association for the Advancement of Colored People made common cause with the ILD when it successfully defended an escaped African-American convict, Jesse Crawford, against extradition to Georgia.

It may only be a matter of time before we see a similar explosion of southern prison tales, though today's public may prove less sympathetic than that of the 1930s. Since 1980, America's prison population has more than tripled, passing the one million mark last year. Annual drug convictions have multiplied tenfold, constituting a hundred thousand new convictions each year. In a country with one of the highest incarceration rates in the world, with prisons in many states under court order to improve conditions, many people (the "public") still call for more prisons, longer sentences, harder time. In May 1995 the state of Alabama reintroduced chain gangs, and now works hundreds of prisoners in chains on its roads; Florida followed suit in December, fifty years after abolishing leg irons; in Louisiana last year, Republican Buddy Roemer made the promise of chain gangs a central feature of his gubernatorial campaign. As in the past, both blacks and whites do time on the chain gang, usually in proportion to their numbers in the overall state prison population (60 percent black in Alabama, 55 percent in Florida). Nevertheless, in states whose population is only one-fourth black the racial implications of the chain gang are inescapable. Both the Southern Christian Leadership Conference (SCLC) and the Southern Poverty Law Center (SPLC), usually associated with civil rights and anti-Klan work, filed suit against Alabama in federal court, claiming the chain gang violated the Eighth Amendment sanction against "cruel and unusual punishment." As a result of the suit Alabama agreed to end the practice of chaining inmates together in coffles of five men. This, however, proved something of a Pyrrhic victory; prisoners still labor against their will in individual shackles.

Editorialists around the country have weighed in on the Pros and Cons of forcing convicts to work the roads in chains, and the television newsmagazines *48 Hours* and *20/20* have run segments on this new "get-tough" policy. From what I see in the media, however, the historical antecedents of the chain gang are poorly understood. Commentators who find this punishment troubling almost always point to its association with slavery. But no intelligent slaveholder would have allowed the state to punish his laborers by making them build roads for someone else. In fact, the chain gang was a distinctive invention of the "New South," not a holdover from slavery days. Ironically, early twentieth-century southern reformers initially offered chain gangs as a humane *alternative* to the then prevailing convict lease system.

During the first forty or fifty years following the Civil War, southern states leased prisoners for private exploitation to coal mines, turpentine farms, sawmills, phosphate pits, and brickyards. Two factors led to this system: the unwillingness to expend scarce resources on building new prisons and the white fears generated by the new rights and assertiveness of former slaves. Many petty crimes that whites would have overlooked during slavery now netted blacks lengthy sentences. Southern liberals who witnessed the convict lease system complained about the inevitable brutality of a system that encouraged the lessees of convicts to work prisoners to the utmost but provided little incentive for humane treatment. If a convict died, another one was always available from the "penitentiary" for the same low price. Critics of leasing also objected to the monetary benefits reaped by favored lessees at the expense of the rest of the public. The solution? Employ convicts to improve the South's dismal roadways. Convict labor should "benefit all the people," these reformers claimed, and in their view prisoners would find a "kind master" in the state. Thus the chain gang on which Robert Burns and Jesse Crawford did hard time was born.

Observers who notice the racial composition of the new chain gangs are on the right track. When southern convicts left the coal mines and turpentine camps for the roads in the early part of this century, 90 percent of them were African-Americans. The visible nature of the chain gang rarely troubled its early advocates, who believed that African-Americans were "benefited by outdoor manual labor." Indeed, the advent of the chain gang coincided with the crystallization of segregation and the spread of black disfranchisement across the South. Like these other white efforts to extinguish once and for all the dreams of freedom and equality generated by emancipation, the chain gang stood as a powerful dramatization of the reassertion of white control over the lives of southern African-Americans. Black men working in chains, overseen by poor whites holding shotguns and authorized to shoot to kill, sent an undeniable message.

White southerners soon abandoned the initial humanitarian impulse that replaced the convict lease with the chain gang, and county road gangs scattered across the South became notorious among blacks and a few concerned whites for their substandard conditions and the vicious punishments meted out to prisoners unable to keep up the pace of work. States maintained little or no oversight of their chain gangs. In the 1930s, for example, three prison commissioners in Atlanta feebly monitored conditions in over 150 county chain gangs in Georgia. When civil rights activist Bayard Rustin spent a month on a North Carolina chain gang in 1947, he reported conditions that had changed little over the decades. Convicts labored, ate, and slept with chains riveted around their ankles. Prisoners worked "under the gun" from sunup to sundown, shoveling dirt at fourteen shovelfuls a minute, a killing pace. They ate bug-infested, rotten food and slept in unwashed bedding, often in wheeled cages nine feet wide by twenty feet long containing eighteen beds. Medical treatment and bathing facilities were unsanitary, if available at all.

Corporal punishment and outright torture—casual blows from rifle butts or clubs, whipping with a leather strap, confinement in a "sweat-box" under the southern sun, and hanging from stocks or bars—followed from the most insignificant transgressions. With the exception of a few "trusties," all the guards and certainly all the wardens in the South were white: thus African-Americans, who remained the majority of chain-gang prisoners, were singled out for punishment. Rustin correctly concluded that the chain gang's ultimate purpose was to degrade and brutalize.

Ironically, in a society committed to segregation from cradle to grave, by the 1930s blacks and whites began to share a brutal solidarity in many of the South's convict camps. The end of leasing and the return of prisoners to public control gradually diminished the traditional southern reluctance to punish poor whites for crimes once prosecuted only if the defendant was black. The chain gang enjoyed a unique status as an interracial institution in the Jim Crow South. Thus one of the harshest institutions of American apartheid ended up falling on the poor of both races, as it does today.

Despite the revelations that came during the 1930s and 1940s, in many states this harsh penal system persisted until the 1960s, when the civil rights movement finally forced a change. Superficially, the chain gangs, bloodhounds, and sweat-boxes of benighted pre–civil rights Dixie now seem remote from the shopping malls, interstates, and suburban sprawl gracing today's "New South." Why then would anyone want to bring them back? The disturbing truth is that the very features that brought the chain gang into disrepute have now become its selling points.

Down to this day southern states have combined extreme fiscal conservatism with high rates of incarceration, which has fallen disproportionately on African-Americans. In other words, white folks want to send black folks to prison but don't want to pay for it. (Of course this is no longer a purely southern phenomenon). After the end of slavery, prisoners were sold back into bondage. This was perfectly legal under the Thirteenth Amendment, which abolished slavery "except for punishment for a crime." Not only did this save the states money, corrections departments actually became revenue generators! The chain gang ended the lucrative lease system, but also proved inexpensive to run and built badly needed new roads across the rural South. And now? Alabama's prisons are overflowing; the always-invoked "public" wants more people sent to prison for longer terms; the chain gang relieves overcrowding. A simple equation: "the big advantage to me is financial," claimed Alabama's prison commissioner, Ron Jones. (Jones was forced to resign when he finally ran afoul of southern "chivalry": he wanted to put women on the chain gang too.)

As prison reformers all over the country point out, the best way to reduce sky-rocketing prison expenditures is to send fewer people to prison. But politicians want to look "tough on crime," and prisoners can't vote. Here is the source of the second powerful political incentive for the reinvention of the chain gang: the public—at least the white public—loves it. Prisoners "should be treated as criminals, as animals, social outcasts, pariahs," are the typical sentiments expressed by letters to the editor in Florida newspapers when the chain gang is discussed. Charles Crist, the ambitious Republican state senator who sponsored the bill authorizing chain gangs in Florida, told me that the "visible and obvious" harshness of the punishment would reduce crime. Unlike his counterparts in Alabama, Crist has little interest in the fiscal implications of the chain gang. He just wants some of the state's sixty thousand prisoners to receive harder punishment. Once, convicts graded and paved roads; now they mostly clear brush from the roadside. The actual work done by prisoners doesn't matter; symbolism is everything.

When Florida's legislature mandated the use of chain gangs starting in December 1995, the new law actually did spark some controversy: should the prisoners be chained together at work or not? Absolutely! proclaimed Crist. That's how they do it in Alabama—five to a chain—and that's what makes it possible to put dangerous felons on the roads, and that's what makes it a brutal and degrading chain gang. Senator Crist also fondly remembers his childhood drives across the Sunshine State, and the powerful moral effect (on him, presumably) of seeing chained men working the roads.

Harry Singletary, the director of Florida's Department of Corrections, disagrees. He believes that convicts should not be chained to one another while at work, and he calls Alabama's experiment with the system a "debacle," designed for media consumption. Indeed, Singletary, while obliged to carry out the law, thinks chain gangs simply provide the illusion that something is being done about crime, but have little "deterrent effect." Singletary, who is African-American and a native Floridian, has less pleasant memories of the old-time chain gang than does Senator Crist. When told that Crist approved of punishing recalcitrant convicts by chaining them to a "hitching post" in the hot sun, as they do in Alabama, Singletary retorted that "they are going to have to get another secretary [of corrections] if they are going to do that."

It is a measure of a distressing consensus that debate has turned on just how cruel this unusual punishment should be rather than whether it should be at all. Moreover, despite its advocates' insistence that the chain gang punishes whites and blacks equally, in states with a large proportion of African-American prisoners, its racial message remains, well, "visible and obvious." Even though Florida decided to work prisoners in individual shackles rather than "on the chain," Singletary remains in the uncomfortable position of carrying out a policy which he and many other African-Americans cannot regard with equanimity. The chain gang stands out as one of the most deeply felt symbols and experiences of white oppression and abuse and as a rebuke to conceptions of fairness and justice in the courts.

For some whites, however, the chain gang has an equally powerful if opposite resonance. Just as die-hard segregationists won points with their constituency by outraging liberal opinion, the more condemnation heaped upon Ron Jones and Alabama's Governor Ron James by the SCLC, the SPLC, the ACLU, and bleeding hearts in New York who read the *Village Voice* the better, as far as its advocates are concerned. In Florida, Charlie "Chain Gang" Crist wears his nickname as a badge of honor. The image of black men working in chains reminds the crowd Crist and Co. play to of a world they think they have lost, a world where tough laws punished crime swiftly and severely, where prisoners paid their "debt to society" in the coin of hard labor, and where the members of the underclass, African-Americans in particular, knew their place. Despite the vociferous denials, this is what the chain gang is all about.

Chapter 169

Breaking Thurgood Marshall's Promise

A. Leon Higginbotham, Jr.

Legal scholar A. Leon Higginbotham, Jr. (1928–1998), served as a federal judge for twenty-nine years. After his retirement as chief judge of the Court of Appeals of the Third Circuit in 1993, he taught at Harvard University and continued to practice law. In 1995, he was awarded the Presidential Medal of Freedom. He was often described as being on the short list for appointment to the Supreme Court. His writings include In the Matter of Color: Race and the American Legal Process *(1978) and* Shades of Freedom *(1996).*

The following selection is reprinted from "Breaking Thurgood Marshall's Promise," New York Times Magazine, 18 January 1998, 28–29. Copyright © 1998 by The New York Times. Reprinted by permission.

Out of 268 first-year students enrolled at the law school of the University of California at Berkeley, only one is African-American. Out of 468 at the University of Texas School of Law, only four are. Embedded in these cold facts is a personal story, of how 47 years ago I witnessed the birth of racial justice in the Supreme Court and how now, after 45 years as a lawyer, judge and law professor, I sometimes feel as if I am watching justice die.

In 1946, when Heman Marion Sweatt, an African-American, was denied admission to the University of Texas School of Law, the state set up a makeshift, unaccredited "law school for Negroes." In 1950, toward the end of my first year at Yale Law School, I watched Thurgood Marshall argue Heman Sweatt's case before the Supreme Court. With controlled outrage, Marshall eloquently asserted the constitutional promise of equality for Sweatt, for all African-Americans and, it seemed, for me personally.

In a unanimous opinion, the Supreme Court held that Sweatt had to be admitted to the whites-only school, but as a Federal judge later noted, he eventually dropped out "after being subjected to racial slurs from students and professors, cross burnings and tire slashings." Indeed, there were some years between 1950 and 1971 when the school's entering classes did not have a single African-American. Throughout the 1960's, Latino students were officially excluded from university organizations. African-Americans were forbidden to live in or even visit white residence halls. As recently as 1980, the U.S. Department of Health, Education and Welfare concluded that Texas's higher-education system remained segregated, in violation of the 1964 Civil Rights Act.

Gradually this situation began to improve. From the 1970's to 1992, the law school adopted various affirmative-action programs for minority students who could compete successfully. Ultimately, about 10 percent of each entering class tended to be Mexican-American and 5 percent African-American. And from the 1970's on, the school produced nearly 2,000 minority lawyers. Many of these alumni assumed leadership positions, among them Ron Kirk, the Mayor of Dallas, and Federico Peña, the Secretary of Energy.

Now, with only four African-Americans in the first-year class, these painstakingly won gains are at great risk. This startling reversal arises entirely from decisions by some Federal judges—appointed by Presidents Reagan and Bush—who seem utterly indifferent to the dangers of turning back the clock of racial progress.

No case better demonstrates these judges' callousness than that of *Hopwood v. Texas.* Cheryl Hopwood, a white woman, along with three white men, claimed that the University of Texas School of Law's affirmative-action program violated the equal-protection clause of the 14th Amendment. The plaintiffs, who had been rejected for admission, alleged that they had a higher grade-point average and test scores than 93 African-American and Mexican-American students who had been admitted.

In 1996, a three-judge panel of the U.S. Court of Appeals for the Fifth Circuit reversed a district court judge and held that the law school could "not use race as a factor in deciding which applicants to admit." Two judges concluded that considering race or ethnicity in admissions would always be unconstitutional—even if it was intended "to combat the perceived effects of a hostile environment," to remedy past discrimination or to promote diversity. The third judge disagreed that diversity could never be a compelling government interest but reasoned that "the admissions process here under scrutiny was not narrowly tailored to achieve diversity." These judges' views are in stark contrast to those of many American educators, among them Nannerl Keohane, the president of Duke University, who testified that "my experience as a teacher at three institutions of higher education and as the president of two others is that diversity benefits students, faculty, institutions and the world of knowledge."

In adopting such drastic reasoning, these three judges—all Reagan or Bush appointees—ignored the history and evidence of discrimination against minorities at the law school, and they ignored some facts of the case—most glaringly, that *Hopwood*'s test scores were higher than those of more than 100 *white* students who were admitted. They also ignored settled precedent. Starting in 1978 with *Bakke v. Regents of the University of California,* the Supreme Court has consistently maintained that student diversity, when properly devised, is a valid justification for race-based affirmative action.

The state of Texas appealed the panel's majority opinion in *Hopwood,* requesting a rehearing before all of its 16 active judges. The request was denied. All nine of the judges who either voted against the rehearing or declined to vote were appointed by President Reagan or President Bush; six of the seven dissenting judges were appointed by President Carter or President Clinton.

The dissenters wrote that the majority's opinion "goes out of its way to break ground that the Supreme Court itself has been careful to avoid and purports to overrule a Supreme Court decision." They added that "the radical implications of this opinion . . . will literally change the face of public educational institutions throughout Texas, the other states of this circuit and this nation."

The majority opinion in *Hopwood* stands in sharp contrast to the role that the Fifth Circuit has played in the civil rights era. In the 1950's and 60's, many Southern officials, white citizens' councils and vigilante groups urged total defiance of the Federal courts' civil rights decrees. Despite the persistent hostility, virtually every Fifth Circuit judge—all appointed by President Eisenhower—repeatedly affirmed the constitutional rights of black citizens, among them Rosa Parks and Martin Luther King Jr.

When Reagan took office, he pledged to bring a "new breed of conservatism" to the judiciary. Under his and President Bush's Administrations, the judiciary became not only far more conservative but also far more white than it had been. Of 83 appointments to the appeals courts, Reagan appointed only one African-American. Bush appointed two, and one of those was Clarence Thomas. (Carter appointed nine African-Americans, and Clinton has appointed five.)

In 1983, during his less conservative days, Clarence Thomas said, "But for affirmative action laws, God only knows where I would be today." Now that he is on the Supreme Court, he repudiates affirmative action and has made it safe for people like Prof. Lino A. Graglia, of the University of Texas School of Law, to assert openly that "blacks and Mexican-Americans are not academically competitive with whites in selective institutions" because "they have a culture that seems not to encourage achievement. Failure is not looked upon with disgrace." Thomas's skewed and hostile views have also paved the way for the ascent of anti-affirmative-action crusaders like Ward Connerly, a driving force behind California's Proposition 209, the philosophy of which seems to be that anything expressly benefiting African-Americans, no matter how benign, useful or good, is inherently suspect and wrong.

Certainly, it is appropriate for a President to consider what he views as the mandate of the voters who elected him and to nominate those who seem to share his judicial philosophy. Still, it's impossible to ignore the tragic impact of the Reagan and Bush appointments.

In a 1989 employment-discrimination case, Justice Harry Blackmun, a Nixon appointee, wondered whether a majority of the Supreme Court "still believes that . . . race discrimination against nonwhites is a problem in our society, or even remembers that it ever was." This question reverberates today in the chilling legacy of the *Hopwood* decision. *Hopwood* has already had a pervasive impact on decreasing minority enrollment in many higher-education institutions. The number of medical-school applications from underrepresented minorities has dropped by 11 percent nationally and 17 percent among students who live in Texas, Louisiana and Mississippi, where the Fifth Circuit now has jurisdiction. The group that represented the plaintiffs in the Texas case recently filed suit to have the affirmative-action program for undergraduates at the University of Michigan declared unconstitutional.

In December 1996, a few months after *Hopwood* was decided, I underwent the first of three open-heart surgeries. Late each evening, after my family and friends had left, I would slip in and out of consciousness and dream of a sign that I saw long ago on the bumper of a rickety cab in Lagos, Nigeria. The sign said, in big, bold letters: NO MORE TIME FOR FOOLISHNESS. The long winter ended, the spring rains came and I got better. But still that sign haunted my dreams. As I returned to the work to which I had dedicated my career, I began to understand—slowly and then clearly—the meaning that sign held for me.

At times, this country seems intent on returning to the foolishness of the past. Donald M. Stewart, president of the College Board, has said that in the wake of court decisions like *Hopwood*, "we're looking at a potential wipeout that could take away an entire generation" of black and Hispanic students. When I think about this potential wipeout, I wonder whether I am still in intensive care, drifting on anesthesia. I ponder: is it a hallucination that in public law schools in California and Texas, the two most populous states in the country, minority enrollment is shrinking almost to the vanishing point? Is the lone black first-year student at Berkeley representative of a dying breed, a tragic echo of James Meredith, who desegregated the University of Mississippi in 1962? How will Texas and California, which are more than a third African-American and Latino, survive with the future shortage of trained minority leadership?

There is a curve of time that separates Heman Sweatt and Cheryl Hopwood. It has been a long while since that spring afternoon in 1950 when, as a first-year Yale law student, I heard the promise of freedom in the voice of Thurgood Marshall. Since then, I have observed commendable progress, lately some tragic retrogression, and now I see even more clearly that, in the long, bloody history of race relations in America, there is no more time for foolishness.

6

Toward a Third Reconstruction

Back to the future: NASA's Mae Jemison, the first black woman astronaut.
(Photo courtesy of NASA.)

Chapter 170

Introduction: Where Do We Go from Here?

Jonathan Birnbaum and Clarence Taylor

> We have to create another people's movement. In America, right now, I think most people—especially young people—are too quiet. We're just too quiet, too complacent. We need to agitate. We need to demand more of national government. . . . In the 60s, we didn't wait on President Kennedy, we didn't wait on President Johnson. We didn't wait on the Congress or the Supreme Court. We created the climate and forced those in high places to respond. There are people who may have the desire to say "no," but by action we can get them to say "yes."
>
> —Representative John Lewis[1]

After the Civil War, southern blacks were left with "nothing but freedom." They were no longer enslaved, but they had no economic rights, no access to the land and credit that would have protected them and their political and civil rights. Without economic protection for blacks, southern whites were able to reimpose a labor system that was only moderately better than slavery. One hundred years later, during the Second Reconstruction, blacks again fought for more than simply political rights. The slogan of the 1963 March on Washington was "Jobs and Freedom." The prize of the vote was important, but African Americans always recognized that more was necessary.

Since the 1980s we've experienced a tremendous resurgence of the conservative right, with conservative Republicans controlling either the presidency or the Congress, effectively capturing control of the country's social policy agenda. As a result, the United States is currently undergoing a gradual rollback of civil rights, including a chipping away of affirmative action programs and Great Society and even New Deal welfare state protections. As part of this resurgent conservatism, we hear claims that the goals of the civil rights revolution have long been accomplished and that now is the time to build a truly colorblind society. But the battle for civil rights, as this book demonstrates, has always been a broader political project. "[T]he black revolution is much more than a struggle for the rights of Negroes," wrote Martin Luther King, Jr. "It is forcing America to face all its interrelated flaws—racism, poverty, militarism, and materialism. It is exposing evils that are rooted deeply in the whole structure of our society. It reveals systemic rather than superficial flaws and suggests that radical reconstruction of society itself is the real issue to be faced.[2]

King, echoing Roosevelt, called for a Bill of Rights for the Disadvantaged.[3] In his 1944 State of the Union address, President Franklin D. Roosevelt had proposed a second Bill of Rights assuring citizens access to useful work and a living wage, food, housing, medical care, old age protection and education. "[T]rue individual freeedom cannot exist without economic security and independence," he said.[4] In 1964, King proposed a similar set of assurances. The 1968 Poor Peoples' Campaign (see chapter 119), which King did not live to see, would have been the opening volley in a battle for broader economic rights. During the 1988 Democratic primaries, Jesse Jackson, continuing the tradition, proposed a worker bill of rights (see chapter 176) and a corporate code of conduct.

"Black power is an engine that drives the great vehicle of social change in America," commented Andrew Kopkind (see chapter 133). Public education was not guaranteed for any group—white or black—in the South before the Civil War. African Americans' demand for public education during Reconstruction led to public education for all. Abolitionism kickstarted the woman suffrage movement. Similarly, during the Second Reconstruction, the spark of the black-led civil rights movement ignited so many other progressive social movements: anti-war, feminism, environmentalism, consumerism, and disability rights, to name a few. The black struggle, in Vincent Harding's phrase, was the "opening wedge" that led to other movements and an expansion of civil rights for all groups. "When the Women's Movement . . . as we know it today, took off in the later part of the 1960s, the debt of inspiration it owed to the black movement was obvious and acknowledged," writes Jenny Bourne, a researcher at London's Institute of Race Relations. "'Black' slogans became 'feminist' slogans, the new perspectives thrown up by the anti-war, civil rights and black power movements harnessed by the [women's movement] served to show up their potential for all oppressed groups. The debt found its way without apology into feminist writings."[5] The backlash against the civil rights movement has been an assault not only on the black struggle but on the movements it inspired.

In the United States, the expansion of black civil rights has played a central role in the progressive social policy agenda. Although the dominant characteristic of the current period is one of backlash, individuals and groups continue the struggle to protect and expand the boundaries of civil rights. The following chapters offer examples from the current discussion that may revive the civil rights project and inspire a Third Reconstruction.

NOTES

1. Interview with Representative John Lewis (D–GA), WBEZ-FM, Chicago (91.5), April 1998.

2. Martin Luther King, Jr., "A Testament of Hope," published posthumously in 1969;

reprinted in *A Testament of Hope: The Essential Writings of Martin Luther King, Jr.*, ed. James M. Washington (New York: Harper and Row, 1986), 315.

3. Martin Luther King, Jr., *Why We Can't Wait* (New York: Harper and Row, 1964).

4. For the text, see Franklin Roosevelt, "Economic Bill of Rights," reprinted in *The United States Constitution: Two Hundred Years of Anti-Federalist, Abolitionist, Feminist, Muckraking, Progressive, and Especially Socialist Criticism,* ed. Bertell Ollman and Jonathan Birnbaum (New York: New York University Press, 1990), appendix B.

5. Jenny Bourne, "Towards an Anti-Racist Feminism," *Race and Class*, Summer 1983, 1. The classic discussion of the connection between the civil rights movement and the U.S. women's movement is Sara Evans, *Personal Politics: The Roots of Women's Liberation in the Civil Rights Movement and the New Left* (New York: Knopf, 1979).

Chapter 171

Time for a Third Reconstruction

Eric Foner

In 1993, after the election of the first Democratic administration in twelve years, several scholars offered suggestions for the incoming president.

Eric Foner, professor of history at Columbia University, serves on the editorial board of the Nation *magazine.*

The following selection, "Time for a Third Reconstruction," is reprinted with permission from the 1 February 1993 issue of the Nation *magazine.*

For other selections by Foner, see chapters 25 and 143.

Last month, the original copy of the Emancipation Proclamation was displayed at the National Archives. Issued on January 1, 1863, the proclamation sounded the death knell of slavery, thereby closing one chapter of American history and opening another, whose central issue was whether freedom for blacks implied genuine equality. Today, 130 years later, the task of bringing the descendants of slaves fully into the mainstream of American life remains to be accomplished.

It is unfortunate that Bill Clinton was out of Washington when the proclamation was exhibited. Had he perused the document and pondered its meaning, he might have been led to reflect on the First and Second Reconstructions—two moments, a century apart, when black and white Americans struggled to breathe substantive meaning into the freedom decreed during the Civil War. Their successes and failures suggest that the time has arrived for a Third Reconstruction, a renewed national effort to address the racial divide that afflicts our society.

The Emancipation Proclamation not only transformed the nature of the Civil War but opened the turbulent period of Reconstruction, in which the national government made its first effort to protect the equal rights of all Americans. Reconstruction is the most misunderstood era of our history. It was long viewed as a time of rampant corruption presided over by unscrupulous Northern carpetbaggers and former slaves unprepared for the freedom that had been thrust upon them. This interpretation helped to justify the subsequent policies of segregation and black disfranchisement in the South and the North's prolonged indifference to white Southerners' nullification of the federal Constitution.

In fact, Reconstruction was a laudable attempt to create, for the first time in our history, an interracial democracy. National civil rights laws and the Fourteenth and Fifteenth Amendments to the Constitution accorded the former slaves equality before the law and granted black men the right to vote.

Beginning in 1868, state and local governments resting on support from black voters and a minority of whites came to power throughout the South. They greatly expanded the states' social responsibilities, establishing public school systems, for example, where none had ever existed. These policies, and the spectacle of black men replacing the old slave-holding elite in offices from justice of the peace to U.S. senator, provoked a campaign of violent opposition led by the Ku Klux Klan that, by 1877, had driven the last Reconstruction government from power.

Not until the civil rights movement of the 1950s and 1960s, often called the Second Reconstruction, did Americans again attempt to implement the unfulfilled social and political agenda of the post–Civil War years. In dismantling legal segregation, restoring to Southern blacks the right to vote and opening doors of economic and educational opportunity from which blacks had been almost entirely excluded, the Second Reconstruction achieved gains even more far-reaching than the first.

Nonetheless, we remain nearly as far from the ideal of a color-blind society as a century ago. As the First Reconstruction drew to a close, Thomas Wentworth Higginson, who had commanded a black regiment during the Civil War, commented, "Revolutions may go backward." Both Reconstructions were times of momentous hopes, followed by retrenchment, reaction and an attempt, sanctioned in the highest offices of the land, to undo much of what had been accomplished.

In both the late nineteenth century and the era of Reagan and Bush a century later, the federal government abandoned its commitment to the principle of equality and an active role in guaranteeing the rights of American citizens. Because it threatened traditions of local autonomy and was so closely associated with the new rights of blacks, the increased power of the federal government during the two Reconstructions generated powerful opposition. In both eras, opponents of equality raised the specter of a federal bureaucracy trampling on the rights of white citizens, warning that government efforts to combat the heritage of discrimination violated the immutable laws of the marketplace and made blacks privileged wards of the state. In both, social theories flourished that explained poverty as a consciously chosen way of life rather than a structural problem affecting the entire economy but for historical reasons most severe among the former slaves and their descendants.

The end of the First Reconstruction was a disaster for black Americans and profoundly affected the course of the nation's development. By 1900, Southern blacks were locked in a system of political, economic and social inequality, and the ideologies of social Darwinism and racism reigned supreme in both North and South. The exclusion of former slaves from the "political nation" left the Solid South under the control of a reactionary elite and shifted the spectrum of national politics significantly to the right.

The verdict is still out on the ultimate fate of the Second Reconstruction. But separate and unequal still rules in our schools, housing, job markets and conditions of life.

Indeed, both Reconstructions foundered, in large measure, because they failed to address the problem of economic equality. The first granted blacks equal rights before the law, but the government's refusal to redistribute land in the South left the freed people with no alternative but to compete as "free laborers" in a society in which all the economic cards were stacked against them. The second failed to confront effectively the economic gap separating black and white Americans.

The workings of the free market will not solve this problem, nor will a general policy of economic growth, whose benefits, history suggests, will not trickle down to the least fortunate. A Third Reconstruction is needed to address directly the economic inequalities that are the accumulated consequence of 250 years of slavery and a century of discrimination.

Today, of course, the nation's racial landscape is far more complex than in the nineteenth century. "Black and white" no longer adequately describes, if it ever did, the makeup of our society. The multiplicity of groups now claiming the status of victimized minority obscures the unique social and economic exploitation black Americans have suffered.

The black community itself is more divided than a century ago. An expanded middle class has arisen in the past generation, while social disintegration stalks the bottom of black society, spawning a pattern of violence that has fueled a rightwing backlash, making the task of addressing racial inequalities all the more difficult.

A national commitment to a Third Reconstruction would require the kind of moral leadership and political courage this generation is unaccustomed to in its Presidents. But let us not forget that emancipation itself was not universally popular. In 1864, some Republicans feared that a reaction against the destruction of slavery would cost their party the next election, and urged that the proclamation be rescinded. If he were to do so, Lincoln replied, "I should be damned in time and eternity." Can we hope for the same courage and sense of historical obligation from the incoming Administration?

Chapter 172

Toward a New Protest Paradigm

Manning Marable

Manning Marable is professor of history and director of the Institute for African American Studies at Columbia University.

The following selection is excerpted from "Rethinking Black Liberation: Towards a New Protest Paradigm," Race and Class, April/June 1997, 8–11. Reprinted with permission of the author.

For other selections by Marable, see chapters 87 and 130.

We are again at a decisive moment in black history, where a new paradigm must be developed to advance the boundaries of our politics. We cannot simply duplicate the strategies and tactics of the civil rights movement of the 1960s, because the issues that confront us are fundamentally different. The internal class composition of the black community has been radically altered and is now characterized by an affluent professional and managerial elite, a black working class with declining incomes, and a black ghetto class of the unemployed and single-parent households which is experiencing a social holocaust. The approach suggested by [Louis] Farrakhan of conservative black nationalism also cannot provide the basis for advancing the movement. Building strong black institutions to provide goods and services black people need is certainly important. But petty capitalist enterprises will not generate the jobs we need to reduce the mass unemployment effectively. Racial separatism does not bring together people from different ethnic and racial backgrounds who nevertheless share common material and social interests. Patriarchy and homophobia serve to divide the progressive community, reducing our politics to the narrow confines of racial identity.

The place to begin the reconstruction of the black liberation movement—as well as the larger progressive, left-of-center movements in the United States—is from the nexus of three crucial sites of struggle: community, class and gender.

By "community," I mean the socioeconomic and environmental context of daily life for most families and households. Nearly all of us live in communities of one kind or another, with their own cultural and geographical dimensions, patterns of social interaction and exchange, and even language and tradition. It is from the site of community that many of us wage struggles in the living space, around the materiality of day-to-day existence: access to decent and affordable housing, public health services, crime and personal safety, the quality of the environment, public transportation, the education of our children. These basic human concerns transcend narrowly defined racial interests: there cannot be an effective program for health care in a community, for example, that addresses only African-Americans. It is where people live that usually defines how they become most active in the civic arena. And if one surveys the actual racial and ethnic composition of most U.S. urban communities, it becomes apparent that neighborhoods are almost never strictly defined by race. Harlem, black America's most famous community, is today more than 40 percent Latino. The largest city of the English-speaking Caribbean is, arguably, Brooklyn. In the next decade Latinos will outnumber African-Americans as the largest group of color in the United States. We must build partnerships across racial identities to serve the broader collective interests of people who live side by side, ride the same buses and subways, send their children to the same substandard schools, and wait for health services in the same overcrowded hospitals and emergency clinics.

By "class," I mean more than the stratification of incomes, or the social status derived from various levels of wealth. Class—the divisions based on the relations and forces of production, and the social consequences of the unequal allocation of property and power—always prefigures the range of social possibilities and life chances, beyond the social realities of gender, race and community. This is not to suggest that either gender or race can be understood as by-products of rigid economic categories, or exist as secondary factors in the class struggle. They aren't. But what history does show is that the way things are produced and distributed within society, the patterns of ownership and divisions of property, prefigure or set in motion certain consequences which, in turn, impact on everything else. During the period of American capitalist hegemony across the globe, especially from 1945 to the late 1970s, part of the surplus was allocated to U.S. workers, who saw their real incomes dramatically improve. Class as a social category almost ceased to be used in mainstream discourse.

In the 1990s the situation regarding class in American life has dramatically changed. For example, families in the upper 5 per cent tax bracket have increased their incomes by 25 per cent since 1979, adjusted for inflation. But for middle-income households, real incomes during the same period declined 1 percent; for low-income households, real wages have declined 13 percent. The income decline was even greater for black and Latino families and for households headed by young adults or single parents. The destruction of jobs and lower wages are a direct result of the globalization of capital, in which businesses relocate overseas in pursuit of low-wage, non-union labor. Even for those workers who have jobs, the pressure of corporate downsizing has created an environment of fear and insecurity. Black and progressive politics need to focus specifically on the issues of employment and a living wage, initiating a public conversation about the importance of work for all people. The Association of Community Organizations for Reform Now (ACORN) recently initiated a "Jobs and Living Wage Campaign," for example, which represents an excellent model of practical class politics. The use of local

and statewide initiatives to increase the minimum wage provides an important vehicle for mobilizing both the unemployed and low-wage workers. These struggles
over jobs and income can also be merged into community-based initiatives around
economic development and urban renewal. A new class-centered activism, combined with the potential revitalization of the AFL-CIO, could generate the basis
for effective multiracial protest.

The basis of the politics of "gender" in the black community is partially the fact
that the primary victims and scapegoats of the Right are women of color and their
children. The demonization of poor and low-income black women is a central
theme in the ideological and policy assault against the entire black community.
When we talk about mobilizing African-American neighborhoods around community concerns, we must recognize that the majority of our households are single
parent families. The majority of neighborhood activists who focus on improving
the quality of public schools, access to decent health care facilities, and the issue
of community safety, are overwhelmingly black women. Struggles for the empowerment of African-American women must be at the very center of how progressive
politics is defined. This includes deepening the struggle against sexism within
black institutions and political organizations, the advancement of black women as
leaders and theoreticians in the overall movement, and greater emphasis on programmatic demands and initiatives speaking to the real issues affecting African-
American women. As long as African-American males define the assertion of
"manhood" as a central goal of their politics, and deny the voices and insights of
their sisters, the black movement will continue to be fragmented and pulled towards the patriarchy of the Right.

Many might suggest that "race" still remains the central site for black struggle.
Of course, "race" as a social category directly manifests itself in community, class
and gender contexts. Where we live, how we work, and our experience of gender
are all profoundly impacted by the inequality of race. Black women's lives and
struggles, as scholars such as Angela Davis, Patricia Hill Collins, and Leith
Mullings have told us, are not mirrored in the perspectives and interests of white
middle-class women. Working people who are black have, not coincidentally, unemployment rates twice those of white workers. Race matters; but race is most
real as a social force when it manifests itself in the social consequences and conditions of inequality and discrimination.

Practical steps which improve the quality of life within communities, such as organizing against police brutality and harassment in our neighborhoods, or taking
measures to reduce the level of gang violence, or mobilizing parents to improve the
curriculum of public schools, all contribute to the empowerment of racial and ethnic
minorities and other oppressed people. Sometimes activism can be effectively channeled through electoral politics, as in voter registration and education campaigns.
But, more frequently, it is through the institutions of civil society, within extended
kinship networks, friends, co-workers on the job, and in our cultural and social organizations, that practical political activism is expressed. All constructive forms of
resistance and collective mobilization by black people directly or indirectly challenge

and undermine institutional racism. When people recognize that through their collective actions they can change the way things are, they truly feel empowered. Liberation begins by winning small battles, day by day, creating greater confidence among the oppressed, building ultimately towards a democratic vision which can successfully challenge the very foundations of this system.

Chapter 173

Why Inter-Ethnic Anti-Racism Matters Now

George Lipsitz

George Lipsitz is professor of ethnic studies at the University of California, San Diego.

The following selection is reprinted with permission from "Like Crabs in a Barrel: Why Inter-Ethnic Anti-Racism Matters Now," ColorLines, Winter 1999, 98–100. Information available from ColorLines, 4096 Piedmont Ave. #319, Oakland, CA 94611; 510/653-3415; colorlines@arc.org.

For another selection by Lipsitz, see chapter 138.

In places near the ocean where merchants sell live crabs, they display their wares in open barrels. When the crabs try to escape by climbing up the sides of the barrel, they always fail. As soon as one starts to climb, it gets pulled back down by the others, who are also trying to escape.

When we try to overcome racism, sexism, homophobia, or class oppression, we often find ourselves in the position of crabs in a barrel. We work as hard as we can, but all our efforts fail to free us. Instead of pulling ourselves up, we only pull someone else down.

It is not hard to figure out why this happens. People with power want us to be divided and to fight each other so we will not unite and fight them. If any of us make gains, they want us to make them at each other's expense instead of demanding a fundamental redistribution of resources and power.

New Model Every Year

This "divide and conquer" strategy has been used more and more in recent years. Malcolm X used to say that racism was like a Cadillac because they came out with a new model every year. There is always racism, but it is not always the same racism. Unlike past segregation and white supremacy which produced a relatively uniform system of exclusion, today's racism employs practices that produce differentiation rather than uniformity, that give excluded groups decisively different relationships to the same oppression.

For example, the opponents of affirmative action make appeals to Asian

Americans, arguing that its dismantling will secure "advantages" for Asians that now go to blacks and Latinos. Anti-immigrant groups try to enlist African Americans in efforts to deprive Asian American and Latino immigrants of social services, health care, and education on the grounds that immigrants are responsible for the declines in economic status and political power experienced by blacks in recent years. Racist legislators intent upon dismantling the political gains won by African Americans over the past three decades invite Latinos to support budget cuts, redistricting, term limits, and other measures designed to undercut the seniority, control over resources, and political influence of black legislators.

At the same time, enemies of rights for women and gays and lesbians seek alliances with men of color. They encourage men from aggrieved racial groups to make gains within their own groups rather than outside them, to gain power at the expense of women and gays and lesbians in their own communities rather than at the expense of wealthy white men with power.

These new divisions can also produce unexpected affiliations and alliances. Attacks on bilingual education and immigrants' rights harm both Latinos and Asian Americans. Irrational and alarmist policies about AIDS stigmatize both homosexuals and Haitians. Puerto Ricans on the mainland are both Spanish speakers from a colonized homeland, like Mexicans, and U.S. citizens, like blacks. Filipinos are non-citizen immigrants from Asia, but they share with Mexicans the experience of being immigrants from a Catholic nation colonized by Spain whose patron saint is the Virgin of Guadalupe.

Limits of Identity Politics

Yet the same forces that create unexpected affinities and alliances can also generate new forms of division and differentiation. All racialized groups face problems because of environmental racism, but Native Americans suffer particularly from cancer, Latinos from polluted air and pesticide exposure, African Americans from lead poisoning, Asian American and Pacific Islanders from underweight births and childhood malnutrition. Unemployment has hit African Americans harder than Asian Americans or Latinos, but women immigrants from Asia, Mexico, and Central America are over-represented in hazardous low-wage jobs.

Under these conditions, inter-ethnic anti-racism is emerging as a tactical necessity. This strategy does not erase purely national or racial identities, nor does it permanently transcend them. There is always room for more than one tactical stance in struggles for social justice, and ethnic nationalism and autonomous single-group struggles will always be legitimate and meaningful under some circumstances. But the current historical moment is generating new forms of struggle, forms eloquently described by scholar-activist Lisa Lowe as "alternative forms of practice that integrate yet move beyond those of cultural nationalism."

Alliances across racial lines offer some obvious advantages. They produce strength in numbers; we are more powerful with allies than we would be alone. If we are there for other people's struggles, there is a greater likelihood that they will be there for us in the future if we need them. By standing up for someone else, we establish ourselves as people with empathy for the suffering of others; it shows that we will not turn our backs on people simply because they seem powerless.

Angela Davis points to the work of workers' centers like Asian Immigrant Women Advocates that address the whole lives of workers—not just their class, racial, or gender identities. These centers combine literacy classes with legal advice about domestic violence and divorce while they address issues about wages, hours, and working conditions.

Because there is no way to improve the lives of Asian American immigrant workers without attending to the concerns of Latinas who often work at their side, and because entrepreneurs from their own ethnic group are often part of the problem, these efforts inevitably lead to inter-ethnic alliances. They lead to cross-class alliances because there is no way to deal with domestic violence as a class-specific or race-specific problem. They also lead to the formation of temporary affinities and alliances across gender, class, and racial lines through tactics like consumer boycotts of goods created under unsafe or unfair working conditions.

Consider also some of the less obvious advantages of inter-ethnic anti-racism. Coordinated actions against racism enable aggrieved groups to focus on the fact of oppression itself rather than merely on the identities of the oppressed. Inter-ethnic anti-racism can shift the focus away from defensive concerns about "minority" disadvantages and toward an analysis of white "majority" advantages, thus helping to define the target.

This might show that racialized groups are not merely disadvantaged, but also taken advantage of. It might make visible the new forms of racialization created day after day in the present, not just those attributable to histories of slavery, conquest, genocide, immigrant exploitation, and class oppression.

Who's Got the Power?

In the final analysis, the most important reason for inter-ethnic anti-racism is that it provides the most effective way for us to see exactly how power works in the world. We will always misread and misunderstand our circumstances if we see things from only one perspective.

Solidarities based on single identity are limited; solidarities based on multiple identities are unlimited. All social movements need some form of organic solidarity. But people who must see themselves as exactly the same in order to wage a common struggle will be poorly prepared for struggles for social justice against a power structure that constantly creates new forms of differentiation among the oppressed.

Yet precisely because no unified identity encompasses anyone's social world, inter-ethnic anti-racist activism offers the opportunity to make struggles for social justice as mobile, fluid, and flexible as the new forms of oppression. They enable us to create places like the ones envisioned by Patrick Chamoiseau's narrator in *Texaco*, an epic novel about anti-racist struggle in Martinique: "those places in which no one could foresee our ability to unravel their History into our thousand stories."

Chapter 174

How the New Working Class
Can Transform Urban America

Robin D. G. Kelley

Robin D. G. Kelley is professor of history and Africana studies at New York University.

The following selection is excerpted by permission from Yo' Mama's Disfunktional: Fighting the Culture Wars in Urban America *(Boston: Beacon Press, 1997), 125–26, 144–50, 158, footnotes deleted.*

For another selection by Kelley, see chapter 65.

The predominantly black, Latino, and Asian American working classes who occupy our cities can win only if they are willing to challenge the problems of the whole city—together. Corporate downsizing, deindustrialization, racist and sexist social policy, and the erosion of the welfare state do not respect the boundaries between work and community, the household and public space. The battle for livable wages and fulfilling jobs is inseparable from the fight for decent housing and safe neighborhoods; the struggle to defuse cultural stereotypes of inner city residents cannot be easily removed from the intense fights for environmental justice. Moreover, the struggle to remake culture itself, to develop new ideas, new relationships, and new values that place mutuality over materialism and collective responsibility over "personal responsibility," and place greater emphasis on ending all forms of oppression rather than striving to become an oppressor, cannot be limited to either home or work.

Standing in the eye of the storm are the new multiracial, urban working classes. It is they, not the Democratic Party, not a bunch of smart policy analysts, not corporate benevolence, who hold the key to transforming the city and the nation. . . . [T]here is no doubt that progressive social policies must be implemented at the federal and state level, and that the terrain of electoral politics cannot be ceded to middle-class suburban voters. But my point is very, very simple. As C. L. R. James himself put it, "The rich are only defeated when running for their lives." I am suggesting that the only way to implement changes, whether at a policy level, a personal level, or a broad cultural level, is through collective struggle. And at the heart of this movement must be working people and the jobless poor. . . .

Labor/Community Strategies against Class-Based Racism

Of course, we cannot stop at the cafeteria or the classroom or workplaces in general. Urban working people spend much if not most of their lives in their neighborhoods, in their homes, in transit, in the public spaces of the city, in houses of worship, in bars, clubs, barbershops, hair and nail salons, in various retail outlets, in medical clinics, welfare offices, courtrooms, even jail cells. They create and maintain families, build communities, engage in local politics, and construct a sense of fellowship that is sometimes life sustaining. These community ties are crucial to the success of any labor movement. . . . History has proven over and over again that in order to generate local support for union struggles, strikes, boycotts, and corporate responsibility campaigns, community-based organizations are key. Let us not forget that the intense class struggles that erupted across the country in the late nineteenth century, on the railroads in 1877, in the mines of the Rocky Mountains and the steel mills in the East and Midwest, and among black washerwomen in the urban South were *community* struggles. It was never a simple matter of labor unions versus employers. During some of those dramatic battles, the local police, families, and even some of the merchants sided with the union, which meant that the employers had to bring in state troops and private Pinkerton agents. The employers were forced to go outside precisely because communities were mobilized. During the 1930s the success of the sit-down strikes in Akron and Detroit, and the struggles of Latina and Asian-Pacific cannery workers in the West, depended on community support; families and friends and sympathetic organizations brought food and blankets, joined picket lines, got the word out, and pooled money to help struggling families survive the loss of a paycheck. Similarly, during the late 1960s and early 1970s, the League of Revolutionary Black Workers and the Revolutionary Union Movement made community organizing a central strategy.

More importantly, working people live in communities that are as embattled as the workplace itself. Black and Latino workers, for example, must contend with issues of police brutality and a racist criminal justice system, housing discrimination, lack of city services, toxic waste, inadequate health care facilities, sexual assault and domestic violence, and crime and neighborhood safety. And at the forefront of these community-based movements have been women, usually struggling mothers of all ages dedicated to making life better for themselves and their children—mothers who, as we have seen, have become the scapegoats for virtually everything wrong with the "inner city." In cities across the United States, working-class black and Latina women built and sustained community organizations that registered voters, patrolled the streets, challenged neighborhood drug dealers, defended the rights of prisoners, and fought vigorously for improvements in housing, city services, health care, and public assistance. Of course, there was nothing new about women of color taking the lead in community-based organizing. A century earlier, black women's clubs not only helped the less fortunate but played a key role in the political life of the African American community. Over a half-century later, when militant, predominantly male organizations like the Black Panther

Party and the Black Liberation Army received a great deal of press, black women carried on the tradition of community-based organizing. If one only looked at South Central Los Angeles in the mid-1960s, one would find well over a dozen such organizations, including the Watts Women's Association, the Avalon-Carver Community Center, the Mothers of Watts Community Action Council, Mothers Anonymous, the Welfare Recipients Union, the L.A. Chapter of the National Welfare Rights Organization, the Central City Community Mental Health Center, the Neighborhood Organizations of Watts, and the South Central Volunteer Bureau of Los Angeles.

These movements were the precursors for contemporary groups such as Mothers ROC (Reclaiming Our Children) and Mothers of East Los Angeles (MELA). Mothers ROC was founded in 1992 by Theresa Allison, the mother of Dewayne Holmes, who helped engineer the historic gang truce in the aftermath of the L.A. rebellion but was falsely convicted on trumped-up charges soon thereafter. Her efforts to overturn his conviction convinced her to form a movement that could challenge the racist and sexist criminal justice system. "We formed Mothers ROC," Allison explained, "to ensure that our children would no longer face the lawyers, judges and courts alone. Our aim is to be the voice of the tens of thousands of young men and women who are locked away in the rapidly growing prison system." Among other things, Mothers ROC has called for an immediate end to the "war on drugs" (recognizing it for what it is: a war on black and Latino youth), the repeal of the "three strikes" law (meaning that three felony convictions, irrespective of the crime, lead to a mandatory life sentence); more funding for public defenders; an end to mandatory minimum laws; and an end to indiscriminate stops, warrantless searches, and the use of electronic databases to identify alleged gang members. In the five years since its founding, Mothers ROC has grown into a nationwide organization with over 100 chapters and a constantly expanding membership.

Similarly, MELA got started as a result of a protracted battle with the prison-industrial complex. Founded in 1984 to fight efforts by the state of California to build a prison in East Los Angeles, MELA built a powerful coalition that not only blocked the prison but kept an oil pipeline and a hazardous waste incinerator from being built in their communities. In an age of deindustrialization and massive joblessness, MELA's resistance to these firms proved to be bold and visionary. While many community leaders were clamoring for jobs at any cost, the women of MELA understood that in the long run no job is worth sacrificing the health and well-being of the entire community. As MELA activist Aurora Castillo put it, "Because we are a poor and Hispanic community they think we will accept the destructive projects if they promise us jobs. But we don't want our children working as prison guards or in incinerators. We need constructive jobs—nurses, doctors, computer specialists, skilled workers, who can make a contribution to our community."

MELA is one of many organizations involved in the struggle for environmental justice. All over the country, especially in the South, women of color are organizing against companies and government institutions responsible for placing landfills, hazardous waste sites, and chemical manufacturers dangerously close to low-income minority communities. The evidence that poor communities of color are singled out for toxic waste sites is overwhelming. One study released in 1987 estimated that three out of five African Americans live dangerously close to abandoned toxic waste sites and commercial hazardous waste landfills. The study also revealed that the largest hazardous waste landfill in the country is located in Emelle, Alabama, whose population is 78.9 percent black, and that the greatest concentration of hazardous waste sites is in the mostly black and Latino South Side of Chicago. A 1992 study concluded that polluters based in minority areas are treated less severely by government agencies than those in largely white communities. Also, federally sponsored toxic cleanup programs, according to the report, take longer and are less thorough in minority neighborhoods.

The effects of these policies have been devastating. Cases of asthma and other respiratory diseases as well as cancer have been traced to toxic waste. Accidents involving the mishandling of hazardous chemicals have ravaged some poor black communities, often with little or no publicity. In July 1993, for example, a ruptured railroad car at General Chemical's plant in Richmond, California, caused a disaster for this overwhelmingly poor black city located just north of Oakland. As journalist and activist Ruth Rosen explained it, the damaged car "spewed a fifteen-mile-long toxic plume of sulfuric acid through surrounding residential communities. People wheezed and coughed, their eyes and lungs scorched by the toxic cloud. Three hours passed before the explosion could be capped. Over the next few days, more than twenty thousand residents sought medical treatment from nearby hospitals." Sadly, the city of Richmond had endured nauseating fumes a few years earlier when fires broke out in a neighboring warehouse owned by Safeway supermarkets.

The environmental justice movement's roots apparently go back to 1982 when black and Native American residents tried to block state authorities from building a chemical disposal site in Warren County, North Carolina. Since then, dozens of local movements have followed suit, including the Concerned Citizens of South Central (Los Angeles), and the North Richmond West County Toxics Coalition. By demonstrating, holding hearings and public workshops, conducting research, and filing suits against local and state governments, these groups have tried to draw attention to the racial and class biases that determine how hazardous waste sites are selected.

One of the pioneers of the movement for environmental justice was Patsy Ruth Oliver, founder and leader of the Carver Terrace Community Action Group. When an investigation revealed that Carver Terrace, a black suburb outside of Texarkana, Texas, had been built on an old toxic waste site and sold to unsuspecting black home buyers, Texas officials asked that the federal government add it to its Superfund cleanup program (a $1.3 billion trust that Congress created to clean up toxic waste dumps). When the Environmental Protection Agency (EPA) came to investigate, they concluded that the soil was contaminated but it posed no danger to the residents. Oliver and her neighbors were outraged, especially after they discovered that the EPA had withheld information suggesting that the residents were, in fact, at risk. Through persistence and protest, Oliver and the Community Action Group were able to force the government to buy them out and help them relocate. Although the people of Carver Terrace lost their homes, it was a significant victory for the movement because they forced the government to acknowledge the seriousness of toxic dumping. Oliver continued to speak out against environmental racism until her death in 1993.

The struggle against environmental racism is integrally tied to workplace struggles, the criminal justice system, the welfare state, and the movements of global capital. Whereas most community- and labor-based organizations limit their focus to an issue or set of issues, even when they are able to see the bigger picture, once in a while there are movements that attempt to fight on all fronts. Such organizations, where they do exist, are often products of the best elements of Third World, feminist, and Black Liberation movements. Rather than see race, gender, and sexuality as "problems," they are, instead, pushing working-class politics in new directions. The exemplary movements include the Center for Third World Organizing, the Southern Organizing Committee for Economic Justice, New Directions, and *Labor Notes*, to name a few.

One of the most visible and successful examples of such a broad-based radical movement is the Labor/Community Strategy Center based in Los Angeles. The leaders of the Strategy Center have deep roots in social movements that go back to Black Liberation and student activism of the 1960s, urban antipoverty programs, farmworkers' movements, organized labor, and popular left movements in El Salvador and Mexico. They have been at the forefront of the struggle for clean air in the Harbor area of Los Angeles—a region with a high concentration of poor communities of color. They have worked closely with Justice for Janitors, providing crucial support to Local 660 of the SEIU. They fought President Bush's proposed "Weed and Seed" program (an urban policy developed in response to the L.A. Rebellion that would provide big tax breaks to entrepreneurs willing to invest in inner cities, and a massive buildup of the police and criminal justice system). They mobilized against Proposition 187, waged a campaign to protect immigrants' rights, and have even engaged in cross-border organizing with Mexican transit workers. . . .

In this tragic era of pessimism and defeat, these grassroots, working-class radical movements go forward as if they might win. While some holier-than-thou leftists might view these movements, and my interpretation of them, as another example of misplaced optimism, I would venture to say that the women and men who have built and sustained these organizations do not have the luxury not to fight back. In most cases, they are battling over issues basic to their own survival—decent wages, healthy environment, essential public services. At the heart of these movements are folks like my mother and the many other working-class women of color, women like Patsy Oliver and Della Bonner, Dania Herring and Theresa Allison, women who have borne the brunt of the material and ideological war against the poor. They understand, better than anyone, the necessity of fighting back. And they also understand that change does not come on its own. As Dr. Martin Luther King, Jr., so eloquently explained:

A solution of the present crisis will not take place unless men and women work for it. Human progress is neither automatic nor inevitable. Even a superficial look at history reveals that no social advance rolls in on the wheels of inevitability. Every step toward the goal of justice requires sacrifice, suffering, and struggle; the tireless exertions and passionate concern of dedicated individuals. Without persistent effort, time itself becomes an ally of the insurgent and primitive forces of irrational emotionalism and social destruction. This is no time for apathy or complacency. This is the time for vigorous and positive action.

The time is now.

Chapter 175

What Works to Reduce Inequality?

Martin Carnoy

Martin Carnoy is professor of education and economics at Stanford University. Among his many works, he is the author of State and Political Theory *(1984), co-author of* Economic Democracy *(1980),* The New Social Contract: The Economy and Government after Reagan *(1983), and* The New Global Economy *(1993), and co-editor of* Decentralization and School Improvement: Can We Fulfill the Promise? *(1993).*

The following selection is excerpted from Faded Dreams: The Politics and Economics of Race in America *(New York: Cambridge University Press, 1994), 223–25. Reprinted with the permission of Cambridge University Press.*

[E]conomic inequality in the United States still has an important racial component and . . . a government with the will to reduce racial inequality can, by its general ideological stance toward race and by specific public policies, achieve that goal. When government has focused its power on racial and ethnic income differences and discrimination in the past, it has had a major impact on the economic conditions of blacks and other disadvantaged minorities. It can have a similar impact if policies combine investment in the education of disadvantaged children and minority college education with expansionary economics. It can have an impact if it combines pro-labor wage and training legislation with the implementation of existing antidiscrimination laws. Government can do all this.

Government has the capability to invest public funds in education and infrastructure in ways that are more favorable to low-income Americans and even more favorable to low-income minorities—focusing public investment on Head Start and on rebuilding cities and providing decent housing rather than on developing military hardware, and phasing out programs that subsidize the already wealthy while expanding programs that increase low-income workers' skills and access to jobs.

Government can affect access to credit for private investments. The two main investments that middle-class consumers make are those in housing and in their children's college education. Credit markets for these investments are exactly the ones that African-Americans have a harder time entering than whites and where government can play a crucial role directly or indirectly to increase access. Government can also favor investment in inner cities, either by reducing regulation on loans to businesses that go into inner cities or by providing direct incentives to such businesses.

Government can support macroeconomic policy that tends to lower general unemployment rates, again favoring the low-income and minority groups who are the most likely to be unemployed when the economy is slack.

Government has the legal power to equalize opportunity in labor markets when there is evidence that discrimination exists. Once the Civil Rights Act of 1965 was passed, the most important issues concerning government action became the act's interpretation by the Supreme Court and its implementation by the Equal Employment Opportunity Commission. Although the Court in the 1980s began to limit the earlier powers of the act, it is still possible for the Justice Department and the EEOC to use earlier standards of class-action failure-to-hire cases instead of the individual discrimination criteria used under Reagan and Bush and to speed up the handling of complaints.

Government can set the standard on wages and employment: blacks were employed in high positions in government a generation before they reached similar positions in the private sector, and black-white wages in government work are more equal even today than in the private sector, which in the current labor market with its increased number of adults earning low wages would affect much more than just youth incomes. Government can raise minimum wages in the private sector. It can also be the employer of last resort, providing short-term employment for disadvantaged youth at reasonable wages.

Government can send an ideological signal that racial inequality as expressed in wage discrimination, political underrepresentaion of minorities, poorer educational treatment for minorities, misleading stereotypes, as well as less individual responsibility for social discipline in minority communities are unacceptable. The great advances for many in the black community at the same time that other blacks face deteriorating social conditions make the politics of sending this signal much more complex than it was in the 1940s and the 1960s. It is especially difficult to develop a package that deals with the poverty/race problem at the same time that it covers a different set of issues for middle-class blacks.

However, the bottom line of any ideological strategy for reducing racial inequality is that the race issue must be on the table. It must be the subject of honest political discourse. This means overturning conservative policies of removing race from out-front political discussion. Overt discussion of racism in political circles has been stigmatized—indeed, many politicians are ready to deem taking racism on as an issue racist. The mainstream politics of race has been pushed into the realm of innuendo and subconscious fears. In this climate, how does government change the signal in order to face up to continued discrimination at the same time that it deals honestly with such issues as street violence, social disintegration, and welfare dependency?

When government is able to combine economic, legal, and ideological actions, it has a ripple effect on inequality beyond the direct impact of the actions themselves. It styles the actions of employers and workers in the private sector as they adjust to changes in the "atmospheric pressure" of the social contract. This is precisely what happened in the 1940s and 1960s, and could happen again.

Chapter 176

A Workers' Bill of Rights

Jesse Jackson and the Rainbow Coalition

Jesse Jackson is the founder and president of the Rainbow/PUSH Coalition. He joined the Southern Christian Leadership Conference (SCLC) in 1965 and was soon assigned the task of expanding the group's operations north, into Chicago. Jackson was later appointed SCLC's director for Operation Breadbasket. He graduated from the Chicago Theological Seminary in 1968 and was ordained as a Baptist minister. In 1971 he set up his own organization, Operation PUSH (People United to Save Humanity), based in Chicago.

Jackson ran for the presidency, under the banner of the Rainbow Coalition, in 1984, winning Democratic Party primaries in South Carolina, Louisiana, and Washington, D.C. He ran again in 1988, garnering 6.6 million votes and finishing second for the Democratic nomination. In 1992, although early polls listed him as the front runner among Democratic voters, he chose not to run. In 1996 Operation PUSH and the Rainbow Coalition merged into the Rainbow/PUSH Coalition. Jackson is the host of Both Sides on CNN, *the author of* Straight from the Heart *(1987), and the co-author of* Legal Lynching: Racism, Injustice, and the Death Penalty *(1996), and* It's About the Money *(2000).*

The following selection is reprinted from "A Workers' Bill of Rights," in Keep Hope Alive: Jesse Jackson's 1988 Presidential Campaign, *ed. Frank Clemente and Frank Watkins (Boston: South End Press, 1989), 105.*

1. Workers Have a Right to a Job

People need jobs and there are jobs which need to be done. We can build the housing, roads and bridges that we need as well as provide care for this nation's people. We can end plant closings without notice and unemployment without hope.

2. Workers Have a Right to a Democratic Union

All workers, including public employees, should be able to organize themselves into democratic unions, have those unions recognized, and work under a collective bargaining agreement.

3. Workers Have a Right to a Living Wage

People who work full time should be able to rise out of poverty on their pay. American families need family wages. Young workers need opportunity.

4. Workers Have a Right to a Healthy Life and a Safe Workplace

Workers need affordable and accessible health care, a right to know the dangers at work, and good faith enforcement by skilled experts of the laws meant to protect their lives.

5. Workers Have a Right to Both Work and Family

No one should be forced to choose between a paycheck and a sick child, or between keeping their job and giving birth.

6. Workers Have a Right to Pension Security

A pension belongs to the worker, not to the company. Every worker is entitled to one as secure as Social Security. Workers should have a voice in ensuring that their pension funds be used in their own interest, not against them.

7. Workers Have a Right to Fair Competition

International trade needs a level playing field. Recognition of the basic democratic fights of workers at home and abroad to organize, bargain collectively, and to have enforced workplace standards is needed. Free labor cannot "compete" with slave labor.

8. Workers Have a Right to Freedom from Discrimination

There also needs to be a level playing field at home—affirmative action for those locked out of better paying jobs and pay equity for those locked into low-wage jobs.

9. Workers Have a Right to Education that Works

Workers need basic education for basic skills, vocational education for current jobs and life-long education for a changing economy.

10. Workers Have a Right to Respect

The contributions of workers, past and present, deserve a prominent place in the education of future workers. Those who give a life of labor deserve to have the companies for whom they work reinvest in their industry, in their community and in their country.

Chapter 177

A Ten-Point Plan

Peter Dreier

Peter Dreier is professor of politics and director of the Public Policy Program at Occidental College.

Poverty & Race, a Washington, D.C.–based newsletter published by the Poverty & Race Research Action Council, devoted its November/December 1997 and January/February 1998 issues to responses to President Bill Clinton's Race Initiative. The following selection is Dreier's contribution, "A Ten-Point Plan," Poverty & Race, November/December 1997. Reprinted with permission of the author.

For other selections by Dreier, see chapters 88 and 181.

Of course we'd like our leaders to set the tone and the climate for change, but we shouldn't expect our Presidents or Congress to initiate the important changes needed to improve race relations in America. As Harriet Tubman, Frederick Douglass, Ida Wells, A. Philip Randolph, Walter Reuther, Martin Luther King, Cesar Chavez and others recognized, improvements in race relations come about when citizens are organized and in motion, demanding justice, not begging for it, forcing government leaders to respond to pressure from below.

What we don't need from [President Clinton's Race Initiative] Advisory Board is a sermon (or a 500-page report) calling for greater understanding, "dialogue" or small pilot programs. Nor do we need another massive study of America's racial situation, such as [Gunnar] Myrdal's *American Dilemma* or the Kerner Commission report.

We don't need a full employment program for sociologists either. Rather, we need a full employment program for America's workers. If there is one truism about race relations, it is that prejudice, bigotry and discrimination decline when everyone who wants to work has a job at decent wages. Although it is simplistic to argue that if you give people a job, hearts and minds will follow, it is certainly true that full employment at decent wages makes interracial co-operation much more likely. Otherwise, competition over a shrinking pie (or the crumbs from the economy's table) will lead to resentments, bitterness and racial tensions. Studies showed that the number of lynchings went up whenever the Southern cotton economy declined. In more recent times, economic hard times are correlated with increases in the murder rate, racial violence and hate crimes.

At a time when the nation's economic prosperity is primarily benefitting the wealthiest 20 percent, we need the Advisory Board to remind us that economic justice is a precondition for racial justice. The Advisory Board should recommend a broad policy agenda that will help unite those Americans on the bottom three-quarters of the economic ladder around a common vision of the American Dream—and a road map explaining how to get there.

Here are 10 ideas for the Advisory Board to consider as its recommendations to President Clinton, Congress and the American people:

1. Require the Federal Reserve to change the definition of "full employment" from 6 percent unemployed to 2 percent unemployed, so that it will no longer boost interest rates whenever working people are doing well, in order to stem Wall Street's misguided fears of inflation.

2. Reform our federal tax structure to return to a more progressive system, especially by raising tax rates on large corporations and very wealthy individuals, so that we have the funds necessary to invest in our nation's future.

3. Invest in a major public works program, similar to the New Deal WPA, to rebuild our nation's crumbling infrastructure of roads, sewers, water systems, bridges, public schools, playgrounds and parks, which would generate millions of jobs in both the public and private sectors.

4. Enact a universal health insurance program and regulate the cost of medical care, so that our nation's children, in particular, will not needlessly go without preventative medical care.

5. Update the nation's labor laws to level the playing field between employees and employers and give America's working people a fair voice in their workplace lives, to replace the current system biased in favor of management.

6. Replace the current campaign finance system of legalized bribery with a system of public financing, to reduce the influence of big money in American politics—ultimately by appointing Supreme Court justices who will vote to overturn the infamous *Buckley v. Valeo* decision that gives wealthy people an unfair advantage in exercising free speech.

7. At a minimum, equalize the funds we spend (per student) on public education between poor and wealthy school districts. Reform our current over-reliance on local property taxes to fund local schools, a system guaranteeing that poor children will receive a poorer education than their wealthier neighbors.

8. Cash in the "peace dividend" we've been expecting since the end of the Cold War by reducing the nation's economic dependence on military spending and putting the money to work solving our nation's economic problems. We need a 10-year plan to convert our nation's scientific and technological over-reliance on the military to civilian uses so that the nation's defense contractors, defense workers (including both civilians and soldiers, who are disproportionately people of color) and communities that have long depended on the Pentagon are not the victims of the Cold War's end.

9. Increase the minimum wage to at least the official poverty level, so that families who work hard will be able to support their children.

10. Bring America's family policies—maternity/paternity leaves, vacation time, child care—up to the level of our Canadian and European counterparts.

Chapter 178

Both Race and Class: A Time for Anger

Dan T. Carter

Dan T. Carter is professor of history at Emory University.

The following selection is reprinted from "Both Race and Class: A Time for Anger," Southern Changes, Summer 1997, 19–22. Reprinted with permission from the Southern Regional Council (www.southernregionalcouncil.org).

For another selection by Carter, see chapter 151.

As we look at the economic changes in the United States over the last quarter century, we can see that a revolution has taken place. Since the late 1970s, there has been a 40 percent increase in real income in the U.S., but over half of this increase has gone to the top one-half percent of America's taxpayers. At the same time, people who make up the bottom 20 percent of income earners have seen a substantial decline in their standard of living. As a result, we have a gap between rich and poor which is greater than at any time since the 1920s.

That gap is growing every year; we are well on our way to the creation of a nation in which a small elite accumulates unimaginable wealth while an increasingly insecure majority struggles to maintain middle-class status, only a step away from a growing underclass of the desperately poor.

What role can a democratic government play in reversing these forces? It seems to me that this is a question of central importance as we think of our future, but it's essentially a non-issue in terms of political debate. Clearly we have lost any sense of the possibility of collective action to reverse these trends.

Why?

I believe it is because we have lost faith in the power of a democratic government to promote equity and justice.

In the 1960s and 1970s, Alabama Governor George Wallace set up half the equation: the federal government—the "central government," as he described it—was always evil. The "government" [he argued] consists of bureaucratic elitists who live off the hard-earned wages of working people and delight in social engineering. Now we know that the mainspring of Wallace's anger toward the federal government lay in its efforts, however timid, to end racial discrimination. But Wallace clearly touched a resonant chord across the nation which went beyond race.

The federal government had fought the Depression, won the Second World War, and laid the foundations for a stable middle class with policies which essentially benefitted that emerging middle class: subsidized housing loans, the GI Bill, Social Security, and a host of other programs. By the 1960s, however, that middle class was restive under the "burden" of taxes and uneasy over the social upheavals of the decade: civil rights, feminism, court protected free speech, a rising crime rate, the inconclusive war in Vietnam, etc. Thus, when Wallace harped on the evils of busing or the rise of a parasitic welfare class—both issues with racial resonance—Americans across the nation proved receptive to his argument that government was part of the problem, not the solution.

In the 1980s, Ronald Reagan carried through where Wallace left off. He continued Wallace's argument that government is inherently "bad," but he made the circle complete by offering a solution: unleashing the beneficent forces of the marketplace. Everything is the best of all possible worlds as long as the government doesn't interfere. The market place alone can adjudicate every economic conflict equitably and render rewards and punishments on the basis of individual achievement.

I'm normally not one for believing that intellectuals have much of an impact on our society. But Godfrey Hodgson's recent book on the triumph of conservatism documents the skillful way in which wealthy right-wing individuals and corporate interests have created a broad network of subsidized think-tanks, grants, fellowship and research sinecures which skillfully promoted their ideological agenda. Nothing is more ludicrous today than conservatives' complaints of a "liberal media." The fact is, the assumptions underlying laissez-faire economics and "free-market" economy dominate public political discussion. And that is true whether we are talking about the print media, Sunday television news programs, the major networks or public television and radio.

It will not be easy to break out of this ideological cul-de-sac. While the economic expansion of the last 20 years has primarily benefitted the wealthy, enough crumbs have trickled down to the middle class to make possible the diversionary focus upon the poor, immigrants, and racial minorities. At the same time, conservatives' success in subverting the role of positive government for working Americans and minorities has led to their increasing cynicism and withdrawal from the political process. In part, they're correct, of course. Government is not working in their interest. The end result of that withdrawal, however, has been the creation of an electorate which is disproportionately white and affluent.

But we have to continue to struggle for racial and economic justice and to change the terms of the debate and to focus on the issues which will arouse the electorate.

It won't be easy to confront racial issues. Despite the progress of the last forty years, this nation remains deeply divided along the color line. The climate of opinion is particularly hostile to affirmative action. In part this is because of the success of conservatives in misrepresenting its purposes and scope and convincing whites—it didn't take much convincing—that discrimination is a thing of the past and that we truly have an open society. We also have to face up to the reality that opposition to compensatory action is deeply rooted in American's notions of "fairness" and equal justice.

Still, I think we can take heart from the fact that there has been a deep shift in the thinking of most white Americans. A quarter-century ago, there would not have been the assumption that there ought to be minority group representation at every level of political and economic life. We have to build upon that shift by challenging the glib arguments used to misrepresent affirmative action.

We should challenge the worship of a handful of standardized tests as though they alone could judge what makes a person qualified for a job or for admission to college or professional school. We have to talk about the ways in which people actually succeed in college, in the workplace, and in life in general.

I'm most familiar with college admission procedures, and I know that my university constantly makes decisions on the basis of a variety of factors other than Standard Achievement Test (SAT) scores. We seek geographical representation. We look for different life experiences from our applicants. We seek students with a range of talents. And, yes, we seek to create a racially and ethnically diverse student body in the belief that there is strength in diversity.

We have to defend the freedom to make those choices in our public life as well.

That, I confess, is still a hard sell.

I think we can be more successful in refuting conservatives' argument that the legacy of centuries of discrimination has miraculously disappeared over the last few years, and the reason minorities continue to lag is simply because they have been paralyzed by the "culture of dependency" fostered by welfare programs. We have to ask those who would throw the poor overboard to sink or swim: "Do you really believe that someone who has grown up in a culture of poverty, who has very limited education, lacks the kind of skills that the marketplace wants, with no financial reserves, no health care, and few resources—do you believe the solution to their situation is simply to throw them to the forces of the market?"

But I want to return to the original point that I made at the outset of our conversation. Discrimination in our society is rooted in both race and class; neither problem can be addressed separately and if we're going to build any kind of effective political coalition, we have to make that linkage clear. Of course right-wing conservatives will cry "class warfare," but that seems a hollow charge coming from a group that has waged relentless war against the weakest and most helpless members of our society.

Just as we must counter the shibboleths of the new racism, we have to challenge the ideological foundations of the new conservatism, driving home the argument that an unrestrained free-market economy does NOT protect the interests of working and middle-class Americans. At the same time, we have to stop passively accepting the big lie that all social investment is wasteful and makes no difference in the lives of the disadvantaged.

I recently spoke to an Atlanta service club about the enormous problems that primary and secondary educators face in impoverished communities. The disadvantages these children face are so great, I argued, that they cannot be overcome by teachers in the classroom, however dedicated. What is needed, I said, was a broad program of support including income assistance, child care, health care, and comprehensive job training for parents trapped in the cycle of poverty. It won't be cheap, I argued, but it is the right thing to do and, in the long run, it will benefit all Americans.

As you can imagine, that didn't go over very well. Afterwards, I was greeted with a chorus of dismay which faithfully echoed what has become the conservative mantra: there is no connection between spending money and improving education or solving social problems.

I like to think that I am a tactful person, but I'm afraid my answer was not very conciliatory. "If that were really true," I replied, "why do we have parents clamoring to get their students into my university at a cost of $25,000 a year when they could send them to community college at $600 a semester?" What you're really saying, I told them, is that money doesn't count when it involves poor kids, but it certainly does when it involves your own.

At the same time, we cannot create the kind of political climate in which needed social investments are made in our society unless we face head-on the "no new taxes" chant that has become dogma to both political parties. And the best way we can do that is by creating a simple, straightforward, progressive tax system stripped of the kinds of convoluted provisions which seem to have rewarded the most rapacious and parasitic individuals and groups within American capitalism.

Having to make this argument does make me realize I'm getting older. No one in the 1960s would have questioned the ethical basis of a progressive tax system, but one of the horrendous accomplishments of the conservative revolution has been to justify various schemes whereby the rich contribute less and less to society, but justify their greed on the basis of some kind of moral superiority, defined of course, by their success in manipulating capital and corrupting the political process.

It is true that middle class Americans have not seen their taxes go down over the last twenty years. But, what Americans need to be reminded is that—despite all the talk of "tax cuts" in the Reagan years—the changes in the tax code in the 1980s brought benefits to a very small portion of the population. The bottom 50 per cent of the population actually saw its taxes increase as rising social security, medicare and excise levies more than offset marginal declines in their income tax rates. There was relatively little change in the tax rate of the population between the 50th and 90th percentile. In contrast, the closer to the top of the pyramid, the greater the reductions in the effective federal tax rates. For the top 10 percent there was a 5 percent reduction in taxes; for the top 1 percent a 15 percent cut. Cumulatively the effect has been to save the wealthiest tax payers billions of dollars over the last fifteen years and to play a significant role in transferring wealth from the working and middle classes to the very wealthy.

Never satisfied, the new rich in this country remind me of the grasping landowner who claimed that he wasn't greedy: he just wanted all the land abutting his farm. And so this summer we are greeted by the sordid spectacle of a Republican congressional majority intent on reducing capital gains taxes to a maximum of 20 percent, even though studies by the Internal Revenue Service show that three quarters of capital gains go to the top one per cent of American taxpayers. (In 1989, 93 per cent of all families received NO capital gains.)

Now is when we really need a little class warfare.

What happened to the notion of the dignity of labor? Where is the morality in a system which decrees that Bill Gates—among the richest men in the world—should pay 20 per cent capital gains tax on the hundreds of millions of dollars he has made from his stocks while the nurse who cares for the sick and the elderly pays 28 per cent income tax on every dollar she makes over $23,000?

I'm certainly not suggesting that we emulate the conservatives by substituting capitalist scapegoats for immigrants, gays, blacks and other minorities. I am saying that people have a right to be angry about a political and economic system which is rigged in favor of the privileged few.

For the last thirty years, conservative demagogues have successfully deflected the anger of middle and working class on the victims of the system rather than the real perpetrators of economic and racial injustice. But there is an opportunity to shift the ideological ground and to begin to build coalitions at the intersection of race and class.

Let me suggest two of the many battlefields where I think advocates of social justice can begin their counterattack.

The first revolves around the issue of childhood poverty. For 30 years, conservative ideologues have revived the 19th century notion of the "undeserving poor" by blaming the victims of poverty for their own plight. But it is difficult to speak about "lazy, shiftless children," or "undeserving toddlers." It seems to me that this is one of the issues around which political coalitions can be built. Certainly in advocating universal children's health care we can bring up the interrelationship between race and economics because we know that Hispanic and African-American children are disproportionately excluded from adequate health care.

Secondly, we can support a revived labor movement. Given the kinds of pressures that working people in the white collar job-force are facing, I believe there is also a potential for that revival. For all the past failures of America's unions, they are the greatest hope we have for building a political base to protect the economic self-interest of working people.

Although blacks, whites, and Hispanics remain segregated in housing, schools, and (to a slightly lesser extent) in higher education, the workforce at the working-class level is going to be integrated simply because of the growing percentage of the Hispanic and African-American population. There is obviously an opportunity here to create an interracial coalition. I don't mean to underestimate the difficulties of revitalizing the labor movement in this country; certainly it will be unlike the industrial, blue-collar movement of the 1930s. And, while racial suspicions still divide workers, I don't think there is any question that flagrant racial prejudice is less in the 1990s than it was in the 1930s and 1940s. So there is at least the potential in the 21st century for an interracial political coalition based upon common class interests.

I've talked a great deal about the role of the federal government on issues of taxation and social investment on a national basis. But the last point I would like to make is that a revival of the politics of social justice has to begin at the grassroots level.

As a black candidate in a newly configured majority-white congressional district in Georgia, Cynthia McKinney would, I feared, lose her bid for re-election in 1996. But she won by a substantial majority and I think she did so by focusing on political issues which cut across racial lines. In local communities as in the McKinney campaign, there are opportunities to build coalitions around issues of child welfare, health care, housing, the inequities of the criminal justice system, and the degradation of our environment.

Above all, we have to remember that authentic political movements always begin at the grassroots level and have their greater impact when we least expect it. It is always hard to predict where, when, or how the next movement for social justice will coalesce and emerge, but we have to learn from our mistakes, build upon our defeats, and move forward with the kind of arguments and proposals that—right now—don't seem to have much prospect of success. Perhaps we can take heart from the words of St. Paul who urged the early Roman Christians to take heart from their troubled past, knowing that "tribulation worketh patience; and patience, experience; and experience, hope. . . ."

Chapter 179

Fear of a Black Feminist Planet

Barbara Ransby

Barbara Ransby, professor of African-American studies at the University of Illinois-Chicago and a regular contributor to Chicago's National Public Radio affiliate, WBEZ–FM, is a long-time community activist. She was one of the conveners of the Black Radical Congress, a 1998 meeting of black academics and activists who discussed reviving the black radical tradition. Ransby is currently completing a biography of Ella Baker.

The following selection is reprinted from "Fear of a Black Feminist Planet," In These Times, 12 July 1998, 20–22. Reprinted with permission of In These Times.

A few months ago, during Black History Month, I was a guest on a black radio station in Chicago. The topic I dared to speak out about was black feminism. I began with the innocuous assertion that black feminism aims not to divide black men and women, as is so often feared, but to challenge us all to be fully human by getting beyond the dominant society's definition of manhood and womanhood. The current gender dichotomy, I said, not only mandates a circumscribed role for my daughter, but tells my son he cannot be sensitive, emotional or nurturing without being considered soft and forfeiting his black manhood. During the call-in segment, I was beset by mostly male callers who expressed vehement hostility to what I had to say.

Why didn't my listeners want to hear it? It's threatening. While many of us in the black community have been able to critique the ways in which black people sometimes internalize racist, anti-black attitudes, we have not been as successful in analyzing the ways in which dominant notions about gender—masculinity, femininity and sexuality—have infected our thinking as well. As a result, the black feminist perspective gets left out of the increasingly male-centered discourse about race and community.

Given the level of hostility toward black women in general, and black feminists in particular, it is significant that we have been included as important players in the Black Radical Congress. Alongside its opposition to racism and class exploitation, the congress is on record in its opposition to sexism, patriarchy and homophobia. In fact, the congress is the first broad-based national coalition of progressive blacks that has included issues of gender and sexuality in the very definition of its purpose. Even though there continues to be a sometimes heated debate about how we understand and define these issues, the consensus of the group is that gender and sexuality must be on the table when discussing black liberation.

This was not always the case. Rethinking who we are as men and women on a fundamental level frightens a lot of people—even those who are prepared to radically reorder society in every other respect. Discussions about sexism and gender politics always have been difficult in the black community. Early black feminists—such as Michele Wallace, author of *Black Macho and the Myth of the Superwoman,* and Ntozake Shange, who wrote the play "For Colored Girls Who Have Considered Suicide/When the Rainbow Is Enuf"—were criticized heavily for expressing some of black women's anger and frustration at the pervasive silence around issues of gender and sexism. While disagreement remains, even in black feminist circles, about the politics articulated in these works, Wallace and Shange should not have been the target of such venomous attacks.

These tensions survive today. Within the current discourse, statistics on black male homicide and imprisonment wholly overshadow comparable statistics about the rising number of African-American women in poverty, in prison and—as a result of male violence—in hospitals or graves. If a black woman discusses sexism, she is accused of being divisive. If she criticizes rapists, batterers or black men who denigrate black women as "bitches and hos" as a form of entertainment, she is accused of attacking all black men and airing our dirty laundry in public.

The "masculinization of blackness," as one of my colleagues has described it, reinforces current misconceptions and half-truths about race and gender and discourages open discourse. Any black woman (or man) who speaks out about sexism, or challenges men to confront the issue, is subject to attack. In the wake of the Million Man March, for instance, a group of black feminists criticized the conservative politics and leadership of the event [see chapter 180—*Eds.*]. They were called names, threatened and castigated as enemies of the race. Even Angela Davis—who is widely revered in the black community as an activist and symbol of '60s militancy—was ridiculed on many black radio stations and on the streets of Harlem for daring to speak out against the march.

Racism within the mainstream, predominately white feminist organizations further fuels the reluctance of many people of color to even engage in a discussion about the larger issues of gender, patriarchy and sexism. Some white feminists have minimized or glossed over racial and class differences in the quest for a universal sisterhood. Black feminists have argued that this tack only reinforces racial and class hierarchies. However, because white feminists are seen as representative of all feminist politics, gender issues often get dismissed as "white" issues within the black community.

No one has fought harder to challenge and confront the racism within the women's movement than black feminists. As feminists, we are laying claim to a term that our more mainstream white counterparts define quite differently. This struggle over the definition of feminism is neither a compromise of principle nor an endorsement of racist or elitist feminists. To say, for example, that one is a Democrat does not imply wholesale endorsement of the current leadership of the

Democratic Party. On the contrary, by identifying ourselves as feminists, we are contesting the meaning of a term that no one has a proprietary claim on.

The history and current reality of black feminism stands in stark contrast to the myths and distortions perpetuated inside and outside the African-American community. In the 19th and early-20th centuries, predating the use of the term "feminist," black women, from educator and church activist Nannie Helen Burroughs to journalist, suffragist and anti-lynching crusader Ida B. Wells-Barnett (and men such as Frederick Douglass), were combating sexism, male chauvinism and the denigration of black women. In her new book on black women blues singers, *Blues Legacies and Black Feminism*, Angela Davis suggests that, as early as the '20s, these artists, grounded in the poor and working class black communities, were also critics of patriarchy, male sexual privilege, homophobia and the subordination of women.

The explicit use of the term "feminist"—or more recently "womanist"—by African-American women began in the '70s and '80s, and was popularized through the writings of self-identified black feminist writers, activists and intellectuals.

So, what's in a name? By identifying ourselves as feminists, we openly proclaim a commitment to fight sexism, homophobia, misogyny and patriarchy, while also continuing to combat racism and class exploitation. As black feminists, we organize around a set of politics informed by the experiences of black people. As bell hooks points out, since black women are disproportionately at the bottom of the class, racial and gender hierarchies in American society, black women as a group have the greatest stake in the greatest degree of change.

A long list of black feminists—including Audre Lorde, Barbara Smith, Beverly Guy-Sheftal, Kimberlé Crenshaw, Evelynn Hammonds, Cathy Cohen, June Jordan, Jill Nelson, Paula Giddings and Marcia Gillespie—have argued that a black feminist vision must address not only multiple forms of oppression, but also, on some level, strive to forge a political alliance across gender, class and racial divides. In the context of these coalitions with black men, white women and other workers, black feminists have refused to rank gender over race or class in a hierarchy of oppression.

And just as black feminists have refused to accept hierarchies of oppression, we have also refused to artificially compartmentalize our experiences as women, people of African descent or workers. However, we recognize the importance of articulating a clear and explicit indictment of sexism. Sexism comes at us through powerful institutions and influences outside of our communities. Unlike white women, we are further humiliated and brutalized by police, social scientists and media pundits, who see us as promiscuous, lazy and stupid. And, even though we don't always want to admit it, sexism exists in the black community as well. Black women are raped, beaten in their homes and grabbed, slapped and beaten in the streets. Popular culture portrays us as gyrating sex objects and as symbols of male success, draped over the hoods of fancy cars or mewing at men's feet in music videos.

Black feminists have never argued that black men are our enemies. Racism and a shared sense of culture and history tie us to black men. At the same time, we have insisted on the right to struggle with our brothers, and each other, about the issue of sexism. The Combahee River Collective, a black feminist organization, at its 1974 founding in Boston, issued a statement that articulated black feminist politics as revolutionary. It has become a manifesto of sorts for many black feminists: "We struggle together with black men against racism, while we also struggle with black men about sexism. We realize that the liberation of all oppressed peoples necessitates the destruction of the political-economic systems of capitalism and imperialism as well as patriarchy."

Black feminist politics are essential to any inclusive agenda for black liberation. On the economic front, black women are often the sole providers and caretakers for black children but are paid less than their employed black male counterparts. With the eradication of welfare and erosion of public housing, black women, children in tow, are being forced into the ranks of the homeless, and into subway tunnels, abandoned buildings, overcrowded shelters and prisons in record numbers. Yet the pernicious myth prevails that black women are getting ahead, at the expense, or in lieu, of black men.

Black feminists are not participating in the Black Radical Congress for cosmetic purposes or to create some type of political smorgasbord. Rather, we offer a political perspective that can, perhaps, help the larger black liberation movement transcend some of its past mistakes. Black feminists offer, not as a perfect model but a principled objective, that inclusive, egalitarian structures are the only legitimate way to build an effective movement for social change. We cannot replicate the same competitiveness, elitism and chauvinism, so prevalent in larger society. We have to forge a different path.

The voices of black feminism, to paraphrase an E. Frances White essay, get us away from a rigid economic determinism that strives to alleviate one layer of oppression, while remaining uncritical of others. We know from painful experiences around the world that to fight for socialism and assume the "woman question" and other issues will take care of themselves is an ahistorical folly.

Just as most of us who identify ourselves as black radicals have come to the conclusion that class and race are inextricably linked in the American context (and throughout most of the world), black feminists have to grapple more seriously with the ways in which gender and sexuality are inextricably tied as well. A black feminist perspective does not offer a narrow, marginal "special interest" politics, nor can it be reduced to individual issues of "identity." Instead, black feminism embodies a revolutionary potential, for both men and women. We see the need to redefine exploitative class relations, dismantle racial hierarchies and, at the same time, redefine what it means to be men, women and sexual beings. Such politics are crucial for any fully liberating vision—if we are not afraid of the challenge.

Chapter 180

Response to the Million Man March

African American Agenda 2000

Nation of Islam leader Louis Farrakhan's call for a Million Man March on Washington to be held 16 October 1995 inspired much commentary and controversy, including the following criticism from a group of black feminists.

The following selection is reprinted from "African American Agenda 2000," 1995.

If ever there was a need for African Americans to come together to demand economic, political and social justice, it is now. Here we stand on the eve of a new century, our communities besieged by drugs, unemployment, crime and violence. We know that many of the men who are planning to answer the call for the Million Man March on Monday, October 16, raised by Minister Louis Farrakhan, the Rev. Benjamin Chavis and others, are doing so to express the frustration and anger we all feel about the push to dismantle hard-fought civil rights laws, affirmative action and the already too fragile support system for people living in poverty. We know that many of the men and women who support this event are also expressing the desire we all feel to stem the rising tide of drugs, crime, violence, and despair that engulfs our communities. But no march, movement or agenda that defines manhood in the narrowest terms and seeks to make women lesser partners in this quest for equality can be considered a positive step. Therefore, we cannot support this march.

Yes, we share the rage and pain and anguish that fuel this march. Yes, it is important that African Americans mobilize. Yes, we must remind this nation of our unswerving commitment to racial and gender justice, to stand in defense of human rights. But our needs are not served by men declaring themselves the only "rightful" leaders of our families, of our communities and of our ongoing struggle for justice. Justice cannot be achieved with a march that excludes Black women and minimizes Black women's oppression. Justice cannot be served by countering a distorted racist view of Black manhood with a narrowly sexist and homophobic vision of men standing "a degree above women."

For more than 400 years African American women and men have stood shoulder to shoulder united in our struggle for justice. Over 100 years ago, Frederick Douglass rejected a version of Black leadership that marginalized women. But at this crucial juncture, the organizers of this march tell us that now is the time for men to step forward and women to step back. They imply that because of men's failure to take responsibility, women have taken on the "burden" of leadership. But, in fact, we still struggle to get women's experiences, concerns and needs addressed and to place women as full and equal partners at the leadership table.

This call for men to take responsibility is not the solution to the rising plague of socially and economically engineered problems that we face. We need to repudiate the Far Right's claim that we rather than racism are the cause of our problems, not echo their rhetoric. Rather than "atonement" for violence against women, it is time to commit to eliminating the sexism and oppression that spawn it. Instead of men marching to atone for their behavior, defend men's rights and define women's roles, we the organizers of African American Agenda 2000 raise the call for men and women to come together and create an inclusive, well-organized social and political movement dedicated to combating racism, sexism, and homophobia and to transforming the lives and conditions of our community. We ask all those who share our commitment to join us.

Chapter 181

What Farrakhan Left Out

Peter Dreier

Peter Dreier is professor of politics and director of the Public Policy Program at Occidental College.

The following selection, originally entitled "What Farrakhan Left Out: Labor Solidarity or Racial Separatism?" is reprinted with permission from Commonweal, *15 December 1995, 10–11.*

For other selections by Dreier, see chapters 88 and 177.

Leaders of organized labor were conspicuously absent from last October's Million Man March. Louis Farrakhan's conservative rhetoric of economic individualism and racial separatism doesn't square with the labor movement's message of class solidarity and racial cooperation. Undoubtedly, however, a significant number of the marchers were union members: Twenty-six percent of black men are unionists.

Beginning with the Depression, civil rights leaders—including A. Philip Randolph, Martin Luther King, Jr., and Jesse Jackson—have recognized that unions and African-Americans share a common agenda. In their view, appeals to racial pride, without a larger vision of economic justice that cuts across racial divisions, are a dead end. Randolph, the founder of the first black trade union (the Brotherhood of Sleeping Car Porters), mobilized civil rights activists during World War II to push the federal government to integrate defense plants and the army. The 1963 March on Washington—famous for King's "I Have a Dream" speech—was Randolph's idea. The labor movement, especially the United Auto Workers, played a key role in organizing and funding the march, and in exerting pressure to enact the Civil Rights Act of 1964 and the Voting Rights of 1965. When King was assassinated in 1968, he was in Memphis to lead a demonstration of predominantly black sanitation workers who were on strike. Jesse Jackson has spent decades walking picket lines and preaching the union gospel of class solidarity among black, white, and Latino workers.

Union strength reached its peak (at 35 percent of the work force) in the United States in the mid-1950s. Unions enabled American workers, especially blue-collar workers, to share in the postwar prosperity and to join the middle class. Union pay scales boosted the wages of nonunion workers as well. Today, unionized workers continue to have higher wages and better benefits than their nonunion counterparts.

But it was not until the civil rights movement of the 1960s that black Americans began to gain their fair slice of these postwar economic gains. The civil rights crusade helped many black Americans move into the economic mainstream. They gained access to good-paying jobs—in factories, government, and the professions—that had previously been off-limits. In unionized firms, the wage gap between black and white workers narrowed significantly. Not so for the gap between union and nonunion workers. According to the Economic Policy Institute, unionized black males earn 19 percent more than blacks in comparable nonunion jobs.

According to Farrakhan, the road to black success is through entrepreneurship: by blacks owning businesses and keeping economic resources in the African-American community. This goal resonates with the American Dream, but it is a far cry from economic reality. Small businesses (including those owned by the Nation of Islam) are difficult to sustain and have a high failure rate. Most blacks, like most whites and Latinos, are wage earners, and will continue to be so for the foreseeable future. And those who have joined or formed unions have better wages, working conditions, and benefits than those who have not.

At the Million Man March, Farrakhan preached personal atonement, up-by-the-bootstraps self-improvement, and a "cooperative effort" to rebuild the inner cities by bringing "government and corporate America" into an "alliance with black organizational, religious, civic, political, and fraternal leaders." Yet tragically absent from his litany was the institution that has played perhaps the largest role in improving the economic condition of black Americans: unions.

While appeals to self-help and racial pride may resonate with African-Americans in our nation's current political climate, they don't address the fundamental problems now facing the black community. To a significant degree, those problems are symptoms of economic distress. Inner-city black America has been especially hard hit by today's harsh economic trends, including the widening gap between rich and poor, corporate downsizing and layoffs, an increase in temporary and part-time work, and the export of decent inner city jobs overseas.

The erosion of America's labor movement is a chief reason for the nation's declining wages and living standards and the nation's widening economic disparities. Today, union members account for only 16 percent of the American work force, the lowest percentage since the Depression. Some of that decline is the result of a shift from the nation's once-strong manufacturing sector to a service-oriented economy; some is due to the anti-union policies and appointments of the Reagan and Bush administrations; but some of it is the result of labor's own failure to organize new workers and new types of workplaces.

Soon after his election in October 1995, the AFL-CIO's new president, John Sweeney, announced a different sort of self-help message: "I am here to tell you that the most important thing we can do—starting right now, today—is to organize every working woman and man who needs a better deal and a new voice." Sweeney wants to rekindle a spirit of militant unionism, focusing in part on sectors now composed disproportionally of minorities, women, and immigrants. His own union, the Service Employees International, has been one of labor's few success stories during the past decade, doubling its membership to 1.1 million by merging with other unions and by organizing janitors and other low-wage workers.

The unions that have made the most headway in recruiting new members in recent years have drawn on themes and tactics from civil rights crusades and grassroots organizing campaigns. The most successful organizing drives have allied unions with church and community groups, such as ACORN and the Industrial Areas Foundation, and have recruited organizers from civil rights, neighborhood improvement, and women's rights groups. Since 1980, according to labor expert Kate Bronfenbrenner of Cornell University, it is workplaces with a higher percentage of minority workers that are more likely to win union elections.

Sweeney has promised to mobilize a wave of union organizing drives, and to recruit a new generation of organizers, especially minority activists. His goal is to expand not only the number of union members, but to increase labor's political clout by training the rank-and-file members, the poor, and minorities.

Most unions, including those with growing minority membership, have been led by white males. This is now beginning to change as well. The recent AFL-CIO convention in New York was noteworthy for the large number of black and Latino delegates and for the fact that the convention voted to expand the AFL-CIO's executive council to increase minority and female representation. As a result, the number of minorities on the board rose from four out of thirty-five (11 percent) to eleven out of fifty-four (20 percent). Under Sweeney, labor's political agenda now looks remarkably similar to those of most progressive African-American organizations. It calls for a new wave of job-creating public investment in the nation's crumbling infrastructure, increasing the minimum wage, protecting social programs, passing national health insurance, expansion of job-training programs, and stronger enforcement of workplace safety regulations and antidiscrimination laws.

In the past two decades, neither organized labor nor the traditional civil rights establishment has had the political clout to secure many victories. But thanks to Sweeney's victory and the Million Man March, there is new excitement among both union and African-American activists. Both have a stake in expending political participation among the bottom half of the electorate. To do so, they need to link their organizing activities and to enunciate a compelling vision of racial and economic justice. But the question remains whether a philosophy of racial separatism and self-advancement or a vision of worker solidarity and racial integration will prevail.

Chapter 182

Clean-Money Campaign Finance Reform

Holly Sklar

Election campaigns have become increasingly costly. Who pays suggests who gains (see chapter 137). In recent years, several forms of campaign finance reform have been suggested to remedy the problem.

Holly Sklar is the author of Chaos or Community? Seeking Solutions, Not Scapegoats for Bad Economics *(1995).*

The following selection is reprinted by permission from "Let's Get Rid of America's Big-Dollar Democracy," Cleveland Plain Dealer, *4 July 1997.*

For another selection by Sklar, see chapter 167.

For more on campaign finance reform, see the Nation *magazine special issue, "Dollar Democracy: Can We Stop It?" 5 May 1997.*

This Independence Day, let's look forward to freeing our government from the grip of big money.

The Declaration of Independence was not about equality for corporate kingpins, liberty for lobbyists and the pursuit of money by politicians. Yet in 1996, the biggest spenders won nine out of 10 seats in our House of Representatives.

Today, we don't have government of, by and for the people. We have a Congress that is increasingly a Congress of, by and for millionaires—the kind of Congress that cuts aid for impoverished children while preserving aid for wealthy corporations.

Take the example of Archer Daniels Midland Corp. According to Common Cause, ADM has given millions to congressional candidates and political parties, and reaped billions in corporate welfare in return. Common Cause says, "every dollar of ADM's profit from corn sweeteners ultimately costs taxpayers $10 in sugar subsidies."

As law professor Jamin Raskin of American University points out, "Less than 1 percent of the people give the vast majority of all money to candidates for Congress."

Maine voters have found a way to declare their independence from big money. Last fall, Maine voters approved a statewide Clean Election Act. Candidates for governor or the legislature who gather a minimum number of $5 contributions and take what's called the "clean money option" receive equal public funding. Supplemental funds are available for clean-money candidates who are outspent by privately financed opponents or targeted by outside groups.

Vermont's legislature acted in May, giving preliminary approval to a measure that would provide public funding in state races. Similar legislation has been filed in Arizona, Illinois, North Carolina, Connecticut, New Mexico and New York City. Other states where such legislation is being drafted or ballot measures are being actively considered include Michigan, Massachusetts, Washington, Missouri, Idaho, Wisconsin, Oregon and Georgia.

Janice Fine was a leading strategist for the Maine initiative and is a board member of Public Campaign, a national organization working for clean-money campaign reform. She says, "If a lawyer gives money to a judge to issue a verdict in his client's favor, we call that bribery. But when wealthy Americans give money to influence politicians, we call that a campaign contribution. We should call it bribery. It's got to stop."

Democratic Sens. Paul Wellstone of Minnesota, John Kerry of Massachusetts, John Glenn of Ohio, Joe Biden of Delaware and Pat Leahy of Vermont have sponsored a bill modeled after the Maine and Vermont initiatives. Candidates who show a minimum level of support and forgo private money would receive public funding and an allotment of free and reduced-price media. The bill would also ban soft-money contributions to the political parties.

The soft-money loophole allows corporations and individuals to give unlimited contributions to political parties for vaguely defined "party building" and "get out the vote drives." These slush funds have multiplied in recent years.

The Democratic Party raised more than $34 million in soft money in the 1991–92 election season and nearly $109 million in the 1995–96 season. The Republican Party raised nearly $50 million in soft money in the 1991–92 season and $127 million in 1995–96.

When advocates of Maine's Clean Election Act first promoted public campaign financing they were told they were dreaming. But they beat big money with grassroots organizing.

Their example shows that Americans everywhere can make our votes count, and replace dollar democracy with real democracy.

Chapter 183

Proportional Representation

Steven Hill

In a winner-take-all election system, how can minorities ever get fair representation? One possibility is through litigious reapportionment struggles. Another option, used in most other democracies, is proportional representation.

Steven Hill, co-author of Reflecting All of Us: The Case for Proportional Representation *(1999), is the West Coast Director of the Center for Voting and Democracy, a nonpartisan organization studying the impact of voting systems on representation and democracy. Hill's commentaries have appeared in the* Nation, Ms., Boston Review, *the* Los Angeles Times, *the* Wall Street Journal, Z Magazine, *and other publications.*

An earlier version of the following selection, "South African Elections Show the Way Toward Racial Fairness," appeared in the Humanist, *July/August 1994, 3–4. Copyright © 1994, 1999 Steven Hill. Published here with the permission of the author.*

For more information about proportional representation, contact the Center for Voting and Democracy, P.O. Box 60037, Washington D.C. 20039; 202/882-7378; e-mail fairvote@compuserve.com; web: www.fairvote.org.

The heady triumph of democracy in South Africa in 1994 was the culmination of a remarkable year for proportional representation (PR), that "other" voting system used by most of the democratic world. In that year alone, and in subsequent years, an astonishing array of countries, organizations, and prominent individuals have flocked to the PR standard, further isolating the few remaining established democracies—the United States included—that continue to use the antiquated winner-take-all system.

The first multiracial elections in South Africa were completed in 1994 using party-list PR. The South Africans never even seriously considered the winner-take-all system because it was universally recognized that the success of their new democracy depended on the degree to which their government reflected the racial and political diversity of their society—never a strong point of winner-take-all systems.

In South Africa, the white minority comprises about 14 percent of the population, with blacks comprising 74 percent, "coloreds" 9 percent, and Asians 3 percent. By comparison, the situation in the United States is exactly reversed, with whites comprising 75 percent, blacks 12 percent, Hispanics 9 percent, Asians 3 percent and Native Americans 1 percent. At times, the clash of race and politics in the United States approaches the intensity of South Africa; yet the United States continues to use a 200-year-old system that routinely denies representation to its racial and political minorities unless one can draw a gerrymandered district around them—not always an easy task, and always a controversial one, especially in the aftermath of recent U.S. Supreme Court rulings overturning districts drawn for racial representation.

The South Africans were smart: they opted for a proportional-representation voting system in which the white minority will not be shut out. Nor will an effective vote be limited only to those who happen to live in the right district. This is because with PR, legislative seats are weighted equally in *multi-member districts*. For example, in a 10-seat district, each seat is worth about 10 percent of the at-large vote. If a party wins 40 percent, it wins four out of 10 seats; 20 percent of the vote wins two out of 10 seats; and if an independent candidate wins 10 percent, he or she would get a seat. Under proportional representation, therefore, a party or candidate need not come in first to win a seat. This means that racial minorities, as well as third, fourth, and more political parties, are significantly empowered in the electoral process.

Winner-take-all systems are notorious for being not very hospitable to third parties or to racial and political minorities. There have been over 1,000 third parties in the history of U.S. politics, but only one of these ever lasted—the Republican Party. This is because votes going to a losing candidate are wasted, even if that candidate garners 49.9 percent of the vote. Voters sense this, and so they often don't vote for the candidate they like but, rather, for the one who stands the best chance of winning—the "lesser of two evils." The winner-take-all system leaves significant blocs of voters unrepresented and renders most political races noncompetitive. Increasingly, many voters don't even bother to vote, which is why the winner-take-all democracies are near the bottom of the list in terms of voter turnout. The United States is next to last in voter turnout, with only 49 percent of eligible voters participating in the 1996 presidential election and even less in off-year elections.

No wonder then that New Zealanders, after using the winner-take-all system for over 140 years, voted in a national referendum in November 1993 to scrap it in favor of the "mixed member" PR system popularized by Germany. In recent years, Japan, Russia, Mexico, and Italy have all adopted a version of the German "mixed member" system, which combines single-member geographic districts like those used in the United States with party-list PR. The trend in the world is toward PR and away from "winner take all." Recently the United Kingdom, the grandmother of all "winner take all" democracies, chose to use PR for elections to the European Parliament, its London city council, and Scotland and Wales voted in national referendums to use proportional systems for their new regional legislatures. A proportional system was chosen as a crucial part of the power-sharing arrangement for the peace agreement in Northern Ireland. A national referendum on PR is slated to occur in Great Britain for electing the House of Commons sometime in the future. Significantly, in the conversion from communism to democracy, all the countries of Eastern Europe adopted some form of PR. Currently, the only governments still using winner-take-all systems are Great Britain, the United States, France (though France does use PR for European elections and local and regional elections), Pakistan, Canada, India and various Caribbean nations. Ukraine, which initially chose "winner take all," has now switched to PR.

In the United States, the move toward proportional representation is gaining steam. Recent developments in voting rights cases in North Carolina, Louisiana, Georgia, and Texas all have pushed PR onto the center stage of national politics. A U.S. Supreme Court ruling, *Shaw v. Reno*, in July 1993 questioned the use of racially gerrymandered districts to ensure the election of minority representatives, opening the gates to a flood of lawsuits. (The Court threw out a majority black district that snakes for 160 miles across North Carolina, no wider than the interstate in places.) This means that many states and localities are now caught between a rock and a hard place: as a result of the Voting Rights Act of 1965 and subsequent amendments in 1982, they have a mandate stating that their legislative bodies *must be* racially inclusive or they may be subject to a voting-rights lawsuit. But now, depending on how they draw their districts to satisfy that voting-rights mandate, they may find themselves subject to lawsuits by either dissatisfied white voters or by racial-minority voters who have been excluded from the gerrymander (thus pitting minority groups against each other).

PR has been proposed as a race-neutral method of remedying minority-vote dilution, one which has the added benefit of circumventing the controversial and partisan process of drawing district lines. Ironically, these developments have brought back into the limelight Lani Guinier, the Clinton administration's rejected nominee to head the Civil Rights Division of the Justice Department. Guinier is widely recognized as the foremost proponent in the United States of alternative voting schemes like proportional representation.

"I think this debate is going to take root," said Guinier in an interview with the *New York Times*, "because I think many Americans, not just racial minorities, feel alienated from politicians who ostensibly represent them. For a premier democracy, our level of [voter] participation is an embarrassment. Some may say that reflects contentment with the status quo. I think it represents . . . rational behavior by voters who realize their votes don't count."

Still, the parameters of the debate in the United States remain quite limited at this point. Few are seriously discussing the adoption of, for instance, the type of PR that has been successfully used to elect the city council of Cambridge, Massachusetts, since 1941. Called "choice voting" (also known as preference voting or single transferable vote), it is a more proportional form of nonpartisan voting than cumulative voting, which has been the preferred option of the voting rights community. With cumulative voting, voters get as many votes as there are candidates. With choice voting, voters rank candidates in their order of preference, and candidates win by reaching the threshold of votes established for each seat. Surplus votes above the threshold are transferred to the next preference on voter's lists, so very few votes are wasted. Besides the Cambridge city council, choice voting is also used to elect the national governments for the Republic of Ireland, Malta, the Australian Senate and the new power-sharing assembly in Northern Ireland. Until the 1950s, choice voting was used by 22 U.S. cities to elect their local governments—including New York, Cincinnati, and Boulder, Colorado—but the system eventually fell victim to a McCarthyite and racist backlash because it resulted in the election of a handful of blacks and Communist Party members. As a result, the history of proportional representation in this country is largely a buried one. Try going to your local library and checking out a book on the subject—most of the available resources are 20 years old or more and are written for an academic audience. In 1993, Columbia University Press published *New Choices, Real Voices* by Douglas Amy, the first lay person's resource on PR to appear in the United States in over 30 years.

The recent global popularity of the German "mixed member" system suggests some interesting possibilities for U.S. voters. The German system's combination of U.S.-style geographic districts with a party-list PR system that elects political parties in proportion to their share of the popular vote would be very familiar to U.S. voters. Voters have two votes in the German system: one for their district representative (just like U.S. voters have now) and one for their desired party. This system has allowed the Green Party to become a potent force in German politics; the Greens have never won any district seats, but they usually win seats in the proportional vote and, in the 1998 national elections won the third highest number of seats and have formed a coalition government with the Social Democratic Party in the Bundestag. This form of PR—as well as any of the other various forms—could easily be adopted in the United States at state and federal levels *without* constitutional amendments, merely by changing applicable laws.

Indeed, grass-roots efforts are springing up to bring about such changes. The Center for Voting and Democracy was established in 1992 to educate citizens about alternatives to the winner-take-all system. The CVD's efforts have spawned local organizations—like Citizens for Proportional Representation in Washington state, FairVote Minnesota, the Fair Ballot Alliance in Massachusetts, and other local groups in Michigan, New Mexico, Vermont, Texas, Massachusetts, Colorado, Oregon, Arizona, California, North Carolina, and Washington D.C.—that are busily educating, lobbying, and otherwise spreading the gospel about PR. In 1996, San Francisco voters rejected a ballot measure that would have elected the city council by choice voting. But the ballot measure won 44 percent of the vote—over 100,000 voters—and important lessons and strategies were learned that will be useful for future campaigns. The task of conversion is daunting, PR advocates say, but they are optimistic that the logic and fairness of PR—particularly when applied to the current confusion swirling around voter-rights cases, racially gerrymandered districts and upcoming battles over incumbent and partisan redistricting—will win out over time.

The United States has one of the world's oldest—and some say most old-fashioned—democracies. Proponents of PR argue that the United States needs a voting system suitable for the twenty-first century, not the eighteenth. A twenty-first century voting system must be able to accommodate a multiracial, multi-partisan society; it must allow a wider range of choices than just Democrat and Republican. The South Africans recognized this and gave themselves the gift of a modern multiparty democracy. Proponents of PR are hoping that the United States will wake up and follow suit. Otherwise, they say, racial tensions in the United States will continue to deteriorate, in no small part as a result of the inherent exclusivity of its winner-take-all voting system.

Chapter 184

We *Can* Educate All Our Children

Constance Clayton

Constance Clayton is the former Superintendent of Schools in Philadelphia.

The following selection, "Children of Value: We Can Educate All Our Children," is reprinted with permission from the 24 July 1989 issue of the Nation *magazine.*

Two different systems of education have been created in our State. One encompasses effective schools holding high expectations for their students and located in affluent or stable communities; the other, ineffective schools which communicate low expectations and aspirations for their students, who are not given full opportunity to succeed. . . . Our society's acceptance of two unequal educational systems is putting us at risk of creating a permanent underclass in New York and our nation. The existence of this underclass will ultimately erode the foundations of our democratic society. We are on our way to becoming two nations—one of the rich and privileged and the other of the poor and disadvantaged. Racism clearly underlies much of the problem. . . . In education, racism is expressed in a variety of ways: inadequate resources to those most in need; perpetuating segregated schools; and in some schools, the tracking of minority students into less rigorous academic programs without regard for individual abilities, interests and potential.

—"The Time for Assertive Action," *Report of the [New York State] Commissioner's Task Force on the Education of Children and Youth At-Risk,* October 1988

The black family and the urban public schools share more than their children. The "plight" of each has been assayed in apocalyptic terms and chronicled in the reports of myriad researchers, panels, commissions and task forces. A new generation of academics has cut its teeth on elaborate analyses written for publication, tenure and self-promotion.

After the critics have retreated into their academic and bureaucratic havens, black families and the metropolitan public schools are left to confront the same situation as before—and more often than not, each other. However, all is not quite the same. In ways sometimes subtle and sometimes not, the researchers have suggested that the plight of the black family and that of the urban public schools are not only related but are causally so. Thus, a seeming conundrum: Is the black family to blame for the plight of the public schools? Or have public schools caused the plight of the black family? Neither happens to be the case, but merely posing the issue in that manner is a phenomenon worth exploring.

The paramount public policy issue today is whether this country accepts as inevitable the existence of a permanent underclass. Encoded in much of the rhetoric of concern about the "plight" of the nation's public schools, and about the family life and home environment of the children who attend these schools, is a considerable degree of ambivalence over a more fundamental question: whether this society seriously intends or even desires to educate the mostly black and Latino children who now occupy the majority of seats in its large urban school systems.

There are those who still question in their hearts the proposition that "all children can learn" and who adhere to the belief that the cultural deficits of some children are too deeply embedded to be overcome. However, that ambivalence also may reflect an intuitive recognition that the absence of a commitment to educate the underclass allows for results that mask significant questions that would otherwise arise about the political economy. As Michelle Fine of the University of Pennsylvania noted, the much-discussed subject of "dropouts" presents an excellent example of this masking:

> What would happen, in our present-day economy, to these young men and women if they all graduated? Would their employment and/or poverty prospects improve individually as well as collectively? Would the class, race, and gender differentials be eliminated or even reduced? Or does the absence of a high school diploma only obscure what would otherwise be the obvious conditions of structural unemployment, underemployment, and marginal employment disproportionately endured by minorities, women, and low-income individuals?

Whatever its bases, the ambivalence about the worthiness of the clientele of the urban schools has structured both the diagnosis and the prescription. First, only failure is perceived as significant. It is highly unlikely that much will be said about the tens of thousands of high-school students who graduated this past June and who will go on to succeed in higher education, the armed forces and the public and private sectors. Their achievements (along with those of the parents and teachers who supported them) will go unheralded, unable to fit into the language of failure.

Second, although couched in terms of parental choice, many of the proposed responses to the "problem" sound very much like a prescription for the abandonment of urban public schools. Whether intended or not, proposals for tuition tax credits, vouchers and metropolitan busing plans would facilitate middle-class flight from the urban "inner-city" public classrooms for seemingly greener pastures in suburban, private and parochial schools.

Proposing abandonment of the public schools would be unthinkable if the children served by those schools were white and middle class, or if the public schools involved were on neatly manicured campuses in well-to-do suburbs. Regardless of their relative performance on conventional measures of achievement, persistence and success, deserting these schools would be deemed an unacceptable response. Rather than being seen as populated by "children at risk," they would continue to be seen as serving and caring for children *of value*.

Perhaps the question answers itself, but it still deserves to be asked: Are there not children of value in the urban public schools? If so, why would we countenance abandonment?

The children-of-value formulation differs from the notion of children at risk. The at-risk designation no doubt began as a well-intentioned attempt to focus attention and resources on those children most in need. This original purpose loses much of its efficacy as the number of those "at risk" approximates, surpasses and then exceeds by far the children judged not to be. In those instances, "at risk" becomes as much a misnomer as the term "minority" in a school that is *majority* black and Latino. The continuing vitality of both appellations can be explained either by linguistic inertia or by a political judgment that the term implies a status so fundamental and lasting as to be impervious to change.

It is important to note, however, that the children-at-risk rhetoric is more than a mere misnomer. The children-at-risk rubric locates the problem at the level of the individual child, with the implicit suggestion that this is where the solution must begin. This notion is often accompanied by dreary statistics on the number of children who live in poor, single parent (generally female-headed) households characterized by high unemployment, low educational attainment and other indicators of marginal or lower socioeconomic status. This litany produces a not-too-subtle and virtually irresistible temptation for schools to join the *if only* chain, a rationale used to explain and excuse less than satisfactory outcomes.

Much of the impetus for school desegregation came from those who believed, conscientiously, that the academic performance of black children could be improved significantly *if only* black children and white children attended the same schools. We know now that even in the absence of second generation problems, desegregation is no panacea.

The generally negative rendition of black family life sent out yet another siren call. If only the children were different (or had different parents from a different social class, race or neighborhood), schools would succeed!

There is at least one major problem with that position: The empirical evidence shows that it is demonstrably wrong. The "effective schools" literature is replete with examples showing that, on the terms by which success is currently measured, there are schools with students of these families that have succeeded in the past and are succeeding now. As the late Ronald Edmonds (belatedly acknowledged as the founder of the effective-schools movement) asked nearly a decade ago:

How many effective schools would you have to see to be persuaded of the educability of poor children? If your answer is more than one, then I submit that you have reasons of your own for preferring to believe that basic pupil performance derives from family background instead of school response to family background. . . . Whether or not we will ever effectively teach the children of the poor is probably far more a matter of politics than of social science and that is as it should be.

That analysis still holds true. Educating the children in urban schools is no mission impossible. Nor is it a mystery. Given the tools, skills and resources, teachers can insure that students become actively involved and, thereby, more effectively involved in learning. Margaret Wang, director of the Temple University Center for Research in Human Development and Education, and others have demonstrated that "adaptive instruction," drawing on new insights from cognitive science and research on teaching, can work when given the chance.

Individual schools can be made to work in terms that are important and measurable. Effective schools share common traits that are identifiable and replicable: a school climate conducive to learning, high expectations, emphasis on basic skills and time-on-task, clear instructional objectives and strong instructional leadership. The mini-industry that has grown up around the effective schools' applied research can now deliver virtually a turnkey operation. Moreover, James Comer and his colleagues at the Yale Child Study Center have demonstrated by example how explicit recognition of the child-development role of the school, coupled with what is known about social and behavioral science and education, can be employed to overcome poor motivation, low self-esteem, discipline problems and even perceived learning disabilities.

School districts, too, can perform better when the will exists. Across the country, new leadership is recapturing urban school districts from disrepair, decay and red ink, rebuilding both infrastructure and instructional programs. Formerly controversial decisions establishing critical minimums for the curriculum, devising new measures and instruments for assessment and evaluation, and ending social promotions have contributed demonstratively to building the framework for educational improvement.

Because we know that classrooms, schools and school districts can work, and we know how to make them work, it is not unreasonable to conclude, as Edmonds did, that the continued "plight" of the urban public schools must reflect an unwillingness to make the fundamental political decision about whether a permanent underclass is acceptable and necessary.

Those whose interests are served by masking the unwillingness of the society to pursue the redistributive policies necessary to deal with the underclass phenomenon often find aid and comfort among educators who have become frustrated by disappointing results from even the most carefully crafted and expertly implemented school improvement programs. Presented with the choice of either accepting responsibility for repeated failure or blaming the parents and children they serve, these educators choose the latter.

Many of us now recognize that behavior as the false choice that it is and refuse to become or to blame the victim. In short, by unmasking and acknowledging the question of perpetuating an underclass, we go about the business of school improvement and education reform fully cognizant of the Sisyphean nature of our task. Simply put, we commit ourselves to educate children who are real, if not ideal; the children we have, rather than the ones we do not.

The school improvement and education reform agenda is both long and concrete. It includes:

- early childhood programs to provide interventions at the point at which they will do the most good and have the most lasting value;
- continuity of instruction efforts to increase time-on-task, increase both student and teacher attendance, reduce "pullout" programs and other school-day interruptions;
- attention to the middle years and the special needs, concerns and developmental processes of those young adolescents who are often overlooked when educators focus upon the elementary and high schools;
- regulatory reform initiatives designed to create an environment freed of the vague drafting, inconsistent interpretation, overlapping jurisdiction and inflexible adult procedures that often combine to prohibit preventive intervention, require premature termination of services and encourage programs designed to be audit-proof even if not pedagogically sound.

Even that partial agenda is ambitious. Its completion would be an accomplishment of considerable magnitude. Nonetheless, such an accomplishment would have a pyrrhic quality unless educators are willing to engage the broad spectrum of issues involving the underclass. Educators could commit themselves to the politically risky course of open advocacy for children, particularly those children whose horizons are being constrained by their conscription into the underclass.

If it is to be authentic, that advocacy would have to be seen as consistent with and falling within the institutional mission of the public school. Thus, an explicit component of that undertaking would have to be to promote social improvement. Once part of the mission, advocacy for social change would be included in both the hidden and the official curriculum. Those who are willing to eschew the teaching of core values or to pretend that no values are being taught now are likely to find this a development of calamitous portents. Teaching would have become truly a subversive activity.

Authentic advocacy would mean breaking with established orthodoxy even when that would entail some version of secular heresy. For example, the current debate around bilingual education assumes a consensus about the rightful place of English as the exclusive national language. Schools could enter the national language debate on the side of those who oppose the explicit or de facto imposition of a national language.

Educators are in a unique position to challenge that consensus by arguing that to treat the language spoken in a child's home as "un-American" or otherwise illegitimate is cultural chauvinism and has nothing to do with education. They must encourage a re-examination of how schools respond to children from non-English-speaking homes. By so doing they will take an important step toward affirming the worth and dignity of the children they must reach to teach.

Most important, advocacy for children will require that educators cease their tacit collaboration with those who suggest that the causes for educational shortcomings reside with individual children or with their parents. Educators can do this by reiterating loudly and clearly the simple yet profound admission offered by Ronald Edmonds:

> We can, whenever and wherever we choose, successfully teach all children whose schooling is of interest to us. We already know more than we need, in order to do this. Whether we do it must finally depend on how we feel about the fact that we haven't [done so] so far.

Whether the children of the underclass, who are becoming the predominant clientele of urban public schools, are allowed to be educationally successful is a matter for society to decide. The future of urban public schools depends less on the development of a new pedagogy than on the emergence of a new politics. Without this, the chances in life of those children will be determined less by their mastery of the three Rs than by their ability to prevail over the myriad obstacles created by a fourth—race; less by former Education Secretary William Bennett's trinity of Cs (content, character and choice) than by the pervasive and confining realities of class.

These realities compel a new relationship between black families and public schools. That relationship would be one dedicated to responding to the urgent problems of race and class and the common ground on which they meet: poverty.

Chapter 185

Algebra as Civil Rights: An Interview with Bob Moses

Peggy Dye

Bob Moses, a popular political organizer and teacher admired for his quiet, self-effacing style, grew up in Harlem and graduated from Hamilton College. Inspired by the example of black students involved in southern sit-ins, he left graduate school at Harvard to work full time with SCLC. Encouraged by local NAACP leader Amzie Moore, he set up the first SNCC voter registration drive, a campaign that led to Freedom Summer (see chapters 107 and 108) and the founding of the Mississippi Freedom Democratic Party (see chapter 109), which challenged the state's all-white delegation at the 1964 Democratic Convention. He is the founder of the Algebra Project, a national program to teach math and computer literacy in the inner city.

Peggy Dye is a New York–based freelance writer who frequently writes on city planning and preservation issues. A series of her articles in the Village Voice *and* Newsday *about the Audubon Ballroom, the Harlem landmark where the Transport Workers Union was founded and Malcolm X was later assassinated, led to a movement that resulted in the partial preservation of the site. She is currently completing a novel about the 1970s New York City fiscal crisis.*

An earlier version of the following selection, "Algebra: The Civil Rights Issue for the 90s," appeared in Newsday, *25 August 1994. Copyright © 1994 Peggy Dye. Published here with permission of the author.*

For more information, write The Algebra Project, 99 Bishop Richard Allen Drive, Cambridge, MA 02139, or call 617/491-0200.

Q: You're famous as the Freedom Summer leader who bused college students to the Mississippi Delta to register black voters in 1964. Today, you called math literacy the civil rights issue of the '90s. What's the connection?

Moses: It's a question of shifting technology. We lived in the '60s with technology that was industrially based. In the '90s, we're in a computer-based technology. That's brought about a profound shift in the literacy requirements for citizenship.

In the 1960s the requirements focused around reading and writing literacy. When we went into Mississippi in the Delta, many of the sharecroppers couldn't read or write. We taught them to do that, and tied it to our [voter registration] campaign. The Mississippi Freedom Democratic Party came out of this.

You need literacy to get freedom. You need your freedom, too—in various degrees—to become literate. But the 1990s have brought in a requirement for quantitative literacy. Computers mean you need people not to crunch numbers—computers do that. You need people to interpret. That gives rise to a school system in which critical thinking about quantitative information is required.

If we don't know how to do that, there won't be any work for us. In this first district for the Algebra Project in New York, [Assemblyman] Roger Green told me there's 80 percent unemployment. So there's an issue for young people. They have no jobs and they don't think they can demand jobs because they don't have any of the tools they need.

Q: How did you start the Algebra Project?

Moses: I got a MacArthur Fellowship in 1982 for my civil rights work and I used that to start the project. Maisha, my daughter, was ready to go into algebra in public school in Cambridge, Mass. But the school didn't give a course in it. I was going to tutor her. I've taught mathematics and my Ph.D. is in the philosophy of math. But Maisha didn't want two "maths"—one at school and one at home. The MacArthur freed me to go into school with her. I gave her and three other students a small tutorial every day.

The next year I looked at the politics of math—who was taking algebra? You had the middle-class and upper-middle-class whites doing algebra, and the minorities and poor whites below grade level. It took another couple of years, but by 1987, Cambridge let us offer the Algebra Project to *all* seventh graders in the public system.

Q: How does the Algebra Project work?

Moses: It stands the usual approach to mathematics on its head. Usually, children begin with symbols in a textbook. They are asked to understand symbols and then to apply them to their world. This doesn't keep most students interested.

In the Algebra Project, we start with the world that children live in. We take some experience, like a subway trip, which the children learn to mathematize, through a protocol of drawing, writing and discussion. They learn to create their own symbols and in the same process, they experience themselves working together in class. They gain a sense of self, and they define their world. That's powerful.

We learned this method in the Delta. We were faced with the issue of empowering sharecroppers who were illiterate, which is what is said about school children today. In the Delta, we discovered that as sharecroppers participated, they gained their own voice, discussing events in daily life that were important to them and devising action plans to do something. Out of this process rose political movement and leadership. Fannie Lou Hamer, for instance, came out of this.

Q: What about white kids? Is the project open to them?

Moses: If there are white kids in the schools, they are in it, too. But in the South, most have fled the system, and more and more in the North, too. There's one area in Eastern Kentucky in the mountains that is all white. But throughout the country, our focus is the same as when we organized around the right to vote. We focus on the sharecroppers, on people at the bottom. They are the people who can most quickly leverage the most change for everybody.

Q: Do New York City kids need a different kind of approach?

Moses: The way we work the project is to have a local group form and take charge. We don't try to implement from afar. Our first invitation here came from Dr. Lester Young when he was an assistant commissioner of state education last year. He asked us if we would consider bringing the project into the city. We said that you must have people from both the community and the school sitting together at the table.

He agreed. A group began to form—a core of about a dozen parents, educators and activists. In the meantime, Lester Young became superintendent for District 13 and the New York Algebra Project decided to pilot the project in this district. We've been holding meetings with parents and the community since last winter and out of that process two schools—Satellite West and P.S. 258—were selected.

The pilot will have 130 sixth graders, their math teachers and parents. We are currently finishing a two-week training of teachers plus some parents, activists, young adult students and a school-board member.

This is a side of organizing that isn't really understood as well as the mobilizing tradition. People know about big campaigns—marches on Washington, for instance. But I come out of a different organizing tradition. We build by bringing a whole community—teachers and parents and kids—together. Organizing is local.

Here, the Algebra Project classrooms will also be open to visitors. It's part of the culture of the project. You want students to feel comfortable being visible and explaining to visitors something they are making.

Q: All this energy comes into a city school system that many say crushes creativity. Is that how you see the system?

Moses: Let's look at it globally. Like all the school systems in major cities, this one is under enormous pressure. Integration has not worked. You have school systems that are public but predominantly minority. Black people have a larger voice in politics but the economic base of the city has eroded, along with the educational base. Then you have technology. How should the school systems be in this age when you have the new technology? You don't have answers. You don't necessarily even have all the questions.

New York City is in the middle of this. The Algebra Project is saying that whatever the transition is going to be, we know that math literacy has to be in place. You have to put a floor under all students. This is the citizenship question.

Q: What is the citizenship question?

Moses: The young people are being faced with the same charges as the sharecroppers—that they don't care about education, that the reason they're not getting education is their fault, that their social conditions are too horrendous, that they've given over to apathy and are dropping out.

The Algebra Project has to work on that constituency and its demanding what it needs. We want to help this generation find their voice in the larger society.

Chapter 186

Pulpit Politics: Religion and the Black Radical Tradition

Michael Eric Dyson

Michael Eric Dyson, senior fellow of the DePaul Humanities Center and professor of religious studies at DePaul University, is the author of Reflecting Black: African American Cultural Criticism *(1993),* Making Malcolm: The Myth and Making of Malcolm X *(1995),* Between God and Gangsta Rap *(1996),* Race Rules: Navigating the Color Line *(1996), and* "I May Not Get There with You": The True Martin Luther King, Jr. *(2000).*

The following selection is reprinted from "Pulpit Politics: Religion and the Black Radical Tradition," In These Times, 12 July 1998, 17–19. Reprinted with permission of In These Times.

The left's well known antipathy to religion derives in no small measure from a sophisticated tradition of misreading Karl Marx's famous statement that religion is the "opiate of the people." But Marx did not detest religious passion; he understood that religion was a crucial human response to oppression and a protest against suffering. In the few sentences that precede his fateful declaration, Marx wrote, "Religious suffering is at the same time the expression of real suffering and also the protest against real suffering. . . . Religion is the sigh of the oppressed creature, the heart of a heartless world, as it is the spirit of spiritless conditions." Clearly, religion was for Marx a symptom of an unacceptable state of affairs that demanded radical change. In the end, though, he was sympathetic to religion's desire to change the world. He wrote in 1881 of the parallel between "the early Christians in their struggle with the Roman Empire" and the coming of "a real proletarian revolution"—even if he disagreed with what they made of it.

It's clear that Marx and Engels—and a whole lot of oppressed folk before and since them—were ticked off by religion's refusal to engage the social and economic forces that harm humans. At best, religion had become passive or otherworldly in the face of suffering; at worst, it had become complicit in human oppression. But typical of the cultural and historical blinders worn by Western radicals and their contemporary American heirs, Marx and Engels overlooked the religious movements outside the orbit of European culture—which not only fought against brutal oppression, but sought to bring both salvation and a little bit of heaven right here on earth.

A striking example is the religion of black Americans. From the days of slavery to the present, black radicalism in the United States has been sustained by black religious ideals of freedom, justice and equality. The black religious tradition proves that radicalism and religious belief together can transform society. While it's a largely Christian tradition, there have been attempts to link spirituality and societal transformation by blacks in religious groups like the Nation of Islam, the Moorish Science Temple, the Black Hebrews, Garveyism, Rastafarianism, neo-African Yorubism, Father Divine's Peace Mission, Egyptocentric Kemeticism, Five-Percenters and so on.

From the very beginning, ever since black folks first converted to Christianity during slavery, there have been suspicions about how adopting the oppressor's religion could free blacks from the yoke of white supremacy. On the one hand, many white slave owners believed that conversion to Christianity would make their slaves docile and obedient. In fact, Frederick Douglass wrote that he met "many good, religious colored people who were under the delusion that God required them to submit to slavery and to wear their chains with meekness and humility."

On the other hand, there were many slaves who believed that their religion gave them the power—and furnished them the principles—to rebel against slavery's psychic and physical restrictions. Indeed, one of the reasons so many slaves converted to evangelical Protestant Christianity is the radical egalitarianism that the religion promoted. During the 1780s and 1790s, Baptists and Methodists provided religious spaces of worship that broke with the racial and social status quo. Some even advocated the abolition of slavery. As Baptists and Methodists became upwardly mobile and more respectable in the 1800s, most rejected the early antislavery pronouncements. But black slaves clung to the egalitarian vision revealed to them, they believed, by God. In any case, by then they'd already started their own churches and were aggressively advocating what religious historians Vincent Harding, Albert Raboteau and Reginald Hildebrand call a "Gospel of Freedom."

Black defiance of white supremacy, then, was nurtured in black churches. Insurgent slave ministers like Gabriel Prosser, Denmark Vesey and Nat Turner led violent revolts against their slave masters, losing their lives but gaining "a better reward"—not because they died in search of heaven, but because they preferred rebellion and death to slavery. Harriet Tubman drew from black religious belief the inspiration to lead hundreds of black souls out of slavery.

The black church was greatly hated and feared by many powerful whites. In 1839, a New Orleans newspaper opined that the black church was "the greatest of all public nuisances and a den for hatching plots against [the] masters." Besides the heroic efforts of Prosser, Vesey, Turner and Tubman, blacks found other ways to resist, some mundane, others more dramatic: work slowdowns, singing spirituals with dual meanings, embracing atheism, urinating in food, aborting babies and committing suicide. While black religious narratives didn't defend all these measures, the black church supported their ultimate aim: to liberate black people from the bondage of slavery and white supremacy.

The history of black religion since slavery has largely been a story of the quest for black freedom from oppressions. Hence, black religion has often been a stimulant and safeguard for the pursuit of a black radical agenda. There's little doubt that Benjamin Mays' contention that the antebellum Negro's idea of God "kept them submissive, humble and obedient" is also true of elements of the black church today. In fact, Mays' prized student Martin Luther King Jr. complained in 1967 that too many black churches were "so absorbed in a future good 'over yonder' that they condition their members to adjust to the present evils over here."

But neither King's early accommodationist protest strategies, nor his latter day radical democratic socialist leanings, erupted out of a historical vacuum. Figures like Bishop Henry McNeal Turner, Bishop Alexander Walter and the socialist preacher Reverend Reverdy C. Ransom had sought to radicalize the black church more than a quarter century before King was born. Moreover, courageous black women have profoundly shaped the black church from its beginnings. As historians Sylvia Frey and Betty Cotton argue, black women formed the black church's revival culture, structured its rituals of worship, gave it secure institutional grounds, spread its religious values between generations and forged the link between the spiritual and the material.

Even in this century, the black church has often been an unsung partner in the struggles of black radicals in the labor movement. In Memphis, Tenn., for example, decades before King led what would be his last march in solidarity with striking sanitation workers, the black church mobilized its forces to help develop a working-class left, to provide a place for white unions to meet and organize when no one else would have them, and to work for better schools and black voting rights. In fact, black religious sentiments were shot through union culture. Black laborers appealed to God to help them, and their white, often racist, counterparts, in their fight to organize. As historian Michael Honey relates, black Southern Tenant Farmers' Union (STFU) organizer John Handcox turned the black gospel song "Roll the Chariot On" into "Roll the Union On," and it became, Honey says, "an anthem for Southern unionism." The connection forged between religiously inspired black workers who organized union drives and their white counterparts suggested the enormous potential of combining the union and the civil rights movements.

Given its grand legacy, the black church seems to have strayed from its radical roots. But that's only half right. It is true, of course, that the largest black denomination, the National Baptist Convention, has been mired in leadership problems. The head of the church, Henry Lyons, has been indicted for misuse of church funds and has come under fire for alleged sexual indiscretion. And the growing social conservatism of black Christians, evidenced in anecdotal reports of their beliefs about abortion, premarital sex, school-prayer and gay rights, bodes ill for a healthy broad-based coalition among progressive groups, especially when some progressives are prejudiced against religion to begin with. But the Rev. Jesse Jackson remains a beacon for progressive black Christian interests, and a vital link to the, admittedly, greatly diminished radicalism of national black politics.

Under these circumstances, I'll suggest five things that we and the current heirs to the radical black religious tradition should do to bring black churches back to their radical roots.

First, we shouldn't give up on the black church, especially not the part of it that continues to agree with crucial elements of the radical black agenda: opposing white supremacy, addressing the failures of welfare reform, forging class solidarity among the working class, shoring up national unions, promoting school reform, defending reparations and affirmative action, advocating environmental justice, supporting full employment, arguing for national health care, opposing the death penalty and demanding the end of police brutality. Those who operate within the radical realm of black religion should join with committed activists throughout black communities to transform our social and political life.

Second, the black church is a sleeping giant with an untapped potential to lobby and mobilize its voter base, a lesson that the often repulsive religious right has already learned. According to a 1984 National Black Election Survey, only 22 percent of blacks attended a church meeting in support of a candidate; 19 percent of churches took up collections for candidates during an election year; 10 percent worked for a candidate through the church. And in a 1983 survey of 1,800 black ministers, only half supported the use of the church as an instrument of social and political change. Of course, I'm not suggesting that radical black democratic energies are exhausted, or even best represented, by what occurs in electoral politics. Nor am I suggesting that grass-roots efforts by black churches, especially those that render crucial social services to local communities, are not equally important expressions of political sentiment. I am saying that there's a great deal of moral, economic, social and political influence being squandered by the black church.

Third, radical black religionists must wage mighty warfare against the profoundly conservative moral, religious and social beliefs of their brothers and sisters in the church and other religious institutions. The white religious right has made detrimental inroads into black religious institutions by appealing to the homophobic passions, patriarchal sentiments and nostalgic hunger for rigid family values that abound in our community. To be sure, many black conservative churches and the Nation of Islam promote such values as well. But the white evangelical invasion of black religious communities seduces blacks with visions of transcendence and neutrality. Even though white conservative evangelicals promote moral and political agendas that are harmful to the black community, black Christians are too often convinced that the Gospel is concerned only about our souls and our personal salvation. To speak of political, sexual, gender or racial issues in a progressive fashion, they say, betrays the Gospel's moral center.

Fourth, radical black religionists must oppose what Interdenominational Theological Center president Robert Franklin terms "positive-thought materialism," which posits that one's own health, wealth and success are the keys to salvation and neglects the social transformation, political activism and moral critique advanced by radical black religion. This religious belief has taken hold of black Americans who have entered the expanding black middle class as a way to justify personal aggrandizement, upward mobility, economic accumulation and material benefits, without being made responsible for how wealth is secured, generated or distributed. Further, it stigmatizes those who aren't healthy, wealthy and successful as inefficient bearers of God's gifts and grace, or as failures in the spiritual realms of prayer and holiness. In any case, they say, the poor are poor because they don't pray right, don't live right, or don't think right. In other words, the problem is individual, not social or collective.

Finally, radical black religion must be race-specific without being race-exclusive. True, in forging coalitions with other progressives, blacks and other racial minorities are often encouraged to surrender the particular claims they might press as a group in deference to a wrong-headed definition of "universalism." This, I believe, is precisely the argument we're now getting from left figures like Todd Gitlin, Michael Tomasky, and to a lesser extent, Richard Rorty. We're told that the scourge of identity politics has torn apart a plausible left movement, and that the insistence on special interests, especially from racial, sexual and gender minorities, has made the sundering of a viable radical politics a fait accompli. But this only makes sense if one ignores the tremendous struggle for human and labor rights that progressive blacks have always backed and given their life blood to. Still, radical black religionists must call upon black folk to accentuate their particularities and varied identities, while at the same time linking their struggles to the fight against homophobia, gender oppression, classism and the like. It's the right thing to do. But it's also a way of enlarging our awareness of the various ways black folk shape their identities and our understanding that all of those ways should be affirmed within our own complexly constituted groups.

Radical black religionists must learn again to become good radical democrats in the public sphere, prophetic pests in the spiritual and moral spheres and insurgent activists in the civic realm. Whatever we do, we should remember to do one thing: translate our beliefs about love into concrete action. Justice, after all, is what love sounds like when it speaks in public.

Chapter 187

Some Truths Are Not Self-Evident

Howard Zinn

Historian and playwright Howard Zinn has taught at Spelman College and Boston University.

The following selection is reprinted from "Some Truths Are Not Self-Evident," Nation, *1–8 August 1987, 87–88. By permission of The Nation Company, Inc. © 1987.*

For other selections by Zinn, see chapters 99 and 108.

This year Americans are talking about the Constitution but asking the wrong questions, such as, Could the Founding Fathers have done better? That concern is pointless, 200 years after the fact. Or, Does the Constitution provide the framework for a just and democratic society today? That question is also misplaced, because the Constitution, whatever its language and however interpreted by the Supreme Court, does not determine the degree of justice, liberty or democracy in our society.

The proper question, I believe, is not how good a document is or was the Constitution but, What effect does it have on the quality of our lives? And the answer to that, it seems to me, is, Very little. The Constitution makes promises it cannot by itself keep, and therefore deludes us into complacency about the rights we have. It is conspicuously silent on certain other rights that all human beings deserve. And it pretends to set limits on governmental powers, when in fact those limits are easily ignored.

I am not arguing that the Constitution has no importance; words have moral power and principles can be useful even when ambiguous. But, like other historic documents, the Constitution is of minor importance compared with the actions that citizens take, especially when those actions are joined in social movements. Such movements have worked, historically, to secure the rights our human sensibilities tell us are self-evidently ours, whether or not those rights are "granted" by the Constitution.

Let me illustrate my point with five issues of liberty and justice:

• First is the matter of racial equality. When slavery was abolished, it was not by constitutional fiat but by the joining of military necessity with the moral force of a great antislavery movement, acting outside the Constitution and often against the law. The Thirteenth, Fourteenth and Fifteenth Amendments wrote into the Constitution rights that extralegal action had already won. But the Fourteenth and Fifteenth Amendments were ignored for almost a hundred years. The right to equal protection of the law and the right to vote, even the Supreme Court decision in *Brown v. Board of Education* in 1954 underlining the meaning of the equal protection clause, did not become operative until blacks, in the fifteen years following the Montgomery bus boycott, shook up the nation by tumultuous actions inside and outside the law.

The Constitution played a helpful but marginal role in all that. Black people, in the political context of the 1960s, would have demanded equality whether or not the Constitution called for it, just as the antislavery movement demanded abolition even in the absence of constitutional support.

• What about the most vaunted of constitutional rights, free speech? Historically, the Supreme Court has given the right to free speech only shaky support, seesawing erratically by sometimes affirming and sometimes overriding restrictions. Whatever a distant Court decided, the real right of citizens to free expression has been determined by the immediate power of the local police on the street, by the employer in the workplace and by the financial limits on the ability to use the mass media.

The existence of a First Amendment has been inspirational but its protection elusive. Its reality has depended on the willingness of citizens, whether labor organizers, socialists or Jehovah's Witnesses, to insist on their right to speak and write. Liberties have not been given; they have been taken. And whether in the future we have a right to say what we want, or air what we say, will be determined not by the existence of the First Amendment or the latest Supreme Court decision but by whether we are courageous enough to speak up at the risk of being jailed or fired, organized enough to defend our speech against official interference and can command resources enough to get our ideas before a reasonably large public.

• What of economic justice? The Constitution is silent on the right to earn a moderate income, silent on the rights to medical care and decent housing as legitimate claims of every human being from infancy to old age. Whatever degree of economic justice has been attained in this country (impressive compared with others, shameful compared with our resources) cannot be attributed to something in the Constitution. It is the result of the concerted action of laborers and farmers over the centuries, using strikes, boycotts and minor rebellions of all sorts, to get redress of grievances directly from employers and indirectly from legislators. In the future, as in the past, the Constitution will sleep as citizens battle over the distribution of the nation's wealth, and will be awakened only to mark the score.

• On sexual equality the Constitution is also silent. What women have achieved thus far is the result of their own determination, in the feminist upsurge of the nineteenth and early twentieth centuries, and the more recent women's liberation movement. Women have accomplished this outside the Constitution, by raising female and male consciousness and inducing courts and legislators to recognize what the Constitution ignores.

• Finally, in an age in which war approaches genocide, the irrelevance of the Constitution is especially striking. Long, ravaging conflicts in Korea and Vietnam were waged without following Constitutional procedures, and if there is a nuclear exchange, the decision to launch U.S. missiles will be made, as it was in those cases, by the President and a few advisers. The public will be shut out of the process and deliberately kept uninformed by an intricate web of secrecy and deceit. The current Iran/*contra* scandal hearings before Congressional select committees should be understood as exposing not an aberration but a steady state of foreign policy.

It was not constitutional checks and balances but an aroused populace that prodded Lyndon Johnson and then Richard Nixon into deciding to extricate the United States from Vietnam. In the immediate future, our lives will depend not on the existence of the Constitution but on the power of an aroused citizenry demanding that we not go to war, and on Americans refusing, as did so many G.I.s and civilians in the Vietnam era, to cooperate in the conduct of a war.

The Constitution, like the Bible, has some good words. It is also, like the Bible, easily manipulated, distorted, ignored and used to make us feel comfortable and protected. But we risk the loss of our lives and liberties if we depend on a mere document to defend them. A constitution is a fine adornment for a democratic society, but it is no substitute for the energy, boldness and concerted action of the citizens.

Chapter 188

We Don't Need Another Dr. King

Patricia Hill Collins

Patricia Hill Collins is professor of African American studies, sociology, and women's studies at the University of Cincinnati. She is the author of Black Feminist Thought *(1991) and* Fighting Words: Black Women and the Search for Social Justice *(1998).*

The following selection is reprinted from "We Don't Need Another Dr. King," New York Times, 19 January 1991. Copyright © 1991 by The New York Times. Reprinted by permission.

"If King were alive, things would be different." "I wish we had a civil rights movement, then we could do something." "We need another King."

These are the voices of the students in my African-American studies class. Despite differences of race, gender and social class, they are upset and outraged when I explain the sobering statistics on domestic and global joblessness, infant mortality, homelessness and hopelessness. They want to eliminate poverty, inequality and injustice.

But while they take Dr. King's vision to heart, these college students simultaneously feel that, when it comes to struggles for social change, they do not matter. Their lives reflect a curious mixture of moral outrage and political disempowerment.

How did this happen? Wasn't getting a national holiday supposed to fix this? Wasn't this generation, born after Dr. King was assassinated, supposed to be inspired by the example of his life?

Poor African-American children, we are told, drop out of school, not because they are trapped in underfunded, inferior institutions, but because they lack positive role models. If low self-esteem is the problem, then learning about Dr. King should be the solution.

But part of the problem is this very drive to sell Dr. King as a role model. Being exposed to positive role models is no guarantee than their ideas and actions will be emulated. Correspondingly, numerous individuals succeed with no obvious role models in sight. Moreover, what happens if a positive role model loses his luster? When the role model becomes discredited, his ideas become increasingly suspect.

The role model approach to social change is no substitute for strategies that challenge unjust employment practices, educational policies and housing customs.

Dr. King wasn't trying to be a positive role model; institutional transformation was his goal.

Another part of the problem is the packaging of Dr. King as a Great Man of History. Even though getting him accepted as such required a protracted struggle—almost by definition, Great Men are white, and Martin Luther King Jr. was black—this approach tells us that Great Men are so powerful that they bring about change all by themselves.

We've all been exposed to this approach—Lincoln freed the slaves, and the like. Now Dr. King is its latest recruit. Social conditions that spur large numbers of people into action are ignored in favor of a Hollywood version of history focusing on one conquering hero. Since a movement for social change is embodied in its leader, death of the leader means death of the movement. By encouraging us to search for positive role models or "kings" to lead us, we feel that we can do little without them.

Focusing on King the Positive Role Model, on King the Great Man of History, on King as "king"—obscured the texture of everyday activism and denies us an understanding of how change occurs. We forget that most activism is brought about by ordinary people like ourselves.

For example, countless anonymous African-American women formed the bedrock of the American civil rights movement. Without their personal struggles, Dr. King would be unknown. Moreover, truly Great Men and Women of History do not foster their own greatness but instead aim to empower others. "The purpose of any leadership is to build more leadership. The purpose of being a spokesperson is to speak until the people gain a voice," observes African-American poet, Nikki Giovanni.

Certainly Dr. King was an extraordinary individual. We definitely would benefit from more individuals with his vision and skills. But the true value of Dr. King's legacy lies not in his greatness but in his ordinariness.

Allowing Dr. King to be like us frees us to see parallels between the struggles in his daily life and those in our own. If one individual can be so central to the massive changes that occurred during his lifetime, then we should be able to effect more modest changes in our own, if we try.

Successful challenges to injustice, poverty and inequality require sustained action by everyday citizens. As the children of Dr. King's dream, we don't need another King to lead us or save us. Instead, we need to believe that we can act like Dr. King in the context of our everyday lives.

Index

Abbott, Robert, 201
Abernathy, Ralph, 442, 574, 577–579
Abolition. *See* Emancipation; Thirteenth Amendment
Abolitionism, 17–19, 36–40, 52, 59, 74, 74–75, 103,
    121, 127, 235, 189, 245, 281, 329, 844, 904–905;
    Liberator on, 53–54; publishing, role of, 86–87;
    woman suffrage and, 255; women and, 50
Abyssinia, 233
Abyssinian Baptist Church, 299–300, 399, 589
Abzug, Bella, 282
Academic freedom, 511
Accommodation, 222–225, 279
ACORN, 882
Acuff, Roy, 740
Adams, John Quincy, 59
Adams, Sam, 495
Adarand v. Pena (1995), 679, 682, 702, 704, 712n. 1
Addes, George, 373
Address, forms of, 194, 211, 451, 480–481
Affirmative action, 22, 368, 410, 650, 655, 678,
    700–701, 708–713, 752 n. 18, 765, 790, 812,
    826–827, 836–839, 843, 853, 865; history, 697–699;
    misrepresentations of, 869–870; Powell on, 682;
    press on, 702–707; for whites, 669–678, 697–699.
    See also Proposition 209
AFL-CIO, 624; Sweeney and, 881–882
Africa, 1, 31, 43, 56–57, 233, 244, 271, 413, 480, 484,
    596, 598; accomplishments of, 51; Delany's explo-
    rations of, 66; *Freedom's Journal* on, 42; slave trade
    and, 9–15
African American Agenda 2000, 878–879
African Methodist Episcopal Church, 111, 116, 131,
    139, 194, 337, 539
African National Congress, 743
Afro-American Association, 618
Afro-American Council, 177
Afro-American League, 177
"Agape and Eros," 465
Agency: of black soldiers, 93, 95; in civil rights, 1; edu-
    cation, blacks and, 109–115; in Emancipation,
    91–97; of slaves, 93–94; of women, 254–255. *See
    also* Great Man Theory of History
Agnew, Spiro, 736, 739–740
Agricultural Adjustment Administration (AAA), 284
Ahmann, Matthew, 496
Aid to Families with Dependent Children (AFDC), 560,
    758, 798–802
AIDS, 826, 854
Alabama, 20, 135, 210, 311, 328, 736; black legisla-
    tors, 146; chain gangs, 832, 834–835; crop lien, 149;
    Dixiecrat party support, 717; environmental racism,
    859; federal supervision for, 544; Klan in, 138; Re-
    construction schools, 115; Southern Manifesto signa-
    torees, 723; woman suffrage, 257–258. *See also*
    Montgomery Bus Boycott; Scottsboro case; Wallace,
    George
Alabama, University of, 490, 731
Alabama Christian Movement for Human Rights,
    478–479
Albany (Ga.) Movement, 487–488, 502, 525
Albany State College, 524
Albemarle Paper Co. v. Moody (1975), 794
Alexander, Will, 284
Algebra Project, 896–898
Algeria, 598
Alien and Sedition Acts, 414–415
Alinsky, Saul, 566
All God's Dangers, 311
Allen, Debbie, 690
Allison, Theresa, 860
All-white primary, 339, 396
Alpha Phi Alpha, 405
Alston, Christopher, 372
Alvord, John W., 113–114
Amalgamated Clothing Workers, 406
Amalgamated Meatcutters Union, 313
Amalgamated Transit Union, 625
Amazons, 249
American Antislavery Society, 24, 52
American Association of Retired Persons, 801
American Bowling Congress, 378
American Civil Liberties Union (ACLU), 279, 323, 567,
    835
American Dilemma, 866
American Dream, 531, 881
American Federation of Labor (AFL), 206, 217,
    218–220, 292–293, 295, 313, 365
American Federation of Labor-Congress of Industrial
    Organizations (AFL-CIO), 624; attacking commu-
    nists, 293, 397; Sweeney and, 881–882
American Federation of Teachers, 625
American Guardian, 310
American Historical Association, 91–92
American Jewish Congress, 496
American Labor Party, 404
American Missionary Association, 226
American Negro Labor Congress, 219–220
American Revolution, 8, 30, 327, 511, 749
American Scottsboro Committee, 279
American Social History Project, 109
American Sociological Review, 689
American Tract Society, 113
American Woman Suffrage Association, 130, 131, 252,
    254
Americans for Democratic Action, 373
Ameringer, Oscar, 310
Ames, Jessie Daniel, 280–282
Amistad (ship), 57

About the Editors

Jonathan Birnbaum is the editor, with Bertell Ollman, of *The United States Constitution: 200 Years of Anti-Federalist, Abolitionist, Feminist, Muckraking, Progressive, and Especially Socialist Criticism* (also available from NYU Press). His work has appeared in the *Guardian, New Politics, Socialism & Democracy, New Political Science,* and other publications. He lives in Illinois.

Clarence Taylor is Professor of History at Florida International University and author of *The Black Churches of Brooklyn* and *Knocking at Our Own Door: Milton Galamison and the Struggle to Integrate New York City Schools.* He was a Fulbright Scholar in Chemnitz, Germany, from 1997 to 1998.